PURCHASING AND SUPPLY MANAGEMENT

TEXT AND CASES

McGraw-Hill Series in Management

CONSULTING EDITORS

Fred Luthans
Keith Davis

McGraw-Hill Series in Marketing

PURCHASING AND SUPPLY MANAGEMENT

TEXT AND CASES

SIXTH EDITION

Donald W. Dobler
Colorado State University
Emeritus

David N. Burt
University of San Diego

THE McGRAW-HILL COMPANIES, INC.
New York   St. Louis   San Francisco   Auckland   Bogotá   Caracas
Lisbon   London   Madrid   Mexico City   Milan   Montreal   New Delhi
San Juan   Singapore   Sydney   Tokyo   Toronto

McGraw-Hill

A Division of The **McGraw·Hill** *Companies*

This book was set in Palatino by The Clarinda Company.
The editors were Karen Westover and Elaine Rosenberg;
the production supervisor was Richard A. Ausburn.
The cover was designed by Rafael Hernandez.
New drawings were done by Vantage Art Inc.
R. R. Donnelley & Sons Company was printer and binder.

PURCHASING AND SUPPLY MANAGEMENT
Text and Cases

This book is printed on acid-free paper.

2 3 4 5 6 7 8 9 0   DOC   DOC   9 0 9 8 7 6

ISBN 0-07-037089-3

Library of Congress Cataloging-in-Publication Data

Dobler, Donald W.
    Purchasing and supply management: text and cases / Donald W.
  Dobler, David N. Burt, —6th ed.
      p.   cm.—(McGraw-Hill series in management)   (McGraw-Hill
  series in marketing)
    Rev. ed. of: Purchasing and materials management. 5th ed. © 1990.
    Includes bibliographical references and index.
    ISBN 0-07-037089-3
    1. Industrial procurement.   2. Purchasing.   3. Materials
management.   I. Burt, David N.   II. Dobler, Donald W.
Purchasing and materials management.   III. Title.
IV. Series   V. Series: McGraw-Hill series in marketing.
HD39.5.D62   1996
658.7—dc20   95-36200

ABOUT THE AUTHORS

DONALD W. DOBLER recently retired as Corporate Vice-President for the National Association of Purchasing Management (NAPM), where he was responsible for its Certification and Education programs. He is also Dean Emeritus of the College of Business at Colorado State University. Earlier in his career, he worked as an engineer for Westinghouse Electric Corporation, and later as Manager of Purchasing and Materials for FMC Corporation at one of its industrial chemical operations. Throughout his career, Don Dobler has been active as a consultant to manufacturing and service organizations in both the operations and the educational/training areas. Since 1979, he has served as editor of the *International Journal of Purchasing and Materials Management,* the scholarly quarterly publication in the field. Dr. Dobler has published widely and is co-editor of *The Purchasing Handbook* and the *CPM Study Guide.* In 1987, he received NAPM's Shipman Gold Medal for distinguished service to the profession. He earned his Ph.D. degree in management from Stanford University.

DAVID N. BURT is National Association of Purchasing Management Professor of Supply Management at the University of San Diego. He is also a consultant for large and midsized manufacturers and service organizations that want to gain the benefits of strategic supply management. Previously, he served as the director of three supply management organizations. His articles have appeared in the *Harvard Business Review, Sloan Management Review, California Management Review, Journal of Marketing Research, International Journal of Purchasing and Materials Management,* and *Thexis.* David Burt is co-director of the University of San Diego's Strategic Supply Management Program, an annual meeting of 75 innovative procurement practitioners from around the world. He is director of the University's undergraduate and graduate programs in purchasing and supply management. Additionally, he is an active member of the NAPM and the Purchasing Council of the American Management Association. Dr. Burt received his Ph.D. degree from Stanford University in 1971, with a major in logistics.

CONTENTS

visits • Management; service • Just-in-time capabilities • The criticality of qualifying sources • Competitive bidding and negotiation • Five prerequisites for competitive bidding • Four conditions favoring negotiation • Two-step bidding/negotiation • The solicitation • Selecting the source

quality requirements • Determination of supplier capability • Defect
prevention versus defect detection • Motivation and control of suppliers •
Process capability analysis • Statistical process control • Supplier
certification • Inspection and quality control • Industrial applications •
The Malcolm Baldrige Award • The Deming Prize • ISO 9000 Quality
Standards • Design of experiments

performance • Purchasing and supply management review • Controlling
the timing factor • Controlling quantity and inventory investment •
Controlling prices and costs of materials • Controlling material quality •
Controlling source reliability • Managing supplier relationships; supplier
councils • Controlling internal coordination • Controlling procurement
efficiency; buyer models • Guidelines for development and use of control
systems • Industry's ten most commonly used measurements • The
CAPS benchmarking program • One firm's progressive approach to
appraisal and control • Reports to management

PREFACE

THE CHANGING BUSINESS SCENE

More major changes have occurred in business and industry during the past few years than in the two preceding decades. World-class competition, criticality of product/marketing timing, environmental objectives, price-based costing, escalating customer demands, and the tremendous emphasis on quality are but a few of the key challenges confronting most U.S. firms today. These developments, in turn, have had a monumental impact on the purchasing function in most organizations.

Clearly, purchasing is a professional activity now in transition. In most leading firms today, the function that used to be called purchasing, or procurement, has expanded to become *supply management*. Often included in this expanded responsibility is the integration of long-term strategic materials planning with the corporate strategic planning process. This approach inherently recognizes the pivotal role played by suppliers—they are the key to successful execution of the buying firm's plans. Purchasing's emerging role—proactive and more strategically oriented—includes participating collaboratively in key material requirements determinations and concomitant supplier qualification and selection activities; and it *focuses* on the management of subsequent supplier relations and performance, with an emphasis on quality.

The new sixth edition of this text incorporates these major developments and paradigm shifts, as the reader will note by the book's new title—*Purchasing and Supply Management*.

FOCUS OF THE BOOK

Historically, this text—now in its fourth decade—has been noted for its practical, yet thorough and rigorous approach to the conduct and management of the purchasing and materials management function. It has focused on the principles and strategies in the field, coupled with the function's interrelationships with the other principal business functions—product design, operations, marketing, and finance.

These essential characteristics are preserved in the sixth edition. And they are integrated with the major new or enhanced responsibilities—proactive environmental monitoring and materials planning; the management of supplier quality; supplier base reduction and management, including partnering agreements and strategic alliances; participation on cross-functional teams for product development, commodity analysis, and supplier sourcing; and so on.

This edition contains two new chapters—"Purchasing: A Profession in Transition" and "Purchasing for Institutions and Governmental Organizations"—and omits the earlier chapter dealing with federal procurement. Five of the chapters have been completely rewritten and most of the remaining chapters have received major revisions. Specific new or expanded and refined topic presentations are noted below.

New Concepts and Topics

- Transition to supply management
- Outsourcing and strategic aspects of make/buy decisions
- Cross-functional teams—and responsibility for purchasing
- Collaborative negotiation
- Management of hazardous materials
- Total Quality Management
- ISO 9000 standards; Baldrige Award; Deming Prize
- CISG; Foreign Corrupt Practices Act
- Impact on purchasing of the European Union and NAFTA
- Ethical and professional standards
- Green purchasing
- Purchasing's role in new product development
- Partnering and strategic alliances
- Purchasing's role in managing quality
- Sourcing with minority business enterprises
- Dealing with cost uncertainty
- Global sourcing
- Just-In-Time systems
- Investment recovery
- Bar coding and inventory identification systems

This edition of the text also includes 34 new cases, in addition to 57 tried and true carryovers, for a total of 91 cases. These real-life situations represent a wide variety of subjects, types, and degrees of sophistication that can be used for various instructional purposes.

USE OF THE BOOK

This is a versatile and flexible book designed for students at several levels. Historically, the book has been used most widely as a basic text at the undergraduate and the MBA levels. It is also used heavily in industrial training programs for practicing purchasing personnel—and as a key reference in preparing for the Certified Purchasing Manager (C.P.M.) examinations. Consequently, the book also finds use as a text for a second level undergraduate course, when supplemented with appropriate journal readings.

Each chapter is designed to "stand by itself." Hence, an instructor can select appropriate chapters to achieve the specific objectives of a given course. Similarly, cases vary in complexity and difficulty and can be used accordingly. Use of the available NAPM videotapes on specialized topics also facilitates this type of customized course design.

The *Instructor's Manual* contains a section that details how the book and the cases can be used to meet specific educational objectives.

ACKNOWLEDGMENTS

The collaboration and assistance of many people are involved in producing a book. The authors are indebted to so many people that individual acknowledgment is impossible. However, we do wish to thank those colleagues who reviewed most of the manuscript during its development and provided many helpful comments and suggestions: Charles F. Bimmerle, University of North Texas; Joseph L. Cavinato, Pennsylvania State University; Don Davis, University of Houston; Robert B. Handfield, Michigan State University; Martin E. Rosenfeldt, University of North Texas; Jay A. Smith Jr., University of Alabama, Birmingham; and Bill Strasen, California State Polytechnic University.

We also wish to express appreciation to those professionals who reviewed and made contributions to selected chapters—specifically, James Caltrider, University of San Diego; Margaret A. Emmelhainz, University of North Florida; Cheryl Johnson, AT&T; Claude Ridens, Industrial Resources; Donn Vickrey, University of San Diego; and Rick Zampell, Hewlett-Packard.

A special word of appreciation is extended to Stephen B. Gordon, Metropolitan Government of Nashville and Davidson County, Tennessee, who authored Chapter 32. Thanks are also expressed to Chan K. Hahn and Daniel J. Bragg, of Bowling Green State University, for their contribution to Chapter 22; and to Kathleen Little, NAPM, for her research, proofing, and indexing work.

Cases and related material for this edition have been drawn from many sources. The authors are indebted particularly to the National Association of Purchasing Management, to the National Association of Educational Buyers, and to Richard L. Mooney of the University Procurement Consulting Group for sharing some of their materials with our readers.

A special debt of gratitude is owed to Elaine Dobler and Sharon Burt. Their understanding and assistance in the preparation of the manuscript made a difficult task distinctly easier. We sincerely thank them both.

Donald W. Dobler

David N. Burt

PURCHASING AND SUPPLY MANAGEMENT

TEXT AND CASES

PART ONE

THE FUNCTIONS OF PURCHASING AND SUPPLY MANAGEMENT

PURCHASING: A PROFESSION IN TRANSITION

What Is a Profession?
A calling requiring specialized knowledge and often long and intensive preparation including instruction in skills and methods as well as in the scientific, historical, or scholarly principles underlying such skills and methods, maintaining by force of organization or concerted opinion high standards of achievement and conduct, and committing its members to continued study and to a kind of work which has for its prime purpose the rendering of a public service.

Webster's Third International

Is purchasing a profession? *Emphatically yes!* Professional purchasing/procurement/supply management[1] personnel contribute at least as much to the success of their organizations as other professionals in areas such as market-

[1]The terms "purchasing" and "procurement" are used interchangeably, although somewhat imprecisely, in many business organizations. The term "supply management" is used increasingly today to encompass the purchasing function and the procurement process—and more. Precise operational and strategic definitions of these terms are developed in Chapter 2. Throughout the book, however, the term "purchasing and supply management" is used to describe this composite business function.

ing, finance and accounting, engineering, and operations. *Specialized knowledge in scientific principles* of commercial, technical, and relationship management is essential. In no other profession are the opportunities to contribute greater. *Intensive preparation*—both in the classroom and through on-the-job experience—is required. The *skills* and *methods* required combine scientific principles with the art of developing and maintaining relationships.

Do the required skills have a *historic* foundation? Professor Harry Page (emeritus, George Washington University) in his draft manuscript on the evolution of purchasing writes:

> Inscribed clay tablets from the 13th Century BC days of the Phoenician traders refer to persons serving as "purchasing agents." The Holy Bible, in the Book of Deuteronomy, provides instruction for buyers in the honest use of weights and measures. Ancient purchase orders, written on parchment scrolls in the days of Julius Caesar, call for delivery of amphoras of wine, honey and oil.[2]

As is true of all modern business functions, many of the *scholarly principles* on which purchasing and supply management are built are taken from economics. Just as supply/demand and marginal analysis form the backbone of economics, the principles of determining the organization's requirements, selecting the optimal source, establishing a fair and reasonable price, and establishing and maintaining mutually beneficial relationships with the most desirable supplier provide the conceptual backbone of the purchasing and supply function. Numerous textbooks and articles in professional publications, including the *California Management Review, European Journal of Purchasing and Supply Management, Harvard Business Review, International Journal of Purchasing and Materials Management, International Journal of Physical Distribution and Logistics Management, Journal of Marketing Research, Sloan Management Review,* and the German language *Thexis,* provide an increasing flow of scholarly information on the supply profession.

The evolutionary nature of management in this field is such that *continued study* and self-improvement are necessary. A number of professional organizations, including the National Association of Purchasing Management, the American Production and Inventory Control Society, the National Contract Management Association, the National Institute of Governmental Purchasing, the Purchasing Management Association of Canada, the Chartered Institute of Purchasing and Supply (U.K.), and the International Federation of Purchasing and Materials Management, are dedicated to the continuing training and upgrading of their members. Today, over forty colleges and universities in the United States offer degree-granting programs in the area of purchasing and supply management.[3] Similar programs exist in Europe, Australia, Asia, and the rest of the Americas.

Does the purchasing profession render a *public service*? *Undeniably, it does!*

---

[2]Letter from Harry Robert Page dated May 12, 1994.

[3]Julie Murphree, "What's New in Formal Purchasing Programs?" *NAPM Insights,* August 1990, 10–11.

The impact of procurement professionals on the quality, cost, and productivity of their organizations is one of the keys to America's competitiveness in the global marketplace. And such competitiveness is the basis of value-adding employment.

Is the profession undergoing changes? Yes—and at an exponential rate! For example, several years ago, one of the authors was a speaker at the Tennant Company's annual manufacturing management conference in Minneapolis. At a dinner for the speakers, we asked a member of the Japanese Management Association, "You treat supply management as a strategic weapon, don't you?" The response was, "Ah, you're very perceptive!" More recently, we visited the head of purchasing at a highly successful multinational firm. This firm had just spent some $7 million studying purchasing and materials practices in Europe and Japan. When asked to share the insight gained, the director of purchasing responded that since this knowledge would give his firm a strategic, global competitive advantage, he was unable to honor our request. Even more recently, a marketing colleague returned from a visit to a major Japanese transplant in the Midwest. His bemused reaction to the visit was, "You're right. Purchasing runs the transplant!"

At organization after organization—whether manufacturing, service, institution, or government—one sees examples of what might be called proactive procurement[4] (stage 3) or strategic supply management[5] (stage 4) as depicted in Figure 1-1. Yet, based on self ratings, the majority of organizations appear to be somewhere else on the continuum shown in Figure 1-1.

The next twenty years will be the most exciting and challenging in the history of purchasing as organizations progress to a "10" in Figure 1-1 *and beyond.* "Kaizen" (continuous improvement) is the word of the day—and all tomorrows! Purchasing and supply management is becoming recognized as a function coequal in corporate importance with design, conversion, marketing, and finance. Compensation of procurement professionals is on a par with other professionals in leading-edge organizations. Purchasing and supply management is becoming (or has become) a critical participant in the organization's strategic planning function. But before we spend more time on the tremendous changes taking place, let's develop a historic perspective of the origins and roots of purchasing.

THE ORIGINS OF PURCHASING AND SUPPLY MANAGEMENT

Purchasing has long been considered one of the basic functions common to all organizations. Curiously, only during the past two centuries has purchas-

---

[4]See *Proactive Procurement: The Key to Increased Profits, Productivity and Quality* by David N. Burt, Prentice-Hall, Englewood Cliffs, N.J., 1984.

[5]See *The American Keiretsu* by David N. Burt and Michael F. Doyle, Business One-Irwin, Homewood, Ill., 1993.

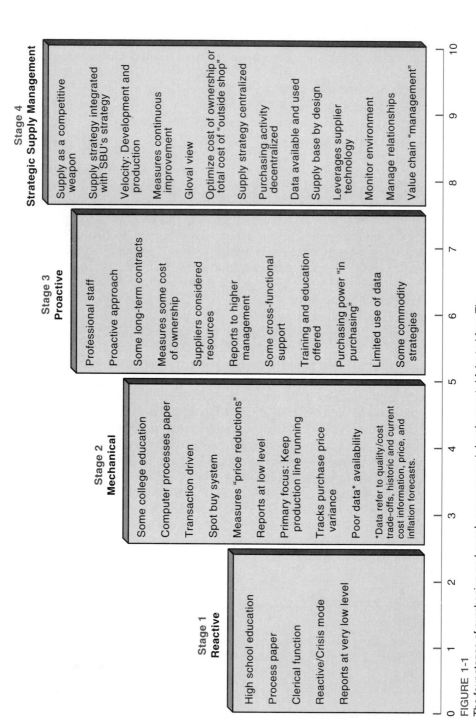

Stage 1
Reactive

High school education

Process paper

Clerical function

Reactive/Crisis mode

Reports at very low level

Stage 2
Mechanical

Some college education

Computer processes paper

Transaction driven

Spot buy system

Measures "price reductions"

Reports at low level

Primary focus: Keep production line running

Tracks purchase price variance

Poor data* availability

*Data refer to quality/cost trade-offs, historic and current cost information, price, and inflation forecasts.

Stage 3
Proactive

Professional staff

Proactive approach

Some long-term contracts

Measures some cost of ownership

Suppliers considered resources

Reports to higher management

Some cross-functional support

Training and education offered

Purchasing power "in purchasing"

Limited use of data

Some commodity strategies

Stage 4
Strategic Supply Management

Supply as a competitive weapon

Supply strategy integrated with SBU's strategy

Velocity: Development and production

Measures continuous improvement

Gloval view

Optimize cost of ownership or total cost of "outside shop"

Supply strategy centralized

Purchasing activity decentralized

Data available and used

Supply base by design

Leverages supplier technology

Monitor environment

Manage relationships

Value chain "management"

FIGURE 1-1
The four stages of purchasing and supply management development. (*Adapted from* The American Keiretsu *by David N. Burt and Michael F. Doyle, Business One-Irwin, Homewood, Ill., 1993.*)

ing been addressed in trade books and textbooks. For example, in 1832, Charles Babbage addressed the topic in his book, *On the Economy of Machinery and Manufacturing.*[6] One of the early books focusing on purchasing was written by H. B. Twyford of the Otis Elevator Company only some eighty years ago. Mr. Twyford was prophetic when he wrote:

> A (purchasing) staff which is entirely unsympathetic with the particular needs of the users of the material will fail to grasp what is one of the most essential things for their department. They will be dealing with papers and accounts instead of with men and things.[7]

It is believed that the first college textbook that focused on purchasing was authored by Howard T. Lewis of Harvard University in 1933.[8] Harvard University has long recognized the importance of purchasing and supply management. Its first course was offered in the 1917–1918 academic year. Today, the *Harvard Business Review* continues Harvard's tradition by publishing numerous timely articles on the subject.

Unfortunately, since senior management's interests historically have focused on marketing, R&D, finance, and operations, purchasing has all too frequently been subordinated to these familiar functions. With many notable exceptions, personnel historically assigned to purchasing had neither the skill nor the aptitude to lead this function to making its full contribution to the success of the organization. Ironically, during this period, purchasing was responsible for a significant portion of the cost of goods sold. Purchased materials were the source of a large share of the firm's quality problems. In many cases, purchasing had more impact on the bottom line than did any other function.

During the 1960s and 1970s, purchasing and materials management frequently used manual "kardex" systems to manage inventory. The buyer's major focuses were *purchase price* and the *prevention of line shutdowns*. A tertiary issue was the management of inventory. The typical department had a series of senior and junior buyers, clerks, an expediter, a purchasing manager, and perhaps several purchasing supervisors, depending on the size of the firm. Then the world of procurement changed.

By the end of the decade of the 1970s, the marketplace had become more international, from both a marketing and a supply point of view. Computers began to help in the management of inventory. Also, the cost of material had become a more important topic as oil embargoes and inflation drove unit costs

---

[6]Charles Babbage, Charles Knight Publishers, London, 1832, pp. 202, 216.

[7]H. B. Twyford, *Purchasing: Its Economic Aspects and Proper Methods*, D. Van Nostrand Co., New York, 1915, p. 56

[8]Howard T. Lewis, *Industrial Purchasing*, Prentice-Hall, Inc., New York, 1933.

up. Concurrently, the amount of automation in the production process increased, thus promoting specialization and driving the unit cost of production down. Senior managers realized that it frequently was less costly to purchase from outside specialized suppliers than to make an item or perform a service internally. All these forces resulted in material costs increasing as a percentage of the cost of goods sold.

These transitions brought about significant changes in purchasing. Purchasing and materials management began taking on a more important role within manufacturing, institutions, service firms, and government. Increased emphasis was placed on the control of inventory. During the early 1980s, many organizations became profitable largely through the careful management of their inventories. These organizations had discovered that inventories cost 25 to 35 percent of the value of the items carried, depending on the cost of capital. Computer-generated material requirements plans (MRP) and improved supplier discipline—including just-in-time inventory[9]—allowed customers to reduce their inventories significantly. New people who were educated in materials, logistics, and computers were recruited into the materials and purchasing function. Purchasing stopped accepting people who could no longer make a *value-added contribution*. "Kardex cards" disappeared, and MRP action reports surfaced. The buyer became a person who was handling higher part loads because of the "efficiency" of the materials management systems. There was no role change to the organization other than a recognition that purchasing and materials management was counted on to make a contribution to the financial success of the organization. Up until this point, when engineering assistance was required to interface with a supplier, manufacturing or design engineering would become involved, obviating the need for engineering expertise by the buyer.

THE TRANSITION TO SUPPLY MANAGEMENT

By the late 1980s material costs made up approximately 60 percent of the cost of goods sold in the United States. The impact of purchasing and materials managers on company assets became very significant *and very visible*. The U.S. manufacturing industry (and many service firms) emulated everything Japanese: kanban, quality circles, just-in-time, and kaizen (continuous improvement). These changes, coupled with electronic purchasing systems and growing recognition by senior management of the crucial role that must be played by purchasing and supply management, provided the stimulus for more change. Purchasing and materials managers began to see the need for two types of resources in their organizations: (1) a team of people who manage the operational and tactical activities of purchasing and materials management

---

[9]With just-in-time inventory, the required materials arrive just at the moment they are needed for incorporation into the item being assembled.

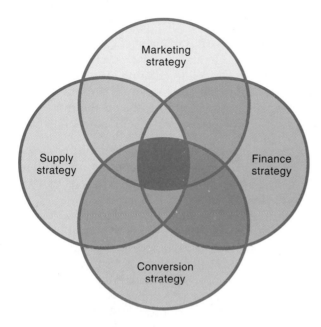

FIGURE 1-2
The elements making up the
strategic business plan.

(materials coordinators) and (2) supply managers who are involved in the development of broader policy aspects of the function.

Supply managers participate in new product development and are responsible for selecting sources, managing costs, developing and nurturing supplier partnerships and strategic alliances, and issuing long-term agreements with carefully selected suppliers. Materials coordinators are responsible for placing orders against these purchase agreements,[10] keeping the production lines running, and also minimizing inventories.

At the most progressive organizations, supply managers also are active participants in the organization's strategic planning process. An organization's supply strategy is becoming recognized as a strategic weapon equal in importance to the firm's marketing, conversion, and finance strategies.[11] These four strategies, when properly integrated, become the organization's strategic business plan, as shown in Figure 1-2.

Two Shifts in Focus

The progression from purchasing to supply management involves two major paradigm shifts: (1) from a focus on internal *processes* to value-adding *benefits* and (2) from a *tactical* to a *strategic* focus.

---

[10]Purchase agreements identify approved sources of supply, prices, and delivery criteria for carefully defined materials and services.

[11]Burt and Doyle, op. cit., p. 5.

Value-Adding Benefits

Historically, the performance of many purchasing managers and their organizations was measured and evaluated on changes in the purchase price of materials, their ability to keep the production line running, and the cost of their department's operation. Today, many world-class organizations expect their purchasing and supply management function to focus on the following five value-adding outputs of proactive procurement or supply management:

- *Quality.* The quality of purchased materials and services should be virtually defect-free [in some cases, 10 or fewer defective parts per million (PPM)]. (At many firms, over 50 percent of all quality defects can be traced back to purchased materials.)
- *Cost.* The purchasing and supply management function must focus on strategic cost management: the process of reducing the *total* cost of acquiring, moving, holding, converting, and supporting products containing purchased materials and services throughout the supply chain.
- *Time.* The purchasing and supply management function and its outside suppliers must play active roles in reducing the time required to bring new products to market. While it is difficult to provide supporting data, most professionals in supply, design, and manufacturing estimate that the time required to bring a new product to market can be reduced by 20 to 40 percent through the establishment and implementation of a world-class strategic supply management system (a "10" in Figure 1-1).
- *Technology.* The purchasing and supply management function has two key responsibilities in the area of technology: (1) It must ensure that the firm's supply base provides appropriate technology in a timely manner. (2) It must ensure that technology which affects the firm's core competencies (the "thing" that gives the firm its unique reason for being) is carefully controlled when dealing with outside suppliers.
- *Continuity of supply.* The purchasing and supply management function must monitor supply trends, develop appropriate supplier alliances, and take such other actions as are required to reduce the risk of supply disruptions.

Strategic Focus

As has been discussed, purchasing's historical focus has been on purchase price and continuity of supply. Supply management adds the following strategic activities:

- *Integration.* The firm's supply strategy must be integrated with the organization's marketing, conversion, and finance strategies and that of the corporation or strategic business unit.
- *Business environment.* Supply management must address the identification of threats and opportunities in the firm's supply environment.

- *Technology.* As discussed in the previous section, supply management must address issues of technology access and control. The firm wants to gain access to technology in its supply base while being careful not to create competitors through outsourcing activities.
- *Component and commodity strategies.* Supply management must develop formalized market-driven supply plans for critical purchased materials and services.
- *MIS.* Supply management must ensure that a timely, cost-effective, and comprehensive information system is in place to provide data required to make optimal supply decisions.
- *Supply base strategy.* Suppliers and the resulting supply base must be carefully developed and managed to ensure that the value chain to which the firm belongs is successful in an increasingly competitive marketplace.
- *Reporting responsibility.* The vice president of purchasing and supply management reports (or will report) to the chief of the strategic business unit, or in some cases to the CEO.
- *Centralization of development and management.* The development and management of the organization's supply strategy will be centralized, while low value-adding supply activities will be decentralized.
- *Use of senior procurement professionals.* The typical manufacturer will assign senior procurement professionals the responsibility of managing five to ten key supply relationships or alliances.
- *Use of professional personnel.* There will be fewer, but far more *professional*, personnel assigned to purchasing/procurement/supply management.

THREE MAJOR DEVELOPMENTS

Cross-Functional Teams

A number of years ago, one of the authors was in charge of a seven-person procurement office responsible for purchasing $20 million in goods and services. The biggest challenge was in dealings with the plant engineer. Virtually all the plans and specifications developed by this organization contained ambiguities which, if not corrected, could result in contract disputes and possible litigation. In order to reduce the time wasted in reviewing and requiring the revision of the plans and specifications, the members of the purchasing team offered to become involved earlier in the design process. The plant engineer summarily rejected this offer. He did not want outsiders "sticking their noses" in his operation.

Not surprisingly, when the plant engineer expressed a desire to become actively involved in the source selection process, he was politely notified to "go play in his own sandbox." Needless to say, such functional biases did *not* reduce cycle time (concept to customer), nor did they reduce costs.

Fortunately, this myopic approach to conducting operations is being replaced by a focus on what's in the best interest of the customer![12] Perhaps the most effective approach today which overcomes the negatives of specialization and departmental walls is the use of cross-functional teams. Such teams tend to be ad hoc organizations brought together to meet specific stated objectives such as the development of a new product or the negotiation of all terms and conditions of an agreement involving representatives of a buying and a selling organization. Others, such as commodity teams, may be ongoing.

Recently, members of the National Association of Purchasing Management were surveyed to study the current and future approach (individual or team) to the following activities:

1 Material requirements review
2 Specifications development
3 Make-or-buy analysis
4 Materials standardization
5 Determination of inventory levels
6 Quality requirements determination
7 Negotiation of price and terms
8 Supplier selection
9 Joint problem solving with suppliers
10 Supplier monitoring and analysis
11 Communication of specification changes
12 Productivity/cost improvements
13 Development of sourcing strategy
14 Market analysis
15 Price forecasting
16 Long-range purchasing planning
17 Determination of purchasing policy
18 Value analysis

The study indicated that a transformation from individual to team responsibility was taking place for all eighteen activities.[13]

A new product development team normally will be chaired by a design engineer or a marketing professional. Other members may come from supply management, manufacturing engineering, operations, quality, and one or more customer and supplier organizations. A negotiating team for a $10 million piece of hospital equipment may be chaired by purchasing, with cardiology, plant maintenance, and finance playing active roles.

Normally, membership on a cross-functional team will be a part-time assignment or will be full time for a specified duration. This approach ensures that the functional experts retain their identification with their functional areas and that

[12]Some eight years ago, a colleague from the Ford Motor Company proudly announced that department walls and functional chimneys were being torn down at Ford.
[13]Lisa M. Ellram and John N. Pearson, "The Role of the Purchasing Function: Toward Team Participation," *International Journal of Purchasing and Materials Management*, Summer 1993, pp. 3–9.

they are kept up to date and are able to report what they have learned to their functional colleagues. This approach also helps ensure the required support by the functional area of decisions made by the cross-functional team(s).

The most important implication of being part of a cross-functional team is that members will have to possess (or develop) excellent team behavioral and leadership skills. The days of John Wayne and the Lone Ranger are over. Cross-functional teams appear to be the way of the future.

Supply Chains

Perhaps the most interesting and challenging aspect of supply management is the development and management of the organization's *supply chain*. This chain is the upstream portion of the organization's *value chain* and is responsible for ensuring that the right materials, services, and technology are purchased from the right source, at the right time, in the right quality. The value chain is a series of organizations extending all the way back to firms which extract materials from mother earth, perform a series of value-adding activities, and fabricate the finished good or service purchased by the ultimate customer. See Figure 1-3.

The development and management of supply chains is one of the most challenging and exciting aspects of supply management. Once a service, commodity, or commodity class has been identified as being critical to the organization's operations, a strategic supply plan must be developed. This strategy must consider the organization's technology road map (which maps out where the organization is headed technologically); its supply base; a list of world-class suppliers for the item(s); plans for selecting and, possibly, upgrading the supplier; objectives for the relationship; and plans for managing and nurturing the relationship. Frequently, a cross-functional team, under the leadership of a supply professional, will be involved in the selection of the desired supplier, negotiation of applicable terms and conditions, and ongoing management of the relationship. This supply professional *must* be both technically and commercially competent.

Supplier Partnerships and Strategic Alliances

Another exciting and challenging change in how business is conducted is progressing in parallel with the development of supply chains: the development of supplier partnerships and strategic alliances. These partnerships and alliances *are not* legal entities, but, rather, mutually beneficial and open relationships wherein the needs of both parties are satisfied.

As shown in Figure 1-4, a customer organization will have many different types of supply relationships in support of its operations. Historically, the vast majority of buyer-seller relationships have been conducted in an arm's-length mode. In many cases, these relationships were adversarial wherein both buyer and seller believed that the only way to "get a good deal" was at the other's expense. Accordingly, much time and effort were involved in zero-sum games.

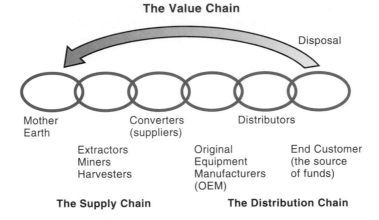

The Value Chain

Disposal

Mother Earth	Converters (suppliers)	Distributors
Extractors Miners Harvesters	Original Equipment Manufacturers (OEM)	End Customer (the source of funds)

The Supply Chain   **The Distribution Chain**

The Supply Chain (Network) Exploded

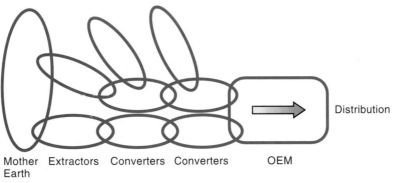

Distribution

Mother   Extractors   Converters   Converters   OEM
Earth

FIGURE 1-3
The value chain.

Common sense and advances in how we conduct business, enlightened self-interest, and the realization that competition is (or should be) between value chains—not between members of a value chain—all combine to motivate buyers and sellers to work in a collaborative mode. The natural outcome is the forming and nurturing of buyer-seller partnerships and, in selected cases, strategic alliances. The key characteristics of such relationships are (1) a compatability of interests; (2) mutual need; (3) a willingness to be open, sharing information as well as the benefits resulting from the relationship; and (4) perhaps of greatest importance, trust.

Much has been written about the challenges and the benefits of such relationships. The relevant point is that professionals from purchasing and supply management assume challenging responsibilities under such relationships. They become the leaders of cross-functional teams responsible for selecting the supply partner, negotiating the terms and conditions of the relationship on issues ranging from price to co-location of personnel and technology sharing, and managing the relationship during its life.

Arm's length relationships			Collaborative relationships	
Vendors	Traditional suppliers	Certified suppliers	Partnership type relationship	Strategic alliances

Lower value added relationships   Higher value added relationships

FIGURE 1-4
A continuum of supply relationships. (*Based on David N. Burt and Michael F. Doyle*, The American Keiretsu, *Business One-Irwin, Homewood, Ill., 1993.*)

This role by purchasing and supply management personnel requires a combination of technical expertise and leadership, communication, and team skills. The challenges are great; the rewards in both job satisfaction and compensation are equally great.

THE FUTURE

Industry, institutions, and government will continue to have a purchasing or supply function—one which grows in importance. Many of the manual tasks presently performed by purchasing will be automated or reassigned so that the personnel in supply management will be concerned with producing high value added, not paperwork. They will become increasingly technically proficient so that they can work with technical customers and suppliers. They truly will become managers of the organization's outside production!

Yet these individuals will have to possess a sound grounding in all the commercial aspects of purchasing and materials management. They will begin work as buyers, not as supply managers. Through application and hard work they will progress to become supply managers—one of the organization's most important professionals!

FOR DISCUSSION

1-1 There are several qualifying elements of a profession. Describe these elements and discuss how purchasing meets the requirements of each one.
1-2 How can purchasing be used as a "strategic weapon"? How do you think this idea will affect the way firms approach purchasing?
1-3 With respect to Figure 1-1, which describes the four stages of purchasing and supply management, what challenges would a firm face in its journey to stage 4?

1-4 According to H. B. Twyford, "A (purchasing) staff which is entirely unsympathetic with the particular needs of the users of the material will fail to grasp what is one of the most essential things for their department." Explain this statement.

1-5 Careful scrutiny is applied to anything that significantly impacts the bottom line of a company. With this in mind, discuss the irony of purchasing's historical role.

1-6 By the end of the 1970s, a chain of events had occurred which caused organizations to recognize that purchasing made a significant contribution to the financial success of a company. Describe that chain of events.

1-7 Explain the functional difference between materials coordinators and supply managers. What do supply managers contribute to the new product development process?

1-8 How does a firm's supply strategy relate to its marketing, conversion, and finance strategies?

1-9 Define and discuss paradigm shifts. How will it be a competitive advantage for a firm to make the shift from *processes* to value-adding *benefits*, and from a *tactical* to a *strategic* focus?

1-10 Why is it important to have the vice president of purchasing report to a chief officer of the company?

1-11 Describe the individual contributions that could be made by a cross-functional team to the following list of activities:

Specifications development	Market analysis
Value analysis	Productivity/cost improvements
Make-or-buy analysis	Determination of inventory levels

Assume the team consists of engineering, manufacturing, and purchasing personnel.

1-12 Discuss the difference between the value chain and the supply chain.

1-13 Effective supply chain management hinges on a comprehensive strategic supply plan. What must be considered when developing a supply plan? Why would the firm's technology road map be an important consideration?

1-14 Supply management professionals are required to possess a broad set of skills. What are some of these skills and why are they important? How have they changed?

1-15 "They (personnel in supply management) will become managers of the organization's outside production." Explain this statement.

CASES FOR CHAPTER 1

THE ROLE OF PURCHASING AND SUPPLY MANAGEMENT IN BUSINESS

KEY CONCEPTS

- Types of purchasing in business
- Purchasing's roles
    A function of business
    Materials and productivity
    Manager of outside manufacturing
- The purchasing function
    Purchasing function versus purchasing department
    Profit potential
    Return on investment
- Relations with other departments
    Purchasing and engineering
    Purchasing and operations
    Purchasing and marketing
    Purchasing and finance
- Evolution of the function, the process, and the organization
    Purchasing
    Procurement
    Supply management
    Materials management
- Synthesis

More major changes have occurred in business and industry during the past few years than in the two preceding decades. These changes, in turn, have produced a multitude of new developments in the organization and practice of activities associated with the acquisition and management of materials. As discussed in the preceding chapter, what used to be called purchasing or procurement clearly is in a stage of transition.

This transition is discussed in detail throughout the book. At this point, however, it is useful to say simply that the major change is one of management philosophy. Many of the individual activities in the purchasing and materials management field that used to be viewed as tactical are now moving rapidly toward the strategic end of the scale. In brief, to a great extent purchasing and materials management is becoming a strategic business function. The term used increasingly to connote this new view is *supply management*.

This second introductory chapter, then, presents an overview of the book's major thrust—purchasing and supply management. The purchasing function is discussed in the first portion, and the broader issue of supply management is reviewed in the latter part of the chapter.

TYPES OF PURCHASING IN BUSINESS

There are two basic types of purchasing in the business world: (1) purchasing for resale and (2) purchasing for consumption or conversion. And both are very different from the types of purchasing activities all of us are involved in as individual consumers. Purchasing for resale is performed primarily by *merchants*. From the beginning of time, this has been their primary responsibility. The quest for goods to sell was the motivating force that led to the discovery of the New World and the riches of the Indies. Ancient merchants spent some of their time dealing with sales problems, but they devoted by far the largest portion of it to the search for suitable purchases of new goods that had market appeal.

The basic problem of the merchant has not changed. Following the techniques of their predecessors, today's merchants determine what consumers want, buy it at a price to which they can add a profitable markup, and sell it to the customer at a satisfactory level of quality and service. For example, if a merchant decides his customers want washcloths when in fact they want sponges, his purchase will be a failure, regardless of any other consideration.

Today's merchants serve as the executive heads of trading firms. Additionally, they serve as the department heads in most merchandising houses, including department stores and mail-order houses. Every department within a merchandising house is normally a profit-centered unit. The buyers who head the units typically are completely responsible for the operation of their departments, including profits and losses. They must decide whether their customers want washcloths or sponges, and then buy what is wanted at a price which will permit resale at a profit.

Purchasing managers who buy materials for consumption or conversion are called *industrial buyers* or purchasers. This term includes buyers for manufacturing firms, service businesses, institutions (schools, hospitals, etc.), utilities, and various government agencies (city, county, state, etc.). Although some of their problems are similar to those of the merchant, for the most part industrial buyers operate very differently in quite different environments. They participate in determining what products their firm should make, what components or parts of these products their firm should manufacture, and which ones should be purchased from outside suppliers. After these decisions have been made, an industrial buyer prepares a long-term strategic purchasing plan for major materials, and researches and monitors appropriate supply markets. He or she plays a major role in qualifying and selecting suppliers, developing mutually profitable ongoing supplier relationships, and coordinating purchases with sales forecasts and production schedules. Most important, these buyers integrate the efforts of their departments with those of the other departments in the firm.

This book is concerned primarily with industrial buyers and how they contribute to the managerial decisions and to the success of their firms.

PURCHASING'S ROLES IN BUSINESS

What is the role of purchasing in business management? Why is it important? To answer these questions, the purchasing function will be observed from three points of view: first, as a function of business; second, as one of the basic elements required to accomplish productive work; and third, as the key department responsible for outside manufacturing.

Purchasing as a Function of Business

Purchasing is one of the basic functions common to all types of business enterprise. These functions are basic because no business can operate without them. All businesses are managed by coordinating and integrating these six functions:

1 *Creation,* the idea or design function, usually based on research
2 *Finance,* the capital acquisition and financial planning and control function
3 *Personnel,* the human resources and labor relations function
4 *Purchasing,* the acquisition of required materials, services, and equipment
5 *Conversion,* the transformation of materials into economic goods and services
6 *Distribution,* the marketing and selling of goods and services produced

The research and design engineering departments, the finance or controller's department, the human resources department, the purchasing department, the production departments, and the sales or marketing department are the common industrial titles of the organizational units responsible for performing these six functions. In institutional and nonindustrial enterprises, the same basic functions must be performed, but they may be identified by different names.

Depending on a company's size, these basic functions may be supervised by a single manager or by individual managers for each function. Regardless of how they are supervised, they are performed by someone in every business. Some small firms, for example, do not have a purchasing department; nevertheless, the purchasing function must still be performed. Sometimes it is performed by the president; at other times it is performed by an executive who administers several basic functions, including purchasing.

By its very nature, purchasing is a basic and integral part of business management. Why is this fact important? For a business to be successful, all its individual parts must be successful. It is impossible for any organization to achieve its *full* potential without a successful purchasing activity. In the long run, the success of a business enterprise depends every bit as much on the purchasing and supply executive as it does on the executives who administer the other functions of the business.

This is not to imply that all purchasing departments are of equal importance to the success of their companies. They are not; their importance varies widely. The importance of any individual business function within a specific organization is dependent on a number of factors. Among these factors are the type of business, its goals, its economic circumstances, and the way the enterprise operates to achieve these goals. In some situations purchasing can function in a perfunctory manner without jeopardizing a company's profit. These situations, however, are exceptions. Similar exceptions can be found in marketing, finance, or any other function of business. For example, in a firm that makes and sells a unique advanced technical product, the marketing department usually does not have weighty responsibilities. Engineering excellence and product performance do more than creative marketing to sell the product. On the other hand, marketing a highly competitive standard product requires ability of the highest order. In such companies, the marketing department has a position of major importance.

It also is interesting to note that the basic functions of business vary in importance within a given firm, over time, as the firm passes through its life cycle. For example, in the early life of the Hewlett-Packard Company (HP), a highly successful producer of precision electronic instruments, design engineering was the dominant function of the company. The company's products were so far advanced technically, and demand for them was so great, that their cost was relatively unimportant. HP products were literally self-selling. Under such circumstances, neither purchasing nor marketing was a major function within the company.

With the passage of time, however, conditions changed. Competent competitors entered the market. Consequently, HP products could no longer be sold at just any price, because the insatiable market for its products disappeared. As a result of these changes, the company had to reevaluate and reorganize its purchasing and marketing functions. As a consequence, purchasing and marketing both became functions of major importance.

Purchased Materials as Elements Required for Productive Work

The basic goal of any industrial activity is the development and manufacture of products that can be marketed at a profit. This goal is accomplished by the appropriate blending of what management authorities historically have called the *five M's:* machines, manpower, materials, money, and management. Materials today are the lifeblood of industry. Materials of the appropriate quality must be available at the right time, in the proper quantity, at the needed location, and at an acceptable total cost. Failure to fulfill any of these responsibilities concerning materials adds to company costs and decreases company profit just as surely as do outmoded production methods, inefficient personnel, and ineffective marketing activities.

Materials have not always been so vital. During the nation's industrial development, the relative importance of the five M's has continually shifted. In the management sense, materials became important around 1900. Before then they were rightfully taken for granted. They were simple, readily available, and cheap. The role of the purchasing function in business can be seen more clearly after exploring the reasons which caused the shift in the relative importance of the five M's.

During the first hundred years of the United States' industrial system, productivity increased very little. The availability of manpower and horsepower exceeded machine power almost one hundredfold. This relationship started to change around 1850. Between 1850 and 1950 an unbelievable increase in productivity took place. In 1850, productive power was divided as shown in Figure 2-1: 2 percent machine power and 98 percent horsepower and manpower. By 1900, this division of power became approximately equal. In 1950, the 1850 power relationship was reversed: 98 percent machine power and 2 percent horsepower and manpower.

Because manpower was the first source of productive power, the initial industrial emphasis was on the human element; labor costs represented the major operating expense. As machines and technology began to develop, management emphasis shifted toward them. As new products, specialized labor, and materials distribution became more complex, emphasis shifted toward scientific management. Still later, as both the complexity of materials and the volume of production skyrocketed, materials became an increasingly important element of cost. Consequently, emphasis naturally shifted toward this element of the five M's.

The introduction of better machines, coupled with progressive management to develop and utilize more sophisticated man-machine systems, made emergence of the factory system possible. This, in turn, sparked many industrial

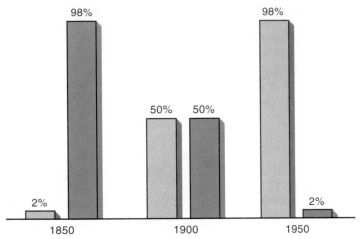

FIGURE 2-1
Power source relationships, 1850 to 1950. The gray columns represent
machine power, and the blue columns represent horsepower and human
labor.

changes—inventions such as the steam turbine, the electric motor, and automatic controls changed the entire complex of manufacturing. Gradually, materials became more complex, mechanization increased, automation emerged,
and labor became more specialized. These changes inevitably led to specialization in manufacturing and the continuing need for more sophisticated and
specialized materials.

As these trends accelerated and the volume of production increased, labor
costs *per unit* decreased. The reduction of unit labor costs increased the relative
cost and importance of materials in the manufacturing process. *Percentagewise,
labor costs went down while materials costs went up.* This change in the value of materials relative to total production costs continues to this day. For example, in 1945
materials represented approximately 40 percent of the manufacturer's total cost
to produce an airplane. In 1955 the materials proportion of total cost increased to
around 50 percent. By the mid-1970s the figure was slightly over 60 percent.[1]

Purchasing as the Manager for Outside Manufacturing

The materials that go into a typical company's products can originate from
either of two sources. The company's production department is the first
source; this department converts raw materials into processed parts. The com-

---

[1] "General Statistics for Industry Groups," *Annual Survey of Manufacturers*, U.S. Bureau of the
Census, Government Printing Office, Washington, D.C., 1970–1990.

pany's purchasing department is the second source. This department not only purchases raw materials, which the production department converts into processed parts, but also purchases finished parts and components. The parts made by the production department are combined in assembly with the items bought by the purchasing department to make the company's final products.[2]

The percentage of industrial components being purchased externally is constantly increasing compared with the percentage being manufactured internally. The trend toward specialization within our factory system inherently creates such a situation. The increasing specialization of technology and labor, the increasing complexity of new materials, and the increasing cost of high-volume specialty machines all tend to cause most industrial firms to buy more and make less. Not even the largest manufacturing concerns have sufficiently high volume requirements to compete with specialty manufacturers in all fields. For example, RCA, one of the nation's largest manufacturers of electronic equipment, buys many of its electronic components. This purchasing action is taken not because RCA cannot make these components, but because it can buy them less expensively from a specialty supplier. Researchers Hamel and Prahalad say the most successful firms identify, cultivate, and exploit their core competencies—they do the things they know how to do the best.[3]

The trend in manufacturing is toward the development of three distinct types of factories. The first type does not make finished end products; it is equipped with costly high-volume specialty machines and produces machined and fabricated parts in large quantities at low unit cost. These parts are sold to numerous factories of the second and third types. The second type of factory, like the first type, does not make finished end products; it makes subassemblies. The required parts for the subassemblies come from factories of the first type, or from the parts it makes, or from a combination of both. The third type of factory makes finished end products. As economic circumstances dictate, this type of factory assembles the finished product from a combination of the parts it makes (usually parts that are unique to its product) and the standard parts or subassemblies it buys from factories of the first and second types.

In the multiple-type factory system of today, then, most firms generally use two distinct sources of supply: *inside* manufacture and *outside* manufacture. The production department is responsible for inside manufacture, including the authority to schedule production in economical quantities, and to do so far enough in advance to have materials available when needed.

---

[2]The Du Pont Company was among the first to recognize the importance of whether a company should make something itself or let its purchasing department buy it. See Ernest Dale, *The Great Organizers*, McGraw-Hill Book Company, New York, 1960, p. 53.

[3]C. K. Prahalad, "Core Competence Revisited," *Enterprise*, October 1993, p. 20.

The purchasing department, on the other hand, has the primary responsibility and authority to source and schedule the delivery of outside production. Purchasing executives have the same managerial interests concerning their outside production as production executives have concerning their internal production. Both must schedule accurately. Production executives are interested in low unit costs and high quality. Purchasing executives are interested in keeping their *suppliers'* costs down. In addition, they are interested in maintaining scheduled deliveries and good quality control to assure that production schedules are met and that customer satisfaction is maximized.

THE PURCHASING FUNCTION

Purchasing Function versus Purchasing Department

Today most firms would agree that the purchasing function should be an integral part of the operation of the enterprise. All the functions of a business must mesh into a unified whole if management is to fulfill its basic responsibility of optimizing company profit. Each function must shoulder its portion of this responsibility.

There is a fundamental distinction, however, between the purchasing function and the purchasing department. They are not necessarily the same. As a function, purchasing is common to all types of business operations. The purchasing department, however, is an organizational unit of a firm whose duties may include responsibility for part or all of the purchasing function—and perhaps additional activities as well. In any case, the purchasing function is usually performed most effectively and efficiently by a centralized unit made up of buying specialists, who at times may work in conjunction with a more comprehensive cross-functional team of specialists.

Based on several recent studies, Table 2-1 shows the activities performed by purchasing departments today. "Buying," as used in the table, includes activities such as interviewing salespeople, negotiating with potential suppliers, analyzing bids, selecting suppliers, issuing purchase orders, handling problems with suppliers, and maintaining appropriate records. A review of the data makes it clear that the *primary* responsibilities of the typical purchasing department today focus on buying activities, materials studies, and purchasing market studies, including some longer-range materials planning. This focus is the product of an evolutionary process spanning the last fifty years.

Prior to the 1950s, more often than not, the purchasing department was a clerically oriented order-placing unit. In the ensuing years, progressive firms shaped their purchasing operations with a *managerial emphasis,* stressing the specialization of individual buying activities, professionalism, and contribution to the firm's profit. During the early to mid-1970s, the managerial orientation was augmented by an emphasis on longer-range *strategic planning* for materials. In many firms, this activity was integrated into the organization's

TABLE 2-1
ACTIVITIES FOR WHICH PURCHASING DEPARTMENTS ARE RESPONSIBLE

Activity	Percentage of departments responsible
Buying activities	100
Materials studies	75
Purchasing/market studies	70
Investment recovery (management of surplus and scrap)	57
Traffic	41
Inventory control	37
Warehousing and stores	34
Receiving	26

Source: H. E. Fearon, *Purchasing Organizational Relationships,* Center for Advanced Purchasing Studies, Tempe, Arizona, 1988. p. 30; and D. W. Dobler, D. N. Burt, and L. Lee, *Purchasing and Materials Management,* McGraw-Hill Book Company, New York, 1990, p. 11.

strategic planning process. Since the early 1990s, the strategic emphasis has been enhanced by purchasing participation in various cross-functional teams for activities such as:

- Product design
- Supplier qualification and selection
- Quality maintenance
- Commodity management

In the more progressive firms, this accelerating strategic emphasis is leading to the development of the *supply management* concept, as discussed in Chapter 1.

Unfortunately, in a relatively small number of firms, the purchasing department is still viewed as a clerically oriented operation. In such cases, the various management responsibilities associated with the purchasing function generally are performed by other functional and upper-level managers. In this book, however, to preclude the need for making numerous qualifying statements, it is assumed that the major portion of the purchasing function is assigned to the purchasing department. Hence, unless otherwise noted, reference to the purchasing department also means the purchasing function.

Profit Potential

How can purchasing increase company profit? For the typical manufacturing firm, purchasing is responsible for spending over half of every dollar the firm receives as income from sales. More dollars are spent for purchases of materials and services than for all other expense items combined, including expenses for wages, depreciation, taxes, and dividends. It is important for management to note that the cost of materials is approximately $2\frac{1}{2}$ times the value of all labor and payroll costs and nearly $1\frac{1}{2}$ times the cost of labor plus all other expenses of running the business. Figure 2-2 illustrates the percentage distribution of the sales dollar for the *average* manufacturing firm.[4] In high-technology firms, such as instrument manufacturers, the cost of materials (34 percent) is well below the composite industry average of 53.2 percent. On the other hand, in the petroleum industry the cost of materials (approximately 84 percent) is far above the composite average. Table 2-2 details materials cost data for these and other major U.S. industries.

The fact that purchasing is responsible for spending over half of most companies' total dollars highlights the profit-making possibilities of the purchasing and supply function. Every dollar saved in purchasing is equivalent to a new dollar of profit. Figure 2-3 illustrates this point. In simplified flowchart form, the figure shows, above the dashed line, key operating accounts that appear on a firm's operating statement. The interaction of these accounts produces a firm's profit margin, defined as:

[4]"Statistics for Industries," *Annual Survey of Manufacturers: 1991*, U.S. Bureau of the Census, Government Printing Office, Washington, D.C., 1993, pp. 1–5, 10, 28. Also *Statistical Abstract of the U.S., 1993*, U.S. Department of Commerce, Bureau of the Census, Government Printing Office, Washington, D.C., 1994, p. 553.

FIGURE 2-2
Percentage distribution of the sales dollar for the average U.S. manufacturing concern in 1991. (Source: Statistical Abstract of the U.S.: 1993, *U.S. Department of Commerce, Bureau of the Census, U.S. Government Printing Office, Washington, D.C., 1993, p. 553;* "Statistics for Industries," Annual Survey of Manufacturers: 1991, *U.S. Bureau of the Census, Government Printing Office, Washington, D.C., 1993, pp. 1–5, 10, 28.*)

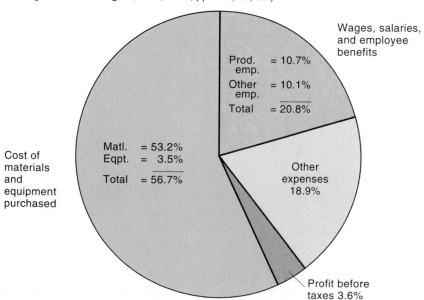

TABLE 2-2
MATERIALS COSTS AS A PERCENTAGE OF SALES INCOME

Industry	Purchased materials (in millions)	Gross sales (in millions)	Materials to sales ratio
Food and kindred products	$242,480.7	$387,600.9	62.6%
Tobacco products	7,551.4	32,031.7	23.6
Textile mill products	38,752.5	65,705.9	59.0
Apparel and other textile products	31,949.8	65,345.0	48.9
Lumber and wood products	43,466.0	70,568.9	61.6
Furniture and fixtures	19,348.8	40,027.3	48.3
Paper and allied products	70,605.0	128,824.1	54.8
Printing and publishing	52,936.2	156,684.6	33.8
Chemicals and allied products	138,060.3	292,325.8	47.2
Petroleum and coal products	132,389.0	158,076.4	83.8
Rubber and miscellaneous products	50,082.7	100,667.9	49.8
Leather and leather products	4,817.6	9,142.2	52.7
Stone, clay, and glass products	27,628.0	59,610.6	46.3
Primary metal industries	84,849.6	132,836.6	63.9
Fabricated metal products	80,126.9	157,077.3	51.0
Industrial machinery and equipment	118,886.2	243,479.4	48.8
Electronic and other electric equipment	80,766.1	197,879.5	45.4
Transportation equipment	209,737.0	364,032.1	57.6
Instruments and related products	43,241.6	127,159.7	34.0
Miscellaneous manufacturing industries	17,250.1	37,131.4	46.5
All industries	1,503,925.4	2,826,207.3	53.2

Source: "Statistics for Industries," *Annual Survey of Manufacturers: 1991*, U.S. Bureau of the Census, Government Printing Office, Washington, D.C., 1993, pp. 1–10.

$$\text{Profit margin} = \frac{\text{net income}}{\text{sales}}$$

Below the dashed line are selected balance sheet asset accounts that, when related to sales, produce one measure of a firm's asset turnover rate, defined as:

$$\text{Asset turnover rate} = \frac{\text{sales}}{\text{total assets}}$$

Top management's performance frequently is evaluated on the basis of the rate of return management is able to earn on the total capital invested in the business. Although return on investment (ROI) can be measured in various ways, one common measurement is:

$$\text{ROI} = \frac{\text{net income}}{\text{total assets}} = \frac{\text{net income}}{\text{sales}} \times \frac{\text{sales}}{\text{total assets}}$$

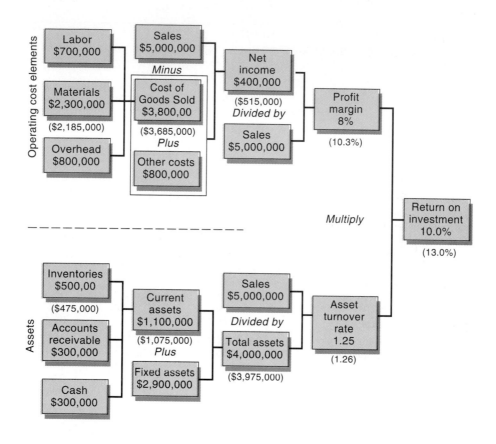

FIGURE 2-3
A graphic view of the relationships of basic elements which influence return on investment. The figures in parentheses reflect a 5 percent reduction in the cost of materials.

Therefore,

$$ROI = \text{profit margin} \times \text{asset turnover rate}$$

A firm's profit margin reflects management's ability to control costs relative to revenue. The asset turnover rate reflects management's ability to effectively utilize the firm's productive assets. Hence, a firm's management can improve ROI (and managerial performance) in three ways: (1) by reducing costs relative to sales, (2) by getting more sales from available assets (or increasing sales proportionately faster than investment), or (3) by some combination of the two. As seen in Figure 2-3, purchasing can contribute to ROI *both* by increasing profit margins and by increasing the asset turnover rate.

The numbers within the boxes shown in Figure 2-3 represent the current operating figures for the Able Company. The parenthetical figures that appear below the boxes represent new operating data resulting from an assumed 5 percent ($115,000) reduction in materials costs. Such a cost reduction would increase profit margins from 8 percent to 10.3 percent, and ROI from 10 percent to 13 percent. This equals a 0.6 percentage point $[(13 - 10)/5]$ improvement in return on investment for each 1 percent reduction in materials costs.

The 5 percent cost reduction used in the example is certainly a realistic expectation in a firm whose purchasing operation may not be particularly progressive or well run. In a well-managed operation, a more reasonable target might be in the 2 to 3 percent area. By inserting experimental figures into the ROI formula, the reader can determine the results and relative attractiveness of other approaches to profit or ROI improvement.

It was noted earlier that every dollar saved in purchasing is equivalent to a new dollar of profit. An additional dollar of income from sales, however, is not a new dollar of profit; applicable expenses must be deducted from the sales dollar to determine the remaining profit.

Returning to the Able Company illustration, a 5 percent reduction in materials costs ($115,000) produced a profit increase of $115,000. If the same profit increase were to be generated by increasing sales, what sales increase would be required? At the existing 8 percent profit margin, the following calculation provides the answer:

$$\text{Profit increase} = \text{new sales} \times 0.08$$
$$\$115,000 = \text{new sales} \times 0.08$$
$$\text{New sales} = \frac{115,000}{0.08} = \$1,437,500$$

This represents a sales increase of 28.8 percent:

$$\frac{1,437,500}{5,000,000} \times 100 = 28.8$$

So, for comparative purposes, in this case, the same absolute profit improvement can be achieved by reducing materials costs 5 percent or by increasing sales 28.8 percent—approximately a 6 to 1 ratio. If the profit margin were greater than 8 percent, the ratio would be somewhat less; if materials costs, as a percentage of sales, were higher, the ratio would be somewhat greater. Profit is the difference between income and outgo. And most progressive managers strive to improve the firm's profit position both by increasing sales revenues and by reducing the various elements of cost.

In practice, though, the cost of materials easily can vary as much as 10 percent, depending on the skill with which the purchasing and supply function is organized and operated. This is why there are usually more opportunities available for reducing purchasing costs 5 percent than there are for increasing sales volume 25 to 30 percent. Also, additional profit from purchasing savings can normally be made without significant increases in expense. If an increase is required, it is usually for only one person to do analytical work. On the other hand, additional profit from increased sales volume normally entails both increases in expenses and increases in the risk of capital. Additional expenses are incurred for such things as an expanded sales force, a larger advertising budget, additional plant capacity, overtime production pay, or some combination of these factors. Additional profit from sales, therefore, entails increased capital risk and increased management effort. Additional profit from purchasing normally entails only increased management effort, plus an occasional modest increase in management expense.

RELATIONS WITH OTHER DEPARTMENTS

A purchasing department is the hub of a large part of a company's business activity. By its very nature, purchasing has continuing relationships with all other departments in the firm, as well as with the firm's suppliers. Purchasing operations cut across all departmental lines. Figure 2-4 provides a graphic illustration of purchasing's many interfaces within the organization.

Purchasing and Engineering

Purchasing, engineering, and operations have many mutual problems. Design engineering, like operations, greatly influences the amount of time purchasing has to handle a procurement assignment. Engineering usually has the initial responsibility for preparing the technical specifications for a company's products and the materials that go into them. To exercise this responsibility effectively, engineering must have the constant help of purchasing and operations. A number of firms have initiated early purchasing and early supplier involvement programs to assist in this effort. The quality, the prices paid for production materials, and the costs to fabricate them are inextricably related to their specifications. Similarly, specifications can be written in a manner that reduces or enlarges the number of firms willing to supply specific items. If profit is to be maximized, the materials specified by engineering must be both economical to procure and economical to fabricate, and they should normally be available from more than one efficient, low-cost producer. And, clearly, the quality must satisfy the ultimate customer.

Purchasing and engineering occasionally differ in their concepts of materials problems. This is understandable. Engineers naturally tend to design conservatively; hence, their specifications may provide amply for quality, safety, and performance. By training, the engineer may be inclined to seek the "ideal" design, material, or equipment without complete regard for cost or timing. The buyer, on the other hand, often believes it is appropriate to reduce the designer's performance goals and safety margins, and to work closer to actual

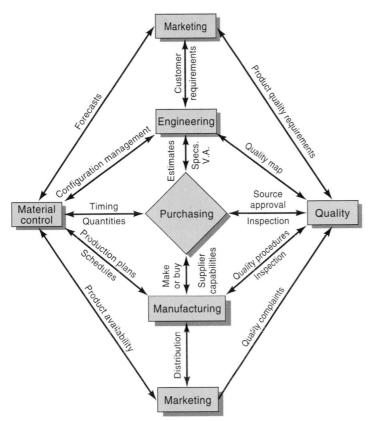

FIGURE 2-4
The many internal interfaces of the purchasing function.

performance requirements. Is an expensive design with a high safety factor necessary if a less costly design with a lower safety factor will do the job? Why use costly chrome plate if brushed aluminum is adequate? Clearly, such conflicting departmental interests cannot always be resolved easily. The answers to such problems are seldom clear-cut. Mutual understanding and a willingness to give and take are required from both sides if mutually satisfactory solutions are to be reached.

Purchasing and Operations

The purchasing-operations relationship begins when the using department transmits its manufacturing schedule or materials requisitions to the purchasing department. Purchasing subsequently translates these documents into a procurement schedule. Purchase timing is often a cardinal difficulty in making this translation. When the user does not allow purchasing sufficient time to purchase wisely, many needless expenses inevitably creep into the final costs of a company's products. When purchasing has inadequate time to properly qualify suppliers, to develop competition, or to negotiate properly, premium prices are certain to be paid for materials. Costly *special production runs* and *premium transportation* costs are two additional factors that frequently result from inadequate purchasing lead time.[5]

The most serious problem stemming from insufficient procurement lead time in manufacturing is a production shutdown. In most process types of operation (chemicals, cement, paint, flour, etc.), either equipment runs at nearly full capacity or it does not run at all. Consequently, material shortages in these industries can be catastrophic, resulting in complete production stoppage. Losses resulting from material shortages in nonprocess industries are not always so disastrous or apparent. A production shutdown in a metal fabricating shop, for example, can be piecemeal. The indirect costs of such shortages, consequently, are often hidden in production costs. One or two machines from a large battery of perhaps fifty can be shut down as a routine occurrence. Conventional accounting records fail to reveal the financial impact of this kind of slow profit-draining inefficiency.

Coordination between purchasing and operations pays off in many ways. For example, a more expensive alternative material that will save the company money can on occasion be selected. This may sound like a paradox. "Pay more and save more"—how can this happen? Savings in manufacturing and assembling costs often can exceed the increased purchase costs. In the normal manufacturing operations of casting, forging, machining, grinding, stamping, and so on, some materials are much more economical to work with than others. For example, the government has saved thousands of dollars by using bronze instead of steel extrusions in aircraft elevator and rudder counterweights. Bronze costs more than steel, but savings in machining time more than offset the increase in material cost. In this case, not only is the direct cost reduced, but as an added benefit skilled machinists and expensive machine tools are freed to do other high-priority work.

Going beyond these day-to-day operational interfaces, purchasing and operations must coordinate effectively to achieve some of a firm's key strategic goals. For example, manufacturing management is striving increasingly to achieve faster "time to market" performance, and to reduce the time required for product changeovers and tool and line setup work. Purchasing must be able to assist in these efforts. They raise issues of getting a faster response from suppliers, working with suppliers to improve their capabilities, and so on. In these types of activities, it is imperative that operations and purchasing and supply management work together closely.

The scenarios just described are but a few of the numerous operating situations that illustrate the continuing and coordinative nature of the purchasing and operations relationship.

---

[5]It is purchasing's responsibility to keep users informed concerning what lead times are for all categories of production materials.

Purchasing and Marketing

All companies recognize the direct relationship between the marketing function and profit. In their enthusiasm to increase sales, however, many companies overlook the leaks in profit that can occur when the sales activity is not properly meshed with the purchasing and production activities.

The purchasing-production-sales cycle has its genesis in a sales forecast. The forecast is the basis for the production schedule, which in turn is the basis for the purchasing schedule. The sales forecast also influences a firm's capital equipment budget, as well as its advertising campaigns and other sales activities.

Prompt communication to production and purchasing of changes in the sales forecast permits these departments to modify their schedules as painlessly and economically as possible. Likewise, changes in the production schedules should be communicated immediately to sales representatives. This action permits sales to alter its distribution schedule in a manner that will not alienate customers. Purchasing must immediately transmit to sales, as well as to other management groups, information concerning increases in material prices. This permits sales to evaluate the effect of price rises in price estimates given for future sales quotations, on current selling prices, and on plans for future product lines.

Purchasing and sales must wisely blend their interests in the delicate area of *reciprocity* (buying from customers). If satisfactory *legal* reciprocal transactions are to be developed, they must be pursued with an understanding of the true costs of reciprocity. Buying from friends can be good business, but not when it is done at the expense of product quality or company profit. In a zest for increased sales, a company can lose sight of the fact that increased sales do not always result in increased profit. Sometimes increased sales result in *decreased* profit if they simultaneously require an increase in purchasing costs.

A purchasing department can be of major help to its sales department by serving as its practical sales laboratory. A firm's purchasing department is the target for many manufacturers' sales operations. Purchasing's files are replete with sales literature, policies, and promotional approaches of a broad range of manufacturers and distributors. Buyers are aware of the personal selling methods that sales representatives have used most effectively on them. They are equally aware of sales practices that fail or that irritate them. Therefore, a company's buyers can be an excellent source of information for developing and refining the company's own sales policies and procedures.

Purchasing and Finance

Purchasing's relationship with finance is different from its relationships with both sales and operations. The difference stems from the fact that cost determinations cannot be hidden in the purchasing-finance relationship as they often can in the other relationships. The importance of good financial planning is highlighted by the fact that poor financial planning is the major cause of business failure. Among the basic data needed by an organization for proper planning of its working-capital and cash flow positions are accurate sales forecasts and accurate purchasing schedules. It is just as important for purchasing to inform finance of changes in its schedule as it is to inform production and sales of these changes.

There are many economic factors that periodically bring about favorable and completely unexpected buying opportunities. For example, a supplier may momentarily have excess capacity because of the cancellation of a large order. During the period that this condition exists, the supplier may sell products at prices designed to recover only out-of-pocket costs.[6] This may be done because it is in the long-term interest of the firm not to reduce its labor force. The potential income from such unexpected buying opportunities must be weighed against the potential income from other alternative uses of the company's capital.

Regardless of the price advantage obtainable, the right time to buy from the standpoint of business conditions is not always the right time to buy from the standpoint of the company's treasury. If the purchasing department makes commitments to take advantage of unusually low prices without consulting the finance department, the company could find itself paying for these purchases with funds needed for other purposes. On the other hand, if the finance department does not strive diligently to make funds available for such favorable buying opportunities, the company may have to pay higher prices later for the same material.

Prompt payment of suppliers is a key contributor to good supplier relations. During the 1970s, for example, Timex had a policy of paying its suppliers the day the supplier's invoice and the receiving report arrived in the accounts payable office. Thus, Timex became a preferred customer of many of its suppliers. During the two material shortage periods of the 1970s, Timex's preferred customer status allowed it to avoid the shortage problems experienced by most firms. Hence, a cooperative relationship between purchasing and finance clearly can impact the development of good supplier relations.

EVOLUTION OF THE FUNCTION, THE PROCESS, AND THE ORGANIZATION

So far, you have been reading about four concepts:

- The purchasing function
- The procurement process
- Supply management
- Materials management

---

[6]A manufacturing concern can be thought of as having two sets of costs: out-of-pocket costs and all other costs. Out-of-pocket costs include direct costs paid for making a specific product. They do not include rent of the factory, taxes, insurance, etc., all of which must be paid whether or not a specific product is made. See Chapter 15.

And none of them has yet been defined with any precision. It is time now to do that—and to show how they relate to each other.

Purchasing

The purchasing function comprises the essential activities associated with the acquisition of the materials, services, and equipment used in the operation of an organization. The major types of activities are:

1 Coordination with user departments to identify purchase needs
2 Discussions with sales representatives
3 Identification of potential suppliers
4 The conduct of market studies for important materials
5 Negotiation with potential suppliers
6 Analysis of proposals
7 Selection of suppliers
8 Issuance of purchase orders
9 Administration of contracts and resolution of related problems
10 Maintenance of a variety of purchasing records

During the early years, the purchasing function tended to be handled in a reactive, "staff support" manner. Subsequently, it was conducted more professionally with a managerial emphasis. But it was still viewed largely as a group of *tactical* activities. In those firms that have not moved toward the development of the procurement or supply management concepts, the importance of the purchasing function has not diminished, but often it is not being fully realized because it still has a tactical, operations-oriented focus.

The firms that have seen the strategic potential inherent in this function have tended to enhance its basic activities by expanding them and developing procurement or supply management operations.

Procurement

The procurement process, or concept, encompasses a wider range of supply activities than those included in the purchasing function. And it typically includes a broadened view of the traditional buying role, with more buyer participation in related materials activities. Specific activities usually included in the process are:

1 Participation in the development of material and service requirements and their specifications
2 Conduct of materials studies and management of value analysis activities
3 Conduct of more extensive material market studies
4 *Conduct of all purchasing function activities*
5 Management of supplier quality
6 Purchase of inbound transportation
7 Management of investment recovery activities (salvage of surplus and scrap)

In essence, procurement tends to be broader and more proactive, with some focus on strategic matters, as compared with the typical implementation of the purchasing concept.

Supply Management

Supply management is a process responsible for the development and management of a firm's total supply system—both the internal and the external components. At an operational level, it includes and expands the activities of the purchasing function and the procurement process. Its major focus, however, is strategic. This is reflected in the activities added to the scope of its responsibilities—all of which have two characteristics: (1) They deal with activities that have great potential for impacting the success of the firm, and (2) they tend to be interdisciplinary in nature and integrate supply actions with those of other key players in the firm.

Specific activities generally included in supply management are:

1 Early purchasing involvement (EPI) and early supplier involvement (ESI) in product design and subsequent specifications development for important items, typically through the use of cross-functional teams
2 *Conduct of all purchasing function and procurement process activities*
3 Heavy use of cross-functional teams in supplier qualification and selection
4 Heavy use of purchasing partnering arrangements and strategic alliances with suppliers—to develop close and mutually beneficial linkages with key suppliers in the value chain and to control quality and costs.
5 Continuous identification of threats and opportunities in a firm's supply environment
6 Development of strategic, long-term acquisition plans for all major materials
7 The monitoring of continuous improvement in the supply chain
8 Active participation in the corporate strategic planning process

The supply management concept, at the present time, represents the most advanced stage in the evolutionary development of the purchasing/procurement/supply sphere of activity. The major characteristic that differentiates it from its predecessors is that it focuses heavily on the strategic aspects of the key elements of a firm's supply system.

Figure 2-5 summarizes the scopes of the three acquisition concepts and illustrates how they relate to each other.

Materials Management

The materials management concept is quite different from the purchasing/procurement/supply management concepts just discussed. It is basically an organization concept that, from a managerial perspective, is designed to enhance

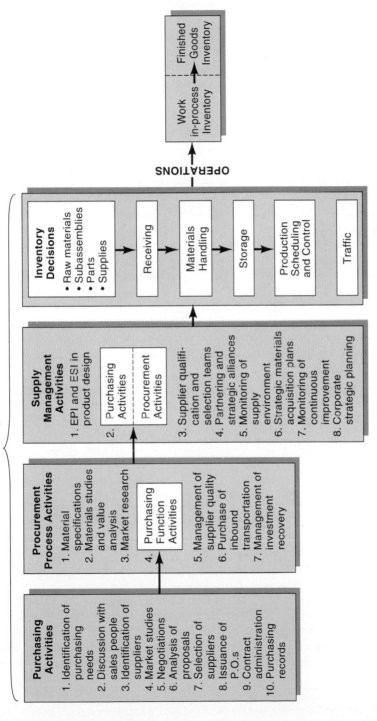

Materials Management

Purchasing Activities
1. Identification of purchasing needs
2. Discussion with sales people
3. Identification of suppliers
4. Market studies
5. Negotiations
6. Analysis of proposals
7. Selection of suppliers
8. Issuance of P.O.s
9. Contract administration
10. Purchasing records

Procurement Process Activities
1. Material specifications
2. Materials studies and value analysis
3. Market research
4. Purchasing Function Activities
5. Management of supplier quality
6. Purchase of inbound transportation
7. Management of investment recovery

Supply Management Activities
1. EPI and ESI in product design
2. Purchasing Activities / Procurement Activities
3. Supplier qualification and selection teams
4. Partnering and strategic alliances
5. Monitoring of supply environment
6. Strategic materials acquisition plans
7. Monitoring of continuous improvement
8. Corporate strategic planning

Inventory Decisions
- Raw materials
- Subassemblies
- Parts
- Supplies

Receiving

Materials Handling

Storage

Production Scheduling and Control

Traffic

OPERATIONS

Work in-process Inventory | Finished Goods Inventory

Tactical Focus ◄————————► Strategic Focus

FIGURE 2-5
The relationship of purchasing/procurement/supply management activities—with materials management and the flow of materials decisions through a firm.

37

coordination and control of the various materials activities. The discussions earlier in the chapter should make it clear that operationally a number of functional interdependencies exist among many of a firm's materials activities, even though they may be located in several different departments. Figure 2-5 shows the flow of materials decisions and related activities through a typical firm—the firm's materials system. A decision or action taken at any point in the materials chain usually impacts a number of other activities or decision points in the chain. Clearly, these activities make up one or more subsystems, which are part of a firm's larger production or operations system. Consequently, most organizations find it necessary to coordinate the various materials activities very carefully.

The required coordination can occur in two ways. First, it may be achieved by developing a straightforward set of reporting, communication, and control procedures designed to enhance coordinated decision making among the involved groups or departments. The second approach involves an organizational rearrangement that consolidates some of the individual materials activities into larger groups for administrative purposes. In this case, coordination typically is easier to achieve because one manager has line responsibility and authority for those activities grouped in his or her operating unit, with the possibility of developing a more effective team-oriented operation.

The materials management form of organization can be utilized with any of the three purchasing and supply management concepts, or a unique combination of them. In fact, today approximately 70 percent of the major U.S. manufacturing firms embrace some operating form of the materials management type of organization.[7] As shown in Figure 2-5, the specific materials activities typically found in a materials management organization are:

1 Purchasing and supply management activities
2 Inventory management
3 Receiving activities
4 Stores and warehousing
5 In-plant materials handling
6 Production planning, scheduling, and control
7 Traffic and transportation

CONCLUSION

An objective analysis of the material in this chapter leads to one inescapable conclusion—namely, that the *potential* importance of the purchasing and supply management function is very great, indeed, for a majority of U.S. business organizations. Purchasing is an essential business function that should make the same level of contribution to a firm's success as the other major business

---

[7]H. E. Fearon, *Purchasing Organizational Relationships*, NAPM Inc., Tempe, Ariz., 1988, p. 17.

functions. Here is just one example—suppliers are essentially an extension of a firm's own productive operations. As such, it is the responsibility of purchasing and supply to ensure that the innovativeness and the quality of material and service provided by these external organizations are at least fully compatible with the requirements of the purchasing firm.

Purchased materials consume over half of the average manufacturing firm's sales revenue. Consequently, the profit potential of effective management of the purchasing and supply activities is enormous compared with other practical management alternatives. For example, in many firms it is possible to reduce aggregate material costs by 4 percent or more. To achieve the same resulting increase in profit, net sales would have to be increased approximately 25 to 30 percent.

Purchasing occupies a pivotal position in a firm's information and decision-making systems. It is the key linkage, along with marketing, between a firm's various product design groups and its ultimate customers. Its work with suppliers produces the information needed by the finance, material control, and quality assurance groups to perform their duties in a timely and effective manner. And, finally, its knowledge of supplier capabilities and its participation in make-or-buy studies provide essential information for management in the manufacturing segment of a firm's operation. In a nutshell, purchasing and supply activities cut across all departmental lines—and, consequently, the function is the hub of much of a firm's business activity.

Over the years, the *purchasing* function has become more complex, more professional, and more encompassing—evolving in many firms into *procurement*, and now into what some leading-edge firms call *supply management*. The shifting focus is from the tactical to the strategic. The philosophy and the resulting practices found in business and industry today are seldom recognizable as a precise implementation of any one of these three concepts. The purchasing and supply function in most companies is a mixture of the three, whose exact character depends on the nature of the firm's products, the competitive environment, the nature and criticality of the firm's materials, its key supply markets, and the firm's management philosophy. The mix typically is somewhat different in each organization. As materials and markets become more complex, and as competition escalates, the resulting purchasing and supply operation tends to become increasingly strategic. Nevertheless, in most firms the *full potential* of the purchasing and supply management function has yet to be developed and realized.

FOR DISCUSSION

2-1 "To a great extent, purchasing and materials management is becoming a strategic business function." Comment on this statement.

2-2 Describe the two types of purchasing in the business world. Discuss the differences between the two. Have you had any experience with either? Explain how your experience relates to the discussion in this chapter.

2-3 How does the purchasing responsibility of an "industrial buyer" differ from that of a "merchant"?

2-4 "Purchasing is more important in an industrial firm today than it was 100 years ago." Discuss.

2-5 What challenges does knowledge of the potential of good purchasing offer you? How can this purchasing course help you?

2-6 Do you think it would be easier for a company to increase its profit by increasing the efficiency of purchasing or by increasing sales? Explain.

2-7 How does efficient purchasing improve ROI? Discuss.

2-8 Economists frequently make the statement that labor costs make up the bulk of industrial expenditures today. Does this contradict the view taken in this chapter? Discuss.

2-9 Discuss the key factors involved in purchasing-production relationships.

2-10 Researchers Hamel and Prahalad have found that the most successful firms identify and exploit their core competencies. What do they mean?

2-11 How can increased purchasing costs sometimes result in greater profit for a company? Is it possible to "pay more and save more"? Explain.

2-12 Discuss the issues involved in the daily operating relationships between purchasing and design engineering.

2-13 Explain how sales and purchasing can help each other by establishing a good relationship.

2-14 "The *potential* importance of the purchasing and supply management function is very great, indeed, for a majority of business organizations." Discuss.

2-15 Discuss how the economic changes in both the United States and abroad are influencing purchasing and supply management's role in business management.

2-16 Discuss the important differences between purchasing and procurement.

2-17 Discuss how the purchasing function, the procurement process, and supply management are related.

2-18 Define and discuss the significance of the materials management concept.

2-19 Compare and contrast supply management and materials management.

2-20 Explain why losses in the purchasing and supply management function are not readily visible but sales and production losses are.

CASES FOR CHAPTER 2

3

OBJECTIVES AND POLICIES

KEY CONCEPTS

- Objectives of purchasing and supply management
    The managerial perspective
    The functional level
    Strategy for specific buying plans
- Basic operating policies
    Policies defining purchasing responsibility
    Policies affecting external relationships and image
    Policies on pricing and supply sources
    Policies concerning ethical practices
    Policies concerning minority business enterprises
- The policy manual

OBJECTIVES

The objectives of purchasing and supply management can be viewed from three levels: (1) a very general managerial level, (2) a more specific functional or operational level, and (3) a detailed level at which precise strategic buying plans are formulated.

From a top managerial perspective, the general objectives have traditionally been expressed as the *five rights* that management expects the department to achieve—the acquisition of materials:

1 Of the *right quality*
2 From the *right supplier*
3 In the *right quantity*
4 At the *right time*
5 At the *right price*

A sixth factor implied in these items includes the desired *services* necessary for optimal supply and utilization of the materials.

Even the casual observer will detect just a bit of the "apple pie and motherhood" syndrome reflected in these five rights. Idealistically, they are all highly desirable. In practice, however, the department can rarely fulfill them all equally, because in some procurements conflicts inherently exist between some of the objectives. For example, the time required for a supplier to design a tool used in manufacturing a specialized high-quality gear to a buyer's specification might not permit the supplier to perform within the specified time frame. So usually some trade-offs must be made. From a practical point of view, supply personnel seek a reasonable balance among them.

From an operating or functional perspective, then, it is necessary to probe more deeply to develop a set of statements that provide practical and useful targets for decision-making purposes. In this sense, the eight basic objectives of purchasing and supply management are identified and discussed briefly below. Each of the items is the topic of one or more chapters later in the book.

1 *To support company operations with an uninterrupted flow of materials and services.* This is the most fundamental of all purchasing and supply objectives. In a logistical sense this is a key reason for the existence of the department. Responsibility for performance of the function typically is located in a single operating unit, thereby facilitating coordination and control of the supply activities.

2 *To buy competitively.* Buying competitively involves keeping abreast of the forces of supply and demand that regulate prices and availability of materials in the marketplace. At times, it also involves an understanding of a supplier's cost structure, coupled with an ability to help improve this cost structure—and then to negotiate price and service arrangements that are fair relative to the supplier's actual costs. A buyer who pays significantly more than his or her competitor does for a given material or service generally is not buying competitively.

3 *To buy wisely.* Buying wisely involves a continual search for better values that yield the best combination of quality, service, and price, *relative to the buyer's needs.* This frequently involves coordination with users in defining the need. It may also involve coordinating and reconciling users' needs with suppliers' capabilities, perhaps through the use of cross-functional design teams, to achieve optimal value considering both issues. A firm that purchases high-grade bond paper for use in internal office communications that could be performed as well with less expensive, softer stock paper usually is not buying wisely. It is the combination of buying com-

petitively and buying wisely that typically contributes most to the profitability of the firm.

4 *To keep inventory investment and inventory losses at a practical minimum.* Although maintaining a large inventory is one way to achieve objective 1, it is also costly. Generally speaking, it costs most firms between 25 and 35 percent of the average inventory value per year for the convenience of having the inventory available. Hence, the supply management job is to achieve a a reasonable balance between the level of inventory required to support operations and the cost of carrying the inventory. Just-in-time production/inventory systems help considerably in achieving this objective.

Through proper buying, packaging, and storing, it is also the department's objective to minimize losses that occur as a result of deterioration, obsolescence, theft, and so on.

5 *To develop effective and reliable sources of supply.* Cooperative suppliers that are willing to work with a buyer to help solve the buying firm's problems and to minimize its materials-related costs are an invaluable resource. Progressive buyers today tend increasingly to "buy suppliers," as opposed to simply "buying products." The identification, investigation, selection, and in some cases development of competent and responsive suppliers is a buyer's paramount responsibility. It is difficult indeed for a firm to perform optimally if it cannot depend on the planned performance of a reliable contingent of suppliers. It is this vital requirement that has led many firms to develop partnering arrangements or strategic alliances with their key suppliers. This can be an effective way of working cooperatively to achieve the objective.

6 *To develop good relationships with the supplier community and good continuing relationships with active suppliers.* Good relationships with suppliers are imperative, and good relationships with potential suppliers are invaluable. The achievement of the preceding objective on a continuing basis is virtually impossible if mutually satisfactory continuing relationships are not maintained. Potential suppliers are much more interested and eager to acquire a firm's business if the buying firm is likely to be a "good customer." And when a purchase contract has been formed with a supplier, the myriad operating problems that inevitably arise throughout the life of the contract are much more easily and effectively solved when the relationship is sound and mutually beneficial. Suppliers naturally direct their research, provide advance information on new products and prices, and in general give better service to such customers.

7 *To achieve maximum integration with the other departments of the firm.* It is essential for buyers to understand the major needs of their using departments, so that these needs can be translated into materials support actions. While these actions vary from firm to firm, they normally require the purchasing and supply operation to support a using department in its major responsibilities. The most common types of support involve

actions such as developing materials standardization programs (in coordination with ongoing design programs), forecasting future prices and general business conditions, performing economic make-or-buy analyses, and serving as a repository of information and data from suppliers regarding new materials, processes, prices, and materials availability.

8 *To handle the purchasing and supply management function proactively in a professional, cost-effective manner.* Management should expect the preceding seven objectives to be achieved in a professional manner at a cost that is commensurate with their value to the total organization. This involves, among other things, the continuous examination of the purchasing process for possibilities to streamline it and enhance its "value-added" capabilities. Firms are increasingly questioning *all* activities, with the objective of eliminating or improving those that only marginally contribute to the effectiveness of the organization.

A part of this composite effort also involves the development of personnel, as well as the creation of operating policies and procedures, that contribute to the accomplishment of departmental objectives in the most cost-effective manner.

These objectives apply in principle to all categories of industrial buying activities: manufacturing concerns, governmental units, schools, hospitals, and all other types of buying units that buy for consumption or conversion. A non-profit activity, of course, cannot seek to "maximize its profit." It can, however, seek to maximize the benefits the organization receives from its appropriated or endowed dollar. A principle common to all types of purchasing activities is to obtain the greatest *value* from each dollar the purchasing department spends.

Under the first objective (uninterrupted materials flow), for example, a manufacturing concern seeks to support its production schedule; the U.S. Navy seeks to support its ships, aircraft, and bases; and a hospital seeks to support its patients. The principles underlying the first objective apply with equal force to all types of organizations. It is the same with the other seven objectives; they apply to all types of industrial buying. The principles are also equally applicable to operations of all sizes, large and small. There are many situations where a slight change in the phraseology of a specific objective is required to make it fit a particular operating environment. The fact remains, though, that only the words change; the principles remain the same.

At the beginning of the chapter, it was noted that purchasing and supply management objectives can be viewed from three levels. The first two levels, managerial and functional, have now been reviewed.

The third level focuses on the detailed objectives that are developed when precise buying plans are made (usually annually) for each of the major categories of materials the firm uses in its operations. These objectives are spawned from the functional-level objectives just discussed, and are applied to fulfill the specific needs associated with each type of purchase. The precise set of objectives for each material typically varies because the usage requirements, the operating conditions, and the markets in which each material is purchased usually are different. Consequently, the specifics and the subtleties of these objectives are discussed later in the book in the technical chapters dealing with topics such as quality, sourcing, pricing, production and inventory planning, development of the buying plan, and so on. At this point, it is sufficient simply to say that all subsequent strategic buying objectives are based on the eight functional objectives just discussed.

BASIC OPERATING POLICIES

What is a policy? A *policy* is a statement that describes in very general terms an intended course of action. After the fundamental objectives of an activity are established, policies are developed to serve as *general guidelines* in making operating decisions that channel actions toward achievement of the objectives. To facilitate this process, a set of operating procedures is subsequently developed that details the *specific actions* to be taken to get the job done.

Before proceeding further, it should be emphasized that this entire book deals largely with matters of policy. Chapters 8 through 12 focus on numerous policies influencing the quality of materials. Chapters 14 through 16 investigate pricing policies. Chapters 22 and 23 consider policies of production scheduling and inventory management, and so on. Every chapter deals with various matters of policy which relate to a specific phase of supply management. The remainder of this chapter is concerned with fundamental *operating* policies—broad policies of particular interest to top management. These policies deal with things such as purchasing authority, external relationships, and the firm's general conduct and image. These policies lie close to the heart of the purchasing and supply management function, yet their influence permeates the entire company operation.

Policies Defining Purchasing Responsibility

Centralization of Purchasing Authority   Generally speaking, in a single-site operation, to decentralize the purchasing function needlessly is to deny a firm some of its potential profit. Centralization of the purchasing function is essential for attainment of both optimum operating efficiency and maximum profit.

Centralization of purchasing, as discussed in this book, is concerned solely with the placement of purchasing *authority*. It has nothing to do with the location of buying personnel. Centralization exists when the entire purchasing function is made the responsibility of a single person. This person is held accountable by top management for proper performance of purchasing activities. Decentralization of purchasing occurs when personnel from other functional areas—production, engineering, marketing, finance, and so on—decide unilaterally on sources of supply or negotiate with suppliers directly for major purchases.

Most companies today view the centralization of purchasing as a logical and desirable evolution of Frederick Taylor's basic concept of the specialization of labor. The extent to which the efficiencies of functional specialization are realized when a firm creates a purchasing or a purchasing and supply department, however, depends largely on the authority delegated to that department. When functioning properly, centralized purchasing produces the following benefits:

1 Duplication of effort and haphazard purchasing practices are minimized by the central coordination of all company purchases.
2 Volume discounts are made possible by consolidating all company orders for the same and similar materials. In addition, a firm is able to develop and implement a unified procurement policy, enabling it to speak with a single voice to its suppliers. In this way, the firm gains maximum competitive advantage from its total economic power.
3 Transportation savings can be realized by the consolidation of orders and delivery schedules.
4 Centralization develops purchasing specialists whose primary concern is purchasing. With training, purchasing specialists inevitably buy more efficiently than less-skilled individuals who view purchasing as a secondary responsibility.
5 Suppliers are able to offer better prices and better service because their expenses are reduced. Their sales personnel have fewer people to call on, fewer orders to prepare, fewer shipments to make, fewer invoices to prepare, and fewer financial records to keep. Under these conditions, supplier goodwill and responsiveness naturally follow.
6 More effective inventory control is possible because of companywide knowledge of stock levels, material usage, lead times, and prices.
7 Line department managers do not have to spend time purchasing. They can devote full time and effort to their basic responsibilities. (When given purchasing responsibility, too often the overriding concern of line managers is to get what they want, when they want it, to the exclusion of all other purchasing considerations.)
8 Fewer orders are processed for the same quantity of goods purchased, thus reducing purchasing, receiving, inspection, accounts payable, and recordkeeping expenses.
9 Responsibility for the performance of the purchasing function is fixed with a single department head, thereby facilitating management control.

Despite the general advantages of centralization, *complete* centralized purchasing is neither always possible nor always desirable. Four types of situations justify some decentralization. The first of these is found in companies that process *single natural raw materials*. Many such firms separate the purchase of the key raw material from the purchase of other materials. Firms in the textile, leather, and tobacco industries are good examples.

In these industries, the raw materials are products of nature that are purchased in unstable markets whose prices fluctuate widely. Buying typically takes place at auctions conducted in small local warehouses. In such markets, a practical knowledge of grades is equally as important as a knowledge of prices. Buyers of these commodities usually guard their specialized know-how with secrecy, frequently handing it down from one generation to the next.

A second situation justifying some decentralization of purchasing authority exists in *technically oriented firms that are heavily involved in research.* In these firms some exceptions to complete centralization are always desirable. Many one-time purchases in the research, design engineering, and related departments can be handled more effectively by professional personnel in these departments. Moreover, the dollar volume of such purchases is usually relatively small.

In the research situation, scientists often do not know exactly what they want. Consequently, they must frequently discuss concepts with one or more suppliers before it is possible to select specific pieces of hardware. The design engineer concerned with developing a prototype must frequently talk with the supplier at the completion of each developmental step. These circumstances dictate giving engineers and scientists flexibility and a small portion of the firm's purchasing authority. *After specifications become firm,* however, the purchasing department should assume full responsibility for procurement.

The third situation justifying a different type of decentralization is found in the *operation of multisite institutional and manufacturing organizations.* This interesting topic is discussed fully in Chapter 6.

Finally, the *purchase of nontechnical odds and ends* also often calls for a partial decentralization of purchasing. Credit card and petty cash fund purchases of less than several hundred dollars are a good example. Decentralizing through the use of these approaches can be a money saver. Most firms estimate that it costs between $50 and $150 to process a formal purchase order. For many small purchases, the cost of the paperwork exceeds the cost of the item purchased. Even though the user may pay more for the item if it is bought in this manner, the extra cost is more than offset by the saving in processing costs.

The danger of losing purchasing control (i.e., efficiency and profit) does not stem from a partial decentralization of the purchasing function per se. Some decentralization is necessary as a matter of common sense. The real danger of loss stems from *excessive* decentralization. What percentage is excessive? Generally speaking, if 95 percent or more of the dollar volume purchased is handled by the purchasing department, decentralization should not be considered a problem. However, the appropriate level of decentralization must be determined for each firm from an analysis of the individual factors involved in its operations. One thing is certain: Operating departments seldom try to assume the functions of a purchasing department if the purchasing department is doing a good job for them.

Before leaving the topic, it is important to mention briefly two emerging trends that relate to the centralization issue. The first, as discussed in Chapter

1, is the increasing use of cross-functional teams in the sourcing process. Because of technical complexity and the competitive emphasis on quality, many major sourcing decisions today are made by a *team* of interdepartmental specialists, with the leadership of a purchasing professional. In this case, responsibility for the purchasing activity remains centralized, but selected tasks of investigation and analysis are delegated to team members.

The second trend involves the separation of strategic and tactical activities in the procurement process. In an increasing number of manufacturing firms, the purchasing contracts for production materials are negotiated and firmed up by a senior buyer in purchasing, and the authority to issue subsequent delivery releases against the contract is delegated to an operating person in production control or an individual close to the operations in the using area. So the strategic purchasing decisions remain centralized, and the operational activities are decentralized.

Implementing Centralization

The Manager of Purchasing and Supply is hereby granted the authority and the responsibility for procurement of all materials, equipment, supplies, and services necessary to maintain the Company as a vigorous, growing, and profitable business enterprise.

Within this authority, the Manager of Purchasing and Supply may delegate to other specific individuals the responsibility for the performance of some of the specific procurement duties.

Only those persons delegated specific written authority are authorized to commit Company funds for materials, equipment, supplies, or services. No other individuals are authorized to commit Company funds for these purposes.

The preceding statement is found in one firm's policy manual. When accompanied with the purchasing manager's subsequent list of individuals to whom specific purchasing authority is delegated, this statement communicates clearly to all company personnel the firm's policy on the acquisition of materials and services.

Most well-managed firms include similar statements in their policy manuals. In addition, an external document is required to communicate the same message to those outside the business—suppliers and others who might do business with the firm. Some type of concise orientation or information booklet usually is prepared for this audience.

In summary, it is essential that appropriate internal and external personnel know and accept the fact that the purchasing department holds full *authority* for negotiating, concluding, and following up purchases. This does not mean that purchasing should not request technical assistance from appropriate operating departments when it is needed. Obviously, it should! As just noted, for technically complex purchases, it is common to utilize a sourcing team that comprises individuals from several departments. The point is that the purchasing department bears the managerial responsibility for the planning and conduct of the procurement actions.

Liaison Responsibility for Major External Contacts   Stemming from this basic policy, most companies issue a series of additional policy statements which give more precise guidance in specific situations. For example, when the head of an operating department wishes to talk with a supplier's sales or technical representative about a potential procurement issue, unless it relates to an ongoing communication, the request normally should be made through the purchasing department. The appropriate buyer then makes the *initial* contact, arranges the appointment, and keeps informed of significant aspects of the following discussions that might influence future purchasing activity.

Selection of Suppliers and Contract Provisions   One of the most important responsibilities of a purchasing organization is to locate and/or develop suppliers that are competent and uniquely qualified to fulfill the buying firm's needs. Staying abreast of the large number of potential suppliers in the marketplace, and their respective capabilities and potential, can be a difficult and time-consuming task if it is done well. Consequently, most firms have a policy that requires buyers to spend a certain percentage of their time searching for, identifying, and investigating potential suppliers in the markets for their most important materials.

Similarly, most departments make it a policy to see all first-time callers from potential suppliers' organizations. Following the initial visit, however, buyers become much more selective in deciding which business callers to see, limiting their interviews to those sales representatives whose firms' products correspond closely with the buying firm's needs.

Despite the cross-functional aspects of sourcing team operations, in most cases the ultimate responsibility for matters of supplier selection, price determination, and the development of specific contractual provisions nevertheless belongs to the purchasing and supply department. As noted earlier, various unique conditions may produce a situation where it is in the firm's best interest to delegate specific purchasing authority. In such cases, however, delegation of the authority should be accompanied with adequate plans and constraints to ensure that the purchasing department does not lose control of its responsibilities. A firm also must make certain that its purchasing department is placed in the best possible bargaining position in subsequent dealings with the supplier.

The Review of Material Specifications and Requests   The purchasing department's responsibility and authority to critically review material specifications and purchase requests is a policy of paramount importance. It must be stated clearly and unequivocally in the firm's policy manual. One company phrases its policy this way:

> The purchasing department and . . . subsidiary purchasing managers have the *duty* and the *authority* to request consideration of specifications or quantity of material requisitioned if, in the opinion of the buyer, the interest of the company or its subsidiaries may be better served. However, any change in the purchase request is pro-

hibited unless it is approved by the person or department initiating the requisition, the bill of materials, or the production plan.

Without the establishment of this basic policy, the profit-making potential of centralized purchasing is severely curtailed. Its importance cannot be overemphasized.

Some companies go even further. They utilize cross-functional design teams that bring appropriate personnel from purchasing and other affected departments, along with selected suppliers, into material specification considerations early in the development process. With this approach, material specifications are, in fact, developed jointly by design engineering (or the using department) and all members of the design team.

In the interest of controlling expenditures, a firm typically delegates the authority to approve routine purchase requisitions only to specified individuals in each using department. This practice establishes the groundwork for a policy requiring that all requests for purchase be submitted in writing. Except in a rare emergency, oral requisitions should not be accepted. This policy obviously eliminates numerous costly communication errors. More important, however, is the fact that it requires operating departments to plan their material requirements more carefully. This in turn results in less ill-advised impulse buying, and it also reduces costly rush buying activities in the purchasing department.

Policies Affecting External Relationships and Image

Most companies spend a great deal of money to develop a favorable public image. Madison Avenue derives its livelihood from the efforts of business executives to convince the public that their companies are "the good guys in the white hats." Irrespective of public relations and advertising expenditures, however, a firm's purchasing and sales departments contribute heavily to the shaping of its public image. Most of a firm's contacts with the business community are managed by these two departments.

The development of sound supplier relations is a major responsibility of the purchasing department, for two reasons. First, good supplier relations contribute to the formation of a good public image. Second, the treatment and service that a supplier gives a customer depends to a great extent on the way the supplier feels about the customer. However the matter is viewed, it is in purchasing's best interest to establish policies that promote favorable relationships with the supplier community. Some of the more important issues are discussed briefly in the following pages.

Salespeople   Perhaps the simplest thing a purchasing department can do to promote favorable supplier relations is to treat all salespeople fairly and courteously. As noted earlier, most companies make it a policy to see all salespeople on the first call, as long as their products are remotely relevant to the firm's needs. To permit more efficient planning and utilization of a buyer's time, many companies establish regular calling hours for suppliers' representatives (perhaps four hours a day, three to five days a week). As a rule, this conserves time for buyers and salespeople alike.

Orientation and Policy Booklets   Careful and complete communication with potential suppliers facilitates the development of good relations. Toward this end, many companies prepare an orientation booklet which is given to all suppliers calling on the purchasing department. Such booklets typically contain a brief description of the company's operations and products or services, a directory of its buyers and the types of materials each buys, and a statement of major purchasing policies and practices that potential suppliers should know about.

The Kaiser Corporation distributes a small booklet which, in addition to explaining the purchasing department's calling hours, sets forth a number of ground rules which affect the company's relationships with suppliers. Several key policies included are[1]:

- Our purchasing departments are the sole agents at the plant who have authority to commit the company to purchases, large or small.
- We prefer to limit the number of our suppliers to an extent that those suppliers will value our business and will endeavor to meet legitimate competition.
- We secure competitive prices whenever possible, giving due consideration to assurance of supply and prompt delivery.
- We buy from suppliers nearest the point of use, other considerations being equal.
- Suppliers' representatives can deal with our plant Purchasing Managers secure in the knowledge that they are protected from any unfair advantage of competing suppliers through "second looks" or personal relationships.

To the extent that orientation booklets apprise a firm's potential suppliers of its basic policies and procedures, they can be very helpful and can prevent exasperating misunderstandings. A buyer must always bear in mind that statements which are *not* made in oral discussions with a supplier's representatives may tell the supplier more than statements that are made. Incomplete communication can give rise to incorrect rumors and speculations highly detrimental to the relationship. For these reasons, many firms follow the policy of communicating relevant purchasing policies to their potential suppliers by means of the written word, stated in a precise yet congenial manner.

Competitive Bids   Although competitive bidding is not used for all purchases, nothing offers more potential danger to a firm's reputation for fair

---

[1]*Welcome to Kaiser Aluminum & Chemical Corporation Purchasing Department*. Kaiser Aluminum & Chemical Corporation.

dealing than a poorly handled competitive-bidding situation. Consequently, most firms establish definite policies to guide all buying personnel in handling bidding activities, both *before* and *after* the issuance of requests for bid.

Despite the fact that no legal requirements compel a private firm to award a contract to the low bidder, the competitive-bidding process itself implies that the lowest qualified bidder will get the contract. It is this expectation that motivates a supplier to compute its costs and assess its competitive position carefully before submitting its bid. To consistently obtain suppliers' best prices on the first bid, a buyer should therefore, in most cases, award the contract to the low bidder. This situation gives rise to two important policies:

1 Sound competitive-bidding practice demands that a buyer be willing to do business with every supplier from whom he or she solicits a bid. The resulting policy states that all suppliers requested to bid must be determined *in advance* to be *qualified* suppliers for the job in question.[2]

2 Whenever the lowest bidder does not receive the contract, the buyer is obligated to explain the decision. A short memorandum to this effect should be filed with the order or with the quotation analysis.

As simple as the preceding policies sound, they can be quite difficult to follow in practice. The fact that very few suppliers are *equally* qualified or motivated to handle a specific purchase makes it virtually impossible to evaluate bidders on the basis of price alone (except for highly standardized, off-the-shelf products). This situation frequently justifies the selection of a firm other than the low bidder. Even though justified, such a decision often is difficult to explain satisfactorily to the unsuccessful bidders who quoted lower prices than the successful bidder. And though a buyer may try to prevent unsuccessful bidders from learning the successful bid price, this is usually impossible. In a competitive industry, "grapevines" are too numerous and too effective to permit the keeping of many price secrets. Thus, even when the decision to award the contract to a high bidder is fully justified by a combined evaluation of quality, service, and price, it can still produce unfavorable supplier relations. Hence, the need for the policies and their enlightened observance is clear.

Chapter 11 stresses the importance of allowing each supplier only one bid on a competitively bid contract. In the interest of fairness, all firms must be accorded the same treatment. The buyer should treat all bid data confidentially and should not divulge one bidder's data to another bidder, either before or after the contract has been awarded. All bidders should be advised of the bid closing date, and no bids should be accepted after that date. If, for extraordinary reasons, the bid date is extended to give an interested supplier more time, it is the buyer's responsibility to notify *all* bidders of the new bid closing date.

---

[2]Exceptions to this policy often exist in governmental purchasing activities; the buying group generally is required to accept bids from all domestic firms that wish to bid.

The rules of common courtesy require the buyer to notify all unsuccessful bidders that the contract has been awarded. This allows those firms to release production capacity that may have been reserved for this potential contract. It is important that bidders be told of their failure to get the contract in a courteous and objective manner. Although a supplier realizes that it cannot get every order, it is likely to be more competitive on future jobs if it is not dissatisfied with its treatment on the current job.

Presale Technical Service   The purchase of certain technical items requires a potential supplier to conduct a presale study of the buyer's specific application of the items to be purchased. Firms in some industries customarily make such studies as part of their regular sales efforts. Selling prices in these industries are set so that the revenue from successful efforts covers the cost of unsuccessful presale studies.

In other industries, however, suppliers' prices provide for very little presale engineering work. Purchasing policy therefore must establish distinct limits with respect to the acceptance of presale technical services. While buyers want all the assistance legitimately available, they cannot afford to place their companies under obligation to a supplier by accepting an unreasonable amount of presale service.[3]

The incurrence of such an obligation usually leads to one of two undesirable results. First, the buyer can place the order with the supplier to whom he or she is obligated; however, some disadvantage may result if another supplier proves to be more desirable. Second, the buyer can place the order with the most favorable supplier, regardless of the obligation to the firm providing the unusual service. Even though the latter may have no legal claim to the order or to compensation for its services, the supplier may frequently feel or say that the buyer has taken an unfair advantage. Whether or not this is true, of course, depends on the explicit agreement reached in prior negotiations. In reality, however, at this point the truth of the matter is of little significance to the buyer. What is important is the fact that as a result of the ensuing rumor, the buyer's firm may be viewed with suspicion by some members of the business community.

Purchasing policy must guard against such problems, however innocently they may arise. Before accepting a supplier's offer to make a presale study, the buyer must estimate the amount of money involved and determine whether the offer is consistent with standard practice in the industry. Any service exceeding normal industry practice should be *purchased* completely apart from the basic purchase of material or equipment.

---

[3]Unfortunately, some salespeople deliberately employ this technique to gain a psychological advantage. If, for any reason, a buyer is under obligation to a seller, the buyer's conscience may well compel him or her to evaluate the relative positions of various suppliers differently than would be the case if he or she were under obligation to none of the suppliers.

Samples   One way to assess the quality of a product is to actually use or test a sample before ordering a significant quantity. In an effort to get a foot in the door, many salespeople request a buyer to accept a free sample of a product and "try it out."

The buyer may find it advantageous to accept such an invitation. It is an inexpensive and effortless way of learning about new, potentially useful products. If the cost of the sample is more than several dollars, however, the buyer should elect to pay for the sample. Such prudence removes any possible obligation that could result from accepting free material.

On the other hand, if the buyer sees no possible value in investigating a sales representative's product, he or she should explain the reason to the sales representative and decline the sample. Once a sample is accepted, the buyer is obligated to see that it gets a prompt and fair test. Further, the supplier is entitled to a complete report of the test as well as an evaluation of the firm's probable use for the product. This procedure requires time and administrative effort. And under the constant pressures of daily business, buyers occasionally tend to handle samples in a haphazard and inconsistent fashion. Yet, nothing irritates a sales representative more than to learn two months later that his or her sample has not even been tested. Such irritation inevitably influences his or her attitude toward the buyer's firm. In the interest of good supplier relations, therefore, a definite policy (and related procedures) should be established to ensure fair and uniform treatment of all samples by all buyers.

Plant and Distribution Center Visits   Every company should require its buyers to visit the operations of major suppliers periodically. Such visits yield three distinct benefits. First, they provide an opportunity for a buyer to learn more about the current technical or manufacturing aspects of the materials he or she buys. Second, these visits enable a buyer to discover a great deal of inside information about specific suppliers. In no other way can buyers become intimately acquainted with their suppliers' strengths and weaknesses or with the unique conditions under which each supplier operates. Third, site visits permit a buyer to develop valuable personal acquaintances and business friendships with suppliers' personnel.

Despite the impersonal nature of most major business decisions, daily business activities and negotiations are conducted by people who prefer to deal with someone they know and like. A buyer who is known personally in a supplier's operation sheds his or her inconspicuous role as a name on the customer mailing list and becomes a living personality. When a buyer has to expedite an order, ask a special favor, or ask a delicate question to which he or she wants a frank answer, there is no substitute for honest and friendly communication on a first-name basis with someone in the supplier's organization. Any purchasing group that fails to recognize this basic truth deprives itself of some of the fun of business, as well as some very tangible benefits.

Policies on Pricing and Supply Sources

Pricing and sourcing decisions represent major activities and outputs of a purchasing and supply operation. They obviously produce a substantial impact both inside and outside the buyer's firm. Consequently, the manner in which these activities are handled and the nature of the decision-making processes are extremely important. For these reasons, it is essential that carefully conceived policies be included in the policy manual to facilitate sound and consistent actions.

Dozens of these policies are discussed in Chapters 11 through 17. Major topics include the use of competitive bidding and the use of negotiation; the number of sources to utilize (single or multiple); the size of sourcing firms; specialty firms; local firms; international firms; distributors and manufacturers; and the selection criteria to be utilized in considering the various options.

This brief discussion is included at this point in the text simply to make the reader aware of the importance of these types of policies in the development of effective relationships with suppliers and potential suppliers.

Policies Concerning Ethical Practices

A business organization has two main windows to the outside world—its sales department and its purchasing department. The activities of these two groups are extremely visible and extremely important in shaping the perceptions of "outsiders" and building the reputation of a firm. We are concerned here with the activities and the behavior of a firm's purchasing and supply personnel. It is sufficient at this point in the discussion simply to say that the activities of a firm's purchasing professionals must be above reproach.

From a perspective internal to the firm, purchasing people also have a unique and an important role to play. A research study conducted by Professor Joseph Cavinato at Penn State University showed clearly that purchasing people do indeed live in "glass houses." After discussing the issue with more than 500 CEOs and upper-level corporate managers, Dr. Cavinato concluded that "the example set by purchasing management personnel is critical in determining how ethical behavior will be defined, implemented, and handled in the firm when problems arise. A clean bill of health in this area is essential to the development of a strong professional purchasing image."[4]

How does a purchasing and supply manager achieve this exemplary ethical behavior among departmental personnel? According to several recent research studies, the two major influencing factors are (1) the development and enforcement of a series of relevant ethics policies and (2) ongoing training and educational experiences. One group of researchers concluded that the existence of

---

[4]Joseph L. Cavinato, "Purchasing Performance: What Makes the Magic?" *Journal of Purchasing and Materials Management*, Fall 1987, p. 14.

formal, written policies dealing with ethical issues in purchasing has a strong, positive impact on the behavior of firms' purchasing professionals.[5]

It appears, then, that field research has made a strong case for the need and the value of policies concerning ethical purchasing practices. These policies are explored in depth in Chapter 31.

Policies Concerning Minority Business Enterprises

During the past decade and a half, this country has witnessed a growing sensitivity on the part of U.S. business firms to their potential roles in helping solve some of the country's major socioeconomic problems. This expanded role as responsible corporate citizens has included extensive participation in a wide variety of youth development programs, secondary and higher education support activities, and community charity efforts, as well as genuine support for affirmative action and equal employment opportunity programs. In addition to these highly visible activities, a less visible—but no less important—thrust has gradually emerged in the form of a variety of minority business procurement programs.

The late 1960s and the early 1970s saw ten years of social unrest in the United States that were unparalleled in recent times. In response to the needs revealed by this situation, the federal government took a number of legislative steps designed to bring more minorities into the mainstream of American economic life. One of these efforts focused on expanded development of qualified minority business enterprises (MBE).[6] Key legislative actions implemented to promote this effort are noted briefly below.

- *1969—Executive Order 11485.* Established the U.S. Office of Minority Business Enterprise within the Department of Commerce, for the purpose of mobilizing federal resources to aid minorities in business.
- *1971—Executive Order 11625.* Gives the secretary of commerce the authority to (1) implement federal policy in support of MBE programs, (2) provide technical and management assistance to disadvantaged businesses, and (3) coordinate activities between all federal departments to aid in increasing minority business development.
- *1978—Public Law 95-507.* Mandates that if a buyer's firm is awarded a *federal* contract that exceeds $10,000, the buyer is required to make "maximum efforts" in awarding subcontracts to small minority businesses.

    If the *federal* contract exceeds $500,000 ($1,000,000 for construction projects), *prior to contract award* the buyer's firm must submit an acceptable buying plan that includes percentage goals for the utilization of minority

---

[5]G. B. Turner, G. S. Taylor, and M. F. Hartley, "Ethics Policies and Gratuity Acceptance by Purchasers," *International Journal of Purchasing and Materials Management,* Summer 1994, p. 46.

[6]A minority business enterprise is defined as any legal entity, organized to engage in commercial transactions, that is at least 51 percent owned, controlled, or operated by one or more minority persons.

businesses. The plan must also detail procedures for identifying and dealing with the minority businesses.

MBE policy requirements are clear for firms that do business with the federal government. The requirements of Public Law 95-507, however, do not apply to firms that deal only in the private sector. Nevertheless, a majority of the country's large firms have supported the concept underlying the minority business development thrust. In 1972 the National Minority Purchasing Council (now renamed the National Minority Supplier Development Council) was formed voluntarily to accelerate the acceptance of minority suppliers through improved communications between majority and minority firms. Most metropolitan areas throughout the country have their own local or regional minority purchasing councils which, as a rule, are strongly supported by the local purchasing management association.

The bottom line of this activity is summarized in the following quotations of two industrial purchasing executives:[7]

> When we help all segments of the business community, we're helping ourselves. American commerce and industry will only be as strong as the segments that make it up. If MBEs are a segment of the total business pie, it's in our interest to assist them, because we are a part of the same pie.
>
> To find the lowest responsible bid that meets the needs of our company, we need to find suppliers and distributors that allow us both to have effective, fair, and considerate competition—and that includes *all* possible sources.

In conclusion, it is fair to say that a majority of firms subscribe to a policy on minority buying that includes all or most of the following elements:

1 The firm intends to award some portion of its business to qualified minority business enterprises.
2 Within practical limits, the firm will supply technical and managerial assistance for a reasonable period of time to help the MBE become a "qualified" supplier.
3 In the long run, the MBE must compete favorably with other potential suppliers on all purchase decision criteria.

THE POLICY MANUAL

It is appropriate at this point to state explicitly an underlying concept which has only been implied in the preceding discussions of policies: If policies are to function effectively, it is imperative that they be placed in written form. A policy is a communication—an important one. It is important that the message reach those who are to receive it as clearly and accurately as possible. The complexity of a modern firm necessitates the establishment of many diverse

---

[7]R. T. Williams, *Doing Business with Minority Vendors*, The Publication Center Inc., Alexandria, Va., 1985, pp. 7 and 8.

policies, all of which cannot possibly be remembered with accuracy. The normal turnover of employees and managers compounds the difficulty. Moreover, because policies are general statements, minor differences in interpretation are inevitable. It is essential, therefore, that care be taken to ensure the accuracy of policy communications.

Consequently, most firms disseminate policy statements to their employees via some type of written policy manual. A policy manual typically has at least two distinct sections, one containing *company* policies and one containing *departmental* policies. The section on company policies spells out in unmistakable terms the responsibility and authority of all departments. It is essential that these policies carry top-management approval and that they be communicated to every department head.

The second section on departmental policies is directed to the personnel of each respective operating department. In the case of purchasing and supply, departmental policies inform personnel of the expected patterns of conduct for major buying activities and for relations with suppliers and other external personnel. The use of a policy manual clearly facilitates consistent basic conduct among all departmental personnel. It is particularly important to foster consistent performance among buyers because their dealings with suppliers can significantly influence the firm's public image. A policy manual also facilitates the training of personnel.

The specific style, format, and contents of purchasing manuals vary widely. Some firms include only policies, while others include policies and procedures. Still others add organization charts, job descriptions, sample departmental forms, and other detailed data which, in total, completely describe the purchasing and supply department's operation. The particular format used is not important. One style may fit one company's need better than another. What is important is that all major policies and operating procedures be committed to writing. They must be stated simply and unambiguously in a manual that is easy to use and that is kept current.

CONCLUSION

What does management expect of a good purchasing operation? It should expect performance that provides an intelligent balance among its basic supply objectives—the *five rights*. Given that purchasing and supply's first responsibility is to support operations with a satisfactory flow of materials, based on a given set of operating and market conditions, its basic charge is to provide optimal value to the organization. It does this by combining in the right proportions the various elements of material quality and cost, tempered with the needed touch of supplier know-how, cooperation, and service. Unfortunately, the difficult part of this balancing act is that the conditions and the requirements change—with time and with different materials. Hence, the optimal purchasing mix changes. This is the challenge for purchasing and supply management in achieving what otherwise would be a reasonably simple set of basic objectives.

Policies are the general guidelines designed to assist these decision makers as they develop plans to "zero-in" on their moving target. The policies channel their actions, as well as those of their non-purchasing colleagues, toward attainment of the desired objectives.

Purchasing and supply policies serve two general functions: (1) They establish the ground rules for the department's relationship with other departments, and (2) they inform purchasing personnel about the expected conduct of departmental activities.

Policies of the first type should establish clearly the centralized purchasing function. They should also specify the function's responsibilities with respect to the development of material specifications, supplier selection, price determination, and contract administration. Policies of the second type should provide guidance for departmental personnel in conducting activities that influence the firm's relationships with external individuals and with external organizations.

A supplier's perceptions about the buyer's firm are important. What suppliers think about the firm's practices, as they reflect such things as competency, honesty, and fair play, definitely influences the type of relationship that develops between the firm and the business community. Some years ago, C. W. McVicar of Rockwell International summed up the idea very well[8]:

> Friendship can even be cultivated by the manner in which a sales representative is told he has lost, or cannot have, an order. These may seem small things, but courtesy, square-dealing, honesty, and straightforwardness beget friendship. They are appreciated by suppliers, and the buyer benefits largely from them. The sales representative who receives brusque treatment is not likely to make an extra effort to render special services, to offer new ideas readily, or to speak as favorably of either the buyer or the company as he would if he felt he had been given fair and courteous treatment.

This sage observation is still sound today—and it will be just as valid after we have entered the twenty-first century.

FOR DISCUSSION

3-1 "Objectives of purchasing and supply management can be viewed from three levels." Identify and discuss the significance of these three levels from a practical point of view.

3-2 Define and explain the "five rights."

3-3 What is the major difficulty in achieving the five rights in practice? Give an example.

3-4 How does the utilization of a strategic alliance with a supplier fit in with the operating-level objectives discussed?

---

[8]George W. Aljian (ed.), *Purchasing Handbook*, McGraw-Hill Book Company, New York, 1966, pp. 3–24.

3-5 What is the difference between "buying wisely" and "buying competitively," as described by the authors?

3-6 Does the use of cross-functional design teams help in achieving any of the operating-level objectives?

3-7 Is the use of a JIT production system a help or a hindrance to accomplishing basic purchasing and supply objectives? Discuss.

3-8 Define a policy.

3-9 How does a policy differ from a procedure?

3-10 Some business executives believe that a company should operate with as few policies and procedures as possible, because they think such things inhibit the creative thinking of managers and employees. Comment on this idea in general. Comment on the idea as it relates specifically to purchasing policies.

3-11 Why is centralizing the purchasing and supply function important? Discuss.

3-12 Assume that you have just become the manager of purchasing and supply for an electric appliance manufacturer employing 2,000 people. You have been asked to rewrite the section of the company's policy manual that includes policies defining the purchasing and supply department's responsibilities. Write the policies as you think they should appear in the company manual.

3-13 Assuming the same conditions as in question 3-12, write a policy for the complete handling of competitive bids in your firm.

3-14 What role should a supplier play as a member of a cross-functional product design team?

3-15 What problems can arise in the handling of presale technical services? Discuss.

3-16 Prepare for your boss (the vice president for purchasing and supply in a medium-size machinery manufacturing firm) a detailed report discussing the concept of centralized purchasing, including its strengths and weaknesses.

CASES FOR CHAPTER 3

Sampson Products Corporation, page 901
Pacific Healthcare, page 876
Mississippi Mutual Life Insurance Company, page 885
Senator Foghorn, page 911
The Old Oak Furniture Company (in the *Instructor's Manual*)

4

OPERATING PROCEDURES

KEY CONCEPTS

- Effective procedures
- General procurement procedures
    Definition, description, and transmission of the need
    Supplier qualification and selection and order preparation
    Order follow-up
    Receipt and inspection
    Invoice audit and order completion
- Purchasing records
    Open orders; closed orders; purchase log
    Commodity record
    Supplier record
    Contract and tool records
- Handling rush orders
- Handling small orders
    Blanket orders; systems contracting
    Contracting/MRP systems
    Telephone/fax orders; electronic systems
    Petty cash and C.O.D. systems
    Purchase credit card system
    Consignment and supplier delivery systems
- Evolving ordering arrangements
    Long term contracts—definite delivery; indefinite delivery
    National agreements

A procedure outlines in detail the specific actions to be taken to accomplish a given task, within the guidelines of any applicable policies. In short, it establishes the way of doing things.

Procurement procedures, and the documents they utilize, serve two fundamental purposes within a firm:

1 They provide the framework and the direction for accomplishing the supply and materials management activities effectively and efficiently.
2 They provide the means for processing information inputs from outside the department to produce output communications needed by individuals in other departments to do their jobs in a coordinated and timely manner. (Figure 4-1 identifies the numerous departments that are affected by procurement procedures.)

Chapters 7 through 27 suggest procedures and policies for the specialized activities discussed in those chapters. The purpose of this chapter is to identify and discuss the basic *operating* procedures, documents, and records that integrate the specialized activities of those chapters into a complete operational purchasing cycle.

In operation, these basic procedures can be implemented manually, by means of a computer-based system, or most commonly by a combination of the two. The next chapter, Chapter 5, discusses the implementation of procurement procedures in a computer-based environment.

GENERAL PROCUREMENT PROCEDURES

A purchasing department buys many different types of materials and services, and the procedures used in completing a total transaction normally vary among the different types of purchases. However, the general cycle of activities in purchasing most operating materials and supplies is fairly standardized. The following steps constitute the typical purchasing cycle:

- Recognize, define, and describe the need
- Transmit the need
- Investigate, qualify, and select the supplier
- Prepare and issue the purchase order
- Follow up the order (including expediting and de-expediting)
- Receive and inspect the material (except in the case of some JIT systems and some partnering agreements)
- Audit the invoice
- Close the order

Figure 4-1 outlines these steps in operational form. More important, it details the minimum flow of communications required for a system to function smoothly and efficiently. These communications may be electronic messages or paper documents, depending on the type of system used. The precise form the electronic message or the documents take varies widely from one

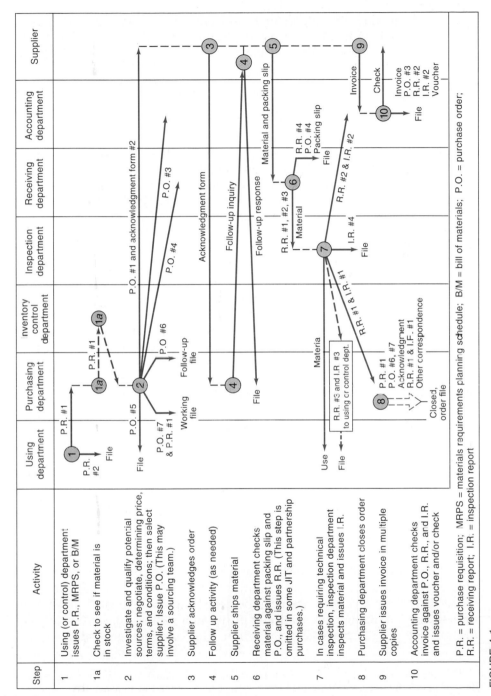

FIGURE 4-1
General procedure and communications flowchart for a typical purchasing cycle.

P.R. = purchase requisition; MRPS = materials requirements planning schedule; B/M = bill of materials; P.O. = purchase order;
R.R. = receiving report; I.R. = inspection report

Step	Activity
1	Using (or control) department issues P.R., MRPS, or B/M
1a	Check to see if material is in stock
2	Investigate and qualify potential sources; negotiate, determining price, terms, and conditions; then select supplier. Issue P.O. (This may involve a sourcing team.)
3	Supplier acknowledges order
4	Follow up activity (as needed)
5	Supplier ships material
6	Receiving department checks material against packing slip and P.O., and issues R.R. (This step is omitted in some JIT and partnership purchases.)
7	In cases requiring technical inspection, inspection department inspects material and issues I.R.
8	Purchasing department closes order
9	Supplier issues invoice in multiple copies
10	Accounting department checks invoice against P.O., R.R., and I.R. and issues voucher and/or check

company to another. The important point to note, however, is that a properly controlled purchase requires extensive communication with numerous work groups. Procurement procedures constitute the framework within which this task is accomplished.

Recognition, Definition, Description, and Transmission of the Need

The need for a purchase typically originates in one of a firm's operating departments or in its inventory control section. The purchasing department is usually notified of the need by one of two basic methods: (1) a standard purchase requisition[1] or (2) a material requirements planning (MRP) schedule. If the need is a one-time purchase, then an engineering bill of materials is sometimes used.

Standard Purchase Requisition The purchase requisition is an internal document, in contrast with the purchase order which is basically an external document. Most companies use a standard, serially numbered purchase requisition form for requests originating in the operating departments. The user generally makes a minimum of two copies. One copy is sent to purchasing; the other is retained in the using department's file. Some companies use as many as nine copies of the requisition for communication with other interested departments. Purchase requisition formats vary widely because each company designs its format to simplify its own particular communication problems. The essential information which every requisition should contain, however, includes a description of the material, quantity, and date required; estimated unit cost; operating account to be charged; the date; and an authorized signature. A typical purchase requisition is shown in Figure 4-2.

Today some progressive firms load into the company's mainframe computer, or its local area network, information and prices for the more commonly used materials. Users can then scan the items through their computer terminals and requisition those desired electronically. The electronic requisition goes directly to the appropriate buyer in purchasing—and the purchasing cycle is under way.[2]

In those firms that maintain their inventory records on a computer, most utilize a programmed inventory monitoring system that identifies the items whose inventory level has reached the reorder point. When the computer detects this condition, it automatically prints an inventory replenishment requisition that goes to purchasing for action. This computer-generated requisi-

---

[1] In manually operated inventory control systems, an additional form—a traveling requisition—is frequently utilized to requisition repetitively used items carried in inventory.

[2] Stephen L. Liccine, "Efficient Processes for Low-Value Purchases and Payables," *NAPM Insights*, August 1994, p. 37.

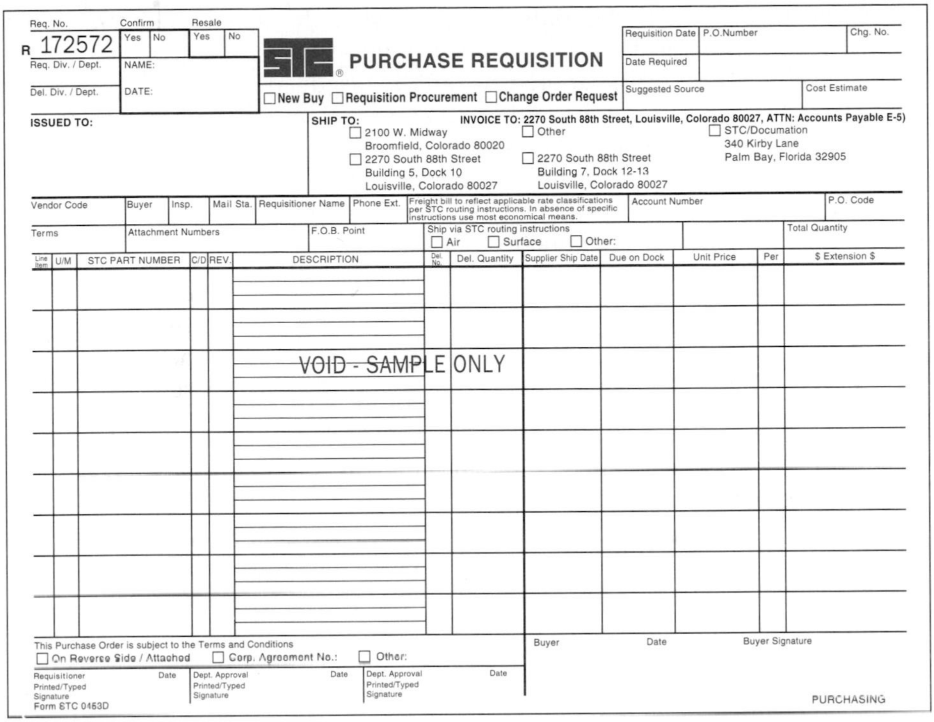
Req. No. R 172572 | Confirm Yes No | Resale Yes No
Req. Div. / Dept. | NAME:
Del. Div. / Dept. | DATE:
STC PURCHASE REQUISITION
☐ New Buy ☐ Requisition Procurement ☐ Change Order Request
Requisition Date | P.O.Number | Chg. No.
Date Required
Suggested Source | Cost Estimate
ISSUED TO:
SHIP TO: INVOICE TO: 2270 South 88th Street, Louisville, Colorado 80027, ATTN: Accounts Payable E-5)
☐ 2100 W. Midway Broomfield, Colorado 80020
☐ 2270 South 88th Street Building 5, Dock 10 Louisville, Colorado 80027
☐ Other
☐ 2270 South 88th Street Building 7, Dock 12-13 Louisville, Colorado 80027
☐ STC/Documation 340 Kirby Lane Palm Bay, Florida 32905
Vendor Code | Buyer | Insp. | Mail Sta. | Requisitioner Name | Phone Ext. | Freight bill to reflect applicable rate classifications per STC routing instructions. In absence of specific instructions use most economical means. | Account Number | P.O. Code
Terms | Attachment Numbers | F.O.B. Point | Ship via STC routing instructions ☐ Air ☐ Surface ☐ Other: | Total Quantity
Line Item | U/M | STC PART NUMBER | C/D | REV. | DESCRIPTION | Del. No. | Del. Quantity | Supplier Ship Date | Due on Dock | Unit Price | Per | $ Extension $
VOID - SAMPLE ONLY
This Purchase Order is subject to the Terms and Conditions
☐ On Reverse Side / Attached ☐ Corp. Agreement No.: ☐ Other:
Buyer | Date | Buyer Signature
Requisitioner Printed/Typed Signature | Date | Dept. Approval Printed/Typed Signature | Date | Dept. Approval Printed/Typed Signature | Date
Form STC 0453D
PURCHASING

FIGURE 4-2
A typical purchase requisition form. *(Courtesy of Storage Technology Corporation.)*

tion replaces what used to be called a "traveling requisition" when the inventory system was operated manually.

Material Requirements Planning Schedule When a design engineer completes the design of a part or an assembly, he or she makes a list of all the materials (and quantity of each) required to manufacture the item. This list is called an *engineering bill of materials.* In firms using computerized production and inventory planning systems, such as an MRP system, the engineering bill of materials is first reconfigured into a *structured multilevel* bill of materials. This structured bill of materials for each item being manufactured can then be used in determining specific material requirements for a given production schedule during a specific time period. The computer program utilizes the reconfigured "bills" along with the production schedules for all items as input—and calculates as output the precise time-phased requirements for each material that will be used in the manufacturing process. This schedule is then sent to purchasing for direct use in obtaining the required materials. It obviously eliminates the necessity of preparing numerous purchase requisitions—and it is ideally suited for use in a multiproduct intermittent manufacturing operation.

Engineering Bill of Materials   In firms that do custom manufacturing work, or for various reasons are involved in unique one-time projects, a similar but less sophisticated approach can be used. When purchase of the required materials is a one-time affair, the engineering bill of materials, along with the production schedule, can be sent directly to purchasing as notification of the production department's need for materials. Total requirements are then obtained by the buyer simply by manually extending the bill of materials for the production quantity scheduled. Thus, communications are simplified and the need for purchase requisitions is eliminated.

Definition and Description of the Need   Chapters 8 and 9 discuss in depth the formulation and utilization of material specifications and standards; Chapter 21 also deals extensively with the various methods of describing quality. Regardless of the form of transmission used, material requirements must be defined effectively, and the most appropriate methods of description should be selected for the situation at hand. The point to be understood here is that *clear, complete, appropriate* definition and description is a joint responsibility of the user and the buyer. One of the reasons why every purchase authorization document should be approved by designated departmental supervisors is to ensure that it is initially reviewed by qualified individuals and subsequently comes to purchasing in correct form. The buyer's responsibility is then threefold. First, he or she checks the document for accuracy and completeness, including internal data such as the account to which the purchase will be charged. Second, the buyer determines that the need has been adequately defined. Finally, he or she must ensure that the appropriate method of description has been used to guarantee a satisfactory purchase for the user and, at the same time, provide all possible latitude in the selection of a supplier.

The Stock Check   With the exception of requisitions that originate in the inventory control section, when purchase requests arrive in the purchasing department, they are checked to see if the requested item is carried in stock. In many cases, a buyer can tell simply by looking at the requisition whether it involves a stock material. If adequate stock is on hand, no purchase is necessary.

Some companies route all requisitions for tools, supplies, and production-type materials to inventory control before they are sent to purchasing. If a sizable percentage of a firm's requisitions involve stores-type items, this procedure expedites the supply process and reduces clerical work in the purchasing department. It also apprises inventory control of the non-stock items that are being ordered repetitively and, therefore, might advantageously be carried in stock.

Supplier Selection and Preparation of the Purchase Order

As soon as a need has been established and precisely described, the buyer begins an investigation of the market to identify potential sources of supply. In the case of routine items for which supplier relationships have already been developed, little additional investigation may be required to select a good source.[3] The purchase of a new or a high-value item, on the other hand, may require a lengthy investigation of potential suppliers. If the item to be purchased is complex or highly technical, the firm may utilize a cross-functional sourcing team, first to qualify potential suppliers—and perhaps eventually to make a team decision about the most desirable supplier.

After qualifying a preliminary group of potential sources, the buyer may employ the techniques of competitive bidding or negotiation, or both. When competitive bidding is used, the buyer initiates the procedure by requesting quotations from a reasonable number of firms with whom the buying group is willing to do business. Although "request for quotation" forms vary widely among firms, typically they contain the same basic information that will subsequently be included on the purchase order. Figure 4-3 provides an illustration.

Once a supplier has been selected, the purchasing department prepares and issues a serially numbered purchase order. In most cases the purchase order becomes a legal contract document. For this reason, the buyer should take great care in preparing and wording the order. Quality specifications must be described precisely. If engineering drawings or other related documents are to be considered an integral part of the order, they should be incorporated clearly by reference. Quantity requirements, price, and delivery and shipping requirements must be specified accurately. In the event that statistical process control or sampling inspection is to be used, conditions of acceptance should be stated or referenced on the order. Similarly, any other important factor affecting the acceptability of the product should be stated precisely. In short, the order should include all data required to ensure a satisfactory contract, and it should be worded in a manner which leaves little room for misinterpretation by either party.

In addition to those provisions that are unique to each contract, most firms also include as a part of every contract a series of terms and conditions that are standard for all orders (typically called "boilerplate"). These terms and conditions are designed to give legal protection to the buyer on such matters as contract acceptance, delivery performance and contract termination, shipment rejections, assignment and subcontracting of the order, patent rights and infringements, warranties, compliance with legal regulations, and invoicing and payment procedures. Each company develops its terms and conditions of purchase in accordance with its own unique needs. Consequently, much variation exists among firms. The terms and conditions which are printed on the back of one firm's purchase order form are reproduced in Figure 4-4.

Most companies prepare their purchase orders on multipart snap-out forms similar to the one shown in Figure 4-5. These multipart forms provide enough copies of the order to satisfy both internal and external communication needs. Although one preparation completes all copies, the various copies of the form

---

[3]In practical purchasing terminology, these types of purchases are termed "rebuys" or "modified rebuys."

REQUEST FOR QUOTATION

STC
(R)

STORAGE TECHNOLOGY CORPORATION
303-673-5151
MATERIAL PROCUREMENT
P.O. BOX 98
2270 SO. 88th ST.
LOUISVILLE, COLORADO 80027

DATE:

REQUEST NUMBER:

INSTRUCTIONS

STORAGE TECHNOLOGY CORPORATION REQUESTS YOUR PROPOSAL (RFQ) ON THE GOODS OR SERVICES LISTED BELOW. PLEASE FURNISH ALL INFORMATION AS REQUESTED. UPON COMPLETION, RETURN RESPONSE AND ONE COPY OF THIS RFQ TO THE BUYER.

TO: ➤

IT IS STORAGE TECHNOLOGY'S INTENTION:
☐ To Make a One-time Buy Only.
☐ To Issue One or More Purchase Orders Over a Period of
☐ To Enter Into a Corporate Agreement to Extend Over a Period of _____

☐ Other _____

PLEASE PROPOSE ON THE ABOVE IN THE FOLLOWING MANNER:
1. ☐ On Exact Quantity Only.
   ☐ From _____ to indicated Quantity, indicating all Price Breaks.
   ☐ On 25%, 50%, and 100% of Quantity.
   ☐ Over _____
2. **MAXIMUM STC LIABILITY IN THE EVENT OF TERMINATION:**
   A) ___ Days Work-in-Process.
   B) ___ Days Material.
3. Other _____

COMPLETE THE FOLLOWING:
Minimum Quantities
Deliverable Per Week _____ Month _____ Payment Terms: _____
Earliest Delivery: _____ F.O.B. Point _____
Deliveries To Be Made From ___ To_____
  Set-Up Costs: _____ Tooling Costs: _____
Deliveries To Be Scheduled _____
Other Costs (please indicate): _____
Specify the Identity of the Individual(s) or Firm (in the event of a local representative) Authorized to Contractually Commit Your Firm in Negotiations and the Execution of Any Resultant Agreement:
Minority Owned & Operated Enterprise   ☐ YES   ☐ NO
THE FOLLOWING ENCLOSURES MUST BE COMPLETED AND RETURNED WITH YOUR PROPOSAL. IF INDICATED BY "X".
☐ Cost Breakdown Requirement   ☐ Certificate of Non-Segregated Facilities
☐ Value Engineering Questionnaire   ☐ Certificate of Employment of Handicapped

DESCRIPTION OF ITEM(S)

ITEM	STC PART NUMBER	DESCRIPTION	EC LEVEL	ESTIMATED USAGE

ADDITIONAL INFORMATION AND REQUIREMENTS
1. ANY PURCHASE ORDERS ISSUED SHALL BE SUBJECT TO AND CITE THE TERMS AND CONDITIONS ON THE REVERSE SIDE OF THIS RFQ. AND ANY EXCEPTIONS TO THESE TERMS AND CONDITIONS MUST BE SUBMITTED IN WRITING AND RETURNED WITH YOUR RESPONSE. ANY PREPRINTED TERMS AND CONDITIONS ON ANY PROPOSAL FORM SHALL BE INVALID AND OF NO EFFECT. TOOLING REQUIRED FOR ANY ORDER SHALL BE SUBJECT TO ATTACHMENT T 100.
2. ALL GOODS OR SERVICES BOUGHT, RENTED, OR LEASED AS A RESULT OF THIS RFQ WILL BE SUBJECT TO THE FOLLOWING ENCLOSED SPECIFICATIONS INDICATED BY "X":

☐ SPEC #3092	☐ SPEC #2925	☐ SPEC #3043	☐ SPEC #26000	☐ SPEC #26001	
☐ SPEC #33118	☐ SPEC #2926	☐ SPEC #21010	☐ SPEC #21002	☐ SPEC #3049	☐ SPEC #QP5003
☐ SPEC #3011	☐ SPEC #3012	☐ SPEC #33200	☐ SPEC #33120	☐ SPEC #23200	☐ SPEC #E52925
☐ SPEC #QP5007	☐ OTHER _____				

3. IT IS STC'S POLICY TO INSURE AN EQUAL OPPORTUNITY FOR ALL QUALIFIED PROSPECTIVE SUPPLIERS. THEREFORE, ALL CONTACTS WITH STC PERSONNEL RELEVANT TO THIS RFQ MUST BE THROUGH THE BUYER. UNAUTHORIZED CONTACTS AT ANY TIME MAY BE THE BASIS FOR DISQUALIFICATION.
4. ALL DRAWINGS, SPECIFICATIONS, PART LISTS, ETC. RECEIVED FROM STC SHALL REMAIN THE PROPERTY OF STC. ANY DISCLOSURE TO THIRD PARTIES WITHOUT AUTHORIZATION BY STC MAY BE THE BASIS FOR DISQUALIFICATION.
5. STC RESERVES THE RIGHT TO REJECT ANY AND ALL PROPOSALS AND TO WAIVE SPECIFIC REQUIREMENTS AT ITS DISCRETION.
6. ALL PRICES PROPOSED MUST BE FIRM FOR _____ DAYS.
7. "ALL PROPOSALS TO BE PHONED IN WITH WRITTEN CONFIRMATION TO FOLLOW."
8. YOUR PROPOSAL, ONE COPY OF THIS RFQ. AND ALL ENCLOSURES REQUIRING RESPONSES MUST BE IN OUR POSSESSION BY _____

A.M.
P.M. _____

IF NOT PROPOSING, PLEASE SO INDICATE AND RETURN ENTIRE PACKAGE TO THE BUYER.

REPLY TO THE ATTENTION OF _____
Material Procurement

FORM STC-0890B

PHONE

FIGURE 4-3
A typical request for quotation form. *(Courtesy of Storage Technology Corporation.)*

Terms and conditions

The following terms and conditions and any specifications, drawings, and additional terms and conditions which may be incorporated by reference or appended hereto are part of this purchase order. By accepting the order or any part thereof, the Seller agrees to and accepts all terms and conditions.

1 The cash discount period available to Buyer shall commence on the date of the receipt of the merchandise or on the date of receipt of the invoice, whichever may be the later.

2 In the event of Seller's failure to deliver as and when specified, Buyer reserves the right to cancel this order or any part thereof without prejudice to its other rights, and Seller agrees that Buyer may return part or all of any shipment so made and may charge Seller with any loss or expense sustained as a result of such failure to deliver.

3 In the event of any article sold and delivered hereunder shall be covered by any patent, copyright, or application therefore, Seller will indemnify and save harmless Buyer from any and all loss, cost, or expense on account of any and all claims, suits, or judgments on account of the use or sale of such article in violation of rights under such patent, copyright, or application.

4 Seller guarantees that the design and performance of all items being purchased conform with the requirements of applicable insurance and government health and safety regulations, including regulations administered by OSHA and EPA.

5 Seller agrees not to use the name of Buyer or to quote the opinion of any of Buyer's employees in any advertising without obtaining the prior written consent of Buyer.

6 Buyer may at any time insist upon strict compliance with these terms and conditions notwithstanding any previous custom, practice, or course of dealing to the contrary.

7 Seller agrees to indemnify, defend, and hold harmless Buyer, its trustees, officers, agents, and employees, of, from, and against any and all claims and demands which may arise in any way out of the furnishing of goods or services hereunder, including, without limitation, claims and demands arising from injury to or death of personnel of Buyer or for damage to the property of Buyer, except those arising by reason of the negligent or willful act of Buyer, its officers, agents, or employees.

8 It is the policy of the Buyer to give favorable consideration to those suppliers who do not discriminate against any employee or applicant for employment because of race, creed, color, or national origin.

FIGURE 4-4
Terms and conditions of purchase appearing on the back of a typical purchase order.

may be printed with slightly different formats as the use of each demands. Seven is the *minimum* number of copies most commonly required. The typical distribution procedure is as follows:

- Copy 1 and copy 2 (the acknowledgment copy) are sent to the supplier.
- Copy 3 informs the accounting department of the purchase. It is used by accounting in checking and issuing payment for the seller's invoice.
- Copy 4 advises the receiving department that it can expect to receive shipment of the order on a particular date. Receiving uses its copy to identify and check the incoming shipment.
- Copy 5 informs the user of the details of the order so he or she can plan the work and budget accordingly.

(2) Req. Number	**(1)**		**(3)**

STC ® **PURCHASE ORDER**

STORAGE TECHNOLOGY CORPORATION
2770 South 88th Street, Louisville, Colorado 80027
(303) 497-5151

RESALE PERMIT *10-13932

Purchase Order Number and Part Number must appear on all packing lists, invoices, outside of containers, and correspondence.

Confirm Yes No   **Resale** Yes No

Req. Div./Dept. No.   Name:

Del. Div./Dept. No.   Date:

Purchase Order No.   Charge No.
Date   Division

ISSUED TO: **(4)**

SHIP TO: (Invoice to: Storage Technology Corp., P.O. Box 98, Louisville, Colo. 80027; ATTN: Accounts Payable) **(5)**

Vendor Code **(6)**	Buyer	Insp.	Mail Sta.	Requisitioner Name	Phone Ext.	Freight bill to reflect applicable rate classification per STC routing instructions. In absence of specific instructions use most economical means.	Account Number **(7)**		P.O. Code
Terms **(8)**		Attachments **(9)**	F.O.B. Point **(10)** ( ) Destination ( ) Shipping Point		Ship via STC routing instructions ( ) Air ( ) Surface **(11)**		Total Material Price **(12)**		Total Quantity

Item	U/M	Part Number	C/D	Rev.	Description	Ind	Via	Del. #	Del. Quantity	Supplier's Ship Date	Due on Dock	Unit Price	Per	Extension
(13)	**(14)**				**(15)**				**(16)**	**(17)**		**(18)**		**(19)**

VOID - SAMPLE ONLY

FORM STC 0446B   **(9)**
☐ On Reverse Side   ☐ Corp. Agreement No.:   ☐ Other:

Buyer   Date   Signature
(20)

VENDOR

Summary of Information Contained:

1. Buying firm and document identification
2. Internal identification
3. P.O. identification
4. Supplier identification
5. Specific shipping destination
6. Internal information
7. Accounting charge
8. Payment terms
9. Additional contract inclusions
10. Point of title transfer
11. Shipping instructions
12. Summary totals
13. P.O. item number
14. Item identification number
15. Item description
16. Delivery quantity
17. Shipping/delivery dates
18. Unit price and measure
19. Extended price × quantity
20. Buyer identification and date

FIGURE 4-5
A typical purchase order form. *(Courtesy of Storage Technology Corporation.)*

- Copy 6 remains in the purchasing department open-order file and is often used for purposes of order follow-up and expediting. (See pages 71–72.)
- Copy 7 becomes the buyer's working document and is filed in purchasing's open-order file.

Some firms organize their personnel into a larger number of specialized work groups and therefore require more copies of the order to complete the communications system. In any event, all parties involved in the transaction should receive a copy of the order. This communication has two objectives: (1) to permit planning and efficient conduct of the individual activities and (2) to integrate the efforts of the individual groups into a smoothly functioning supply operation.

After an order has been issued, changes in company requirements frequently require a change in the contract. In such cases, the buyer issues a *change order*, following the same procedures as were followed for the original order. When accepted by the supplier, the change order either supplements or replaces the original order.

Acknowledgment and Follow-Up of the Order

In most cases, the original copy of the purchase order which is sent to the supplier constitutes a legal "offer" to buy. No purchase "contract" exists, however, until the seller "accepts" the buyer's offer. The seller's acceptance can take one of two forms: (1) performance of the contract or (2) formal notification that the offer is accepted.

The purpose of sending the supplier an acknowledgment form along with the purchase order is twofold. First, it is a form that can be completed conveniently and returned to the buyer, acknowledging acceptance of the order. At the same time, the supplier can indicate whether or not it is able to meet the desired delivery date. If a supplier ships the ordered item immediately from stock, it frequently disregards the acknowledgment form.

If shipment is *not* made immediately, an acceptance should be sent to the buyer. Although the acknowledgment form usually serves this purpose, some sellers prefer to use their own forms, which state their terms and conditions of sale. In either event, the buyer should check the acceptance closely to see that the supplier has not taken exception to any provisions of the order. If the seller's acceptance terms are different from those on the buyer's order, the law holds that they will automatically be incorporated in the contract unless they materially alter the intent of the offer, or unless the buyer files a written objection to their inclusion. In cases where the seller's and the buyer's terms are in direct conflict, the law omits such terms from the contract, leaving settlement of the differences to private negotiation or legal adjudication.[4] In view of the posture adopted by the courts on this matter, it is amply clear that a buyer must review suppliers' order acceptances with great care.

The purchasing department's responsibility for an order does not terminate with the making of a satisfactory contract. Purchasing bears full responsibility for an order until the material is received and accepted.

Even though a supplier intends to meet a required delivery date, many problems can arise to prevent it from doing so. When there is a reasonable chance that the supplier may not stay on schedule, important orders with crit-

[4]This subject is discussed in depth in Chapter 30.

ical delivery dates should receive active follow-up attention. At the time such orders are placed, the buyer should determine specific dates on which follow-up checks are to be made.

Regardless of the specific system used, follow-up communication with the supplier usually takes one of two forms. A fax or a telephone call is typically used for most critical orders. Routine follow-up for the less critical orders is usually accomplished by mailing or faxing a preprinted inquiry to the supplier.

In some firms, follow-up procedures are conducted by the buyer handling the order. In others, follow-up activities are conducted by a separate expediting group. This subject is discussed in Chapter 6.

Although relatively few in number, some firms maintain a force of follow-up personnel in the field. Such firms typically purchase a great deal of critical material or major equipment on very tight delivery schedules. To ensure that all material is available when needed, these firms track critical purchases by having traveling follow-up representatives personally visit suppliers' plants. In some situations these field personnel have the additional responsibility of attempting to speed up (expedite) or even delay (de-expedite) delivery as the buyer's timing requirements undergo unexpected changes.[5]

Receipt and Inspection

The next step in the traditional purchasing cycle is receipt and inspection of the order. When a supplier ships material, it includes in the shipping container a packing slip which itemizes and describes the contents of the shipment. The receiving clerk uses this packing slip in conjunction with his or her copy of the purchase order to verify that the correct material has been received.[6]

After a shipment has been inspected for quantity and for general condition of the material, the receiving clerk issues a receiving report. In some cases, the report is prepared on separate receiving department forms. However, the trend in most companies today is to reduce the clerical work by using an on-line computer-based system, coupled with bar code order identification, or by preparing a receiving report form during the same typing or printing operation that prepares the purchase order. In the latter situation, a receiving report form is included in the snap-out purchase order form. A typical form is shown in Figure 4-6. To complete the report, the receiving clerk merely records the identification and receiving figures in the appropriate spaces included on the form.

---

[5]The term "expedite" is used rather loosely in industry. In a more precise sense, "follow-up" involves activities to ensure delivery as scheduled. To "expedite" involves actions to achieve an earlier delivery than that originally planned. To "de-expedite" is to attempt to delay delivery beyond the original schedule.

[6]A complete discussion of the procedures to be followed when short or damaged shipments are received is found in Chapters 24 and 25.

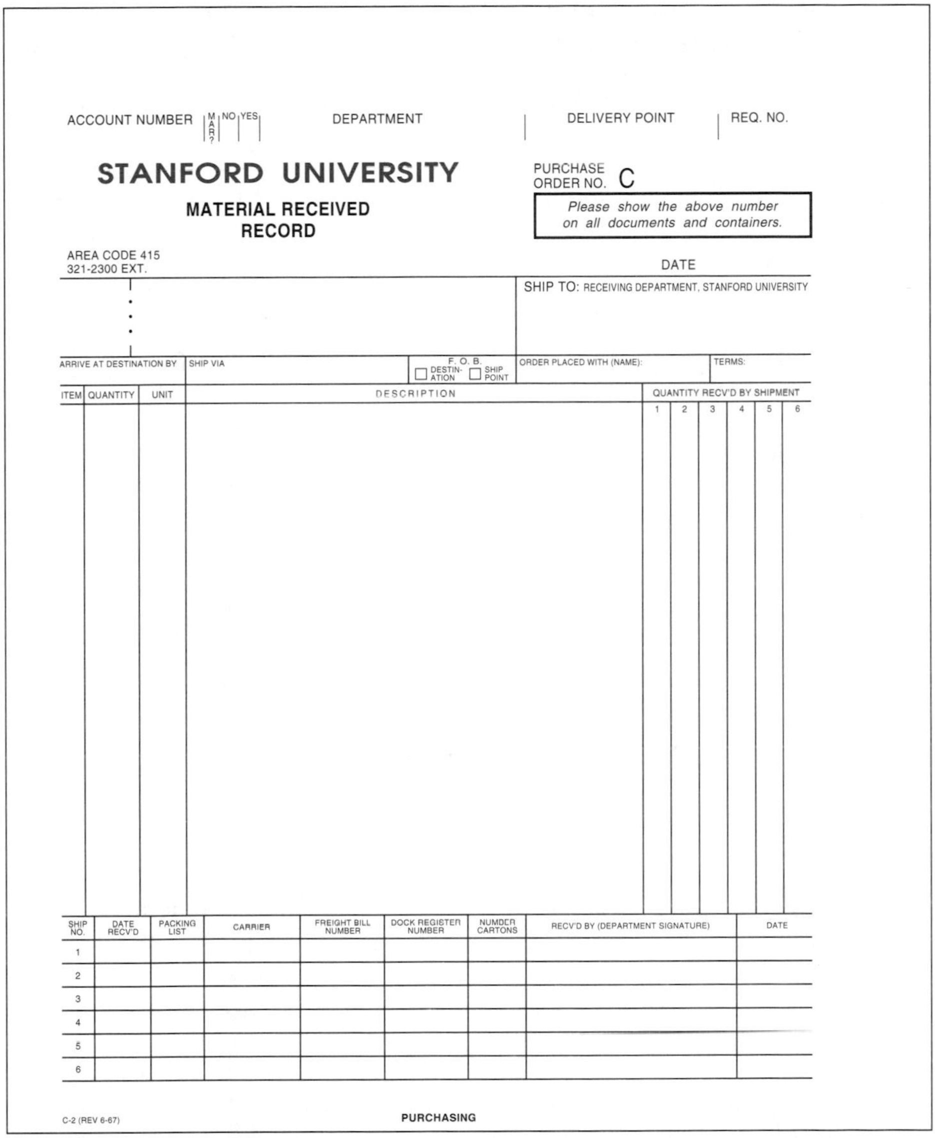

ACCOUNT NUMBER | MAR? | NO | YES | DEPARTMENT | DELIVERY POINT | REQ. NO.

STANFORD UNIVERSITY

MATERIAL RECEIVED RECORD

PURCHASE ORDER NO. C

Please show the above number on all documents and containers.

AREA CODE 415
321-2300 EXT.

DATE

SHIP TO: RECEIVING DEPARTMENT, STANFORD UNIVERSITY

ARRIVE AT DESTINATION BY	SHIP VIA	F. O. B. ☐ DESTIN-ATION ☐ SHIP POINT	ORDER PLACED WITH (NAME):	TERMS:

ITEM	QUANTITY	UNIT	DESCRIPTION	QUANTITY RECV'D BY SHIPMENT 1	2	3	4	5	6

SHIP NO.	DATE RECV'D	PACKING LIST	CARRIER	FREIGHT BILL NUMBER	DOCK REGISTER NUMBER	NUMBER CARTONS	RECV'D BY (DEPARTMENT SIGNATURE)	DATE
1								
2								
3								
4								
5								
6								

C-2 (REV 6-67) PURCHASING

FIGURE 4-6
A receiving report form, reflecting a purchase order format different from that shown in Figure 4-5. *(Courtesy of Stanford University.)*

Copies of the receiving report are typically distributed as follows:

- Copy 1 is used by the purchasing department in closing out its working file of the order.
- Copy 2 is used by the accounting department in reviewing the order for payment.

- Copy 3 is sent to the user as notification that the material has arrived, or as a delivery copy if immediate delivery is made. (If another notification system is used, this copy can be omitted.)
- Copy 4 is retained in the receiving department's operating record file.

Before some shipments can be accepted, technical inspection is necessary. (A discussion of these procedures is found in Chapter 24.) In some companies, distribution of the receiving report is withheld until the technical inspection report has been prepared. In other companies, distribution of the receiving report precedes distribution of the inspection report. Some firms send an inspection report to every department that gets a receiving report, so their records of *actual* receipts will be complete. Other companies provide copies only to purchasing, accounting, and inspection.

Three developments in recent years have modified the traditional receiving policy in some firms. The use of *certified suppliers* in some JIT and some partnering purchasing arrangements has led to the elimination of the receiving inspection function for such purchases. Instead, incoming shipments are routed directly to the point of use, bypassing receiving. In such cases, the buying organization relies completely on the quality control and operating accuracy of the supplying firm. The third development is the advent of the purchase credit card. In many firms that use company credit cards for small purchases, the purchased item does not go through receiving because of its relatively low value.

The Invoice Audit and Completion of the Order

Occasionally, a supplier's billing department makes an error in preparing an invoice, or its shipping department makes an incorrect or incomplete shipment. To ensure that the purchaser makes proper payment for the materials actually received, sound accounting practice dictates that some type of review procedure precede payment to the supplier.

A typical procedure involves a simultaneous review of the purchase order, the receiving report, and the invoice. By checking the receiving report against the purchase order, the purchaser determines whether the quantity and type of material ordered was in fact received. Then by comparing the invoice with the purchase order and receiving report, the firm verifies that the supplier's bill is priced correctly and that it covers the proper quantity of acceptable material. Finally, by verifying the arithmetic accuracy of the invoice, the correctness of the total invoice figure is determined.

Auditing invoices is a repetitive, time-consuming task that should be handled as efficiently as possible. It should also be conducted soon after receipt of the invoice to permit the accounting department to make prompt payment and obtain any applicable cash discounts. As mentioned in Chapter 2, prompt payment also supports the firm's efforts to establish and maintain good supplier relations. Because of the labor cost involved in auditing invoices, many companies do not verify the accuracy of low-dollar-value invoices.

Invoice auditing is technically an accounting function. And when possible, it is prudent to separate the responsibility for authorizing payment for an order from the responsibility for placing the order. Theoretically, the purchasing department's job is completed when the material covered by a purchase order has been received in the plant and is ready for use. In practice, however, some firms assign the invoice auditing responsibility to accounting, while others assign it to purchasing.

In the purchase of complex or technical materials, operationally it makes sense to assign the auditing task to the buyer who handled the order. This individual is familiar with the materials and their technical nomenclature, with prices and contract provisions, and with all ensuing negotiations. Invoices for such orders often are difficult to interpret and evaluate without a detailed knowledge of these things. Auditing invoices for the purchase of most standard materials, on the other hand, is a routine task that should be assigned to appropriate accounting personnel. A majority of most firms' orders fall in this category.

Figure 4-1 indicates that the purchasing department closes its purchase order file before the invoice is audited. This is usually the case if accounting audits the invoice. When purchasing audits the invoice, its records are closed after the audit. Closing the order simply entails a consolidation of all documents and correspondence relevant to the order; the completed order is then filed in the closed-order file. In most firms, a completed order consists of the purchase requisition, the open-order file copy of the purchase order, the acknowledgment, the receiving report, the inspection report, and any notes or correspondence pertaining to the order. The completed order file thus constitutes a historical record of all activities encompassing the total purchasing cycle.

PURCHASING DEPARTMENT RECORDS

The files of a purchasing department contain an endless flow of operating data. Despite its huge volume, much of this information can be useless in daily operations unless it is organized in a manner which makes it readily accessible. Although the unique needs of each purchasing department dictate the specific structure of its records system, the following basic records are essential for the effective operation of most purchasing departments:

- A record of open orders
- A record of closed orders
- Purchase log
- Commodity record
- Supplier record
- Contract record
- Special tool record

Record of Open Orders

All buyers need immediate access to information concerning the status of their outstanding orders. The record system can be maintained on a computer, in hard-copy form, or as a combination of the two. Because reference to these orders most frequently requires identification by the supplier's name, the record system customarily is indexed alphabetically by suppliers' names. Within each supplier's subfile, orders are arranged in ascending numerical sequence.

Although practice varies widely, each order record commonly contains the purchase requisition, the working copy of the order, the returned acknowledgment information, follow-up data, and all notes and correspondence that pertain to the order. Some companies also include competitive bids in the order file. Others prefer to keep bids in a separate price file or with the commodity record. When the bid is not included in the order file, the order record must contain a cross-indexing reference.

Some firms also maintain a separate numerical file or log of purchase requisitions. Such a file makes it easy to locate a purchase order needed to answer questions from a requisitioner who can identify the order only by requisition number. In such situations, it is essential to note the purchase order number on the requisition.

Record of Closed Orders

The closed-order file provides a historical record of all completed purchases. It frequently serves as a useful reference when questions arise concerning past orders and when certain historical data are needed to guide future decisions. Specific inclusions of the file were discussed previously.

It is difficult to generalize about the length of time such records should be kept. While government contract records should be kept indefinitely, most firms retain their other closed orders from three to seven years. Normally, any order files kept longer than this should be retained only on a highly selective basis. In a large firm, records retention is costly. Therefore, if commodity and supplier records are properly maintained, only unique and high-value orders are generally worth keeping longer than the four-year period required for legal purposes.[7]

Purchase Log

Every purchasing department should maintain an ongoing record, in numerical sequence, of all purchase orders issued. The record need not be elaborate, but it should contain the purchase order number, the status of the order, the supplier's name, a brief description of the material purchased, and the total value of the order. Such a record summarizes the commitments for which the purchasing executive is responsible. In the event that the working copy of an order is lost, basic data concerning the purchase can be found in the log. The log further serves as a convenient record from which summary administrative

---

[7]The Uniform Commercial Code, Article 2, Section 2–725, states that "an action for breach of any contract for sale must be commenced within four years after the cause of action has accrued."

data can be extracted concerning such matters as the number of small orders, rush orders, and total orders issued; the volume of purchases from various suppliers; the value of outstanding commitments; and so forth.

The purchase logs of some firms consist of a sequential list of purchase orders recorded in a journal or in the computer data base. Other firms accomplish the same objective simply by filing, in numerical sequence, the follow-up copy or an additional copy of the order.

Commodity Record

The file of commodity records constitutes a vast reservoir of materials data that makes efficient "mass production purchasing" possible. A commodity record card or computer file should be maintained for each major material and service that is purchased repetitively. Typically included in the record is a complete description of the material or service, with full reference to necessary engineering drawings and specifications which might be filed elsewhere. Also included should be a list of approved suppliers and their price schedules. Competitive quotations may be included in the file, although it is more common to summarize bid data in the record, note a cross reference to the original quotation, and place all quotations in a separate file.

The preceding data provide a buyer with the basic information initially required in a repetitive purchase investigation. In making the purchase decision, the buyer supplements this information with numerous qualitative considerations concerning individual suppliers, such as their current work loads, internal problems, quality performance, and so on. Some companies, however, also include in the record a complete purchase history for the item. For every purchase, the purchase order number, purchase quantity, price, delivery performance, and quality performance are recorded. In deciding how much detailed information to keep in its commodity record, each firm must weigh the value of the information against the cost of transcribing it.

Supplier Record

To provide quick access to information about suppliers, most companies centralize such information in a single record file. A separate card or computer record is maintained for each major supplier. In this record is recorded the address, telephone number, and the names of personnel to contact on specific matters of inquiry. Selling terms and routing instructions for shipping purposes also usually are included. Although the practice varies, many firms additionally summarize in this record the supplier's delivery and quality performance, as well as the annual volume of materials purchased from the supplier.

In a matter of seconds, these records enable a buyer to obtain a wealth of summary information about any important supplier.

Contract Record

Today most firms are purchasing an increasing number of items on a long-term contractual basis. In such cases, it is usually convenient to consolidate all contracts in a separate file. In addition to providing immediate access to all contract documents, this file also apprises all buying personnel of the materials that are purchased in this manner. If the number of contracts is large, it is desirable also to list them in summary form to provide a bird's-eye view of all contract purchases and their expiration dates.

Special Tool Record

Many companies have no need for this record. However, such a record is essential to those firms that purchase many items requiring special tooling for their manufacture. On some orders the purchaser buys the required dies, jigs, fixtures, and patterns; on others the supplier owns them. By maintaining a record of special tools, the buyer can summarize for quick reference the special tools owned, the age and location of each, and the essential mounting and operating characteristics of each.

RUSH ORDERS

Every department executive tries to develop an orderly and systematic pattern of operation that efficiently utilizes the resources of that department. In a well-run purchasing department, systematic analysis and processing of most orders is completed in two to four days after the purchase request is received.

How should purchasing handle the emergency needs that inevitably arise in any business operation? Clearly, a special procedure for processing *rush* requisitions is needed. The key elements of such a procedure are discussed in the following paragraphs.

Even in the case of emergencies, it is unwise to accept oral requisitions—in person or over the telephone. Too much chance for erroneous interpretation of the requirement exists. The requisitioner should state the need in writing and, preferably, deliver it to the buyer in person. For purposes of identification, emergency requisitions can be printed on paper of a different color, or they can be identified with a visible emergency sticker. Typically, the buyer should process these requisitions immediately and telephone emergency orders to the supplier. In no case, however, should an order be placed without assigning it a purchase order number. For most purchases, a confirming purchase order subsequently should be mailed to the supplier. In cases where the emergency is less urgent, the buyer may process such requisitions at appointed times twice daily (say, at 10:30 a.m. and 2:30 p.m.).

Purchasing's basic responsibility is to the departments it serves—its internal customers. Yet purchasing should not permit users to take unfair advantage of its emergency service. Only justifiable requests should receive this service.

Rush orders always cost more than if they were handled through the normal purchasing system. Higher prices frequently are paid because rush purchases are not investigated as thoroughly as those handled in the normal routine, and premium-cost transportation typically is used. Furthermore, the interruption of a buyer's scheduled work by the emergency request invariably produces inefficiency in normal purchasing department activity.

Consequently, steps should be taken to discourage all rush orders that arise because of poor planning in the using departments. In practice, three approaches have proved successful. The *first* involves a concerted effort to *coordinate the activities of the using group or production scheduling and purchasing*. Some companies require that realistic order points for inventory materials be established jointly by production scheduling and purchasing. In other firms operating on a job-order basis, purchasing is required to issue periodic lead time reports to users for all major classes of materials. A *second* approach, designed to reduce unjustifiable requests, *requires the requisitioner to obtain approval from a general management executive* for all emergency requisitions. A modification of this approach requires an after-the-fact review of all rush orders by top management. Still *another approach assesses the requisitioning department a predetermined service charge* for each emergency requisition processed.

THE SMALL-ORDER PROBLEM

Small orders are a perennial problem in *every* organization—and a serious problem in some. Examination of a typical company's purchase order file reveals that a sizable percentage (sometimes up to 80 percent) of its purchases involve an expenditure of less than $250. In total, however, these purchases constitute a small percentage (seldom more than 10 percent) of the firm's annual dollar expenditures.

For example, 75 percent of Conoco's purchase orders are for expenditures of less than $500, and 50 percent are for less than $100.[8] The Intel Corporation found that its purchasing department spent 66 percent of its time managing 1.7 percent of the firm's expenditures.[9]

Clearly, no manager wants to devote more buying and clerical effort to the expenditure of less than 10 percent of his or her funds than to the expenditure of the other 90 percent. Yet this frequently is what happens. The very nature of business requires the purchase of many low-value items. Nevertheless, small orders are costly to buyer and seller alike. It costs a seller only a few cents more to process a $1,000 order than it does to process a $10 order. The following sections discuss various methods a purchasing manager can use to minimize the small-order problem.

[8]Gordon Regan, "Conoco Procurement Card Program," presentation to the Executive Purchasing Roundtable, Phoenix, Ariz., Feb. 28, 1994.
[9]Roger A. Whittier, "How Intel's Purchasing Now Uses Plastic to Generate Cost Savings," *Supplier Selection and Management Report*, May 1994, p. 13.

Centralized Stores System

A stores system is the first approach typically used to reduce the volume of small-order purchasing activity. When experience shows that the same supply items are ordered in small quantities time after time, the logical solution is to order these items in larger quantities and place them in a centralized inventory for withdrawal as needed. An analysis of repetitively used production materials leads to the same action for the multitude of low-value items. If usage of an item is reasonably stable, an optimum order quantity can be computed using a basic economic order quantity approach. There is, of course, a limit to the number of items and the financial investment a firm can place in inventory.

Blanket Order System

A stores system solves the small-order problem only for items that are used repetitively. A *blanket order* system helps solve the problem for the thousands of items a firm cannot carry in inventory, as well as some that it does carry.

Briefly, the general procedure used for this type of purchase is as follows. On the basis of an analysis of past purchases, the buyer determines which materials should be handled in this manner. After bidding or negotiation, the buyer selects a supplier for each item, or family of items, and issues a blanket order to each supplier. The order includes a description of each item, a unit price for each item when possible, and the other customary contract provisions. However, no specific order quantities are noted. The blanket order typically indicates only an estimated usage during the period of coverage (usually one to three years). It also states that all requirements are to be delivered upon receipt of a release from the buyer or other authorized person. On receiving a requisition for one of the materials, the buyer merely sends a brief release form to the supplier. On the release form are noted the blanket order number, the item number, and the quantity to be delivered. Receiving reports are filed with the original order, and at the end of the month are checked against the supplier's monthly invoice. At the end of the period, the order may be renewed or placed with another firm, depending on the supplier's performance record.

Many companies develop their own unique modifications of the basic procedure. For example, instead of advising suppliers of order releases by means of a written form, some companies simply issue releases to local suppliers by telephone or fax. By noting such releases on the order, the buyer still retains adequate control. Some firms are experimenting with the use of electronic data interchange releases.

In the event that material is needed immediately (and the supplier is nearby), some firms allow the using department to pick up the material without notifying the purchasing department. The employee obtaining the material simply endorses and enters the proper accounting charge on the sales receipt, a copy of which is sent to the buyer. This document then serves as the receiving report. This procedure is particularly applicable to the frequent purchase of various repair parts, when specific needs are not known until the faulty equipment is dismantled. It also works well for purchasing special processing services, such as heat-treating and plating, when the service is required quickly but cannot be planned in advance. This variation of the basic blanket order procedure can easily be abused and possibly can lead to petty fraud. It is therefore important to entrust its use only to responsible operating personnel and periodically to review the endorsed sales receipts.

The blanket order system offers six important benefits:

1 It requires many fewer purchase orders and reduces clerical work in purchasing, accounting, and receiving.
2 It releases buyers from routine work, giving them more time to concentrate on major problems.
3 It permits volume pricing by consolidating and grouping requirements.
4 It can improve the flow of feedback information, because of the grouping of materials and suppliers.
5 Because some suppliers will stock material for prompt delivery, this system may reduce the buyer's lead times and inventory levels.
6 It develops longer-term and improved buyer-supplier relationships.

To function effectively in the long run, however, any blanket order system must provide adequate internal control. Absence of the control element encourages petty fraud and poor supplier performance. The elements essential to effective control are:

1 A numbered purchase order, including proper internal accounting charge notations
2 A record of authorized delivery releases
3 Bona fide evidence of receipt of the material

Despite the fact that blanket order systems offer both the buying and the supplying organizations a number of important benefits, historically they have been used by fewer firms than might be expected. A recent study conducted by *Purchasing* magazine found that approximately 25 percent of the firms surveyed used a blanket order type of contracting system extensively for their small purchase needs. Increased usage was forecast in view of growing demands for more effective utilization of industrial resources.[10]

Systems Contracting

At this point a few words need to be said about systems contracting. Though frequently used as a basic purchasing strategy, as well as an approach for minimizing the small-order problem, systems contracting, in reality, is simply an extension and more sophisticated development of the blanket order purchasing concept. Some firms call it "stockless" purchasing.

---

[10]Susan Avery, "MRO Buyers Take on Challenges of the 90s," *Purchasing*, Apr. 24, 1994, pp. 52–55.

As its name implies, systems contracting involves the development of a corporatewide agreement, often a one-to-five year requirements contract, with a supplier to purchase a large group or "family" of related materials. The items to be purchased are usually described in detail in a "catalog" that becomes part of the contract. Estimated usage usually is included, along with a fixed price for each item and an agreement by the supplier to carry a stock of each item adequate to meet the buyer's needs. Various types of supplies and commonly used operating items, typically purchased from distributors, are the materials most often covered by these types of agreements.[11]

In addition to the benefits of blanket order purchasing, a major objective of systems contracting is to minimize both the buyer's and the supplier's administrative costs associated with the purchases. The operating procedures of the two firms are integrated to the extent practical. For example, users in the buyer's various operating locations usually send their purchase requisitions directly to the supplier holding the contract for the item. The requisition thus serves as the purchase order. The supplier then simply maintains a list of such shipments on a "tally sheet," identifying each by the requisition number (or a supplier-assigned number), and periodically (monthly or semi-monthly) submits the tally sheet to the buyer for payment in lieu of an invoice.

These types of integrated procedures and shortcuts typically develop a closer relationship between the two firms and reduce paperwork and associated costs markedly. The buyer's inventories and carrying costs obviously decline as well.

Term Contracting System Coupled with MRP

On page 65 the engineering bill of materials was discussed as a device for communicating production material needs to the purchasing department. Some firms that use an MRP computer-based scheduling system have carried this concept one step further, moving closer to achievement of a "paperless" purchasing operation.

The engineering bill of materials first is converted into a "structured," or tiered, bill of materials that can be used for production planning purposes. The logic of an MRP system then converts these bills of materials into aggregate requirements schedules for each part used in the products being manufactured. Using these precise MRP schedule requirements, some firms utilize a two-step approach to eliminate both the purchase requisition and the purchase order. First, the buyer establishes a long-term contract (one year or longer) with a supplier for each part. Second, material needs are transmitted directly to suppliers simply by sending them updated copies of the weekly (or monthly) material requirements schedule. The MRP schedule thus serves as *both* the purchase requisition and the purchase order (or release). Suppliers

---

[11]For a good discussion of systems contracting in MRO buying, see J. A. Lorincz, "Systems Contracts Put Control in MRO Buying," *Purchasing World*, May 1986, pp. 51–54.

simply deliver to the schedule. At the Boston Gear Works, for example, this approach works smoothly, involving purchasing personnel only on a management-by-exception basis after the initial purchase contracts are developed.[12]

Telephone/Fax Order System

Most companies now use a telephone or fax ordering system to reduce the paperwork associated with small-order purchasing. Under this system, when the purchasing department receives a requisition, it does not prepare a formal purchase order. Instead, the order is placed by telephone or fax, and the requisition is used in the receiving procedure.

Although many variations of this system are in use, it is important that the requisition form be designed to provide all data necessary for internal communications and control. One company uses a six-part form which includes all data normally included on a conventional purchase order. When the order is placed, one copy of the requisition is sent to the requisitioner, one goes to accounting, one remains in purchasing, and three copies are sent to receiving. When the material arrives, all receiving data are noted on the latter copies. One of these copies is sent to accounting, one is sent to purchasing, and the final copy either goes to the requisitioner or remains in a permanent receiving file.

One large firm in the electrical industry reportedly places most of its *small* orders by telephone—this translates to approximately 60 percent of *all* orders placed during the year. The system goes one step further in the elimination of paperwork; the firm's suppliers send no invoices for telephone purchases. A firm price is determined during the initial telephone conversation and is recorded on the requisition. When the material is received as ordered, the accounting department issues payment on the basis of the purchase requisition.

Electronic Ordering Systems

A number of electronic communication systems currently are available to transmit material purchase requests without writing orders or talking on the telephone. The hardware in a commonly used system consists of a magnetic card reader connected to a telephone in the purchaser's office and an interpreting unit connected to a telephone in the supplier's office. With this system, the buyer simply places a purchase requisition, in magnetic card form, in the card reader and dials the supplier's telephone number. The requisition data are then transmitted over telephone lines to the supplier's interpreting unit.

Another approach in this evolving process utilizes a computer terminal as the input device at the buyer's site. The terminal is tied to a telephone line through a modem. The data signal is then communicated via the telephone line to a printer or other receiving device at the supplier's site.

---

[12]John Fitts, "On the Road to Paperless Purchasing," *Purchasing World,* May 1982, pp. 48–50.

Such electronic systems will have limited use for *general* purchasing activity until a buyer's major suppliers acquire the necessary equipment and operating systems. Rapid growth in usage, however, *is* occurring among industrial supply firms. In situations where buyers find their use feasible, such systems can expedite the purchasing process, reduce paperwork, and simplify internal accounting and control. They are particularly applicable to the purchase of repetitively used items whose recurring orders can be placed using the same card or input source. Clearly, the use of an electronic ordering system requires a blanket order or similar contractual arrangement with the supplier.

The next step in the evolutionary development of this concept—computers talking to computers—is now a reality in a growing number of firms across the country. The topic of electronic data interchange (EDI) is discussed in the next chapter.

Petty Cash and C.O.D.

Most firms today use a *petty cash* fund for making small one-time purchases. For this purpose, many firms define "small" as under $100. It is often less expensive for an individual user (or a purchasing delivery employee) to buy minor items personally and pay for them from a petty cash fund than it is to buy them through the conventional purchasing system. Any inefficiencies that may arise because of a lack of buying skill are more than compensated for by the administrative savings resulting from not placing a purchase order.

Some firms also find it economical to make small one-time purchases on a C.O.D. basis. Material can be ordered by telephone and paid for on arrival. Payment can be made using petty cash or a departmental check written on an account set up for such purchases.

Purchase Credit Card

The use of corporate credit cards by employees for MRO purchases has become commonplace during the past few years. In addition to eliminating the need for most purchase orders, this buying technique reduces the purchasing cycle time, improves purchasing relations with operating departments, provides much faster payment to suppliers, and significantly reduces the workload in the accounts payable department.

Here is how the system usually works. First, purchasing makes arrangements with a known and respected group of suppliers for company credit card purchases. Usually, though not always, a blanket order contract is negotiated with the supplier to make the arrangement attractive, because the supplier will have to pay the credit card company or its bank a service fee for each purchase made. For this reason, purchasing reduces the number of suppliers used and consolidates certain types of purchases with each firm. Through this leveraged action, some companies have reported price reductions of up to 15 percent on the items covered by the blanket order.[13]

Internally, credit cards are issued to operating department personnel selected by their supervisors. Each card carries the appropriate departmental accounting charge number, along with a dollar purchase limit, usually ranging from $500 to $2,000. Subsequent purchases must be approved by the department supervisor—and can be made in person or by telephone or fax. Billing arrangements made with most suppliers call for invoicing on a monthly basis, with a copy to the appropriate department head.

Although this type of credit card system offers the buying firm a number of benefits, it also entails some additional exposure to risk: (1) The firm inevitably loses some control over what is actually purchased on the card; (2) it is sometimes possible for card holders to bypass departmental authorization and control; and (3) there is always the possibility that card use will provide some opportunities for petty fraud. On the other hand, purchasing can maintain indirect control in three ways: (1) It selects the suppliers where the card can be used, usually those with which the firm has had a long-term relationship; (2) with the help of department supervisors, it determines who receives cards; and (3) it sets the purchase limit for each card.

To date, most firms that use a carefully designed credit card system are pleased with the results.

Supplier Stores/Consignment System

If a purchaser buys a large enough volume of certain materials from a single supplier, the supplier sometimes can afford to staff a small "store" at the purchaser's plant and operate it on a consignment basis. Some suppliers find that annual purchases of approximately $100,000 justify such a branch operation. Users then simply go to the store and sign for their purchases. At the end of the month the company is billed for its purchases just as if the user had "gone downtown" to buy the material.

This system clearly is not a short-term arrangement. The purchaser, therefore, must take great care in selecting the supplier and in negotiating the terms of the agreement.

Supplier Delivery System

The supplier delivery system is somewhat similar to a supplier stores system, but it is more feasible for firms with a smaller volume of purchases. Many suppliers who are not willing to set up a store at the buyer's plant are willing to stock numerous miscellaneous materials and make daily or semiweekly deliveries. The buyer typically reviews and accumulates purchase requisitions for such materials. The supplier's delivery person then picks them up on the

---

[13] Whittier, op. cit., p. 14.

specified day, and at the same time delivers the material ordered on the preceding batch of requisitions. This continuous shuttle service provides reasonably fast delivery and also reduces the purchaser's paperwork and inventory problems. Properly designed, the system can provide for adequate accounting control.

A variation of this approach is used by Bethlehem Steel's Burns Harbor plant. This organization uses what it calls a "single-sourced bin-stocking" concept. For related families of inventory items, Bethlehem single-sources them with a proven supplier, covering the arrangement with a blanket order. The supplier checks Bethlehem's inventory bin levels once a week, replenishing the supply of any item that has reached the reorder point. This ongoing inventory control/delivery service by 21 MRO item suppliers has saved Bethlehem approximately $1.3 million per year through leveraged price reductions, significantly reduced its MRO inventory, reduced the number of purchase orders by approximately 41,000 per year, and improved material delivery time immensely.[14]

EVOLVING ORDERING ARRANGEMENTS

Purchasing and supply managers long have been interested in reducing the time and administrative cost involved in ordering, receiving, and paying for materials that are used repetitively in a firm's operation. In progressive firms, the purchasing and supply unit focuses on adding value, not time-consuming paperwork. This section describes briefly several approaches that many firms use to help achieve this basic objective.

Long-Term Contracts—Annual and Multiyear

Because of the economies of scale, large-quantity buyers generally purchase their high-dollar-value materials under long-term contracts. Today, contracts extending up to three years, sometimes five, are commonly used for the purchase of regular production materials. Such contracts eliminate duplicate yearly supplier investigations and purchasing administrative efforts. Lower prices and total purchase costs are the natural result.

In addition to the cost benefits which accrue from the economies of scale, long-term contracts provide the buying firm other benefits. For example, under such contracts, the seller is assured a large volume of business. It may adopt just-in-time manufacturing techniques or agree to carry inventories for the buyer. Consequently, the buying firm can reduce its inventory. When the seller knows the buyer's delivery schedule well in advance, distribution costs and production costs both can be reduced. Some of this saving should be passed along to the buyer. In times of scarcity, the buyer is assured of a reliable

---

[14]Jean Graham, "A Simple Idea Saves $8 Million a Year," *Purchasing*, May 21, 1992, pp. 47–49.

source of supply, as well as the best possible protection against unjustified price increases. Because long-term contracts are negotiated only once every several years, buying personnel are freed for other productive work such as supplier management, purchasing research, value analysis, and so on. The sophisticated buyer schedules major contracts to expire at approximately equal intervals throughout the year to balance his or her workload.

The use of multiyear contracts is increasing. As markets for certain materials become more volatile and availability becomes more uncertain, long-term contracts can offer significant advantages for both the buyer and the seller. Larger volumes, over longer periods of time, justify additional supplier investment in research, training, and tooling, thus contributing to lower unit costs and prices. Many of these contracts have an automatic renewal feature which is operationalized unless one of the parties objects. Such contracts frequently are called "evergreen" contracts.

Some of the contractual arrangements that buyers commonly use to cope with variable demand and varying delivery schedules are discussed below.

Definite Delivery-Type Contracts   When production schedules for the entire period of a contract are known, definite quantities for delivery on definite dates can be established. A contract with these provisions is called a *definite delivery-type contract.* This is the ideal type of ordering arrangement when such a degree of certainty is present.

Indefinite Delivery-Type Contracts   In some cases, production schedules cannot be planned precisely; hence, the quantities of materials required and their times of use, or both, are unknown. Materials and services for the support of such operations must be contracted for on an indefinite delivery schedule. There are three basic types of indefinite delivery contracts. In order of preference for the best pricing, they are (1) *definite quantity contracts,* (2) *requirements contracts,* and (3) *indefinite quantity contracts.*

Definite Quantity Contracts   These provide for the purchase of definite quantities of materials or services—whose time of use is uncertain. The contract therefore specifies that instructions regarding delivery schedules will be provided later. Because the quantities are known, however, favorable prices are possible for this type of agreement.

Requirements Contracts   These contracts provide for the purchase from one supplier of *all* of a buyer's requirements, for a stipulated time period, for specified materials or services for a designated operation or activity. Requirements contracts typically are used in applications such as the support of a firm's automotive repair shop, with parts being purchased from a specific parts dealer during the life of the agreement. To be certain that this type of contract is both legal and mutually satisfactory, the contract should provide for a *minimum quantity* the buyer is committed to take, and it should stipulate that neither party can terminate the contract during its life, as long as performance is satisfactory and as long as the buyer's requirements continue to exist. Without such provisions, requirements contracts have been found by courts to be unenforceable.

Indefinite Quantity Contracts During an agreed-upon period of time, these contracts provide for the delivery of a specific category of materials or services. Quantities and delivery dates are indefinite, but the buyer is committed to purchase between designated high- and low-quantity limits.

The indefinite quantities associated with both indefinite quantity contracts and requirements contracts preclude optimum pricing. However, the contracts represent a total volume of business that, although indefinite, is large enough for suppliers to want and to price competitively to obtain.

Scheduling order releases for these three types of indefinite delivery-type contracts usually is delegated to the using department, often the production scheduling group. In some cases releases are issued automatically by a buyer's MRP system directly to the supplier's MRP system.

National Agreements

National agreements are used by many firms that have two or more operating locations. Such an agreement usually takes the form of a long-term contract with a supplier for the purchase of material that is used regularly at a number of different operating sites. The item purchased can range from light bulbs to personal computers to production materials. At firms such as Hewlett Packard, national contracts are awarded by the corporate purchasing organization. At other firms, such as the General Electric Company, the operating location with the largest volume of purchases for the item in question usually is assigned responsibility for sourcing the corporation's domestic requirements.[15]

National contracts provide a number of benefits—continuity of supply, consistent quality, material standardization throughout the organization, reduced prices, lower inventory levels, reduced delivery costs, and improved efficiency for the corporationwide procurement staff. Such contracts normally provide price protection for both the buying and selling organizations by means of an escalation formula that usually is tied to the supplier's basic costs of production. Consequently, prices may increase or decrease during the life of the contract, depending on the behavior of the selected price or cost indexes.

"National contracts require considerable time to establish and administer. Purchasers must continually monitor the performance of selected suppliers, the market conditions concerning price and availability, and how the selected supplier compares with competitors."[16] Nevertheless, the benefits of such agreements offset the cited costs many times over.

---

[15]For a more comprehensive discussion of national contracts, see Ed Patrick, "The Nuts and Bolts of National Contracts," *NAPM Insights*, April 1990, p. 5.
[16]Ibid.

CONCLUSION

Every business unit develops a series of procedures to assist operating personnel in carrying out the policies and plans of the unit. In total, these procedures establish the ground rules for the daily activities of the department.

The *specific* procedures employed by each firm should be designed to meet the unique needs of that firm. *Generally* speaking, properly designed procedures should accomplish four objectives:

1 Accomplish each task satisfactorily with a minimum of time, effort, and paperwork.
2 Effectively communicate and coordinate the efforts of one work group with another.
3 Minimize overlapping efforts and group conflicts by clearly designating responsibility for each step of the procedure.
4 Permit effective management by exception.

It is important, too, to consider the external dimension of the procedures issue. The nature of the procedural interface that is established with a supplier is defined by the form of relationship that is developed with the firm. This area is undergoing a rapid evolutionary change as acquisition needs of purchasing firms become more dynamic. Driven by the need to continuously seek value enhancement, most firms are utilizing more creativity in the ways they approach firm-to-firm relationships *and transactional linkages.*

FOR DISCUSSION

4-1 One executive has said that the development of many of her company's procedures was a waste of time. Could there be any merit to this statement? Why do executives develop procedures and record them in procedure manuals? Explain.

4-2 What basic objectives should a good procedure fulfill?

4-3 List and discuss the steps in the purchasing cycle.

4-4 What improvements can you make to the procedures illustrated in Figure 4-1? Explain.

4-5 Explain how stock replenishment requisitions are developed in firms that use computer-based inventory management systems.

4-6 Write a procedure for auditing invoices.

4-7 Design a commodity record card (include related requirements). Design a contract record summary sheet.

4-8 Design a supplier record card (include related requirements). Design a special tool record.

4-9 How are bills of material used to notify purchasing of impending production material requirements?

4-10 Assume that you are a maintenance supplier buyer. A maintenance foreman calls you to inquire about a purchase order you placed two weeks ago. The foreman has lost his copy of the order, but he does have his copy of the requisition. How would you locate your copy of the purchase order to get the information he requests? Explain.

4-11 What is the value of maintaining a purchase log?

4-12 Discuss receiving practices in firms that use JIT production/purchasing systems.

4-13 Write a procedure to be used in handling telephone orders.

4-14 What does a purchasing executive mean by the "small-order problem"? Explain.

4-15 Discuss the rush order problem. How should rush orders be handled?

4-16 Explain briefly the various techniques that might be used to help solve the small-order problem.

4-17 How does a blanket purchase order system work? What are its advantages? What are its disadvantages?

4-18 How does systems contracting differ from blanket order purchasing?

4-19 How does a purchase credit card system work? What are its advantages and disadvantages?

4-20 What impact do you think the computer will have on the small-order problem of most businesses?

4-21 Discuss briefly the various types of long-term contracts.

4-22 What is an "evergreen" contract?

4-23 Discuss briefly the use of a national agreement.

CASES FOR CHAPTER 4

Blozis Company, page 784
Tokisan Corporation, page 925
The Office Supplies Hassle, page 875
WVC Industrial Chemicals Company, page 934
The Oakland School District, page 873
Metropolitan University (in the *Instructor's Manual*)

5

COMPUTER-BASED
SYSTEMS/EDI

KEY CONCEPTS

- A computerized materials management system
    Inventory control and purchase requisitions
    Purchase orders and change orders
    Follow-up and expediting
    Receiving, inspection, and stores requisitions
    Invoices and payment
    Management reports
- Impact on daily operations
- Impact on decision making and productivity
    Analytical applications
    Data base applications
    Expert systems applications
    Communications applications
- Electronic data interchange
    Standards requirements
    Third-party networks
    EDI and bar coding

The significance of computerization for purchasing and materials management is readily understood when one considers the amount of purely administrative work involved in the procurement cycle of the average company. Literally thousands of requisitions, requests for quotation, purchase orders, change orders, status reports, receiving records, invoices, and other documents must be processed and recorded.[1] Today, a computer-based system for handling these activities is a necessity. As one team of authors has described it, "A computer is in effect a huge file, a superfast calculating machine, and a printer rolled into one. It stores basic data in its memory and translates the data for procurement action."[2]

The preceding chapter discussed the basic procedures, documents, and records typically found in most firms' procurement operations. Although computerized systems were mentioned occasionally, the discussion was set primarily in the context of a manual operation using traditional office equipment and clerical methods. This chapter discusses the characteristics of a computer-based procurement system, along with the changes it brings to the department in performing key activities.

Effective use of a computer offers a purchasing or materials manager a number of important advantages. Because of its ability to process huge volumes of data rapidly, a computer can do much of the routine clerical work, thus freeing departmental personnel from many dull repetitive tasks. This means that a department can operate with fewer clerical people, or that existing personnel can spend their time on more creative purchasing work.

Most managers agree that the *primary advantage* a computer offers a buyer or a materials planner is the immediate availability of much more complete data for use in making cost-effective materials-related decisions. Because of its speed, a computer can supply virtually instantaneous reports which otherwise might take a small army of clerks weeks to prepare and update. The timeliness of such reports enables a materials executive to manage by exception and to do a more effective and more profitable job of purchasing and managing the flow of materials throughout the operation.

A COMPUTERIZED MATERIALS MANAGEMENT SYSTEM

When a system is computerized, the basic activities of the procurement process remain essentially the same as when the system was operated manually. What changes is the way in which the activities are performed.

In a computer-based system, for the most part, the same records that are maintained in a manual system are stored in disc or tape files that are readily accessible to the computer's central processing unit (CPU). Although the specific format and data contents vary among systems, the records readily available to the computer for display or processing typically are:

- Open-order file
- Order/parts behind schedule file

---

[1]Margaret A. Emmelhainz, "Computers in Purchasing/EDI," Chapter 4, *The Purchasing Handbook*, 5th ed., McGraw-Hill Book Company, New York, 1992, p. 106.

[2]S. F. Heinritz, Paul V. Farrell, Larry Giunipero, and Michael Kolchin, *Purchasing: Principles and Applications*, 8th ed., Prentice Hall, Englewood Cliffs, N.J., 1991, p. 87.

- Supplier record file
- Material (commodity) record file
- Inventory record file

These computer files usually contain the same detailed data (and perhaps more) that was discussed in the design of manual operating procedures in the preceding chapter.

Every company that automates its materials activities utilizes the computer in a slightly different manner. The data inputs vary from firm to firm, as do the desired data outputs. The form and timing of various reports depend to a great extent on the operating needs of each particular firm. Generally speaking, however, the *basic* materials activities which can be performed well by a computer-based system are the same in all cases. They are:

1 Maintenance of inventory records
2 Computation of order quantities
3 Preparation of purchase requisitions for inventory items
4 Preparation of requests for quotation
5 Preparation of purchase orders
6 Maintenance of order status records
7 Distribution of accounting charges
8 Automatic preparation of follow-up memos
9 Posting of delivery and quality records, by part and by supplier
10 Preparation of numerous operating reports for management
11 Provision of decision support system information
12 Auditing of invoices and preparation of checks for payment
13 Electronic data interchange communications

Three types (and sizes) of hardware are used today in computer-based purchasing operations. The *first* is a large mainframe system that purchasing shares with most other operating units in the organization. In most cases, the input terminals are located at the appropriate purchasing work stations and are linked to the processing hardware, which is usually located elsewhere in a centralized computer center. The *second* type of system frequently found in purchasing departments today is built around the use of a minicomputer. As its name implies, the mini is simply a miniature version of larger mainframe units. This type of system frequently (but not always) is dedicated for use in the purchasing and materials management activities of the firm. Operationally, this system functions much like a mainframe system, usually with better accessibility but with reduced memory and capacity. *Finally,* purchasing and supply operating systems in some firms, particularly smaller companies, are often handled adequately by a network of microcomputers (PCs) that constitute purchasing's own freestanding system. Some of these units may have the capability to access larger corporatewide data bases that are part of the firm's mainframe system. In any case, in recent years the growth in capacity and speed of PCs has been phenomenal.

In all these systems, authorized personnel communicate directly with the computer data base through the terminal for purposes of entering and recalling data, as well as performing calculations and other machine processing activities. Through the use of computer security codes, each individual's data access is usually restricted to that portion of the data base he or she needs to use in performing his or her job.

Figures 5-1 and 5-2 show in schematic form the general operation of an online computerized materials management system.

FIGURE 5-1
Schematic diagram of the materials ordering activity in a computerized materials management system.

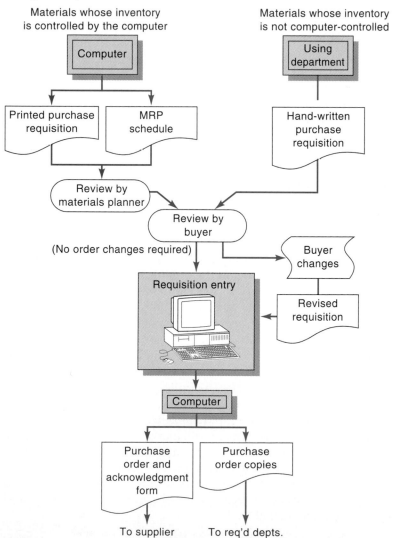

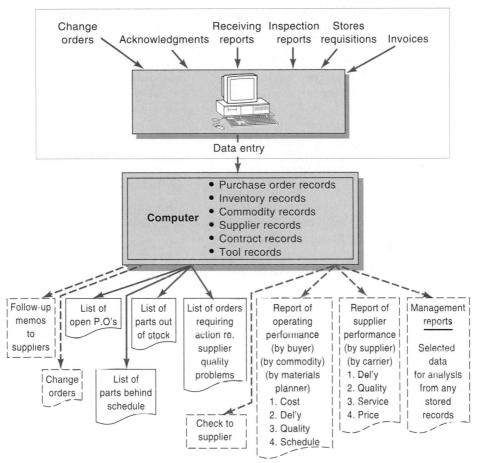

FIGURE 5-2
Schematic diagram of the activities subsequent to placement of the purchase order in a computerized materials management system.

Inventory Control and Purchase Requisitions

In an automated materials system, all inventory and part records (including engineering drawings and bills of material) are filed in memory accessible to the CPU. For each part either one record or several different records can be maintained. In either case, certain standard information is included, such as the part number, its name, required descriptive data, historical usage data, and the current inventory balance. Additionally, price data from recent purchases as well as price quotation information are also on file. Just as in a manual system, the file memory contains such information as supplier names and addresses, shipping terms, quality and delivery performance data, purchase history, and open orders.

Each time the machine posts a stores withdrawal requisition for a particular part, it updates the balance on hand and compares this figure with a specified reorder point figure. When the balance falls below this level, the computer prints out a purchase requisition. The quantity that the machine orders may be a predetermined order quantity or the quantity required by a planned period production schedule.

In the case of items controlled by an "order point" inventory control system, software is available to compute the most economical quantity, just as a buyer might do manually. Quantity calculations are based on predetermined figures for inventory carrying costs and acquisition costs, and on current figures for part usage and price; these data are filed in memory.[3] Thus, the computer automatically produces printed purchase requisitions which contain most of the information (including the appropriate accounting charge) that normally would appear on a manually prepared requisition. For the buyer's use, the requisition also can contain monthly usage data for the past year, a listing of past purchase orders and prices, and a summary of the most recent price quotations from different suppliers.

The computer, however, cannot determine the urgency of a firm's need for a part. Consequently, for other than normal delivery requirements, exact shipping dates, order follow-up dates, and carrier designations must be specified by the buyer. For this reason and for purposes of control, an automated system usually provides for a review of all purchase requisitions by the material planner and by the buyer. In the event that production needs fluctuate, the planner changes the requisition accordingly before sending it to the buyer. The buyer analyzes the requisition in terms of potential suppliers' performances under current conditions. He or she also considers future quantity and quality requirements, as well as other intangible factors, and makes any changes deemed appropriate. At this point, a purchase order number is also assigned.

Note that all purchase requisitions for parts whose inventory is *not* controlled by the computer must be finalized manually by the buyer. From this point on, however, a purchase order (P.O.) can be created and handled in the automated materials system without difficulty.

Purchase Orders and Change Orders

For computer-generated requisitions, if the buyer makes no changes, the purchase order can be prepared simply by adding the name of the desired supplier and a purchase order number—and instructing the computer to print out the requisition in the form of a purchase order. When data are added and changes are made to the requisition, or in the case of manually generated requisitions, all new data are keyed directly into the computer

---

[3]This discussion focuses on the use of an order point inventory control system. The operation can be automated just as easily for items that are controlled under a cyclical review or MRP system of inventory control. The cyclical review system frequently is used extensively in companies that cannot accurately forecast production demands more than a month or two in advance. In fact, computerization of inventory control in such cases reduces clerical costs of operating the inventory control system immensely.

through a terminal with the instruction to print out the corresponding purchase order.

At the same time the computer prepares the purchase order to be mailed to the supplier, it can produce an acknowledgment form for the supplier, copies of the purchase order for internal distribution, and forms to be used as the receiving and inspection reports. While producing purchase orders, the computer also produces and files in memory a cumulative list of all outstanding purchase orders. This becomes the major "working" order file.

In the event an order is changed after it has been issued, a change order form is prepared by the buyer and processed by the computer. This and subsequent documents are processed by the machine in the same way as the original purchase order. With accompanying documents, they simply replace the original order.

Follow-Up and Expediting

The file of open purchase orders can be processed as frequently as desired to produce current information for purchasing personnel. Today most firms update open orders once a day to provide purchasing with up-to-the-minute status reports.

One of the most important outputs of the open-order processing operation is the follow-up communication. At the time a purchase requisition is converted into an order, the buyer instructs the computer to print out a follow-up memo at specified dates prior to the scheduled delivery date. Such a system assures periodic review of every purchase order, regardless of departmental workload or employee absenteeism. The computer, as instructed, faithfully reproduces follow-up memos, according to a predetermined format; hence, mailing these communications is the only clerical effort required of purchasing personnel. Upon receipt of a supplier's response, the buyer or expediter gives attention only to those orders requiring further follow-up work.

Orders whose delivery is behind schedule are brought to the attention of the buyer by a "behind schedule" report.

Receiving, Inspection, and Stores Requisitions

When an order is received, the receiving clerk (or a terminal operator) utilizes a remote terminal to enter the conventional receiving information directly into the computer's order record. This activity often is facilitated with a bar code scanning operation. Simultaneously, the machine produces the printed reports required for the use of other company personnel. Receiving reports thus can be generated in multiple copies for the buyer, the materials planner, and other using departments. For those orders requiring technical inspection, inspection reports are produced in conventional form and are processed periodically by the computer to update the open-order file and the inventory record file.

As previously indicated, stores requisitions that are prepared in conventional form are entered through a terminal and processed periodically to update inventory records.

Daily updating of the open-order records and the parts inventory records, coupled with the computer's speed, permits the preparation of numerous daily operating reports to facilitate the buyer's job. Four commonly used reports are:

- List of open purchase orders
- List of orders or parts that are behind schedule
- List of parts that are out of stock
- List of orders or parts that require action because of supplier quality or related problems

Such reports are of tremendous value to individual buyers. They provide a buyer with a summary of critical, up-to-the-minute information about his or her orders that is virtually impossible to obtain manually. These summary reports also permit the buyer to manage by exception—that is, to concentrate efforts on those orders requiring attention in time to prevent the development of serious purchasing problems.

Invoices and Payment

When an invoice for an order is received, it is keyed directly into the computer through a terminal. The computer then audits the invoice by comparing the item, the quantity, and the price with corresponding information recorded in the updated purchase order (and receiving) files. The computer also verifies the price extension. Any discrepancies are noted on an output error list. If no discrepancies are found, the unit signals a printer to write a check to the supplier for the amount of the invoice less any applicable discounts.

Accounting charges for the order can be distributed in the conventional manner from a printed copy of the purchase order, or they can be distributed by the computer. If the accounting system is computerized, distributions can be made by the machine during the processing of the accounting records.

Management Reports

In its initial design, an automated materials management system can be developed to accumulate various data useful to managerial personnel for decision making and control purposes. The computer's speed permits monthly or weekly analysis and summary of much information that is outside the realm of feasibility in a manually operated system. While managers in different firms may desire different types of reports, most supply executives want to evaluate the performance of suppliers, carriers, and commodities, as well as their own individual personnel and departments.

It is entirely possible to purchase or develop computer software to provide periodic reports of each supplier's and carrier's performance with respect to such things as volume of business, late deliveries, rejected shipments (because of poor quality), transit damage, or price trends. Such reports can even be broken down by product lines, in the case of multiproduct suppliers. Likewise, the computer can prepare reports on the performance of individual buyers, materials planners, and departments. Such reports can include figures on number of orders, blanket orders and materials handled, dollar volume of orders by commodity, percentage of open orders, prices paid versus target prices, percentage of late deliveries, percentage of rejected shipments, percentage of schedules missed, etc. Some companies even develop formulas for determining performance indexes for suppliers and buyers and have the computer automatically compute the indexes monthly. The computer offers materials executives an endless number of possibilities for developing data to improve management decisions and control.

THE IMPACT OF A COMPUTER-BASED SYSTEM ON DAILY OPERATIONS

The first observable change a computer-based system makes in the traditional purchasing office routine is in the generation and processing of purchase requisitions. As a rule, a majority of the firm's purchase requisitions are prepared by the computer, including virtually all the requisitions for materials carried in inventory. Items whose inventory cannot be controlled effectively by a computer on a continuing basis are primarily those with extremely unstable usage patterns. Requisitions for these items as well as for "new buys," normal "one-time" purchases, and certain emergency and critical items usually continue to be generated manually.

A second, and related, change produced by an automated system focuses on the utilization of people. A computer-based system frees buyers and other professional personnel from a vast amount of routine work associated with the initiating and processing of requisitions. One company found that prior to the installation of an automated system, the average buyer spent nearly 50 percent of his or her time processing purchase requisitions. After installation of the system, requisition processing required only a fraction of this time. Automation thus permitted the typical buyer to devote a majority of the time to creative buying activities such as supplier investigation, negotiation and problem solving, value analysis, and various types of purchasing research.[4]

Another difference, with significant managerial implications, is that the system regularly provides buyers and managers with a large variety of new and

---

[4]For an interesting variety of case study experiences, see (1) Steve Springer, "The Role of the PC in the Purchasing Environment," *The Hoosier Purchaser*, March/April 1988, pp. 12–13; (2) T. F. Dillon, "Caterpillar Connects with EDI," *Purchasing World*, August 1986, pp. 62–64.

valuable detailed control data. One aircraft manufacturer found that use of the report data enabled it to reduce delays in manufacturing by effectively controlling late shipments. It was also able to reduce its inventory investment, reduce average material costs, do a better job of planning cash flows, improve its cost accounting control, and increase the speed and effectiveness of the total procurement operation.

Still another change is seen in the relationships developed between purchasing and other materials activities. These relationships, particularly with production control, are somewhat closer under an automated system. The computer is the common bond which draws all materials activities into an integrated system. This situation promotes the development of a materials management type of organization. Even where the traditional forms of organization persist, buyers find themselves working more closely with their counterparts in the production control department. The design of the system and the speed with which it functions minimize buck-passing between the two and tend to make specific materials problems company problems, rather than departmental problems.

Finally, compared with a traditional purchasing operation, the general tenor of activities in an automated department is upgraded and focuses more sharply on the managerial and creative responsibilities of the purchasing function. Fewer clerks and expediters are required. The buyer's role, if developed as a logical extension of the old one, involves more analytical work and more purchasing research.

IMPACT ON DECISION MAKING AND PRODUCTIVITY

Microcomputers (PCs) are found in virtually all business offices today, including purchasing and supply management offices. In the latter case, micros are used primarily to increase the productivity and effectiveness of procurement personnel. The increase is accomplished in two ways:

1 By making it possible for individuals to do more thorough *analytical* work that leads to more effective materials decisions
2 By making it possible simply to increase the volume of work that can be handled—hence, increasing the individual's productivity

Three types of microcomputer applications are found most frequently in the materials environment—analytical, data base, and communications.

Analytical Applications

The most common technique used in the various analytical applications is "spreadsheet" analysis. A *spreadsheet* (developed either on paper or on a PC) is simply a matrix of rows and columns into which relevant data elements are inserted for different operational alternatives (e.g., suppliers, operating plans, and so on). Many of the data elements for each alternative are related mathematically, and it is the PC's ability to make such calculations quickly that makes it so useful for this type of analysis.

Spreadsheet analysis is used most commonly in purchasing offices for activities such as:

1 The evaluation of competitive bids
2 The analysis of various quantity discount purchase alternatives
3 Cost-price analysis for different potential suppliers
4 Make-or-buy analysis
5 The quantifiable aspects of value analysis.

In all these various analyses, many of the data elements are variable as they relate to each other (different quantities, different service, different costs and prices, and so on), and they typically vary among alternative suppliers, plans, and so on. So the job of the analyst is to make the calculations, develop comparable data among the alternatives (compare apples to apples), and then analyze the findings to determine the best course of action. The value of a PC-based spreadsheet analysis in this work is obvious.

"What if" analysis is a similar type of spreadsheet application that can give management extremely useful data for planning purposes. This approach, in effect, simulates the operation of a total system under different operating conditions. For example, a materials manager might conduct an inventory system simulation. Suppose he or she wants to know the effects on costs and service of reducing the inventory levels of certain commodity classifications, or of developing various supplier stocking arrangements for certain materials, or of developing a JIT purchasing plan with selected suppliers—"what if" we did such and such? Once the system is modeled on the spreadsheet, the manager can change a given variable, and within seconds the computer will show the impact of the modification on the entire system.

Data Base Applications

When the data records maintained in the computerized operating system are originally designed, practical considerations typically limit the amount of information to be contained in each record. In the course of their work, however, certain buyers or buying groups may have unique needs for more detailed or refined information about certain suppliers, operations, data needed for forecasting, and so on. A microcomputer or a networked micro system in the department can be used to expand selected operating data files for such purposes.

Records that frequently are enhanced in this way include those dealing with materials and market variables, suppliers, services, quotations, and contracts. When such records are expanded by using a PC, it is important to integrate the system carefully with the purchasing operating system and to provide adequate data security so that unauthorized individuals cannot modify the basic record.

Expert Systems Applications[5]

A fledgling technology is emerging that utilizes both the analytical and data base PC applications—"purchasing expert systems." Expert systems are computer programs that solve problems by emulating the problem-solving behavior of human experts. These systems are developed by knowledge engineers who conduct interviews with one or more experts to capture their knowledge and problem-solving logic regarding a specific problem. The engineers then construct a computer model using artificial intelligence programming languages.

An expert system consists of a knowledge base and an "inference engine." The knowledge base contains program goals, facts generally agreed upon by the experts, and "rules of thumb" that an expert would use in making decisions. The inference engine represents the expert's problem-solving approach and uses the contents of the knowledge base to reach conclusions. Expert systems then provide decision support to managers by means of a computer-based question and answer session. Thus, an expert system uses information obtained from consultation with experts, the department's own data base, and possibly external data bases to make recommendations to purchasing and supply management.

This technology is still in embryonic form as far as purchasing use is concerned. Although it appears to hold promise for improving the effectiveness of purchasing decisions in the future, only a few large firms use it at the present time. IBM, for example, is reported to save $1.5 million per year through its use of an expert system program in buying injection moldings.

Communications Applications

PC software is commonly available to provide "electronic mailbox" and "electronic bulletin board" capabilities, as well as word processing capability. Many purchasing departments use electronic mail communications among personnel within the department, as well as with users in operating departments. The bulletin board feature can be used to communicate material lead-time changes, price changes, information about supplier problems, and similar types of information that purchasing and other individuals throughout the organization need to know.

As in all departments, word processing capability can be a real time-saver in purchasing. The repetitive preparation of various reports, requests for quotation, and so on, in which some data remain constant from one preparation to

---

[5]This discussion is based on Robert L. Cook, "Expert Systems in Purchasing: Applications and Development," *International Journal of Purchasing and Materials Management*, Fall 1992, pp. 20–27.

the next while other data change, represents an excellent opportunity to increase productivity by using this PC capability.[6]

ELECTRONIC DATA INTERCHANGE

Once a firm has an effective computer-based purchasing system in operation, a logical extension of that system is to link it, in one way or another, with the order-handling computer system of selected suppliers. The term generally given to this type of buyer-supplier communications operation is *electronic data interchange—EDI*. In an evolutionary sense, EDI simply is an advanced step in the continuing drive toward the development of a "paperless" purchasing operation that began with techniques such as the blanket order, systems contracting, consignment purchasing, and various data-phone techniques discussed in the preceding chapter.

In its purest sense,

> EDI is the direct electronic transmission, computer to computer, of standard business forms, such as purchase orders, shipping notices, invoices, and the like, between two organizations. In a purchasing environment, documents are transmitted "over the wire," eliminating the need to generate hard copies and to distribute them manually. By utilizing EDI, a buyer and a supplier are operating in a near real-time environment, which can reduce material delays by shortening procurement lead times.[7]

Types of Operations

In practice, applications based on the EDI concept take several forms. The first step in many firms is the transmission of data from a dedicated terminal in the buyer's operation to a terminal (and perhaps printer) in the supplier's operation. Technically, this is not a pure EDI operation because a terminal operator is required to input data generated by the buyer's automated purchasing system, and an operator frequently is required to receive the data at the supplier's location. Nevertheless, in this type of proprietary system transmission is instantaneous and most of the key benefits accrue to both organizations.

Another similar application, terminal to computer, involves transmission from the buyer's terminal to the supplier's electronic mailbox at its computer site. In this case, operation is about the same as in the preceding example, except no operator is required at the receiving site. However, it is necessary to ensure that the supplier's system is ready to receive the communications before transmission is begun.

---

[6]Detailed discussions of PC applications in purchasing are found in (1) Stephen Wildstrom, "In Search of the Paperless Contract," *Business Week,* Aug. 29, 1994, p. 14; (2) Springer, op. cit., pp. 12–13; (3) Jeff Pinkerton, "Using Spreadsheets as a Purchasing Tool," *Purchasing World,* October 1986, pp. 34–36.

[7]Robert M. Monczka and Joseph R. Carter, "Implementing Electronic Data Interchange," *Journal of Purchasing and Materials Management,* Summer 1988, p. 2.

The last stage, in what is sometimes an evolutionary process, is computer-to-computer communication. Both the buyer and the supplier have electronic mailboxes into which the other party can deposit purchase orders, acknowledgments, invoices, and related communications. Because neither party has access to the internal files of the other, the integrity of proprietary data is maintained. This system represents operational development of the concept to its fullest extent; the two firms' computers literally talk with each other in a standardized language. Figure 5-3 shows in simplified schematic form the flow of communications in this system, as compared with a traditional hard copy system.

Standards Requirements

For the two firms' computers to communicate with each other effectively, they must "talk the same language." To accomplish this requirement operationally, it is necessary for both firms to use certain standard procedures. These technically based requirements involve two types of procedures—communication standards and message standards.

Communication Standards   Communication standards provide guidelines for the *transmission* of electronic data. These standards help to ensure that the message is received and can be processed by the receiver. Issues covered include[8]:

- The speed at which the data can be transmitted
- The timing of the placement or retrieval of information to or from the mailbox
- The requirement for passwords and the coding of data
- The matching of equipment to be used

Message Standards   Message standards provide guidelines for the *content* of the data to be transmitted. These standards help to ensure that the meaning of the data is clear to both parties. The standards cover[9]:

- Definition of words and codes
- Meanings for specific terms of trade
- Methods of identifying specific products and terms
- Essential elements to be included in the transmission

To permit the development of EDI relationships among large numbers of different buying and supplying firms, it is important that essentially the same message standards be used by all firms. Consequently, a variety of industry groups have developed standards for their industries. Most of these standards

[8]Margaret A. Emmelhainz, "Electronic Data Interchange in Purchasing," *Guide to Purchasing,* NAPM Inc., New York, 1986, p. 6.
[9]Ibid.

TRADITIONAL TRANSMISSION OF DOCUMENTS

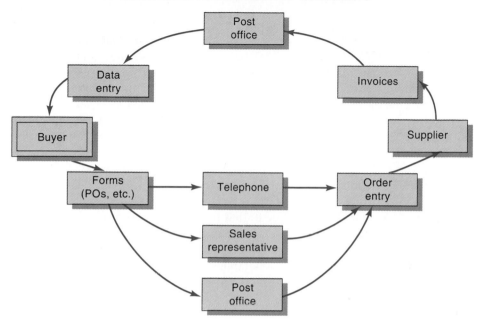

ELECTRONIC TRANSMISSION OF PURCHASING DOCUMENTATION

Direct Transmission

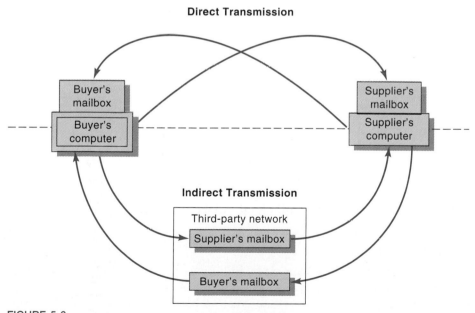

Indirect Transmission

FIGURE 5-3
Simplified schematic of communication flows in traditional and electronic transmission systems.
(Source: *Based on Margaret A. Emmelhainz, "Electronic Data Interchange in Purchasing,"* Guide to Purchasing, *NAPM Inc., New York, 1986, pp. 10–11.*)

are based on a structure developed by the Transportation Data Coordinating Committee (TDCC), which was subsequently expanded and refined by the American National Standards Institute (ANSI). The current set of standards most commonly used by industrial purchasers and sellers is identified as ANSI X12, which includes all TDCC-developed standards. For international commerce, the most commonly used standard is the European Electronic Data Interchange for Administration, Commerce, and Trade, which is better known as EDIFACT. Special software is required to translate ANSI X12 into EDIFACT, and vice versa. These standards accommodate virtually all forms of purchasing-related documents.

Each buying firm's computer system typically generates its purchasing data in an internal format that is unique to that firm. Hence, prior to domestic electronic transmission the internal data format must be translated into the ANSI X12 format. This translation into the standard format is generally done through the use of commercially available software. Once the data are translated into a standard format, the message is communicated to the supplier. This communication can be accomplished either directly (buyer to supplier) or through a third-party network.

Third-Party Networks

A third-party network firm functions as a central communications clearinghouse, much as a central check clearinghouse functions in the banking industry. It accepts the buyer's purchase orders, separates them by supplier, and at the appropriate times transmits them to the computer in each supplier's organization. In addition, a third-party network firm can provide certain value-added functions such as control reporting, standards translation, media conversion, and other transmission-related functions.

If a buyer is working in the EDI mode with only one or a small number of suppliers, the buying and the selling firms usually can manage the translation and communication standards requirements satisfactorily. As EDI purchasing agreements expand to include a number of suppliers, these logistical management problems increase correspondingly and soon become impractical to handle. In this situation, third-party network firms usually are employed to manage the transmission processes of the interfacing companies. The lower portion of Figure 5-3 diagrams the resulting information flows.

EDI and Bar Coding

An EDI operation can be enhanced by linking to it a bar coding system. When the supplier receives the buyer's electronic order or order release, it contains information the supplier can use to create a bar code shipping label. At the time of shipment this label is scanned by the supplier to generate a packing slip and an electronic advance shipping notice (ASN) that is transmitted to the buying firm. When the shipment arrives at the buyer's receiving dock, the bar code label can be scanned and compared with the ASN for identification purposes, and subsequently used in the receiving and internal communication processes. This technique expedites and increases the accuracy of the receiving operation.

The use of bar coding is discussed in greater detail in Chapter 24.[10]

Benefits

Once an EDI system is in place and functioning properly, it produces a number of clear-cut operating benefits for the buying firm. An obvious reduction in paperwork and related administrative requirements contributes noticeably to increased productivity. Because data are transmitted directly between computers, accuracy of the data throughout the process typically is increased. For the same reason, more complete and faster feedback of order status information is possible. Finally, and perhaps most important, purchasing lead time is reduced. This reduces a firm's "time to market" for its products, and it also produces additional time that can be utilized for planning, solving problems, and so on. The net result frequently is the reduction of troublesome materials and operations delays.

There is little doubt that the EDI approach will be utilized increasingly in the future for purchases that involve a number of standard inventory items obtained from a given supplier, or for repetitive high-volume purchases of production materials (standard or special) that can be supplied by one or a small number of firms.[11]

CONCLUSION

During the past two decades, we have witnessed the evolution of one of the most important trends in the history of organized society—the increasingly sophisticated use of computers. Although these amazing electronic devices have found applications in virtually every type of human endeavor, the business sector is a major beneficiary.

Within a business operation, no functional area is likely to benefit more from computerization than the materials activities. In addition to its capabilities for processing enormous quantities of data, producing timely management reports, and developing EDI operations, a computer provides another capability that is particularly important to management. Its speed in performing mathematical computations produces a quantitative analytical capability infinitely greater than that possible in a manual system. Consequently, numerous operations research techniques and "what if" models now can be used to analyze materials problems to generate data for planning purposes. Managers

[10]For a thorough treatment of this topic, see Joseph R. Carter and Gary L. Ragatz, "Supplier Bar Codes: Closing the EDI Loop," *International Journal of Purchasing and Materials Management,* Summer 1991, pp. 19–23.

[11]For a more detailed discussion of EDI, see Ven Sriram and S. Banerjee, "Electronic Data Interchange: Does Its Adoption Change Purchasing Policies and Procedures?" *International Journal of Purchasing and Materials Management,* Winter 1994, pp. 31–40.

can investigate alternative plans with quantitative precision and, hence, make decisions based on more factual data and more informed assumptions and judgments than was previously possible.

Managers must not lose sight of the fact, however, that a computer is only as capable as the people who design the software and the systems in which it is used. Finally, it is essential to remember that the integrity of the output is no greater than the quality and integrity of the data the computer-based system is asked to process.

FOR DISCUSSION

5-1 Discuss how the basic activities of the procurement process change after a manual system is converted to a computerized system.

5-2 What are the *basic* records contained in virtually all computerized materials management systems?

5-3 Explain how an automated purchasing system such as that shown in Figures 5-1 and 5-2 works in practice.

5-4 How does a computer determine when the order point has been reached in an automated inventory control operation? Explain how this computer capability is used in developing other operating elements of an automated purchasing system.

5-5 "The uninformed person sometimes envisions an automated purchasing system as one in which most purchasing personnel are simply replaced by a computer." Comment. Discuss the impact computerization has on departmental staffing requirements.

5-6 In what ways does a buyer's job change when his or her company computerizes the purchasing operation?

5-7 Discuss in detail the benefits a purchasing department might expect to obtain from computerizing its operation. What problems or disadvantages might be expected?

5-8 It is frequently said that managers and buyers can truly "manage by exception" in a purchasing department that is automated. What is your reaction to this statement?

5-9 "The design and speed of an integrated computer-based purchasing operation minimize buck-passing between purchasing and production control personnel." Comment.

5-10 How can a PC be used in a purchasing department?

5-11 Explain how purchasing productivity can be increased by the use of microcomputers.

5-12 Give a detailed illustration of how a buyer might use "what if" analysis in his or her work.

5-13 What is an expert system? How does such a system work in practice?

5-14 What is EDI? How does it work in practice?

5-15 Why do standards need to be developed for effective EDI use? Explain the two types of standards used.

5-16 Discuss the role of third-party network firms in EDI operation.

5-17 Explain how bar coding can be used in conjunction with an EDI operation.

CASES FOR CHAPTER 5

Julberg, Inc., page 833
New Valley Power Corporation, page 867

6

ORGANIZATION

In any group activity, three principal factors largely determine the level of performance attained by the group as a whole:

- The capabilities of the individuals
- The motivation of the individuals
- The organizational structure within which the individuals function

This chapter focuses on the last factor.

The first two factors are obvious to most business people. However, to many people the third is less clear. In the case of purchasing, the function's location in the management hierarchy of a firm is important, for this decision either facilitates or limits the influence purchasing policies and actions can have on the firm's total performance. Within the department itself, the form of organization selected influences the types and levels of expertise developed and also, to a great extent, the effectiveness with which the talents of individuals are utilized.

The starting point in thinking about various potential organization structures is a delineation and an analysis of the work to be done by the unit—the responsibilities and activities discussed on pages 114–115. In small firms, these duties may be handled by a purchasing or supply manager and one or two assistants; everyone wears several hats. In large organizations, the department may consist of 100 to 300 purchasing and supply professionals.[1] The possibilities for various types of specialization in this type of organization are great indeed.

LOCATION OF THE PURCHASING AND SUPPLY FUNCTION IN AN INDUSTRIAL ORGANIZATION[2]

A firm's organizational structure reflects management's basic attitudes toward the major activities involved in its operation. Where should the purchasing and supply function fit in a firm's organizational structure? A recent study of the *Fortune 1000* firms reveals the reporting relationships shown below[3]:

Percent of firms	Purchasing reports to
34%	President or executive vice president
25	Vice president of manufacturing
29	Other functional vice presidents
12	Other units

The two most commonly found alternatives are shown schematically in Figures 6-1 and 6-2.

---

[1]Large multiplant firms may employ up to 1,000 or more buyers.

[2]The discussion in this chapter is set in a manufacturing environment because the various organizational approaches are most fully developed in that setting. The concepts discussed, however, are just as applicable in the nonmanufacturing environments of service-oriented institutions and government. The only thing that changes is the terminology.

[3]Harold E. Fearon, *Purchasing Organizational Relationships*, NAPM, Inc., Tempe, Ariz., 1988, p. 28.

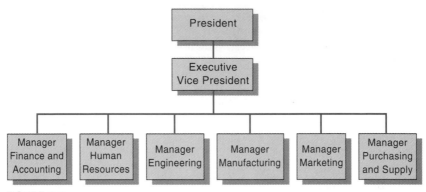

FIGURE 6-1
Skeleton organization for a medium-sized firm, with purchasing and supply as a top-level function.

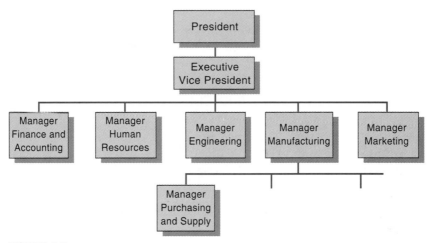

FIGURE 6-2
Skeleton organization for a medium-sized firm, with purchasing and supply as a second-level function.

In a given firm, how does one tell whether purchasing and supply is a top-level function that should report to a general management executive, as do marketing and manufacturing, or a subfunction that should report to one of the top functional executives? Answers to these questions can be determined only by finding the answers to several more basic questions. How important is the purchasing and supply management activity to the total company operation? Will the company suffer significantly if it does not perform as effectively as it might? How important is it that purchasing activities be coordinated closely with engineering and finance activities? Is it essential that material costs be tightly controlled?

Due to the varied nature of different firms' products and operations, answers to the preceding questions differ among firms. The importance of purchasing and supply management in any specific firm is determined largely by four factors:

1 *Availability of materials.* Are the major materials used by the firm readily available in a competitive market? Or are some key materials bought in volatile markets subject to periodic shortages and price instability? If the latter condition prevails, creative performance by analytical purchasing professionals is required; this typically is a top-level group.

2 *Absolute dollar volume of purchases.* If a company spends a large amount of money for materials, the sheer magnitude of the expenditure means that top-flight purchasing can usually produce significant profit. Small unit savings add up quickly when thousands of units are purchased.

3 *Percent of product cost represented by materials.* When a firm's materials costs are 40 percent or more of its product cost (or its total operating budget), small reductions in material costs increase profit significantly. Top-level purchasing and supply management usually pays off in such companies.

4 *Types of materials purchased.* Perhaps even more important than the preceding considerations is the amount of control purchasing and supply personnel actually have over materials availability, quality, costs, and services. Most large companies use a wide range of materials, many of whose price and service arrangements definitely can be influenced by creative purchasing performance. Some firms, on the other hand, use a fairly small number of standard production and supply materials, from which even a top-flight purchasing and supply department can produce little profit, despite what it does, as a result of creative management, pricing, and supplier selection activities.

Value analysis and purchasing-engineering coordination activities produce handsome profits for a company like General Electric. On the other hand, the types of materials required by some companies leave little room for savings to be produced by such creative effort. A manufacturer of conventional storage batteries, for example, would appear to have little need for sophisticated value analysis work after product designs have been refined several times.

Economic analysis and other profit-oriented activities conducted by purchasing research groups likewise are much more lucrative when dealing with some materials and markets than with others. Purchasing for a technical research and development organization, for example, is often primarily a service activity. In such a firm, material costs and market trends are not the important concerns they are in a production-oriented firm.

When business operations are viewed in the light of the preceding criteria, it is evident that many firms can benefit from a high-caliber, creative purchasing and supply department. In such companies this function should be a top-level, profit-making function that receives close attention from general management. In other firms, purchasing performs primarily a service activity for a major operating function. In such cases, purchasing properly should report to that functional executive. Similar types of considerations dictate the location of all departments in an organization. In most companies, for example, engineering and marketing are top-level functions; in some companies, however, they perform a secondary function and are organized accordingly.

ORGANIZATION FOR PURCHASING AND SUPPLY MANAGEMENT IN A SINGLE-PLANT COMPANY

A Basic Approach to Organization

The nature of purchasing activity permits effective use of the functionalization concept. Purchasing and supply work divides naturally into five distinct classifications, each of which encompasses a fairly wide range of activities. In most cases the classifications can be further divided into more specialized tasks, each of which still involves working with different problems, different products, and different suppliers. This happy circumstance permits the attainment of a high degree of specialization, without creating motivational problems for most purchasing or supply personnel.

The five classifications of work found in a purchasing operation are:

1 *Management.* Management of the purchasing and supply function involves all the tasks associated with the management process, with emphasis on the development of policies, procedures, controls, and the mechanics for coordinating purchasing operations with those of other departments. On an exception basis, it also involves the management of unique supplier and commodity problems.

2 *Buying.* This includes a wide variety of activities, such as working with users to help develop requirements and specifications, reviewing requisitions, analyzing specifications, investigating suppliers, analyzing supplier capabilities, interviewing salespeople, studying costs and prices, analyzing bids, negotiating, and selecting suppliers.

  Some firms have expanded the buying job and now see it as "supplier management." This additional responsibility involves continuing work with a supplier to improve supplier capability and performance, particularly in the quality area.

3 *Follow-up and expediting.* Order follow-up activity involves various types of supplier liaison work, such as reviewing the status of orders, writing letters, telephoning and faxing suppliers, and occasionally visiting suppliers' plants.

4 *Strategic planning and research work.* A well-developed purchasing and supply management operation has an unending number of research projects and systems studies requiring specialized knowledge and analytical ability. The more an organization has progressed toward a supply management focus, the more emphasis it places on these strategic activities.

  The core activities in this area include economic, industry, and supply market studies; development of material buying strategies; development of supply base and partnering plans; product research and value analysis work; and operating and information systems analysis.

5 *Clerical activities.* Every department must write orders and must maintain working files, catalog and library materials, and records for commodities, suppliers, prices, and so on.

The precise manner in which purchasing work is subdivided and grouped depends on the size of the department, which in turn depends on the size of the company. The size of the purchasing and supply department typically runs somewhat over 1 percent of the total company work force in small firms to substantially less than 1 percent in large firms (1.2 to 0.7 percent is a frequently cited range).

In a small company, say 150 employees, purchasing and supply frequently is a two-person department. The manager handles all work in the first four classifications, and a secretary performs the clerical work. As the size of the department increases, additional personnel are usually assigned joint buying and follow-up duties. At this point, buyers begin to specialize on the basis of broad classifications of the commodities they buy, and each typically does his or her own follow-up and expediting work. As the department grows, buyers continue to specialize in increasingly narrower commodity classifications. Eventually, the follow-up and expediting work may be withdrawn from the buyers and assigned to expediters, who may specialize in somewhat the same manner as buyers. Continued growth often results in the addition of one or more staff personnel who specialize in the various kinds of strategic supply project work.

The Typical Organization Structure

Figure 6-3 illustrates a typical structure for the internal organization of a purchasing and supply department in a medium-sized firm.[4]

Manager of Purchasing and Supply The chief purchasing and supply executive assumes various titles in different companies, such as manager of purchasing, director of purchases, manager of purchasing and supply, or, occasionally, purchasing agent. In a small department, he or she usually performs major buying activities as well as the required management duties. As the department grows, most of the manager's time is devoted to management and strategic issues, except for the negotiation of a few major contracts.

Buyers Buyers and their assistants perform the actual buying activity and work directly with suppliers. Each buyer, and assistant if the job requires one, handles a specific group of materials.

---

[4]A common modification of this basic pattern entails the assignment of expediting personnel and clerical personnel to each buying group. This kind of structure is a "pure" commodity-type organization. It reduces the possibility of divided responsibility among buyers and expediters, and some firms feel that it tends to increase employee job satisfaction. On the other hand, this type of organization can be more costly and less flexible, especially in small companies.

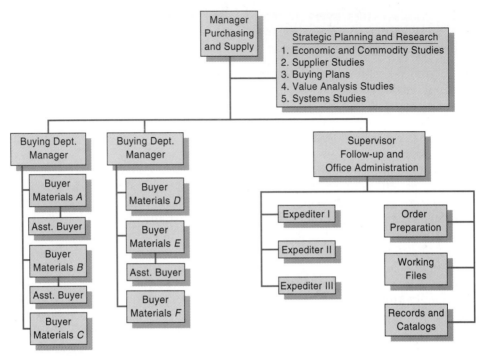

FIGURE 6-3
A typical basic structure for the internal organization of a single-plant purchasing and supply department in a medium-sized firm.

For buying purposes, materials can be grouped in two ways: (1) materials whose purchase requires similar buying skills and technical knowledge can be grouped together (market focus), or (2) materials that are used in the same finished product (or by the same operating department) can be grouped together. The former practice is the more common. Grouping materials that have similar buying and technical characteristics permits a buyer to become a technical specialist. For example, he or she may specialize in buying electronic parts, metal castings, or abrasive materials. In most firms today this is highly desirable. As materials continue to become more complex, specialized knowledge of their characteristics, manufacturing processes, and markets is indeed required to purchase them intelligently. Table 6-1 illustrates a classification of materials used in a typical production operation. For assignment to buyers, these classifications are organized into larger groups on the basis of required buying skills. Exact groupings depend on the size of the department and the volume of material usage.

If a buyer's materials are grouped by similarity of end use, one buyer may buy some or all of the parts for finished product A, and another buyer may buy the parts for finished product B. Or one buyer may handle the materials used by the fabrication department and another may handle the components

TABLE 6-1
A CLASSIFICATION OF MATERIALS USED IN A TYPICAL MANUFACTURING OPERATION

1	Abrasives	18	Machine tools
2	Adhesives	19	Office furniture and equipment
3	Bearings	20	Office supplies
4	Castings	21	Packaging material
5	Chemicals	22	Paint
6	Coal	23	Plastic parts
7	Containers	24	Powdered metal parts
8	Electrical and electronic components	25	Printed materials
9	Electrical and electronic assemblies	26	Power sources
10	Electrical cable and wire	27	Pumps
11	Fasteners	28	Rubber goods and parts
12	Forgings	29	Safety clothing
13	Fuel oil	30	Sheet metal parts
14	Hardware	31	Shop supplies
15	Laboratory supplies	32	Stampings
16	Lubricants	33	Tooling
17	Machined parts		

for the assembly department. Generally speaking, when materials are grouped by end use, the buyer buys a wider range of items and becomes less of a specialist than would be the case under the preceding method. This arrangement also produces some duplication of effort because several different buyers invariably buy some of the same types of materials.

A major advantage of grouping materials by end use, however, is the fact that buyers do not become immersed in their own technical specialities. They have a tendency to identify to a greater extent with the product or the department for which they are buying. In these circumstances, the buyer frequently feels that he or she is an integral part of a *specific* production effort. Companies favoring this form of organization believe that the loss of technical buying specialization is more than compensated for by the added effectiveness of the purchasing-production team effort that results. The extent to which this is actually true in a specific situation depends on the range and complexity of materials purchased by each buyer and the effectiveness achieved by the team effort.

Buying Supervisors   The size of the buying staff and the complexity of the purchases handled determine the need for buying supervision. In some departments eight or ten buyers can report directly to the department manager or to a line assistant. In other cases, each commodity buying group is headed by a senior buyer who reports to the chief purchasing and supply executive. Possibly the most common arrangement is depicted in Figure 6-3. In this case, buyers are organized into larger groups on the basis of similar commodity characteristics. An intermediate manager, who reports to the chief executive, is assigned to each group (sometimes called a buying department).

These managers are variously titled senior buyers, assistant purchasing agents, purchasing agents, or buying department managers, consistent with the title of the top purchasing executive. The duties of these individuals typically encompass both managerial and actual buying activities.

Expediters The most common form of organization for the follow-up and expediting activity is shown in Figure 6-3. Formation of a separate expediting department permits a high degree of specialization; additionally, it facilitates an even distribution of the workload and efficient utilization of expediting personnel.

However, there is a wide difference of opinion concerning the most effective arrangement for handling the expediting activity. Some firms require each buyer to do his or her own expediting. Because of the buyer's status and intimate knowledge of the order, these firms believe that a buyer can obtain more effective results from suppliers than can someone of lesser status in the organization. More important, companies using this approach want the buyer to assume *total* responsibility for each of his or her orders. They feel the buyer can do this best by personally participating in all phases of the purchase. Additionally, if a buyer is responsible for all phases of an order and for all supplier contacts, it is easier to measure and control his or her performance.

Since much follow-up and expediting is routine work, however, it often represents an inefficient use of a buyer's time. Some companies therefore develop a hybrid organization. To achieve the benefits of specialization, they assign the follow-up and expediting function to a separate expediter. So that the buyer can retain full control of his or her orders, though, each expediter is assigned directly to one buyer (or a buying group). Thus, the expediter does his or her work as directed by the buyer, and the buyer is held fully accountable for his or her orders. In practice, the expediter usually handles all routine follow-up inquiries and calls on the buyer for assistance with the difficult or delicate expediting problems.

Strategic Planning and Research Staff The number of staff specialists employed depends on the size of the department, the complexity of its operation, and the extent to which the firm has progressed toward a supply management focus. Theoretically, in making prepurchase investigations good buyers should perform many of the activities such staff specialists are hired to do. However, most companies now realize that under the pressure of daily operations, most buyers simply do not have time to conduct all desired analyses in adequate depth. This is particularly true for complicated purchases and for strategic planning activities. This fact, coupled with an awareness of the benefits that specialization can produce in planning and research, has led many firms to organize these strategic activities functionally within a special staff group. The specific activities of this group are discussed in the chapters dealing with purchasing research, development of the buying plan, and value analysis. For these activities to yield optimum benefits, it is essential that their organization and implementation be carefully planned from a *companywide* point of view.

Organization by Product or Project

Few single-plant companies are large enough to support a separate purchasing group for each major product line the firm manufactures. A few large firms making a limited number of major products, however, do organize the total purchasing activity on the basis of product or project. General Motors is one of these companies.[5] In such firms each product division is largely autonomous and to a great extent operates its own manufacturing facility, complete with all supporting functions. The basic objective of this type of organization is to develop a group of employees whose interests and identification with a specific *production effort* transcend their identification with a functional department. This attempt to motivate individuals and to develop a smoothly coordinated team effort is based on the same reasoning as that involved in grouping buyers' materials by end use. Viewing the total operation from the standpoint of each *product manager,* this form of organization permits more effective coordination and control of all operating functions contributing to his or her production responsibility.

As top management views the purchasing activity, however, this decentralized form of organization can in some cases possess two disadvantages. First, when the autonomous divisions use many of the same materials, savings can be lost through the failure to consolidate requirements and exploit the company's full buying potential. Second, some duplication of buying effort always exists. Given a fixed number of buying personnel, this means that the firm is not taking full advantage of the potential benefits afforded by increased buyer specialization that would be possible under a consolidated purchasing effort. The seriousness of these two disadvantages largely depends on the size of the individual product divisions.

ORGANIZATION FOR PURCHASING AND SUPPLY MANAGEMENT IN A MULTIPLANT FIRM

To this point, the discussion has focused largely on single-site purchasing and supply operations. We turn now to these activities in multisite organizations. A multiplant firm faces one additional organizational question that does not concern most single-plant companies: To what extent should purchasing and supply management activity be centralized at the corporate level? In practice, virtually every firm answers this question differently. Some firms centralize the activity almost completely, doing the buying for all sites at a central headquarters office. Others decentralize the function entirely, giving each site full

---

[5]For an interesting discussion of General Motors' product line organization, see T. E. Drozdowski, "At BOC They Start with the Product," *Purchasing,* Mar. 13, 1986, pp. 62B5-62B11.

authority to conduct all of its purchasing activities. Still other firms—the majority of them—develop an organization somewhere between these two extremes. Each extreme approach offers significant benefits that are discussed below.

Advantages of Multiplant Centralization

Greater Buying Specialization Perhaps the greatest benefit of centralization stems from the fact that it permits greater technical specialization among buyers. This leads to the development of more knowledgeable and more highly skilled buying personnel. Thus, centralization enables a firm to do a better technical job of buying, or it permits a job of buying comparable with that under decentralization to be accomplished with fewer buyers. It also provides for the capable buying of major capital equipment and construction services which are required only intermittently by any single site, but which on a companywide basis represent a continuing purchasing activity.

In most companies, the importance of specialized buying cannot be overvalued. The complexity of industrial materials increases constantly. A buyer who does not fully comprehend the significance of a material's major technical and manufacturing characteristics cannot perform effectively. If buyers fail to perform with technical competence, the important buying decisions will ultimately be made in the using departments, and buyers will be relegated to a glorified clerical status.

Consolidation of Requirements Just as single-plant centralization facilitates the consolidation of plant requirements, multiplant centralization facilitates the consolidation of material requirements at the corporate level. In most situations, such consolidation results in larger purchases from a smaller number of suppliers, yielding more favorable prices and increased supplier service. Increased purchase volumes also permit the negotiation of highly profitable *long-term* contracts for many production materials.

Easier Purchasing Coordination and Control When all company purchasing activities are consolidated in one office, procedures for coordinating and controlling individual segments of activity can be effected more quickly and with less paperwork. Consolidation permits more direct administration and control of such important policies as those affecting supplier selection procedures, supplier relations, purchasing ethics, budget compliance, and the consistency of general purchasing practices among the various buying groups. In general, under this type of organization, the chief supply executive finds it easier to control the total efficiency of the corporate purchasing activity.

Effective Planning and Research Work The existence of a centralized group to handle corporatewide purchasing requirements provides the concentrated staff know-how to improve purchasing and supply research work. Virtually all purchasing planning needs—from internal systems design to strategic materials planning—can be conducted in more depth with greater efficiency for all purchasing operations throughout the corporation.

Advantages of Multiplant Decentralization

Easier Coordination with Operating Departments   From an operating standpoint, the greatest advantage of decentralization is that it facilitates the coordination of purchasing activities with the activities of using departments within each site operation. When a complete purchasing unit is located at each operating site, buying personnel are close to the users' operating problems and develop a much better feel for unique plant needs and their implications in the purchasing area. Buyers can personally discuss purchasing matters with using supervisors any time they wish. Value analysts and technical coordinators can work daily with engineering personnel whenever necessary. Also, a plant purchasing department can develop a much closer working relationship between suppliers' technical representatives, buyers, and plant engineers than is possible under a centralized organization.

In brief, under a decentralized arrangement, purchasing personnel can participate more fully as members of a specific purchasing-operations team.[6]

Speed of Operation   A purchasing department located at the plant clearly can respond more quickly to users' needs. The transmittal of information from plant to headquarters by means of a conventional paperwork system typically lengthens the purchasing procedure by one or two days. Of course, telephone, fax equipment, and computer links can be used in many cases, but often these are not practical as a regular method of communication. If most operating needs could be adequately planned, and plans always functioned according to schedule, the time delay factor would be a minor problem. In a dynamic business situation, however, unforeseen events cause enough deviations from schedule so that this is rarely the case.

Effective Use of Local Sources   If a firm's plants are geographically dispersed, it can be difficult for a centralized purchasing department to locate and develop potentially good suppliers near each plant. At times this difficulty deprives a plant of various technical and purchasing benefits resulting from close working relationships between plant personnel and suppliers. If plants are separated by great distances, decentralized purchasing departments in many cases may also be able to reduce material transportation costs by the wise use of local suppliers.

---

[6]To prevent each site from losing its identification in a *centralized* purchasing office, some companies using centralization locate a "plant coordinator" for each plant in the purchasing office. The coordinator's job is to act as a liaison between plant users and centralized purchasing; he or she looks after the particular procurement interests of his or her plant.

Plant Autonomy   A fundamental principle of management holds that the delegation of responsibility must be accompanied by the delegation of adequate authority to carry out that responsibility. A plant manager who is given full responsibility for the operation and profit performance of a plant can properly contend that he or she should have full authority over the expenditures for materials. Decentralization of purchasing gives a plant manager this authority.

Although entirely valid, the preceding idea implies that a plant manager has no control over material expenditures if purchasing is centralized. This need not be true. While a plant manager has no line control over a centralized purchasing and supply department, many firms develop coordinating committees to correct purchasing situations that are unsatisfactory to plant management. If these are established within the proper framework, a plant manager, through such a mechanism, can exercise satisfactory indirect control over the performance of a centralized purchasing operation.

Purchasing Councils

To minimize one of the major disadvantages of decentralized purchasing, many firms use *purchasing councils*. In a decentralized operation, a purchasing council is simply a coordinating group made up of purchasing managers and selected senior buyers from each of the firm's plants. Council members meet periodically to coordinate policies and buying activities, to consolidate purchases for selected major materials, and to stay abreast of the latest trends and their implications for the corporation.

The Eaton Company, headquartered in Cleveland, Ohio, utilizes a decentralized purchasing function in its various operating units. And it supplements the operation with three different types of purchasing councils—commodity councils, councils for specific issues, and councils for similar business units. Eaton's director of purchasing explains, "We created the council network as a way to bring the business units together from the standpoint of the buying expertise we have in the company."[7]

Factors Affecting Feasibility and Desirability of Centralization

Three factors determine how feasible or desirable centralization of the purchasing function may be in a given situation: (1) similarity of the classes of materials used in each of the plants, (2) size of each plant's purchasing department, and (3) distance separating the individual plants.

Similarity of Materials Usage   If a firm's plants use entirely different materials, centralization of purchasing offers only minimal benefits; the

---

[7]"Keeping Up with the Times—Purchasing Councils," *Purchasing Executive's Bulletin*, Nov. 25, 1988.

major benefits of increased specialization and requirements consolidation cannot be achieved. In such cases, potential disadvantages of centralization usually outweigh the advantages gained from better coordination and control.

Most firms, however, generally have a greater similarity of materials usage among plants than is at first apparent. To make specialization profitable, the various plants do not have to use exactly the same *items*. The important thing is the similarity of *types* of materials (or markets). Specialization of buyers is accomplished on the basis of material (or market) *classifications*. Most firms find that their plants *do* use a number of the same *classifications* of materials.

The J. I. Case Company provides a classic illustration of this. Some years ago, when Case was considering a reorganization of its purchasing operations, it found that only about 5 percent of the 16,000 items it purchased were used by more than one of its five plants (each plant makes a different line of products—agricultural machinery, industrial tractors, materials-handling equipment, and construction equipment). However, analysis of these items by material classification revealed that of the total 191 classifications of material, over 75 percent were used by at least several plants. Further study of the situation led the Case Company to centralize its purchasing operation, whereas the initial decision had been to decentralize because of the dissimilarity of the items purchased.[8]

Plant Department Size   As a general rule, centralization is more advantageous when a firm's individual plant purchasing departments are not large. If plant purchasing operations are large, a high degree of buyer specialization may already have been achieved. Similarly, the benefits to be gained from consolidating requirements of large departments are less significant than those gained from consolidating the requirements of small plants. This is not to say that consolidation of large departments does not yield benefits. It usually does. The benefits, however, are not as significant as in the case of small departments, and they are frequently outweighed by the offsetting disadvantages.

Geographic Dispersion of Plants   The closer a firm's plants are situated geographically, the easier centralization becomes. Conversely, if much centralized buying is done, the more widely the plants are dispersed, the more serious the disadvantages of centralization become. Even if a centralized purchasing office has direct telephone and fax service to the production scheduling offices at each plant, when a plant is 1,000 miles distant, the problems of communication and coordination with that plant are difficult indeed.

[8]For a complete account of the Case Company's reorganization, see "J. I. Case Switches to Centralized Purchasing," *Purchasing Week,* May 6, 1963, pp. 18–19.

TRENDS IN INDUSTRY

Centralization and Decentralization

While the purchasing and supply organizations of some multiplant firms are found at both ends of the centralization continuum, most are located somewhere between these two extremes. The NAPM study cited earlier found that 60 percent of the *Fortune 1000* firms employ a combined centralized/decentralized form of organization, 26 percent a centralized form, and 14 percent a straight decentralized form.[9] The trend clearly appears to be toward the general type of organization shown in Figure 6-4. This organization includes elements of both centralization and decentralization. Its objective is to reap the major benefits offered by both approaches.

A centralized purchasing and supply management office is established at the corporate level, with the chief purchasing/supply executive usually reporting to the president or executive vice president. Duties of the centralized office typically include strategic planning, research, and specialized buying. Economic and industry analyses, technical commodity research, strategic materials planning, systems planning, and government contract regulation work are the most common types of planning and research activities. Buying activities conducted centrally vary widely from firm to firm; however, they focus on the material classifications for which highly specialized buying and requirements consolidation produce the greatest profit. In addition, many of the important long-term contracts are negotiated centrally on a companywide basis. Plant purchasing departments then issue orders against these contracts in accordance with their needs.

In most cases, the relationship between the central purchasing office and the plant purchasing departments is a "functional" relationship. This means that each plant has its own purchasing department, whose manager usually reports directly to the plant manager. By explicit agreement, however, the plant purchasing department relinquishes to the central purchasing department certain planning and buying responsibilities. The central department generally has no line authority over the plant manager of purchasing, but typically it does have the authority to determine specifically which materials will be purchased locally and which centrally. The central department also serves in a coordinating capacity by formulating and enforcing basic purchasing policy and by designing purchasing systems and procedures for all plants.

Long-Range Materials Planning

The increasing need in recent years for thorough long-range materials planning has increased the attention given to the strategic materials planning activ-

---

[9]Fearon, op. cit., p. 28.

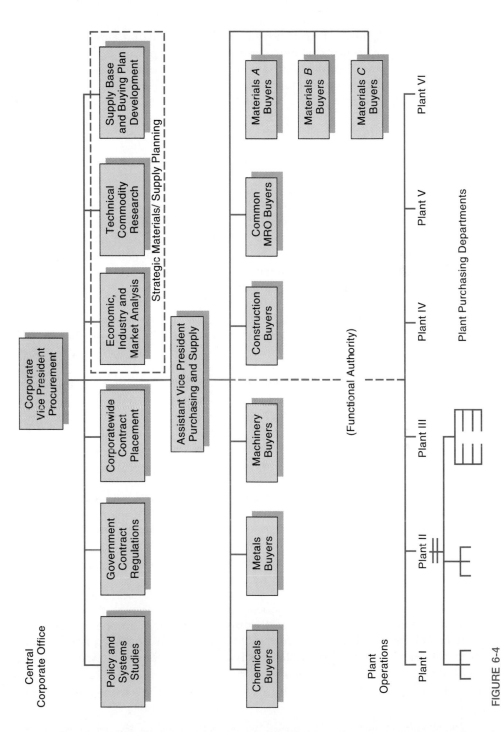

FIGURE 6-4
A multiplant purchasing and supply organization with some activities centralized and some decentralized.

ity. A growing number of firms have consolidated existing activities or have established a new central planning group at the corporate level to conduct these economic and technical investigations on a continuing basis. This phenomenon, coupled with a general increase in the volume of long-term contract buying, has produced a noticeable expansion of centralized purchasing and supply management efforts in some industries. Clearly, this evidences a centralization of strategic activities and a partial decentralization of tactical and operating activities.

An Illustration[10] The Hewlett-Packard Company (HP) provides an interesting and somewhat unique illustration of several of the trends emerging in industry today. For years HP has thrived and grown while employing a strict policy of autonomy and accountability for each of its manufacturing divisions. In recent years, however, the firm created a corporate procurement and materials management group. The function of this central group is to provide support and guidance for the decentralized procurement groups at each of the divisions. HP currently has more than 1,000 buyers companywide, with approximately 180 purchasing people employed in the central procurement operation. The major responsibilities of the central group are:

1 To develop companywide forecasts for all divisions' component usage.
2 To qualify suppliers for critically important materials. This is done with a number of "commodity teams" staffed by central office specialists.
3 To help develop and manage corporate contracts for materials used by multiple divisions in excess of $200,000 per year.
4 To provide support to individual divisions for international procurement.
5 To monitor the companywide procurement system, including supplier performance, on a continuing basis.
6 To manage the data bases of component specifications and part control numbers.
7 To provide leadership for the development of corporate procurement strategy.

Note that the central group does not buy anything, per se. It serves uniquely in both leadership and staff supporting roles, in an operating system that is still decentralized to a great extent. Again, this approach is consistent with the trend to centralize strategic activities and decentralize the operating activities.

---

[10]R. M. Faltra, "How HP Buys Electronics," *Electronics Purchasing*, a special report, March 1987.

Cross-Functional Teams

A recent research study conducted jointly by the Center for Advanced Purchasing Studies and the Graduate School of Management at Michigan State University "revealed that almost 80 percent of the U.S. firms surveyed plan to emphasize the use of cross-functional teams to support procurement and sourcing decisions over the next three years."[11] Throughout American business today, the concept of drawing on the coordinated expertise of a group of people from different functional areas to investigate and resolve operating issues as a "team" appears to have caught on.[12]

In the procurement area, this development clearly will have a long-run impact on the purchasing and supply management organization structure. The discussion up to this point in the chapter, however, has focused on the conventional organization structures that have predominated in American industry for a number of years, because it is still too early to predict exactly what affect the increasing use of teams will have on the formal organization on a national scale. Nevertheless, it is useful here to define more precisely the areas in which cross-functional teams are being utilized today, or are expected to be utilized within the next several years.

A research study conducted by two professors at Arizona State University has produced some revealing insights into the current and expected use of cross-functional teams in the purchasing and supply management area.[13] Professors Lisa Ellram and John Pearson surveyed 600 members of the National Association of Purchasing Management with respect to cross-functional team participation in 18 activities normally considered to be areas of significant responsibility for purchasing and supply management personnel. They asked purchasing and supply managers the extent to which "teams" participated in these activities in 1993—and also the extent to which teams were expected to participate in 1995. The results of their research are shown in Table 6-2.

In summary, the researchers found that in American industry there is an increasing emphasis on cross-functional responsibility for most aspects of the purchasing function. There is a definite trend toward team responsibility for the 18 key decision issues investigated in the study. This does not mean, however, that the purchasing function's responsibilities are being diminished. Purchasing and supply, in fact, is becoming more heavily involved in some areas in which it previously had minimal responsibility—for example, the development of material specifications and the firm's material standards program.

---

[11]Robert M. Monczka and Robert J. Trent, *Cross-Functional Sourcing Team Effectiveness*, NAPM Inc., Tempe, Arizona, 1993, p. 7.

[12]See J. R. Katzenback and D. K. Smith, *The Wisdom of Teams: Creating the High Performance Organization*, Harvard Business School Press, Cambridge, Mass., 1993.

[13]Lisa M. Ellram and John N. Pearson, "The Role of the Purchasing Function: Toward Team Participation," *International Journal of Purchasing and Materials Management*, Summer 1993, pp. 3–9.

TABLE 6-2
PERCENTAGE OF FIRMS IN WHICH TEAMS HAVE A MAJOR RESPONSIBILITY IN KEY
MATERIALS DECISION ISSUES

Materials activities	Percent of firms	
	1993	Expected 1995
Internal issues		
1 Review material requirements	22.9	40.5
2 Develop specifications	17.1	38.1
3 Analyze make-or-buy data	30.0	54.8
4 Standardize materials	26.2	53.8
5 Determine inventory levels	14.8	34.8
6 Determine quality requirements	24.3	52.9
External issues		
7 Negotiate price/terms	8.6	23.3
8 Participate in supplier selection	32.9	54.8
9 Problem-solve with supplier	37.6	52.4
10 Gather information from supplier	16.2	34.3
11 Communicate specification changes	16.2	28.6
12 Contribute to productivity/cost improvements	23.8	49.0
13 Develop sourcing strategy	20.0	43.3
14 Gather market information	11.4	28.6
Planning and strategy issues		
15 Make price forecasts	7.1	15.2
16 Do long-range purchasing planning	13.8	29.5
17 Determine purchasing policy	8.6	24.3
18 Conduct value analysis studies	27.1	47.1

Source: Adapted from Lisa M. Ellram and John N. Pearson, "The Role of the Purchasing Function: Toward Team Participation," *International Journal of Purchasing and Materials Management,* Summer 1993, pp. 7–8.

In practice, the involvement of cross-functional personnel in these activities appears to be emerging through the evolution of five major types of cross-functional teams:[14]

1 Commodity procurement strategy team
2 Sourcing team
3 Supplier performance evaluation team
4 Supplier certification team
5 New product development team

[14]For an interesting discussion of how some firms use various types of teams, see Mary Siegfried, "Understanding Teams by What They Do," *NAPM Insights,* July 1994, pp. 50–52; and "How Five Experts Turned Concurrent Engineering Theory into Action," *Supplier Selection & Management Report,* November 1992, pp. 7–11.

Commodity Procurement Strategy Teams   This is one of the more important teams because of the strategic nature of its responsibility. It generally is a permanent team whose responsibility is to evaluate the supplier base for a commodity group, including the specific capabilities of each firm relative to current and expected requirements of the buying firm. The team's objective is to rationalize the supplier base, solve specific problems, and develop a strategic purchasing plan for the given commodity or family of items.

For illustrative purposes, return for a moment to the Hewlett Packard Company illustration. The seventh item in Hewlett Packard's list of central procurement responsibilities—that of developing corporate procurement strategy—is clearly one of the group's most important functions. In HP this is accomplished by means of a group of "commodity procurement strategy teams." Each team is made up of members from various operating divisions from the areas of research and development, manufacturing, quality assurance and control, and purchasing. Each team is headed by a commodity manager from the central procurement group and focuses on a strategic group of materials purchased through a corporate contract. The team evaluates suppliers on the basis of technology, quality, cost, responsiveness, and delivery—and then decides which suppliers will get what portion of the business.

As the approach is developing in practice, different firms use somewhat different techniques, but the concept is fundamentally the same. The General Motors Corporation, for example, utilizes a similar approach with its "purchasing steering committees" and its "commodity buying teams."[15]

Sourcing Teams   Some sourcing teams function much like a commodity strategy team, but the responsibilities of most are somewhat more limited. A sourcing team usually focuses on the investigation and selection of one or more sources for a given material. The material may be used in a new product, or it may be a rebuy item for which the firm has experienced quality or other types of problems. Some sourcing teams have an ongoing life, but a majority are temporary teams.

Supplier Performance Evaluation Teams   This is usually a permanent team whose responsibility is to develop a set of performance measures and criteria to be used in monitoring the performance of key suppliers. Cross-functional participation is vital in developing the evaluation system. Operationally, each team member typically monitors the performance of a group of suppliers whose important operating or product characteristics relate most closely to his or her discipline.

Supplier Certification Teams   In practice, this type of team is temporary in some firms and ongoing in others. The basic responsibility of the team is to

---

[15] T. E. Drozdowski, "Purchasing at GM Restyles for the '90s," *Purchasing*, Oct. 24, 1985, pp. 56–60.

work with selected suppliers to help them attain the performance level required by the buying organization to achieve "certified" status. This typically involves factors such as product quality level, cost improvement, service and delivery performance, consistency, and so on.

New Product Development Teams   This unique and important team usually includes members from design engineering, manufacturing, marketing, quality, purchasing and supply, and frequently one or more supplier representatives. The team's responsibility is to analyze possible alternative configurations, develop the product's design specifications, and select the materials from which it will be made. The team usually is dissolved when the design for the product is complete. Through coordination of the different types of expertise of team members, a product cost reduction of up to 30 percent is not uncommon.[16]

A Concluding Observation about Teams   As noted earlier, at this time there is little uniformity in industry with respect to the design, the use, and even the perceived value of teams.[17] Some leading-edge firms utilize teams heavily—others only sparingly. Different firms develop different types of teams, and many use the same team in different ways. Some firms use a sourcing team as part of their new product development team; others use a separate team for developing supplier alliances; many continue to use their traditional negotiating teams; and so on. However, evidence at the moment points toward an increasing use of various procurement teams in the future—and there likely will be some crystallization of the types of teams and approaches to their use. As firms continue to *reengineer* their major operating units, including the purchasing function, a changing organization structure and the development of teams are bound to be among the products of the effort.

The Michigan State research study mentioned earlier identified five team characteristics that affect the success of cross-functional sourcing teams:[18]

1 Higher levels of internal and external decision-making authority
2 Participation of suppliers when required
3 Effective team leadership
4 Availability of key organizational resources
5 Higher levels of effort put forth on team assignments

While one would intuitively concur with these findings, the first three are particularly worthy of note with respect to the topic of organization. If suc-

---

[16]Siegfried, op. cit., p. 52.

[17]Two interesting articles that shed more light on this subject are J. P. Womack and D. T. Jones, "From Lean Production to the Lean Enterprise," *Harvard Business Review*, March–April 1994, pp. 93–103; and David Fagiano, "Don't Throw the Baby Out with the Bathwater," *Management Review*, August 1994, p. 4.

[18]Robert J. Trent and Robert M. Monczka, "Effective Cross-Functional Sourcing Teams: Critical Success Factors," *International Journal of Purchasing and Materials Management*, Fall 1994, pp. 6–10.

cessful teams have a high level of authority concerning specific purchasing actions, it is imperative that purchasing and supply management be represented on the team by a strong, knowledgeable professional who possesses effective interpersonal skills. It is also important that the purchasing function provide solid policy and operational guidelines for the team. Purchasing guidance is required, too, in the utilization of selected suppliers on the team. Finally, one would expect team leadership in a reasonable number of cases to come from purchasing and supply management representatives. This again underscores the need for purchasing people to possess solid leadership and interpersonal abilities.

THE MATERIALS MANAGEMENT CONCEPT

To this point, the discussion has dealt mostly with the organization of the purchasing and supply management function. In designing an organization structure for a total plant, management must decide how to group and coordinate the other activities whose major interest also focuses on the company's acquisition and utilization of materials. In addition to purchasing, the departments that are primarily concerned with materials are inventory (materials) control, receiving, stores, production scheduling, and traffic. To which functional executives should these departments report?

Chapter 2 discussed the materials management concept and its growing application in American industry. Historically, firms have divided responsibility for the various materials activities among two or three functional departments (i.e., purchasing, production, and marketing). This division of responsibility makes it difficult to coordinate the interrelated activities of the materials-oriented departments. More important, it makes effective identification and control of *total* materials costs extremely difficult, if not impossible. The materials management concept, and its related form of organization, has evolved in response to these needs.

Materials management provides an *integrated systems approach* to the *coordination* of materials activities and the *control* of total materials costs. It advocates assigning to a single operating department all major activities which contribute to the cost of materials. The objective is to optimize performance of the materials *system*, as opposed to suboptimizing the performance of individual operating units that are parts of the materials system. Although there are differences among firms, a common organization of materials activities that stems from the materials management concept takes the general form shown in Figure 6-5.

Materials Management In Practice

Over the past twenty years, the organization structure shown in Figure 6-5 has become the "classical" materials management model. Various studies during this period, however, not only have identified a number of variations from the

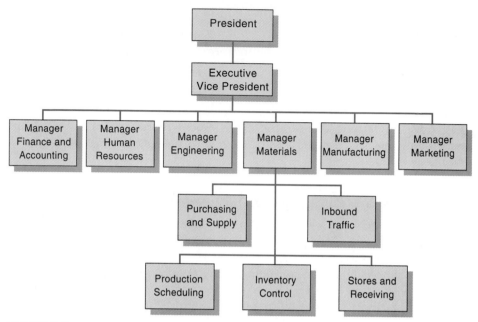

FIGURE 6-5
The general structure of an organization employing the materials management concept.

basic model, but have determined that the variations tend to cluster into a small number of specific patterns.[19] These patterns reflect two basic differences from the classical materials management model: (1) the level to which and the executive to whom the materials manager reports and (2) the specific functions included in the materials department.

One of the definitive studies was conducted by Jeffrey Miller and Peter Gilmour of the Harvard Business School.[20] This study covered 206 firms of various sizes in a cross section of manufacturing industries. With respect to the reporting level, the study found that in 53 percent of the firms the materials manager reports to a general management executive—i.e., the president (or general manager), the executive vice president, or the vice president for administration. In other words, with respect to reporting level, these firms follow the classical model. On the other hand, in 43 percent of the firms the materials manager reports to the manager of manufacturing. In these firms the materials function is a second-level activity. (Four percent of the materials managers in the study report in a second-level position to the controller or the manager of finance.)

---

[19]For details, review the following studies: (1) Harold E. Fearon, *Purchasing Organizational Relationships*, NAPM, Inc., Tempe, Ariz., 1988, pp. 17, 36; (2) Ronald Baer and John Centimore, "Materials Management: Where It Stands—What It Means," *Purchasing*, special reprint, no date.

[20]Jeffrey Miller and Peter Gilmour, "Materials Managers: Who Needs Them?" *Harvard Business Review*, July–August 1979, pp. 143–153.

Results of the study were less clear concerning the specific functions included in the materials management department. However, three organizational clusters seem to emerge:

1 Approximately 50 percent of the firms include in the materials management department the functions shown in the classical model. A few also include the physical distribution function.
2 Slightly more than 25 percent of the firms utilize the classical model, but exclude production and inventory control from the materials management department.
3 Slightly less than 25 percent of the firms include in the department all of the classical model functions except purchasing. In these cases, purchasing usually reports individually to a general management executive.

The Supplier Management Concept Several years ago, General Motors' Buick-Oldsmobile-Cadillac Group (BOC) restructured its total operation on the basis of a consolidated product line organization—luxury vehicles, specialty vehicles, premium vehicles, and power train products.[21] Each of these four product lines has one integrated team totally responsible for the product, "bumper to bumper . . . cradle to grave." Included in each team is a materials management group responsible for the following functions:

- Production control
- Material control and transportation
- Supplier development and certification
- Supplier management

Clearly, the BOC organization includes all the functions in the classical materials management model—and just a bit more. Note that the purchasing function has been divided into two parts: (1) supplier development and certification and (2) supplier management. After a supplier has been selected, the first group works with the firm helping it develop manufacturing and quality capabilities until it passes the BOC test for supplier "certification." After the supplier becomes certified, the "supplier manager" (the former buyer) assumes responsibility for continued work with and management of the supplier relationship.

The purpose of this expanded purchasing role is twofold. The first objective is to bring suppliers up to a certified level of performance by making a significant front-end investment in this activity before a supplier is really accepted as part of the BOC team. The second objective is to provide a closer, more intensive working relationship between the buyer and appropriate individuals in the supplier's organization. In this setting, the buyer truly functions as a supplier relationship manager, responsible for continued supplier improvement in capability and performance, particularly in the area of quality and reduced total costs.

---

[21]T. E. Drozdowski, "At BOC They Start with the Product."

In this type of operation, the production planner's role is also expanded somewhat. The planner now assumes responsibility for managing the *daily flow* of material into the plant. In addition to the normal scheduling work, this includes issuing purchase releases directly to the supplier, along with telephone follow-up and expediting work with the supplying organization. For this reason, on the production planning side of the house, this arrangement is also referred to as the "supplier scheduler" concept.

Use of this concept is not confined to multisite organizations, or to those utilizing a materials management structure. However, the concept intrinsically fits well with the materials management philosophy. In any case, an increasing number of firms are expanding the buying activity somewhat along these lines.

The Buyer-Planner Concept   Within the structure of a materials management organization, some firms have taken a different approach. These organizations have expanded the buyer's job, but in the opposite direction. In effect, they have merged the jobs of the buyer and the production control materials scheduler. The new job, aptly described by its title, is that of "buyer-planner."

The *buyer-planner* is responsible for determining materials requirements, developing materials schedules, making order quantity determinations, and handling all the activities associated with the buying function. The concept is a logical extension of the basic materials management idea, simply applied at a micro level in the department. It is particularly applicable in a manufacturing operation utilizing an MRP-type system.

The concept has been adopted at a moderately increasing rate the past few years, particularly in intermittent manufacturing operations. Firms that use it report three major benefits: (1) a smoother materials flow, (2) improved coordination with key suppliers, and (3) increased productivity.

The fact that the approach eliminates one major interface (buyer/production planner), and its attendant problems, tends to smooth the materials flow. Additionally, a buyer-planner develops a better understanding of the total materials cycle. These two factors in combination usually increase the efficiency of the planning-buying activity. At the same time, because the buyer-planner sees the total materials requirements picture over an extended period of time, he or she frequently is able to match requirements more closely with a supplier's manufacturing capabilities and constraints. Lot sizing can be considered also from the supplier's point of view in developing order release schedules.

Practical Benefits   How do practicing managers view materials management? On the whole, very positively; approximately 70 percent of the nation's major manufacturing firms utilize it in one form or another. Mr. Norman Beckert, Director of Corporate Procurement for the Boise Cascade Corporation, summarizes his observations in the following statement:

> The current reasons for developing a materials management operation are many. Materials management certainly enables a company to better utilize control tools, to cut across functional lines, and to enhance inter-departmental coordination in the

materials area. Materials management makes a profit contribution that is measurable because of the direct management of inventory, production control, purchasing, and traffic, and has a clear potential to contribute cost reductions in all these areas. Most important, with proper authority given to the function, materials management is the most direct means of reconciling conflicting objectives in the performance of materials subfunctions, because decisions can be made with the total materials position in mind.[22]

Effect on The Purchasing and Supply Management Organization

What effect does the adoption of a materials management organization have on purchasing? It has no effect on the purchasing function per se. Likewise, internal organization of the purchasing and supply department, in most cases, changes very little.[23] The position of the chief purchasing or purchasing and supply executive changes significantly, however, if he or she previously reported to a general management executive. This position automatically moves down the executive hierarchy one level. Under the new organization, the purchasing and supply manager reports to a materials manager, who now occupies his or her previous location on the organization chart.

Although the materials manager has responsibilities that are considerably broader than purchasing, purchasing and supply is the focal point of activity in the new department. For this reason, a competent purchasing executive, as well as an equally competent production control manager, is a logical candidate to fill the materials manager's position when the transition is made. In firms that have made the transition, approximately the same number of materials managers have moved up from purchasing as from production control.

CONCLUSION

The fundamental purpose of organization is to provide a structure that facilitates the motivation of people and the coordination of their efforts toward the common goals of the firm. A poorly designed structure can inhibit such accomplishments, just as a well-designed structure can facilitate them.

Location of the purchasing and supply management department within a firm's organizational hierarchy is determined very simply by one factor—management's perception of the importance of the function. In a majority of manufacturing firms this function or the materials function reports to a top-management executive, but in a sizable minority it is seen as a second-level function.

In addition to the complexity of the markets and the value and complexity of the materials purchased, the type and amount of specialized expertise in

[22]C. Norman Beckert, "Purchasing Organization," Chapter 2, *The Purchasing Handbook*, McGraw-Hill, Inc., New York, 1992, p. 61.

[23]To facilitate coordination of buyers and production control schedulers, materials groupings may be modified so that a given buyer and a given scheduler tend to handle the same materials.

purchasing also influence its profit potential—and its importance. Hence, over the long term, the position of purchasing and supply in the hierarchy can be influenced heavily by the department's internal pattern of organization. How purchasing chooses to specialize is important. It can specialize buying activities by material categories, and it can specialize by operating function (e.g., buying, expediting, purchasing research, value analysis, and so on). In practice, all but the smallest departments do some of both. But, with limited staff, each staffing decision represents a trade-off. The manager must decide which type of expertise (material or functional) is most useful to the firm at a given time and develop the organization accordingly. These needs, however, change from time to time.

This is why very few firms have organizational structures that are exactly alike. Each design represents a compromise solution to the different problems in each firm. It is for this reason, for example, that many multiplant firms decentralized purchasing in the 1960s; then, with the changing conditions of the late 1970s, moved back toward more centralized purchasing; and now during the 1990s are again decentralizing a number of the day-to-day buying activities.

Hence, managers constantly seek to maximize utilization of the capabilities of their human resources, following the sage observation of Dr. Harry Hopf:[24]

> That a business cannot permanently occupy levels of effectiveness higher than those clearly determined by the capacity of its executives is self-evident; but it is not generally understood that the influence of a superior organization upon the accomplishments of mediocre executives can raise the enterprise to heights not otherwise attainable.

FOR DISCUSSION

6-1 What factors distinguish a good organization from a poor organization?

6-2 Where in a single-plant manufacturing company's organizational structure should the purchasing department be located? Explain.

6-3 Some business executives say that overorganization is just as bad as underorganization. What is your reaction to this idea? Explain.

6-4 Assume that you have been asked to study a plant's purchasing and supply management department and to recommend an ideal organization to the manager. Describe exactly what you would do and how you would conduct the study.

6-5 Discuss the pros and cons of a project-oriented purchasing organization.

6-6 On what bases are materials grouped for buying purposes? Explain the strengths and weaknesses of each approach.

6-7 How and by whom should the expediting function be conducted in a purchasing and supply department? Explain.

[24]Harry A. Hopf, as quoted by Ernest Dale, *Planning and Developing the Company Organization Structure,* American Management Association Research Report 20, New York, 1952, p. 17.

6-8 Under what conditions is centralization of the purchasing function in a multiplant company probably not a good idea?

6-9 Discuss the advantages and disadvantages of centralized purchasing and supply management in a multiplant company.

6-10 Is centralized multiplant purchasing and supply likely to expand or decline in the decade ahead? Explain.

6-11 Cross-functional procurement teams are used with increasing frequency today. Explain how they are used. What are the primary advantages of their use?

6-12 Discuss the purpose and operation of a new product development team.

6-13 Discuss the purpose and operation of a commodity procurement strategy team.

6-14 What are the major factors that contribute to the success of a cross-functional team?

6-15 What implications do the factors in question 6-14 have for purchasing and supply personnel?

6-16 Generally speaking, what is the major difference between a sourcing team and a commodity procurement strategy team?

6-17 If a firm adopts the materials management concept, what impact does this action have on its organization structure?

6-18 Discuss the supplier management concept.

6-19 Discuss the buyer-planner concept.

6-20 From an operating point of view, discuss the pros and cons of the materials management concept.

CASES FOR CHAPTER 6

Northeastern Equipment Company, page 869
Blozis Company, page 784
Smith-Jones Electronics Corporation, page 915
G.A.R. Manufacturing Company (in the *Instructor's Manual*)

PART TWO

TWO

THE GENERATION
OF REQUIREMENTS

7

PURCHASING'S ROLE IN NEW PRODUCT DEVELOPMENT

KEY CONCEPTS

- Early purchasing and supplier involvement
- The design process
  The investigation phase
  Defining the new product
  Select components, technologies, and supplies
  Stress testing and failure analysis
  The development phase
  The production phase
  Engineering change management
- How to expand purchasing and supply management's role
  Design or project teams
  Materials engineers
  Co-location
- Buyers who interface successfully with engineers

The first six chapters provide the framework and conceptual foundation of the procurement process. This process consists of four key components:

- Determining what to buy (the requirements determination process).
- Determining from whom to buy (the source selection process).
- Determining what price to pay (the pricing process).

- Managing the resulting contract to ensure that the supplier performs according to the terms of the contract (contract management). As purchasing progresses to supply management, this fourth component expands considerably to include the maintenance and nurturing of value-adding supplier relationships.

The first phase of the procurement process (determining what to buy) is the most critical of the four. *Some 80 percent of the total cost is either designed in or excluded during this phase!* Professional sourcing, pricing, and contract management may be able to effect some savings of both cost and time, but usually no more than 20 percent of the total available through sound procurement.

This chapter and the next three address the requirements process as it applies to production materials. Chapter 18 will address purchasing's role in the procurement of capital equipment. Chapter 19 addresses purchasing's role in the procurement of services.

EARLY PURCHASING AND SUPPLIER INVOLVEMENT

In many progressive firms, the design of new products is conducted by a team representing a number of functional areas. Product planning, design engineering, reliability engineering, purchasing, manufacturing engineering, quality, finance, field support, marketing, and, frequently, carefully selected suppliers and customers are involved, as appropriate.

Anecdotal evidence indicates that the development of new products by such cross-functional teams and the use of concurrent engineering[1] have the potential of significantly improving three key issues: time, quality, and cost.[2] The turnaround of many troubled manufacturers during the recent decade was the result of replacing departmental walls with teamwork among those who should be part of the design process. Purchasing is moving to earlier involvement in the new product development process because of the important contributions it can make in the areas of quality, cost, and timely market availability. This early involvement commonly is referred to as *early purchasing involvement (EPI)*.

The lack of effective, cooperative teamwork among the groups noted frequently has been accompanied by quality problems, cost overruns, forgone all-in-cost savings,[3] major scheduling problems, and new products which are

---

[1]Concurrent engineering is a process in which functional specialists execute their parts of the design as a team concurrently instead of in separate departments serially.

[2]Charles O'Neal, "Concurrent Engineering with Early Supplier Involvement: A Cross-Functional Challenge," *International Journal of Purchasing and Materials Management*, Spring 1993, pp. 3–9.

[3]"All-in-cost" is a summation of purchase price, incoming transportation, inspection and testing, storage, production, lost productivity, rework, process yield loss, scrap, warranty, service and field failure, and customer returns and lost sales associated with the purchased item. The term "all-in-cost" is similar to "total cost of ownership" and simply "cost." All recognize that the purchase price of an item is merely one component of the total cost of buying, owning, and using a purchased item.

late to enter the marketplace. Further, early recognition of problems is difficult or impossible in the absence of cooperative teamwork. Extensive redesign, rework, and retrofit operations are common when operating in the traditional functional mode. Ultimately, the absence of teamwork results in products which are a continuing burden to the firm's long-term competitiveness.

Cost overruns and forgone cost savings frequently result when the designers (or the design team) fail to consider the supply base's design, manufacturing, quality, and cost capabilities. For example, during the early 1980s, design engineers at GE's Jet Engine Division frequently designed materials to be purchased from outside suppliers under the mistaken belief that the outside suppliers had the same manufacturing and process capabilities as GE. In fact, this was not the case; outside suppliers frequently did not possess the same equipment and processes. The results were cost growth and schedule slippages as the suppliers, through a trial and error process, attempted to meet GE's specifications. Frequently, it became apparent that these specifications could not be met and a costly and time-consuming process of reengineering would be required.[4]

A similar example of costs resulting from the failure to consider supply implications during design involves IBM. In 1993, IBM's PC units' sales were just over $8 billion, with earnings of about $200 million (2.5 percent). By contrast, Compaq's profits were $462 million on sales of $7.2 billion (6.4 percent). According to *Business Week*, "At least one reason . . . seems clear, IBM still does not use common parts across its product families." Another contributor to lower profits was IBM's failure to shift away from pricey Japanese compo nents as the value of the yen rose.[5] It was noted that IBM recognized that its supply management system had been the source of significant cost overruns and forgone dollar savings. This recognition resulted in the appointment of a new Vice President of Procurement in 1994.

Scheduling problems frequently are the result of the late delivery of required parts. When supply considerations are not addressed during new product development, unique nonstandard components may be specified. Such components frequently require longer lead times than do standard items. The use of nonstandard items often results in the inability of the manufacturer to react quickly to changes in market demand, frequently resulting in lost sales. In order to reduce its reaction time to changes in demand, IBM is now replacing unique components with standard "commodity" ones.[6] In addition to being more readily available, such commodity components tend to be far less expensive than the unique items they replace.

The global marketplace and global competition coupled with advanced communication systems and computers have generated an environment

---

[4]Personal interview with Gene Walz, Materials Manager, General Electric, Jet Engine Division, June 1983.
[5]Ira Sager, "IBM: There's Many a Slip . . . ," *Business Week,* June 27, 1994, pp. 26–27.
[6]Ibid.

where "time to market" and first to market have significant competitive advantages. Clearly, the need to reduce development time has forced companies to look for new methods to compete. The use of purchasing professionals earlier in the product development cycle is a key means to reducing time to market.

In the early 1990s, the Chrysler Viper went from concept to production in thirty-six months, against an industry norm of sixty months. Chrysler did not achieve this goal alone. It got a lot of support from its suppliers. "They were as much a part of the Viper team as anyone . . . suppliers are an integral part of the team," says Dave Swietlik, the man in charge of procurement for the Viper program. "Their processes drive design."[7]

When a cross-functional team has the responsibility for the development of new products, a concurrent approach to the myriad of tasks involved is taken. This avoids the traditional (and time-consuming) passage of a project from concept development to design to manufacturing engineering to purchasing to manufacturing to marketing to field support. Such a sequential approach requires even more time and personnel resources when changes have to be made. The cross-functional team uses a concurrent approach wherein the team members work together and collaborate throughout the process.

This chapter addresses four key issues: (1) early purchasing and supplier involvement; (2) the process of designing and developing new products, with emphasis on purchasing's role in the process; (3) several approaches to increasing purchasing's role in the new product development process; and (4) a description of buyers who interface successfully with engineers during the new product development process.

THE DESIGN PROCESS[8]

Design is the progression of an abstract notion to something having function and fixed form. The desired levels of quality and reliability must be "engineered in" during the design phase of the new product. "Suppliers must have access to product design as early as humanly possible in the design process to assure optimal use of any special skills or processes they can contribute."[9] *The design stage is also the optimum point at which the vast majority of the cost of making an item can be reduced or controlled.* If costs are not minimized during the design stage, excessive cost may be built in permanently, resulting in expensive, possibly noncompetitive, products that fail to fully realize their profit potential.

These days, one hears a great deal about designing for manufacturability; however, invariably, the focus is the firm's *internal* manufacturing process. But when those responsible for design ignore the manufacturing process and

---

[7]Ernest Raia, "The Chrysler Viper: A Crash Course in Design," *Purchasing,* Feb. 20, 1992, p. 48.
[8]Much of this section is based on *The American Keiretsu* by David N. Burt and Michael F. Doyle. The material is used with the permission of the authors and their publisher, BusinessOne-Irwin.
[9]John A. Carlisle and Robert C. Parker, *Beyond Negotiation: Redeeming Customer-Supplier Relationships,* John Wiley & Sons, Chichester, U.K., 1989, p. 127.

technological capabilities *of outside suppliers,* problems with quality, time-to-market, configuration, control, and cost are the inevitable result. If optimal design performance is to be achieved, suppliers must be active from the beginning, when they can have a major impact on performance, time, cost, and quality. Selected suppliers should participate in feasibility studies, in value engineering, and in prototype, failure, and stress analysis, among other product development tasks.

There is a growing trend among manufacturers such as Kawasaki and Toyota and, more recently, Chrysler to develop an "envelope" of *performance specifications* for suppliers. For example, instead of determining the materials, manufacturing processes, and engineering drawings for a seat for one of its motorcycles, Kawasaki specifies the environmental conditions and the maximum weight which the seat must withstand together with a drawing showing how the seat is to attach to the motorcycle frame. The suppliers' engineering and CAD/CAM[10] tools, not the buying firm's, are then dedicated to designing selected components. This approach allows engineers at the buying firm to focus on the development of more sophisticated core technologies and proprietary systems. The customer firm's engineers do not prepare engineering drawings for nonstrategic components. However, they review and approve the supplier's designs. Such action not only redirects critical engineering resources to higher value activities, but places responsibility for manufacturability and quality with the supplier.

In order to involve suppliers effectively and early, manufacturing companies should invite carefully selected suppliers' engineers into their own engineering departments.[11] (Such co-location of key supplier company engineers has long been practiced in Japanese industry.) Manufacturers should allow key suppliers to review the design of the entire subassembly before committing to it. Not only does this tease out new ideas, but it also helps the supply partner understand the customer's real needs—and likely future needs.

> At Tennant we have found that involving our suppliers at the design stage has improved our products. Since they are the experts in their fields, they prevent us from making mistakes, help us save money and time, and help us do it right the first time.[12]

The changing competitive environment forces much more planning, coordination, and review to take place during the design and development process than previously was the case. Complexity of product lines must be addressed. Lower levels of complexity result in higher schedule stability, a necessary prerequisite to just-in-time manufacturing. Feasibility studies, computer simulations, prototype analysis, failure analyses, stress analyses, and value engineering all must be conducted in an effort to develop *producible,* defect-free products quickly.

---

[10]Computer-assisted design/computer-assisted manufacturing.
[11]Source selection is discussed at length in Chapters 11 and 12.
[12]Roger L. Hale, Ronald E. Kowal, Donald D. Carlton, and Tim K. Sehnert, *Made in the USA,* The Tennant Company, Minneapolis, 1991, p. 69.

The new product development process has undergone a tremendous change during the past few years. The process is described in Figures 7-1a, b, and c and is discussed below.*

The Investigation of Concept Phase (Figure 7-1a)

There are several types of new product design. The first is that used for a totally new product. This is the least-used approach since completely new products are the exception. Most new product design is actually an adaptation or an expanded feature set for a previous design. Advancing technology, process improvements, and market expansion drive the majority of new product design activity. The process described is equally applicable to a totally new product or a "new improved one."

Defining the New Product The design and development process begins with the investigation phase. First, the product is defined. This function is normally performed with considerable marketing involvement and has been formally titled "customer focused product and process development" at some firms, or "quality function development" at others.[13] Marketing authority Regis McKenna is quoted as saying:

> Companies need to incorporate the customer into product design. That means getting more and more members of an organization in contact with the customer—manufacturing and design people, as well as sales and marketing staff. You can, for example, have customers sitting in on your internal committee meetings.[14]

One of a buyer's key responsibilities is to acquire, assimilate, digest, and share information concerning new or forthcoming developments in the supply markets for which he or she is responsible. Interviews with present and potential suppliers, visits to suppliers (with emphasis on their research and development and production activities), attendance at trade shows, weekly reviews of relevant literature, and discussions with colleagues at local National Association of Purchasing Management and American Production and Inventory Control Society meetings help the buyer remain current. Through such activities, the buyer will become aware of new products and new technologies which may be of interest. This information may help product managers in marketing and senior design personnel responsible for identifying and developing new products. While being careful to screen out inappropriate information, the buyer should share potentially attractive information with marketing and engineering.

---

*Some leading firms prepare a report at the end of a new product development project to document the major lessons learned—ones which can be applied to future projects.

[13]The interested reader is referred to "The House of Quality" by John R. Hauser and Don Clausing, *Harvard Business Review,* May–June 1988, pp. 63–67.

[14]Interview with Regis McKenna by Anne R. Field, "First Strike," *Success,* October 1989, p. 48.

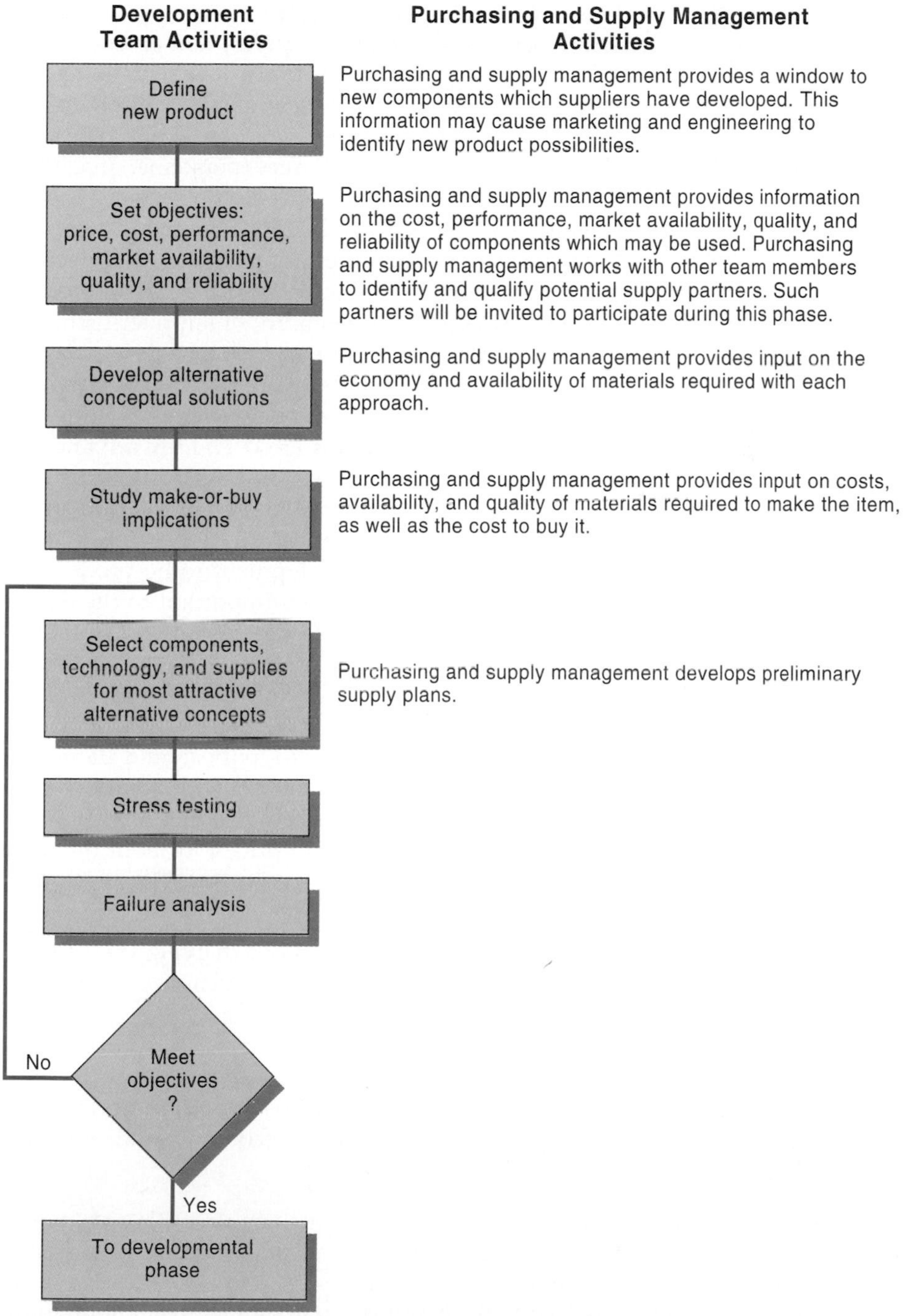

Development Team Activities	Purchasing and Supply Management Activities
Define new product	Purchasing and supply management provides a window to new components which suppliers have developed. This information may cause marketing and engineering to identify new product possibilities.
Set objectives: price, cost, performance, market availability, quality, and reliability	Purchasing and supply management provides information on the cost, performance, market availability, quality, and reliability of components which may be used. Purchasing and supply management works with other team members to identify and qualify potential supply partners. Such partners will be invited to participate during this phase.
Develop alternative conceptual solutions	Purchasing and supply management provides input on the economy and availability of materials required with each approach.
Study make-or-buy implications	Purchasing and supply management provides input on costs, availability, and quality of materials required to make the item, as well as the cost to buy it.
Select components, technology, and supplies for most attractive alternative concepts	Purchasing and supply management develops preliminary supply plans.
Stress testing	
Failure analysis	
Meet objectives ? — No / Yes	
To developmental phase	

FIGURE 7-1a
The modern design and development process, investigation phase. (Source: *Burt, Norquist, and Anklesaria,* Zero-Base Pricing: Achieving World Class Competitiveness through Reduced All-in-Cost, *Probus Publishing, Chicago, Ill., 1990.*)

Statement of Objectives   Next, a statement of needs, desires, and objectives is developed. Needs are based on marketing's perception or knowledge of what customers want (or the customer's direct input if the customer is a member of the design team), balanced against the company's objectives and resources. Needs that are potentially compatible with the firm's objectives (profit potential, sales volume, and so on) and resources (personnel, machines, and management) are considered for development. Product objectives, including performance, price, quality, and market availability, are then established and become the criteria that guide subsequent design, planning, and decision making. The well-informed buyer is the key source of information on the cost, performance, market availability, quality, and reliability of supplier-furnished components which may be used in the new product.

The planned product life cycle typically includes not only the original product but several future products that will incorporate improvements in design, function, features, and so on. These new products are driven by advances in technology, design, and/or materials; competitive offerings; and customer expectations. These desired advances frequently are known at the time of the original product design, but they are not included in the design, since the technology does not exist, or requires additional development to be production-ready. This product feature design "wish list" is very important to the design engineer since he or she most closely understands the design trade-offs and compromises that were included in the original design. This "wish list" of technology requirements is extremely important. Unfortunately, most firms do not document these technical interests that eventually drive a subsequent iteration through their product development process. Not only should these data be documented, but they must become an important focus for a supply partner's R&D efforts. Quick development will drive new product offerings that add additional sales volume, frequently at premium prices, for both the manufacturer and supplier.

Development of Alternatives   Alternative ways of satisfying these needs, desires, and objectives should be developed and then evaluated against the criteria established in the preceding step.

There is an unfortunate tendency to proceed with the first approach that appears to meet a need, although less obvious alternatives may yield more profitable solutions. Alternative approaches should be evaluated on the basis of suitability, producibility, component availability, economy, and customer acceptability.

- *Suitability* refers to technical considerations such as strength, size, power consumption, capability, maintainability, and adaptability. Engineering has primary responsibility for these issues.
- *Producibility* is the ease with which a firm can manufacture an item. In the past, designs needed to be changed to accommodate the firm's or its suppliers' ability to produce the item economically. Problems arose when the

needed changes were implemented. Early manufacturing engineering involvement in the design is needed to ensure the producibility of items made internally, while early supplier involvement helps ensure the producibility of items furnished by suppliers.

- *Component availability* is the time at which components are available, while *component economy* describes the cost of the item or service. Component availability and economy are the responsibility of purchasing.
- *Customer acceptability* is defined as the marketability of an item to potential customers.

The selection of components, technologies, and suppliers for the most attractive conceptual solutions is a complex process. At progressive firms such as GE, Hewlett-Packard, and Chrysler, the selection process is a team effort, with design engineering providing the majority of the staffing and the team leadership.

Often, an engineer has a need that must be filled—a power transmission gear ratio, a structural component, a capacitance, a memory requirement. This need can usually be met in more than one way, and yet many times the engineer may not be aware of the options available. In this case, a buyer may be able to supply suggestions. A gear, for example, might be machined of bronze or steel, die cast in aluminum or zinc, molded from plastic, or formed by powder metallurgy. All these options may meet engineering's constraints while offering a wide range of cost, availability, and reliability choices.[15] Purchasing and potential suppliers can provide information on the economy and availability of the materials and subassemblies to be purchased under each approach.

As practiced by leading firms today, *early supplier involvement (ESI)* is a component of an early purchasing involvement program. With ESI, suppliers are carefully prequalified to ensure that they possess both the desired technology and the right management and manufacturing capability. Thus, the technological benefits of early supplier involvement can be obtained, with due consideration to the commercial aspects of the relationship—the best of both worlds.

When a component or subsystem is to be developed by an outside supplier under an ESI program, two or three potential suppliers normally will be requested to design and develop the required item. Potential suppliers are given performance, cost, weight, and reliability objectives and are provided information on how and where the item will fit (interface) in the larger system. These potential suppliers must develop quality plans during the design of the item to ensure that the item will be producible in the quality specified. Selection of the "winning" supplier is a team effort, with purchasing and supply management, design engineering, reliability engineering, product planning, quality, manufacturing, finance, and field support participating.

---

[15] Jim Esterby, "Design Stage Is the Best Time to Prevent Quality Problems," *Purchasing*, Dec. 8, 1983, p. 78A1.

Performance, quality, reliability, and cost are all considered during the selection process. When a carefully crafted supply partnership or strategic alliance for the item or the commodity class (e.g., fasteners, resistors, safety glass) exists, the supply "partner" alone will be invited to design and develop the required item.

Early purchasing and supplier involvement can reduce the well-known start-up problems that occur when the design and the supplier's process capability are poorly matched. Ideally, supplier suggestions will be solicited and the matching of design and manufacturing process will take place during the investigative phase of the design process. "The technical support suppliers provide in the early stages of design is a critical—some say *the* critical—factor in squeezing the material costs out of a product, improving quality, and preventing costly delays."[16]

Make-or-Buy Analysis The make-or-buy issue should be addressed for all new items which can be either purchased or produced in-house. Every job release and every purchase request implies a decision to make or to buy. Purchasing and supply management plays a key role in the make-or-buy process by providing information on the cost, quality, and availability of items, as discussed in Chapter 10.

Select Components, Technologies, and Supplies Several options may meet engineering's constraints while offering a wide range of cost, availability, and reliability choices. Purchasing personnel and selected suppliers provide information on the availability of the materials and subassemblies to be purchased under each approach.

The early involvement of quality engineers allows advanced quality planning to commence in a timely manner. Quality standards are developed to ensure that components and products being designed can be produced at the quality specified.

The selection of required standard components is facilitated by the availability of a current internal catalog of standard items and sources which have been prequalified.[17] The use of such a catalog simplifies the design engineers' job while simultaneously supporting the efforts of materials management to standardize the items used. The use of standard materials, production processes, and methods shortens the design time and lowers the cost of designing and producing an item. In addition, standardization reduces quality

---

[16]Marilyn J. Cohodas, "Make the Most of Supplier Know-How," *Electronics Purchasing*, July 1988, p. 38.

[17]This catalog is developed and maintained by the joint efforts of design engineering, reliability engineering, purchasing, and manufacturing engineering. It reflects the technical and commercial implications of the items included. The catalog typically classifies components as low, medium, or high risk, in an effort to dissuade design engineers from using high-risk components in new products. The internal catalog is in contrast to a supplier's catalog, which, while simplifying the engineer's efforts to describe an item, places the firm in an unintentional sole-source posture.

problems with incoming materials, inventories, administrative expenses, inspection, and handling expenses, while obtaining lower unit costs.

The selection of technologies is a complex issue due to inherent cost/benefit trade-offs and functional orientations. Engineers are eager to incorporate the latest technology. The marketplace often richly rewards those who are first to market with innovative products; therefore, there is a strong case for incorporating new technology or processes before they are perfected. But the cost of such a decision can be high. Not only does such an approach result in a proliferation of components to be purchased and stocked, but it frequently results in the use of items whose production processes have not yet stabilized; quality problems, production disruptions, and delays frequently result, all increasing project risk. Engineering, quality, purchasing, and manufacturing personnel must ensure that both the costs and benefits of such advanced developments are properly considered. The design team should design new products to the requirements of the customer, not necessarily to the state of the art.

Stress Testing and Failure Analysis   Once candidate component and subsystem items have been identified, they are subjected to stress testing and failure analysis. Failures are caused by failure mechanisms which are built into the item and then activated by stresses. Studying the basic stresses and the failure mechanisms they activate is fundamental to the design of effective reliability tests. The correct design approach is to find and eliminate the fundamental causes of failure. This means that the most successful stress tests are ones that result in failures. Successful tests are also ones that are tailored to look for particular failure mechanisms efficiently, by selectively accelerating the tests.

Every failure has a cause and is a symptom of a failure mechanism waiting to be discovered. The tools of failure analysis are both statistical and physical; used together, they are a potent means for detecting the often unique fingerprint of the underlying source of the failure.

The Development Phase

The rapid advances in computer technology and software have made the feasibility of large-scale, complex computer simulations possible. Manufacturers typically conduct extensive computer simulations to identify interferences, fit issues, functionality, algorithmic logic accuracy, and so forth, prior to the development of prototypes. As the technology continues to advance, computer modeling and simulation may replace prototype development.

Notwithstanding these technical advances, breadboard and/or hardware prototypes commonly are developed so that the design team may conduct tests on the integrated system to eliminate performance and quality problems. The selected approach is reviewed in detail for feasibility and likely risk. Efforts are taken to reduce risk to acceptable levels by developing and testing prototypes.

Prototypes   Following the model in Figure 7-1b, the first complete prototypes of the new product are designed, built, and tested. Documentation such as materials lists, drawings, and test procedures is created. It is not unusual to repeat this phase more than once, perhaps building the first prototype in the laboratory to test the design and the second generation in manufacturing as a test of the documentation. The design should not exit this phase until a prototype has met all the design goals set for it, although it may not be possible to demonstrate the reliability goal because of the small number of prototypes available to test.

FIGURE 7-1b
The modern design and development process, development phase. (Source: *Burt, Norquist, and Anklesaria,* Zero-Base Pricing: Achieving World Class Competitiveness through Reduced All-in-Cost, *Probus Publishing, Chicago, Ill., 1990.*)

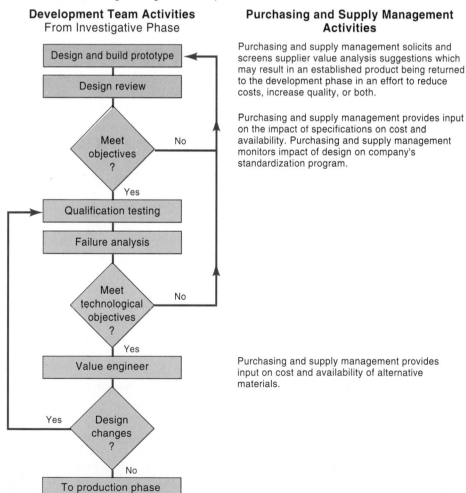

Development Team Activities
From Investigative Phase

Purchasing and Supply Management Activities

Purchasing and supply management solicits and screens supplier value analysis suggestions which may result in an established product being returned to the development phase in an effort to reduce costs, increase quality, or both.

Purchasing and supply management provides input on the impact of specifications on cost and availability. Purchasing and supply management monitors impact of design on company's standardization program.

Purchasing and supply management provides input on cost and availability of alternative materials.

Design Reviews   The design review is the point at which the new design can be measured, compared with previously established objectives, and improved. Purchasing and supply management participates in design reviews and provides information on the effect of specifications and the availability of items that are standard production for, or are inventoried by, suppliers. The buyer must ensure that the specification or other purchase description is complete, is unambiguous, and provides necessary information on how items furnished under it are to be checked or tested. The buyer should be satisfied that the purchase description is written in terms relevant to and understandable by potential suppliers.

Qualification Testing   Qualification tests are conducted on the prototype equipment. There are two different types: (1) margin tests and (2) life tests. *Margin tests* are concerned with assuring that the threshold of failure—the combination of conditions at which the product just begins to malfunction—is outside the range of specified conditions for the product's use.

Life tests are intended to find patterns of failure which occur too infrequently to be detected by engineering tests on one or two prototypes. These tests differ from margin tests primarily in the number of units tested and the duration of the test.

Failure Analysis   The stress testing and failure analysis techniques described in the investigation phase are applied to the prototype.

Meet Objectives?   The design team determines whether the prototype meets the objectives established in the investigation phase. If the prototype fails this analysis, it reenters the design process and a new or upgraded prototype is developed.

Value Engineering   Prior to releasing a design to production, it should be reviewed to engineer-out unnecessary costs through the application of the techniques described in Chapter 28, "Value Analysis/Value Engineering."

The Production Phase

Manufacturing and Production Plans   In the production phase, as shown in Figure 7-1c, the manufacturing plan and the procurement plan (frequently in the form of a bill of materials) are finalized. As a result of its early involvement in the design and specification development process, purchasing also should be able to develop contingency plans that will satisfy the firm's needs if the first source doesn't work out. The appropriate plans are now formalized and implemented.

Knowledge Transfer   Manufacturing engineering applies experience from similar projects and new developments from other manufacturers to the pro-

Development Team Activities
From Developmental Phase

Purchasing and Supply Management Activities

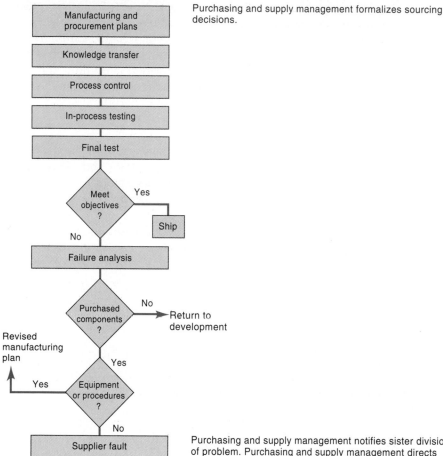

Purchasing and supply management formalizes sourcing decisions.

Purchasing and supply management notifies sister divisions of problem. Purchasing and supply management directs suppliers to develop and implement corrective action plan. Purchasing and supply management, quality, and manufacturing, as appropriate, work with supplier to correct problem.

FIGURE 7-1c
The modern design and development process, production phase. (*Adapted from: Burt, Norquist, and Anklesaria,* Zero-Base Pricing: Achieving World Class Competitiveness through Reduced All-in-Cost, *Probus Publishing, Chicago, Ill., 1990.*)

duction process. Manufacturing engineers also work with suppliers to share new and improved production techniques.

Process Control   Contrary to popular opinion, the design is not finished when the transfer from development to production takes place—quite the contrary. Unfortunately, changes at this stage of product development are very costly and tend not to be evaluated with the same thoroughness as the original alternatives. Finding a quick fix typically is the order of the day, preferably a fix that does not require extensive retooling or scrap. Still, there are some legitimate reasons why changes in the design occur after release to production. For example, there may be phenomena that occur so infrequently that they are not discovered until a large number of products are manufactured. Another reason for changes at this point is that with the pressure to develop new products in a shorter time, *concurrent design* is often practiced. This means that a new manufacturing process is developed simultaneously with a new product using that process, rather than sequentially. This is a risky approach, but one that is gaining popularity because it saves time and results in earlier new-product release.

When manufacturing problems arise, whether in the buyer's or the supplier's manufacturing operations, there is a tendency to look for a quick fix. One type of solution is to adjust the manufacturing process to minimize the problems, rather than to change the design. Perhaps this approach is taken because the process documentation is internal and not shipped to the customer along with the product. More likely, such changes in manufacturing processes are made because the process is under the jurisdiction of production and consequently the change does not require design engineering's approval. This approach can create problems. The situation can deteriorate to the point where there is a customized process for each product—nothing is standard—and the process is out of control most of the time. When design rules and process parameters are both being varied at the same time, the situation quickly becomes too complex to understand or control, and quality suffers. The correct solution is to optimize the process, get it under control, and keep it that way. Then the designs can be modified so that they fit the standard process, producing stable and predictable yields day after day.

In-Process and Final Testing   There are two objectives for in-process testing: (1) to eliminate defects before much value is added to the product and (2) to adjust or calibrate the performance in some way. Final product testing ensures that the item meets its performance objectives.

Every failure has a cause and is a symptom of a failure mechanism waiting to be discovered. For example, if failure analysis identifies a purchased component as the source of the failure, further analysis is required to determine whether: (1) faulty equipment or procedures are to blame or (2) the problem resides with the supplier. Failure analysis also may identify a latent defect in the product's design, requiring redesign.

Engineering Change Management

Any changes in components or the product itself may have profound effects on its cost, performance, appearance, and acceptability in the marketplace. Changes, especially at the component or subassembly level, can have a major effect on manufacturing. Unless changes to the configuration of an item or its components are controlled, manufacturers may find themselves in trouble. They may possess inventories of unusable raw materials or subassemblies. They may possess materials that require needlessly expensive rework to be adapted to a new configuration. Or they may produce an end item that will not meet the customer's needs. Uncontrolled changes generally mean that quality and reliability requirements have been compromised without appropriate retesting.

Engineering change management, a discipline which controls engineering changes, has been developed to avoid such problems.[18] How often engineering change management is required is a matter of managerial judgment. But for most modern technical items, engineering change management is a necessity. In some cases, it will be imposed on the manufacturer by the customer. Using this approach, changes are controlled and recorded. Marketing and all activities involved in the purchase, control, and use of purchased materials are told of any proposed changes to the item's characteristics. These organizations then comment on the effect of the proposed change. Such control and coordination is especially important when production scheduling and the release of purchase orders are controlled by a material requirements planning system.

There are many ways to organize an engineering change management group. Ideally, an engineering change management board is established with engineering, manufacturing, marketing, production planning, inventory management, and purchasing represented. When a materials management organization exists in the firm, a senior representative of production planning and inventory control is a logical candidate to chair this board. It is crucial that purchasing and the function responsible for materials control be involved in the review of proposed engineering changes for three reasons: (1) to provide input on the purchased materials implications of a proposed change, (2) to discuss the timing of proposed changes in order to minimize costs associated with unusable incoming materials, and (3) to be aware of forthcoming changes so that appropriate action can be taken with affected suppliers.

Adherence to this or a similar design process is key to the firm's success in the development of new products. Product quality, cost, and availability all must receive proper attention. Engineering, manufacturing, marketing, quality assurance, and purchasing all have vital roles to play in the design process.

HOW TO EXPAND PURCHASING AND SUPPLY MANAGEMENT'S ROLE

This chapter has described the design and development process with early purchasing and supplier involvement. In too many firms, the design engineer

---

[18]Engineering change management controls the changes to a product's design—specifically, its form, fit, and function.

attempts to address not only the technical and functional issues of design and development, but also manufacturing considerations, marketing implications, and the procurement considerations of economy and availability. Many of these individuals enjoy interacting with suppliers on both technical and commercial issues. And most believe they are serving their employer's best interest—even when making sourcing and specifications decisions that turn out to be suboptimal in the long run.

Purchasing and supply management personnel have their work cut out for them. They must develop and maintain cooperative relations with engineering *that protect the profitability of the firm.* Early purchasing and supplier involvement is an essential ingredient of the program to maximize a firm's profitability.

> Purchasing must be proactive. It must create a demand for its services within the design function by generating ideas with respect to potential suppliers and materials during the product design stage. . . . A survey conducted in the early 1990s confirms the importance to the new product development process of purchasing personnel gaining technical credibility in their relationship with design engineers and suppliers alike.[19]

Purchasing and supply management personnel must understand the orientation and dedication of the typical design engineer. Obviously, an ability to speak the engineer's language is very helpful. In a study conducted by one of the authors, it was found that purchasing personnel who think in the same manner as engineers have a much higher success rate when dealing with engineers than do other individuals. Such thought processes can be identified through established testing procedures.[20]

Whenever feasible, purchasing and supply management personnel should provide advice on the commercial implications of designs under consideration in a positive and constructive manner. Buyers must learn to co-opt their engineering counterparts by providing value and service. Purchasing then is seen as a partner which takes care of business problems, thereby allowing engineers to concentrate on technical issues. Several successful approaches to obtaining the desired level of purchasing input during the design process now are described.

Design or Project Teams

As has been discussed, when the importance of a project or program warrants, a dedicated project team is the ideal means of ensuring early purchasing and supply management involvement.

---

[19] S. P. Guy and B. G. Dale, "The Role of Purchasing in Design: A Study in the British Defense Industry," *International Journal of Purchasing and Materials Management,* Summer 1993, p. 29.

[20] See "Personal Factors in the Purchasing Engineering Interface" by J. Anklesaria and David N. Burt, *Journal of Purchasing and Materials Management,* February 1988.

Materials Engineers

Individuals with an engineering background are good candidates for buying positions whose responsibilities require involvement with design engineering. Some purchasing organizations divide buying responsibilities into two specialties: (1) materials engineering and (2) the buying activities of sourcing, pricing, and negotiating. The material/liaison engineer is responsible for coordinating with design engineering, for prequalifying potential sources (usually with the assistance of quality assurance), and for participating in value engineering and value analysis.

Co-Location

This approach calls for the placement of members of the purchasing staff in locations where design engineering and development work is done. These individuals are available to assist design engineers by obtaining required information from prospective suppliers and advising designers on the procurement implications of different materials and suppliers under consideration.

BUYERS WHO INTERFACE SUCCESSFULLY WITH ENGINEERS

The buyer is the key to successful early purchasing involvement in the new-product development process. Management directives, policies, and procedures supporting early purchasing involvement all help. But it is only when design engineers realize that the early involvement of a professional buyer is a productive asset, and not a nuisance, that EPI makes its full contribution.

The buyer who recognizes the importance of being involved early in the process can acquire the necessary skills and knowledge to be seen and accepted as a contributor. Courses in the development and interpretation of engineering drawings, as well as in a wide variety of technologies, can be taken via correspondence, night school, or a few degree-granting programs.* Sales personnel love to talk and will gladly help a willing listener gain technical insight into their products. Visits to suppliers' operations provide further insight and understanding.

CONCLUSION

The design and development of new products is one of a firm's most crucial activities. Profitability and even survival are affected. Purchasing and the firm's suppliers have major contributions to make during this process. A number of successful firms involve purchasing and suppliers up front because of contributions they can make in the areas of quality, cost, and time to market.

*A small but growing number of universities now offer an integrated procurement and engineering management program.

FOR DISCUSSION

7-1 What impact can early purchasing involvement have on the following new product development issues?
Quality
Cost
Scheduling
Time to market

7-2 "Ultimately, the absence of teamwork results in products which are a continuing burden to the firm's long-term competitiveness." Explain.

7-3 Discuss how and when selected suppliers can help to achieve optimal design performance.

7-4 What is one method of delegating the design of nonstrategic components to selected suppliers?

7-5 What is one of the buyer's key responsibilities during the investigation phase? How can he or she accomplish this?

7-6 What is the importance of a statement of objectives in the product development cycle? What information can purchasing contribute?

7-7 When evaluating alternative design approaches, what must be considered? Define each consideration.

7-8 What assessment are firms hoping to make when prequalifying a supplier?

7-9 Explain the cost/benefit trade-offs inherent in technology selection. What is a good rule of thumb to use when making this selection?

7-10 Discuss the objectives of stress testing and failure analysis. What happens when the objectives are not met, according to Figure 7-1a?

7-11 What are the three principal reasons for purchasing to be involved with engineering change management?

7-12 What is purchasing's role during the design review?

7-13 Describe three approaches to expanding purchasing's role in new product development.

7-14 Technical credibility can help purchasing develop and maintain cooperative relationships with engineering. Why is this important? What are some ways purchasing can acquire this credibility?

CASES FOR CHAPTER 7

Mazda Electronics, page 848
Elite Electronics (in the *Instructor's Manual*)
Fauquier Gas Company, page 816
The Dear John Mower Company, page 806
Dynamic Aircraft, page 811
Signal-Tek Corporation, page 912
Hy Tech (in the *Instructor's Manual*)

8

PURCHASE DESCRIPTIONS AND SPECIFICATIONS

The purchase description forms the heart of the procurement. Whether or not a purchase order or contract will be performed to the satisfaction of the buying organization frequently is determined at the time the purchase description is selected or written, specifying the quality requirements. In no other form of communication is there a need for greater clarity and precision of expression.

QUALITY DEFINED

Quality frequently is defined as "fitness; merit; excellence." This is the definition most people have in mind when they think of quality. The Rolls Royce is taken for granted to be a quality automobile. The diamond is accepted without question to be a quality gem. People generally believe that "high quality" is something desirable in itself.

In industrial and institutional purchasing, quality has an entirely different meaning. Here quality is related to suitability and cost (not price),[1] rather than to intrinsic excellence. The best quality is that which can be purchased at the lowest cost to fulfill the need or satisfy the intended function for which the material is being purchased.

Quality has no meaning in purchasing except as it is related to function and ultimate cost. A few examples will clarify this point. A new PC may be the fastest machine available, but if your application can't take advantage of the speed, then it is not the appropriate PC. Because of its high price, in most cases it would be needlessly wasteful to use silver as an electrical conductor, even though its conductivity is approximately 9 percent greater than that of copper. The high cost of labor for painting would make it foolish to attempt to save money on the price of the paint without considering its lasting qualities.

This chapter discusses the important aspects of written descriptions of quality and their impact on good purchasing. Such purchase descriptions serve a number of purposes, among them to:

- Communicate to the buyer in the purchasing department what to buy
- Communicate to prospective suppliers what is required
- Serve as the heart of the resulting purchase order
- Establish the standard against which inspections, tests, and quality checks are made

Purchase descriptions directly affect the quality and performance of the item purchased and the price paid. For example, unnecessarily tight tolerances result in needlessly high production costs and prices for purchased materials. Performance specifications that describe the function to be performed without specifying the materials and procedures to be used allow potential suppliers to propose alternative approaches to satisfying the requirement. When purchasing with performance specifications, the buyer benefits through a "competition of concepts," frequently with significant savings. Many firms pay a "fair and reasonable" price for materials; however, they do not always pay the "right" price. The right price is paid only when the "right" material is

---

[1]Price is only one element of cost, as is discussed in Chapter 7.

specified and after all reasonable efforts to improve the purchase descriptions have been exhausted.

Purchase descriptions fall into two broad categories: detailed specifications and other purchase descriptions.

DETAILED SPECIFICATIONS

Specifications are the most detailed method of describing requirements. Various types of design specifications are the detailed descriptions of the materials, parts, and components to be used in making a product. Hence, they are the descriptions that tell the seller exactly what the buyer wants to purchase. Because they impact the activities of engineering, operations, purchasing, and quality, optimum specifications vitally influence the contribution made by all these departments to the firm's success.

In a manufacturing firm, when specifications are fixed, the final design of the product is also fixed. When the final design is fixed, the product's competitive stance and its profit potential are also fixed. It is estimated that 75 to 85 percent of avoidable total costs are controllable at the design stage. Consequently, early involvement of purchasing and supplier professionals is essential in the firm's effort to reduce total cost.[2]

Developing proper specifications is an important management task. The task is difficult because it involves many variables, including the problem of conflicting human sensitivities and orientations. Many departments are capable of contributing to design; however, they frequently are thwarted from fully doing so because of conflicting views. Before the optimum in design can be achieved, these major conflicting views must be reconciled. For example, to gain a competitive advantage, the marketing department normally desires unique and nonstandard features in a product. Engineering sometimes desires features of design excellence which contribute little to sales potential and which may complicate the manufacturing process. Operations, to achieve its goals of low unit costs and relatively long production runs, favors materials that are easy to work and designs which result in the smallest possible number of items in the product line. Such natural departmental differences regarding design problems can be resolved only by perceptive and skillful management.

Reduced costs usually result in increased profit. Direct attempts to reduce labor costs normally result in strong counterpressures. Labor unions and individual workers are innately suspicious of attempts to save money by reducing labor costs. Hence, when an attempt is made to reduce these costs, regardless of its justification, labor troubles often follow. Cost reduction in the design area sometimes also generates opposition. But through imaginative and creative thinking, costs in this area typically can be reduced more easily than in any other area. This is why the design area is an extremely fruitful field for man-

[2]David N. Burt and Michael F. Doyle, *The American Keiretsu,* BusinessOne-Irwin, Homewood, Ill., 1993. p. 158.

agement cooperation and coordination between engineering, operations, and purchasing and supply management.

Basic Importance of Specifications

The cost of materials alone clearly dictates that their selection is an important consideration during product design. As noted, the costs of many materials are firmly engineered into a product's specifications during the design stage. This is the first (and sometimes the only) point at which numerous costs can be reduced and controlled. If costs can be, but are not, reduced at this point, it is possible that they will be built into the product permanently and will be hidden forever in the firm's cost accounting records. They will not show up on the firm's profit and loss statement as a loss; rather, they will continue indefinitely as an unnecessary and undetected profit drain.

As will be discussed in Chapter 28, "Value Analysis/Engineering," all is not lost if all unnecessary costs are not eliminated at the design stage. Markets, materials, and methods are constantly changing; hence, a second look to modify, simplify, or improve specifications will always be necessary, justified, and profitable. However, it is at the time of original design that the greatest dollar savings from both specifications and standardization are possible.

Preparing specifications for a product involves four major considerations:

1 Design considerations of function
2 Marketing considerations of consumer acceptance
3 Manufacturing considerations of economical production
4 Procurement considerations of markets, materials availability, supplier capabilities, and cost

As previously pointed out, it is not uncommon for these considerations to conflict with one another. Consequently, top management must provide the encouragement and direction that will motivate all departments to cooperate and seek a company solution, rather than departmental solutions. A design capable of solving the functional problem perfectly might very well present difficult production problems of machining or fabricating. A design could function well and be easy to produce, but present insoluble problems of materials procurement and pricing. All too frequently a product design is functionally sound, production is economical, and procurement is effective—but the consumer does not want to buy the product! Some years ago a major automobile manufacturer built a car that was superbly engineered and very economical to operate. These were the two qualities the manufacturer thought the consumer wanted most. This turned out to be an erroneous assumption. Because the car lacked some of the style features of its competitors, it did not sell well, and the manufacturer lost almost half its previous share of the total automobile market.

Interdepartmental conflicts of interest are seldom as grave as the extremes just cited. Although department managers do disagree occasionally, compromises usually can be worked out when the various aspects of the problem are understood and the organizational mechanism for resolving such conflicts has been established.

How Balanced Specifications Are Developed

Too often design engineers and production engineers resolve between themselves all four of the major considerations of specifications preparation, without consulting purchasing or the other concerned departments. This is regrettable because professional engineers seldom have the commercial experience and the market information required to resolve the procurement considerations of specifications. In their attempts to do so, they frequently develop stringent specifications that do not provide sufficient latitude to allow effective competition. In an article entitled "Three Essentials of Product Quality," management consultants Jack Reddy and Abe Berger write: "In most plants, management assumes that specs are correct and that stated tolerances are necessary. In our experience, this assumption is false; a significant fraction of valuable processing time in plants is inefficiently employed in refining products to unnecessarily tight specifications."[3]

When specifications conflicts arise, final authority for the decision should rest with the department having responsibility for the product's performance. This is usually the design engineering department. However, this is not a justifiable reason for engineering unnecessarily to subordinate the design considerations of manufacturing, procurement, quality, and marketing. From a company viewpoint, the right specifications are those that blend the requirements of all departments. Only such specifications can satisfy the goals of top management—i.e., increased sales, decreased costs, and the added corporate security which comes with an increasingly strong competitive position.

To develop specifications that properly balance product quality characteristics and product cost, management must coordinate the firm's technical and business skills. Four approaches can be used: (1) early purchasing and supplier involvement, (2) the formal committee approach, (3) the informal approach, and (4) the purchasing coordinator approach.

Early Purchasing and Supplier Involvement   As we saw in Chapter 7, more and more, progressive firms involve purchasing and potential suppliers during the early stages of new product development. Such early involvement optimizes the development of specifications since the technical and commercial issues are addressed at a point where there is maximum objectivity and flexibility. This can improve product quality and reliability, while compressing development time and reducing total material cost.[4] Prospective suppliers are provided rough function-fit specifications. As the item's configuration takes form, more definitive specifications evolve.

[3]*Harvard Business Review,* July–August 1983, pp. 153–159.
[4]Burt and Doyle, op. cit., p. 116.

As more and more firms embrace the use of cross-functional teams in the development of new products, early purchasing and supplier involvement becomes an inherent component of the process that culminates in the development of specifications. Progressive firms find that this approach is an important element in their quest for quality at realistic costs.

The Formal Committee Approach   This approach recognizes that a good specification is a compromise of basic objectives. A specifications review committee is established, with representatives (as appropriate) from design engineering, production engineering, purchasing, marketing, operations (including production control), quality, and standards. When a new product design is proposed, all members of the committee receive copies of all drawings, bills of materials, and specifications. No design becomes final until it is approved by the committee. One electronics firm estimates that it saves over $1 million annually by using such a team to evaluate new specifications in this way.

The Informal Approach   This method emphasizes the concept of a buyer's responsibility to "challenge" materials requests. At the same time, top management urges designers to request advice from buyers and work with them on all items that may involve commercial considerations. Emphasis at all times is placed on person-to-person communication and cooperation between individual buyers and designers. Using this approach, a company-oriented, cost-conscious attitude is developed at the grass-roots level throughout the organization.

The Purchasing Coordinator Approach   One or more positions are created in the purchasing department for individuals, frequently called *materials engineers*, to serve in a liaison capacity with the design department. Typically, the materials engineer spends most of his or her time in the engineering department reviewing design work as it comes off the drawing boards. The materials engineer searches for potential purchasing problems in an attempt to forestall them before they become serious. This approach is highly structured, as well as expensive. It also is very effective. Therefore, it should be used whenever coordination problems stemming from the technical nature of a firm's product or from the magnitude of its cost justify such an investment.

The reader should not infer from this discussion any intent to derogate the work of the design engineer. None is intended. Often, for reasons of policy, tradition, or expediency, the design engineer is required to make decisions alone that could be made more effectively in collaboration with others. Nevertheless, billions of dollars are lost annually through the adoption of unnecessarily stringent specifications at the design stage.

Writing Specifications

After the design of a product is determined, the next step is to translate the individual part and materials specifications into written form. The need for clarity and precision of expression is important in all business communications. Nowhere is it more important than in the communications emanating from purchase contracts.

Optimal performance in all departments is contingent on good specifications. To meet the needs of all departments, a specification must satisfy many requirements:

- Design and marketing requirements for functional characteristics, chemical properties, dimensions, appearance, etc.
- Manufacturing requirements for workability of materials and producibility
- Inspection's requirements to test materials for compliance with the specifications
- Stores' requirement to receive, store, and issue the material economically
- Purchasing and supply management's requirement to procure material without difficulty and with adequate competition from reliable sources of supply
- Production control's and purchasing's requirement to substitute materials when such action becomes necessary
- The total firm's requirements for suitable quality at the lowest overall cost
- The total firm's requirement to use commercial and industrial standard material whenever possible and to establish company standards in all other cases where nonstandard material is used repetitively

Procurement Importance of the Specification

One of the basic requirements of a good specification is to satisfy the procurement consideration of clear, concise, and unambiguous communication. Clarity in written expression is not always easy to achieve. One company recently lost $65,000 on a closed-circuit television installation because its written specifications misled the supplier into believing that a more expensive installation than the buyer really wanted was specified.

In addition to achieving clarity, care must be exercised to ensure that specifications are not written around a specific product, so as to limit competition. Several years ago, a fire chief wrote into the specifications for a new fire truck the requirement that the truck's 12-cylinder engine be produced by the manufacturer of the truck. This completely restricted competition, since only one manufacturer of fire engines manufactured 12-cylinder engines in its own plant. Had the fire chief specified what was wanted in terms of performance characteristics, such as speed and acceleration, competition would have been plentiful. This example typifies one of industry's most common forms of specifications abuse, i.e., slanting specifications to one manufacturer's product, thus reducing or precluding competition. In this particular case, fortunately, the situation had a happy ending; the purchasing department challenged the specifications, and the fire chief agreed to rewrite them in a form permitting maximum competition. A significant savings resulted from this change.

As previously discussed, specifying unreasonable tolerances is another common specification difficulty. Unnecessary precision pyramids costs! It costs more to make materials to close tolerances, it costs more to inspect them, and more rejects typically result. The best method of avoiding such unnecessary costs is to adhere to the most economical method of manufacture while using standard specifications wherever possible. For example, in procuring 1,000 drive pulleys for use in vacuum-sweeper motors, the first decision would be to determine whether the pulleys could be manufactured satisfactorily by a casting process. Although this method dictates the use of looser tolerances, in large volumes its unit cost is considerably lower than that of a second alternative, machining the pulley from bar stock. The second decision would be to select an industrial standard for the part, regardless of the method of manufacture used. This decision leads directly to a consideration of standardization, an issue which is addressed in the next chapter.

There are three principal types of detailed specifications: commercial standards, design specifications (generally accompanied by engineering drawings), and material and method-of-manufacture specifications.

Commercial Standards

Recurring needs for the same materials have led industry and government to develop commercial standards for these materials. A commercial standard is nothing more than a complete description of the item standardized. The description includes the quality of materials and workmanship that should be used in manufacturing the item, along with dimensions, chemical composition, and so on. It also includes a method for testing both materials and workmanship. Commercial standards are a cornerstone of the mass production system; therefore, they are important to efficient purchasing and to the standard of living in the United States.

All nuts, bolts, pipes, and electrical items that are made to standard specifications can be expected to fit all standard applications, regardless of who manufactured the item. Materials ordered by standardized specifications leave no doubt on the part of either the buyer or the seller as to what is required. Standard specifications have been prepared for many goods in commercial trade. National trade associations, standards associations, national engineering societies, the federal government, and national testing societies all contribute to the development of standard specifications and standard methods of testing. Commercial standards are applicable to raw materials, fabricated materials, individual parts and components, and subassemblies.

Purchasing by commercial standards is somewhat similar to purchasing by brand name. In both methods, the description of what is wanted can be set forth accurately and easily. With the exception of proprietary products, most widely used items are standard in nature; hence, they are highly competitive and readily available at reasonable prices. There are many users of standard products; therefore, manufacturers who make them can safely schedule long, low-cost production runs for inventory. They do not need specific sales commitments before production. They know that materials will be ordered under these standard specifications when they are needed.

Inspection is only moderately expensive for materials purchased by commercial standards. Commercial standard products require periodic checking in addition to sight identification to assure buyers that they are getting the quality specified.

Commercial standard items should be used whenever possible. They contribute greatly to the simplification of design, purchasing procedures, inventory management, and cost reduction. Copies of standard specifications can be obtained from a number of government, trade association, and testing association sources. In fact, the easiest way to get a particular specification is to ask a manufacturer to provide a copy of the standard specification of the material or product that it recommends for the buyer's intended need.

Design Specifications

Not all items and materials used in industry are covered by standard specifications or brands. For many items, therefore, a large number of buying firms prepare their own specifications. By so doing, these buyers broaden their field of competition. All manufacturers capable of making the item described in the buyer's specifications are potential suppliers.

By preparing its own specifications, a company can often avoid the premium prices of brand name items and the sole-source problems of patented, copyrighted, and proprietary products. When preparing its own specifications, a company should attempt to make them as close as possible to industry standards. If any special dimensions, tolerances, or features are required, every effort should be made to attain these "specials" by designing them as additions or alterations to standard parts. This action will save time and money.

Describing requirements with chemical or electronic specifications, or with physical specifications and accompanying engineering drawings, entails some risk. For example, if a buyer details for a paint manufacturer the exact chemical specifications of the paint desired, the buyer assumes complete responsibility for the paint's performance. Should the paint fade in the first month, it is the buyer's responsibility. If a buyer specifies for a metal fabricator the exact dimensions wanted in a part, the buyer assumes all responsibility for the part's fitting and functioning. Should it develop that a part, to fit and function properly, must be 26.045 inches long, rather than 26.015 inches as specified in the purchase order, the responsibility for failure rests solely with the buyer.

The cost of inspection to assure compliance with company-prepared specifications can be high. The very nature of the materials purchased under this method of description tends to require special inspection.

Engineering Drawings

Engineering drawings and prints occasionally are used alone, but more typically in conjunction with other physical purchase descriptions. Where precise shapes, dimensions, and spatial relationships are required, drawings are the most accurate method of describing what is wanted. Despite their potential for accuracy, exceptional care must be exercised in using them. Ambiguity, sometimes present in this method of description, can produce costly repercussions. All dimensions, therefore, must be completely covered, and the descriptive instruction should be explicit.

Engineering drawings are used extensively in describing quality for construction projects, for foundry and machine shop work, and for myriads of special mechanical parts and components. There are four principal advantages in using drawings for description: (1) They are accurate and precise, (2) they are the most practical way of describing mechanical items requiring extremely close tolerances, (3) they permit wide competition (what is wanted can easily be communicated to a wide range of potential suppliers), and (4) they clearly establish the standards for inspection.

Material and Method-of-Manufacture Specifications

When this method is used, prospective suppliers are instructed precisely as to the specific materials to be used and how they are to be processed. The buyer assumes full responsibility for product performance. Further, the buyer assumes that his or her own organization has the latest knowledge concerning materials, techniques, and manufacturing methods for the item being purchased. In this case, purchasers see no reason to pay another company for this knowledge.

Material and method-of-manufacture specifications are used extensively by the armed services and the Department of Energy. A modified version of these specifications is used by industry. Large buyers of paint, for example, frequently request manufacturers of a standard paint to add or delete certain chemicals when producing paint for them. Large steel buyers make the same type of request when purchasing special steels. Chemical and drug buyers, for reasons of health and safety, sometimes approach full use of the material and method-of-manufacture technique in describing quality. Also, these specifications are used most appropriately in those situations where technically sophisticated buyers in large companies deal with small suppliers having limited research and development staffs. Normally, however, this technique is little used in industry because it puts such great responsibility on the buyer. It can deny a company the latest advancements in both technical development and manufacturing processes. Specifications of this type are expensive to prepare. Inspection generally is very expensive.

There are two important features of this method of description. First, the widest competition is possible, and thus good pricing is assured. Second, since the product is nonstandard, the antidiscriminatory provisions of the Robinson-Patman Act pose no barrier to obtaining outstanding pricing and service.

OTHER PURCHASE DESCRIPTIONS

Performance Specifications

A performance specification, in theory, is the perfect method of describing a requirement. Instead of describing an item in terms of its design characteristics, performance specifications describe in words, and quantitatively where possible, what the item is required to do. This type of description is used extensively in buying highly technical military and space products. For example, the product wanted could be a missile capable of being launched from a submarine with a designated speed, range, and accuracy. Or it could be a telemetering system capable of tracking and reporting missiles or satellites during their flight. Potential suppliers are told only the performance that is required. Though performance is specified in precise detail, suppliers are not told how the product should be manufactured or what material should be used in its manufacture.

Performance specifications are not limited to such complex items as spacecraft. Electronics, aircraft, and automobile companies, for example, frequently use this method to buy such common materials as electrical wire, batteries, and radios. A performance specification for wire may require it to withstand a given temperature, have a designated resistance to abrasion, and have a given conductivity capability. No mention is made in the specifications of what materials are to be used or how the wire is to be manufactured or insulated to give it the required characteristics. Manufacturers are free to make these choices as they see fit.

Industry uses performance specifications extensively to buy expensive, complicated machines and machine tools. Today, more production machines are replaced because of technological obsolescence than because of wear. Therefore, in buying such a machine, a firm should make every effort to obtain the ultimate in technological advancement. Often this can be done best by using performance specifications. To reduce and control the expense associated with this approach to describing requirements, descriptions should be written as explicitly as possible. Also, the product being purchased should be sectionalized into the greatest practical number of distinct components, with potential sellers required to quote on each component. This practice helps solve the difficult problem of comparing sellers' prices by allowing comparison of individual components.

There are two primary advantages of describing quality by performance specifications: (1) ease of preparing the specifications and (2) assurance of obtaining the precise performance desired. For complex products, it is by far the easiest type of specification to write. It assures performance, and if the supplier is competent, it assures inclusion of all applicable new developments.

Proper supplier selection is essential when performance specifications are used. In fact, the ability to select capable and honest suppliers is prerequisite to the proper use of performance specifications. Because the supplier assumes the entire responsibility for designing and making the product, quality is entirely in its hands. If the supplier is not capable, it cannot apply the most advanced technical and manufacturing knowledge. If it is not honest, materials and workmanship may be inferior. When using performance specifications, buyers must solicit competition among a number of capable sellers. Capable suppliers ensure quality; competition ensures reasonable prices.

Function and Fit Specifications

Such purchase descriptions are a variation of performance specifications and are used in *early supplier involvement (ESI)* programs. With this approach, the design team describes the function(s) to be performed and the way the item is to fit into the larger system (e.g., automobile, computer, etc.), together with several design objectives (cost, weight, reliability). As ESI becomes more common, this approach to describing requirements undoubtedly will increase in popularity. With careful prequalification of suppliers, there are no significant disadvantages with this approach.

Brand or Trade Names

When manufacturers develop and market a new product, they must decide whether or not to brand it. Branding or differentiating a product is generally done to develop a recognized reputation and thus gain repeat sales, protect the product against substitutes, maintain price stability, and simplify sales promotion.[5] The primary reason most manufacturers brand their products is to obtain repeat sales. Consumers develop a preference for brands. Therefore, branded products can generally be sold at higher prices than unbranded products of similar quality. A brand represents the manufacturer's pledge that the quality of the product will be consistent from one purchase to the next. A buyer can be certain that a reputable manufacturer will strive to keep this pledge. For example, Xerox introduced its Total Satisfaction Guarantee Program in 1990. "Typical of the guarantee is a replacement product if the user is not completely satisfied."[6] Violation of the pledge carries the severest penalty possible—consumer rejection of the manufacturer's product.

Brand name products are among the simplest to describe on a purchase order. Thus, they save purchasing time and reduce purchasing expense.

---

[5]Manufacturers also produce merchandise for wholesalers and retailers who market it under their own private brands. In such arrangements the manufacturer is relieved of marketing and promotional responsibilities.

[6]Kate Evans-Correia, "Are Guarantees Proof of Product Quality?" *Purchasing*, Sept. 23, 1993, p. 95.

Inspection expense is also low for branded products. The only inspection required is sight verification of the brand labels. The brand is the quality ordered. The higher prices usually paid for name brands thus are offset to some extent by reduced description preparation and inspection costs.

A supplier's success in maintaining a consistent quality level is greatest in those situations where production and quality control are under its own supervision. If a supplier buys an item from several manufacturers (each exercising its quality control), the quality variation in all probability will be larger than if the supplier made the item or bought it from a single source. For this reason, it is important for buyers to know who is responsible for the production and quality control of all branded products they buy. In situations where tight quality control is essential, multiple sources of production should be avoided if possible.

It is often said that when a buyer purchases by brand name he or she eliminates competition by limiting the purchase to a single source of supply. If a buyer had to limit purchases to a single brand from a single source, this would represent a major disadvantage of purchasing by brand name. In fact, however, there are very few situations in which only one brand is acceptable for a given purpose. A profitable market for any item in a competitive enterprise economy attracts other manufacturers to make the item. Competition, therefore, is available by brands just as it is by other types of quality descriptions. In addition, the same branded product may be available from different wholesalers or jobbers who are willing to compete on price and service to get a buyer's order.

Competition among brands is usually attained by specifying "brand A or equal" on the bid forms. What does "or equal" mean? This question generates many arguments. Realistically, it means materials that are of equal quality and are capable of performing the function intended. Equal quality means similar quality of materials and similar quality of workmanship. Comparing the quality of materials is relatively easy, but comparing the quality of workmanship is particularly difficult. Here such nebulous considerations as precision of production, fit and matching of adjacent parts, types of finish, and shades of color must be resolved. The key to the "or equal" consideration is "Can the 'equal' perform the function for which the specified brand is desired?" If it cannot, it certainly is not equal; if it can, it is equal.

One practical way of resolving the "or equal" problem is to let the user department decide which products are equal before prices are solicited. Only companies whose products are accepted by using departments as equal are requested to submit prices. This technique helps avoid wounded feelings among potential suppliers. It also permits requisitioning departments to make more objective decisions.

In some situations, purchasing by brand name can be made more effective by including in the purchasing description additional references or limitations. For example, if the buyer suspects that other materials can perform the desired function, reference in the description should give prospective suppliers the opportunity to offer such other materials for consideration. When limitations concerning physical, functional, and other characteristics of the materials to be purchased are essential to the buyer's needs, they should be clearly set forth in the brand name description. For example, in many purchases of equipment, interchangeability of repair parts is essential. When this is the case, this limitation should be spelled out in the brand name description. The invitation for bids or requests for proposal should reserve the right to examine and test the proffered item should an "or equal" product be offered.

For small quantities, brand buying is excellent.[7] The primary disadvantage of purchasing by brands frequently is higher price. Many categories of branded items sell at notoriously high prices. Antiseptics and cleaning compounds are common examples of such items. For these, another type of purchase description is preferable. When purchased by detailed or performance specifications, savings often exceed 50 percent. In recent years, buying drugs by generic name rather than by brand has resulted in spectacular savings for many hospitals; savings up to 70 percent are not uncommon.

Samples

Samples have been called the lazy person's method of describing requirements. When samples are used, the buyer does not have to look for an equal brand, pick a standard specification, or describe the performance wanted. Samples are neither the cheapest nor the most satisfactory method of purchase. Usually the money saved in description costs is substantially exceeded by the money spent on inspection costs. It usually is difficult to determine by inspection that the product delivered is, in fact, the same as the sample. Quality of materials and quality of workmanship are generally exceedingly difficult to determine from routine inspection. Therefore, in many cases, acceptance or rejection becomes a matter of subjective judgment.

Samples generally should be used only if other methods of description are not feasible. Color and texture, printing, and grading are three broad areas in which other methods of description are not feasible. A precise shade of green, for example, is difficult to describe without a sample. Proposed lithographic work is best judged by the supplier's proofs. Establishing grades for commodities such as wheat, corn, and cotton by samples has proved to be the best method of describing these products.

Market Grades

Grading is a method of determining the quality of commodities. A grade is determined by comparing a specific commodity with standards previously

---

[7]Brand buying is mandatory in some situations. Common examples are when a supplier's production process is secret, when its workmanship exceeds all competitors', or when testing competitive items is too costly.

agreed on. Grading is generally limited to natural products such as lumber, wheat, hides, cotton, tobacco, food products, and so on. The value of grades as a description of quality depends on the accuracy with which the grades can be established and the ease with which they can be recognized during inspection. There are, for example, thirteen grades of cotton, each of which must be determined from an examination of individual samples. Trade associations, commodity exchanges, and government agencies all expend great effort in establishing and policing usable grades.

In buying graded commodities, industrial buyers often use personal inspection as a part of their buying technique. Just as individuals select by inspecting the shoes, dresses, and shirts they buy, so industrial buyers select by inspecting some of the commodities they buy in primary markets. There can be a significant difference between the upper and lower grade limits of many commodities. The difference is so great in some that materials near the lower limit of the grade may be unacceptable. Hence, inspection is critically important in buying many materials by market grade. Brewers and millers, for example, usually inspect all the grains they buy. Inspection is necessary if they are to obtain raw materials of the quality needed to produce a finished product of consistent quality.

Beef is an excellent illustration of the wide quality spread that can exist within a grade. Normally, 700-pound steers dressed and graded as "U.S. Prime" have a spread of roughly 40 pounds in fat content between the beef at the top of the grade and beef at the bottom of the grade. Such a wide spread may be a minor consideration to the purchaser of a 1-pound steak. However, to the industrial food service manager buying millions of pounds of beef, the difference can be thousands or hundreds of thousands of dollars.

Qualified Products

In some situations, it is necessary to determine in advance of purchase whether a product can meet specifications. These situations normally exist when: (1) it takes too long[8] to conduct the normal post-purchase inspections and tests that are required to ensure quality compliance, (2) inspection to ensure compliance with the quality aspects of the specifications requires special testing equipment that is not commonly or immediately available, and (3) the purchase involves materials concerned with safety equipment, life survival equipment, research equipment, or materials described by performance specifications.

When advance qualification is indicated, suppliers are prequalified by a thorough review and test of the entire process by which they ensure compliance with their specifications. After qualification, the products of the approved

---

[8]The federal government and some large industrial firms have defined "too long" as a period exceeding 30 days.

suppliers are placed on what is called a *qualified products list (QPL)*. Approved products are described by trade name, model number, part number, place of manufacture, and similar identifying data on the QPL.

Combination of Methods

Many products cannot adequately be described by a single method of description. In such cases, a combination of two or more methods should be used. For example, in describing the quality desired for a space vehicle, performance specifications could be used to describe numerous overall characteristics of the vehicle, such as its ability to withstand certain temperatures, to perform certain predetermined maneuvers in space at precise time sequences, and to stay in space for a specific period of time. Physical specifications could be used to describe the vehicle's configuration as well as the television cameras and other instruments it will carry. Commercial standards or brand names might be used to describe selected pieces of electrical or mechanical hardware used in the vehicle's support systems. A chemical specification could be used to describe the vehicle's paint. Finally, a sample could be used to show the color of this paint.

Few products are as complex as space vehicles; nevertheless, an increasing number of industrial products require two or more methods of quality descriptions. For instance, something as commonplace as office drapes could require chemical specifications to describe the cloth and fireproofing desired, physical specifications to describe the dimensions desired, and samples to describe the colors and texture desired.

Methods Used in Practice

A survey of a wide range of manufacturing companies indicates that purchase requirements in these companies are described as follows:

Method	Percent of total items purchased
Brand name*	25
Commercial standards	26
Specifications	31
Combination	8
All other methods	10
	100

*Ninety-one percent of the purchasing executives buying brands stated they were able to get competition when purchasing by this method. Competition came from competitive brands accepted as equal and from competitive sources selling the same brand.

Regardless of the method(s) used to describe purchase requirements, only the minimum quality needed for the product to perform the function intended should be specified. Overspecifying and including restrictive features in purchase descriptions cause delays and increase costs. The section of the purchase order including purchase descriptions should also include all applicable warranties.

HOW TO SELECT THE RIGHT APPROACH
TO DESCRIBING REQUIREMENTS

While the decision on what type of purchase description to use may appear to be simple, many factors complicate the issue. For small, noncritical procurements, brand names frequently best describe requirements. The use of a brand name as a purchase description is appropriate (1) to obtain the desired level of quality or skill when these are not described easily, (2) to gain the benefits of wide advertising of the brand name item that would aid in promotion of the purchaser's end product, or (3) to accommodate users who have a bias or prejudice (whether founded or unfounded) in favor of the brand. Such prejudices can be virtually impossible to overcome.

When brand names or samples are inappropriate methods of describing requirements, some type of specification will be employed. When selecting or developing the specification, consideration must be given to the importance of competition and the desirability of avoiding unnecessarily restrictive criteria.

Once a need has been identified and functionally described, and when the size of the contemplated purchase warrants, procurement research and analysis should be conducted to investigate the availability of commercial products able to meet the buyer's need. This research and analysis also should provide information to aid in selecting a procurement strategy appropriate to the situation. Procurement research and analysis involves obtaining the following information, as appropriate:

- The availability of standard products suitable to meet the need (with or without modification)
- The terms, conditions, and prices under which such products are sold
- Any applicable trade provisions or restrictions or controlling laws
- The performance characteristics and quality of available products, including quality control and test procedures followed by the manufacturers
- Information on the satisfaction of other users having similar needs
- Any costs or problems associated with integration of the item with those currently used
- Industry production practices, such as continuous, periodic, or batch production
- The distribution and support capabilities of potential suppliers

CONCLUSION

Specifications play an important role in the search for the right quality and the right value. They also assist in resolving the design conflicts which exist between engineering, manufacturing, marketing, and procurement. Specifications serve as the heart of the resulting purchase order or contract.

FOR DISCUSSION

8-1 Many firms pay a "fair and reasonable" price for materials; however, they do not always pay the "right" price. Explain.

8-2 Discuss the role which both the design department and selected suppliers should play in a company's cost-control efforts.

8-3 Discuss the importance of specifications.

8-4 Why should product design be a cross-functional effort? What are the impacts on profit, control, and quality?

8-5 What are the four major considerations involved in the development of specifications?

8-6 Why should a specification not be written around a specific product?

8-7 Discuss the benefits and weaknesses of commercial standards.

8-8 When using commercial standards, what is the relation between quality and inspection and cost?

8-9 When would you recommend the use of a company-prepared specification? What are the advantages and disadvantages?

8-10 Why does a performance specification not describe chemical or physical properties? What should it include? What are the potential problems with performance specifications?

8-11 How can purchasing by brand name be made more effective? Discuss ways to safeguard against a supplier's substitute, or "equal" product.

8-12 Market grades are typically associated with commodities. Could other products also be graded?

8-13 What is a qualified product list? When are QPLs necessary?

8-14 Which factors must you consider when selecting the right approach to describing requirements?

CASES FOR CHAPTER 8

Fauquier Gas Company, page 816
Dynamic Aircraft, page 811
The Big "O" Company, page 783
SMC Turbines, page 914
The Peach Computer Company, page 879
OCR, Inc. (in the *Instructor's Manual*)
Gotham City Buys Fire Engines (in the *Instructor's Manual*)
The Case of the Unruly Spider (in the *Instructor's Manual*)

9

STANDARDIZATION

KEY CONCEPTS

- Standardization
  Standardization defined
  The broad implications of standardization
  How standardization reduces costs
- Simplification
  Simplification defined
  The consequences of not simplifying
  The usefulness of a materials catalog
- Awakening interest in standardization
  Kinds and sources of industrial standards
  International standards
  Metric conversion
  Organizing a successful standardization program

STANDARDIZATION

Standardization Defined

In business practice, the concept of standardization is applied in two different areas. The first is concerned with the standardization of things—their size, shape, color, physical properties, chemical properties, performance characteristics, and so on. The present chapter investigates this usage of the standardization concept, which frequently is called "industrial standardization." The second application deals with the managerial aspects of business activity—standardizing such things as operating practices, procedures, and systems. This type of standardization, frequently termed "managerial standardization," is discussed in the chapters that deal with managing purchasing and supply activities.

Although minor differences are found in practice, *industrial standardization* can be defined as "the process of establishing agreement on uniform identifications for definite characteristics of quality, design, performance, quantity, service, and so on." A uniform identification that is agreed on is called a *standard*.

Two historical incidents illustrate the importance of standardization. Eli Whitney is best known to most Americans for his invention of the cotton gin, but his contribution to the development of standardization was a much greater accomplishment. The cotton gin is an important machine, but standardization is the prerequisite to mass production and mass prosperity.

Whitney's work on standardization started in 1801, when he accepted a contract to furnish 10,000 muskets to the United States government. It appeared that Whitney had fallen behind on his contract. He was summoned to Washington by Thomas Jefferson to explain his delay. The explanation is a little-known but extremely important landmark in American history. Whitney took with him a box containing the parts of ten muskets. On a table before his congressional interrogators, he separated these parts into piles of stocks, barrels, triggers, firing hammers, and so on. He asked a congressman to pick a part from each pile. Whitney then assembled these parts into a finished musket, repeating the process until all ten muskets had been assembled.

After his demonstration, it was easy for Whitney to explain his apparent delay. Rather than furnishing a proportional number of guns each month, as an artisan gunsmith would have done after individually making the parts for each gun and then assembling each gun in turn, Whitney had been working to design machine tools and dies with which he could mass-produce parts which were interchangeable with each other. He had standardized the parts. When his machine tools were completed, he was able to produce the 10,000 muskets in a period of time during which an artisan gunsmith could have produced only a few muskets. This effort gave birth to the techniques of mass production.

In short, Whitney discovered that by standardizing parts, the skills of artisans could be transferred to machines that could be operated by less-skilled labor. This, in turn, reduced the need for highly skilled labor, which, at the time, was in extremely short supply. Even more important, this practice introduced mass production and sizable industrial growth to the United States.

The burning to the ground of Baltimore's business district in 1904 clearly illustrates the need for standards in urban living. Like the battle that was lost for the lack of a horseshoe nail, Baltimore was lost for the lack of standard firehose couplings. Washington, New York, and Philadelphia all responded to Baltimore's cry for help. When their equipment arrived in Baltimore, however, the rescuers just stood by helplessly. There was no way to connect the different-sized hose couplings to Baltimore's fire hydrants.

The Broad Implications of Standardization

There are three basic systems of production: job-shop or batch production, line or continuous production, and process production. The systems themselves can represent degrees of industrial progress. This is not to imply that in all cases progress lies in advancing from the job-shop to the process system of production. Each of these systems has its own applications and benefits. However, whenever feasible, production should progress from a less technologically sophisticated to a more technologically sophisticated system. Such a move will produce greater economic gains.

This concept of advancement is well understood in industry, although it is not always equally well applied. Less well understood is the fact that production systems are heavily influenced by standardization. If Eli Whitney introduced mass production in the United States, Henry Ford made it universal. Ford, however, misinterpreted one important relationship of standardization to mass production: He visualized mass production to mean a standard product produced on an assembly line. Ford thought he spoke correctly when he said, "The customer can have any color car he wants as long as it is black." Actually, he missed the full implication of mass production. Mass production is the production of many diverse products, assembled from standardized parts which themselves have been mass-produced.

A West Coast manufacturer who produces only a few hundred machines yearly for picking apples, harvesting beans, and picking tomatoes comes closer to the concept of true mass production than did Henry Ford. This firm produces only a few machines of a given type. It designs specialized machines from standardized parts which are mass-produced. The design engineers of this company are fully aware that their job entails more than designing specific machines which can perform functions that will make farming more efficient. To sell this company's unique machines at prices customers can pay, the machines must be designed from standard parts and assemblies that are themselves mass-produced.

Billions of dollars are saved by companies through standardization. A survey of the American National Standards Institute (ANSI) lists the following examples:

- A maker of business machines spends about $90,000 a year on standards work. It estimates annual savings at $500,000.
- A manufacturer of electronic equipment spends $24,000 annually on standards to save $125,000.
- A division of a major lubricating-equipment maker believes it saves $3.50 for every $1.00 spent on standards work.
- Two major standards projects of a certain manufacturing concern are tank design and minimum piping. Total savings equal $500,000.

- An engineering firm saves $25,000 per year, mostly on engineering and drafting time, through standards. The cost is $2,000.

How Standardization Reduces Costs

The use of standards permits a firm to purchase fewer items, in larger quantities, and at lower prices. Thus, fewer items are processed and stocked. This reduces purchasing, receiving, inspection, and payment costs. Stocking fewer items makes controlling inventories easier and less costly. The use of standardized approved items drastically reduces the number of defects in incoming materials. Consequently, the purchase of standardized materials saves money four ways: lower prices, lower processing costs, lower inventory carrying costs, and fewer quality problems.

Conversely, the use of nonstandard items, commonly referred to as "specials," almost always assures a firm of higher total acquisition and carrying costs. Additionally, because for specials there frequently is no history of manufacturing experience, using them can result in problems such as unknown quality, uncertain delivery schedules, and lack of uniformity.

Recently, Japanese manufacturers have joined the standardization bandwagon. For example, Mr. Tadashi Arai, a screw engineer of Nissan Motor Company's research and development center southwest of Tokyo, is repudiating his life's work. He is quoted as saying, "I used to derive happiness from designing different types of things." Mr. Arai points to a Plexiglas board displaying 100 screws used in Nissan cars. Now, emblazoned over the display is a new message: "Behold! This Is Our Bulky State." His team's new mission: to cut the variety of fasteners in Nissan vehicles—some 6,000 in all—by half.

"If we use fewer different screws, plant workers can save time changing the heads on their power tools," he explains, drilling an imaginary bolt with his index finger. "We can save 50 seconds per car. And one second equals one yen."[1]

SIMPLIFICATION

Simplification, a corollary of standardization, is another term for which recognized authorities have varying definitions. Most frequently, simplification means reducing the number of standard items a firm uses in its product design and carries in its inventory. For example, one company formerly used twenty-seven different kinds of standard lubricating greases in the maintenance of its machinery. Analysis showed that in some cases the same grease could be used for several different applications and that a total of only six kinds of grease were needed. Hence, through simplification the number of standard greases used was reduced from twenty-seven to six. Similar analysis showed that the number of standard bearings and fasteners used in production could be

---

[1]Clay Chandler and Michael Williams, "A Slump in Car Sales Forces Nissan to Start Cutting Swollen Costs," *The Wall Street Journal,* Mar. 3, 1993, p. 1.

reduced by half. Reductions of this scope are commonplace. Here are some other typical examples:

- A large electrical manufacturer reduced its number of standard washers from 1,350 to 150 varieties.
- Another large company saves $250,000 yearly from simplifying its standard typewriter desks, formerly purchased at prices ranging from $60 to $500.
- Still another company saves $217,000 yearly from standardizing and simplifying the paper towels used throughout its multiplant operations.
- The United States Navy saves several million dollars yearly from simplifying its stock of ball bearings.

The preceding examples illustrate that simplification can indeed produce big savings. Simplification savings result primarily from reduced inventory investment, more competitive prices, greater quantity discounts (because of larger-volume purchases and the use of blanket orders), and reduced clerical and handling costs (because fewer different items have to be handled and controlled).

Some authorities consider simplification an integral part of standardization, rather than a corollary of it. They visualize the simplification process as taking place primarily at the design level, rather than at the stocking level. They think in terms of simplifying (or reducing) the number of related items that are approved as standards in the first place.

Results of No Simplification Program

Recently, a procurement system review was performed by one of the authors for a California instrument manufacturer. The firm was suffering from low sales volume brought on, in large part, by quality problems. In addition, the high cost of goods sold resulted in anemic profits. Purchasing and supply management was not involved in the design and development of new products. It soon became apparent that many of the firm's problems could be attributed to the absence of a simplification program, and that both of the cited problems were directly affected by this absence.

Engineers responsible for developing new products had no systematic way of drawing on the firm's previous experience with purchased materials. A connector, capacitor, or gate array designed into a product last year may have had either of two shortcomings: a low level of quality or a low level of reliability.[2] The designer of a new product frequently specified the same problem materials. This led to more waste in production and more avoidable field failures.

---

[2]"Quality" has many definitions. As used in this book, *quality* is conformance to specifications that result in a product which meets customers' expectations, not the number of features or degree of sophistication of the product. *Reliability* is the degree of confidence or probability that an item will perform a specified number of times under prescribed conditions. This topic is discussed in detail in Chapter 21, "Managing for Quality."

The absence of a simplification program affected the cost of goods sold in another way. In many instances, design engineers were specifying new materials that were similar, but not identical, to materials already in use for other products. This proliferation of materials resulted in small-quantity buys, usually at higher unit prices than would have resulted from higher-volume consolidated purchases. Further, unnecessarily high inventory carrying costs resulted.

Materials Catalog

A current, easily accessible materials catalog of approved standard items is the logical output of a standardization/simplification program. The catalog greatly aids the firm's design efforts. The availability of such a catalog virtually eliminates the possibility that designers will utilize materials which previously caused problems.

A Success Story

Several years ago, the corporate materials management department of a computer manufacturer began developing a catalog of approved parts. This catalog has been developed by the joint efforts of design engineering, reliability engineering, purchasing, and manufacturing engineering. It is a result of team effort which considers both the technical and commercial implications of the items included. The internal catalog is in contrast to a given supplier's catalog which, while simplifying the engineers' efforts to describe an item, places the firm in a single-source posture.

All items in the catalog have undergone and passed extensive quality analyses. All suppliers have been carefully qualified to ensure that they have the ability to continuously supply high-quality materials. This catalog is made available to the design engineers who are responsible for the development of new products. These engineers are able to incorporate parts from this catalog without further approval. If they want to use a part which is not approved in the catalog, or which has a marginal technical or supplier rating, engineering management and supply management must agree on the use of the item. The development of the catalog has been expensive, but the rewards have been far greater. A dramatic reduction in quality problems with purchased materials and significant price and inventory cost reductions have been enjoyed. The catalog is electronically based and is made available on a real-time basis.

Unfortunately, often there is no systematic way to measure the progress of standardization/simplification efforts, to quantify their impact on the bottom line, or to recognize and reward those responsible. For this reason, standardization efforts need to be systematized within manufacturing firms; these efforts need to be conscious and ongoing.[3]

---

[3]Robert M. Monczka and James P. Morgan, "Strategic Sourcing Management," *Purchasing*, June 18, 1992.

AWAKENING INTEREST IN STANDARDIZATION

American industry is expanding its use of standardization noticeably. The American National Standards Institute reports that its number of American National Standards increased 75 percent during the 1970s.[4] The increasing speed of scientific and technological advancement now mandates the establishment of standards at the time new products are developed. Standardization after the fact is so expensive and difficult to administer that predesign or current design standardization is essential. New computer-aided design (CAD) systems provide considerable assistance in this regard.

As might be expected, the government imposes standardization requirements for major purchases. Prime military contractors are required to develop standardization programs for systems and major items of hardware purchased. Under this requirement, prime contractors also must stipulate to the government their procedures for imposing adequate standardization requirements on their subcontractors. Incentive awards are given to those contractors who use the smallest feasible number of different components in a system's design and who select the maximum feasible number of standardized items that are already in the military supply system.

The European-based International Organization for Standardization (ISO) has several hundred specialized committees that develop a wide variety of standards which are promulgated by ISO and usually are accepted worldwide. Many of these standards are adaptations of standards from the American National Standards Institute, the German Institute for Standards, the British Standards Institute, and other national standards organizations around the world.

Kinds and Sources of Industrial Standards

In industry, there are three basic kinds of materials standards: (1) international standards, (2) industry or national standards, and (3) company standards. If a designer or user cannot adapt a national or international standard for his or her purpose, the second choice is to use a company standard. If the required part is truly a nonrepetitive "special," then use of a standard is impossible.

Where can one get standard specifications? Specifications for items that have been standardized can be obtained from the organizations that have developed them, such as those listed below:

- ISO
- National Bureau of Standards
- American National Standards Institute
- American Society for Testing and Materials
- American Society for Quality Control
- Society of Automotive Engineers

---

[4]*1980 Annual Report*, The American National Standards Institute, New York, Aug. 1, 1981, p. 9.

- Society of Mechanical Engineers
- American Institute of Electrical Engineers
- Federal Bureau of Specifications
- National Lumber Manufacturers' Association

A catalog of United States standards, international recommendations, and other related information is published annually and distributed without charge by the American National Standards Institute.[5] The Institute is a federation of more than 100 nationally recognized organizations, trade associations, and technical societies, or groups of such organizations. Its members can gain ANSI assistance in developing any standard desired. Recommendations for establishing a standard can be made at any time. If, after appropriate research and debate, ANSI approves the recommended standard, it will be adopted as a United States standard.

Both the civilian and military departments of the United States government participate in standardization work that greatly assists industry. For example, the National Bureau of Standards (NBS), among other things, was established to serve "any firm, corporation, or individual in the United States engaged in manufacturing or other pursuits regarding the use of standards."

International Standards

The need for international standards is fundamental; by eliminating technical trade barriers, international standards facilitate increased international trade and prosperity. The ISO 9000 series of quality standards, now used voluntarily worldwide, is a good illustration. (This topic is discussed in detail in Chapter 21.)

In 1979, Congress passed the United States Trade Act to implement the Multilateral Trade Agreements, which, among other provisions, include an international standards code. Thirty signatory nations, including the United States, the European Economic Community, the Nordic countries, Canada, New Zealand, and Japan, currently use the code.

Establishing the Multilateral Trade Agreements, the mechanism used to create international standards, was relatively easy. However, actually getting international standards adopted in some cases will be a long and difficult task. Consider just a few of the existing difficulties. The United States is only in the early stages of implementing metric standards. Although metric standards are used in both Europe and Japan, product dimensions have not been standardized, so parts from these countries are not yet interchangeable. Standardizing electric power characteristics is a very difficult problem; for example, voltage requirements for electrical equipment vary significantly between the United States and Europe. In short, countries around the world currently have widely different standards for virtually everything, from safety to ecology.

---

[5]ANSI, 1430 Broadway, New York, N.Y., 10018.

Nevertheless, simply because there is no quick or easy way to get international standards adopted does not mean that progress will not be made. The economic stakes associated with the development of international standards are so high—in terms of increased international trade and prosperity—that progress, albeit slow, is inevitable. Because private organizations, national and regional governments, and other international organizations are all involved in the adoption process, political infighting is inescapable. This, of itself, precludes fast action.

The following facts are presented to give a feeling for some of the current progress being made in the development of international standards. The American National Standards Institute represents the interests of the United States' voluntary standards system in programs carried out by non-treaty organizations,[6] such as the International Organization for Standardization (ISO), the International Electrotechnical Commission (IEC), and the Pan American Standards Commission (COPANT). ISO and IEC are the most important of over fifteen active international voluntary standards organizations. ANSI is a participating member in more than 800 international technical committees, subcommittees, and working groups. ANSI also holds the secretariat for a number of critically important committees. For example, it holds the post of secretariat for the ISO committee on plastics standardization. This group developed a standard glossary of technical terms and characteristics in French, English, German, and Russian. Producers and buyers of plastics in the world market now have a common reference point for doing business. This kind of progress eases the problems faced by American purchasing managers who buy abroad. Further progress in developing international standards will produce similar benefits for purchasing managers in all industrialized countries.

In summary, the concept and the advantages of international standards are widely recognized and accepted. Progress toward their implementation is being made. As in most international efforts, however, progress is slow.

Metric Conversion

Metric system measurements are among the important international standards. At one time, ANSI believed that adoption of the metric system, formally called the International System of Units (SI),[7] by U.S. industry was just about a dead issue. However, this is no longer the case; ANSI now considers adoption of a major portion of the metric system possible. *There is no doubt that the United States places itself at a competitive disadvantage by remaining the world's only*

---

[6] The United States Trade Act of 1979 provides for ANSI to represent U.S. interests in nongovernmental international standards organizations.

[7] The International System of Units was defined and given official status by the Eleventh General Conference of Weights and Measures in 1960.

major industrialized, nonmetric country. Many companies competing in the global marketplace have found that overseas customers are reluctant to accept inch-based products. It is generally agreed that conversion to the metric system would increase United States exports by a minimum of $2 billion annually.[8]

There are three primary obstacles thwarting speedy metric conversion: (1) cost, (2) the apathy of some industries, and (3) the fact that many U.S. firms are indifferent to the issue because they do not engage in foreign trade. Actually, the conversion cost is unknown, but it has been estimated to be as high as $20 billion.

Regardless of obstacles, there is evidence that the country is slowly adopting the metric system. In many fields, America has already gone metric. The shutters of thousands of 8-, 16-, and 35-millimeter cameras daily click across America. Work is done daily in hundreds of repair shops on thousands of foreign automobiles manufactured to metric standards in foreign countries. General Motors' conversion to metric is over 90 percent complete.[9] U.S. pharmaceutical companies went metric over fifteen years ago, and the electronics industry has used the metric system since 1954.

In December 1975, Congress passed the Metric Conversion Act. Although the act provided only for voluntary action, monitored by the United States Metric Board, interested persons and associations had a focal point around which they could rally and exchange implementation plans and ideas. Additionally, the Department of Defense, under DOD Directive 4210.18, has established definite policies to implement the metric system within the DOD. The United States is NATO's largest member. It is the only member not using the metric system, making the establishment of NATO standards exceedingly difficult. The failure to establish such standards is dangerous from a defense point of view, as well as expensive.

How is the United States Metric Board progressing with its voluntary program? "Slowly," according to a survey of typical U.S. industrial firms. Products made to metric measurements now account for only 6 percent of U.S. sales. Far more common are soft conversion products—that is, products made to U.S. measurements but labeled with metric equivalents. Will everything eventually be metric? "Not likely," the Metric Board says. The change is strictly voluntary, and conversion is likely to occur only after the development of economic incentives such as those that now exist for firms engaged in foreign trade. With increasing world shortages of materials and with expanding world technology, more and more U.S. firms probably will be slowly forced to establish international markets for both the sale of their products and the purchase of their materials.

[8]National Bureau of Standards, *Special Bulletin 330.*
[9]"Coming: Fewer Types, Greater Economy for Purchasers," *Purchasing World,* February 1981, p. 44.

Organizing a Standardization Program

A standardization/simplification program can be organized in various ways. Because so many departments are affected by standards decisions, however, a committee effort is the most commonly used approach. A standards committee normally consists of representatives from engineering, purchasing, operations, marketing, and transportation. This committee typically is charged with the responsibility for obtaining input from all user departments, reconciling differences between them, and making the final standards decisions. Theoretically, a member from any department could serve as head of the committee. Purchasing and supply management is particularly well qualified to head the committee in companies where materials complying with national standards or maintenance, repair, and operating (MRO) items form a large portion of the company's total purchases. In companies that manufacture highly differentiated technical products assembled from parts made to company standards, engineering is well qualified to head the committee.

The form of organization used, or who heads it, is not of major importance. It is important, however, that a firm has an effective standards program and that it attains the substantial benefits standardization affords. Regardless of the organization employed, the purchasing and supply management department occupies a focal point in the process. It is only in purchasing that duplicate requests for identical (or nearly identical) materials, overlapping requests, and "special buy" requests from all departments become visible. Hence, no program for standardization can be optimally successful unless purchasing and supply management is assigned a major role in the program.

CONCLUSION

Many firms still do not fully appreciate the concepts embraced in standardization and its corollary, simplification. Nevertheless, the philosophies underlying these concepts played an important role in bringing the United States to a position of industrial might. It seems highly probable that these same philosophies will continue to be important in the future. Aided by increased automation, coupled with computer-aided design and computer-aided manufacturing systems, standardization seems to be part of the answer to meeting the lower costs of some foreign competitors.[10] By further standardizing its component parts, its processes, and its operations, U.S. industry can refine and streamline the system that made it a dominant industrial power. Such refinement should permit the production of additional lines of low-cost, high-quality, differentiated products that will be competitive in the world marketplace.

---

[10]Recall the discussion and illustrations in Chapter 2 which depicted the direct relationship between reductions in material costs and increases in profit margins and return on investment.

FOR DISCUSSION

9-1 What are the two areas of application for standardization?

9-2 Discuss the significance of Eli Whitney's invention of interchangeable parts to modern manufacturing.

9-3 What are the three basic systems of production? What do they represent?

9-4 Explain why Henry Ford's early system of production fell short of a true implementation of mass production.

9-5 How might the use of standardization permit a firm to experience a reduction in costs?

9-6 In what way is simplification a corollary to standardization?

9-7 Describe how the absence of a simplification program in a firm can affect the cost of goods sold.

9-8 What is ISO? What is ANSI? What assistance might they be able to give to a developing firm?

9-9 What are the three basic types of materials standards currently in use in industry?

9-10 How might a materials catalog aid in the use of standardization in engineering design efforts?

9-11 Discuss the possible benefits of systematizing the standardization efforts within firms.

9-12 Discuss some of the difficulties encountered in attempting to establish international standards.

9-13 What are the three primary obstacles the United States faces in adopting metric conversion? What are the risks of not converting?

9-14 Which departments of a firm are normally involved in a standardization program?

9-15 Why is it essential that purchasing be involved in the standardization program of a firm? How can management involve purchasing?

CASES FOR CHAPTER 9

10

OUTSOURCING AND MAKE-OR-BUY DECISIONS

Today manufacturing focus means learning how not to make things—how not to make the parts that divert a company from cultivating its skills—parts its suppliers could make more efficiently.

Ravi Venkatesan[1]

Manufacturing strategy is about creating operating capabilities a company needs for the future.

R. H. Hayes and G. P. Pisano[2]

KEY CONCEPTS

- Strategic decisions
     Core competencies
- Tactical decisions
- Factors influencing make-or-buy decisions
     The time factor ⎫
     The capacity factor ⎬ Cost considerations
     Control of production or quality
     Design secrecy
     Unreliable suppliers
     Suppliers' specialized knowledge and research
     Small-volume requirements
     Limited facilities
     Work force stability
     Multiple-sourcing policy
     Managerial and procurement considerations
- The volatile nature of the make-or-buy situation
- Administration: procedures and personnel

---

[1]Venkatesan, "Strategic Sourcing: To Make or Not to Make," *Harvard Business Review,* November–December 1992, p. 98.

[2]Hayes and Pisano, "Beyond World-Class: The New Manufacturing Strategy," *Harvard Business Review,* January–February 1994, p. 84.

These two views set the stage for discussion of a topic that historically has been referred to as the *make-or-buy* decision. More recently, the term *outsourcing* has evolved to connote the buy side of the issue.

When a firm considers which components or subsystems it should make and which it should buy, it should analyze the issue at two levels—strategic and operational or tactical. The strategic, obviously, is the more important of the two as far as the future of the firm is concerned. So this initial analysis has a forward-looking, futuristic aura about it.

This chapter focuses initially on the strategic analysis and later on the tactical analysis.

STRATEGIC DECISIONS

The starting point most firms use in conducting the strategic analysis is to identify the major strengths of the firm—and then build on them. What is it we really do well—better than most firms? Do our strengths lie in certain design skills, unique production skills and equipment, different types of people skills? A thorough investigation of these types of questions is what many people today call identifying the firm's existing *core competencies*. The next step in the process is to look at the current and expected future environment in which the firm operates—the competition, the governmental regulatory climate, the changing characteristics of sales and supply markets, and so on. The bottom-line question management must answer, then, is: "Precisely what business do we really want to be in to maximize the use of our core competencies as we proceed into the future?"

Once a clear answer to this question has been formulated, expected competency requirements necessary for future operations must be identified. These are then compared with existing core competencies to determine which ones need to be refined and which ones need to be supplemented with related competencies that must be developed to create a competitive advantage. Two researchers place these ideas in sharp focus when they say "senior managers must conceive of their companies as a portfolio of core competencies rather than just as a portfolio of businesses and products."[3] The products and the nature of the business flow from the core competencies.

In considering what to make and what to buy, then, the decisions should cultivate and exploit the firm's core competencies. The items that should be made in-house are those that require capabilities that are closely linked with the core competencies and are mutually reinforcing, as opposed to those that can be separated. This is the fundamental strategic consideration that guides the original make-or-buy decisions that ultimately shape the character of the firm.[4]

[3]C. K. Prahalad, "Core Competence Revisited," *Enterprise,* October 1993, p. 20.
[4]Hayes and Pisano, op. cit., p. 84.

If one steps back to assess the current situation in American industry, it is clear that the concept of "lean manufacturing" is widely embraced for competitive purposes. This means that such firms increasingly buy more and make less. A rule of thumb used by some firms is to outsource subsystems and components unless they fall into one of the following three categories:[5]

1 An item that is critical to the success of the product, including customer perceptions of important product attributes
2 An item that requires specialized design and manufacturing skills or equipment—and the number of capable and reliable suppliers is extremely limited
3 An item that fits well within the firm's core competencies or within those the firm must develop to fulfill future plans

Components or subsystems that fit into one of these categories are considered strategic—and are produced in-house if possible. The analytical procedure used in making these decisions is straightforward and is shown in the following simplified illustration.

Deal first with subsystems of the product:

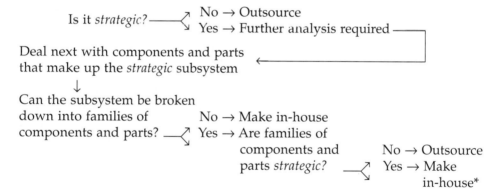

If the analysis to this point indicates that a "make" decision is desirable from a strategic point of view, before the decision is made several additional factors must be analyzed. These practical considerations focus on a comparison of the firm's present situation with that of potential suppliers with respect to the matters of design, manufacturing, and quality capabilities. Similarly, relative costs and volume requirements also need to be compared and evaluated

[5]This discussion is based on material in Venkatesan, op. cit., pp. 100–103.
*In some cases, in the short run it is not possible to make such an item in-house. This may be due to budget constraints, capability problems, capacity limitations, and so on. In these cases, until the problem is resolved, the item must be outsourced under a carefully crafted and managed strategic alliance.

as supplementary information to be used in conjunction with the strategic analysis in reaching a final decision.

This, then, is the approach used at the strategic level of analysis to determine whether a firm should make an item or outsource it. These are the crucial decisions that to a great extent shape the destiny of the firm.

Let us turn now to subsequent make-or-buy decisions that are made at the operating level.

TACTICAL DECISIONS

After the strategic "make" and outsourcing decisions are finalized, and as operations progress, a number of situations inevitably arise that require additional make-or-buy analyses at something less than a strategic level. Unsatisfactory supplier performance in the case of some outsourced items, changing sales demands, restricted manufacturing capacity, and the modification of an existing product are just a few of the operating factors that generate these needs. As a general rule, from a "make" perspective these tactical make-or-buy situations involve items for which the firm already possesses most of the necessary production resources. Small investments in tooling, minor equipment, or a few additional personnel usually are all that would be needed to do the job in-house. Consequently, these investigations tend to be driven by operating considerations of efficiency, control of quality and reliability, cost, capacity utilization, and so on.

In any case, the make-or-buy possibility requiring only a modest expenditure of funds in the event of a "make" decision is the type most commonly encountered by supply managers. A decision of this type usually does affect a firm's resource allocation plans; however, its effect on the firm's future is minimal compared with a decision requiring a major capital investment.[6] Although the decision requiring a nominal expenditure of funds does not require *direct* top-management participation, *it does require coordinated study by several operating departments*—perhaps using a team approach. Top management's responsibility is to develop an operating procedure which provides for the pooling and analysis of information from all departments affected by the decision. In other words, *management should ensure that the decision is made only after all relevant inputs have been evaluated.*

FACTORS INFLUENCING MAKE-OR-BUY DECISIONS

Two factors stand out above all others when considering the make-or-buy question at the tactical level: *cost** and *availability of production capacity*. A good make-or-buy decision, nevertheless, requires the evaluation of many less tan-

---

[6]For a good discussion of this topic, see Michiel Leenders and Jean Nollet, "The Grey Zone in Make or Buy," *Journal of Purchasing and Materials Management*, Fall 1984, pp. 10–15.

*As previously discussed, cost refers to "all-in-cost" or total cost.

gible factors, in addition to the two basic factors. The following considerations influence firms to make or to buy the items used in their finished products or their operations.

Considerations Which Favor Making

1 Cost considerations (less expensive to make the part)
2 Desire to integrate plant operations
3 Productive use of excess plant capacity to help absorb fixed overhead
4 Need to exert direct control over production and/or quality
5 Design secrecy required
6 Unreliable suppliers
7 Desire to maintain a stable work force (in periods of declining sales)

Considerations Which Favor Buying

1 Suppliers' research and specialized know-how
2 Cost considerations (less expensive to buy the part)
3 Small-volume requirements
4 Limited production facilities
5 Desire to maintain a stable work force (in periods of rising sales)
6 Desire to maintain a multiple-source policy
7 Indirect managerial control considerations
8 Procurement and inventory considerations

Cost Considerations

In some cases cost considerations indicate that a part should be made in-house; in others, they dictate that it should be purchased externally. Cost is obviously important, yet no other factor is subject to more varied interpretation and to greater misunderstanding.

A make-or-buy cost analysis involves a determination of the cost to make an item—and a comparison of this cost with the cost to buy it. The following checklist provides a summary of the major elements which should be included in a make-or-buy cost estimate.

To Make

1 Delivered purchased material costs
2 Direct labor costs[7]
3 Any follow-on costs stemming from quality and related problems
4 Incremental inventory carrying costs
5 Incremental factory overhead costs

---

[7]It is assumed that all inspection costs associated with the "make" operation are included in the direct labor costs.

6 Incremental managerial costs
7 Incremental purchasing costs
8 Incremental costs of capital

To Buy

1 Purchase price of the part
2 Transportation costs
3 Receiving and inspection costs
4 Incremental purchasing costs
5 Any follow-on costs related to quality or service

To see the comparative cost picture clearly, the analyst must carefully evaluate these costs, considering the effects of time and capacity utilization in the user's plant.

The Time Factor   Costs can be computed on either a short-term or a long-term basis. Short-term calculations tend to focus on direct measurable costs. As such, they frequently understate tooling costs and overlook such indirect materials costs as those incurred in storage, purchasing, inspection, and similar activities. Moreover, a short-term cost analysis fails to consider the probable future changes in the relative costs of labor, materials, transportation, and so on. It thus becomes clear that in comparing the costs to make and to buy, the *long-term view* is the correct one. Cost figures must include all relevant costs, direct and indirect, and they must reflect the effect of anticipated cost changes.

Since it is difficult to predict future cost levels, *estimated average* cost figures for the total time period in question are generally used. Even though an estimate of future costs cannot be completely accurate, the following example illustrates its value.

Suppose the user of a particular stamped part develops permanent excess capacity in its general-purpose press department. The firm subsequently decides to make the stamped part which had previously been purchased from a specialized metalworking firm. Because this enables the firm to reactivate several unused presses, the additional cost to make the item is less than the cost to buy it. However, the user finds that the labor segment of its total cost is much higher than the labor segment of the automated supplier's cost. Should labor costs continue to rise more rapidly than the other costs of production, the user's cost advantage in making the part may soon disappear. Thus, an estimate of future cost behavior can prevent a "make" decision that might well prove unprofitable in the future.

The Capacity Factor   When the cost to make a part is computed, the determination of relevant overhead costs poses a difficult problem. The root of the problem lies in the user's *capacity utilization factor*. As is true in most managerial cost analyses, the costs relevant to a make-or-buy decision are the *incre-*

mental costs. In this case, *incremental costs are those costs which would not be incurred if the part were purchased outside.* The overhead problem centers on the fact that the *incremental overhead* costs vary from time to time, depending on the extent to which production facilities are utilized by existing products.

For example, assume that an automobile engine manufacturer currently buys its piston pins from a distant machine shop. For various reasons, the engine producer now decides that it wants to make the piston pins in its own shop. Investigation reveals that the machine shop is loaded to capacity with existing work and will remain in that condition throughout the foreseeable future. If the firm decides to make its own piston pins, it will have to either purchase additional machining equipment or free existing equipment by subcontracting to an outside supplier a part currently made in-house. In this situation, the incremental factory overhead cost figure should include the variable overhead caused by the production of piston pins, *plus* the full portion of fixed overhead allocable to the piston pin operation.[8]

Now assume that the same engine manufacturer wants to make its own piston pins and that it has enough excess capacity to make the pins in its machine shop with existing equipment. Investigation shows that the excess capacity will exist for at least the next two or three years. What are its incremental overhead costs to make the pins in this situation? *Only* the variable overhead caused by production of the piston pins! In this case, fixed overhead represents sunk costs which continue to accumulate whether piston pins are produced or not. The total machine shop building continues to generate depreciation charges. Heat, light, and janitorial service are still furnished to the total machine shop area. Also, property taxes for the machine shop remain the same regardless of the number of machines productively employed. The firm incurs these same fixed costs regardless of the make-or-buy action it decides on. Such costs, under conditions of idle capacity, are *not* incremental costs and, for purposes of the make-or-buy decision, must be omitted from computation of the cost to make a new part.

The concept can also be observed from a slightly different point of view in the graphic representation of Figure 10-1. Note that a $12\frac{1}{2}$ percent increase in production volume (an increase from 80 to 90 percent of capacity) can be achieved by a total cost increase of only 10 percent. This favorable situation results simply because the $12\frac{1}{2}$ percent increase in production is accomplished by activating unused capacity. Fixed overhead costs are incurred irrespective of the decision to make piston pins by utilizing unused capacity.

Finally, consider a third common situation in which the same engine manufacturer wants to make its own piston pins. Investigation in this case reveals that enough excess capacity currently exists in the machine shop to permit

---

[8]In the event that piston pin production replaces production of another part, the piston pin operation should carry the same absolute amount of fixed overhead that was carried by the part replaced. In the case where new equipment is purchased to produce piston pins, the piston pin operation should be charged with the additional fixed overhead arising from acquisition of the new equipment.

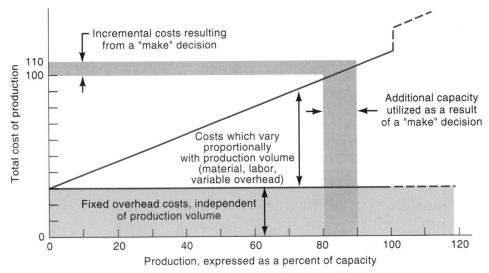

FIGURE 10-1
A representative case illustrating the incremental costs resulting from a "make" decision when operating at 80 percent of production capacity.

production of the piston pins. However, management expects a gradual increase in business during the next several years, which will eliminate all excess capacity by the end of the second year. How should the make-or-buy decision be approached in this particular case?

As always, the starting point of the analysis is an estimate of the costs to make versus the costs to buy. For the first 1½ to 2 years, the cost to make piston pins will not include fixed overhead because excess capacity exists. Beyond two years, however, the cost to make must include fixed overhead; if piston pins are not made, increased production of some other part will, in the normal course of business, carry its full share of fixed overhead. One alternative is to consider the make-or-buy decision separately for each of the two time periods. While the analysis may indicate that it is profitable to make the pins in both cases, it will probably reveal that it is profitable to make the pins only for the first two years and to buy them beyond that date. In this case, several qualitative factors must be investigated to determine the practical feasibility of a split course of action. If the split course of action does not appear feasible, a second alternative is to compute a weighted average cost to make the pins during both time periods. The cost data can then be used in considering the total make-or-buy question.

In practice, an infinite number of situations exist between the two extremes of excess capacity and full capacity. There is no simple, absolutely accurate solution to any of these problems. Each situation must be analyzed in its own dynamic context.

In summary, an analyst should be guided by several basic ideas. First, *incremental costs* are virtually always the costs germane to the managerial decision-making process. Second, the determination of a realistic cost to make an item requires a realistic estimate of the future conditions of capacity. When capacity can be utilized by existing business or by alternative new projects, incremental overhead costs to make a new item must reflect total overhead costs. During any period when this condition does not exist, the incremental overhead to "make" consists only of variable overhead. When conditions of capacity normally oscillate frequently between partial load and full load, it is likely that the make-or-buy decision for a new project of substantial duration will turn largely on considerations other than comparative cost.

Precautions in Developing Costs   If a firm decides to buy a part that it has made in the past, it must exercise particular care in interpreting the quotations it receives from potential suppliers. Some suppliers may prepare the quotation carelessly, with the mistaken idea that the user does not really intend to buy the part. Other suppliers may bid unrealistically low in an attempt to induce the user to discontinue making the part in favor of buying it. Once the user has discontinued its "make" operation, resumption of the operation in the future may be costly. Thus, the user may be at the mercy of the supplier in case the supplier later chooses to increase the price.[9] It is essential that the buyer carefully evaluate the reliability of all quotations in his or her attempt to determine a realistic estimate of the total cost to buy the part.

In estimating the cost to make a part, an analyst must ensure that the firm possesses adequate equipment and technical know-how to do the job. Moreover, in an industry where technological change occurs rapidly, a firm can find its equipment and know-how competitively outmoded in a few short years. Thus, the factor of obsolescence should also be given adequate consideration in determining the ultimate costs of equipment and personnel training.

The proper equipment to make an item may sometimes be easier to acquire than the properly skilled manpower. Large-volume requirements, complex skill requirements, or unique geographic locations can precipitate shortages of adequately skilled manpower. In preparing cost-to-make estimates, the local manpower situation must be evaluated. Should it be necessary to import adequately skilled personnel, total labor costs can substantially exceed initial estimates.

In the case of a "make" decision, it is equally important to investigate the availability and price stability of required raw materials. Large users of particular materials generally find the availability and price structure of these materials much more favorable than do small unspecialized users. Wise analysts ensure that their estimates for raw material are realistic.

Finally, in estimating the cost to make a part for the first time, the analyst must also investigate several practical production matters. The first deals with

---

[9]A partnering arrangement or a long-term requirements contract may be used to help control such price increases.

the cost of unacceptable production work. What is the expected rate of rejected and spoiled parts? Equally important, what learning curve can the production department reasonably expect to apply? Answers to these questions may vary substantially, depending upon the complexity of the job and the type of workers and equipment available. The resulting influence on the make-buy cost comparison can be considerable, however, and realistic answers should be sought.

Control of Production or Quality

Consider now some of the factors other than costs that influence make-or-buy decisions. Two conditions weigh heavily in some firms' decisions to make a particular part—control of production and control of quality.

Production Requirements   The need for close control of production operations is particularly acute in some firms. A company whose sales demand is subject to extreme short-run fluctuations finds that its production department must operate on unusually tight time schedules. This kind of company often produces a small inventory of those parts used in several different products. However, it produces to individual customer order the parts unique to a particular product or customer specification. Sales fluctuations for products using unique parts therefore influence the planning and scheduling of numerous assembly and subassembly operations, as well as single-part production operations. Efficient conduct of assembly operations thus depends on the firm's ability to obtain the unique unstocked parts on short notice.

Most suppliers serving a number of customers cannot normally tool up and fit an order for a unique part into existing schedules on a moment's notice unless it is operating under some type of JIT or partnering arrangement. If a user cannot tolerate suppliers' lead-time requirements, its only other major alternative is to control the part production operations itself. Thus, by making the item, the user acquires the needed control. It is possible to quickly revise job priorities, reassign operators and machines to specific jobs, and require overtime work as conditions demand.

Some firms also choose to make certain critical parts to assure continuity of supply of these parts to succeeding production operations. This type of integration guards against production shutdowns caused by supplier labor problems, local transportation strikes, and miscellaneous supplier service problems. These are particularly important considerations when dealing with parts that feed an automated production operation whose downtime is tremendously expensive. If such action reduces the risk of a production stoppage, it may well justify the incurrence of extra materials costs.

Quality Requirements   Unique quality requirements frequently represent a second condition requiring control of part production operations. Certain parts in technical products are occasionally quite difficult to manufacture.

Compounding this difficulty, at times, is an unusually exacting quality specification the part must meet. In certain technological fields or in particular geographical areas, a user may find that the uniqueness of the task results in unsatisfactory performance by an outside supplier. Some companies find that their own firm is in a better position to do an acceptable production job than are external suppliers.

A user normally understands more completely than an outside supplier the operational intricacies connected with usage of the part. Therefore, if the using firm makes the part itself, there can be greater coordination between the assembly operation and the part production operation. Conducting both operations under one roof likewise eliminates many communications problems which can arise between a buyer and supplier whose operations are geographically separated. Finally, large users often possess technological resources superior to those of smaller suppliers. Such resources may be needed in solving *new* technical problems in production.

For example, one producer of hydraulic systems makes a practice of subcontracting production of some of the valves used in its systems. The production of one particular subcontracted valve involved difficult interior machining operations as well as tight quality requirements. Of the supplier's first four shipments, the systems manufacturer rejected 80 percent of the valves for failure to meet quality specifications. During the ensuing months, the systems manufacturer worked closely with the subcontractor in an attempt to solve the quality problem. With the passage of time, however, it became clear that the systems manufacturer was contributing considerably more to solution of the problem than was the supplier. Eventually, the systems firm decided to make the valve. Although production of the valve still remained a difficult task, the systems manufacturer was able to develop the techniques necessary to produce a valve of acceptable quality, with a greatly reduced reject percentage.

Design Secrecy Required

Although their number is small, a few firms make particular parts primarily because they want to keep secret certain aspects of the part's design or manufacture. The secrecy justification for making an item can be found in highly competitive industries where style and cost play unusually important roles. Also, a firm is more likely to make a key part for which patent protection does not provide *effective* protection against commercial emulation.

If design secrecy is really important, however, a firm may have nearly as much difficulty maintaining secrecy when it makes a part as it would when a supplier makes it. In either case, a large number of individuals must be taken into the firm's confidence, and once information leaks to a competitor, very little can be done about it. Nevertheless, a firm can usually control security measures more easily and directly in its own plant. In either case, however, the element of trust is extremely important. World-class firms work hard to create an atmosphere of trust surrounding both internal and external activities.

Unreliable Suppliers

A few firms decide to make specific parts because their experience has shown that the reliability record of available suppliers falls below the required level. The likelihood of encountering such a situation thirty years ago was infinitely greater than it is today. Competition in most industries today is so keen that grossly unreliable performers do not survive the competitive struggle. With one major exception, unreliable delivery or unpredictable service is confined largely to isolated cases in new, highly specialized lines of business where competition has not yet become established. Such businesses are usually characterized by low sales volumes, the requirement of highly specialized production equipment, or the unique possession of new technological capabilities.

The one major exception mentioned above is the case of the buyer who provides only an insignificant fraction of a specific supplier's total volume of business. Even the most reputable suppliers are forced at times to short-change very small accounts in order to give proper attention to their major accounts. Regardless of the reasonableness of the cause, however, consistently unreliable performance by a supplier is sufficient grounds for shifting suppliers or possibly reconsidering the original make-buy decision.

Suppliers' Specialized Knowledge and Research

A primary reason underlying most decisions to buy a part rather than make it is the user's desire to take advantage of the specialized abilities and research efforts of various suppliers.

Lest the preceding discussion of "make" decisions distort the total procurement picture, bear in mind that the typical American manufacturing firm spends more than 50 percent of its sales dollar for purchases from external suppliers. Modern industry is highly specialized. No ordinary firm, regardless of size, can hope to possess adequate facilities and technical know-how to make a majority of its production part requirements efficiently. Large corporations spend millions of dollars on product and process research each year. The fruits of this research and the ensuing technical know-how are available to customers in the form of highly developed and refined parts and component products. The firm that considers forgoing these benefits in favor of making an item should, before making its final decision, assess carefully the long-range values that accrue from industrial specialization.

Small-Volume Requirements

When a firm uses only a small quantity of a particular item, it usually decides to buy the item. The typical firm strives to concentrate its production efforts in areas where it is most efficient and in areas it finds most profitable. The work of designing, tooling, planning, and setting up for the production of a new part is time-consuming and costly. These fixed costs are recovered more easily from long production runs than from short ones. More often than not, the small-volume user consequently searches for a potential supplier who specializes in production of the given part and can economically produce it in large quantities. Such specialty suppliers can sell to a large number of users in almost any desired quantity at relatively low prices.

Small-volume production of *unique, nonstandard* parts may likewise be unattractive to external suppliers. Every supplier is obligated to concentrate first on its high-volume, high-profit accounts. Thus, cases may develop in which a user is virtually *forced* to make a highly nonstandard part it uses in small quantities. Generally speaking, however, as the part tends toward a more common and finally a standard configuration, the tendency to buy increases proportionally.

Limited Facilities

Another reason for buying rather than making certain parts is the physical limitation imposed by the user's production facilities. A firm with limited facilities typically attempts to utilize them as fully as possible on its most profitable production work. It then depends on external suppliers for the balance of its requirements. Thus, during peak periods a firm may purchase a substantial portion of its total requirements because of loaded production facilities, and during slack periods, as internal production capacity opens up, its purchases may decrease markedly.

Work Force Stability

Closely related to the matter of facilities is the factor of work force stability. A fluctuating production level compels a firm to face the continual problem of contracting and expanding its work force to keep in step with production demands. Significant continuing fluctuation, moreover, adversely affects the quality of workers such a firm is able to employ. The less stable an operation, the more difficult it becomes to retain a competent work force.

At the time when a firm sizes the various segments of its production operation, many make-buy decisions are made. One factor which often bears heavily on the decision is the firm's desire to develop an interested, responsible group of workers with a high degree of company loyalty. Awareness that stable employment facilitates the attainment of this objective sometimes prompts a firm to undersize its production facility by a slight margin. Its plan is to maintain as stable an internal production operation as possible and to buy requirements in excess of its capacity from external suppliers. This policy is most effective in firms whose products require a considerable amount of general-purpose equipment in the manufacturing operation. Equipment, as well as personnel, that can perform a variety of different jobs provides the internal flexibility required to consolidate or split work among various production areas as business fluctuates. This capability is necessary for the successful implementation of such a policy, because as business increases, it is not feasible to place small orders for a large number of different parts with outside suppliers. It is much more profitable to farm out large orders for a small number of parts.

Firms that successfully solve their work force problems in this way frequently create problems in the purchasing area. External suppliers are, in effect, used as buffers to absorb the shocks of production fluctuations. This action transfers many of the problems associated with production fluctuations from the user to the supplier. The supplier's ability to absorb these production shocks is therefore an important consideration. In some instances it may be able to absorb them reasonably well; in others, it may not.[10] In all cases, however, the supplier prefers, as does the user, to maintain a stable production operation. Consequently, many suppliers are not interested in the user who buys only its peak requirements. The question naturally arises: Will a supplier ever be motivated to perform well for a buyer who uses the supplier only for surplus work? This question should be considered carefully before a "buy" decision of this type is made.

Multiple-Source Policy

Some firms occasionally make *and* buy the same nonstandard part. This policy is followed for the explicit purpose of having available a reliable and experienced second source of supply. Firms adopting a make-and-buy policy recognize that they may not always be able to meet their internal production schedules for certain parts. In case of an emergency, an experienced outside source is usually willing to increase its delivery of the part in question on a temporary basis until the situation is under control.

Managerial Control Considerations

Companies occasionally buy and make the same part for the purpose of developing managerial control data. Some firms use outside suppliers' cost and quality performance as a check on their own internal production efficiency. If internal costs for a particular part rise above a supplier's cost, the user knows that somewhere in its own production system some element of cost is probably out of line. An investigation frequently uncovers one or more problems, some of which often extend to other production areas. Consequent improvements may therefore exhibit a compounding effect as they reach into other operations where inefficiencies might otherwise have gone undetected.

---

[10]Two factors largely determine a supplier's ability to absorb fluctuating order requirements from a user. They are:

1 The similarity of the work involved in producing a particular user's requirement and in producing other customers' orders. The more similar the requirements are, the less is the expense of special planning and setup work for a particular user.

2 The extent to which other customers' orders offset the peaks and valleys in the supplier's production operation. The more stable the supplier's total production operation is, the less disturbing is the effect of an occasional fluctuating account.

Procurement and Inventory Considerations

A "buy" decision produces several significant benefits in the management of purchasing and inventory activities. For purchasing, such a decision typically means that it has fewer items to buy and fewer suppliers to deal with. Usually, though not always, when a component is made in-house a number of different materials or parts must be purchased outside to support the "make" operation. A corresponding buy decision usually involves only one or two suppliers and a relative reduction in the associated buying, paperwork, and follow-up activities. The same relative reduction in workload is passed on to the receiving, inspection, stores, and inventory management groups. Typically, inventory investment is also reduced.

One of the goals of most purchasing departments today is to achieve a reduction in the supplier base, simply to facilitate more effective purchasing and supplier management.

THE VOLATILE NATURE OF THE MAKE-OR-BUY SITUATION

Although make-or-buy investigations begin with a cost analysis, various qualitative factors frequently portend more far-reaching consequences than does the cost analysis. Therefore, a make-or-buy decision correctly approached considers the probable *composite effect* of all factors on the firm's total operation.

A thorough investigation is complicated considerably by the dynamics and uncertainties of business activity. Certain factors can hold quite different implications for a make-or-buy decision at different points in time and under different operating conditions. As pointed out, changing costs can turn a good decision into a bad one in a very short period of time. And future costs, complicated by numerous demand and capacity interrelationships, are influenced substantially by such variable factors as technological innovation and customer demand. The availability of expansion capital also influences make-or-buy decisions. An "easy money" policy, a liberal depreciation policy, or liberal government taxing policies tend to encourage "make" decisions. Contrary policies promote "buy" decisions. These federal policies fluctuate with economic and political conditions.

The tendency toward "make" decisions in order to stabilize production and work force fluctuation is usually greater in small firms than in large ones. In some small shops the loss of just a few orders results in the temporary layoff of a sizable percentage of the work force until additional orders can be obtained. Generally speaking, larger organizations do not have such severe problems because their fluctuations in production volume relative to total capacity are smaller. As large firms adopt compensation plans that move toward a guaranteed wage structure, however, they too will feel a similar pressure to favor "make" decisions.

Finally, the labor-relations climate within a firm can influence its make-or-buy decisions. A hostile union may seize the opportunity to irritate management as a result of the decision to buy an item previously made in-house. An amicable labor-management climate may evoke a very different union reaction.

To summarize, the point very briefly stated is this: Beware of rigid formulas and rules of thumb that claim to produce easy make-or-buy decisions. The make-or-buy question is influenced by a multitude of diverse factors that are in a constant state of change. Under such conditions, few easy decisions turn out well in both the short and the long run. Moreover, the relevant factors vary immensely from one firm to another. For these reasons, every company should periodically evaluate the effectiveness of its past decisions to generate information helpful in guiding future courses of make-buy action.

ADMINISTRATION OF MAKE-OR-BUY ACTIVITIES

It is not difficult to find otherwise well-managed firms in which many tactical make-or-buy decisions are inadvertently delegated to an operating person in inventory control or production control. It should now be apparent that this is a poor practice. In the first place, such a person normally does not have adequate information with which to make an intelligent decision from a companywide point of view. Second, even if adequate information were available, this type of person typically lacks the breadth of experience to evaluate fully the significance of the information and the resultant decision.

In most cases, make-or-buy decisions should be made, or at least reviewed, at a managerial level. The decision maker must be able to view such problems with a broad companywide perspective. Many progressive firms use a team or committee approach to analyze make-or-buy alternatives. The important point to keep in mind is that all departments that can contribute to the decision, or that are affected by it, should have some voice in making it. A team or committee accomplishes this directly. In other cases, a formal mechanism must be established which facilitates, and perhaps requires, all interested departments to submit relevant data and suggestions to the decision maker. Moreover, to ensure thoroughness and consistency, the system must detail the cost computation procedures to be used and assign cost investigations to specific operating groups.

In addition to providing an operational framework within which make-or-buy alternatives are investigated, a review system is necessary. The system should provide procedures for three important additional activities: (1) the entry of projects into the study system, (2) maintenance of essential records, and (3) a periodic audit of important decisions.

Procedures should be established as part of a firm's product development program, compelling high-value and strategically oriented parts in new products to enter the make-or-buy analysis process. In some cases, this analysis can be effectively integrated with preproduction value engineering investigations. Similarly, existing production parts should be subjected to a systematic review which searches for borderline make-or-buy items warranting careful study.

Regardless of the source of entry, all make-or-buy investigations should be classified as "major" or "minor," based on the value and strategic nature of the part. In one firm all items involving expenditures under $25,000 are classed as minor. Subsequent studies of minor items involve personnel from production, purchasing, quality control, and occasionally design engineering. Major items entail expenditures over $25,000, and additionally involve personnel from finance, marketing, and other production areas.

Certain summary records are essential to full utilization of the data developed in make-or-buy investigations. The record should be designed to serve as a useful future reference. A brief discussion of all factors pertinent to the decision that was made should be included, as well as the primary reasons for the decision. Assumptions about future conditions should be stated. And an accurate summary of cost data should always be included. Records of this type provide the information required when a firm is forced to make quick decisions about subcontracting work under peak operating conditions, or about bringing work back into the shop when business slumps. Accurate records can mean the difference between a profitable decision based on *facts* and a hopeful decision based on intuition and hunches.

Finally, investigation records provide the basic data for postdecision audits.

CONCLUSION

If one takes a broad view of the American industrial scene over the past several decades, three characteristics stand out clearly: (1) Firms are becoming more aware of the strategic dimension of the make-or-buy decision; management is more proactive in identifying and exploiting the firm's core competencies as organizations adopt a lean manufacturing strategy; (2) as technology has advanced, most manufacturing firms have become much more specialized—in the words of researchers Peters and Waterman, they "stick to their knitting";[11] and (3) the cost of materials, expressed as a percentage of total product cost, has continued to increase in many industries. These three factors lead to the inevitable conclusion that, in the aggregate, American firms are buying more and making less. Planned or unplanned, the trend continues to develop. In a nationwide *Purchasing* magazine survey, 41 percent of the responding purchasing executives said that their firms have moved significantly to the buy side of the make-buy equation, as compared with just a few years ago.[12] General Electric is a prime example.[13]

Yet, at the managerial level, many successful firms have not handled the recurring make-or-buy issue in a well-organized, systematic manner. Instead, many have elected to deal with specific cases on an ad hoc basis as they arose.

---

[11]T. J. Peters and R. H. Waterman, *In Search of Excellence*, Harper & Row Publishers, New York, 1982, pp. 292–305.
[12]Somerby Dowst, "The Winning Edge," *Purchasing*, Mar. 12, 1987, pp. 52–60.
[13]"Why GE Makes as Little as Possible," *Electronics Purchasing*, Mar. 1992, pp. 25–27.

This situation is understandable, yet ironic. In earlier years when the cost-price squeeze was less severe for many firms, poor decisions in this area did not affect earnings noticeably. Yet, in the aggregate, make-or-buy decisions do significantly affect a firm's ability to utilize its resources in an optimal manner.

Past practices are changing. Three forces will continue to stimulate this change:

- *Pressures on profit margins* are severe, and will continue to increase—resources must be utilized more effectively.
- *Firms continue to become more highly specialized* in products and production technology, producing greater cost differentials between making and buying for many users.
- *Computer modeling capability* is becoming commonplace; make-or-buy evaluation and control systems can be developed and handled quasi-automatically with this capability.

Just as materials management organizations, MRP systems, and JIT systems have developed over the past several decades, so will implementation systems for recurring make-or-buy analysis. Interaction of the three factors noted above will produce refined make-or-buy operating systems in many firms in future years.[14]

FOR DISCUSSION

10-1 What issues does make-or-buy analysis at the strategic level focus on?

10-2 How does make-or-buy analysis at the operating level differ from make-or-buy analysis at the strategic level?

10-3 What is meant by the term "a firm's core competencies"?

10-4 Do all make-or-buy investigations require the same type of analysis? Explain.

10-5 Outline the basic procedure followed in making a make-or-buy analysis at the strategic level.

10-6 Develop in detail a procedure to be followed in conducting a make-or-buy cost analysis. (Include explanations necessary for the reader's full understanding of the procedure.)

10-7 List and briefly discuss the major difficulties that may be encountered in making a valid make-or-buy cost analysis.

10-8 Why may fixed overhead expenses in a specific plant be an incremental cost in the case of one make-or-buy cost investigation and not in the case of a similar investigation made at a later date in the same plant? Explain.

10-9 Refer to Figure 10-1. How do you explain the fact that a $12\frac{1}{2}$ percent increase in production produces only a 10 percent increase in production cost?

---

[14]Readers interested in a detailed examination of the make-or-buy issue should review the classical study conducted some years ago by J. W. Culliton, *Make or Buy?* Research Study 27, Graduate School of Business Administration, Harvard University, Boston, 1942, 4th reprint, 1956.

10-10 Are make-or-buy decisions influenced by the learning curve concept?

10-11 It has been said that make-or-buy decisions are much more critical in companies whose production operations are highly automated than in others. What is your reaction to this statement? Explain.

10-12 Compared with the situation ten years ago, are firms buying (versus making) more or less today? Discuss.

10-13 Some business executives advocate vertical integration of production operations because this approach can eliminate payment of a profit to various middlemen. What is your reaction to this argument?

10-14 List and briefly discuss the major factors which tend to influence make-or-buy decisions in the direction of buying.

10-15 List and briefly discuss the major factors which tend to influence make-or-buy decisions in the direction of making.

10-16 Some companies claim that they can transfer much of the shock of sales fluctuations normally felt in the production operations to their suppliers. How can this be done? What problems frequently result when a firm attempts to do this?

10-17 Outline a plan for the administration of make-or-buy activities.

10-18 The text states that most make-or-buy decisions are volatile in nature. What is meant by this statement? Explain.

10-19 To whom should a company assign the responsibility for make-or-buy decisions? Explain.

10-20 Discuss the acceptance and application of make-or-buy analysis in U.S. industry.

CASES FOR CHAPTER 10

PART THREE

SOURCING

11

SOURCES OF SUPPLY: PART I

To produce the best products worldwide you need more than ideas, designs and specifications. You need to choose the very best suppliers. . . . [1]

Your products are only as strong as your weakest supplier.[2]

KEY CONCEPTS

- Two categories of supply
- The importance of source selection
- Development and maintenance of the supplier base
    Sources of supplier information
    Supplier development
    Supplier goodwill
    Partnerships/collaborative purchasing
    Supplier management
- Strategic and tactical issues in supplier selection
    Early supplier involvement
    Number of suppliers; share of supplier's business
    Buying locally/nationally/internationally
    Manufacturer or distributor
    Green purchasing
    Minority- and women-owned business enterprises
    Ethical considerations
    Dishonest suppliers
    Reciprocity
    Miscellaneous considerations

[1] *Xerox Commodity Teams,* October 1986, p. 3.
[2] "Tenant Examines Purchasing Quality," *Purchasing,* Jan. 16, 1992.

TWO CATEGORIES OF SUPPLY

A firm has two categories of suppliers: (1) the firm itself and (2) outside suppliers. Prior to addressing this issue, world-class firms conduct a strategic analysis of what their core competencies are—the skills and processes which are the basis of their success and competitive advantage. As Prahalad and Hamel say, "Core competencies are the wellspring of new business development."[3] If an item or service represents a core competency or supports or interfaces with such a competency, then the source of supply normally will be the firm itself. If there are important reasons to outsource (e.g., financial constraints, etc.), then a carefully crafted and managed strategic alliance should be established with the appropriate supplier.

The widespread use of concurrent engineering as described in Chapter 7 has resulted in a major change in the timing of the source selection process. As shown in Figure 11-1, the traditional approach to design, sourcing, and manufacturing calls for sourcing to take place after design and development are completed. The concurrent approach requires the key suppliers who will be involved in the design and development of new products under early supplier involvement to be carefully screened and selected prior to, or in parallel with, the design and development process. The mechanics of sourcing under both approaches are fairly similar. The concurrent approach requires that the cross-functional team responsible for new product development (or a subgroup, frequently called the sourcing team) be responsible for source selection. As will be discussed in Chapter 12, the traditional approach to sourcing also frequently involves members of several functions (purchasing and supply management, design engineering, manufacturing engineering, quality, finance, etc.), but usually in a much less structured mode.

After determining the requirement's possible relationship to the organization's core competencies, nonstrategic materials and services must undergo a further review, as discussed in the previous chapter. If the decision is to buy, then selection of outside suppliers, as discussed in this and the next two chapters, takes place.

THE IMPORTANCE OF SOURCE SELECTION

A Good Supplier: An Invaluable Resource

A good supplier is an invaluable resource to the organization requiring its product or service. Such suppliers make a direct contribution to a firm's success. They can assist their customers with product development, value analysis, and timely delivery of the desired level of quality. Good buyer-seller relations facilitate the buyer's efforts to gain superior performance, extra service,

---

[3]For more insight into this important strategic issue, see "The Core Competence of the Corporation" by C. K. Prahalad and Gary Hamel, *Harvard Business Review*, May–June 1990, pp. 79–91.

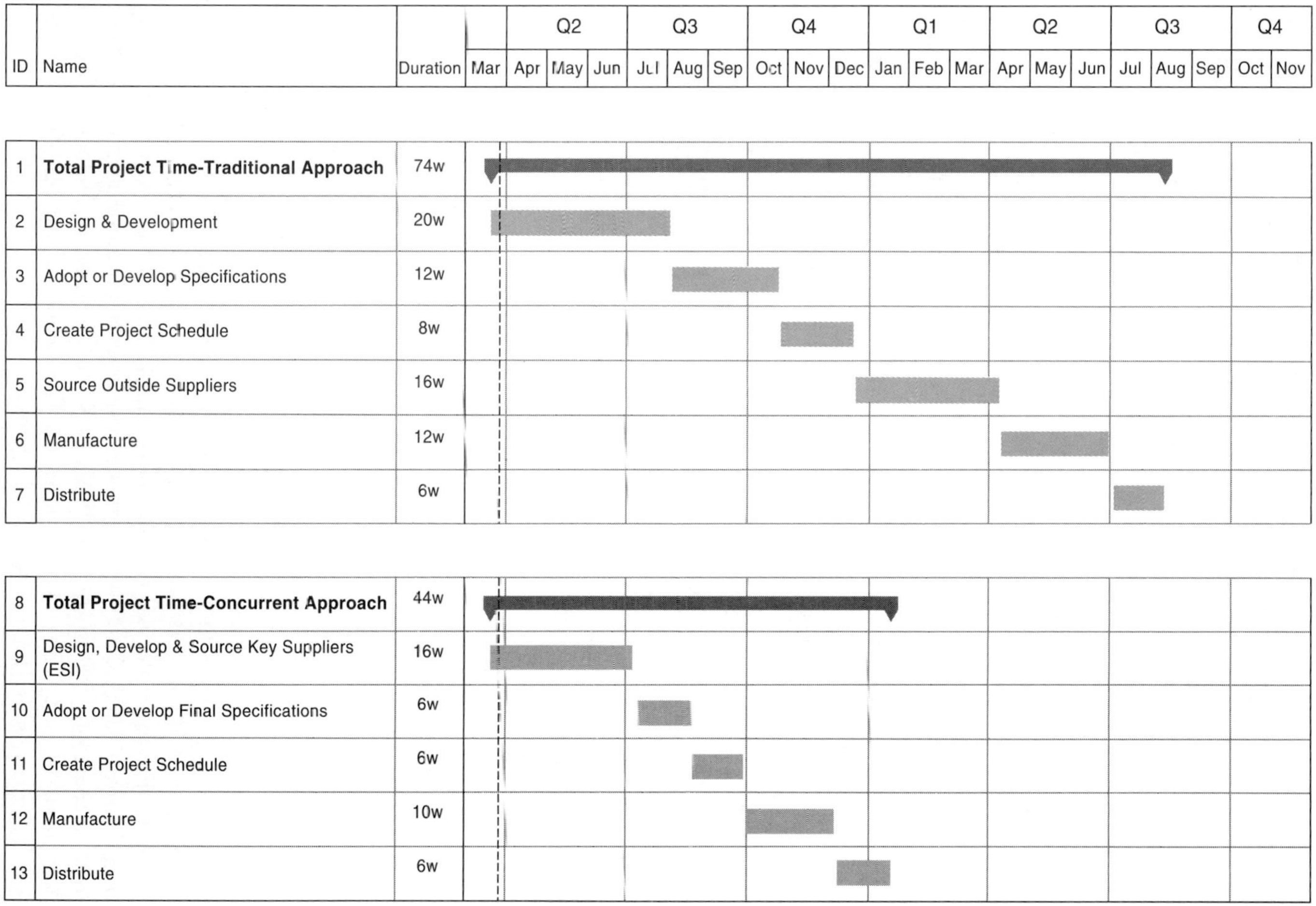

ID	Name	Duration	Q2			Q3			Q4			Q1			Q2			Q3			Q4	
			Mar	Apr	May	Jun	Jul	Aug	Sep	Oct	Nov	Dec	Jan	Feb	Mar	Apr	May	Jun	Jul	Aug	Sep	Oct	Nov
1	**Total Project Time-Traditional Approach**	74w																					
2	Design & Development	20w																					
3	Adopt or Develop Specifications	12w																					
4	Create Project Schedule	8w																					
5	Source Outside Suppliers	16w																					
6	Manufacture	12w																					
7	Distribute	6w																					

ID	Name	Duration	Q2			Q3			Q4			Q1			Q2			Q3			Q4	
8	**Total Project Time-Concurrent Approach**	44w																					
9	Design, Develop & Source Key Suppliers (ESI)	16w																					
10	Adopt or Develop Final Specifications	6w																					
11	Create Project Schedule	6w																					
12	Manufacture	10w																					
13	Distribute	6w																					

FIGURE 11-1
Two approaches to design, sourcing, and manufacture. (Source: *This figure was developed by Rich Zampel of the Hewlett-Packard Corporation.*)

cooperation on cost reduction programs, and a willingness to share in new processes and procedures.

Selection and management of the right supplier is the key to obtaining the desired level of quality, on time, and at the right price; the necessary level of technical support; and the desired level of service. Buyers must take six important supplier-oriented actions in order to satisfy this responsibility. The buyers must:

- Develop and maintain a viable supplier base
- Address the appropriate strategic and tactical issues
- Ensure that potential suppliers are carefully evaluated and that they have the potential to be satisfactory supply partners
- Decide whether to use competitive bidding or negotiation as the basis of source selection
- Select the appropriate source—or be the team leader responsible for this task
- Manage the selected supplier to ensure timely delivery of the required quality at the right price

The first two of these responsibilities are the subject of this chapter. The third, fourth, and fifth responsibilities are the subject of Chapter 12. Supplier management is addressed in Chapter 20.

DEVELOPMENT AND MAINTENANCE OF THE SUPPLIER BASE

An adequate supplier base is essential to the economic well-being of a firm. Such a base is as much a resource as are research scientists or skilled production personnel. The supplier base is especially critical in high-technology industries and in industries where scarcity of materials is a potential occurrence.

When developing the supplier base, it is essential that those responsible for the development and implementation of the supply base plan ensure that the plan meets existing and future needs. They must coordinate closely with marketing and new product development to ensure that they are aware of any possible shifts in product lines and product technology changes.

One of the interesting transitions taking place in purchasing and supply management is the shift from enlarging the firm's supply base to downsizing the base. For example, Xerox reduced its supply base by 92 percent in the early 1980s—from 5,000 to 400 suppliers. Chrysler has winnowed its supplier base from a mass of 2,500 in the late 1980s to a lean, long-term nucleus of 300. At the moment, suppliers love working for Chrysler, and for obvious reasons: The company's production volume is growing rapidly. Chrysler includes suppliers in development activities from day one and listens eagerly to their suggestions for design improvements and cost reductions. Chrysler has also replaced its adversarial bidding system with one in which the company designates suppliers for a component and then uses target pricing (as will be discussed in Chapter 15) to determine with suppliers the component prices and how to achieve them. Most parts are sourced from one supplier for the life of the product.[4]

Determination of the optimal size of the supply base is a strategic issue. The supply base strategy is driven by quality, cost management, technology access, and the firm's ability to substitute the management of supplier relationships for the effects of marketplace competition.

Although some buyers rely on memory and experience for knowledge of sources of supply, competent buyers more correctly rely on the department's own records, published material, and personal contacts. Sources of information concerning suppliers are plentiful. The following information sources should prove helpful to a buyer in establishing a list of potential suppliers.

Sources of Supplier Information

Supplier Purchasing Information File Purchasing and supply management departments should keep supplier information files on past and present suppliers which include the name of each supplier, a list of materials available from each supplier, the supplier's delivery history, the supplier's quality record, the supplier's overall desirability, and general information concerning the supplier's plant and management. In addition to a departmental file, buyers usually maintain a personal supplier file for their own use. Supplier information files are important because many purchasing operations are repetitive; hence, it would be poor management indeed if buyers spent time repeatedly recapturing information which was once available to them but had been needlessly lost.

Supplier Catalogs Because catalogs are a commonly used source of supplier information, many purchasing and supply management departments maintain a catalog library. Here users examine the catalogs to locate the materials they need. The firm's buyers also use catalogs to determine potential sources of supply and, on occasion, to estimate prices.

Large firms frequently employ a full-time librarian for indexing and keeping their catalogs up-to-date. Without an indexing system, using manufacturers' and jobbers' catalogs can be excessively time-consuming. In addition to catalogs, purchasing libraries traditionally include a commodity file, a supplier name file, appropriate trade publications, and purchasing textbooks. A few libraries now have fully indexed microfilm catalogs containing information on many suppliers—primarily those in the electronics and aerospace industries.

---

[4]James P. Womack and Daniel T. Jones, "From Lean Production to the Lean Enterprise," *Harvard Business Review*, March–April 1994, p. 97.

Trade Registers and Directories   *Thomas' Register of American Manufactur-ers* is typical of several widely known trade registers and directories. These registers contain information on the addresses, number of branches, and affiliations of all leading manufacturers. Financial standings of firms are also frequently given. The registers are indexed by commodity, manufacturer, and trade name or trademark description of the item. Kompass Publications in Europe provides similar information for European firms.[5]

Trade Journals   Trade journals are another excellent source for obtaining information about possible suppliers. Advertisements in trade journals are often a buyer's first contact with potential suppliers and their products. Among the magazines in the purchasing field, *Purchasing* and *NAPM Insights* are perhaps the best known and most widely read trade journals. Both contain purchasing, general management, and economic information that is valuable to all buyers and all purchasing managers. Specialized trade journals are available for more specific information about specific industries. For example, a buyer in the aircraft industry would routinely read *Aviation Week;* a buyer in the steel industry would routinely read *Iron Age.*

The Yellow Pages   Another commonly known directory is the classified yellow pages section of telephone directories. This source of information is frequently of limited value to industrial buyers because local telephone books list only local companies. However, buyers can readily obtain telephone books for all major cities from the telephone company. The size and capability of companies are also difficult to determine, as management and financial data are normally not included in the advertisements. The yellow pages do, however, have the virtue of being well indexed. Also, they can serve as a useful starting point if other sources have proved fruitless or if local sources are desired.

Filing of Mailing Pieces   Many mail advertisements are worth saving. These should be given a file number, dated, and indexed by the name and number of each publication. When buyers seek a new source, they can then refer to the index and review the appropriate brochures and booklets.

Some purchasing and supply management departments ask prospective suppliers to complete a simple form giving basic information about themselves and their products. This information, which includes company name, address, officers, local representatives, and principal products, is kept in a set of loose-leaf notebooks or in a computer file. By referring to these standardized data, a buyer can obtain immediate, current information about potential new sources.

Sales Personnel   Sales personnel are excellent sources for information about suppliers and materials. Not only are they usually well informed about

---

[5]Kompass Publications, Ltd., Windson Court, East Grimstead House, East Grimstead, Sussex, RH19-IXD, England.

the capabilities and features of their own products, but they are also familiar with similar and competitive products as well. By the very nature of their specialized knowledge, salespeople can often suggest new applications for their products which will eliminate the search for new suppliers. From their contacts with many companies, salespeople learn much about many products and services, and all this information is available to the alert, receptive buyer. This is a key reason why sales personnel should always be treated courteously and given ample time to make their sales presentations. To deny them this opportunity is to risk the loss of valuable information, including information concerning new and reliable sources of supply.

Trade Exhibits   Regional and national trade shows are still another way by which buyers learn about possible sources of supply. The use of exhibits as a means of sales presentations is increasing. Exhibits provide an excellent opportunity for buyers to see various new products and modifications of old products. They also offer buyers an opportunity to compare concurrently similar products of different manufacturers. Regional trade exhibits are sponsored periodically by many manufacturers, distributors, and trade organizations. For example, a large distributor of scientific apparatus and glassware holds annual trade exhibits in major cities throughout the country; electronics distributors hold similar exhibits. Invitations to these exhibits are sent to all interested purchasing and technical personnel in the area. Although buyers must often find time to visit trade exhibits after working hours, doing so is usually worthwhile. Exhibits offer a buyer an excellent opportunity to expand his or her knowledge of new products, new potential suppliers, and new ideas.

Company Personnel   Personnel from other departments in a buyer's firm can often provide purchasing with helpful information about prospective suppliers. Through their associations in professional organizations, civic associations, and social groups, these employees often learn about outstanding suppliers. Scientific, technical, and research personnel who use sophisticated materials or services always have many valuable suggestions to make regarding possible sources of supply. From their attendance at conventions and trade exhibits, and from their discussions with associates, these personnel are particularly well informed regarding new products, new methods, and new manufacturers.

Other Purchasing and Supply Management Departments   Purchasing and supply management departments in other firms can be helpful sources of information regarding suppliers. Information exchanged among individuals from these departments can be mutually beneficial for all participating companies; therefore, this source of information should be actively developed.

Local purchasing management associations, such as the local affiliates of the National Association of Purchasing Management, the Purchasing Management Association of Canada, the National Institute of Governmental Purchasing, and the National Association of Educational Buyers, publish a list of their members. One of the basic objectives of a purchasing management association is that its members help each other in every possible way. Accordingly, members usually will do everything possible to help fellow members locate and evaluate new sources of supply. However, they will not, and they should not, exchange pricing information. That would be both unethical and illegal.

Supplier Development

The competition for world-class suppliers has already begun. In many instances, the purchasing firm may be unable to identify a world-class supplier that is willing (or able) to meet its needs. If the requirement is sufficiently important, the buying firm will select the most attractive supplier(s) and then develop the supplier into one capable of meeting its present and future needs. Training in project management, teamwork, quality, production processes, and purchasing and supply management may prove to be a worthy investment. Such training has been provided by several leading customer firms for well over a decade.

The Importance of Supplier Goodwill

Business has long recognized that customer goodwill is a valuable asset. In fact, customer goodwill has legal recognition, and it is carried as an asset on many company balance sheets. Business is just beginning to realize that supplier goodwill is also an important company asset. A company develops customer goodwill by selling acceptable products at a fair price, supported by good service with the customers' interests in mind. The buying firm develops supplier goodwill by being open, impartial, and scrupulously fair in all its dealings with suppliers.

A company's purchasing organization should motivate its suppliers to participate in a mutually profitable buyer-seller relationship. To create such motivation fully, it is essential that both buyer and seller completely understand the mutual advantage of a continuing relationship. Such a relationship permits the seller to learn the intricacies of the buyer's operations, and vice versa. The seller learns about the buyer's business problems—manufacturing, inventory, receiving, and overall operational problems. As the relationship develops, the supplier typically can reduce its direct selling effort; consequently, it can afford to direct additional effort to the study of mutual problems that may reduce prices. The end result of good supplier relations is a meshing of the operations of both companies. The seller's production and distribution facilities in reality become an extension of the buyer's production line.

In 1976, two U.K. authorities presented several arguments for what they called "voluntary collaboration,"[6] or partnerships:

- Every time a new set of partners comes together, a learning process is required. The potential for communication difficulties is much greater during early transactions than during later ones.
- Changing market conditions and changing technology that affect the buying process require adaptation on the part of buyers and sellers. Such adaptation can be much less painful under conditions of an ongoing and mutually beneficial relationship where the parties have teamed to adapt together.
- The likelihood of quality problems and late deliveries is greatly reduced in a continuing relationship.
- Open relationships can help to cushion bad times. Customers and suppliers who value each other, based on long-term relations and respect, are more likely to come to each other's aid during times of adversity.
- Suppliers learn from the behavior of an aggressive, price-optimizing purchaser. Such buyers will find it more difficult to obtain delivery of the required goods on time than will buyers who have developed continuing relations with their suppliers.
- Opportunistic buyers are more subject to shocks resulting from capacity or supply problems encountered by the supplier than are buyers who maintain continuing relations with their suppliers.
- Opportunistic buyers should expect less effective performance from suppliers who believe that they have little to lose in the way of follow-on business.

More recently, another group of researchers advanced three significant cost-based arguments against the traditional short-term competitive-based approach to source selection.[7]

- Significant cost reductions in manufacturing operations typically are achieved through the development and implementation of methods improvements and technological innovations. Such accomplishments generally require significant research and development expenditures and/or capital investment. Clearly, an uncertain business environment and the potential loss of business are negative factors in the management analysis of these types of opportunities. Suppliers tend to view such a situation as too risky, and perhaps too costly, and will be reluctant to make these types of long-term commitments without some assurance of obtaining an adequate return on investment. Consequently, major opportunities

[6]David H. Farmer and Keith MacMillan, "Voluntary Collaboration vs. 'Disloyalty' to Suppliers," *Journal of Purchasing and Materials Management*, Winter 1976, pp. 3–8.
[7]Chan K. Hahn, Kyoo H. Kim, and Jong S. Kim, "Cost of Competition: Implications for Purchasing Strategy," *Journal of Purchasing and Materials Management*, Fall 1986, p. 6.

for cost reduction through R&D and capital investment typically are severely limited.

- The use of multiple-sourcing and competitive-bidding strategies requires that a buyer provide potential suppliers with fully developed and precisely described product specifications. In order to ensure uniformity of product quality, the buyer must insist that suppliers conform strictly to the specifications. Consequently, suppliers are not likely to take the initiative in considering modifications that may improve product quality or reduce production costs, since their commitment is tied only to the current contract. In essence, possible productivity improvement through value analysis/engineering is severely limited.
- Furthermore, by frequently changing suppliers, a buyer deprives his or her current supplier of the chance to reduce its production cost through the extended learning curve effect that accompanies many production activities. With accumulated experiences from continuing production, a supplier obviously would be in a better position to achieve certain improvements that could well result in reduced costs.

Partnerships

Many of the above forces favor the establishment of long-term relationships between buying and supplying organizations. These relationships are commonly called *partnerships*.

A *supply partnership* is a collaborative relationship between a buyer and seller which recognizes some degree of interdependence and cooperation on a specific project or for a specific purchase agreement. The partnership calls for the sharing of forecasted demand and cost data, and *must* contain an element of trust and respect between the parties. Note that the term "supply partnership" implies neither the presence nor the absence of a single-source relationship. That is, the buying firm may have one, two, or three "partners" for the same item, although the trend is toward single sourcing.

Long-term partnering agreements encourage suppliers to invest research and development dollars in order to propose technologically current, cost-effective, and high-quality solutions to the buying firm's needs. Properly priced life-of-product agreements encourage suppliers to invest in the equipment, training, and appropriate management systems required to be an efficient, low-cost producer. The buyer benefits from such an agreement in many ways: low "all-in-cost" (total cost), a dependable source of supply, and a partner familiar with his or her needs.

Such partnerships are a major departure from the more traditional and, frequently, quasi-adversarial relationships with suppliers. The buying firm must be open about its true needs (e.g., technology, quantities, and schedules). The buyer must agree to protect the supplier partner from sudden changes which might leave the supplier with unusable raw materials or finished goods. Trust must be developed and possible reform action enhanced. And as will be seen in Chapter 20, a different set of supplier management skills must be developed and applied.

The Ford Motor Company is a leading advocate of supplier partnerships. Ford has found that its supplier partners invest in better tools and equipment, better methods, and far more training than under previous short-term adversarial relationships. As a result, quality, cost reductions, and flexibility (responsiveness) have all increased drastically.

Supplier partnerships do not just happen. Planning and the expenditure of effort on the part of both parties are required. Intel Corporation likens a supplier partnership to a marriage. The buying company must avoid marriage (partnership) without courtship. Intel stresses "formal supplier partnerships which feature written co-objectives and regular meetings between senior executives of Intel and its suppliers."[8]

There is, however, a downside to partnering. Mr. Joe Sandor, a senior manager in corporate purchasing at Sara Lee Corporation, reported that a study by Bain & Co. of approximately 100 *Fortune 500* companies indicated that for 58 percent of the respondents, partnering failed to meet expectations; 34 percent said it met them; and only 8 percent said that it surpassed their expectations.[9]

Mr. Sandor listed the following six dangers associated with partnering. (*Note:* Mr. Sandor's concerns are italicized. The implementations for purchasing and supply managers are in parentheses.)

- *Partnering is a way to reduce purchasing staffs.* (Designing, developing, and managing supplier partnerships requires as much as or more time and attention than the traditional nonpartnership approach to purchasing and, therefore, calls for a reallocation of personnel, not downsizing.)
- *Partnering can lead to complacency.* (The stories of buyers being taken advantage of by their supply "partners" are too numerous to count. The buyer cannot go to sleep at the switch; he or she must actively manage the relationship through continuous measurement and a sharing of expectations.)
- *Partnering can weaken leverage.* (Since competition, which provides the buyer with leverage or clout, is reduced or absent, the buyer must substitute the management techniques described in Chapters 17 and 20 for the beneficial effects of market competition.)
- *Purchasing and audit control can be lost.* (Such lost control occurs only in poorly structured and managed partnerships.)
- *Success can lead to excess.* (Not every product or commodity class and not every supplier lends itself to partnerships. The costs and benefits of each potential supply relationship must be weighed carefully.)
- *Every supplier wants to be your partner.* (At times this seems to be the case, even though many suppliers aren't clear about the meaning of the term

---

[8]Somerby Dowst, "The Right Suppliers Have the Right Stuff," *Purchasing,* Jan. 30, 1986, p. 95.
[9]Joe Sandor, "Partners Face Early Divorce," *Purchasing,* June 4, 1992, p. 20.

"partnership." Many suppliers do not possess the capabilities or the willingness to become partners, as the term was described above.)

Supplier Management

The challenging issue of managing suppliers is dealt with in detail in Chapter 20. At this point, however, it is essential to recognize that the buyer has many responsibilities associated with the management of his or her suppliers. Satisfying these responsibilities should ensure that suppliers perform as required or that appropriate corrective action is taken to upgrade or eliminate them from the firm's supplier base.

In addition, purchasing and supply management must, on a periodic basis, analyze its suppliers' abilities to meet the firm's long-term needs. Areas that deserve particular attention include the supplier's general growth plans, future design capability in relevant areas, the role of purchasing and supply management in the supplier's strategic planning, potential for future production capacity, and financial ability to support such growth.

If present suppliers appear to be unlikely to be able to meet future requirements, the firm has three options: (1) It may assist the appropriate supplier(s) with financing and technological assistance, (2) it may develop new sources having the desired growth potential, or (3) it may have to develop the required capability internally.

STRATEGIC AND TACTICAL ISSUES IN SUPPLIER SELECTION

The buying firm must consider many factors in selecting sources of supply. This section of the chapter investigates several areas of concern.

Early Supplier Involvement

Over ten years ago, a study conducted by *Purchasing* indicated that when suppliers are involved early in the buyer's design process, they can apply their expertise in the following nine areas:[10]

- Material specifications
- Tolerances
- Standardization
- Order sizes
- Process changes in supplier's manufacturing
- Packaging
- Inventory

---

[10]Somerby Dowst, "Better-Forged Links Bring in Better Designs," *Purchasing,* Sept. 6, 1984, pp. 67–75.

- Transportation
- Assembly changes in buyer's plants

Today, early supplier involvement (ESI) is an accepted way of life at many progressive firms. As noted in an article in *Purchasing*, "Not only is ESI desirable, it's absolutely necessary for establishing the high level of trust demanded by long-range projects."[11]

The *Purchasing* article advances four reasons cited by purchasing executives for utilizing ESI:

- Get supplier inputs before the design is frozen.
- Capitalize on the latest technology.
- Save time since design cycles are getting shorter.
- Let the supplier know that it is part of the team.

ESI normally, but not always, results in the selection of a single source of supply. At most progressive companies, this selection process is the result of intensive competition between two or three carefully prequalified potential suppliers. The company selected becomes the single source of supply for the life of the item using its material.

Number of Suppliers

Should one, two, or more suppliers be used? In addition to the reasons discussed in the prior sections on partnering and ESI, the major argument for placing all of a firm's business with *one supplier* is that in times of shortage, this supplier will give priority to the needs of a special customer. Additionally, single sources may be justified when:

- Better pricing results from a much higher volume (economies of scale)
- Quality considerations dictate[12]
- The buyer obtains more influence—clout—with the supplier
- Lower costs are incurred to source, process, expedite, and inspect
- The quality, control, and coordination required with just-in-time manufacturing require a single source

Selection of a single source of supply is also favored when:

- Significantly lower freight costs may result

---

[11]James Dairs, Manager of Transportation Programs at G.E.'s Plastics Group, Pittsfield, Mass., quoted in "The Winning Edge" by Somerby Dowst, *Purchasing*, Mar. 12, 1987, p. 57.

[12]Dr. Edwards Deming, the long-time dean of America's quality gurus, long advocated that buyers should strive to have one good source of supply in an effort to upgrade the quality of their products. Deming recommended that we "end the practice of awarding business on the basis of the price tag. Instead, depend on meaningful measures of quality, along with price. Move toward a single supplier for any one item, on a long-term relationship of loyalty and trust." *The Deming Guide to Quality and Competitive Position* by Howard S. Gitlow and Shelly J. Gitlow, Prentice-Hall, Inc., Englewood Cliffs, N.J., 1987, p. 51.

- Special tooling is required, and the use of more than one supplier is impractical or excessively costly
- Total system inventory will be reduced
- An improved commitment on the supplier's part results
- Improved interdependency and risk sharing result
- Time to market is critical[13]

Dual or multiple sourcing may be appropriate:

- To protect the buyer during times of shortages, strikes, and other emergencies.
- To maintain competition and provide a back-up source. Through the award of 70 percent of the volume to one supplier and 30 percent to a second supplier, economies of scale are obtained from the "big supplier" while the "little supplier" provides competition. Many Japanese firms use this approach. Any time the big supplier "misbehaves," its volume is reduced and given to the smaller supplier. (An interesting approach to discipline!)
- To meet local content requirements for international manufacturing locations.
- To meet customer's volume requirements.
- To avoid lethargy or complacency on the part of a single-source supplier.
- When the customer is a small player in the market for a specific item.
- When the technology path is uncertain.
- In areas where suppliers tend to leapfrog each other technologically.[14]

The single-multiple-source issue has been around since time immemorial. For noncritical procurements the buyer or sourcing team can make reasoned decisions that are in the best interest of the firm. For critical procurements, the buyer or sourcing team should conduct a thorough study—in effect, a cost/benefit analysis. This analysis should be forwarded to the executive committee or chief operating officer, together with a recommendation. Such decisions are larger than the purchasing and supply management department, the commodity team, or the cross-functional team responsible for source selection. These decisions may affect the success—or even the survival—of the firm.

Share of Supplier's Business

Many highly regarded firms try not to be more than 15 to 25 percent of any one supplier's business. They reason that if their purchases represent too large

---

[13]Bob Bretz, former director of Corporate Purchasing for Pitney Bowes and 1994 Shipman Medalist, indicates that "'single sourcing' is much simpler. There's less effort on the part of the seller and it's easier to resolve issues." Patrick Robert Bretz, quoted in Patrick Flanagen, "The Rules of Purchasing Are Changing," *Management Review*, March 1994, p. 30.

[14]Several large corporations use a dual or multiple approach to sourcing items with dynamic technology. See "Buyers Beef Up Supplier Management Skills," *Purchasing*, Oct. 21, 1993, p. 28.

a share of the supplier's business and they discontinue a product or purchase an item from another supplier, they could put the initial supplier in a very difficult financial situation.

Buying Locally

Sometimes community relations require greater use of local sources than can be justified solely by economic factors. One large hospital in a city of approximately 700,000 people, for example, has found that it must purchase at least half its materials requirements within the community; otherwise, local business people will not support the fund-raising campaigns needed by the hospital to obtain part of its required operating budget.

Local buying sometimes can be justified solely on an economic basis. A local supplier often can furnish smaller quantities of materials at lower prices than could be obtained from distant sources. Local suppliers also can maintain and finance a well-balanced inventory of materials for continuing local users. Working with local sources of supply and encouraging them to be capable suppliers is a part of progressive purchasing.

Two basic considerations are involved when deciding to buy locally or nationally. First, large-dollar purchases should be placed at sources as close to the manufacturer as possible to obtain optimum prices and discounts. Second, small- and medium-dollar purchases should be placed with local sources when price differentials are small or when such action is necessary to keep materials physically available in the immediate area.

Most buyers prefer to patronize local sources whenever such action is prudent. A Stanford University research study found that approximately three-fourths of 152 buyers surveyed indicated a preference to buy from local sources whenever possible. Many of them were willing to pay slightly higher prices to gain the advantage of better service and immediate availability of materials offered by some local suppliers.

Local suppliers often can be made more effective if buyers from several firms coordinate their requirements. For example, a large number of oil companies actively drill for oil and gas in the area around Bakersfield, California. Because it is costly to shut down a producing well, historically each drilling company carried its own inventory of expensive valves, pumps, and similarly critical production components. A few years ago, buyers from each oil company involved met to discuss the possibilities of eliminating this costly, duplicate expense. They concluded that if the local suppliers would carry reasonable levels of the expensive items of inventory now carried by each oil company, and if the suppliers would guarantee around-the-clock delivery of these items in case of emergency, everyone would benefit economically. The suppliers were willing to render this kind of service for a reasonable profit. Now, instead of each oil company carrying, for example, a $25,000 valve which it may never use, the selected supplier carries one of these valves which is available to all companies. The price for the valve is slightly higher than when it was carried in the storeroom of each company. However, savings from lower valve inventories and from less valve obsolescence have reduced total costs for all companies substantially from their former level. Thus, this arrangement results in worthwhile gains for both the oil companies and the local suppliers.

Just-in-time manufacturing requires dependable sources of defect-free materials which arrive within ˎ very tight time frame. Suppliers to JIT customers are meeting their requirements in three ways: (1) They are locating close to their customers;[15] (2) suppliers are implementing responsive manufacturing systems; and (3) they are taking aggressive action to control the transportation of their materials to their customers.

In summary, local buying has the following advantages:

1 Closer cooperation between buyer and seller is possible because of close geographical proximity. JIT deliveries are thus facilitated.
2 Delivery dates are more certain since transportation is only a minor factor in delivery.
3 Lower prices can result from consolidated transportation and insurance charges. A local supplier, in effect, brings in many local buyers' orders in the same shipment.
4 Shorter lead times frequently can permit reductions or the elimination of inventory. In effect, the seller produces just-in-time.
5 Rush orders are likely to be filled faster.
6 Disputes usually are more easily resolved.
7 Implied social responsibilities to the community are fulfilled.

Buying Nationally

National buying has the following advantages:

1 National sources, as a result of the economies of scale, can in some situations be more efficient than local suppliers and offer higher quality or better service at a lower price.
2 National companies often can provide superior technical assistance.
3 Large national companies have greater production capacity and therefore greater production flexibility to handle fluctuating demands.
4 Shortages are less likely with national companies because of their broader markets.

Buyers should give careful consideration to both the advantages and disadvantages of buying locally and buying nationally. In those situations where economic and technical considerations justify the selection of local sources, it is the policy of most companies to buy locally. If this is not the case, national suppliers should be used.

---

[15]For example, Chrysler builds additional buildings on-site and leases them to its suppliers. Robert M. Faltra, "How Chrysler Buyers Make Quality a Standard Feature," *Electronics Purchasing,* vol. 101, July 10, 1986, p. 62A15.

Buying Internationally

This important buying consideration is discussed in detail in Chapter 13. It is mentioned here only to note that it is an important factor in supplier selection.

Manufacturer or Distributor?

In deciding whether to buy from a manufacturer or distributor, a buyer's considerations should focus largely on the distributor's capabilities and services, not on its location. In the steel industry, for example, distributors pay the same prices for steel as other buyers. Distributors, however, buy in carload lots and sell in smaller quantities to users whose operations do not justify carload lot purchases. The distributors realize a profit because large lots sell at lower unit prices than small lots. If buyers wish to purchase steel directly from the mill and bypass the distributor, they are perfectly free to do so; however, when they do, they usually forgo certain special services that a competent distributor is equipped to offer. Distributors, for example, have cutting and shaping tools, and skilled personnel to operate them. They maintain large, diverse inventories. They also are able to perform numerous customer services.

When the materials ordered from a distributor are shipped directly to the user by the manufacturer (a *drop shipment*), an additional buying decision becomes necessary. In this situation, the distributor does not handle the materials physically; it acts only as a broker.[16] Under such circumstances, a buyer is strongly motivated to buy directly from the manufacturer—if the manufacturer will sell to him or her.

Buyers should be aware that distributors stock many manufacturers' products. Hence, ordering from a distributor can significantly reduce the total number of orders a buyer must place to fill some of his or her materials requirements. If there were no distributors, orders for production as well as maintenance, repair, and operating (MRO) requirements would all have to be placed directly with many different manufacturers. This obviously would increase direct purchasing costs. Furthermore, for every additional purchase order placed, an additional receiving, inspection, and accounts payable operation is created.

In the final analysis, the manufacturer-distributor decision centers on one critical fact: The functions of distribution cannot be eliminated. The buyer needs most of these functions; therefore, the buyer should pay for them once—but he or she should not pay for them twice. Either the distributor or the manufacturer must perform the essential distribution functions of carrying the inventory, giving technical advice, rendering service, extending credit, and so on. The buyer must decide for each individual buying situation how to best purchase the functions needed. The buyer must answer the question: Is it my

---

[16]Manufacturers' representatives, who usually deal only in technical items, also effect deliveries by drop shipments, and they act as brokers. Manufacturers' reps also aid a buyer by being able to furnish numerous product lines from a single source.

company, the distributor, or the manufacturer that can perform the required distribution services satisfactorily at the lowest cost?

"Green" Purchasing

Environmentally sensitive purchasing can make good business sense. Many of us have heard of the story of young Henry Ford. It seems that Mr. Ford was very explicit in the dimensions and quality of the lumber used in constructing the packing crates his suppliers used to ship parts to Ford. One day, one of the suppliers asked a Ford employee why a throwaway packing crate had to be made to such explicit specifications. The answer was "because we use the wood to build the floor boards of our Model T." Was Mr. Ford an environmentalist or a good businessman? Quite obviously, he was both!

Environmentally sensitive purchasing has two components: (1) the purchase of materials and items which are recyclable and (2) the environmental and liability issues associated with the use and discharge of hazardous materials—anywhere in the supply chain.

Recycled Materials   David Biddle, executive director of the Public Recycling Officials of Pennsylvania, writes in a recent *Harvard Business Review* article:

> Top managers of companies like American Airlines, Bell Atlantic, and Coca-Cola have made buying recycled products and investing in green R&D part of their overall business strategies. They've cut down on waste, increased profit margins, and, in some cases, truly closed the recycling loop.[17]

> The Buy Recycled Business Alliance is a group of firms including Bank of America, American Airlines, Bell Atlantic, Coca-Cola, and Anheuser-Busch which are on its steering committee of 33 companies. . . . In less than one year, the steering committee members alone have accounted for $3 billion in purchases of recycled-content products and materials. . . . By the end of 1995, the business alliance hopes to sign 5,000 companies as members.[18]

The purchasing organization is well positioned to play a key role in green purchasing. Well-informed buyers should be aware of recycled materials which may meet the firm's needs. Purchasing professionals at large firms may be instrumental in developing suppliers who will use recycled materials in their production process. In some cases, the buying firm may need to enter into a long-term contract in order to provide the supplier assurance that it will be able to recoup the investment required to use recycled materials. And purchasing and supply management, through its membership on cross-functional design teams and on value analysis/value engineering committees, can champion the consideration of recycled materials.

---

[17]David Biddle, "Recycling for Profit: The New Green Business Frontier," *Harvard Business Review*, November–December 1993, p. 146.
   [18]Ibid., p. 148.

Environmental and Liability Issues Purchasing and supply management, the firm's environmental engineer (or environmental consultant), and the firm's attorney should study the firm's value chain to identify the possible uses and disposal methods for environmentally hazardous substances and materials. It is entirely possible, for example, that a supplier who disposes of hazardous waste in an environmentally unsafe manner, while producing a product for the buying firm, may subject the buying firm to financial liability, should the supplier have limited financial resources. Current statutes cover present and previous operators and owners.

Additionally, purchasing has a responsibility to ensure that a supplier's salvage and disposal contractors meet OSHA standards both prior to award and during performance under the contracts. One way of dealing with this challenging issue is to require the supplier to post adequate performance and liability bonds. This topic is discussed in detail in Chapter 26.

Minority- and Women-Owned Business Enterprises

Many forces motivate a buying firm to develop and implement programs designed to ensure that minority- and/or women-owned businesses receive a share of the firm's business. These motivators include federal and state legislation, set-aside quotas in government appropriations, the actions of regulatory bodies such as the state public utilities commission, chambers of commerce, civil rights activists, and a firm's "corporate social consciousness." Perhaps one of the most significant motivators is the recognition by a firm's management that *its customer base* includes minority- and women-owned business enterprises and their employees. In addition to a sense of social responsibility, MWBE should be focused on bottom-line profitability and good business sense.[19]

A minority business enterprise is a business that is at least 51 percent owned, controlled, and operated by one or more U.S. citizens belonging to a recognized minority group. The recognized minority classification includes:

- Asian Pacific Americans
- Native Americans
- African Americans
- Hispanic Americans
- Subcontinent Asian Americans[20]

A women-owned business enterprise is one which is at least 51 percent owned, controlled, and operated by one or more women. The term MWBE is

[19]Debbie Newman, Patricia Richards, and Linda Butler, "Shared Commitment to MWBE Development," *NAPM Conference Proceedings*, Tempe, Ariz., 1994, p. 300.
[20]Eberhard E. Scheuing, Debra K. Goldmann, and Michael C. Rogers, "Benchmarking MBE Practices to Revitalize Minority Sourcing," *NAPM Conference Proceedings*, Tempe, Ariz., 1994, pp. 28–29.

used in this section to refer to any program that enhances or encourages the award of purchase orders, contracts, and subcontracts to any or any combination of minority- or women-owned business enterprises.

Some firms combine both minority- and women-owned business enterprises under one program, others have separate programs, and still others may have only a minority business enterprise (MBE) program. While the mechanics of such programs are similar, much more research has been conducted on MBE programs. Further, anecdotal evidence indicates that these programs are more resistant to successful implementation. There appear to be more misconceptions concerning MBE suppliers than any other group of potential suppliers. Accordingly, this section will focus on these potential suppliers in an effort to dispel these misconceptions. Dr. Eb Scheuing and two associates write:

> Many MBEs fall into the small business category and are thus, at times, subject to stereotyping and misconceptions about their ability to serve an organization's needs. Such *misconceptions* may include notions that:
>
> > MBEs are unsophisticated
> > MBEs are unreliable
> > MBEs have insufficient capacity
> > MBEs have inadequate equipment
> > MBEs perform substandard work
> > MBEs charge more
> > MBEs do not provide what we need
>
> The facts clearly refute such misconceptions, once they are presented to purchasing decision makers. Most MBEs are every bit as sophisticated and reliable as their majority counterparts. They often possess adequate capacity or are able to expand to meet a customer's needs. The free enterprise system would not allow them to stay in business if they performed substandard work or did not utilize state-of-the-art equipment. MBEs are also often quite competitive and responsive as suppliers, particularly in spot buying situations where smaller purchases are involved that frequently receive limited attention from major suppliers. And they provide a broader range of goods and services than is commonly known. It is accordingly a key purpose of the Councils that represent minority business enterprises to overcome these knowledge barriers and misconceptions and present the impressive capabilities of MBEs to purchasing decision makers.[21]

Three major blockages exist in the successful implementation of MWBE programs:

- Inadequate knowledge of qualified MWBE potential suppliers
- Internal resistance to such programs
- Purchasing and supply management's objectives and rewards: In many firms, a buyer is recognized and rewarded for timely delivery of the right

[21]Ibid., p. 29.

quality, at the right time, at a low price; not for meeting desirable social objectives.

Inadequate Knowledge   One way to identify MWBE potential suppliers is through the use of published directories. For example, the 95-year-old Thomas Publishing Company, which publishes reference books used by manufacturers and others to identify potential suppliers, recently initiated a service to identify minority- and women-owned suppliers for some 3,500 product categories.[22] Another way to find MWBE suppliers is to work with local chambers of commerce and local, state, and federal government agencies.

Internal Resistance and Inadequate Reward Systems   A 1990 study sponsored by the National Association of Purchasing Management's Center for Advanced Purchasing Studies addresses several problems encountered by women-owned (WBE) suppliers. The two key problems identified were *undercapitalization* and *buyer attitudes toward WBEs*. The WBE respondents "believe that buyers have negative attitudes toward WBE's, thus making it difficult for WBE's to 'get their foot in the door.' "[23]

At many buying firms, the blockages of internal resistance and purchasing's inadequate reward system have been addressed by a corporate initiative to award a specified percentage of business to MWBEs under these programs. A senior executive (frequently the CEO or COO) designates the dollar-volume award objective(s) as a high priority and makes the objective(s) known to all appropriate personnel. Performance evaluations for these personnel (including members of the procurement system) reflect the individual's attitude and successes under the program.

Meetings are held with appropriate managers. The CEO or COO explains that it is the executive board's policy that the company will increase MWBE purchases by X percent. Officials of firms with successful long-running MWBE programs frequently attend to comment on their experiences and to offer suggestions.

On occasion, it may be desirable to provide financial and technical assistance to MWBEs. The financial assistance can take the form of advance or progress payments, the underwriting of loans, direct loans, and loaned equipment. Technical assistance may include technical training and/or the loan of one or more engineers or quality personnel.

On significant dollar procurements, many firms have an aggressive MWBE subcontracts program (with specific objectives) in an effort to increase awards to such suppliers by the firm's larger suppliers. Experience has indicated that such programs require careful management and auditing.

Large firms with successful MWBE programs frequently appoint an executive, full- or part-time, to evaluate other MWBE programs and develop and

---

[22]"Supplying a Minority or Female Supplier," *Wall Street Journal*, Sept. 21, 1993, p. B1.
[23]Carol L. Ketchum, "CAPS Study on Women-Owned Suppliers," *NAPM Insights*, April 1990, p. 9.

implement the firm's own program. During implementation of the program, the responsible executive develops and releases publicity on the corporate goals and achievements. The firm recognizes—even promotes—those who are doing the best job of locating and sourcing with MWBE suppliers.

Outstanding MWBE suppliers should be recognized periodically, along with the firm's other outstanding suppliers.

> Outreach to minority- and women-owned businesses in this environment makes good business sense. These MWBEs have proven they can be innovative, creative, and competitive when placed on equal footing with all of America's businesses. Failing to recognize the contribution of this segment of the business community is a critical error in today's and certainly this country's future economic environment.[24]

Ethical Considerations

Buyers must be aware of potential conflicts of interest when selecting suppliers. A conflict of interest exists when buyers must divide their loyalty between the firm which employs them and another firm. In purchasing and supply management, this situation usually occurs when a buyer is a substantial stockholder in a supplier's firm or when he or she makes purchases from close friends and relatives. Conflicts of interest are discussed more fully in Chapter 31. The subject is introduced here solely to remind the reader that such conflicts always should be avoided in all source selection decisions.

Buyers should keep themselves as free as possible from unethical influences in their choice of suppliers. It is very difficult to maintain complete objectivity in this matter, for it is only human to want to favor one's friends. On occasion, friends can make unusually good suppliers. They will normally respond to emergency needs more readily than suppliers without a strong tie of personal friendship. On the other hand, buyers tend not to discipline friends who perform poorly to the same degree as they do other suppliers.

Gifts which are intended to influence buying decisions have no place in a professional purchasing and supply management department. In most states commercial bribery is a criminal offense. Lunches with salespeople customarily are not considered gifts for the purpose of influencing decisions. Traditionally, they are judged to be a means of providing more time for the buyer and seller to discuss business problems. Beyond this point, the issue of undue influence may be raised. It is for this reason that many companies prohibit their buyers from accepting any gift beyond a simple meal. Regarding meals, firms should provide expense accounts for members of their purchasing departments. This permits buyers to reciprocate with salespeople in paying for lunches, thus eliminating any suspicion of undue influence. Chapter 31 addresses ethical issues in greater detail.

---

[24]Newman et al., op. cit., p. 302.

Dishonest Suppliers

Dishonest sellers exist in the industrial world just as they do in the consumer world. This may surprise some readers, for it is logical to assume that dishonest suppliers would not tackle experienced industrial buyers, but they do. Dishonest suppliers, therefore, can be a problem in source selection. A recurring technique used by dishonest suppliers is to contact a buyer by telephone, usually stating that the buyer has been referred to them by a top corporate executive—commonly one who cannot be contacted quickly or one who is located in another city. A typical story centers upon an unfortunate person who must liquidate the family stationery business immediately. The entire inventory of office supplies is offered at very low prices. If the buyer takes the offer, and many do, the result is always the same: poor quality, high prices, and late delivery. How many buyers take such offers? Several studies indicate that from 12 to 15 percent of buyers, at one time or another, have been swindled by dishonest suppliers. It's caveat emptor, without a doubt—even in the industrial world.

A buyer's best protection against dishonest suppliers is the practice of thorough and prudent investigation before becoming seriously involved with a supplier. This type of professional purchasing performance, blended with a liberal dose of common sense, should keep buyers on safe ground in most cases.

What can buyers do if they are swindled by a dishonest seller? From a practical standpoint, in most cases, they have little legal recourse, but they should attempt to expose such sellers. They should contact the nearest better business bureau and the postal inspector if mail solicitation is involved. They should also inform the district attorney and the local purchasing association. Dishonest sellers cannot operate in the light of publicity. The reluctance of victims to admit that they have been swindled is one of a dishonest seller's greatest protections.

Reciprocity

When buyers give preference to suppliers that are also customers, they are engaging in a practice known as *reciprocity*.[25] The practice can be illegal, and the line between legal and illegal reciprocal practices frequently is very thin. A key criterion used by the courts in determining illegality is the degree to which reciprocal activity tends to restrict competition and trade. Hence, those who engage in reciprocal practices must do so with care and legal consultation.

---

[25]Reciprocity becomes more insidious when it involves more than one tier of suppliers. For example, A is asked to buy from B, not because B is A's customer, but because B is C's customer, and C is A's customer, and B wants to sell to A. Obviously, it is possible for reciprocal relationships to extend to four or more tiers.

The following cases clearly illustrate illegal practices. One of the nation's largest shippers was convicted of illegal reciprocity as a result of threatening to withdraw business from a large railroad if the railroad did not use a braking system manufactured by a subsidiary of the large shipper. Another large company was convicted of unlawful reciprocal dealing under its announced policy of "I will buy from you if you buy from me." Under this policy, by means of its economic power the company forced other companies to purchase its products at higher than market prices under the threat of losing the firm's high-dollar business. *In contrast, it is entirely legal to buy from one's customers at fair market prices, without economic threat, and without the intent of restricting competition.*

Most buyers disapprove of the practice of reciprocity, even when legal, because it restricts their ability to achieve competition among potential suppliers. Thus it usually constrains purchasing's opportunity to increase profit by reducing the cost of materials. Those opposed to reciprocity cite the following dangers:

- Reciprocity does not follow sound principles of buying and selling on the fundamental criteria of quality, price, and service.
- Companies may relax their competitive efforts in technical and production areas as a result of reduced competition. Consequently, purchasing costs may be higher.
- Sales departments may develop a false sense of security, resulting in deterioration of a firm's selling effort.

In addition,

- New customers may be hard to find because of preestablished relationships with competitors.
- Company reputations may be impaired because of bad publicity resulting from reciprocity. Consequently, sellers of new, advanced products and processes will not waste their time with companies known to be tied up with reciprocal agreements.
- Conspiracy and restraint-of-trade situations can develop, with their attendant legal dangers. The Antitrust Division of the Justice Department is taking the position that purchasing and supply managers are responsible for their own illegal actions regarding reciprocity; they can no longer transfer these responsibilities to top management.

Consequently, most U.S. firms proclaim a reciprocity policy similar to this one: "When important factors such as quality, service, and price are equal, we prefer to buy from our customers."[26]

Buyers find, however, that combinations of quality, service, and price are seldom exactly equal. If quality and price are equal, then the supplier would

---

[26]Some firms use vague phrases such as "Buy from customers when doing so will contribute to the greatest economic good of the firm."

be selected solely on the basis of service. Service is seldom equal except for standard off-the-shelf items because, as was discussed earlier, in the majority of cases it is a supplier's capabilities that are being purchased, not commodities. To test the validity of this conclusion, readers should ask themselves questions such as the following and also should consider how many times they believe the answers would be the same for different suppliers:

- Does the supplier have an effective value analysis program for its products?
- To what extent will the supplier provide engineering and design assistance?
- To what extent does the supplier have a service-shop organization that is available to me?
- Are repair parts available locally? On short notice? Will the supplier make available reserve production facilities to meet my emergency demands?
- To what extent will the supplier plan shipments to minimize my inventory?
- To what extent will the supplier help me cut acquisition costs such as qualifying visits, telephone calls, spoilage, and waste?

The proponents of reciprocity contend that it is simply good business. They believe that if a buyer buys from a friend, both the buyer and the friend will profit in the long run. They maintain that service is better from suppliers who are also customers. They argue that reciprocity is a legitimate way to expand a company's markets. For example, a battery manufacturer states that it only makes good sense to buy the brand of automobile that uses its company's batteries.

Companies manufacturing high-volume, highly competitive, standardized products are more susceptible to reciprocal pressure than companies manufacturing highly differentiated products. Industries most susceptible to reciprocal pressures typically include transportation, petroleum, steel, and cement.[27] Industries less susceptible to such pressures include those involved with electronic data processing equipment, electronics, and defense systems.

In the final analysis, reciprocity is neither a marketing problem nor a purchasing problem; rather, it is a management problem. If management believes that it can expand its markets permanently and add to the firm's profit *legally* by reciprocity, then this is the decision management should make. Conversely, if management believes profit will be increased by buying without the constraints of reciprocity, then that is the policy management should adopt. Although reciprocity can benefit a firm, no economist would argue that it benefits a nation's total economy.

---

[27]As might be suspected, the firms in these industries tend to have the greatest interest in reciprocity. In many cases, however, large firms have altogether disbanded their reciprocity organizations under threat of antitrust violations. See Martin T. Farris, "Purchasing Reciprocity and Antitrust Revisited," *Journal of Purchasing and Materials Management*, Summer 1981, pp. 2–7.

Miscellaneous Considerations

By the very nature of business, managers move up the executive ladder from functional to general management positions. Thus, it should not be surprising that all firms have a specific functional orientation or bias depending on the functional backgrounds of their top executives. Some firms have a marketing orientation; others have a production, financial, or engineering orientation. Competent buyers seek out suppliers having management orientations that best blend with the requirements of their own firms.

In searching for a new supplier, it is possible that a routine supplier evaluation might result in the selection of an efficient supplier who is also the major supplier of the buyer's major competitor. This could create an extremely dangerous situation. During periods of shortages, economic pressures assuredly would cause a seller to favor its older, large customers at the expense of its newer, less important customers. Obviously, a buyer should avoid such a situation.

In selecting suppliers, buyers also should consider the seller's general product mix and the types of markets served. These factors should fit well with the needs of the buyer's own company. How do the supply curves of the seller match the demand curves of the buyer? Would a long-term relationship be economically beneficial to both? Clearly, a buyer seeks positive answers to such questions.

CONCLUSION

The buyer's first responsibility in source selection is to develop and manage a viable source base. Once such a base is available, the buyer or sourcing team can focus on selecting the *right* source of supply, the subject of the next chapter.

FOR DISCUSSION

11-1 Describe the analysis that should take place prior to the selection of an outside source. Explain how "core competencies" relate to sourcing.

11-2 Consider Figure 11-1. Given that the mechanics of sourcing are similar under both approaches, what are the structural and philosophical differences between the two?

11-3 "A good supplier is an invaluable resource to the organization requiring its product or service." Explain this statement.

11-4 What are three pitfalls of opportunistic buying?

11-5 Why should a company develop and maintain a dependable supplier base?

11-6 How can a purchasing department motivate its suppliers to participate in a mutually profitable relationship? Should the seller know about the buyer's business problems?

11-7 Explain the statement "The end result of good relations is the meshing of operations."

11-8 What are the characteristics of a "supply partnership"? What are the dangers associated with partnering?

11-9 Does early supplier involvement exclude competition? Discuss.

11-10 When making single-/multiple-source decisions, buyers should handle noncritical and critical procurements differently. Why?

11-11 Explain the 70/30 approach to dual sourcing. What are some potential drawbacks to using this approach?

11-12 Evaluate the advantages and disadvantages of buying from a local source of supply.

11-13 Identify the factors to be considered when choosing between a distributor and a manufacturer.

11-14 What are some of the liability issues that buyers should be aware of when they engage in "green purchasing"? What are some ways of dealing with these issues?

11-15 Identify three major roadblocks to the successful implementation of MWBE programs, and discuss possible ways to overcome them.

11-16 What is reciprocity? Discuss the legality of this practice. What are the potential dangers of reciprocity? Whose problem is it?

CASES FOR CHAPTER 11

12

SOURCES OF SUPPLY: PART II

KEY CONCEPTS

- Responsibility for source selection
    - Commodity teams
- Evaluating a potential supplier
    - Type of evaluation needed
    - Preliminary surveys
    - Financial condition
    - Plant visits
    - Management; service
    - Just-in-time capabilities
    - The criticality of qualifying sources
- Competitive bidding and negotiation
    - Five prerequisites for competitive bidding
    - Four conditions favoring negotiation
    - Two-step bidding/negotiation
- The solicitation
- Selecting the source

RESPONSIBILITY FOR SOURCE SELECTION

While purchasing and supply management has the ultimate responsibility for selecting the "right" source, the process is handled in many ways. Procedurally, the simplest approach is when the *buyer alone* conducts the analysis and makes the selection. A second common approach calls for the use of a *cross-functional team* consisting of representatives of purchasing and supply management, design engineering, operations, quality, and finance. The third common approach is the use of a *commodity team,* which we will discuss next.

Commodity Teams

Many progressive firms use commodity teams to source and manage a group of similar components. Ideally, a commodity is a shopping basket of similar items that are purchased together from one source (or small group of sources) in order to maximize value, efficiency, leverage, and so forth for both the buyer and the seller.

Commodity teams frequently consist of buyers, materials engineers, and production planners. Larger commodity teams include a commodity manager (normally from purchasing and supply management) and representatives of materials, design and manufacturing engineering, quality, and finance. Commodity teams are essentially a type of cross-functional team. The principal difference between them is that commodity teams tend to be fairly permanent, while cross-functional teams tend to be one-time assignments.

EVALUATING A POTENTIAL SUPPLIER

After developing a comprehensive list of potential suppliers, the buyer's next step is to evaluate each prospective supplier individually. By a process of elimination, a selected list of potential suppliers is developed with whom the buying company may be willing to do business. Unless a decision has been made to employ a single source of supply, as discussed in Chapter 11, the supplier list should be complete enough to bring to bear every type of competition desired, including:

- Technological and quality competition, resulting from identifying potential suppliers who excel in good ideas, engineering planning, design, material quality, and production techniques
- Price competition resulting from identifying the lowest-cost producers or distributors
- Service competition, resulting from identifying those suppliers that are especially anxious to get contracts and that are willing to add "plus" values over and above functional value (quality) and price

What kind of company makes the best supplier? It would be difficult to improve on the definition given by Professor Wilbur England of Harvard University:[1]

> A good supplier is one who is at all times honest and fair in his dealing with the customers, his own employees, and himself; who has adequate plant facilities, and know-how so as to be able to provide materials which meet the purchaser's specifications, in the quantities required, and at the time promised; whose financial position is sound; whose prices are reasonable both to the buyer and to himself; whose management policies are progressive; who is alert to the need for continued improvement in both his products and his manufacturing processes; and who realizes that, in the last analysis, his own interests are best served when he best serves his customers.

Type of Evaluation Needed

The type of evaluation required to determine supplier capability varies with the nature, criticality, complexity, and dollar value of the purchase to be made. It also varies with the buyer's or buying team's knowledge of the firms being considered for the order. For many uncomplicated, low-dollar-value purchases, an examination of the information already available in the departmental library (such as the supplier information file, catalogs, and brochures) is sufficient.

For complex, high-dollar-value, and perhaps critical purchases, additional evaluation steps are necessary. These steps can include surveys conducted by mail, telephone, or both—and then visits to the facilities of two or three carefully selected potential suppliers. As necessary, visits are followed by even more detailed analyses of the most promising suppliers' managerial, quality, and service capabilities. For an extremely difficult purchase, a supplier evaluation conference frequently is held at the buyer's plant to discuss the purchase. From such a discussion, it is usually easy to differentiate among those suppliers who understand the complexities of the purchase and those who do not. By eliminating those who do not, the search for the right supplier is further narrowed.

Preliminary Surveys

If an examination of existing data indicates that a firm appears to be an attractive supplier for existing or anticipated requirements, a telephone or mail survey should be conducted to obtain additional information. Such a survey should provide sufficient knowledge of the supplier to make a decision to include or exclude the firm from further consideration; clearly, this should precede any plant visits. The survey is based on a series of questions which cover

---

[1]Wilbur B. England, *Procurement Principles and Cases,* 5th ed., Richard D. Irwin, Homewood, Ill., 1967, p. 405.

the following areas: the principal officers and titles, bank references, credit references, the annual history of sales and profit for the past five years, a referral list of customers, the number of employees, the space currently occupied, expansion plans (including sources of funds), the current production defect rate for similar products, the number of inspectors used, the date when statistical process control was adopted, and a list of all equipment and tools which would be used to manufacture, test, and inspect the purchase in question.

Financial Condition

Preliminary investigation of a potential supplier's financial condition often can avoid the expense of further study. These investigations are conducted by a qualified buyer or professional from the finance department. A review of financial statements and credit ratings can reveal whether a supplier is clearly *incapable* of performing satisfactorily. Financial stability is essential for suppliers to assure continuity of supply and reliability of product quality. Imagine the difficulty of getting: (1) a financially weak supplier to maintain quality, (2) a supplier who does not have sufficient working capital to settle an expensive claim, or (3) a financially unsound supplier to work overtime to meet a promised delivery date.

In addition to informing a buyer or the sourcing team about a supplier's capability to perform a contract, financial information can be useful in other ways as well. Financially strong firms are usually managerially strong; hence, they generally make good suppliers. An analysis of a firm's balance sheet and operating statement is helpful in numerous ways. For example, on discovering that a firm's financial condition has started to deteriorate, a buyer should tighten quality monitoring and consider either searching for a new supplier or reducing the size of the orders given to the distressed firm. Increasing profit margins alert a professional buyer to the fact that it may be possible to obtain price reductions—if the buyer has the purchasing skills and economic leverage to get such reductions. Falling profit margins may indicate that price rises are probable. In this case, the supplier either is becoming less efficient or is losing sales and working at lower percentages of capacity. In either case, price rises are likely, and they are certain if demand for the product is relatively inelastic.

Integrated firms with ample supplies of raw materials and adequate production equipment and capability make highly desirable suppliers. Even during depressed economic conditions, these firms have to make only minimum cash payments to outsiders; thus, they usually have ample resources available to serve their customers. On the other hand, firms that have to purchase their supplies on a hand-to-mouth basis or lease their buildings and equipment can, even in mild recessions, suffer cash squeezes that can affect quality, service, and prices.

Firms with sound working capital positions—that is, those that have enough cash to purchase required materials, pay employees, and extend credit as necessary to customers—can be particularly desirable suppliers. On the other hand, firms with weak working capital positions may be satisfactory suppliers only when business is good.

Buyers are not expected to be trained financial analysts. However, competent buyers should be able to interpret financial reports and to make intelligent comparisons from them. The financial information buyers routinely need is found in corporate annual reports, 10-K reports, Moody's Industrials, Dun and Bradstreet (D & B) Reports, D & B *Key Business Ratios,* and occasional consultations with a supplier's banker.

Dun and Bradstreet[2] publishes a booklet entitled *Key Business Ratios;* this annual publication is free. For each industry, this booklet cites the fourteen financial ratios that D & B considers most important in determining a firm's credit status. By comparing these ratios with those of the potential suppliers, purchasing can determine which firms are most likely to be reliable or unreliable suppliers, from a financial point of view. For example, a firm that ranks high in its industry on all fourteen ratios should be an outstanding supplier candidate. Conversely, firms ranking low in most of the ratio categories should be avoided. (See Appendix A for financial ratio calculations.)

Quality Capability

A critical factor to examine is the firm's quality capability. If the prospective supplier's process capability is less than the buying firm's incoming quality requirements, the supplier typically is not worthy of further investigation. An obvious exception is the case in which no supplier possesses the required process capability. In this case, the two firms will have to work together to improve the supplier's process capability. This critical issue is discussed in detail in Chapter 21.

Plant Visits

By visiting a supplier's plant or distribution facility, the sourcing team can obtain firsthand information concerning the adequacy of the firm's technological capabilities, manufacturing or distribution capabilities, and its management's technical know-how and orientation. Depending on the importance of the visit, the company may send representatives from only purchasing and engineering; or it may also include some combination of representation from finance, operations, quality assurance, marketing, and industrial relations. Occasionally, top management may also participate in the visit and the evaluation. When the concurrent approach to the design of new products is utilized, appropriate members of the cross-functional team conduct the visit and evaluation. As noted, in this case the timing for such visits is at the earliest stage of the design and development cycle so that the selected supplier(s) can contribute its expertise to the development process.

---

[2]D & B's address is 99 Church Street, New York, N.Y. 10007.

In planning plant visits, only a few outstanding potential suppliers' plants should be chosen for observation due to the time and costs involved. In addition to observing production equipment and operations, there are other compelling reasons for plant visits. It is vital, for example, to determine a supplier's managerial capabilities and motivation to meet contractual obligations. The buying firm wants suppliers whose management is committed to excellence. To make such a determination properly requires an overall appraisal. Among the factors to be addressed are:

- Attitude and stability of the top- and middle-management teams
- R&D capability
- Appropriateness of equipment
- Effectiveness of the production control, quality assurance, and cost control systems
- Competence of the technical and managerial staffs

Other important factors include:

- Morale of personnel at all levels
- Industrial relations
- Willingness of the potential supplier to work with the buying firm
- Quantity of back orders
- Effectiveness of purchasing and supply management and materials management operations

And past performance:

- Past major customers
- General reputation
- Letters of reference

The plant visit should be planned carefully to provide the required level of knowledge and insight into the potential supplier's operations, capacity, and orientation. The efficiency with which the plant visit is planned and conducted reflects on the buying organization. To provide the reader with a sense of the detail in which some plant visits are conducted, one firm's evaluation form is reproduced in Appendix B of this chapter. This evaluative instrument is used by a high-tech firm that utilizes a number of single-source partnering arrangements.

Although it varies with the firm's size and organizational structure, the *initial orientation meeting* typically is attended by the sourcing team members and their management counterparts from the potential supplier's organization. In smaller firms, the president often leads the supplier group. In this session, the sourcing team provides general information and explains the interests of its company: its kind of business, a brief history, kinds of products, the importance of the item(s) to be purchased, and volume, quality, and delivery requirements.

The prospective supplier usually is requested to provide additional information on the company's history, current customers, sales volume, and financial stability. If classified or confidential data might be involved during design and production operations, the sourcing team must review the supplier's security control system.

In the quality area, the buyer and his or her sourcing teammates should attempt to understand the *supplier's attitude* toward quality by asking questions such as: How do you feel about zero defects and total quality management? Are you ISO 9000 certified? Do you employ the design of experiments during new product development? Do you employ statistical process control? Have you adopted a total quality commitment plan? How do you measure customer satisfaction? Show us how you've implemented these concepts. Do you have a quality manual? Copies of the manual and the policy should be reviewed by the buying team's quality representative. The potential supplier also should be asked to describe *its own* supplier quality control program. The more technical aspects of supplier quality are addressed in Chapter 21.

An increasing number of firms, including Motorola and many other leading-edge manufacturers, require that potential suppliers be registered under the appropriate ISO 9000 quality standard(s). It is important that the buyer and members of the sourcing team understand that ISO 9000 is a series of process standards, and that an ISO certificate is not necessarily a guarantee of high product quality.[3]

If the sourcing team is satisfied with the results of the introductory meeting, a tour of the facilities typically is made. Prior to the tour, the sourcing team should get permission to talk freely with various individuals working in the operation, not just hand-picked managers.

The potential supplier's management often assumes that satisfactory operating controls are in place. In reality, however, experience frequently shows that some of these controls may not have been implemented, or that they may have been discontinued. When management describes these things, the sourcing team should respond, "That sounds excellent, we'd like to see them." The team should also check controls by asking such questions as, "How do you ensure that the most current drawing is in use?" "How do you segregate rejected materials?"[4]

As a cross-check on specific information obtained in the initial meeting, perceptive team members often ask shop and staff personnel similar types of questions. When the potential supplier's managers are not present, operating personnel should be asked about *their* understanding of the firm's quality systems, schedules, cost control efforts, and related requirements. Workers can also be asked about working conditions and turnover, about the firm's commitment to quality, about quality tools, and about training.

When observing plant equipment, the sourcing team should determine whether the equipment is modern, whether it is in good operating condition,

---

[3]"Does the ISO 9000 Need Fixing?" Industry Forum Supplement to the June 1994 issue of *Management Review*.

[4]Warren E. Norquist, Director of Worldwide Purchasing and Materials Management, Polaroid Corporation, personal interview, October 1987.

whether tolerances can be held consistently, and what the output rates are. The sourcing team also should look for special modifications or adaptations of equipment; these things often provide clues to the ingenuity of operating management personnel.

The first impression of a supplier's operation is generally obtained through observing the housekeeping of the plant itself. Is it clean and well organized? Are the machines clean? Are the tools, equipment, and benches kept orderly and accessible? Good housekeeping tends to be an indication of efficiency. Many sourcing team members responsible for source selection believe it is reasonable to expect that a firm displaying pride in its facilities and equipment will also take pride in the workmanship that goes into its products.

During the visit, responsible sourcing team members should investigate production methods and efficiencies. Is a just-in-time system utilized to a significant extent? Is material moving freely from storage to production areas? Are there any production bottlenecks? Is the production scheduling and control function organized and functioning well? Is reserve production capacity available? Is it available on a regular or an overtime basis? Does the potential supplier have a competent maintenance crew? And, finally, the sourcing team should determine whether inventory levels for both production materials and finished goods are adequate for the company's needs.

Employee attitudes are extremely important. In the long run, production results often depend more on people than on the physical plant. Do the employees seem to work harmoniously with one another and with their supervisors? Are they interested in quality and in improving the products they make? Is enthusiasm at a reasonable level? In short, do the people take pride in their jobs and in the firm—or do they view it as an eight-to-five clock-punching operation?

Management   Normally, a buyer's first contact with a potential supplier is with a sales representative. A properly trained representative knows his or her product thoroughly, understands the buying firm's requirements, gives useful suggestions to the buyer and appropriate members of the buying team, commits the company to specific delivery promises, and follows through on all orders placed. This type of sales representative indicates that the supplier's firm is directed and managed by responsible and enterprising executives. A well-managed firm seldom experiences the instability that results from continual labor problems and always strives to reduce its cost. Such a company can be a good supplier.

When the buying firm purchases an off-the-shelf item which a supplier has manufactured using its own design and tools, it is primarily buying a *product*. However, when the firm purchases a high-dollar-value item made to its own unique specifications, for which the firm may or may not furnish special, high-cost tooling, *then the buying firm is buying far more than just a supplier's production capability.* Technical competence in itself does not assure that a firm will be a good supplier. Rather, technical competence must be blended with good business management to ensure that a firm has the ability to be a "good source of supply" in the fullest sense of the term.

In the final analysis, it is a firm's *technical ingenuity* and *managerial ability,* coupled with its *financial strength,* that determines how effectively its physical and cash resources will be employed.

Service   "Service" is a term that varies in meaning, depending on the nature of the product being purchased. Specifically, good service always means delivering on time, treating special orders specially, filling back orders promptly, settling disputes quickly and fairly, and informing buyers in advance of impending price changes or developing shortages. In some situations, it means exceptional post-sale service. Service also can include actions such as stocking spare parts for immediate delivery, extending suitable credit arrangements, or warranting the purchased item's quality and performance to a degree beyond that normally required. In the aggregate, good service means that a supplier will take every reasonable action to ensure the smooth flow of purchased materials between the supplying and buying firms.

What kinds of companies can provide the best service? Service is usually measured by a supplier's ability to comply with promised delivery dates, specifications, and technical assistance. How do forward-looking companies feel about the service they expect from their suppliers? A leading valve manufacturer has said, "We want a supplier to do more than simply quote prices from an engineering drawing. We want the supplying firm to know the parts thoroughly, so that it can use specialized knowledge of processing alternative designs and alternative materials to help us cut costs. We make it quite clear that cost-saving ideas can win a contract."

Another firm states its position this way: "We feel our approach in recognizing our specialty suppliers' expert knowledge and letting them work with responsible people in our organization has paid off handsomely. We have effectively expanded our purchasing knowledge and gained experience that might have taken years with another approach."

An electrical company holds the following view concerning specialty suppliers: "Common sense should tell us that they know more about the design and building of their products than we do. So it's only natural for us to draw on their skill and experience in coming up with a better end product of our own."

Just-in-Time Capabilities

When properly implemented, a just-in-time (JIT) system results in the following *supply chain* benefits: reduced inventory, increased quality, reduced lead time, reduced scrap and rework, and reduced equipment downtime.[5] The benefits of JIT protect and enhance the success of firms that embrace it. Unfor-

---

[5]Caron H. St. John and Kirk C. Heriot, "Small Suppliers and JIT Purchasing," *International Journal of Purchasing and Materials Management,* Winter 1993, p. 12.

tunately, too frequently a key prerequisite to successful implementation of such a system is ignored: JIT requires virtually defect-free incoming purchased materials.

Many American manufacturers still operate under a materials manufacturing system which tolerates a 1 to 3 percent defective rate in incoming purchased materials. This level of quality translates to 10,000 to 30,000 defects per million incoming parts. With JIT, often there is no inventory of purchased goods awaiting inspection. There is, at most, a small inventory of purchased goods in the storeroom awaiting manufacture. Typically, there is no more than an hour's supply of items which have been processed through station C waiting to move through work station D. *Inventory is squeezed out of the total system to detect waste, errors, and inefficiencies.*[6] However, it is a common misconception that the objective of JIT is the reduction or elimination of inventory at the buying plant. In fact, under JIT, reductions in inventory *throughout the entire supply chain* are a means of identifying unsound procedures which result in waste.

Defects in purchased materials obviously disrupt such a system and result in lost production. Typically, JIT systems can tolerate incoming defect levels of only 500 or fewer parts per million (PPM). This level of quality has been found to be essential if the using firm is to enjoy the major benefits of JIT.

In addition to requiring virtually defect-free incoming materials, JIT requires a high degree of integration of the customer's and supplier's operations. The inevitable changes in a customer's production plans and schedules affect the supplier's schedules. Experience has demonstrated that dependable, single-source partnerships are virtually essential if the required level of integration is to result.

A firm that is considering the adoption of JIT manufacturing must focus on its suppliers' abilities and willingness to meet the stringent quality and schedule demands imposed by the system. The sourcing team must carefully investigate a potential supplier's capability as a JIT manufacturer. Michael McGrath has identified four stages of a supplier's typical progress into a JIT program. These stages are depicted in Figure 12-1.[7]

The Criticality of Qualifying Sources

By now, the cynical reader probably is thinking, "Come on. Qualifying suppliers can't be this critical or this complex!" A 1983 *Harvard Business Review* article cites the following example which demonstrates that, yes, qualifying sources carefully is essential:

A leading copier manufacturer developed a new machine requiring 1,500 purchased parts, and buyers were given three months to find qualified bidders to supply these

---

[6] JIT systems are discussed extensively in Chapters 22 and 23.
[7] Michael McGrath, "Guidelines for Assessing Supplier JIT Capability," *Electronics Purchasing,* June 1988, p. 37.

SUPPLIER CHARACTERISTICS	STAGE 1 "Exploration"	STAGE 2 "Acceptance"	STAGE 3 "Pilot project"	STAGE 4 "Full implementation"
Overall Measurements:				
Knowledge of concepts	Hazy or no awareness	Understood	Applied	Teachers
Management commitment	Uncommitted	Superficial	Evaluating	Drivers
JIT customers	None	Talks with one or two	Contracts with several	Majority of output
Manufacturing Process:				
Quality programs	Not formalized	Quality circles	PPM targets	Low PPM achieved
Capacity flexibility	Very inflexible	Discussing options	Flexible work force	Flexible automation
Pull mechanisms	Shortage lists	Sales orders	Some Kanbans	All Kanbans
Batch sizes	Monthly to quarterly	2 weeks	Weekly	Daily
JIT purchasing	None	Talking with suppliers	Some JIT	Majority JIT
Supply Process:				
Delivery frequency	Monthly	2 weeks	Weekly to daily	As required
Delivery quality variance	Uncontrolled	5%	1%	Low PPM
Delivery quantity variance	±10%	±5%	±1%	None
Delivery time variance	±Weeks	±Days	±Hours	None

FIGURE 12-1
Chart your supplier's JIT progress.

parts. In an attempt to obtain the lowest costs and still meet delivery schedules, the buyers selected 500 different suppliers. After the buyers had placed the orders, a survey team determined the qualifications of the suppliers making the 30 most critical parts, and [subsequently] reported that only six suppliers could deliver parts consistently manufactured to specification, at the cost quoted. As it turned out, the company required a costly two-year program to correct the problems created during the three-month rush of placing orders without benefit of adequate information about supplier qualifications.

Buyers and purchasing managers are often given unrealistically tight schedules. In addition, they are usually isolated from engineering and quality control staff whose services they frequently need to fulfill their mission of buying at the lowest cost from qualified suppliers. Major problems often arise when buyers try to assess a supplier's qualifications. Some of the information needed requires detailed sampling and analysis of the supplier's manufacturing process, and this has to be done by quality control engineers in close cooperation with the supplier's technical personnel at the supplier's plant.[8]

COMPETITIVE BIDDING AND NEGOTIATION

Once a buyer or the sourcing team has identified the potential suppliers to be invited to submit bids (or proposals), a decision must be made whether to use competitive bidding or negotiation (or a combination of the two) as the basis for source selection. When competitive bidding is used by private industry, requests for bids are traditionally sent to three to eight potential suppliers depending on the dollar size and complexity of the purchase. Requests for bids ask suppliers to quote the price at which they will perform in accordance with the terms and conditions of the contract, should they be the successful bidder. Government buyers generally are not able to restrict the number of bidders to only eight. Rather, all suppliers desiring to bid are permitted to do so (for large purchases, the numbers are literally in the hundreds). Under competitive bidding, industrial buyers generally, *but not always*, award the order to the lowest bidder. By law, government buyers are routinely required to award the order to the lowest bidder, provided the lowest bidder is deemed qualified to perform the contract.

Five Prerequisites

The proper use of competitive bidding is dictated by five criteria. When all five criteria prevail, competitive bidding is an efficient method of source selection and pricing. The criteria are:

1 The dollar value of the specific purchase must be large enough to justify the expense, to both buyer and seller, that accompanies this method of source selection and pricing.
2 The specifications of the item or service to be purchased must be explicitly clear to both buyer and seller. In addition, the seller must know from actual previous experience, or be able to estimate accurately from similar past experience, the cost of producing the item or rendering the service.
3 The market must consist of an adequate number of sellers.
4 The sellers that make up the market must be technically qualified and *actively want* the contract—and, therefore, be willing to price competitively to get it. Frequently, criteria 1, 2, and 3 prevail, yet there is no real competition because the sellers are not anxious to bid. Backlogs of work in some potential suppliers' plants may prevent competition. Under such circumstances, additional orders would entail overtime operation and its

---

[8]Jack Reddy and Abe Berger, "Three Essentials of Product Quality," *Harvard Business Review*, July–August 1983, pp. 157–158.

attendant problems of scheduling difficulties and premium wage payment. Under such circumstances, if bids are made at all, they are at prices
that include numerous contingencies.

5 The time available must be sufficient for using this method of pricing—
suppliers competing for large contracts must be allowed time to obtain
and evaluate bids from their subcontractors before they can calculate
their best price. Bidders must also have time to perform the necessary
cost analysis required within their own organization and to assure themselves of reliable sources of materials. The time required for preparing,
mailing, opening, and evaluating bids is usually considerably longer than
those unfamiliar with this system would expect. Thirty days is not an
uncommon time.

Four Conditions When Competitive Bidding Should Not Be Used

In addition to satisfying the preceding five prerequisites, four other conditions
should *not* be present when employing competitive bidding as the means of
source selection:

1 Situations in which it is impossible to estimate costs with a high degree of
certainty. Such situations frequently are present with high-technology
requirements, with items requiring a long time to develop and produce,
and under conditions of economic uncertainty.

2 Situations in which price is not the only important variable. For example,
quality, schedule, and service may well be negotiable variables of equal
importance.

3 Situations in which the purchasing firm anticipates a need to make
changes in the specification or some other aspect of the purchase contract.
When unscrupulous suppliers anticipate changes, they may "buy in"
with the expectation of "getting well" (and even wealthy) on the resulting changes.

4 Situations in which special tooling or setup costs are major factors. The
allocation of such costs and title to the special tooling are issues best
resolved through negotiation.

If these nine conditions are satisfied, then competitive bidding usually will
result in the lowest price and is the most efficient method of source selection.
To ensure that the lowest prices are obtained, the competing firms must be
assured that the firm submitting the low bid will receive the award. If the purchasing firm gains a reputation for negotiating with the lowest bidders *after*
bids are opened, then future bidders will tend *not* to offer their best prices initially, believing that they may do better in any subsequent negotiations. They
will adopt a strategy of submitting a bid low enough to allow them to be
included in any negotiations. But their initial bid will not be as low as when

they are confident that the award will be made to the low bidder without further negotiation.[9]

When all these prerequisites to the use of competitive bidding are not satisfied, the *negotiation process* should be employed to select sources and to arrive at a price.

Several progressive purchasing and supply management professionals offer two additional arguments which favor the use of negotiation over competitive bidding for critical procurements:

1 The negotiation process is far more likely to lead to a complete understanding of all issues of the procurement. This improved understanding greatly reduces subsequent quality and schedule problems.
2 Competitive bidding tends to put great pressure on suppliers to reduce their costs in order to be able to bid a low (but profitable) price. This cost pressure may result in sacrifices in product quality, development efforts, and other vital services.

Normally the competitive bidding system itself, when all the prerequisite criteria prevail, evaluates quite accurately the many pricing factors bearing on the purchase being made. These factors include determinants such as supplier production efficiency, willingness of the seller to price this particular contract at a low profit level, the financial effect on the seller of shortages of capital or excesses of inventories, errors in the seller's sales forecast, and competitive conditions in general.

Because the proper uses of competitive bidding appear to be widely misunderstood, this system of pricing is frequently abused by both industry and government. Government officials, because of political pressures from Congress, tend to overuse competitive bidding. The reason for such behavior is easily understood. By stressing competitive bidding as the best method of pricing, and by allowing all constituents the opportunity to compete, regardless of their qualifications, politicians can avoid disputes with their constituents. When competitive bidding is used in industry, too often buyers hold steadfastly to the unsound premise that purchasing judgment is not required. In reality, however, planning the preliminaries correctly for competitive bidding takes purchasing judgment of the highest order.

If the preliminary planning of tight specifications, proper selection of competing suppliers, correct quantities, precise delivery schedules, adequate time for placing bids, and general economic analysis is done correctly, selecting the successful bidder after the bids are evaluated is generally a routine matter. Except in unusual circumstances, the low bidder should receive the order. Purchasing judgment and analytical planning should normally be exercised *before* competitive bids are requested, not after the bids are in.

---

[9]On occasion, a buyer may intend to use the initial proposal solicitation process to identify firms with which he or she plans to conduct follow-on negotiations. In this case, professional ethics as well as good business judgment dictate that the initial solicitation state clearly that follow-on negotiations will be conducted.

The general belief that adequate competition is a sound method of obtaining the right source and price is correct. However, the belief that competitive bidding assures adequate competition is wrong. Competitive bidding assures adequate competition and the right price only when the mandatory five criteria for this method of pricing prevail and the four cited situations are not present. Too often industry and government alike err in using competitive bidding to buy highly technical products with vague specifications. This practice inevitably leads to faulty cost estimates and contingency pricing. The contingency pricing on the part of suppliers is the result of the poor purchasing judgment of the buying firm, which is guilty of incorrectly using a good and effective purchasing tool under inappropriate circumstances. It is also an error to use competitive bidding for purchases involving high engineering, setup, and testing costs.

Buyers must remember that sellers frequently will bid on any product or service they are asked to bid on. It is not the seller's responsibility to tell a buyer that the wrong method of source selection and pricing is being used. However, if sellers do not have adequate cost information, do not fully understand the specifications, or already have large backlogs, they will factor into their bid prices contingencies for labor costs, materials costs, and all other possible costs they can think of. For example, if a supplier is not sure how many hours it will take to complete a job, its bid may be based on the estimated maximum number of hours. Sellers are not at fault for making high competitive bids to protect themselves just because buyers are naive enough to use an incorrect method of source selection and price determination. Caveat emptor! (Buyer beware!) To buy wisely is the buyer's responsibility. Competitive bidding improperly used is not buying wisely. Competitive bidding properly used is an excellent method of selecting the right source and obtaining a fair price. Generally speaking, this method of sourcing and pricing is most applicable to highly standardized products that are widely used and produced abundantly for stock by many manufacturers and for standard services.

Two-Step Bidding/Negotiation

On occasion, large, technically oriented firms and the federal government use a modified type of competitive bidding called "two-step bidding." This method of source selection and pricing is used in situations where *inadequate specifications* preclude the initial use of traditional competitive bidding. In the first step, bids are requested only for technical proposals, without any prices. Bidders are requested to set forth in their proposals the technical details describing how they would produce the required materials, products, or services. After these technical bids are evaluated and it is determined which proposals are technically satisfactory, the second step follows.

In the second step, requests for bids are sent only to those sellers who submitted acceptable technical proposals in the first step. These sellers now compete for the business on a price basis, as they would in any routine, competitive-bidding situation. The price is determined in either of two ways: (1) Award may be based solely on the lowest price received from those competing, or (2) the price proposals for the accepted technical approaches may be used as the beginning point for *negotiations*. It is important that the buyer specify *at the outset* which of the two procedures will be used.

THE SOLICITATION

Once a decision has been made whether to use competitive bidding or negotiation as the means of selecting the source, an *invitation for bids (IFB)* or a *request for proposal (RFP)* is prepared. The IFB or RFP normally consists of a purchase description of the item or service required, information on quantities, required delivery schedules, special terms and conditions, and standard terms and conditions. The legal implications of these documents and processes are discussed in Chapter 30.

When an RFP is used in anticipation of cost negotiations with one or more suppliers, the buyer should request appropriate cost data in support of the price proposal. The buyer must also obtain the right of access to the supplier's cost records that are required to support the reasonableness of the proposal. *The cost data and the right of access must be established during the RFP phase of the procurement, at a time potential suppliers believe that there is active competition for the job.* Details of the negotiation process are explored in Chapter 17.

SELECTING THE SOURCE

In many instances, one prospective supplier is obviously superior to its competition—and selection is a very simple matter. Unfortunately, though, the choice is not always so clear. In these cases, a numerical weighted-factor rating system can greatly facilitate the decision process.

A weighted-factor system calls for two activities: (1) the development of factors (selection criteria) and weights and (2) the assignment of ratings. The first step, identification of the key factors to be considered in the selection decision, along with their respective weights, typically is accomplished by a committee of individuals involved in the purchase (individuals from operations, design, and purchasing). An illustration of the approach is shown in Table 12-1.

Step 2 requires the assignment of numerical ratings for each of the competing firms. These assessments are based on the collective judgments of the evaluators after studying all the data and information provided by the potential suppliers, as well as that obtained in field investigations.

In effect, a weighted-factor rating system breaks a complex problem down into its key components and permits analysis of each component individually. The approach is widely used in practice and generally leads to a fair and reasonably objective result.

TABLE 12-1
AN ILLUSTRATION OF THE WEIGHTED-FACTOR RATING APPROACH

Factors	Maximum rating (weights)	Supplier		
		A	B	C
Technical:				
Understanding of the problem	10	9	9	7
Technical approach	20	19	16	16
Production facilities	5	4	5	3
Operator requirements	3	2	3	2
Maintenance requirements	2	2	2	2
Total	40	36	35	30
Ability to meet schedule	20	20	16	15
Price	20	16	20	15
Managerial, financial, and technical capability	10	10	8	8
Quality control processes	10	9	8	9
Rating total	100	91	87	77

CONCLUSION

The procurement process has four major components. One of the most crucial is the selection of the right source. The right source provides the right quality, on time, at the right price, and with the right level of service.

Selection of the right source is more important today than ever before, since more firms are entering into long-term partnerships with a single source of supply. The benefits of such partnerships are many, but the risks are great. Careful selection of suppliers and the professional management of the relationships are essential.

FOR DISCUSSION

12-1 What are the advantages of using commodity teams for source selection and management?

12-2 What types of competition may be desired during source selection?

12-3 What factors affect the type of evaluation to be employed?

12-4 In what ways is an analysis of the potential supplier's financial condition useful?

12-5 Where can the required financial data be located?

12-6 When should a plant visit be made? Who should make the visit?

12-7 What information should be shared during the introductory meeting phase of a plant visit?

12-8 What are the reasons for conducting a tour of the supplier's facilities? What areas typically receive more attention?

12-9 How does buying a standard product differ from buying a high-dollar-value item made to the firm's own unique specification?

12-10 Define and discuss your concept of service.

12-11 How does just-in-time manufacturing affect source selection? What are the implications for inventory reduction under JIT?

12-12 What are the five prerequisites to using competitive bidding? Under what four conditions should competitive bidding not be employed?

12-13 Purchasing professionals offer two arguments in favor of the use of negotiation over competitive bidding for critical procurements. Describe and discuss these two arguments.

12-14 Describe the abuses of competitive bidding by both government and industry. Discuss a major misconception that many buyers have about competitive bidding.

12-15 Does competitive bidding assure adequate competition? Explain your answer.

12-16 Describe two-step bidding. When is it used?

12-17 What extra requirement should a buyer impose when an RFP is used in anticipation of cost negotiations? Discuss.

12-18 Describe the weighted-factor rating system approach to source selection.

CASES FOR CHAPTER 12

Collier Company I, page 800
Selection of a Pressure Vessel Manufacturer, page 905
Sampson Products Corporation, page 901
Lion Industries, page 844
Microcomp, Inc., page 850
Pegasus Technologies, page 881
Black Motor Company (in the *Instructor's Manual*)
Great Western University (in the *Instructor's Manual*)
Alpha Omega Corporation (in the *Instructor's Manual*)

APPENDIX A:
FINANCIAL STATEMENT ANALYSIS*

The following information is useful during preliminary sourcing. These ratios and measures are useful for analyzing company-specific trends and for making comparisons among competing suppliers. Comparative data for specific industries may be obtained from Dun and Bradstreet or Robert Morris Associates.

Liquidity Measures Liquidity refers to a company's ability to pay its bills when they are due and to provide for unanticipated cash requirements. In general, poor liquidity measures imply short-run credit problems. From a supply-management perspective, short-run credit problems could signal possible decreases in quality or difficulties in meeting scheduled deliveries. Three common liquidity measures are:

*This Appendix was prepared by Donn W. Vickrey of the University of San Diego.

1 **Working capital** = Current assets – Current liabilities

Working capital measures the amount of current assets that would remain if all current liabilities were paid.

2 **Current ratio** $= \dfrac{\text{Current assets}}{\text{Current liabilities}}$

The current ratio is a standardized measure of liquidity. In general, the higher the ratio the more protection a company has against liquidity problems. However, the ratio can be distorted by seasonal influences and abnormal payments on accounts payable made at the end of the period.

3 **Quick ratio** $= \dfrac{\text{Quick assets}}{\text{Current liabilities}}$

The quick ratio is a standardized measure of liquidity in which only assets that can be converted to cash quickly (e.g., cash, accounts receivable, and marketable securities) are included in the calculation.

Funds Management Ratios   The financial position of a company depends on how it manages key assets such as accounts receivable, inventory, and fixed assets. As a business grows, the associated expansion of these items can lead to significant cash shortages—even for companies that maintain profitable operations. As implied previously, short-term cash problems may signal future decreases in quality or delays in scheduled deliveries. Six frequently used measures of funds management are:

1 **Receivables to sales** $= \dfrac{\text{Accounts receivable (net)}}{\text{Sales}}$

In the absence of detailed credit information, the receivables-to-sales ratio can be used to analyze trends in a company's credit policy.

2 **Average collection period** $= \dfrac{\text{Accounts receivable}}{\text{Sales}} \times 365$

The average collection period is used to assess the quality of a company's receivables. The average collection period may be assessed in relation to the company's own credit terms or to the typical credit terms of firms in its industry.

3 **Average accounts payable period** $= \dfrac{\text{Accounts payable}}{\text{Purchases}} \times 365$

The average accounts payable period is used to assess how well a firm manages its payables. If the average days payable is increasing, or large in relation to the credit terms offered by the company's suppliers, it may signal that trade credit is being used as a source of funds.

4 **Inventory turnover** $= \dfrac{\text{Cost of goods sold}}{\text{Average inventory}}$

The inventory-turnover ratio indicates how fast inventory items move through a business.

5 **Average days in inventory** $= \dfrac{365}{\text{Inventory turnover}}$

The average days in inventory is a simple conversion of the turnover ratio to a more intuitive measure of inventory management.

6 Fixed asset turnover $= \dfrac{\text{Sales}}{\text{Average fixed assets}}$

net sales/average net fixed assets. The fixed asset turnover provides a crude measure of how well a firm's investment in plant and equipment is managed relative to the sales volume it supports. Unfortunately, interpreting the fixed asset turnover ratio is not always a straightforward proposition. For example, a decrease in the firm's turnover ratio could result from poor management of fixed assets *or* from an investment in new technology (e.g., computer integrated manufacturing).

Profitability Measures   Profitability refers to the ability of a firm to earn positive cash flows and to generate a satisfactory return on shareholders' investments. Profitability measures provide an indication of a firm's long-term viability. Profitability measures may be used to infer quality in the sense that, to generate a satisfactory return, a firm must ensure that it provides quality products from year to year. Profitability measures may also be used, to some extent, to infer a company's pricing policies. Thus, they may be useful for negotiating contract prices and, in particular, the profit portion of such prices.

1 Profit margin $= \dfrac{\text{Net income}}{\text{Sales}}$

The profit margin percentage measures the amount of net income earned on a dollar of sales.

2 Gross profit margin $= \dfrac{\text{Gross margin}}{\text{Sales}}$

The gross margin percentage measures the gross profit earned on each dollar of sales. Thus, this ratio may be used to infer the typical markup percentage used by a supplier.

3 Return on assets $= \dfrac{\text{Net income}}{\text{Average total assets}}$

Return on investment measures how efficiently assets are used to produce income.

4 Return on equity $= \dfrac{\text{Net income}}{\text{Average stockholders' equity}}$

Return on equity measures the percentage return on the stockholders' average investment.

Measures of Long-Term Financial Strength   The ability to deliver quality products over time is contingent on the long-term financial strength of the supplier. Difficulties meeting long-term obligations may also signal insolvency. The disruptions caused by insolvency can cause major delays in shipments, decreases in quality, or complete inability to perform.

1 Debt to equity $= \dfrac{\text{Total liabilities}}{\text{Stockholders' equity}}$

Since debt requires periodic interest payments and eventual repayment, it is inherently more risky than equity. The debt-to-equity ratio measures the proportion of the company that is financed by creditors relative to the proportion financed by stockholders.

2 Times interest earned $= \dfrac{\text{Operating profit before interest}}{\text{Interest on long-term debt}}$

The times-interest-earned ratio measures the extent to which a company's operating profits cover its interest payments. A low times-interest-earned ratio may signal difficulties in meeting long-term financial obligations.

APPENDIX B:
ILLUSTRATIVE PLANT SURVEY

After conducting preliminary surveys of potential suppliers of critical materials, equipment, or services, it frequently is desirable to conduct a plant visit to the one or two most attractive candidates. The purpose of such visits is to gain firsthand knowledge of the supplier's facilities, personnel, and operations. Such a visit normally is conducted by a team from the purchasing firm. Each member will study his or her area of expertise at the potential supplier's operation.

The plant survey shown in Figure 12-2 is used by one high-tech manufacturer. The evaluation form calls for yes or no answers to specific questions and evaluation ratings for all questions, asking the team member to evaluate how well the supplier is doing in a given area. The evaluation ratings are described below.

Rating	Description
10	The provisions or conditions are extensive and function is excellent.
9	The provisions or conditions are moderately extensive and function is excellent.
8	The provisions or conditions are extensive and are functioning well.
6/7	The provisions or conditions are moderately extensive and are functioning well.
4/5	The provisions or conditions are limited in extent but are functioning well.
2/3	The provisions or conditions are moderately extensive but are functioning poorly.
1	The provisions or conditions are limited in extent and are functioning poorly.
0	The provisions or conditions are missing but needed.

Assume that the purchasing firm's quality assurance (Q.A.) manager is rating a potential supplier on the sections entitled Quality Management (pages 262-263) and Quality Information (pages 263–264). When these phases of the study are complete, the Q.A. manager is in a position to assign an average or overall rating for Quality Management on the first sheet of the survey (page 259).

Such an evaluation is used in at least two ways: (1) It now is possible to compare competitors' operations, with major emphasis on quality, and (2) actual or potential problem areas for an otherwise attractive supplier may be identified. The purchasing firm then may require that the area of concern be corrected or upgraded before award, or as a condition of award.

Company Name _____

Address _____

Phone _____

Management Officials:

Name   Position

_____   _____

_____   _____

_____   _____

_____   _____

_____   _____

Type of Manufacturing Service or Products:

_____

_____

FACILITIES

Employee breakdown:

Total plant area, sq. ft. _____   Design engineering _____

Number of buildings _____   Manufacturing engineering _____

Type of buildings _____   Research and development _____

Total number of employees _____   Purchasing _____

Sales volume $ _____

OVERALL RATINGS

Design Information   ( )   Quality Information   ( )

Procurement   ( )   Calibration   ( )

Material Control   ( )   Inspection of Completed Material   ( )

Manufacturing Control   ( )   Final Acceptance   ( )

Quality Management   ( )

Work Schedule

Hours _____ Shifts _____ Days Work _____

Percent of present production to full capacity _____%

Condition of production equipment _____

Report prepared by _____ Title _____ Date _____

FIGURE 12-2
Plant survey.

DESIGN INFORMATION

Control of design and manufacturing information is essential for the control of product. It consists of making sure that operating personnel are furnished with complete technical instructions for the manufacture and inspection of the product. This information includes drawings, specifications, special purchase order requirements, engineering change information, inspection instructions, processing instructions, and other special information. A positive recall system is usually considered necessary to ensure against use of superseded or obsolete information.

How well do procedures cover the release, change, and recall of design and
manufacturing information, including correlation of customer specifications, and how well are procedures followed?   (   )
How well do records reflect the incorporation of changes?   (   )
How well does quality control verify that changes are incorporated at the
effective points?   (   )
Is the design of experiments employed to ensure robust designs prior to the
release of designs to manufacturing and purchasing and supply manage-
ment?   (   )
How well is the control of design and manufacturing information applied to
the procurement activity?   (   )
Is there a formal deviation procedure, and how well is it followed?   (   )
Does your company have a written system for incorporating customer
changes into shop drawings?   (Y/N)
Does your company have a reliability department?   (Y/N)
Are reliability data used in developing new designs?   (Y/N)
Is quality history fed back to engineering for improvements in current or
future designs?   (Y/N)
Does Q.A. review new designs?   (Y/N)
Does your company have a sample or prototype department?   (Y/N)
Does Q.A. review sample prototypes?   (Y/N)
Is this information used in developing shop inspection instructions?   (Y/N)
Are customer specifications interpreted into shop specifications?   (Y/N)
Do drawings and specifications accompany purchase orders to suppliers?   (Y/N)
Are these reviewed by Q.A.?   (Y/N)
Are characteristics classified on the engineering documents as to impor-
tance?   (Y/N)
Does Q.A. review new drawings with the intent of designing gauging
fixtures?   (Y/N)

PROCUREMENT—CONTROL OF PURCHASED MATERIAL

It is essential for the assurance of quality that outside suppliers meet the standards for quality imposed on the firm's own operations department. Sources should be under continuous control or surveillance. Incoming material should be inspected to the extent necessary to assure that the requirements have been met.

How well are potential suppliers evaluated and monitored?   (   )
How well are quality requirements specified?   (   )
How well are inspection procedures specified, and how well are they fol-
lowed?   (   )

How adequate are inspection facilities and equipment? ( )
Have you certified (approved) key suppliers' design manufacturing and
quality processes so that their shipments to you do not require inspection
and testing? ( )
How adequate are "certifications" which are used in lieu of inspection? ( )
How well are certifications evaluated by independent checking? ( )
How well are inspection results used for corrective action? ( )
Do you have an incoming inspection department? (Y/N)
(If yes, list personnel) Inspectors _____ Supervisory _____
Quality Engineers _____
Are purchase orders made available to incoming inspection? (Y/N)
Is there a system for keeping shop drawings up-to-date? (Y/N)
Are written inspection instructions available? (Y/N)
Is sample inspection used? (Y/N)
Is gauging equipment calibrated periodically? (Y/N)
Is gauging equipment correlated with suppliers' equipment? (Y/N)
Are suppliers' test records used for acceptance? (Y/N)
Are commercial test records used for acceptance? (Y/N)
Is material identified to physical and chemical test reports? (Y/N)
Are records kept to show acceptance and rejection of incoming material? (Y/N)
Does your company have a supplier rating system? (Y/N)
Is it made available to the purchasing department? (Y/N)
Is the supplier notified of nonconforming material? (Y/N)
Does your company have an approved supplier list? (Y/N)
Does your company survey supplier facilities? (Y/N)
Does the incoming inspection department have adequate storage space to
hold material until it is inspected? (Y/N)
Is nonconforming material identified as such? (Y/N)
Is nonconforming material held in a specific area until disposition can be
made? (Y/N)
Who is responsible for making disposition of nonconforming material? _____

MATERIAL CONTROL

Control of the identity and quality status of material in-stores and in-process is essential. It is not enough that the right materials be procured and verified; they must be identified and controlled in a manner that will assure they are also properly used. The entire quality program may be compromised if adequate controls are not maintained throughout procurement, storage, manufacturing, and inspection.

How adequate are procedures for storage, release, and movement of material, and how well are they followed? ( )
How well are incoming materials quarantined while under test? ( )
How well are materials in-stores identified and controlled? ( )
How well are in-process materials identified and controlled? ( )
How well are materials in inspection identified and controlled? ( )
How adequate are storage areas and facilities? ( )
How well is access to material controlled? ( )
How well do procedures cover the prevention of corrosion, deterioration, or
damage of material and finished goods? How well are they followed? ( )
How well are nonconforming items identified, isolated, and controlled? ( )

MANUFACTURING CONTROL

In-process inspection, utilizing the techniques of quality control, is one of the most satisfactory methods yet devised for attaining quality of product during manufacture. Because many quality characteristics cannot be evaluated in the end product, it is imperative that they be achieved and verified during the production process.

How well are process capabilities established and maintained?	( )
How well is in-process inspection specified? How effectively is it performed?	( )
How adequate are inspection facilities and equipment?	( )
How well are the results of in-process inspection used in the promotion of effective corrective action?	( )
How adequate are equipment and facilities maintained? How adequate are housekeeping procedures, and how well are they followed?	( )
Does your company have a process inspection function?	(Y/N)
(If yes, list on a separate sheet inspectors, supervisory and quality engineering personnel.)	
To whom does process inspection report? _____	
Are inspection stations located in the production area?	(Y/N)
Are shop drawings and specifications available to inspection?	(Y/N)
Is there a system for keeping the documents up-to-date?	(Y/N)
Are written inspection instructions available?	(Y/N)
Is there a system for reviewing and updating inspection instructions?	(Y/N)
Is sample inspection used?	(Y/N)
Do production workers inspect their own work?	(Y/N)
Are inspection records kept on file?	(Y/N)
Is inspection equipment calibrated periodically?	(Y/N)
Is all material identified (route tags, etc.)?	(Y/N)
Is defective material identified as such?	
Is defective material segregated from good material until disposition is made?	(Y/N) (Y/N)
Are first production parts inspected before a job can be run?	(Y/N)
Is corrective action taken to prevent the recurrence of defective material?	(Y/N)
Who is responsible for making disposition of nonconforming material?	

Does your company use:

X-bar and R charts?	(Y/N)
Process capability studies?	(Y/N)
Are standards calibrated by an outside source that certifies traceability to NBS?	(Y/N)
Are standards calibrated directly by NBS?	(Y/N)
Are packaged goods checked for proper packaging?	(Y/N)

QUALITY MANAGEMENT

The key to the management of quality lies in philosophy, objectives, and organization structure. The philosophy forms the primary policy and should include the broad principles common to good-quality programs. The objectives should be clearly stated in specific terms and should provide operating policies which guide the activity of the quality program. The organizational structure should clearly define lines of authority and responsibility for quality from top management down to the operating levels.

Does the potential supplier embrace total quality management?   (   )
How adequate is the quality philosophy, and how well is it explained in
   operating policies and procedures?   (   )
How adequate is the technical competence in the quality discipline of
   those responsible for assuring quality?   (   )
How well does the organizational structure define quality responsibility
   and authority?   (   )
How well does the organizational structure provide access to top manage-
   ment?   (   )
How adequate is the documentation and dissemination of quality control
   procedures?   (   )
How adequate is the training program, including employee records?   (   )
The quality department reports to:
Name _____ Position _____
Other functions reporting at the same level are _____
Does the quality department have:
   Written quality policy and procedures manual?   (Y/N)
   Written inspection instructions?   (Y/N)
   A quality engineering department?   (Y/N)
   Person or persons who perform vendor surveys?   (Y/N)
   Incoming inspection department?   (Y/N)
   In-process inspection department?   (Y/N)
   Final inspection department?   (Y/N)
   A quality audit function?   (Y/N)
   A gauge control program?   (Y/N)
   A gauge control laboratory?   (Y/N)
   Other quality laboratories?   (Y/N)
     (If yes, specify type) _____
   A quality cost program?   (Y/N)
   A reliability department?   (Y/N)
To whom does the inspection department report? _____
Who is responsible for analyzing customer complaints and goods
   returned for defective quality? _____
Does the quality department use statistical tools (control charts, sampling   (Y/N)
   plans, etc.)?
Explain _____
Is government source inspection available to your plant?
Resident _____ Itinerant _____ No _____

QUALITY INFORMATION

Records should be maintained of all inspections performed, and the data should be periodically analyzed and used as a basis for action. Quality data should always be used, whether it be to improve the quality control operation by increasing or decreasing the amount of inspection, to improve the quality of product by the initiation of corrective action on processes or suppliers, to document certifications of product quality furnished to customers, or to report quality results and trends to management. Unused or unusual data are evidence of poor management.

How well are records of inspections maintained?   (   )
How adequate is the record and sample retention program?   (   )
How well are quality data used as a basis for action?   (   )
How well are quality data used in supporting certification of quality fur-
   nished to customers?   (   )
How well is customer and field information used for corrective action?   (   )
How well is it reported to management?   (   )

CALIBRATION—INSPECTION AND TESTING

Periodic inspection and calibration of certain tools, gauges, tests, and some items of process control equipment are necessary for the control and verification of product quality. Controlled standards, periodically checked or referenced against national standards, will assure the compatibility of vendor and vendee measurements. Inaccurate gauges and testers can compromise the entire quality control program and may result in either rejection of good material or acceptance of defective material.

How well do internal standards conform to national standards or customer
   standards?   (   )
How well are periodic inspections and calibrations specified?   (   )
How adequate are calibration facilities and equipment?   (   )
If necessary, is traceability to NBS adequate?   (Y/N)
If external calibration sources are utilized, how adequate is the program and
   how well is it executed?   (   )
Does your company have a gauge control function?   (Y/N)
   (If yes, list personnel.)
Does your company have written instructions for operating inspection and
   test instruments?   (Y/N)
Are all inspection instruments calibrated at periodic intervals?   (Y/N)
Are records of calibration kept on file?   (Y/N)
Is there a system to recall inspection instruments when they are due for cal-
   ibration?   (Y/N)
Are the inspection instruments used by production calibrated?   (Y/N)
If so, are these instruments removed from use until they can be repaired or
   recalibrated?   (Y/N)
Are shop masters calibrated at periodic intervals to secondary standards
   traceable to NBS?   (Y/N)

INSPECTION OF COMPLETED MATERIAL

Does your company have a final inspection function?   (Y/N)
   (If yes, list inspection, supervisory, and quality engineers on a separate
   sheet.)
To whom does the final inspection department report?_____

Are shop drawings and specifications available to inspection? (Y/N)
Is there a system for keeping the documents up-to-date? (Y/N)
Are written inspection instructions available? (Y/N)
Is there a system for reviewing and updating inspection instructions? (Y/N)
Is sample inspection used? (Y/N)
Are inspection records kept on file? (Y/N)
Are records of inspection results used for corrective-action purposes? (Y/N)
Is inspection equipment calibrated periodically? (Y/N)
Is all material identified (route tags, etc.)? (Y/N)
Is defective material identified as such? (Y/N)
Is defective material segregated from good material until disposition is
  made? (Y/N)
Is reworked material submitted for reinspection? (Y/N)
Who is responsible for making disposition of nonconforming material? _____

FINAL ACCEPTANCE

Final inspection, testing, and packing are critical operations necessary to assure the acceptability of material. The specifications must form the basis for these activities. And to the extent that certifications or in-process inspections are used, in lieu of final inspection, records of those activities should be reviewed to verify conformance.

How well are specifications used in determining the acceptability of mate-
  rial? (   )
How well are certifications and in-process inspection records used in the
  final acceptance decisions? (   )
How adequate are inspection procedures? How well are they followed? (   )
How adequate are inspection facilities and equipment? (   )
How well are inspection results used for corrective action? (   )
How adequate are packing and order-checking procedures? How well are
  they followed? (   )

13

INTERNATIONAL/GLOBAL SOURCING

Boundaries are shrinking and disappearing, and what's becoming apparent is that global purchasing and domestic purchasing are flowing, blending, and converging into one stream.

R. Jerry Baker[1]

Operating in an increasingly interconnected world, leading companies perceive competition as global and are moving to implement an integrated strategy worldwide. Global competitors are learning to develop and manufacture products that can be introduced and marketed simultaneously in many countries. In doing so, they are sourcing technology, materials, and components from sites and suppliers located throughout the world.

Carl R. Frear, Lynn E. Metcalf, and Mary S. Alguire[2]

---

[1]Baker, "The World, A Bigger Place," *NAPM Insights*, July 1993, p. 2.
[2]Frear, Metcalf, and Alguire, "Offshore Sourcing: Its Nature and Scope," *International Journal of Purchasing and Materials Management*, Summer 1992, p. 2.

KEY CONCEPTS

- The benefits and risks of international and global sourcing
    Why purchase international goods and service?
    Problems associated with international procurement
    Common definitions
- Starting an international/global sourcing program
- Supply channels
    International intermediaries
    International procurement offices
    Direct purchasing
- Identifying potential international suppliers
- Qualifying potential international suppliers
- Preparing for direct relations
    Intercultural preparation
    Interpreters
    Technical and commercial analysis
- Currency and payment issues
    Currency
    Letters of credit
- Recent international developments
    The European Community
    The North American Free Trade Agreement (NAFTA)
- Countertrade
- Internationalization of the procurement process

Purchasing products and services of foreign origin can be extraordinarily challenging. On the one hand, virtually all of the practices and procedures described in this book are applicable. At the same time, many new issues must be addressed if a sourcing team is to ensure that its organization receives the right quality, in the right quantity, on time, with the right services, at the right price.

In recent years, the term "foreign sourcing" has largely been replaced with "international sourcing": the process of purchasing from suppliers outside of the firm's country of manufacture. At a number of leading firms, international sourcing is being replaced with a broader international approach called "global sourcing." Professors Monczka and Trent define global sourcing as "the integration and coordination of requirements across worldwide business units, looking at common items, processes, technologies, and suppliers."[3]

[3]Robert M. Monczka and Robert J. Trent, "Global Sourcing: A Development Approach," *International Journal of Purchasing and Materials Management*, Spring 1991, p. 3.

THE BENEFITS AND RISKS OF INTERNATIONAL SOURCING

Why Purchase International Goods and Services?

International sourcing requires additional efforts when compared with domestic sourcing, but it can yield large rewards. One of the complexities of buying goods and services of foreign origin is the wide variability among the producing countries in characteristics such as quality, service, and dependability. Quality, for example, may be very high in products from one country but inconsistent or unacceptably low in products from a neighboring land. With this caveat in mind, let us look at six common reasons for purchasing goods and services from international sources.

Quality   Discussions with purchasing managers lead to a surprising conclusion: a key reason for international sourcing is to obtain the required level of quality. Although this factor is declining in significance, buyers in a variety of industries still look to international sources to fulfill their most critical quality requirements.

Timeliness   A second major reason for purchasing international goods and services is, in general, the dependability of the supplier in meeting schedule requirements. Once initial difficulties of the new business relationship have been overcome, many international sources have proved to be remarkably dependable. In this area, too, the performance of American suppliers has improved markedly during the last several years and, in all likelihood, will continue to become more reliable and more service-oriented. The growing use of flexible manufacturing systems and the increasing use of tightly controlled production planning systems, as discussed in Chapter 22, should enable American firms to equal or exceed the performance of many of their foreign competitors in the near future.

Cost   International sourcing generates expenses beyond those normally encountered when sourcing domestically. For example, additional communications and transportation expenses, import duties, greater costs when investigating the potential supplier's capabilities (see Chapter 12), and so forth, all add to the buying firm's total costs. To illustrate the point, one major computer manufacturer uses a rule of thumb that a foreign material's price must be at least 20 percent lower than the comparable domestic price to compensate for these additional costs. *Nonetheless,* after all of the additional costs of "buying international" are considered, in the case of many materials it frequently is possible to reduce the firm's *total cost* of the material through international sourcing.

Product and Process Technologies   No country holds a monopoly on new technology. International sources in some industries are more advanced technologically than their domestic counterparts. Not to take advantage of such product or process technologies can result in a manufacturer's losing its competitive position vis-á-vis manufacturers that incorporate the new technologies.

Broadening the Supply Base   Professional buyers want to develop and maintain an adequate supply base for required materials. It may be necessary to develop international suppliers in order to have a competitive supply base. In some cases, there may not be a qualified domestic source.

Countertrade   Many countries require their nondomestic suppliers to purchase materials in their country as part of the sales transaction. These arrangements commonly are called barter, offsets, or countertrade. The tying of *sales into a country* with *the purchase of goods from that country* makes both marketing and procurement far more challenging than when pure monetary transactions are involved. For a firm to compete and make sales in many countries, increasingly it is necessary to enter into agreements to purchase items made in those countries. This topic is discussed in greater detail on pages 289 to 293.

Problems Associated with International Procurement

The American Standard of Living   In a broad sense, the biggest risk in buying goods and services of foreign origin is the long-term impact on the U.S. standard of living. Stephen Cohen and John Zysman in their provocative book, *Manufacturing Matters,* argue that the ability of the American economy to maintain high and rising wages under conditions of openness to international competition is *not* enhanced by abandoning production to others.[4] Akio Morita, the former chairman of Sony, warns America: "Unless U.S. industry shores up its manufacturing base, it could lose everything. American companies have either shifted output to low-wage countries or come to buy parts and assembled products from countries like Japan that can make quality products at low prices. The result is a hollowing of American industry. The United States is abandoning its status as an industrial power."[5]

In contrast to the situation described by these gentlemen, progressive purchasing and supply managers at leading firms such as Xerox, Tennant, General Electric, Texas Instruments, and the Ford Motor Company work with their *domestic* suppliers to develop them into world-class manufacturers that compete successfully with nondomestic manufacturers. Thus, the buying firm, the supplier, and the American economy all benefit.

Culture and Communications   Perhaps the largest obstacles to developing mutually profitable business relations with international sources are the cul-

[4]Stephen Cohen and John Zysman, *Manufacturing Matters,* Basic Books, Inc., New York, 1987.
[5]Ibid., p. 60.

tural differences between the buyer and the seller. The nature, customs, and ethics of individuals and business organizations from two different cultures can raise a surprising number of obstacles to successful business relations. What is considered ethical in one culture may not be ethical in another. The intention of filling commitments, the implications of gift giving, and even the legal systems differ widely.

Language frequently poses a significant barrier to successful international business relations. Differences in culture, language, dialects, or terminology may result in miscommunication and cause problems. Both parties may think they know what the other party has said, but true agreement and understanding often may be missing. Think, for instance, of the confusion the simple word "ton" can create. Is it a short ton (2,000 lb), a long ton (2,240 lb), or a metric ton (2,204.62 lb)? The use of textbook English in practice raises innumerable interesting problems. For example, in the Far East, the word "plant" is interpreted to mean only a living organism, not a physical facility.

Payment Terms and Conditions   From the buyer's point of view, the preferred method of payment is after receipt and inspection of the goods. However, it is customary in many countries for advance payments to be made prior to commencing work. Such a provision ties up the purchaser's capital. Letters of credit also are common in international commerce. Again, the purchaser's funds may be committed for a longer period of time than if a domestic source were involved, and a cost is incurred in obtaining the letter of credit.

The absence of fixed exchange rates can be a problem; it creates at least four potential situations, as described below.

Case 1   A contract calls for *payment in a foreign currency.* The exchange rate moves against the U.S. dollar during performance of the contract. For example, assume that a contract was awarded to a supplier in Germany for 1 million deutsche marks (DM 1 million). Assume further that the rate of exchange was U.S. $1.00 = DM 1.5; that is, one U.S. dollar purchased 1.5 deutsche marks at the time the contract was awarded. Ignoring all other costs, the dollar cost to the U.S. buyer would be

$$\frac{\text{DM } 1,000,000}{\text{DM } 1.5/\$} = \$666,666.66$$

Assume that the U.S. dollar weakens to the point that $1.00 buys only DM 1. The cost in dollars then becomes

$$\frac{\text{DM } 1,000,000}{\text{DM } 1.0/\$} = \$1,000,000$$

This is an increase of $333,333.33, or a 50 percent increase in the cost of the item in U.S. dollars. Note that the German supplier is no better off, since it receives only DM 1 million, while the U.S. purchaser has suffered the 50 percent increase in the cost of the item in *U.S. dollars.*

Case 2 A contract calls for *payment in a foreign currency* (DM), and the exchange rate improves for the U.S. dollar so that $1 now buys DM 2. The cost of the item in U.S. dollars now is

$$\frac{\text{DM } 1,000,000}{\text{DM } 2/\$} = \$500,000$$

The American buyer has reduced its costs from the initial likely amount of $666,666.66 to $500,000.00, a 25 percent saving.

Case 3 The contract is with an international supplier, *with payment in U.S. dollars,* and the dollar weakens. Assume that when the contract was awarded, the rate of exchange was U.S. $1 = DM 1.5; the cost of the item was DM 1 million, or $666,666.66. Were there no change in the rate of exchange, the supplier would convert the $666,666.66 received into DM 1 million. Unfortunately for the supplier, the dollar has weakened so that $1 will buy only DM 1. Now, when the supplier receives its $666,666.66 and has this converted to deutsche marks, it receives only DM 666,666.66, a $33\frac{1}{3}$ percent reduction from what it expected under the former exchange rate. Quite obviously, the supplier will be very unhappy and may translate this either to nonperformance or to a demand for a price increase.

Case 4 The contract is with an international supplier *with payment in U.S. dollars.* The dollar strengthens. As with case 3, the contract called for a payment of $666,666.66. Assume that the rate of exchange changed so that $1 U.S. purchases DM 2. When the supplier receives its $666,666.66 and has it converted to marks at the current rate, it will receive 666,666.66 × 2 = DM 1,333,333.32, a windfall gain of DM 333,333.33. While the German supplier may be delighted, the American buyer should be less enthusiastic.[6]

Long Lead Times Variable shipping schedules, unpredictable time requirements for customs activities, the need for greater coordination in international purchasing, strikes by stevedores and maritime unions, and storms at sea (which can cause both delays and damage) usually result in longer lead times. Air freight may be used to offset some of the problems of variable shipping schedules, but at a significant increase in cost.

Additional Inventories The quantity of additional inventory needed when purchasing from foreign sources can be difficult to determine. Quite often, however, the additional inventories are not as large as one might expect. Nevertheless, inventory carrying costs must be added to the purchase, the freight, and the administrative costs to determine the true total cost of buying

---

[6]The reader interested in strategies for handling fluctuating exchange rates should read J. R. Carter and S. K. Vickery, "Managing Volatile Exchange Rates in International Purchasing," *Journal of Purchasing and Materials Management,* Winter 1988–1989, pp. 13–20.

from international sources. Occasionally, when a U.S. industry is producing at full capacity, it is possible to get both faster delivery and lower prices from international sources. Routinely, however, additional lead times, which traditionally exceed thirty days, must be considered in planning foreign purchases when surface transportation is involved. It should be noted that some buyers do *not* add buffer stocks, relying on air freight in case of emergencies.

Quality   As previously mentioned, international suppliers frequently are utilized because many of them can provide a consistently high level of quality. But problems do exist. The United States is the only major nonmetric country in a metric world. This frequently leads to manufacturing *tolerance problems*. Additionally, nondomestic suppliers tend to be less responsive to necessary design changes than do their domestic counterparts. In many cases, there is the risk that production outside of the U.S. firm's control can result in "off-spec" incoming materials. Potential rework or scrap costs could add substantially to the total cost of doing business with international suppliers.

Social and Labor Issues   "In Europe and the U.S., unions and some politicians are pushing for retaliatory measures against exporting countries where workers lack clout and labor laws are either weak or routinely flouted. And retailers (such as Levi, Nordstrom, Wal-Mart, and Reebok) discern a greater tendency by some customers to shun production from sweatshops."[7] Documentaries by the news media of working conditions in some international plants have made U.S. retailers sensitive to working conditions in those plants. It seems highly likely that domestic manufacturers will soon have similar concerns with their international suppliers.

Higher Costs of Doing Business   The need for translators, communications problems, the distances involved in making site visits, and so on all add to the cost of doing business with international suppliers. Port-order services are more complicated because of currency fluctuations, methods of payment, customs issues, and the utilization of import brokers and international carriers. Inadequate local (international) logistical support functions such as communication systems (telephones, telexes, and fax machines), transportation systems, financial institutions, and so forth can complicate communications and product distribution.

Common Definitions

International purchasing involves a number of unique documents, activities, and taxes. This section provides the normally accepted definitions for the most important of these items. These definitions are abstracted from a

---

[7]G. Pascal Zachary, "Levi Tries to Make Sure Contract Plants in Asia Treat Workers Well," *Wall Street Journal*, July 28, 1994, p. 1.

National Association of Purchasing Management publication authored by N. A. DiOrio.[8]

Import Duties   When goods are dutiable, three types of rate may be assessed: ad valorem, specific, or compound rates. An *ad valorem rate,* which is the type of rate most often applied, is a percentage of the appraised value of the merchandise, such as 5 percent ad valorem. A *specific rate* is a specified amount per unit of weight or other quantity, such as 5.9 cents per dozen. A *compound rate* is a combination of both an ad valorem rate and a specific rate, such as 0.7 cents per pound plus 10 percent ad valorem.

Dutiable or Free of Duty   Rates of duty for imported merchandise may also vary depending on the country of origin. Certain rate concessions are reflected in the tariff schedules for merchandise from least-developed countries. Most merchandise is dutiable under the most favored nation (MFN) rates of the tariff schedules. Merchandise from countries to which the MFN rates have not been extended is dutiable at the full or "statutory" rates of the tariff schedules.

Free rates are provided for many items in the tariff schedules. Duty-free status is also available under various condition exemptions. One of the more frequently applied exemptions from duty occurs under the Generalized System of Preferences. GSP-eligible merchandise qualifies for duty-free entry when it is from a beneficiary developing country and meets other requirements.

Assists   U.S. Customs requires that any "assist" supplied by the buying firm for use in connection with the production of goods imported into the United States is dutiable and must be declared. Assists include (a) components or similar items incorporated in the imported goods; (b) tools, dies, molds, and so on, used in their production; (c) engineering, development plans, and sketches performed or provided outside the buying country by other than the buying firm's employees.

Rulings on Imports   The U.S. Customs Service makes its decision as to the dutiable status of merchandise when the entry is liquidated after the entry documents have been filed. When advance information is needed, the buyer should not depend on a small "trial" or "test" shipment since there is no guarantee that the next shipment will receive the same tariff treatment. An importer, or importer's broker, may get advance information on any matter affecting the dutiable status of merchandise by contacting the director of the port or district where the merchandise will be entered.

Customs Penalties   In most instances, the clearance of shipments through U.S. Customs is handled by *customs brokers* who serve as buyer's agents. Cus-

[8]N. A. DiOrio, "International Procurement," *Guide to Purchasing,* National Association of Purchasing Management, Tempe, Ariz., 1987, pp. 11–12.

toms brokers generally conduct freight forwarding services in addition to their customs activities. Although brokerage fees vary according to the pricing policy of the customs brokers, arrangements can be negotiated based on a fixed fee for each shipment handled. Normal buying practice is to instruct the international supplier (1) to consign the shipment and (2) to airmail the original and required import documents to the selected customs broker.

Customs Invoice   A customs invoice is a special document or invoice, prepared by the seller, on a form supplied by the U.S. Treasury which may be obtained from any U.S. Consulate. It is used to clear merchandise through U.S. Customs. It must be distinguished from the commercial invoice.

Pro Forma Invoice   This document is used largely for banking purposes. It is an abbreviated invoice sent in advance of a shipment, usually to enable the buying firm to obtain an import permit or an exchange permit, or both. The pro forma invoice gives a close approximation of the weights and values of a shipment that is to be made.

In the absence of a commercial or customs invoice at the time of entry to U.S. Customs, a pro forma invoice may be filed and a bond given for the presentation of the required invoice within a prescribed period.

Packing List   The purchase contract should require a specified number of packing lists to facilitate the identification and movement of the order and checking of containers and contents. The lists should detail the contents with descriptions, weights and measures, and markings.

Bill of Lading   As in the case of domestic shipments, a bill of lading is a receipt issued by a carrier for merchandise to be delivered to a party at some named destination. It is (1) a contract for shipment of merchandise; (2) a receipt for merchandise; (3) a document of title to the merchandise; (4) a document of freight charges (where indicated); and (5) a guide to the carrier's staff in handling the shipment.

An *ocean bill of lading* covers the movement of goods by water and may be issued in either a "straight" form or an "order" form. When a straight form is used, the consignee *must* be named in the bill. When an order form is used, either the consignee or a designee can be named. Steamship lines insist on surrender of an original bill of lading on both straight and order consignments. *Air waybills* are generally issued by air carriers in nonnegotiable form, and the carrier will effect delivery to a straight consignee only.

Inspection Certificate (When Required)   An inspection certificate is a document normally prepared by an independent entity other than the exporter to attest to the condition, quality, or quantity of goods being shipped. It is requested by the importer as a means of assuring that the goods contracted for are those that the exporter has shipped.

Certificate of Origin (When Required)   Certain commodities require a document certifying the country from which the goods originated as distinct from the country from which they were immediately exported. U.S. Customs regulations prescribe the conditions under which this certificate is required for entry.

GETTING STARTED

Raul Casillas, of the Alps Manufacturing organization, suggests:[9]

> To help determine if a part, product, or process is a candidate for international sourcing, ask the following questions:
>
> - Does it qualify as "high-volume" in your industry?
> - Does it have a long life (two to three years)?
> - Does it lend itself to repetitive manufacturing or assembly?
> - Is demand for the product fairly stable?
> - Are specifications and drawings clear and well defined?
> - Is technology not available domestically at a competitive price and quality?
>
> If the answer to all six questions is yes, then the buyer may want to evaluate the support network within his or her firm, asking the following questions:
>
> - Is there engineering support to efficiently facilitate engineering change orders when they do occur?
> - Will the buyer be able to allow sufficient time to phase out existing and "pipeline" inventory?
> - Will the buyer's firm take the responsibility for providing the necessary education and training for those that will have to interact with and support foreign suppliers?
> - Is the firm prepared to make a financial commitment for expensive trips to the supplier?
> - Is management willing to change the approach, in some cases even the policy, of how business and related transactions are conducted?
> - Is the buyer aware of the environment—i.e., current and forecasted exchange rates, general impact of tariff schedules, available technologies, and products from other countries, as well as their political climates, and leading economic indicators both in the U.S. and abroad?

If the answers to both sets of questions are all positive, international sourcing may be a realistic possibility for the buyer. A significant number of negative responses indicates the potential for real problems if an international sourcing arrangement is developed. Before a positive decision is made, however, the buyer needs to explore several issues with top management. First, do the required procedural and policy changes mesh satisfactorily with the firm's existing mode of operation? More important, is the international sourcing con-

---

[9]Raul Casillas, "Foreign Sourcing: Is It for You?" *Pacific Purchaser*, November–December 1988, p. 9.

cept, and its underlying rationale, compatible with the firm's long-term plans? It is important that the program contribute positively to achievement of the firm's long-range goals—and that the commitment be made as something more than a short-term-strategy decision.

SUPPLY CHANNELS

International Trade Intermediaries

Once a decision has been made to consider goods of international origins, the simplest way to get started is through the use of an intermediary. Selection of the appropriate intermediary is a function of availability and of the services required. The use of such intermediaries typically adds a significant cost to the overall cost of the transaction, but in most cases their use avoids many unforeseen problems.[10] The buyer who is venturing into international sourcing is well advised to solicit the advice of colleagues from the local purchasing management association. Some typical intermediaries are described below:[11]

- *Import merchants* buy goods for their own account and sell through their own outlets. Since they assume all the risks of clearing goods through customs and performing all the intermediate activity, their customers are relieved of import problems and, in effect, can treat such transactions as domestic purchases.
- *Commission houses* usually act for exporters abroad, selling in the United States and receiving a commission from the foreign exporter. Such houses generally do not have goods billed to themselves, although they handle many of the shipping and customs details.
- *Agents* or *reps* are firms or individuals representing international sellers. Since their commission is paid by the seller, their primary interests are those of the exporter. They generally handle all shipping and customs clearance details, although they assume no financial responsibility of the principals.
- *Import brokers* act as "marriage brokers" between buyers and sellers from different nations. Their commissions are paid by sellers for locating buyers and by buyers for finding sources of supply, but they are *not* involved in shipment or clearance of an order through customs. They also may act as special purchasing agents for designated commodities on a commission basis. Like agents, import brokers do not assume any of the seller's fiscal responsibility.
- *Trading companies* are large companies which generally perform all the functions performed individually by the types of agencies previously listed. The worldwide operations and know-how of such firms offer

---

[10]Dick Locke, "Get the Purchasing Channel You Want," *Electronics Components*, October 1993, p. U–12.
[11]N. A. DiOrio, op. cit., p. 7.

significant advantages and convenience. The use of Japanese trading companies is particularly advantageous to U.S. importers since the Japanese government exercises a high degree of control over their operations. Standard directories and trade publications list such firms, their capabilities, and areas of service.

- *Subsidiaries,* such as NEC Americas and Hitachi Americas, have been established by international manufacturers to facilitate international sales in the United States. They are staffed with people who speak the local language. They serve to buffer the buyer from both language and time zone problems. They offer to set prices in dollars and deliver the material to the buyer with all duties paid. Unfortunately, they are remote from the manufacturing and marketing decision makers and can be blockers in the flow of technical information. One experienced international authority finds that these subsidiaries add 5 to 35 percent for their services.[12]

International Procurement Offices

When an organization's purchases in a foreign country or region warrant (e.g., $10 million to $20 million per year), consideration should be given to establishing an international procurement office (IPO). Such an organization quickly becomes familiar with qualified sources, thereby expanding the buying firm's potential supplier base. IPO personnel can evaluate suppliers personally, negotiate for price and other terms, and monitor quality and job progress through direct site visits. IPO personnel are in a position to develop and maintain better information on local conditions such as materials shortages, labor issues, and governmental actions than are U.S.-based buyers. The IPO facilitates payments to the suppliers, provides on-site support at the supplier's site if problems arise, and provides logistical support. IPOs normally are staffed by expatriates who have worked for the U.S. manufacturer—usually in a technical role. IPOs normally are established as cost centers, charging a 1 to 2 percent markup for their services. Competition from other channels (foreign trade intermediaries and direct relations) tend to keep the IPOs efficient. The one weakness of IPOs which has been observed is their tendency to represent the local supplier's interests more than those of the U.S.-based purchasing firm.

Direct Purchasing

Dealing directly with the supplier usually will result in the lowest *purchase price* (including transportation and import duties). It eliminates the markups of international trade intermediaries. But it requires an investment in travel, communications, logistics, and interpretation of costs. Direct relations with the

---

[12]Locke, op. cit. Mr. Locke formerly was a director of international sourcing at Hewlett-Packard and is founder of the San Francisco-based Global Procurement Group.

supplier should be undertaken only after carefully conducting a cost/benefit analysis. It is important to note that conditions in developing countries often are not similar to those in the United States. Buyers should anticipate problems. For example, China, India, South America, and Eastern Europe have fewer faxes, telexes, P.C.s, and so on than do firms in North America, Western Europe, and Pacific Rim countries.

After the buying firm has gained confidence in the quality of the imported materials, and volume increases, the firm typically attempts to discontinue the use of international trade intermediaries for major procurements. Its major motivation is to avoid the intermediary's markup. The buyer should inform its supplier of this new policy—and then visit each of the manufacturers, *without the intermediaries,* to negotiate new contracts. While cost and the desire for direct dealings on technical issues may motivate the buying firm to deal directly with the supplier, the final decision will be made at the supplier's headquarters. The buyer should anticipate resistance by both the intermediaries and their manufacturers. But this resistance normally can be overcome. In some cases, new suppliers may have to be developed due to the tight ties the international trade intermediaries may have with the existing supplier. Before taking such action, the buyer must ensure that his or her company is set up to handle items such as traffic, customs clearance, and international payments.[13]

Direct purchasing requires the involvement of the company in all aspects of the transaction; when properly conducted, it eliminates the added profit of the middleman. Outside agencies may be engaged to perform specialized services. For example, *customs brokers* can be used to handle entry requirements, *export brokers* to handle foreign clearances, and *freight forwarders* to arrange for transport. Such agents do not take title to the goods. They are used by most direct purchasers whose scale of activities does not warrant such in-house capability.

Identifying Potential Suppliers   Potential direct international suppliers can be located through a wide variety of sources. A list of sources of information on potential international suppliers is contained in the Appendix of this chapter. International trade intermediaries are also an excellent source of information. Unfortunately, these organizations have a vested interest in maintaining their position in the supply channel. The best way to prepare to bypass the intermediary is to develop direct contacts with key players at the division performing the design, manufacture, and marketing of the item or commodity class. The buyer should provide performance feedback *directly* to the supplier. The buyer should tell the intermediary that he or she wants to visit with the supplier's key personnel the next time they are in the country or the next time the key personnel are in the buyer's country. Dick Locke says to:

> use this meeting to provide performance feedback and to explain your company's purchasing goals and values. Take care not to appear to be an unreasonable com-

---

[13]Richard G. Novotny, "Global Search," *Electronic Buyers' News,* Dec. 19, 1988, p. 34.

pany to work with, even if you must deliver a critical message. Work to make foreign visitors to your company feel as welcome as possible.

As part of the strategy, consider the timing of your request. The ideal time is when you are considering a change in suppliers or are selecting a supplier for a new project. The possibility of a major increase in business will give you more leverage.

If you're dealing with a new supplier, state your intention to deal directly right from the start. Once a subsidiary or rep has started to handle your business, they are difficult to dislodge. It's easier to change your mind and start dealing through reps than the other way around.

Once your company has established a relationship with the business and technical staff of the supplier, make the request to deal more directly. You might be requesting to deal through an IPO, or you might be asking to deal directly. This request should go to the supplier's sales management, and specifically to an individual whom you already know.

Be prepared to give reasons. These might be that you need a lower cost and believe that both parties can benefit by removing intermediaries. Another might be that the rep or subsidiary doesn't add enough value to the transaction to justify the markups it must be charging.[14]

Qualifying Potential International Suppliers

Prior to investing additional energy in dealing with an international supplier, two issues should be addressed: *country and regional stability* and the *potential supplier's financial condition.*

Country and Regional Analysis

For approximately $750, Dun & Bradstreet will prepare a Country Analysis Report for its clients, including some 70 pages of in-depth research, information on both the current and historical economy and government, import and export practices, trading partners and monetary policies.

Most experts recommend a survey of a region as well as the company and country because such factors as political and monetary stability, currency transfer laws, and trade and product liability policies may be crucial to doing business there.

. . . The client should also ask what is needed to engage in commerce in a particular country. Credit professionals cite such factors as: required documentation for transactions, the transportation and distribution infrastructure, religious customs, quality standards and existing regulations that may restrict sale of the client's product or service. Will there be overseas agents to facilitate a deal? How reliable and experienced are they? Many a deal has been derailed by such cross-border questions as whether the desired country prohibits sales of products whose *components* originated in a certain country.[15]

The buyer or buying team is cautioned not to judge the creditworthiness of the potential supplier by the ability of its key personnel to speak fluent Eng-

---

[14]Locke, op. cit., p. U–11.
[15]Heidi Jacobs and Barbara Ettorre, "Evaluating Potential Foreign Partners." Cited by permission of publisher. From *Management Review,* October 1993, p. 60. American Management Association, New York. All rights reserved.

lish. A careful financial analysis (as discussed in Chapter 12) must be conducted. Jacobs and Ettorre list the following sources of information for such analyses: Dun & Bradstreet (800-234-3867), Gradon America (800-466-3163), Owens On Line (800-745-4656), Justitia International Inc. (203-589-1698), and Piguet International (203-584-8088). A random sample of prices in 1993 was $47 to $275, depending on the country and complexity.[16]

> International credit specialists also caution their clients to familiarize themselves with the Foreign Corrupt Practices Act, which bars U.S. companies from engaging in bribery and other practices when doing business overseas.[17] (See Chapter 30.)

Preparing for Direct Relations

Preparation for direct relations includes all the issues raised in Chapters 11 and 12, as well as intercultural preparation, the hiring of a competent translator, and an exhaustive technical and commercial analysis.

Intercultural Preparation   Virtually all purchases from international suppliers are the result of negotiations. The success of each of these negotiations is influenced, in part, by the American negotiator's ability to understand the needs, and ways of thinking and acting, of representatives of international firms.

In addition to the conventional preparation for any negotiation, it is essential to conduct an extensive study of the culture(s). It is important to emphasize that this study should focus on the culture, not the language. When there are language differences between cultural groups, many busy American executives believe that a competent interpreter is all that is necessary to overcome these differences. But the use of interpreters, while allowing communication to take place, does not obviate the need for an understanding of the non-American's culture. Even when one overcomes the natural barriers of language difference, it is still possible to fail to understand and be understood.

The ability to understand a non-American's cultural background is of great practical advantage for several reasons. U.S. negotiators perform more effectively if they understand the cultural and business heritage of their counterparts—and the effect of this heritage on their counterparts' negotiation strategies and tactics. Also, it puts the non-American off his or her guard. He or she expects most Americans to be clumsy and able to do business only in the American way. Sage Publication's 1970 *Culture's Consequences*, Edward and Mildred Hall's *Understanding Cultural Differences* (1990, Intercultural Press), and Dow Jones Irwin's *Big Business Blunders* are good investments and good reading. Talk with others who have experienced living or working in the culture. Learn what the holidays are, what the units of measure are, what the currency exchange is, what topics are taboo, and so on.

---

[16]Ibid., p. 61.
[17]Ibid., p. 60.

Another aspect of cultural preparation becomes important in cases where there is a strong likelihood of continuing relations (i.e., one or more transactions that would require a year or more for completion). Under such circumstances, the non-Americans (accompanied by their spouses) frequently visit the U.S. firm. The American hosts should go to considerable lengths to become acquainted with their counterparts (and their spouses) on a social basis. Americans should entertain the visitors in their homes (a rarity in Europe and the Far East). This will give the Americans and their spouses an opportunity to develop good relations with their counterparts. This bank of goodwill, while not a means of co-opting the foreign supplier, projects a desire and willingness to understand, which frequently proves to be invaluable during subsequent transactions.

One other aspect of cultural preparation needs to be emphasized: It takes much longer to negotiate with non-Americans. This is especially true if the international firm has not had extensive exposure to U.S. business practices and specifications. The longer time required is due to the different organization and mode of operation of most non-American businesses. In the case of European firms, it usually takes at least twice as much time, and up to six times as long is often required for Far East firms. The American negotiator must be aware of the requirement for additional time—and plan accordingly. He or she must be patient and thick-skinned when progress is slow.

Interpreters

Bilingual business discussions obviously require a third party—an interpreter. A good interpreter ably used will speed negotiations. An ineffective interpreter, or one ineptly used, can convert even simple matters into interminable wrangles, and complex discussions may simply grind to a halt amid a haze of miscommunication. "One or two words with a double meaning can certainly change the entire content of a statement,". . . . Executives experienced in international trade usually have learned these lessons, if only by trial and error. However, with the economy's rapid globalization, many executives recently have found themselves thrown willy-nilly into multilingual negotiations. The inexperienced thus risk wasting inordinate amounts of time for very little gain while acquiring the necessary communication skills.[18]

Technical and Commercial Analysis   Before dealing with identified candidate suppliers, the buying team should:

- Review the specifications and drawings.
- Determine in great detail what the quality requirements are.
- Identify specific production scheduling requirements.
- Determine (as a group) what percentage of the annual requirements for the item can be placed offshore.

---

[18]Hal Porter, "Interpreters: What They'll Do for You," *Across the Board,* October 1993, p. 14.

- Determine requirements for special packaging.
- Identify likely lead times.
- Develop a clear idea of the price objective.
- Prepare a briefing on the buyer's firm. Frequently, much effort will be expended selling the potential suppliers on doing business with the buying firm. The briefing should include:

  Information on the relevant product line and related lines

  Actual and forecasted sales volume

  Customers

  Market share

  Unclassified corporate strategy information

  Annual reports

  An indication of why the buyer is soliciting the potential international supplier's interest (quality? price?)

The trade council of each supplier's country should be visited before the team departs. The buyer should take along samples (or photos) of required materials.

The Initial Meeting

It is essential to visit potential suppliers and review their facilities. Experience has shown that the controller of the target supplier usually occupies a very influential position. To gain his or her support, the buyer or buying team should describe how the supplier firm will get paid! The buying firm's technical people clearly must be part of the visiting team. The potential supplier will be judging the buying firm just as much as the buyer will be judging the potential supplying firm.

Currency and Payment Issues

Currency   Locke and Anklesaria write that:

U.S. purchasing departments are at a disadvantage compared to their more sophisticated counterparts . . . in countries [which] deal in foreign currencies as a matter of course. . . . U.S. buyers' unfamiliarity in dealing in foreign currencies leads to higher costs in two ways. First, they attempt to put all currency risk on the supplier, which causes the supplier to include charges for hedging, or to add an extra margin for contingencies into the price. Second, in an attempt to avoid dealing in foreign currencies, buyers use suppliers' U.S. subsidiaries and representatives, who will accept payment in dollars, but who also charge high markups.

 . . . Buyers and finance staffs of firms should understand when to buy in foreign currencies and when to buy in U.S. dollars. They should know the measures to take to avoid major increases in dollar cost and to be flexible enough to get decreases when possible. They should understand methods of reducing short term risk through hedging. They should have analytical tools available to help them choose between various hedging strategies.

   The biggest advantage comes from the choice of the best pricing currency (the currency in which prices are set). The payment currency (you may actually pay an equivalent amount of a different currency) does not make a big difference in prices. To choose a pricing currency, you must answer two questions.

   First, what are you buying? Product prices can be divided into cost driven and market driven categories. Cost driven prices are those where the supplier can set prices based on his/her costs. Market driven prices are those where prices are set on a world market, usually in U.S. dollars, and the supplier cannot sell at a higher price. Second, where is the product built? Some countries have currencies that are pegged to the U.S. dollar. Other currencies float freely. If a currency is truly pegged to the dollar, there should be no need for currency protection. The table below shows the possibilities.

Floating Currency, Cost Driven Product

These products are typically custom or semicustom products. An example would be a printed circuit assembly from Japan or Europe. By pricing in the supplier's currency, the supplier is relieved of the currency risk. This should enable a buyer to negotiate a lower initial price than if the supplier were to take on the risk. It is better to start with the lower price, because one doesn't know if the dollar will strengthen or weaken. The buying firm can protect itself against dollar cost increases by low cost hedging; an escape clause is needed in the purchase agreement.

Floating Currency, Market Driven Product

These products are typically commodities whose price is nearly the same anywhere in the world. Examples are gold, oil, and DRAMs. For this type of product, a buyer should not hedge. The buying firm is better off negotiating one worldwide price and maintaining the price the same around the world. This works best if the firm has a purchasing presence in various regions, so that hedging does not work

BEST BUYING CURRENCY

Pricing driver \ Type of currency	Pegged currency	Floating currency
Cost-based product	Dollars or supplier's currency	Supplier's product
Dollar market-based product	Dollars	Dollars

as it does with cost driven parts. If the dollar strengthens, the price in another currency goes up.

Pegged Currency, Cost Driven Product

Countries with pegged currencies are generally smaller ones. They include Taiwan, Thailand, Hong Kong and Korea. There is little need to hedge these currencies, because they are unlikely to move against the dollar. In addition, the foreign exchange market is thin and not well developed. Instead of hedging, a buyer should have an escape clause in the contract, because these currencies do make occasional controlled changes in value against the dollar. . . .

Pegged Currency, Market Driven Product

If the market is dollar based, these products need not be hedged. Similar techniques to those used for market driven products from floating currency countries are the best choice.

Hedging

Hedging protects the dollar value of a future foreign currency cash flow. The reason to hedge is to protect against major swings in the value of a purchase. A buyer can achieve this via forward or futures contracts or via currency options. The buyer would enter into contracts to sell dollars for foreign currency at the time the supplier is paid. It's easiest to think in terms of using the foreign currency that was purchased in the hedge to pay the supplier, but this is not what happens. There is a profit or loss on a hedge contract that takes place behind the scenes. This profit or loss is applied to a material price variance that results from exchange rate changes and offsets higher or lower part costs.

Forward contracts give a fixed cost for foreign currency and therefore for foreign currency purchasing. If the interest rates in the foreign country are higher than they are in the US, the forward rate is at a discount to the spot rate, and this reduces the dollar cost still more.

Forward contracts also have the advantage of being suitable for internal transactions. If the buying company exports to the country it is buying in, and wants to sell in local currency, purchasing in local currency reduces the company's currency exposure. The purchasing flow of funds offsets the sales office flow of funds. If an internal forward agreement is made between the two departments, only the difference between the two flows needs to be hedged at banks.

Options allow a buyer to take advantage of an increase in the value of the US dollar but protect against a decrease. Unfortunately, they are expensive. A six month option on a volatile currency typically costs about 5% and most people choose not to buy them. An added difficulty is that option prices for the European style options that buyers need are not well listed in financial newspapers.

Risk of Buying in Dollars

Dollars are not the safe course that many are led to believe. A dollar buyer may start off with a higher price than necessary. If the dollar weakens, he or she is paying even more. A more sophisticated competitor would be paying less. A supplier's competitors will soon let buyers know that they are paying too much. Other channels of distribution could also open up. Finally, supplier promises of fixed dollar pricing are often broken when the value of the dollar declines.

Length of Hedging

Hedging for too long a period with forward contracts can lead to the same problems as buying in dollars. If the dollar increases in value, a buyer will be paying too much. Hedging for too long with options is expensive, because the option premium increases with time. Three months of orders plus three month lead time gives six months hedging, a typical period.

Risks in Hedging

Hedging does involve some risks, but they are limited and can be controlled with simple attention to the fundamentals. Risk arises from forecast inaccuracy, and can lead to unexpected price variations, either up or down. If a company overforecasts purchases and hedges with forwards, there will be larger profit or loss on the hedge than the variance on part cost. With overforecasts, there will be a loss on forward contracts if the dollar strengthens and a gain if the dollar weakens. The total unexpected gain or loss will be approximately the percent overforecasted times the percent that the dollar changed. For example, a 20% overforecast and a 15% currency strengthening will result in a 3% (15% of 20%) extra cost of the parts.

With underforecasts, some of the parts must be purchased at the spot rate without an offsetting hedge. If the dollar weakens, they will be more expensive and if it strengthens, they will be cheaper.

Choosing a Hedging Strategy

The biggest gains in currency management will come from choosing the right currency. A good negotiator should be able to get an initial price reduction of 5% or more against a volatile currency like the yen or the mark. The next most consequential decision is whether or not to hedge. Not hedging opens the buyer to dollar price swings that are often as much as 20% in six months. This uncertainty is unacceptable to most companies.

The third decision is to choose a hedging strategy.[19]

In a recent article, Joseph Carter and his coauthors demonstrated the benefits of choosing a hedging strategy based on a Bayesian statistical analysis of probable outcomes. In this study, Carter shows that choosing a hedge strategy would have saved 3.6 percent compared with paying in the supplier's currency.[20]

---

[19]Richard Locke, Jr., and Jimmy Anklesaria, "Selection of Currency and Hedging Strategy in Global Supply Management," *Proceedings,* International Conference of Purchasing and Materials Management, Atlanta, Ga., May 1994, pp. 294–299.

[20]Joseph R. Carter, Shawnee Vickery, and Michael P. D'Itri, "Currency Risk Management Strategies for Contracting with Japanese Suppliers," *International Journal of Purchasing and Materials Management,* Summer 1993, pp. 19–25.

Payments   Payments to an international supplier are simplified when a trade intermediary or an IPO is involved. When payment is to be made directly by the buying firm to the supplier, a letter of credit frequently is used.

Letters of Credit   As part of the negotiations, many international suppliers will request that the purchaser obtain a letter of credit from its bank. A letter of credit is an instrument issued by a bank at the request of a buyer. It promises to pay a specified amount of money upon presentation of documents stipulated in the letter. The letter of credit is not a means of payment, but merely a promise to pay. Actual payment is accomplished through a draft, which is similar to a personal check. It is an order by one party to pay another party. Documents commonly stipulated in the letter of credit include the bill of lading, a consular invoice, and a description of goods. In effect, if the purchaser defaults, then the bank has to foot the bill. Thus, any risk of payment is transferred to the bank. Frequently, the international supplier will use the purchase order (contract) together with the letter of credit as security when obtaining a loan for working capital for the required labor and materials.

Letters of credit are classified three ways:

- *Irrevocable versus revocable* An irrevocable letter of credit can be neither canceled nor modified without the consent of the beneficiary.
- *Confirmed versus unconfirmed* A bank which confirms the letter of credit assumes the risk. The best method of payment for an exporter in most cases is a confirmed, irrevocable letter of credit. Some banks may not assume the risk, preferring to take an advisory role. Such banks and their correspondents believe that they are better able to judge the credibility of the issuing bank than the exporter.
- *Revolving versus nonrevolving* Nonrevolving letters of credit are valid for one transaction only. When relationships are established, a revolving letter of credit may be issued.

Obtaining a letter of credit may take three to five business days. A detailed application must be completed. Since a letter of credit is an extension of credit from the bank, it is processed much as a loan is processed. If no line of credit has been previously established with the bank, the applicant must prepay the specified amount. Typical charges involved include an application fee—0.008 percent on a $125 minimum—plus a negotiation charge—0.0025 percent on a $110 minimum. In case of cancellation, a charge of $100 is common.

RECENT INTERNATIONAL DEVELOPMENTS

While international political and economic change is the nature of the world, two developments will have an especially significant impact on international purchasing: the European Union and the North American Free Trade Agreement.

The European Union[21]

Wednesday, October 13, 1993, Sally Jacobsen of the Associated Press reported:

At long last, the European Community has the green light to go ahead with its grand design for political and monetary union, with a common foreign policy and a single currency by the end of the decade.

. . . The treaty calls for common foreign, security and, eventually, defense policies, and a common central bank and single currency by 1999. It gives the community more powers in education, industry and health.[22]

William L. Richardson, former director of Commercial Services for British Steel, Inc., in London, made the following comments while addressing the 78th International Purchasing and Materials Management Conference in San Antonio in May of 1993:

. . . For the American purchaser, the European Single Market offers considerable opportunities and it makes purchasing easier. . . . First, it will strengthen or create new effective alternatives to existing large manufacturers, be they in the U.S.A., Japan, or elsewhere. Second, it makes purchasing easier by virtue of the creation of European standards where [currently] as many as 12 different national standards can exist. This is a huge aid to the cost of reducing and simplifying the quality and performance comparisons purchasers have to make when evaluating the advantages of different supply sources.

If the U.S.A. fears the European Single Market, it is a misplaced fear. In a sense Europe has looked at the U.S.A., seen how America has created a giant manufacturing base and said to itself, what is it that prevents us Europeans from achieving similar growth and prosperity? The European answer is, first, to tear down its own internal barriers and then to open up its market to world trade fairly conducted within international law.[23]

Richard L. Pinkerton, in the conclusion to his article reporting on the history and evolution of the European Community and the implications for purchasing managers, writes that:

Purchasing managers should be prepared to join their firm's EC strategy/tactics team. Each purchasing professional must investigate the specific EC technical directives and the implications of the ISO 9000 standards as they apply to his or her firm.[24] Subsequently, the development of implementation plans should be undertaken as an integral part of the firm's overall EC strategy and plan.

In many respects, the standardization directives and programs of EC 92 will facilitate trade with Europe by reducing a number of different codes into a single code. Not only does this "harmonization" reduce the need for 12 different sets of paper

---

[21]The European Community, now called the European Union, consists of the following countries: Austria, Belgium, Britain, Denmark, Finland, France, Germany, Greece, Holland, Ireland, Italy, Luxembourg, Norway, Portugal, Spain, and Sweden.

[22]Sally Jacobsen, "Europe Finally to Be United, but Federation Is a Loose One," *The Arizona Republic,* Oct. 13, 1993, p. A10.

[23]Quoted in "Voices from Europe" by Richard L. Pinkerton, *NAPM Insights,* July 1993, p. 27.

[24]See Chapter 21 for a detailed discussion of the ISO 9000 series standards.

work, including border documents, and for a variety of rules and regulations, it should also reduce the costs of products bought and sold. Additionally, a more efficient and uniform European transportation system is expected to develop. Although some product variation will always be present as a result of differing styles, tastes, languages, and other cultural nuances among the member nations, it is very clear that Europe is moving toward essentially the same type of free market that currently exists in the United States. Sourcing should be accomplished more quickly, with fewer suppliers, as customers in all 12 countries utilize a common set of standards and procedures, coupled with the growth of mass distribution centers.

To develop this scenario one step further, consider the possible future inclusion in the EC of the eastern European countries and the Commonwealth of Independent States. This action clearly is a realistic possibility within the next decade or two. Such an eventuality, in all likelihood, means that "greater Europe" will not only write the rules for international trade, these countries will also dominate it.[25]

The North American Free Trade Agreement

In June 1990, President Bush (of the United States) and President Salinas (of Mexico) endorsed the idea of a comprehensive U.S.-Mexico Free Trade Agreement in order to guarantee that the positive effects of export growth and industrial competitiveness, which had already begun, would continue to expand. By 1991, Canada joined the talks, leading to the three-way negotiation known as the North American Free Trade Agreement, or NAFTA. This agreement was designed to create a Free Trade Area (FTA) comprising the United States, Canada, and Mexico. Consistent with WTO rules, all tariffs will be eliminated within the FTA over a transition period. NAFTA involves an ambitious effort to eliminate barriers to agricultural, manufacturing, and service trade; to remove investment restrictions; and to protect intellectual property rights effectively. In addition, NAFTA marks the first time in the history of U.S. trade policy that environmental concerns have been directly addressed in a comprehensive trade agreement. By accelerating the integration of the three markets, NAFTA should enable North American businesses to produce goods that are more competitive compared with goods produced in Asia and in the European Union and will allow North American consumers to benefit from a greater selection of higher-quality, lower-priced goods.[26]

Implications   Canada and the United States have long been sources of supply to each other. Modern-day Mexico has pockets of expertise that are world-class. Many U.S. buyers already avail themselves of Mexican sources of supply.

---

[25]Richard L. Pinkerton, "The European Community—'EC 92': Implications for Purchasing Managers," *International Journal of Purchasing and Materials Management,* Spring 1993, p. 25.
[26]*NAFTA, the Beginning of a New Era,* Business America (partial extract), Aug. 24, 1992, National Trade Data Bank, Mar. 27, 1994.

When a global analysis of potential suppliers reveals that it makes sense to develop a world-class supplier in Mexico, a joint venture with carefully developed plans, objectives, action plans, and milestones is the appropriate way of developing the supplier. (Obviously, these principles apply to the development of suppliers in many parts of the world.) This approach brings together the social, political, and economic strengths of the supplier with the knowledge, technology, systems, and commercial expertise of the international buyer.

COUNTERTRADE

The term "countertrade" refers to any transaction in which payment is made partially or fully with goods instead of money. Countertrade links two normally unrelated transactions: the sale of a product into a foreign country and the sale of goods out of that country. Countertrade requirements normally are imposed by foreign governments in an effort to gain foreign exchange or foreign technology.[27] An example of the persuasiveness of countertrade is reflected in Figure 13-1, which depicts the suppliers involved in McDonnell Douglas's MD-11 program.

Laura Forker, in her 1991 report on countertrade, reports the following advantages and disadvantages:

Countertrade's Advantages

Companies involved in countertrade frequently have enjoyed a variety of marketing, financial, and manufacturing advantages that have resulted in increased sales, increased employment, and enhanced company competitiveness. By accepting goods or services as payment instead of cash, countertrade participants have been effective in: (1) avoiding exchange controls; (2) selling to countries with inconvertible currencies; (3) marketing products in less-developed, cash-strapped countries (with centrally planned economies) that could not make such purchases otherwise; and (4) reducing some of the risks associated with unstable currency values. In overcoming these financial obstacles, countertrading firms have been able to enter new or formerly closed markets, expand business contacts and sales volume, and dampen the impact of foreign protectionism on overseas business.

Countertrade has also engendered good will with foreign governments concerned about their trade balances and hard currency accounts. Finally, Western participants in countertrade have enjoyed fuller use of plant capacity, larger production runs, and reduced per-unit expenses due to the greater sales volume. Their expanded sales contacts abroad have sometimes led to new sources of attractive

---

[27]The interested reader is encouraged to read *Creative Countertrade: A Guide to Doing Business Worldwide* by Kenton W. Elderkin and Warren E. Norquist, Ballinger Publishing Co., Cambridge, Mass., 1987, and the more recent study by Laura Forker: "Countertrade: Purchasing's Perceptions and Involvement," Center for Advanced Purchasing Studies/National Association of Purchasing Management, Inc., Tempe, Ariz., 1991. Single copies are available gratis by written request to the Center for Advanced Purchasing Studies, P.O. Box 22160, Tempe, Ariz. 85285-2160.

Global engineering
Main MD-11 subcontractors

■ Douglas Aircraft, Long Beach

□ Other McDonnell Douglas locations

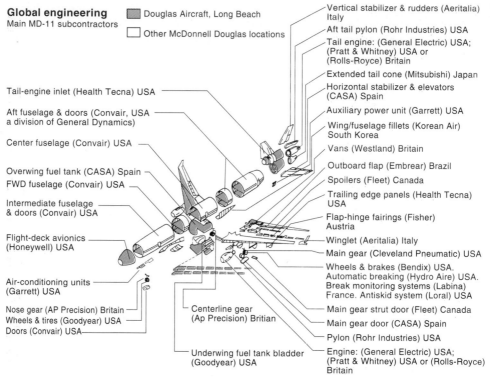

Vertical stabilizer & rudders (Aeritalia) Italy

Aft tail pylon (Rohr Industries) USA

Tail engine: (General Electric) USA; (Pratt & Whitney) USA or (Rolls-Royce) Britain

Extended tail cone (Mitsubishi) Japan

Horizontal stabilizer & elevators (CASA) Spain

Auxiliary power unit (Garrett) USA

Wing/fuselage fillets (Korean Air) South Korea

Vans (Westland) Britain

Outboard flap (Embrear) Brazil

Spoilers (Fleet) Canada

Trailing edge panels (Health Tecna) USA

Flap-hinge fairings (Fisher) Austria

Winglet (Aeritalia) Italy

Main gear (Cleveland Pneumatic) USA

Wheels & brakes (Bendix) USA. Automatic breaking (Hydro Aire) USA. Break monitoring systems (Labina) France. Antiskid system (Loral) USA

Main gear strut door (Fleet) Canada

Main gear door (CASA) Spain

Pylon (Rohr Industries) USA

Engine: (General Electric) USA; (Pratt & Whitney) USA or (Rolls-Royce) Britain

Tail-engine inlet (Health Tecna) USA

Aft fuselage & doors (Convair, USA a division of General Dynamics)

Center fuselage (Convair) USA

Overwing fuel tank (CASA) Spain

FWD fuselage (Convair) USA

Intermediate fuselage & doors (Convair) USA

Flight-deck avionics (Honeywell) USA

Air-conditioning units (Garrett) USA

Nose gear (AP Precision) Britain
Wheels & tires (Goodyear) USA
Doors (Convair) USA

Centerline gear (Ap Precision) Britian

Underwing fuel tank bladder (Goodyear) USA

FIGURE 13-1
An example of countertrade. (Source: The Economist, *Sept. 3, 1988.*)

components and, at other times, to valuable outlets for the disposal of declining products. Countertrade has opened up many new opportunities for American firms willing to become involved in it.

Countertrade's Disadvantages

Experienced companies have encountered a number of problems, however, that are either unique to or exacerbated by countertrade. Countertrade negotiations tend to be lengthier and more complex than conventional sales negotiations and must be conducted at times with powerful government procurement agencies that enjoy negotiating strength. Additional expenses in the form of brokerage fees and facilities, other transaction costs, and higher procurement costs reduce the profitability of countertrade deals. Difficulties with the quality, availability, and disposal of goods taken as payback have been reported by a number of authors. And countertrade introduces pricing problems associated with the assignment of values to products and/or commodities received in exchange. Commodity prices can vary widely over the lengthy negotiation and delivery periods, and trading partners may differ as to the worth of particular products. All these drawbacks result in higher risk and greater uncertainty about the profitability of a countertrade deal.

Offsets entail further concerns in the form of technology transfer requirements, local procurement conditions that favor local suppliers, and rigidities that offsets introduce into the buying process. The result for Western firms is often increased competition. Offset customers can become competitors later on. And some offset requirements divert a Western firm's resources to less-than-optimal suppliers. These additional costs must be considered when a proposed deal is being evaluated.[28]

Definitions

Barter   This form of transaction preceded the use of money. Goods are exchanged for other goods with no money involved. This is the simplest form of countertrade. If goods are bartered to save on transportation costs, the arrangement is called a swap.

Offset   Under this form of transaction, some, all, or even more than 100 percent of the value of the sale is *offset* by the purchase (or facilitation of purchases by others) of items produced in the buying country. Offsets are categorized as direct and indirect. A *direct offset* involves close technological ties between the items sold and purchased. For example, when the government of Australia purchased helicopters made by Boeing, Boeing agreed to buy ailerons for the 727 from an Australian supplier. An *indirect offset* involves the purchase or facilitation of sales of commodities unrelated to the purchasing country. When the Swiss purchased F-5 aircraft, the manufacturer (Northrop) facilitated sales of Swiss elevators and other non-aircraft products in North America. Offsets normally are limited to the sale of military-related goods and services.

Counterpurchase   With this type of transaction, unrelated goods are exchanged. The U.S. manufacturer purchases goods in the foreign country from a supplier who is paid in local currency by the buyer of the manufacturer's goods. Counterpurchase normally involves two separate, but linked, contracts: one for purchase and one for counterpurchase.

Buy-Back/Compensation   Buy-back (or compensation) is an agreement by the seller of turnkey plants, machinery, or other capital equipment to accept as partial or full payment products produced in the plants and/or on the capital equipment.

Purchasing and Supply Management's Role in Countertrade

Historically, procurement has been dragged screaming to a countertrade transaction by the firm's marketing people who are intent on making a sale. One of the authors was involved in such transactions during the 1970s. Little thought

---

[28]Forker, op. cit., pp. 11–12.

was given to the American seller's countertrade obligations until the purchasing government brought economic and political pressure to bear. At this point, the U.S. firm's buyers frantically began to see what could be purchased in the foreign country. A very uncomfortable relationship developed between the customer and the seller.

Both marketing and procurement people must recognize that they need to work as a team if countertrade is to operate to the firm's benefit. When countertrade is used to facilitate sales, purchasing and supply management should be involved *up-front*. Buyers should review the items their company requires. Similar requirements must be levied on the firm's suppliers so that they are in a position to assist the manufacturer in meeting its present or potential obligations.

Creative Countertrade

Elderkin and Norquist define traditional countertrade as focusing "on existing goods to be brought out of the host country and sold in existing world markets. Traditional countertrade must deal with the limitations of fitting what already exists into unresponsive markets."

"Creative countertrade," on the other hand, with its focus on creating future goods for *new market niches*, has greater flexibility and wider possibilities. Creative countertrade is broader than traditional countertrade. It includes not only traditional countertrade, but also international investment and international joint venture activities. It carefully analyzes the needs of all the major parties, including the potential development of new international suppliers, and creatively applies existing business tools to answer these needs.

Traditional countertrade provides quick-fix solutions to ongoing trade problems. But it lacks the depth and longer time horizons of creative countertrade. It seems likely that progressive firms will embrace creative countertrade as a means of both increasing sales and developing new dependable sources of supply.[29]

Internationalization of the Procurement Process

A firm's approach to international sourcing normally progresses from a reactive mode to a proactive one. Under reactive international sourcing, the firm reacts to opportunities in the supply marketplace. If an internationally produced good or service is the most attractive buy, then it is purchased.

As the firm embraces a proactive approach to procurement, it develops supply strategies and supply plans for its requirements. The development of these strategies and plans calls for the analysis of all possible sources of supply— both domestic and international. The principles introduced in this chapter

---

[29]Elderkin and Norquist, op. cit., pp. 122–123.

allow the buyer to determine the optimal source of supply, whether domestic or international.

CONCLUSION

International/global procurement is one of the most challenging aspects of purchasing and supply management. Many new problems are involved for the buying firms. Perhaps the most perplexing issue is that of balancing the purchasing firm's short-term interest with America's long-term need to be competitive.

FOR DISCUSSION

13-1 What is the number-one reason for international sourcing? What are five other reasons?

13-2 Describe the biggest risk in buying foreign-made goods and services.

13-3 What is the largest obstacle to developing mutually profitable business relations with foreign sources? Discuss.

13-4 Describe four possible outcomes of variable exchange rates on an international purchase.

13-5 What are key contributors to longer lead times when purchasing internationally?

13-6 Discuss the nature of social and labor issues that domestic manufacturers will likely face with their international suppliers.

13-7 Identify the sources of higher costs of doing business internationally.

13-8 Define import duties, assists, and customs invoices.

13-9 What is the simplest way to start purchasing goods of international origin?

13-10 List and describe five international intermediaries.

13-11 What are the advantages of establishing an IPO?

13-12 Why would a purchaser prefer to buy directly from an international supplier? How would such a purchaser proceed?

13-13 What two issues should be addressed when qualifying potential international suppliers? Why?

13-14 What three things should be done in preparation for direct relations with international sources?

13-15 Why is it important to understand a non-American's cultural background?

13-16 What is hedging? Why is it practiced? Discuss the advantages and disadvantages of hedging.

13-17 When are letters of credit typically required? How are they classified?

13-18 What impact will the European Community (now known as the European Union) have on international sourcing?

13-19 Describe countertrade. What are its major advantages to a U.S. manufacturer? Disadvantages?

CASES FOR CHAPTER 13

The Dutzel Diesel Case, page 810
National Machine and Electronics, page 863
SDC Corporation, page 904
The Wide, Wide World of Purchasing (in the *Instructor's Manual*)

APPENDIX:
INTERNATIONAL SOURCES

Because a high percentage of buyers now utilize international suppliers, information concerning foreign markets and companies is available from an increasing number of sources. Some of them are:

- *International Business Practices,* January 1993. U.S. Department of Commerce in Cooperation with Federal Express Corporation. U.S. Government Printing Office, Washington, D.C. 20402. Contains business organizations, useful contacts, commercial policies, taxation, international property rights for 117 countries, plus general guides.
- *The World Factbook 1993* by Central Intelligence Agency, Superintendent of Documents, P.O. Box 371954, Pittsburgh, Pa. 15250-7954. Phone: 202-783-3238. A complete economic and geopolitical data source on all the countries of the world, including a beautiful color map set and an appendix on international organizations and groups.
- *Destination Japan: A Business Guide for the 90's,* prepared by Eric Kennedy, the Japan Export Information Center (JEIC), U.S. Department of Commerce, and the International Trade Administration, December 1991. U.S. Government Printing Office, Washington, D.C. 20402-9328.
- *NAFTA: The North American Free Trade Agreement: A Guide to Customs Procedures,* January 1994. Customs Publication No. 571, Department of the Treasury, U.S. Customs Service, Washington, D.C. Order from the U.S. Government Printing Office, Washington, D.C. 20402-9328.
- *The China Business Guide,* January 1994. The U.S. Department of Commerce and the International Trade Administration, U.S. Government Printing Office, Washington, D.C. 20402-9328.
- The United States Department of Commerce, 1615 H Street, N.W., Washington, D.C. 20233. Has many publications of foreign agents, distributors, and buyers.
- Foreign commercial attachés, who are located in foreign embassies and consulates throughout the United States.
- American commercial attachés, who are located in U.S. embassies and consulates abroad.
- *Trade Directories of the World,* Croner Publications, Inc., 21105 Jamaica Ave., Queens Village, N.Y. 11428.
- The New York Chamber of Commerce and Industry, 99 Church Street, New York, N.Y. 10007.

- The International Federation of Purchasing and Materials Management, Amsterdam, the Netherlands.
- The United States Counsel of the International Chamber of Commerce, 1212 Avenue of the Americas, New York, N.Y. 10036. Publishes many pamphlets of interest to buyers.
- The international departments of all large banks have considerable material on foreign buying.

Other sources of information include *Europages* (the principal business directory for Europe: 9, Avenue de Friedland, Paris, France F-75008), current business publications, catalogs, associations, newspapers, local chambers of commerce, official trade commissions and government agencies represented in many major cities in the United States, international banks, trade boards, and colleagues in the buyer's industry.

14

PRICING PRINCIPLES

KEY CONCEPTS

- General economic considerations
    - Conditions of competition
    - Variable-margin pricing
    - Differences between products
    - Six categories of cost
    - Regulation by competition
- Price analysis
    - Competitive price proposals
    - Regulated, catalog, and market prices
    - Historical prices
    - Independent cost estimates
- Purchasing design work
- All-in-cost/Total cost of ownership
- Documenting a price analysis
- Discounts
    - Trade discounts
    - Quantity discounts
    - Seasonal discounts
    - Cash discounts
- Legal implications of pricing

Obtaining materials at the right price is important; it literally can mean the difference between a firm's success or failure. Professional buyers interpret the right price to mean a price that is fair and reasonable to both the buyer and the seller. Unfortunately, there is no magic formula for calculating precisely what constitutes a "fair and reasonable price." The right price for one supplier is not necessarily the right price for any other supplier, either at the same time or at different points in time. To determine the right price for any specific purchase, a number of constantly changing variables and relationships must be evaluated. This chapter discusses the most important of these variables and their relationships.

GENERAL ECONOMIC CONSIDERATIONS

Conditions of Competition

Economists of the classical school speak of a competitive scale that includes three fundamental types of competition: pure, imperfect, and monopoly. At the one end of the scale is *pure (or perfect) competition.* Under conditions of pure competition, the forces of supply and demand alone, not the individual actions of either buyers or sellers, determine prices.[1]

At the other end of the competitive scale is *monopoly.* Under conditions of monopoly, one seller controls the entire supply of a particular commodity, and thus is free to maximize its profit by regulating output and forcing a supply-demand relationship that is most favorable to the seller.

The competitive area between the extremes of pure competition and monopoly is called *imperfect competition.* Imperfect competition takes two forms: (1) markets characterized by few sellers and (2) those in which many sellers operate. When there are just a few sellers, an *oligopoly* is said to exist. The automobile, steel, and tobacco industries are examples of oligopolies. Generally, oligopolistic firms produce relatively few different products.

In contrast to oligopolies, the second form of imperfect competition exists where many sellers produce many products. This form of competition does not have a distinctive name. Most of the products sold in this market are *differentiated* (distinguished by a specific difference), although some are not. Sellers, however, spend big bucks along with major promotional efforts to persuade buyers that their products are different. This is the market in which the majority of the products made in the United States are traded. These economic principles are portrayed in Figure 14-1.

In practice, the three categories of competition are not mutually exclusive; actually, they overlap considerably. When one considers both the buying and

---

[1]Pure competition exists only under the following circumstances: The market contains a large number of buyers and sellers of approximately equal importance. The products traded are homogeneous (a buyer would not desire one particular seller's product over any other's). The buyers and sellers always have full knowledge of the market. The buyers always act rationally, and sellers are free to enter and to leave the market at will.

Types of Competition	Imperfect competition			
	Monopoly	Oligopoly	Differentiated competition	Perfect competition
Degree of Competition	One seller	Few sellers	Many sellers of similar products	Very many sellers of similar or identical products
Approximate Percent of Transactions	5	├ ─ ─ ─ ─ ─ ─ 70 ─ ─ ─ ─ ─ ─ ┤		25

FIGURE 14-1
Competitive scale.

the selling sides of the total market, it is apparent that the number of market arrangements between individual buyers and sellers is very large indeed.

It is frequently suggested that oligopolists conspire and act together as monopolists to thwart price competition. The facts, however, indicate that price conspiracies among oligopolists are not the normal order of business. Although the U.S. Department of Justice does uncover a few conspiracies every year, any buyer who has purchased in oligopolistic markets knows that both price and service competition can be intense. Chevrolet strives intensely to outsell Ford, and vice versa. This is not to say that oligopolistic industries do not periodically exercise monopolistic tendencies to their own advantage. They do. For example, in times of recession, it requires only a basic knowledge of economics, not a conspiracy, for oligopolies to lower production rates and thus direct a balance of the forces of supply and demand in their favor.

It should be noted that oligopolistic industries frequently hold firmly to their prices for long periods and appear noncompetitive. This appearance may be deceptive, however. Frequently, in order to gain a competitive advantage without notice, oligopolists shift their competitive efforts to other areas, such as service. Sellers may agree to perform such additional services as carrying customers' inventories, extending the payment time of their bills, or absorbing their freight charges. Such indirect price reductions often are not advertised.

Consequently, the amount of service a firm is able to obtain usually correlates directly with the perception and skills of its purchasing personnel. Foreign competitors also greatly influence the freedom of U.S. oligopolies to raise their prices above fair market prices. For example, the freedom of U.S. automobile, steel, and electronic companies to raise prices is noticeably restrained because of foreign imports. For a number of items, specialty suppliers also compete effectively with oligopolies. Consequently, the competent buyer who learns to operate successfully within the practices of oligopolistic industries can definitely influence the firm's total cost of materials.

It is important to understand that oligopoly is not characteristic of industry as a whole. Most firms and industries operate somewhere in the area of imperfect competition. Millions of people, working in thousands of factories, produce hundreds of thousands of products substantially without governmental or any other outside direction. The firms that make up this market exercise almost complete control over their prices, and price conspiracies in this market are extremely rare. In fact, aside from utilities, transportation, and some manufacturing industries, the concentration of oligopolistic power is rare.

Most Prices Are Subject to Adjustment   It is because most firms are free, within broad limits, to adjust their prices at will that competent buyers can obtain better prices in direct proportion to their ability to analyze costs, markets, and pricing methodologies. Prices can be negotiated very little with firms in the markets of pure competition or monopoly. They can be negotiated a great deal with firms operating in the markets of imperfect competition. The question then is: What proportion of the nation's total market falls within the area of imperfect competition? What percentage of a buyer's total purchases are subject to price flexibility?

Studies made at the Graduate School of Business at Stanford University show the nation's economy to be approximately 70 percent free. The results of similar studies by other authorities support this conclusion. Buyers in most purchasing situations, therefore, have considerable latitude for negotiating both price and service with their suppliers. At the same time, however, every buyer should guard against the inducement of illegal price concessions. Buying personnel must understand the operation of federal and state restraint of trade laws. (See Chapter 30.)

Variable-Margin Pricing

Most industrial firms sell a line of products rather than just a single product. Very few firms attempt to earn the same profit margin on each product in the line. Most firms price their products to generate a satisfactory return on their whole line, not on each product in the line. Such a variable-margin pricing policy permits maximum competition on individual products. The profits from the most efficiently produced and "successfully priced" items are used to offset the losses or the lower profit margins of the inefficiently produced items.

An understanding of the theory of variable-margin pricing is essential if buyers are to obtain the right price. Because it is usually advantageous to them, whenever possible sellers use average profit margins for pricing orders. In some cases, this practice results in prices that sophisticated buyers realize are too high—particularly when low-cost, efficiently produced items are being purchased. Invariably when average margins are used, prices considerably above fair prices result for large, long-term purchases. When dealing with large, multiproduct firms which utilize this pricing approach, a buyer must also know which of the items purchased are high-margin and which are low-margin items. This fact is learned by noting the differences in volumes, manufacturing skills, and costs of the various producers.

The following case illustrates the practical concepts of the preceding discussion. A large, high-technology research firm successfully negotiated a $2.8 million annual contract for medical and scientific supplies. At the outset, the seller proposed that the contract be priced at cost plus the firm's annual gross profit margin of 19 percent. After several hours of negotiation, the contract was priced at cost plus a 6 percent profit margin. Had the buyer not understood the concept of variable-margin pricing, and not known which items the seller produced efficiently, this contract would have cost his company an additional $320,000.

In their search for optimum prices, competent buyers are aided by analyzing the pricing methods of both full-line and specialty suppliers. Regrettably, only buyers from a few progressive firms actually make such in-depth analyses of the entire product line of the industries in which they do business. Rather, most buyers focus their analyses on just one product at a time (the product presently being purchased). Buyers are rewarded by directing their efforts toward the development of savings produced by recurring long-term cost reductions, rather than focusing on savings from short-term cost reductions. In short, optimal pricing comes to buyers who understand the pricing processes for complete product lines, in all firms, in all industries from whom they buy.

In the long run, a firm must recover its costs or go out of business. In the long run, for any given item, the price is roughly equal to the cost of the least efficient producer who is able to remain in business. *In the short run,* however, prices in the free, competitive segment of the economy (roughly 70 percent of the whole) are determined primarily by competition, that is, by supply and demand, and not by costs.

Differences between Products

There are many basic differences between the kinds of products marketed in the various segments of the economy. Some products in the competitive segment are *undifferentiated* products (not distinguished by specific differences), and others are *differentiated*. In some cases, the products are intrinsically different (differentiated); in others, manufacturers are successful in making their similar products appear different from those of their competitors. Even in those cases where a product cannot be made different in substance, producers can still get premium prices if they can persuade buyers *to believe* that their products are superior. Some producers spend huge sums of money on sales personnel and advertising to accomplish such a purpose. In the jargon of the economists, "They attempt to make the demand curve for the products of their firm somewhat inelastic." If their efforts are successful, they can charge higher prices for their products. On the other hand, if their efforts are defeated by the counterefforts of competitors, as is frequently the case, price competition comparable to that in pure competition can result. Grocers, for example, are well acquainted with this economic fact.

For both differentiated and undifferentiated products, producers compete on quality and service as well as price. The consumer market is more susceptible to producers' advertising claims than the industrial market; therefore, the major portion of advertising effort is directed toward the consumer market. Nonetheless, industrial buyers must be aware of advertising and sales tactics and be very careful that they determine quality from an analysis of facts, not from unsupported claims.

Six Categories of Cost

A buyer knows that price = cost + profit. He or she must understand variable, fixed, semivariable, total, direct, and indirect costs, and how these costs influence prices. Profit is addressed in Chapter 15.

Variable Costs   These are items of cost that *vary directly and proportionally with the production quantity* of a particular product. Variable costs include direct labor wages, the cost of materials, and a small number of overhead costs which the supplier incurs in filling an order. For example, if a specific cutting tool costs $10 and lasts for 100 cuttings, each cut represents a variable cost of 10 cents. If three cuts were required in machining a specific item, the variable cost for cutting would be 30 cents. Thus, variable costs represent money sellers can keep if they do not perform a specific contract, and money they must pay if they do perform it.

Fixed Costs   Fixed costs *do NOT vary with volume,* but rather change over time. Fixed costs are costs sellers must pay simply because they are in business. They are a function of time and are not influenced by the volume of production. For example, if the lathe that held the cutting tool in the preceding example depreciates at the rate of $250 a month, this is a fixed cost. The seller has this $250 expense every month, whether or not any turnings are made during that period. Fixed costs generally represent either money the seller has already spent for buildings and equipment or money the seller will have to spend in the future for unavoidable expenses such as taxes and rent, regardless of the plant's volume of production. Other fixed costs include advertising and research and development, which may be increased or decreased from one time period to another, regardless of production volume.

Semivariable Costs   Generally, it is not possible to classify all production costs as being either completely fixed or completely variable. Many others, termed semivariable costs, fall somewhere between these extremes. Costs such as maintenance, utilities, and postage are partly variable and partly fixed. Each is like a fixed cost, because its total cannot be tied directly to a particular unit of production. Yet it is possible to sort out specific elements in each of these costs that are fixed as soon as the plant begins to operate. When the fixed portion is removed, the remaining elements frequently do vary rather closely in proportion to the production volume. For example, if a plant is producing an average of 5,000 items a month, it might have an average light bill of $700 a month. Should the number of units produced be increased to 8,000, the light bill might increase by $100 to $800. The $100 increase is not proportional to the production increase, because a certain segment of the light bill is fixed whether any production occurs or not. Above this fixed segment, however, light costs do vary in a fairly consistent relationship with production volume.

Total Costs   The sum of the variable, fixed, and semivariable costs comprises the total costs. As the volume of production increases, total costs increase. However, the cost to produce *each unit* of product decreases. This is because the fixed costs do not increase; rather, they are simply spread over a larger number of units of product. Suppose, for example, that a single-product firm has the following cost structure:

Variable costs, per unit	$ 2.25
Fixed costs, per month	1,200.00
Semivariable costs:	
Fixed portion, per month	450.00
Variable portion, per unit	0.30

Under these circumstances, Table 14-1 shows how unit costs change as volume changes. To understand fully the intricacies of the volume-cost-profit relationship it is essential to understand variable, fixed, and semivariable costs.

Because it is difficult to allocate costs specifically as fixed, variable, and semivariable, accountants generally classify costs in two categories—direct costs and indirect costs. These are discussed briefly below.

Direct Costs   These are costs that are specifically traceable to or caused by a specific project or production operation. Two major direct costs are direct labor and direct materials. Although most direct costs are variable, conceptually, direct costs should *not* be confused with variable costs; the two terms are rooted in different concepts. The former relates to *traceability* of costs to specific

TABLE 14-1
VOLUME-UNIT COST RELATIONSHIPS

Monthly production units	Variable costs	Fixed costs	Semivariable costs Fixed	Semivariable costs Variable	Total cost	Unit cost
500	$1,125	$1,200	$450	$150	$2,925	$5.85
1,000	2,250	1,200	450	300	4,200	4.20
1,500	3,375	1,200	450	450	5,475	3.65
2,000	4,500	1,200	450	600	6,750	3.375
2,500	5,625	1,200	450	750	8,025	3.21

operations, while the latter relates to the *behavior* of costs as volume fluctuates. The salary of a production supervisor, for example, can be directly traceable to a product even though he or she is paid a fixed salary regardless of the volume produced. Returning to the illustration of the cutting tool, if a firm pays a worker 15 cents for making the three cuts required for each item, direct labor costs are 15 cents. If the value of the piece of metal being cut is 85 cents, direct costs for the item are $1.00.

Indirect Costs (Overhead) These are costs that are associated with or caused by two or more operating activities "jointly," but are not traceable to each of them individually. The nature of an indirect cost is such that it is not possible (or practical) to measure directly how much of the cost is attributable to a single operating activity. Indirect costs can be fixed or variable, depending on their behavior (e.g., the portion of energy consumption that varies with the level of production is a variable overhead). So, it is important that the reader not confuse indirect costs with fixed costs.

Regulation by Competition

From a buyer's point of view, competition is the mainspring of good pricing. As previously discussed, most producers do not have the same real costs of production. Even when their costs are the same, their competitive positions can be quite different. Hence, their prices can also be quite different. Consider the following example. Assume that a buyer is ready to purchase 10,000 specially designed cutting tools. The buyer sends the specifications to five companies for quotations. All five respond. For the sake of simplicity, assume that direct costs in these five companies are identical. Assume further that each company uses the same price-estimating formula; overhead is figured as 150 percent of direct labor, and profit is calculated as 12 percent of total cost. Each company could then lay out its figures as follows:

Cost of materials	$12,000	
Cost of direct labor	3,000	
Cost of overhead*	4,500	(150 percent of direct labor)
Total cost	$19,500	
Profit	2,340	(12 percent of total cost)
Price	$21,840	

*To simplify the example, assume all overhead is classified as fixed; that is, it remains constant over a given range of production.

Even with all the controlling figures fixed, the companies more than likely would not quote the same price, because *the cost of production and profit are only two of the factors a seller considers in determining price.* In the final analysis, it is the factors stemming from competition that determine the exact price each firm will quote. That is, when faced with the realities of competition, the price any specific firm will quote will be governed largely by *its need for business* and by *what it thinks its competitors will quote,* not by costs or profits.

Who is responsible for final determination of the price to be quoted? Generally, it is the chief marketing executive; in some cases, it is the president of the company. Pricing is one of the most important management decisions a firm must make. As an objective, a firm tends to seek the highest price that is compatible with its long-range goals. What is the possible price range for the order in the preceding example? The out-of-pocket (variable) costs for this order are $12,000 for materials and $3,000 for direct labor, a total of $15,000. This is the lowest price any company should accept under any circumstances. The highest price is $21,840, based on the assumption that a profit in excess of 12 percent is not in the long-range interest of the firm. (Such a profit may attract additional competition to enter this market, which in turn would erode the profitability of the market.)

What could cause one of the firms to consider a price of $17,000? Keen competition among suppliers could. On the other hand, keen competition among buyers could drive the price higher. This is why competition, as a leveler, is such a dominant factor in pricing. If the firm had been unable to obtain a satisfactory volume of other business, it would gladly take this order for a price of $17,000. As a result of the order, the $15,000 out-of-pocket costs would be covered, the experienced work force could be kept working, and a $2,000 contribution could be made to overhead. Remember that the fixed overhead would continue whether or not the firm received this order.

In the long run, a firm must recover all costs or go out of business, for in the long run, plant and machinery must be maintained, modernized, and replaced. *In the short run,* however, it is generally better for a firm to recover variable costs and some portion of overhead rather than undergo a significant decline in business. This would not be true, of course, if such additional business would affect the pricing of other orders the firm has already filled or is going to fill.

Business in good times is not ordinarily done at out-of-pocket prices. A more traditional situation would be for each of the five firms to bid prices above the total cost figure of $19,500. How much above this figure each would bid would depend on the specific economic circumstances and expectations applicable to each firm. Those firms hungry for business would bid just slightly above the total cost figure of $19,500. Those with large backlogs and growing lists of steady customers (and therefore not in need of new business in the short run) would bid a larger profit margin (perhaps 14 percent). Sellers can be expected to evaluate competitive situations differently, depending on how much they want or need the business. Therefore, even with the simplifying assumption of identical costs, it is reasonable to expect bids in this situation to range from approximately $19,700 (1 percent profit) to $21,840 (12 percent profit). Prices close to out-of-pocket costs could be offered if the seller were attempting to obtain a desirable, prestigious account, or if the supplier desired to gain experience in a situation wherein additional large orders are expected to follow.

Varying Profit Margins   A seller must recover *all* costs from his or her total sales to make a profit. However, *each* product in the line does not have to make a profit, and all accounts do not have to yield the same profit margin. Bearing these thoughts in mind, the principal cost/competition implications of pricing can be summarized as follows: *Sound pricing policy dictates that sellers, in accordance with their interpretation of the prevailing competitive forces, quote prices that are high enough to include all variable costs and make the maximum possible contribution toward fixed costs and profit.*

Similarly, sound pricing policy dictates that, for any given purchase, buyers should use their knowledge of products, markets, costs, and competitive conditions to estimate the price range at which sellers can reasonably be expected to do business. Finally, with this information, a knowledge of the value of the buyer's ongoing business to a seller, and an appreciation of the value of this specific order, the buyer applies all relevant purchasing principles and techniques to purchase at prices as close as possible to the bottom of the estimated price range.

PRICE ANALYSIS

Some form of price analysis is required for every purchase. The method and scope of analysis required are dictated by the dollar amount and circumstances attending each specific purchase. *Price analysis is defined as the examination of a seller's price proposal (bid) by comparison with reasonable price benchmarks, without examination and evaluation of the separate elements of the cost and profit making up the price.*

A buyer has four tools which can be used to conduct a price analysis: (1) analysis of competitive price proposals; (2) comparison with regulated, catalog, or market prices; (3) comparison with historical prices; and (4) use of independent cost estimates.

Competitive Price Proposals

Chapter 12 described the conditions which should be satisfied before using competitive bidding as a means of selecting the source of supply. When this approach is employed, and the following additional conditions are satisfied, then the resulting low bid normally provides a fair and reasonable price:

- At least two qualified sources have responded to the solicitation.
- The proposals are responsive to the buying firm's requirements.
- The supplier competed independently for the award.
- The supplier submitting the lowest offer does not have an unfair advantage over its competitors.
- The lowest evaluated price is reasonable.

The buyer cannot apply this approach to pricing in a mechanical manner. He or she clearly must use common sense and ensure that the price is reasonable when compared with past prices, with independent estimates, or with realistic rules of thumb.

Regulated, Catalog, and Market Prices

Prices Set by Law or Regulation   When the price is set by law or regulation, the supplier must identify the regulating authority and specify what the regulated prices are. With regulated prices, some governmental body (federal, state, or local) has determined that prices of certain goods and services should be controlled directly. Normally, approval of price changes requires formal review, hearings, and an affirmative vote of the regulatory authority. No supplier may charge more or less than the approved price.

Catalog Price   An established catalog price is a price that is included in a catalog, a price list, or some other form that is regularly maintained by the supplier. The price sources must be dated and readily available for inspection by potential customers. The buyer should request a recent sales summary demonstrating that significant quantities are sold to a significant number of customers at the indicated price before accepting a catalog price.

Market Price   A market price results from the interaction of many buyers and sellers who are willing to trade at a given (market) price. The forces of supply and demand establish the price. A market price is generally for an item or a service that is generic in nature and not particularly unique to the seller. Normally the daily market price is published in local newspapers or trade publications which are independent of the supplier.

Historical Prices

Price analysis may be performed by comparing a proposed price with historical quotes or prices for the same or similar item. It is essential to determine that the base price was fair and reasonable (as determined through price analysis) and is still a valid standard against which to measure the offered price. The fact that a historical price exists does not automatically make it a valid basis for comparison. Several issues must be considered:

- How have conditions changed?[2]
- Were there one-time engineering, setup, or tooling charges?
- What should be the effect of inflation or deflation on the price?
- Will the new procurement create a situation in which the supplier should

---

[2]The Bureau of Labor Statistics in Washington, D.C., provides thousands of different price indexes every month. Available are indexes by stage of processing, industry, and individual commodity grades. A commonly used series for these purposes is the producer price index (PPI). Also import and export price indexes broken down in the major subcategories are available. These indexes allow the price analyst to adjust historical prices by appropriate changes over time.

enjoy the benefits of learning? (The concept of learning curve analysis is discussed in Chapter 15.)

Independent Cost Estimates

When other techniques of price analysis cannot be utilized, the buyer may use an independent cost estimate as the basis for comparison. The buyer must determine that the estimate is fair and reasonable.[3] If price analysis is impractical or if it does not allow the buyer to reach a conclusion that the price is fair and reasonable, then cost analysis, the subject of the next chapter, should be employed.

PURCHASING DESIGN WORK

When a buyer contracts for the design as well as the manufacture of a special component, he or she must be careful not to create a future supplier relations problem. One facet of the potential problem centers on the matter of ownership of the special design. Another facet concerns the supplier's recovery of sunk costs in design work and tooling.

When a supplier agrees to design and manufacture a special component, or to develop a special process, who owns the resulting design— the supplier or the buyer? Who has the right to apply for a patent on the item? Further, who owns the special tooling the supplier must obtain to produce the item? The answers to these basic questions should be specified unequivocally in the purchase contract. By taking this precaution, the buyer can avoid the uncertainties and distasteful misunderstandings which at times accompany such purchases.

The purchase price stated in the contract should reflect the decision regarding ownership of the design and tooling. From a buyer's standpoint, the most desirable method of pricing is one which separates the supplier's charges into three categories: (1) price for design and development work, (2) price for special tooling and equipment, and (3) price for manufacturing. Under these circumstances, both parties know precisely what the buyer is paying for and what should be obtained in return.

If a buyer can purchase design work and tooling completely apart from the manufactured components, the contract is usually clear-cut and no problems ensue. The buyer can do whatever he or she wishes with the design or tooling without infringing on the prerogatives of the supplier. Other things being equal, this is by far the most desirable type of contract. It makes the buyer less dependent on a single supplier who chooses to operate in a short-term-profit-maximizing mode in lieu of a partnership mode; it gives the buyer more leverage which can be used in stimulating competition among additional potential suppliers.

---

[3]The development and use of independent cost estimates is described in detail in Chapter 4 of *Zero Base Pricing™: Achieving World Class Competitiveness through Reduced All-in-Cost*, by D. N. Burt, W. Norquist, and J. Anklesaria, Probus Publishing, Chicago, 1990.

As anyone with good business sense would suspect, some suppliers are unwilling to accept contracts for continuing business on the basis just described. A shrewd supplier may well prefer to develop a proprietary product and, for a limited period of time, establish itself in a monopolistic position. It is this type of contract that generates supplier relations problems. Clearly, the buyer does not want to remain a captive customer of one supplier indefinitely. On the other hand, in the interest of fairness, the buyer is obligated to see that the supplier is adequately compensated for its original design and development work. Therefore, if the supplier will not divulge design and tooling costs, the buyer should write the purchase contract in a manner which compels the supplier to price the job so as to recover these costs within a reasonable period of time (usually within a year). For example, the contract might guarantee the purchase of a specified number of units, or it might state that the job will be opened for bid on an annual basis.

Although the original supplier has an inherent advantage over future bidders, it is nevertheless essential that the buyer state at the outset the intention to open the job to competition as soon as the original contractor has recovered the sunk costs and earned a reasonable profit. This approach is in keeping with the buyer's responsibility to treat all suppliers fairly, and at the same time to seek out the efficient, low-cost producer.

ALL-IN-COST

The modern professional buyer is concerned with obtaining the lowest "all-in-cost"—that is, the total acquisition and usage cost of the procurement to the buying firm. "Total cost of ownership" is another term commonly used to describe this concept. Price is only one of the components of all-in-cost. Other components are costs associated with transportation, storage, and administration, as well as the costs resulting from defective materials entering the conversion process. Defective materials costs include rework, lost productivity, and total costs incurred to the point the item is scrapped. In addition, postmanufacturing costs in the areas of warranty, service, and field failure costs resulting from defective materials should be included in all-in-cost.

> THE PROFESSIONAL BUYER RECOGNIZES THAT
> PRICE IS ONLY A COMPONENT OF ALL-IN-COST!

DOCUMENTING A PRICE ANALYSIS

A price analysis report is a written summary of the analysis for a given procurement. The report is prepared for each major procurement to summarize the basis for the buyer's conclusion that a price is fair and reasonable. It is included in the purchase order or contract file.

The report may be a separate document, particularly if there is to be no negotiation conference. If competitive bidding was used to select the source and the price, an abstract of the bids received will suffice. The findings of the price analysis may be incorporated in the price negotiation memorandum as part of the explanation of the prenegotiation objective and as part of the justification for the resulting price. There are strong arguments, however, for requiring a written report of price analysis before the negotiation. The discipline of writing the report requires the buyer to sift through the data, reconstruct the process and its events, restate key issues and decisions, and state conclusions based on these findings.

The price analysis report should indicate:

- Information that was considered
- Weight given to each piece of information and why
- Logic supporting the determination that an offeror's price is or is not reasonable
- Soundness of that logic

The length and detail in a price analysis report depends on the nature of the procurement. Similarly, the specific elements included depend on what it takes to establish reasonableness and what is available.

DISCOUNTS

Discounts frequently are considered to be a routine, prosaic part of pricing. Perceptive buyers, however, recognize that this is not always the case. As will be illustrated in the discussion to follow, discounts can sometimes succeed as a technique for reducing prices after all other techniques have failed. The four most commonly used kinds of discounts are *trade discounts, quantity discounts, seasonal discounts,* and *cash discounts.*

Trade Discounts

These discounts are reductions from list price allowed various classes of buyers and distributors to compensate them for performing certain marketing functions for the original seller (the manufacturer) of the product. Trade discounts are frequently structured as a sequence of individual discounts (e.g., 25, 10, and 5 percent), and in such cases they are called *series discounts.* Those who perform only a part of the distribution functions get only one or two of the discounts in the series. If the retail price of an item with such discounts is $100, the full discounted price is calculated as follows: 25 percent of $100 = $25; 10 percent of ($100 − $25) = $7.50; 5 percent of ($100 − $25 − $7.50) = $3.38. The manufacturer's selling price, then, is $100 − $25 − $7.50 − $3.38 = $64.12.

An industrial buyer who purchases through distributors must, as a result of the very nature of series trade discounts, be certain that the buy is from the right distributor (i.e., the distributor obtaining the most discounts). The general guideline for a buyer is to get as close to the manufacturer as is practical. For example, a large buyer normally should not purchase paper requirements from a janitorial supply house which usually does not obtain all discounts in the series for paper. If an account is sufficiently large, the buyer should purchase from a paper distributor who normally does obtain all discounts in the series. Such a supplier can, at the same profit margin as the janitorial supply house, offer buyers lower prices. Buyers with very large accounts should purchase directly from paper manufacturers.

Quantity Discounts

These price reductions are given to a buyer for purchasing increasingly larger quantities of materials. They normally are offered under one of three purchasing arrangements:

1 For purchasing a specific quantity of items at one time
2 For purchasing a specified dollar total of any number of different items at one time
3 For purchasing a specified dollar total of any number of items over an agreed-upon time period

The third type of quantity discount noted above is called a *cumulative discount*. The period of accumulation can be a month, a quarter, or, more commonly, a year. For large-dollar-value, repetitive purchases, buyers should always seek this type of discount. Also, because unplanned increases in business occur with regular frequency, buyers should include in all quantity discount contracts a provision that if the total purchases made under the contract exceed the estimated quantities, then an additional discount will be allowed for all such excesses.

The quantity discount concept originally stemmed from the unit cost reductions inherent in large-volume manufacturing operations. In a traditional mass or batch production operation, a large production run of a single product spreads the fixed costs over the number of items produced and results in a lower production cost per item. With the continuing improvement of flexible manufacturing systems, however, the dilution of fixed setup costs becomes rather small compared with other product-specific cost elements. Consequently, if a quantity discount is based solely on the distribution of setup and order processing costs over the volume of production, there is clearly a declining incentive for such a supplier to offer this form of quantity discount.

Seasonal Discounts

Based on the seasonal nature of some products (primarily consumer products), their producers commonly offer discounts for purchases made in the off-season.

Cash Discounts

In many industries, sellers traditionally offer price reductions for the prompt payment of bills. When such discounts are given, they are offered as a percentage of the net invoice price. When suppliers extend credit, they cannot avoid certain attendant costs, including the cost of tied-up capital, the cost of operating a credit department, and the cost of some bad-debt losses. Most sellers can reduce these costs by dealing on a short-term payment basis. Therefore, they are willing to pass on part of the savings to the buyers in the form of a cash discount.

Buyers should be aware of the importance of negotiating the highest possible cash discount. The most commonly used discount in practice is 2 percent 10 days, net 30 days. In industries where prompt payment is particularly important, cash discounts as high as 8 percent have been allowed. A cash discount of 2/10, net 30 means that a discount of 2 percent can be taken if the invoice is paid within 10 days, while the full amount should be remitted if payment is made between 10 and 30 days after receipt of the invoice.

A 2 percent discount, viewed casually, does not appear to represent much money. In one sense, however, it is the equivalent of a 36.5 percent annual interest rate. Because the bill must be paid in 30 days and the discount can be taken up to the tenth day, a buyer not taking the discount is paying 2 percent of the dollar amount of the invoice to use the cash involved for 20 days. In a 365-day year, there are 18.25 twenty-day periods (365/20 = 18.25). A 2/10 discount translates into an *annual* discount rate of 36.5 percent (2 percent times 18.25).[4] If a firm does not have sufficient cash on hand to take cash discounts, the possibility of borrowing the needed money should be investigated. Under normal conditions, paying 10 to 15 percent for capital that returns 36.5 percent is good business. Capable buyers understand the time value of money. In some situations, generous cash discounts can be obtained either for prepayment or for 48-hour payment.

Various other types of cash discounts are in use. One common type is the *end-of-month (EOM)* dating system. This system of cash discounting permits the buyer to take a designated percentage discount if payment is made within a specified number of days after the end of the month in which the order is shipped. If materials are shipped on October 16 under 2/10 EOM terms, a 2 percent discount can be taken at any time until November 10.

Lower prices, in the form of higher cash discounts, are an ever-present source of price reduction which buyers should always explore. Frequently, sellers who will not consider reducing the prices of their products will consider allowing higher cash discounts. Such action accomplishes the identical result for the buyer. For example, a major petroleum company recently was able to gain a 6 percent price reduction on the purchase of a complex testing machine—a machine the manufacturer had never before sold below its listed

---

[4]A complete analysis of this situation must include the opportunity cost of early payment. If a firm's internal cost of capital is 15 percent/year, the *net* saving generated by the 2/10, net 30 discount is 36.5 percent − 15 percent, or 21.5 percent on an annualized basis.

$92,000 selling price. The $5,520 price reduction was achieved by the buyer's offering to pay one-half of the purchase price one week in advance of the machine's delivery to his company's testing laboratory.

LEGAL IMPLICATIONS OF PRICING

Pricing cannot always be decided solely on the basis of economic considerations. Legislation and court decisions, both federal and state, sometimes influence pricing. The major pricing laws are discussed in Chapter 30, "Legal Considerations."

CONCLUSION

Obtaining the *right* price is one of a buyer's important responsibilities. When focusing on price, the buyer is concerned with the *total cost,* or all-in-cost, of the item or service being purchased.

FOR DISCUSSION

14-1 Describe the three fundamental types of competition identified by the classical school of economics.

14-2 Discuss the pricing strategy of oligopolistic industries and the efforts they employ to maintain competitiveness.

14-3 Which classical market structure provides the best environment for price negotiations? Explain.

14-4 What is variable-margin pricing?

14-5 List and briefly describe the six categories of cost. Which ones are used in making an incremental cost analysis?

14-6 As the volume of production increases, the cost to produce each unit of product decreases but total cost increases. Why?

14-7 How might it be against the long-range interest of a supplier to establish a large profit margin?

14-8 What impact does a flexible manufacturing system have on quantity discount theory? Discuss.

14-9 What are the four tools a buyer can use to conduct price analysis?

14-10 What are some of the issues involved in historical price considerations?

14-11 Discuss the problems involved in purchasing design work.

14-12 Describe the concept of all-in-cost. How would you measure it?

14-13 Why should a buyer prepare a written report documenting his or her price analysis?

14-14 List and describe the four most commonly used discounting practices.

14-15 Why do some buyers pursue cash payment discounts so vigorously? Explain.

CASES FOR CHAPTER 14

Hardy Company, page 828
Collier Company I, page 800
Branson Electronic Company (A and B in the *Instructor's Manual*)
Templeton Engine Company, page 922
Nationwide Telephone, page 865
A Problem of Price, page 891
World-Wide Industries, page 932
Campbell Typewriter Corporation (in the *Instructor's Manual*)

15

COST ANALYSIS

KEY CONCEPTS

- Cost analysis
  Cost analysis defined
  The capabilities of management
  The efficiency of labor
  The amount and quality of subcontracting
  Plant capacity
- Sources of cost data
  Potential suppliers
  Supply partners
  Cost models
- Direct costs
  Direct labor
  Direct materials
- Learning curves
  The cumulative curve and the unit curve concepts
  Application of learning curves
  Pitfalls in using learning curves
- Tooling costs
- Indirect costs
  Engineering overhead
  Materials overhead
  Manufacturing overhead
  General and administrative
  Selling
  Recovering indirect costs
- Activity-based costing/management
- Target costing
- Profit

COST ANALYSIS

Cost analysis should be employed when price analysis is impractical or does not allow a buyer to reach the conclusion that a price is fair and reasonable. Cost analysis generally is most useful when purchasing nonstandard items and services.

Cost Analysis Defined

We have seen that price analysis is a process of comparisons. *Cost analysis* is a review and an evaluation of actual or anticipated costs. This analysis involves the application of experience, knowledge, and judgment to data in an attempt to project reasonable estimated contract costs. Estimated costs serve as the basis for buyer-seller negotiations to arrive at mutually agreeable contract prices.

The purpose of cost analysis is to arrive at a price that is fair and reasonable to both the buyer and the seller. Estimates can be made with the help of one's engineering department or by analyzing the estimates submitted by the seller. To analyze a seller's costs, a buyer must understand the nature of each of the various costs a manufacturer incurs. The buyer must compare the labor hours, material costs, and overhead costs of all competing suppliers as listed on their cost-breakdown sheets. Most important, he or she must determine the reasons for any differences, focusing on three principal elements of cost: direct, indirect (overhead), and profit. These cost elements were defined and discussed in the preceding chapter.

A buyer should always be conscious of the fact that costs vary widely among manufacturing firms. Some firms are high-cost producers; others are low-cost producers. Many factors affect the costs of specific firms, as well as the cost of individual products within any given firm. Some of the most important elements affecting costs are:

- The capabilities of management
- The efficiency of labor
- The amount and quality of subcontracting
- The plant capacity and the continuity of output

Each of these factors can change with respect to either product or time. For this reason, a specific firm can be a high-cost producer for one item and a low-cost producer for another. Similarly, the firm can be a low-cost producer one year and a high-cost producer another year. These circumstances make it extremely important for a buyer to obtain competition among potential suppliers. Competition can be a buyer's key to locating the desired low-cost producer.

The Capabilities of Management

The skill with which management plans, organizes, staffs, coordinates, and controls all the personnel, capital, and equipment at its disposal determines the efficiency of the firm. Managements utilize the resources available to them with substantially different degrees of efficiency. This is one basic reason why finding the correct supplier (and price) is so profitable for astute buyers.

The Efficiency of Labor

Anyone who has visited a number of different firms surely has noticed the differences in attitudes and skills that exist between various labor forces. Some are cooperative, take great pride in their work, have high morale, and produce efficiently, while others do not. The skill with which management exercises its responsibilities contributes greatly to these differences between efficient and inefficient labor forces. Buyers are well rewarded for pinpointing suppliers with efficient labor forces.

The Amount and Quality of Subcontracting

When a contract has been awarded to a supplier (the *prime contractor*), the supplier frequently subcontracts some of the production work required to complete the job. The supplier's subcontracting decisions are important to a buyer because they may involve a large percentage of prime contract money. The first decision a prime contractor must make regarding subcontracts is which items should be made and which specific items should be bought. Should the prime contractor decide to buy some of those items which can be made more efficiently, and vice versa, the buyer suffers financially. Even if the prime contractor makes the correct "make" decision, it still is responsible for selecting those subcontractors which are needed for the "buy" items.

Subcontractor prices and performance directly influence the prices the buyer pays the prime contractor. Hence, the prime's skills in both making and administering its subcontracts are of great importance to the buyer. For this reason, buyers must periodically review their major suppliers to ensure that they have effective purchasing and subcontracting capabilities of their own.

Plant Capacity

A plant's overhead costs are directly influenced by its size. A plant can get too large for efficient production and, as a result, lose its competitive ability. On the other hand, plants with large capital investments, or those manufacturing products on a mass production basis, can be too small to attain the most efficient production levels. A buyer must be alert to detect firms whose operations are adversely affected by size.

Plant output is clearly one of the controlling elements in the cost/profit picture. Table 15-1 illustrates this concept numerically. Note how volume affects profit when variable costs change because of inefficient use of facilities beyond optimum plant capacity. Note also that while total profit continues to increase as production output increases, beyond a certain output profit increases at a decreasing rate. This relationship is an important one for buyers to keep in mind.

SOURCES OF COST DATA

There are three primary sources of cost data: (1) from potential suppliers as a precondition of submitting proposals and bids, (2) from suppliers with whom the firm has developed preferred or strategic supplier relationships/partnerships, and (3) cost models.

Cost Data as a Precondition of Bidding

When a buyer anticipates that cost analysis will be required, he or she should include a request for a cost breakdown with each request for quotation. This is the proper time to make such a request, *not after* negotiations have started. Suppliers cannot complain that making this breakdown is an extra burden at this time, since they must perform such an analysis to prepare their bids. A simple procedure used by a number of progressive firms for obtaining cost breakdowns is to include the following statement with their request for quotations: "The buyer will not consider any quotation not accompanied by a cost breakdown." Not all suppliers readily provide cost-of-production information; however, the number refusing to do so for nonstandard items is becoming rel-

---

TABLE 15-1
HOW PRODUCTION VOLUME AFFECTS FIXED COSTS, VARIABLE COSTS, AND PROFIT

Production quantity	Selling price	Sales revenue	Fixed costs	Variable costs	Total cost	Total profit	Profit per unit of added production
0	$20	$ 0	$4,000	$ 0	$4,000	−$4,000	$15
100	20	2,000	4,000	500	4,500	− 2,500	15
200	20	4,000	4,000	1,000	5,000	− 1,000	15
300	20	6,000	4,000	1,500	5,500	+ 500	15
400	20	8,000	4,000	2,000	6,000	+ 2,000	15
500	20	10,000	4,000	2,500	6,500	+ 3,500	15
600	20	12,000	4,000	3,000	7,000	+ 5,000	14
700*	20	14,000	4,000	3,600	7,600	+ 6,400	12
800*	20	16,000	4,000	4,400	8,400	+ 7,600	10
900*	20	18,000	4,000	5,400	9,400	+ 8,600	

*Plant begins to strain capacity and administrative capabilities. The result is less efficient operation; i.e., overtime is required, less experienced workers are utilized, scheduling and handling of materials becomes less efficient, and variable costs per unit rise. Consequently, although profit continues to increase beyond a production quantity of 600, it increases at a decreasing rate.

atively small. An example of a typical cost breakdown request form is shown in Figure 15-1.

Cost Data from Partners

As firms develop open relationships built on trust and collaboration, the purchasing firm will share information on forecasts, schedules, the way purchased items integrate into its product or process, etc. The supply partner will share information on its design, production, and quality processes and on its *design and production costs.*

Cost Data from Cost Models

On some occasions, it may not be possible to obtain cost data from the supplier. In other cases, the cost data obtained may appear unrealistic or support prices which are unacceptable. Under these conditions, it may be necessary for the purchasing firm to develop its own cost models to estimate what the supplier's costs *should be.* The development of such models requires the application of both accounting and industrial engineering skills, and is beyond the scope of the presentation in this chapter. It is sufficient at this point simply to say that this approach, though not extensively used by small and medium-sized firms, is commonly used by leading-edge firms that have the technical resources available.[1]

DIRECT COSTS

Except in industries with heavy fixed capital investments, direct costs are normally the major portion of total costs. As such, they generally serve as the basis on which sellers allocate their overhead costs. The astute buyer, therefore, must carefully investigate a seller's direct costs. *A tiny reduction here (because they are relatively large) is worth more (price-wise) to the buyer than a major reduction in the percentage of profit* (which is relatively small). Referring to Table 15-2, a 25 percent reduction in the $8 direct labor cost of situation 1 to the $6 direct labor cost of situation 2 results in a $6.05 ($33.88 − $27.83) reduction in price. A 25 percent reduction in profit would result in only a 77-cent reduction in price (0.25 × $3.08 = $0.77).

Direct Labor

During the development and production phase of a new item, a supplier typically experiences a heavy design and production engineering effort. These

---

[1]The interested reader is referred to Chapter 8 of *Zero Base Pricing™: Achieving World Class Competitiveness through Reduced All-in-Cost,* D. N. Burt, W. Norquist, and J. Anklesaria, by Probus Publishing, Chicago, 1990.

COST ANALYSIS	CHECK APPROPRIATE BOX ESTIMATED COST ☐ HISTORICAL COST ☐ PERIOD COVERED:		
NAME OF SUPPLIER	INQUIRY OR PURCHASE REQUISITION NO.		
ADDRESS (Street, City, State)	QUANTITY	AT $　　EACH	AMOUNT $
ARTICLE			
TERMS AND DISCOUNT　　　　NET TOTAL OF QUOTATION $			
ANALYSIS OF COST AS OF _____, 19___ INDICATE WHETHER: COST PER ITEM☐ OR TOTAL COST ☐			

ITEM	AMOUNT	PERCENT OF COST
1. DIRECT MATERIAL		
2. LESS SCRAP OR SALVAGE		
3. NET DIRECT MATERIAL		
4. PURCHASED PARTS - FROM SUBCONTRACTORS		
5. DIRECT PRODUCTIVE LABOR　　　HOURS AT $		
6. DIRECT FACTORY CHARGES:		
(A) TOOLS AND DIES		
1. DIRECT WAGES　　　HOURS AT $		
2. TOOLING BURDEN		
3. MATERIALS		
(B) SPECIAL MACHINERY		
(C) MISCELLANEOUS		
7. INDIRECT FACTORY EXPENSES (Burden), ON BASIS OF　　See Note[a]		
8. ENGINEERING AND DEVELOPMENT EXPENSES - DIRECT:		
(a) SALARIES AND WAGES　　HOURS AT $		
(b) BURDEN		
(c) OTHER		
TOTAL MANUFACTURING COST		
9. GENERAL AND ADMINISTRATIVE EXPENSE:		
PERCENT OF　　　　　　　　　　See Note[b]		
10. SELLING EXPENSE　　　　　　See Note[c]		
11. CONTINGENCIES　　　　　　　See Note[d]		
12. OTHER EXPENSES　　　　　　See Note[e]		
13.		
14.		
15.		
16.		
17.　　　TOTAL COST		
18. SELLING PRICE		

19. (a) Are the wage rates used in estimating the direct labor of the unit cost break-down
　　the same as those now prevailing?
　(b) If "No," explain difference and indicate approximate amount thereof.

20. (a) What operating rate has been used in calculating the above estimate?
　　　Hours of operation per week?
　(b) At what rate is your plant now operating?
　　　Hours of operation per week?

　　　_____　　_____
　　　　(Supplier)　　　　　(Signature and title)

　　　_____
　　　　(Date)

a State basis of allocation.
b State nature of expenses included and basis of allocation.
c State nature of expenses included and amount of advertising, if any, separately, and basis of allocation.
d Explain in detail.
e State nature of expenses, basis of allocation, and why related to the cost of this item.

FIGURE 15-1
Example of a typical request for a cost breakdown.

TABLE 15-2
DIRECT COSTS AND PRICES

Cost elements	Situation 1	Situation 2
Material	$ 8.00	$ 8.00
Direct labor	8.00	6.00
Fixed overhead at 150 percent of direct labor	12.00	9.00
Manufacturing cost	$28.00	$23.00
General and administrative overhead at 10 percent of manufacturing cost	2.80	2.30
Total cost	30.80	25.30
Profit at 10 percent of total cost	3.08	2.53
Price	$33.88	$27.83

efforts will peak and then decrease. As they do, tooling and setup efforts increase, peak, and decline. Machining, assembly, and test effort then become the predominant users of labor. A buyer should be cognizant of these factors and should analyze a bidder's estimate to ensure that it is based on proper planning, applying reasonable expectations of efficiency in this regard.

When analyzing direct manufacturing labor estimates, the buyer should pay particular attention to the following:

- Allowances for rework
- Geographic variations
- Variations in skills

Allowances for Rework   A buyer should carefully review a bidder's estimate of rework costs. Modern production techniques now make it possible to drastically reduce scrap rates. Effective purchasing by a supplier's organization can reduce the defect rates on incoming materials as much as 95 percent. The combined effect of reduced incoming quality problems and improved production and quality systems should reduce a supplier's requirement for rework markedly.

Geographic Variations   Wage rates vary significantly from one part of the country to another. A buyer must ensure that the wage rates proposed are, in fact, the wage rates applicable in the areas where the work is to be performed. The Bureau of Labor Statistics provides current wage rates for different trades in different locations.

Variations in Skills   The buyer, with assistance from the firm's industrial engineering or production departments, should review the types of labor skills proposed, to ensure that they are relevant and necessary for accomplishment of the required tasks.

Direct Materials

Direct materials are consumed or converted during the production process. Sheet metal, fasteners, electrical relays, and radios for automobiles are all examples of direct materials. In most cases, such materials normally are purchased from a wide variety of suppliers. And in some cases, the materials may have been produced or partially processed in other plants or divisions of the supplier's operation. The resulting costs should be scrutinized carefully for internal transfer charges and markups.

Further analysis of proposed materials costs frequently reveals a difference between the buyer's cost estimate for a given bill of materials and the bidder's estimate for the same bill. In such cases, the buyer should request supporting data from the supplier. In some cases, the labor component of the proposed materials costs should reflect a learning effect as more units are produced (this topic is discussed shortly). In any case, careful analysis and discussion should help identify the source of the variance.

LEARNING CURVES

In many circumstances, labor and supervision become more efficient as more units are produced. The *learning curve* (sometimes called the *improvement curve*) is defined as an empirical relationship between the number of units produced and the number of labor hours required to produce them. Production managers can use this relationship in scheduling production and in determining manpower requirements for a particular product over a given period of time. Buyers can use the relationship to analyze the effects of production and management "learning" on a supplier's unit cost of production.

Traditionally, the learning curve has been used primarily for purchases of complex equipment in the aircraft, electronics, and other highly technical industries. Recently, its use has spread to other industries. The learning curve is useful in both price and cost analysis. It is probably most useful in negotiations, as a starting point for pricing a new item. In addition to providing "buyer's insurance" against overcharging, the learning curve is also used effectively by government and commercial buyers in developing (1) target costs for new products, (2) make-or-buy information, (3) delivery schedules, and (4) progress payment schedules for suppliers.

The Cumulative Curve and the Unit Curve

In practice, two basic forms of the learning curve exist. The first curve, "the cumulative average cost curve," is commonly used in price and cost analysis.

This curve plots cumulative units produced against the average direct labor cost or *average labor hours required per unit for all units produced.* The second, "the unit or marginal cost curve," is also used in labor and cost-estimating work. The unit curve plots cumulative units produced against the *actual labor hours required to produce each unit.* Figure 15-2 illustrates and compares the two types of curves.

Selection of the learning curve technique to use tends to be based on an organization's past experience. Ideally, whether one should use a cumulative or a unit curve is a function of the production process itself. Some operations conform to a cumulative curve; others conform to the unit curve. The only way to know which to use is to record the actual production data and then determine which type of curve fits the data the best. The relationship is strictly an *empirical* one.

FIGURE 15-2
Comparison of a cumulative average learning curve A and a unit learning curve B, plotted on an arithmetic grid.

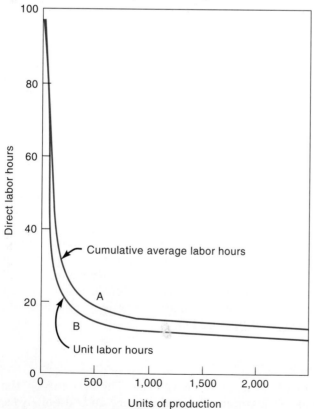

Target Cost Estimation

If a new product is custom-made to unique specifications, what should be paid for the 50th item? The 500th item? Obviously, costs should decline—but by how much? Analysis of the learning curve provides an answer. Cost reductions and estimated prices can be obtained merely by reading figures from a graph.

The learning curve is a quantitative model of the commonsense observation that the unit cost of a new product decreases as more units of the product are made because of the learning process. The manufacturer, through the repetitive production process, learns how to make the product at a lower cost. For example, the more times an individual repeats a complicated operation, the more efficient he or she becomes, in both speed and skill. This, in turn, means progressively lower unit labor costs. Familiarity with an operation also results in fewer rejects and reworks, better scheduling, possible improvements in tooling, fewer engineering changes, and more efficient management systems.

Suppose a buyer knows that it took a supplier 100 hours of labor to turn out the first unit of a new product, as indicated on Figures 15-3 and 15-4. The supplier reports that the second unit took 80 hours to make, so the average labor requirement for the two items is 180 ÷ 2 = 90 hours per unit. The production report for the first four units is summarized in Table 15-3.

Observe that the labor requirement dropped to 74 hours for the third unit and to 70 hours for the fourth unit. Column 4 shows that the average number

FIGURE 15-3
A 90 percent cumulative average learning curve, plotted on an arithmetic grid.

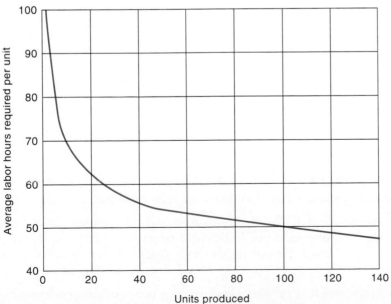

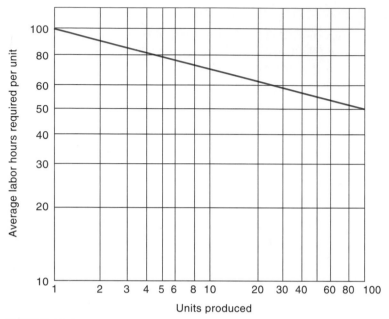

FIGURE 15-4
The 90 percent cumulative average learning curve of Figure 15-3, plotted on a log-log grid.

TABLE 15-3
NINETY PERCENT CUMULATIVE LEARNING CURVE DATA

Unit produced	Labor hours required	Cumulative labor hours required	Average labor hours required per unit
1st	100	100	100.0
2d	80	180	90.0
3d	74	254	84.7
4th	70	324	81.0

of labor hours required for the first four units was 81 hours per unit. Investigation of the learning rate shows the following relationships:

- As production doubled from one to two units, *the average labor hours required per unit* dropped from 100 to 90, a reduction of 10 percent.
- As production doubled from two to four units, *the average labor hours required per unit* dropped from 90 to 81, a reduction of 10 percent.

Figure 15-3 indicates that the same learning rate continues as production of the new item increases. Each time production doubles, the average labor requirement for all units declines by 10 percent. Thus, the product is said to have a 90 percent learning rate, or a 90 percent learning curve. Note that this is based on the *cumulative average* learning curve phenomenon. The basic point revealed by the learning curve is that *a specific and constant percentage reduction in the average direct labor hours required per unit results each time the number of units produced is doubled.* It is an established fact that specific learning rates occur with reasonable regularity for similar groups of products in many different industries.

Studies made in the aircraft, electronics, and small electromechanical subassembly fields indicate that learning rates of 75 to 95 percent are typical. However, learning curves can vary anywhere within the practical limits of 50 to 100 percent. As more units are produced, the effect of a constant learning rate on unit costs gradually diminishes. After several thousand units, the absolute reduction in cost from learning becomes negligible. Note in Figure 15-3 how the curve flattens out as the number of units produced increases. This is why learning curve analysis is of greatest value for new products.[2]

Most analysts prefer to plot the data for learning curves on log-log graph paper, as in Figure 15-4. The logarithmic scales on both the horizontal and vertical axes convert the curve of Figure 15-3 into a straight line (because a log-log grid plots a constant rate of change as a straight line). The straight line is easier to read, and it also simplifies forecasting since a constant learning rate always appears as a straight line on log-log coordinates. To verify the fact that both graphs represent the same thing, look at the number of hours needed to produce 100 units in Figures 15-3 and 15-4; both figures indicate about 50 hours per unit.

In addition to determining the direct labor component of price, the labor hour data also have the following purchasing applications.

Estimating Delivery Times   Since the learning curve can be used to forecast labor time required, it is possible to estimate how many units a supplier can produce over a specified time with a given labor force. This information can be extremely helpful to a buyer in scheduling deliveries, in planning his or her firm's production, and in identifying suppliers who obviously cannot meet desired delivery schedules.

Supplier Progress Payments   Since the learning curve reflects changing labor costs, it provides a basis for figuring a supplier's financial commitment on any given number of units. This information is important because suppli-

---

[2]Different types of labor generate different percentages of learning. Assembly-type labor generates the most rapid improvement and fabrication-type labor the least. Fabrication labor has a lower learning rate because the speed of jobs dependent on this type of labor is governed more by the capability of the equipment than the skill of the operator. The operator's learning in this case is confined to setup and maintenance times. In some situations, therefore, when a precise analysis is desired, a learning curve should be developed for each category of labor. Also, it should be noted that different firms within the same industry experience different rates of learning.

ers often operate in the red during the initial part of a production run, until learning can reduce costs below the average price. Buyers can minimize supplier hardship by using the learning curve to break down an order into two or more production lots—each with successively lower average prices—and then set up progress payments based on the supplier's costs.

Application of Learning Curves

Before applying a learning curve to a particular item, a buyer must be certain that learning does in fact occur at a reasonably constant rate. Many production operations do not possess such properties. Gross errors can be made if a learning curve is misapplied; therefore, buyers must be alert to the following problems.

Nonuniform Learning Rates   Learning curve analysis is predicated on the assumption that the process in question exhibits learning at a reasonably constant rate. Direct labor data from such a process should plot in a straight line on a log-log grid. If a straight line cannot be fitted to the data reasonably well, the learning rate is not uniform and the technique should not be used.

Low-Labor-Content Items   Continued learning occurs principally in the production of products entailing a high percentage of labor. The learning opportunity is particularly high in complex assembly work. On the other hand, if most work on a new item involves machine time, where output tends to be determined by machine capacity, there is little opportunity for continued learning.

Small Payoffs   Obtaining historical cost data to construct a learning curve entails much time and effort, particularly when a supplier uses a standard cost accounting system. Therefore, learning curve analysis is worthwhile only if the amount of money which can be saved is substantial.

Incorrect Learning Rates   Learning varies from industry to industry, plant to plant, product to product, and part to part. Applying one rate just because someone in the industry has used it can be misleading. Intelligent use of learning curves demands that learning rates be determined as accurately as possible from comparable past experience.

Established Items   If a supplier has previously made the item for someone else, a buyer should not use the learning curve even if the product is nonstandard and new to the buyer. Since most of the learning has already been done on previous work, any additional cost reduction may well be negligible.

Misleading Data   Not all cost savings stem from learning. The economies of large-scale production spread fixed costs over a larger number of output units, thus reducing the unit cost of the item. However, this phenomenon has nothing to do with the learning curve.

An Example of Learning Curve Application: The Cumulative Average Curve The following simplified example shows a basic application of the cumulative average learning curve concept in labor cost analysis and contract pricing.

The ABC Corporation has purchased 50 pieces of a specially designed electronic component at $2,000 per unit. Of the $2,000 selling price, $1,000 represents direct labor. An audit of product costs for the first 50 units established that the operation is subject to an 80 percent cumulative average learning curve. What should ABC pay for the purchase of 350 more units?

Solution

1 Using log-log paper, plot 50 units (on the horizontal axis) against $1,000 direct labor cost on the vertical axis (see Figure 15-5).
2 Double the number of units to 100 on the horizontal axis and plot against a labor cost of $800 (80 percent as high as the original $1,000 cost).
3 Draw a straight line through the two cost points. The line represents an 80 percent learning curve, constructed on the basis of labor cost data for the first 50 units of production.
4 Locate 400 units on the horizontal axis (the total expected production of 50 original units plus 350 new ones). Read from the curve the labor cost of approximately $510. This is the *average* expected labor cost per unit for the total production of 400 units.
5 To find the labor cost for 400 units, multiply 400 × $510, the direct labor cost per unit. The total is $204,000.
6 Subtract the labor paid in the original order to determine the labor cost of the new order of 350 units. Hence, subtract $50,000 (50 × $1,000) from $204,000. The answer is $154,000, the labor cost which should be paid for the new order of 350 units: $154,000 ÷ 350 units = $440 per unit labor cost, as compared with the original $1,000 per unit.
7 Now determine the cost for materials, overhead, and profit on the 350 units. Add this figure to the labor cost determined in step 6 to obtain the total price ABC should pay for the additional 350 units.

An Example of Learning Curve Application: The Unit Curve The preceding application dealt with the use of a *cumulative average* learning curve. To illustrate the application of a *unit* learning curve, consider the following hypothetical situation.

Assume that a manufacturer receives an order to produce 515 units of a new product. After the necessary production and tooling design work is com-

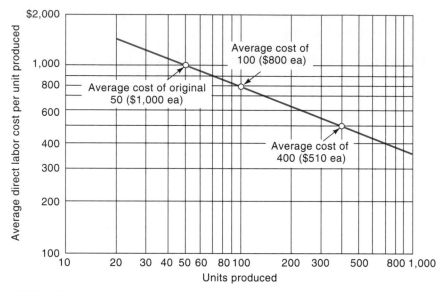

FIGURE 15-5
Estimating labor cost for the new contract.

TABLE 15-4
THE MANUFACTURER'S PRODUCTION DATA

Column 1 Unit produced	Column 2 Labor hours required to produce the corresponding unit in col. 1	Column 3 Labor hours required as a percent of those required for the preceding unit
1	60	—
2	51	85.0%
4	43	84.3
8	37	86.0
16	31	83.8
32	26	83.9

pleted, the manufacturer begins production. Prior experience with moderately similar products leads the manufacturing manager to believe that a
unit learning curve phenomenon probably will be experienced as production operations proceed.

To investigate this possibility, for the first 32 units produced, he records
the production data shown in Table 15-4, columns 1 and 2. Then he makes
the calculations shown in column 3. As production doubled (1 to 2, 2 to 4, 4
to 8, etc.), in each case it is clear that a significant learning effect was experienced. (The 2nd unit took 85 percent of the time required by the 1st unit,
the 4th unit required 84.3 percent of the time required by the 2nd unit, and
so on, as indicated in column 3). Although the rate varies slightly, the manager concludes that a unit learning curve of approximately 85 percent is a

good indicator of the manner in which the process will behave during the production of the remainder of the order. (That is, that the 64th unit will require 85 percent of the time required by the 32nd unit, that the 128th unit will require 85 percent of the time required by the 64th unit, and so on.)

Consequently, he constructs the curve on a log-log grid—and reads directly from the graph that the 512th unit will require approximately 13.6 direct labor hours for its production. Similar determinations for all units produced permit him to calculate the total number of labor hours for the complete job. Using this information, he can schedule production efficiently, as well as estimate the total labor cost the job will incur.

TOOLING COSTS

Most procurement authorities advocate that the buyer pay for and take title to special tooling. Such an approach allows the buyer maximum control. Analysis of production costs is easier, and the tooling can be moved if circumstances dictate.

There should be an inverse relationship between the investment in tooling and the number of hours required to produce a unit of output. The buyer should ensure that the supplier plans to use sufficient tooling to minimize labor hours, but at the same time avoids investments which are not recovered through labor savings.

INDIRECT COSTS

Indirect costs represent 30 to 40 percent of many suppliers' total costs of production. Five of the most common indirect cost pools are engineering overhead, materials overhead, manufacturing overhead, general and administrative expense, and selling expense.

Engineering Overhead

This is the cost of directing and supporting the engineering department and its direct labor staff. Costs include supervisory and support labor, fringe benefits, indirect supplies, and fixed charges such as depreciation.

Materials Overhead

This category of overhead usually includes the indirect costs of purchasing, transporting incoming materials, receiving, inspection, handling, and the storage of materials.

Manufacturing Overhead

This category includes all production costs except direct materials, direct labor, and similar costs that can be assigned directly to the production of an item.

Manufacturing overhead includes:

- The cost of supervision, inspection (some firms charge quality assurance or inspection as a direct cost), maintenance, custodial, and related personnel costs
- Fringe benefits such as social security and unemployment taxes, allowances for vacation pay, and group insurance
- Indirect supplies such as lubricating oils, grinding wheels, and janitorial supplies
- Fixed charges, including depreciation, rent, insurance, and property taxes
- Utilities

General and Administrative

General and administrative (G&A) expenses include the company's general and executive offices, staff services, and miscellaneous activities.

Selling

Selling expenses include sales salaries, bonuses and commissions, and the normal costs of running the department.

Recovering Indirect Costs

The supplier allocates overhead costs to specific operations. Normally, this allocation is based on a product's age in terms of its life cycle. For instance, mature products generally incur lower G&A expenses than new products, which require more development and marketing effort. This allocation results in the use of an overhead rate for each indirect cost pool. The rate is determined by management personnel who select an appropriate base (or allocation vehicle) and then develop the ratio of the indirect cost pool dollars to that base. For example, the following allocation formula might be used for manufacturing overhead:

$$\frac{\text{Manufacturing overhead pool dollars}}{\text{Manufacturing direct labor hours}} = \frac{\$5{,}000{,}000}{1{,}000{,}000} = \begin{array}{c}\$5 \text{ per direct} \\ \text{manufacturing} \\ \text{labor hour}\end{array}$$

Overhead rates are generally established annually, typically before the start of the accounting period.

When determining the reasonableness of overhead rates, a buyer should not look only at the rate. He or she must consider the reasonableness of the indirect costs in the overhead pool and the appropriateness of the overhead allocation base. Since rates typically are established annually, the buyer should also ensure that the allocation rate used by a supplier is applied consistently.

Activity-Based Costing/Management

Activity costing can be traced back to the late 1700s. During the intervening 200 years, management focused on labor costs, since they represented over 50 percent of total costs. The allocation of overhead costs based on the number of hours required to produce a product was relatively realistic and certainly easy.

But as direct labor costs have shrunk to 10 percent or so of total costs, they have become a less logical and realistic basis on which to allocate indirect costs. During the 1980s, a band of accounting academics, led by Professors Robert Kaplan and Robin Cooper of the Harvard Business School and Clare-mont McKenna College, respectively, developed what has become known as activity-based costing (ABC)—a tool which more accurately identifies and allocates indirect costs to the products they support. Recently, ABC has evolved into activity-based management (ABM).

ABC or ABM can be used to identify opportunities to reduce the supplier's indirect costs. ABC goes beyond identifying and allocating these indirect costs to products: It identifies the drivers of these costs. Some examples of cost drivers are the number of orders, length of setups, specifications, engineering changes, and liaison trips required. This identification allows management to identify and implement cost savings opportunities. Quite obviously, if the supplier's management does not implement the required changes, an alert buyer from purchasing and supply management can "encourage" such action.

TARGET COSTING

In a recent *Wall Street Journal* article, management guru Peter F. Drucker wrote of five deadly business sins—avoidable mistakes that will (and in many cases have) harm(ed) a business.

Drucker's third deadly sin is *cost-driven pricing*. He argues, "The only thing that works is *price-driven costing.* . . . The only sound way to price is to start out with what the market is willing to pay . . . and design to that price specification."[3] Dr. Drucker's comments are as applicable to procurement as they are to marketing.

Some forty years ago, the Ford Motor Company employed price-based costing in the development of its highly successful Mustang. The car was designed to retail at $1,995. This pricing objective drove design engineering to focus on cost, as well as performance and aesthetics. In turn, this drove engineers and purchasing and supply management to identify target prices for items to be purchased from suppliers. Members of these two functions then worked with their potential suppliers to develop processes and procedures to produce the required materials and components at these target prices. Curiously enough, American management largely reverted to cost-based pricing during the inter-

---

[3]Peter F. Drucker, "The Five Deadly Business Sins," *Wall Street Journal*, Oct. 21, 1993, p. 14.

vening forty years, while its Japanese competition adopted price-based cost-ing. Dr. Drucker points out that "cost based pricing is the reason there is no American consumer-electronics industry anymore."[4]

It is heartening to see Chrysler (and a few other manufacturers) replace its "adversarial bidding system with one in which the company designates sup-pliers for a component and then uses target pricing . . . to determine with suppliers the component prices and how to achieve them."[5]

PROFIT

There are no precise formulas which can be used to help form a positive judg-ment concerning the right price, of which profit is one component (price = cost + profit). There are, however, certain basic concepts of pricing on which schol-ars and practitioners do agree. One objective of sound purchasing is to achieve good supplier relations. This objective implies that the price must be high enough to keep the supplier in business. The price must also include a profit sufficiently high to encourage the supplier to accept the business in the first place, and, second, to motivate the firm to deliver the materials or services on time. What profit does it take to get these two desired results? On what basis should it be calculated?

If profit were calculated on a percentage-of-cost basis, the high-cost, inefficient producer would receive the higher profit (in absolute terms). To make matters even worse, under the cost concept of pricing, producers who succeeded in lowering their costs by attaining greater efficiency would be "rewarded" by a reduction in total profit. For example, if an efficient producer has costs of $1,000 and a fair profit is agreed to be 10 percent of cost, its profit would be $100. If an inefficient producer has costs of $1,500, its profit on the same basis would be $150. If by better techniques the efficient producer should lower its costs to $800, the reward would be a $20 loss in profit—from $100 to $80. Obviously, the concept of determining a fair profit as a fixed percentage of cost is unrealistic.

Another concept on which profit might be determined is the relationship of capital investment required to produce the profit. Profit might be calculated as a percentage of capital investment. However, under this system, it would still be possible for the inefficient producer to receive the greater reward. For example, suppose firm A makes a capital investment of $2 million to produce product X. Firm B, on the other hand, invests only $1 million in its plant to produce product X successfully. From the buyer's point of view, there is no reason why firm A, simply because of its greater investment, should receive a higher profit on product X than firm B. Firm B, in fact, is utilizing its invest-ment more efficiently. Thus, profit calculated as a fixed percentage of a firm's

[4]Ibid.

[5]James P. Womack and Daniel T. Jones, "From Lean Production to the Lean Enterprise," *Har-vard Business Review*, March–April 1994, p. 97.

capital investment is not a satisfactory method for a buyer to use in determining a fair profit.

In a competitive economy, the major incentive for more efficient production is greater profit and repeat orders. A fair profit in our society cannot be determined as a fixed percentage figure. Rather, it is a flexible figure that should be higher for the more efficient producer than it is for the less efficient one. Low-cost producers can price lower than their competitors, while simultaneously enjoying a higher profit. Consequently, one of a buyer's greatest challenges is constantly to seek out the efficient, low-cost producer.

Considerations other than production efficiency can also rightly influence the relative size of a firm's profit. Six of the most common considerations are discussed briefly below.

1 Profit is the basic reward for risk taking as well as the reward for efficiency; therefore, higher profits justifiably accompany extraordinary risks, whatever form they take. For example, great financial risk usually accompanies the production of new products. For this reason, a higher profit for new products is often necessary to induce a seller to take the risk of producing them.

2 A higher dollar profit per unit of product purchased on small special orders is generally justified over that allowed on larger orders. The justification stems from the fact that the producer incurs a fixed amount of setup and administrative expense, regardless of the size of the order. Consequently, the cost of production for each unit is greater on small orders than on large orders. Since producers incur this cost at the request of the buyer, they usually demand a proportionately higher absolute profit before accepting an order which forces them to use their facilities in a less efficient manner than they might otherwise do.

3 Rapid technological advancement creates a continuing nationwide shortage of technical talent. The cost in dollars and time of training highly technical personnel frequently makes it necessary to pay a higher profit on jobs requiring highly skilled people.

4 In the space age, technical reliability can be a factor of overriding importance. A higher profit is generally conceded as justified for a firm that repeatedly turns out superbly reliable technical products than for one producing less reliable products. Good quality control, efficiency in controlling costs, on-time delivery, and technical assistance that has resulted in better production or design simplification all merit profit consideration.

5 On occasion, because of various temporary unfavorable supply-demand factors (e.g., excessive inventories, a shortage of capital, a cancellation of large orders), a firm may be forced to sell its products at a loss in order to recover a portion of its invested capital quickly or to keep its production facilities in operation.

6 A firm that manufactures a product according to the design and specifications of another firm is not entitled to the same percentage of

profit as a firm that incurs the risk of manufacturing to its own design. In the first instance, the manufacturing firm is assured of a sale without marketing expense or risk of any kind, provided only that it fulfills the terms of the contract. In the second instance, the manufacturing firm is without assurance that its product can be sold profitably, if at all, in a competitive market.

In summary, there is no single answer to the question: What is a fair profit? In a capitalistic society, profit generally is implied to mean the reward over costs that a firm receives for *the measure of efficiency it attains* and the *degree of risk it assumes*. From a purchasing viewpoint, profit provides two basic incentives. First, it induces the seller to take the order. Second, it induces the seller to perform as efficiently as possible, to deliver on time, and to provide all reasonable services associated with the order. Except in those temporary cases where a firm is willing to sell at a loss, the profit is too low if it does not create these two incentives for the seller.

CONCLUSION

Armed with an understanding of cost principles, the buyer now is in a position to conduct an analysis of a potential supplier's proposal. This analysis is a major step in preparing for negotiations, as described in Chapter 17.

FOR DISCUSSION

15-1 What are the four principal elements affecting cost? Describe the effects of each element on cost.

15-2 Describe the factors that buyers must review when they select a seller that engages in subcontracting.

15-3 How might the application of experience, knowledge, and judgment to data assist in an attempt to project contract costs?

15-4 What are the three sources of cost data? Under what circumstances should cost models be used?

15-5 How can a reduction in direct cost generate more of a price savings for the buyer than a similar percentage reduction in the seller's profit?

15-6 What must the buyer consider when he or she analyzes direct manufacturing labor estimates?

15-7 Discuss the two basic types of learning curves and their applications.

15-8 What is the learning rate if each time the production rate doubles, the average labor requirement for all units declines by 20 percent?

15-9 Why might a person working on a punch press exhibit a lower rate of learning than one working in a complex assembly operation?

15-10 How might the purchasing department apply learning curves?

15-11 What are some examples of misapplied learning curve use?

15-12 List some factors that contribute to a supplier's "learning."

15-13 List and describe the most common indirect cost pools. What determination should a buyer make regarding these indirect costs?

15-14 What is the objective of activity-based costing? Why has it become a more logical and realistic approach to cost allocation?

15-15 Explain target costing. What important role does purchasing and supply management have in implementing target costing?

15-16 Why might it be discouraging for an efficient producer to have its profit for a job based solely on its costs?

15-17 Discuss some of the considerations, other than production efficiency, that can influence the relative size of profits.

CASES FOR CHAPTER 15

Frich Turbo Engine Company, page 818
A Problem of Price, page 891
Hartinco, Inc. (in the *Instructor's Manual*)
Black Motor Company (in the *Instructor's Manual*)
Collier Company II (in the *Instructor's Manual*)
Naval Operating Base, Arkladelphia (in the *Instructor's Manual*)
Branson Electronic Company—A and B (in the *Instructor's Manual*)

DEALING WITH COST UNCERTAINTY: TYPES OF COMPENSATION AGREEMENTS

KEY CONCEPTS

- Introduction to compensation agreements
- Contract cost risk appraisal
    - Technical risk
    - Contract schedule risk
- General types of contract compensation agreements
    - Fixed price contracts
    - Incentive contracts
    - Cost-type contracts
- Specific types of compensation agreements
    - Firm fixed price contracts
    - Fixed price with economic adjustment contracts
    - Fixed price redetermination contracts
    - Incentive arrangements
    - Cost plus incentive fee arrangements
    - Cost plus fixed fee arrangements
    - Cost plus award fee
    - Cost without fee
    - Cost sharing
    - Time and materials
    - Letter contracts and letters of intent
- Considerations when selecting contract types

A wide selection of contract compensation arrangements is necessary to provide the flexibility needed for the procurement of a large variety of materials and services. The compensation arrangement determines (1) the degree and timing of the cost responsibility assumed by the supplier, (2) the amount of profit or fee available to the supplier, and (3) the motivational implications of the fee portion of the compensation arrangements. The following examples are introduced in an effort to portray visually the seller's and, in turn, the buyer's problem of dealing with uncertainty.

Example 1: Low Level of Uncertainty   In this example the seller's likely cost for a project is $1,000,000. The seller is confident that the lowest possible cost will be $950,000 and the highest cost $1,050,000. This information is portrayed in Figure 16-1. One can see that the seller is virtually certain that costs will be within the range of $950,000 to $1,050,000, with the most likely outcome near $1,000,000.

If the seller adds 10 percent for profit to the most likely cost outcome, it will be willing to agree to a firm fixed price of $1,100,000. Note that the supplier's actual profit will be in the range of $150,000 (if actual costs are $950,000) to $50,000 (if actual costs are $1,050,000). The most likely profit is $100,000 [$1,100,000 (the price) − $1,000,000 (the most likely cost outcome)]. In this example, the use of a firm fixed price contract (as discussed below) seems appropriate.

Example 2: High Level of Uncertainty   In this example, assume that the range of likely cost outcomes is much wider—say, $500,000 to $1,500,000. (Such an extreme range of cost outcomes is highly unlikely but is used here to introduce the concept that the type of compensation agreement should be appropriate for the amount of uncertainty present.) Again, the most likely cost outcome is $1,000,000. This example is portrayed in Figure 16-2.

FIGURE 16-1
Probability of cost outcome: low level of uncertainty.

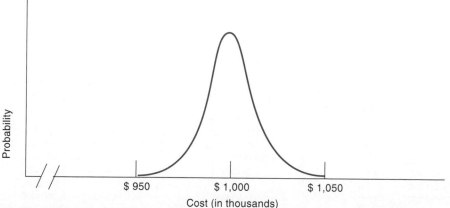

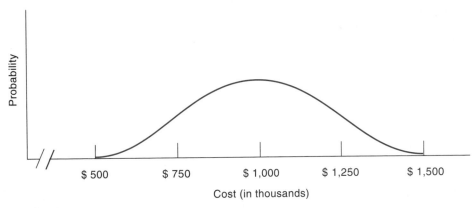

FIGURE 16-2
Probability of cost outcome: high level of uncertainty.

Most sellers are very risk averse: that is, they are unwilling to accept large amounts of uncertainty unless they are able to transfer the uncertainty to the buyer in the form of higher prices. In this case, the seller studies the distribution of likely cost outcomes and concludes that, 9 times out of 10, the actual cost will be $1,400,000 or less. Accordingly, if the buyer is unwise enough to insist on using a firm fixed method of compensation, the seller may demand a firm fixed price of $1,540,000 [$1,400,000 plus $140,000 (10 percent profit on this cost)].

Table 16-1 portrays the supplier's profit under various cost outcomes for this second example. It is fairly obvious that if the buyer could assume the risk inherent in this procurement, a lower price would be possible—except in the extreme case in which actual costs exceeded approximately $1,540,000.

Let us assume that the buyer and supplier agreed to a cost plus fixed fee contract with a target cost of $1,000,000 and a fixed fee of $50,000. Note that the fee is relatively low: 5 percent of target cost. This is so the supplier will not incur any risk. Table 16-2 portrays the price to be paid by the buyer under different cost outcomes.

The sophisticated reader may say: "Interesting. But a fee or profit of $50,000 on a cost of $500,000 (see line 1, Table 16-2) is 10 percent. That's too high, con-

TABLE 16-1
PROFIT OUTCOME AT VARIOUS ACTUAL COSTS
(Firm Fixed Price of $1,540,000)

Actual cost	Actual profit	Fixed price
$ 500,000	$1,040,000	$1,540,000
1,000,000	540,000	1,540,000
1,400,000	140,000	1,540,000
1,500,000	40,000	1,540,000

TABLE 16-2
PRICE OUTCOME AT VARIOUS ACTUAL COST OUTCOMES
(Fixed Fee)

Actual cost	Fixed fee or profit	Price paid
$ 500,000	$50,000	$ 550,000
1,000,000	50,000	1,050,000
1,400,000	50,000	1,450,000
1,500,000	50,000	1,550,000

sidering that there's no cost risk! Why not apply a fixed percent fee to costs?" Such an approach is shown in Table 16-3. One does not have to be a rocket scientist to see that such an approach motivates the supplier to increase costs since the higher the cost, the higher the fee!

Without going into further detail at this point, it should be apparent that selection of the right type of compensation arrangement can save money. Insightful readers may be asking themselves: "What would happen if, instead of paying a fixed fee or a fixed percent of cost, we were able to incentivize the supplier to control costs?"

The buyer has a range of compensation arrangements designed to meet the needs of a particular procurement. At one end of this range is the firm fixed price contract where the supplier assumes all cost responsibility and where, therefore, profit and loss potentials are high. At the other end of this range is the cost plus fixed fee contract where the supplier has no cost risk and where the fee (profit) is fixed, usually at a relatively low level. In between these two extremes are numerous incentive arrangements that reflect a sharing of the cost responsibility.

CONTRACT COST RISK APPRAISAL

The degree of cost responsibility a supplier reasonably can be expected to assume is determined primarily by the cost risk involved. It is to the buyer's advantage to estimate this risk prior to negotiations. Since the majority of contracts are "forward priced," that is, priced prior to completion of the work,

TABLE 16-3
FEE AND PRICE OUTCOMES AT VARIOUS COST OUTCOMES
(With Profit a Fixed % of Cost)

Actual cost	Fee (10% of actual cost)	Price paid
$ 500,000	$ 50,000	$ 550,000
1,000,000	100,000	1,100,000
1,400,000	140,000	1,540,000
1,500,000	150,000	1,650,000

some cost risk is involved in each of them. The degree of cost risk involved will depend on how accurately the cost of the contract can be estimated prior to performance. The accuracy of the cost estimate and the degree of cost risk usually are a function of both technical and contract schedule risk.

A buyer should insist on a fixed price contract unless (1) the risks will result in a contract price containing large reserves for contingencies that may not occur, or (2) the risks result in reliable suppliers refusing to agree to a fixed price contract because a significant loss might be incurred, or (3) the use of a fixed price contract could result in the supplier "cutting corners" in order to avoid taking a loss.

Technical Risk

Technical risk is that risk associated with the nature of the item being purchased. Appraisal of technical risk includes analysis of the type and complexity of the item or service being purchased, stability of design specifications or statement of work, availability of historical pricing data, and prior production experience. Analysis of technical risk in a complex system may include appraisals by a team with members from the user group, the engineering staff, and the purchasing and supply management group. Think, for example, of the technical risk involved in the Apollo mission to put a man on the moon: leaving the earth's gravity, sustaining life in a gravity-less environment, landing on an unknown surface structure of the moon's crust, and reentering the earth's stratosphere without burning up.

Technical risk is reduced as the job requirements, production methods, and pricing data become better defined and the design specifications or statement of work becomes more stable. Research and development contracts, in particular, have a rather high technical risk associated with them. This is due to the ill-defined requirements that arise from the necessity to deal beyond, or at least very near, the limits of the current technology.

Contract Schedule Risk

In addition to technical risk, schedule risk must be assessed in determining the supplier's cost risk. Preferred procurement practice calls for forward pricing of contract efforts. This practice attempts to anticipate material and labor cost increases during performance of the contract. These estimates, along with possible schedule slippage, are always subject to error.

GENERAL TYPES OF CONTRACT COMPENSATION ARRANGEMENTS

Compensation arrangements can be classified into three broad categories: (1) fixed price contracts, (2) incentive contracts, and (3) cost reimbursement contracts.

Fixed Price Contracts

Under a fixed price arrangement, the supplier is obligated to deliver the product called for by the contract for a fixed price. If, prior to completion of the product, the supplier finds that the effort is more difficult or costly than anticipated, the supplier is still obligated to deliver the product. Further, the supplier will receive no more than the previously agreed-on amount. The amount of profit the supplier receives will depend on the actual cost outcome. There is no maximum or minimum profit limitation in fixed price contracts. A fixed price arrangement is normally used in situations where specifications are well defined and cost risk is relatively low.

Incentive Contracts

Incentive contracts are employed in an effort to motivate the supplier to improve cost and possibly other stated requirements such as schedule performance. In an incentive contract, the cost responsibility is shared by the buyer and the seller. This sharing addresses two issues: (1) the desire to motivate the supplier to control cost and (2) an awareness that if the supplier assumes all or most of the risk when significant uncertainty is present, a contingency allowance will be required, thereby inflating the contract price.

Incentive contracts are of two types: (1) fixed price incentive and (2) cost plus incentive fee. With a fixed price incentive contract, the ceiling price is agreed to (or fixed) during negotiations. Under the cost plus incentive fee arrangement, the supplier is reimbursed for all allowable costs incurred, up to any prescribed ceiling. Obviously, the supplier's cost accounting system must meet commonly accepted standards and be open to the customer for review. In addition, the supplier receives a fee designed to motivate it to meet the buyer's cost and other stated objectives.

Cost-Type Contracts

Under a cost-type arrangement, the buyer's obligation is to reimburse the supplier for all allowable, reasonable, and allocable costs incurred, and to pay a fixed fee. Again, the supplier's cost accounting practices must meet commonly accepted standards and be open to the customer. Most cost arrangements include a cost limitation clause that sets an administrative limitation on the reimbursement of costs. Generally, under a cost-type arrangement, the supplier is obligated only to provide its "best effort." Usually, neither performance nor delivery is guaranteed. Cost-type arrangements are normally used when:

- Procurement of research and development involves high technical risk
- Some doubt exists that the project can be successfully completed
- Product specifications are incomplete
- High-dollar, highly uncertain procurements such as software development are involved

SPECIFIC TYPES OF COMPENSATION ARRANGEMENTS

There are a number of specific types of compensation arrangements under each of the above categories.

1 Fixed price compensation arrangements:
- Firm fixed price
- Fixed price with economic price adjustment
- Fixed price redetermination

2 Incentive arrangements:
- Fixed price incentive
- Cost plus incentive fee

3 Cost-type arrangements:
- Cost reimbursement
- Cost sharing
- Time and materials
- Cost plus fixed fee
- Cost plus award fee

The applicability, elements, structure, and final price computation for the various compensation arrangements are discussed in the following paragraphs.

Firm Fixed Price Contracts

The most preferred contract type, if appropriate for the procurement, is the firm fixed price contract. A firm fixed price (FFP) contract is an agreement to pay a specified price when the items (services) specified by the contract have been delivered (completed) and accepted. The contracting parties establish a firm price through either competitive bidding or negotiation. Since there is no adjustment in contract price after the work is completed and actual costs are known, the cost risk to the supplier can be high.

An FFP contract is appropriate in competitive bidding where the specifications are definite, there is little schedule risk, and competition has established the existence of a fair and reasonable price. An FFP contract also can be appropriate for negotiated procurements if a review reveals adequate specifications and if price and cost analysis establish the reasonableness of the price.

As previously stated, under an FFP contract there is no price adjustment due to the supplier's cost experience. Because the supplier has all cost responsibility, the actual outcome will show up in the form of profit or losses. Therefore, the supplier has maximum incentive to control costs under an FFP contract. If the supplier incurs expenses beyond the buyer's obligation, the seller must find the required funds elsewhere. Conversely, if the supplier reduces costs, all savings contribute to the supplier's profit. This dollar-for-dollar relationship between expenditures and profit is the greatest motivator of efficiency

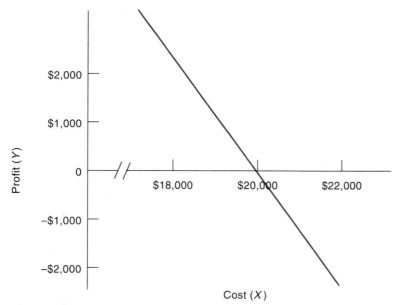

FIGURE 16-3
Firm fixed price contract—$20,000.

available. An FFP contract has only one contract compensation arrangement element: total price. Although negotiations may involve the discussion of costs and profit, the contractual document reflects only total price. This structure can be seen in Figure 16-3, which depicts an FFP contract for $20,000.

In this example, cost is shown as the independent variable (x-axis), and profit, since it is a function of cost, as the dependent variable (y-axis). The graph depicts the one-to-one relationship between costs and profit by showing that as costs increase by $1, profit decreases by $1.

Computing the final price in an FFP-type contract is a simple matter. If a $20,000 firm fixed price contract is negotiated, on contract completion the supplier will receive $20,000 whether costs were $15,000 or $25,000 or any other amount.

It should be noted that a fixed price does not always stay fixed. A supplier who is losing money *may* request and get some relief, if any of the following apply:

1 The customer in some way has contributed to the loss.
2 The customer badly needs the items and other suppliers are not willing to provide them at the established price.
3 The supplier has unique facilities and time is too short to do anything but to get the product at an increased cost from the initial supplier.

As previously discussed, early supplier involvement (ESI) with a decision to rely on one supplier during and after development results in many benefits based on the early matching of process and product. But ESI may result in cost overruns and higher costs if the supplier can't perform at the fixed price due to unforeseen (usually technical) reasons. It should be recognized that when a supplier fails to perform under a fixed price contract and the buyer is forced to turn the business into a cost plus type of contract, the supplier has damaged its chance for future business with the customer and other potential customers. The buyer, on the other hand, can use the prospect of continued future business to keep the price well below what the supplier's leverage of the moment might suggest.

Variations of the FFP contract have been developed to meet special circumstances. One such variation is the FFP level-of-effort contract. This arrangement calls for a set number of labor hours to be expended over a period of time. The contract is considered complete when the hours are expended, although normally a report of findings is also required. The FFP level-of-effort contract is appropriately used when the specification is general in nature and when no specific end item (other than a report) is required. This arrangement is most frequently used for research and development efforts under $100,000 and for "get our foot in the door" consulting contracts.

Fixed Price with Economic Price Adjustment Contracts

Fixed price with economic price adjustment (FPEPA) contracts are used to recognize economic contingencies, such as unstable labor or market conditions which would prevent the establishment of a firm fixed price contract without a large contingency for possible cost increases or decreases in the unit cost of labor and/or materials. An FPEPA contract is simply an FFP contract that includes economic price adjustment clauses. Such provisions are common when purchasing items containing precious metals and construction services.

Economic price adjustments (EPA) or escalator/de-escalator clauses provide for both price increases and decreases to protect the buyer and supplier from the effects of economic changes. If such clauses were not used, suppliers would include contingency allowances in their bids or proposals to eliminate or reduce the risk of loss. With a fixed contingency allowance in the contract price, the supplier is hurt if the changes exceed its estimate, and the buyer will overpay if the input unit cost increases do not materialize.

An economic price adjustment clause may be used for fixed price–type arrangements resulting from both competitively bid and negotiated contracts. Price adjustments normally should be restricted to contingencies beyond the control of the supplier. Under an FPEPA contract, specific contingencies are left open subject to an EPA clause, and the final contract price is adjusted, depending on what happens to these contingencies. Where cost pass-through or escalator clauses cover specific materials and/or labor, the buyer should be sure that the price increase does not occur until the higher-cost material is used or until the labor contract increase takes effect.

The use of economic price adjustment clauses varies with the probability of significant price fluctuations. Their use also increases when purchasing strategy favors early supplier involvement, longer-term contracts, fewer supplies, and more single-source suppliers. An economic price adjustment clause should recognize the possibility of both inflation and deflation in determining price adjustments. Further, labor and material costs subject to economic adjustment must reflect the effects of learning on both labor and material costs. It takes considerable purchasing skill to use economic price adjustment clauses well. Decisions must be made on what items to include and which price/cost index or benchmark is best for each item.

The cost elements to adjust are high-value raw materials, specific high-value components, and direct labor. The professional buyer generally should oppose including costs within the supplier's control such as development, depreciation, fixed expenses, other overhead items, and profit in the base subject to escalation.

In selecting indexes for price adjustment clauses, the following rules are suggested:

- Select from the appropriate Bureau of Labor Statistics category.
- Avoid broad indexes; use the lowest-level classification which includes the item.
- Develop a weighted index for materials in a product.
- Select labor rate indexes by type and location.
- Define energy indexes by fuel type and location.
- Analyze the past history of each proposed index versus the actual price change of the item being indexed.

Using a broad index can produce strange results. One marketing executive used the producer price index (PPI) to adjust the purchase price of electronic apparatus, not recognizing that the PPI consists of about 40 percent food and fuel components with only 3 percent electronics input.

The details of the economic price adjustment clause must be thought through with various scenarios in mind. When will adjustments be made? Under what conditions can the contract be renegotiated? How will it be audited? By whom?

Fixed Price Redetermination Contracts

These contracts provide for a firm fixed price for an initial contract period with a redetermination (upward or downward) at a stated time during contract performance [FPR (prospective)] or after contract completion [FPR (retroactive)]. The FPR (prospective) is usually used only in those circumstances calling for quantity production or services where a fair and reasonable price can be negotiated for initial periods but not for subsequent periods. The FPR (retroactive) is used in those circumstances where, at the time of negotiation, a fair and reasonable price cannot be established and the amount involved is so small and the performance period so short that use of any other contract type would be impractical.

The data shown in Table 16-3 on page 339 are also applicable to an FPR contract. As was observed, the supplier is motivated to increase costs, since the higher the cost, the higher the fee!

Incentive Arrangements

Firm fixed price (FFP) and cost plus fixed fee (CPFF) contracts are extremes of the range of contract compensation arrangements since in either case all of the cost responsibility falls on only one party. In between these two extremes are a number of contract arrangements where the cost responsibility is shared between the customer and the supplier. These are called incentive-type contracts.

Incentives are applied to contracts in an attempt to motivate the supplier to improve performance in cost, schedule, or other stated parameters. By far the most frequent application of incentives is in the area of cost control. However, this is not the only type of incentive. The specific type of incentive applied depends on the desired outcome. For example, if the primary interest is in developing a high-performance read head, it would be logical to reward the supplier for development and production of a read head which exceeds the minimum specifications. If the same read head were needed to meet a crash development effort, schedule may be the basis of an incentive. For the same read head, funds may be a real constraint due to budgetary limitations, and a production unit cost incentive would be appropriate. If a combination of performance and cost objectives were of concern, a multiple-incentive contract could be developed.

In this text, the discussion of incentive arrangements is limited to cost incentives. The focus will be on the two most frequently applied cost incentive compensation arrangements: the fixed price incentive (FPI) contract and the cost plus incentive fee (CPIF) contract. A general discussion of how a simplified incentive contract is structured precedes analysis of the specific elements and structure of these two compensation arrangements. The elements of a simplified incentive contract include (1) the target cost, (2) the target profit, and (3) the sharing arrangement.

Target Cost   The target cost for an incentive contract is that cost outcome which both the buyer and the supplier feel is the most likely outcome for the effort involved. The target cost should be based on costs that would result under "normal business conditions." Although the target cost is thought to be the most likely, it is recognized that the probability of the supplier's final costs being very close to the target cost is low. After all, if there were a high probability that the target cost would be close to the final cost, a firm fixed price contract would be appropriate. The target should be that cost point where both parties agree that there is an equal chance of going above or below the target.

Target Profit   In addition to a target cost, a target profit is developed. The target profit in an incentive contract is a profit amount that is considered fair and reasonable, based on all relevant facts, as discussed in Chapter 15.

Allocating Costs above or below Target   Since an incentive contract recognizes that the target most likely will *not* be met, a method of allocating cost increases above or decreases below target is necessary. The method is a sharing arrangement that reflects the sharing of the cost responsibility between the buyer and the supplier. This arrangement should reflect the cost risk involved as evidenced by the magnitude of potential increases and decreases for the specific effort. In addition, the sharing arrangement must address two questions: "What percent of the savings below target will be required to motivate the supplier to perform as efficiently as possible?" and "What percent of the cost overrun—cost above target—charged to the supplier (in the form of lower profit) will cause the supplier to perform as efficiently as possible?"

How is the magnitude of a potential cost increase or decrease established? It is developed through an assessment of possible cost outcomes, based on varying circumstances a supplier might face during contract performance. In addition to developing a target cost and profit outcome, the parties establish cost outcomes and associated profits for a "best case" and a "worst case" situation. The best-case cost outcome is referred to as the most optimistic cost (MOC) point, and its related profit is referred to as the most optimistic profit (MOPr) point. The worst-case cost outcome is referred to as the most pessimistic cost (MPC) point, and its profit is referred to as the most pessimistic profit (MPPr) point.

The difference between the target point and the most optimistic point provides the buyer with the magnitude of a potential cost decrease. The difference between the target point and the most pessimistic point provides the buyer with the magnitude of a potential cost increase. One normally would not expect these magnitudes to be equal, since the potential for things to go wrong is usually higher than the potential for things to go better than expected. Another way of looking at the magnitude of potential cost increase is that it provides an estimate of the cost risk a supplier faces if the target cost is not met. This cost risk and the supplier's assumption of this risk are reflected in the sharing arrangement.

An Example   The example below shows how an incentive contract is structured. The following cost and profit outcomes were agreed on by the buyer and the seller:

	Estimated dollars (in thousands)	Price (in thousands)
Target cost (TC)	$1,000	
Target profit (TPr)	80	$1,080
Most optimistic cost (MOC)	800	
Most optimistic profit (MOPr)	120	920
Most pessimistic cost (MPC)	1,200	
Most pessimistic profit (MPPr)	0	1,200
Ceiling price	1,200	1,200

This example is portrayed in Figure 16-4.

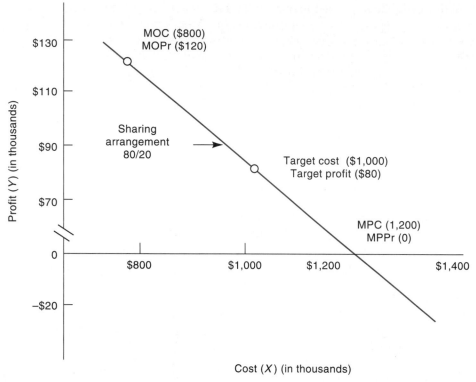

FIGURE 16-4
Fixed price incentive fee.

Computing of the final payment under an incentive arrangement is more complex than under either an FFP or CPFF contract. Under an incentive arrangement, the supplier's profit will be adjusted to reflect performance in the cost area. If the supplier has incurred costs above target, the target profit will be decreased by the supplier's share of the cost above target cost up to the ceiling price. Conversely, if the supplier's costs are below target, its profit is increased. The final price outcome (cost plus profit) would then be the final cost plus or minus the supplier's share of the cost savings or cost increase.

Cost Plus Incentive Fee Arrangements

CPIF contracts combine the incentive arrangement and the cost plus fixed fee arrangement. Under a CPIF arrangement, an incentive applies over part of the range of cost outcomes. The fee structure resembles a cost plus fixed fee contract at both the low-cost and high-cost ends of the range, as shown in Figure 16-5. Thus, if cost were $800,000 or less, the fee would be $120,000. If cost were $1,400,000 or more, the fee would be $20,000.

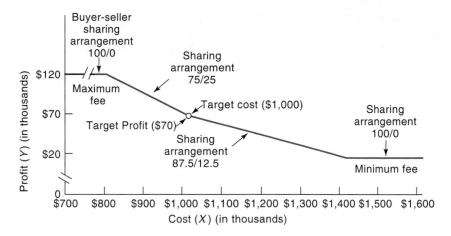

FIGURE 16-5
CPIF arrangement.

The diagram shows a CPIF arrangement that is structured and based on the following negotiated cost and fee outcomes:

Target cost	$1,000,000
Target profit	70,000
Optimistic cost	800,000
Optimistic and maximum profit	120,000
Pessimistic cost	1,400,000
Pessimistic and minimum profit	20,000
Sharing below target (customer/supplier)	75/25
Sharing above target (customer/supplier)	87.5/12.5

A cost plus incentive fee arrangement is used in those circumstances where the cost risk warrants a cost-type arrangement but where an incentive can be established to provide the supplier with positive motivation to manage costs. CPIF arrangements are most suitable for advanced development efforts and for initial production runs. In these circumstances, risk may be too high to warrant use of a fixed price arrangement or an FPI arrangement, but not high enough to require a CPFF arrangement to get a reliable supplier.

The CPIF contract is structured very similarly to the FPI compensation arrangement. Cost and fee outcomes are established for target, most optimistic, and most pessimistic points. These cost and fee outcomes are used to establish the sharing arrangement for cost decrease and increase situations. The difference between the structure of the FPI and CPIF arrangements is that under the CPIF arrangement, the contract converts to a CPFF contract at both the most optimistic and the most pessimistic fee points.

The computation of the final price to be paid to the supplier on contract completion follows the same steps as in the fixed price incentive arrangement. However, in a CPIF contract a comparison is made between computed fee and minimum and maximum fees prior to the calculation of the final price. For example, using the CPIF contract structured in Figure 16-5, the buyer would compute the final price, based on a final cost of $700,000, as follows:

Target cost	$1,000,000
Target profit	70,000
Maximum fee	120,000
Minimum fee	20,000

1 Cost savings = target cost − final cost
$300,000 = $1,000,000 − $700,000
2 Supplier's share of cost savings = cost savings × supplier share
$75,000 = $300,000 × 0.25
3 Computed fee = savings fee + target fee
$145,000 = $75,000 + $70,000

Since there is a maximum limitation on fee, a comparison is made between the computed fee and the maximum fee. In this case, the supplier receives only the maximum fee, $120,000.

4 Final price = final cost + maximum fee
$820,000 = $700,000 + $120,000

The CPIF contract is an incentive arrangement that converts to a CPFF contract at both the maximum and minimum fee points. This type of contract provides the supplier some incentive to control cost outcomes in the area over which the sharing arrangements apply, called the range of incentive effectiveness.

Cost Plus Fixed Fee Arrangements

Under a CPFF contract, the buyer agrees to reimburse the supplier for all allowable, reasonable, and allocable costs that may be incurred during the performance of the contract. Moreover, the buyer agrees to pay the supplier a fixed number of dollars above the cost as the fee for doing the work. The fee changes only when the scope of work changes. Under the CPFF, the supplier has no incentive to reduce or control costs.

The contractual elements of this arrangement include an estimated cost and a fixed fee. The estimated cost represents the best estimate of the customer and the supplier for the work involved. The fixed fee is the amount of fee the supplier will receive regardless of cost outcome. Because the supplier has no cost risk under a CPFF contract, the profit potential is relatively low. Normally there is a limit on the customer's total liability.

The buyer should remember that the final cost should be audited. Purchasing and supply management departments spend hours negotiating the right to inspect the actual invoices for material and the hours worked. Many, however, don't conduct an appropriate audit. It is a good use of time to look at the details even though one might not expect to find any inappropriate charges. The knowledge gained will often prove helpful in future negotiations.

Computing the final payment due the supplier under a CPFF contract is simply a matter of adding the incurred costs (assuming that an audit has found them to be reasonable, allowable, and allocable) to the fixed fee. In the case of a CPFF contract with an estimated cost of $1,000,000 and a fixed fee of $50,000, some possible final contract price outcomes are shown below:

	Possible outcomes (in thousands)			
Final cost	$800	$900	$1,000	$1,200
Fixed fee	50	50	50	50
Price to be paid to the supplier	$850	$950	$1,050	$1,250

The buyer must remember that in a cost-type contract, the limit is on the fee, not on total customer obligation. Obviously, the CPFF-type contract should be used only when the buyer cannot get a more favorable arrangement or when the presence of great uncertainty and risk would result in inclusion of a large contingency in a firm fixed price contract. The CPFF contract also is appropriate in circumstances where the technical and schedule risks are so high that the cost risk is too large for the supplier to assume. This type of contract is designed chiefly for use in research or exploratory development when the uncertainty of performance is so great that a firm price or an incentive arrangement cannot be set up at any time during the life of the contract. Costs normally are audited by the buyer before final payment.

Cost plus Award Fee (CPAF)   This type of contract was pioneered by NASA when the agency was purchasing highly complex hardware and professional services in support of the space program. The CPAF is very applicable to the procurement of software developed for the buying company, and for janitorial, landscaping, and similar services where the ability to reward the supplier for nonquantitative aspects of its performance on a subjective basis makes good business sense. The award fee is a pool of money established by the buyer to reward the supplier on a periodic basis for the *application of effort in meeting the buyer's stated needs*. The key difference between the award fee and other fees is that the supplier's receipt of the fee is based on the buyer's *subjective evaluation* of how well the supplier applies its *efforts* in meeting the buyer's needs. The subjective aspect provides a flexibility to contracting situations in an uncertain environment. When properly used, the award fee benefits both the buyer and the supplier. Superior performance receives superior rewards in the form of a superior fee. The award fee also introduces an element of flexibility since the buyer can change the areas receiving supplier attention by providing advance guidance for any performance period. The award fee gives the buyer's management a flexible tool with which to influence performance.

Cost without Fee   Nonprofit institutions, such as universities, usually do research work for both government and industry, without the objective of making a profit. Such research is done under cost-type contracts without a fee. Because universities do much of the nation's pure research, as distinguished from applied research done by industry, a growing number of contracts of this type are being used. Naturally, the universities recover all overhead costs, which generally include facilities costs and remuneration for personnel who work on the contracts. In recent years, high-technology firms have increased their use of this contract type.

Cost Sharing   In some situations, a firm doing research under a cost type of contract stands to benefit if the product developed can be used in its own product line. Under such circumstances, the buyer and the seller agree on what they consider to be a fair basis to share the costs (most often it is 50-50). The electronics industry has found this type of contract especially useful.

Time and Materials   In certain types of contracts, such as those calling for repairs to machinery, the precise work to be done cannot be predicted in advance. For instance, it cannot be known exactly what must be done to a large malfunctioning pump aboard a ship until it is opened and examined. Perhaps only a new gasket is required to put it in good working order. On the other hand, its impeller could require a major job of balancing and realignment. The time and materials contract is one method of pricing this type of work. Under this type of contract, the parties agree on a fixed rate per labor hour that includes overhead and profit, with materials supplied at cost.

Suppose a mechanic working on the ship's pump is paid $30 per hour. Assume also that overhead is calculated as 100 percent of the labor cost and profit is set at 10 percent of total cost. A billing rate for this mechanic for one hour would be calculated as follows:

Direct labor cost, per hour	$30
Overhead at 100 percent of labor	30
Total cost	$60
Profit at 10 percent of total cost	6
Billing rate, per hour	$66

If it took the mechanic two days (16 hours) to repair the pump, using $320 worth of material, the job price would be $1,376 (16 × $66 + $320).[1] Profit should be paid only on labor and overhead costs. Some sellers have been known to compute profit on materials, sales taxes, and so on.

A variation of the time and materials type of contract is called a labor-hour contract. In this type of contract, materials are not supplied by the seller; however, other costs are agreed to as in time and materials contracts.

Letter Contracts and Letters of Intent   Letter contracts are used in those rare situations in which it is imperative that work start on a complex project immediately. Letter contracts are *preliminary contractual authorizations* under which the seller can commence work immediately. The seller can prepare drawings, obtain required materials, and start actual production. Under letter contracts, the seller is guaranteed reimbursement for costs up to a specified amount. Letter contracts should be converted to definite contracts at the earliest possible date.[2]

Considerations When Selecting Contract Types

With such a wide variety of contract types available, a buyer must exercise considerable care in selecting the best one for a particular use. If a bid or a quoted price is reasonable, this will help the buyer decide to use a firm fixed price contract. On the other hand, if the fairness of the price is in doubt, a fixed price contract could entail excessive expense to the buyer and would be a poor choice. If price uncertainty stems from unstable labor or market conditions, fixed price with escalation may be a solution. If the uncertainty is due to a potential improvement in production effort, an incentive contract may be the best answer. Plainly, the many factors that affect procurement costs can themselves guide the buyer in his or her selection of the best type of contract for a given purchasing situation.

The specific nature of the materials, equipment, or services to be purchased also can frequently point up advantages of one contract type over another. The more complex or developmental the purchased item, the greater the risks and difficulties in using a fixed price contract. Any uncertainty in design affects a seller's ability to estimate costs, as does a lack of cost experience with a new item. The details of any given purchase will themselves indicate the magnitude of the price uncertainties involved. A full understanding of these uncer-

---

[1]The alert reader will observe that this is really a cost plus percentage of cost contract. If the mechanic is a good worker, he might complete the job in 10 hours ($60 profit to his employer). If he is a poor worker, he could take 20 hours, and his employer would receive $120 in profit. Obviously, buyers must exercise close control over this type of contract to be sure that inefficient or wasteful methods are not used.

[2]For more on this topic, see "Using Letters of Intent to Provide a Framework for Relationships with Suppliers" by William A. Hancock, January 1994, in *The Purchaser's Legal Adviser* published by Business Laws, Chesterland, Ohio (800-759-0920).

tainties permits buyers to allocate the risks more equitably between their firm and the supplier's firm through the proper choice of contract type.

Timing of the procurement quite frequently is a controlling factor in selection of the contract type. Allowing potential suppliers only a short time to prepare their bids can reduce the reliability of the cost estimates and increase prices. A short delivery period usually rules out the effective use of incentive contracts. On the other hand, a long contract period allows time to generate and apply cost-reducing efficiencies, an ideal situation for an incentive contract. The facts of each procurement must be considered individually in determining which contract type the buyer should use.

Business practices in specific industries frequently can provide additional clues as to the best choice of contract type. The construction industry, for example, traditionally accepts a wider range of competitive fixed price jobs than the aerospace industry. The lumber industry accepts prices established by open auctions. Architects and engineers frequently will not enter into price competition with one another for architectural or engineering services; neither will some management consulting firms compete with one another on price. Business factors such as these help determine the best contract type in a great many purchasing situations.

The scope and intensity of competition definitely can influence the type of contract to use. If competition is intense and the prices bid are close, then the buyer can justifiably feel that the prices are fair and reasonable and use a firm fixed price contract. On the other hand, if competition is not adequate and the buyer has doubts concerning the reasonableness of prices, an incentive or cost contract may be appropriate.

In short, *the buyer's basic preference for a firm fixed price contract is just the starting point for an analysis of alternative compensation choices.* As the buyer considers all available compensation types, he or she must weigh the preference for fixed prices against the risks involved, the time available, the degree of competition involved, experience with the industry involved, the apparent soundness of the offered price, the technical and developmental state of the item being purchased, and all the other technical and economic information that affects the purchase transaction. Determination of the best compensation agreement for a given situation requires a careful analysis of all the factors relevant to that situation.

CONCLUSION

A buyer can, in most instances, enter into a firm fixed price contract even when significant cost risk is present. But if risk is high, the buyer usually will experience either of two equally unsatisfactory results: (1) The contract price will include a large contingency or (2) the supplier could incur a loss. The possibility of a loss may result in (1) reduced quality in an effort to minimize the loss, (2) a request to renegotiate, (3) refusal to complete the work, (4) insolvency, resulting in the loss of a good supplier, or (5) a "grin and bear it" approach.

The selection of the contract compensation arrangement to be used for a specific contract is an important determination. The selection must be based on the cost risk involved and the circumstances surrounding the procurement. The compensation agreement selected must result in a reasonable allocation of the cost risk and should provide adequate motivation to the supplier to assure effective performance. In addition, the compensation arrangement selected must be compatible with the supplier's accounting system. Sound application of these compensation methods will significantly reduce expenditures when cost risk is present.

FOR DISCUSSION

16-1 What three issues are addressed by a compensation arrangement? Explain what is meant by "motivational implications" of a compensation arrangement.

16-2 The buyer has a range of compensation arrangements designed to meet the needs of a particular procurement. What two types of contracts are at the extremes of this range?

16-3 What is meant by "cost risk"? What two elements contribute to the calculation of cost risk?

16-4 Identify and define the three categories of compensation arrangements. Give examples of specific arrangements in each category.

16-5 Using Figure 16-3, explain why firm fixed price contracts are the greatest motivators of efficiency.

16-6 When using an economic price adjustment clause, which cost elements should be included? Which costs should be opposed?

16-7 What is the potential danger of using a fixed price redetermination contract? See Table 16-3.

16-8 What is the objective of using an incentive arrangement? What are the elements of an incentive contract?

16-9 Discuss the irony involved in setting cost targets.

16-10 Explain how the final price outcome is derived under an incentive contract. How does this motivate the supplier to perform as efficiently as possible?

16-11 Explain the comparison that is made in a cost plus incentive fee arrangement prior to calculating the final price. Why is this necessary?

16-12 Explain the structure of a cost plus fixed fee contract. What should a buyer do to ensure the legitimacy of the final cost?

16-13 What is the difference between an award fee and other contractual fees? Discuss the advantages of award fees from the perspectives of the supplier and the buyer.

16-14 Under what situation might both the buyer and seller agree to engage in cost sharing?

16-15 Discuss some of the considerations that must be employed when selecting a particular contract type.

CASES FOR CHAPTER 16

17

NEGOTIATION

KEY CONCEPTS

- Objectives of negotiation
- When to negotiate
- The buyer's role in negotiation
    The buyer acting alone
    The buyer as team leader
- The negotiation process
    Preparation
    Establishing objectives
    The dynamics of negotiation
    The four phases of face-to-face negotiation
- Negotiating techniques
    Universally applicable techniques
    Traditional techniques
    Collaborative negotiation
- Negotiating for price
    Price analysis negotiation
    Cost analysis negotiation
- Documentation
- Characteristics of a successful negotiator

Negotiation is one of the most important as well as one of the most interesting parts of professional purchasing. In industry, and at most levels of government, the term "negotiation" frequently causes misunderstandings. In industry, negotiation is sometimes confused with "hassling" and "price chiseling." In government, negotiation is frequently visualized as a nefarious means of avoiding competitive bidding and of awarding large contracts surreptitiously to favored suppliers.

Webster's dictionary defines *negotiation* broadly as "conferring, discussing, or bargaining to reach agreement in business transactions." To be fully effective in purchasing, negotiation must be utilized in its broadest context—as a decision-making process. In this context, negotiation is a process of planning, reviewing, and analyzing used by a buyer and a seller to reach acceptable agreements or compromises. These agreements and compromises include all aspects of the business transaction, not just price.

Negotiations differ from a ball game or a war. In those activities, only one side can win; the other side must lose. In successful negotiations, both sides win something. Popular usage calls this approach "win-win negotiating." The "winnings," however, are seldom equally divided; invariably, one side wins more than the other. This is as it should be in business—superior business skills merit superior rewards.

OBJECTIVES OF NEGOTIATION

Several objectives are common to all procurement/sales negotiations:

- To obtain the quality specified
- To obtain a fair and reasonable price
- To get the supplier to perform the contract on time

In addition, the following objectives frequently must be met:

- To exert some control over the manner in which the contract is performed
- To persuade the supplier to give maximum cooperation to the buyer's company
- To develop a sound and continuing relationship with competent suppliers
- To create a long-term partnership with a highly qualified supplier

Quality

In most cases, the buyer's objectives require him or her to obtain the quality specified by design engineering or by the user group. In some cases, however, quality itself may be a variable. For example, assume that the cost per unit, with a guarantee of no more than 100 defective parts per million incoming parts, is $5. Further, assume that the cost per unit with a guarantee of no more than 10 defective parts per million is $10. Does the higher unit price result in higher or lower total costs? Quite obviously, a highly advanced and accurate management information system must be available to provide the necessary data to allow the buyer to make an optimal decision.

Fair and Reasonable Price

In the majority of cases, the establishment of a fair and reasonable price for the desired level of quality becomes the principal focus of the negotiation process. This aspect of negotiation ranges in complexity from the use of price analysis to the more complex analysis of the potential supplier's cost elements. While the buyer focuses on obtaining a fair price, this must be done within the context of obtaining the lowest total cost, as previously discussed.

On-Time Performance

Inability to meet delivery schedules for the quality and quantity specified is the single greatest supplier failure encountered in purchasing operations. This results primarily from (1) failure of requisitioners to submit their purchase requests early enough to allow for necessary purchasing and manufacturing lead times and (2) failure of buyers to plan the delivery phase of negotiations properly. Because unrealistic delivery schedules reduce competition, increase prices, and jeopardize quality, it is important that buyers negotiate delivery schedules which suppliers can realistically meet, without endangering the other requirements of the purchase.

Control

Deficiencies in supplier performance can seriously affect, and in some cases completely disrupt, the operations of the buyer's firm. For this reason, on important contracts buyers should negotiate for controls which will assure compliance with the quality, quantity, delivery, and service terms of the contract. Traditionally, controls have been found to be useful in areas such as man-hours of effort, levels of scientific talent, special test equipment requirements, the amounts and types of work to be subcontracted, and progress reports.

Cooperation

Cooperation is best obtained by rewarding those suppliers who perform well with future orders. In addition to subsequent orders, however, good suppliers also expect courtesy, pleasant working relations, timely payment, and cooperation from their customers—*cooperation begets cooperation.*

Continuing Relations

When negotiating with suppliers, a buyer should recognize that current actions usually constitute only a part of a continuing relationship. Negotiating conditions which permit buyers to take unfair advantage of sellers invariably, with time, change to conditions which allow sellers to "hold up" buyers. For this reason, the buyer must realize that any advantage not honestly won will, in all likelihood, be recovered by the supplier at a later date—probably with interest. Thus, as a matter of self-interest, buyers must maintain a proper balance between their concern for a supplier's immediate performance on the one hand and their interest in the supplier's long-run performance on the other.

In summary, the objectives of negotiation require investigation, with the supplier, of every area of negotiable concern—considering both short-term and, normally, long-term performance. The buyer's major analytical tools for negotiating prices were discussed in the preceding chapters—such things as price, cost, and learning curves. Additional negotiating tools, as well as the development of strategy and tactics for negotiation, are discussed throughout this chapter.

WHEN TO NEGOTIATE

Negotiation is the appropriate method of purchasing when competitive bidding is impractical. Some of the most common circumstances dictating the use of negotiation are noted below:

- When *any of the five prerequisite criteria for competitive bidding are missing.*
- When many *variable factors bear* not only on price but also *on quality* and *service.* Many high-dollar-value industrial and governmental contracts fall into this category.
- When *early supplier involvement* (as described in Chapter 7) is employed.
- When the business *risks and costs* involved *cannot be accurately predetermined.* When buyers seek competitive bids under these circumstances, excessively high prices inevitably result. For self-protection, suppliers factor every conceivable contingency into their bids. In practice, not all these contingencies occur. Hence, the buyer unnecessarily pays for something not received.
- When a buyer is *contracting for a portion of the seller's production capacity,* rather than for a product the seller has designed and manufactured. In such cases, the buyer has designed the product to be manufactured and, as an entrepreneur, assumes all risks concerning the product's specifications and salability. In buying production capacity, the buyer's objective is not only to attain production capability but also to acquire such control over it as may be needed to improve the product and the production process. This type of control can be achieved only by negotiation and the voluntary cooperation of suppliers.
- When *tooling and setup costs represent a large percentage of the supplier's total costs.* For many contracts, the supplier must either make or buy many costly jigs, dies, fixtures, molds, special test equipment, gauges, and so on. Because of their special nature, these jigs and fixtures are primarily limited

in use to the buyer's contract. The division of special tooling costs between a buyer and a seller is subject to negotiation. This negotiation includes a thorough analysis of future buyer or seller use of the tools, the length and dollar amount of the contract, the type of contract to be used, and so on.

- When *a long period of time is required to produce the items* purchased. Under these circumstances, suitable economic price adjustment clauses must be negotiated. Also, opportunities for various improvements may develop— for example, new manufacturing methods, new packaging possibilities, substitute materials, new plant layouts, and new tools. Negotiation permits an examination and evaluation of all these potential improvements. Competitive bidding does not. What supplier, for example, would modify its plant layout to achieve increased efficiency without assurance of sufficient long-term business to cover the cost involved and assurance of a reasonable profit for the effort?
- When *production is interrupted frequently* because of numerous change orders. This is a common situation in fields of fast-changing technology. Contracts in these fields must provide for frequent change orders; otherwise the product being purchased could become obsolete before completion of production. The ways in which expensive changes in drawings, designs, and specifications are to be handled and paid for are subjects for mutual agreement arrived at through negotiation.
- When a *thorough analysis is required to solve a difficult make-or buy decision.* Precisely what a seller is going to make and what it is going to subcontract should be decided by negotiation. When free to make its own decision, the seller often makes the easiest decision in terms of production scheduling. This may well be the most costly decision for the buyer in terms of price.
- When the *products of a specific supplier are desired to the exclusion of others.* This can be either a single or a sole sourcing situation. In this case, competition is minimal or totally lacking. Terms and prices, therefore, must be negotiated to prevent unreasonable dictation by the seller.

In all ten of these cases, negotiation is essential; and, in each case, quality and service are as important as price.

THE BUYER'S ROLE IN NEGOTIATION

Depending on the type of purchase, a buyer plays one of two distinct roles in negotiation. In the first role, he or she is the company's sole negotiator. In the second, the buyer heads a team of specialists which collectively negotiates for its company.

The Buyer Acting Alone

For recurring purchases of standard items, regardless of their dollar amounts, the buyer invariably acts alone. Typically, for this type of purchase, a negotiation conference is held in the buyer's office with the supplier's sales manager (the seller's sole negotiator). These two persons alone negotiate all the important terms and conditions of the contract.

A buyer's "solo negotiation" is not limited to periodic formal negotiating sessions. Rather, such negotiations continue on a daily basis with both current suppliers and visiting vendors who wish to be suppliers. Consider several typical examples. A supplier calls on the telephone and informs the buyer that prices are to be raised 20 percent within sixty days. The buyer responds with the thought that production in her company's plant is slack and that a price rise as high as 20 percent could well trigger a "make" decision, in lieu of what is now a "buy" decision. The buyer is negotiating!

A seller's value analyst discovers a substantially less expensive method of manufacturing one of the buyer's products. However, there is one drawback: An expensive new machine is required for the job. The supplier's sales representative informs the buyer of the discovery. The buyer and an engineer study the concept; it is a good one. The two thank the sales representative for introducing the new idea. At the same time, the buyer explains that his company is financially unable at this particular time to invest in the required new machine. Further, the buyer conjectures that if the seller's company were to purchase the machine, then the buyer without doubt could get his company to reconsider the rejected long-term contract the seller proposed last year. Informal, unplanned negotiations are being conducted.

A salesperson calls, and the buyer says, "I have been thinking about your contract with us. Under the contract, our purchases now total roughly $60,000 per year, primarily for valves. But your company also manufactures a number of fittings that we use. If these fittings were combined with the purchase of the valves, what benefits would your company be able to grant us?" Another informal negotiation is under way.

The preceding year a buyer purchased $300,000 worth of liquid oxygen in individual cylinders from a single supplier. Because of its high dollar value, the buyer began to analyze oxygen usage requirements thoroughly. In this analysis, an interesting fact was discovered. By installing a bulk storage tank at the buyer's plant (at a cost of $160,000) and having the stores personnel deliver the required liquid oxygen to the shops, $70,000 per year could be saved. When the supplier's salesperson called, she was informed of the buyer's study and was given the buyer's worksheets for her review and study. Negotiations were under way, and the price of liquid oxygen would soon be reduced.

The Buyer as Team Leader

The complexity of a purchasing contract usually correlates directly with the complexity of the item being purchased. For high-value, technically oriented contracts (such as those developed for the purchase of high-technology products, capital equipment, and much research and development work), and for the development of long-term relationships where the supplier's production flows into the buying firm's operation, the buyer typically is no longer qualified to act as a sole negotiator. The buyer's role, therefore, shifts from that of sole negotiator to that of negotiating team leader. A typical team consists of from two to eight members, depending on the complexity and importance of the purchase to be made. Team members are selected for their negotiating knowledge and their expertise in the technical or business fields needed to optimize their team's negotiating position. Customarily, members are from fields such as design engineering, manufacturing engineering, cost analysis and estimating, finance, production, traffic, purchasing and supply management, and legal affairs.

In the team approach to negotiation, the buyer usually serves as the leader of the team (and is called the negotiator). In this capacity, he or she functions as the coordinator of a heterogeneous group of different specialists who can be expected to view similar matters differently. As head of the team, the negotiator must weld the team members into an integrated whole. By careful planning, the leader must draw on the specialized knowledge of each team member and combine this expertise with his or her own. To accomplish this, *it is very important that an overall strategy be developed by the team and that each team member be assigned a specific role*. Additionally, mock negotiations should be included as one of the final steps in team preparation. Mock negotiations normally constitute the best possible insurance to preclude the team's committing *the most costly error of negotiation*—that of the members speaking out of turn and thus revealing their firm's position to the seller's team. In this way, the buyer develops a sound, unified approach to uncover, analyze, and resolve (from a companywide point of view) all the important problems applicable to the contract under negotiation.

THE NEGOTIATION PROCESS

In the broadest sense, negotiation begins with the origin of a firm's requirements for specific materials or services. As discussed in Chapter 8, the ultimate in purchasing value is possible only if design, production, purchasing and supply, and marketing are able to reconcile their differing views with respect to material specifications. Buyers must always think in terms of total cost and total value, not in terms of price alone.

Actual two-party negotiation begins with a buyer's requests for proposals from potential suppliers. It develops as the negotiator carefully evaluates these proposals and prepares for discussion of the important issues that may arise in the impending negotiation conference. The negotiation process ends with the resolution of all issues that actually do arise during the negotiation conference.

The negotiation process consists of three major phases: *preparation*, the *establishment of objects*, and *face-to-face discussions* which result in agreement on all items and conditions of a contract, or a decision not to enter into an agreement with the potential supplier.

Preparation

Probably *90 percent or more of the time involved in a successful negotiation is invested in preparing for the actual face-to-face discussions*. The negotiator must (1) possess or gain a technical understanding of the item to be purchased, (2) analyze the buyer's and seller's relative bargaining positions, (3) have conducted a price or cost analysis (as appropriate), and (4) know the seller.

Know the Item or Service   The negotiator does not need to understand all the technical ramifications of the item being purchased. But it is essential that he or she have a general understanding of what is being purchased, the production process involved, and any other issues that will affect quality, timeliness of performance, and cost of production. The negotiator should understand the item's intended use, any limitations, and the existence of potential substitutes. The buyer should be aware of any prospective engineering problems which may arise. The negotiator should be aware of the item's procurement history and likely future requirements. Ideally, the buyer will be familiar with any phraseology or customs relevant to the industry.

The Seller's Bargaining Strength   The seller's bargaining strength usually depends on three basic factors: (1) how badly the seller wants the contract, (2) how certain he or she feels of getting it, and (3) how much time is available to reach agreement on suitable terms.

The buyer should encounter no difficulty in determining how urgently a seller wants a contract. The frequency with which the salesperson calls and general market conditions are positive indicators of seller interest. Sellers' annual profit and loss statements, as well as miscellaneous reports concerning backlog, volume of operations, and trends, are valuable sources of information about individual sellers. Publications such as the Department of Commerce's "Economic Indicators," *The Federal Reserve Bulletin*, industrial trade papers, and local newspapers provide a wealth of basic information about potential suppliers and their industries in general.

The less a seller needs or wants a contract, the more powerful its bargaining position becomes. The presence of an industry boom, for example, places it in a strong position. On the other hand, when a seller finds itself in a general recession or in an industry plagued with excess capacity, its bargaining position is decidedly weakened.

If a seller learns that its prices are lower than the competition's or learns from engineering or production personnel that it is a preferred or sole source of supply, it naturally concludes that its chances of getting the contract are next to certain. In these circumstances, a supplier may become extremely difficult to deal with during negotiations. In extreme situations, it may be unwilling to make any concessions whatever. When this happens, the negotiator sometimes has only one alternative—to accept the supplier's terms.

When trapped by such circumstances, a negotiator can threaten delay to search for other sources. Such threats are likely to be ineffective, unless the seller knows that alternative sources are actually available and interested in the business. An alternative threat which may be effective when patents are not involved is the threat to manufacture the needed item in the buyer's plant. When made realistically—when the supplier believes the buyer has the technical capability, the determination, and the capacity to make the product—this threat usually gains concessions.

A firm's negotiating position is always strengthened when the company has a clear policy that permits only members of its purchasing department to discuss pricing, timing, and other contractual terms with sellers. Most prenegotiation information leaks that give sellers a feeling of confidence about getting a contract occur in the technical departments of a firm. Such leaks can be extremely costly, and because they are often undetected by general management, they can be a continuing source of profit loss.

Short lead times drastically reduce the buyer's negotiating strength. Conversely, they significantly increase the seller's bargaining strength. Once a supplier knows that a buyer has a tight deadline, it becomes easy for the supplier to drag its feet and then negotiate favorable terms at the last minute when the buyer is under severe pressure to consummate the contract.

The Buyer's Bargaining Strength   The buyer's bargaining strength usually depends on three basic factors: the *extent of competition* present among potential suppliers, the *adequacy of cost or price analysis*, and the *thoroughness with which the buyer and all other members of the buying team have prepared* for the negotiation.

Intensive supplier competition always strengthens a buyer's negotiating position. Competition is always keenest when a number of competent sellers eagerly want the order. General economic conditions can bear heavily on the extent to which a firm really wants to compete. A firm's shop load, its inventory position, and its back-order position are typical factors that also bear heavily on the ever-changing competitive climate.

When necessary, a buyer can increase competition by developing new suppliers; making items in-house rather than buying them; buying suppliers' companies; providing tools, money, and management to competent but financially weak suppliers; and, above all, hiring highly skilled negotiators.

The Adequacy of Cost or Price Analysis   A comprehensive knowledge of cost analysis and price analysis is one of the basic responsibilities of all negotiators. When an initial contract is awarded for a portion of a supplier's production capacity rather than for a finished product, cost analysis becomes vital. In this situation, the negotiators are not prepared to explore with the supplier the reasonableness of its proposals until after a comprehensive analysis of all applicable costs has been completed. Cost analysis in such purchases, in a very real sense, is a substitute for direct competition. For follow-on contracts, and for contracts for common commercial items, price analysis is usually sufficient to assure the buyer that prices are reasonable. In the aggregate, *the greater the amount of available cost, price, and financial data, the greater the buyer's chances for successful negotiation.*

Know the Seller A professional buyer and members of the negotiating team should endeavor to know and understand both the prospective supplier firm and its representatives. Buyers at a leading East Coast firm prepare for critical negotiations by reviewing financial data and articles dealing with their prospective suppliers. The buyers and all negotiating team members know how the supplier's business is faring, key personnel changes, and so on. This level of preparation pays dividends when conducting face-to-face negotiations!

The Thoroughness of Buyer and Negotiating Team Preparation Knowledge is power. The more knowledge the negotiator acquires about the theory and practice of negotiation, the seller's negotiating position, and the product being purchased, the stronger his or her own negotiating stance will be. A negotiator without a thorough knowledge of the product being purchased is greatly handicapped. A negotiator is similarly handicapped if he or she has not studied and analyzed every detail of the supplier's proposal. Whenever feasible, *before requesting bids*, the negotiator should develop an estimate of the price and value levels for the items being purchased. Knowledge of current economic conditions in the market for the product in question is also an essential element of preparation.

Prior to the main negotiating session, all members of the negotiating team must evaluate all relevant data and carefully assess *their own* and *their supplier's strengths* and *weaknesses*. From this assessment, they develop not only a basic strategy of operation, but also specific negotiating tactics. Alert suppliers readily recognize negotiators who are not prepared. They gladly accept the real and psychological bargaining advantage that comes to them from lack of preparation by members of the buyer's negotiating team.

Establishing Objectives

The outcome of contract negotiations hinges on relative buyer-seller power, information, negotiating skills, and how both perceive the logic of the impending negotiations. Each of these controlling factors can be influenced by adroit advanced planning. This is why *proper planning is without question the most important step in successful negotiations.*

Having prepared for negotiations, the next step is to establish objectives. Negotiation objectives must be specific. General objectives such as "lower than previous prices," "good delivery," or "satisfactory technical assistance" are inadequate. For each term and condition to be negotiated, the negotiating team should develop three specific positions: (1) an objective position, (2) a minimum position, and (3) a maximum position. Using the cost objective as an example, the minimum position is developed on the premise that every required seller action will turn out satisfactorily and with minimum cost. The maximum position is developed on the premise that a large number of required seller actions will turn out unsatisfactorily and with maximum cost. *The objective position is the negotiator's best estimate of what he or she expects the seller's actual costs plus a fair profit should be.*

In developing concrete objectives, actual dates are established for delivery schedules, actual numerical ranges for quality acceptance, and actual dollar levels for applicable elements of cost. The major elements of cost which traditionally are negotiated—and for which objective, maximum, and minimum positions are developed—include *quantity of labor, wage rates, quantity of materials, prices of materials, factory overhead, engineering expense, tooling expense, general and administrative expense,* and *profit.* In addition to determining his or her own position for each major element of cost, the buyer and the negotiating team members must estimate the objective, maximum, and minimum positions of the seller. Determining the seller's maximum position is easy; it is the offer made in the seller's proposal.

In addition to costs, specific objectives should be established for all items to be discussed during the negotiation, including:

- All technical aspects of the purchase
- Types of materials and substitutes
- Buyer-furnished material and equipment
- The mode of transportation
- Warranty terms and conditions
- Payment terms (including discount provisions)
- Liability for claims and damage
- F.O.B. point
- General terms and conditions

Other objectives may include:

- Progress reports
- Production control plans
- Escalation/de-escalation provisions
- Incentive arrangements
- Patents and infringement protection
- Packaging
- Title to special tools and equipment
- Disposition of damaged goods and off-spec materials

The Dynamics of Negotiation

Typically, the two parties' positions appear as shown in Figure 17-1. The seller's positions are generally all higher than the corresponding positions of the buyer. The closer the two objectives are initially, the easier the negotiations. As negotiations proceed, the seller tends to make concessions from its maxi-

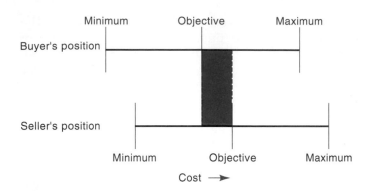

"Essence" or "heart" of negotiation

FIGURE 17-1
Negotiating positions.

mum position toward its objective. Simultaneously, the buying firm's negotiators reduce their demands, moving from the minimum position toward the objective.[1] Usually, little difficulty arises during this preliminary skirmish. This is not to say that this part of the negotiation process is easy or that it does not take time. Normally, vigorous testing is required to convince each party that the other is actually at his or her objective. Each party attempts to convince the other that the objective has been reached before this has, in fact, occurred.

As each party approaches its objective, negotiation becomes difficult. The distance between the buyer's objective and the supplier's objective can well be called the "essence" or "heart" of the negotiation. (See Figure 17-1.) Any concession made by either party from its objective position will appear unreasonable to him or her based on the previous analysis of the facts. Changes in position, therefore, must now be the result of either logical persuasion and negotiating skills (entailing further investigation, analysis, and reassessment of the facts) or the pressure of brute economic strength.

It is in the area of objective persuasion that the skillful negotiator stands out. He or she makes progress by uncovering new facts and additional areas of negotiation that permit the supplier to reduce its demands. For example, an analysis of the supplier's manufacturing operations might reveal that if lead time were increased by only one week, the job could be done with fewer machines making longer production runs. This change could substantially reduce the supplier's setup and scheduling costs, thus permitting a price reduction. Additional lead time might be made available by a slight modification in the buyer's production schedule. The cost of making this

---

[1]If the negotiator believes there is a possibility of actually achieving the minimum position, he or she should open with a position below this point—*provided such a position can be logically supported.*

change could well be much less than the seller's savings from the longer production runs. Thus both parties would profit from the change. It is this type of
situation that competent negotiators constantly seek to discover and exploit in
their attempt to close the gap between the seller's objective and their own.
Such situations have the highly desirable effect of benefiting each party at no
expense to the other party.

In some sole-source negotiations, the seller's objective is to maximize its
position at the expense of the buyer. In these situations, a continuing relationship is of secondary interest to the seller; therefore, it uses its bargaining
strength to maximize price, rather than to achieve a mutually advantageous
contract that will lead to continued business. The buyer who senses such a situation should start negotiations by attacking the reasonableness of the seller's
cost breakdown, using his or her own prepared cost estimates as the basis for
such contentions. In the absence of competition, this is a buyer's most logical
and most effective plan of action. If the supplier refuses to divulge its cost
data, the negotiator has only three available courses of action. He or she can
appeal to the seller's sense of reason, pointing out the potential negative long-
run implications of such actions; a second approach is to fight force with force
by threatening to use substitutes, or to redesign and manufacture the product;
and a third alternative is to further develop and refine the firm's cost estimating models and utilize them more forcefully in pursuing the original course of
negotiating action.

When faced with this type of problem, the negotiator must attempt to bring
the supplier's price as close to the objective as possible. In the short run, the
buyer usually pays the seller's price. In the long run, the buyer works toward
the development of competing sources, substitute products, and compromises
with the supplier.

If a seller's negotiation objective is to resolve issues as quickly as possible,
employing logical analysis rather than economic bargaining power, it is sometimes reasonable for the buyer to start negotiations by proposing his or her
actual objective as the counteroffer to the seller's proposal. In fact, in industrial
situations where continuing relationships are the rule, each successive negotiation brings the objectives of both parties ever closer together. Under these
conditions, buyers and sellers need develop only their objective positions;
there is no need for maximum and minimum positions.

The Four Phases of Face-to-Face Negotiations

Fact Finding During the *initial meeting* with the potential supplier, the
professional negotiator and the negotiating team limit discussions to fact
finding. Any inconsistencies between the supplier's proposal and the buyer's
information are investigated. Fact finding should continue until the negotiator
has a complete understanding of the supplier's proposal. Questions of a *how,*

what, when, who, and *why* nature are used by the negotiator. Experience has shown that when the negotiator limits this initial meeting to fact finding, a satisfactory agreement normally results with a minimum of hassle and disagreement. During the fact-finding process, the negotiator should gain a better understanding of both the supplier's interests and the supplier's strengths and weaknesses. The buying and selling representatives should disclose their interests—not their positions. Altogether too much time is wasted in haggling over positions. Professional negotiators quickly learn their opposite's interests, not their positions. It is much easier to satisfy interests than it is to move one's opposites off their positions. *On completion of the fact-finding process, the negotiator should call for a recess.*

The Recess   During the recess, the negotiating team should reassess its relative strengths and weaknesses, as well as those of the supplier. It may also want to review and refine its cost estimate. The team then should review and revise its objectives and their acceptable ranges. Next, the team should organize the agenda it desires to pursue when the two teams return to the negotiating table.

All negotiations center on specific issues. One of the difficult tasks of negotiation is to define fully the important issues which are to be included on the agenda and then to be sure that the discussion is confined to these issues. Most authorities believe that the issues should be discussed in the order of their probable ease of solution. With this priority system, an atmosphere of cooperation can develop that may facilitate solving the more difficult issues.

Narrowing the Differences   When the formal negotiations reconvene, the negotiator defines each issue, states the facts (and any underlying assumptions), and attempts to convince the supplier's representative(s) that the negotiator's position is reasonable. If agreement cannot be reached on an issue, the negotiator moves on to the next issue. Frequently, discussions on a subsequent issue will unblock an earlier deadlock.

During this phase of the negotiating process, *problem solving* and *compromise* are used to find creative solutions where both parties win. The buying team's manufacturing engineers may identify a more cost-effective process than the supplier had planned to use. Small acceptable changes in packaging, schedule, or tolerances; offers by the customer to furnish a material or an item of equipment; and payment terms (including possible advance payments) can unblock negotiations to the benefit of both parties.

In most instances, it is possible to reach a satisfactory agreement through the use of these procedures. If a satisfactory agreement cannot be reached, the negotiating team has the choice of adjourning (an attractive alternative for the buyer if another supplier is waiting in the wings) or moving on to hard bargaining.

Hard Bargaining   Hard bargaining, the last resort, involves the use of take-it-or-leave-it tactics. Its use is limited to one-time or adversarial situations where long-term collaborative relationships are *not* an objective. The negotiating team should carefully and professionally review and revise its objectives and, if absolutely necessary, give the supplier the option of accepting or rejecting its final proposal. The experienced negotiator does not bluff unless willing to have the bluff called. Unless a one-time purchase of an item already produced (e.g., an automobile on a dealer's lot) is involved, the wise negotiator avoids having the seller feel that it has been abused or treated unfairly. Such feelings set the stage for future confrontations, arguments, unsatisfactory performance, and possible claims.

TECHNIQUES

Negotiation techniques (tactics) are the negotiator's working tools. The negotiator uses them to achieve his or her strategic goals. In the hands of a skillful negotiator, these tools are powerful weapons. In the hands of a novice, they can be dangerous booby traps. Competent negotiators, therefore, spend a great deal of time studying and perfecting the use of these techniques. There are so many negotiating techniques that all cannot be discussed here. Those selected for discussion adequately represent the techniques that have proved to be most important and most effective.

The objective of negotiation is agreement. Even though agreement is the fundamental goal of negotiation, negotiations occasionally end without agreement. In the short run, reaching no agreement is sometimes better than reaching an unsatisfactory agreement. Generally speaking, however, experienced negotiators seldom let negotiations break down completely. They do not intentionally maneuver or let their opponents maneuver themselves into take-it-or-leave-it or walkout situations unless they are involved in a one-time or adversarial relationship.

Negotiating techniques may be divided into three categories: (1) those that are universally applicable, (2) those that are applicable to *traditional* (and, frequently, adversarial dealings), and (3) those that are applicable to *collaborative relationships.*

Universally Applicable Techniques

These are techniques which are applicable to all negotiations, whether arm's length or collaborative ones.

"Murder Boards" and Mock Negotiations Experienced negotiators frequently finalize their preparation through the use of "murder boards" and mock negotiations.

A murder board consists of senior purchasing and supply management, finance, manufacturing, quality, engineering, and general management personnel. The negotiating team presents its agenda, objectives, and tactics for the forthcoming negotiations. Members of the murder board dissect the negotiating plan in an effort to identify avoidable problems.

Mock negotiations allow the members of the negotiating team to prepare for the negotiation through a simulation of what is likely to occur. Other members of the organization (preferably from general management) play the roles of the supplier's negotiating team members during a simulated negotiation.[2]

Murder boards and mock negotiations enhance the negotiating team's level of preparation. Further, the processes result in general management's being aware of the negotiating team's agenda, objectives, and tactics. Should the subsequent negotiations deadlock, management is in a position to step in and revitalize critical negotiations.

Use Diversions   On the human side of negotiations, the negotiator who knows the seller personally, or has carefully studied his or her personal behavior patterns (as should be the case), has an advantage. When tempers start to get out of hand, as they occasionally do, the experienced negotiator quickly diverts attention away from the issue at hand. At such times a joke, an anecdote, or a coffee break can be an effective means of easing tensions. This type of diversion is usually more easily accomplished when the participants know what situations are most irritating to the other.

Use Questions Effectively   The wise use of questions is one of the most important techniques in negotiation. By properly timing and phrasing questions, the negotiator can control the progress and trend of the negotiation. A perceptive question can forcefully, yet tactfully, attack the supplier's position. Similarly, the negotiator can effectively defend his or her own position by asking the seller to evaluate certain carefully chosen data the buyer has developed.

The technique of answering questions properly sometimes is as important as the technique of asking them properly. The successful negotiator knows when to answer, when not to answer, when to answer clearly, and when to answer vaguely. Not all questions require an answer. Many questions are asked for which the seller knows there is no answer; therefore, a reply is not really expected.

The correct answer to questions in negotiation is not governed by the same criteria governing the correct answer to questions in most other situations. For negotiation questions, the correct answer is the answer that furthers either the negotiator's short-term tactics or long-range strategy. Labor leaders and politicians are experts at asking and answering questions. Their questions and their answers are made to correlate with their strategic plans (strike platforms, party platforms, and so on). To an uninformed observer, it often appears that the answers given by politicians and labor leaders do not relate to the questions that they are asked. These observations are only partially correct. When answering questions, politicians and labor leaders tell their listeners what they

---

[2]See David N. Burt, "Simulated Negotiations: An Experiment," *Journal of Purchasing and Materials Management*, Spring 1982, pp. 6-8.

want them to know about their platforms, whether or not the response fully answers the questions asked.

Successful negotiators realize that negotiation sessions are not like the classroom, where precise answers earn high marks. In negotiation, the purpose of questions and answers is not to illustrate to the seller how smart the negotiator is. Rather, it is to ferret out the seller's objectives and to learn as much as possible about how the seller's representatives intend to maneuver to achieve them. For this purpose, precise answers are sometimes the wrong answers. The correct degree of precision is dictated by the particular circumstances of each negotiation.

Use Positive Statements   As with sophisticated questions, perceptively used positive statements can favorably influence the course of negotiations. For example, assume a buyer knows that certain questions will evoke an emotional reaction from the seller. The questions are asked, and an opportunity is created for the proper use of a positive statement. A competent negotiator would say something like this: "I see your point, and I understand how you feel about this matter. Your point is well taken." Contrast the effect of this type of positive response with that of an emotional, negative response in which the buyer tells the seller that he or she is "dead wrong." When a buyer tells a seller that the seller's viewpoint is understood and considered reasonable, even though the buyer does not agree with it, the seller is certain to consider the buyer's viewpoint more objectively.

Machiavelli, in *The Prince*, gave the world some unusually sage advice concerning the use and misuse of positive statements: "I hold it to be proof of great prudence for men to abstain from threats and insulting words toward anyone, for neither . . . diminishes the strength of the enemy; but the one makes him more cautious, and the other increases his hatred of you, and makes him more persevering in his efforts to injure you."[3]

Be a Good Listener   Generally speaking, salespeople thoroughly enjoy talking. Consequently, buyers should let them talk. While talking, they very often talk themselves into concessions that a buyer could never gain by negotiation. Listening, per se, recognizes a basic need of a seller. Additionally, listening carefully to a seller's choice of words, phrases, and tone of voice, while at the same time observing his or her gestures and other uses of body language, can be rewarding. From observing such actions, a buyer can gain many clues regarding a seller's negotiating position.

Be Considerate of Sellers   A small number of negotiation experts contend that negotiations are best won by negotiators who are as brutal and as arbi-

---

[3]Niccolo Machiavelli, *The Prince*, Great Books of the Western World, Encyclopedia Britannica, 1982, vol. 23.

trary as possible. Although some evidence supports this viewpoint, it is definitely a minority one.

Unquestionably, there are some purchasing situations in which a merciless frontal assault can be a proper and successful negotiating technique. However, for the vast majority of firms—those that seek profitable, continuing relationships with the seller—a more considerate and reasoned technique is recommended. Buyers lose no negotiating advantages whatsoever by being fully considerate of sellers personally, by letting them save face, and by reasonably satisfying their emotional needs.

Traditional Techniques

Much negotiating literature is based on traditional—even adversarial (win-lose)—approaches. Two effective books addressing this approach are Gerald Nierenberg's *The Complete Negotiator*[4] and Herb Cohen's *You Can Negotiate Anything.*[5] Two of the traditional tactics which deserve emphasis are to keep the initiative and to never give anything away.

Keep the Initiative   The buyer should strive never to lose the initiative automatically obtained when the supplier's proposal is received and reviewed. There is a good deal of truth in the old saying that a good offense is the best defense. The buyer should constantly "carry the game" to the supplier, keep the supplier on the defensive by confronting its representatives with point after point, making the supplier continually justify its position. For example, if the supplier states the cost of materials in dollars, the buyer should ask the seller's representative to justify the figures with a bill of materials, appropriate scrap rates, and a full explanation of the manufacturing processes to be used. The more the buyer bores in and the more pressure he or she maintains, the better will be the buyer's bargaining position. If the supplier's position seems sound, the buyer can offer a counterproposal. In either case, the buyer starts with the initiative, and should work hard to retain it.

Never Give Anything Away   As a matter of strategy, a successful negotiator periodically lets the seller maneuver him or her into accepting one of the seller's proposals. This does not mean that the negotiator gives something away. He or she never "gives anything away." The buyer always expects to get a concession in exchange. On the other hand, the buyer does not feel obligated to match every concession made by the seller. Consequently, in the exchange process, the successful negotiator makes fewer concessions than his or her less successful adversary. By a continuation of this exchange process, a position

---

[4]Nierenberg, *The Complete Negotiator*, Nierenberg & Zeif Publishers, New York, 1986.
[5]Cohen, *You Can Negotiate Anything*, 2d ed., Bantam Books, New York, 1982.

close to the objectives of both parties is usually reached. Mutual concessions benefit both parties, and a contract so negotiated is *mutually* advantageous; but it is not *equally* advantageous.

Collaborative Relationships

The most widely read book ever written on negotiations is *Getting to Yes* by Roger Fisher and William Ury.[6] The authors introduce what they call "the principled negotiation method of focusing on basic interests, mutually satisfying options, and fair standards, resulting in a wise agreement."

Fisher and Ury's method calls for the use of four powerful techniques:

- Separate the people (negotiators) from the problem (quality, price, etc.).
- Focus on interests, not positions.
- Invent options for mutual gain.
- Insist on using objective criteria.

Experience demonstrates that applying these techniques to collaborative (or win-win) negotiations will result in both wise agreements and the basis of success for long-term relationships. Many of these relationships blossom into preferred partnerships and even into strategic supply alliances.

Separating People from the Problem   The negotiator is *not* dealing with abstract representatives, but rather with human beings. If possible, he or she should get to know the individuals representing the seller before the negotiation begins. Americans tend to be too anxious to rush into negotiations without getting to know and understand the supplier's representatives. We have much to learn from members of other cultures. Most spend a good amount of time becoming acquainted with those with whom they are to negotiate before entering into the formal phase of negotiations. These negotiators find ways to meet the seller's representatives informally. If possible, they arrive early before the negotiation is scheduled to begin and stay late after it ends.

Successful negotiators divide the negotiation into two components: *the people issue* and *the technical issues* such as quality, time, price, etc.

People issues require the negotiators to understand where the other party is coming from. In effect, the negotiators must walk in the shoes of the seller's representatives. Professional negotiators work at ensuring that they understand the other party—frequently rephrasing what they have heard to ensure understanding. They frequently ask the seller's representatives to describe in *their* own words what the buyer or buying team has said.

Emotions also get in the way of successful negotiations. Both parties to a negotiation have a right to get upset or angry and to express such emotions.

---

[6]Fisher and Ury, *Getting to Yes*, first published by Houghton Mifflin Company in 1981 and now published by Penguin Books, New York.

The wise negotiator lets the seller's representatives let steam off without taking offense or allowing the negotiation to become disrupted.

The most constructive negotiations—the ones which well may be the basis of a beneficial long-term relationship—occur when the representatives of the buying and selling organizations work together in a search for a fair agreement in which both sides are better off than if there were no agreement.

Focus on Interests   During the fact-finding phase of face-to-face negotiations, the professional buyer learns the seller's interests while disclosing his or her own interests. During the third phase (narrowing the differences), both parties work at reconciling and satisfying interests, not positions. Since both buyer and seller normally have multiple interests, it is wise to identify all of them and then work at developing a solution (agreement) which satisfies most or all of them. This approach calls on creativity and frequently results in increasing the size of the pie—the package of benefits to be shared by the two parties.

Invent Options for Mutual Gain   Fisher and Ury's third principle flows from the use of creativity to develop many options. When both parties become involved in creativity or brainstorming, they generate creative solutions wherein both parties benefit. Two rules of thumb are (1) develop many options and (2) remain in option generation past the point of comfort. Many of the most creative ideas require time and even discomfort to develop. Only after a list including one or more truly creative ideas has been developed should the negotiators attempt to select from the list.

Use Objective Criteria   When a long-term relationship is an objective of both parties, the use of objective criteria will avoid much positional negotiation—and the possibility of disrupting or destroying the relationship. For example, if price is the issue under discussion, then possible objective criteria include (1) the supplier's agreed-to allowable costs plus a reasonable profit and cost determination (2) by a cost model, (3) by a market-based pricing methodology, or (4) by target (design-to-cost) pricing. (Remember, these issues were all discussed in the previous chapter.) Having identified four possible objective criteria, the issue now becomes a discussion of which criteria, or combination of them, should be applied.

Benefits Are Not Divided Equally   In some purchasing circles, a common misunderstanding exists that successful negotiation means an equal buyer-seller distribution of the benefits. While both buyer and seller should benefit from a well-negotiated contract, the benefits are seldom divided 50-50. Traditionally, 60 to 70 percent of the benefits of a typical negotiated contract go to the more skillful negotiator, leaving 30 to 40 percent for the less skilled negotiator.

NEGOTIATING FOR PRICE

Historically, price is the most difficult of all contract terms to be negotiated. Based on its high relative importance and its complexity, negotiation for price will be used as an example to illustrate what is involved in negotiating all the terms of the contract. If the reader understands what is involved in negotiating price, he or she can easily visualize what is involved in negotiating other issues.

When negotiating price, the negotiator must concurrently consider the type of contract to be used. Contract type and the negotiation of price are directly related; hence, they must be considered together.

To assure buying at favorable prices, buyers strive to develop the greatest practical amount of competition or enter into fact-finding discussions with representatives of preferred suppliers or "partners" about their costs and cost drivers. Whenever it is possible, therefore, the initial step for a buyer seeking successful negotiation(s) based on competition is to get an adequate number of bids or proposals from among those potential suppliers who are genuinely interested in competing for the contract.[7] In negotiated purchasing, requests for proposals usually ask for not only total price but also a complete break-down of all attendant costs.

For every negotiated purchase, either price analysis or cost analysis, or both, is required. Which analysis is best to use and the extent of the analysis required are determined by the facts bearing on each specific purchase being negotiated. Generally speaking, price analysis is used for lower-dollar-value contracts and cost analysis for higher-dollar-value contracts. A discussion of the applicable uses of both price analysis negotiation and cost analysis negotiation follows.

Price Analysis Negotiation

Price analysis negotiation (often referred to simply as "price negotiation") is the most commonly used approach when negotiating for price. Some proponents of cost negotiation disparage price negotiation, referring to it as "unsophisticated" and "emotional." In the many cases where price negotiations are undertaken in an unprofessional manner, such criticism is fully justified. Banging on the table and shouting "I want lower prices" or "I can get it cheaper from B" is certainly not professional price negotiation.

On the other hand, in many specific cases where pricing data are developed and utilized with professional skill, price negotiation can be just as advantageous as cost negotiation, or more so. Compared with cost negotiation, price negotiation has three distinct advantages: (1) negotiation time is shorter, (2)

---

[7]The term "bids" is traditionally used in competitive bid purchases. Consequently, bids used in negotiated purchases are sometimes referred to as "proposals," to clearly identify the buy as a negotiated purchase. However, the terms are frequently used interchangeably.

support of technical specialists is seldom needed, and (3) pricing data are relatively easy to acquire.

The traditional sources from which buyers get pricing data are federal government publications, purchasing trade publications, newspapers, and business journals. Competing suppliers are excellent sources of pricing data. They can provide the buyer with price lists, catalogs, numerous special pricing data, and formal price quotations. From these competing supplier data, the buyer can readily determine two very important facts: *the nature of the market* (competitive or noncompetitive) and *the extent of supplier interest* in this particular purchase. As discussed in Chapter 14, historical pricing data and engineering estimates also provide a sound basis for price analysis.

Price Comparison   The negotiator's first step in price analysis is to determine the extent of market competitiveness and supplier interest. The second step is to examine in detail the absolute and relative differences existing among the various prices quoted by the competing suppliers. From this examination, a buyer detects that differences in prices among suppliers exist but does not learn the causes of these differences. The search for causes begins in the purchasing department's supplier information file.

The bid prices of the competing suppliers are compared with past prices of similar purchases from the supplier information file. The causes of all significant variations are pinpointed and analyzed. Adjustments are made for changes in factors such as specifications, quantities ordered, times of deliveries, variations which have taken place in the general levels of business activity and prices, and differences which may have resulted from learning experience. After these adjustments are made, the negotiator (sometimes with the help of an engineering estimator or a price analyst) determines whether or not the prices offered are reasonable. From this determination, the negotiator decides on the target price to use for his or her negotiating position.

Trend Comparisons   Historical prices paid for purchases of similar quantities can be analyzed to disclose helpful price trend information. For example, if prices have been increasing, it is reasonable to expect that the seller will attempt to maintain a similar pattern of increase. Hence, by carefully analyzing the reasons for all price increases, the negotiator can structure a bargaining position on the basis of any invalidities uncovered.

Similarly, the negotiator can analyze decreasing prices to determine whether the price decrease is too little or too much. If the buyer determines that the decrease is too large, he or she must determine whether the trend is creating, or is likely to create, quality or service problems in contract performance. If the decrease is too little, then the buyer must determine whether the benefits of improved production processes are being proportionally reflected in lower prices.

Even a level price trend offers opportunities for price analysis. For example, the negotiator may ask whether level prices are justified, considering the many manufacturing improvements which have been made. Did the supplier charge too much initially? Has the supplier's competitive position in the industry changed? If the negotiator's analysis indicates that costs have fallen because of reductions in the supplier's cost for materials or because of improvements in the production processes, his or her negotiating position is clear. The buyer negotiates for pro-rata reductions reflecting these changes.

Cost Analysis Negotiation

As previously stated, price analysis negotiation is more commonly used than cost analysis negotiation. In cost negotiations, each applicable cost element is negotiated individually, i.e., design engineering cost, tooling cost, direct materials cost, labor hours, labor rates, subcontracting, overhead cost, other direct costs, profit, and so on. Cost analysis negotiation (commonly referred to as "cost negotiation") is steadily growing in use. It has been used successfully for decades by many large firms such as General Electric, Ford, and Polaroid, and in recent years it has been employed increasingly by small and medium-size firms.

When preferred supplier or strategic supply relationships are utilized by a firm, careful detailed analysis of the supplier's costs (both present and projected) replaces the role of competition in the marketplace. Both buyer and seller must see themselves as members of a value chain competing *with other value chains* for the customer's purchasing dollar. Thus, discussions about costs, cost allocations, cost drivers, cost reductions, possible cost avoidance, and profits must be seen in context: *If our portion of the value chain becomes noncompetitive, then we will fail to attract the customer's purchase dollars and we both lose!* Discussions can and often do get heated—conflict can be healthy—but the discussions should be conducted in the context of what is in the *joint* best interests of the two parties. In reality, they should see themselves as members of the same team.

DOCUMENTATION

Personnel turnover and the frailties of the human memory make accurate documentation of the negotiation essential. The documentation must permit a rapid reconstruction of all significant considerations and agreements.

Documentation begins in the purchasing office with the receipt of a purchase requisition and continues with the selection of potential suppliers and their proposals. Documentation of the actual negotiation must be adequate to allow someone other than the buyer to understand what was agreed to, how, and why. Burt, Norquist, and Anklesaria suggest the following format for the documentation of negotiations:[8]

---

[8]David N. Burt, Warren E. Norquist, and J. Anklesaria, *Zero Base Pricing™: Achieving World Class Competitiveness through Reduced All-in-Cost*, Probus Publishing, Chicago, 1990, chap. 13.

Subject   This is a memorandum designed for many readers with different orientations. This section, together with the introductory summary, should give the reader a complete overview of the negotiation, including information such as the supplier's name and location, the contract number, and a brief description of what is being purchased.

Introductory summary   The introductory summary describes the type of contract and the type of negotiation action involved, together with comparative figures from the supplier's proposal, the buyer's negotiation objective, and the negotiated results.

Particulars   The purpose of this section is to cover the details about what is being bought and who is involved in the procurement. This should be done without duplicating information that was included in the subject section.

Procurement situation   The purpose of this section is to discuss factors in the procurement situation which affect the reasonableness of the final price.

Negotiation summary   This section shows the supplier's contract pricing proposal, the buyer's negotiation objective, and the negotiation results, tabulated in parallel form and broken down by major elements of cost and profit. Whether these are shown as summary figures for total contract value, summary for the total price of the major item, unit price for the major items, or some other form of presentation depends on how negotiations were conducted. The general rule is to portray the negotiation as it actually took place.

CHARACTERISTICS OF A SUCCESSFUL NEGOTIATOR

The characteristics of successful negotiators should now be clear. These people are skillful individuals, with broad business experience. They possess a good working knowledge of all the primary functions of business, and they know how to use the tools of management—accounting, human relations, economics, business law, and quantitative analysis. They are knowledgeable about the techniques of negotiation and the products their firms buy. They are able to lead conferences and to integrate specialists into smoothly functioning teams. In addition to being well educated and experienced, successful negotiators excel in good judgment. It is good judgment that causes them to attach the correct degree of importance to each of the factors bearing on the major issues. Combining their skills, knowledge, and judgment, they develop superior tactical and strategic plans. Additionally, they consider problems from the viewpoint of the firm as a whole, not from the viewpoint of a functional manager.[9]

[9]In recent years women have entered the purchasing and materials management profession in increasing numbers. These new professionals have proved themselves capable in all phases of the profession—especially negotiation.

Fully successful negotiators share three common attributes:

1 All realize that specialized training and practice are required for an individual to become an effective negotiator. Although some people have stronger verbal aptitudes than others, no one is born with negotiating knowledge and skills.
2 All habitually enter into negotiations with higher negotiating goals than their counterparts, and generally they achieve them.
3 All are included, or are destined to become included, among an organization's most highly valued professionals.

CONCLUSION

Negotiation is free enterprise at its very best. When *traditional* negotiations (*win-lose*) are appropriate, negotiation matches the skills of determined buyers against those of equally determined sellers. Both explore ways to achieve objectives that tend to optimize the self-interest of their organizations. In short, in such circumstances negotiation is a powerful purchasing tool which competent buyers use to achieve maximum value at minimum cost. By rewarding efficiency and penalizing inefficiency, the negotiation process not only benefits the negotiating firms, but also benefits the nation's economy as a whole.

At the same time, in different circumstances the increasingly common *collaborative* approach to negotiations that is required with "preferred suppliers" and "strategic alliance partners" substitutes a *win-win* approach. With this approach, both parties are better off entering into the negotiated deal than not to reach agreement. But this approach substitutes for the forces of marketplace competition the expertise of the buying and selling firms' representatives (and, subsequently, their firms) at identifying and squeezing unessential costs out of the coupling of the two operations. Thus, costs must be driven to their lowest possible levels (without adversely affecting quality) in order to ensure the survival and success of the buyer and seller's value chain in the marketplace.

FOR DISCUSSION

17-1 What does negotiation mean in purchasing? Why is it often confused with "hassling" and "price chiseling"?
17-2 "Superior negotiating skills merit superior reward." Do you agree with this statement? Why or why not?
17-3 Enumerate the six objectives common to most negotiations. Should a negotiation team pursue all objectives while negotiating?
17-4 Under what circumstances should negotiation be used in preference to competitive bidding?
17-5 Compare and contrast the terms "informal negotiation" and "mock negotiation."

17-6 What must a negotiator do to properly prepare for face-to-face negotiation? Why is preparation so important?

17-7 Discuss three factors which influence a seller's negotiating strengths and weaknesses.

17-8 Discuss three factors which influence a buyer's negotiating strengths and weaknesses.

17-9 In the process of negotiation, after both sides reach their negotiation objectives, progress becomes difficult. Why? How are such difficulties resolved?

17-10 What are the four phases of face-to-face negotiation? What is the objective of the fact-finding phase?

17-11 What are the three categories of negotiating techniques? Give examples of techniques in each category.

17-12 Identify the difference between cost and price negotiation. When should you use cost negotiation? What is the appropriate context for cost negotiations with a preferred, or strategic, supplier?

17-13 Why is price the most difficult of all contract terms to negotiate?

17-14 Describe how the documentation for a given negotiation is typically organized. What purpose does the documentation serve?

17-15 What are the characteristics of a successful negotiator?

CASES FOR CHAPTER 17

PART **FOUR**

SPECIAL PURCHASES

18

PURCHASING CAPITAL EQUIPMENT

KEY CONCEPTS

- Differences in the procurement of capital equipment
    Nonrecurring purchases
    Nature and size of expenditure
    Considerations in source selection: operating characteristics, engineering
       features, economic analysis, qualitative considerations
    Team selection of equipment
- Life cycle cost analysis
- Procedure for the purchase of capital equipment
- Purchasing's role in capital equipment procurement
    Information and liaison service
    Specification development and bids
    Qualitative analysis
    Economic analysis
    Negotiation, contract preparation, and administration
- The used equipment market
    Types of sources
    Reasons for purchasing used equipment
    Cautions in purchasing used equipment
- Leased equipment
    Types of leases
    Factors favoring leasing
    Disadvantages of leasing
    Cost analysis—the decision process

The purchase of capital equipment differs substantially from the purchase of production materials and supplies. Such items as pianos, pumps, standard electric motors, microcomputers, materials-handling trucks, and office furniture are typical examples of *general-purpose* capital equipment. Things such as power-generating equipment, specialized machine tools, unique production machinery, and chemical processing equipment are examples of *special-purpose* capital equipment, designed for unique applications. Because of the specialized applications and complex nature of the equipment, development of specifications for this latter category of capital items usually requires a great deal of interaction between technical personnel in the buying and the selling firms. For the same reasons, the effective life of the equipment frequently is determined by technological obsolescense factors.

For accounting purposes most firms classify both categories of equipment as noncurrent assets, which are capitalized and depreciated over the course of their economic lives.

DIFFERENCES IN THE PROCUREMENT OF CAPITAL EQUIPMENT

Nonrecurring Purchases

The purchase of a particular piece of capital equipment typically occurs only once every three to five years or so. For example, one buyer recently purchased a unique high-temperature electric furnace for use in her company's research and development laboratory. Since the furnace is used only periodically for experimental work, it is very likely that another purchase of this kind of equipment will not be made in the foreseeable future.

On the other hand, a few industrial operations require the use of many identical machines in the production process. For example, in petroleum and chemical processing plants, the product is transported by pipeline throughout most of the production operation. This requires dozens, at times hundreds, of similar pumps which vary only in size and details of construction. To keep capital expenditures at a fairly uniform level from year to year and to minimize maintenance costs, pumps are often replaced on a continuing basis, rather than all at once. Although relatively uncommon, this type of capital equipment purchase assumes some of the characteristics of conventional production purchasing.

A unique feature of most capital equipment purchases is the lead-time requirement. While some types of capital equipment are standard off-the-shelf products, many are not. Much production machinery and prime moving equipment are built (at least in part) to operate under specific conditions peculiar to each purchaser's operation. Consequently, manufacturing lead time is usually a matter of months or perhaps years. The production of a large steam turbine generating unit, for example, may require negotiating and expediting work substantially different from that normally required in production purchasing.

Nature and Size of Expenditure

An expenditure of company funds for capital equipment is an investment. If purchased wisely and operated efficiently, capital equipment generates profit for its owner. Because it exerts a direct influence on the costs of production, the selection of major capital equipment is a matter of significant concern to top management.

Although capital equipment prices cover a wide range, the purchase of most major equipment involves the expenditure of a substantial sum of money. The purchase price for a piece of equipment, however, is frequently overshadowed in importance by other elements of cost. Since a machine is often used for ten years or more, total costs of operation and maintenance during its lifetime may far exceed its initial cost. Hence, the *total life cost* of a machine, relative to its productivity, is the cost factor of primary importance.[1] Estimating operating and maintenance costs which will be incurred in future years is not easy; frequently these costs vary from year to year. Consequently, discussions involving the choice between several alternative machines often center on the probable accuracy of specific cost estimates.

The timing of many capital purchases often presents a paradoxical situation. Typically, the general supply capabilities of capital equipment producers do not adjust quickly to changes in levels of demand. Thus, because most firms' capital equipment purchases are made rather infrequently and can often be postponed, producers of industrial capital goods frequently find themselves in a "feast or famine" type of business. When a potential purchaser's business is good, it needs additional production equipment to satisfy customers' burgeoning demands. But because other purchasers are in the same situation, the buyer also may find capital equipment prices rising in a market of short supply. Conversely, when a buyer's business is down and additional production equipment is not needed, capital equipment is in plentiful supply, often at reduced prices.

Considerations in Source Selection

When purchasing capital equipment, selection of a supplier is governed largely by four general considerations: (1) operating characteristics of the equipment, (2) engineering features of the equipment, including compatibility with existing equipment, (3) a total economic analysis, and (4) various qualitative considerations.

---

[1]This type of analysis is also called *life cycle costing*. The term and the concept were originally developed and refined in military procurement. Subsequently, industry adopted the concept and now it is widely used in most industries. This topic is discussed in more detail shortly.

Operating Characteristics   This is by far the most influential factor in selecting the supplier for a particular production machine. Once the user and appropriate engineering personnel clearly establish the function the equipment is to perform, design and operating capability are paramount in selecting the specific machine to be purchased.

Design and operating features for a given type of equipment can differ markedly among the machines available from different suppliers. For this reason, the number of suppliers willing to produce a machine capable of meeting every aspect of a purchaser's operating requirements is frequently limited. This, of course, is more likely to be the case for specialized equipment than for general-purpose equipment. Nevertheless, this is one reason why a purchasing department usually finds its freedom of source-selection activities constrained considerably in obtaining capital equipment as compared with buying production materials.

Engineering Features   Closely related to the equipment's operating characteristics are its engineering features. *These features must be compatible with the buyer's existing equipment, process, and plant layout;* they must also be in accordance with standards established by state and federal regulatory agencies such as the Occupational Safety and Health Administration (OSHA) and the Environmental Protection Agency (EPA). A few major engineering considerations are noted below.

- *Specific process capabilities.* Is performance compatible with that of existing machines, thus minimizing process coordination problems? Will use of the new machine produce capacity imbalance problems?
- *Physical size and mounting dimensions.* Will the machine fit into existing available space satisfactorily? Can it be tied in to existing supporting structures without difficulty?
- *Flexibility.* Can the equipment be moved and relocated without excessive difficulty?
- *Power requirements.* Can existing power supplies be used?
- *Maintenance.* Are lubrication fittings and adjusting mechanisms conveniently located? Is any special maintenance required that cannot be handled by existing maintenance programs?
- *Safety features.* Does the machine have any unsafe features? Does it meet OSHA standards, and is its general safety level comparable with that of existing equipment?
- *Pollution characteristics.* Does the equipment perform in accordance with EPA requirements concerning pollution and contamination discharge levels?

The general questions to be answered are: How does this piece of equipment fit in with the existing operation? Will many costly modifications be involved in adapting the equipment to the existing system?

Economic Analysis After several acceptable machines have been identified, a thorough evaluation of their relative merits is undertaken. The task is a complicated one. An analysis of the major operating alternatives includes a comparative economic analysis of the potential new machines, and also a comparison of each with the alternative of using the existing equipment now in operation. In all cases, the analysis of each machine must relate its total expected life cost to its total expected productivity. The cost analysis is done most commonly utilizing the *life cycle costing* technique (see page 391). These results, in turn, can be expressed using several different measures of profitability.

Although it has serious limitations, the *payback* approach is still widely used throughout American industry. As its name implies, the objective of payback analysis is to determine the number of years a machine requires to pay for itself from additional earnings generated by its increased level of operating efficiency. This is a useful measure for evaluating a potential purchase in light of a firm's liquidity position. However, it must be supplemented with one of the discounted cash flow–based measures that gives a more complete picture of a machine's total profitability over the life of the equipment investment. The *time adjusted rate of return* on investment is one such technique that is used by some firms. Among several other widely used approaches is the *net present value method*.[2]

Before the total investigation proceeds too far, a formal proposal justifying the need for additional capital equipment should be prepared for top management. Although the proposal must consist of more than an economic analysis, a complete quantitative analysis showing the potential profitability of the various alternatives should constitute a major section of such a proposal.

Qualitative Considerations Certain qualitative factors concerning potential suppliers are important in making any purchase. However, not all the factors important in selecting sources for production materials weigh as heavily in selecting sources for capital equipment. Capital equipment purchases require a different type of cooperative relationship between the buyer and the seller. It is important, initially, that a supplier be willing to work with the buyer's technical personnel to ensure a good fit of equipment to operating need. After the purchase, the buyer may need help with installation, start-up, adjustment, and so on. In fact, adjustment or calibration may be a continuing need, depending on the type of equipment and the buyer's in-house capability.

At some future date, the buyer may also require a warranty adjustment. Especially important is an assessment of the supplier's policy and cooperativeness with respect to the supply of replacement parts and service for the equipment, particularly later when the equipment is superseded by a new model. These types of factors represent one group of qualitative issues that a

---

[2]The reader interested in a detailed treatment of this topic should review any current text dealing with financial management. Particularly good are E. F. Brigham, *Financial Management—Theory and Practice*, 3d ed., Dryden Press, New York, 1991, chap. 3; and S. B. Block and G. A. Hirt, *Foundations of Financial Management*, rev. ed., Richard D. Irwin, Inc., Homewood, Ill., 1991, chaps. 9 and 11.

buyer considers in making a capital equipment purchasing decision, with each case posing its own unique requirements. Generally speaking, however, the buyer focuses on somewhat different considerations than when a continuous stream of production materials is being purchased.

Another group of qualitative considerations the capital equipment buyer is concerned with are those indicating a supplier's ability to produce reliable equipment that performs in accordance with specifications. This implies the definite need for an assessment of the supplier's technical and production capabilities. As the situation demands, a good buyer uses various approaches and personnel in making such an assessment, including plant visits and technical discussions with the supplier's personnel. However, buyers should not overlook the simple technique of investigating a supplier's reputation among present customers. This is an invaluable source of information that is easy to tap.

Generally speaking, qualitative considerations do not play a primary role in the selection of a supplier for capital equipment. They are usually considered in the final analysis, after the major factors have been weighed. The qualitative factors are the straws that tip the balance one way or the other for the several potential suppliers who rank high on combined technical and economic considerations.

Joint Selection of Equipment

It should now be clear that the final selection of capital equipment should be a joint undertaking by all departments having a legitimate interest in the decision. To facilitate this process, larger firms frequently utilize a buying team composed of representatives from operations, process engineering, plant engineering, finance, and purchasing and supply management, depending on the nature of the purchase.[3] In smaller firms, this coordination may be achieved less formally by a series of meetings among the appropriate functional individuals; in this case, purchasing's capital equipment buyer often serves in a coordinating or administrative role. In either case, because capital equipment represents a long-range investment, a general management executive frequently makes the final purchasing decision, based on recommendations from this interdepartmental group.

Because the operations manager is responsible for the efficiency of the total production operation, his or her views logically carry a great deal of weight in the selection of production equipment. It is good to bear in mind also that the importance of the human element should not be overlooked. More than one purchasing and supply manager has discovered that because the head of the department where the equipment is to be used is directly affected by the decision, the enthusiasm or reluctance of his or her acceptance may have a direct bearing on the

---

[3]For a broadly based discussion of this topic, see Lisa M. Ellram and John N. Pearson, "The Role of the Purchasing Function: Toward Team Participation," *International Journal of Purchasing and Materials Management*, Summer 1993, pp. 3–9.

efficiency of the equipment in actual use! Consequently, the operations manager may well choose to bring the appropriate supervisor into the decision also. The technical contribution to be made by process engineering and plant engineering representatives is clearly an important one, for the reasons previously outlined.

The finance department has three primary interests in capital equipment purchases and leases. First, this department usually administers the firm's capital budget; it is therefore concerned with the allocation of funds for the proposed purchase. If the budget contains a provision for such equipment, all is well; if not, a priority question must be resolved. Second, the finance department has the responsibility of deciding how to finance such purchases. Is enough cash available? Can a long-term loan be arranged? Will it be necessary to raise the money through a bond issue? For large purchases, the answers to these questions bear heavily on the final decision. Third, the finance department should review and evaluate the economic analysis of alternative machines and potential leases. In some firms, the finance department conducts the original analyses; in others, they are made by engineering or purchasing. In any case, the finance department typically administers these activities in connection with its capital budgeting responsibility.

After the technical and economic analyses have been completed, the purchasing group develops and evaluates the qualitative factors relevant to the decision. After the supplier is selected, purchasing handles the negotiations and carries out the conventional purchasing responsibilities.

LIFE CYCLE COST ANALYSIS

How important is the *price* of a new piece of productive equipment? The answer is, it depends. It depends on a number of factors that vary widely with the design and usage of the equipment, as well as the number of years it will be in service (coupled with various economic inflation factors). In addition to the original delivered cost of the machine, its total cost to the owner includes such cost factors as those associated with installation, ongoing adjustment and calibration, energy and labor for operation, routine maintenance, major overhauls, downtime, and eventual disposition of the machine (net cost or salvage value). As a rough rule of thumb, in industry today the delivered price of a piece of productive equipment seldom exceeds 50 percent of the eventual total cost of ownership of the asset—and is generally substantially less.[4]

The price of anything that one buys is important. But in the case of capital equipment, it is usually less important than the sum of all the *follow-on* costs that eventually accompany the purchase, particularly if the equipment is expected to have a reasonably long life. In any case, the important requirement in capital equipment purchasing is to conduct a life cycle cost analysis to put

---

[4]Researchers Michael Leenders and Harold Fearon find that most industrial equipment falls in the 20 to 60 percent range; Leenders, Fearon, and England, *Purchasing and Materials Management,* Richard D. Irwin, Inc., Homewood, Ill., 1993, p. 574.

all the cost factors in the correct perspective. It is not uncommon for the operating and maintenance costs of a less expensive machine to exceed those of a somewhat higher-priced machine to the extent that, in total, the higher-priced machine is a significantly better buy.

Conceptually, the life cycle costing concept is quite simple. It seeks to determine the *total* cost of performing a given function during the useful life of the equipment performing the function. It focuses on the total cost of ownership rather than on initial price.

In practice, however, the concept frequently is not so easy to apply. A number of the anticipated costs are not known with certainty; many will occur in the future, and many will be based on estimates of labor rates, energy costs, and downtime requirements during maintenance and overhaul. The extent to which these costs can be estimated accurately depends on three factors: (1) the experience and sophistication of the manufacturer in making its performance estimates, (2) the buying organization's experience with similar types of equipment, and (3) the sophistication of the buyer's economic forecasting group.

Despite the practical difficulties, in most cases organizations that utilize the life cycle costing concept have learned to make the required estimates with an acceptable degree of accuracy. The procedure followed in conducting a life cycle cost analysis is summarized below.

1 Determine the operating cycle for the equipment—types of operation, routine maintenance, overhaul, sequence, and so on, detailing how the machine functions or what will be done in each step of the cycle.
2 Identify and quantify the factors that affect costs—power consumption and rates at various levels of operation, labor requirements and rates, maintenance requirements and rates, average time between failures, time between overhauls, average downtime cost, and so on.
3 Calculate all costs at current rates and prices.
4 *Project costs to the future dates at which they will be incurred,* adjust for expected inflation or deflation, consider estimated salvage value, and complete the life cycle cost matrix.
5 *Discount all future costs and benefits to their present values.*
6 Sum all costs and benefits to obtain the total life cycle cost, expressed in *present value* terms.

The generalized formula for making the calculations described in steps 5 and 6 is:[5]

$$TCO = (A) + \left(NPV \sum_{i=1}^{n} Ci\right) - NPV\ Sn$$

[5]Marvin R. Fischer, "The Acquisition of Capital Assets," *The Purchasing Handbook,* McGraw-Hill Inc., New York, 1992, chap. 22, p. 661.

where TCO = total cost of ownership

A = delivered acquisition cost

NPV = net present value

Ci = total operating costs incurred in year i
Sn = salvage value in year n

PROCEDURE FOR PURCHASING CAPITAL EQUIPMENT

The major differences between capital equipment purchasing and production purchasing have now been identified and discussed. At this point the entire procedure is outlined briefly to illustrate how the differences fit into the over-all decision-making plan.

1 For more than 75 percent of the capital equipment purchases, recognition of the need arises in the using department. Typically, this is in one of the operations departments or in the general management area.
2 Rarely is the need for capital equipment absolute; acquisition can usually be postponed until conditions for purchase become favorable. Although the initial inquiry may come to purchasing in the form of a requisition, more often than not the purpose at this point is only to obtain general information about the equipment in question, not to make an immediate purchase. The purchasing and supply department consequently obtains general sales and performance literature, together with approximate price and delivery information.
3 The using department studies the preliminary information obtained by purchasing and determines the feasibility of pursuing the matter further.
4 If the decision is affirmative, a buying team may be formed. Detailed specifications then should be drawn up jointly by the using and engineering departments, with input from purchasing. Specifications should spell out unambiguously the required design or performance characteristics necessitated by the current operating situation.

   As a rule, the user needs to discuss various aspects of the equipment with manufacturers' representatives. A manufacturer's sales engineer can often provide valuable suggestions regarding application of his or her firm's equipment in the user's unique situation. Moreover, in the case of complex applications, the sales engineer frequently offers to make an engineering study as a service to the buyer. This activity normally is coordinated by the buyer assigned to the job.
5 When the investigation is complete and specifications are firm, the purchasing and supply management department may take one of two courses of action, depending on the type of equipment being purchased.

If it is possible to do so, the buyer often arranges a side-by-side demonstration, on the buyer's premises, of selected suppliers' products that meet the specifications. The purpose is to provide a hands-on comparative testing opportunity for using personnel and members of the buying team. Based on the results of this performance comparison, the team then develops a list of acceptable machines and potential suppliers. Subsequently, purchasing requests formal proposals from the selected suppliers. This approach works well when buying standard products that are transportable. At times, the sequence of the demonstration and bidding activities may be reversed to provide a smaller and more selective demonstration event if matters of practicality or purchasing strategy indicate a preference for this approach.

When buying equipment for which on-site demonstrations are not possible—things such as mainframe computers, industrial drying ovens, and custom-designed machines—purchasing initiates a different course of action. In this case, two-step bidding might well be used. First, technical proposals are requested. After the most attractive bidders have been identified, the buying team typically visits the selected group of potential suppliers to talk with appropriate technical and managerial personnel and to study similar types of equipment in operation at the supplier's facility. Subsequently, the bidding field may be narrowed further and final bids requested. In the event that only one or two suppliers can produce an acceptable machine, the buyer may have decided initially to negotiate the purchase.

6   An economic analysis of the various feasible alternatives is made at this point. The analysis can be made by any of the departments involved in the review. Frequently it is made by purchasing or finance, based on operating, technical, and cost information provided by the engineering, using, and purchasing departments.

7   The required facts are now ready for evaluation. In a large organization this is done by the buying team. In some smaller firms it is done informally by the departments participating in the decision. The end result of the evaluation should be the preparation of a written report justifying the recommendation that a certain machine be purchased. Included in the report should be a description of where and how the machine will be used, why it is required, and what the estimated figures are for its utilization and its life. Also included should be cost data for the existing operation and for the several alternatives considered. Financial computations concerning the rate of return on investment (or other similar measures of profitability), together with any qualitative comments from the participants, should constitute the last section of the report.

8   The written report is submitted to top management for a decision.

9   If the decision is positive, the purchasing department proceeds to conclude the purchase.

PURCHASING AND SUPPLY MANAGEMENT'S ROLE IN CAPITAL EQUIPMENT PROCUREMENT

At this point, the reader undoubtedly has concluded that the purchasing and supply department plays a distinctly different role in the acquisition of capital goods than it does in the acquisition of production materials. In the procurement of capital equipment, purchasing acts to a great extent in a service capacity as a gatherer of information, a process coordinator, a purchasing consultant to management, and finally a contract administrator.

Source of Information

No department is in a better position than purchasing and supply to keep abreast of the general developments occurring in major equipment industries. Through daily contact with both salespeople and current trade literature, alert buyers pick up considerable information of value to operating department managers. In a large company, one buyer may specialize solely in machinery and capital equipment purchasing. A good purchasing operation makes a point of regularly relaying information concerning new developments in the capital equipment area to appropriate operating executives.

Once a requisition has been initiated, of course, it is purchasing's responsibility to locate competent suppliers and secure the information required by the user in making a preliminary analysis. Suppose the quality control manager, for example, wants to buy an expensive microscope. With his or her knowledge of the market, the capital equipment buyer can easily obtain the basic data needed for analysis. Moreover, a good buyer should be able to arrange a side-by-side display or demonstration of major competitive models so quality control personnel can test and compare them.

Liaison Service

During investigation of various manufacturers' equipment, an operating manager frequently finds it advantageous to discuss technical details with a machine manufacturer's representative. A customary (and sound) practice is for the appropriate buyer to act as a liaison in arranging meetings between potential suppliers and operating departments. As a rule, the capital equipment buyer should sit in on these meetings, or at least keep informed of significant developments. It is his or her responsibility to ensure that no premature commitments are made by line departments; likewise, the buyer must at all times be aware of the current status of all negotiations if he or she is to function effectively in the buyer's role.

In these types of preliminary discussions, as noted earlier, a manufacturer's sales engineer may offer to make a preproposal applications study as a service to the buying organization. Sellers in *some industries* customarily make preliminary technical studies as part of their regular sales efforts. Both parties realize that such supplier participation is entirely voluntary and that the related expenses are those normally encountered in stimulating sales. Selling prices in these industries are set so that the revenue from successful efforts covers those situations where preproposal efforts do not result in eventual sales. In other industries, the cost of preproposal studies is not covered fully by the selling price.

Purchasing professionals, therefore, should always be cautious with respect to the acceptance of presale engineering work. The buyer naturally wants all the assistance available. But in some cases presale engineering studies can entail excessive costs and place the buyer under obligation to the seller. The wise buyer avoids this kind of obligation. Before accepting a seller's offer for such a study, the buyer should find out how much money is involved and determine whether the offer is consistent with standard practice in the industry. If the costs exceed normal industry practice—yet the study is clearly worthwhile—the buying firm should consider contracting and paying for the study itself. By separating the purchase of the study from the purchase of the machine, the buyer ensures against the incurrence of an unwise obligation.

Specification Development and Bids

One of the advantages of formally establishing a buying team is the fact that more *cooperative* action usually is generated in attacking the buying problem. This can be extremely useful in development of the equipment specifications, particularly when the buyer is genuinely involved. As a part of this involvement, when specifications are nearing completion and invitations for bid are to be issued, a good buyer should also function in the role of an informal auditor. Although technical requirements predominate, the buyer should make every effort to see that specifications are written as functionally as possible. Most users hold biases for and against specific types of equipment. It is not unusual to find pilots who want to fly only McDonnell-Douglas airplanes, or printers who believe they obtain good work only on a Micron press, or machinists who believe that Cincinnati machine tools maintain the most precise tolerances. Every effort should be made to exclude such personal biases from the specifications. The nature of many capital equipment requirements limits the number of possible suppliers in the first place. This number should not be further reduced by arbitrarily excluding certain types of equipment on the grounds of prejudice alone.

To function effectively in this role, the buyer should have participated in most of the technical discussions between the company's line personnel and the various manufacturers, and he or she must have a basic understanding of the significance of the technical problems involved. The buyer's job is still one of challenging questionable specification inclusions. Ironically, however, a buyer's success in this endeavor depends less on technical knowledge than on skill in understanding and dealing with people. In the realm of technical matters, the buyer is at a disadvantage because he or she is dealing with professionals in this area. Therefore, the long-range approach should focus on an attempt to *gain the cooperation of technical managers.* The buyer must persuade them that unbiased functional specifications serve the company's best interests.[6]

Once specifications are completed, the buyer is responsible for arranging comparison demonstrations and for securing bids from a reasonable number of qualified suppliers.

Qualitative Analysis

Some suppliers are more qualified than others. The degree of qualification should be considered carefully by the review team in deciding which machine to buy. Purchasing normally gathers and analyzes such information for the group. The buyer must first determine, usually with engineering assistance, the level of a supplier's *technical* and *production* capabilities. This is of utmost importance.

Second, the buyer must assess the supplier's *capability* and *willingness* to provide any engineering service required during the installation and start-up of the new equipment. This is an extremely important financial consideration when complex, expensive equipment such as steam turbines, numerically controlled machine tools, and so on is involved. Closely related to this factor is the necessity of training operators. What service is the supplier willing to provide in this area?

Another important consideration is the reliability of a supplier in standing behind its guarantees. Once the equipment is installed, unexpected problems beyond the purchaser's control sometimes add significantly to the total cost of a machine. Finally, what is the supplier's policy on providing replacement parts? When the purchased machine is superseded by a new model, what will be the availability of obsolete parts? The policy of one pump manufacturer, for example, is to produce a small stock of replacement parts for obsolete equipment once every six months. The semiannual production policy of this manufacturer, combined with its low inventory levels, forces some customers to carry unreasonably large stocks of major replacement parts. The other costly alternative for the customer is to risk occasional breakdowns, which might leave a machine out of service as long as three or four months, waiting for the next run of parts.

In practice, unfortunately, such considerations frequently play a minor role in the initial selection of equipment, only to assume major proportions at a later date. It is the purchasing and supply management department's responsibility to evaluate potential suppliers in light of these qualitative factors and to bring significant considerations of this kind before the evaluating group for adequate appraisal. After a machine is purchased, the wise buyer works

---

[6]Some years ago, Humana Inc. successfully implemented a unique capital equipment purchasing system that utilizes an interdepartmental panel to develop equipment specifications, evaluate equipment, and select suppliers. The cooperative action achieved in specification development is unusual. For a detailed discussion, see "Capital Equipment Buying—A Joint Decision," *Purchasing World*, January 1981, pp. 86–89.

closely with the maintenance department in keeping and interpreting historical records (part by part) of machine performance. Data of this kind are valuable in making similar future analyses.

Bid Tabulation and Economic Analysis

When bids are received, the buyer tabulates them and makes any adjustments
necessary so they can be interpreted on a comparable basis by the group
responsible for the final recommendation.

As noted previously, the finance department frequently assumes responsibility for conducting the total profitability study, because administration and
control of such activities are clearly related to the capital budgeting function.
The authors' view, however, is that once management has selected the types of
analysis to be used, the purchasing department might well perform the analyses more easily and effectively than the finance department. Such analyses are
a logical extension of the purchasing department's bid analysis activities.
Clearly, the buyer is familiar with any bid complications. Through his or her
involvement in the preceding technical discussions, the buyer should also
understand any technical problems involved in estimates for maintenance and
operating costs. Thus, one individual with a fairly complete understanding of
the total cost situation could perhaps most effectively prepare, interpret, and
present the complete package of price, cost, and profitability data for the
group's consideration.

Negotiation, Contract Preparation, and Administration

After top management has approved a proposal for the purchase of capital
equipment, the buyer assumes his or her customary responsibility for negotiating the final price, delivery, and related terms of the contract. The purchase
order or contract should be written with particular care, specifying the responsibility of both parties for equipment performance and postsale activities.
Acceptance testing and inspection methods, acceptance timing, machine
specifications and performance standards, and guarantee conditions should be
clearly stated. Similarly, supplier responsibility for postsale services pertaining
to installation, start-up, operator training, maintenance checks, and replacement parts should be spelled out clearly so there is no question about what is
expected.

In the event that the purchase involves a lengthy manufacturing period, a
special follow-up and expediting program should be developed. This may call
for periodic plant visits and in-process inspection of the work. Responsibility
for monitoring this activity often rests with the purchasing department.

It can be seen, viewing the situation in total, that purchasing's role in the
acquisition of capital equipment assumes a considerably greater staff orientation and a lesser decision-making orientation than is customary in the procurement of standard production materials.

A Summary of Purchasing's Role

The following key points summarize purchasing's role in a typical capital equipment purchase.[7]

- Participate in the preliminary discussion phase, including solicitation of information and budgetary estimates.
- Assist in preparation of the organizational funding authorization request (including make or lease versus buy analysis).
- Review and request clarification of specifications.
- Coordinate the development and qualification of potential suppliers, including various qualitative analyses.
- Compile required commercial terms and conditions.
- Prepare and process the request for proposal.
- Coordinate the analysis of supplier proposals, including the economic analyses and the resolution of any exceptions to specifications.
- Arrange for side-by-side demonstrations, if practical.
- Plan, coordinate, and conduct negotiations as necessary.
- Prepare and execute final contract documentation.
- Manage any third-party consultant's activities (if consulting services are required).
- Maintain project records and status including:
    Request for proposal (issuance and receipt)
    Purchase commitments
    Changes pending and authorized
    Expediting log, including final receipt and acceptance
- Coordinate and conduct contract inspection/expediting services.
- Coordinate purchase contract closeout.
- Critique and document supplier's performance.
- Maintain records of price and delivery trends for future procurements.

USED EQUIPMENT

A buyer is by no means restricted to the purchase of new capital equipment. Purchases of used machinery, in fact, constitute an important percentage of total machinery sales.

Reasons for Purchasing Used Equipment

A purchaser may consider buying used equipment for several reasons. First, the cost of used machinery is substantially less than that of new equipment. Analysis of payback or return on investment may well reveal that a piece of used equipment is a better buy than a new machine. Even if this is not the

---

[7]This summary is based on material presented in Fischer, op. cit., p. 665.

case, a firm's financial position may dictate the purchase of a lower-priced machine. Second, used equipment frequently is more readily available than new equipment. In some situations, availability may override all other considerations.

A third and very common reason for the purchase of used equipment is that used equipment adequately satisfies the purchaser's need, in which case there is no point in buying new equipment. In cases where operating requirements are not severe, a used machine in sound condition frequently provides economical service for many years. In the event that equipment is needed for standby or peak-capacity operation, or for use on a short-lived project, more often than not used equipment can satisfy the need very well.

The Used Equipment Market

Used equipment becomes available for purchase for a number of legitimate reasons. When a firm buys a new machine, it frequently disposes of its old one. Although the old machine may be obsolete relative to the original owner's needs, it is often completely adequate for the needs of many potential buyers. If significant changes are made in a firm's product design or production process, it may be advantageous to obtain more specialized production equipment. Finally, some used equipment becomes available because the owner lost a particular contract or has discontinued operation altogether.

Whatever the reason, a great deal of used equipment is available and commonly is purchased from one of four sources: (1) used equipment dealers, (2) directly from the owner, (3) brokers, and (4) auctions. In recent years, the majority of these purchases have been made from used equipment dealers who specialize in buying, overhauling, and marketing certain types of equipment. Dealers are usually located in large industrial areas, and, as a rule, they periodically advertise the major equipment available.

Used Equipment Dealers   These dealers typically specialize in certain kinds of equipment and sell two types of machines—"reconditioned" machines and "rebuilt" machines. Generally speaking, a reconditioned machine carries a minimal dealer warranty and sells for approximately 40 to 50 percent of the price of a similar new machine. The machine usually has been cleaned and painted, broken and severely worn parts have been replaced, and the machine has been tested under power. A rebuilt machine typically carries a more inclusive dealer warranty and sells for perhaps 50 to 70 percent of a new machine's price. A rebuilt machine usually has been completely dismantled and built up from the base. All worn and broken parts have been replaced, wearing surfaces have been reground and realigned, the machine has been reassembled to hold original tolerances, and it has been tested under power.

Sale by Owner   Some owners prefer to sell their used equipment directly to the next user because they think they can realize a higher price than by selling to a dealer. Some buyers also prefer this arrangement. It permits them to see the machine in operation and learn something about its usage history before making the purchasing decision.

Brokers   A broker is an intermediary who brings buyers and sellers together but generally does not take title to the equipment sold. Brokers sometimes liquidate large segments of the equipment of a complete plant. Occasionally, an industrial supply house or a manufacturer's agent will act as a broker for a good customer by helping the firm dispose of an odd piece of equipment which has a limited sales market.

Auctions   Auction sales represent still another source of used equipment. Several types of auction firms are in operation. Some actually function as traders, buying equipment and selling from their own inventory. More common, however, are the firms which simply provide the auction sale service. Their commission is usually somewhat less than a broker's commission. Generally speaking, buying at auction is somewhat more risky than the other supply sources because auctioned machines usually carry no warranty, and rarely is it possible to have the machine demonstrated. In some cases, however, machines can be purchased at auction via videotape or closed-circuit TV; this permits the buyer to see the machine operating in a distant plant.

Cautions in Purchasing Used Equipment

The age-old adage of *caveat emptor*—let the buyer beware—is particularly applicable when purchasing used equipment.

It is difficult to determine the true condition of a used machine and to estimate the type and length of service it will provide. For this reason it is wise to have one buyer specialize in used equipment. Moreover, it is virtually essential to enlist the cooperation of an experienced production or maintenance specialist in appraising used equipment. It is always sound practice to check the reputation of a used equipment supplier and to shop around, inspecting several machines before making a purchase. Whenever possible, a machine should be observed under power through a complete operating cycle. Finally, a prospective buyer should determine the age of a machine. If not available in the seller's records, the age of a machine can be traced through the manufacturer simply by serial number identification. The combined knowledge of age and usage history is a key guide in predicting the future performance of a used machine.

In preparing a purchase order for used capital equipment, care must be taken to include all essential data. In addition to an adequate description of the machine, an order should specify the accessories included, warranty provisions (if any), services to be performed before shipment, and financing as well as shipping arrangements.

Generally speaking, sellers do not provide service for used equipment after the purchase. All transportation, handling, installation, and start-up costs, as well as risk, are usually borne by the purchaser.

LEASED EQUIPMENT

In addition to the possibilities of purchasing new or used capital equipment to satisfy a firm's requirements, a buyer has a third alternative—that of *leasing* the equipment. In recent years, leasing indeed has become big business. It is now a $190 billion industry whose volume of business has doubled in the last five years. It is estimated that approximately 20 percent of the new office and industrial equipment used in American business today is leased.[8] Generally accepted reasons underlying this trend appear to be the heavy demand for capital in most firms, relatively high interest rates, and the fact that in an inflationary economy depreciation usually fails to produce sufficient funds to replace all the capital equipment that needs replacing.

Types of Leases

If one looks at leases in terms of the basic purposes for which they are used, most fall into one of two categories—operating leases and financial leases.

An *operating lease*, as the name implies, is used by most firms as a vehicle to facilitate business operations. The focus typically is on operating convenience and flexibility. Frequently, a firm has a temporary need for equipment to be used in the office or on a special production or maintenance job. It requires the use of the assets but is not interested in owning them. In some cases, the need stretches beyond the temporary period, but the firm still is not interested in ownership and the risks and responsibilities that accompany it. Equipment obtained by means of an operating lease may fit such a firm's needs well. Most operating leases are *short term,* for a fixed period of time considerably less than the life of the equipment being leased.

A *financial lease,* in most cases, is used for a very different purpose. While operating equipment is obtained by means of a financial lease, the primary motivation for using this type of lease is to obtain financial leverage and related longer-term financial benefits. A financial lease, relatively speaking, is a *long-term* lease that usually covers a time period just a bit shorter than the approximate life of the equipment being leased. Many financial leases are non-cancellable.

Factors Favoring Leasing

The primary potential advantages of leasing are identified and discussed briefly in the following paragraphs.

Operating and Managerial Convenience   While there are different types of leasing organizations, most leasing firms that industrial buyers deal with are *full-service* lessors. This means that the leasing organization owns the

---

[8] R. S. Reichard, "Tax Reform May Spur Leasing," *Purchasing World,* December 1986, pp. 52–53.

equipment, has its own continuing source of financing, and is prepared to assume all the responsibilities of ownership for the lessee. Hence, the lessee has full use of the equipment and can concentrate on its regular business operations, without having to worry about maintenance, special service, and other administrative tasks associated with equipment ownership. In the case of complex equipment requiring highly specialized technical support, this can become a benefit of major importance.

Operating Flexibility With relatively short-term leases for selected pieces of operating equipment, a lessee is not locked into long-term commitments because of large capital investments. It can maintain maximum flexibility in its operations to respond to changing business conditions and subsequent production requirements. It can use a leasing arrangement to meet temporary operating needs with relative ease, and in the same manner it can test new equipment prior to making a longer-term purchasing decision.

Obsolescence Protection Leasing substantially reduces the risk of equipment obsolescence. In many businesses, particularly those using high-tech equipment, some machines become technologically obsolete in a very short period of time. When leasing such things as data processing equipment, for example, an arrangement usually can be made with the lessor to replace or upgrade the old equipment. This can be an extremely important consideration in a highly competitive industry.

Financial Leverage A major advantage of leasing expensive equipment stems from the fact that a leasing decision typically replaces a large capital outlay with much smaller, regularly timed payments. This frees working capital for use in meeting expanded operating costs or for investment in other segments of the business operation.

Viewing the lease strictly as a financing mechanism, generally it also provides a cash flow advantage over a conventional bank loan financing arrangement. Most equipment leases can be stretched over a longer payment period, thus reducing the relative size of the monthly payments.

Balance Sheet Structure In an accounting sense leasing, as compared with a capital equipment purchase, permits the lessee to record the financial commitment in a statement footnote rather than as additional debt on the balance sheet. Consequently, the firm's debt structure as shown on the balance sheet appears to be more favorable than it really is. Although this accounting technicality produces only a cosmetic effect, some lessees view this as an advantage.

Income Tax Considerations If a lease fulfills the Internal Revenue Service requirements for a "true lease," from an accounting point of view lease payments are recorded as an operating expense. Thus, as long as lease payments exceed the value of allowable depreciation (if the asset were owned), an additional tax shield is provided for the lessee. Comparatively speaking, the amount of taxable income is reduced by the difference between the lease expense payments and allowable depreciation expenses. So if a lessee plans on obtaining this tax benefit, it is important to compare the proposed lease payments with the corresponding allowable depreciation figures (if the asset were owned) over the life of the lease—to ensure that the anticipated positive relationship actually exists.

It is important to bear in mind, also, that the IRS has established rather stringent guidelines to distinguish between a true lease and a lease which is really intended to be a disguised conditional sales contract. Whenever it appears that the actual intent of the parties is simply to use the lease as a financing arrangement for a subsequent purchase of the equipment, no incremental tax benefit is allowed.

A related but separate action, the Tax Reform Act of 1986, has had a significant influence on the lease/buy decision for some firms. The 1986 tax law eliminated the investment tax credit and modified the allowable depreciation preferences, forcing many firms into an alternative minimum tax position. The combined effect of these two provisions has made it more costly, from a tax perspective, for some capital-intensive firms to buy capital equipment. Although the situation is different for each firm, experience to date indicates that the 1986 law has made leasing a more attractive alternative for many firms.

A recent survey conducted by *Purchasing* magazine places the current views of buyers in perspective. "When asked why they would rather lease certain kinds of equipment, buyers pointed to two things: cash and technology."[9] In other words, the availability of increased working capital and protection against equipment obsolescence appear to be major drivers in making the lease/buy decision today.

Factors Weighing against Leasing

Cost   As a general rule, the primary disadvantage of leasing is its cost. "Margins" are typically higher on leases than interest rates are on direct loans. This is understandable, because in addition to covering financing charges, the lessor must also bear all the risks associated with ownership (including obsolescence and inflation risks). The typical financial lease runs for approximately three-quarters of the equipment's estimated useful life, and monthly fees total approximately 120 to 135 percent of the purchase price.

Control   A second disadvantage arises from the fact that the lessor retains control of the equipment. This loss of control often places restrictions on the

---

[9]Kate Evans-Correia, "Buyers Find Savings by Leasing Equipment," *Purchasing*, Aug. 19, 1993, p. 73.

manner in which the equipment is operated; it also requires that the lessee allow the lessor access to the equipment for inspection and maintenance. There are usually times when such control by the lessor creates inconveniences for the lessee. Closely related to this fact is the possibility that the lessee may have its purchasing prerogatives constrained with respect to the purchase of operating supplies for the leased equipment. A lessor normally wants to have the equipment operated with its own supplies. In the event that use of other manufacturers' supplies could conceivably impair the machine's performance, the lessee usually agrees to such an arrangement.

To Lease—or to Buy?

Cost Comparison   Because the cost aspect of leasing is its primary disadvantage, it is imperative for a buyer to make a comparative analysis of the cost to lease and the cost to own. A discounted cash flow analysis of the two alternatives over the life of the lease is the most accurate and straightforward approach to use.

Procedurally, the same approach is used in this analysis as is used in making a life cycle cost analysis (see page 391). Basically, all cost and savings factors for the lease alternative are identified and quantified—and then projected to appropriate future dates when they actually will be incurred. This produces a cost matrix over the life of the lease. All future costs are then discounted to their present values and subsequently summed to express the total cost in present value terms. The same procedure is followed for the "buy" alternative. Total present value costs can then be compared directly to determine the additional true cost (or saving) associated with the leasing alternative.

The Decision   The lease-or-buy decision should be made just like any other sound purchasing decision is made. First, the merits of the alternative products must be assessed relative to the buying firm's functional needs. The total cost of each is then considered in light of the preceding functional analysis. To these factors are added the relevant qualitative considerations that may vary among suppliers, markets, economic conditions, and so on. A decision is then made on the basis of the relative cost/benefit assessments. In the case of a lease-or-buy decision, this process can be summarized in the following four steps:

1 Determine the *operating* (including financing considerations) advantages and disadvantages of leasing and of owning. Input from operations, finance, and purchasing is required.
2 Compare the two alternatives and answer the question: From an operating point of view, is leasing the preferred alternative?
3 If leasing is preferable, calculate and compare the *present value costs* of the two alternatives.
4 Make the decision: Are the operating benefits of leasing worth the additional cost?

More often than not, the final decision will center on a determination of whether the extra cost entailed in leasing is justified by the avoidance of the major risks and responsibilities associated with ownership.[10]

CONCLUSION

In most firms capital equipment is not purchased every day—but when it is, such purchases represent important management decisions. As a rule, these purchases are major investments—investments that lead to improved productivity or to the manufacture of more competitive products that increase sales in the marketplace.

The role of the purchasing department is distinctly different in this type of buying activity than it is in production buying. In the procurement of capital equipment, purchasing personnel function in a creative capacity as facilitators, coordinators, contract administrators, and purchasing consultants to management. Specifications must be precise and complete, and they must be written as functionally as possible. Economic analyses should utilize appropriate techniques, they must be thorough, and they must be based on accurate data. The contract must be equally precise and complete. There should be no doubt about installation and start-up responsibilities, performance requirements, test and inspection methods, related postsale responsibilities, and warranties.

The buyer contributes directly to the accomplishment of some of these activities. More important, however, is his or her responsibility to orchestrate the total performance. The buyer's main job is to ensure that everything happens as it should and when it should.

FOR DISCUSSION

18-1 Explain how capital equipment purchases differ from purchases of production materials and supplies.

18-2 Discuss the role the purchasing and supply department plays in capital equipment purchasing.

18-3 Prepare a summary list of activities for which a buyer should be responsible in a major capital equipment purchase.

18-4 Discuss the major factors in selecting a source from which to purchase capital equipment.

18-5 What qualitative considerations relative to supplier capabilities are important in capital equipment purchasing? Compare these qualitative considerations with those important in production purchasing.

18-6 Explain the concept of life cycle cost analysis.

18-7 Outline a procedure for conducting a life cycle cost analysis.

18-8 Write a generalized formula for calculating total life cycle cost. Discuss.

---

[10]For a comprehensive analysis of the lease/buy question, see W. L. Ferrara, J. B. Thies, and N. W. Dirsmith, *The Lease-Purchase Decision*, The National Association of Accountants, New York.

18-9 Why is a *total* economic analysis of alternative machines important in purchasing capital equipment?

18-10 In capital equipment purchasing, which usually is more important—the price of the equipment or its expected operating costs? Discuss.

18-11 Why should a present value analysis be conducted in making a life cycle cost analysis? Discuss.

18-12 Discuss the reasons why a company might want to purchase a used machine rather than a new machine.

18-13 Discuss the differences between a reconditioned machine and a rebuilt machine.

18-14 *Caveat emptor*—in buying used equipment. What does this mean? Discuss.

18-15 What risks are involved in purchasing used equipment? Discuss.

18-16 Is economic analysis applicable in evaluating a used machine compared with a new machine? Discuss.

18-17 Discuss the major types of equipment leases.

18-18 Discuss the advantages and disadvantages of leasing capital equipment.

18-19 Discuss the impact of high interest rates on the lease-or-buy decision.

18-20 What impact did the Tax Reform Act of 1986 have on the typical firm's lease-or-buy decision? Discuss.

CASES FOR CHAPTER 18

Capital Equipment Purchasing, page 792
The County Water Works, page 802
Standard Tele-Link Corporation, page 919
Gotham City Buys Fire Engines (in the *Instructor's Manual*)

19

PURCHASING SERVICES

The procurement of services is an activity of increasing importance. Expenditures on services by commercial firms, not-for-profit organizations, and government increase each year. In some cases, services procurement represents more than 25 percent of the organization's expenditures. Purchased services play key roles in the successful operation of these organizations. In many instances, *the impact of the services themselves on the success of the organization's operation is far greater than the impact of the dollars spent.* Services ranging from architectural engineering, promotion and advertising, and the development of software, to the maintenance and repair of production equipment are of critical importance to the operation of the organization. More mundane purchases such as cafeteria and janitorial operations impact the morale of all employees.

A tidal wave of "outsourcing" of services is taking place in America and abroad. Services which are not at the core of the organization's competencies, such as management information systems, payroll, travel services, delivery services, even the procurement of MRO supplies and services, are being outsourced to service providers. These suppliers have the expertise and economies of scale to allow them to provide the services at the same or higher quality level than the purchasing firm and at a lower total cost.

Obtaining services is one of purchasing's most challenging responsibilities. In no other area is there a more complex interdependency between the purchase description (statement of work), method of compensation, source selection, contract administration, and a satisfied customer.[1]

HIDDEN OPPORTUNITIES

Warren Norquist, former vice president of International Materials Management at Polaroid, has involved his staff in many of the following nontraditional procurements:

- Print ad production
- General consultants
- Computer consultants
- Computer network management
- Design of exterior of products
- Television ad production
- Outplacement agencies
- Training consultants
- Network TV time
- Market research

- Financial auditors
- Training courses
- Per diem help
- Placement agencies
- Technical consultants
- Spot TV and radio time
- Telephone customer service
- Annual reports
- Logistics and inventory control

Mr. Norquist's experience is that when qualified personnel are involved in the planning and procurement of such services, savings of approximately 25 percent are enjoyed with equal or improved quality and service.[2]

---

[1] This material is based on *Zero Base Pricing™: Achieving World Class Competitiveness through Reduced All-in-Cost* by David N. Burt, Warren E. Norquist, and J. Anklesaria, Probus Publishing, Chicago, 1990.

[2] Burt, Norquist, and Anklesaria, op. cit., p. 177.

In addition, an increasing number of proactive procurement operations now purchase services such as:

- Utilities
- Disposal services
- Insurance
- Guard service
- Fire protection
- On-site contracting services

THE STATEMENT OF WORK

As is true in the procurement of production requirements and capital equipment, the most critical ingredient to a successful procurement of services is the development and documentation of the requirement—the *statement of work (S.O.W.)*. And as is true with production requirements and capital equipment, *one of the keys to success is the involvement of qualified purchasing personnel at this point in the procurement process.* In fact, professional buyers know that most of their service customers lack training and experience in the development of service requirements or specifications. Accordingly, a buyer can provide invaluable assistance during this phase of the procurement. In many instances, professional buyers invite two or three carefully prequalified potential contractors to aid in the development of the statement of work. Such early involvement aids the internal customer in fully understanding the organization's true needs. At the same time, the potential contractor gains insight into the nature and level of effort required.

The statement of work identifies what the contractor is to accomplish. The clarity, accuracy, and completeness of the S.O.W. determine, to a large degree, whether the objectives of the contract will be achieved. The S.O.W. clearly identifies first the primary objective and then the subordinate objectives, so that both the buyer and seller know where and how to place their emphasis. Those responsible for developing the S.O.W. must ask themselves questions such as: Is timeliness, creativity, or artistic excellence the primary objective?

One of the objectives of writing a statement of work is to gain understanding and an agreement with a contractor concerning the specific nature of the technical effort to be performed. Satisfactory performance under the contract is a direct function of the quality, clarity, and completeness of its statement of work.

The S.O.W. also impacts the administration of the contract. It defines the scope of the effort, that is, what the contractor does and what the buyer receives. The manner in which the scope is defined governs the amount of direction that the buyer can give during the contract's life.

A well-written statement of work enhances the contractor's performance in pursuit of S.O.W. objectives. Before writing it, those responsible must develop a thorough understanding of all the factors that will bear on the project and that are reflected in the S.O.W.

Planning the Statement of Work

A statement of work frequently is described as a document that details a strategy for contractor and buyer accomplishment of the objectives of a project. But before any strategy can be developed, certain basic questions must be answered and understood:

- What are the objectives of the project?
- Where did the objectives come from, who originated them, and why were they originated?
- What is the current status, including resource and schedule constraints, of the effort?
- Based on current status, what is the risk factor associated with the achievement of project objectives?

The planning phase of S.O.W. preparation is aimed at a thorough investigation of the *why* and *what* of the project. The following checklist will assist the program manager and the buyer in this determination.

- Identify the resource, schedule, and compensation constraints for the project.
- Identify all buyer and contractor participation needed for the project, and define the extent and nature of their responsibilities. All buyer support, such as buyer-furnished equipment, materials, facilities, approvals, and so forth, should be specifically stated.
- Challenge the tasks identified, including sequencing and interrelationships of all required tasks. For example, on a janitorial services contract, should the contractor be required to wash (versus completely erase) blackboards every evening or only once a week? On a landscape maintenance contract, should the contractor be required to furnish expendables such as fertilizer? In effect, those responsible should apply the value analysis techniques described in Chapter 28.
- Identify contractor delivery requirements at specified points in time; include details about the type and quantity of any deliverables.
- Identify specific technical data requirements such as plans, specifications, reports, and so on.

Writing the Statement of Work

As a result of a thorough planning effort, the individuals writing the S.O.W. have determined the tasks and details that need to be included. These must now be documented.

Writing a quality statement of work is not an easy task. The S.O.W. must maintain a delicate balance between *protecting the buyer's interests* and *encouraging the supplier's (contractor's) creativity* during both proposal preparation and contract performance. For example, when purchasing janitorial services, some well-intended buyers specify the number of personnel which the contractor must supply, in the rather questionable belief that this provision will guarantee satisfactory performance. But such action blocks the supplier's creativity and generally results in needlessly high prices. The use of a carefully developed S.O.W. which specifies the required performance and procedures for monitoring (inspecting) the contractor's performance allows the contractor to apply its experience and creativity—usually at a significant savings. To further complicate the task, those developing the S.O.W. must remember that it will be read and interpreted by customer and contractor personnel of widely varying expertise.

The following issues deserve special attention on a case-by-case basis. Required provisions may be in either the S.O.W. or special terms and conditions included by the buyer in the request for proposal and the resulting contract.

- *A performance plan.* The contractor must be required to develop a nonsubjective, quantifiable blueprint for providing the services. Staffing, equipment, and supplies should all be identified. After developing the blueprint, all required processes must be identified by the contractor.
- *Quality monitoring system.* The contractor should be required to establish fail-safe measures to minimize quality problems.
- *Personnel plan.* The contractor is required to develop and maintain recruiting and training programs acceptable to the buyer.
- *Performance and payment bonds.* The contractor must provide performance and payment bonds equal to x percent of the value of the contract amount.

SELECTING SERVICE CONTRACTORS

Selecting the "right" source is much more of an art when purchasing services than when purchasing materials. Based on the complexity of many service procurements and the unexpected problems that tend to arise, it normally is prudent practice to select only established, reputable firms. Exceptions may be made occasionally in cases involving promising minority suppliers who have not yet established a "reputation." Unless the potential supplier possesses some truly unique skill or reputation, competition typically is employed. In some service markets, however, experienced buyers find that the competitive process is not completely effective because of the structure of the market. This issue is discussed later in the chapter.

When a large number of potential contractors is available, the buyer and the customer normally reduce this list to three to five firms. The purchasing/customer team interviews prospective contractors' management, talks with previous customers, and checks out employees through random interviews. The buyer then invites proposals from only the potential suppliers with which the buying firm would be comfortable doing business.

During the evaluation process, emphasis should be placed on the *total* cost and *total* benefits to the buying organization. Assume, for example, that two architect-engineering (A-E) firms are under consideration for the development of plans and specifications for a new building estimated to cost approximately $10 million. Firm X has a reputation of designing functional buildings whose costs are relatively low. Firm Y, on the other hand, has a reputation of designing more elaborate and aesthetically more attractive buildings whose costs tend to run about 10 percent more than X's. For the sake of illustration, however, assume that firm X's professional fees tend to run about 12 percent more than Y's. Figure 19-1 illustrates these cost differentials and shows the overriding influence of construction costs in the complete analysis. Hence, in this case, the contractor's design fee is a relatively minor item in the total cost package.

In addition to the traditional concerns about a prospective contractor's financial strength, management capability, experience, and reputation, the area of *technical capabilities* requires special analysis. An article in *Purchasing World* identifies the following issues that should be addressed when selecting a contractor for computer maintenance. This list of issues is introduced simply as an example of the depth of analysis required when selecting a contractor for this specialized service.

- Will the contractor maintain *all* the equipment in your computer installation?
- Can the contractor *quickly* correct the problem?
- How close to your facilities is the contractor's field engineering office?
- Does the contractor specialize in your type of equipment?
- Does the contractor have a prescribed schedule of service calls?
- Does the contractor have troubleshooting escalation procedures, skilled field engineers, and ready availability of spare parts?
- If there is any possibility of having to move the computer equipment, does the contractor have proven successful experience moving computers?
- Does the contractor offer equipment brokerage?
- Does the contractor have the technical ability to make low-cost modifications to your equipment? If so, can the firm support the resulting system?
- Will the contractor service refurbished equipment?
- Does the contractor have high hiring standards, require appropriate training, and equip field service personnel with appropriate tools and equipment?

FIGURE 19-1
Total costs for the construction project.

	Firm X	Firm Y
Construction cost	$10,000,000	$11,000,000
Design fee	739,200	660,000
Total cost	$10,739,200	$11,660,000

- Does the contractor supply maintenance documentation?
- Will the contractor develop custom products for your special needs?
- Is the contractor flexible in meeting your specific requirements?[3]

The selection of suppliers for repair services depends on the situation. The best way to cope with emergency repairs is to anticipate them. Vehicles, office machines, and plant equipment do break down. Sewer lines do get clogged. In many cases, it is possible, and certainly desirable, to establish the source and the price or dollar rates for such services *before* the emergency occurs.

When purchasing transportation services, consistent on-time pickup and delivery, equipment availability, and service to particular locations typically are more important than price.[4]

Competitive prices should be solicited every two or three years for recurring services. Such action tends to avoid complacency and helps to maintain realistic pricing. *More frequent changes in contractors often cause too many service disruptions.*

The Ideal Services Supplier

The ideal services supplier listens to what users complain about most and then designs service products that supply the market's missing ingredients. Satisfaction is built into service products rather than added as an afterthought. Employees of "ideal" services providers are given every conceivable form of automation to help them deliver a consistently satisfactory service product. The ideal services supplier invests to increase both employee productivity and customer satisfaction.

If such an "ideal" services supplier or contractor is not available, the purchasing firm should consider the development of a long-term relationship with a supplier willing and able to grow into an "ideal" provider.

PRICING SERVICE CONTRACTS

Procurement authority Louis J. DeRose writes that "the competitive process is not truly efficient in services markets. It is constrained by three forces and factors of supply":

- One of the strongest factors influencing competition and prices—a continuing or cumulative supply—is absent.
- Interchangeable services generally are not available due to the personal effort and involvement of the supplier.
- "The supply of services is more easily restricted or restrained than it is for commodities or products."

---

[3] "How to Choose a Computer Maintenance Service," *Purchasing World*, August 1987, p. 73.
[4] James R. Stock and Paul H. Finszer, "The Industrial Purchase Division for Professional Services," *Journal of Business Research*, February 1987, p. 3.

It is for these reasons, DeRose writes, "that buyers must negotiate service agreements."[5] Yet there are some situations where competitive bidding is an effective method of determining both source and price. A janitorial services contract for which competition is intense is an example. Again, the professional buyer's judgment plays a key role: Are all of the conditions required for the use of competitive bidding (as discussed in Chapter 11) satisfied? Are time and qualified resources available to prepare for and conduct negotiations? Are purchasing's internal customers prepared to play a constructive role in professional negotiations? In many instances, negotiation often results in better pricing and the supply of a more satisfactory service.

Too frequently, the pricing of service contracts is not tailored to motivate the supplier to satisfy the organization's *principal* objective. Once the primary requirement (artistic excellence, timeliness, low cost, and so on) is identified, the buyer must ensure that the resulting contract motivates the supplier to meet this need. When conditions require, the contract should reward good and penalize poor service.

Professional Services

Architect-engineering firms, lawyers, consultants, and educational specialists are representative of the individuals and firms which provide professional services. The professional buyer pays particular attention to the relationship between the price mechanism (e.g., firm fixed price, cost plus incentive fee, fixed price with award fee, and so on) and the contractor's motivation on critical professional services contracts. For example, fixed price contracts reward suppliers for their cost control. Every dollar that the supplier's costs are reduced results in a dollar of additional profit.

Assume that you were selecting an individual or a firm to prepare a fairly complex personal income tax return for a gross income of $125,000. Firm C advertises that it will prepare any tax return, regardless of its difficulty, for a guaranteed maximum of $200. Firm D offers rates of $75 per hour. Discussion with a representative of firm D indicates that approximately five hours will be required to prepare your return. If forgone tax savings are considered as a cost, which firm is more likely to provide the service at the lowest *total* cost? The use of firm D will cost an estimated $375 ($75 × 5 hours), or $175 more than firm C. Assuming that C and D had similar hourly costs, it is likely that D would spend about two hours more preparing the tax return. Most individuals with a $125,000 income would pay the extra $175 in hope of offsetting the outlay with a larger tax saving.

Cost-type contracts should be considered when there is significant uncertainty concerning the amount of effort that will be required or when there is insufficient time to develop a realistic S.O.W. Obviously, the dollar amount involved must warrant the administrative cost and effort involved. For smaller

---

[5]Louis J. DeRose, "Not by Bids Alone," *Purchasing World*, November 1985, p. 46.

dollar amounts, a time and materials or labor-hour contract should be considered to avoid contingency pricing. Such contracts require close monitoring to ensure that the specified labor skill is furnished and that the hours being billed are in fact required.

Administratively, it may be impractical to use anything other than a fixed price contract or an hourly rate price for relatively small professional services contracts. Even on larger dollar amounts, the supplier's reputation may allow the use of a fixed price contract. But buyers should be aware of the potential effect of the pricing mechanism on the contractor's performance.

Technical Services

Technical services include such things as:

- Research and development
- Software development
- Machine repairs
- Printing services
- Advertising and promotion
- Heating and air-conditioning maintenance
- Elevator maintenance
- Pest control
- Energy management
- Accounting and bookkeeping services
- Payroll services
- Mailroom services
- Copyroom and message services

R&D services normally are purchased through one of two methods of compensation: a fixed price for a level of effort (e.g., fifty days) or a cost plus fixed or award fee. Software development lends itself to cost plus award fee contracts. This approach rewards excellent performance and punishes poor performance while ensuring the contractor that its costs will be reimbursed and at least a minimum fee will be received.

In a competitive market, once a good S.O.W. is available for services such as printing, promotional services, and the development of technical manuals, competition should be employed to select the source and determine the price, using a fixed price contract.

Operating Services

Janitorial, security, landscaping, and cafeteria operations are typical operating services. Experience has shown that obtaining effective performance of such services can be very challenging for administrators. Accordingly, the compensation scheme should reward the supplier for good and penalize it for poor service. Such an approach to pricing greatly aids in the administration of the contract and results in a far higher level of customer satisfaction.

Insurance, plant and equipment maintenance, and anticipated emergency services should be sourced and priced through the use of competition of *carefully prequalified* suppliers. Unanticipated emergency repairs normally are purchased on a "not-to-exceed" time and materials basis (as described in Chapter 16).

CONTRACT ADMINISTRATION

The four keys to successful service contract administration are (1) a sound S.O.W., (2) selection of the "right" source, (3) a fair and reasonable price, and (4) aggressive management of the contract. The administration of many service contracts can be a very challenging responsibility. The buyer needs to monitor and have a realistic degree of control over the supplier's performance. Crucial to success in this area is the timely availability of accurate data, including the contractor's plan for performance and the contractor's actual progress. The buyer *must* proactively manage the relationship to ensure success. Chapter 20 describes in detail the actions required to ensure timely, high-quality performance.

CONSTRUCTION SERVICES

The purchase of new facilities is a commitment for the future. Quality, productivity of the new plant, the time required to effect the purchase, and cost all must be considered. Aesthetic requirements, time requirements, and the availability of highly qualified designers and builders all will tend to influence the selection of a purchase method.

There are five common methods of purchasing construction; however, it is unlikely that any one of the five methods will consistently be the proper choice for all building requirements. Figure 19-2 provides a graphic presentation of the various steps involved in each method, from start to completion of a construction project.

Conventional Method

This is the most frequently employed approach to buying building construction in the United States. With this approach, design of the required facility is performed by architects and engineers without the involvement of a builder. Design of the facility is completed before potential contractors are requested to submit bids. Two separate organizations are responsible: one for the design work and one for the construction phase of the project.

Many architects are not noted for being cost-conscious. Nevertheless, the cost factor can be controlled in several ways. A common approach involves employment, on a consulting basis, of a "cost-control architect" who is concerned solely with cost reduction. Naturally, the general architect typically does not appreciate having his or her work reviewed. However, use of a consulting architect undeniably tends to make the primary architect more cost-conscious.

If a consulting architect is not used because of the general architect's sensitivity, alternative methods of cost control are available to the buyer. For example, for major interior furnishings, the architect or interior decorator can be required to specify three manufacturers' products which can be purchased by competitive bids (any one of the specified products being satisfactory). The

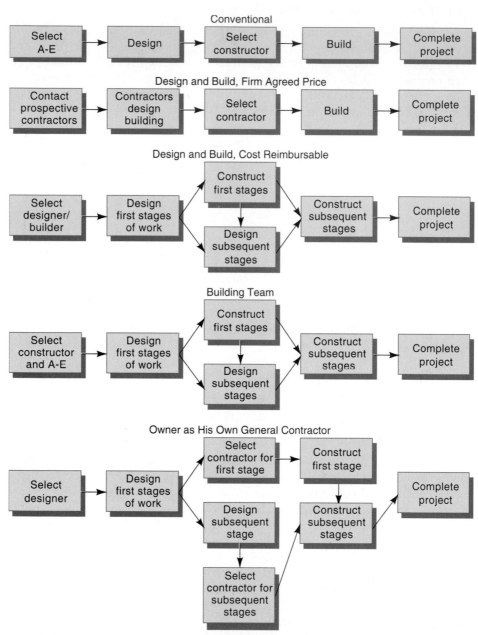

FIGURE 19-2
Sequence of steps involved with alternative methods of purchasing construction.

actual purchasing can be done by the organization, the architect, or the interior decorator. The three-bid requirement itself assures competitive pricing. As an added bonus, this practice helps eliminate conflicts of interest, unreasonable personal bias, and the specifying of low-volume, proprietary items.

Design and Build, Firm Agreed Price Method

This approach could be described as construction with gratuitous design. The owner determines the basic facility requirements, such as size, temperature, electrical, mechanical, and so on. These requirements become the basis of a performance specification. This specification is furnished to carefully pre-qualified builders who, with their prospective subcontractors, prepare a bid package consisting of a *design and price proposal.* The purchasing firm awards a firm agreed price contract for construction to the builder whose bid is most attractive.

Design and Build, Cost-Reimbursable Method

With this method, only one contract is awarded for both design and construction. Design is accomplished by architects and engineers employed by the general contractor. Thus, the builder has ample opportunity to influence the design of the required facility. With this approach, construction of a work element (excavation, structural work, and so on) proceeds when the design of the element has been completed. It is not necessary to await design of the total project since one firm is responsible for both the design and the construction phases. This approach is particularly useful when a structure is required within a very short time period and the design and build, firm agreed price method is not applicable.

Building Team

With this approach, the owner retains both a designer and a builder concurrently. In contrast to the conventional method, the builder is retained during the design phase and is expected to contribute information on costs, procedures, and time requirements to the designer. As the A-E completes the plans and specifications for a work element, the builder either accomplishes the work with its own crews or obtains prices from several specialists and awards the work to the qualified subcontractor making the best offer (price, time, and quality considered). As with the other methods, the general contractor oversees and integrates the efforts of the subcontractors.

The Owner as a Contractor

With this method, the owner contracts directly for the various work elements and performs the functions of integrating and controlling that would other-

wise be accomplished by a general contractor. Since purchase orders and contracts are awarded on a work element basis, it is possible for construction to
proceed prior to completion of the total design phase.

Research conducted by one of the authors on these five methods shows that
the conventional method is, by far, the most costly approach to purchasing
construction. Savings of approximately 25 percent were found to result when
the design and build, firm agreed price method was used rather than the conventional method. Savings of 9 percent resulted when either the design and
build, cost-reimbursable or the building team method was used in lieu of the
conventional method. Savings of about 5 percent resulted when the owner
acted as his or her own general contractor.

The amount of time from first contacting the designer or builder until completion of the facility usually is as important as the price paid. Availability of
the required facilities varies significantly with the methods used. On a typical
130,000-square-foot manufacturing plant, 16 months were required with the
conventional method; 11.5 months with the design and build, firm agreed
price method; 12 months with both the design and build, cost-reimbursable
method and the building team method; and 15.5 months when the owner
acted as the general contractor.

Professional buyers know that selection of the most appropriate method of
purchasing plant facilities can significantly reduce the cost and time required
to purchase new facilities. Their early involvement in such projects is a key to
saving both time and money.

Construction Purchasing Entails Unique Problems

Construction purchasing is a highly specialized field. Of particular importance
is the fact that proper financial, legal, and planning actions must be undertaken to prevent possible losses. For example, an organization sometimes discovers that after completion of a new building it has a mechanic's lien filed
against it. In such cases, the organization has typically paid the general contractor, but the general contractor has not paid its subcontractors. Under the
law, if a "general" does not pay its "subs," the owner of the building is financially responsible.

The proper financial and legal steps that must be taken differ among states
and municipalities; hence, the *specific* steps to be taken must be determined
individually in each case. In general, though, the first step that must be taken
is to carefully analyze the financial status of all prospective contractors before
awarding any contracts. Next, the buyer should consider the desirability of
utilizing such protective devices as bid, performance, and payment bonds,[6]
liquidated damages contract clauses; and the development of construction cost
estimates by the organization's own engineering personnel (perhaps with the

---

[6]Some organizations require performance bonds on all construction contracts, at times mis-
takenly believing that performance bonds per se assure quality performance.

assistance of a specialized consultant). Finally, legal protection is achieved when the organization properly files all required completion and related reports, at the appropriate times, at the appropriate courthouses.

Construction Insurance   Because construction is a high-risk business, the insurance a buyer requires the contractor[7] to carry is very important. All construction contracts should stipulate specific insurance responsibilities. For example, such a contract clause might require the contractor, at its expense, to maintain in effect during performance of the work certain types and minimum amounts of insurance coverage, with insurers satisfactory to the buyer.

In addition, the contract should specify that prior to the performance of any work, the contractor must provide certificates of insurance as evidence that the required insurance is actually in force—and that it cannot be canceled without ten days' written notice to the buying organization. Failure to require any of the foregoing insurance provisions could be very costly.

CONCLUSION

The procurement of services is one of purchasing's most interesting and challenging assignments. Large sums of money are involved. Of equal or greater importance, successful operation of the organization is affected by the effectiveness with which key services are purchased.

FOR DISCUSSION

19-1 Define and discuss your concept of the "procurement of services." How does the procurement of services differ from that of materials?

19-2 Purchases of services are growing faster than purchases of materials. Why is this area growing so fast? What are the implications for purchasing personnel?

19-3 Why should a service be performed by the firm itself? Mention the variables involved in this decision.

19-4 Which purchasing method (negotiation or competitive bidding) should be used for complex or specialized services? Discuss.

19-5 What is a statement of work? Why is the statement of work so important in services procurement?

19-6 Enumerate the elements a buyer should identify in the planning phase of developing a statement of work.

19-7 Identify issues that should be addressed when selecting a services contractor.

19-8 Describe an "ideal services provider."

19-9 "The competitive process is not truly efficient in service markets." Do you agree with this statement? Why or why not?

---

[7]In the construction business, the supplier is typically referred to as the "contractor."

19-10 When developing a fair and reasonable price, what are the major differences between services and materials contracts?

19-11 In purchasing a professional service, which method of compensation should be selected: a fixed price contract or a cost plus award fee contract? Why? Discuss the advantages and disadvantages of each method.

19-12 Describe the five common methods of purchasing construction.

19-13 The most costly approach to buying construction is the "conventional" method. Why do you think it is the most widely used?

19-14 How could the early involvement approach save money and time when purchasing construction? How about with purchasing technical services?

19-15 What types of bonds should be considered when purchasing construction?

19-16 What insurance issues should be considered?

CASES FOR CHAPTER 19

PART **FIVE**

CONTRACT ADMINISTRATION

20

POSTAWARD ACTIVITIES AND THE MANAGEMENT OF SUPPLIER RELATIONS

KEY CONCEPTS

- Ensuring understanding
- Preaward conference
- Monitoring and controlling project progress
    - Gantt charts
    - CPM and PERT
    - Closed loop MRP systems
- Monitoring and controlling total supplier performance
    - Supplier performance evaluation
- Motivation
    - Punishment
    - Rewards
- Assistance
    - Training
    - Quality audits and procurement system reviews
    - Problem solving
- Supplier surveys
- Partnerships
    - Managing the relationship
- Appendix A: Supplier reporting requirements for unique major projects
- Appendix B: How critical path scheduling works
- Appendix C: Supplier questionnaire
- Appendix D: Internal evaluation

Historically, the postaward phase of procurement has been a weak one in many purchasing operations. Large inventories were available to accommodate quality problems and late deliveries. Multiple sources of supply often allowed the buyer to live with little supplier management. But this mentality cost the buying firm dearly. Shorter production runs under a multiple-sourcing policy frequently resulted in higher prices, lower quality, and the receipt of items which were not completely identical. Late deliveries resulted in production disruptions, higher production costs, and broken delivery commitments to the firm's customers.

Just-in-time (JIT) manufacturing creates even more need for professional postaward management. Under JIT, large inventories are no longer available to cushion the results of weak management at this stage in the process. JIT requires the receipt of consistently interchangeable items. Tight schedule integration between supplier and customer must be maintained. These forces combine to make buyer-supplier partnerships virtually essential. Such partnerships require the buyer to take a proactive approach to managing the supplier relationship.

Professional supply relations management is a vital ingredient in several other settings: defense subcontracts, construction contracts, and the purchase of essential services.

This chapter discusses the many activities a buyer must perform to ensure that the quality specified in the contract is received on time and that relations with key suppliers are managed carefully.

ENSURING UNDERSTANDING

The foremost prerequisite to successful postaward and relationship management is a sound understanding by both parties of all aspects of the program. Early supplier involvement, as described throughout this text, greatly facilitates the development of this understanding.

PREAWARD CONFERENCE: THE STAGE HAS BEEN SET

When the dollar magnitude or the complexity or criticality of the work to be performed dictates, professional buyers will have held a conference with the prospective supplier immediately prior to award of the contract. The buyer's management team—consisting of the buyer, subcontract administrator or expediter, design engineer, manufacturing engineer, internal customer, quality engineer, and inspector(s), as appropriate—should have met with the supplier's team. The issues discussed will have been addressed in technical terms in the request for proposal and the proposed contract. *The preaward conference is the vehicle the professional buyer and his or her team use to ensure that these provisions are fully understood and implemented.* The following items, as appropriate, should have been addressed:

- All terms and conditions
- Delivery or operations schedule
- Staffing and supervision
- Site conditions, work rules, safety (if appropriate)
- Invoicing procedures and documentation (for incentive and cost contracts)
- Materials purchase procedures (for incentive, cost, and time and materials contracts)
- Background checks and security clearances
- Insurance certificates
- Permits
- Possible conflicts with other work
- Submission of time sheets (for incentive, cost, and T&M contracts)
- Buyer responsibilities. Buyer-supplied items such as tools, equipment, facilities, and so on. Timeliness of buyer reviews and approvals for studies, reports, plans and specifications, and so on must be established and accepted by both parties.

Major one-time projects, such as large construction or site development jobs, have their own, fairly unique, reporting requirements. These are described in Appendix A of this chapter.

MONITORING AND CONTROLLING PROJECT PROGRESS

Suppliers are responsible for the timely and satisfactory performance of their contracts. Unfortunately, a buyer cannot rely entirely on the supplier to ensure that work is progressing as scheduled and that delivery will be as specified. Poor performance or late deliveries disrupt production operations and result in lost sales. Accordingly, purchasing must monitor supplier progress closely to ensure that desired material is delivered on time. The method of monitoring depends on the lead time, complexity, and urgency of the order.

At the time a purchase order or contract is awarded, the buyer should decide whether routine or special attention is appropriate. On many orders for noncritical items, simply monitoring the receipt of receiving and inspection reports may be adequate. On others, telephone confirmation that delivery will be as specified may be sufficient. (See Chapter 4.) But on orders for items critical to the scheduling of operations, more detailed procedures are in order.

When evaluating a supplier's progress, the buyer is interested in *actual* progress toward completing the work. Data about progress may be obtained from a variety of sources: production progress conferences, field visits to the supplier's plant, and periodic progress reports by the supplier.

In some instances, the supplier is required by the terms of the contract to submit a phased production schedule for review and approval. A phased production schedule shows the time required to perform the production cycle—planning, designing, purchasing, tooling, plant rearrangements, component manufacture, subassembly, final assembly, testing, and shipping.

In many cases, the buyer may include a requirement for production progress information in the request for proposal (RFP) and in the resulting contract. The ensuing reports frequently show the supplier's actual and forecasted deliveries, as compared with the contract schedule; delay factors, if any; and the status of incomplete preproduction work such as design and engineering, tooling, construction of prototypes, and so on. The reports also should contain narrative sections in which the supplier explains any difficulties, and action proposed or taken to overcome the difficulties. In designing the system, the buyer should ask himself or herself, "What is really essential information?" in an effort to prevent the system from becoming a burden instead of a tool for good management.

Production progress reports do not alleviate the requirement to conduct visits to the supplier's plant or the work site on crucial contracts. The right to conduct such visits must be established in the RFP and the resulting contract. On critical contracts, where the cost is justified, it may be desirable to establish a resident plant monitor at the supplier's facility to monitor the quality and timeliness of the work being performed.

When it is determined that an active system of monitoring the supplier's progress is appropriate, the first step in ensuring timely delivery is to evaluate the supplier's proposed delivery schedule for attainability. In their planning and control activities, most suppliers utilize a variety of graphic methods for portraying the proposed schedule, and then for monitoring progress against it. These are useful management tools that can also be reviewed and evaluated by the buying team. These visual presentations are forceful and usually can be updated economically. Two progress planning and control techniques commonly used for important projects and jobs are now briefly discussed.

Gantt Charts

Gantt charts are the simplest of the charting techniques for planning and controlling major projects and the materials deliveries that flow from them. Gantt charting requires that (1) first, a project must be broken into its elements; (2) next, the time required to complete each element must be estimated and eventually plotted on a time scale; (3) the elements must then be listed vertically in time sequence, determining which elements must be performed sequentially and which concurrently; and (4) finally, actual progress is charted against the plan on the time scale.

In addition to the detailed charts maintained by the supplier, the buyer can also construct a master chart to use in controlling the job. In this case, the supplier is asked to submit weekly or monthly progress data which are posted to the buyer's master chart. Figure 20-1 illustrates a typical Gantt chart of this type.

The Gantt chart, then, portrays the plan, schedule, and progress together in one easy-to-use chart. It shows the status of project elements, or activities, and identifies which are behind or ahead of schedule. Unfortunately, Gantt charts

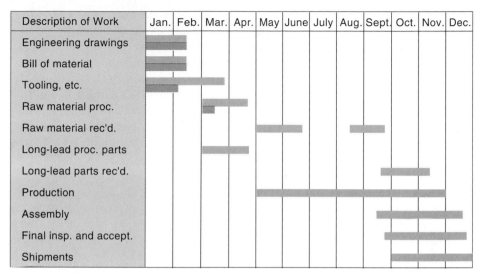

Description of Work	Jan.	Feb.	Mar.	Apr.	May	June	July	Aug.	Sept.	Oct.	Nov.	Dec.
Engineering drawings												
Bill of material												
Tooling, etc.												
Raw material proc.												
Raw material rec'd.												
Long-lead proc. parts												
Long-lead parts rec'd.												
Production												
Assembly												
Final insp. and accept.												
Shipments												

Key: planned ▮▮
    actual ▮▮

FIGURE 20-1
Production schedule and progress chart (Gantt chart).

fail to provide the full impact of an activity's being behind or ahead of schedule, and they do not provide sufficient detail to detect some schedule slippages in a timely manner.

As long as the project is not too large or complex, Gantt charts work fine. As the number of *interdependent* activities increases, however, a Gantt chart fails to tell the buyer one important fact he or she needs to know to manage the project efficiently. If slowdowns occur as work progresses on the various parts of the project, is the timing of some activities more critical than others? The answer is yes—and the Gantt chart does not tell the buyer which ones! For every project, large or small, there is one group of interrelated activities that make up the so-called *critical path;* if any of these activities falls behind schedule, the total project will not be completed on time. It is these potential bottleneck activities that the buyer must manage very carefully. To overcome this Gantt chart deficiency, a computer-based technique called critical path scheduling has been developed to provide this required management capability.

CPM and PERT

Critical path scheduling is a tool that can be used to manage project buying activities, construction projects, and research and development projects, to name just a few. The technique can be used for these and other complex projects of a one-time nature whose magnitude justifies its relatively high cost compared with more conventional methods such as the Gantt chart. It is useful for planning, monitoring, and controlling complex projects composed of a large number of *interrelated* and *interdependent* activities.

The critical path approach quantifies information about uncertainties faced by the activities responsible for meeting a predetermined time schedule. The very process of analyzing these uncertainties focuses the manager's attention on the most critical series of activities in the total project from a timing perspective—those that constitute the "critical path." The critical path activities must be accomplished sequentially, thus representing the chain of activities that require the most time from start to finish of the project. When these are pinpointed, the manager can develop an appropriate control strategy to optimize the operating results.

When used for controlling contract performance, the posting of progress data permits the buyer to compare actual accomplishments with those planned. He or she can then determine the likely implications of slippages, with respect to critical path time requirements, and work with the supplier to correct or minimize the resulting problems.

A variety of specific techniques have been derived from the basic critical path scheduling concept. The best known of these are *critical path method* (CPM) and *program evaluation and review technique* (PERT). CPM was originally developed in 1955 by the du Pont and Remington Rand companies for use in coping with complex plant maintenance problems. PERT emerged in 1958 through the joint efforts of the United States Navy, the Booz, Allen & Hamilton consulting firm, and the Lockheed Missile and Space Division in connection with the Polaris weapons program. With the passage of time, PERT and CPM have become very similar in concept. Currently, they differ only with respect to various details of application.

In practice, the application of CPM/PERT generally is accomplished with a computer program. It uses network diagrams to show time and dependency relationships between the activities that make up the total project. The purpose of the technique is to keep all the "parts" arriving on schedule so that the total project can be completed as planned. Using CPM/PERT data outputs, the buyer can evaluate possible trade-offs if supplier resources are reallocated in alternative ways to improve the chances of meeting the time schedule. This technique can quickly determine the results of alternative courses of action, thus making a choice of decisions available.

Most important, the CPM/PERT technique is both a planning and a control tool. The fact that the individual activities of a project are structured into a network requiring time and sequence determination is critically important; it is the basis for all subsequent monitoring and control activity. Use of the technique forces the buyer to conduct this step-by-step planning in advance, and to periodically reexamine the logic of the decisions as the dynamics of the operation unfold.

The mechanics of critical path scheduling are briefly described with an example in Appendix B, at the end of this chapter.

Closed Loop MRP Systems

Many progressive manufacturers use a closed loop MRP system (as described in Chapter 22) to schedule and control production, inventory levels, and deliveries from outside suppliers. Supplier-furnished data can be used by the individuals controlling the firm's incoming materials schedules as they monitor their system reports. Daily or weekly status reports flow from the supplier to the scheduler, who then inputs the data for the next MRP run. (A growing number of firms link their suppliers' computer-based systems into their own computer system so that real-time data are available to both parties.) If supplier-furnished data indicate that the supplier's delivery dates will result in a disruption of the buyer's schedule, the appropriate scheduler or buyer can take action to modify the supplier's schedule or to adjust the firm's own production schedule, as appropriate.

MONITORING AND CONTROLLING TOTAL SUPPLIER PERFORMANCE

The use of supplier performance evaluation systems is on the rise. A recent survey conducted by *Purchasing* magazine shows that most of the major manufacturing firms either have established formal supplier-evaluation programs (59 percent) or are in the process of doing so (30 percent).[1]

Many progressive buying organizations monitor their major suppliers' performance at both a contract and an aggregate level. This information is used to control a supplier's contract performance, and it is also used during source selection for follow-on procurements to ensure that only satisfactory performers are considered. "Formalized supplier evaluation programs have never had better odds for success than today. Total quality management (TQM) programs are giving rise to the major organizational changes that will enable purchasing professionals to step into the corporate limelight and orchestrate the development of the supply base."[2]

Supplier Performance Evaluation

After a major supplier has been selected and the buyer-supplier relationship has begun to develop, it is important to monitor and assess the supplier's overall performance. The purpose is to enhance the relationship and thereby control performance.

Many evaluation teams use a three- to six-month moving average for the aggregate evaluation of a supplier's performance. For example, with a six-

[1] T. Minahan, "Big Buyer Keeps Eye on Supplier," *Purchasing*, Jan. 16, 1992, p. 94.
[2] A. Millen Porter, "Supplier Evaluation Revisited," *Purchasing*, Oct. 24, 1991, p. 58.

month window, a supplier's rating in June is an average of all the ratings accumulated between January and June. The moving average allows suppliers to start over at some point. Their mistakes don't haunt them forever. They're motivated to improve. The length of the window is important and should be case-specific. A shorter window may be ineffective because it lets suppliers off the hook too easily. A longer window may be punitive and self-defeating.[3]

In its research study, "Evaluation of Supplier Performance," the National Association of Purchasing Management investigated three types of evaluation plans: the *categorical plan*, the *weighted point plan*, and the *cost ratio plan*. Each of these plans is reviewed briefly in the following pages.

Categorical Plan   Under this plan, personnel from various departments of the buyer's firm maintain informal evaluation records. The individuals involved traditionally include personnel from purchasing, engineering, quality, accounting, and receiving. For each major supplier, each evaluator prepares a list of performance factors which are important to him or her. At a monthly or bimonthly meeting, each major supplier is evaluated against each evaluator's list of factors. After the factors are weighted for relative importance, each supplier is then assigned an overall group evaluation, usually expressed in simple categorical terms, such as "preferred," "neutral," or "unsatisfactory." Figure 20-2 portrays a typical supplier performance evaluation form used in the categorical plan. This simple qualitative plan is easy to administer and has been reported by many firms to be very effective.

The Weighted Point Plan   Under this plan, the performance factors to be evaluated (often various aspects of quality, service, and price) are given "weights." For example, in one circumstance, quality might be weighted 25 percent, service 25 percent, and price 50 percent. In another, quality could be raised to 50 percent, and price reduced to 25 percent. The weights selected in any specific situation represent buyer or buying team judgments concerning the relative importance of the respective factors.

After performance factors have been selected and weighted, a specific procedure is then developed to measure actual supplier performance on each factor. Supplier performance on each factor must be expressed in quantitative terms. To determine a supplier's overall rating, each factor weight is multiplied by the supplier's corresponding performance number; the results (for each factor) are then totaled to get the supplier's final rating for the time period in question.

---

[3]"From Concept to Kickoff," *Purchasing*, Oct. 24, 1991, p. 65.

Supplier _____   Date: _____

Summary Evaluation, by Department	Preferred	Neutral	Unsatisfactory
Purchasing	_____	_____	_____
Receiving	_____	_____	_____
Accounting	_____	_____	_____
Engineering	_____	_____	_____
Quality	_____	_____	_____

Performance Factors

Purchasing
	Preferred	Neutral	Unsatisfactory
Delivers on schedule	_____	_____	_____
Delivers at quoted prices	_____	_____	_____
Has competitive prices	_____	_____	_____
Is prompt and accurate with routine documents	_____	_____	_____
Anticipates our needs	_____	_____	_____
Helps in emergencies	_____	_____	_____
Does not unfairly exploit a single-source position	_____	_____	_____
Does not request special consideration	_____	_____	_____
Currently supplies price, catalog, and technical information	_____	_____	_____
Furnishes specially requested information promptly	_____	_____	_____
Advises us of potential troubles	_____	_____	_____
Has good labor relations	_____	_____	_____
Delivers without constant follow-up	_____	_____	_____
Replaces rejections promptly	_____	_____	_____
Accepts our terms without exception	_____	_____	_____
Keeps promises	_____	_____	_____
Has sincere desire to serve	_____	_____	_____

Receiving
	Preferred	Neutral	Unsatisfactory
Delivers per routing instructions	_____	_____	_____
Has adequate delivery service	_____	_____	_____
Has good packaging	_____	_____	_____

Accounting
	Preferred	Neutral	Unsatisfactory
Invoices correctly	_____	_____	_____
Issues credit memos punctually	_____	_____	_____
Does not ask for special financial consideration	_____	_____	_____

Engineering
	Preferred	Neutral	Unsatisfactory
Has past record on reliability of products	_____	_____	_____
Has technical ability for difficult work	_____	_____	_____
Readily accepts responsibility for latent deficiencies	_____	_____	_____
Provides quick and effective action in emergencies	_____	_____	_____
Furnishes requested data promptly	_____	_____	_____

Quality
	Preferred	Neutral	Unsatisfactory
Provides high-quality material	_____	_____	_____
Furnishes certification, affidavits, etc.	_____	_____	_____
Replies with corrective action	_____	_____	_____

FIGURE 20-2
Supplier performance evaluation form, categorical plan.

The following hypothetical case illustrates the procedure. Assume that a purchasing department has decided to weight and measure the three basic performance factors as follows:

Weight	Factors	Measurement formula
50%	Quality performance	= 100% − percentage of rejects
25%	Service performance	= 100% − 7% for each failure
25%	Price performance	$= \dfrac{\text{lowest price offered}}{\text{price actually paid}}$

Assume further that supplier A performed as follows during the past month. Five percent of its items were rejected for quality reasons; three unsatisfactory split shipments were received; and A's price was $100/unit, compared with the lowest offer of $90/unit. Table 20-1 summarizes the total performance evaluation calculation for supplier A.

This procedure can be used to evaluate any number of different suppliers whose performance is particularly important during a given operating period. The performance of competing suppliers can be compared quantitatively, and subsequent negotiating strategies developed accordingly. The user should always remember that valid performance comparisons of two or more suppliers require that the same factors, weights, and measurement formulas be used *consistently* for all suppliers.

In contrast to the categorical plan, which is largely subjective, the weighted point plan has the advantage of being somewhat more objective. The exercise of subjective judgment is constrained more tightly in the assignment of factor weights and the development of the factor measurement formulas. The plan is extremely flexible, since it can accommodate any number of evaluation factors that are important in any specific case. Also, the plan can be used in conjunction with the categorical plan if buyers wish to include important subjective matters in the final evaluation of their suppliers.

Various research studies have noted, however, that a weighted point plan must be developed with care. The estimates of factor importance must be con-

---

TABLE 20-1
ILLUSTRATIVE APPLICATION OF THE WEIGHTED POINT PLAN
Supplier A Monthly Performance Evaluation

Factor	Weight	Actual performance	Performance evaluation
Quality	50	5% rejects	50 × (1.00 − 0.05) = 47.50
Service	25	3 failures	25 × [1.00 − (0.07 × 3)]= 19.75
Price	25	$100	$25 \times \dfrac{\$90}{\$100} = 22.50$
			Overall evaluation: = 89.75

sistent from one situation to the next, and they must be consistent with the performance measurement formulas used because of the obvious interaction between them.[4]

Cost Ratio Plan   This plan evaluates supplier performance by using the tools of *standard cost* analysis that business people traditionally use to evaluate a wide variety of business operations. When using this plan, the buying firm identifies the *additional* costs it incurs when doing business with a given supplier; these are separated as costs associated with the quality, service, and price elements of supplier performance. Each of these costs is then converted to a "cost ratio" which expresses the additional cost as a percent of the buyer's total dollar purchase from that supplier. These three individual cost ratios are then totaled, producing the supplier's overall additional cost ratio. For purposes of analysis, the supplier's price is then adjusted by applying its overall cost ratio. The adjusted price for each supplier is then compared with the adjusted price for other competitive suppliers in the final evaluation process.

For example, assume that for one supplier the quality cost ratio is 2 percent, the delivery cost ratio is 2 percent, the service cost ratio is –1 percent, and the price is $72.25. The sum of all cost ratios is 3 percent; hence, the adjusted price for this supplier is $[72.25 + (0.03 \times 72.25)] = \$74.42$. This is the price used for evaluation purposes vis-à-vis other suppliers.

Although the cost ratio plan is used by a number of large progressive firms, on the whole it is not widely used in American industry. Operationally speaking, it is a complex plan. It requires a specially designed, companywide, computerized cost accounting system to generate the precise cost data needed for effective operation. Consequently, the majority of purchasing departments employing a quantitative type of evaluation rely on the simpler but effective weighted point plan—typically, modified specifically to meet their own unique circumstances.

For these reasons, the cost ratio plan is not discussed in detail in this book. Nevertheless, it is an excellent concept that has the ability to provide the most precise evaluation data of the three plans discussed. For firms using sophisticated information systems, the cost of designing and implementing the cost ratio plan typically is repaid many times by savings resulting from more precise analysis of supplier performance.

All three of the plans discussed—categorical, weighted point, and cost ratio—involve varying degrees of subjectivity and guesswork. The mathematical treatment of data in two of the plans often tends to obscure the fact that the results are no more accurate than the assumptions on which the quantitative data are based. In the final analysis, therefore, supplier evaluation must represent a combined appraisal of facts, quantitative computations, and value

---

[4]For example, see Kenneth N. Thompson, "Scaling Evaluative Criteria and Supplier Performance Estimates in Weighted Point Prepurchase Decision Models," *International Journal of Purchasing and Materials Management*, Winter 1991, pp. 27–28.

judgments. It simply cannot be achieved effectively by mechanical formulas alone.

Cost-Based Supplier Performance Evaluation A number of firms are experimenting with various types of cost-based evaluation plans, similar to the cost ratio plan. Such plans address the issue of how to measure overall supplier performance on a total cost basis. In addition to rationalizing lowest total cost performance suppliers, such plans demonstrate that supplier nonperformance costs can be measured. Recognizing the supplier as an integral member of the organization, competitive strategy requires the development of a system that provides supplier accountability and control while maintaining dependable, competitive suppliers. As buying organizations continue to secure longer-term supplier relationships, the ability to quantify performance becomes increasingly important. Companies can use such methodology as a contract monitoring tool when incorporated into long-term agreements.[5]

Professors Monczka and Trecha describe the details of such a system in the Spring 1988 issue of the *Journal of Purchasing and Materials Management*.[6]

MOTIVATION

Two common approaches are used in motivating suppliers to perform satisfactorily: punishment and reward. Many progressive buyers use a combination of both approaches.

Punishment

Quite obviously, the greatest punishment for unsatisfactory performance (if the area of litigation and punitive damages is ignored) is *not* to award contracts for future requirements. This is a powerful motivator, especially during periods when buyers reduce the number of suppliers with whom they do business. A less drastic approach called the "bill back" is especially appropriate when dealing with a "partnership" supplier or a defense contractor. Under the bill back, incremental costs resulting from quality problems or late deliveries are identified and then billed back to the appropriate supplier. Some progressive buyers have increased the motivational effect of the bill back by sending the bill to the supplier's chief operating officer so that he or she is aware of problems within the supplier organization.

---

[5]Robert M. Monczka and Steven J. Trecha, "Cost-Based Supplier Performance Evaluation," *Journal of Purchasing and Materials Management,* Spring 1988, p. 7.
[6]Ibid., pp. 2–7.

Rewards

The biggest reward for satisfactory performance is follow-on business. Additionally, as with raising children or dealing with "significant others," recognition also is a powerful stimulant to future successful performance. Recently, an Arizona purchasing manager divided her suppliers into three categories: outstanding, acceptable, and marginal. She wrote an appropriate letter to the CEO of each supplier firm. The results of her efforts were rewarding. The outstanding group performed even better! Most of the CEOs from the second and third groups requested meetings to discuss what they could do better to earn *an outstanding letter!*

General Electric's Major Appliance Group in Louisville, Kentucky, publicly recognizes its most successful suppliers. Such suppliers are encouraged to share their recognition with their employees. The employees are encouraged to continue their efforts to improve quality and productivity. Many suppliers reward their outstanding employees with a trip to GE's Appliance Park to see how their products are used (and to visit nearby Churchill Downs, home of the Kentucky Derby).

Each year, the Major Appliance Group selects its 100 "best" suppliers. This selection is based on a combination of service, responsiveness, value analysis suggestions, cost, and related factors. Each representative and CEO attends the Supplier Appreciation Group's Day. Over 50 senior GE managers also attend. Each of the 100 outstanding suppliers receives a plaque acknowledging its status and contribution. GE publicizes this list in appliance and purchasing magazines, to the delight of those listed.

The Ford Motor Company, like GE, believes in recognizing its successful supplier partners. Ford's quality, engineering, manufacturing, and purchasing departments rate their suppliers based on an extensive system survey, defect prevention activities, delivery performance, technical capabilities, and management.

High ratings result in increased follow-on business. But public recognition also plays a big role in motivating suppliers. Ford publicly recognizes its highest-rated suppliers in the *Wall Street Journal* by identifying those suppliers who have received the firm's exalted "Q1" status (see page 476).

ASSISTANCE

Progressive firms have discovered that two types of assistance to suppliers pay big dividends: *training* and *problem solving.*

Training

Firms such as Xerox, Texas Instruments, GE, and Tennant have learned the benefits of providing training to their suppliers in the areas of statistical process control (SPC), just-in-time (JIT) manufacturing, and total quality commitment

(TQC). These progressive firms recognize that their ability to purchase the required levels of quality, delivered on time, requires supplier firms with competence in these areas. By the time this book is in print, the authors estimate that these and other purchasers also will provide essential training to their suppliers in the techniques of modern purchasing and supply management.

Quality Audits and Procurement System Reviews

As organizations realize their interdependence with their suppliers, they are becoming more proactive in ensuring that their suppliers' quality systems and procurement systems operate effectively. Quality audits are described in Chapter 21.

A supplier's procurement system affects its quality, cost, technology, and dependability. In theory, competition rewards suppliers that have efficient procurement systems with *survival* and *profit,* and it penalizes suppliers with inefficient systems. But such theory may take years to show results. Further, as firms move from reliance on market competition to partnerships, the implications of inefficient supplier procurement systems become even more frightening. The procurement system review provides a framework which a buying firm may follow when reviewing and assisting its key suppliers to upgrade their procurement systems. The review is conducted in a constructive, cooperative atmosphere. Details of this concept are described in the presentation "The Purchasing Manager's Guide to Improved Status, Cooperation, Leadtime, and Staffing," contained in *Freedom of Choice,* published by the National Association of Purchasing Management.

Problem Solving

Most progressive firms provide technical and managerial assistance to their suppliers when quality and related problems are encountered. Progressive buyers have replaced the attitude "It's their contract and it's their problem" with the knowledge that the buying firm's success is dependent on its suppliers' success.

SUPPLIER SURVEYS

An often overlooked aspect of successful supplier management is the solicitation of supplier feedback. As quality guru Philip B. Crosby writes, "You need to demonstrate your understanding and willingness to clean your own house before asking the supplier to clean his."[7] Crosby suggests soliciting answers from suppliers to the following questions:

---

[7]Crosby, "Seven Steps for Producing a Useful Supplier Survey," *Purchasing,* Sept. 6, 1984, p. 126 A31. This topic is discussed in detail in Chapter 29.

- How knowledgeable are our buyers?
- How accurate are our engineering specifications?
- How clearly do we state our quality requirements?
- How timely are our payments?

The Ford Motor Company utilizes a supplier survey at least once a year. Ford purchasing personnel feel that the feedback obtained has played a significant role in improving supplier relations and in ensuring that high-quality materials are received on time. Appendices C and D, at the end of this chapter, contain questionnaires designed to capture supplier input. Such surveys normally are conducted by an independent third party such as an audit firm or a procurement consultant.

PARTNERSHIPS

Experience in recent years demonstrates that the most successful supplier management results when the buyer and the supplier view their relationship as a "partnership." Partnerships are based on mutual interdependency and respect. Supplier partnerships begin with careful source selection during the product design and development process. At this point, the buying firm needs a dependable supplier to provide the required design and technological input if a marketable, profitable product or a satisfactory service is to result. In turn, the supplier needs a responsible customer for its products and services. Professional buyers need the supplier as much as (or more than) the supplier needs them. This interdependence grows as a project moves from design into production. Unexpected problems arise which require a "We shall overcome" attitude by the partners. During production, the buyers and suppliers must mesh their schedules, requiring another phase of cooperation.

Respect permeates the partnership and replaces the adversarial attitude present in too many buyer-seller relationships. It has not been that many years since many buyers treated their suppliers with distrust and contempt. Today, this attitude has been replaced with programs such as "Partners in Progress."

The *ultimate* in partnerships is a vertical integration of buyer and supplier, wherein two independently owned entities pool their resources for as long as the relationship benefits both parties. Lengthy contracts, change orders, and other legalistic and defensive procedures are replaced by one- or two-page memoranda of agreement.[8]

Purchasing professionals have moved a long way from the old adversarial ways of doing business with suppliers. But it will take many years of successful partnerships before this level of vertical integration becomes the norm.

[8]For additional insight into this issue, see "Reopening the Vertical Integration Case" by David N. Burt and Michael F. Doyle, *Harvard Business Review*, March–April 1989, pp. 190–191.

Managing the Relationship

As previously discussed, any purchasing and supply management department normally will have a continuum of supplier relationships from arm's length through partnerships to strategic alliances. The latter two relationships will be relatively few in number, but all will be critical to the well-being of the buying firm. These are the relationships which require careful managing.

A progressive approach has been developed by David Nelson, vice president of purchasing, Honda America Manufacturing (HAM). Every key supply relationship has a relationship manager to ensure that the relationship meets Honda's present and future needs. Additionally, an ombudsman is appointed for each relationship. This individual is available to the supplier, should it feel that it is not being treated fairly by HAM.

Several actions must be taken to ensure the success of each partnership or strategic relationship. For example:

- The cross-functional teams from both the buying and the selling firms must receive training in being constructive cross-functional team members.
- The interfirm team composed of representatives of both firms must jointly receive training and development in cross-functional team skills.
- The two firms must develop an integrated communication system responsive to the needs of both parties in their area of cooperation.
- Plans to increase trust between the two organizations must be developed and implemented.
- Arrangements for co-location of key technical personnel and for periodic visits to each other's facilities must be developed and implemented.
- Plans must be developed and implemented for training on issues, including the designing of variance out of products and processes, quality, procurement, value analysis and engineering, strategic cost analysis, activity-based management, etc.
- Measurable quantifiable objectives must be established in areas, including quality, cost, time, technology, etc.
- The results of such improvement efforts must be monitored and reported to appropriate management.

It is in the interest of both the buying and supplying firms for the buyer to support the supplier's operations:

"Suppliers are given huge support in meeting their productivity, quality, and cost goals," says David Nelson. "Working with suppliers is a full-time job for the Honda engineers assigned to purchasing." He believes this will become common practice as more firms—U.S., as well as Japanese—move to adopt a "lean production philosophy."[9]

---

[9]"Profile: Honda's Dave Nelson," *Purchasing*, July 18, 1991, p. 32A1.

CONCLUSION

Without question, supplier management is a critical and challenging activity. Perhaps the most challenging aspect is the evolution from managing or controlling the supplier to managing the partnership or the relationship. New attitudes and skills are required. As Theodore Levitt wrote in the *Harvard Business Review*, supplier partnerships require the same amount of attention as a good marriage.[10] But the many benefits of successful partnerships make the efforts worthwhile.

FOR DISCUSSION

20-1 What are the possible results of late deliveries of critical materials?

20-2 Does JIT manufacturing call for more or less emphasis on supplier management? Why?

20-3 What is the foremost prerequisite to successful supplier management?

20-4 Describe and discuss the objectives and potential topics for a preaward conference.

20-5 What are logical sources of data on the supplier's actual progress?

20-6 What is the simplest progress charting technique? Describe it.

20-7 Describe critical path scheduling. When is it applicable?

20-8 How can closed loop MRP systems aid in controlling a firm's incoming materials?

20-9 Identify and describe three supplier performance evaluation plans.

20-10 How can a buyer motivate suppliers to perform satisfactorily?

20-11 Should industrial firms facilitate the training of their suppliers? If so, in what areas? Why?

20-12 What is the procurement system review? How can it help the buying firm?

20-13 Phililp Crosby suggests that we clean our own house before asking the supplier to clean its house. What questions does Crosby suggest the purchasing firm address?

20-14 Describe a supplier partnership.

20-15 Discuss the responsibilities of a supply relationship manager.

CASES FOR CHAPTER 20

Printed Circuits Components for a JIT Factory, page 886
Lion Industries, page 844
Randall Corporation, page 893
SMC Turbines, page 914
Placido Engine Company, page 884
AAA, Inc., page 773

---

[10]Levitt, "After the Sale is Over," *Harvard Business Review*, September–October 1983, pp. 87–93.

SDC Corporation, page 904

Alpha Omega Corporation (in the *Instructor's Manual*)

Hydrosub's Unfloatable Amphibious Assault Vehicle (in the *Instructor's Manual*)

The Tidewater Gas and Electric Company (in the *Instructor's Manual*)

Diatech versus RPM (in the *Instructor's Manual*)

Florida Retail Company (in the *Instructor's Manual*)

APPENDIX A: SUPPLIER REPORTING REQUIREMENTS FOR UNIQUE MAJOR PROJECTS

During the preaward conference, arrangements are made for the timely receipt of the following data, as appropriate in a given situation.

- *A program organization chart.* For a large job, the supplier designates its program manager and shows the key members of the organization by name and function. The program manager's functional authority should be clearly defined.
- *Milestone plan.* For a complex project, this plan identifies all major milestones on a time-phased basis, including those of the supplier's major subcontractors.
- *Funds commitment plan* (incentive and cost reimbursement contracts only). This plan shows estimated commitments on a dollar versus month basis and on a cumulative dollar versus month basis.
- *Labor commitment plan.* This plan shows estimated labor loading on a labor-hour versus labor-month basis.
- *Monthly progress information.* This report should be submitted ten days after the close of each month. The report should contain as a minimum:

    —*A narrative summary of work accomplished* during the reporting period, including a technical progress update, a summary of work planned for the next reporting period, problems encountered or anticipated, corrective action taken or to be taken, and a summary of buyer-seller discussions.

    —*A list of all action items,* if any, required of the buyer during the forthcoming performance period.

    —*An update of the milestone plan* showing actual progress against planned progress.

    —*An update of the funds commitment plan* showing actual funds committed against the planned funds by time (incentive and cost reimbursement contracts only).

    —*A report on any significant changes* in the supplier's program personnel or in the financial or general management structure, or any other factors that might affect performance.

—*A missed milestone notification and recovery plan.* The supplier should notify the buyer by phone within twenty-four hours after discovery of a missed major milestone or the discovery of an anticipated major milestone slip. The supplier should provide the buyer with a missed milestone recovery plan within seven working days after notification.

Such data can be costly to compile and should be required only when it has been determined that their cost and the cost associated with using them to manage an order will result in a net saving or the likely avoidance of a schedule slippage. The subcontract manager, on a case-by-case basis, must determine what level of detail is necessary.

APPENDIX B: HOW CRITICAL PATH SCHEDULING WORKS

Critical path scheduling begins with the identification and listing of all significant activities involved in the project to be planned and controlled. When the list of activities is complete, the sequential relationship between all activities is determined and shown graphically by constructing an activity network (see Figure 20-3a). The network shows the time required to complete each activity, and it explicitly indicates the relationship of each activity to all other activities. Finally, it establishes the sequence in which activities should be scheduled for efficient completion of the total project. Some activities can be paralleled, allowing many different jobs to be carried on simultaneously; other activities must be placed in series to allow step-by-step completion of interrelated tasks. The complete interrelationship of all project activities is the important feature that distinguishes critical path analysis from Gantt and other bar chart planning techniques.

Construction of the network permits determination of a project's *critical path*—the chain of activities requiring the most time for completion from start to finish of the project. Once the critical path is determined, the planner can identify precisely and completely the activities that require close control. He or she can also determine which activities permit the greatest latitude in scheduling and can, if necessary, most easily relinquish manpower to more urgent jobs. An activity network also highlights the activities that can be expedited most effectively in case a stepped-up pace becomes necessary.

Figure 20-3 illustrates the mechanics of network development. This simplified example shows a partial network of the major subcontracted activities involved in the construction of a new laboratory. Engineering and purchasing activities prior to site preparation have been omitted for reasons of simplification. The example shows only the major activities to be completed after the site has been excavated and prepared for the concrete subcontractor.

1 Column 1 (Figure 20-3b, page 446) lists the major activities to be completed.

2 Figure 20-3a shows the activities in network form. The required interdependencies and sequencing of operations have been determined and reviewed with the project engineer and the various subcontractors. Each arrow in the diagram represents an *activity* that will be conducted during

444

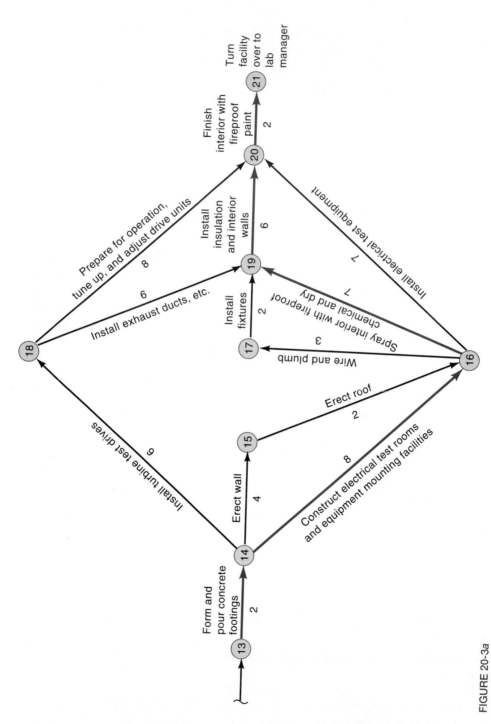

FIGURE 20-3a
Simplified critical path network for subcontracted activities of a laboratory construction job.

specific period of time (e.g., the start of an activity and the completion of an activity).

3 Careful estimates of the time required to complete each activity have been made by the respective contractors and are noted next to the appropriate arrows.*

4 The critical path (longest chain of activities) consists of the activities 13-14-16-19-20-21; it will take 25 weeks to finish the project. The critical path is determined by totaling the time requirements for individual activities put together in every conceivable path from start to finish of the project. The critical path is the one requiring the longest time. Using the given time estimates, it is impossible to complete the project in less time.

5 At this point, the objective is to determine the amount of "slack time" (extra time, or leeway) existing in each of the noncritical paths. This is done by first developing the figures in column 2 (the earliest start and completion dates for each activity) and then those in column 3 (the latest possible start and completion dates for each activity) of Figure 20-3b.

The earliest start and completion date for each activity is determined by starting with the first activity and totaling the time requirements of the various paths through the network. If we say that the earliest start date for 13-14 (the concrete work) is today (the 0 point in time), the earliest completion date for 13-14 is the end of week 2 (0 + 2 = 2). Therefore, the earliest start date for both 14-15 and 14-16, which cannot begin before 13-14 is completed, is the end of week 2. The earliest completion date for 14-16 is the end of week 10 (2 + 8 = 10), and for 14-15 it is the end of week 6 (2 + 4 = 6). The earliest start date for 15-16 is the end of week 6, and the earliest completion date is the end of week 8 (6 + 2 = 8). What is the earliest start date for the electrical wiring and plumbing activity 16-17? Is it the end of week 8 or week 10? Clearly, it is the end of week 10, because the wiring cannot be started until the electrical test rooms and mounting facilities are completed. The analysis continues in this manner through the entire network until column 2 is complete.

The latest possible start and completion date for each activity (column 3) is determined in exactly the reverse manner. Begin with the completion date for the final activity and work backward through the network, determining the latest completion and start dates that can be used for each activity without delaying completion of the project. All activities on the

---

*The PERT technique is often used for jobs whose time requirements cannot be accurately estimated. For this reason PERT requires three time estimates for each activity: (1) t_l = longest time required under the most difficult conditions (expect once in 100 times), (2) t_s = shortest time required under the best conditions (expect once in 100 times), (3) t_m = most likely time requirement. The expected time t_e, the figure actually used on the network, is a weighted average computed as

$$t_e = \frac{t_l + t_s + 4t_m}{6}$$

Activity (1)	Earliest (2)		Latest (3)		Slack (4)
	Start	Complete	Start	Complete	
13-14 Form and pour concrete footings	0	2	0	2	0
14-16 Construct electrical test rooms and equipment mounting facilities	2	10	2	10	0
16-19 Spray interior with fireproof chemical and let dry	10	17	10	17	0
19-20 Install insulation and interior walls	17	23	17	23	0
20-21 Finish interior with fireproof paint	23	25	23	25	0
14-15 Erect walls	2	6	4	8	2
15-16 Erect roof	6	8	8	10	2
16-17 Install electrical wiring and plumbing	10	13	12	15	2
17-19 Install fixtures	13	15	15	17	2
14-18 Install turbine test drives	2	8	5	11	3
18-19 Install exhaust ducts, etc.	8	14	11	17	3
16-20 Install electrical test equipment	10	17	16	23	6
18-20 Prepare for operation, tune up, and adjust drive units	8	16	15	23	7

FIGURE 20-3b
Data for Figures 20-3a and 20-3c.

FIGURE 20-3c
Network of Figure 20-3a drawn against a slack scale.

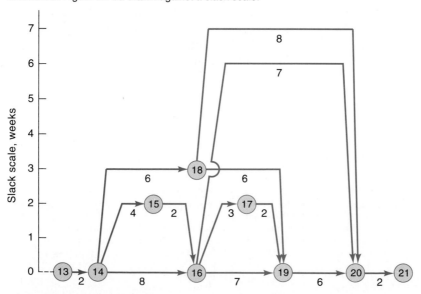

critical path will have identical "earliest" and "latest" dates. This is not true, however, for the noncritical path activities.

The latest completion date for the final painting activity (20-21) is the end of week 25, and the latest start date is the end of week 23 (25 − 2 = 23). Therefore, the latest completion date for 18-20 is the end of week 23, and the latest start date is the end of week 15. Notice, however, that the latest completion date for 14-18 is not the end of week 15. Activity 14-18 must be completed by the latest start date for activity 18-19, which is the end of week 11 (23 − 6 − 6 = 11). This procedure, then, is followed back through the network to complete column 3.

6 The purpose in developing columns 2 and 3 is to determine the amount of *slack time* in each noncritical, or slack, path (column 4). The slack time existing for a particular activity is simply the difference between the earliest start date and the latest start date (or between the earliest completion date and the latest completion date). This important factor represents leeway which can be used in scheduling the slack path activity most efficiently in light of other demands for facilities and manpower.*

7 Figure 20-3c represents the network in Figure 20-3a drawn against a vertical slack scale. Its purpose is merely to show, at a quick glance, how much slack is available in each slack path activity. Such a chart frequently serves as a good visual planning aid.

The preceding discussion has dealt only with the rudiments of the critical path planning concept. In practice, performance is monitored, and progress data are periodically compared with the original plan. The technique is therefore an effective control device as well as an aid in making future planning decisions as changes in plans occur. The projects to which the technique is applied in practice are often made up of several thousand activities. After the initial network is constructed for such projects, a computer program is written or adapted for use, and the mechanics of preparing and monitoring progress reports are accomplished by computer.

The illustration depicted in Figure 20-3 considers the planning and controlling activities only with respect to the factor of time. Some techniques of critical path analysis add to this the factor of cost. These techniques integrate the two important variables in a single system, permitting virtually total managerial control.

A wise manager always raises two questions about the practicality of any planning or control concept: How accurate is it? and How much does it cost? Like other planning techniques, critical path analysis is no more accurate than the data it manipulates. As for cost, some companies find it profitable; others do not. Generally speaking, the greatest profit potential for such a system lies in its application to projects too complex for adequate planning with bar charts. The basic question a firm must answer is: How important is the ultimate control the system affords? When management puts a price tag on this variable, it then can determine whether or not adoption of the system is likely to be profitable.

---

*Column 4 indicates that both activities 14–15 and 15–16 have two weeks' slack. Notice that this is an either-or situation. Two weeks' slack cannot be utilized in both activities; two weeks represents the total combined slack for both activities.

Its current popularity indicates that a large number of users find critical path analysis profitable primarily because it forces suppliers to do more planning than they otherwise would do. Numerous governmental and industrial buyers require subcontractors to submit a critical path network (for major events, or "milestones") with their bids on subcontract and construction jobs. Some companies have found that the technique can pay off even without the use of a computer, although it is rare today to find a firm without access to a minicomputer or microcomputer adequate for the job.

APPENDIX C:
SUPPLIER QUESTIONNAIRE

The Purchasing and Internal Audit Departments at _____ have developed a short questionnaire to determine weaknesses and strengths of our procurement and payable functions. To ensure creditability, all suppliers being requested to complete this form were selected by Internal Audit. We would appreciate your taking a few minutes and completing the form. While you need not identify yourself, we would appreciate a generic description of the product or service you provide—see question #7. A self-addressed postage-paid envelope is enclosed for your convenience.

1. Do you find the purchasers you interact with at _____ to possess the necessary expertise to evaluate your products or services fairly?
    _____ Yes _____ No
2. Are you accorded a prompt and courteous interview in the Purchasing Department?
    _____ Yes _____ No
3. When requested to respond to written bids, is your firm allowed sufficient time?
    _____ Yes _____ No
4. On a scale of 1 to 5, 5 being the highest, how would you rate the ethics (honesty, willingness to listen to both sides of an issue, impartiality, etc.) of members of the Purchasing Department?
    Circle one: 1   2   3   4   5
5. Are invoices paid on time? _____ Yes _____ No
6. Do you receive a prompt response when calling regarding a delinquent payment?
    _____ Yes _____ No
7. Please identify the product or service you provide—examples: laboratory equipment/supplies, agricultural-related products, computer equipment/supplies, etc.
    _____
    _____
    _____

8. Are there any additional comments you have relative to the operation of the purchasing and accounts payable functions at _____ ?
    _____
    _____
    _____

Please return the completed questionnaire to: _____. We would appreciate a return date by _____. Your comments will be appreciated. Thank you!

APPENDIX D: PURCHASING QUESTIONNAIRE FOR SUPPLIERS

The following is a series of statements about purchasing at _____. Please offer your perceptions of _____ purchasing effort as it compares with other companies to which you sell. Simply check the appropriate box to the right of each question.

	Strongly agree	Agree somewhat	Neither agree nor disagree	Disagree somewhat	Strongly disagree
1. The purchasing department displays a high level of professionalism.	☐	☐	☐	☐	☐
2. The firm provides clear specifications/requirements as to what goods or services it requires.	☐	☐	☐	☐	☐
3. The supplier selection process takes longer and is more cumbersome than that of most companies.	☐	☐	☐	☐	☐
4. The firm seems to select its suppliers based on a combination of factors (price, quality, delivery reliability, etc.), rather than price alone.	☐	☐	☐	☐	☐
5. Purchase terms and conditions are more demanding than for most customers.	☐	☐	☐	☐	☐
6. The firm maintains an adversarial relationship with its suppliers.	☐	☐	☐	☐	☐
7. Purchasing department personnel have sufficient knowledge of the items they procure.	☐	☐	☐	☐	☐
8. The supplier selection process seems arbitrary and capricious.	☐	☐	☐	☐	☐
9. Purchasing personnel are demanding negotiators.	☐	☐	☐	☐	☐
10. Purchasing personnel are fair negotiators.	☐	☐	☐	☐	☐
11. The firm requires more paperwork to process an order than most customers.	☐	☐	☐	☐	☐
12. The percentage of rush/special orders is about the same as that of other customers.	☐	☐	☐	☐	☐

	Strongly agree	Agree somewhat	Neither agree nor disagree	Disagree somewhat	Strongly disagree
13. Once orders have been placed, the firm issues more changes to orders than most companies.	☐	☐	☐	☐	☐
14. Purchasing personnel check on the status of open orders more than most companies.	☐	☐	☐	☐	☐
15. Compared with most customers, the firm spends a good deal of effort controlling the quality of the goods it receives.	☐	☐	☐	☐	☐
16. Orders are placed by operating personnel (rather than purchasing personnel) more than most companies.	☐	☐	☐	☐	☐
17. Our sales force is likely to target operating personnel, rather than purchasing personnel, to promote my company's goods/services.	☐	☐	☐	☐	☐
18. The firm is timely in the payment of its purchases.	☐	☐	☐	☐	☐
19. The firm seems "bureau-cratic" to deal with.	☐	☐	☐	☐	☐
20. The firm could receive better purchasing services by negotiating sole supplier relation-ships.	☐	☐	☐	☐	☐
21. Operating division personnel are more involved in the purchasing decision than at most compa-nies.	☐	☐	☐	☐	☐
22. Purchasing makes an attempt to establish a long-term relationship with its suppliers.	☐	☐	☐	☐	☐
23. Purchasing and operating division per-sonnel will often inquire independently about the same order.	☐	☐	☐	☐	☐

21

MANAGING FOR QUALITY

KEY CONCEPTS

- Total quality management (TQM)
- Basic concepts of quality
- The role of purchasing and supply in quality management
    Specification of quality requirements
    Determination of supplier capability
    The current view of quality—defect prevention versus detection
    Motivation and control of suppliers
- Quality management concepts
    Process capability analysis
    Statistical process control
    Supplier certification
    Inspection and quality control
- Industrial applications
- National and international quality recognition
    The Malcolm Baldrige Award
    The Deming Prize
    ISO 9000 quality standards
- Design of experiments

Chapter 8 discussed how to determine and how to specify quality. This chapter discusses a more encompassing issue—total quality management (TQM) and purchasing's responsibility for managing supplier quality within a TQM system.

TOTAL QUALITY MANAGEMENT

During the 1970s and early 1980s the quality of many products turned out by American industry left a great deal to be desired. As some have said, the producers in Japan, Singapore, and other Pacific Rim countries were literally "eating our lunch." But times have changed! A great "quality awakening" has surged through U.S. business during the past decade or so. And one of the key concepts generated as a result of this thrust is a management approach called *total quality management.*[1]

There seems to be no universally accepted definition for TQM—different firms understand and implement it somewhat differently. However, the International Organization for Standardization offers the following definition:[2]

A management approach to an organization centered on quality, based on the participation of all its members and aiming at long-term success through customer satisfaction, and benefits to the members of the organization and to society.

The key elements that appear to be common to most definitions are:

- The notion that quality is everybody's responsibility
- The commitment and active participation of all individuals in the organization
- Continuous improvement of quality
- Satisfaction of the customer

The concept is based on the notion that people *want* to contribute, and that management should create a climate in which this can happen easily. The idea is reminiscent of Douglas McGregor's Theory Y of the 1950s.[3]

The operating experience of two successful TQM firms provides some additional insight into the basic definition.[4]

1 The **A. T. Cross Company** gives every production employee the power to reject any imperfect part at any time during the production process.

---

[1]During this period, a stream of new management approaches has emerged: total quality management, total quality control, total quality leadership, continuous process improvement, continuous quality improvement, business process improvement, and business process reengineering. Each of these methods is intended to result in systematic improvement of an organization's performance through process change.

[2]As quoted by Greg Hutchins, *ISO 9000*, Oliver Wight-Publications, Inc., Essex Junction, Vt., 1993, p. 4.

[3]An interesting exploration of the development of TQM is found in John Bessant, Paul Levy, Bob Sang, and Richard Lamming, "Managing Successful Total Quality Relationships in the Supply Chain," *European Journal of Purchasing and Supply Management*, March 1994, pp. 7–17.

[4]These two experiences are synthesized from discussions in James F. Cali, *TQM for Purchasing Management*, McGraw-Hill Inc., New York, 1993, pp. 29–31.

When the product reaches the customer, it is protected by the firm's lifetime mechanical guarantee.

2 The **ITT Defense** firm's TQM effort focuses on meeting the needs of customers through employee participation in quality assurance. The employee-generated vision of ITT Defense follows:

WE ARE ITT DEFENSE

- We are the best in the world at what we do.
- We take pride in our technology, teamwork, and integrity.
- Our employee, customer, and supplier teams strive for continuous improvement through mutual trust and open communication.
- Our customers rely on us to provide the best, and we deliver.

The ultimate goal of ITT's TQM effort is that it will cease to have its own identity, as continuous improvement philosophies and principles become the normal business approach. However, a TQM steering committee composed of unit general managers is responsible for developing and maintaining the TQM *philosophy* throughout the company.

James F. Cali describes a typical TQM operational model in his TQM research study. An adaptation of this model is shown in Figure 21-1.[5]

So how does the purchasing and supply function fit into a TQM system? In most cases, it plays a critical role in making the entire program work effectively. Most quality experts now agree that a majority of the problems and related costs associated with a firm's product quality are caused by the quality level and the variability of incoming materials used in the manufacturing process.[6] This fact, coupled with the additional fact that the cost to find and repair a quality problem escalates tremendously as an item progresses through the chain of production activities, brings the issue into sharp focus. Consider the following cost data developed by General Electric.[7]

ESTIMATED COST TO FIND AND REPAIR A QUALITY PROBLEM

Incoming purchaser inspection	= $0.03
Fabrication inspection	= $0.30
Subassembly test	= $3.00
Final assembly test	= $30.00
Point of product service	= $300.00

---

[5]Ibid., p. 64.

[6]While a majority of a firm's quality problems commonly can be attributed to purchased materials and subassemblies, the root cause of most of these problems is in the design and resulting specifications of the items and their production processes. Purchasing professionals have two areas of responsibility in this design/quality issue: (1) They and invited suppliers must work cooperatively with the firm's design engineers to design appropriate quality characteristics into the materials to be purchased, and (2) this same group must ensure that suppliers design variability out of their production processes to the extent that is practical.

[7]Cali, op. cit., p. 36.

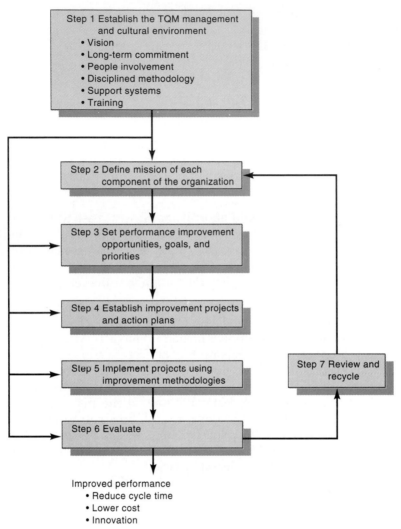

FIGURE 21-1
A generalized total quality management model.

It is very clear that quality consultant Joseph Juran is correct when he writes: "The assurance (for good quality) must come from placing the responsibility on the supplier to make the product right and supply proof that it is right."[8] Consequently, purchasing and supply management becomes the "point" player—the playmaker—in a firm's TQM program. Purchasing and supply management bears the major responsibility for managing supplier *quality.*

[8]As quoted by Paul Moffat in "Quality Assurance," *The Purchasing Handbook,* McGraw-Hill Inc., 1992, chap. 13, p. 421.

BASIC CONCEPTS OF QUALITY

As noted in Chapter 8, there are several different views of quality, depending on one's perspective. It is important to understand the significance of these different concepts before proceeding further. Basically, quality can be defined in three ways:

1 In absolute terms
2 Relative to a perceived need
3 As conformance with stated requirements

In *absolute terms*, quality is a function of excellence, intrinsic value, or grade, as determined over time by society generally or by designated bodies in specialized fields. Hence, most people consider gold to be a high-quality precious metal. In a more utilitarian sense, "prime" beef is generally considered to be among the highest-quality meats in the meat market. While few absolutes endure the test of the ages, for a given period of time in a given culture, most people hold absolute views about the quality of many things.

In business and industrial activities, generally quality is first defined in terms of *relationship to a need* or a function. In these cases the important thing is not the absolute quality of an item, but the suitability of the item in satisfying the particular need at hand. Thus, design engineers, users, and buyers attempt to develop a material specification in which the quality characteristics of the specified material match closely with the quality characteristics needed to satisfactorily fulfill the functional requirements of the job. Consequently, in the *development* of product or material specifications, quality is defined relative to the need.

Once the specifications have been finalized, the specific requirements have been set for those who subsequently work with the specifications. For these people, especially purchasing personnel and suppliers, quality is defined very simply—*conformance with the stated requirements*. A buyer's responsibility, and a supplier's job, is to deliver material whose quality conforms satisfactorily with specification requirements.

The last two definitions of quality, then, are the ones with which this chapter deals. As purchasing works with users and suppliers in the development of material specifications, it is concerned with quality relative to a functional need. In dealing with suppliers' output quality levels, purchasing is concerned with quality in the sense of its conformance to requirements.

As pointed out in several of the preceding chapters, in recent years top management's expectations for the purchasing function have changed markedly. In progressive firms, purchasing's role has shifted significantly from "buying materials" to "managing supply." And as noted in the preceding section, one of the most important elements in managing supply is managing the quality levels of the materials shipped by those suppliers. Once material specifications are firm, purchasing's major responsibility is to ensure that qualified suppliers are selected, and then that they perform consistently at the desired quality levels. The partnering concept discussed in the preceding chapter is one of the approaches that can be utilized to facilitate management of this key responsibility.

THE ROLE OF PURCHASING AND SUPPLY MANAGEMENT IN QUALITY MANAGEMENT

Many of us have seen the sign in many manufacturing shops: *Quality Must Be Built into the Product*. In line with our previous discussion, one of the most important responsibilities of a buyer is to ensure that suppliers have the *ability*, the *motivation*, and *adequate information* to produce materials and components of the specified quality in a cost-effective manner. In fulfilling this responsibility, a buyer can, to a great extent, control the quality and related costs of incoming material.

Generally speaking, four factors determine the long-run quality level of a firm's purchased materials:

1 Creation of complete and appropriate specifications for quality requirements
2 Selection of suppliers having the technical and production capabilities to do the desired quality/cost job
3 Development of a realistic understanding with suppliers of quality requirements, and creation of the motivation to perform accordingly
4 Monitoring of suppliers' quality/cost performance—and exercise of appropriate control

Purchasing and supply management is directly responsible for factors 2 and 3, and it should play a strong cooperative role in the first and fourth factors.

Material Specifications

A sound material specification represents a blend of four different considerations: (1) design requirements, (2) production factors, (3) commercial purchasing considerations, and (4) frequently marketing factors. When dealing with the commercial considerations, purchasing personnel should make the following investigations with respect to quality:

- Study the quality requirements.
- Ensure that quality requirements are completely and unambiguously stated in the specifications.
- Investigate their reasonableness, relative to cost.
- Ensure that specifications are written in a manner that permits competition among potential suppliers.
- Determine whether the desired quality can be built into the material by existing suppliers.
- Ensure the feasibility of the inspections and tests required to assure quality.

For some materials and components, such investigations are relatively simple. For others, they are extremely complex, involving highly technical considerations. Some firms, for example, include "reliability or quality engineers" on the purchasing staff to assist with analysis of the more complex problems. When technical quality problems arise, a reliability engineer and the buyer jointly review the specifications to determine the appropriateness of the quality requirements. Working in a coordinating capacity, they make their recommendations to the design engineer, directing to his or her attention the potential quality problems arising from commercial considerations.

As discussed previously, many firms now utilize a cross-functional product development team in the overall design process. This approach is ideal for integrating the views of purchasing, as well as the other appropriate functions, in the specification development process. In some cases it is desirable to involve appropriate designers or application engineers from the supplier's organization in the specifications development process before the specs are finalized. Early cooperative involvement of these individuals frequently provides technical and manufacturing input from the supplier's perspective that is useful in reducing costs or in avoiding subsequent processing and quality problems in the supplier's operation. This type of cooperative activity is becoming more common in progressive buying organizations today. Clearly, purchasing is responsible for planning and coordinating this type of supplier involvement.

Selection of Suppliers

Most firms can minimize their material quality problems simply by selecting competent and cooperative suppliers in the first place. The following paragraphs discuss briefly some of the methods used to achieve this objective.

Product Testing   One practical approach used in determining potential suppliers' quality capabilities is to test their products before purchasing them. The quality of most purchased materials can be determined by *engineering tests* or by *use tests*. Usually such tests can be conducted by the buying firm; when this is not practical, commercial testing agencies can be used.

The object of product testing is twofold: (1) to determine that a potential supplier's quality level is commensurate with the buyer's quality needs, and (2) where feasible, to compare quality levels of several different suppliers. This permits the development of a list of qualified suppliers which the buyer can compare on the basis of the quality/cost relationship.

Buyers frequently utilize their own operating departments for the performance of use tests. It is not uncommon, for example, for a buyer to test several brands of tires on his or her firm's vehicles during the course of regular operations. Although still feasible, use testing of most *production* parts and components is more difficult because tests often cannot be conducted until the buyer's finished product is placed in service. In many cases, though, the buyer's sales force is able to obtain feedback data on operating performance from customers. In such cases, various kinds of use tests can be conducted to compare the performance of different suppliers' components.

Regardless of the method used, purchasing usually needs the cooperation of other departments in setting up and conducting the tests. Consequently, the buyer typically functions as an organizer and an administrator in coordinating the efforts of others.

A word of caution is appropriate, however, for the practitioner unskilled in experimental testing. Test results for products being compared must be obtained through well-designed experiments that permit *valid* comparisons. For example, mileage data on two sets of tires, each taken from a different truck, are not comparable if the two trucks were operated under significantly different conditions. The variables in the testing situation must be controlled to the extent that the results are truly comparable. A "comparison of apples with oranges" is of little value in the decision-making process.

Unfortunately, in conducting use tests without the benefit of controlled laboratory conditions, it may be difficult to generate truly comparable test data. Consequently, experience and judgment play an important role in determining the extent to which test results are comparable and, hence, useful. At times, interpretation of test data may also require a basic knowledge of statistical inference. While many buyers have this background, it is essential to recognize when the help of an experienced statistician is required.

In firms that have testing laboratories for their engineering and research work, the purchasing department has an additional resource to support its quality management activity. Such laboratories can take much of the experimental and interpretive burden off purchasing's shoulders. In addition, they are usually equipped to conduct more precise and sophisticated tests with greater speed and ease than use testing allows. An example will illustrate the point. One of IBM's computer-manufacturing plants has an electronic testing laboratory used primarily for research and development work. The laboratory, however, also serves the purchasing department. Before new electronic components are purchased for assembly into IBM products, a sample of each new component is subjected to rigorous tests in this laboratory to determine whether its performance characteristics meet the company's quality specifications.

Firms without testing laboratories frequently use one of the many commercial testing laboratories located throughout the country. A directory of these laboratories, indicating their locations and their types of services, is published annually by the U.S. Department of Commerce.

Proposal Analysis   A second point at which purchasing can assess a potential supplier's quality capabilities is in the proposal analysis. Firms indicate in their proposals, either directly or indirectly, how they intend to comply with the quality requirements of the purchase. The buyer must be especially alert in detecting areas of misinterpretation or possible areas of overemphasis by the prospective supplier that could result in excessive costs. In purchases where quality requirements are critical, the trend today is to *require* potential suppliers to state *explicitly* how they plan to achieve the specified quality level with consistency.

Capability Survey   For those potential suppliers whose written proposals survive the buyer's analysis, the next step in evaluating quality capabilities is an on-site capability survey. Because of the time and expense involved, most companies conduct this survey only for their more important purchases and for government contracts requiring it. In inspecting a prospective supplier's facilities and records, and in talking with management and operating personnel, the buyer's investigating team attempts to ferret out answers to questions such as these:

1 What is the firm's basic policy with respect to product quality and quality control?
2 What is the general attitude of operators and supervisors toward quality? Does the firm utilize a TQM program, quality circles, some type of zero defects program, or other emerging quality programs that focus attention on the attitudes and responsibilities assumed by each individual for high-quality work?[9]
3 Does the prospective supplier use design of experiments to reduce process variation?
4 What is the prospective supplier's engineering/production experience and ability with respect to this specific type of work?
5 Is the production equipment capable of consistently producing the quality of work required?
6 Exactly how is the firm organized to control quality, and to what extent does the quality assurance organization receive management support? Does the quality staff report to operations management personnel or to general management personnel?
7 What specific quality control programs, techniques, and test equipment does the prospective supplier employ? Is statistical process control utilized effectively?

These questions make it clear that an effective survey usually cannot be conducted by a buyer alone; rather, the endeavor must be a *team effort*. Specialists from design and process engineering, quality assurance, and sometimes maintenance are needed to give professional interpretation to the facts the survey uncovers. The buyer's major responsibility in such an endeavor is

---

[9]For two unique discussions about the individual's responsibility for quality, see (1) William Ouchi, "The Q-C Circle," *Theory Z*, Addison-Wesley Publishing Co., Reading, Mass., 1981, pp. 261–268; and (2) Robert M. Smith, "Zero-Defects and You," *Management Services*, January–February 1966, pp. 35–38.

to organize and coordinate the efforts of these specialists and to make a composite evaluation of the potential supplier, considering the findings of all team members.

Motivation and Control—The Current View of Quality

To this point, the discussion has focused largely on ways in which a purchasing and supply department can contribute to quality assurance *prior* to the placement of business with a particular supplier. The next logical question is: What can be done to ensure suppliers' quality performance *after* they have been added to the firm's supplier base?

During the past decade and a half, U.S. industry's answer to this question has changed markedly. This change was precipitated to a great extent by the quality challenge posed by Japanese industry in world markets during the 1980s. Ironically, as a result of the influence of W. Edwards Deming, the noted American quality expert, Japanese manufacturers maintained extremely high standards for the precision and the performance of their products. They were able to do this primarily because of their ability to control part and component quality at a consistently high level. In working with the Japanese, Deming contended that the vast majority of defective or poor products produced in manufacturing operations are directly traceable to poor-quality input materials—parts and components. These, in turn, in many cases are the result of poorly coordinated design specifications.[10]

Defect Detection System   To control the quality of production materials entering a manufacturing or assembly operation, American industry historically has utilized a defect detection concept. That is, after a batch of items has been produced at one step in the process, the items are inspected to identify the ones that do not meet the design specification. Those that do not are reworked or scrapped, and the good items pass on to the next processing operation. Frequently, though not always, a similar inspection activity is also conducted after this operation, and so on through the entire manufacturing process until a finished product is produced. This concept is depicted graphically in Figure 21-2.[11]

Three basic problems are inherent in the defect detection type of operation. First, there tends to be some duplication of inspection activity, both within the supplier's manufacturing operation and between the buyer's and the supplier's operations. Second, a very large number of items are inspected. Third, *and most important*, defective items are found only after they are finished (or

---

[10]For an interesting article on this subject, see Richard G. Newman, "Insuring Quality—Purchasing's Role," *Journal of Purchasing and Materials Management,* Fall 1988, pp. 14–21.

[11]Figures 21-1 and 21-2 are developed from material in Gordon K. Constable, "Statistical Process Control and Purchasing," *Freedom of Choice,* National Association of Purchasing Management, Tempe, Ariz., 1987, p. 15.

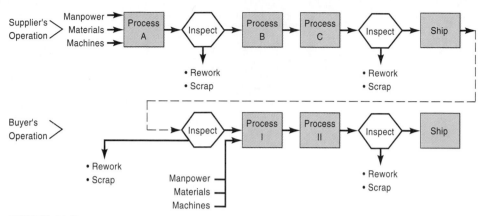

FIGURE 21-2
Defect detection concept.

semifinished)—after the mistakes have been made and after substantial processing costs have been incurred. Hence, the design of such a system makes it inefficient and expensive. And in the interest of cost control and the maintenance of production schedules, there is frequently a tendency to cut back on inspection and to reduce the standards, resulting in the acceptance of some off-spec items. The bottom line is that in many firms using this system, quality levels tend to be inconsistent and perhaps lower than originally planned.

Defect Prevention System To alleviate the problems inherent in most defect detection systems, Deming proposed the use of a *defect prevention* system. The idea is to detect the operating (process) problems that produce defective items before many defectives are produced. This approach monitors the output of a process as it occurs and identifies unacceptable process changes soon after they occur. When an unsatisfactory situation is identified, the process is stopped and the operating cause (tool wear, machine adjustment, operator error, and so on) is determined. Appropriate corrective action on the operating system is then taken to prevent the production of more defectives.

The specific technique used to detect such process changes is called *statistical process control (SPC)*. The theory and the operating details of SPC are discussed on pages 467–471. For the moment it is sufficient to say that in practice the technique is relatively easy to apply and it operates with a high degree of reliability. A defect prevention system utilizing SPC is shown in simplified graphic form in Figure 21-3.

Critique In summary, it is important that a buying organization develop some type of system that monitors a supplier's quality performance. Historically, defect detection systems have been widely used, but they are expensive and results frequently are not as effective as desired. While such systems will continue to be used in a number of applications, the trend has moved rapidly

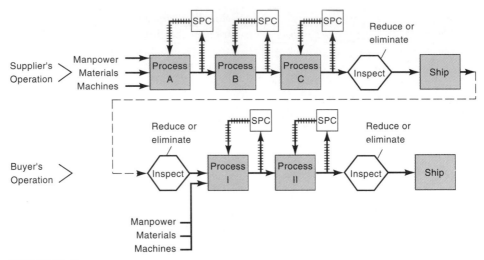

FIGURE 21-3
Defect prevention concept.

toward the use of an SPC type of defect prevention system. Philip Crosby summarizes the attitudes in American industry well in the following statement:[12]

> A prudent company makes certain that its products and services are delivered to the customer by a management system that does not condone rework, repair, waste, or nonconformance of any sort. These are expensive problems. They must not only be detected and resolved at the earliest moment, they must be prevented from occurring at all.

Once an SPC system is in place, benefits of improved quality control capability and reduced costs of quality flow to both the buyer and the supplier. Properly implemented, it should be a win-win situation that tends to improve buyer-seller cooperation and set the stage for a continuing relationship that is mutually beneficial.

Defect Avoidance   At this point in the discussion it is appropriate to call to the reader's attention the work of Mr. Kekki Bhote, who is known for his practical work with the design of experiments (DOE). Through DOE applications prior to the final stabilization of a production process, it is often possible to reduce process variation significantly, thus enhancing the uniformity of product quality. Additional discussion of Mr. Bhote's work is found in the Appendix at the end of this chapter.

[12]Philip B. Crosby, *Quality Is Free*, Mentor New American Library, Times Mirror, New York, 1979, p. 106.

Motivation   A *cooperatively* developed defect prevention system, including appropriate training of suppliers' personnel by the buying firm, creates a situation that should enhance a supplier's motivation to perform satisfactorily for the buyer. The anticipated prospect of follow-on business in a longer-term continuing relationship normally provides a significant incentive for the supplier to perform well in the quality area.

Appropriate public recognition of exceptional supplier quality performance is another technique that often is used to provide visibility for a supplier who has earned it, as well as a psychological stimulus to continue the good work. The Ford Motor Company's Q1 Preferred Quality Award program is a good illustration of this technique. It is discussed in more detail on p. 476.

The broader issue of motivating suppliers is discussed extensively in the preceding chapter, which deals with the complete realm of buyer-supplier relationships. Motivation in the quality area is an integral part of that total effort.

QUALITY MANAGEMENT CONCEPTS

All buyers should have at least a rudimentary understanding of quality systems, process capability analysis, and statistical process control concepts. As pointed out in the preceding section, a progressive firm views its quality system and the supplier's quality system as two parts of a single integrated system. The buyer is the middle person in this operation. He or she first must be able to cooperate with in-house quality people intelligently in designing and making operating decisions about the firm's quality system. Next, because the buyer is the key communication link with suppliers, he or she must be able to deal with them effectively on a wide variety of quality issues. Recurring matters include things such as additional SPC training requirements for supplier personnel; interpretation of SPC control charts for given orders; the costs associated with use of various sampling inspection plans, and who should bear them; and decisions about the disposition of unsatisfactory product and related cost responsibilities, to name just a few.

For these reasons, this section deals with fundamental quality assurance concepts as they relate to the things a good buyer should know.

Process Capability Analysis

No operations activity can produce identical results time after time. This is true even for machine-based production processes. Every process possesses some natural variability due to such things as machine part clearances, bearing wear, lubrication, variations in operator technique, and so on. In the language of statisticians, these are "chance" or "common" causes that produce *random variations* in the output. Over time, this natural variability in the output of a process will produce a distribution of outputs around the mean quality level. In many cases this distribution approximates the normal bell-shaped curve. The difference between the two extremes of the curve, the high and low values, is defined as the *natural tolerance range* of the process. As long as the process is properly adjusted and is not affected by any outside nonrandom forces—as long as the process is "in control"—the distribution it produces is predictable, as shown in Figure 21-4.

If a buyer's desired range of quality for a given purchased part is compatible with the natural tolerance range of a potential supplier's production process, the supplier should have little difficulty in providing the buyer with parts that meet specifications. On the other hand, when the buyer's required quality range is narrower than the natural capability range of the process, the supplier is bound to produce some unacceptable parts.

Alert buyers recognize the direct economic relationship between their specified quality requirements and the producer's ability to perform consistently at the specified level. In the case of a nonstandard item, the capable buyer, before selecting a supplier, must determine (1) whether the potential supplier in fact knows what the natural capability range for its production process is; (2) if so, whether the buyer's *desired* range of quality is compatible with the supplier's natural capability range; and (3) if so, how the supplier plans to monitor the process to ensure that it stays in control so that it will consistently produce satisfactory output. The following examples should clarify this concept.

In Figure 21-5a, assume that a buyer wants to purchase 100,000 metal shafts 1 inch in diameter, with a tolerance of ±0.005 inch. Assume further that the supplier has studied its process, stabilized it, and knows its natural capability for this type of job to be 1 inch ± 0.004. Examining Figure 21-5a, the buyer sees that as long as the supplier's process operates normally and remains centered on 1.0 inch, every piece produced will fall within his or her acceptable range of quality. In this example, then, if the supplier is able to keep the process in control, this situation appears to represent a sound purchase for the buyer from a quality point of view.

FIGURE 21-4
The output distribution of a process that is "in control."

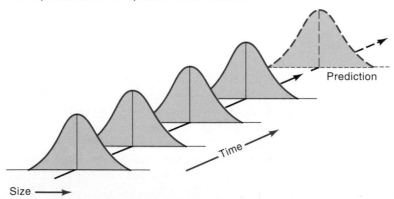

Prediction

Time

Size ⟶

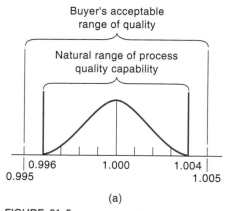
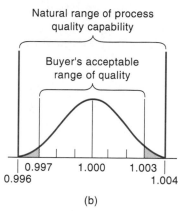

FIGURE 21-5
An illustrative comparison of quality requirements with process capability. (Process frequency distribution curves for shafts are shown.)

Assume now that the buyer wants to purchase 100,000 shafts 1 inch in diameter, with a tolerance of ±0.003 inch. Examination of Figure 21-5b reveals that, dealing with the same supplier, under normal operating conditions the production process cannot entirely satisfy the buyer's requirement. Some shafts will be produced with diameters less than 0.997 inch and some with diameters larger than 1.003 inches. It is important for the buyer to understand this type of situation. Unusable shafts, whether reworked or scrapped, must be paid for. In the long run, it will be the buyer who pays. Assuming that the buyer's requirements cannot be compromised, he or she is faced with two alternatives:

1 Negotiate with the supplier to determine whether the natural range of process capability can be narrowed economically to a point nearer the buyer's requirements.
2 Seek another supplier whose process can meet the requirements more economically.

Process Capability Index   Another way of expressing a process's capability relative to a buyer's specific design requirement is by means of a *process capability index* (Cp). This index is defined as

$$Cp = \frac{\text{buyer's absolute design tolerance}}{\text{natural capability range of the process}^{13}}$$

[13]In practice, the natural capability range of the process frequently is *estimated* by taking the mean output quality value ±3 standard deviations of the output values. In the case of normally distributed output values, this means that the process capability range includes 99.7 percent of the expected population values. In other words, there are 3 chances in 1,000 that the process output will fall outside the estimated process capability range.

Some firms with high precision requirements estimate the natural capability range of a process by using the mean output value ±4, ±5, or ±6 standard deviations. In the latter case, there is approximately 1 chance in a million that the process output will fall outside the estimated process capability range.

A *Cp* value of 1 indicates that the capability range of the process matches *exactly* the quality range required by the buyer. From a practical point of view, this is a very marginal fit for the buyer. A value of more than 1 reveals excess process quality capability, while a value of less than 1 indicates insufficient process capability.

Consider the examples in Figure 21-5.

$$Cp \text{ (a)} = \frac{1.005 - 0.995}{1.004 - 0.996} = \frac{0.01}{0.008} = 1.25$$

$$Cp \text{ (b)} = \frac{1.003 - 0.997}{1.004 - 0.996} = \frac{0.006}{0.008} = 0.75$$

In case (a), the $Cp = 1.25$, indicating that the quality capability of the process, if it stays centered, exceeds the buyer's requirement. In case (b), the $Cp = 0.75$, showing clearly that the process is not capable of satisfying the buyer's quality requirement. In the vernacular, for case (a) the process is "capable"; for case (b) the process is "incapable."

The preceding discussion makes one important assumption—that the manufacturer's process average can be adjusted to line up with the center point (the target value) of the buyer's specification (as is the case in Figure 21-5). In some operating situations this is not always possible. Suppose, in the situation discussed in Figure 21-5a, that after a great deal of experimentation the best process average the supplier was able to achieve was 0.999 inch. This condition is depicted in Figure 21-6.

One can see by inspection of the sketch that there is adequate excess quality capability at the upper end of the scale (1.005–1.003), but at the lower end there is no excess (0.995–0.995). Any movement of the process distribution to the left will produce out-of-spec shafts.

So we see that one additional factor is important in making a process capability analysis—the location of the process average relative to the buyer's tar-

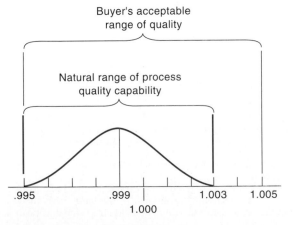

Buyer's acceptable
range of quality

Natural range of process
quality capability

.995   .999   1.003   1.005
          1.000

FIGURE 21-6
An illustrative comparison of quality requirements with process capability when the process mean is not centered.

get specification value. That means that the previously calculated capability index (*Cp*) must be adjusted for the off-center location of the process average. The adjusted *Cp* is called the *process capability/location index (Cpk)*. It can be calculated as follows:

$$Cpk = Cp(1 - k) \qquad \text{where } k = \frac{\text{buyer's target value} - \text{process mean}}{\text{buyer's absolute design tolerance} \div 2}$$

For the situation in Figure 21-6, the location index is

$$k = \frac{1.000 - 0.999}{(1.005 - 0.995)/2} = \frac{0.001}{0.005} = 0.2$$
$$Cpk = 1.25(1 - 0.2) = 1.25 \times 0.8 = 1.0$$

The *Cpk* value is interpreted just like the *Cp* value; less than 1 indicates an incapable process, and a value greater than 1 indicates a capable process. In this case the fit is marginal because of the absence of any leeway on the lower end of the distribution.

Statistical Process Control (SPC)

The preceding discussion about the natural process capability range was based on the premise that the supplier could keep the process operating in a stable manner—that is, "in control."

At this point in the discussion, it is necessary to point out that in addition to the random variations which occur naturally in any process, during the course of operation some *nonrandom* variations caused by external factors also occur. At times a machine goes out of adjustment, cutting tools become dull, the hardness or workability of the material varies, human errors become excessive, and so on. When these things happen, they usually take the process "out of control." What really happens is that *the quality capability of the process changes because of these unplanned events.* The process output distribution changes. It may spread out, increasing the range; it may shift up or down, altering the mean and the extreme values; or a combination of these things may occur. The end result is that the characteristics of the distribution no longer can be predicted—statistically, *the process is out of control.*

As noted earlier in the chapter, the statistical process control technique has the ability to detect these process shifts due to outside forces, or assignable causes, as they occur. When such changes are detected, the process is stopped and an investigation is initiated to find the cause of the problem. An operator who is familiar with the process and the equipment typically can locate the problem fairly quickly. This technique thus enables the operator to detect the problem, make necessary corrections, and continue operation, with the production of few, if any, defective products.

So after a buyer locates a potential supplier whose process capability matches his or her needs, the final step in the process is to persuade the supplier to use an SPC system that will keep the process in control and ensure the consistency of the process's output quality.

The following paragraphs discuss the basics of SPC theory and application.

Control Charts   Several different types of control charts are used for different kinds of applications. The most common, however, are the $\overline{X}$ and R control charts for variables. These typically are applied in situations where the quality variable to be controlled is a dimension, a weight, or another measurable characteristic. Operationally, the two charts are used together. The $\overline{X}$ chart monitors the absolute value, or the location, of the process average; and the R chart monitors the spread (range) of the output distribution, that is, the piece-to-piece variability.

Figure 21-7 illustrates an $\overline{X}$ and an R chart in simplified form. Before the charts are constructed for operating use, *the process must be studied carefully to determine that it is, in fact, stable*—that it is in statistical control. This is usually done by quality assurance and maintenance specialists and often is a time-consuming experimental task. Once the process has been stabilized—that is, its operation is influenced only by natural, random variations—its natural capability range can be determined and process control limits can be calculated.

At this point, the operating procedures are established. Usually the operator will inspect a small sample of output units every 15 minutes or so. Sample size typically runs between 3 and 5 units. The idea is to sample sequentially produced units in a manner that tends to minimize the quality variation within a given sample subgroup, and to maximize variation between the periodic sample subgroups.

The measurements are recorded as they are taken in the upper portion of the table shown below the R chart. (For illustrative purposes, hypothetical shaft dimension data from the example in Figure 21-5 are included in the first three subgroup columns.) The measurements for the *subgroup sample* are then summed and the average, $\overline{X}$, is computed. The range for the subgroup is also determined and entered in the table. After 20 to 25 subgroups have been inspected, enough data are available to provide good estimates of the process average and spread. At this point, an average of the subgroup $\overline{X}$ values is computed ($\overline{\overline{X}}$), and an average of the subgroup R values is computed ($\overline{R}$). The $\overline{X}$ value represents the mean value of the average shaft diameter sizes determined in each subgroup; *this is the value used as the process average on the $\overline{X}$ chart.* The $\overline{R}$ value represents the mean value of the range of the shaft diameter sizes found in each subgroup; *this is the value used as the average range on the R chart.*

In most applications, $\overline{X}$ *control chart limits are set at* $\overline{\overline{X}} \pm 3$ standard deviations of the $\overline{X}$ values (3 sigma limits). Parenthetically, the reader should note that the frequency distributions used in constructing control charts are distributions of averages, not distributions of the individually measured values produced by the process. This fact ensures the existence of a normal distribution

$\bar{X}$ Chart

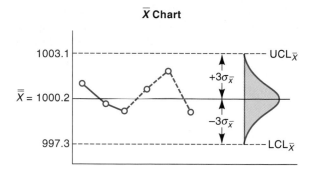

R Chart

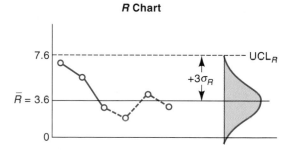

Subgroup No.		1	2	3						20
Time		8:00	8:15	8:30						
Individual sample measurements in 0.001"	1	999	997	998						
	2	997	1003	1000						
	3	1002	1003	1001						
	4	1004	998	999						
	5	1003	998	998						
Sum		5005	5000	4996						
$\bar{X}$ (average)		1001	1000	999.2						
R (range)		7	6	3						

$\Sigma \bar{X}_{20 \text{ subgps.}} = 20{,}004$

$\bar{\bar{X}} = \dfrac{20{,}004}{20} = 1000.2$

$\Sigma R_{20 \text{ subgps.}} = 72$

$\bar{R} = \dfrac{72}{20} = 3.6$

FIGURE 21-7
An illustration of $\bar{X}$ and R charts in simplified form.

of control chart values when the process is in control.[14] Thus, the 6 sigma range (±3 sigma limits) of the chart encompasses 99.7 percent of the $\bar{X}$ values that will result from the process operation as long as only natural random process variations are occurring.

The 3 sigma control chart limits can be determined by calculating the standard deviation of the $\bar{X}$ values, multiplying by 3, and subtracting and adding to $\bar{\bar{X}}$. In practice, however, this calculation has been simplified by the construction of a

[14]The statistical central limit theorem states that the *means of small samples* tend to be normally distributed, regardless of the type of distribution from which the individual sample values are taken.

table of constant factors (for various sample sizes) that can be applied to $\bar{R}$ (and $\bar{\bar{X}}$) to obtain the control limit values directly. This can be done quickly and easily.

The same rationale and procedure apply to the construction of R chart control limits. In this case, however, it should be noted that only the upper control limit is of practical significance in operation.

After the control charts are constructed, *as the operation continues data are plotted and the charts are interpreted.* As shown in Figure 21-7, the operator plots both the $\bar{X}$ value and the R value on their respective charts following his or her inspection and computations for each subgroup sample.

In the majority of cases, interpretation of the charts is a relatively simple matter. Any points falling outside the control limits usually indicate the existence of nonrandom variation. (If the process were actually in control, this would happen only 3 times in every 1,000 subgroup inspections.) The appearance of other nonrandom patterns may also be observed. For example, an unusually large number of points in sequence on the same side of the average line may indicate a shift in the process average or an expansion of the spread. As a rule of thumb, a run of seven points usually indicates an out-of-control situation. Clear-cut trends of points in one direction may indicate a tool wear or adjustment problem. As noted previously, when the operator suspects an out-of-control situation, he or she stops the process and investigates the potential problem.

The Personal "Buy-In" Statistical process control is not a new concept. Its origins date back to the 1920s when Walter Shewhart, of Bell Laboratories, conceived the idea and first began to experiment with the use of control charts. Subsequently, a significant number of manufacturing firms used the SPC concept during the 1940s and the 1950s. For various reasons, interest in the concept waned and it was not until Deming's work in the late 1970s that it was dusted off, refined, and resold to American industry.

There is one major difference, however, between the way SPC is practiced today and the way it was practiced in the "old days." The difference is personal commitment by the operator using the technique in his or her operation.

In the early days all quality control activities, including SPC, were handled by QC specialists. The quality engineer did the inspection, charting, and so forth—and the operator did the production work. There was little integration of the two activities, and often an adversarial climate developed. Today, the focus is on operator involvement. The operator does his or her own inspecting, recording, and charting. Then the operator interprets the charts and decides what to do. The operator is responsible for the quality of his or her own production. The idea is to give the operator the tools to do the complete job, including quality control, and then stimulate the development of his or her pride in the output of the job.

Training By now, the importance of training should be obvious. Clearly, all operations people who are going to utilize SPC must be thoroughly trained. One who doesn't understand the concept well is not going to use it enthusiastically or properly. Similarly, supervisory personnel need to understand it equally as well as the operators. Staff support personnel, including buyers, who interface with the SPC function need a different kind of understanding. They need to understand the rudiments of the concept and the applications aspects as they are utilized in their jobs.

Finally, general management personnel must understand not only how SPC works, along with its benefits, problems, and costs to the organization; management must lead the charge. It is management's responsibility to inculcate the defect prevention philosophy into the business life of the organization.

The last point to be made is this: These efforts must be conducted not only in the buyer's organization, but in the supplier's organization as well. And generally it is the buyer's responsibility to see that the supplier's programs are properly designed, conducted, and funded.

Application Limitations   A word should be said about the practical limitations of SPC usage. Although the defect prevention concept is now widely accepted, statistical process control is not a panacea for all quality problems. It works better in some situations than others. It is ideally suited for application in continuous or semicontinuous manufacturing operations. It also works well in some standardized office and clerical operations. From a process point of view, the key is standardized repetitive operations. Consequently, SPC is not well suited to some types of job shop operations, particularly low-volume jobs and those that are not completely standardized. The process itself has to be capable of attaining a stabilized state and then continuing in operation long enough to justify the cost of implementing the SPC system.

Like many other managerial control techniques, the use of SPC is sometimes limited by cost considerations. In some cases, on-line measurement may be very difficult to do and, hence, fairly costly. In other cases involving low-value products, the cost of on-line inspection and charting may exceed the benefits it produces. The decision to use SPC in a given case should be made on the basis of the expected benefits weighed against the cost to obtain the benefits.

Supplier Certification

The concept of supplier certification has been practiced by a number of progressive firms for years. However, the increased emphasis on quality and the renewed interest in SPC in recent years have sharpened the focus on the real values of a certification program. The concept of supplier certification fits very logically with supplier quality and partnering arrangements.

The certification concept simply recognizes the fact that a supplier's quality system and a buyer's quality system are two parts of a larger quality system, and that through integration of the two the total costs associated with quality can be reduced. The objective, in addition to maintaining desired quality levels, is to reduce duplicate efforts in inspection and related QC activities. Certification agreements take many forms, ranging from a simple supplier's guarantee of quality to a formally negotiated document that specifies the responsibilities of both parties for specifications, process design inspection procedures, SPC applications and training, reporting and correction procedures, and so forth.

Although certification programs vary widely from firm to firm, the general approach to certification involves three steps:

1 Qualification
2 Education
3 The certification performance process

Qualification   Because of the mutual trust and dependence that exists in a certification relationship, a supplier is not considered for certification until the buying organization has had a fairly lengthy positive experience with the firm. In addition to quality and reliability performance, the buyer again verifies the broader supplier characteristics that are important to the relationship—management philosophy, financial stability, R&D capability, shop organization and management, manufacturing support capabilities, including purchasing, etc.

The technical qualification requirements for certification typically are rigorous. They start with product and process design, tightened process capability studies, and a stringent quality capability survey to ensure mutual agreement on the quality system the supplier will employ. Applications for potential design of experiments and statistical process control are identified and the procedures are detailed. At this point in the process, the buyer's quality personnel work with their counterparts in the supplier's organization to fine-tune the system and develop the procedures to be used in final inspection.

Education   Two types of supplier education typically are required: (1) The first deals with the buying organization's structure, people, mode of operation, and the resulting expectations for a certified supplier's performance; (2) the second focuses on specific quality concepts and techniques that may be new to the supplier, but that are needed for successful operation—things such as various applications of SPC, unique inspection measurement techniques, the philosophy of TQM, and so forth.

The extent to which education is required obviously varies from supplier to supplier. The important point, however, is that the buying firm must assume responsibility for ensuring that the education function is accomplished. In some cases, this education must continue up the supply chain to the supplier's suppliers.

The Certification Performance Process   To use an old operations expression, this is where "the rubber meets the road." The supplier must now demonstrate that it can meet the buyer's requirements for certification.

After the manufacturing and assembly processes are stabilized and the quality assurance system is in place, the supplier's test period is begun. Initially the supplier's output is subjected to 100 percent inspection, often by both parties. This process facilitates the identification and correction of unanticipated problems. When the predetermined quality level has been maintained for a specified period of time, full inspection is replaced by sampling inspection of declining severity as quality levels are maintained. At some point in the process, the supplier provides key SPC control charts to the buyer for continued analysis. And periodically the buyer's quality expert visits the supplier's plant to ensure that control tests are being conducted appropriately. This process is continued for a period of perhaps six months to several years, depending on the specifics of a given operation, until the predetermined quality performance requirements have been fulfilled.

Once a supplier has gained certification, the buyer's goal is to do very little, if any, inspection of incoming materials. When possible, material is delivered directly to the point of use after the required receiving activities. Periodically, however, the buying organization checks supplier performance in one of several ways: (1) by reviewing the supplier's process control charts for critical manufacturing operations, (2) by using a minimal sampling inspection program, (3) by reviewing test reports from the buyer's laboratories, and (4) by periodic visits to the supplier's plant.

One authoritative research study found that today 35 to 55 percent of U.S. medium- and high-tech firms use certification programs for key suppliers.[15] Firms that have used certification programs generally have experienced favorable results. Inspection costs typically are reduced, while quality levels usually remain high. Most suppliers take pride in being included on a customer's certification list. They are also aware that good performance places them in a favored position to receive additional business.

Inspection and Quality Control

Even with the increasing use of SPC systems today, most firms maintain a traditional inspection department. Not all of a firm's suppliers use SPC for all items, for a variety of reasons, so traditional incoming inspection capability is still necessary. In addition, some selected operations in both the buyer's and the supplier's plants may still require either 100 percent or sampling inspection. This is particularly true in some cases following certain types of assembly or final assembly operations. In any case, to some extent inspection activities are still part of a buyer's world—and for this reason, the topic is discussed briefly in the next few paragraphs.

Receiving and Inspection Procedure   If a shipment is coming from a certified or a JIT supplier, it may go directly to the point of use, bypassing the traditional receiving and inspection operations. In a majority of cases, however, when a purchase order is issued, the receiving and inspection departments both receive copies of the order, which specifies the inspection the material is to receive. When a shipment arrives, receiving personnel check the

---

[15]Joseph R. Carter and Ram Narasimhan, *Purchasing and Materials Management's Role in Total Quality Management and Customer Satisfaction*, Center for Advanced Purchasing Studies, Tempe, Ariz., 1993, p. 23.

material against the supplier's packing slip and against the purchase order to ensure that the firm has actually received the material ordered. This is the basis for subsequent invoice/payment approvals. The receiving clerk then inspects the material in a nontechnical manner (looking for shipping damage and so on) to determine its general condition. Finally, a receiving report is prepared on which the results of the investigation are noted. In some cases, no further inspection is required. In the case of more complex materials, a copy of the receiving report is forwarded to the inspection department, advising it that material on a given order has been placed in the "pending inspection" area and is ready for technical inspection.

The inspection department performs the specified technical inspection on a sample or on the entire lot, as appropriate, and prepares an inspection report indicating the results of the inspection. If the material fails to meet specifications, a more detailed report is usually completed describing the reasons for rejection. Rejected material, in some cases, is clearly useless to the buying firm, and the purchasing department immediately arranges with the supplier for its disposition. In other situations, the most desirable course of action is less clear-cut. The purchaser often has three alternative courses of action:

1 Return the material to the supplier.
2 Keep some of the more acceptable material and return the rest.
3 Keep all the material and rework it to the point where it is acceptable. (From a strategic point of view, this is not a good alternative. It says to the supplier that it is permissible to ship off-spec material, and it can be interpreted as an invitation to do it again.)

Cases involving rework are usually sent to a materials review board for study and decision. A typical board is composed primarily of personnel from production, production control, quality, and purchasing. After the board reaches its decision, the appropriate papers are sent to the buyer, who concludes final cost negotiations with the supplier.

Technical Inspection   Before a contract or a purchase order is issued, quality control personnel, in conjunction with engineering and purchasing, should decide what type of inspection the incoming material will require to ensure that it meets specification requirements. If the supplier is certified, perhaps no inspection will be required. If the supplier is using SPC in the item's production, it may be sufficient simply to review the supplier's control charts for selected processing operations to determine if further inspection is required. In other cases sampling inspection may be desirable,[16] and in still other situations

---

[16]Industry uses a wide variety of statistical sampling plans. Two of the more commonly used sources are Dodge and Romig, *Sampling Inspection Tables—Single and Double Sampling,* John Wiley & Sons, Inc., New York; and Freeman, Friedman, Mosteller, and Wallis, *Sampling Inspection,* McGraw-Hill Publishing Company, New York. The Dodge and Romig tables are designed specifically to minimize total sampling. *Sampling Inspection,* by Freeman et al., contains plans which are particularly useful in inspecting material coming from statistically controlled production processes. These plans tend to minimize the "consumer's risk" of accepting off-spec material.

100 percent inspection may be required.[17] In all cases, a technical inspection plan should be prepared by quality personnel—and key information from this document should be communicated to the supplier in the purchase order or a related contractual document. In this way, appropriate people in both organizations are fully aware of the procedures to be followed and can work together toward that end.

HOW INDUSTRY DOES IT

The following paragraphs provide some insight into the quality management activities found in several progressive U.S. firms. The purpose of this section simply is to highlight and summarize key approaches and experiences as they relate to the concepts discussed earlier in the chapter.

Xerox Corporation[18]

Xerox was the 1985 winner of *Purchasing Magazine*'s Professional Excellence in Purchasing award. Xerox utilizes a materials management form of organization in which three geographically based line purchasing units and four specialized staff support units all report to the corporate manager of materials management. One of the four staff units is Materials Quality Assurance. This group works directly with buyers and suppliers to ensure the continued flow of specified quality materials into Xerox plants. Key elements of the operation are discussed below.

1 In all cases where it is practical, the firm *requires its major part and component suppliers to utilize statistical process control* in their manufacturing operations. Xerox quality assurance (QA) staff people assume the responsibility and the cost for training suppliers in the use of SPC and related inspection and QC techniques.
2 To provide continuing follow-up support, *a Xerox QA staffer is assigned to work with each major supplier* (and the appropriate buyer) in helping resolve quality problems. As a rule this QA specialist visits his or her assigned suppliers frequently—from once a week to once a month, depending on the need.
3 Xerox is committed to *a strong supplier certification program.* Approximately 50 percent of the materials purchased come from suppliers that have been certified. In a majority of these cases, materials are not subjected to incoming technical inspection.

    Early in the certification process a number of "concurrence sessions" are held with the supplier. Key factors such as material specifications,

---

[17]In many types of inspection activities involving human operation or judgment, experience indicates that 100 percent inspection may detect only 80 to 95 percent of the defects present. Consequently, when quality is extremely critical, a second inspection operation may be required.

[18] Somerby Dowst, *Purchasing Magazine Medal of Professional Excellence,* Cahners Publishing Co., June 27, 1985.

tolerances, processing operations, SPC applications, and inspection are explored thoroughly. Both parties must come to an acceptable "concurrence" before the certification process continues.

4 Based on continuing Xerox manufacturing experience, *each supplier receives a monthly report on its quality,* taken from a consolidated report covering Xerox's entire supplier base.

It is clear that this organization is committed to high-quality procurement on a worldwide basis. Its approach, at least philosophically, is one of buyer-supplier cooperation and partnership.

Ford Motor Company[19]

"The quality revolution at Ford falls squarely under the heading of supplier relations." Beginning in the early 1980s, communications with suppliers carried the theme of Ford's new operating philosophy, which, in a nutshell, was "to pursue never-ending improvement in the quality and productivity of products and services throughout the company, its supply base, and its dealer organizations."[20] The key elements of the Ford program are noted below.

1 The first step in the program was to *reduce the number of suppliers* purchasing had to deal with. The base has been reduced over 25 percent since the program started. Presently, approximately 90 percent of Ford's expenditures for production parts for North American operations are concentrated with about 300 suppliers. In addition, Ford relies on *longer-term single-sourcing agreements* in dealing with most of these suppliers.

2 Part of *the longer-term relationship with these suppliers involves them more closely and earlier* in new product planning, design, specifications, and production.

3 Strong *emphasis is placed on supplier use of SPC systems.* Initially Ford *encouraged* suppliers to use SPC, and the company included SPC as a factor in its overall supplier performance evaluation program. Less than two years later, Ford suppliers were *required* to utilize SPC systems in their production operations.

In implementing this requirement, Ford assumed responsibility for training suppliers' personnel. Today it has conducted or cosponsored over 250 SPC seminars that have trained nearly 10,000 individuals from suppliers' organizations.

4 As noted earlier, another important element of Ford's overall quality program is its Q1 *Preferred Quality Award Program for suppliers.* Suppliers that meet the stringent Q1 requirements are rewarded with public visibility in

[19]James A. Lorincz, "Job-One Is Being Done with Statistical Process Control," *Purchasing World,* September 1985, pp. 34–38.
[20]Ibid., p. 34.

national news publications. Figure 21-8 is a reproduction of a full-page presentation that appeared in a recent issue of the *Wall Street Journal*. Such suppliers also receive preferential treatment in new part development programs and a preferred position in source selection.

Ford's purchasing function obviously plays an important role in the total corporate quality management effort.

Tennant Company[21]

The Tennant Company's philosophy is that a supplier is responsible for the quality of material delivered to Tennant, and that purchasing is responsible for the supplier's performance. The quality management program of the firm has achieved remarkable results in just a few short years. Major elements and results of the program are summarized below.

1 The process begins with *a rigorous materials and process qualification program* that includes the following activities.
  a All new engineering drawings are reviewed by a "new product development team" which includes both purchasing and quality engineering. Purchasing is responsible for the early involvement of suppliers at this point, if appropriate.
  b Next, prototype and sample parts undergo a thorough inspection by QC personnel.
  c Thorough reliability testing of all new items is then conducted by engineering.
  d If all results are positive at this point, the potential supplier's processes are subjected to a thorough process capability analysis.
2 After a supplier has come on line, *all shipments pass through receiving inspection and often through the traditional technical inspection* activities, depending on the supplier's past performance.
3 If quality problems develop, a *"supplier corrective action team" is formed* to monitor the supplier's performance and to work with appropriate individuals in the supplier's firm to identify and correct the problems. Representatives from purchasing, quality engineering, and product engineering make up the team.
4 More recently, Tennant has *initiated an SPC program*, both in-house and in its suppliers' operations. Tennant assumes the responsibility for training its suppliers in SPC techniques.

The results of Tennant's total quality program have been monitored closely. They are indeed gratifying. Tennant has been able to increase its quality levels

---

[21]*Tennant Company Supplier Requirements and Information Manual,* Tennant Company, Minneapolis, Minn., August 1984; "Tennant Company—Quality in Purchasing," *Purchasing World,* June 1988, p. 36.

THANKS FOR THE QUALITY.

Active Tool & Manufacturing Co.
- Active Industries, Inc.
  Elkton, MI
- Sebewaing Industries Division
  Sebewaing, MI

Ada Metal Products
- C.T. Charlton Group
  Lincolnwood, IL

Aisan Industry Co., Ltd.
- Anjo Plant
  Anjo, Aichi, Japan

Allied-Signal, Inc.
- Bendix Electronics
  Controls Products
  Chatham, ONT., CN

Almco Steel Products Corporation
  Bluffton, IN

BASF AG/Sterling Group
- BASF Corp./Sterling Chemicals, Inc.
  Texas City, TX

The Budd Company
- Wheel & Brake Division
  Ashland, OH

Cirtek Corporation
  Flint, MI

Colonial Rubber Works
  Dyersburg, TN

Color Custom, Inc.
  Warren, MI

Colt Industries, Inc.
- Stemco Truck Products Division
  Longview, TX

Crescive Die & Tool, Inc.
  Saline, MI

Dana Corporation
- Weatherhead Division
  Columbia City, IN

Dexter Corporation
- Dexter Plastics Division
  Grand Prairie, TX

Dow Chemical Company
- Texas Division
  LaPorte Plant
  LaPorte, TX

Edgewood Tool & Mfg. Co.
- Ann Arbor Assembly Corporation
  Ypsilanti, MI

Exxon Corporation
- Exxon Chemical Company
  Baton Rouge, LA

Fawn Plastics, Inc.
  Middlesex, NC

Federal-Mogul Corporation
- Switches, Inc.
  Juarez, MX

Gilreath Enterprises
- Gilreath Mfg., Inc.
  Michigan Division
  Howell, MI

Goetze Corporation of America
- Muskegon Piston Ring Company
  Muskegon, MI

Handy & Harman
- Handy & Harman Automotive Group, Inc.
  Dover Division
  Dover, OH

Hatch Stamping Company
  Chelsea, MI

The Hill and Griffith Co.
  Cincinnati, OH

ITT Corporation/ITT Automotive
- ITT Milrod Metal Products
  Mississauga, ONT., CN

Jason, Incorporated
- Janesville Products
  Norwalk, OH

The Lobdell-Emery Manufacturing Co.
  Alma, MI
  Winchester, IN
- Greencastle Manufacturing Co.
  Greencastle, IN

Magna International, Inc.
- Decoma International
  Rollstamp
  Richmond Hill, ONT., CN
  Vernomatic
  Downsview, ONT., CN

NOK Corporation
- Fukushima Plant
  Fukushima, Japan

Phillips Plastics Corp.
  Phillips, WI
  Medford, WI

Pullman Industries, Inc.
  Pullman, MI

SGS-THOMSON
- Microelectronics, Inc.
  Brianza, Italy

Siemens Corporation
  Regensburg, W. Germany

Sparton Corporation
- Kent Products Division
  White Cloud, MI

Special Machine & Engineering, Inc.
- Grant-Durban, Inc.
  Belleville, MI

Thiem Corporation
- Foundry Materials Division
  Oak Creek, WI

Trinova Corporation
- KMC Division
  Sterling Engineered Products
  Henderson, KY

Walbro Precision Plastics
  Bad Axe, MI

Worthington Industries, Inc.
- Hamilton Plastics
  Mason, OH

The **Q1** Preferred Quality Award is a special tribute to suppliers who are helping us produce the highest quality American cars and trucks. This is based on an average of wner-reported problems in a series of surveys of '81, '82, '83, '84, '85, '86 and '87 models designed and built in North America.

The companies whose names appear on this page join a select group of **Q1** preferred quality suppliers. To the new recipients, we'd like to say thanks for your time, energy and commitment to make Quality Job 1.

Quality is Job 1.

Ford • Lincoln • Mercury • Ford Trucks

FIGURE 21-8
One approach to recognizing preferred quality suppliers.

significantly, and at the same time the firm has reduced its total cost of quality approximately 50 percent. For a number of its component parts, in three years the firm's failure rates have dropped from the 8–9 percent level to the 1–3 percent level. During the same period, Tennant's overall cost of quality dropped from 2 percent to approximately 1 percent, through reduced rework and failure costs, coupled with fewer stockouts and related costs.[22]

NATIONAL AND INTERNATIONAL QUALITY RECOGNITION

The Malcolm Baldrige National Quality Award

On August 20, 1987, President Ronald Reagan signed into law the Malcolm Baldrige National Quality Act. The act called for establishment of a national quality award that would provide a comprehensive framework of guidelines an organization could use to evaluate its quality program and its quality improvement efforts.

Additionally, the award was designed to provide recognition for U.S. organizations that had demonstrated excellence in the attainment and management of quality. Each year firms compete for this recognition in three categories:

1 Large manufacturing companies or subsidiaries
2 Large service companies
3 Small manufacturing or service companies

Up to two firms per year can be recognized in each category. The performance criteria used in the competition are outlined in Figure 21-9.

On balance, the program has been extremely popular, and certainly has elevated the awareness and interest of American business people in the importance of quality. Most managers recognize that quality improvement is a developmental process which takes time, and that there are seldom any quick fixes. But, clearly, the Baldrige Award format provides a helpful road map. Additionally, previous award winners are required to share their success stories with other interested firms.

The Deming Prize

In appreciation for Dr. W. Edwards Deming's contributions to Japanese industry, in 1951 the Japanese technical community established this prestigious award that bears Dr. Deming's name. Like the Baldrige Award, the Deming Prize is designed to recognize organizations' achievements in the field of quality, but it includes a unique emphasis on the use of statistical techniques.

Unlike the Baldrige Award, any firm that meets the requirements is eligible to receive the award—and at the present time the Deming Prize is open to

[22]Ibid., p. 36.

1.0 Leadership   100 points
   1.1 Senior executive leadership
   1.2 Quality values
   1.3 Management for quality
   1.4 Public responsibility
2.0 Information and analysis   70
   2.1 Scope and management of quality data information
   2.2 Competitive comparisons and benchmarks
   2.3 Analysis of quality data and information
3.0 Strategic quality planning   60
   3.1 Strategic quality planning process
   3.2 Quality goals and plans
4.0 Human resource utilization   150
   4.1 Human resource management
   4.2 Employee involvement
   4.3 Quality education and training
   4.4 Employee recognition and performance measurement
   4.5 Employee well-being and morale
5.0 Quality assurance of products and services   140
   5.1 Design and introduction of quality products and services
   5.2 Process quality control
   5.3 Continuous improvement of processes
   5.4 Quality assessment
   5.5 Documentation
   5.6 Business process and support service quality
   5.7 Supplier quality
6.0 Quality results   180
   6.1 Product and service quality results
   6.2 Business process, operational, and support service
      quality results
   6.3 Supplier quality results
7.0 Customer satisfaction   300
   7.1 Determining customer requirements and expectations
   7.2 Customer relationship management
   7.3 Customer service standards
   7.4 Commitment to customers
   7.5 Complaint resolution for quality improvement
   7.6 Determining customer satisfaction
   7.7 Customer satisfaction results
   7.8 Customer satisfaction comparison

Total = 1,000 points

FIGURE 21-9
Baldrige Award performance criteria. (Source: *National Institute of Standards and Technology, 1991.*)

overseas firms as well as Japanese firms. The evaluation checklist focuses on the ten performance categories shown below. It is generally thought that the evaluative criteria within this structure are specified in a way that provides for significant use of interpretive judgment by the evaluators.

1 Policy and objectives
2 Organization and operation
3 Education and extension
4 Assembling and disseminating information
5 Analysis

6 Standardization
7 Control
8 Quality assurance
9 Effects
10 Future plans

ISO 9000 Quality Standards

The International Organization for Standardization (ISO), as its name implies, is an international body composed of members representing standards organizations from ninety-one countries throughout the world.[23] Headquartered in Geneva, Switzerland, ISO comprises more than 180 technical committees that cover a wide range of industry sectors and products. The objective of the organization is to promote the development of standards, testing, and certification in order to encourage the international trade of goods and services.[24] Over the years, ISO has promulgated thousands of standards in the pursuit of this objective.

The global emphasis on economic competitiveness, the unification of the European market, and a broad array of different quality standards among countries led to concentrated ISO work in the quality area during the early 1980s. The product of this work was the issuance of the ISO 9000 series of *quality system* standards in 1987.

These standards, contrary to the belief of some observers, are not product standards—they do not deal with the quality of products. Rather, they are process standards that deal with the systems that produce the products. A firm that adopts the ISO 9000 standards is required to document what its quality management procedures are for each element in the standards—and then be able to prove to the ISO auditor that these procedures are in fact followed in practice. In the words of one auditor: "I'm not going to tell you how to run your business. I'm just going to make sure that you are doing what you say you are going to do."[25] So it is possible for a manufacturer to comply with the ISO 9000 standards and still produce a mediocre quality product. If properly applied, however, what the standards do guarantee is that the manufacturer *consistently* follows its documented procedures. Obviously, most firms' procedures will be designed to assure at least a reasonably high-quality product for

---

[23]The American National Standards Institute (ANSI) is the U.S. member of ISO.
[24]Hutchins, *ISO 9000*, p. 3.
[25]Martin Ramsay, "ISO 9000: The Myths and Misconceptions," *The Cincinnati Purchaser*, September–October 1992, p. 5.

competitive purposes—but one should understand what the standards are designed to do and what they are not designed to do.

The ISO 9000 series is actually made up of five separate standards: ISO 9000, 9001, 9002, 9003, and 9004. Standards 9000 and 9004 are interpretive guidelines, and the remaining three are the standards for different types of business operations, as noted below.[26]

- *ISO 9000.* Provides guidelines and definitions used to select the standard most applicable for a given organization—a road map to the other standards.
- *ISO 9001.* Provides a quality assurance model for assuring conformance in *design, development, production, installation,* and *servicing.* This is the most comprehensive standard and is intended for use by firms that design and develop their own products.
- *ISO 9002.* Provides a quality assurance model for conformance in *production* and *installation.* This standard is appropriate for firms that manufacture products to another firm's design specifications and have no responsibility for servicing.
- *ISO 9003.* Provides a model for conformance in *final test and inspection* procedures, appropriate for use in firms such as commodity suppliers, etc.
- *ISO 9004.* Provides guidance in the establishment and internal documentation of a quality system. It assists in identifying and developing the relationships between inputs necessary to assure quality.

Countries that adopt the ISO 9000 series of standards usually use their own identification symbols for the standards to provide consistency with the country's nomenclature for its existing national standards. The United States, for example, calls the ISO 9000 series its Q90 series to provide consistency with existing ANSI/ASQC standards used in the United States. (Q90, 91, 92, 93, and 94 correspond with ISO 9000, 9001, 9002, 9003, and 9004 standards, respectively.) The specific quality system elements utilized in the various ISO 9000 standards are shown in Figure 21-10.

Impact on Purchasing and Supply Managers   The ISO 9000 standards have two types of implications for purchasing and supply people—and both are important. For better or for worse, the standards are becoming a competitive weapon in global business. Nearly 30,000 firms in Europe have adopted the ISO 9000 standards, as well as another 1,000 in other parts of the world. And it appears that the numbers will continue to increase. Consequently, if an American firm wants to do business in the global marketplace, the chances are good that it will have to be ISO 9000–registered. When a firm goes through the registration process, purchasing is involved. Note elements 3, 5, 6, 7, 10, 13, 14, and 15 in Figure 21-5 for starters. Although purchasing's involvement may be

---

[26]For a more complete discussion of the individual standards, see John Nolan, "Understanding ISO 9000," *NAPM Insights,* September 1992, pp. 28–29.

Elements	ISO 9001 (20 Reqts.)	ISO 9002 (18 Reqts.)	ISO 9003 (12 Reqts.)
1 Management responsibility	x	x	x
2 Quality system	x	x	x
3 Contract review	x	x	—
4 Design control	x	—	—
5 Document control	x	x	x
6 Purchasing	x	x	—
7 Purchaser-supplied product	x	x	—
8 Product identification traceability	x	x	x
9 Process control	x	x	—
10 Inspection and testing	x	x	x
11 Inspecting, measuring, and test equipment	x	x	x
12 Inspection and test status	x	x	x
13 Control of nonconforming product	x	x	x
14 Corrective action	x	x	—
15 Handling, storage, packaging, and delivery	x	x	x
16 Quality records	x	x	x
17 Internal quality audits	x	x	—
18 Training	x	x	x
19 Servicing	x	—	—
20 Statistical techniques	x	x	x

FIGURE 21-10
Quality system elements, ISO 9000 standards.

peripheral in some of these activities, it will be heavily involved in things such as assessment of subcontractors, responsibility for the quality of purchased products, integrity of the procurement data system, and so on. This, then, is ISO 9000's first implication for purchasing.

While the standard does not require that a registered firm's suppliers also be ISO 9000–registered, a number of indirect factors point in this direction—thus producing a possible second implication for buyers. ISO 9004 notes that any material, components, or assemblies that become part of the firm's final product have a direct effect on the quality of the finished product. Consequently, it encourages a close relationship with suppliers, including continuing communications and efforts to develop continuous improvement. Certainly requiring supplier certification or perhaps ISO 9000 registration would be the next logical steps for a buyer to take.

In fact, a recent survey by *Electronics Purchasing* reveals that by 1996 69 percent of its readers expect to require their major suppliers to be ISO 9000–registered. One of Hewlett-Packard's materials managers supports this trend, saying, "ISO-registered suppliers are less costly for us to manage."[27] Other firms' buyers have had similar experiences, and note additionally that the disciplined self-evaluation involved in applying for ISO registration almost always

[27]John Kerr, "The Day the Auditors Come," *Electronics Purchasing*, January 1993, pp. 35–37.

produces significant performance and reliability improvement in the supplier organization.

CONCLUSION

Purchasing and supply management's responsibility is fulfilled only when materials of the specified quality are available and ready for production use—not before. Quality management is a major component of purchasing's supplier performance management responsibility. Quality failures lead directly to costly difficulties that reduce productivity, profit, and often market share. To preclude such losses, purchasing and supply should participate creatively in the corporate quality management program. To contribute most effectively to the organizational effort, purchasing's role in the program should include (1) participation in the development of specifications; (2) participation in the selection of appropriate quality control, inspection, and test requirements; (3) the selection and motivation of qualified suppliers; and (4) the subsequent monitoring and nurturing of the ongoing buyer-supplier relationship.

The concluding thought for this chapter is expressed well by Philip Crosby:

> Given the chance to explain quality management to people who will listen, it is possible to make a case for becoming deeply involved. No other action a manager can take will generate improved operations, increased profits, and reduced costs so quickly with so little effort.[28]

FOR DISCUSSION

21-1 Define the concept of total quality management.

21-2 What is purchasing's role in TQM?

21-3 What are the key elements of a TQM operation? Discuss.

21-4 Define quality.

21-5 Discuss the role the purchasing department should play in a firm's overall quality program.

21-6 What is the purchasing department's interest in its firm's material specifications, as far as quality is concerned?

21-7 How do use tests differ from engineering tests? What role should the purchasing and supply department play in the handling of use tests? What role should it play in the handling of engineering tests?

21-8 What specific precautions should be observed by the person conducting a use test?

21-9 What can a buyer tell about a potential supplier's quality capability from an analysis of its proposal for a particular job?

21-10 What is a quality capability survey? How is it conducted? What role does the purchasing department play in a capability survey?

---

[28]Crosby, *Quality Is Free*, p. 14.

21-11 What is Cp? What is Cpk? Discuss.

21-12 How does a buyer use Cpk? Discuss.

21-13 A statement is made in the text to the effect that the buyer is responsible for positively motivating the supplier with respect to quality. What is meant by this statement? What specific courses of action might a buyer take in carrying out the responsibility implied in this statement?

21-14 Buyers frequently visit suppliers at their plants. Is there any reason why a buyer might want to ask a supplier's representative to visit him or her at the buyer's own plant? Explain.

21-15 One large company feels strongly that individual buyers should be responsible for the performance of their suppliers. Accordingly, in the annual merit review for promotion, one of the points on which buyers are evaluated is the performance rating of their suppliers. Discuss the strengths and weaknesses of this policy.

21-16 Generally speaking, what should a top-notch buyer know about his or her firm's quality department? How is this knowledge related to the actual buying job?

21-17 Explain the difference between receiving inspection and technical inspection. What generally determines whether an incoming material should be subjected to receiving inspection, technical inspection, or both?

21-18 What is a defect detection system? Discuss.

21-19 What is a defect prevention system? Discuss.

21-20 What is statistical process control?

21-21 What role does SPC play in the work of a purchasing and supply department?

21-22 What is process capability analysis? How is the natural process capability range determined?

21-23 What is an $\overline{X}$ chart? How is it constructed?

21-24 What is an R chart? How is it constructed?

21-25 Who should be responsible for plotting and maintaining control charts? Discuss.

21-26 Explain how $\overline{X}$ and R charts are used.

21-27 Discuss the role of training in SPC implementation.

21-28 "In the long run, all costs of inspection and all costs of producing unusable products are borne by the purchaser." Comment.

21-29 In a medium-sized automobile engine manufacturing plant, all personnel associated with the inspection of incoming materials report to the manager of the purchasing and supply department. Discuss possible strengths and weaknesses of this organizational arrangement.

21-30 Briefly discuss the concept of supplier certification. What possible dangers do you see in the use of this concept by a purchasing department?

21-31 Outline the basic elements of a supplier certification program.

21-32 Discuss the Baldrige Award.

21-33 Discuss the Deming Prize.

21-34 What is ISO 9000? How is the United States involved with it?

21-35 What are the implications of ISO 9000 for buyers?

21-36 Identify and discuss the various parts of ISO 9000.

21-37 Describe in general terms how the DOE concept is used in improving the quality of a manufactured product.

CASES FOR CHAPTER 21

Drive Shaft Decision: Case A, page 809
Placido Engine Company, page 884
Generation Disk Systems Inc., page 825
OCR Inc. (in the *Instructor's Manual*)
The Case of the Unruly Spider (in the *Instructor's Manual*)
SDC Corporation, page 904

APPENDIX: DEFECT AVOIDANCE THROUGH DESIGN OF EXPERIMENTS

As we all recognize, it is better (and usually easier) to avoid defects than to detect them. While SPC is useful in detecting process changes, it is far more effective and less costly to design defects out *before entering production*. In the 1970s, the Japanese concluded that "SPC in production was 'too little and too late.'"[29]

Kekki Bhote is a former corporate consultant on quality and productivity improvement for Motorola, Inc., the first company to win the prestigious Malcom Baldrige National Quality Award. Mr. Bhote played a key role in Motorola's transformation to one of America's world-class manufacturers. Mr. Bhote writes:

> The secret weapon of Japan's quality is the Japanese industry's widespread use of design of experiments. The objective here is to discover key variables in product and process design well ahead of production; to drastically reduce the variations they cause (and only then keep the reduced variation under control with SPC); and to open up the tolerances on the large number of unimportant variables so as to reduce costs. DOE can also be used as a problem-solving tool (the very best problem-solving tool) on old products that were not subjected to the preventive disciplines of DOE before production.[30]

The principles and mechanics of using the design of experiments (DOE) in designing variation out are described in Mr. Bhote's book. This key concept is portrayed in Figure 21-11a and b. Figure 21-11a portrays variation in process and product resulting from the application of conventional quality methods. Note that acceptable variation is in the range of 20–40 [30 ± 3σ (the ideal)] for a *Cp* of 1.0 where

$$Cp = \frac{\text{specification width}}{\text{process width}} = \frac{20}{20}$$

[29]Kekki R. Bhote, *Strategic Supply Management*, AMACOM, New York, 1989, p. 169.
[30]Ibid., p. 170.

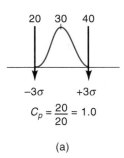 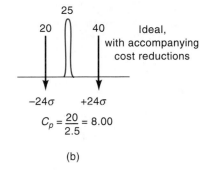

FIGURE 21-11
Illustration of the application of DOE.

Note that this yields a product which meets the specified target 30 ± 10; that is, acceptable products will vary over the range 20 to 40.

Through the application of DOE, it is possible to reduce this variation (as portrayed in Figure 21-11b). In this example, the product meets the specified target (30) with variation over the much narrower range of 23.75 to 26.25 with a $Cp = 8.00$.

Does reduced variation make a difference? Emphatically yes! A few years ago, Ford and Mazda assembled similar transmissions from the same blueprint. Ford's components all met spec: That is, they were within the range of $\pm 3\sigma$ for a Cp of 1. Ford's parts were all "acceptable." "In spec" was the mind set. The parts had *no defectives.*

The parts produced by Mazda displayed no variation: They were virtually identical! Mazda's definition of quality was entirely different. Mazda focused on no difference instead of no defects. As a result, its system (transmission) performed better than Ford's. Needless to say, customer satisfaction with the Mazda transmission was much higher than with Ford's—even though both transmissions were built from the same blueprint parts which met the same specification.

Not only is customer satisfaction increased through the application of DOE, but costs are actually reduced since noncritical variables can have their tolerances relaxed, resulting in lower costs. Bhote observes that the time required to achieve a Cp of 5.0 and higher is three weeks or less with well-designed experiments.

MATERIALS MANAGEMENT ACTIVITIES

22

PRODUCTION PLANNING

KEY CONCEPTS

- Fundamentals of production planning
- Modern production planning systems
    Aggregate planning and master scheduling
    Material requirements planning (MRP)
    Capacity requirements planning (CRP)
    Control of shop floor activities
    Management considerations
- Evolution of planning systems
    Closed loop MRP system
    MRP II system
- Impact of MRP systems on purchasing and supply
    Buyer-planner concept
    Supplier scheduler concept
    Contract buying
    Supplier flexibility and reliability
    Relationships with suppliers
- Just-in-time systems (JIT)
    The concept
    Applications
    Impact on purchasing and supply

As was discussed in Part One, the production planning and control function is part of the materials management organization in approximately half of those firms utilizing the materials management concept. Regardless of the organizational arrangement, however, the interface between procurement and production planning is extremely important.

One of the major responsibilities of the production planning group is the determination of timing and volume requirements for materials used in the manufacturing operation. These decisions, along with the communication lead time, have an obvious impact on the purchasing and inventory management operations. If the item has not already been sourced, the thoroughness of the market analysis, the number of sources solicited, the quality of the negotiations, and the total cost of the material are all influenced by the production planning actions. Even if the item has been presourced, supplier scheduling and a host of related quality and logistical issues are affected by the planning decision. For these reasons, it is essential that procurement personnel understand and coordinate effectively with production planning.

Over the past two decades, production planning and control has evolved into a highly specialized and often sophisticated activity. A number of books have been devoted to the technical aspect of the subject.[1] The purpose of this chapter is to examine only the fundamental activities involved in production planning—and to relate them to procurement activities.

THE FUNDAMENTALS OF PRODUCTION PLANNING

The objective of the production planning and control function is to coordinate the use of a firm's resources and to synchronize the work of all individuals concerned with production in order to meet required completion dates, at the lowest total cost, consistent with desired quality.

Historically, all firms conducted their production planning and control activities manually, with the use of a variety of Gantt charts and specialized visual scheduling/control boards. Today, most firms utilize some type of computer-based system to perform essentially the same types of activities in a more comprehensive, semiautomatic manner. Regardless of the specific operating system used, an effective production planning and control operation must accomplish five general activities:

1 Preliminary planning
2 Aggregate scheduling
3 Detailed production scheduling

---

[1]Several comprehensive works are John E. Schorr, *Purchasing in the 21st Century,* Oliver Wight Ltd. Publications Inc., Essex Junction, Vt., 1992; Oliver W. Wight, *The Executives' Guide to Successful MRP II,* Wight Publications Inc., Essex Junction, Vt., 1982; *Material Requirements Planning,* IBM Corporation, undated; J. E. Schorr and T. F. Wallace, *High Performance Purchasing: Manufacturing Resource Planning for the Purchasing Professional,* Wight Publications Inc., Essex Junction, Vt., 1986.

4 Release and dispatching of orders
5 Progress surveillance and correction

Preliminary Planning   After the initial product design and process design work are completed by the respective engineering groups, the preliminary planning work begins. The product's engineering bill of materials is restructured for compatibility with the firm's planning system. *For the given product (or special job)*, analysts then determine the specific material requirements, standard labor and machine requirements, and tooling requirements. And in the case of most intermittent manufacturing operations, one or more work-flow routings through the shop are determined.

Aggregate Scheduling   The next step in the process is scheduling—first, aggregate scheduling and, then, detailed production scheduling. As orders and forecasts are generated, they are matched against and fit in with the facility's overall capability. Aggregate scheduling is simply a first-pass, broad-brush determination that shop capacity—equipment and people—and required materials probably can be made available through careful, detailed scheduling work.

Production Scheduling   The ensuing step is the detailed production scheduling work. The aggregate planning work is broken down into specific product models and configurations, and for each the detailed manufacturing steps are scheduled into specific work centers or on specific machines. Start and completion dates for each operation or set of related operations are assigned, indicating the desired production priorities. Specific material and tooling requirements for the job are determined, as is the specific shop routing for the job.

Release and Dispatching of Orders   The work completed to this point in the process has developed an operating plan. When the order is released to the shop, the plan becomes operational and the order is dispatched from one operating unit to the next until it is complete. One of the key functions in this activity is to review the production priorities established in the prior scheduling activity. Any desired changes can be made at this point.

When the order is released, it is accompanied by a packet of paperwork and instructions. The packet typically contains such things as the engineering drawings and perhaps the bill of materials, tooling and material requisitions or computer entry instructions, a routing sheet, and detailed operations instructions for the production people. It may also contain instructions for charging labor and moving the job from one operation to the next.

Progress Surveillance and Correction   The last step in the process is the control function. Progress at each stage of the operation is monitored and fed back to the shop dispatcher and the production scheduler, who compare actual performance with the plan. Significant deviations from schedule typically require some type of corrective action—rerouting, rescheduling, the use of overtime work, and so on. These decisions, if fairly routine in nature, typically are made by production planning and control personnel. If a serious trade-off of resources or priorities is involved, marketing and manufacturing personnel may also enter the decision-making process.

MODERN PRODUCTION PLANNING SYSTEMS

The preceding discussion sketched briefly the fundamental activities that must be accomplished in planning and controlling production operations effectively. In practice, manufacturing firms conduct these activities in a variety of ways— some with great detail and precision, others with less sophistication. As competition in the marketplace has become increasingly keen, however, firms have been forced to meet higher performance standards and to do so cost-effectively. This economic reality, coupled with the availability of relatively inexpensive computing capability, has spawned a new era in production planning. Within just a few years, a progressive firm without a sophisticated, computer-based production planning and control system will be a rarity.

Although numerous different systems are evolving, both as custom-designed and standard commercial software packages, most utilize essentially the same basic elements. Figure 22-1 portrays, in flowchart form, the basic operating elements found in most current computer-based production planning systems.

Aggregate Planning and Master Scheduling

The development of a viable aggregate plan and a coordinated master production schedule is the starting point for the use of a detailed computer-based planning system.

The *aggregate plan* is based on the expected receipt of a certain number of orders for a given family of products during the planning period. For the near term, a number of firm orders typically are in hand. As the planners peer further into the future, they use various forecasting techniques to determine an approximate aggregate demand for the product family. The most commonly used forecasting approaches are:

- Bottom-up analysis, utilizing the opinion, judgment, and market surveys of field sales personnel
- Time series analysis
- Exponential smoothing techniques
- Regression and correlation analysis

Forecasting activities typically are conducted or coordinated by a specialized staff group and generally are handled as a responsibility separate from the computerized planning system activities.

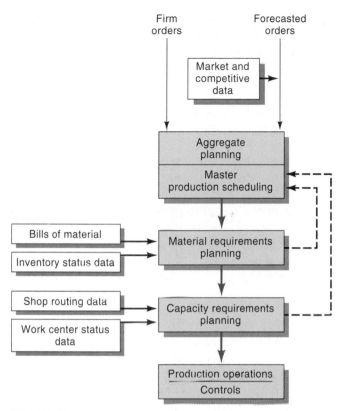

FIGURE 22-1
A basic flowchart for a modern production planning system.

Development of the aggregate plan itself is usually a top management responsibility. General management, sales management, and manufacturing management personnel jointly develop the initial version of the plan, based on the known and expected order data.

With the assistance of senior production planning personnel, in most firms the plan is developed for a period of from six to twelve months. To be effective, the schedule must cover a time span that exceeds the cumulative lead time of the finished product. The plan must be firmed up for a reasonable period of time, simply because overall production volume cannot be changed abruptly without incurring significant unplanned costs. Every production volume utilizes a given mix of labor, materials, and equipment. When the output rate is changed, a new optimal mix must be achieved by readjusting the usage rate of the various resources. In the longer term this is possible by replanning the variables—the employment level, the use of overtime, the use of subcontracting, and the variation of inventory levels. In the short run this usually is difficult to do efficiently.

The *master production schedule (MPS)* is developed directly from the aggregate plan—and is the instrument that drives the firm's entire production system. The aggregate plan establishes an overall level of operations that balances the plant's capability with external sales demand. The master schedule translates the aggregate plan into specific numbers of specific products to be produced in identified time periods.

The relationship between the master schedule and the aggregate plan is shown in Figure 22-2. In this hypothetical illustration, an appliance manufacturer's aggregate plan for refrigerator production is shown at the top of the figure. (When this plan is added to the firm's aggregate plans for ranges, washing machines, and dryers, the firm's total production capacity will have been utilized for the year.) Note that the master production schedule breaks down the aggregate production of refrigerators into the production of seven specific models, time-phased by quantity per month for the planning period of a year. For example, the 500 units planned in January consist of 200 Model A Standards, 50 Model A Deluxe units, 200 Model B Standards, and 50 Model B Deluxe units. The master schedule for the rest of the year was constructed in the same manner.

FIGURE 22-2
Illustrative relationship of the aggregate plan and the master production schedule.

Aggregate Plan for Refrigerators

Month	Jan.	Feb.	Mar.	Apr.	May	June	July	Aug.	Sept.	Oct.	Nov.	Dec.
Number of refrigerators	500	500	600	700	700	800	800	700	600	500	400	400

Master Production Schedule for Refrigerators

Month	Jan.	Feb.	Mar.	Apr.	May	June	July	Aug.	Sept.	Oct.	Nov.	Dec.
Business model												
• Standard	—	100	—	200	—	200	—	150	—	100	—	100
• Heavy duty	—	100	—	100	—	100	—	100	—	50	—	50
Model A												
• Standard	200	100	300	150	300	200	350	200	250	150	150	100
• Deluxe	50	—	50	—	100	—	100	—	50	—	50	—
• Executive	—	100	—	150	—	200	—	150	—	100	—	100
Model B												
• Standard	200	100	200	100	200	100	250	100	250	100	150	50
• Deluxe	50	—	50	—	100	—	100	—	50	—	50	—

The next step in the development of the master schedule is to evaluate its feasibility by simulation, checking the availability and balance of required materials and capacity resources. If bottlenecks or imbalances are encountered, the schedule is modified by trial and error until an acceptable arrangement is found. Many computerized planning systems have this simulation capability built in, as will be seen shortly.

Once an acceptable schedule is determined, its outputs—the volume and timing of the production of specific products—become the inputs required for the subsequent detailed computer planning work that drives the production, inventory, and purchasing operations.

Before moving on to this part of the discussion, however, it is necessary to say just a word about timing and modification of the original plan. The time interval used in master scheduling obviously varies from firm to firm; it depends on the types of products produced, the volume of production, and lead times of the materials used. However, weekly periods are probably most commonly used, followed by biweekly and monthly intervals. So, within the time frame of a six- to twelve-month aggregate plan, the master schedule typically is updated weekly to reflect changing sales demands and perhaps internal problems that require rescheduling. If the system is to work effectively, it is essential that the schedule be updated regularly. After each update, many firms follow the policy of holding the next four weeks' schedule *firm,* providing only modest flexibility for adjustment in the schedule for weeks 5 through 8, and providing considerable flexibility for change in the schedule for weeks 9 through 12.[2]

Material Requirements Planning

Material requirements planning (MRP) is a technique used to determine the quantity and timing requirements of "dependent demand" materials used in the manufacturing operation. The materials can be purchased externally or produced in-house. The important characteristic is that their use be directly dependent on the scheduled production of a larger component or finished product—hence, the term "dependent demand." For example, a refrigerator door is a dependent demand item in the production of a refrigerator.

The material requirements planning and the capacity requirements planning (CRP) segments of the production planning system are the responsibility of the production planning and control group. In practice, the actual number-crunching and paperwork generation usually is accomplished by computer.

Production planning personnel are responsible for structuring and formatting the product bills of material eventually contained in computer memory. The same group is responsible for setting up the part and component inventory status records (perpetual inventory records) that are also computerized. In addition to the current inventory balance, an inventory status record typically contains the timing and size of all open (scheduled) orders for the item,

---

[2]Some firms use time frames of five or six weeks rather than four weeks.

the lead time, safety stock levels, and any other information used for planning purposes. When this preliminary planning work is completed, material requirements for a given time period can be generated.

Although details of the software operation may vary, generally speaking, the MRP segment works as follows. It takes the master production schedule output for a given product and calculates precisely the specific part and component requirements for that product during the given period of operation. This is done by "exploding" the product bill of material (listing separately the quantity of each part required to make the product) and extending these requirements for the number of units to be produced. Since a given part often is used in more than one finished product, the process is repeated for all products. Then all products' requirements for a given part can be summed to obtain the total requirement for the part during the given period of operation.

For illustrative purposes, return to the refrigerator example in Figure 22-2 for a moment. Assume that all the refrigerator models produced, except the Model B Deluxe, use one standard 1-horsepower electric motor. Because of an additional freezing compartment, Model B Deluxe uses two standard 1-horsepower motors. For the month of January, the MRP system would determine that the manufacturing operation requires 550 standard 1-horsepower electric motors.

Returning now to our general discussion of the MRP processing activity, after a part's requirements for the operating period are calculated, the computer compares these requirements with the inventory balance, considering open orders scheduled for receipt, to determine whether a new order needs to be placed.

The output of the MRP system, then, can be the following items:

1 Current order releases to purchasing (or to previously selected suppliers), with due date requirements.
2 Planned order releases to purchasing for ensuing periods (considering inventory balance, scheduled requirements, and lead-time requirements).
3 Current and planned order releases for in-house production, with completion date requirements.
4 Feedback to the master production scheduler, in case operating changes or supplier performance has produced material availability problems.
5 With revised output from the master production schedule, the MRP system will replan and schedule the material requirements.

A more detailed illustration of an MRP system's operating logic is provided in the following section.

MRP Logic and Format[3] As utilized today, most versions of MRP act as information processing systems which seek to develop and maintain a set of

---

[3]Based on Daniel J. Bragg and Chan K. Hahn, "Material Requirements Planning and Purchasing," *Journal of Purchasing and Materials Management,* Summer 1982, pp. 18–20. Used with permission of the authors.

orders that support the production plan, while simultaneously maintaining inventories within the production system at reasonably low levels. Orders within an MRP system fall into two categories: (1) open orders which have been released but have not yet arrived and (2) planned orders which are developed in anticipation of future releases. As previously noted, each category can contain both purchase orders and shop orders.

The processing logic of MRP centers on the development of a materials planning record for each item. Figure 22-3 illustrates a typical planning record based on the data contained in the master production schedule, bill of materials, and inventory record file shown at the top. The top row of each record shows the "gross requirements," or anticipated usage of the item projected into the future. The second row shows all current "open orders (scheduled receipts)," with each order assigned to the time period in which it is expected to arrive. The "on hand" row projects the inventory balance into the future. This is calculated by determining the impact of gross requirements (planned withdrawals) and open orders (planned receipts) on the inventory balance. The current inventory balance is shown to the left of period 1. The bottom row shows the "planned order releases" for the item, with each order assigned to the time period when it should be released.

The development of the planning record is based on three fundamental concepts which form the essence of the MRP-based approach to materials planning and control. They are:

- Dependent demand
- Inventory/open order netting
- Time phasing

Dependent demand takes the multistage product into account in the planning for individual items. Clearly, the decisions to acquire purchased materials should be based on anticipated production plans. These decisions include both quantity and timing considerations. Dependent demand logic is used to calculate the gross requirements for each planning record. This projected usage includes the planned production of all other products which require the item being planned.

The inventory/open order netting concept is used to develop the "on hand" balance row of the planning record. Efficient use of inventory implies that current stocks should be largely depleted prior to the acquisition of additional inventory. The netting process accomplishes this by allocating current inventory and open orders to the earliest requirements. When the on-hand balance falls below zero, additional stock must be ordered. This process not only signals the need to plan an order but also determines when the order should arrive. This "need date" becomes the due date for the order.

Time phasing utilizes lead-time information and need dates. The "planned order releases" row of the planning record shows time-phased orders, whose placement dates are offset from the need dates of the orders by the lead time of the item. Each order, if released in the time period designated by the

Master Production Schedule				
Week	1	2	3	4
Production	100	150	170	130

Inventory Record File			
Item	(B)	(C)	(D)
On hand	100	0	150
Lead time	1	1	2
Open orders:			
Quantity	–	100	170
Due week	–	1	2

Bill of Materials

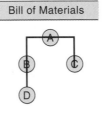

		Week			
Item A		1	2	3	4
Master production schedule		100	150	170	130

Item B		1	2	3	4
Gross requirements		100	150	170	130
Open orders (scheduled receipts)		– = 0	150 0̶	170 0̶	130 0̶
On hand	100 +	0	0 −1̶5̶0̶	0 −1̶7̶0̶	0 −1̶3̶0̶
Planned order releases		150	170	130	0

Item C		1	2	3	4
Gross requirements		100	150	170	130
Open orders (scheduled receipts)		100	150 0̶	170 0̶	130 0̶
On hand	0	0	0 −1̶5̶0̶	0 −1̶7̶0̶	0 −1̶3̶0̶
Planned order releases		150	170	130	0

Item D		1	2	3	4
Gross requirements		150	170	130	0
Open orders (scheduled receipts)		0	170	130 0̶	0
On hand	150	0	0	0 −1̶3̶0̶	0
Planned order releases		130	0	0	0

FIGURE 22-3
A typical MRP planning record.

planned order row, should arrive exactly at the time it is needed by a following production stage.

Utilization of the three basic concepts can be observed in the simplified illustration of Figure 22-3. The bill of materials diagram shows that item B is a fabricated part that is manufactured using D as a raw material, and that B is used as a component of A. The dependent demand concept is seen in the gross requirements data; the planned usage of B matches the planned production of A, in both quantity and timing.

The netting process calculations determine the need for additional orders to be planned. For item B, in week 2, 150 units are needed. Since the on-hand quantity of 100 is used to meet week 1 requirements, an order release for 150 units is shown in week 1. Time phasing maintains the timing difference between the planned order and its need date; this is the item's lead time. In this case the lead time is one week. A similar process is used to develop the remaining orders in the "planned order releases" row. For item D, for example, the process is repeated, the only difference being that D is dependent on B.

MRP not only plans for each order, but also allows the replanning of orders. Replanning is generally necessary when the status of an item is changed due to new information. An example of a status-changing event could be notice of a late delivery. Using item D as an illustration, an open order currently is planned to arrive in week 2. If this order is known to have an altered delivery date of week 3, the current plan should be adjusted (replanned) to reflect this new information. The impact of this change can be traced to every other item by reversing the processing logic and working from bottom to top rather than from top to bottom.

The impact of the shortage also can be reduced by adjusting the orders for the other items. Take item B, for example. The planned order release in week 2 is no longer feasible and should be shifted into week 3. The requirement that was to be covered by this planned order can no longer be supported. It should also be shifted into the next week, thus affecting the master production schedule.

Hence, the MRP system generates a complete set of planned orders for all manufactured parts and purchased materials based on the information inputs. Clearly, the validity of the plan produced by the system is dependent on both accurate and timely lead-time information from purchasing personnel. At the same time, if system planning is done far enough in advance (and rescheduling activity is kept to a minimum), the advance knowledge about specific material requirements certainly can facilitate planning and conduct of the buying activities.

Capacity Requirements Planning

The next step in the production planning process is capacity requirements planning (CRP). The function of the CRP segment of the process is to convert the shop orders produced by the MRP system into scheduled workloads for the various factory work centers. In addition to the MRP system output, two other sets of data inputs are required to do this: (1) shop routing data and (2) work center status data. These inputs for CRP operation are analogous to the bill of materials and inventory status inputs for MRP operation.

In an intermittent production operation, the manufacture of each product or component requires that a series of specific machine or human operations be performed on the item as it progresses toward completion. These required operations define the "route" the item must travel through the manufacturing facility. Sometimes more than one routing sequence is possible. In any case, one of the required preliminary planning activities is to develop one or more shop routing plans for each product and component produced in-house. In addition to the physical routing plans, standard processing time requirements must be determined for each operation in the sequence—and included in the shop routing data file. In a continuous manufacturing operation, these activities usually are simplified by the design and layout of the production facility.

The work center status data file maintains a perpetual record of the capacity—equipment and human—that is available (and committed) in each of the factory's work centers. Capacity typically is measured in standard man or machine hours per time period.

With shop routing data and work center status data files loaded in computer memory, the CRP system is ready for operation. Recall that during the development of the master production schedule, a preliminary analysis of work center capacity was done prior to firming up the schedule. While this "rough cut" produced approximate data accurate enough for overall scheduling purposes, it is not precise enough for the detailed work-loading job at hand. So—with the MRP-generated current and planned shop order releases now known with certainty for a given time period—a second pass is made. The CRP program first obtains the necessary routing and timing data for each scheduled order—and then checks the appropriate work center status files to determine if the required capacity is available. Frequently the proposed plan does not mesh satisfactorily with the availability and timing of capacity existing in the required work centers. In this case, the CRP activity becomes an iterative process, and replanning continues until realistic work center loads are developed. The variables that can be manipulated by the system and the planner to achieve a reasonable balance typically include:

- Alternative routings
- Personnel reallocation
- Use of overtime
- Inventory-level variations
- Use of alternative tooling
- Use of subcontracting

Occasionally an impossible scheduling situation is encountered. In this case the system communicates to the scheduler the need for selected capacity modification or for a revision of the master schedule. Most of the time, however, a reasonable fit can be achieved. The normal output of the system in these cases is:

1 Verification of the planned orders from the MRP system

2 Work center load reports that reflect the priorities established by the MRP system

This information subsequently is used in the final stage of the planning and control process.

Control of Production Activities

According to a time-honored adage, "The proof of the pudding is in the eating." The validity and the usefulness of the detailed planning done to this point in the process will now be seen as it is applied to production operations in the shop.

The output of the MRP and CRP systems is transmitted to the manufacturing organization in the form of order releases and a dispatch list. Referring again to Figure 22-3, the planned order releases shown on line 4 of the planning record, when released as the date moves into the current period, officially become the open orders (scheduled receipts) shown on line 2 of the planning record. Before releasing an order, the planner must make one final check to ensure that the priority sequencing of the order is still valid, that capacity is still available, and that materials are available. If all factors are not "go," release may be delayed rather than having the order held up after it is started in the shop.

When an order is released, typically it is accompanied by a packet of materials and instructions required to complete the job. Included are such things as engineering drawings, bills of materials, route sheets, move tickets, materials requisitions, labor charge forms, and so on. Depending on the extent to which the entire system is computerized, some of these functions may be handled through the use of on-line terminals.

The dispatch list, containing a series of order releases, is prepared by the planner and may cover a time period ranging from a day to a week. It goes to the appropriate work center foreman, who schedules his or her machines and people in accordance with the due dates specified for each order on the list.

If daily dispatch lists are used, the foreman generally has little discretion in scheduling the jobs in the work center. On the other hand, if the list covers several days of work or more, the foreman has an increasing amount of latitude in his or her detailed scheduling activities. This provides a better opportunity to maximize the operating efficiency of the work center. Perceptive planning and scheduling by the foreman usually can minimize setup and material move costs and maximize the utilization of equipment and labor. Consequently, it is important that planners coordinate the development of their dispatch lists closely with the appropriate foremen in an effort to optimize both planning control and shop efficiency. A team-type spirit and effort usually produce the best results.

As noted earlier, control is an essential element if the entire process is to work effectively. In most operations this is accomplished at two levels. First, as a job progresses, status and related information are fed back to the planner from either the operator or the foreman on the job. Information reported typically includes order status, anticipated delays, materials shortages, and rework and scrap data. As appropriate, such feedback occurs either daily or when a job is started and completed. Some firms report only on an exception basis. In continuous manufacturing operations, such reporting typically is done less frequently at predetermined checkpoints in the process. In any case, such information is used by the planner to determine if replanning or other corrective action is necessary to meet the firm's sales commitments.

In addition to order status types of control reports, most systems also require one or more types of capacity control reports. The most commonly used one is an input/output report, typically developed weekly. This type of report usually shows the hours of work planned for a given work center, the number of hours actually worked on the planned jobs, and the difference between the two. Significant deviations from plan can produce obvious problems in the CRP and subsequent scheduling activities. Hence, in most operations, this type of control is essential.

Reporting and monitoring methodology varies among firms. Some are totally computerized, with computer graphics output, while others use a combination of computer and manual communication and charting techniques. The use of Gantt charts and schedule/control boards is still fairly common.

In most organizations, control is also exercised at a second level—personal control right on the shop floor. One or more dispatcher/expediters, usually assigned to the production planning and control group, spend most of their time on the floor visually following jobs through the manufacturing operation. This individual's job is threefold: (1) to ensure the integrity of the job priority plan—that is, that the routing and scheduling instructions for jobs are implemented reasonably; (2) to ensure reasonable capacity control—that is, that the hours scheduled in the various work centers are actually being worked; and (3) to help the operating people solve unexpected planning and scheduling difficulties. As problems arise, the dispatcher/expediter works with the various foremen in helping to resolve them. This person is the planning group's representative on the shop floor. Within reason, he or she has the authority to suggest certain micro planning and scheduling changes that may be able to resolve a problem directly and expeditiously.

To summarize, the production planning activities all come together on the shop floor to initiate and control the production operations. Overall responsibility for *control* of operations usually is vested with the production planning and control manager or the materials manager. In firms without a materials management department, the manufacturing manager is sometimes responsible. The control function usually has both a centralized and a decentralized component. Order release, dispatching, and formal status control are the responsibility of the centralized production planning and control group. Decentralized informal control on the shop floor is the joint responsibility of dispatcher/expediter personnel and the line foremen responsible for the actual production operations. Viewed in another sense, it is the responsibility of the foremen to do the micro work center scheduling and to run each production operation so that planned completion dates are met. It is the responsibility of production planning and control to keep work flowing through the shop at a steady rate, focusing always on order priority control and capacity control.

Two Management Considerations

It is appropriate at this point to reiterate two important concepts that may have gotten buried in the details of our discussion of the total planning system.

The first concerns the *multilevel nature of the operation of the production planning system*. A review of Figure 22-1 perhaps will recall the fact that, for the most part, the aggregate planning and the master scheduling activities are top-management and staff responsibilities. On the other hand, most activities associated with the material requirements planning and capacity requirements planning activities are primarily the responsibility of production planning and control personnel. Finally, the control of production operations themselves is a joint responsibility of production planning and control personnel and supervisory operating personnel. For a system to function effectively, the coordinated efforts of all three groups are required.

The second concept focuses on the *dynamic nature of the total production planning system*. Although time periods vary for different organizations, a majority of firms utilizing a comprehensive computer-based planning system work from an aggregate plan structured for the coming year. The master schedule subsequently covers the same year's period, but typically it is further delineated by month and by week. Material and capacity requirements are also structured in weekly "time buckets." In order to maintain a current plan that correctly reflects changing sales demands and internal scheduling and capacity constraints, the entire operation typically is replanned on a weekly basis. So the firm, semifirm, and flexible portions of the total operating schedule simply drop the week just past and encompass one new week as replanning occurs each week. Some systems utilize a technique in which only selected portions of the operation that are influenced by changing conditions are replanned; this approach has some obvious logistical advantages. Regardless of the specific technique used, however, the important point is that the dynamic nature of the planning system keeps it current on at least a weekly basis. And from a practical point of view, this is the feature that makes such a system so valuable to a large complex firm operating in a competitive environment.

EVOLUTION OF MRP AND MRP II SYSTEMS

As innovations are accepted and refined in the business world, inconsistencies in the use of terminology and variations of the concept inevitably emerge with the passage of time. Such has been the case with MRP and its subsequent derivatives. The following paragraphs describe briefly the evolution of MRP and its progeny, MRP II.

The computer-based material requirements planning technique found its first significant industrial usage in the early 1970s. Though it became known as MRP, for a number of years it was used primarily to generate orders for parts and materials that related to a specific demand schedule. Later, users found that with some refinement it could be used as a scheduling technique. It could be used to feed back schedule change data and subsequently reschedule existing orders to maintain valid material and shop order dates. Hence, it became a much more valuable tool.

However, from a production planning point of view, MRP still left something to be desired because it was unable to deal with the capacity variable. Before long, though, necessity proved to be the mother of invention, because soon a capacity requirements planning module was developed and linked to the original MRP module. With further development of the master production schedule concept, in many firms the bulk of the planning activities shown in Figure 22-1 were integrated into a single planning and scheduling package. Today, with the exception of the aggregate planning and the production operation controls segments, this entire integrated package is identified as a *closed loop MRP system*. Thus, the concept and the terminology have both changed with time.

The last step, to date, in this evolutionary process is an expanded system known as *MRP II—manufacturing resource planning*. This system simply adds two new capabilities to a closed loop MRP system. The most significant addition is the financial interface. This module provides the ability to convert operating production plans into financial terms, so the data can be used for financial planning and control purposes of a more general management nature. Related to this feature, the second addition provides a simulation capability that makes it possible for management to do more extensive alternative planning work in developing the marketing and business plans. This can be done by asking "what if" types of questions—that is, by modifying an operating variable and receiving a systemwide response to the proposed operating change.

As MRP and MRP II systems developed in different firms, they often included somewhat different levels of capability. For example, some MRP systems did not originally include comprehensive CRP capability and did not function fully as a closed loop system. When MRP II capability subsequently was developed, it included these features that previously were missing. As a result of this situation, coupled with the fact that MRP II is more comprehensive in nature, many users see MRP II as the "umbrella" system, with MRP as a major component of that system.[4]

---

[4]For an interesting discussion of MRP II development, see Troy Juliar, "Completing the Mix: Materials Management and MRP II," *Purchasing Management,* February 1987, pp. 6–11.

IMPACT ON PURCHASING AND SUPPLY

Sooner or later, most manufacturing firms will use some type of MRP-based system as a central component of their production planning system. If present experience is a reasonable indicator of the future, purchasing operations will be affected in the following important ways:[5]

1 Expanded use of the buyer-planner or the supplier scheduler concept
2 Expanded use of contract buying
3 Necessity of greater supplier flexibility and reliability
4 Development of closer relationships with suppliers, including more part-nering arrangements
5 Increased accuracy and timeliness of materials records

Buyer-Planner and Supplier Scheduler Concepts   The very nature of an MRP operation places the planner in close, continuing contact with material requirements and their frequently changing schedules. Typically, the planner has a more sensitive feel than the buyer for the probable usage pattern of most materials. Consequently, to improve efficiency of the planning-buying activity, as well as communications with suppliers, many firms have used one of several organizational schemes that utilize the planner as the supplier contact person for day-to-day material flow activities.

The buyer-planner concept is one commonly used approach. This organizational arrangement was discussed in Chapter 6, and will be reviewed only briefly here. In essence, the buyer's job and the planner's job are combined into a single job done by one individual. This person obviously handles a smaller number of items than were originally handled by either the buyer or the planner. The buyer-planner is responsible for determining material requirements, developing material schedules, making order quantity determinations, issuing all material releases to suppliers, and handling all of the activities associated with the buying function. Thus, in this integrated role, the buyer-planner maintains close contact with various supplier personnel.

Another popular approach is simply to assign to the planner the responsibility for dealing directly with suppliers in releasing and following up materials orders. In this arrangement, the buyer handles all the normal purchasing responsibilities except requirements releases against existing contracts. The planner handles this latter function—and becomes the buying firm's supplier contact on all day-to-day material scheduling matters. Most firms refer to this arrangement as the *supplier scheduler concept*.

In a recent survey of present MRP users, researchers found that approximately 55 percent of the firms utilize the supplier scheduler concept and that

---

[5]An MRP-type system also generates output that can be utilized easily and effectively as input for an electronic data interchange (EDI) system. Consequently, as EDI operations become more widely used, MRP systems will tend to facilitate their use.

30 percent use the buyer-planner organizational arrangement. Only 15 percent of the firms utilize the traditional pattern of operation.[6] It seems clear that a continued expansion of the use of these two concepts will accompany MRP development in the future.

Contract Buying   Because an MRP system requires the placement of frequent orders for relatively small quantities of materials, it obviously would be inefficient, if not impossible, to make a new buy for every weekly requirement. The alternative, of course, is to place annual or longer-term contracts with suppliers for the required materials—and then simply issue a telephone or an MRP schedule release against the contract, as the production operation requires.

Not only is this buying approach required in an MRP-scheduled operation, but as a general rule it is excellent buying practice. It permits more careful purchasing planning and more thorough market and supplier research—and it needs to be done only once every year or two for each material. In addition, such contracts usually produce attractive pricing arrangements and improved supplier relations. This topic is discussed at length in Chapter 27, "Developing and Managing the Buying Plan."

Supplier Flexibility and Reliability   Because of the weekly updating of most MRP systems, coupled with the frequent rescheduling that sometimes occurs, a supplier has to be more than reasonably flexible. Even if a supplier has the buyer's MRP schedule with weekly or biweekly requirements for the next two months, the irregularity of demand and the short notice given on schedule changes present a difficult operating situation for most suppliers. Resolution of the potential problems requires careful cooperative planning and usually some compromises by both parties.

It is obvious that supplier reliability is a must. The buying firm typically carries some inventory, but not as much as in the traditional operating situation since one of the objectives of the system is to reduce inventory levels. Hence, there is much less cushion in the system to handle the problems of late deliveries and off-spec materials.

The bottom line of these two stringent operating requirements is that supplier selection is a critical, yet a more difficult, task.

Closer Relationships with Suppliers   The use of contract buying and the need for unusual supplier flexibility and reliability create an operating situation in which the buyer-supplier relationship must be closer and more cooperative than it might normally be. As discussed in the earlier chapters on sourcing, this type of operating situation requires the ultimate in coordination, cooperation, and teamwork. A mutual understanding of each other's operations and problems is essential in achieving this type of effectiveness. It liter-

[6]J. E. Schorr and T. F. Wallace, op. cit., p. 150.

ally is an informal partnership operation—and it must turn out to be a win-win deal.

The buyer-planner or the supplier scheduler must stay in close touch with the supplier's counterpart on a week-to-week basis as far as scheduling and delivery matters are concerned. And the buyer (or buyer-planner) must handle the broader issues of the relationship with appropriate supplier sales and technical personnel on a regular and timely basis.

Materials Records   As one reviews the MRP segment of the production planning system, it is readily apparent that the accuracy of the system will be no better than the accuracy of the data used in its calculations. If the system is to work effectively, records such as specifications, bills of materials, supplier lead times, receiving reports, inventory balances, and so forth must be as near 100 percent accurate as possible.

JUST-IN-TIME PRODUCTION PLANNING

Although originally pioneered by Henry Ford, the just-in-time manufacturing concept has been refined and developed over the past several decades in Japanese industry. The purpose of this recent concerted effort was to improve quality and reduce costs to help Japanese business become more competitive in world markets for selected product lines. The resounding success of the Japanese effort prompted a growing number of U.S. firms to develop and implement modified versions of the system in this country.

The just-in-time concept is considered by many to be a technique used for reducing inventories. In reality, it is much more. The complete JIT concept is an operations management philosophy whose dual objectives are to reduce waste and to increase productivity. It is true, however, that operationally speaking the basic theme of the JIT concept is that *inventory is evil*. Inventory is considered to be undesirable for three reasons:

- It hides quality problems.
- It hides production inefficiencies and productivity problems.
- It adds unnecessary costs to the production operation—carrying costs of approximately 25 to 35 percent of the inventory value per year.

Inventories of production materials permit suppliers' quality deficiencies to be covered up, and in-process inventories permit off-spec work in-house to be given less attention than it should. This occurs simply because the unacceptable items can be replaced with good items from inventory while those that are unacceptable are being reworked. The same rationale applies to schedule slippages caused by inefficiencies in the workplace and in the system itself. The end result, claim JIT proponents, has been a tendency among U.S. managers and their employees to accept mediocre, second-rate work as the norm.

Hence, in an effective JIT application the operating policy is to minimize production inventories and work-in-process inventories by providing each work center with just the quantity of materials and components needed to do a given job at the exact time they are needed. In an ideal situation, each unit of output would be produced just as it is needed at the succeeding work station. In reality, of course, this ideal is not achieved. But, within reason, it is a viable objective in many organizations. Practically speaking, the result is a reasonably continuous flow of small-lot production. At the supply end of the operation, those materials that are procured in a JIT mode are delivered frequently by suppliers in fairly small quantities. Deliveries may range from twice a day to once a week.

Consequently, throughout the entire system, with only minimal inventories on hand to cover for poor-quality materials and workmanship, the focus is on consistently high-quality material and in-process work. Without it, the system breaks down.

To summarize, then, the basic operating plan is to gear production and final assembly as closely to sales demand as possible. Individual production operations are also geared more closely together. This is accomplished either by means of a product-type layout of equipment and work centers[7] or by means of a material-pull, "Kanban" type of material movement system[8] in a process-oriented layout. Finally, the firm's total production operation, through its purchasing activities, is geared as closely as practical to key suppliers' production operations. So—the characteristic of small-lot flow can be traced through the entire system from a supplier's plant, through the buyer's plant, out into the finished goods distribution system. The actuating element is sales demand, which *pulls* the various stages of in-process work and materials through the complete system.

A JIT Illustration

Figure 22-4 provides a flow diagram of the major production operations in an electronic instrument manufacturing plant, both before and after the firm implemented a JIT system.

The top portion of the figure shows the original operation. After incoming material was received, counted, and logged into the system, it went through a standard visual receiving inspection operation where potential quality prob-

---

[7]A *product-type layout* is one in which the various types of equipment required to make a given product are arranged adjacent to each other so that operations occur sequentially, in line, from one end of the manufacturing process to the other. An automobile assembly plant is a good example of product layout. A process-type layout groups similar types of equipment together, without regard for the flow of the product being manufactured—e.g., all lathes are grouped together, all boring machines are grouped together, and so on. A traditional job shop exemplifies this type of layout.

[8]A *Kanban material production and movement system* is simply one in which no more than approximately an hour's supply of material is produced in one run in each work center—and the next production run does not occur until the material is called for by the succeeding operation. It is this feature of the operation that produces the *small batch* and *pull-flow* characteristics of the system.

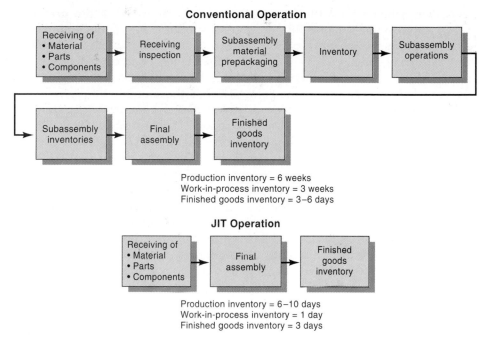

FIGURE 22-4
How JIT was implemented in one U.S. firm.

lems were detected, and perhaps submitted to quality assurance for further detailed inspection. The next step was to prepackage the materials, parts, and components that would subsequently be used in putting together a given subassembly. This was done for each subassembly produced to facilitate stock picking for the later assembly work. Most production inventories were thus stored in this subassembly kit form. After subassembly operations occurred, subassembly units were then inventoried until later used in a product's final assembly operation. Approximately a week's finished goods inventory for most products was maintained at the plant.

The lower portion of Figure 22-4 shows the dramatic change that occurred as a result of JIT implementation. The receiving inspection and quality control technical inspection operations for purchased materials were completely eliminated. *The responsibility for incoming quality was placed with the purchasing department and delegated to each supplier organization.* This required a reasonable amount of supplier education. In most cases purchasing and QC worked with suppliers to develop and install statistical process control (SPC) systems in their manufacturing operations. SPC control charts were then required to be submitted with each shipment of delivered material.

The next major change occurred on the shop floor. The facility originally utilized a specialized process-type layout, similar to a large job shop. This was revised to achieve a modified product-type layout. Although the firm produced approximately half a dozen different product lines, enough similarity between products existed to permit the use of several product-flow types of facilities arrangements. This layout permitted the use of an open-type storage system adjacent to the production operations themselves. So incoming materials were delivered directly to the point of use in the shop.

Production scheduling subsequently was based completely on units of finished product, rather than on the production of subassemblies. This made it practical to eliminate the subassembly prepackaging and storage activities, as well as the subassembly operations themselves. The firm's closed loop MRP system was still used to generate requirements and overall schedules, but it was necessary to "smooth" the master schedule to facilitate the reasonably continuous, small-lot production. Consequently, the total shop now resembles a continuous manufacturing operation much more than its previous job shop character.

As shown underneath each of the two flow diagrams, inventory levels were reduced greatly. Production inventory was decreased approximately 70 percent, and in-process inventories were dropped from about a fifteen-day supply to a one-day supply. Finished goods inventory was reduced by about 40 percent. Hence, the total float figure declined from approximately fifty days to twelve days—and the firm reports that quality problems have declined noticeably.

In summary, the following elements tend to characterize most successful JIT operations[9]:

1 The JIT concept is most applicable to manufacturing operations that produce a relatively small number of different products in at least a quasi-continuous environment.

2 Product demand must be reasonably predictable, and requirements must be generated accurately. A closed loop MRP system can be used to do this, but typically the master production schedule must be smoothed on a daily basis.

3 Statistical process control typically is used in both the buyer's and suppliers' organizations to ensure tight control of material and production quality. This is vital to the functioning of the low-float, small-volume, relatively smooth-flowing operation.

4 Production operation setup requirements must be able to be reduced to relatively short times. Most firms target for tool changes and equipment setups of less than ten minutes. Without this capability, small-batch and smooth-flow production of different models or different products cannot be accomplished efficiently.

---

[9]The following articles provide good in-depth analyses of JIT applications: Chan K. Hahn, Peter A. Pinto, and Daniel J. Bragg, "Just-in-Time Production and Purchasing," *Journal of Purchasing and Materials Management*, Fall 1983, pp. 2–15; C. H. St. John and K. C. Heriot, "Small Suppliers and JIT Purchasing," *International Journal of Purchasing and Materials Management*, Winter 1993, pp. 11–16; P. A. Dion, P. M. Banting, S. Picard, and D. L. Blenkhorn, "JIT Implementation: A Growth Opportunity for Purchasing," *International Journal of Purchasing and Materials Management*, Fall 1992, pp. 32–38.

5 Purchasing must be able to reduce materials replenishment lead times. This usually is accomplished by reducing the four major elements of lead time—internal paperwork and ordering time, supplier queue and manufacturing time, transportation time requirements, and incoming receiving and inspection requirements.

6 Successful JIT operation suppliers must be able to be flexible to meet the buying firm's stringent, short-fused material requirements—and they must be reliable to the nth degree.

These considerations lead logically to a discussion of the impact of a JIT system on the purchasing operation.

JIT's Impact on Purchasing and Supply

Purchasing and supply plays a key role in any JIT operation. *Whether a JIT production system works or not depends on how well purchasing does its job in selecting and managing suppliers.*

Obviously, it is not practical to procure all materials on a JIT basis. Most successful JIT firms buy from 5 to 10 percent of their individual materials—those that account for 60 to 75 percent of the firm's materials expenditures and those that are space-intensive—in a JIT mode. This keeps the administrative part of the job manageable.

Finding reliable suppliers that are willing to comply with a JIT buyer's stringent requirements typically is not an easy task. Consequently, purchasing usually utilizes two basic strategies:

- A specific plan to reduce the number of suppliers utilized, using single and dual sources in many cases
- Extensive use of long-term contracting

Evaluation and qualification of JIT suppliers clearly is a critical and time-consuming activity.

The very nature of a JIT purchasing operation requires, and in fact usually creates, a closer, more cooperative relationship between the buying and supplying firms. Hence, from a practical point of view a reduced supplier base is a necessity—and a longer-term contract is the primary incentive that attracts a supplier to consider the arrangement. Only with knowledge of the buyer's long-term requirements schedule can a supplier schedule production and size inventories so that replenishment lead time can be reduced, while simultaneously providing both flexible and reliable service.

As noted earlier, the basic objective of the "partnering" relationship is to reduce costs, improve efficiency, and increase profitability for *both* organizations. The development of scheduling guidelines and parameters, the implementation of SPC quality systems, and the conduct of value analysis work on the purchased items must be done jointly in a team-type environment. To assist in all of these activities, the buyer often makes greater use of *perfor-*

mance specifications to encourage the supplier to exercise as much creativity as possible.[10]

Reducing the delivering carrier's transportation time is also an important objective. Consequently, suppliers located near the buyer's operation may offer a distinct advantage. The most important strategy in this element of the equation, however, is to work out a longer-term contractual JIT arrangement with a small number of selected carriers. This type of transportation service can be purchased in the same manner material is purchased from a JIT supplier. This topic is discussed further in Chapter 25, "Traffic."

A final impact of JIT is seen in the form of a shift in the workload within the purchasing and supply department. The buyer's job now involves more responsibility for contract administration and supplier management than previously. The tight delivery schedules, the emphasis on control of quality and performance, and the joint resolution of problems with suppliers require this. At the same time, the nature of the JIT buying operation now requires less routine, nitty-gritty buying work. In effect, the JIT buyer's job tends to require a broader range of professional and managerial skills than typically was the case previously.

CONCLUSION

The interface between procurement and production planning is an extremely important one. Production planning decisions influence the parameters within which purchasing does its work. At the same time, the effectiveness with which purchasing does its job directly influences the success of the production planning system.

In recent years, with the aid of computerized systems, production planning has evolved into a highly specialized and sophisticated activity. Closed loop MRP systems, MRP II systems, and JIT systems all significantly affect the design and implementation of a firm's purchasing and supply systems. To a great extent, purchasing strategies used in prior years must be modified, and in some cases replaced with new approaches, to create the supply environment required to support and sustain these evolving planning systems.

In this dynamic environment it is imperative that the procurement and production planning functions be developed in close coordination because of the interdependencies they share—and that operationally they be coordinated effectively on a day-to-day basis.

FOR DISCUSSION

22-1 Why should a purchasing professional understand something about production planning and control?

---

[10]For a detailed discussion of the buyer-seller relationship, see C. R. O'Neal, "The Buyer-Seller Linkage in a Just-in-Time Environment," *Journal of Purchasing and Materials Management,* Spring 1989, pp. 34–40.

22-2 "An effective production planning and control operation must accomplish five general activities." Identify these activities and discuss each briefly.

22-3 What is aggregate planning? Discuss its significance in the production planning process.

22-4 How is the information used in the aggregate planning process developed? Discuss briefly.

22-5 What is the relationship between the aggregate plan and the master schedule?

22-6 Describe how the material requirements planning module works and what it does in a modern production planning system.

22-7 What does the capacity requirements planning module accomplish in a production planning system? Discuss.

22-8 Frequently the proposed production plan does not mesh satisfactorily with the availability and timing of the capacity existing in required work centers. What variables may be manipulated by the planner to achieve a reasonable balance between the proposed requirements and available capacity? Discuss.

22-9 In a typical firm using an MRP system, how far into the future is the production schedule firm? Discuss briefly.

22-10 When an order is released to the shop for production, what materials typically accompany it? Discuss.

22-11 What is meant by "the multilevel nature of the operation of the production planning system"? Discuss.

22-12 What is a closed loop MRP system? Draw a flowchart and discuss.

22-13 What is the difference between a regular MRP system and an MRP II system? Discuss.

22-14 Identify and discuss the impacts of an MRP system on a purchasing and supply department's operation.

22-15 Describe how the buyer-planner concept works.

22-16 Describe how the supplier scheduler concept works.

22-17 Describe how a just-in-time production system works.

22-18 According to JIT proponents, why are inventories undesirable?

22-19 Identify and discuss the key characteristics of a JIT production operation.

22-20 How does a firm's purchasing operation contribute to the success of its JIT production operation? Discuss in some detail.

22-21 Can an MRP system and a JIT system be used together? Explain.

22-22 "The interface between procurement and production planning is an extremely important one." What is your reaction to this statement? Discuss in depth.

CASES FOR CHAPTER 22

23

INVENTORY MANAGEMENT

KEY CONCEPTS

- Functions of inventories
- Types of inventories
- Analysis of inventories
    - ABC concept; 80/20 analysis
    - Dependent and independent demand
    - Inventory costs
- EOQ concept
    - Incremental costs
    - Quantity discounts
- Types of control systems
    - Cyclical/Fixed order interval system
    - Flow control system
    - JIT inventory system
    - MRP inventory system
    - Order point/Fixed order quantity system
    - Two-bin system
- Applications and comparisons of various systems

The preceding chapter set the tone for a review of inventory management. The production planning systems just discussed determine to a significant extent the size of a firm's inventories, as well as the types of approaches that can be used in managing them. As the production planning function has become more sophisticated in recent years, so too has its operating twin, inventory management.

Several statistics clearly point up the significance of this function. In most manufacturing firms today, inventories constitute the second-largest category of assets shown on the balance sheet, exceeded only by physical facilities and equipment.[1] Inventories frequently account for as much as 30 percent of the firm's invested capital.

A second startling figure is uncovered when one ferrets out and totals the annual costs of carrying a given inventory. While the figure varies considerably from firm to firm, numerous studies made by manufacturing firms and consultants reveal that a typical manufacturer incurs inventory carrying costs of from 20 to 40 percent of average inventory value. This means that a medium-sized firm pays in indirect costs approximately $300,000 per year merely for the convenience of having a million-dollar inventory in its warehouse. This figure is significantly greater than is apparent to the average business person.

THE FUNCTIONS OF INVENTORIES

The preceding discussion of the JIT concept highlighted very sharply the disadvantages inventories can bring to a manufacturing operation. In many circumstances, however, inventories do have some redeeming values—they are not all bad. The trick is to obtain the best of both worlds at a reasonable cost.

Generally speaking, inventories make possible smooth and efficient operation of a manufacturing organization by *decoupling individual segments* of the total operation. *Purchased-part* inventories permit activities of purchasing and supply personnel to be planned and conducted somewhat independently of shop production operations. By the same token, these inventories allow additional flexibility for suppliers in planning, producing, and delivering an order for a given part.

Inventories of *parts and components produced in-house* in an intermittent operation decouple the many individual machines and production processes from various subassembly and assembly activities. This typically enables management to plan production runs in individual production areas in a manner which utilizes manpower and equipment considerably more efficiently than if all were tied directly to the final assembly line. In addition, *finished goods* inventories perform the function of decoupling the total production process

---

[1]D. J. Armstrong, "Getting Things Done: Sharpening Inventory Management," *Harvard Business Review,* November–December 1985, p. 42.

from distribution demands, allowing on a broader scale the development of similar efficiencies of production. These inventories also help *balance the firm's supply with the market forces of demand.*

Thus, well-planned and effectively controlled inventories can contribute to the effective operation of a firm and to a firm's profit. The basic challenge is to determine the inventory level that works most effectively with the operating system or systems existing within the organization—and that realistically is the most feasible in dealing with given suppliers and material markets.[2]

If the inventory issue is viewed through the eyes of various operating department managers, an interesting situation appears. The *marketing manager* tends to favor larger inventory stocks to assure rapid assembly and delivery of a wide range of finished product models. This capability obviously can be used as an effective sales tool. The *production manager* is inclined to go along with the marketing manager, but for quite a different reason. He or she argues for higher inventory levels because they allow more flexibility in daily planning; unforeseen problems in producing a given component can be mitigated if productive efforts can easily be transferred to another component for which the required raw materials are on hand. Likewise, a reasonable inventory of the required items *ensures against production shutdowns* due to delivery problems, supplier problems, and stock-outs, thus avoiding the incurrence of high production downtime costs. These arguments reveal the flip side of the arguments favoring a JIT system.

The *financial officers* of the firm, on the other hand, argue convincingly in favor of very low inventory levels. They point out that the company's need for funds usually exceeds availability and that reduced inventories free sorely needed working capital for other uses. They note also that total indirect inventory carrying costs drop proportionately with the inventory level. The *purchasing and supply manager* is the final participant; he or she is concerned with the size and frequency of individual orders. Purchasing often favors a policy of placing fewer and larger orders. Unless contractual arrangements with routine delivery-release systems can be worked out with suppliers, fewer and larger orders usually increase the total inventory level. At the same time, however, they tend to minimize operating problems with suppliers, and in some cases they may reduce unit material prices. Large-volume buying also permits more *efficient utilization of buying personnel* and more effective advance planning for major activities such as market studies, supplier investigations, and so on. Thus, it is clear that each departmental executive supports his or her position with legitimate justification.

Concepts and techniques useful in analyzing the inventory issue in order to arrive at sound policy decisions are the focal point of our investigation in this chapter.

---

[2]For an interesting discussion of the JIT system and the value of inventories, see George Newman, "As Just-in-Time Goes By," *Across the Board*, October 1993, pp. 7–8.

DEFINITION OF INVENTORIES

Although inventories are classified in many ways, the following classification is convenient for use in further discussion of the topic:

1 *Production inventories.* Raw materials, parts, and components which enter the firm's product in the production process. These may consist of two general types: (1) special items manufactured to company specifications and (2) standard industrial items purchased "off the shelf."
2 *MRO inventories.* Maintenance, repair, and operating supplies which are consumed in the production process but which do not become part of the product (e.g., lubricating oil, soap, machine repair parts).
3 *In-process inventories.* Semifinished products found at various stages of the production operation.
4 *Finished goods inventories.* Completed products ready for shipment.

In most manufacturing companies, production and MRO inventories together represent the major segment of total inventory investment.

Let us now place the discussion in perspective. Inventory planning occurs at several levels in an organization and covers various time spans. Our concern in this chapter focuses on the planning and control of production and MRO inventories in a short-run situation, involving weekly, monthly, and in some cases quarterly or yearly decisions. Hence, the discussion assumes that the longer-range activities of sales forecasting, product modification, aggregate planning, and master scheduling have for the moment been completed. Our investigation begins at this point in the planning cycle.

INVENTORY ANALYSIS

The inventory of a typical industrial firm includes as many as 5,000 to 50,000 different items. Initial planning and subsequent control of such an inventory is accomplished on the basis of knowledge about *each* of the individual items and the finished products of which each is a part. Consequently, the starting point for sound inventory management is the development of a complete inventory catalog, followed by a thorough ABC analysis.

Inventory Catalog

After all inventory items have been completely described, identified by manufacturer's part number, cross-indexed by user's identification number if necessary, and classified generically for indexing purposes, some form of inventory catalog should be prepared for use by all personnel.[3] Careful preparation and maintenance of such a catalog pays two important dividends.

---

[3]Most firms have a companywide materials standardization program. The materials included in the inventory catalog should all have been accepted as company "standards." This topic is discussed further in Chapter 9, "Standardization."

An inventory catalog serves, first, as a medium of communication. It enables personnel located in many different departments to perform their jobs more effectively. A design engineer, for example, may have a choice between using either of two standard parts in an experimental design; an inventory catalog quickly tells whether either part is carried in inventory and may be available immediately for use in the experimental work. Suppose the item in question is to be used in large quantities on the production line. If one of the alternative parts is a stock item and the other is not, the engineer knows immediately that procurement time and cost will probably be lower for the part which already is being purchased and used elsewhere in the plant.

As a further example, envision a mechanic who has just removed a faulty bearing from a major production machine that has broken down. Upon examination, the mechanic finds the manufacturer's name and part number stamped on the edge of the bearing. Unfortunately, though, the storeroom clerk cannot help, because that particular bearing is not carried in stock. If the mechanic or a supervisor consults the inventory catalog, however, they may well find that a satisfactory substitute bearing, carried under another manufacturer's part number, is in stock. Proper cross-indexing in the inventory catalog can inform users about common interchangeable parts, a typical situation with many MRO supplies.

A second significant benefit produced by an inventory catalog accrues to the inventory control operation itself. This benefit takes the form of more complete and correct records through the reduction of duplicate records for identical parts. A purchasing department often buys the same part from several different suppliers, under various manufacturers' part numbers. Unless control requirements dictate otherwise, identical parts from all suppliers should be consolidated on one inventory record. A simple situation? Perhaps, but one is amazed to find in highly reputable companies many similar cases in which two or more inventory records bear different numbers for the same part. A carefully constructed catalog significantly reduces the possibility of such problems.

ABC Analysis; The 80–20 Concept

As soon as an inventory is identified and described, the manager must determine the importance and the dollar value of each individual inventory item. This calls for a study of each item in terms of its price or cost, usage (demand), and lead time, as well as specific procurement or technical problems. Without the data provided by such a study, an inventory manager normally does not have enough information to determine the best allocation of departmental effort and expense to the tasks of controlling thousands of inventory items.

A study of several hundred medium-sized West Coast manufacturing firms conducted by the authors reveals the data illustrated in Figure 23-1. This figure shows that in the typical firm a small percentage of the total number of items carried in inventory constitutes the bulk of the total dollars invested in inventory. In the study cited, 10 percent of the inventory items account for approximately 75 percent of the investment, and only a quarter of the items make up approximately 90 percent of the total investment. The remaining 75 percent of the items constitute, roughly, only 10 percent of the inventory investment. While these figures vary somewhat from one firm to another, the magnitude of variation usually is not great. Several similar studies in large corporations have produced strikingly similar results, leading to what some firms call the *80–20 phenomenon* (20 percent of the items account for 80 percent of total inventory investment). Historically, some firms have termed this phenomenon the *Pareto principle*, based on the law of "the vital few and the trivial many," developed by the Italian economist Vilfredo Pareto around the turn of the twentieth century.

Among different companies this type of analysis is known by several different names, *ABC analysis* or *Pareto analysis* being the most common. In practice, such an analysis can be made on the basis of either the average inventory investment in each item or the annual dollar usage of each item. The analysis is easy to conduct once inventory has been properly identified and usage

FIGURE 23-1
Graphic analysis of production and MRO inventories.

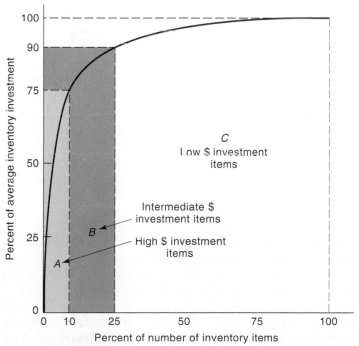

records have been maintained for a complete operating cycle. First, *all items are simply ranked in order of their average inventory investment* (or dollar usage). The total of these values (average inventory investment or annual usage) for all inventory items is then computed. The value of each item is next expressed as a percentage of the total. By going down the list and successively cumulating the individual percentages for each item, one can determine which items make up the first 75 percent of inventory investment, the first 90 percent, and so on. If it is convenient to use the three arbitrary classifications noted above, they can be labeled *A, B,* and *C,* respectively, and each inventory item becomes an *A, B,* or *C* item.

The value of such an analysis to management is clear. It provides a sound basis on which to allocate funds and time of personnel with respect to procurement management and the refinement of control over the individual inventory items. Obviously, no supply manager wants to spend as much time and effort managing the items that make up 20 percent of the investment as is spent on those making up the remaining 80 percent. In this sense, management may take several forms. It may involve minimizing acquisition cost, maximizing service and reliability, minimizing inventory investment, minimizing indirect costs associated with inventory, or utilizing personnel effectively. The concept clearly permeates a number of departmental operations—purchasing, production control, stores, and accounting, for example.

In practice, a never-ending problem is that of adequately planning for handling the thousands of low-value *C* items. In many cases, availability and reliability for these items are just as important as they are for the *A* and *B* items. Even with good purchasing planning, because of the sheer number of *C* items, low-value nuisance purchases frequently require more time than should be allotted to them. Consequently, they reduce the amount of time available to purchasing and supply personnel for supplier studies, value analysis, and other creative work involving high-value *A* and *B* items.

A problem that has grown out of the discussion in the preceding paragraph focuses on another potential dimension of the *ABC* classification. Some firms have observed that in addition to the varying dollar magnitude (or turnover) represented by each material in the three categories, the *criticalness* of each material to the firm's operation also varies and is important from the standpoint of managerial control.

To provide additional guidance for supply managers, James A. G. Krupp, director of corporate materials for Echlin Inc., suggests that each material might also be classified according to its service or operating importance on a three-point scale: 1—critical, 2—medium, and 3—noncritical. Thus, a less important *A* material would be designated an *A*-3 item, while a critical *C* material would be identified as a *C*-1 item. Depending on the circumstances in a specific situation, it is possible that the *C*-1 item might require more stringent management attention than the *A*-3 item. In any case, some firms have adopted this two-digit classification system to provide additional managerial guidance.[4]

An effective inventory management system must help resolve the problems identified in the preceding paragraphs.

Dependent and Independent Demand

To do the job well, an inventory manager needs one additional bit of information about each of the items in inventory—is the demand (usage) for the item "dependent" or "independent"?

An item is said to exhibit *dependent demand* characteristics when its use is directly dependent on the scheduled production of a larger component or parent product of which the item is a part. Hence, in a plant producing automobile engines the demand for engine block castings is a dependent demand; once the production schedule for a group of engines is established, the planner knows with certainty that one block will be required for each engine. Conversely, the demand for cutting oil used by the machines on the line cannot be calculated accurately from the production schedule and bills of materials; thus, cutting oil is said to have an *independent demand*. Generally speaking, in an assembly or fabrication-type operation, most production inventory items will have a dependent demand, while MRO and similarly used items will have an independent demand.

Although the distinction seems relatively simple, it is important for the inventory manager to know whether an item exhibits a dependent or an independent demand. Certain inventory control systems function more effectively with one type of item than with the other.

COSTS ASSOCIATED WITH INVENTORIES

From a managerial point of view, two basic categories of costs are associated with inventories: (1) inventory carrying costs and (2) inventory acquisition costs. These plus a related variable cost are discussed in the following paragraphs.

Carrying Costs

Carrying material in inventory is expensive. Prior to the relatively recent periods of higher interest rates, a number of studies determined that the *annual cost* of carrying a production inventory averaged approximately 25 percent of the value of the inventory. The escalating and volatile cost of money in recent years, however, has increased the typical firm's annual inventory carrying

---

[4]For a complete discussion of this interesting approach, see James A. G. Krupp, "Are ABC Codes an Obsolete Technology?" *APICS—The Performance Advantage*, April 1994, pp. 34–35.

cost to a figure between 25 and 35 percent of the value of the inventory. Five major elements make up these costs in the following manner:

1	Opportunity cost of invested funds	12–20%
2	Insurance costs	2– 4%
3	Property taxes	1– 3%
4	Storage costs	1– 3%
5	Obsolescence and deterioration	4–10%
	Total carrying costs	20–40%

Let us briefly examine these carrying costs.

1 *Opportunity cost of invested funds.* When a firm purchases $50,000 worth of a production material and keeps it in inventory, it simply has this much less cash to spend for other purposes. Money invested in productive equipment or in external securities earns a return for the company. Conceptually, then, it is logical for the firm to charge all money invested in inventory an amount equal to that it could earn if invested elsewhere in the company. This is the "opportunity cost" associated with inventory investment.

2 *Insurance costs.* Most firms insure their assets against possible loss from fire and other forms of damage. An extra $50,000 worth of inventory represents an additional asset on which insurance premiums must be paid.

3 *Property taxes.* As with insurance, property taxes are levied on the assessed value of a firm's assets; the greater the inventory value, the greater the asset value, and consequently the higher the firm's tax bill.

4 *Storage costs.* The warehouse in which a firm stores its inventory is depreciated a certain number of dollars per year over the length of its life. One may say, then, that the cost of warehouse space is a given number of dollars per cubic foot per year. And this cost conceptually can be charged against inventory occupying the space.

5 *Obsolescence and deterioration.* In most inventory operations, a certain percentage of the stock spoils, is damaged, is pilfered, or eventually becomes obsolete. No matter how diligently warehouse managers guard against these occurrences, a certain number always take place. With new products being introduced at an increasing rate, the probability of obsolescence is increased accordingly. Consequently, the larger the inventory, typically the greater the absolute loss from this source.

Generally speaking, this group of carrying costs rises and falls nearly proportionately with the rise and fall of the inventory level. Further, the inventory level is directly related to the quantity in which the ordered material is delivered. When the complete order is shipped at one time, the larger the order quantity, the higher the *average* inventory level during the period covered by the order. Hence, costs of carrying inventory vary nearly directly with the size of the delivery quantity. This relationship is illustrated by the *CC* curve in Figure 23-2.

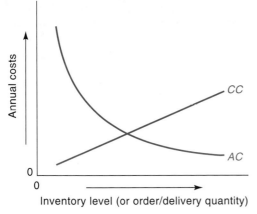

FIGURE 23-2
Relationship of inventory-related costs to
inventory level (AC = acquisition costs;
CC = carrying costs).

If a firm has estimated its approximate inventory carrying cost, as a percentage of inventory value, the *annual* inventory carrying costs that would be
generated by delivery quantities of various sizes can be calculated as follows:

$$(\text{Carrying cost per year}) = (\text{average inventory value}) \times \left(\begin{array}{c} \text{inv. carrying cost as} \\ \text{a \% of inv. value} \end{array} \right)$$

$$\left(\begin{array}{c} \text{Carrying cost} \\ \text{per year} \end{array} \right) = \left(\begin{array}{c} \text{average inventory} \\ \text{in units} \end{array} \right) \times \left(\begin{array}{c} \text{material unit} \\ \text{cost} \end{array} \right) \times \left(\begin{array}{c} \text{inv. carrying} \\ \text{cost as a \%} \\ \text{of inv. value} \end{array} \right)$$

$$CC = \frac{Q}{2} \times C \times I$$

where CC = carrying cost per year for the material in question
Q = order or delivery quantity for the material, in units[5]
C = delivered unit cost of the material
I = inventory carrying cost for the material, expressed as a percentage of inventory value

Acquisition Costs

Looking at inventory costs in another light, a different set of indirect materials
cost factors emerges. These factors all contribute to the cost of generating, pro-

[5]When the entire order is delivered in one shipment, Q for the order and Q for the delivery are
the same number. When the order is delivered in several shipments, Q per delivery is smaller than
Q for the order. In this case, Q for the delivery should be used in the formulas to calculate carrying cost.

cessing, and handling an order, along with its related paperwork. Examples of these costs are listed below and can be thought of as inventory acquisition costs.

1 A *certain portion of wages and operating expenses* of such departments as purchasing and supply, production control, receiving, inspection, stores, and accounts payable—those departments whose personnel devote time to the generation and handling of the order

2 *The cost of supplies* such as engineering drawings, envelopes, stationery, and forms for purchasing, production control, receiving, accounting, and so forth

3 *The cost of services* such as computer time, telephone, fax machines, telegraph, and postage expended in procuring material

When considering this group of acquisition costs, observe that they behave quite differently from carrying costs. Acquisition costs are not related to inventory size per se; rather, they are a function of the number of orders placed or deliveries received during a given period of time.

One simplified example will illustrate this point. Suppose a buyer in the purchasing and supply department receives a requisition for a special fabricated part used in the manufacture of one of the firm's products. Assume further that the part has been purchased before and that price quotations from three or four shops are on file. The buyer first reviews the present inventory situation and probably checks with production control to see if any significant changes are anticipated in future production. Drawings and specifications of the part are then reviewed to refresh his or her memory regarding required tooling and other technical details of the purchase. Next, the buyer reviews the quotations to determine why the order was placed with supplier A last time. Before deciding if supplier A should again receive the order, the buyer must also review supplier performance data. Finally, the buyer decides which supplier should receive the order and subsequently inquires about the firm's current shop loads and any other matters that have arisen during the investigation. It is entirely possible that a negotiation session may also be required.

In total, the buyer's investigation may require anywhere from an hour to several days. The total cost of the buyer's time to the company will be the same whether the purchase order is written for 20 parts or 200 parts. This process may result in the development of a term contract with the supplier, in which case the buyer's effort is spread over all deliveries of the item during the life of the contract. If this is not the case, however, the next time the buyer receives another requisition for this part, he or she will go through somewhat the same process, generating almost the same indirect cost for the company.

The largest segment of the acquisition cost element is made up of these types of indirect labor and overhead costs, generated in purchasing and in the other departments that subsequently become involved in handling some activity associated with the purchase. The cost of supplies and services consumed in the placement and handling of an order typically varies directly with the number of orders placed. While these costs are significant, they are considerably less so than the human and related overhead cost figures just discussed. Although the variable acquisition cost per order varies widely among firms, depending on the specific cost inclusions, today the range appears to run from approximately $50 to $125 per order.

If a firm experiences a certain annual usage of an item, the number of orders placed during the year will decline as the individual order quantity increases, thus generating lower *annual* acquisition costs. The experience of numerous firms over the years reveals that this relationship is not linear, but that it follows the approximate contour of the *AC* curve shown in Figure 23-2.

If a firm's cost accounting department can estimate its approximate acquisition cost *per order*, the *annual* acquisition costs that would be generated by order quantities of various sizes can be calculated as follows:

$$\left(\text{Acquisition cost per year} \right) = \left(\begin{array}{c} \text{number of orders} \\ \text{placed per year} \end{array} \right) \times \left(\begin{array}{c} \text{acquisition cost per} \\ \text{order} \end{array} \right)$$

$$AC = \frac{U}{Q} \times A$$

where AC = acquisition cost per year for the material in question
U = expected annual usage of the material, in units
Q = order or delivery quantity for the material, in units[6]
A = acquisition cost per order or per delivery for the material[6]

Economic Order Quantity Concept (EOQ)

If one has to make decisions about managing an inventory, it is useful to understand the behavior of the inventory-related cost factors just discussed. These factors often help a manager determine which items should or should not be carried in inventory, what inventory levels should be carried for specific items, and what order quantities are appropriate for given items.

The latter part of the chapter discusses several types of systems that can be used in managing an inventory. In each case one of the short-term operating questions that must be answered is: How much of the item should be ordered? Among the factors that often enter this decision process is a concept known as

---

[6]When the entire order is delivered in one shipment, the Q value and the A value for the order are the same as for the delivery. However, in the case of a term contract, Q and A values should be calculated on the basis of each delivery. Thus, purchasing expenses incurred in generating the order and administering the contract should be spread over the deliveries so that A = the acquisition cost per delivery, and Q = the delivery quantity. This approach produces the most useful A value, and it is also consistent with the approach used in calculating inventory carrying costs.

EOQ—the notion of an economic order quantity. As its name suggests, this concept holds that the appropriate quantity to order may be the one that tends to minimize all the costs associated with the order—carrying costs, acquisition costs, and the cost of the material itself.

Concentrating for the moment on the first two costs, Figure 23-2 shows clearly that as the order or delivery quantity increases, carrying costs rise—and at the same time acquisition costs decrease. To see the total picture more clearly, if carrying costs and acquisition costs are added together over the order quantity range shown on the graph, the total indirect materials cost curve, TC, is produced. This transformation is shown in Figure 23-3. The economic order quantity concept simply says that the sum of all the indirect costs associated with inventory will be minimized on an annual basis if the material, for which the graph is drawn, is ordered (or delivered) consistently in the quantity that corresponds with the low point on the TC curve. This is the *economic order quantity.*

Note that the low point on the total cost curve coincides with the point at which the carrying cost curve intersects the acquisition cost curve. This makes it easy to develop the basic formula that can always be used to calculate a material's *basic* EOQ. Recall the two simple cost formulas developed for annual carrying costs and annual acquisition costs on pages 525 and 527. These can now be used to develop the EOQ formula.[7]

[7]A more straightforward mathematical solution can be obtained using differential calculus: (1) Write the equation for the total cost curve; (2) differentiate the equation; (3) find the minimum value of the function by setting the derivative equal to 0 and solving for Q.

FIGURE 23-3
Graphic representation of the EOQ concept (*AC* = incremental acquisition costs; *CC* = incremental carrying costs; *TC* = total incremental costs).

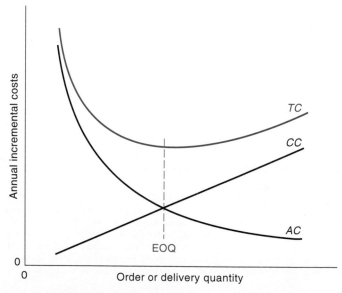

EOQ occurs when

$$\text{Annual carrying cost} = \text{annual acquisition cost}[8]$$

$$CC = AC$$

$$\frac{QCI}{2} = \frac{UA}{Q}$$

Solving for Q:

$$Q^2CI = 2UA$$

$$Q = \sqrt{\frac{2UA}{CI}}$$

This formula, then, is the fundamental mathematical representation of the EOQ concept. It can be modified to accommodate numerous special conditions, but in practice it probably finds its most effective application in this form.

Professor Daniel Jones, who has researched various lot sizing concepts, says that the EOQ concept can be used in conjunction with a variety of inventory management systems, including JIT. He writes: "When the EOQ model is properly employed, there is little difference between lot sizes based on the JIT model and the EOQ model." He points out that all relevant incremental costs must be included when using the EOQ model. This is perhaps an obvious observation, but one that he finds frequently is violated in practice.[9]

So, despite some criticisms, the EOQ concept continues to be a versatile and useful tool if it is properly applied.

Incremental Costs and Stability Note that the vertical axis in Figure 23-3 is labeled "annual *incremental* costs." It is appropriate at this point to emphasize the fact that the costs which are relevant in making an EOQ analysis are incremental costs. *Incremental costs are those costs that actually change as a result of a particular operating decision.* For example, if the decision to issue more purchase orders during the year actually increases supply and service costs, these are incremental costs. If it requires the addition of a buyer or clerical person to

---

[8]See footnotes 5 and 6 for use of the EOQ formula in the case of term contracts with multiple deliveries.

[9]As reported by Daniel Jones in "Don't Let JIT Overrule EOQ," *Supplier Selection and Management Report*, June 1991, p. 10.

handle the load, the additional payroll costs are incremental costs. *Incremental costs are either variable costs or opportunity costs* that represent a forgone opportunity to utilize an asset in some other productive way.

By their very nature, most of the inventory carrying costs discussed are incremental costs and are reasonably stable. The distinction is less clear when dealing with inventory acquisition costs. Judgment is usually required in estimating the portion of the human effort that represents a legitimate opportunity cost. In any case, EOQ produces valid results only when the *I* and *A* cost factors are largely incremental, and when the usage and unit cost elements, as well as *I* and *A*, are reasonably stable over the operating period.

Material Prices and Quantity Discounts   In the discussion of EOQ analysis to this point, it has been assumed that material prices and transportation costs were constant factors for the range of order quantities considered. In practice, some situations occur in which the delivered unit cost of a material decreases significantly if a slightly larger quantity than the originally computed EOQ is purchased. Quantity discounts, freight rate schedules, and perhaps anticipated price increases may create such situations. These additional variables can also be included in the basic formula, but from a practical point of view usually they can be handled more easily with a separate simple calculation.

Using *Q* computed with the basic formula, such alternative quantity decisions can be made quickly and accurately. By simply comparing annual material cost savings, resulting from the purchase of the additional quantity, with the additional inventory carrying costs occasioned by the increased purchase, the most economical decision quickly becomes evident. With a limited amount of practice, a buyer can determine in a matter of seconds whether material cost savings exceed carrying costs for the additional inventory.

Other Uses of the EOQ Concept

A final word should be said about *general* usage of the EOQ concept. Even though our discussion has been set entirely in the purchasing environment, the EOQ concept logically has broader application as well.

A very common situation in which the concept is used is the determination of economic production lot sizes in a manufacturing operation. Consider the formula a moment ($Q = \sqrt{2UA/IC}$), and look at the individual factors in light of both the purchasing and the production operations. In converting the formula for production use, the annual usage and carrying cost factors are the same as they were in the purchasing application. The unit cost factor, however, is no longer delivered price; instead, it consists of direct labor and materials and production overhead costs. Production acquisition cost is similar to purchasing acquisition cost, except that production setup cost replaces most of the purchasing and related departmental wage and operating costs.

Buyers should also consider (from a supplier's point of view) the formula in this form when determining lot sizes on term contract purchase orders going to various types of job shop suppliers. A supplier's costs and subsequent product price are obviously influenced by the size and frequency of such orders.

TYPES OF INVENTORY CONTROL SYSTEMS

To this point in the discussion, we have considered background concepts that are useful in formulating fundamental aspects of the plans to manage inventories. The discussion now turns to the specific operating systems that can be used.

Generally speaking, four types of inventory control systems are in use: (1) the cyclical or fixed order interval system, (2) the JIT approach, (3) the MRP-type system, and (4) the order point or fixed order quantity system. Each system monitors and controls inventory levels. And each system, based on its own unique characteristics, provides the inventory manager with information that helps answer the two basic questions of *when* to order and *how much* to order.

Cyclical or Fixed Order Interval System

The cyclical system, or fixed order interval system as it is sometimes called, is the oldest and simplest of the systems now found in use. Years ago, when most businesses were small and uncomplicated, this control system was used in all types of operations—manufacturing, service, wholesale, and retail. With the exception of one variation called "flow control," the cyclical system is not widely used today except in smaller and medium-size operations.

Operationally, the system works like this. It is a *time-based* operation which involves *scheduled periodic reviews* of the stock level of all inventory items. Looking at it in a manufacturing setting, when the stock level of a given item is not sufficient to sustain the production operation until the next scheduled review, an order is placed to replenish the supply. The frequency of reviews is determined judgmentally and varies with the degree of control desired by management; *A* items might be reviewed weekly (or more often), *B* items monthly or bimonthly, and *C* items quarterly or semiannually.

Stock levels can be monitored by physical inspection, by visual review of perpetual inventory record cards, or by automatic computer surveillance. In most operations, a perpetual inventory record is maintained,[10] either by computer or manually, except in simple flow-controlled shops (which will be examined shortly). As is discussed in the next chapter dealing with warehousing operations, physical stock counts are required once or twice a year to reconcile actual values with book values in all systems utilizing perpetual inventory records.

---

[10]A perpetual inventory record for a material controlled in a closed stores system is maintained simply by posting receipts from invoices or receiving reports and disbursements from stores material requisitions or similar withdrawal authorizations. In most firms today, perpetual records are computer-based.

The first operating question—*when to order*—is answered or controlled by the review dates established by the inventory manager. If material usage has remained reasonably stable, an order (or a release against an order) is usually placed each time the item is reviewed.

The order date decision is also impacted by the quantity previously ordered, so let us consider the second question also—*how much should be ordered?* The quantity to be ordered generally is determined by three factors: the number of days between reviews, the anticipated daily usage during the cycle period, and the quantity actually on hand and on order at the time of the review. One of the primary reasons this system is used is to control high-value items closely and to maintain a relatively low investment in inventory. Hence, the order quantity typically is the quantity required to cover only the ensuing period, with allowance for order lead time. Occasionally a two- or three-period supply is ordered, but not as a rule.

Consequently, as its name implies, the system works in cyclical fashion, with an order typically placed at each review date for a quantity large enough to cover the ensuing cycle plus the order lead time. A small safety stock is generally carried, based on the observed lead time variability. Inventory levels and tightness of control are thus determined by the establishment of the period of the cycle. High-value *A* and *B* items typically are placed on short cycles and *C* items on longer cycles.

This system can be used with both dependent demand and independent demand materials. It works most effectively in an organization that has a continuous operations function, manufacturing or service, in which demand is fairly stable and can be predicted with reasonable accuracy. Additionally, it is probably the most efficient system to use for independent demand items that experience irregular or seasonal demand and for any items whose purchases must be planned months in advance because of infrequent supplier production schedules. In these cases it tends to keep inventory levels lower than would be possible with the other applicable systems. When used for materials with these characteristics, however, the system must be augmented with a minimum balance figure which signals the need for an early reorder in the case of a sharp usage increase.

To conclude, the cyclical system finds its greatest usage in organizations that have large numbers of independent demand items to control, or in relatively simple process operations where dependent item demand can be projected easily from the production schedule. When used for dependent demand items in an intermittent manufacturing operation, it becomes difficult to determine cycle period demands if many products are involved or if individual items are used in several different products. The bill of materials explosion and time-phasing capabilities of an MRP system must all be handled manually in the cyclical system. As product complexity increases, this becomes a virtual impossibility, so historical demand data tend to become the basis for order quantity determination—and this soon leads to unreasonably high inventory levels because of the uncertainties associated with near-term demand. For these reasons, *MRP systems have replaced most cyclical systems in intermittent manufacturing operations.*

Flow Control System   The "flow control" method of managing inventories is a special variation of the cyclical system. This special method is applicable in continuous manufacturing operations that produce the same basic product in large quantities day after day. Most materials used in such an operation are purchased on term contracts and scheduled for daily or weekly delivery throughout the term. The production cycle is often a day or less in duration, and, in effect, material flows through the plant in continuous streams. Inventory floats consequently can be kept quite low, thus requiring a minimum investment in production inventory.

In such an operation, an open stores system is used for most production materials, and the individual items are stored on the line near the point of use. Stores personnel visually review the level of all material stocks daily and report any imbalances to the purchasing or production control department. Changes in production schedules must be relayed immediately to buyers so that delivery schedules can be revised accordingly.

The Just-in-Time (JIT) Approach

The just-in-time concept was explored in detail in the preceding chapter. It was pointed out there that, in total, JIT is an operating management philosophy. Based on that philosophy, a number of specific operating techniques have been developed—techniques for manufacturing operations, for production planning, and for inventory management. Those dealing with inventory management are the products of the JIT decisions made in the manufacturing and the planning areas.

The operating concept of the system is to gear factory output tightly to distribution demand for finished goods, to gear individual feeder production units tightly together, and to gear the supply of production inventories tightly to the manufacturing demand schedule. This means that all inventories in the system, including production inventories, are maintained at absolutely minimal levels.

It should be emphasized at the outset, however, that as a practical matter most firms utilizing the JIT concept do so for no more than 5 to 10 percent of the materials handled by the purchasing and supply activity, regardless of the extent of the commitment in the manufacturing operation. This means that the production inventory items handled in the JIT inventory system are primarily high-value *A* items. All these items are purchased on a long-term contractual basis, with small-volume deliveries scheduled as frequently as once or twice a day up to once or twice a week.

If one were to observe a JIT operation strictly from an inventory point of view, it would look very much like a flow control operation, with material flowing into and through the plant operation in continuous streams. In fact, it functions much like a flow control operation, only more tightly and more stringently controlled. From strictly an inventory point of view, the systems have almost identical objectives. Many JIT materials are delivered directly to the production operation and are stored close to the point of use; others are handled in a conventional closed stores operation.

From a practical point of view, a JIT inventory system in its purest sense is workable only in continuous manufacturing and processing operations or in intermittent operations that produce a small number of standard products and, because of this fact, are similar to continuous operations. Most, if not all, of the materials handled are dependent demand items.

How are the *when* and *how much* questions answered? As discussed in the preceding chapter, the buyer and the supplier work together closely on the matters of delivery volumes and scheduling. The buying firm's production schedule drives the entire process. The detailed production schedule typically is firmed up for one or two weeks at a time, and in more general terms for a month or so ahead. Specific daily requirements for JIT materials can be determined from this schedule and are relayed directly to the contracting supplier. The exact size and frequency of each delivery is worked out jointly in an attempt to minimize the buyer's incremental inventory-related costs and, at the same time, to maintain an efficient and practical operation for the supplier. As a general rule, the buyer does not identify a specific safety stock component in the firm's inventory figure. Depending on the material, the buying firm typically works on an inventory of several days' to a week's supply. As is the case in a flow control system, stores personnel on the shop floor visually monitor stock levels at least daily and communicate potential overage or shortage problems to the appropriate buyer.

To this point, our discussion has covered only the 5 to 10 percent of a firm's production materials that typically are handled by its JIT purchasing and inventory management system. What about the remaining 90 to 95 percent of the items? As a rule, they are handled in the more conventional manner by one of the other standard systems—namely an MRP or an order point system.

Material Requirements Planning (MRP) System

The preceding chapter, "Production Planning," detailed how closed loop MRP systems function as complete production planning and control systems. The material requirements planning module is an integral part of such a system. Through its bill of materials explosion and aggregation process, this element of the system generates on a weekly basis the projected materials requirements for all the finished products included in a firm's updated master production schedule for the coming two- to three-month period.

Taking the projected gross requirements for a given material during the planning period, the logic of the MRP module then calculates the net requirements by subtracting on-hand inventory and any scheduled receipts of the item as production is scheduled to progress through the planning period. This produces a "time-phased" purchase order requirement to be released at a calculated future date. (The reader may wish to review this logic by referring to Figure 22-3 on page 500.)

The inventory that is carried in the system is a function of three factors: (1) the quantity purchased when each order is placed, (2) the purchase lead time specified by the buyer, and (3) any safety stock that is routinely carried. The objective of time-phasing the order point is to keep the inventory as close to zero as is practical until the material is actually needed for production. Consequently, using an MRP system, the average inventory levels of most materials are relatively low over the long term.

In the case of some materials, no safety stock is carried. In other cases a one- to two-week supply may be carried as a hedge against uncertainties such as possible fluctuations in demand, variations in supplier lead-time requirements, or anticipated scrap or reject rates. Variations in supplier lead-time requirements also may be covered by simply extending the lead-time figure used in calculating the order release date; in this case safety stock would be reduced correspondingly. These safety stock and lead-time hedge values typically are determined judgmentally on the basis of past experience with specific materials and suppliers.

The *when to order* question, then, is answered by the logic of the system. Deciding *how much to order* is in part a judgmental issue. The most common approach, as was the case in the cyclical system, is to order the quantity required during the planning period—the "lot for lot" approach. This method typically tends to minimize the inventory in the system. At times, however, the lot-for-lot approach may produce an order quantity that is too small to be economical. Because of high acquisition costs or production setup costs, order size may have to be larger. In this case, the EOQ or a related least-cost calculation is frequently used to obtain a more appropriate order quantity figure. A number of other decision rules are sometimes used, but those just mentioned appear to be the most common.

The MRP system is designed for use with dependent demand items—that is, production materials. The only way it can handle an independent demand item is by tying such an item's use into a product bill of materials. For production tools and certain other MRO supplies, it is sometimes possible to do this in an approximate way by estimation. But the system's most important use, by far, is with dependent demand materials in an intermittent manufacturing operation. An MRP system can be adapted for use in a continuous or a processing-type operation, but it does not fit such operations well and usually it offers few significant advantages over the other types of systems.

Order Point or Fixed Order Quantity System

The order point system, historically known as the *fixed order quantity system*, is another inventory control system that has been used for years in this country by both manufacturing and nonmanufacturing organizations. The system recognizes the fact that each item has its own unique optimum order quantity, and it is therefore based on *order point* and *order quantity* factors, rather than on the time factor.

Operation of an order point system requires two things for each inventory item:

1 The *predetermination of an order point*, so that when the stock level on hand drops to the order point, the item is automatically "flagged" for reorder purposes. The order point is computed so that estimated usage of the item during the order lead-time period will cause the actual stock level to fall to a planned minimum level by the time the new order is received. Receipt of the new order then increases the stock level to a preplanned maximum figure.

2 The *predetermination of a fixed quantity to be ordered* each time the supply of the item is replenished. This determination typically is based on considerations of price, rate of usage, and other pertinent production and administrative factors.

The automatic feature of the system is achieved by maintaining a perpetual inventory record for each item. The computer, or an inventory clerk in the case of a manual system, continues to post all material issues until the balance of an item falls to its order point. At this point the system notifies the appropriate buyer, who replenishes the stock in a quantity that takes the inventory to its planned maximum level. During the course of operation, the ongoing inventory level is thus maintained between the planned minimum and maximum values.

The predetermined order point, then, tells the buyer *when* to order. In most organizations the order point is determined in the following manner: First, basic operating data about demand and lead time must be obtained. Next, a decision must be made about the desired service level. For most materials, most firms target for 100 percent—that is, they don't want to run out of stock before the new order arrives. At this point in the discussion, the process can be described most easily with the use of a simple illustration. Suppose the following data have been determined for a given inventory item:

Purchasing lead time = 1 week (very stable; little chance of variation)

Material usage = 50 units per week, with ±10 percent variation over the long run

So: Maximum usage during lead time = 55 units
                   Average usage during lead time = 50 units
                   Minimum usage during lead time = 45 units

Figure 23-4a shows a simplified, or idealistic, inventory movement pattern for the material in question, with the usage rate constant at the maximum level of

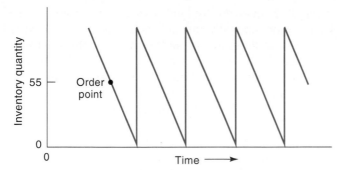

FIGURE 23-4a
Illustrative simplified inventory movement pattern for a given
material, with a maximum usage rate.

55 units per week. If the buyer does not want to run out of stock, at what
inventory level should the new order be placed? If lead time is known to be
one week, and the *maximum* usage has been determined to be 55 units per
week, the new order clearly should be placed when the stock level falls to 55
units. Under these conditions, the new order will arrive just when the stock
level reaches zero. So—the order point is 55 units.

Now, what happens when the usage rate runs around 50 units per week, as
it does much of the time? The inventory movement pattern shown in Figure
23-4a then becomes the dashed sawtooth pattern shown in Figure 23-4b. With
an order point of 55 units, as long as the *average* usage rate of 50 units per
week prevails, the new order will arrive when 5 units (55 – 50 = 5) are still left
in stock. This brings us to the definition of safety stock. In an order point system, set up as just described, *safety stock* is normally defined as *the maximum
lead-time usage minus the average lead-time usage.* In this case, then, the order
point is 55 units and the basic safety stock is 5 units.

FIGURE 23-4b
Preceding movement pattern with an average usage rate, showing
safety stock determination.

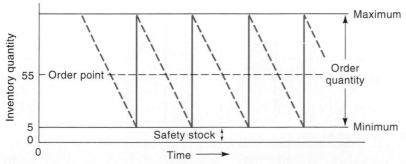

In operation, over a period of time, this means that the low point of the inventory sawtooth pattern will occasionally fall to 0 as the new order arrives (55 − 55 = 0); and when usage is at its lightest, the low point of the sawtooth will be as high as 10 units when the new order arrives (55 − 45 = 10). Most of the time, the low point of the sawtooth will fluctuate between these two extremes, with occurrences concentrated around the safety stock value of 5, which is also defined as the *theoretical* planned minimum. Figure 23-5 depicts this situation hypothetically.

Now that the question of *when* to order has been answered, how does the buyer determine *how much* to order? Any number of decision rules can be used, but the most common approach is to determine the EOQ value. A fixed order quantity system is a natural for EOQ application. The EOQ value can be calculated automatically almost instantaneously with a computer-based order point program. In a manual system, tables of EOQ values can be precalculated and prepared for the near-instantaneous use of inventory clerks. Nomographs and preprogrammed hand-held calculators can also be used easily and quickly. More general decision rules sometimes used by experienced managers are to order a one- to four-week supply of *A* items, a one- to two-month supply of *B* items, and a four- to six-month supply of *C* items.

The major advantages of an order point system are (1) unlike the cyclical and the JIT approaches, the EOQ concept can be applied easily in this system, so each material can be procured in the most economical quantity; (2) this preplanned approach utilizes the time and efforts of people efficiently—purchasing and inventory control personnel automatically devote attention to a given item *only when the item requires attention;* and (3) within limits, control can easily be exerted to maintain inventory investment at a target level simply by varying the planned maximum and minimum values.

On the other side of the coin, the system also has some serious limitations.

- The most serious problem in using an order point system stems from the fact that it works on the basis of historical rather than actual demand

FIGURE 23-5

Typical inventory movement pattern for a reasonably stable material, with a fixed order quantity.

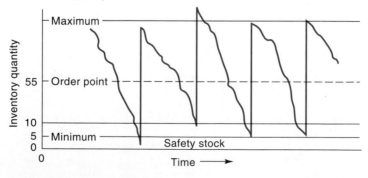

data. Therefore, the order point cannot be time-phased to correspond with actual demand requirements. This means that over the long term, an order point system almost always produces a higher average inventory level than would a comparable MRP system.

- The system functions correctly only if each of the materials exhibits reasonably stable usage and lead-time characteristics. When these factors change significantly, a new order point and a new order quantity must be determined if the system is to fulfill its objectives. Consequently, although it can be adapted, the system becomes costly and cumbersome to operate effectively when applied to materials with highly unstable demand and lead-time patterns.

Bearing in mind the advantages and disadvantages just discussed, it is appropriate to note that an order point system can be used equally well with both independent and dependent demand items. In a *dependent demand* manufacturing environment, a time-phased MRP system is far superior to an order point system because of its use of actual demand data and its ability to maintain average inventories at significantly lower levels. However, if it is not practical to use MRP for low-value *C* items, an order point system can be used very effectively, and the increased inventory levels will affect total costs very little. In managing *independent demand* inventories, a well-designed order point system has no peer—it works extremely well.

As pointed out earlier, an order point system is versatile—it can be used in any type of operation from manufacturing to service. For school districts, hospitals, banks, and numerous other service-oriented institutions, virtually all inventory items exhibit independent demand characteristics. And as one would suspect, order point systems are used in a vast majority of these types of operations.

Two-Bin System A variation of the basic order point system is found in the operation of the simple two-bin system. The distinguishing feature of this system is the absence of a perpetual inventory record. In practice, the stock is physically separated into two bins, or containers. The lower bin contains a quantity of stock equal to the order point figure. This, typically, is just enough stock (or slightly more) to last from the date a new order is placed until the incoming material is received in inventory. The upper bin contains a quantity of stock equal to the difference between the maximum and the order point figures. At the outset, stock is used from the upper bin; when this supply is depleted, it signals the clerk that the order point has been reached. At this point an order is placed, and material is used from the lower bin until the new stock is received. Upon receipt of the new order, the proper quantities of material are again placed in the two bins.

This method demonstrates very simply the fundamental concept which underlies the basic order point system.

The two-bin method is widely used in all types of operations in handling low-value hardware and supplies whose usage is not recorded on a perpetual record. The major advantage of the method is the obvious reduction of clerical work. Issues do not have to be posted to determine the proper reorder time. Receipts, however, are usually posted to reveal significant changes in usage or lead time. A possible disadvantage of the system in some cases is the requirement of additional storage facilities and perhaps some practical difficulty in keeping the two stocks properly separated.

To generalize, it should be pointed out that none of the systems or their adaptations discussed in this chapter are mutually exclusive. *Several or all of them may be used advantageously for different materials in a single firm.*

SYNTHESIS AND CONCLUSION

Production planning and inventory management activities for the past five years or so have been in a significant state of change. New and evolving systems have spawned new and increasingly sophisticated planning and control capabilities. In some cases, the more traditional inventory control systems have been replaced for certain types of applications—in other cases they have not. Table 23-1 draws together in summary form the most significant applications features of the various systems in use today.

It is becoming increasingly difficult for most firms to control inventories effectively. One major reason for this is the expansion of product lines and models. A second key reason is that more and more components going into the typical firm's products are being *purchased* as fabricated parts, rather than being produced from basic materials in the firm's own shops. This means, in many firms, that the number of inventory items to be managed is constantly growing. And because of the increasingly technical nature of materials today, the number of dollars that may be invested in inventory is growing at an even faster rate than the number of items.

In its daily operation, inventory control should be largely a series of clerical or computerized activities, carried on within a carefully defined and controlled framework. The routinization of the daily operation, however, often camouflages the importance of sound management in this area.

At this point in the discussion, there should be little doubt that the basic responsibility for inventory control should lie with top management. The effects of poor inventory management, unfortunately, are not directly visible on the operating statement as a composite cost of inventory management. Nevertheless, in most organizations these indirect costs, dispersed and hidden throughout the operating statement, can have a significant impact on profit. For this reason, top management should carefully formulate and periodically review the basic policies and operating plans that constitute the framework within which the daily inventory control operation functions.

FOR DISCUSSION

23-1 What function do inventories serve in a manufacturing concern? Discuss both the advantages and disadvantages.

TABLE 23-1
COMPARISON OF INVENTORY CONTROL SYSTEMS' CHARACTERISTICS AND APPLICATIONS

Type of system/ characteristics	Order point	Cyclical	MRP	Flow control	JIT
Maintains low inventory level	fair	fair/good	good/excellent	excellent	excellent
Application to items, type of demand	• all types • particularly good for independent demand	all types	primarily dependent demand	primarily dependent demand	dependent demand
Application to type of operations	• all types of manufacturing operations • particularly good for service operations	• all manufacturing operations • service operations	primarily intermittent manufacturing operations, with great product variety	continuous manufacturing operations, with little product variety	continuous manufacturing, with moderate product variety
Demand data used	historical	• actual in simple operations • historical in complex operations	actual	actual	actual
Time-phased order point?	no	• yes in simple operations • no in complex operations	yes	yes	yes
Computer required?	optional	optional	yes	optional	optional
Bill of materials explosion/ aggregation capability	no	no	yes	yes	yes
Administrative effort required	minimal	moderate	moderate	heavy	heavy

23-2 Managers and firms that promote the use of the JIT concept state in no uncertain terms that "inventories are evil." What is your view of this statement? How does the statement relate to your answer to the preceding question?

23-3 Detail in step-by-step form how you would conduct an ABC analysis of an inventory. As a materials manager in an organization, discuss how you would utilize the results of the ABC analysis.

23-4 How can an ABC classification system be modified to recognize the service and operational importance of some C items?

23-5 Explain what is meant by the terms "inventory carrying costs" and "inventory acquisition costs."

23-6 In making an EOQ calculation, the text states that all costs included should be "incremental costs." Why? Discuss. Define an incremental cost.

23-7 What is "opportunity cost," and why should it be included as an inventory carrying cost?

23-8 Suppose your firm utilizes three-year contracts for the purchase of most of its major materials. Explain how you would use the EOQ concept in this situation. How does this application differ from the use of EOQ in a single delivery purchase?

23-9 Can the economic order quantity approach be used just as easily with all four basic control systems (cyclical, JIT, MRP, and order point)? Explain.

23-10 What is the difference between a dependent demand and an independent demand inventory item?

23-11 In determining a firm's incremental acquisition cost per purchase order, should the salary of the purchasing manager and the senior buyers be included? Explain.

23-12 How might quantity discounts be considered in making an EOQ computation in practice? Explain.

23-13 Discuss briefly the major features of the cyclical ordering system. What are the primary advantages and disadvantages of the system?

23-14 What is a flow control system? Under what conditions might you consider the use of a flow control inventory management system? What are the advantages and disadvantages in using such a system?

23-15 How does a flow control system differ from a JIT inventory control system? Discuss.

23-16 Explain briefly how the order point system operates. From an operating point of view, what are the major advantages and disadvantages of using an order point system?

23-17 Compare and contrast the use of an order point system with the use of an MRP system.

23-18 Explain how an MRP system operates. How is an MRP system able to keep inventory levels relatively low?

23-19 Under what operating conditions can an MRP system be utilized most effectively?

23-20 What is the economic order quantity concept? Explain the theory underlying the concept.

23-21 What is meant by a time-phased order point? Explain.

23-22 Assume that you have just been hired to develop an inventory system for a company which in the past has given little attention to the management of inventories. Prepare an outline of the approach you would use in attempting to carry out this assignment. Discuss each point on your outline in some detail, indicating the information you would need, the problems you would expect to encounter, and any other pertinent factors management would be interested in when evaluating your approach to the problem.

23-23 In an order point system, how is safety stock determined?

23-24 Referring to the example on page 536 what would the order point and safety stock values be if the lead-time figure were 1 week ±20 percent?

23-25 List and discuss the chief limitations of EOQ theory.

CASES FOR CHAPTER 23

24

WAREHOUSE AND STORES MANAGEMENT

KEY CONCEPTS

- Responsibilities of receiving and stores
- Receiving procedures and control
- Bar coding
- Identification of materials
    External systems
    Internal systems
- Stores systems and procedures
    Closed system
    Open system
    Random-access storage system
- Storing of materials
    Methods and equipment
    Automated storage and retrieval system
    Layout
- Organization

Receiving and storage are important flow control activities in the materials management chain. Regardless of the efficiency with which all preceding materials activities have been conducted, to a significant extent receiving and stores determine the degree to which the operating units will be supplied satisfactorily.

Because the purchasing and supply department is normally responsible for materials until they are ready for use, it is essential that purchasing managers understand the fundamentals of receiving and stores operations. Additionally, in a majority of U.S. industrial and institutional organizations, receiving and stores departments are either placed under the jurisdiction of the purchasing department or grouped with purchasing and related activities in a materials management department.[1] Whether a firm adopts the materials management concept extensively or not, receiving and stores are a vital element in its total materials system. Effective coordination with the purchasing, inventory management, and traffic functions is imperative.

RESPONSIBILITIES OF RECEIVING AND STORES

Receiving and stores operations provide both service and control functions. First, they generally organize and control the flow of materials into the production operation. Second, the stores organization acts as a custodial and controlling agency. It is responsible for the safety and physical control of a substantial portion of a firm's current assets. And, finally, for many items the existence of a stores operation permits quantity buying and the attendant savings in price, paperwork, and handling.

Specific Responsibilities

A receiving department is responsible for the receipt, identification, and general inspection of most incoming materials. It also notifies the interested individuals of the arrival and condition of the material.

Subsequently, the stores department is responsible for appropriate physical storage of all production materials, some in-process inventory, and most MRO items. In some firms, stores also handles finished goods storage.

The stores manager must develop a system for classifying, marking, and locating all materials so they are readily accessible and, at the same time, protect them against pilferage, unauthorized usage, and unnecessary damage or deterioration. In a closed system, the department must also control physical issuance of material and provide effective service for the operating units.

Cost Implications

Receiving and stores activities *indirectly* influence product costs in several ways. Inventory carrying costs stemming from deterioration, damage, and pilferage of materials, as well as related indirect labor costs, are controllable to a great extent by these managers. Additionally, an alert stores organization can help reduce costs of obsolescence by developing systems to detect slow-moving and inactive materials. Efficient use of scarce storage space can also reduce costs.

---

[1] Harold F. Fearon, *Purchasing Organizational Relationships*, NAPM Inc., Tempe, Ariz., 1988, p. 36.

At the same time, a stores operation typically impacts a firm's *direct* labor costs. Strategically located storage facilities that provide prompt service for operating personnel help reduce the unproductive time of these people. Individuals and machines waiting for the delivery of material add nothing to the productive effort of the organization.

RECEIVING OF MATERIALS

Receiving is essentially a clerical operation. Because many clerical activities are regarded as "routine," however, the importance of the receiving function often is underrated. Only at the receiving desk do the purchasing control documents meet the physical materials themselves. Most problems or errors in a purchasing transaction should come to light during the receiving operation. If the problem (quantity shortage, damaged materials, incorrect items shipped, and so on) is not detected and corrected during the receiving operation, the cost to correct the mistake later is always higher. For example, if a shortage is not discovered at the time of receipt, any combination of departments can be drawn into the problem later. Hours frequently are spent trying to determine what "really happened"—and then in rectifying the situation. Thus, hours are required to correct an error that could have been corrected at the receiving desk in minutes.

The *receiving report*, completed upon receipt of a shipment, is the only document a firm has that details the material it actually received. It also contains important supplier information—delivery timing, shipment damage, reject percentage, split shipments, and so on. This document is used as the basis for invoice payment, for continued purchasing negotiation, and for closing the order. Accuracy is therefore essential. Clearly, poor receiving performance can produce costly consequences. For this reason, receiving should be supervised by a person who is reasonably familiar with the physical characteristics of the materials and who is capable of exercising sound judgment in situations where a choice of alternatives must be made.

Receiving Procedure

A typical receiving procedure consists of four steps:

1 *Unloading and checking the shipment.* The number of containers unloaded from the carrier's vehicle is checked against the carrier's manifest (freight bill) to make certain the full consignment has been delivered. All containers are also inspected for external damage; any damage found is inspected by the carrier's representative and noted on the receipt which the receiving clerk signs. Failure to follow this procedure before accepting a shipment can relieve the carrier of all liability, except liability for concealed damage not evident until the container is unpacked.

2 *Unpacking and inspecting the material.* A receiving clerk is held responsible for three verifications. First, he or she checks the material received against the seller's packing slip and against a copy of the firm's purchase order to verify that the correct items have been shipped. Second, the quantity of the shipment is verified in the same manner. Finally, the clerk inspects the general condition of the material to determine whether any external damage was incurred during shipment.

3 *Completion of the receiving report.* The paperwork system used varies significantly from firm to firm. In some companies a multipart receiving report form is produced as a by-product when the purchase order is generated. When the receiving clerk has finished the inspection, he or she completes this form by recording the quantities of the items received, indicating those that are still open, and noting any other useful information on the form. In other firms that utilize a computerized purchasing/inventory system, the clerk records the receiving data on the receiving report or a short form, from which a data entry clerk keys the data directly into the computer system. The system then updates the order and inventory records and may also generate a receiving report in either hard copy or electronic form.

   Regardless of the system used, four operating groups generally require notification that the material has been received: the requisitioner, the purchasing department, the accounting department, and the inspection department if technical inspection is required.

4 *Delivery of the material.* For non-stock materials, the receiving department is usually responsible for delivery—directly or via an internal delivery service. In the case of inventory materials, the practice varies. In some firms the receiving department is responsible for internal deliveries, while in others this function is performed by an internal transportation service. In still others, stores clerks are responsible for picking up their own materials.

   Upon delivery of the materials, the recipient customarily signs the receiving report or a delivery receipt, relieving the receiving clerk of further responsibility for the material.

It should be noted at this point in the discussion that in some firms not all delivered materials go through the receiving operation. Some JIT purchasing shipments, some materials purchased from certified suppliers, and most credit card purchases are delivered directly to the point of use, bypassing receiving. This situation is discussed further in the section dealing with an open stores system.

Bar Coding

Anyone who has shopped in a supermarket knows that bar coding is used extensively for product identification in the wholesale and retail food business.

Only in recent years, however, has industry used it to any significant extent. Today approximately 20 percent of the country's industrial firms use the technology to some extent in their receiving, inventory control, or work in process tracking operations. Although the use of bar coding is still limited in most industrial operations, applications are estimated to be growing at a rate in excess of 25 percent per year.[2] Hence, it is appropriate to introduce the concept briefly at this point in the discussion.

"In its briefest form, a bar code label is simply a unique license plate. This license plate accesses a data file containing information about the labeled object."[3] The size and arrangement of the solid bars and spaces on the label represent the object's part or product number in coded form. When read with a laser scanner, the bars and spaces reflect a light pattern that is converted into electrical pulses that a computer decodes and uses to access the part number's file in its memory.

More than a dozen bar code symbologies are in use today, with four predominating: (1) Code 39, (2) Interleaved Two-of-Five, (3) Universal Product Code, and (4) Codabar. The Interleaved Two-of-Five code is most commonly used in industrial stores and inventory operations, and the Universal Product Code is the standard used in the grocery business.[4] Figure 24-1 provides a sample of each.

If incoming material shipments are bar coded, the receiving operation in a computer-based purchasing/inventory system can be refined beyond the one just described. The step in the process at which receiving data are entered into the computer system can usually be simplified. The data entry clerk now can access the item's inventory record simply by scanning the bar code, rather than keying the information in manually.[5] This improves both the speed and the accuracy of the operation immensely. If material can be packaged and recorded in standard quantities, the total operation can be refined even more. Some purchasers arrange to have suppliers apply the bar code label to the material or its container before shipment. Others apply their own preprinted labels at the receiving desk, and some generate the labels by computer as the material is being received.

Depending on the nature of a given firm's receiving activities and the design of its computer information system, the potential for improvement of productivity and accuracy can be substantial through development and use of an appropriate bar coding operation.

---

[2]E. J. Walter, "Bar Code Boom Extending through Industry," *Purchasing World,* February 1988, p. 39; Bruce S. Richmond, "Warehouse Trends and Technology," *NAPM Insights,* November 1993, p. 44.

[3]David C. Allais, "Code 49—What Is It? Why Do We Need It?" *Purchasing World,* February 1988, p. 40.

[4]Susan Avery, "Bar Codes Take Off from Factory Floor," *Purchasing,* Nov. 7, 1991, p. 52.

[5]If the original purchase order is also bar coded, the order can be accessed in the open order file as well. Some firms do this to facilitate tracking of the order through the procurement cycle. See Caroline Reich, "Putting Bar Codes to Work," *Purchasing World,* August 1987, pp. 57–61.

| Universal Product Code | Interleaved Two of Five | FIGURE 24-1 An illustration of two commonly used bar codes. |

IDENTIFICATION OF MATERIALS

Stores operations involve the physical aspects of materials handling and storage. From a management perspective, however, the stores manager and the materials manager are concerned first with the design and control of the systems utilized in conducting stores activities. Developing a system for effective identification of materials carried in stores is a major responsibility confronting these managers.

A firm's stock catalog, prepared by the inventory management group, lists and describes every item normally carried in inventory. These descriptions, however, usually are somewhat imprecise and awkward for use in identifying materials during daily operations. Although all standard purchased items can be identified by suppliers' part numbers, different suppliers use vastly different numbering systems. This makes it virtually impossible for a purchaser to develop a satisfactory material identification system based on suppliers' part numbers. Consequently, a firm with a sizable production and MRO inventory is compelled to develop its own numerical identification system for its materials. When the system is complete, the inventory catalog usually is arranged and indexed by the *purchaser's own* part numbers, and includes a reference to the supplier's part number for each purchased item. Although the catalog can be cross-indexed in various ways, at a minimum it should be cross-indexed by generic name of the items and perhaps also by suppliers and their part number.

The objective is to develop an unambiguous identification system, with adequate item description, that facilitates clear communication among all users.

Identification Systems

In a broad sense, there are two types of material identification systems—those designed primarily for *external use* and those designed for *internal use*. The systems designed for external use have as their objectives the facilitation of sales transactions (buyers and suppliers using common identification codes) and material reporting activities required in international trade. As the name implies, internal systems are designed with enough detail to communicate unequivocally the identification and description of materials to all using departments within the organization—from design engineering to operations to purchasing and supply to accounting.

Can the same system be used for both external and internal purposes? It may be possible, but few if any firms do. The basic difficulty is that most firms want their internal systems to contain as much detail as possible to fulfill their own unique needs. And systems used for external purposes tend to be somewhat more attenuated, focusing on product and material *types*, rather than on specific items, detailed characteristics, and so on.[6]

External Systems

The two external systems most commonly used in international business are:

- The Harmonized Commodity Description and Coding System
- The Export Commodity Control Numbers (ECCN) system

The *Harmonized* system provides a set of descriptions and six-digit codes for commodity identification, description, and reporting. It also contains an option for the addition of four more digits to provide more local detail. This is perhaps the most widely used of the two international systems.

The *Export Commodity Control Numbers* system consists of product numbers that take the form of a five-character alphanumeric code. This system is used primarily for security-sensitive materials requiring export control.[7]

Internal System Design

Literally hundreds of similar but unique internal material identification systems are used in American industry today. However, most firms follow some

---

[6]For readers interested in other standardized coding systems, it should be noted that two government-oriented systems exist in the United States. The National Institute of Governmental Purchasing (NIGP) has developed its Commodity/Service Code System that is designed for public purchasing operations. Additionally, the General Services Administration has developed the Federal Supply Classification system for use in identifying and coding materials commonly used by federal government agencies.

[7]For a more thorough discussion of standard commodity coding systems, see George A. Johnson, CFPIM, "Setting the Standard: Commodity Coding Systems," *NAPM Insights*, April 1993, p. 5.

type of *symbolic approach* in designing the system. Symbolic systems can be either *numerical* or *mnemonic*.

A numerical system typically assigns a six- to ten-digit code number to each item. The first several numbers usually indicate the classification to which the item belongs, the next several numbers typically indicate the subclass, and the last three numbers are usually uncoded. The following example illustrates the concept:

2	137	019	508
General Class	Generic Class	Subclass	Specific Item Number

This ten-digit code number is one firm's stock number for a ¼- by ¾-inch stainless steel square-neck carriage bolt. The first digit indicates that the item is a purchased part, in accordance with the following general classification:

1 Raw materials
2 Purchased parts
3 Manufactured parts
4 Work in process
5 MRO supplies

The next three digits indicate the generic classification of the item. In this case it is a fastener, code number 137; it might have been a bearing, a pulley, a pump, or an electric motor. All items are generically classified by their nature and carry a number from 000 to 999.

The next three digits indicate the subclass to which the item belongs. In this case, number 019 is a carriage bolt with a square neck. It might have been a machine screw, a rivet, or a nut. All fasteners are subclassified into a class bearing a number from 000 to 999.

The last three digits indicate the specific part number of the item. In this case, all part numbers under 500 designate plain steel, and numbers over 500 represent various alloys; 508 is stainless steel, ¼ by ¾ inch. Other dimensional details can be determined only by referring to the inventory catalog.

This example and similar systems provide a complete and ordered framework within which all materials can be identified uniquely. As a rule, each company devises its own specific system to suit the needs of its own particular materials. A ten-digit number is long and cumbersome; a six-digit system is much easier to use if it provides adequate definition and contains enough unused numbers to accommodate future growth. A few companies structure their systems around finished products rather than generic classification. The subdivision distinctions can be made as fine or as broad as desired. A major factor to consider in these decisions is the value the additional system refinement provides the user.

A mnemonic system functions much like a numerical system. However, it combines numeric and alphabetic notations in its symbols. For example, the preceding carriage bolt might be described this way in a mnemonic system:

P   Fa   BCS   508

P denotes a purchased part; Fa is a fastener; BCS stands for bolt, carriage, with a square neck; and 508 represents the specific number of the bolt.

Mnemonic systems, particularly where a small number of items are involved, frequently make visual identification easier because they are more descriptive and are often shorter. As more and different types of items are added to the inventory, however, this advantage diminishes because the number of good symbols is limited. Telephone companies encountered this coding problem some years ago. As a result, all major firms have converted telephone calling codes from mnemonic to numeric.

Some firms identify the stock parts manufactured to their own engineering specifications by using the *engineering drawing number* as the part number. This system is effective because it is simple and it directly references the technical data source for the part. Moreover, it simplifies interdepartmental communications because all departments can easily use the same system. On the other hand, the system has the disadvantage of not having sequential numbers assigned to items in the same generic class. Drawing numbers usually are assigned sequentially as new designs are created, regardless of the type of product involved. Additionally, since this system covers primarily manufactured parts, a separate system must be devised to handle purchased parts and components.

Physical Identification

Even though a satisfactory identification system is developed, physical identification of materials in the storeroom may still be a problem. The first step in minimizing this problem is to record the storage location of all items in the inventory catalog. When a storeroom is properly laid out, every storage location has a numerical designation. Using a conventional system (non-random-access), each inventory item should be assigned a specific storage location. These locations can be noted in the catalog or in a separate storage locator index so that anyone can locate any material with ease.

Each storage bin should be labeled with its part number. In some cases, an abbreviated description of the item may be helpful. All items that are not readily identifiable on sight should be tagged or marked with the part number by the storekeeper. On nonstandard items, suppliers can frequently mark an item during the manufacturing or shipping operation. Castings, stampings, and forgings are good examples of items that can be marked permanently for little or no extra cost. Some materials, such as steel plate, bars, special bolts, and so on, are difficult to mark, but intercompany groups have made good progress in standardizing identification markings for such materials. One scheme involves the use of a standard color code; the ends or edges of the material are simply marked with the appropriate color to facilitate quick identification.

STORES SYSTEMS

Two basic systems can be used in physically controlling stores materials: (1) a closed stores system and (2) an open stores system. The application of each depends on the nature and requirements of a specific production operation. As a general rule, most firms use one system for certain materials and the second system for others.

Closed System

As its name indicates, a *closed stores system* is one in which all materials are physically stored in a closed or controlled area. Wherever possible, the general practice is to maintain physical control by locking the storage area. As a rule, no one other than stores personnel is permitted in the stores area. Material enters and leaves the area only with the accompaniment of an authorizing document. This system is designed to afford maximum physical security and to ensure tight accounting control of inventory material.

Records   In years past, each storekeeper was responsible for maintaining an inventory record for each of the items under his or her control. All receipts and withdrawals were posted on a "bin tag" which eventually became the firm's permanent record of activity for a given material.

Today, virtually all firms maintain centralized perpetual inventory records independent of storeroom stock cards. In most firms these records are computerized. Receipts are posted to the perpetual record from suppliers' invoices or from the firm's receiving reports.[8] Withdrawals from stores are normally authorized and posted from one of three sources. The most common source is the stores requisition, which is made out by the user and signed by an authorized supervisor. Thus, the central record provides a running balance for each major inventory item.

A second commonly used source in continuous and intermittent manufacturing operations is a periodic release (usually weekly) of production requirements. The production scheduling group analyzes and aggregates production schedules for the coming period and forwards a list of the aggregated material requirements to purchasing and stores. This document then authorizes the release of the specified materials from the closed stores operation.

A third source of withdrawal authorization used in some job-shop-type operations is the engineering bill of materials. These lists of materials are

---

[8]In some cases, this is done by means of a bar code scanning operation, as described in a previous section.

developed along with the design drawings. After the design engineering work for a job has been completed, production control schedules the job and arranges for the release of the required materials to the shop. Instead of preparing a set of stores requisitions for these materials, production control may simply reproduce the engineering bill of materials and send a copy to stores as the document authorizing release of the materials. For effective use, this system requires clear and complete identification of all materials on the engineering bill of materials. For the materials involved, a single company-wide inventory numbering system is a necessity when this system is used.

When the materials required for a job are to be withdrawn from stores over a period of time, using bills of materials as withdrawal authorizations presents a problem. Unless a daily report of withdrawals for the job is prepared, it is difficult for the central inventory record section to keep its records current, because the stores department must retain its copy of the bill of materials until all withdrawals are made.

This problem can be circumvented, however, by using a material apportioning system. Under this system, the bill of materials goes first to the inventory record section, where the total requirement for each material needed on a job is deducted from the current inventory balance. The required amount is set aside, or apportioned (on the perpetual record), so it will not be allocated for use on another job before the current requirement materializes in the shop. When the apportioned material is actually used, the apportioned quantity on the inventory record is charged off to the job. The apportioning system, of course, can be used to assure material availability for specific jobs regardless of the method used to authorize stores withdrawals. The system is widely used among firms with job-shop-type operations.

Every firm uses many low-value inventory items. To maintain a perpetual inventory record for all low-value items may cost more than the control provided by such a record is worth. To obtain a record of approximate usage, it is much cheaper to have the stores clerk record all receipts on a bin tag. To indicate when an item should be ordered, a bin level mark or some form of the two-bin control system can be used. For small items, many firms simply place the lead-time usage quantity (plus safety stock) in a plastic bag; when the clerk has to use stock from the bag, he or she knows it is time to reorder. This method is frequently used for nuts, bolts, and other low-value hardware. If the accounting charge can be determined at the time an order is issued, the accounting department can pick up the proper distribution code from the purchase order. If not, the accounting department usually develops a method by which the expenditure can be allocated equitably among the users.

Physical Inventory   No matter how diligently a storekeeper performs the custodial job or how carefully an inventory control clerk maintains records (computerized or manual), some discrepancy between the actual and the book balances of inventories is bound to occur. The system is operated by people, and people occasionally make mistakes. For this reason, every inventory item should be counted physically and checked against its book balance at least once a year. The books subsequently are adjusted to match the actual count. Most companies create an "inventory short and over" account to absorb such discrepancies; this account is eventually closed into the manufacturing overhead account.

Use of a bar coding receiving/inventory system can markedly reduce the time required to take the physical inventory. If the inventory items or their storage locations have been previously bar coded, the task can be accomplished with a portable laser scanner and hand-held data terminal. The scanner is used to identify the item, and the count is entered into the data terminal, which is later uploaded into the computerized inventory system.

From a scheduling point of view, the physical inventory can be conducted in one of three ways:

1 *Fixed annual inventory.* Many companies take physical inventory annually at the close of the fiscal year. This necessitates shutting down the production operation and organizing a special crew for the inventory job.

2 *"Cycle count" or continuous inventory.* At the beginning of each year some firms divide their inventory into fifty-two equal groups and assign one of the fifty-two groups to be physically counted each week. Thus, the physical inventory operation goes on continuously without interrupting the production operation or upsetting storeroom activities.

3 *Low-point inventory.* Some companies take physical inventory irregularly, whenever the stock level of an item reaches its lowest point.

All three methods are widely used; the selection of the most appropriate one depends largely on conditions in each individual business. The fixed annual inventory can be troublesome because it is a major task which must be accomplished in a short period of time. However, it is ideal for seasonal businesses or for businesses that completely close down for an annual vacation or equipment maintenance check.

The cycle count inventory approach has two major advantages. It can be planned and worked into scheduled activities without a shutdown. And it can be conducted in an orderly and relaxed manner, which is conducive to accurate work. It has the additional advantage of early detection and elimination of basic causes of errors that might otherwise continue throughout the year. This approach also facilitates efficient utilization of stores personnel. In many storerooms, withdrawals are heavy early in the day and much lighter later on. Thus, when the stock clerks' normal work slacks off, they always have a backlog of inventory work to do.

The low-point approach minimizes the time required for actual inventory work because of the small quantities of materials involved. However, it has the disadvantage of producing an irregular inventory schedule, which tends to peak the workload for stores personnel.

Finally, before developing the details of any physical inventory method, a company should consult the accounting firm that audits its books. A company must be able to demonstrate to auditing firms, and to local and federal tax officials, that the method finally selected is capable of producing accurate inventory reports.

Storeroom Location   In laying out a manufacturing operation, a layout engineer attempts to develop an efficient work flow that minimizes the transportation and handling of materials. This means that materials should be stored as close to their point of use as is feasible. Hence, the use of decentralized storage facilities frequently reduces manufacturing costs.

On the other hand, the centralization of storage facilities also yields significant benefits. From a managerial point of view, the major advantage of centralization is that it facilitates control of the total stores operation—manpower, materials, space utilization, and equipment. Whenever an activity is divided and conducted as a number of separate subactivities, supervision and coordination of the total operation become more difficult. Up to a point, the larger the storage area, the more efficiently space and equipment can be used. Similarly, a larger operation facilitates the balancing of individual workloads and permits more efficient utilization of personnel.

A firm normally attempts to use both centralized and decentralized locations in its total stores operation. The objective is to secure the major advantages of both approaches to the extent possible in a particular situation. Most plants attempt to centralize as much material as is practical. The result, for example, may be two or three large storerooms strategically located near different manufacturing areas, the exact number depending on the size and nature of the production operation. When possible, heavy or bulky materials that are costly to handle should be stored adjacent to the point of use. For example, in a processing plant it is quite common to find one or two large centralized storerooms handling small production items, packaging materials, tools, and MRO supplies. Located throughout the plant adjacent to the point at which they are used in the process are numerous stacks of large bags and drums containing such things as chemicals and additives.

Open System

The open system represents the second major type of stores system. Its widest use is in highly repetitive, mass production types of operations that exhibit a continuous and predictable demand for the same materials. Most JIT manufacturing systems exemplify this situation.

In plants using the *open stores system,* no storeroom as such exists; each material is stored as close to its point of use as is physically possible. Materials are stored in bins, on shelves, in racks, on pallets, in tote boxes, and so on, much as they would be stored in a storeroom. However, the storage configuration at each work station is arranged to fit the available space. Storage facilities are completely open, and any worker has access to any storage facility.

After material is received, stores personnel are usually responsible for delivering it to the production areas. They are further responsible for working out satisfactory physical storage arrangements with the production supervisors. After the material has been delivered, production supervisors assume responsibility for materials stored in their areas.

The open system is designed to expedite production activities. It places little emphasis on the physical security of materials. In ideal applications, there is considerable justification for this approach because the material is used relatively quickly, and it is not subject to a high rate of deterioration, obsolescence, or theft.

An automobile assembly plant offers the clearest example of an open stores system. Here, daily production is high, and purchased parts and subassemblies flow into the plant in a steady stream. For higher-cost, bulky items, deliveries from suppliers may be scheduled several times a day. As a result, average inventory is extremely low relative to plant output. Such systems place unusually exacting demands for close cooperation on personnel in production control, purchasing, and the supplier and carrier organizations.

The open system also places less emphasis on the accounting control of materials. Materials are usually put into production without the use of a requisition or a control document. No perpetual inventory records are kept in an open system. To determine the *actual* usage of a material during a given period, it is necessary to take a physical count of the material at the end of the period and to compare this figure with the similar beginning-period figure, adjusted for material receipts during the period. Hence, accounting charges are determined indirectly rather than directly. As a result, the system provides control over material usage only if it is used in conjunction with an accounting system employing "standard cost" techniques.

To conclude, the open system is most applicable in situations where a repetitive production operation produces standardized products, and in JIT types of operations. Materials handled in an open system should not be subject to pilferage, nor should they be easily damaged. If production requires delicate or pilferable items, they probably should be controlled in a closed storeroom. Generally speaking, an open system is more likely to function successfully if it is not applied to a large number of items. Firms applying such a system to several hundred items typically experience better results than those applying it to several thousand items.

Random-Access Storage System

The random-access storage system is a unique type of closed stores system, used by a relatively small number of large firms. In this system, no material has a fixed storage location. When an item enters the storeroom, it is stored in the first available bin or shelf suitable for its storage requirements. When the item is withdrawn from stores, the storage space is available for any other incoming item having similar physical storage requirements. All materials are thus stored at random locations throughout the warehouse. This means, for example, that a stock of nine 20-horsepower electric motors may be located at nine different places in the storage area. However, *similar types and sizes of storage equipment* are grouped together. This has the effect of dividing the warehouse into areas of materials that are similar in size and storage requirements.

How does the storekeeper find an item once it has been stored? In a typical system, when an item enters the storeroom a record is created for it in the memory of the system's self-contained computer. This record contains the storage location (each location is numbered) assigned to the item. When a stores requisition is received for an item, an operator can access the item record through a terminal and obtain either a printout or a video screen display showing the item's storage address. In some systems, the item record can also be accessed by the command of another computer—such as one in production planning's system—linked to the storage system's computer. In any case, this sophisticated type of control system makes possible the development of an automated storage/retrieval system—a topic which will be discussed shortly.

The random-access storage system clearly is most adaptable in relatively large operations. It requires a computer-based intelligence system and usually an expensive operating system. The system also has several significant disadvantages. For example, tight physical control of materials may be more difficult to achieve. Stores clerks seldom become familiar with the total stock of any item, simply because they lose the close visual contact they have with their materials in a conventional system. In the event of a storage location input error or a computer malfunction, the item itself may literally be lost for an indefinite period of time. A second drawback is that when a physical inventory is taken, it clearly becomes a major time-consuming project.

On the positive side, if properly designed and operated, a random-access storage system possesses two important advantages. First, it utilizes space much more efficiently than a fixed-location system. In arranging storage facilities, space for a fluctuating inventory level does not have to be left vacant for each material. Second, the system provides great flexibility. The same storage facilities can easily accommodate different materials, shifts in inventory mix, and unexpected increases in the stock level of an existing material.

STORING OF MATERIALS

Few things irritate a production supervisor more than an inefficient, poorly organized warehouse. A good layout and good storage methods yield the following benefits:

1 Ready accessibility of major materials, permitting efficient service to users
2 Efficient space utilization and flexibility of arrangement
3 A reduced need for materials handling equipment
4 Minimization of material deterioration and pilferage
5 Ease of physical counting

Methods and Equipment

Today, most firms emphasize the need to minimize inventories and non-value-added support activities. Attainment of these objectives often calls for smaller warehouses and more efficient layout and stores operations. Consequently, stores management is being pressed for continuing improvements in the warehousing and physical supply operation.[9]

Planning   Regardless of size, planning is the key to consistent and efficient stores operation. What types and combinations of storage equipment should be used? How should the warehouse be laid out? These are key planning questions that must be answered.

The initial step in answering the first question is to compile a list of information about the materials to be stored. Using a current inventory catalog, the following data should be listed for each item carried:

1 How much space (and what configuration) is required to store the item properly?
2 How many units are normally withdrawn at once? Should the item be stored singly, in pairs, in dozens?
3 What is the maximum number of units to be stored at one time?
4 What type of storage facility best suits the item (considering such things as weight, shape, and handling)?
5 What handling equipment is necessary to transport the item?
6 How often is the item withdrawn from stores?
7 Where is the item most frequently used in the production operation?

The numbers and types of storage facilities currently required can be determined fairly definitely if these seven questions are answered for all materials. At the same time, estimates of future needs should be made. By comparing future requirements with current requirements, a solution to the current problem can often be designed to include enough flexibility to permit relatively easy adaptation of the facilities to future needs when that time arrives.

Equipment   Eight general types of equipment are commonly used in storing materials:

1 Pallets and skids
2 Open and closed shelving
3 Cabinets (with or without counters)
4 Bins
5 Stacking boxes
6 Special storage racks
7 Gravity feed racks
8 Outdoor platforms and racks

---

[9]John B. Nofsinger, "New Realities and Advances," Warehouse Trends and Technology section, *NAPM Insights,* November 1993, pp. 42–43.

Figures 24-2 and 24-3 illustrate several storage installations using some of the common types of storage and materials handling equipment.

Most industrial warehouses used to be equipped with wooden shelving and storage facilities. Wooden facilities still offer several advantages. Wood is softer than metal and provides safer storage for delicate items which might be dropped or scuffed in the bin. Wooden facilities can also be built to special configurations and can generally be installed quickly and inexpensively.

Wooden facilities are quite inflexible, however, and this causes problems as an operation expands or as storage needs change. To overcome this disadvantage, most companies today use steel equipment of the "knock-down" variety. This equipment is designed so that it can be assembled and reassembled in shelf or bin form in numerous different standardized shapes and sizes. Although steel equipment is more expensive initially, its long-run advantages usually outweigh the additional cost. Its configuration and location flexibility gives steel equipment a major advantage over wooden equipment. Steel equipment has the additional advantages of strength and fire resistance; it is also easy to keep clean.

Automated Warehousing   For a growing number of firms, the automated warehouse is now a reality. A combination of the random-access storage con-

FIGURE 24-2

A two-level storage facility using a combination of metal shelving, bins, and cabinets. Materials handling equipment shown consists of roller conveyors joined by a belt conveyor. *(Courtesy of Lyon Metal Products Inc.)*

FIGURE 24-3
Wooden pallets being used to provide efficient storage for heavy, unwieldy industrial valves.
The materials handling equipment is a gasoline-powered forklift type of stacking truck.
(Courtesy of the Clark Equipment Company.)

cept, highly sophisticated storage/retrieval machines, and a computerized control system has produced today's *automated storage/retrieval system* (AS/RS).

The storage facility frequently is a 30- to 80-foot high-rise structure, constructed of open steel columns. Typically it is configured into storage cubicles of different sizes and utilizes various types of standardized pallets and containers for storage. Figure 24-4 illustrates two different types of installations. A number of warehouse stock clerks are replaced with automated storage/retrieval machines that are mounted either on captive floor rails or on conventional wheels. The tall, masted vehicles have a lifting platform with a shuttle that stores and retrieves palletized or containerized loads on both sides of the aisle.

These vehicles normally are controlled remotely by a computer, although they can be controlled manually. Hence, this type of operation is simply an extension of the random-access storage concept to include computer direction of mechanized vehicles used in the actual storage and retrieval of materials.

FIGURE 24-4
Automated warehouse installations, using computer-operated, captive-rail storage/retrieval machines.
(a) Palletized installation. (Note the storage operation in progress.) The materials handling vehicles in the foreground are computer-controlled "Robocarrier" vehicles. They are precision battery-powered vehicles that "track" a network of guidepath wires embedded in the floor. *(Courtesy of Eaton-Kenway.)*

Operating efficiency can be increased even more by linking the production planning computer system with the AS/RS control computer. In this case, required production materials are automatically located and mechanically "picked" from storage by a computer command initiated by a computer-released production schedule in the production planning department.

In addition to increased operating efficiency, these automated "skyscraper" facilities possess two other advantages. First, they utilize warehouse space (the "cube") exceptionally well, which is welcome news to any financial manager concerned about the cost of buildings and real estate. Second, they drastically reduce warehouse labor requirements and operating costs. The other side of the coin, obviously, is that this equipment requires a large initial investment—and high-volume usage to make it profitable. For these reasons, only a limited number of large firms utilize these systems today.

FIGURE 24-4
(b) Containerized installation. (*Courtesy of Eaton-Kenway.*)

Storage Methods An important objective of all stores operations is to minimize deterioration and spoilage. It is common practice, particularly when dealing with materials that tend to deteriorate or become obsolete, to issue old material ahead of new material. Numerous schemes can be devised for accomplishing this. A very simple solution, however, is illustrated in Figure 24-5.

Figure 24-5 represents stacked boxes of material. As material is withdrawn, it is taken from the left end of the stack, moving progressively to the right. When new shipments arrive, they are stored on the right. Thus, by moving from left to right, older material is used first, leaving newer material for future use. This technique is commonly referred to as storage for "first-in, first-out" usage.

Special protection is occasionally required for some items. If metal parts are subject to rust or corrosion, they should be stored in dry areas. In some cases, they should be covered with suitable rust-inhibiting compounds. Since dust is harmful to certain items, airtight containers or drawers may be suitable for storage of such items if they cannot be purchased in inexpensive sealed containers.

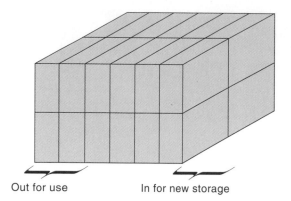

FIGURE 24-5
Storage scheme for first-in, first-out usage.

Out for use   In for new storage

Some liquids are sensitive to heat and cold; certain granulated materials are sensitive to moisture. Such items should be stored in suitable locations.

Obviously, items subject to pilferage should be stored in locked cabinets or other secure areas to reduce temptation and subsequent losses.

Units of Issue   A warehouse does not always issue a material in the same units in which it is purchased. Steel, for example, is usually purchased in tons or pounds and issued in sheets, bars, or feet. Some boxed materials are purchased by the gross and issued by the dozen. Record-keeping and pricing errors sometimes occur when specific units of issue are not clearly established for such materials.

To avoid possible communication difficulties, the *standard unit of issue* for a material is usually defined as the *smallest quantity likely to be issued*. The inventory record should be maintained in terms of the standard unit, and stores requisitions should state withdrawals in the same terms. Errors can be avoided by using the same unit of issue for similar materials. Likewise, units of issue involving calculations, such as square feet or board feet, should be avoided whenever possible. In cases where the unit of issue is not obvious to operating personnel, it should be marked clearly on the stock bin and on the inventory record.

Some items, such as powdered materials, nails, screws, and numerous small items, can be dispensed more efficiently by weight than by actual count. In such cases, weight-to-unit conversion tables should be developed so that records can be maintained in the same units as issues are made.

Layout

Good warehouse layout attempts to achieve five objectives:

1 A straight-line flow of activity through the storage areas with minimum backtracking

2 Minimum handling and transportation of materials

3 Minimum travel and waste motion for personnel
4 Efficient use of space
5 Provision for flexibility and expansion of layout

It is virtually impossible to attain all objectives completely. However, a carefully planned compromise solution can usually satisfy most layout objectives reasonably well.

The initial criteria used in laying out most warehouses are the size, shape, and type of material to be stored. First, items must be analyzed to determine their storage facility requirements—then those with similar requirements are grouped together. From this analysis, the total requirement *for each type of storage equipment* can be determined. Once this determination is made, it can be analyzed in conjunction with a floor plan of the available space. By making scaled templates of the equipment, various arrangements can be simulated on the floor plan until the one that most nearly satisfies the basic objectives is found.

Storage Location Address   A well-worn but appropriate slogan seen in many warehouses is "A place for everything and everything in its place." A "place for everything" can be planned. Keeping "everything in its place," though, is not always an easy job. The development of a good storage location address system provides assistance to those who try to keep everything in place.

There are numerous ways of addressing storage locations. One widely used system is illustrated in Figure 24-6. This system arranges the warehouse in "blocks" of storage units, much as a city is laid out in blocks of houses. Each block is identified by a lateral block letter and a longitudinal block letter. Within each block, every row of shelves is given a number. Each row is divided vertically into columns and horizontally into shelves. A particular bin is identified by reading the letters and numbers in the following sequence: lateral block, longitudinal block, row, column, and shelf.

Blocks and rows should be identified clearly with painted signs. Columns and shelves are always read starting from the lower left corner. Frequently, the shelves are not labeled because shelves are added and taken away from time to time as storage requirements change.

Every item carried in stores thus has a specific storage location address. These location addresses should be listed in the inventory catalog if possible; if not, they should at least be listed in a stores location index.

ORGANIZATION

The stores and receiving jobs are closely related. Therefore, the receiving activity usually is placed under the supervision of the stores manager. As noted earlier, in a majority of U.S. industrial firms, stores either reports to the purchasing and supply department or is grouped with purchasing in a materials management department. There are two strong arguments for such an organizational arrangement:

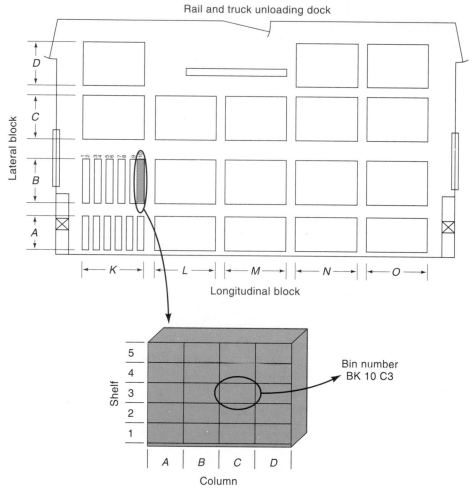

FIGURE 24-6
A common system used in addressing storage locations.

1 The stores activity is a materials-oriented activity; therefore, it should report to a department whose primary interest and expertise also lie in materials and supply operations. Supervisory personnel thus will recognize and be equipped to deal with the materials and supply problems encountered in receiving and stores.

2 Receiving is the last step in the material acquisition process, and stores is the last step in the material supply process. From the standpoint of the *total control of materials* these activities should be included with the rest of the materials activities. From an operating point of view, such a materials organization facilitates coordination between the related materials activi-

ties. Specifically, it ensures that the relationships between stores, inventory control, and purchasing will receive proper attention, as will the important factor of indirect material costs.

Some firms place the stores activity under the production department. In a few cases, it is placed under a factory superintendent; in others, it reports to the production control manager; and in still others, it reports to the general production manager. Two common justifications for this form of organization are:

1 Production management is responsible for running the production operation smoothly and for meeting product delivery dates. Production should therefore have control of its immediate material supply group to ensure smooth delivery of material to the production work stations.

2 Receiving and stores disbursement activities should not be supervised by the department that buys and authorizes payment for the same materials. Collusion and embezzlement are discouraged when stores and receiving personnel report to a manager outside the purchasing and supply department.

Both preceding sets of arguments are valid, although the authors believe that in most firms the arguments supporting a materials management structure are significantly more compelling.

In making the organization decision, management's primary concern should be fulfillment of *three basic objectives:* (1) to optimize the effectiveness of the total procurement and supply process by utilizing and coordinating the capabilities of the individual elements of the system; (2) to ensure that materials are in good condition and are available where and when needed to meet operating requirements as scheduled; and (3) to accomplish these objectives and related activities at an optimal cost.

CONCLUSION

Receiving and stores play a more important role than is sometimes recognized in supporting and facilitating a firm's production operations. Receiving is responsible for expeditious receipt and general inspection of materials, as well as for a thorough review and comparison of all relevant documentation with the materials. Stores is responsible for identification and safe, efficient physical handling and storage of materials.

The receiving operation is an important control point in a firm's materials system. This is the only point at which the purchasing control documents actually meet the materials themselves. Subsequently, stores assumes responsibility for the physical care and control of the firm's inventory. Since this material represents from 15 to 30 percent of the organization's total invested capital, this responsibility is a significant one, to say the least.

In addition to the custodial and material control aspects of the responsibility, these functions directly influence costs. The manner in which receiving and stores activities are conducted clearly influences inventory carrying costs and, to some extent, the direct labor costs of production.

FOR DISCUSSION

24-1 "Receiving and stores activities indirectly influence product costs in several ways." Comment on this statement.

24-2 Why is receiving a more important activity than it sometimes appears to be?

24-3 Outline and discuss briefly a typical receiving procedure.

24-4 In what types of operating situations is the receiving activity often bypassed? What are the benefits of doing this? What are the potential problems?

24-5 Prepare a complete flowchart for a receiving procedure to be used in a plant where inventory control is handled entirely on a computer. Supplement your flowchart with a brief description of the various documents you use and an explanation of their significance.

24-6 What is a bar code? Explain how a bar coding operation works.

24-7 How can bar coding be used effectively in a materials management operation? Discuss.

24-8 As bar code usage becomes more widespread, what problems might accompany this development? Discuss.

24-9 Discuss briefly the responsibilities of a typical stores department.

24-10 **a** What problems exist when a company attempts to use suppliers' part numbers in its material identification system?

    b What problems does a company encounter when it develops its own material identification system but develops the system only for its major production materials?

24-11 Discuss briefly the differences between an external and an internal materials identification system.

24-12 **a** Explain how a numerical material identification system works.

    b Explain how a mnemonic material identification system works.

    c Devise and explain an eight-digit numerical system which could be used for identifying production materials used in an automobile assembly plant.

24-13 **a** Explain how a closed stores system operates. How is accounting control maintained? Under what conditions should a closed stores system be used?

    b Explain how an open stores system operates. How is accounting control maintained? Under what conditions should an open stores system be used?

24-14 Discuss the use of a perpetual inventory record in both the closed and open stores systems.

24-15 Explain how a random-access storage system works.

24-16 What are the key characteristics of an automated storage/retrieval system?

24-17 Are warehouses becoming larger or smaller in today's industrial environment? Explain.

24-18 Prepare a step-by-step procedure for use in conducting an annual physical inventory of materials. Make rough sketches of any forms required and include any instructions necessary for clerical personnel.

24-19 Describe and discuss the merits of the three scheduling methods which might be used in conducting a physical inventory of materials.

24-20 a Discuss the advantages and disadvantages of centralized warehouse facilities.

b Discuss the advantages and disadvantages of decentralized storage facilities.

24-21 Assume that you have been given the responsibility of making a study of an existing warehouse and of taking charge of its reorganization. Outline and explain briefly the approach you would use in planning this undertaking.

24-22 What are the objectives of good warehouse layout? Explain.

24-23 Prepare for your boss a short report summarizing your analysis of the major factors involved in determining how stores and receiving should fit into the company organization.

CASES FOR CHAPTER 24

25

TRAFFIC

KEY CONCEPTS

- Carrier selection and routing
    Domestic shipping terms/F.O.B. terms
    International shipping terms/Incoterms
    Modes of transportation
    Types of carriers: common, contract, and private
    Regulation and deregulation
    Class rates and commodity rates
- Expediting and tracing shipments
- Loss and damage of freight
- Demurrage
- Freight bill audits
- Transportation strategy
    Purchasing transportation services
    Strategic alliances with carriers
    Cost reduction projects
- The role of purchasing and supply in traffic

The traffic function, particularly inbound traffic, is an integral part of the materials management function. Traffic's importance is magnified by the fact that, for most firms, transportation cost and service factors significantly affect the total cost of materials. They also influence the efficiency of the production

570

operation and, ultimately, the firm's ability to compete in the marketplace. Current estimates indicate that U.S. industry spends over $700 billion per year for transportation services.[1] By any measure, this is big business.

Managers are concerned not only with their own transportation bill, but also with their competitors' transportation bills. Assume, for example, that steel prices are approximately the same at two different mills. If the first mill can deliver steel for less than the second because it has lower transportation costs, it has a distinct advantage over its competitor. If customers pay the freight charges, the first mill can expect to get proportionately more orders; if the mills pay the freight, the first mill will net a higher unit profit. For this reason, industrial traffic managers must stay attuned to the dynamics of the marketplace and its quasi-regulatory environment.

The traffic function in an industrial firm includes responsibility for:

1 The transportation of incoming shipments
2 The transportation of outgoing shipments
3 Major internal transportation of materials and products on the firm's property
4 Participation in hearings before regulatory agencies, congressional committees, and other governmental bodies on matters affecting the cost and quality of transportation services

The primary traffic issues faced by buyers involve *inbound shipments*. Hence, this chapter focuses on these issues as they relate to the purchasing and supply management function. The chapter pinpoints the things a buyer should understand about traffic to do an effective purchasing job.

Transportation costs can be high; in some companies they average as much as 20 to 40 percent of the product cost. In the steel, lumber, cement, and heavy chemical industries, for example, transportation frequently represents one of the largest elements of total cost. At the other end of the spectrum, in some light manufacturing firms transportation costs sometimes total less than 1 percent of product cost. Electronics and pharmaceutical producers are good examples. Thus, transportation costs vary greatly, depending on the nature of the materials a firm uses. The importance of the traffic management function consequently varies from one industry to another.

Irrespective of cost, transportation *service* is frequently a critical factor in the purchasing and supply process. If shipments fail to arrive when scheduled, serious operating delays may ensue. Moreover, the general efficiency of a total supply program can be affected significantly by the type of cooperation obtained from carriers. On matters of materials handling methods, shipment tracing and expediting, and the allowance of various in-transit privileges, carrier cooperation is essential.

Transportation services should be purchased much as any material or service is pur-

---

[1]Based on data in Peter Bradley, "Carriers Feel the Squeeze," *Purchasing*, Mar. 17, 1994, pp. 37–43.

chased. After careful investigation of potential carriers, the selection decision should be based on thorough evaluation of service, quality, and price.

CARRIER SELECTION

A purchaser normally can obtain the option to specify the carrier and the routing to be used in transporting the purchased material. When this prerogative exists, a buyer should view it as part of his or her overall purchasing responsibility. Unfortunately, too many buyers forfeit this profit-generating opportunity by simply noting, "Ship best way."

Shipping Terms

Domestic Shipments   The shipping terms included in a sales contract determine who has the legal right to specify the carrier and the routing. More precisely, shipping terms define the point at which a buyer takes title to the goods. This, in turn, defines who is responsible for selecting the carrier, paying the freight charges, handling negotiations with the carrier, and filing any necessary loss or damage claims. In short, the owner of the material holds all rights and responsibilities that accompany ownership. Numerous shipping terms can be used, but the most common used for domestic shipments are:

1 F.O.B. buyer's plant (destination)
2 F.O.B. seller's plant (origin)
3 F.O.B. seller's plant, freight allowed to buyer's plant

The abbreviation *F.O.B.* historically meant "free on board"; legally, the F.O.B. designation defines the point of title transfer. Under the first arrangement, title to the material passes from the seller to the buyer when the carrier delivers the material at the buyer's plant. Because the seller retains ownership of the material during transit, it has the legal right to select the carrier as well as the responsibility for paying the freight charges. Under the second arrangement, the buyer takes title when the carrier accepts the material for shipment at the seller's plant. In this case, the buyer assumes responsibility for carrier selection and payment of freight charges. The third arrangement is similar to the second, so far as legal liability is concerned; however, the shipper agrees to reimburse the buyer for the freight charges.

Buying under the terms of F.O.B. seller's plant is common practice today; approximately 60 to 90 percent of all major shipments are purchased under these terms.[2] Buyers utilizing this approach want control of an order during transit. Many feel that they can do a better job of carrier selection and routing than their suppliers can. This is frequently true, because many small shippers simply are not properly staffed to make such decisions for all of their geo-

---

[2]Ernest Gilbert, publisher of *Inbound Traffic Guide,* "Problems in Purchasing Transportation," NAPM 67th International Purchasing Conference, Los Angeles, May 10, 1982. See also Julie J. Gentry, *Purchasing's Involvement in Transportation Decision Making,* CAPS/NAPM, Tempe, Ariz., 1991, pp. 17–18.

graphically dispersed customers. Many purchasers also develop long-term relationships with carriers, just as they do with suppliers. Hence, the routing of each major production material, from various points across the country, is but one element of a total transportation purchasing program which is designed to serve the purchaser's long-range interests. Consequently, the buyer usually wants the prerogative of carrier selection because he or she plans to develop certain types of relationships with specific carriers. Additionally, when a manufacturer controls both incoming and outgoing shipments, it can enjoy economies of scale.

There are situations, however, in which a supplier will be better informed than the buyer about traffic conditions and about the services offered by specific carriers in the supplier's area. In such cases, the perceptive buyer works with the supplier and utilizes the latter's capabilities to the fullest extent.

Some buyers prefer to buy F.O.B. their plant. They reason that by so doing they shift the burden of locating effective carriers to the supplier and do not have to concern themselves with the details of transportation investigations. Likewise, since the supplier has agreed to pay the freight charges, the buyer does not have to worry about costs of transportation. And, finally, in the event that problems arise from shipping damage, the buyer is not responsible for the time-consuming negotiation with the carrier which often ensues. Operating in this manner, a buyer may believe he or she is assured of acceptable carrier performance before the supplier is paid. Unfortunately, this type of reasoning contains two fallacies. In the first place, there is no assurance that the supplier will accept the responsibility of finding an "effective" chain of carriers. The buyer, in effect, abdicates his or her responsibility for buying effective transportation service. Second, even though the supplier pays the freight bill, in the long run freight charges are included and passed on to the buyer in the material selling price. Ultimately, the buyer pays the transportation bill and also bears any extra costs resulting from poor carrier selection.

International Shipping Terms   Most firms today do at least some international buying, and many are heavily involved in global sourcing. Consequently, purchasing and supply people should be familiar with international shipping terms, better known as *Incoterms*. Incoterms are rules dealing with the international transportation of materials and are published by the International Chamber of Commerce, headquartered in Paris; they are recognized as the international standard. The thirteen terms are grouped into four categories, and each describes the obligations of the supplier and the buyer with respect to packing materials for shipment, obtaining import or export licenses, delivery, payment for carriage and insurance, and the risk of loss.[3] The Incoterms currently in use are summarized briefly in Table 25-1.

---

[3]Beth Perdue, "Perdue on Law: Cutting the Risks of Buying Abroad," *Electronics Purchasing,* January 1993, p. 20.

TABLE 25-1

DEFINITION AND CLASSIFICATION OF INCOTERMS

	General definition		Specific incoterm
Group E:	Goods are made available at the supplier's named site. Buyer assumes all responsibility for transportation, cost, and risk beyond this point.	EXW	Ex works (supplier's site).
Group F:	Supplier delivers goods to specified carrier location. Buyer assumes all costs and risks associated with the main carriage and beyond.	FCA	Free carrier at a named place. Supplier clears goods for export.
		FAS	Free alongside ship (on dock). Buyer clears goods for export.
		FOB	Free on board (on ship). Supplier clears goods for export.
Group C:	Supplier contracts for main carriage and assumes all costs to the destination country. Buyer assumes all risks during main carriage, plus cost of delivery from destination dock to buyer's site.	CFR	Cost and freight to the port of destination. Supplier clears goods for export.
		CIF	Cost, insurance, and freight to the port of destination. Same responsibilities as CFR, except supplier is responsible for insurance during main carriage.
		CPT	Carriage paid to the named destination. Supplier clears goods for export.
		CIP	Carriage and insurance paid to the named destination. Same responsibilities as CPT except supplier covers insurance during main carriage.
Group D:	Supplier assumes all risks and costs to the specified destination.	DAF	Delivered at frontier (country border) at a specified location, but before the customs border of the adjoining country. Supplier clears goods for export.
		DES	Delivered ex ship at specified port of destination. Goods are available aboard ship, uncleared for import.
		DEQ	Delivered ex quay (dock) at the named port of destination. The duty can be paid or unpaid, depending on the agreement.
		DDU	Delivered duty unpaid at the specified place of destination.
		DDP	Delivered duty paid at the specified place of destination. Supplier bears all risks and costs, including duties, taxes, and other charges of delivering the goods, cleared for import.

Just like shipping terms become part of the contract for a domestic purchase, Incoterms become part of the contract for an international procurement. And clearly they have a significant impact on the *delivered* cost. It is important, too, to ensure that the Incoterms specified in the contract match identically the payment terms specified in the letter of credit the buyer uses for payment to the international supplier.

Modes of Transportation

The bulk of U.S. intercity freight traffic is moved by rail, motor freight, water carrier, and pipeline. The railroads have continually lost ground to the motor freight industry since World War II. Today they haul approximately 30 to 35 percent of the country's freight—down 50 percent from 1947—while the truckers haul in excess of 40 percent. During the same period freight movement by air has increased at a fantastic rate, but it still amounts to only about 1 to 2 percent of all freight moved.

A surprisingly large number of transportation methods are available. Most buyers, at one time or another, utilize a majority of the following methods:

1 Parcel post
2 Private parcel delivery service
3 Bus service
4 Air cargo
5 Rail freight, carload (CL) and less than carload (LCL)
6 Motor freight, truckload (TL) and less than truckload (LTL)
7 Freight forwarder
8 Coastal, intercoastal, and inland water freight
9 Intermodal carriage (piggyback and fishyback)
10 Pipeline

Generally speaking, a buyer of transportation finds that methods providing fast delivery cost more than slower methods. For example, a West Coast firm buys heavy machine parts from a firm in Philadelphia. The parts can be shipped by water, by rail, by truck, or by some combination of these methods. If shipment is by truck, delivery time is approximately eleven days. By intercoastal steamship, delivery takes roughly twice as long. Depending on the specific part, however, the water freight rate ranges from 20 to 50 percent lower than the truck rate.

Exceptions to this rule, of course, do exist. A buyer may discover some isolated cases where a faster mode is also cheaper. For instance, for many years the air freight rate between San Diego and San Francisco for some materials was less than the rail rate! Other similar exceptions undoubtedly exist.

When approaching a shipping problem for the first time, wise purchasers initially compare rates and delivery times of the feasible alternative shipping methods. Buyers should bear in mind, however, that certain indirect cost factors may be just as important as the freight rate itself. Packaging and crating costs may vary from one mode to another. Also, the size and frequency of shipment is determined by the mode. Consequently, the necessity for warehousing and the cost of maintaining inventory may vary from one mode to another. Clearly, the buyer is concerned with *total costs* influenced by transportation, not direct transportation costs alone.

Parcel Post Very little industrial freight travels by parcel post. However, this rather expensive service is a relatively fast and convenient method of shipping small packages. The U.S. Postal Service has placed the following size and weight limits on parcel post shipments:[4]

Weight limit = 70 pounds for all zone destinations
Size limit = 108 inches combined length and girth for
all zone destinations

Air parcel post (Express Mail) service is also available for one- or two-day delivery at substantially higher rates. Shipping limits for air service are 70 pounds and 108 inches.

Private Parcel Delivery Service Privately operated parcel delivery services provide important door-to-door delivery services for packages up to 150 pounds. Most of these firms operate in interstate commerce, although some operate only intrastate or intracity. In recent years private parcel delivery services have grown rapidly in number and size, primarily because of their flexibility and strong service orientation. Typically it is possible to arrange for one- or two-day delivery with these carriers, most of which move their long-haul shipments by air. United Parcel Service and Fed Ex are outstanding examples of this type of firm. Business customers have generally responded favorably to the wide range of specialized and custom-tailored services available.

Bus Service Intercity bus transportation is another method used occasionally for shipping easily manageable packages over relatively short distances. Most bus lines accept packages larger than parcel post size, provided one person can handle them without difficulty. Although this too is an expensive service, delivery is usually fast for distances less than 200 miles because of the numerous scheduled runs between major cities. In an emergency situation the buyer sometimes finds this service to be extremely valuable. Some of its value,

---

[4]These parcel post limitations were in effect January 1, 1995. They may be changed from time to time by the Post Office Department.

however, may be negated by the necessity for local delivery or pickup of the shipment at the bus terminal.

Air Cargo   Although air cargo movements have increased tremendously in recent years, high rates still prohibit regular use of air service for most industrial purchasers. As a general rule, freight rates are approximately twice as high for air cargo as for LCL and LTL movements. The continued development of high-capacity jet freighters, however, may permit further rate reductions in the future.

Because air travel produces a smooth ride compared with other methods of moving freight, it is an exceptionally good way to transport delicate equipment or perishable commodities. Because of this fact, if ground handling is not too rough, packaging and crating requirements for materials may be reduced substantially if they are shipped by air. This cost reduction partially offsets the higher freight rate in some cases.

One selling point emphasized by most air cargo carriers is the fact that the short delivery time afforded by air shipment permits a purchaser to carry smaller inventories. The rationale underlying this point is entirely valid. The final decision, however, still involves an analysis of *total* costs. Each purchaser must make his or her own analysis and determine in which cases a net saving in fact results.

Rail Freight   Rail shipments move as full carload (CL) shipments or as less than carload (LCL) shipments. For ordinary materials, a CL movement is considered to be approximately 30,000 pounds or more. When hauling a dense commodity such as grain, however, the figure might range from 60,000 to 100,000 pounds. The CL volume is usually sufficient to fill a car, so the car does not have to be opened until it reaches its destination. CL shipments move at a freight rate that is substantially below (in some cases approximately one-half) the LCL rate. As will become evident in the following paragraphs, rail LCL shipment frequently does not compete favorably with motor freight shipment. For this reason, the volume of LCL shipments is declining for most railroads. *By and large, the railroad's major business today is transporting bulk materials.*

To make effective use of CL movements, the shipper and purchaser should each have conveniently located spur tracks and loading facilities. If a purchaser has to unload a railcar at the freight yard and truck the material to its plant, the cost of double handling frequently makes it less costly to utilize a single truck haul all the way from the supplier's plant. On the other hand, *for LCL shipments*, the rate usually includes pickup and delivery service, provided the shipment moves more than 300 miles.

A railroad's major advantage over its trucking competitors is in the area of long intercity hauls. A railroad must make a huge investment/in equipment, rolling stock, and trackage. While its fixed costs are high, its variable operating costs are relatively low. Once a train is loaded and rolling, it costs little more to move it 1,000 miles than to move it 100 miles. Hence, on long hauls, its total operating cost per ton-mile typically is lower than that of its motor freight competitors. For shipments moving less than 1,000 miles, the reverse situation occurs.

Railroads offer CL shippers two privileges that prove extremely valuable in some types of business: (1) in-transit privileges and (2) diversion and reconsignment privileges.

In-transit privileges, generally speaking, give a shipper the right to stop a shipment en route, unload it, perform certain processing operations on the material, reload the processed material, and continue the shipment at the original freight rate (subject to a modest additional charge). The economics of the total operation become clear when one observes that freight rates on processed materials are usually significantly higher than on corresponding raw materials. This means, for example, that a tank fabricator in Kansas City might purchase a car of steel in Chicago, ship it to Kansas City, fabricate tanks from the carload of steel, and then ship the tanks on to a customer in Denver. In doing this under a fabrication-in-transit agreement, the tank fabricator pays almost the same freight rate on tanks shipped from Kansas City to Denver as it paid on the steel shipped from Chicago to Kansas City.

A similar type of agreement allows shippers to delay a shipment and use the railcar as a temporary storage facility until they wish to continue the movement.

Diversion privileges permit a shipper to divert a car in transit to a new destination. This can be a very convenient prerogative when unexpected conditions in a multiplant company call for the shipment of an extra car of material to plant X, rather than to plant Y as scheduled. *Reconsignment privileges* allow the shipper to go a step further; it can also consign the car to a new customer, or consignee, at the same or at a different location. In certain types of businesses these privileges can be used to very definite advantage.

Rail carriers also provide other privileges, for little or no additional cost. One of these services is pickup or loading at two separate points with a single delivery at destination. They also provide for a single pickup with delivery and unloading at two separate points. These privileges can be of particular value to multiplant companies.

Motor Freight   In this industry shipments move on either a truckload (TL) or less than truckload (LTL) basis. TL rates are substantially lower than LTL rates. In contrast with rail freight movement, a load of 20,000 to 30,000 pounds of ordinary material typically makes up a full truckload. The definition of a "full truckload," however, varies somewhat among commodities and among carriers.

Comparison of truck rates with rail rates reveals that, in general, the difference between them depends on the length of the haul and the weight of the load. On movements of less than 1,000 miles, truck rates often are lower than rail rates. On long hauls, however, the reverse typically is true, notably for heavy, low-grade bulk materials.

A point of interest to purchasing and supply personnel centers on the difference between weight requirements for TL and CL shipments. Suppose a buyer is considering shipping a 20,000-pound order by rail, LCL. If truck shipment is feasible, a TL rate probably will apply. In most cases, the TL rate will be considerably lower than the LCL rate. A similar situation may exist when shipment weights are somewhat below 20,000 pounds. The freight bill for a 17,000-pound shipment which is moved and billed as a full truckload may well be lower in total than if it were actually billed as 17,000 pounds and moved at the higher LTL rate.

The most important advantage a truck line possesses over a rail line is its operating flexibility. For short hauls it has no peer. In contrast with a train, a truck is a small, flexible, self-contained unit. It can be loaded easily and less expensively (because less bracing is required) at a shipper's plant. Once on the road, a TL shipment can proceed directly to its destination. It does not have to wait in various classification yards across the country, as a railcar does, to be switched to a new train that moves it over the next leg of its journey. As a consequence, in almost all cases, motor freight delivery is faster than rail freight delivery.

For a short haul of 300 miles an LTL shipment should arrive in a day, while an LCL shipment typically requires three or four days. As the length of the haul increases, the truck advantage becomes less pronounced. Finally, on transcontinental CL hauls delivery performance tends to be about equal. Some of the aggressive railroads now offer improved service, on a limited basis, between selected metropolitan areas having high-density traffic movements. This service takes two forms: (1) fast "hi-ball" freight trains which bypass classification yards and (2) scheduled "merchandise cars" which move immediately on through trains.

Freight Forwarder   The operations of rail freight forwarders are designed to provide a service to firms buying materials in less-than-carload lots. For distances over 300 miles, freight-forwarding shipments should normally move much faster than ordinary LCL shipments, closely paralleling CL and LTL delivery service. Freight forwarders' rates, in virtually all cases, are at least as low as LCL and LTL rates, and on long hauls they are usually significantly lower.

A freight forwarder operates much like a broker. The firm accepts only less-than-carload shipments. Such shipments are then combined into a full load and shipped by rail at the CL rate. Thus, the forwarder's operating margin is the difference between the rate the firm charges and the CL rate it pays for shipment. Long hauls are therefore most profitable for the freight-forwarding firm. They frequently permit the firm to reduce its rate below the LCL level and still generate a reasonable profit.

Air freight forwarders operate in much the same way. Some air freight forwarders now offer a combination of air and surface movement for their shipments. These can be used to advantage when direct air shipments are not feasible or when the combination provides advantageous movement at a lesser cost than direct air service.

Coastal, Intercoastal, and Inland Water Freight   Domestic shipping lines, operating on inland as well as on coastal and intercoastal waterways, represent one of the earliest forms of American freight transportation. Because of infrequent sailing schedules and relatively slow speeds, water transportation is by far the slowest of all transportation methods. To compensate for slow deliveries, water carriers offer considerably lower rates than their rail and truck competitors.

The federal government considers domestic shipping lines to be a vital part of the American Merchant Marine. It therefore protects their existence in various ways. For example, it legislates protection against competition from more cheaply operated foreign ships, makes capital equipment available at reduced prices, and partially subsidizes the harbors and docking facilities they use. Such actions permit domestic water carriers to remain financially sound and still quote freight rates substantially below competing rail and truck carriers.

Water transportation is frequently used by strategically located firms for moving raw materials, heavy items, and low-value materials, when shipments can be planned well in advance of operating requirements. In computing total shipping costs, the user should be aware that water freight rates do not include pickup and delivery service. The cost of transporting material to and from dockside must be added to the water carrier's quoted rates. Water carriers charge on the basis of weight or volume, depending on which yields the greater revenue. Consequently, shipping costs for bulky, low-density materials, relative to corresponding rail costs, are higher than for high-density materials.

Intermodal Carriage   Combination methods of freight transportation—commonly called piggyback and fishyback—made their initial appearance on the commercial transportation scene during the mid-1950s. In both cases the cargo is loaded in truck trailers or large standardized containers at the shipper's plant. In using *piggyback,* a truck tractor pulls the trailer or container from the plant to rail loading yards, where the trailer or container is placed on a flatcar. The long intercity haul is then made by rail. At the destination, truck tractors pick up the trailers or containers and deliver them to the purchaser's plant.

This method of transportation actually combines the major advantages of both truck and rail movement. It utilizes the flexibility of trucks on pickup, delivery, and short off-line hauls, and it takes advantage of the railroads' favorable cost and speed performance on long hauls. This method of shipment usually cuts down loading and handling time, and it also frequently results in faster delivery for the purchaser. At times it results in a lower rate, particularly when shipment is made from or to plants without rail sidings.

In its earlier days, truck/rail intermodal movement suffered somewhat from a poor service image. In recent years, however, both modes have worked hard to correct this situation. Most railroads now segregate intermodal traffic from other freight operations, mechanizing intermodal terminals and offering more regularly scheduled intermodal trains. These efforts clearly have paid off. Truck/rail intermodal shipments have increased more than 100 percent during the past decade.[5]

Fishyback is similar to piggyback, except that it combines the use of truck and water carriers rather than truck and rail. While the main objective of piggyback is to utilize the strong features of both truck and rail movement, the major objective of fishyback is to reduce the extremely high costs of loading and unloading individually crated items aboard ship. Fishyback replaces the handling of thousands of individual items with the handling of a relatively small number of previously loaded trailers or large standardized containers.

Pipeline   Pipelines are used primarily in transporting petroleum products, chemicals, and water. However, they are also being used increasingly for transporting cereal, coal, and certain ores. Movement of these materials is accomplished by pulverizing the solid material, mechanically suspending it in water, and pumping the solution through a pipeline. Although pipelines of this kind are considered common carriers and are regulated by the Interstate Commerce Commission, they have very specialized uses when viewed as part of the total freight transportation picture.

Types of Carriers

A transportation buyer should be familiar with the basic legal status of the carriers with which he or she deals. The federal government recognizes three types of carriers: (1) common, (2) contract, and (3) private.

Common Carriers   A common carrier serves all customers but carries only the types of freight for which it is certified. Some truck certificates, for example, explicitly exclude specific types of freight, while others include only certain very limited types. The bulk of industrial freight moves by common carrier. The preceding discussion, with the exception of postal service, has dealt with freight movement by common carriers.

Regulation and Deregulation   The Interstate Commerce Act of 1887, although targeted at regulation of the railroads, gives the federal government the right to regulate—in the public interest—almost all common carriers engaging in *interstate* traffic. A host of subsequent legislation reinforces the

---

[5]For more detailed discussions, see (1) Peter Bradley, "Intermodal Takes a Leap," *Purchasing*, Apr. 16, 1992, pp. 61–63; and (2) Peter Bradley, "Intermodal Fights Perception Gap," *Purchasing*, June 17, 1993, pp. 30–33.

basic intent and supplements the authority of the original act. Most notable among these additions are:

- *Motor Carrier Act of 1935.* Established trucking industry regulation.
- *Civil Aeronautics Act of 1938.* Established airline industry regulation.
- *Department of Transportation Act of 1966.* Created a cabinet-level department (DOT).

All rail, motor, and intercoastal water common carriers are regulated by the federal Interstate Commerce Commission (ICC). Ships in international commerce are regulated by the Federal Maritime Commission (FMC). Prior to deregulation, air common carriers were regulated by the Civil Aeronautics Board (CAB). The regulatory agencies operate under the Department of Transportation, a cabinet-level department of the executive branch of the federal government.

Fundamentally, the regulating agencies do two things. First, they prescribe *a body of operating regulations* which constitute the legal framework within which carriers operate their businesses. The ICC, for example, issues all "certificates of public convenience and necessity." The certificates give truck lines the authority to haul freight in a designated geographic area or over certain specific routes. No truck can operate as an interstate common carrier without a certificate. Second, they act as *controllers of the freight rate structure* to ensure that no carrier charges rates which discriminate against other carriers or against customers. All common carrier rates must be approved and filed with the ICC. Most states have state agencies which function in a similar manner for all carriers engaged in *intrastate* transportation.

During the late 1970s, a strong effort was initiated to *deregulate* the U.S. transportation system. This movement culminated in the passage of four additional legislative acts, all designed to reduce governmental control and promote freer market competition in the transportation industry. The key legislation includes:

1 Air Cargo Act of 1977
2 Staggers Rail Act of 1980
3 Motor Carrier Act of 1980
4 Shipping Act of 1984

In reality, this legislation did not deregulate the industry—rather, it produced a form of "re-regulation." The primary impact on the transportation industry has been fourfold:

1 Carriers in all four modes (rail, motor, air, and water) possess substantially increased flexibility to modify freight rates and services without regulatory intervention.
2 For air and motor carriers, entry into the business and acquisition of specific routes are much easier to achieve.
3 For rail carriers, low-cost federal loans are available to upgrade facilities and equipment.

4 Water carriers have considerably more freedom to enter joint ventures with other carriers, producing unique, containerized intermodal services for inland shippers.

All common carriers now have the ability to adjust freight rates rather freely within a broad range. Rail carriers, for example, are permitted to raise rates up to 175 percent of their variable costs, plus possible additional inflation offsets. Motor carriers and freight forwarders can adjust rates up to 10 percent per year, on the basis of the previous year's rates. Perhaps the greatest benefit of the legislation to motor carriers is the "ease-of-entry" provision for service and routes. Although a trucker still must obtain a certificate of public convenience and necessity, the procedure is greatly simplified. An applicant simply must be able to demonstrate that the firm is "fit, willing, and able" and that the proposed service is responsive to a public need.

From the transportation buyer's point of view, the full effect of deregulation remains to be seen. Clearly, the legislation has produced greater competition— competition among carriers in a single mode and also among carriers in competing modes. Hence, buyers find most carriers to be much more marketing-oriented and more willing to negotiate different types of price and service arrangements. The development of national transportation contracts (with correspondingly reduced rates) for multiplant buyers has become a very profitable alternative.[6]

The element of increased competition cuts both ways. Typically it produces benefits for most buyers located in high-density traffic areas. For buyers located in low-density traffic areas, however, it has produced some negative consequences. Although more carriers are in operation, service to customers on many low-volume, low-profit routes has been curtailed or dropped by a number of carriers. Additionally, a number of weaker and less efficient carriers have felt the brunt of the "survival of the fittest" environment. A dozen or so major carriers and an uncounted number of smaller ones have either closed their doors or experienced bankruptcy.[7]

Contract Carriers A contract carrier does not provide service to the general public; it operates only under negotiated contractual agreements with specific customers. Although all contract carriers are regulated by the same agencies as common carriers, generally speaking their regulation is less strin-

---

[6]All transportation buyers should be familiar with the Negotiated Rates Act of 1993 (NRA93). One section of this act requires that motor carrier *contracts* take the form of a written agreement, separate from the bill of lading receipt. The intent of the act is "to limit the potential for unwarranted future undercharge claims" by carriers in financial trouble. In addition to the requirement for a written document, NRA93 also details significant content requirements for motor carrier contracts. For a detailed discussion of NRA93, see John M. McKeller, "New Legislation for Shippers— NRA93," *NAPM Insights,* June 1994, p. 16.

[7]Interesting discussions of the effects of deregulation are presented in T. S. Robertson, S. Ward, and W. M. Caldwell, "Deregulation: Surviving the Transition," *The Harvard Business Review,* July–August 1982, pp. 20–24; John Fitts, "Deregulation Offers Opportunities and Dangers," *Purchasing World,* June 1981, pp. 48–52; and Joseph L. Cavinato, "Buying Transportation," *Guide to Purchasing,* NAPM, Tempe, Ariz., 1986, pp. 3–7.

gent. Each carrier must obtain an operating permit and also must file a schedule of minimum rates with the appropriate agency.

As a rule, most carriers that operate solely as contract carriers have no loading or terminal facilities. Consequently, their operating costs are usually somewhat lower. This also means that, by and large, contract carriers handle only truckload shipments. Unlike the liability of a common carrier, which is fixed by law, the liability of a contract carrier depends entirely on the contractual arrangement made with the customer.

An interesting provision of the deregulation act now permits a contract carrier also to hold a common carrier certificate, and vice versa. Hence, a carrier holding both types of certificates can combine "common" and "contract" loads on the same vehicle.

Private Carriers   Private carriers are not subject to regulation by the ICC. A private carrier transports material that the carriage firm owns. Some industrial firms have thus become private carriers by operating their own fleets of trucks. A common problem such firms encounter in hauling their own production materials, though, is that of running the truck empty on one leg of the trip. Consequently, this type of private carrier generally tries to haul finished goods to customers traveling one way, and production materials to the plant going the other. However, in such an operation scheduling becomes a major problem. Likewise, in the industrial relations area the company may find that it has an additional union—the Teamsters—to deal with. Thus, becoming a private carrier puts the firm in the trucking business as well as the manufacturing business, and it cannot escape certain problems unique to the transportation industry.

Purchasing people need not concern themselves with the plethora of legal details surrounding carrier operation, but they should be aware of the general framework within which carriers operate. Keeping out of legal difficulties in the transportation business is a complex problem in itself. Furthermore, the law holds a shipper equally liable with the carrier for violation of federal transportation regulations. Consequently, it behooves buyers of transportation services to have a general knowledge of the regulatory acts that influence the transportation segment of their responsibilities.

Freight Rates

The structure of freight rates in the U.S. transportation industry appears to be little short of chaotic. Unlike most business operations, the price charged for hauling freight usually does not bear a consistent relationship to the carrier's actual cost of providing the service. The difficulty of allocating operating costs to specific products carried, coupled with the plethora of rates that represent historical precedents, contributes to the inconsistent and confusing rate structure which now exists.

A brief review of the rough-and-tumble era during which railroads were laying the foundation for the nation's transportation system provides a clear explanation of how the complex rate system originated. The miscellany of rates developed during that period were, for the most part, created independently of each other as various needs arose. Little thought was given at that time to the rate structure for the total transportation system. Individual rates were based largely on "what the traffic would bear" and were conditioned by numerous economic and political pressures coming from different areas of the country.

Rates established today are based on cost to a greater extent than in past years. However, the following factors, some of them very subjective, are all considered in present-day rate making, which still appears to be much more an art than an exact science.

- Value of the service to the shipper
- Cost to the carrier of providing the service
- Special services involved, such as transit privileges
- Volume of traffic movement involved
- Rates on similar articles moving under similar conditions
- Rates of competing carriers
- Competitive conditions existing in the *shipper's* industry

Class Rates and Commodity Rates Generally speaking, freight moves under one of two types of rates: (1) class rates or (2) commodity rates. It was originally impossible to establish a rate for every individual commodity shipped. Consequently, similar commodities were grouped in classes, and rates were established for each *class* of commodity. These rates became known as *class rates*. Commodity classifications have since become standardized to ensure uniform treatment by all carriers. For rail transportation, the *Uniform Freight Classification* is the document used to determine which class rating is appropriate for a given shipment. In the trucking industry, the *National Motor Freight Classification* is the guide used for shipment classification purposes.

A *commodity rate* is a unique rate created for the shipment of *a given material* in large quantities between specified origin and destination cities. The material must be shipped in CL or TL lots on a continuing basis. Commodity rates normally are significantly lower than class rates—and are established to give special treatment to particular commodity movements that have economic or competitive importance in a certain market.

In practice, although a majority of the *number of shipments* move under a class rate, a majority of the *dollar volume* moves under commodity rates. A transportation buyer who wants to apply for a commodity rate generally proceeds in the following manner:

1 The buyer contacts the major carrier involved, explains the problem, and requests the carrier to initiate a proposal on his or her behalf.
2 If the carrier agrees, carrier representatives prepare a complete proposal for the requested commodity rate and submit it to the standing rate committee of the carrier's cooperative rate-making association.

3 This committee studies the proposal and accepts or rejects it. If the proposal is accepted, the new rate is written and filed with the ICC.
4 If the proposal is rejected, the case can be appealed to an executive group of the rate-making association.
5 If the proposal is again rejected, final appeal can be made directly to the ICC for a hearing of the case.

One thing is clear: Even in today's environment, rate making and commodity classification are extremely specialized activities. It is not uncommon for a well-qualified general traffic manager to call on a specialist for assistance.

Designating Carrier and Route

Not only do freight rates differ significantly between the modes of transportation which might be selected for a given shipment, but, since deregulation, they vary markedly among carriers and among the various routes over which the shipment might move. Hence, to minimize shipping costs, it is important that the right mode, carrier, and routing be designated.

To many transportation buyers, the service factor is a more important consideration than cost in designating a specific carrier and routing. Service offered by different carriers can vary as much as that of different suppliers. In the case of a motor freight shipment, on long hauls a buyer may have the choice of using a dozen or more connecting carriers. Usually, he or she tries to involve as few separate carriers in the move as possible in order to reduce the number of transfers required. When a shipment passes from one carrier to another at the boundary of the first carrier's operating territory, the transfer can be made with varying degrees of efficiency. The time actually lost during the transfer depends on running schedules and transfer facilities of the lines involved.[8]

A city in the Rocky Mountain area, for example, is served by three major motor carriers from Chicago. Because of differences in schedules and facilities at intermediate transfer points, normal delivery times for the alternative carriers range from three to six days. This difference can be quite significant if a firm operates with low inventories or needs an emergency shipment.

On many railroad runs between two points, the carrier can use several alternative routes. There is the fast, direct route, and usually there is a slower, circuitous route designed to serve communities located off the direct route. So long as the carrier operates both routes, it can move unrouted shipments over either one. However, the railroad frequently sends unrouted shipments via the circuitous route to achieve a better load distribution among its trains. The informed buyer avoids this possibility by specifying the routing to be used.

---

[8]Between New York and Los Angeles there are over 300 possible rail carrier combinations. The number of possible truck combinations from New York to Los Angeles has never been calculated; there are thousands of possibilities.

A final reason for controlling carrier selection involves a principle well understood by purchasing people. If a firm distributes its transportation business among a few selected carriers, in adequate volumes, it is possible to develop very favorable long-term relationships with the carriers. Relationships of this kind can be valuable to the buyer in many ways. When the buyer needs the best service possible for occasional urgent shipments, a favored and friendly carrier is much more inclined to provide the desired service willingly. Likewise, such a carrier is more prone to settle claims promptly and to provide assistance with cost reduction projects.

EXPEDITING AND TRACING SHIPMENTS

When it is imperative that a buyer receive a tightly scheduled shipment by a particular date, he or she may wish to *expedite* the shipment. In these cases, the buyer advises the carrier of the situation *prior* to shipment and requests that arrangements be made for faster than normal movement. Most carriers are willing to expedite shipments if a purchaser requests the service only when really necessary. Like the proverbial boy who cried wolf too often, the buyer who makes frequent and unnecessary use of this service soon finds that the carrier pays little attention to repetitious demands.

Tracing is the process of following a shipment *after* its departure to obtain a record of the various steps of its movement. A purchaser finds that this activity occasionally is required to bring in an overdue shipment; it is inevitable that some shipments become misdirected or lost. In critical situations, tracing is necessary to ensure prompt delivery and continuity of manufacturing operations. Effective tracing work is contingent on a rather detailed understanding of how various carriers handle their freight. In conducting expediting and tracing work, a buyer may simply contact a carrier's general agent and ask him or her to handle the detailed investigation. If the matter is urgent, the buyer may have a traffic specialist from his or her firm also participate in the detailed investigation with the carrier's personnel.

The ease with which a shipment can be traced depends largely on two things: (1) the completeness and accuracy of the shipping information possessed by the tracer and (2) the shipping records maintained by the carrier.

As an example, the following information is helpful in tracing a CL shipment:

- Description of material
- Date shipped
- Car number
- Train number
- Route
- Shipper
- Consignee
- Origin
- Destination

In tracing an LCL shipment, additional information typically required is the number of pieces, weight, waybill number, and the first transfer point for the shipment.

Rail CL shipments can be traced fairly easily because most railroads keep records of CL shipments by car initial and number. *Passing reports* are also maintained along the line, so that a particular car usually can be traced without difficulty from one classification yard to the next as it progresses along its route.

Rail LCL tracing is sometimes difficult. Some railroads keep records of the loading of LCL shipments; others do not. Where records are available, tracing can be accomplished. When no records are maintained, tracing is a nebulous task because of the guesswork involved, and frequently it is impossible.

Freight forwarders usually trace their own CL shipments. Forwarders maintain records which permit them to cross-check any shipment to the railcar in which it moved.

Motor TL shipments can be traced quite easily because records are kept on every trailer. A trailer travels directly from origin to destination, with perhaps several tractor changes, and can be traced through its various checkpoints along the route.

Motor LTL shipments, as a rule, can be traced fairly easily. Most truck lines maintain a record of every LTL shipment handled.

Air cargo carriers, for the most part, keep records of individual shipments. When a plane takes off, most carriers teletype or fax its entire manifest, giving individual shipment identification, to the destination stations. Consequently, tracing can usually be accomplished without difficulty.

Water carrier shipments can be located easily because once loaded, they remain aboard the ship until it reaches its destination. The important point, however, is to ensure that the shipment is taken aboard in the first place! Occasionally, cargo is left behind because more material is delivered to the dock than the vessel can carry. In tracing, however, there should be no mystery as to whether cargo was in fact loaded, because the first mate (or a subordinate) is required to sign the waybill when the cargo is actually taken on board.

Private parcel delivery service shipments as a rule can be traced easily. But this capability does vary among firms. Most firms have improved this service markedly in recent years.

Parcel post shipments cannot be traced unless they are registered or insured. The postal service keeps records of individual shipments only when they are registered or insured.

Clearly, the completeness of the shipping records maintained by any carrier determines the ease with which tracing can be accomplished. In those firms that have computerized records systems, tracing is usually a simple matter.

In recent years some carriers, notably the progressive trucking firms, have developed an exceptionally valuable service for key customers. Through a computer terminal located in the customer's office, they provide direct access to their computer information system containing trailer loading, routing, scheduling, and movement data, as well as tariff and classification information. Thus, without leaving the office it is possible for a buyer to trace his or her shipments and compare actual movement with the schedule, to audit the freight bill, and to obtain selected information for management reporting purposes. Other carriers provide the same type of tracing service, though less personalized, by means of an 800-number telephone inquiry service.

LOSS AND DAMAGE OF FREIGHT

Shipments sometimes get lost or arrive in damaged condition. Normally, a carrier is legally responsible for a shipment from the time it is loaded aboard the vehicle until it is unloaded at the destination. To obtain a satisfactory settlement for lost shipments, the purchaser should initiate the following procedures: If a shipment does not arrive within a few days of its expected delivery date, the buyer should contact the *supplier* to determine definitely that the material was shipped—and if it was, also to obtain necessary tracing information. The buyer should then contact the carrier and request that the shipment be traced. If the shipment cannot be located, a loss claim for a specific amount of money should be filed in writing with the carrier. It is mandatory that all claims be filed within nine months after the loss, or they may be disallowed. In the interest of prompt investigation and settlement, the sooner the claim is filed, the better.

Damage

A shipment can incur two types of damage in transit: (1) apparent damage and (2) concealed damage. If a shipment appears to be damaged or partly missing, these facts should be noted in writing before the shipment is accepted. This can be done on the delivery receipt or the freight bill. Generally, the carrier's driver signs the exception on the copy left with the consignee, while the consignee's receiving clerk signs the exception on the copy retained by the carrier. The purchaser should then contact the carrier's freight agent and request him or her to inspect the damage and prepare an inspection report.

Occasionally, damage is concealed and not discovered until a shipment is unpacked. When this happens, the unpacking operation should be discontinued immediately upon detection of damage. The purchaser should contact the carrier's freight agent when the damage is found, in no case more than fifteen days after delivery, and request an inspection of the shipment. The merchandise, as well as the packing material and container, should be left undisturbed for the agent's inspection. Most firms use an instamatic camera to photograph the damaged item in its partially unpacked condition to provide evidence in support of the claim that subsequently will be filed. Claim settlement is dependent on satisfactory determination of the party responsible for the damage. Consequently, it is to the purchaser's advantage to preserve all evidence for the carrier's inspection.

The following data are usually submitted in support of a damage claim filed with a carrier:

- The statement of claim, itemized and submitted on a standard claim form available from the carrier

- The carrier's inspection report
- A certified copy of the invoice indicating the value of the shipment
- The paid freight bill
- The original bill of lading

In the case of concealed damage, a statement from the supplier may also be required.

A claim should always be filed as quickly as practical after the damage is known. The probability of obtaining a favorable settlement usually is greater while the facts of the case are still fresh and clear.

Responsibility for filing a claim rests *with the owner of the material at the time damage occurred*. Consequently, if the damaged material was shipped F.O.B. supplier's plant, the purchaser bears this responsibility. On the other hand, if the shipment was made F.O.B. purchaser's plant, the supplier is responsible for assembling supporting data and filing the claim. In either case, the purchasing firm must do most of the work preparatory to the actual filing of the claim because its personnel discovered the damage and it has possession of the material.

It is very difficult for a claimant, even by resorting to legal action, to recover the full cost of concealed damage from a carrier. A claimant must present evidence that the material was properly packed to withstand the normal rigors of shipment and that the merchandise was in undamaged condition at the time it was delivered to the carrier. A claimant also must show that loss or damage was not sustained after delivery while the shipment was in its custody. These are sometimes difficult matters to prove. The wise buyer, therefore, makes every effort to settle such claims out of court. The development of a good business relationship with carriers and a cooperative attitude in following carriers' regulations for reporting and inspecting damage can pay handsome dividends.

DEMURRAGE

When a purchaser receives a carload of material, the railroad allows the firm approximately two days to unload the car. If the purchaser retains the car beyond the allowable period, the carrier assesses a *demurrage* charge. The reason for such a penalty is clear. A freight car is a piece of productive equipment for the railroad; as long as it sits idle on a customer's siding it produces no revenue.

Straight demurrage charges are assessed in the following manner. After a car is received and properly placed for unloading, the purchaser is given forty-eight hours beyond the next 7:00 a.m. to unload the car. For instance, if the railroad delivers and positions a car at 1:00 p.m. Monday, the purchaser has until 7:00 a.m. Thursday to unload the car. For each day the buyer keeps the car after 7:00 a.m. Thursday, he or she must pay a demurrage charge. Although rates fluctuate with the supply and demand for cars, charges typically run $20 to $30 per car per day for the first week, and $60 or more per car per day thereafter. Saturdays, Sundays, and holidays are considered free days and are excluded from demurrage computations.

If a firm does much purchasing in carload lots, it may wish to enter into an *average demurrage agreement* with the carrier. Under such an agreement, one demurrage debit is assessed for each day one car is held beyond the allowable time period; one demurrage credit is allowed for each car released during the first twenty-four hours of the allowable forty-eight-hour period. Each month the purchaser is billed for the debits in excess of its credits.

Clearly, a purchasing department should consult with the department responsible for car handling and unloading when it schedules carload shipments. Good coordination at this point can produce an orderly flow of cars that does not exceed the manpower and physical facilities available for unloading. Sound planning in this area minimizes congestion on the receiving docks, reduces demurrage charges, and reduces labor overtime costs.[9]

FREIGHT BILL AUDITS

A purchaser of transportation services has the right to audit its freight bills and submit a claim for overcharges within a three-year period after the date of delivery. Most firms find it profitable to audit freight bills. Although such an audit is only prudent business practice, the complexities of freight classifications and rates provide a clue to a more compelling motive for scrutinizing freight bills.

The voluminous and complex commodity classification structure produces literally thousands of rates under which different materials move between different geographical points. It is not uncommon, even for a skilled rate clerk, to make an error in commodity description or commodity classification. This results in an incorrect rate determination. For example, "fiberglass insulating blocks packed loosely in boxes" take one rate, while "fiberglass insulating shapes other than blocks packed loosely in boxes" take another rate. In thumbing through the Uniform Freight Classification, one finds literally thousands of similar cases illustrating even finer distinctions between two classifications. It is, therefore, an understandably common occurrence for most firms to receive a significant number of freight bills that are incorrect simply because the carrier's billing department unintentionally applied the wrong rate. If the item is purchased repetitively, errors of this kind may be repeated and a firm's loss compounded.

A firm's freight bills can be audited by its own traffic specialist(s) or by an external consultant. During the last several decades, numerous specialized audit bureaus and traffic consultants have developed profitable businesses by

---

[9]While most companies object to paying demurrage charges, at times a boxcar can serve effectively as a rolling warehouse. In certain situations, it may be profitable to pay planned demurrage charges and use a car for storage purposes.

auditing their clients' freight bills on a 50 percent commission basis. Under this system the consultant audits all the purchaser's freight bills free of charge. If incorrect bills are detected, the consultant prepares and processes a claim with the carrier, and the purchaser pays the consultant 50 percent of the net recoverable overcharges. The fact that more than two dozen independent rate consultants operate in the San Francisco area alone attests to the significance of this problem.

TRANSPORTATION STRATEGY AND COST REDUCTION

If one takes a broad view of effective management and cost control in the transportation area, two basic approaches become evident. First, and certainly most important, is the development of a strategy for the buying of transportation—an *integrated* plan for the purchase of transportation services to meet *all* of the organization's major needs. Second is the identification and conduct of the more traditional cost reduction projects that have high payoff potential for the organization.

Purchasing Transportation Services

A statement made early in the chapter bears repeating: "Transportation services should be purchased much as any material or service is purchased." Although the logic of this observation seems obvious, only a minority of the firms in the country actually do it! If a single commodity accounts for even 5 percent of a firm's total cost of materials, its purchase should be handled with thorough research and analysis—that is, professionally. Transportation is just such a commodity for virtually every purchaser in the country.

Until the 1980s, this concept was not easy to implement effectively. Competition was constrained by regulation, and as a result, most carriers simply did not think in terms of developing competitive service-oriented arrangements with their customers. Deregulation changed that. Today virtually all carriers compete vigorously and are interested in negotiating arrangements that are mutually advantageous.

Intelligent purchasing dictates the development of an integrated one- to three-year transportation buying plan. This begins with a macroscopic analysis of inbound (and outbound) materials movements with respect to origin and destination points. After determining the approximate annual tonnage movements between general areas of the country, specific carriers are identified that might be able to handle such movements. From this point forward, the procedure is much like that involved in any supplier evaluation. Subsequently, the top group of carriers is invited to submit proposals for the firm's business on a contractual basis for the next several years. Specific factors considered in the carrier evaluation process are:

1 Financial stability and profitability
2 Equipment capability

3 Number and location of terminals and break-bulk centers

4 Quality programs; ISO 9000 registered?

5 Percentage of shipments that would have to be interlined

6 Average transit times between the major origin and destination areas

7 On-time performance record

8 Various elements of service available

9 Cooperativeness in working on service improvement and cost reduction projects

10 Effectiveness of the tracing system; direct access to the computer information system via buyer's terminal

11 Claims to freight bill ratio performance record

12 Claim settlement ratio performance record

13 Shipping rates for the contract period

The number of carriers required is then determined, depending on the buyer's tonnage movement configuration. If the geographic configuration permits, normally two or three carriers are used for the contract period! And the business is divided among them in a manner that produces optimal incentives for performance.

In most cases, the closeness of the buyer-carrier relationship produces improved understanding, cooperation, and reliability of service. In virtually all cases, the rates are significantly lower than they would have been working on an order-by-order basis. In the case of contract arrangements with motor carriers, rate discounts of 25 to 50 percent are reported consistently.[10]

Partnering Arrangements   In 1990 American President Companies (APC) started double stack container rail service from Woodhaven, Michigan, to Ford Motor Company's assembly plant in Hermosillo, Mexico. APC coordinated all the information, transportation, and inventory handling necessary to pick up parts and components from suppliers and load them into containers for delivery on a JIT basis to the Hermosillo plant. The movement included coordination over four railroads and with Mexican customs officials for delay-free clearance. At the plant, Ford built a state-of-the-art stack train terminal to smooth the flow of sequenced parts into assembly operations. APC provided cranes and management to break down the containers. Then the partners collaborated to return the containers to the United States carrying components produced in the Maquiladora region.[11]

This elaborate partnering arrangement was one of the early strategic alliances in the logistics field. It has all the characteristics of good buyer-supplier partnerships discussed in Chapter 11—concentration on a long-term relationship, the development of synergy by working together cooperatively, and the sharing of information, risks, and benefits. To be successful, however, such a partnership does not have to involve a mammoth project. Some purchasers

---

[10]R. S. Reichard, "Discounts and Price Shading Continue," *Purchasing World*, April 1988, p. 28.

[11]Donald J. Bowerson, "The Strategic Benefits of Logistics Alliances," *Harvard Business Review*, July–August 1990, p. 36.

develop partnering relationships with small package delivery services. Traffic volumes of $50,000 to $100,000 per year have been reported to reduce total transportation costs up to 60 percent.[12] So even though partnering arrangements are used most often in the purchase of materials and products, they can be equally effective in working with transportation and logistics suppliers.

Project-Oriented Cost Reduction Possibilities

A skilled traffic specialist can contribute substantially to the reduction of delivered materials costs. In addition to the freight bill auditing program discussed earlier, four types of projects should be considered: (1) the use of unique multimodal shipping arrangements, (2) freight reclassification studies, (3) commodity rate investigations, and (4) pool car arrangements.

Multimodal Arrangements   Since the advent of piggyback and fishyback, buying organizations have devised innumerable unique cost-saving intermodal arrangements. Some firms have even found that a combination of rail and barge carriage is advantageous for selected coast-to-coast runs.[13]

One innovative arrangement, possible only in a relatively deregulated environment, is reported by the Ball Corporation.[14] Ball is an eastern manufacturer of glass, among a wide variety of other products. One of the key ingredients in glassmaking is soda ash, a dense, bulky commodity produced primarily in southwestern Wyoming. Because of the product weight, shipping distance, and shipping volume, the soda ash transportation cost was a significant element in Ball's final product cost.

Ball's initial cost reduction effort was targeted at the one railroad geographically positioned to serve the soda ash supplier. Unfortunately, after extensive attempts Ball was unable to negotiate a satisfactory shipping rate with the railroad. Subsequently, however, joint efforts with the supplier produced a unique solution to the problem. The soda ash is now hauled, under contract, by a truck line from the supplier's plant to another railroad located approximately 200 miles distant. With the use of a newly renovated transfer station, the soda ash is transferred to the cars of the second rail line, which hauls it to the Ball plant. Even with the double handling and the unusual expenses involved, Ball was able to generate an attractive cost saving on the total arrangement—a product of creativity and buyer-supplier-carrier cooperation.

Reclassification Projects   The numerous, closely related commodity classifications which have been devised for rate-making purposes present a

---

[12]Timothy D. Larson, "Buying Small Package Delivery Services," *NAPM Insights,* November 1993, pp. 14–15.

[13]S. A. Reese, "Cargo: How to Get It from There to Here," *Pacific Purchasor,* September 1987, pp. 20–24.

[14]Peter J. Walters, "The Purchasing Interface with Transportation," *Journal of Purchasing and Materials Management,* Winter 1988–1989, p. 23.

fertile field for cost reduction investigation. Because many items shipped do not fit neatly into a single classification, the elements of interpretation and judgment play a significant role in the final assignment of a classification number to a given item. Similarly, the method in which a material is packed influences the risk involved in transporting it and, consequently, the classification to which it is assigned.

An alert rate specialist frequently is able to negotiate the reclassification of certain materials into lower-rated classes. Ironically, this can often be accomplished merely by revising written descriptions of materials or by slightly modifying packing methods.

For example, one traffic manager in a small plant was successful in getting a regularly purchased casting reclassified as a lower-rated material. Upon investigation, he discovered that several different classifications were applicable to the casting; the classifications differed only with respect to the way in which the casting was crated. By eliminating only one board from the original crate, the lower-rated classification was fully applicable. This was done, and the reclassification was approved by the carrier. The savings on this simple project amounted to more than 10 percent of the transportation cost.

Commodity Rate Investigations As noted previously, commodity rates exist as exceptions to class rates and are usually lower than class rates. Quite often, however, no commodity rate exists for the particular item a purchaser ships from a given city. If shipments are repetitive and the volume is reasonably large, or if economic or competitive reasons justify it, the purchaser should negotiate with a carrier in an attempt to obtain a commodity rate. It is sometimes possible, too, for several small buyers to consolidate their regular shipments of like materials and attain a volume sufficient to justify the establishment of a commodity rate.

The case of a large San Francisco firm illustrates the point. Although the firm purchased a large number of castings from a Chicago foundry, the volume was not sufficient to justify the establishment of a commodity rate. Consequently, the traffic manager studied the casting requirements of other manufacturers in the area. Fortunately, he found several that patronized Chicago foundries. By coordinating their plans, he and the traffic managers from the other firms worked out a shipping schedule which permitted them to combine shipments of similar castings to attain a large and consistent volume. A subsequent rate negotiation yielded a commodity rate for these shipments which was 40 percent below the previously paid class rate.

In a more widely publicized case, one large California winery, unable to negotiate what it considered to be a satisfactory commodity rate on East Coast shipments, designed and built a ship for the sole purpose of shipping its wine in bulk. This action gave the winery a significant shipping cost advantage over its competitors. However, as often happens with innovations, the loss of this large traffic movement prompted the railroad to establish a lower commodity rate for the remaining California wineries, to forestall further traffic losses.

Quite apart from the consideration of rates, the additional costs of special handling and packing required for transportation of fragile or unusual items can be excessive. In the case of frequent, large-volume shipments of such items, a buyer may find it profitable to modify the design of a conventional railcar (or trailer) for exclusive use in shipping this material. Through negotiation, the carrier or the supplier may agree to provide this service at minimal or no cost.

Pool Car Arrangements   It is also possible for several buyers to consolidate their requirements for dissimilar items into one single shipment. The individual buyers' small shipments would each ordinarily move under LCL class rates. By combining the small shipments, however, it is often possible to move the *pooled* shipment under a lower CL class rate. Cost-conscious transportation specialists make a point of knowing about other firms that patronize suppliers located in the same areas and are quick to take advantage of pool car opportunities. At the same time, alert suppliers should know about the availability of pool cars. This is one situation about which the seller may have better transportation information than the purchaser.

PURCHASING'S ROLE

Two things are clear. First, the typical buyer who has a basic understanding about the buying of transportation is in a position to do his or her job in a more enlightened manner. Second, the buying of transportation is a specialized task best handled by a buyer trained in the specialty.

The purchasing and supply department and the traffic department must work together. Their most important task is to jointly establish their firm's strategy with regard to the basic plan for buying transportation, shipping terms and conditions to be utilized, and supplier development activities. Wise buyers consult frequently with traffic specialists on matters of carrier designation and routing; they also request estimates of realistic delivery times and costs via different methods when either is critical. Additionally, buyers must coordinate their efforts with those of traffic personnel with respect to expediting and tracing activities, the filing of loss and damage claims, and the scheduling of major incoming carload shipments. Finally, where appropriate, buyers and traffic specialists should work together in identifying and conducting transportation cost reduction projects.

CONCLUSION

Many people are not aware of the keen competition that exists in the transportation industry. Truck, rail, air, and water carriers all compete vigorously for tonnage. Deregulation has made it possible for carriers in the same mode to compete much more actively for business on the basis of a variety of innovative price and service options. Contract carriers utilize only a schedule of minimum rates; hence, buyers often can save money by using competitive bidding or negotiating with these carriers as well as common carriers. Partnering arrangements clearly are another possibility. Progressive buyers understand the potential of this market and take full advantage of its competitive nature.

FOR DISCUSSION

25-1 What activities typically are included in the traffic function?

25-2 What should be the operating relationship between purchasing and traffic?

25-3 "Transportation services should be purchased much as any material or service is purchased." Analyze and discuss this view.

25-4 What is the significance of the shipping terms (F.O.B. terms) which appear on a purchase order issued by the buyer?

25-5 Some firms prefer to buy F.O.B. supplier's plant. What do you see as the major arguments for and against this policy? Discuss.

25-6 What are Incoterms? Why are they important?

25-7 Define briefly the four groups of Incoterms.

25-8 Which Incoterm minimizes the risk and work required for a buyer? Why?

25-9 Which Incoterm minimizes the risk and work required for a supplier? Why?

25-10 When a buyer specifies the method of transportation to be used in shipping an order, he or she has at least a dozen different choices in some cases. List and discuss the significant factors the buyer should consider when viewing the possibility of shipping by each of the following methods:
   a Parcel post
   b Intercity bus service
   c Air cargo

25-11 Answer question 25-10 with respect to the following methods of transportation:
   a Freight forwarder
   b Intercoastal or inland water freight
   c Piggyback and fishyback
   d Pipeline

25-12 Recognizing that there may be many specific exceptions, if you were to state a general rule, under what conditions is it usually most advantageous to use rail freight, and under what conditions is it usually most advantageous to use truck freight?

25-13 Is intermodal carriage increasing or decreasing in volume? Why do you think this is occurring?

25-14 List and discuss the major types of carriers as viewed by the federal government for regulatory purposes.

25-15 Which federal regulatory agency has jurisdiction over the activities of each type of carrier listed in answer to question 25-14?

25-16 What is the significance of the Staggers Rail Act of 1980? Of the Motor Carrier Act of 1980? Of the Shipping Act of 1984?

25-17 From a buyer's point of view, what has been the impact of the government's deregulation activities?

25-18 It has been said that in many cases there appears to be little logical relationship between the freight rates in effect for different commodities. What are some of the general reasons which might help to explain this situation?

25-19 What is the difference between a class rate and a commodity rate? Explain.

25-20 Is it very likely that a shipper will ever be billed incorrectly for the transportation service rendered by a carrier? Explain.

25-21 **a** Define the term "expedite."
   b Define the term "trace."
   c Under what conditions might a shipper or a purchaser engage in either of these activities?

25-22 Outline step by step the procedure you would use in developing an integrated transportation buying plan for your firm.

25-23 In what way might a manufacturing firm employ the services of a traffic consultant or an audit bureau? Explain.

25-24 Outline in detail a receiving procedure which a firm might use to ensure proper handling of lost and damaged shipments.

25-25 **a** Define the term "demurrage."
   b Explain the different types of demurrage agreements under which a firm may operate.

25-26 Discuss in detail the various things a firm might do to reduce its transportation costs.

25-27 Why do some purchasers attempt to develop strategic alliances with carriers? Why do so few buying firms do this?

25-28 What is the purchasing and supply department's role in the traffic function? Explain.

CASES FOR CHAPTER 25

Transportation Service, page 926
Robotics Inc., page 899
The Privileged Fly, page 889

26

INVESTMENT RECOVERY: THE MANAGEMENT OF SURPLUS MATERIALS AND ENVIRONMENTAL CONSIDERATIONS

KEY CONCEPTS

- Problems and opportunities
  Ecology, energy, strategic materials shortages, recycling, profit
- Primary sources of surplus
  Scrap and waste
  Obsolete and damaged stocks
  Obsolete and damaged equipment
- Organization for the management of surplus
  Investment recovery departments; Salvage and reclamation units
  Role of materials management and purchasing and supply management
- Disposal of surplus
  Potential users and buyers
  Contractual considerations
- Buying surplus material
  Advantages
  Specialized dealers
  Knowledge of markets
- Managing and disposing of hazardous materials
  Regulatory acts
  Specific problems
  Approaches to managing the problems
  Hazardous waste disposal
- The need for national materials policies

PROBLEMS AND OPPORTUNITIES

For most people, surplus is not an inspiring topic. It may bring to mind thoughts of old pup tents, mess kits, gas masks, and other military paraphernalia. Even industrial surplus seems to imply mistakes in overprocurement, wasteful production processes, and inefficiencies in general. To make matters worse, surplus is often associated unglamorously with junk heaps. Consequently, surplus is seldom considered an exciting business activity, and it rarely receives the management attention it deserves. This is regrettable, because a firm's total cost of production is the sum of the costs of labor, materials, and overhead *minus* any return from the successful sale or use of all kinds of surplus materials.

To put the topic in a somewhat different light, consider the following view. "Recycling surplus, obsolete, and scrap material into productive channels is an important multi-billion dollar worldwide business. A well managed recovery operation is important whether the incentive for the recovery and reduction of idle investment is conservation of natural resources, the recycling of used materials, or the development of a source of added revenue from otherwise nonproductive assets."[1] All three objectives can be achieved simultaneously.

Profit Opportunities

In spite of the lack of glamour associated with surplus materials, effective disposal of surplus can be very profitable. For example, a large aircraft manufacturer recently increased its annual revenue from surplus sales by over $980,000 after reorganizing and refining its approach to surplus disposal. Similarly, a large oil company recovered $286,000 the first year it reprocessed sludge and sediment that was formerly discarded as valueless. Several years ago Monsanto Chemical Company restructured its surplus equipment disposal program, which is a full-time activity for one of its purchasing groups. The firm's experience to date is that "on average, the return on investment [in this program] is ten to one."[2]

Investment recovery at Minnesota Mining and Manufacturing Company, the Scotch tape giant, is so profitable that the firm devotes a fifteen-member department to the activity. In 1988 the department generated $34.5 million in sales; this accounted for 3.7 percent of 3M's domestic pretax profit that year.[3]

---

[1]Edward B. Maupin III, "Investment Recovery: The Management of Scrap and Surplus," *The Purchasing Handbook*, McGraw Hill, Inc., 1992, chap. 18, p. 546.

[2]C. C. Lewis, "Monsanto Chemical's Purchasing Is Smaller and Stronger," *CPI Purchasing*, August 1987, p. 31.

[3]"Companies Uncover Hidden Funds Selling Old Stuff Garage-Sale Style," *The Wall Street Journal*, Sept. 27, 1989, p. B-10.

Environmental Problems

In the 1970s, the United States determined it should reclaim the purity of its air, water, and living environment. The reduction or elimination of the causes of pollution and the conservation of natural resources became major national objectives. These objectives impinged directly on the materials manager's responsibilities for recovering idle investment from capital surpluses and for recycling surplus materials back into economic channels. Thus, the image and the scope of surplus operations, and the materials manager's responsibility for this activity, changed perceptibly.

Because minerals constitute such a significant part of the overall environmental and natural resources problem, they will be discussed in the following paragraphs to bring the surplus problem into focus from a macroscopic point of view.

Strategic Materials Problem

Most Americans are concerned about the energy problem and understand the environmental problem; however, many do not seem to comprehend the strategic minerals problem. This lack of understanding is regrettable, because this problem has far more serious implications than the energy problem. To function as an industrial society, the United States *must* have thirty-six strategic minerals. The country is presently dependent on foreign sources for twenty-two of these minerals. To make matters even more serious, a high percentage of our imports of many of these strategic metals come from the former U.S.S.R. and South Africa—hardly the most reliable sources of supply. Approximately 92 percent of the chromium consumed in the United States is imported. Other critical materials imports include tantalum and manganese, 97 percent; cobalt, 93 percent; platinum group, 88 percent; nickel, 77 percent; and tungsten, 50 percent. *In comparison, oil imports typically total in the neighborhood of 40 to 50 percent.* In the face of such circumstances, the necessity to conserve and reuse strategic scrap metals is clear.

Recycling Benefits

Consider the critical facts depicted in Table 26-1.[4] Recycling steel, aluminum, lead, zinc, and copper scrap, compared with processing virgin ores, results in energy savings averaging 76 percent. In an era of energy shortages, this is indeed a desirable source of savings.

In addition to energy savings, recycling yields many other desirable benefits. For example, several years ago the Environmental Protection Agency reported to Congress that when 1,000 tons of steel are produced from recycled scrap rather than from virgin ore, the following benefits accrue: 6.7 million gal-

[4]*Phoenix Quarterly,* Institute of Scrap Iron and Steel, Summer 1981, p. 9.

TABLE 26-1
ENERGY SAVINGS AVAILABLE THROUGH THE RECYCLING OF SELECTED METALS

Metal	Energy required to produce 1 ton of metal from primary ore, kwh/ton	Energy required to produce 1 ton of metal from scrap, kwh/ton	Energy savings, kwh/ton	Energy savings, %
Aluminum	51,379	2,000	49,379	96
Copper	13,532	1,726	11,806	87
Iron/steel	6,481	1,784	4,697	74
Lead	7,910	3,176	4,734	60
Zinc	19,044	7,031	12,013	63

lons of water are saved; 104 tons of air pollution effluents are avoided; and 2,754 tons of mining wastes are avoided.

In total, therefore, *recycling reduces energy requirements, reduces gaseous and solid pollutants, and conserves raw materials.*

Related Problems

The purpose of this chapter is to discuss the specific surplus responsibilities of purchasing and materials managers. In a broad sense, however, surplus materials problems go far beyond the responsibilities of these managers. Important illustrations include problems such as balancing the cost of environmental, health, and safety regulations against the nation's need for critical minerals; weighing the benefits of nuclear energy against its possible dangers; and developing a foreign policy designed to preclude the pitfalls of foreign supply disruptions and price fixing.

Of lesser but still significant importance are tangential surplus problems, such as the disposal of hazardous materials, the control of toxic substances, and the need for insurance to protect firms from pollution accidents. Although supply and materials managers do not have direct responsibility for most of these types of surplus problems, an understanding of these macroscopic issues can help them in solving their specific surplus problems.

PRIMARY SOURCES OF SURPLUSES

Industrial surpluses are defined as those materials which are in excess of a firm's operational requirements. Surpluses typically originate from three primary sources: (1) scrap and waste; (2) surplus, obsolete, or damaged stocks; and (3) surplus, obsolete, or damaged equipment. Each is discussed in the following paragraphs.

Surplus from Scrap and Waste

Some surplus from production processing is inevitable. Not all production materials are wholly consumed in most manufacturing processes; frequently, a residue is left. For example, one company stamps disks from copper strips. From this operation, at least 15 percent of the copper left cannot be used elsewhere in the firm's operations. This excess, called *scrap*, must be disposed of as surplus. It is impossible to eliminate this type of surplus; however, by intelligent planning and effective production controls it can be minimized.

Surpluses also result from the inefficient use of production machinery, carelessness, and poor purchasing. This type of surplus is called *waste*. Effective management does everything possible to keep waste at a minimum.

Obviously, the least costly method of controlling surplus of all types is to eliminate it at the source. This is why cost reduction programs that eliminate surpluses before they occur are so profitable.

The largest single category of salable surplus material is scrap metal.[5] Nationwide, the estimated value of this scrap is well over $16 billion. Because of its high dollar value, the disposal of this large quantity of scrap is a significant element in the nation's economy. Scrap metal is also an essential material in the operation of one of the nation's largest industries—the steel industry.

The magnitude of the impact of recyclable scrap on U.S. manufacturing industries is seen clearly in the following statistics. As a general rule today, purchased scrap comprises approximately 40 percent of the steel produced in this country, 40 percent of the copper, 30 percent of the aluminum, 50 percent of the lead, 30 percent of the nickel, 20 percent of the zinc, and 30 percent of the paper.[6]

The proper recovery and disposal of scrap from *precious metals* also is a growing source of profit and conservation. These metals are especially important today because of their increasing rates of usage by the electronics, precision instruments, health care, photography, and chemical industries.

By comparing its results with those of other firms doing similar work, a firm can determine with reasonable accuracy the standard scrap rates for its production processes. When actual scrap rates vary from predetermined standards, or when learning experience does not reduce scrap losses, corrective action should be taken. Scrap losses should decrease with learning for the same reasons that production times decrease with learning. The learning curve concept, as discussed in Chapter 15, also applies to scrap rates. The curve that portrays the relationship between scrap rates and time is called the *efficiency curve*. It is based on the theory that scrap losses will decline at a predictable percentage rate as production operatives and supervisors gain experience in

---

[5]Traditionally, the word "scrap" is used to mean ferrous metals that are suitable for resmelting to produce iron and steel products. The word "metals" is used to identify surplus nonferrous materials.

[6]"Scrap: The Hidden Source of Metals," *Purchasing*, Oct. 13, 1988, p. 48B4.

manufacturing any specific product. Like the learning curve, the efficiency curve can be used as an effective negotiating tool.

Surplus from Obsolete or Damaged Stocks

It is unreasonable to expect that sales forecasting and planning will always be absolutely accurate. In cases of overanticipation, material excesses above actual requirements inevitably result. An automobile company, for example, may predict that consumers want seats of real leather, for which they will be willing to pay an extra charge. Time may prove, however, that most consumers in fact prefer fabric or imitation leather, at no extra charge, thus leaving the manufacturer with a surplus of real leather that must be disposed of.

Changes occur constantly in the designs and specifications of fast-moving technological products. As a consequence, obsolete products and their parts constitute a continuing source of surplus materials. Production planning normally takes place well in advance of the date production actually starts. At any time prior to the beginning of the manufacturing operation, either technical or product changes can completely alter the schedule of materials required for any specific production run. Even after production begins, changes in highly technical items often make some materials in inventory obsolete. The ease with which technological advancement can generate surpluses is highlighted by the single fact that in many firms today over 50 percent of the products they sell did not even exist ten years ago.

Excessive "forward buying" is another common source of surplus materials. Some firms forward-buy only under specific economic circumstances; others forward-buy as a matter of routine company policy. Regardless of the reason for using this method of buying, it entails the hazard of surplus generation from obsolescence, deterioration, or excessive inventory.

Planned overbuying and overproduction represent still other sources of surplus stocks. Some firms, such as machinery and automobile manufacturers, produce more parts for specific models of equipment and automobiles than they may sell because of what is called the *life of type problem*. Frequently, it is more economical for an automobile manufacturer to produce an oversupply of certain replacement parts for new cars while the production line for those cars is in operation (and pay for their storage for as long as the manufacturer accepts the responsibility of furnishing replacement parts for this model) than it is to pay the high start-up costs entailed in reestablishing production facilities for the same parts some years later.

Any warehousing operation, regardless of how efficiently it is controlled, also accumulates some surpluses from breakage, deterioration, and errors in record keeping.

Surplus from Obsolete or Damaged Equipment

All machine tools and equipment at some point in their life become surplus for one of two primary reasons: They wear out, or they become technologically obsolete. In today's rapidly advancing technological world, major machine tools seldom wear out; more frequently they are replaced because they have become technologically obsolete.

In addition to machine tools and plant equipment, most firms also have a large capital investment in office equipment and in the physical plant itself. Competent management makes every practical effort to extend the life of the firm's capital equipment as long as possible, but ultimately, because of obsolescence, breakdowns, the introduction of new products, or new methods of production, replacement of all capital assets—even buildings—becomes mandatory.

Supply Management Ferrets out Surpluses

Progressive purchasing and supply management departments do not wait passively for production or some other department to declare equipment surplus. Rather, in cooperation with the other departments, they review company operations with the objective of determining if any capital equipment should be declared surplus. Suppose, for example, that a firm operates sixteen large truck-mounted cement mixers. Analysis discloses that the firm can operate efficiently with fifteen. One mixer is declared surplus and is sold. This action produces two kinds of benefits: It reduces depreciation, taxes, and operating costs—and it increases profits.

Part-time operations are especially fruitful areas for the identification of surplus equipment. For example, Stanford University found that the Stanford Press, which operated its presses and ancillary printing machines only 20 to 30 hours per week, could not compete with printing shops which ran their machines 60 to 120 hours per week. By purchasing its printing from firms that operated their equipment full time, the university not only reduced the costs for its printed materials, but also generated cash from the sale of printing equipment that was no longer needed.

Inventories are another prime source for generating surpluses. For example, when old equipment is taken out of service, some of the repair parts stocked solely for that equipment remain in inventory. Additionally, dead inventory stock accumulates for a variety of other reasons as the dynamics of a firm's operations and its product lines change. In many firms, surpluses such as these go undetected. Progressive supply managers, however, develop programs that facilitate their speedy identification and disposition.

ORGANIZATION FOR THE MANAGEMENT OF SURPLUS

Investment Recovery Departments

Some firms identify the operating group as their "salvage and reclamation" unit. Because this function has grown in importance in most firms, however, many have expanded and sophisticated its level of activity—and have graced the operation with a new and more appropriate title, the *investment recovery* department.

Whatever the unit is called, nearly all manufacturing firms (large and small) and many nonmanufacturing firms should have such a functional activity organized and in operation. Depending on the quantity and value of the salvageable material involved, the unit can operate on either a full- or a part-time basis. Many small firms, unfortunately, fail to establish such an operating unit simply because they believe their volume of surplus does not justify a full-time operation.

Industry loses millions of dollars annually by neglecting the investment recovery function. For example, a large electrical company, by reorganizing its salvage operation, recently increased it yearly savings by over 20 percent to roughly $1,200,000. A large university started an investment recovery program and had sales of over $200,000 and savings of over $130,000 in the program's first year. A bank created additional profits of over $95,000 per year by correctly salvaging its wastepaper! Many other firms could benefit similarly, but they fail to recognize the profit potential of salvage and reclamation activities.

Assume that an obsolete motor-generator set is to be disposed of. If there were no salvage operation, the department head would dispose of the equipment "as is." With the existence of a salvage operation, the first determination to be made would be whether the machine could be sold as an operating machine, either in its present condition or after some minor repair work was done.[7] If it could not be sold as an operating machine, the second determination would be to decide on the economic feasibility of disassembling it and segregating it into its component parts and/or into its various kinds of metals, such as copper, steel, or aluminum. The component parts of some used machines can be valuable either for stock purposes or for sale. If the decision is against disassembly, the machine would be sold "as is" for its scrap metal value. Each of the alternatives will produce a different net revenue. Selling the machine in operating condition *usually* produces the greatest return, while selling it "as is" for scrap produces the least. Some firms with high-dollar-value surpluses include in their investment recovery departments recycling or recovery equipment, such as balers, shredders, and metal separators.

How to salvage materials can sometimes be a challenging analytical exercise. A university, for example, had an old chapel organ to sell. Unfortunately, the market for used organs of this vintage was almost nonexistent, and the high bid was $10,000. The surplus and salvage manager thought the organ could be sold for more. Further analysis proved he was right. For $3,000, the organ was disassembled into its component parts. The tin from the pipes was sold for $30,000; the remainder of the organ was sold for $3,200.

Overall company salvage expense frequently can be reduced greatly by preplanning and instituting simple operating procedures. For example, sorting surplus metals by type can often be accomplished inexpensively simply by

---

[7]Major repairs generally are best left to dealers who specialize in repair work.

providing suitably marked containers *at the point of accumulation.* This easy procedure increases scrap value. For example, if high-carbon-steel cutting tools are mixed with less expensive grades of metal scrap, the money realized from selling the mixed scrap as a single lot will be considerably less than that which would result from selling the cutting tools as one lot and the remainder of the scrap as another. To simplify sorting of this type, barrels of different colors can be used for different kinds of scrap metals. Similarly, surplus paper, cardboard, and similar surplus materials should be segregated during accumulation by using the method that will bring the highest selling price.

An investment recovery unit typically handles all three kinds of surplus: scrap, surplus stock, and surplus equipment.

The Role of the Materials Management and the Purchasing and Supply Departments

The materials cycle is not complete until all surplus materials are disposed of in the most productive manner. Consequently, in firms with a materials management department, the investment recovery function often reports to the firm's materials manager. In some operations having large dollar surpluses, however, the investment recovery unit reports directly to the plant manager or a staff assistant. Yet, in a majority of the cases the investment recovery unit is assigned to the purchasing department. A broadly based 1988 NAPM/CAPS study reported that in 57 percent of the firms studied, purchasing was responsible for the investment recovery function.[8]

Why is this odd responsibility assigned to purchasing? Usually, no other department in the firm is as well qualified to perform the task. The professional and managerial skills required for a successful disposal operation are also required to do a good job of buying. No other department of a firm is as concerned with or as informed about materials, their markets, and related operating practices as the purchasing department.

The purchasing department routinely buys a large variety of raw materials, component parts, and equipment. It has knowledge about who makes these materials, what other firms use them, how they are used in its own firm, and how much they cost. This is the precise knowledge needed to sell surpluses of these materials successfully. Also, a relatively large number of buyers in the metal industries regularly buy some form of scrap or other surplus material for their own manufacturing purposes. The vice president for materials in one of the nation's largest steel companies told the authors that he considers the purchasing of scrap metal to be the *key profit responsibility* of his purchasing department. In this and similar situations, purchasing personnel are particularly knowledgeable about the markets in question. Daily contact with industry representatives, coupled with the reading of purchasing and trade journals, keeps them informed of surplus trends in a variety of markets. Additionally,

---

[8]Harold E. Fearon, *Purchasing Organizational Relationships,* NAPM/CAPS, 1988, p. 14

buyers frequently sell a significant portion of their firms' surpluses back to the suppliers from whom they were purchased.

DISPOSING OF SURPLUS PROFITABLY

When material is declared surplus, the materials management, purchasing, or investment recovery unit, as appropriate, is informed. Following this action, disposal is made by one of seven methods:

1 Use within the firm
2 Return to the supplier
3 Direct sale to another firm
4 Sale to a dealer or broker
5 Sale to employees
6 Donations to educational institutions
7 Some combination of the preceding methods

Use within the Firm

At a well-known multiplant pump company, lists describing surplus materials and equipment available for use within the firm are circulated to all divisions. If no request for use is forthcoming from U.S. divisions, the lists are sent to the firm's overseas subsidiaries.

After restructuring and refining its surplus equipment disposal program, Monsanto Chemical discovered an interesting phenomenon. It found that its single largest customer for surplus equipment was its own engineering purchasing group, which supports the design and modification of production operations in all of the firm's domestic and foreign plants.[9]

At a large automobile manufacturing company, the disposal of fixed assets for all U.S. plants is the function of a three-person staff in the central office. When a surplus develops, it is the responsibility of the local plant manager to inform his or her division manager. The latter contacts all divisional facilities to determine whether the equipment can be used. If it cannot be used within the division, the matter is referred to the three-person disposal staff in the central office. This staff then initiates a companywide screening program that sometimes involves overseas divisions as well. If the screening steps fail to turn up a user, the local plant is given authority to sell the equipment as surplus.

Use within the firm is always the most profitable form of surplus disposal. For relatively new equipment this type of disposal realizes 100 percent of the original cost, whereas returns to suppliers typically yield 80 to 90 percent of original cost, and sales to dealers and brokers only 10 to 40 percent.

[9]C. C. Lewis, "Monsanto Chemical's Purchasing Is Smaller and Stronger," *CPI Purchasing*, August 1987, p. 31.

Return to Suppliers

If the surplus material cannot be used within the firm, the return-to-supplier method of disposal is generally the next best method. Suppliers typically allow the return of both new and used surpluses as a courtesy to good accounts. Salable materials returned from inventory are traditionally accepted at original cost, less a nominal restocking charge. Since different firms have different levels of technical requirements, suppliers can frequently resell even obsolete inventory items at full price.

Scrap metals can sometimes be returned to suppliers, depending on the size of the buyer's account, the metal involved, its degree of contamination, and the current economics of the scrap market. When scrap is scarce, many suppliers routinely require the return of scrap as a precondition of further sales. Particular attention should be paid to the so-called exotic metals, which include most nonferrous metals, alloy steels, and tool steels. Usually these metals can be sold to the supplier at prices much higher than are attainable in the open market.

Supplier policies regarding the return of used equipment to the manufacturer or dealer from whom it was purchased vary widely with the economics of the used equipment market and the sales policies of manufacturers.

Selling to Other Firms

Some companies sell surplus materials and equipment directly to other firms. Sales of equipment to other firms depend primarily on the condition of the equipment, pricing considerations, and the availability of similar equipment from other sources. Equipment sales made directly to a user typically result in a better price than sales made to dealers or brokers.

Sales of production surpluses are most profitable when the surplus of one company is the raw material of another. For example, if a firm can sell its waste paper back to the paper mill, it generally will get the highest price and cause the least pollution.

Selling to Dealers and Brokers

Surplus dealers and brokers (referred to as "dealers") constitute an excellent outlet for surplus materials. When a firm advertises surplus materials for sale, dealers often respond. Transactions with dealers are usually "where is, as is," and most of the time they are for cash. Surplus machine tool dealers, for example, operate in two ways: by auction, which usually involves selling a plant's entire equipment inventory; or by purchase of small lots. For auctions, the dealer receives a commission and seldom does more to the equipment than show it to bidders. For small-lot transactions, however, the dealer pays the owners cash, and then often reconditions or rebuilds machine tools before selling them. Normally, it is not profitable for the original owner to recondition equipment before selling it.

Although cooperative action among purchasing people to sell surplus materials is rare, such a situation does exist among members of the Cleveland Association of Purchasing Management. This group has a surplus commodity service available to its members. Purchasing and materials managers send their lists of surplus commodities to the association office. The association approves the list, writes a covering letter, reproduces both, and distributes the information to all its members.

Interplay among dealers is more widespread than among purchasing associations. Through the Machinery Dealers' National Association, its members have what amounts to a single inventory pool. One dealer, for example, may have a customer for equipment not in its stock, but by knowing what other dealers have on hand, the first dealer can make a sale from another dealer's inventory. All dealers learn what other dealers have on hand from an equipment listing that is published periodically by the association. Association members find such a reciprocal arrangement advantageous, because even the largest dealer cannot stock everything.

Selling to Employees

Many firms make it a practice to sell both the products they manufacture and their surpluses to their employees. If the surpluses are the result of overstocking or obsolescence and the materials are in new or good condition, or if they are odds and ends of scrap desired by "do-it-yourself" employees, this can be a satisfactory method of disposal. On the other hand, if the surpluses are not in fully satisfactory condition, such sales, regardless of their attractive prices, can create resentment in employees toward their employers. Used automobiles can be an especially dangerous item of equipment to sell to employees.

Because of the numerous potential disadvantages involved, many sophisticated firms will not sell *used* surpluses (especially equipment) to their employees. Besides possible dissatisfaction, selling to employees often entails excessive paperwork, and it always involves an administrative burden in an effort to ensure complete impartiality among employees. High administrative costs have caused some firms to set minimum dollar amounts for sales to employees. Other firms, to avoid administrative costs, give their employees surplus materials having only a nominal value.

Donations to Educational Institutions

Federal and state tax laws in some cases can create another profitable basis for disposal of surplus materials: giving them away. At the present time, colleges and schools acutely need machine tools and other types of industrial materials for instructional use. Although recent tax laws have reduced the tax benefits allowed for gifts to educational and other nonprofit institutions, desirable benefits sometimes still exist. Because the applicable tax laws and regulations are complicated, before making large gifts potential donors should consult their tax advisers to determine exactly what benefits are available.

Contracting Considerations

Generally speaking, the following contractual considerations apply to the three major categories of materials that are sold as surplus.

Scrap metals, depending on existing economic conditions, are best disposed of by either a short- or a long-term contract made with a local scrap dealer. The dealer getting the contract should be selected after an investigation of at least three dealers. Because of the breadth of scrap market activities, a purchasing department should generally experience little difficulty in interesting three or more capable dealers who will compete vigorously for the business. Also, the highly competitive nature of the scrap business usually keeps the variation in bid prices within a narrow range. Local dealers have an operating and transportation advantage over more distant competitors; also, they can provide more frequent pickups and more personalized contract service. Published market prices are available for many varieties of scrap, and these prices are frequently used as the bases for long-term contract prices. Bid prices are normally used for short-term contract prices.

Surplus stock that cannot be returned to the supplier is best disposed of by sale to jobbers or secondhand dealers. Such sales are most frequently made on a competitive bid basis, and competition for these materials is usually keen.

Surplus equipment typically can be disposed of most effectively by obtaining competitive bids from dealers. However, on occasion negotiation is used. Intense competition is traditionally developed after a firm acquires a select group of dealers who are interested in bidding for its surplus equipment on a continuing basis. Fixed prices to dealers are satisfactory when a selling firm is sure of the equipment's fair selling price. Auction is frequently used as a quick and convenient method of disposing of large quantities of equipment. Occasionally, advertisements in trade journals or trade papers prove effective in selling this category of surplus.

BUYING SURPLUS MATERIAL

Purchasing departments not only *sell* surplus material; at times they also *buy* it. Purchasing managers often can find real bargains by shopping among surplus dealers. These dealers can supply almost anything—from transistors to molding machines. The wide range of surplus goods now available to those looking for good buys is best illustrated by the yearly displays at the Institute of Surplus Dealers Trade Show. Exhibitors' booths are filled with an impressive variety of power tools, packaging materials, grinding wheels, pressure-sensitive tapes, electronic parts, and a multitude of other products.

The Advantages

Most surplus dealers stress low price as their main selling point; however, a few extol the advantages of *immediate availability,* which is often an even more valuable advantage to a buyer. A company building a prototype product, for example, can often pick up suitable material immediately from a surplus dealer, whereas it might have to wait weeks or months to get the same material new.

Purchases of surplus equipment may also represent sound buying decisions in the following situations:

- When the equipment is to be used infrequently, such as for standby service
- When the equipment fills a one-time need
- When the equipment is to be used for maintenance, pilot, or experimental work
- When the equipment is to be used by students or apprentices
- When the buyer's firm is not able to finance new equipment

Specialized Dealers

The rapid increase in the variety and volume of surplus products has led naturally to the emergence of an increasing number of specialized dealers. Alben Packaging Corporation, for example, specializes in the sale of surplus paper and packaging materials. Specialists in hydraulic parts, nylon rope, bearings, marine supplies, machine tools, and many other fields are replacing those dealers who formerly sold everything.

Even some dealers who specialize, however, still handle a wide range of materials. A few dealers, such as The Tunnel Machinery Exchange, stand ready to equip an entire plant. "If you want to set up a factory to manufacture fluorescent light fixtures," an executive of Tunnel has said, "Tunnel Machinery Exchange can supply presses, molding machines, office equipment, typewriters—everything you need."

Knowledge of Markets Required

Surplus material purchases typically offer buyers significant cost savings. When buying technical products whose design is subject to rapid change, however, knowledge of the market and expected market trends is mandatory. In mid-1981, for example, *Purchasing World* reported the advantages of purchasing used computers.[10] Just two months later a *Wall Street Journal* article reported that "used computers may not be much of a bargain if prices of new ones continue to dive."[11] In the article, Adolph Monosson, board chairman of American Used Computer Company (the largest used-computer dealer in the United States), predicted that sales for used computers would peak in 1983, then drop precipitously. He stated that advancing technology would soon drive the price of new computers down so fast that used equipment would no longer be an attractive alternative. Although this example occurred well over

---

[10]"Used Computers: A Cost-Saving Alternative," *Purchasing World,* July 1981, pp. 57–79.
[11]"Used Computers," *The Wall Street Journal,* Sept. 17, 1981, p. 1.

a decade ago, it illustrates an extremely important point. The rapidly changing conditions, characterized in these two articles, emphasize the fact that the effective purchase of used technical products requires perceptiveness, analytical skill, and accurate market data—it is no business for a novice! Likewise, buying new designs and models of the same products requires similar capabilities.

Where to Find Surplus Dealers

Buyers looking for a dealer—for either buying or selling—can contact the New York office of the Institute of Surplus Dealers. This office lists all members and their various specialties.[12] Two regional associations can provide similar information: the Associated Surplus Dealers in Los Angeles and the National Surplus Dealers Association in Chicago. The Institute of Scrap Iron & Steel, Inc., in Washington, D.C., can supply a list of dealers who buy and sell all types of ferrous metals.[13] The Machinery Dealers National Association has a free *Buyers Guide* which lists surplus and salvage dealers throughout the United States.[14] Twice a month, the *McGraw-Hill Equipment Bulletin* provides a listing of used, surplus, and rebuilt equipment which has been advertised for sale in twenty-five magazines.[15]

MANAGING AND DISPOSING OF HAZARDOUS MATERIALS

There is a dramatic shift underway in how companies see the environment and how they are responding to new environmental challenges. These trends are irreversible and their message is clear. Companies that ignore the environment do so at the risk of their own survival.[16]

—Michael H. Jordan, CEO
Westinghouse Electric Corporation

The fact remains: our planet is ailing. Billions of pounds of hazardous chemicals are being released into our rivers and skies, holes in the ozone layer grow larger, and ever-larger mountains of waste are being generated. The truth is, environmental efforts and the needs of business are not mutually exclusive. One can dovetail with the other if businesses integrate environmental concerns and initiatives into their planning processes.[17]

—IDA Management Journal

[12]Institute of Surplus Dealers, 254 Manhattan Avenue, New York, N.Y. 11211.
[13]Institute of Scrap Iron and Steel, 1627 K Street N.W., Washington, D.C. 20006.
[14]Machinery Dealers National Association, Box 19128, Washington, D.C. 20036.
[15]*McGraw-Hill Equipment Bulletin*, Box 900, New York, N.Y. 10020. Single copies free.
[16]Michael H. Jordan, "Chairman's Message," *Environmental Performance Update*, Westinghouse Electric Corporation, Pittsburgh, Penn., September 1994, p. 1.
[17]"Going Green: How Three Firms Make Environmental Initiatives Pay," *Just in Time: IDA Management Journal*, July–August 1994, p. 4.

These two quotations set the tone for this concluding section of the chapter. Responsible business practices that involve hazardous materials start with (1) the generation of requirements for and the purchase of such materials—and proceed to (2) compliance with "right-to-know laws" [the promulgation of Material Safety Data Sheets (MSDS)], (3) emergency planning, (4) training of the materials handlers and users, and finally (5) disposal of the hazardous waste and leftover materials. Purchasing and supply professionals are most commonly involved in activities (1), (2), and (5).

As noted earlier in the chapter, during the 1970s cleaning up the air, water, and land became a national priority in the United States. Since that time a multitude of laws and regulations have been enacted to help achieve this objective. In addition to the establishment of the Environmental Protection Agency (EPA), some of the key legislation is summarized below.[18]

- The *Occupational Safety and Health Act* (OSHA), among many other things, regulates communication of hazards to employees through the use of MSDSs, and through the training of employees on the handling and use of hazardous materials.
- The *Resource Conservation and Recovery Act* (RCRA) regulates all aspects of wastes from generation to final disposal.
- The *Comprehensive Environmental Response, Compensation, and Liability Act* (CERCLA or Superfund) regulates releases of hazardous substances into the environment and requires cleanup of disposal sites.
- *The Hazardous Materials Transportation Uniform Safety Act of 1990* is the primary law covering the transportation of hazardous material.
- The *Superfund Amendments and Reauthorization Act* of 1986, better known as the *Emergency Planning and Community Right to Know Act*, requires the development of a plan for emergency response and, under certain conditions, the submission of MSDSs for hazardous materials to local planning groups.

Violation of these laws is a serious affair. The maximum corporate penalty for violation is $500,000 per incident, plus up to five years imprisonment.[19] And in recent years the laws have been enforced rigorously.

The Specifics of the Problem

More than 33,000 materials are considered to have some type of potentially hazardous impact on users or handlers. These materials are classified as a "hazardous substance," an "extremely hazardous substance," or "hazardous waste." Hazardous waste is defined by the CERCLA Act as "toxic, ignitable,

---

[18]Tammy Schwerman, "HazMat Handle with Care: Safe Handling," *NAPM Insights*, July 1992, p. 10.
    [19]See ibid, p. 11; and Donna Delia-Loyle, "Here's Help for the HazMat Headache," *Global Trade*, January 1992, p. 22.

corrosive, or dangerously reactive substances." And it is reported that U.S. organizations produce more than 210 million tons of hazardous waste each year.[20]

It is not surprising, then, to find that most firms generate some type of hazardous waste, and over half produce a significant volume. The fact that such common materials as paint thinner, many cleaning materials, insecticides, some glues, and gasoline are classified as hazardous materials underscores the fact that few organizations are completely exempt from hazardous material regulations.[21]

The bottom-line significance of this discussion for these firms is that a hazardous waste "generator" has a *"cradle to grave"* responsibility for this hazardous material. That is, the firm that uses the material or produces the hazardous waste has the responsibility for safe use or handling of the material from its creation until it either is completely destroyed or otherwise becomes inert. A user or generator cannot delegate its responsibility! Since some hazardous materials do not degrade for thousands of years, the practical implications are tremendous. Merely contracting for a firm to safely dispose of the materials does not relieve the original user of its ultimate cradle-to-grave responsibility, regardless of the care with which the contractor discharges its duties.[22]

Potential Courses of Action

How does an organization go about minimizing the hazardous waste problem? The most effective action clearly is to *reduce or eliminate the generation of hazardous waste* in the first place. The starting point is in the product design process. Purchasing representatives, along with other team members, can stress the use of environmentally friendly materials to the extent that it is practical. The same concept carries through to the requirements for different types of processing operations. To the extent possible, these should be "green" operations. The same basic approaches can be used in selecting and working with suppliers. This topic is discussed more extensively in the section on "green purchasing" in Chapter 11.

Recycling and reusing certain materials is a practice that has been used for a number of years and often reduces the volume of objectionable materials significantly. *Cleaning chemicals* to remove hazardous contaminants is another approach used rather widely. Yet another approach to "cleanse" a chemical is to use it in a chemically reactive process that will neutralize it. For example, an

---

[20]Gordon F. Bloom and Michael S. Morton, "Hazardous Waste Is Every Manager's Problem," *Sloan Management Review,* Summer 1991, p. 80.

[21]For a brief but interesting discussion of this topic, see Richard A. Hoover, "And You Thought You Were Exempt," *The Wright Stuff,* March 1993, pp. 1–3.

[22]For a thorough exploration, see Ernest T. Lee, "Contracting for Hazardous Materials Disposal," *79th Annual International Purchasing Conference Proceedings,* NAPM, Tempe, Ariz., 1994, pp. 59–64.

acidic liquid that is a waste product of a given manufacturing process may be used to neutralize the caustic waste stream produced by another processing operation.

In a recent NAPM survey, approximately 70 percent of the respondents stated that their firms actively pursue a formal environmental policy that includes reducing, reusing, or recycling their waste products. This fact provides some indication of the seriousness with which American industry is approaching this issue.[23]

After all elimination and reduction approaches have been considered, the major remaining alternative is to "dispose" of the hazardous waste in an environmentally safe manner.

Hazardous Waste Disposal

More often than not, the purchasing and supply operation is assigned the responsibility of handling the disposal of hazardous waste—for the same reasons it is assigned the responsibility for the disposal of scrap and surplus materials. Basically, two approaches can be used in disposing of hazardous materials, along with the packaging or containers in which some of the materials were originally shipped.

1 Purchasing may outsource the entire operation to a specialized contractor or consulting firm in this business. This includes any laboratory testing required prior to shipment, packaging, transportation, contracting with a hazardous material disposal site, and record keeping and administrative requirements.
2 Purchasing may work directly with a transporter licensed by the Department of Transportation (or federal and state EPAs) to haul the hazardous material—and handle the other functions itself. Or, of course, it can handle only a part of the other functions and subcontract some along with the transportation activity.

A *Purchasing* magazine survey of the top 100 purchasing organizations in the United States found that approximately 60 percent of these large firms followed the first alternative—that of outsourcing the entire hazardous waste disposal operation. Additionally, most observers believe that firms with only small hazardous waste requirements find outsourcing to be their best solution as well. It is estimated that by the year 2000, with the continued emphasis on environmental protection, hazardous waste consulting and disposal will grow to a $25 billion per year industry.[24]

One additional fact turned up by the *Purchasing* study is that 81 percent of the hazardous waste treated at the specialized sites is incinerated. That is, the

[23]Patricia Ellett, *Government Relations Issues Membership Survey No. 2*, NAPM, Tempe, Ariz., 1993, p. 2.
[24]Tom Stundza, "A Toxic Challenge: No Clear Solution," *Purchasing*, Mar. 19, 1992, p. 58.

waste is "dry-cleaned," thickened, and burned, sometimes using other wastes as fueling agents.

How does a purchasing and supply department proceed in deciding how it will handle the hazardous waste assignment? Denis Riordan, chairman of Inter Continental—a freight brokerage and project management firm—suggests a broad three-step approach in establishing the program.[25]

- First, purchasers must define exactly what type and how much hazardous waste is involved.
- Second, staff knowledge and expertise is evaluated to determine internal capabilities.
- Finally, after making these appraisals, the two basic options are studied carefully—and an optimal approach for the given situation is determined.

CONCLUSION

Materials for U.S. industry originate from three basic sources—*domestic, foreign,* and *surplus.* To the extent practical, surplus is the preferred source since it provides so many unique advantages. Examples are reduced costs for transportation, processing, and energy; reduced emissions that form gaseous and solid pollutants; and reduced usage of new materials. Consequently, surplus materials always should be well managed, and they should be used whenever it is feasible to do so.

Although mineralogists do not agree precisely when the earth's key mineral supplies will be exhausted, they do agree that the supply is finite, and that at some future dates the various supplies will be exhausted. The seriousness of this situation was highlighted by President Reagan's warning in 1982: "It is now widely recognized that our nation is vulnerable to sudden shortages in basic raw materials."[26] Assuredly, so serious a situation dictates that the United States develop policies that specifically address this national problem.

New *domestic materials policies* are needed to replace current policies that tend to be conflicting and counterproductive. Transportation costs, health costs, safety costs, environmental costs, land preservation costs, and so forth, should be evaluated in terms of the nation's total materials requirements and its ability to pay for these requirements. Only such an evaluation can reconcile the total cost and noncost factors impinging on the nation's overall raw materials problem.

New *foreign materials policies* are needed to secure the nation's supply of critical minerals from foreign sources. Analysts recognize that secure foreign sources of many raw materials are essential to assure the nation's economic prosperity, its future economic growth, and its national defense.

---

[25]Denis Riordan, "Moving Hazardous Waste," *NAPM Insights,* November 1990, p. 24.
[26]White House speech, Feb. 19, 1982.

Because both the industrialized and the developing nations are using increasing quantities of scarce minerals, the world is becoming engaged in a resources struggle. As the seriousness of this struggle becomes more clearly recognized, and as new scarce materials policies are implemented, additional opportunities will open up for progressive supply managers. By development of timely conservation-oriented programs that maximize the value of surpluses bought and sold for their individual firms, purchasing and supply managers can make a genuine contribution. They can increase corporate profits, contribute to the reduction of U.S. dependence on foreign sources for basic materials, reduce the balance of payments deficit, and contribute to the nation's continuing prosperity.

FOR DISCUSSION

26-1 Explain why surplus materials are important to the individual firms that create them.

26-2 What impact can surplus materials have on the national economy?

26-3 What effect does a well-managed surplus materials program have on the environment?

26-4 Are national environmental objectives and a manufacturing firm's business objectives generally compatible? Discuss.

26-5 What department in most companies do you feel is best qualified to handle surplus disposal? Why?

26-6 Some observers say that the sales department is the logical place to locate the scrap disposal function. Discuss.

26-7 Discuss how surplus materials are created in the U.S. economy. Can these surpluses be controlled?

26-8 How does national economic planning relate to the effective utilization of surplus materials?

26-9 Explai ι why some companies engage in planned overbuying, thus possibly creating a disposal-of-surplus problem.

26-10 What are some of the problems in attempting to use surplus material throughout a large multiplant company?

26-11 If you were the purchasing manager for the prime contractor for a Mach 3 commercial airliner, what thoughts would you have about the disposal of scrap metals that will be used in this 2,000-mile-an-hour plane?

26-12 Explain why some purchasing managers follow scrap prices with such great interest.

26-13 Explain and discuss the traditional ways most firms dispose of scrap.

26-14 Discuss the advantages and the possible hazards of buying surplus capital equipment.

26-15 Discuss the impact you think the world's increasing scarcity of raw materials will have on the management of surpluses after the year 2000. Discuss the additional opportunities this impact will open to supply managers.

26-16 Assume that you are the manager of a large firm's investment recovery department. Outline in general form the plan you would use in deciding how to dispose of surplus capital equipment after it comes to your department for handling.

26-17 Referring to the preceding question, outline a general plan for handling and disposing of scrap metal from the production shops.

26-18 What are MSDS documents? For what purposes are they used?

26-19 What role do OSHA regulations play in a firm's management of hazardous materials?

26-20 What is meant by the term "cradle to grave" responsibility? Discuss briefly.

26-21 What is meant by the term "green purchasing"?

26-22 Assume that you are a purchasing and supply manager for a medium-size manufacturing firm. You are asked to develop a policy for disposal of the firm's hazardous waste products. Prepare an outline covering the steps you would go through in developing this policy. Discuss the key elements of your approach.

26-23 How does an organization go about minimizing its hazardous waste problem? Discuss briefly.

26-24 Discuss the principal surplus materials problems which supply managers can do very little to solve.

CASES FOR CHAPTER 26

SEVEN

GENERAL MANAGEMENT
RESPONSIBILITIES

27

DEVELOPING AND MANAGING THE BUYING PLAN

The first purchasing agent's position was created to provide a service for the people managing the primary operating functions of the firm. In time, the buying activity became a specialized, then a professionalized, staff function. Until the last decade or two, however, the job of most buyers in the purchasing department began when they received a purchase requisition from one of the operating units. In other words, the purchasing function typically operated in a *reactive* manner. When a materials need arose, purchasing reacted to it.

Today, progressive industrial purchasing and supply management departments operate differently. Most organizations have learned that a majority of their material needs over the course of a four- to twelve-month period can be determined in advance with acceptable accuracy. Not all material needs can be forecast, but many can. Hence, most purchasing managers and their senior buyers develop an annual buying plan for their key materials when it is practical to do so.[1] Included in this plan is the use of a variety of volume buying and longer-term contracting techniques. Thus, progressive purchasing and supply departments are *proactive*—that is, they make things happen. In this case, they prepare a flexible "game plan" before specific materials needs arise.

The development and management of these plans is the subject of this chapter.

THE PLANNING APPROACH

The Firm's Annual Operating Plan

In preparation for each new fiscal year most firms construct a firmwide *annual operating plan*. A forecast of the scope and magnitude of key operating activities is the starting point for development of the plan. In a manufacturing firm this is the *sales forecast*—which usually consists of a total annual figure that is further divided into quarterly and monthly estimates by product line. The sales forecast is then translated into an aggregate production plan and master schedule, taking into consideration finished goods inventory levels as well as desired in-process inventory levels for specific items. For obvious reasons, near-term forecast data can be converted into a production schedule with more accuracy, for shorter time periods, than is possible when the planners peer farther into the future.

All materials planning subsequently flows from the preliminary master production schedule. Likewise, operating plans at the group and departmental levels emanate, in a more general way, from this same source. Planning work to this point sets the stage for the budget planning which follows. Figure 27-1 diagrams this general process in terms of the generation of a simplified organization budget.

---

[1]In some cases, more general plans are made to cover periods of from one to three years. See Doug Johnson, *Purchasing's Role in Strategic Planning*, NAPM—Hawaii, Mar. 17, 1994, p. 7.

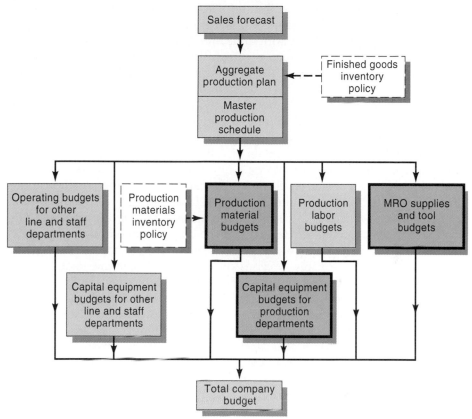

FIGURE 27-1
Major constituents of a total company budget.

The Materials Budget   The basic materials budget, then, is a product of the sales forecast and a planned volume of production. Since sales forecasts are rarely completely accurate, though, actual production levels inevitably deviate from planned levels. When deviation occurs, the basic budget is in error for those items whose costs vary with the level of production—namely, direct material and labor requirements. This unavoidable situation has led most companies to adopt some form of flexible budgeting. The *flexible budget* makes use of supplementary data which adjust variable costs in accordance with the production level actually experienced.

Since the materials budget is based on an estimated level of production, preparation of a *detailed* annual materials budget is practical only for those products whose sales can be forecast reasonably accurately, or for materials that are used in a variety of products whose aggregate demand can be forecast. This means that many companies find it impossible to develop a materials budget for the full year ahead, and that others may be able to budget only selected key materials (perhaps JIT and Class A inventory items). Nevertheless, whenever possible, most supply departments find it profitable to develop a materials budget in terms of both units and dollars.

When the preliminary production schedule is available, it can be converted into a materials budget with the use of the appropriate product bills of material. Conversion simply entails an extension of materials requirements for each product, followed by a consolidation of individual material requirements if the material is used in more than one product. At this point the budget is expressed in units. Conversion of units into dollars is normally accomplished by applying either standard cost data or estimated cost figures.

When a materials budget is to be expressed in terms of dollars, the purchasing and supply manager is normally called on to provide the budget department with two types of information: (1) estimates of material *prices* during the coming year and (2) plans for the specific *timing* of purchases. This information gives the finance department the data required to draw up a realistic schedule of cash requirements for each operating period.

In purchasing, reasonably precise knowledge of materials requirements over an extended period of time facilitates forward buying and permits the advantageous use of contract purchasing and blanket order purchasing techniques. Quantity discounts also can be utilized more effectively. Inventory investment, and its associated risks, likewise can be reduced by advance planning of requirements. *Materials budgets provide maximum purchasing lead time.* This benefit permits the careful selection of qualified suppliers, negotiation without the pressure of deadlines, and a better chance to obtain maximum value for each dollar spent. Additional lead time also produces savings by the use of routine rather than premium transportation, by a reduction in expediting costs, and by a smoothing of the purchasing workload. Supplier relationships can be improved and costs can be reduced because time is available to mesh purchasing requirements with the supplier's production schedule more effectively.

The next step in the process is the development of a detailed *annual buying plan* for each major material or category of materials. Before discussing this topic, however, it is first essential to review the nature of volume and timing decisions.

Volume and Timing Decisions

Volume and timing decisions are influenced by a number of factors, including the type of market in which the purchase is to be made. The first significant variable is the stability of the market.

Stable Markets Materials purchased in stable markets are the multitude of standard, off-the-shelf industrial products, supplies, and hardware (e.g., standard electric motors, pumps, valves, bearings, chemicals, tools, nuts, bolts). In the *long run*, in a reasonably competitive economy the general forces of supply and demand tend to determine the price levels at which these standard products will be sold. In conducting daily business, however, a buyer is more concerned with short-run market conditions. And in the *short run*, shelf prices of these materials are relatively insensitive to the general forces of supply and demand. In the short run, about the only way a buyer can influence the prices he or she pays for these types of items is through some type of volume buying arrangement that permits a supplier to reduce its production or distribution costs.

Nonstandard components and materials, which constitute a substantial portion of most manufacturers' purchases, represent a special situation. Many nonstandard items are bought from numerous small machine shops, foundries, and similar job-shop producers. Consequently, the supply of these items adjusts fairly quickly to the general level of demand. As far as the buyer is concerned, the result in most cases is a reasonably stable supply and price situation. Because of the number and the flexibility of suppliers, the price a buyer pays for such materials is determined largely by the effect of his or her unique demand on the suppliers' costs of production.

Unstable Markets   Unstable markets exhibiting substantial short-run fluctuation of the supply and price factors exist for numerous raw materials. Typical examples of such commodities are crude rubber, copper, tin, zinc, lead, scrap iron, burlap, wool, cotton, hides, wheat, flour, and vegetable oils. The supply of such raw materials is frequently influenced by political forces, weather conditions, actions of speculators, and similar unpredictable factors. As a result, the short-run prices of such commodities may be extremely sensitive to the general forces of supply and demand.

In most cases, the market is supplied by a large number of producers, and the buying action is conducted by a large number of relatively small purchasers. This means that the actions of an *individual buyer* have little effect on the equilibrium price in the market. The market price of such commodities often varies substantially from week to week and month to month, as is indicated by the price charts for several commodities shown in Figure 27-2.

Timing of Purchases   When considering the timing of purchases, buyers are interested first in assuring their firms an *adequate supply* of material and second in acquiring the material at an *optimal price*, considering quality and service requirements. As a general rule, timing is not a critical matter from either point of view when the purchase is made in a market that tends toward price stability. There are exceptions, of course. For example, a professional buyer always tries to anticipate general price increases arising from wage and other cost increases in his or her suppliers' industries. Likewise, the buyer keeps a close eye on the level of general demand for key suppliers' products. If general demand for a particular supplier's product increases sharply, a tem-

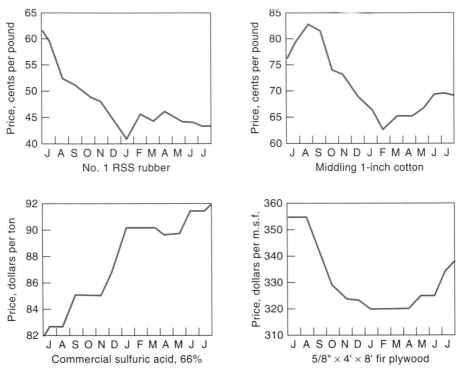

FIGURE 27-2
Illustration of commodity price movements for selected commodities.

porary shortage may develop until demand again tapers off or until production capacity has increased to satisfy the increased level of demand.

Timing is a much more important matter when a purchase is made in a market that tends to be unstable. Careful observation and analysis of market conditions are essential if buyers hope to satisfy their price and supply objectives. Although normally buyers cannot influence the *market price*, they can, by their timing of purchases, control to some extent the *price they pay.*

In recent years, demand for certain raw materials, and the products derived from them, has tended to increase more rapidly than supply. This phenomenon has frequently produced periodic shortages and an increase in the number of materials markets that are characterized by periodic instability. Expansion of multinational business activity and international purchasing, coupled with the volatility of some foreign political environments, has tended to compound the problem of market instability. This situation is particularly evident in markets heavily affected by countries located in the Middle East, Latin America, and Africa. Hence, the timing of purchases made in a growing number of these markets has become increasingly important—a situation which likely will continue into the foreseeable future.

Buying Policies Related to Volume and Timing   In a broad sense, a buyer can utilize one of two basic buying approaches: (1) purchase according to current known requirements, or (2) purchase primarily according to supply market conditions. If the first approach is used, the purchasing schedule is based strictly on the volume of the firm's current needs and largely disregards the behavior of the market in which the purchase is made. If a buyer adopts the second policy, in addition to considering anticipated needs he or she bases purchase timing decisions, in part, on the behavior of the market. In this case, two types of buying activity can be employed: (1) hand-to-mouth buying and (2) forward buying. Each type of buying activity is discussed briefly in the following paragraphs.

Buying to requirements, as the name implies, is a buying policy designed to cover only a firm's materials requirements that are definitely known. Although the time coverage varies from firm to firm for obvious reasons, a period of from one to three months is most common in practice. Most firms use a rolling production forecast that is translated into a firm schedule on either a monthly or a quarterly basis. Buying to requirements generally is the most conservative of the various alternatives and is considered by many firms to be the soundest approach when dealing in a market involving price risks.

Forward buying is the practice of buying materials in a quantity exceeding specified current requirements, but not beyond the actual foreseeable requirements. Even though not known with precision, it is reasonably certain that a longer-term production need for the material does exist. Any purchases beyond this point fall into the speculative buying category. Forward buying can be used in stable markets or in unstable markets where prices appear to be rising. One potential hazard in forward buying, however, is the possible price risk involved, depending on the volatility of the market in which the purchase is made. Intelligent forward buying clearly requires a careful professional analysis of numerous market factors. The buyer must also consider the additional inventory carrying costs and the attendant tie-up of working capital that accompany forward-buys, unless contractual arrangements can be made for the supplier to carry part of the inventory.

Hand-to-mouth buying is the practice of buying material to satisfy current operating requirements in quantities smaller than those normally considered economical. As the term indicates, the production operation literally exists on a hand-to-mouth supply of materials. This buying policy is used primarily in an unstable market that is falling or in situations where demand for specific items may decline or terminate on short notice, for any number of reasons. This approach is *unlike* a small-delivery JIT operation that is based on a longer-term contractual arrangement. When employing a hand-to-mouth buying policy, each purchase is contracted separately at the current material price.

Because of the many variables involved in any specific buying situation, from a precise timing point of view there is no clear-cut definition of the dividing lines between the individual buying policies discussed. However, in order

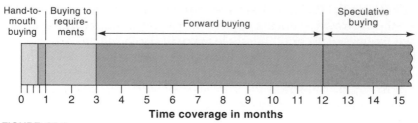

FIGURE 27-3
Buying policies in approximate relation to time.

to place these policies in some concrete time perspective, they are defined in a general way as shown in Figure 27-3.

The Annual Buying Plan

After a preliminary materials budget has been developed for the coming year, buying plans are then developed for the same period. A precise buying plan should be structured for *each major material or category of materials.*

Demand Analysis   For dependent demand materials, the annual demand for each can be estimated by aggregating the requirements of all products using the given material. For independent demand materials and MRO items, an approximate annual demand figure can be estimated based on prior usage and expected plans for the coming year. At this point, an all-inclusive ABC analysis should be conducted to quantify with reasonable accuracy the high-value materials for the coming year's operation. As a general rule, the 80-20 phenomenon holds for most organizations. That is, approximately 80 percent of the firm's purchase dollars will be expended in buying approximately 20 percent of the materials the firm uses.

Buying plans should be constructed for most materials, but for obvious reasons, it is particularly important that plans for the top 20 percent or so of the materials be developed using careful detailed analyses. The 80 percent of the materials that account for approximately 20 percent of the firm's expenditures typically are grouped by general classifications, and a plan is made for each group of similar items.

Market Analysis   The next step in making a buying plan is to assess the market in which the item will be purchased. Since a buyer's major *initial* concerns are availability and price, the anticipated supply and demand factors, along with their expected stability, must be reviewed. The results of this analysis can be compared with the buyer's estimated quarterly demand requirements to determine whether any potential supply problems exist. At the same time, potential changes in the pricing situation can be estimated by comparing supply-demand data and data from general economic forecasts with comparable data from the preceding period. Such an analysis should disclose the likely impact of capacity utilization and cost factors on suppliers' pricing actions.[2]

Supplier Analysis   The next level of the analysis focuses on specific suppliers in the market. At this point in the process, the objective is to review generally the past performance of current suppliers to determine whether any significant problems exist. At the same time, a *general* review of other potential suppliers can be done to determine whether any particularly attractive possibilities should subsequently be investigated more closely. The result of such an analysis can lead to several possible courses of action:

- Current suppliers are completely satisfactory, and no further analysis is required.
- Current suppliers are not completely satisfactory, so a subsequent search for one or more new suppliers should be undertaken.
- The material in question should be submitted for a value analysis study to determine whether specification modifications are possible, to the extent that effective sourcing of the item can be simplified.

Purchasing Research   These analyses required for the preparation of a buying plan—demand analysis, market analysis, supplier analysis, and perhaps value analysis—are, in effect, fairly specialized types of purchasing research work. Operationally they can be accomplished in several ways. Some firms' purchasing and supply departments include these activities as part of a senior buyer's job. In these organizations, each buyer does his or her own purchasing research work for the materials he or she handles. In a majority of the more progressive firms, however, this purchasing research work is assigned to a group of staff specialists who are specifically trained in these activities. And in a growing number of the leading-edge firms, this group of specialists is composed of cross-functional representatives that make up an ongoing commodity procurement strategy team for a given material.

In most firms, in recent years individual buyers have tended to purchase an increasing number of varied items. And in many cases, these are complex items produced by more complex manufacturing processes. Consequently, many firms have found that the mounting pressure of daily buying activities tends to leave the buyer without adequate time to conduct all the necessary purchasing research investigations. Instead of simply adding more buyers to the department, many firms have resolved the problem by creating a staff of purchasing research specialists or a cross-functional commodity team. This

[2]In most markets that are important to a buying firm, doing a detailed analysis and forecast is a complex undertaking, much beyond the scope of this book. The interested reader, however, is encouraged to review the following thorough treatment of the subject in Robert J. Bretz, "Forecasting," *The Purchasing Handbook*, McGraw-Hill, Inc., New York, 1992, Chap. 15, pp. 465–493.

separation of tactical and strategic responsibilities, it is claimed, solves the problem more efficiently, because it ensures time and capability for adequate depth research and it eliminates duplications of research effort.

Buying Plan Objectives and Target Modes of Operation   Chapter 3 discussed various purchasing and supply management objectives and noted that they are developed for use at three different levels—managerial activities, functional operations, and detailed buying plan development. This section discusses the third level—those detailed objectives and operating targets that are formulated as a part of the buying plan *for each major material.*

In developing a buying plan, objectives and target modes of operation should be established within each of the broader *functional objectives* of the department. The following series of questions are classified in this manner and can be used as a checklist in developing the plan.

To Develop Effective Suppliers

1 Is the supplier base reduced to the lowest practical level? How many suppliers should be used? Multiple source? Single source?
2 Should an ongoing partnering relationship be developed with the supplier?
3 How important is it that the supplier be a low-cost producer?
4 Are there any unique service requirements?
5 How important are reliability and cooperativeness?
6 How important are transportation costs and services?

To Buy Competitively

1 Should the purchase be competitively bid? Should it be negotiated?
2 Should the material be purchased on a term contract? What is the preferred contract period?
3 Are short-term supply-demand shifts important? Should hand-to-mouth or forward buying be used?
4 What price is being paid? What should be the target price in the new buying period?
5 What value improvements should be sought in the new buying period?
6 Should a life cycle cost analysis be made?
7 What terms of payment are preferred?

To Optimize Material Availability and Investment

1 Should a JIT purchasing arrangement be developed?
2 What should be the average inventory level target? What should be the target service level?
3 Are storage capacity constraints a problem?

4 Should systems contracting, blanket orders, or purchase credit card buying methods be used?

5 Should a supplier stocking plan or a consignment buying plan be used?

To Buy Quality Effectively

1 Does the material specification fit the need effectively? Is the specification as flexible as is practical? Should purchasing be involved in firming up the specification?

2 Is the specification compatible with the supplier's capability? Should the supplier be involved in firming up the specification?

3 Should SPC be used? Should quality assurance personnel work with the supplier's quality assurance people in developing the QC/inspection system? Should statistical sampling be used? Which plan?

4 What value improvements should be sought in the new buying period?

To Coordinate Effectively with Users

1 Does this item require further standardization work?

2 Do items 1 and 2 from the preceding quality objective require further coordination with using departments?

3 Is further liaison required with the user during the new buying period?

In developing the various elements of a new material buying plan, whenever a change is made from the preceding buying plan, a brief written discussion of the reason for the change is appropriate. This type of justification forces the buyer or the team to rethink the analysis to verify its correctness—and the document also should explain clearly to the authorizing manager the rationale for the proposed new course of action.

Finally, it should be noted that in most cases the specific objectives and modes of operation for the annual buying plans will be somewhat different for each material. The markets, the suppliers' capabilities, and the characteristics of the materials and their usage are all quite different. Consequently, it is reasonable to expect that the key elements of the buying plans will also be different.

BUYING STRATEGY

A buyer's basic elements of strategy for managing each material are embodied in the various buying plans developed. Additionally, from a *departmental perspective,* the purchasing and supply management team must develop an overall strategy for handling its buying responsibilities *in the aggregate.* As a general rule, this strategy includes three elements:

1 *Contract buying.* Most firms typically attempt to develop annual or longer-term contracts with suppliers for materials that represent 60 to 80 percent of the firm's annual purchasing expenditures.

2 *Minimizing small orders.* A well-managed firm attempts to minimize the number of small orders placed.

3 *Managing the "in-between" materials.* Good management attempts to optimize value relative to total cost for those medium- and lower-value materials that are purchased primarily in response to requisitions from inventory and operating departments.

Contract Buying

Properly used, contract buying can yield a number of significant benefits. The major advantages flow from the continuing collaborative relationship that can be developed with the supplier during the contract period. Such a relationship facilitates the development of improved control of material quality and costs as well as delivery and service arrangements. A long-term agreement also usually produces a significantly better pricing arrangement than is possible for shorter-term, smaller-volume purchases.[3]

From an internal managerial point of view, term contracting has several important advantages. Since the supplier review and selection effort is undertaken only once every year or two, the buying organization can utilize a review team of specialists to conduct a comprehensive, detailed investigation of the market and individual potential suppliers. Thus, both efficiency and effectiveness are improved. Likewise, paperwork is reduced and ongoing ordering efficiency is increased.

Term contracting clearly can be utilized most effectively in markets that are reasonably stable and predictable. Although an incentive or cost-type contract is sometimes used, typically such agreements are structured with a firm fixed price contract or a fixed price with escalation/de-escalation clause–type contract. Contract buying is used for as many of the high-value items as is practical, simply because it can provide a more manageable, cost-effective buying situation. Many of the progressive firms target approximately 80 percent of their dollar expenditures for contract buying.

Minimizing Small Orders

Ironically, in many otherwise well-managed purchasing departments small orders account for a disproportionately high percentage of the purchase orders placed. It is not uncommon to find half or more of the orders issued to be for purchases of less than $250. This type of purchasing activity is extremely inefficient. It is a poor use of clerical time and an even poorer use of buyers' time. Consequently, perceptive managers develop a buying strategy that minimizes this type of operating situation.

A number of techniques can be used to reduce the volume of small orders to a practical level. Many firms use systems contracting and blanket orders

---

[3]Many firms now develop partnering relationships with selected suppliers for these types of purchases.

effectively to reduce both the required purchasing and clerical effort and, at the same time, improve price and service performance. Credit card purchases and special low-value "field order" or "short order" forms can also be used to accomplish similar results. And in some cases, frequently used low-value items can be placed in inventory and easily pay for their additional carrying costs. Chapter 4 discusses these and other small-order management techniques in detail.

Managing the "In-Between" Materials

Many B and some C category materials do not possess a stable enough demand to warrant the use of contract buying, or the markets in which they are purchased are too unstable to make contract buying practical. In the case of these materials, purchases are usually made in response to specific purchase requisitions. Sometimes requirements contracts, systems contracts, or blanket orders can be used to improve buying effectiveness, but more commonly each buy is made on an individual basis.

If a buyer determines that a rising or a falling market clearly exists, hand-to-mouth buying and forward buying strategies might be used, as shown in Figure 27-4.

By using a forward buying strategy during a rising market, the average price actually paid on the cycle upswing *should be significantly less* than the average market price during the period. If hand-to-mouth buying is used on the downswing, the average price paid *will approximate the average market price* during the period, if the purchase intervals are fairly short.

On the other hand, if a buyer's strategy is to *minimize price risk* during the entire cycle—particularly in an unpredictable market—a hand-to-mouth strategy in both up and down periods will tend to produce an average price paid that is close to the average market price during the complete cycle. This situation is portrayed in Figure 27-5.

FIGURE 27-4
Timing purchases to take advantage of market action: forward buying in a rising market; hand-to-mouth buying in a falling market.

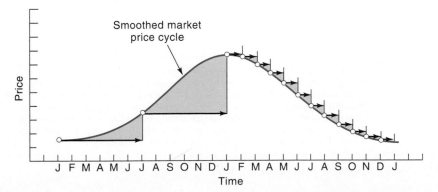

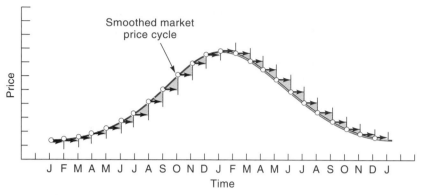

FIGURE 27-5
Timing purchases to minimize price risk: hand-to-mouth buying in both rising and falling markets.

Hedging

When purchasing raw materials and commodities, hedging is another technique used to *minimize the risk associated with fluctuating market prices.* However, the technique can be used only in buying materials for which an organized commodity exchange exists.

An organized commodity exchange is a marketplace where a particular commodity is bought and sold in substantial quantities. At many of the exchanges, both "cash" transactions and "futures" transactions take place. A *cash transaction,* as the words imply, involves a current exchange of cash for the physical commodity. A *futures transaction* involves a current purchase or sale, at a quoted price, for which the physical commodity will be delivered at a specified date in the future. With the passage of time, the current cash price for a commodity and its futures price often fluctuate together, approximately paralleling one another.[4] It is the futures transaction that is essential in a hedging operation.

If the reader refers to the market section of the *Wall Street Journal,* or a similar financial publication, he or she will find a listing of the numerous commodity markets. Futures markets operate for many of these commodities, such as cotton, cocoa, coffee, sugar, hides, rubber, wool, and various metals, grains, and oils.

---

[4]The most important single factor to the hedger is the difference between the cash price and the futures price, commonly called the *basis.* In a completely competitive situation where supply and demand are in balance, the futures price would be expected to exceed the cash price by the total cost of carrying the commodity in storage until the future date. Because supply and demand typically do not remain in balance long for free market commodities, the difference between futures and cash prices is influenced considerably by the way buyers evaluate present and anticipated supply-demand conditions. This explains why the basis for a given commodity varies with time, reflecting something less than a parallel relationship between the movement of the cash and the future prices.

For the industrial buyer, hedging is a technique that can provide protection against market price declines during the period when his or her firm is processing a raw material preparatory to selling it in another form as a finished product. With this financial worry removed, the manufacturer is free to concentrate on normal production and sales activities.

For example, suppose a chocolate manufacturer has signed a contract to sell a large candy manufacturer ten carloads of refined chocolate syrup each month for the next year. The contract stipulates that chocolate syrup will be sold at a price based on the market price of raw cocoa *at the time of delivery of the chocolate syrup.* What happens to the chocolate manufacturer, then, if it buys raw cocoa at $0.26 per pound, and one month later, when it delivers the refined chocolate made from this cocoa, the market price for raw cocoa has fallen to $0.21 per pound? The firm has to sell the refined chocolate at a lower price than was intended when the cocoa was purchased. Consequently, the chocolate manufacturer's profit margin is reduced, or perhaps entirely eliminated. To protect against such an occurrence, the manufacturer might choose to engage in a hedging operation. Such a hedge would consist of the following market transactions:

1 First, the firm *buys raw cocoa* in the cash market (to use in making chocolate syrup). At the same time, it *sells a futures contract* in the futures market for the same quantity of raw cocoa, to be delivered shortly after it expects to sell the refined chocolate. (Note that the firm does not own any cocoa at this time which it could deliver at this future date.)
2 At the time the firm *sells the refined chocolate*, it also *buys a futures contract for cocoa* to cover the futures contract it originally sold and would soon have to deliver.

The protection offered by the hedge is based on the premise that should raw cocoa cash market prices drop during the manufacturing period (resulting in a reduced selling price for chocolate), futures prices will also drop proportionately. Thus, although the producer takes a loss by selling its chocolate at a reduced price, it makes an approximately equal profit by covering its futures contract at a similarly reduced price. Bear in mind that in this example the selling price of chocolate maintains a constant relationship to the purchase price of raw cocoa. An important prerequisite to the use of hedging requires that the purchaser's finished product be sold in a market where prices move approximately parallel to the prices of the purchased raw material. These concepts are illustrated numerically in the simplified example and in Figure 27-6 that appears on page 638.

So—while the chocolate manufacturer lost $5,000 on its manufacturing activity because of the 5 cent/pound drop in cocoa prices, it was able to offset this loss with a $5,000 gain by hedging in the futures market, thus preserving its normal profit margin on the sale of the refined chocolate. Had the price of cocoa risen from January 15 to February 15, the situation would have been reversed. The firm would have shown an extra profit in its manufacturing

Cash activities	Futures market activities

January 15:
Cash market *purchase* of 100,000 pounds of *raw cocoa* at $0.26/pound =
       100,000 × $0.26 = $26,000
	January 15:
	Sells a March *futures contract* for 100,000 pounds of raw cocoa at $0.275/pound =
	       100,000 × $0.275 = $27,500

January 15 to February 15: Purchaser incurs manufacturing costs (*including normal profit*) of $0.43/pound = 100,000 × $0.43 = $43,000	

February 15:*
Sells refined chocolate (equivalent of 100,000 pounds of cocoa) to customer at $0.64/pound =
       100,000 × $0.64 = $64,000
	February 15:
	Buys a March *futures contract* for 100,000 pounds of raw cocoa at $0.225/pound =
	       100,000 × $0.225 = $22,500

Net gain on manufacturing activity =
  $64,000 − ($26,000 + $43,000) = **− $5,000**
	Net gain on activity in March futures cocoa market =
	    $27,500 − $22,500 = **+ $5,000**

*The raw cocoa market price has dropped $0.05/pound since January 15. Had it not dropped, refined chocolate would have sold for $0.69/pound on February 15.

FIGURE 27-6
Simplified illustration of a perfect hedge.

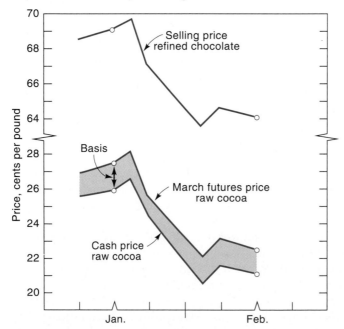

operation because of the price increase, but it would have suffered a loss on its futures transaction; thus, the firm would still experience no net gain or loss as a result of fluctuating market prices.

The preceding case is a simplified example of a perfect hedge, which, to reiterate, is based on two assumptions:

1 The selling price of the buyer's finished product will move exactly parallel to the cash market price of its major raw material.
2 Futures prices will move exactly parallel to cash market prices.

In practice, these conditions exist only imperfectly. The degree of perfection found in the relationship depends largely on specific market conditions and on the characteristics of each specific seller's market. The hedger nearly always gains or loses *some* money on a hedging transaction because the spread between futures and cash prices and the spread between product selling price and material purchase price both vary somewhat with time. However, this by no means invalidates the technique. Provided the relationships show reasonable stability, hedging can in many cases provide good protection against the risk of *wide* price swings. To use hedging successfully, buyers must be skilled enough to estimate the magnitude of possible gain or loss through "basis" variation. Their decision to hedge (or not to hedge) rests on a comparison of this factor with an assessment of the probable magnitude and direction of cash market price fluctuations.

STRATEGIC MATERIALS PLANNING

Strategic planning is concerned with the development of a firm's plans for its long-term material requirements, as contrasted with its plans for foreseeable, near-term requirements—the former extending five to ten years ahead, and the latter one to two years. Strategic planning thus focuses management's attention on *long-term competitiveness and profitability,* rather than on short-term bottom-line considerations.

Until a decade or so ago, conventional corporate planning wisdom held that a firm's long-range planning cycle began with an analysis of its products, its markets, and its competition—and then worked back through the various operating and staff departments, as shown in Figure 27-7a. Historically, purchasing or materials management departments seldom participated in this process until the long-term plans were firm and subsequently translated into annual operating plans. This process worked satisfactorily as long as materials were readily available at competitive prices. In recent years, however, scarcity of some resources, intensive worldwide competition, and increasing international and environmental uncertainties have produced a marked change in this approach.

Many firms now find themselves faced with a significant list of critical materials that may not be *readily available at competitive prices* in the years ahead. Consequently, it is necessary to identify the potentially critical materi-

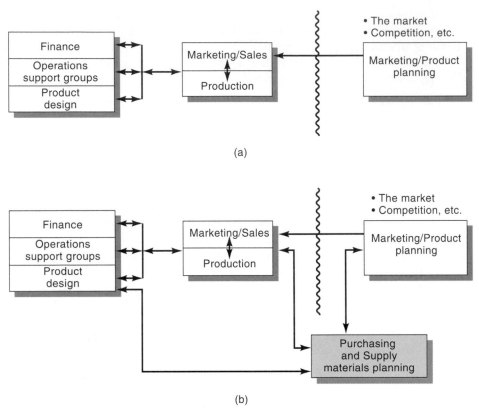

FIGURE 27-7a and 27-7b
Simplified models of information flows in the corporate strategic planning process. (a) Traditional
model. (b) Model including materials planning.

als early in the planning process—and to analyze each issue thoroughly enough
to determine whether a serious problem does in fact exist. In many firms this situation has led to a modification of the corporate long-range planning process,
as shown in Figure 27-7b. The process now begins as it did originally, but it
brings together almost immediately both *product demand* and *material supply*
considerations, recognizing the respective dynamic market environment of
each.

The unique characteristic of strategic materials planning is its focus on the
impact that *changes in the external environment* might have on the firm's materials needs and procurement policy. Dr. Robert Spekman's generalized model of
the strategic procurement planning process highlights the significance and the
interactive nature of this characteristic. (See Figure 27-8.)[5]

[5]Robert E. Spekman, "A Strategic Approach to Procurement Planning," *Journal of Purchasing
and Materials Management,* Winter 1981, pp. 2–8.

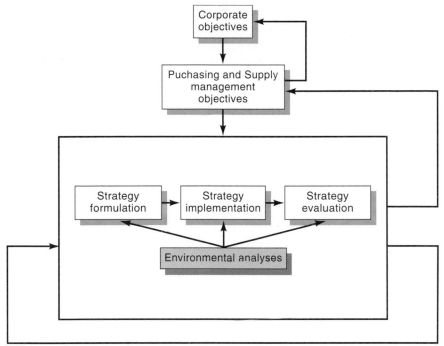

FIGURE 27-8
A model of the strategic procurement planning process.

Strategic materials planning involves both economic and technical investigations. On the domestic and relevant foreign scenes, forecasts of general economic (and political) conditions are made, and studies of specific industries and commodity markets are undertaken. Price trends and technological developments in industries producing interchangeable materials are studied in an attempt to forecast future conditions in competitive industries. These forecasted conditions are then related to the firm's future needs. This type of analysis permits an assessment of current purchasing policy and points up the possible need for changes which may require careful advance planning. Technical investigations dovetail into two major programs which frequently are conducted on a companywide basis—*value analysis* and *make-or-buy analysis.*

The end product of a strategic materials planning investigation can take three forms:

1 Agreements with one or more suppliers to provide agreed-on material requirements for specific future time periods—i.e., mutually satisfactory long-term contractual arrangements or partnering arrangements. (This may require mutual support for the development of additional supplier capability.)

2 A decision to phase out the use of a given material and replace it with a more satisfactory or more easily obtainable material. This decision clearly must be coordinated with a preliminary value analysis study to determine its feasibility, and likely will be followed with more detailed value analysis work.

3 A decision to make the item in-house, eliminating dependence on suppliers and external conditions, which may be excessively difficult if not impossible to control.

CONCLUSION

Procurement planning stands at the heart of our purchasing operation: without it, all of our efforts would be opportunistic, and we almost certainly would overlook important opportunities to contribute to company profitability.[6]

This statement was made by an experienced purchasing executive, in a new job assignment, after successfully transforming his new firm's purchasing department from a reactive to a proactive operation. In a broad sense, it serves as a testimonial to the purpose of this chapter.

In developing a firm's buying strategies and its annual buying plans, a perceptive manager generally will employ most of the buying objectives, policies, and techniques discussed in this chapter. And although planning is both an art and a science, skill in properly blending the use of these management tools in practice is acquired only through experience as one gains familiarity with specific materials and markets.

FOR DISCUSSION

27-1 What role does the purchasing department play in a company's budgeting procedures?

27-2 What is meant by the terms "stable market" and "unstable market"? List six materials that are purchased in each type of market. Explain why the price of rubber fluctuates substantially, while the price of steel in the short run fluctuates very little.

27-3 Discuss the significance of the timing of purchases. (Include a discussion of the factors which affect the timing of purchases.)

27-4 What is forward buying? Explain.

27-5 What are the major reasons for forward buying? Discuss each briefly.

27-6 What is hand-to-mouth buying? When would you use it?

27-7 What is meant by the term "buying to requirements"?

27-8 In practice, what is the most difficult part of implementing the concept shown in Figure 27-4? Explain.

[6]Frank L. Bauer, "Managerial Planning in Procurement," *Journal of Purchasing and Materials Management*, Fall 1977, pp. 3–8.

27-9 What is an annual buying plan? Why is an annual buying plan used?

27-10 What is the most difficult part of conducting a "market analysis" for an important material in developing the material's annual buying plan? Discuss.

27-11 Assume you are a buyer for a firm that produces the ore used to make a high-value industrial chemical. The firm operates a large hard-rock mine one-quarter of a mile under ground. It uses large quantities of various structural steel members and steel "roof bolts" to keep the mine tunnels safe and open for traffic.

Describe in detail the steps you would go through in making an annual buying plan for structural steel and roof bolts.

27-12 "All good buyers engage in purchasing research." Explain.

27-13 Why do some companies find it desirable to institute a formal purchasing research program? Explain.

27-14 What are the major values of separating the strategic from the tactical activities in the purchasing operation?

27-15 Why is annual or longer-term buying used? What are the advantages? What are the potential problems?

27-16 In developing a two-year contract for a major material used in your firm's operation, which types of contracts might be used? Discuss.

27-17 Explain how a hedging activity is conducted.

27-18 What is the "basis"? Why is it important in a hedging operation?

27-19 In a commodity market, what is the maximum value a futures price will reach relative to its corresponding cash price? Explain.

27-20 Identify a type of manufacturing organization that could benefit significantly from having a hedging specialist in its purchasing department. Discuss.

27-21 How does strategic materials planning differ from other purchasing planning techniques? Why is it used?

27-22 Explain what is happening in Figure 27-7. Why would a firm want to implement the concept depicted in Figure 27-7b?

27-23 What benefits might a firm expect to receive from the use of strategic materials planning?

CASES FOR CHAPTER 27

28

VALUE ANALYSIS/ENGINEERING

KEY CONCEPTS

- What is value analysis?
- Value engineering vis-à-vis value analysis
- Design analysis
    Value analysis checklist
    Functional cost approach
    Brainstorming
    Use of suppliers
- Cost analysis
- The value analysis study
- Examples of value analysis
    Production parts and assemblies
    Packaging
    Systems/service applications
- Conditions conducive to value analysis
- Organization and administration
    Specialized staff approach
    Cross-functional team/committee approach
    Staff training approach
    Quality circles
    Carrier's view of VA
- Reporting value analysis

WHAT IS VALUE ANALYSIS?

Approximately thirty years ago, the *Reader's Digest* published an article entitled "The Biggest Thing Since Mass Production." The article described how dramatic dollar savings were produced for consumers and taxpayers by a new industrial technique called value analysis. In reality, this "new" concept had its genesis during the war years of the early 1940s. During the intervening years acceptance of the concept grew. By the mid-1960s, value analysis was established as the cornerstone of most purchasing research and *cost* reduction programs in major manufacturing firms. Since that time, enthusiasm for the concept has waxed and waned, diminishing in popularity usually until periods of material shortages and escalating prices again highlight its profit potential. Today, nearly three-quarters of all American industrial firms have some type of value analysis program in operation.[1]

During World War II many critical materials and components were difficult to obtain, and most manufacturers were required to specify numerous substitutions in their design and production activities. Harry Erlicher, then vice president of purchasing for the General Electric Company, observed that many of the required substitutions during this period resulted not only in reduced costs but also in product improvement. Consequently, Mr. Erlicher assigned to L. D. Miles the task of developing a systematic approach to the investigation of the *function/cost* aspect of *existing* material specifications. Larry Miles not only met this challenge successfully, but subsequently pioneered the scientific procurement concept General Electric called "value analysis."

In 1954 the U.S. Navy's Bureau of Ships adopted a modified version of General Electric's value analysis concept in an attempt to reduce the cost of ships and related equipment. In applying the concept, the Navy directed its efforts primarily at *cost avoidance during the initial engineering design stage* and called the program "value engineering" (VE), even though it embodied the same concepts and techniques as GE's value analysis (VA) program. In an operational sense, however, the two terms typically are used synonymously in industry today—only the timing differs. Hence, throughout this book the term "value analysis" is used, and it carries the same conceptual meaning as the term "value engineering," except for the practical matter of timing.

The techniques of value analysis represent a potentially powerful set of tools which can be used by management in controlling material costs. The fundamental objective of all value analysis activities is the procurement (or manufacture) of materials representing the "best buy" in terms of the *function* to be performed. In this sense the idea certainly is not new; it is synonymous with a longstanding objective of good purchasing. The unique feature of current value analysis programs, however, lies in the *systematic* and *thorough* approach used in attaining this objective.

---

[1]Somerby Dowst, "Buyers Say VA Is More Important Than Ever," *Purchasing,* June 26, 1986, p. 64.

Value Engineering Vis-à-Vis Value Analysis

As practiced in U.S. firms for many years, value analysis techniques were most widely used in programs designed to engineer unnecessary costs out of *existing* products. Finally, the more progressive firms began to follow the Navy's lead by establishing what they too called "value engineering" programs—programs that applied the value analysis concept during the early stages of the *new* product design process. And, clearly, this is the first point at which it should be applied. This is where the greatest benefits are produced for both the firm and its customers.

What is the mix of value analysis and value engineering applications in American industry today? No one really knows. But the number of both programs has grown markedly in the last decade, with value engineering programs setting the pace.

The VE concept finds its most unique use in two kinds of companies—those that produce a limited number of units of a very expensive product and those that mass-produce products requiring expensive tooling. In these types of companies, value analysis of an item already in production is often impractical because it is then too late to incorporate changes in the product economically. In manufacturing certain electronic instruments used in defense systems, for example, the production run is often so short that it precludes the effective use of value analysis after production has been initiated. In fact, the Federal Acquisition Regulations now stipulate that most major defense procurement contracts must be subjected to value engineering studies *prior* to initial production.[2]

A somewhat different situation that produces similar operating results is found in firms mass-producing automobiles. For example, in manufacturing the body panel for a car, once the design is fixed and the dies are purchased, it is normally too costly to change them, even though value analysis studies might subsequently disclose design inefficiencies.

Value engineering utilizes all the techniques of value analysis. In practice, it involves very close liaison work between the purchasing and supply, production, and design engineering departments. This liaison is most frequently accomplished through the use of product design teams or various procurement and production coordinators, who spend considerable time in the engineering department studying and analyzing engineering drawings as they are initially produced. Once coordinators locate problem areas, value analysis techniques are employed to alleviate them.[3]

---

[2]For an interesting discussion of how the Department of Defense utilizes value engineering, see "DOD Honors ASD Value Engineering Program," *Skywriter,* August 1991, p. 7.

[3]For a complete discussion of this topic see D. W. Dobler, "How to Get Engineers and P.A.'s Together," *Purchasing,* Aug. 12, 1963, pp. 55–58; P. V. Farrell, "Purchasing and Engineering," *Purchasing World,* November 1980, pp. 48–51; and D. N. Burt, *Proactive Procurement,* Prentice-Hall Inc., Englewood Cliffs, N.J., 1984, chap. 2.

VA/VE TOOLS

Although different companies stress different variations of the fundamental idea, *two general conceptual tools are basic to the operation of a VA/VE program:*

1 Design analysis of the required product, part, or material
2 Cost analysis of the required product, part, or material

Design Analysis

Design analysis entails a methodical step-by-step study of all phases of the design of a given item in relation to the *function* it performs. The philosophy underlying this approach is not concerned with appraisal of any given part per se. Rather, the appraisal focuses on the function which the part, or the larger assembly containing the part, performs. This approach is designed to lead the analyst away from a traditional perspective which views a part as having certain accepted characteristics and configurations. Instead, it encourages the analyst to adopt a broader point of view and to consider whether the part performs the required function both as effectively and as efficiently as possible. Both quality and cost are objects of the analysis.

One technique many firms use in analyzing component parts of a subassembly is to dismantle, or "explode," the unit and then mount each part adjacent to its mating part on a pegboard or a table. The idea is to demonstrate visually the functional relationships of the various parts. Each component can thus be studied as it relates to the performance of the complete unit, rather than as an isolated element. Analysis of each component in this fashion attempts to answer four specific questions:

1 Can any part be *eliminated* without impairing the operation of the complete unit?
2 Can the design of the part be *simplified* to reduce its basic cost?
3 Can the design of the part be changed to permit the use of simplified or less costly *production methods?*
4 Can less expensive but equally satisfactory *materials* be used in the part?

When viewed in this manner—from the standpoint of composite operation and cost—possibilities for making component design simplifications frequently are more apparent than is possible under the original design conditions. This in no way reflects unfavorably on the work done initially by the design engineer. The discovery of such potential improvements is simply the product of an analysis with a substantially broader orientation than that possessed by the original designer. An organized VA/VE study usually utilizes a number of individuals with different types of backgrounds, experience, and skill impossible to combine in the person of a single designer. Resulting design changes often permit the substitution of standardized production operations for more expensive operations requiring special setup work. In some cases, considering the volume of parts to be produced, an entirely different material or production process turns out to be more efficient than the one originally specified.

The specific manner in which a value analyst approaches the problem of design analysis is a highly creative matter which differs from one analyst to another. Each possesses unique analytical abilities and develops unique patterns of thought. Some companies, however, require analysts to follow one or more general approaches which are designed to stimulate and organize their efforts. Those commonly used are (1) the value analysis checklist, (2) the functional cost approach, (3) the use of brainstorming, and (4) the use of suppliers.

The Value Analysis Checklist Most companies develop some type of checklist to systematize a value analyst's activity. Literally hundreds of questions and key ideas appear on these lists.[4] Some of them are highly specialized for particular types of products. Illustrative of the more general questions is the following checklist suggested by the National Association of Purchasing Management.[5]

First, determine the *function* of the item, then determine:

1 Can the item be eliminated?
2 If the item is not standard, can a standard item be used?
3 If it is a standard item, does it completely fit the application, or is it a misfit?
4 Does the item have greater capacity than required?
5 Can the weight be reduced?
6 Is there a similar item in inventory that could be substituted?
7 Are closer tolerances specified than are necessary?
8 Is unnecessary machining performed on the item?
9 Are unnecessarily fine finishes specified?
10 Is "commercial quality" specified? (Commercial quality is usually most economical.)
11 Can you make the item less expensively in your plant? If you are making it now, can you buy it for less?
12 Is the item properly classified for shipping purposes to obtain lowest transportation rates?
13 Can cost of packaging be reduced?
14 Are suppliers being asked for suggestions to reduce cost?

In using this or similar checklists, an analyst evaluates the component under investigation with respect to each item on the checklist. When a question is found to which the answer is not entirely satisfactory, this becomes a starting point for more detailed investigation. The checklist focuses the analyst's attention on those factors which past experience has proved to be potentially fruitful cost reduction areas.

---

[4]For an interesting list of suggestions, see Dave A. Lugo, "Boost Your Creativity with Divergent Thinking and Checklists," *NAPM Insights,* May 1994, p. 12.
[5]*Basic Steps in Value Analysis,* a pamphlet prepared under the chairmanship of Martin S. Erb by the Value-Analysis-Standardization Committee, Reading Association, NAPM, Tempe, Ariz., pp. 4–18.

The Functional Cost Approach An additional question which appears on some checklists may be worded something like this: "What does it cost to perform the function done by this part?" or "Does the importance of the function to be performed justify the cost of performing it?" The idea underlying these and similar questions actually constitutes a separate approach to value investigation.

As value analysts in a particular industry gain experience, they quickly establish benchmark costs for performing certain functions characteristically encountered in their industry. For example, it may cost approximately x cents to join two pieces of metal of given sizes if the joint is to perform under conditions of mild vibration. On the other hand, it may typically cost approximately y cents to make the same joint if it must perform under conditions of excessive vibration. In another case, a manufacturer may find that on the average it costs z dollars to circulate coolant through a totally enclosed motor of a given size, under certain operating conditions.

The important point is this: After analyzing certain types of equipment day after day, good value analysts learn in a general way approximately what it costs to perform certain functions. As these kinds of data are accumulated, costs of particular functions appearing on new jobs can be compared with historical benchmarks. If the cost seems excessive, the analyst investigates further to determine the reason. The cost may well be justified due to differences between the new unit and past units on which the benchmarks were based. If this does not appear to be the case, the analyst continues to search for a lower-cost method of performing the function.

For some parts, comparative analysis of similarly processed items may highlight unusually high-cost items. For example, formed or fabricated metal parts typically cost less per pound as the weight of the part increases. For all similar fabricated parts, an analyst might construct a graph on which the weight of each piece is plotted against its price per pound. Any items not conforming reasonably well with the resulting curve would be good candidates for more detailed analysis.

One important feature of this general approach is the idea of comparing current performance with typical past performance. A second and perhaps more important feature of the approach is the concept that the cost of performing a function must be reasonably proportionate to the value of the function itself.

The Use of Brainstorming A third technique which often is used in conjunction with either of the preceding approaches is the classical brainstorming approach. *Brainstorming* is a process designed to stimulate creative thinking. A group of individuals with different backgrounds meets for the purpose of generating ideas useful in solving a particular problem. Emphasis is placed on the free-wheeling generation of ideas, which are recorded as soon as they are made. During this period no one in the group evaluates any ideas, since the objective at this point is to develop spontaneous and positive ideas. The theory underlying this approach to problem solving recognizes that many of the ideas spontaneously generated are completely infeasible. However, the theory holds that some of these ideas trigger thoughts from others in the group that lead to different and often very useful ideas. During a period of sixty minutes as many as several hundred ideas are sometimes recorded. Even if only several workable ideas emerge from the session, a good chance exists that one or two can be developed into a satisfactory solution to the problem.

The potential use of this technique for approaching value analysis problems should be apparent. Once the facts of a problem are thoroughly defined and understood, some companies call on several representatives from the appropriate departments to participate in a brainstorming session. After the session, the resulting ideas are analyzed for feasibility and for cost. The promising ideas are subsequently turned over to an analyst for further development.

Some companies utilize this technique as an integral part of the total value analysis procedure, although not every firm subscribes to extensive use of brainstorming. Some feel that in certain cases a greater number of practical ideas frequently can be generated with the expenditure of fewer man-hours by permitting analysts to work independently.

The Use of Suppliers An increasing number of major manufacturing firms subscribe to the idea that the primary responsibility of the purchasing and supply department is to manage "outside manufacturing." This fundamental concept implies the development of a continuing relationship with major suppliers—and a partnering arrangement with some of them. Functioning in this type of environment, suppliers frequently prove to be extremely valuable assets in a firm's total value analysis effort. More than one firm has found that a majority of its value analysis savings come directly from suggestions of suppliers who have been asked to participate in its value analysis program.

The Chrysler Corporation, for example, initiated a voluntary value analysis/cost reduction program for its suppliers several years ago. The objective was for each supplier to value-analyze one or more of its key products sold to Chrysler, and to submit the resulting value analysis suggestions for consideration. During the first two years of the program, Chrysler received more than 3,400 suggestions which materialized into projects that saved approximately $136 million.[6]

Perhaps this fact is not too surprising. After all, as a rule, a supplier knows more about its product and its potential capabilities than do most of the firm's customers. A supplier's technical knowledge, combined with broad experience in applying its product to hundreds of operations, frequently qualifies the firm to participate in most companies' value analysis programs.

A supplier's assistance can be enlisted in various ways that fit into two basic categories: (1) by informal participation and (2) by participation in a

---

[6]Ernest Raia, "Advantage Chrysler: Supplier Ideas Save Automaker Millions," *Purchasing*, June 4, 1992, p. 43.

"supplier workshop." When using the informal approach, a firm usually has numerous high-priority value analysis projects exhibited on display boards, with all parts completely identified and tagged as to current cost. The purchasing and supply executive invites current and potential suppliers to study particular exhibits at their leisure for the purpose of offering possible cost reduction or quality improvement suggestions for items each might furnish. If a supplier can provide a lower-cost item that performs satisfactorily, or if it suggests feasible design modifications which permit the use of a lower-cost item, the firm is rewarded with additional business.

A similar approach is used by some firms when they ask suppliers to bid on an item. A simple supplier value analysis checklist is included with the specifications in each bid request. As illustrated in Figure 28-1, suppliers are encouraged to utilize their creativity and experience to obtain a competitive edge in the bidding process. If the checklist reveals bidders who use different production methods and different materials, or have similar low-cost proprietary products, chances are maximized for the generation of unique cost-saving ideas.

A second approach entails the use of periodic, formally organized supplier workshops. A group of perhaps fifty technical and managerial representatives from suppliers' firms is invited to the purchaser's plant for a one- or two-day workshop. The sessions typically include an introduction to the purchaser's new products, general company plans and their effects on suppliers, basic buying policies, and selected major value analysis problems. An important segment of the program is a tour of the buyer's production facilities. Here top-level supplier representatives have an opportunity to see how and where their products are used by the purchaser. Additionally, suppliers can be requested to study specific value analysis exhibits, as is done in the informal approach.

An enhancement of this approach was used by General Motors' Oldsmobile Division. As part of the program, the division hired a consulting firm to present a "how to do it" supplier seminar in value analysis. What purchasing management was saying to its major suppliers was: "We want all the help you can provide. Here are the functions we need, the way our customer wants them. Here are the value analysis methods to help you maximize your capabilities to meet our needs." Guidance was specific. "Always improve quality. When possible improve costs."[7] The results from Oldsmobile's first seminar of this type were rewarding—first-year cost reductions totaled approximately $1 million. And the company expected the greatest benefits in the years ahead.

It should be emphasized that solicitation of supplier assistance in a value analysis program is based on the premise that creative suppliers will be compensated for their efforts by receiving additional business or by sharing in the cost savings they help generate. Most companies find either approach to sup-

[7]Larry Miles, "Dynamic Vendor Programs: They Work," *Purchasing World*, August 1984, p. 58.

SUPPLIER CHECKLIST FOR VALUE ANALYSIS STUDY

Part name and number _____

Estimated annual usage _____

Buyer _____

Questions	Yes	No	Recommendations
Do you understand the part function? Could costs be reduced by relaxing requirements: ■ Tolerances? ■ Finishes? ■ Testing? ■ By how much?			
Could costs be reduced through changes in: ■ Material? ■ Ordering quantities? ■ The use of castings, stamping, etc.? ■ By how much?			
Can you suggest other changes that would: ■ Reduce weight? ■ Simplify the part? ■ Reduce overall costs?			
Do you feel that any of the specifications are too stringent?			
How can we help alleviate your greatest element of cost in supplying this part?			
Do you have a standard item that could be substituted for this part?			

Other suggestions? _____

_____

Supplier _____   Date _____

Address _____

Signature _____   Title _____

Additional comments may be added on the back of this sheet.

FIGURE 28-1

An illustrative value analysis checklist used to stimulate supplier participation in the value analysis program. (Source: *Lea Tonkin, "No Purchasing Department Is Too Small for Value Analysis,"* Purchasing World, *June 1982, p. 87.*)

plier participation profitable. In the case of the supplier workshop or seminar, improved supplier relations frequently emerge as a bonus benefit.

Cost Analysis

It is no secret that many manufacturers do not base the selling prices of their products entirely on costs. In some cases, the complexities of multiproduct cost accounting make it virtually impossible to determine the exact cost of producing and marketing a specific product. In other cases, firms may follow a variable-margin pricing policy, whereby the markup on certain types of products is greater than on others. Still other firms may follow the industry leader in establishing product prices.

Whatever the reason, industrial buyers realize that many of the prices they pay do not accurately reflect the cost of the product. Moreover, unless the buying firm has real clout and substantial knowledge of production costs, in some cases it may not know whether its buyer is in fact paying a fair price. As far back as 1928, C. F. Hirshfeld, then chief engineer of the Detroit Edison Company, advocated the practice of cost analysis to assist the buyer in this quandary.[8] The concept was subsequently adopted widely throughout the automobile industry. Elsewhere it received only sporadic support until the value analysis movement again spotlighted its potential value.

As currently practiced, cost analysis involves the investigation of a supplier's probable costs of producing a given product. The analyst constructs estimated elemental costs for materials, labor, manufacturing overhead, and general overhead. When totaled, these figures represent the theoretical total cost incurred by an efficient producer. An experienced analyst, with the use of wage data, material price lists, and various industry time standards, can determine a total theoretical cost which reasonably approximates the actual cost. To this figure is added a reasonable profit margin. Although the calculated price is not exact, it provides the buyer with a powerful negotiating tool. By using this calculated price as a target, a buyer can place a selling firm in a position of having to point out any errors in the development of the figure, or else justify its own quoted price with supporting cost data.

As the reader now knows, the use of cost analysis is not confined to value analysis work. Its basic use is in negotiating an original procurement. In recent years, however, cost analysis has become an extremely useful adjunct of value analysis, playing two major roles:

1 Cost analysis is conducted for currently purchased items whose costs appear excessive. In such cases, the information developed from cost

[8]C. F. Hirshfeld, "Engineers in the Purchasing Department," *Mechanical Engineering,* vol. 50, no. 11, November 1928, pp. 848–849.

analysis is used as a basis for further price negotiation with the supplier.

2 Cost analysis also serves as a means of locating high-cost parts which should be subjected to design analysis. During the course of a cost analysis, some high-cost elements are frequently isolated for the first time. Subsequent design analysis often leads to specification and production modifications and ultimately to reduced costs.

The Value Analysis Study

Let us take a moment at this point to draw together the foregoing discussions in a simple procedural model of the typical value analysis study. Although many companies have developed well-organized formal VA/VE programs, it should be obvious now that value analysis studies can be conducted formally by organized groups or informally by individuals such as buyers, engineers, production personnel, and so forth. In either case, the *elements* of the study are the same. Obviously, the depth and breadth of the analysis are influenced by the size and composition of the team making the study. Figure 28-2 illustrates in simplified form the elements of the overall value analysis study.[9]

EXAMPLES OF VALUE ANALYSIS

The following examples illustrate the types of modifications and savings that VA/VE can produce.

Production Parts and Assemblies

While analyzing the components of a particular small motor, the value analyst for an electric motor manufacturer questioned the construction of the belt guard. The guard, shown in Figure 28-3, was a two-piece assembly made of expanded metal and sheet steel. The expanded metal was blanked to shape and then hand-welded to a metal frame which had also been blanked to shape. After studying the part and its functional requirements, the analyst recommended an equally suitable guard which could be completely produced from sheet metal in a single press-forming operation. The new guard was subsequently adopted and produced at a cost of approximately 20 percent of the cost of the old guard. Thus, a design change permitted less expensive material as well as less costly production methods to be used, producing a substantial annual saving for the motor manufacturer on this simple item.

The part shown in Figure 28-4 illustrates how another very simple design change permitted the realization of a substantial saving in both material and production time. This part, which looks something like a bolt with a flat circu-

---

[9]This model is based on a discussion of the value engineering job plan in *Value Engineering*, prepared by the Value Engineering Department, Lockheed-Georgia Company, Lockheed Aircraft Corp., pp. 12–15.

Elements of the Study   **Activities of the Study**

| Information phase | 1. Define and price the function [10]
2. Obtain and interpret all the facts | What is it?
What does it do?
What does it cost? |

| Speculation phase | 1. Generate new ideas [11]
2. Determine alternative solutions | How else can the job be done?
At what cost? |

| Analysis phase | 1. Determine and compare feasibility
2. Determine and compare suitability
3. Determine and compare costs | Is this better than that?
How much better?
Why? |

| Decision and action phase | 1. Review key alternatives with all departments and suppliers concerned
2. Select best alternatives
3. Get departmental and managerial approvals
4. Prepare new specifications | |

| Evaluation phase | 1. Audit effectiveness of the selection
2. Use operating experience to effect further improvement | |

FIGURE 28-2
A generalized procedural model of the value analysis study.

[10]Most items perform more than one function—usually a *basic* function plus several *supporting* functions. Experience has shown that often the basic function constitutes 20 to 25 percent of the cost of the item and supporting functions account for the rest of the cost. Consequently, it is important to clearly identify these two types of functions. Use of the FAST (function analysis system technique) diagram approach provides an easy way to organize functions and subfunctions in their logical relationships. Details are available in (1) Carlos Fallon, *Value Analysis*, Wiley Interscience Publishers, 1991; and (2) Gary Long, *VA/VE Workship Workbook*, Society of American Value Engineers, Sept. 24, 1993, Phase One and Phase Two.

[11]In addition to the techniques discussed in the preceding pages for generating new ideas, Dr. Alvin Williams and his colleagues suggest a number of other techniques that readers may find helpful. For details see Alvin J. Williams, Steve Lacey, and William C. Smith, "Purchasing's Role in Value Analysis: Lessons from Creative Problem Solving," *The International Journal of Purchasing and Materials Management*, Phoenix, Ariz., Spring 1992, pp. 37–41.

FIGURE 28-3
A belt guard before and after value analysis.

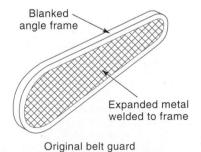

Blanked angle frame

Expanded metal welded to frame

Original belt guard

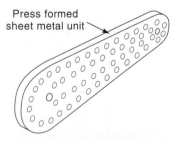

Press formed sheet metal unit

Modified one-piece belt guard

FIGURE 28-4
A value-analyzed machine part.

lar head, is a rotating machine part. The grooved stem must fit precisely with its mating parts. When the part was originally designed, stringent tolerances were specified for both the head and the stem. This design requirement dictated that the part be machined from larger bar stock the size of the head. Consequently, a large amount of stock was wasted in the lengthy machining process. An investigation of the part's function, however, revealed that the head tolerances could be loosened considerably without affecting the operation of the part. This meant that a less costly production method could be used. It was possible to produce the part by first cold-heading a piece of bar stock the size of the smaller stem and then performing the required finishing machining operations. Cost of the added operation was more than offset by material, labor, and time savings.

Figure 28-5 shows how Walter Kidde & Company applied value analysis to a small, relatively simple assembly. Note that cost savings were obtained using three different approaches:

1 *Elimination* of the dual-mounting screw configuration and the left- and right-hand coupling reduced cost through *design simplification.*
2 Changing the cover from a brass stamping to molded thermosetting plastic reduced cost through the *use of less expensive material.*
3 *Substitution* of a pulley machined from bar stock for the pulley machined from a casting further reduced cost through the use of *less costly manufacturing methods.*

Additional examples of production parts which have been value-analyzed are shown in Figure 28-6.[12]

Packaging

Some firms' products and production operations afford very little opportunity to value-analyze production parts. Consider, for example, a steel mill or a plant producing automobile batteries. Companies of this type use very few production parts. Moreover, the value analysis potential of those parts that are

---

[12]For a detailed discussion of these value analysis techniques, see the classical value analysis text by Lawrence D. Miles, *Techniques of Value Analysis and Engineering,* 2d ed., McGraw-Hill Book Company, New York, 1972, chaps. 3 and 4.

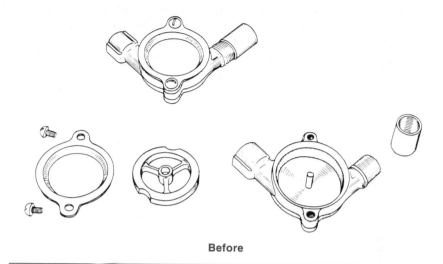

Before

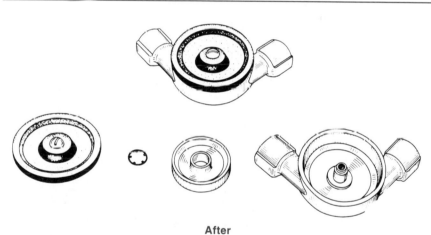

After

FIGURE 28-5
A value-analyzed assembly. After going through two cost reduction studies, the assembly (used to direct steel cable through an angle-top) was value-analyzed with these results: Left- and right-hand coupling was eliminated (bottom); cover was changed from brass stamping to plastic; special tapping operation was eliminated by using one captive screw to hold cover (tapped hole was made concentric with body recess); pulley was made as a screw machine piece rather than a machined casting, and held captive to the body to ease field installation; only one assembly was used for two sizes of cable; and specialty suppliers with high-speed equipment were used. Costs on the unit dropped 60 percent. *(Reprinted with the permission of* Purchasing *magazine.)*

used is restricted because of technical constraints imposed by the requirements of the process or the finished product. Even so, it is amazing to see how companies of this type locate problems *outside the production area* which lend themselves to value analysis. The general field of packaging is an extremely fruitful area in many companies.

FIGURE 28-6
Examples of value analysis producing spectacular cost reductions. *(Reproduced with the permission of* Business Management *magazine, formerly* Management Methods *magazine.)*

HOW VALUE ANALYSIS SLASHES COSTS

Weights mounted on a rotor ring were curved to match the ring curve. Did it need this feature? No. Using a straight piece, the cost dropped from 40¢ to 4¢.	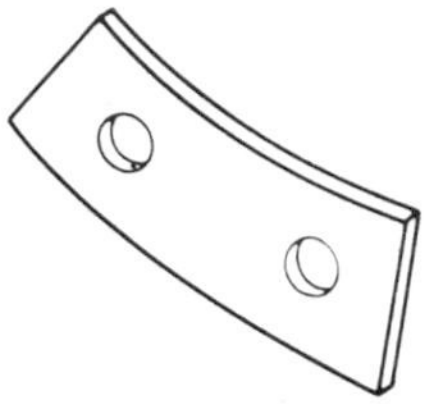 **40¢**	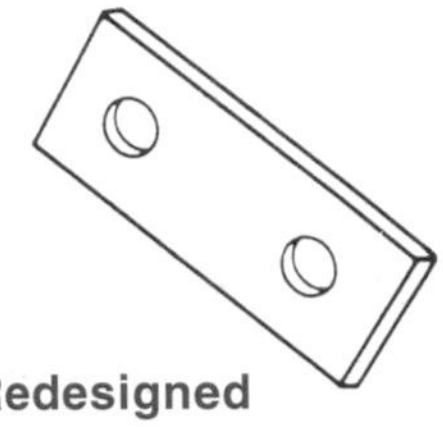 **Redesigned** **4¢**
Field coil supports were machined from stock, but the original design blended nicely into a casting operation. The change resulted in lowering the cost from $1.72 to 36¢ each.	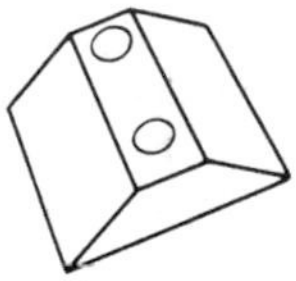 **Machined** **$1.72**	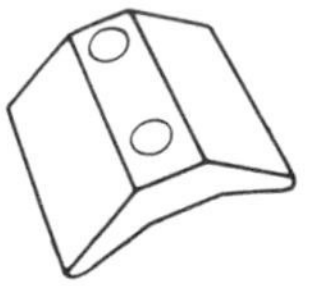 **Cast** **36¢**
This insulating washer was made from laminated phenolic resin and fiber. Machined from individual pieces of material, it cost $1.23. A supplier with specialty equipment now fly-cuts the parts, nesting them on full sheets, at 24¢ each.	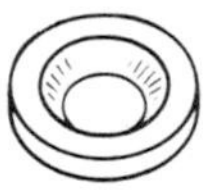 **Machined** **$1.23**	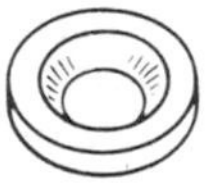 **Fly-cut** **24¢**
Standard nipple and elbow required special machining to fit a totally enclosed motor. Casting a special street "L" with a lug eliminated machining and a special assembly jig. The cost dropped from 63¢ to 38¢.	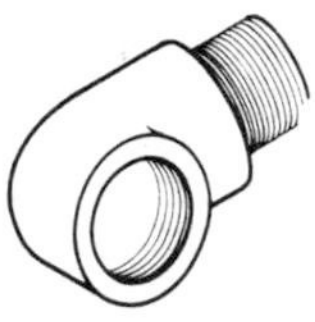 **63¢**	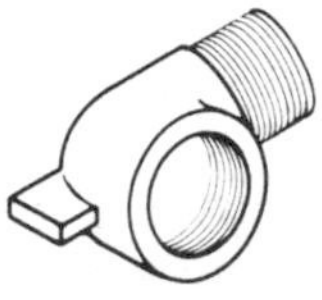 **Redesigned** **38¢**
An insulator costing $4.56 was originally porcelain, leaded extra heavy. Now molded from polyester and glass, it is lighter and virtually indestructible. New cost: $3.25.	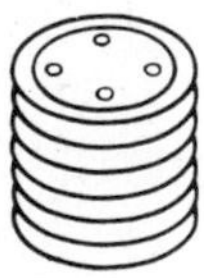 **$4.56**	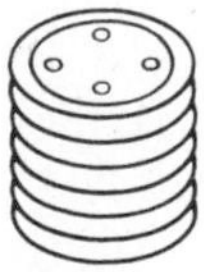 **New material** **$3.25**

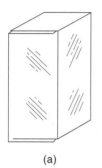 

(a)   (b)

FIGURE 28-7
Box design before and after value analysis.

The nail-making department of one of the United States Steel Corporation's division plants provides a good example. This division originally shipped its nails to customers in wooden kegs. Value analysis of the packaging method produced a seven-part corrugated-cardboard box that did the job better than the keg and saved the firm over $500,000 per year. Subsequent analysis of the seven-part box resulted in the use of a two-part box which saved the company an additional $118,000 per year.[13]

A second very simple example occurred some years ago in a number of companies that packaged their products in light cardboard boxes (e.g., breakfast food, sugar, and soap producers). Originally, on the top and the bottom of the box the closure flaps completely overlapped each other, as in Figure 28-7a. When many firms analyzed the functions the box performed, they found that the strength provided by a full overlap was not required. Consequently, many redesigned their containers to provide only a partial overlap, as shown in Figure 28-7b. Such a simple modification as this in some cases reduced a firm's cardboard requirement by 5 percent, saving hundreds of thousands of dollars because of the large quantity of boxes used.

The final example in the packaging area comes recently from the "golden arches" company—McDonald's. Perseco, the private firm that buys all of McDonald's packaging materials, value-analyzed the boxes and wrapping paper used in packaging the finished product—hamburgers, french fries, etc. When it came to the "quarter pounder with cheese," the VA team recommended using a smaller sheet of insulated wrap—11 inch × 12 inch, rather than the 11½ inch × 13 inch previously used. The new wrap worked just fine (no quarter pounders fell out!), the recommendation was adopted, and McDonald's saved $1.6 million the next year.[14]

---

[13]*Cost Reduction through Value Analysis: Conference Leader's Guide,* prepared by the Purchasing and Industrial Engineering Departments, Columbia-Geneva Steel Division of United States Steel Corporation, section on Shipping and Handling Applications.
[14]Daniel Liehr, "Value Analysis: 1993 (Quarter Pounder W/Cheese to Go)," *Purchasing,* June 3, 1993, p. 62.

The Broader Applications

When firms first started using value analysis, the original emphasis was almost entirely on applications to parts, subassemblies, and packaging in manufacturing operations. Fundamentally, however, the value analysis concept really defines a creative, systematic thought process that can be applied to problem solving in a wide variety of areas. Hence, over the years, as one might suspect, value analysis has been applied to a broad range of activities and procurement-related problems outside the manufacturing area. Applications range from the design of operating systems, to the development of corporate reengineering projects, to the procurement of services and transportation. The following cases illustrate the point.[15]

When one firm began planning a new warehouse, a major element for analysis was the type of racks and shelving to be used. The original plan called for conventional closed shelving and cabinets. An analysis that focused on the storage functions to be performed revealed that in many cases, open wire grid racks and shelving would do the job very well. So the final plan developed was for an ultramodern facility that included both open and closed storage equipment, based on specific functional needs. The results were (1) a substantial saving in initial equipment costs; (2) simplification of fire sprinkler system requirements and a considerable reduction of the system cost; and (3) most important, reduction of insurance premium costs by more than $100,000 per year because of the reduced fire hazard that resulted from the modified plan.

In another case, purchasing officials from the state of New Mexico applied value analysis effectively to a systems problem. Several state agencies periodically mailed large numbers of a variety of standard documents to state residents. Processing, mailing, and postage costs were high. A value analysis team, including operating personnel, a buyer, a systems analyst, and an equipment supplier, studied the entire operation from a functional point of view. The result of their efforts was a modified system that now saves the state in excess of $250,000 per year. Major operating changes included (1) redesign of many of the forms and a significant reduction in the number of forms utilized; (2) production of a number of the forms on the in-house computer output mailing system, as opposed to purchase from a commercial printer, reducing material, inventory, and mailing preparation costs; and (3) program changes in the computer-operated mailing system that permitted the insertion of several documents going to the same address in one envelope, thus reducing supply, labor, and postage costs.

In all types of applications, micro and macro, the focus is on *function*. How can the function be performed at the specified quality level, at the lowest total cost?

[15]Edward J. Walter, "Value Analysis—It's Not Just Parts," *Purchasing World*, February 1988, pp. 31–38.

CONDITIONS CONDUCIVE TO VALUE ANALYSIS

A broad view of American industry reveals vast differences among its thousands of production operations and among the myriad products manufactured. Because of these differences, value analysis holds considerably more cost reduction potential for some firms than for others. Generally speaking, the factors discussed in the following sections determine the usefulness of the value analysis concept to a particular organization.

Design Analysis

Design analysis can be used to greatest advantage under the following conditions:

1 Design analysis is predicated on the assumption that material specifications can be changed. Therefore, the first condition of application requires that a firm's material specifications *not* be tied down rigidly by its products or operations. The greater the flexibility in the specifications, the greater the potential value of this technique.
2 A design analysis program can be most easily supported when a firm produces, on a recurring basis, a large number of different products. Further, the probability of finding untapped cost reduction areas is greater when each of these products is made up of a large number of complex components.
3 Greatest benefits accrue when a material is used in large quantities, by virtue of either a high rate of usage in one product or a lesser rate of usage in each of several products.
4 The opportunity to effect significant changes is greater when product designs have not been highly refined by similar analyses during earlier stages of development. Thus, if specifications are originally developed by the use of extensive interdepartmental participation or by computer-assisted design, opportunities to produce savings through subsequent design analysis are reduced. Conversely, when a product design is modified frequently, opportunities for savings usually increase.
5 From the value analyst's point of view, a nonstandard item presents more lucrative possibilities for design change than does a standard item whose design has been refined by its manufacturer.
6 The technique is most applicable to a product for which a single design change can be effected without altering the performance of a large number of related components of the product.
7 The chance for profitable design change for a given product increases as the availability of alternative production materials increases.

Cost Analysis

When strong price competition exists between suppliers, competitive forces tend to keep prices in line with costs. Under these conditions, most suppliers have value-analyzed their own products, and cost analysis by the purchaser usually uncovers very few high-cost components. The buyer therefore finds cost analysis most effective when dealing with nonstandard materials or with standard materials whose markets do not exhibit rigid price structures. Likewise, greatest benefits accrue to a buyer when dealing in large quantities of materials.

ORGANIZATION AND ADMINISTRATION OF VALUE ANALYSIS

When a company initially decides to establish a VA/VE program, it must answer two questions: (1) Who should be responsible for developing, leading, and controlling the program? (2) What mechanisms should be used to facilitate communication and coordination between the various departments included in the effort?

In the case of a value engineering program, the answers are very straightforward. Development and control of the program usually both reside in the design engineering department. And a cross-functional product development team usually provides the coordination and communication required among the various departments.

In the case of a value analysis program, however, there are no pat answers to these questions. The more clearly top-level executives understand the total value analysis concept, the more clearly they realize that value analysis should really be everybody's business. In one sense, value analysis is a state of mind—a way of looking at business life. Maximum potential can be realized from a value analysis program only if everyone in the plant is value-conscious, and then only if management properly taps these potential resources. Consequently, while sound organization is essential to the success of a value analysis program, the total effects of organization per se are not as far-reaching as those stemming from the successful creation of value-conscious attitudes among all the people in the organization.

It is not surprising, then, to find extreme variation among companies in their organization for value analysis. Because of product and operational differences, each firm's need for value analysis differs. Consequently, each company may choose to emphasize certain aspects of value analysis and largely neglect others. This decision may, in turn, influence the subsequent decision concerning administrative policy. If a firm elects to concentrate on cost analysis, for example, there probably will be a strong inclination to center authority for the program in the purchasing and supply department, because of purchasing's extensive role in this activity. On the other hand, if design analysis is the focal point of the program, the engineering department may logically play the more dominant role in its development and promotion.

Studies of current practice indicate that among firms with successful value analysis programs, three basic organizational approaches are most common: (1) the specialized staff approach, (2) the cross-functional team approach, and (3) the staff training approach.

Specialized Staff Approach

The most widely used type of value analysis program among *large companies* is one built around a group of highly trained value analysts who function in a staff capacity. In some situations the analysts constitute a separate staff agency reporting to a general management executive; occasionally, the group reports to a top-level engineering design manager. Most frequently, however, the value analysis staff is attached to the purchasing and supply department.[16]

In some cases purchasing administration of the program simply can be traced to the fact that the purchasing department was largely responsible for initiating value analysis. Aside from this, two important factors underscore the logic of such an arrangement. First, *every buyer must be a value analyst in his or her own right.* Formal value analysis is simply an extension of the job every buyer should do when placing an order. Since the basic nature of the value analysis function ties in closely with the purchasing function, a close organizational relationship for administrative purposes logically follows. Second, *the purchasing department is normally the most cost-conscious department in a company as far as production materials and components are concerned.* Its objectivity in evaluating the cost and performance of materials is usually unencumbered with the biases and goal conflicts which often hamper some departments that are totally performance-oriented. It should be noted that this factor also supports the argument for the independent status of value analysis, that is, assignment of the function directly to a general management executive.

In any case, in the specialized staff approach, most detailed analyses and recommendations are made by the staff analysts. This requires cooperation and assistance from buyers and design engineers. Any specification changes, however, are normally negotiated by the buyer and the engineer, based on the analyst's recommendations. While the manager of value analysis has no direct authority to enforce any staff recommendations, he or she does have a certain amount of indirect leverage. This leverage evolves from the fact that the recommendations are made by impartial and qualified analysts who frequently are also experienced engineers. Added to this is the fact that the value analysis staff usually enjoys a close relationship with higher management.

One medium-sized manufacturing plant which uses the specialized staff approach finds that a background in both purchasing *and* engineering or production is ideal for a value analyst. In this firm it takes a new analyst approximately six months to produce cost savings that exceed his or her salary. After approximately a year, however, the firm reports that most value analysts produce at least five times their salary in savings annually.

The General Electric Company, where value analysis originated, continues to be one of the acknowledged leaders in the field. Several years ago GE initiated a new approach for generating candidate products for analysis in its VA pro-

---

[16]See the classical study by Stanley S. Miller, "How to Get the Most out of Value Analysis," *Harvard Business Review,* January–February 1955, pp. 123–132; and L. S. Miles, *Techniques of Value Analysis and Engineering,* 2d ed., McGraw-Hill Book Company, New York, 1972, chap. 8.

gram. Its motor division factory now uses a "customer advisory panel" to identify product problems, in much the same manner as a marketing focus group, with significant attention to detail. To date, the program has worked well.[17]

In describing the General Electric program in his book, Larry Miles states that GE has found the specialized staff approach to be the most successful method of VA operation.[18] Westinghouse Electric Corporation and Ford Motor Company also conduct similarly designed programs. During the early years of its program's operation, in one year alone, Westinghouse effected savings totaling more than $7.5 million.[19]

The Cross-Functional Team/Committee

A second approach used in both large and small firms today involves committee administration and team conduct of the value analysis program. This approach, or some variant of it, predominates among smaller firms.

A typical value analysis committee usually is composed of four to eight people, including senior representatives from areas such as operations, engineering, purchasing and supply, marketing, and general management. The committee may be headed by a senior functional representative, frequently from purchasing or general management, or by a full-time "value coordinator" assigned to the top-management staff.

In most companies, the suggestions for projects to be analyzed may come from any department. One firm requires each department head to submit ten potential value analysis projects to the committee every month. Another firm solicits suggestions from all employees, tying this activity into its broader employee suggestion system, which provides financial awards for those whose suggestions are developed into actual cost-saving operations.

However the suggestions are acquired, the value analysis committee then reviews them and selects the promising ones for detailed analysis. At this point, the committee approach differs radically from the specialized staff approach. In most committee-administered programs, the detailed value analysis work is conducted by an ad hoc team of operating personnel chosen from participating departments. It is not uncommon for a project to be assigned jointly to a buyer, a design engineer, and a production supervisor. Analysis is done individually and jointly until the team is ready to submit the results of its study to the value analysis committee for review and decision.

Use of the team/committee approach does not prohibit the use of specialized value analysts. Many firms use this approach, however, because they consider it to be an ideal way to develop a team approach to value analysis. Con-

---

[17]"GE Redesigns Its 56 Frame Motors with Buyer Help," *Purchasing*, Dec. 12, 1991, p. 90.

[18]Lawrence D. Miles, "Purchasing Productivity Improvement through the Use of Value Analysis," NAPM 67th International Purchasing Conference, Los Angeles, May 11, 1982.

[19]For an interesting discussion about the early development and implementation of a value analysis program in one of America's giant corporations, refer to A. H. Phelps, "Westinghouse Cost Reduction," *Purchasing*, June 1951, p. 108.

sequently, they usually prefer to involve as many operating personnel as possible in the detailed analytical work. The obvious bonus accruing from such involvement is that each operating participant becomes a better value analyst, carrying this ability and attitude back to his or her daily work in design, production, or purchasing and supply.

Thus, the committee acts as the authority and the coordinating medium for the total value analysis program. A potential weakness of this approach, so far as the total program is concerned, sometimes lies in a committee's inability to elicit support and cooperation. Consequently, for successful operation, a committee-administered program must have active management support, a strong committee chairperson, and a clear-cut operating procedure which facilitates the enforcement of decisions.

The Staff Training Approach

The philosophy underlying the staff training approach to value analysis grows out of the same idea that leads some companies to involve operating personnel in detailed value analysis work. Companies subscribing to the staff training approach believe that value analysis yields maximum benefits only when it is practiced by all key operating personnel. Consequently, this approach aims primarily at developing an understanding of the concept and a working knowledge of techniques among most professional and operating personnel responsible for specifying, buying, and using production materials.

The value analysis organization in this case consists of a small staff group which reports to general management. The activities of this group focus on value analysis training. The group is responsible for developing a total value analysis training program and for conducting individual value analysis training sessions. In one company, forty hour-long training sessions are conducted for small groups of participants. An individual's initial training experience is followed up every year or so with a short refresher session in which new techniques and ideas are demonstrated, discussed, and practiced.

Most companies adopting this approach have no staff groups of specialized value analysts. To achieve value analysis cost savings, they rely entirely on a continuous training program and on the *individual application* of this training by participating personnel in all departments, particularly engineering, operations, and purchasing and supply.

To supplement the staff training approach and the committee approach, some companies publish a monthly "value analysis bulletin" which has the following goals:

- To create a cost-conscious attitude on the part of employees and to develop a team spirit in the approach to value analysis
- To give examples of successful value analysis projects to employees so they can see "how to do it"
- To give recognition to individuals who have submitted good ideas

It is sometimes difficult to obtain employee acceptance of such a publication. If done successfully, however, it can produce outstanding results because it strikes at the heart of all cost reduction program goals—*individual* motivation.

Quality Circles   The quality circle concept is a natural vehicle to use in implementing the staff training approach. Hailed by the Japanese as one of the keys to that nation's exploding productivity, quality circle activity is a broadly based application of Theory Z participative management. Its objective is extensive involvement of all employees in making company decisions that affect them, the workplace, and company productivity.

Each quality circle typically consists of approximately a dozen people who work together in any area of the organization—from the production line to the front office. Participation is voluntary, and groups usually meet once or twice a week for one to two hours; each group selects its own leaders. Topics for discussion and investigation cover any company matter of concern to group members—work procedures, material problems, environmental issues, and so on. Circle members study, plan, and solve their problems together as a team. When necessary, specialized expertise or staff assistance is provided by management.

Clearly, this broadly based "people-management" concept and the basic philosophy underlying value analysis both hold one important common goal: *individual concern* and *individual motivation* that lead to *group pride* and cohesive *group action*. Logically, then, some companies have found that value analysis training and value analysis projects integrate effectively with their ongoing quality circle activities. Of those firms that have embraced the quality circle concept, not all have linked it with value analysis. Some who have, however, report outstanding results. F. A. Boyle of Honeywell, for example, reported annual savings in excess of $1 million in his firm.[20]

Carrier's Approach to Value Analysis

To conclude this section dealing with a firm's organization for conduct and delivery of VA services, a brief look at the Carrier Corporation's view of the subject provides a concise summary. Carrier, now a part of the United Technologies organization, is the world's largest manufacturer of heating, ventilating, and air-conditioning equipment; it has forty plants located around the globe.

In this far-flung empire, value analysis reigns supreme—and is housed administratively in Carrier's headquarters purchasing department. The Carrier organization utilizes all three of the major organizational VA approaches just discussed. At headquarters the central VA group has the following responsibilities:

1 To function as a specialized VA staff to conduct value analysis studies on selected major items used corporatewide

---

[20]*Purchasing World,* November 1980, pp. 48–51; and D. N. Burt, *Proactive Procurement,* Prentice-Hall Inc., Englewood Cliffs, N.J., 1984, chap. 2.

2 To develop VA teams in each of the forty plants to conduct value analysis studies, with suppliers, of unique items at the grass-roots level

3 To conduct VA workshops and training sessions throughout the organization to support the grass-roots-level value analysis activities

Clearly, here is a firm whose top management believes in the potential of value analysis—and has provided the support to make it happen.[21]

Reporting Value Analysis

A firm should determine the magnitude of the savings generated by each dollar it invests in its value analysis program. Such a control measure obviously is useful to management. Most firms therefore develop a reasonably complete cost reporting system.

Some organizations go even further. They tabulate and sometimes publish value analysis savings for each department and each individual. Through this increased visibility they attempt to promote the value analysis program and stimulate increased value analysis effort throughout the organization.

There is considerable difference of opinion, however, concerning the use of reporting systems that detail departmental or individual savings. While some firms find that publication of such data serves as an effective incentive for their individual employees, others find just the opposite. Those opposed maintain that in many cases the credit for a value analysis saving cannot clearly be given to one or even several individuals. They contend that many people usually contribute to the final solution. This view is supported by the fact that some firms have experienced employee dissatisfaction resulting from inequitable recognition and an occasional inflation of savings favoring certain analysts or departments. Nevertheless, it is generally agreed that some form of personal guidance and encouragement is helpful in motivating the individuals involved. This means that the reporting system must provide enough detail to apprise a supervisor of the general acceptability of each individual's value analysis performance.

CONCLUSION

Value analysis is a significant element in most firms' purchasing research activities—and it possesses tremendous profit-making potential. However, if its potential is to be realized, those responsible for administration of the value analysis program must adopt a broadly based management point of view. This is essential because value analysis is a companywide activity whose purpose is to optimize returns to the *total* business operation.

In practice, the value analysis activity cuts across numerous functional lines of authority. For this reason, the activity must be organized and administered

---

[21]Ernest Raia, "Why Carrier's Hot about VA," *Purchasing,* June 3, 1993, pp. 50–53

with care. Varying historical traditions and orientations in different firms may point to different administrative approaches. In its most basic form, the administrative problem becomes one of *human relations and motivation* more than anything else. In a broad sense, value analysis is simply a unique way of looking at business life. Management must not overlook the fact that, in the long run, it is the attitude of the participants that largely determines the degree of success achieved by any program. Value analysis concepts must be *understood, accepted,* and *practiced* by a majority of the various functional specialists involved in the program if such a program is to be fully effective.

As industrial technology advances, during the years ahead an increasing number of larger firms will utilize robotics and computer-assisted design and manufacturing devices. As higher levels of analytical capability are built into these devices, resulting product designs will become more efficient at the outset than is generally the case today. Hence, some value engineering capability will, in effect, be transferred to the automated design process. The anticipated result is that this evolutionary trend gradually will reduce the need for detailed value analysis of product design as it is practiced today. Consequently, as we move into the next century, the value analysis emphasis in some firms will likely shift toward cost analysis and more broadly based conceptual applications.

FOR DISCUSSION

28-1 Do many firms use value analysis? Discuss.

28-2 What is value engineering? How does it differ from value analysis?

28-3 Discuss the basic objectives of value analysis.

28-4 What is cost analysis, and how is it used in a value analysis program?

28-5 What is design analysis, and how is it used in a value analysis program?

28-6 What would you say to a disgruntled design engineer who does not want to participate in your firm's value analysis program because he or she believes it infringes on the prerogatives of design engineering?

28-7 "Value analysis is more of a human relations and motivation problem than anything else." Discuss this statement.

28-8 Comment on Chrysler's approach to VA.

28-9 Discuss the specific techniques used in design analysis.

28-10 Go to a local fast-food restaurant and order a popular sandwich. After enjoying the sandwich, value-analyze the wrapper or container the sandwich came in. (Do a good job—and perhaps your VA suggestion can be parlayed into another sandwich!)

28-11 Dismantle a desk stapler (or similar convenient object) and value-analyze it. Before starting, outline the total procedure to be followed, the records to be kept during the process, and the report to be submitted on completion of the analysis. For all parts, estimate costs as closely as possible, using data in your library and data which may be available from local businesses.

28-12 Experiment with brainstorming by value-analyzing a multipart object in this way: Six people form one group and work jointly, using the brainstorming technique, in value-analyzing the object. Six other people form a second group. Each of these individuals will value-analyze the same object by himself or herself. After finishing, these six individuals will meet and select the best of the individual solutions. Each group should prepare a report on its job. At a class meeting, the two groups will review their activities in detail and present their findings. The class will then compare and evaluate the two approaches. See question 28-11 for procedural details.

28-13 Why can suppliers be helpful in value analysis programs? How can they be used? Does this use of suppliers in any way violate your concept of good business ethics?

28-14 Suppose you have decided that you would like to involve some of your key suppliers in your firm's value analysis program. As the purchasing manager, prepare a plan for this project that you would submit to your boss for approval.

28-15 Earlier in the book, the concept of early supplier involvement was discussed. Operationally, how does this relate to value analysis?

28-16 Suppose you are the purchasing manager for a small manufacturing firm. How would you determine whether or not a value analysis program might pay off in your plant? Outline your investigation in step-by-step fashion, and discuss.

28-17 Referring to question 28-16, suppose you thought that value analysis would be profitable. Prepare a proposal to submit to the general manager, attempting to convince him or her that the firm should establish a value analysis program. Detail the type of program you suggest, stating any assumptions you wish to make about the company and its products.

28-18 Discuss the advantages and the disadvantages, as you see them, of each of the organizational approaches used in implementing a value analysis program.

28-19 Do a brief analysis of Carrier's approach to value analysis.

28-20 In your opinion, what are the advantages of locating a value analysis program in the purchasing and supply department for administrative purposes? What are the disadvantages?

28-21 What is a FAST diagram? How can it be used in VA/VE work?

28-22 What are quality circles? How do quality circles relate to value analysis?

28-23 How can value analysis be used in a nonmanufacturing organization?

CASES FOR CHAPTER 28

29

APPRAISAL, CONTROL, AND REPORTS

KEY CONCEPTS

- Control concepts
    Problem prevention
    Problem detection
    Postaction control process
- Appraising and controlling procurement performance
    Problems in controlling purchasing performance
    A basic approach to control of purchasing and supply
    The purchasing and supply management review
    Controlling the timing factor
    Controlling quantity and inventory investment
    Controlling prices and costs of materials
    Controlling material quality
    Controlling source reliability
    Managing supplier relationships
    Supplier councils
    Controlling internal coordination
    Controlling procurement efficiency
    Buyer models
- Guidelines for development and use of control systems
- How industry does it
    Ten most commonly used measurements
    The CAPS benchmarking program
    One firm's progressive approach to appraisal and control
- Reports to management

How do managers know when their departments are performing satisfactorily? How do they know whether departmental objectives are being achieved? On what basis do they set priorities in allocating resources to improve performance? This chapter deals with the answers to these questions. Appraisal and control of operations is the last step in the management process.

CONTROL CONCEPTS

Experienced managers know that two approaches should be used in performing the control phase of the management job—*problem prevention* where possible, followed with a *monitoring system that detects problems* that slip through the prevention net.

Problem Prevention

Problem prevention, or *preaction control* as some call it, is standard operating procedure for all airline pilots. Before the airplane leaves the ground, engines, alternators, pumps, various operating systems, and other vital pieces of equipment are tested to ensure that they function as they should. *The control mechanism is built into the procedure* before the action occurs. Similarly, in a purchasing and supply operation, a number of problem prevention techniques are built into the department's operating policies and procedures. A few of the more common ones are listed below.

1 Each buyer is authorized to commit the firm to a limited number of dollars per purchase order. Beyond that limit, supervisory approval is required.
2 In competitive bidding situations, bidding between at least three suppliers may be required on all orders in excess of x dollars, and between at least five bidders on all orders in excess of y dollars.
3 Policy may require that a job be negotiated if certain specified conditions exist.
4 Policy may require that for certain types of purchases all suppliers must utilize an SPC system.
5 The methodology for conducting a supplier's process capability analysis may be specified in one of the firm's procedures.

Thus, this means of preventive control through the use of carefully constructed policies and procedures is designed to facilitate correct or effective action by purchasing and supply personnel *the first time*. This approach, coupled with appropriate training, supervisory guidance, and motivation, is perhaps a manager's most effective control technique. In the preceding chapters of the book, a wide range of these concepts has been presented. By design, the first twenty-eight chapters have established the foundation for preaction control.

Problem Detection

The second, and most visible, segment of a manager's total control responsibility is the postaction control operation. The purpose of a *postaction control system* is to *monitor performance* and to *detect any problems*—some of which are bound to occur in a dynamic operating system in which human judgment and supplier behavior are but two of the variables. As soon as problems are detected, the system should provide for corrective action quickly to minimize nonstandard operation or output. This type of after-the-fact control process consists of four activities:

1 Establishing a workable *standard* of performance
2 Developing procedures that *feed back* actual performance data to the manager
3 *Comparing* actual performance with the standard and *evaluating* the results
4 Taking *corrective action* when necessary

Of the four activities, establishing a realistic standard that is accurate and readily accepted by operating personnel usually is the most difficult. The variability of job requirements is the culprit. Although output standards can be set fairly easily for repetitive jobs, as job duties become varied and require more creativity, determination of a workable standard becomes increasingly difficult. Similarly, in establishing standards for material prices, the uncertainties associated with the market and with suppliers' cost structures obviously introduce problems of estimation that can be difficult to handle with accuracy.

This chapter focuses on the development and implementation of postaction control systems in purchasing and supply operations.

APPRAISING AND CONTROLLING PURCHASING AND SUPPLY PERFORMANCE

Appraisal and control of supply performance has always been important in a well-managed firm, but in today's environment it is more important than ever. Such market factors as increasingly stringent global competition, the extreme emphasis on quality, and the push to bring products to market faster all exert legitimate and increased pressure on a firm's purchasing and supply operation. Another important element resulting from these market factors is the changing relationship between buying and supplying firms. Today they must work together in a closer collaborative mode, sometimes in alliance relationships—and this produces an increasing interdependence between the firms. This coupled with the drive for continuous improvement mandates the development of effective performance measures that can be used as the basis for proactive assessment and control of operations.

In developing a system to monitor and control supply performance, the logical starting point is to review and perhaps revise the objectives of the department. Aggregate departmental objectives should be broken down by major material category or by buying group because, as noted in Chapter 27, different objectives frequently are established for the handling of different materials. Once the performance objectives—those relating to quality, price/cost, quantity, timing, supplier relations, and so on—are clear, the critical activities where control and cooperative work with suppliers are most important can be determined.

Problems in Controlling Purchasing Performance

When an analysis of these detailed objectives is made in a typical purchasing operation, it reveals one unfortunate fact. Most of the critical control points lie in a single activity—the buying activity. As a rule, a given commodity buyer's or buying team's job encompasses a number of extremely variable activities. Additionally, performance in most of these areas is hard to measure in quantitative terms. Hence, the very nature of the purchasing function makes it unusually difficult to establish meaningful performance standards. Consequently, the development of a reliable control system is not an easy task.

The intangible nature of purchasing's *primary* responsibilities often prohibits the direct measurement of purchasing accomplishment. Most standards and measurements therefore focus on secondary factors that are *indirect* indicators of true accomplishment. The secondary factors that can be measured (e.g., quality rejection rate and price paid) are useful in determining *trends* of performance. In appraising the absolute level of accomplishment, however, secondary factors may or may not be useful. The validity of each factor must be assessed in each specific case; it varies with materials, markets, and suppliers.

A Basic Approach to the Control of Purchasing and Supply

Because of the difficulties encountered in developing precise purchasing control systems, many companies have adopted a fairly broad approach to the evaluation and control of their purchasing and supply activities. Such an approach includes three different types of assessments:

1 *A qualitative assessment of a number of broad managerial responsibilities—a management review.* This assessment includes factors such as the capabilities of personnel; the soundness of the organization structure; scope of the purchasing and supply job; purchasing plans, policies, procedures; and so on. The theory underlying the use of such an evaluation is that these factors control the *potential* level of a department's performance; as such, they are useful indirect indicators of performance.

2 *An appraisal of buying and supply effectiveness.* Effectiveness in this sense is defined as the degree of success experienced in achieving a firm's primary buying and supply objectives. To evaluate this success, attempts are made to establish performance targets (standards) for the measurable *sec-*

ondary factors that relate to *primary* buying objectives. Recognizing that a single factor may not provide an accurate indication of creative buying performance, most companies develop a cross-check by measuring several factors that relate to the same primary objective. For example, buying performance relative to the price/cost objective can be checked from two standpoints: (1) Actual prices paid can be compared with target prices, and (2) targets for cost savings resulting from negotiation and from value analysis can be established and actual savings compared with these targets. Thus, two measurements provide a cross-check on the same primary objective—price/cost. A similar approach can be used in evaluating buying performance relative to each of the other basic objectives.

3 *An assessment of purchasing efficiency.* "Effectiveness" in buying and "efficiency" in buying are two distinctly different elements. Control of efficiency involves evaluation of workloads, personnel utilization, operating costs, and processing times as related to specific volumes of purchasing operations. Clearly, a purchasing executive wants to achieve a high degree of operating efficiency—*but not at the expense of buying effectiveness.* The latter element offers far more opportunity for cost savings than the former.

The Review—Appraising Managerial Performance

The broad appraisal of managerial effort is, in essence, a management review of the purchasing and supply operation. Because of the subjectivity involved in this kind of evaluation, it usually can be conducted most effectively by someone outside the purchasing and supply department. Individuals normally called on to conduct such reviews are private consultants, staff systems specialists, staff management engineers, and internal staff auditors. This does not mean that purchasing management should not make such evaluations. On the contrary, to improve the operation, internal management should continuously ask itself the same types of questions that management consultants ask.

The areas investigated and the types of questions raised during the evaluation are similar to those discussed in the previous section of the book. Without repeating the details, the list that follows outlines the general areas of inquiry.

1 *Scope of the purchasing and supply function.* How important does management consider the purchasing and supply activity in the firm's total operation? Is purchasing properly located in the organizational hierarchy? Does purchasing participate in the formulation of policies on forward buying, JIT, and inventory levels? To what extent does purchasing participate in long-term strategy and make-or-buy decisions, in the materials standards program, in the value analysis program, in the quality management program?

2 *Evaluation of purchasing managerial personnel.* Are purchasing managers adequately qualified? Do they fully understand the economic and busi-

ness intricacies of their company and industry? Are they qualified administrators? Do they have adequate knowledge of relevant materials and manufacturing processes? Do they have adequate knowledge of the suppliers and markets with which they deal?

3 *Organization.* Does the department have a complete and current organization chart? Is all purchasing activity centralized in the purchasing department? Have clear lines of responsibility and authority been established? Is sufficient authority delegated along with responsibility? Are the operating activities logically grouped for purposes of functional operation, coordination, and control? Has the department developed adequate job descriptions and employee qualifications for its jobs? Is adequate organization planning being done to meet future needs?

4 *Personnel.* Do employees' qualifications match job requirements? Are adequate selection criteria used in hiring personnel? What job training is given personnel? What professional development training is afforded and required of personnel? What planning and preparation are done for the advancement and replacement of personnel? Are compensation levels adequate to retain competent personnel? Is the employee turnover rate reasonable?

5 *Policies.* Is a well-defined basic purchasing policy, outlining purchasing responsibility and authority, well known and accepted throughout the company? Is a well-developed policy manual in use? What policy has been adopted regarding purchasing research activities (economic and market research, commodity research, systems research)? Do buyers concentrate time and effort on materials proportionate to their respective dollar-volume values?

Is adequate advance materials planning done to permit effective purchasing and term contracting? Are proactive annual or multiyear buying plans used? Are cross-functional teams utilized in any of the purchasing activities? Do satisfactory policies exist for the following activities: new supplier identification, supplier evaluation and selection, use of competitive bids, use of negotiation (cost analysis and price analysis), and supplier relations? Have satisfactory policies been developed concerning the use of single and multiple sources as well as partnering relationships? Are terms of purchase, routing of shipments, SPC, and types of inspection (and coordination with suppliers) properly covered by policy statements?

6 *Procedures.* Have all procedures been automated to the extent reasonably possible? Is a well-developed procedure manual in use (simple, clear, complete)? Have procedure flowcharts been developed? Are all forms well-designed, simple, and effective? Are procedures in operation that effectively coordinate purchasing with using departments, quality assurance, the data processing division, finance, inventory control, receiving and stores, traffic, and engineering (as regards EPI, ESI, and VA/VE work)?

Are adequate procedures used to handle rush orders and small orders? Are sound procedures in existence for such activities as negotiation, competitive bidding, supplier selection, and order follow-up? Are complete procedures available for controlling the receiving activity and for handling loss and damage claims? Do adequate stores procedures exist for receiving, storing, and disbursing materials? Have procedures been developed for evaluating capital equipment purchase alternatives? Are sound procedures used in managing inventory, in determining order quantities, and in determining safety stock levels?

7 *Records and reports.* Are adequate records maintained to facilitate effective purchasing (emphasis on commodity records and supplier records)? Do operating records contain necessary data for control purposes? What reports are submitted to purchasing management to facilitate managerial control by exception? How frequently are such reports submitted? What reports are submitted to top management?

The first two areas, *scope of the function* and *evaluation of managerial personnel,* are vital to the long-range health of the purchasing organization. However, development and changes in the first area, and to some extent in the second, are conditioned heavily by a firm's management philosophy—and typically occur rather slowly. On the other hand, the other five areas are tightly interwoven with the department's short-term operation. Consequently, in progressive organizations a systematic evaluation of the first two areas usually occurs *every three to five years,* with the latter five areas receiving more frequent reviews—perhaps *every one to two years.*

Controlling Buying Effectiveness

In most cases, a manager needs feedback on at least a monthly basis, and frequently more often, to do a good job of controlling buying effectiveness. The operating situation is dynamic, and corrective action or a change in strategy usually should be accomplished fairly quickly. In addition, an *annual review* of the effectiveness measurements is also useful as a foundation for the development of the ensuing year's buying plan.

A number of different performance factors can be measured to provide a basis for appraising and controlling buying effectiveness. The factors differ in importance among companies, depending on the nature of the business and the materials purchased. Most firms, therefore, do not use *all* the measures discussed in this section. Similarly, to pinpoint certain problems more precisely, some firms find it desirable to divide certain individual measurements into several more detailed measurements. *Each firm selects a manageable number of measurements that are tailored to its particular needs.*[1]

In the following discussion, measurement factors are classified according to the *primary* purchasing objectives whose attainment they help achieve.

---

[1] For a good overview of this topic, see Jim Morgan and Robert Monczka, "Today's Measurements Just Don't Make It," *Purchasing,* Apr. 21, 1994, pp. 46–50.

Controlling the Timing Factor A purchasing and supply department's first responsibility is to support the firm's line operations. The following measurements indicate how effectively this responsibility is fulfilled.

1 Identification and percentage of major suppliers that meet on-time delivery requirements.
2 Percentage of overdue orders. To provide more direct control, a weekly or more frequent list of overdue orders can be reported.
3 Average lead-time report by material and supplier.
4 Number of production stoppages caused by late deliveries.
5 Actual expediting expense compared with budgeted expediting expense.
6 Premium transportation costs paid.

Targets (standards) against which most of these measurements are compared are based on historical performance and subjective assessments of possible improvement. An initial categorization of these data by material classification usually provides an adequate basis from which subsequent control action can be taken.

Controlling Quantity and Inventory Investment Closely related to the preceding measures of operations support effectiveness are the following three measures:

1 Percentage of stock-outs caused by poor JIT performance.
2 Number of production stoppages caused by poor JIT performance.
3 Actual stock supply "service level" compared with a target service-level figure.

Other measurements useful in controlling the quantity factor are:

4 A chart showing target and actual inventory levels in the aggregate and by major material classification. This chart is most useful when supplemented with a chart showing inventory turnover rates (annual material usage divided by average inventory) for the same material classifications. When analyzed together, these charts point up imbalances between inventory carrying costs and material acquisition costs.
5 A report of "dead stock" materials in stores, resulting from overbuying or requirements changes. The report should be classified by major material classes, listing the items in each class and their respective dollar values.
6 A list of supplier stocking arrangements that have been negotiated and an estimate of resulting inventory savings.

Controlling Prices and Costs of Materials The following techniques provide a cross-check on the reasonableness of prices paid for materials.

1 The number of partnering arrangements and the estimated annual cost savings from them should be tracked over time.
2 The number of long-term contracts utilized and the estimated savings produced by them should be tracked over time.

- Percentage of purchasing expenditures covered by long-term contracts

3 Target prices should be established for most major materials. Prices actually paid can then be charted against the target figures to display any significant differences. Targets commonly used are:

- A "should be" price based on a competitive market analysis of cost, quality, and design
- Historical prices, adjusted for inflation and other relevant factors
- Standard cost figures developed jointly by accounting and purchasing personnel
- Producer prices (wholesale) and commodity prices published by the Department of Labor and the Department of Commerce
- GSA prices for MRO and office purchases, published by the General Services Administration

4 A materials budget, utilizing standard price data, can be used to achieve the same result. However, the preceding technique provides a more direct measurement which can be interpreted more easily and more quickly.

5 A firm can develop its own weighted average "price paid" indexes for major classes of materials. If developed on a comparable basis, these indexes can be charted against various national commodity price indexes such as the producer price index (PPI) published by the Bureau of Labor Statistics. Such comparisons reveal cases in which a firm's materials costs may be rising or declining more than market prices during an inflationary or deflationary period. Viewed over time, the *trend* of the buyer's own weighted index can also provide useful control information.[2]

6 A growing number of firms have developed measurements to identify unique follow-on costs that stem from doing business with specific suppliers. The factors most commonly measured are:

- Supplier quality nonperformance costs
- Supplier delivery nonperformance costs
- Supplier service nonperformance costs

These measurements reveal unique elements of cost, in addition to price, associated with purchases from a given supplier.

7 Periodic cost-savings figures can be charted individually for savings arising from such activities as consolidated volume buying in multiplant operations, negotiation, value analysis design changes, value analysis material changes, cost analysis, supplier suggestions, changing suppliers, packaging improvements, and transportation cost reduction projects.

The development of accurate figures for such projects sometimes poses a problem because of the variables involved. Numerous individuals,

---

[2]The General Motors Corporation's use of price targets and Bureau of Labor Statistics price indexes to provide an independent measurement of purchasing performance is discussed in an excellent article by its director for international trade. See Patrick L. Hanafee, "Use of Price Indexes in MRO Buying," *Journal of Purchasing and Materials Management,* Spring 1981, pp. 2–9.

teams, and departments often contribute to the solution of a single prob-lem—and all should receive credit for the accomplishment. Additionally, at times questions arise concerning the magnitude of savings figures and the validity of the time period used in computing repetitive savings. For these reasons, it is wise to have a separate auditing group coordinate the development of the actual figures. The credibility of the effort depends on the credibility of the figures.

Further, if cost-savings data are used to compare the performance of one buyer or buying group with that of another, usually they must be adjusted to reflect differences in the *potential* for cost savings between those people or jobs being compared. For example, there is usually more opportunity to generate major cost savings when buying specially designed production components than when buying standard office supplies.

8 The number of new product development teams in which one or more buyers and/or suppliers are involved is a useful measure. Although specific cost savings typically are not determined, the volume of this activity over time usually is a good proxy for the resulting manufactur-ing and material cost savings.

9 Gains and losses from forward buying activities should be reported peri-odically to determine forecasting effectiveness. Again, a major problem is the determination of a standard figure to use as a basis for comparison. Typically, prices actually paid during a period are compared with the average market price during the period. While this is a feasible approach, in reality it produces only approximate savings figures. A more precise approach would compare prices paid with prices that would have been paid had the conventional buying schedule been followed. However, this approach requires more clerical effort than typically can be justified.

10 A report of the percentage of purchase orders that are issued without firm prices provides another basis for controlling material costs.

All the preceding measurements can be classified and subclassified in vari-ous ways to pinpoint responsibility for the problems or benefits they reveal. The most useful initial classification, however, is by major material group-ings—then perhaps by buyer, using department, and supplier.

Controlling Material Quality   The following measures are most commonly used to monitor buyers' and suppliers' performance in the area of quality.

1 The number of partnering arrangements and a listing of the quality improvements they have produced is a useful general measure of quality improvement.

• The percentage of purchasing expenditures covered by partnering arrangements is also useful as a trend measurement.

2 The number (and trend) of ISO 9000–registered suppliers can be a good indirect measure of quality.

- The percentage of major suppliers that are ISO 9000–registered is a useful trend measurement.

3 Once material specifications have been established, the most direct measure of quality performance is the percentage or number of delivered materials that are rejected by the inspection and operating departments.
4 Another measure is to track the number of suppliers that have achieved and maintained a "certified supplier" status with the buying firm.
5 For firms utilizing statistical process control, it is useful to track the number of suppliers using SPC, the number of individual SPC applications per supplier, and the number of quality problems detected when reviewing suppliers' SPC control charts in inspection.
6 To check on the improvement of quality specifications, a record can be maintained showing the number and type of design changes and material changes resulting from joint VA/VE work. A record of supplier involvement in these activities can also be maintained.
7 A final indirect measure of quality performance is a record of the extent to which cross-functional supplier qualification and selection teams are used.

Controlling Source Reliability   The following measurements can be used to indicate the reliability of major suppliers:

1 A report of changes in major suppliers, with the rationale for each change.
2 Reports dealing with percentage of late deliveries and percentage of rejected items can be further analyzed and classified by supplier.
3 Percentage of orders on which incorrect materials were shipped.
4 Percentage of orders on which incorrect quantities of materials were shipped.
5 Percentage of orders on which split shipments were made.
6 Some firms combine these and other measurements, by means of a formula, into a single supplier rating which is published and used for control purposes. This approach is discussed in detail in Chapter 20.
7 To provide close control of partnering and single-source suppliers of nonstandard materials, a periodic report should be made summarizing for each supplier the percentage of rejected materials, the percentage of late deliveries, lead times, cost reductions, and the dollar volume of business handled.
8 The quality of transportation service offered by various carriers can be appraised partially by maintaining records of transit times, damaged shipments, and carrier suggestions for quality and cost improvements.

Managing Supplier Relationships   This intangible factor is extremely difficult to control because of the numerous nebulous activities that combine to shape suppliers' opinions. However, a periodic supplier survey is useful and probably is the most common method used to monitor performance in this area. The survey typically is conducted by means of a mail questionnaire. Although responding suppliers normally remain anonymous, various techniques can be used to relate responses to material classifications or to buyers for control purposes. The following questions appear on one firm's questionnaire:

1 Are your sales representatives always received in a friendly, courteous, businesslike manner by our purchasing personnel?
2 Are your personnel kept waiting in our reception room longer than is necessary?
3 Do our buyers devote full attention to the interview, with only a reasonable number of distractions?
4 Are you allowed a sufficient amount of time in each interview?
5 Do our buyers solicit your suggestions and ideas?
6 Are you urged by our buyers to develop new ideas and methods that will help *both* firms cut costs?
7 Do the buyers with whom you do business have a satisfactory knowledge of the items they purchase?
8 Do you believe that our buyers are concerned excessively with price considerations?
9 Do you consider our buyers' negotiation techniques to be satisfactory?
10 Are our buyers overly critical of your products and services?
11 Do you believe that our buyers all have high ethical standards?
12 How could we make better use of your firm's know-how and experience?
13 Do you always receive fair treatment in your dealings with our purchasing personnel?
14 Do we place too many rush orders with you?
15 Do we expect only services that are reasonably justified?
16 How would you rate our purchasing department as compared with other firms' departments with which you are familiar?
17 With which buyers do you normally come in contact?
18 We would appreciate any additional comments or suggestions.

Supplier Councils Closely related to the management of supplier relationships is the use of *supplier councils.* To help in evaluating purchasing performance, a number of leading firms have developed one or more supplier councils. Such a council is composed of a representative group of suppliers (ten to twelve top-level managers) from a firm's "preferred" supplier base that works with the buying firm's top management (six to eight people) to develop improved relationships and supply practices. A council typically meets two to four times a year to explore specific buyer-supplier issues. For example, the John Deere organization's objectives for its supplier council are to:[3]

---

[3]"John Deere Harvester Works and Waterloo Works Establish a Supplier Council," *Supply Management News,* Winter 1992/1993, p. 1.

- Detect and resolve problems based on supplier identification of problems which add cost to purchased material and components
- Improve quality through continuous improvement of processes, components and assemblies, and services
- Improve communications between each factory unit of Deere and its suppliers
- Identify and implement strategies that will make Deere a world-class customer

Controlling Internal Coordination   A purchasing and supply department can partially determine how successfully it coordinates its efforts with those of other departments by evaluating the effectiveness of certain joint activities (e.g., the joint development of materials standards with users, joint value analysis investigations with engineering, joint establishment of order quantities with production control). Unfortunately, these assessments tend to be somewhat haphazard and difficult to make. Moreover, they cover only a few isolated cases out of the many potential possibilities for coordination.

Consequently, many purchasing and supply units now conduct periodic surveys of the departments they serve to supplement their own subjective assessments of performance in this area. By means of a *biennial questionnaire,* one firm asks its using departments the following questions:

1 Does the purchasing department regularly provide you with a list of estimated lead times for the items you use?
2 Do you believe that the buyers who handle your requirements know enough about the key items to make intelligent purchasing decisions?
3 Is the quality of material the purchasing department obtains for you always suitable for your needs?
4 Does the buyer who handles your requirements periodically visit personally with your departmental staff?
5 Is he or she familiar with the operations and problems of your department?
6 Does he or she assist you in planning your materials requirements?
7 Does he or she keep you informed regarding delays, estimated delivery dates, and so on for materials that you have requisitioned?
8 Does he or she periodically bring a supplier's representative to your department to discuss cost-saving proposals?
9 Are you always treated in a friendly, courteous, businesslike manner by purchasing and supply personnel?
10 Do you believe that buyers are taking advantage of cost-saving ideas and recommendations of suppliers?
11 Do you think that buying personnel continually urge suppliers to develop new methods and ideas that will help you cut your costs and improve your operations?
12 Do the materials you requisition usually arrive on time?

13 How often do buyers arbitrarily change the quality specifications on your purchases without consulting you?

14 How long does it take, on the average, for the stores department to fill your requisition for items that are carried in inventory?

15 Additional comments and suggestions.

The success of interdepartmental coordination is evidenced by the extent to which using departments follow published purchasing policies and procedures. To check on this phase of coordination, some firms periodically have buyers formally evaluate using departments' performance on such matters as unauthorized negotiations with suppliers, cooperativeness in reducing material costs by changing specifications and suppliers, allowance for sufficient purchasing lead time in planning requirements, correctness and completeness of requisitions, and so on.

When used together, the preceding three techniques provide a reasonably good measurement of purchasing's performance in the area of service to and coordination with its internal customers.

Composite Audit of Buying Performance   To supplement the use of *selected techniques* from the preceding lists, some firms continually audit a small random sample of completed purchase orders or contracts in each major material classification. Such an audit typically is conducted on a weekly basis and entails a *careful evaluation of total buying performance*. Each order or contract reviewed is scrutinized closely to determine whether the buyer (1) used the appropriate method of purchase, (2) conducted a thorough price analysis, (3) consolidated order requirements advantageously, (4) handled bids properly, (5) selected the supplier wisely, (6) devoted sufficient value analysis effort to the order, and (7) obtained the appropriate quality of material.

When conducted on a continuing basis, such an audit frequently detects newly developing problems more quickly than do the other techniques using aggregate measurements. Moreover, the psychological effect of the audit usually stimulates buyers to higher and more consistent levels of performance.

The Value of Statistical Trends   Valid and accurate *absolute* standards are difficult to determine for many of the preceding measurements. Even so, most firms find it helpful to *compare present performance with past performance.* Although a firm has no assurance that past performance occurred at an optimal level, such a comparison does indicate the *trend* of performance and serves as a basis for setting priorities and developing plans for future improvement. In addition, graphing each measurement over a period of time is an excellent method of portraying performance to facilitate quick visualization and comprehension of progress.

The need for careful interpretation of the preceding statistical measurements cannot be overemphasized. Many of the performance measures are interrelated in such a manner that improvement of one factor may contribute to poorer performance of another factor (e.g., the relationship of material quality measurements and delivery time measurements in the case of certain materials or suppliers). Further, the behavior of numerous operating variables such as production demands, departmental workloads, suppliers' problems, and so on significantly influences short-run performance. The purchasing and supply manager must look beyond the statistics themselves carefully to determine their true meanings and significance.

Controlling Procurement Efficiency

Every purchasing manager wants to achieve a high degree of buying effectiveness and, at the same time, utilize the department's resources as efficiently as possible. A number of measurements can be used only as guides in controlling departmental efficiency, but they must be used in a very general way. Too much emphasis on efficiency can easily decrease buying effectiveness. The challenge is to determine the optimal level of operating efficiency that still permits personnel to do a thorough, proficient job of buying. Because this problem can never be solved completely, few *absolute* standards of efficiency are used in practice. Purchasing and supply management customarily compares *trends* of efficiency measurements with *trends* of effectiveness measurements in an attempt to determine the optimum combination which yields a maximum net purchasing profit.

Buying Efficiency   Although many different statistics are used to reflect buying efficiency, some combination of the following measurements is most common. Most of the measurements can be broken down by buying group, by buyer, and by commodity, as is most useful for control purposes.

Workload Measurements

1 *Number of noncontract purchase orders issued per period* (and per working day). Useful related information is:

   - Number of new requisitions per period
   - Number of open contracts requiring administration
   - Number of blanket order releases per period

2 *Purchasing processing time report.* Many firms periodically sample the orders issued to determine the percentage of purchase requests processed in one day, two days, three days, and so on. This report provides data useful in detecting imbalanced workloads and purchasing bottlenecks. Moreover, it provides another indication of purchasing service to the using departments.

3 *Number of new long-term contracts per period.* This is an extremely important statistic for purchasing management. First, as discussed in Chapter

27, it indicates the extent to which the department has engaged in studying major material needs and has developed commensurate long-term buying plans to meet those needs. Second, the technique reduces total buying time requirements and subsequently the aggregate departmental workload. Total value of all term contracts should also be expressed as:

- A percent of total dollars purchased per period

4 *Number of purchase orders placed against long-term contracts per period.* This statistic, coupled with the blanket order release figure, indicates the extent to which such negotiated arrangements are used to reduce buying time. An additional useful statistic is:

- The percent of total number of orders placed per period

5 *Average number of dollars expended per purchase order per buying group.* Changes in this value provide an indication of buyers' abilities to control low-value purchases. More important, when used in conjunction with the average number of purchase orders issued per day, this statistic helps a manager plan *workloads* and *staffing requirements* as operating conditions change.[4]

6 *Frequency of purchase order size.* Every month (or quarter) some firms sample the orders issued to determine the percentage of orders for purchases under $100, the percentage of orders for purchases between $100 and $500, and so on for the various value classifications they find useful. When possible, it is usually useful to categorize the data also by material classification and by supplier.[5]

These data are extremely useful to purchasing management. They provide specific information required for controlling the allocation of buying time, for initiating standardization projects, for initiating stock-level changes, for developing more effective consolidation of requirements, and for making more effective use of blanket orders, credit card purchasing, and so forth.

7 *Number of rush orders issued per period.* Although this statistic cannot be completely controlled by buyers, it indicates to some extent how effectively rush order control procedures preserve buying efficiency. The number of rush orders also indicates how satisfactorily the routine system is working. Additional useful information is:

- Percent of total number of orders placed per period
- Premium transportation costs incurred

8 *Number of change orders issued during the period.* In addition to measuring the stability of design characteristics and demand, this statistic also par-

---

[4]The experience of several governmental purchasing units reveals that on the average their buyers process between 1.7 and 2.2 requisitions per buyer per hour.

[5]In automated records systems, a complete tabulation of summary data can be obtained inexpensively as a by-product of normal operation.

tially measures the thoroughness with which original buying activities are conducted. Obviously it is a workload measure, as well.

Social Responsibility Measurements

1 *Dollar purchases to small businesses per period*
2 *Dollar purchases to minority businesses per period*

These two measurements are useful for two reasons. First, if the buying firm does business with the federal government, it probably will be required to supply these data as part of the contractual agreement. Completely apart from government contracting requirements, many firms have made commitments of social responsibility to place certain volumes of business with small and minority-owned firms when it is practical to do so. Hence, data provided by these measurements can be utilized directly in such programs.

Departmental Operating Cost Measurements

1 *Purchasing department operating costs per period.* Most firms use a departmental operating budget categorized by nature of expenditure (salaries, travel, telephone, and so on) and by work group. Actual expenditures can thus be expressed in several ways:

- Actual expenditures versus budgeted expenditures
- Operating cost as a percent of material purchase expenditures
- Operating cost as a percent of the firm's operating budget
- Operating cost per purchase order issued

2 *Number of purchasing employees.* This figure may be expressed as:

- A percent of the organization's total number of employees

3 *Employee turnover rate per period.* The following formula typically is used:

$$\frac{\text{Number of terminations per year}}{\text{Average number of departmental employees}} \times 100$$

The statistics included in the first two operating cost measurements have very little meaning by themselves.[6] They vary as much as several hundred percent from one firm to another. It is their *trends* over time that are important to management from the standpoint of control. When their trends are carefully analyzed in conjunction with the trends of other efficiency and effectiveness statistics, they can provide a good indication of the relationship between

---

[6]Good buying efficiency in terms of cost per purchase order may in reality represent only a decrease in the dollar amount of each purchase order and an accompanying increase in the number of purchase orders issued. Similarly, a reduction in the cost of committing each purchase dollar may merely be the result of spending more than necessary for some of the items purchased.

departmental cost and such factors as business volume, material quality, and total material costs.

General Information

1 *Purchases per year* in dollars
2 *Company sales per year* in dollars
3 *Dollar purchases ÷ dollar sales* = percent per year

It is useful for purchasing management to know what percent of the firm's sales dollar is expended for materials—and what variations occur from year to year. As was discussed in the first chapter, this statistic provides some insight into the potential impact purchasing can exert on a firm's net profit. Indirectly, too, it provides a clue to the level of departmental budget support that might be justified.

Efficiency of Personnel The following techniques and records are helpful in controlling performance in this area.

1 *Performance standards for clerical jobs.* It is entirely feasible to develop per-formance standards that are acceptable to employees for the repetitive jobs in purchasing, receiving, stores, and inventory control.[7] Although most standards for such work are not as precise as factory standards, they can nevertheless be used very effectively in controlling the volume of clerical performance over the period of a week or longer.[8]
2 *Study of time utilization for nonrepetitive jobs.* Although satisfactory perfor-mance standards (for the volume of work done) can rarely be developed for jobs requiring creative intellectual activity, a manager can take a step in this direction which definitely facilitates control. The work habits of buyers and managers (including the chief purchasing executive) should be studied periodically to detect inefficiencies in their patterns of activity.

   A work sampling study, for example, can accurately reveal to a buyer the proportion of his or her time devoted to the various activities of the job. Such data may well indicate that too much time is being spent on rel-atively inconsequential matters. This awareness perhaps would call for a reallocation of his or her time. It might also lead to a study and modification of various office and paperwork systems that tend to require the buyer to perform in this manner. In fact, inefficiency in a purchasing office frequently is due more to the use of inefficiently designed systems

---

[7]Of the numerous available techniques, work sampling is the most commonly used today for determining clerical performance standards.

[8]During the past few years, a large insurance firm (with an increasing workload) has reduced the number of clerical jobs in its 3,500 district offices by approximately 35 percent. It has achieved this $5 million annual saving solely by refining procedures and systems and by establishing stan-dards for repetitive clerical jobs.

(management's responsibility) than to ineffective or lackadaisical performance by employees.

3 *The use of models for staffing purposes.* Based on specific operating experience, today growing numbers of firms are developing fairly precise workload models for buyers with different types of responsibilities. The objective is to develop a series of models that establish a standard workload for each type of buyer in the organization. The quantitative data required in the model usually are determined jointly by buyers and managers, based on past experience and judgmental estimates. As the departmental workload expands or contracts, then, the aggregate figure can be divided by the standard workload for a given type of buyer to determine the number of buying positions involved. One firm's buyer models are reported in *The Purchasing Handbook* and are outlined for illustrative purposes in Figure 29-1.[9]

FIGURE 29-1
Illustrative buyer models for workload/staffing estimates.

MODEL 1 BUYER

Buys:	• New subcontracted systems, new forgings, new castings.
Assumptions:	• Buyer has 5 to 7 years experience, is working on systems or parts with 30 weeks lead time, and is buying for 3 programs.
Workload:	• Buyer can handle 25 active part numbers and 3 new requisitions per week.

MODEL 2 BUYER

Buys:	• State-of-the-art products with special testing and data requirements.
Assumptions:	• Buyer has 3 to 5 years purchasing experience, is working on parts with 24 to 30 weeks lead time, and is buying for 5 programs.
Workload:	• Buyer can handle 75 active part numbers and 5 new requisitions per week.

MODEL 3 BUYER

Buys:	• Special parts made to customer specification without special testing.
Assumptions:	• Buyer has 2 or more years experience, is working on parts with 8 weeks lead time, and is buying for 10 programs.
Workload:	• Buyer can handle 340 active part numbers and 30 new requisitions per week.

MODEL 4 BUYER

Buys:	• Standard parts.
Assumptions:	• Buyer has 1 or more years experience, is working on parts with 3 weeks lead time, and is buying for 15 programs.
Workload:	• Buyer can handle 450 active part numbers and 100 new requisitions per week.

[9]Robert B. Ackerman, "Evaluating Purchasing Performance," *The Purchasing Handbook,* McGraw-Hill, Inc., New York, 1992, chap. 11, p. 341.

Receiving and Stores   The key measurements used in planning workloads and controlling efficiency in receiving and stores are noted below.

1 *Average number of incoming shipments received daily.*
2 *Average time required to receive and process an incoming shipment.*
3 *Average number of stores requisitions processed daily.*
4 *Stores loss, obsolescence, and damage report.* A periodic report listing damaged, obsolete, and lost items (traced to stores activities) is helpful in appraising the efficiency of storage methods and handling procedures.
5 *Periodic personal inspection of storage areas.* The stores operation should be inspected periodically to ensure that materials are properly marked, easily located, and adequately stored and protected. Such an inspection also permits an appraisal of safety procedures and general housekeeping practices.

Guidelines for Development and Use of Measurement and Control Systems

At this point in the discussion, it is appropriate to summarize a few key guidelines that are important in the development and implementation of purchasing measurement and control systems. The following seven guidelines are a synthesis of the experience and judgment of a number of practicing managers over a decade or so of experimentation, failures, and successes.

1 Performance measurement systems are a tool of good management—not a substitute for it. The effectiveness of the system will not exceed the perceptiveness and the sensitivities of the managers operating it.
2 A measurement system should be designed to support the individual buyer or the buying team in doing a better job. Correspondingly, these individuals should participate in designing the system and in establishing the standards that affect them and their work.

   Communication is vital in implementing an effective operating system. The system must be clearly understood by all who use and are affected by it.
3 The degree of sophistication of the system should be based on the specific needs of the organization. As long as the system provides the major information required for control—the simpler the better.
4 The cost of a measurement and control system should be balanced against the management value of its output. When the cost of an incremental unit of output exceeds its usefulness, the system should be redesigned and cut back to the point of equilibrium.
5 The measurements of efficiency and effectiveness must be separated. Efficiency measures reflect the resource utilization of the department and tend to be quantitative in nature. Effectiveness measures focus on how well people do their jobs and often involve subjective assessments to some extent. While efficiency is important, buying effectiveness offers far

more opportunity for improved organizational performance.

6 A small number of precise measures typically are more useful than a larger number of less precise approximations. Validity and accuracy are essential for effective use of the results.

7 Systems that measure past performance are of value primarily in providing information and experience that can be used for improvement in the future. Thus, the most effective systems are found in an environment that provides a positive stimulus for the buyer to use the output of the system constructively.

HOW INDUSTRY DOES IT

To this point in the chapter, a fairly large number of potentially useful measurements have been discussed briefly and categorized in accordance with major purchasing and supply objectives. As noted at the outset, no firm uses all these measurements. *Each firm selects those that it believes are most useful for its own assessment purposes, and develops its own managerial appraisal and control program.*

In this section three examples of actual industry practice are discussed briefly to provide a basis for comparison with the previous discussions.

Ten Most Commonly Used Measurements

Each year, NAPM's Center for Advanced Purchasing Studies (CAPS) invites approximately sixty top-level purchasing executives from *Fortune* 500 companies to attend its Executive Purchasing Roundtable. For three days at the Roundtable these purchasing professionals discuss a variety of important issues that impact their firms and industries—and the purchasing profession.

One of the topics explored in depth at a recent Roundtable session was the matter of performance measurements for purchasing and supply operations. From that discussion emerged a list of the most frequently used measurements by the *Fortune* 500 firms represented at the Roundtable. The top ten measurements are summarized below.[10]

1 Material cost reductions produced by joint buyer-supplier efforts, categorized by material and supplier

2 Percent of major suppliers that deliver on time, noted by material

3 Percent of orders received within a specified number of days of the due date, noted by material

4 Internal customer satisfaction

5 Material cost savings generated from centralized and consolidated buying activity

---

[10]NAPM/CAPS Executive Purchasing Roundtable, Phoenix, Ariz., Feb. 28 and Mar. 1–2, 1993.

6 Material quality defect rate categorized by material and supplier
7 Documented improvements attributed to strategic supplier partnerships
8 Average supplier lead time, by major materials
9 Percentage of major suppliers "certified" to the buying firm's standards
10 Number of long-term contracts in place, along with dollar volume

The CAPS Benchmarking Program

A benchmark is a point of reference that serves as a standard against which operating data can be compared. In 1989, NAPM's Center for Advanced Purchasing Studies initiated a manufacturing and service industry benchmarking program for purchasing operations. Typically, a cross-section of fifteen to twenty firms *from a given industry* participate with the CAPS organization by providing their operating performance data for nineteen benchmark measurements. For each measurement, CAPS identifies three values—the high, low, and mean—that constitute the typical operating benchmark and the range for company performance *in that industry.*

Thus, a given firm can obtain from CAPS the benchmark data for its industry and compare its own performance with the benchmarks for the nineteen measurements[11]—and answer the question, "How are we doing compared with other firms?" As one might suspect, for a given measurement the high-to-low range of values typically is fairly wide, and clearly there are substantial explainable differences among industries. Nevertheless, such comparisons are useful to a firm's supply management people in a general way in identifying strengths as well as potential problem areas that might be improved to move the firm toward more effective performance.

The nineteen standard cross-industry benchmarks measured by CAPS for approximately twenty-two industries are listed below.[12] (CAPS also provides five industry demographic measurements with the benchmarks.) Note that approximately half are efficiency measurements, while half are essentially effectiveness measurements.

1 Purchase expenditure dollars as a percent of sales dollars
2 Purchasing expense as a percent of sales dollars
3 Purchasing expense as a percent of purchase dollars
4 Purchasing employees as a percent of total company employees
5 Sales dollars per purchasing employee
6 Purchase expenditure dollars per purchasing employee
7 Purchase expenditure dollars per professional purchasing employee
8 Active suppliers per purchasing employee

---

[11]Only the aggregate benchmark data are provided; data from the original participating firms are kept confidential.
[12]"CAPS Summary Benchmark Data, 1993–1994," Center for Advanced Purchasing Studies, Tempe, Ariz., February 1994.

9 Active suppliers per professional purchasing employee
10 Purchase dollars spent per active supplier
11 Purchasing expense per active supplier
12 Change in number of active suppliers during the year
13 Percent of purchases spent with minority-owned suppliers
14 Percent of purchases spent with women-owned suppliers
15 Percent of suppliers accounting for 90 percent of the purchase dollars
16 Purchase order cycle time
17 Percent of purchase dollars processed through EDI
18 Percent of total goods purchased handled by the purchasing department
19 Percent of total services purchased handled by the purchasing department

One Progressive Firm's Approach to Appraisal and Control

One progressive *Fortune* 500 firm links its departmental *performance evaluation* effort with its annual purchasing and supply *planning program.* The idea is to tie its assessment and subsequent control efforts closely to its detailed operating plan for the year—to monitor the effectiveness of its implementation activities and to make appropriate modifications in the following year's plan.

Although this *specific* approach is not widely used, it is illustrative of the *general type* of planning and evaluation approach utilized by an increasing number of forward-looking organizations. An outline of the essential elements of the plan is detailed below.

An Overview of One Company's Approach to Planning and Evaluating Purchasing Performance

I *Elements of the purchasing planning and evaluation program*
  1 An annual detailed departmental plan and self-evaluation (responsibility of each division or plant purchasing manager)
  2 An annual performance review and evaluation by *general management* (responsibility of each division or plant general manager)
  3 A purchasing function performance audit by an "outside" audit team every three years

II *Departmental plan and self-evaluation*
  1 The "rolling" *three*-year plan
    • First, ensure availability of key materials
    • Set *general* targets for:
      Quality
      Delivery   } For the top
      Price   80 percent of
      Overall supplier performance and relationship   purchase dollar
      (alliance, certification, SPC, JIT, service, etc.)   volume

2 Precise *annual* targets
  - Establish *specific* targets for the coming year for each factor listed in item II-1, on a material-by-material (or category-of-material) basis.
3 Detailed plans for achieving item II-2
  - Outline specific actions to be taken, and by whom, including such things as:
    a Material specification development—on selected items EPI/ESI is utilized, or a value-analysis-type study is conducted by an interdepartmental team, to determine optimal spec requirements.
      (1) Make-or-buy analysis is conducted when appropriate.
      (2) Special tooling and capital equipment is included when appropriate.
    b Standardization—when practical, a smaller number of parts and components is established as "standard" by an interdepartmental team.
    c Activities 3a and b are also conducted on an interdivisional basis when appropriate.
    d The consolidation of interdivisional purchases is done by means of corporate contracts, blanket orders, etc.
    e A cost and operating analysis of inbound transportation is conducted.
    f Consistent utilization of a supplier performance evaluation program, when necessary to achieve II-2 and II-3.
    g A planned effort to involve selected suppliers in the company's ongoing value analysis program, when it is potentially profitable to do so.
    h A thorough annual buyer performance evaluation—and assessment of needs.
    i A review of required expertise, technical support, and specific training requirements.
→**4** Departmental self-evaluation
    At the end of each year, based on the details of that year's plan, a thorough evaluation of the preceding year's performance is conducted—on an item-by-item and material-by-material basis.
  - As a result of the analysis, recommendations are generated for inclusion in next year's plan.
→**III** *General management review and evaluation*
  1 At the end of each year, the general manager to whom each purchasing/supply manager reports must:
    - Review the three-year departmental plan
    - Review the departmental plan for the year just past
    - Review specific performance results (information provided as a result of the departmental self-evaluation)
    - Make specific recommendations for improvement to be included in next year's plan

- Based on the preceding activities, provide his or her own rating of department performance on a point-by-point basis
2 Later, when available, the general manager reviews the modified three-year plan and the annual plan for the coming year—and provides feedback to the purchasing manager.
IV *Outside audit*
1 Every three years a performance review is performed by a team of three to five purchasing professionals from outside the unit being audited. The team chairman may be an outside consultant. Audit activities are based on:
- Recommendations from the preceding audit
- Analysis and recommendations from the preceding annual evaluation by the department and by the general manager
- Areas surfacing in a preceding discussion with the general manager
- Findings that develop during the course of the audit
2 The typical time requirement for the review/audit is approximately one week.

Two features of this approach are especially noteworthy. First, in addition to its detail and thoroughness, it uses as its benchmarks the *preceding year's operating plan*, rather than more generic departmental objectives and targets. Second, and perhaps most important, is the fact that *upper-management* people *play an active and well-defined role in both the planning and the performance evaluation processes*. This augurs well for the strategic role purchasing and supply plays in the firm.

REPORTS TO MANAGEMENT

The measurements discussed to this point provide purchasing and supply managers with the detailed data required to appraise and control purchasing activities. The chief purchasing and supply executive, in turn, should summarize the most significant features of this information in periodic reports to top management. Reports for top management should serve two purposes. First, they should provide *new information that management can use in controlling company operations* and in planning future company activities. Second, reports should keep management informed about *key purchasing operations,* and they should apprise management of purchasing's *contribution to the total company effort*.

Consequently, purchasing reports to management should take two forms. **The first report** is usually issued monthly (or biweekly) and contains the following type of information:

1 *A summary of general business conditions* in the major markets the company patronizes
2 *A list of specific price increases or decreases* for the major materials purchased
3 *A summary of trends in lead-time requirements* for major materials
4 *A list of materials that may be in short supply* and a statement outlining the purchasing and supply strategy for coping with each individual problem

This report is designed to inform management of conditions in the materials area that potentially could have a serious impact on the company's total operation.

The second report, usually issued quarterly (or monthly), apprises management of matters dealing primarily with purchasing performance and administrative programs. Typically, it contains the following kinds of information:

1 *A summary of how well purchasing and supply has performed* during the period. This summary should include indications of both purchasing effectiveness and purchasing efficiency. In the section on effectiveness, it is usually desirable to summarize supplier quality and reliability improvements and cost savings resulting from negotiation, supplier initiatives, value analysis, and so forth. The summary figure for savings may be reported as a percentage of total annual purchasing expenditures.

2 *Selected but very brief operating statistics* that are useful to management. Typically, the following items are included: number of department employees and department operating cost, number of new supplier partnering agreements during the period, number of purchase orders issued during the period, number and value of outstanding contracts, and total dollars committed during the period (usually broken down by major material classifications).

3 *A brief discussion of department status and problems.* This section should summarize progress made on projects and undertakings previously reported. It should also point up existing problems in the supply function and indicate what action is being taken to alleviate them.

4 *Future plans.* Plans for significant procurement projects and administrative activities should be summarized to provide clear communication with management on matters which management may want to coordinate with other plans.

Reports to top management should contain only timely information that is of definite value to the recipient. Functional managers at times have difficulty in discriminating between the data they need to appraise and control performance of their departments and the data management needs to appraise and control the operations of the total firm. Whenever possible, data should be presented graphically to facilitate interpretation. The objective of management reports is to present key departmental data in concise form so that they can be quickly and clearly understood.

CONCLUSION

Performance evaluation and control constitute the last step in the management process. No matter how well the preceding planning and procurement work may have been done, much of it can be rendered largely ineffective if the control element fails to function well. Failure may result from a poorly designed system or from poor execution by management.

During the past decade, control of the procurement function has become even more important than it was previously. Competition has become keener for most firms as a result of increasing pressures from the cost-price squeeze. Additionally, the cost of materials, as a percent of total product cost, continues to increase for most organizations. Compounding these problems for some firms are volatile markets and prices that create planning difficulties and periodic material shortages. These three factors have combined to make thorough evaluation and tight procurement control an absolute essential for many organizations.

The silver lining of these ominous clouds is the fact that most firms now have a sophisticated computer-based information system for their procurement operations. If planned properly when the system and the data base are designed, it is possible for a computer-based system to "massage" a large amount of data and produce numerous timely performance evaluation reports. Hence, despite the fact that purchasing is innately difficult to control, more thorough and less expensive control can be achieved under these conditions.

FOR DISCUSSION

29-1 Define and discuss the use of preaction control.

29-2 Define and discuss the use of a postaction control system. What are the objectives of postaction control?

29-3 What general criteria should a manager use in determining the points at which to control the performance of his or her organization? Explain.

29-4 "Establishing a realistic performance standard against which to compare actual performance is usually the most difficult part of the control process." Explain this statement.

29-5 List and discuss the major problems involved in controlling purchasing performance.

29-6 Explain the difference between purchasing efficiency and purchasing effectiveness. Which is more important? Explain.

29-7 Why is a management review of the purchasing and supply department useful in controlling departmental performance? Explain.

29-8 How does the use of a JIT system affect a purchasing department's control system? Explain.

29-9 How can producer price index data be used in the development of a purchasing performance control system? Explain.

29-10 How does a supplier's use of an SPC system affect a buyer's traditional quality monitoring system? Explain.

29-11 Assume that as a purchasing and supply manager you have just received a production report which indicates that your department has caused an excessive number of material stock-outs and an excessive number of production stoppages due to material shortages. Outline in step-by-step fashion exactly how you would proceed to correct the situation. What additional facts must you know? Discuss.

29-12 Develop three additional questions that could be used advantageously on the supplier relations survey questionnaire shown in the text.

29-13 Develop three additional questions that could be used advantageously on the departmental internal coordination survey questionnaire shown in the text.

29-14 What is a supplier council? Explain how it works.

29-15 What potential weaknesses do you see in the use of a supplier council?

29-16 Why is it difficult to appraise purchasing efficiency?

29-17 How would you develop a buyer model for use in making purchasing department staffing estimates? What problems would you expect to encounter?

29-18 What problems arise in establishing value analysis cost-saving targets (or standards) for buyers? What problems arise in administering such a control program? Discuss.

29-19 Assume you are a purchasing and supply department manager. Outline how you would proceed to establish and place in operation performance standards for the clerical personnel in the purchasing office. Discuss not only what you would do but also the problems you anticipate and how you would overcome them.

29-20 What is the CAPS benchmarking program? From a user's point of view, what do you see as its strengths and weaknesses?

29-21 What do you think is the major benefit of the planning and assessment approach described on page 692–694?

29-22 Develop a reporting system for the supply manager of a steel-fabricating firm (employing 110 people) to use in reporting to the company president. Design the system completely, including forms and any explanations required.

29-23 What impact does utilization of a computer have on a manager's ability to evaluate and control purchasing operations?

CASES FOR CHAPTER 29

The Centennial Company, page 798
Golden Buffalo, Inc., page 827
Eagle Machine, Inc., page 814

30

LEGAL CONSIDERATIONS

KEY CONCEPTS

- The Uniform Sales Act
- The Uniform Commercial Code
- Status of an agent
- The purchase contract
    Offer and acceptance
    Consideration; competent parties; legality
- Inspection and rejection rights
- Title
- Warranties
- Order cancellation and breach of contract
    Liquidated damages
- JIT contracts
- Arbitration
- Honest mistakes
- Patent infringement
- Restraint of trade laws
- Product liability and purchasing
- International considerations
    Convention on the International Sale of Goods
    The Foreign Corrupt Practices Act
- The buyer's responsibility

In professional life most purchasing professionals seldom, if ever, become involved in litigation. Yet their daily activities are subject to two major areas of the law—the law of agency and the law of contracts. A purchasing manager or a buyer acts as an agent for his or her firm. Legally, this relationship is defined and governed by the law of agency. When a purchaser buys materials and services from other firms, each purchase involves the formation of a purchase contract. Should a serious disagreement arise between the purchaser and the supplier, the dispute would normally be settled by a court of law or, if the contract provides for arbitration, by an arbitrator. In either case, the dispute would be resolved in accordance with the law of contracts.

A purchasing manager's basic responsibility is to conduct the firm's procurement business as efficiently and expeditiously as possible. Buying policies and practices are therefore predicated primarily on business requirements and business judgment, rather than on legal considerations. As Professor Dean Ammer has aptly stated, "A highly legalistic approach is both unnecessary and unprofitable." From a business standpoint, contractual disputes can normally be resolved much more effectively and with less cost by negotiation. A lawsuit almost always alienates a good supplier. Additionally, the outcome of any court case is usually uncertain; otherwise there would be little need for court action. Litigation is also costly, even in the event of a favorable decision. The total cost of legal fees, executive time diverted to the dispute, and disrupted business operations is seldom recovered from damage awards. For these reasons, in settling disputes, most business firms utilize litigation only as a last resort.

The fact that a purchasing executive tries to avoid litigation, however, does not mean that he or she can overlook the legal dimensions of the job. On the contrary, a basic knowledge of relevant legal principles is essential to success. Unless a purchasing manager understands the legal implications of his or her job—and actions—legal entanglements are almost certain to crop up from time to time.

The purpose of this chapter is to review briefly some of the principal legal concepts as they relate to a purchasing professional's responsibilities. The chapter does not attempt to provide a complete discussion of these concepts. Most purchasing people should acquire some depth in the field through selected studies in commercial law.

DEVELOPMENT OF COMMERCIAL LAW

Historically, each state developed its own body of statutes and common law to deal with the problems prevalent in its particular spheres of activity. This ultimately led to the creation of a series of commercial laws that varied widely from state to state—a situation that obviously produced difficulties for businesses involved in interstate commerce.

In an attempt to promote uniformity among the laws applicable to business transactions, the American Bar Association created a committee known as the National Conference of Commissioners on Uniform State Laws (NCCUSL). The assignment of this group was to codify (i.e., set forth in writing) the laws applying to various business transactions. Its first product was the Uniform Negotiable Instruments Law, followed by the Uniform Stock Transfer Act, the Uniform Conditional Sales Act, the Uniform Bills of Lading Act, the Uniform Warehouse Receipts Act, and the *Uniform Sales Act.*

The work of purchasing professionals has been influenced most heavily by the Uniform Sales Act, which contributed substantially to the uniformity of laws affecting sales and contracts. Unfortunately, however, in practice the act still left much to be desired. It permitted each state considerable latitude in applying its own laws of contract, and decisions on legal interpretations still varied widely among state courts. Moreover, only about three-quarters of the states adopted the Uniform Sales Act.

Recognizing the need for modernization, and noting the sporadic adoption of the act in the face of increasing interstate trade, the NCCUSL joined with the American Law Institute in the early 1940s to formulate a new uniform code. The resulting code, entitled the *Uniform Commercial Code* (UCC), was published in 1952; refined versions of the code followed, with the most recent being published in 1991. Although the UCC deals with a wide range of commercial activities, Article 2 deals specifically with the sale and purchase of goods. The UCC does not apply to the purchase of services.

A fundamental difference between the UCC and the Uniform Sales Act lies in the basic underpinnings of the acts themselves. The Uniform Sales Act determined many rights and obligations of contract parties on the basis of title; that is, such decisions depended heavily on which party had title to the material. The UCC, on the other hand, determines rights and obligations on the basis of fairness and reasonableness in the light of accepted business practice. Thus, the code is geared more closely to the needs and circumstances found in daily business operations.

Today, the UCC has been adopted by all the states except Louisiana.[1] It has effectively eliminated a majority of the important differences that existed between the commercial laws of the various states and has also provided new statutory provisions to fill many of the gaps in the prior laws. It should be noted, however, that the code is silent on some matters covered by earlier laws. Consequently, unless superseded by provisions of the UCC, earlier laws dealing with matters such as principal and agent, fraud, mistakes, coercion, and misrepresentation continue in effect and supplement the provisions of the code.

Topics treated throughout the rest of the chapter therefore reflect the provisions of the UCC where applicable, as well as the provisions of earlier laws not displaced by the code.

---

[1]Louisiana has enacted only parts of the UCC.

BASIC LEGAL CONSIDERATIONS

Status of an Agent

In the legal sense, an *agent* is a person who, by express or implied agreement, is authorized to *act for* someone else in business dealings with a third party. Regardless of the job title, this is precisely what purchasing managers and buyers do. A "purchasing agent" is not a legal party to his or her business transactions, but rather serves as an intermediary. In this capacity, the law requires the agent to be loyal to the employer (the principal) and to perform his or her duties with diligence, dedication, and capability. Because the purchasing agent has agreed to act for the benefit of the employer, the law permits the employer to hold its purchasing agent(s) personally liable for any secret advantages gained for himself or herself or for any aid given to competitors.

The authority under which a buyer functions is granted by the employer. Since the law requires him or her to operate within the bounds of this authority, it behooves every buyer to know as precisely as possible the types of transactions in which he or she can and cannot legally represent the firm. In practice, the amount of authority delegated to buyers varies significantly among companies. Hence, it is difficult for sales representatives to know the exact limits of a particular buyer's authority. Consequently, under the law, a buyer operates under two types of authority—*actual authority* and *apparent authority*. Although a salesperson may not know the buying agent's actual authority, if both act in good faith the law says that the sales representative can reasonably assume that the buyer has apparent authority comparable with that of similar agents in similar companies.

The significance of "apparent authority" becomes evident upon examination of a buyer's legal liability. For example, if an agent acts outside his or her actual authority *but within what can reasonably be inferred as his or her apparent authority,* the seller generally can hold the agent's firm liable for the agent's action. However, the firm, in turn, can legally bring suit against the agent for acting beyond the limit of his or her actual authority. On the other hand, if an agent exceeds the limits of both his or her actual and apparent authority, a seller usually cannot hold the firm liable, but may be able to hold the agent personally liable for the action. In both of these situations, however, if the seller knows at the time of the act that the agent is exceeding his or her authority, the seller generally has no legal recourse against the agent or the firm.

Just as purchasing professionals occupy the legal status of buying agents for their firms, sales representatives similarly hold the status of selling agents for their firms. Buyers and purchasing managers, however, usually are classified as *general* agents, while salespeople typically are classified as *special* agents, having somewhat more restricted authority. Consequently, *in most cases a salesman or saleswoman does not have the authority to bind a company to a sales contract or to a warranty.* The courts usually hold that, unless otherwise stated, as special agents sales representatives have authority only to solicit orders. It is important that buyers recognize this fact. On important jobs, to ensure that a legally binding contract does in fact exist, a buyer should require acceptance of the order by an authorized company officer, normally one of the supplier's sales managers who customarily serve as the company's general agent for this purpose.

The Purchase Contract

Although a legalistic approach to purchasing is in most cases unnecessary, every buyer nevertheless must protect his or her company against potential legal problems. The buyer's major responsibility in this regard is to ensure that each purchase contract is satisfactorily drawn and legally binding on both parties. To be valid and enforceable, a contract must contain four basic elements: (1) agreement ("meeting of the minds") resulting from an offer and an acceptance; (2) consideration, or mutual obligation; (3) competent parties; and (4) a lawful purpose.

Offer and Acceptance   When a buyer sends a purchase order to a supplier, this act usually constitutes a legal offer to buy materials in accordance with the terms stated in the order. Agreement does not exist, however, until the supplier accepts the offer; when this occurs, the law deems that a "meeting of the minds" exists regarding the proposed contract. In the event that a buyer requests a quotation or a bid from a supplier, the supplier's quotation usually constitutes an offer. Agreement then exists when the buyer accepts the quotation (often by subsequently sending a purchase order to the supplier).

Under the Uniform Sales Act, the law required acceptance of an offer in terms that were identical with the terms of the offer—the mirror image concept. The UCC, however, eliminates this stringent requirement. The code states that "conduct by both parties which recognizes the existence of a contract is sufficient to establish a contract or sale although the writings of the parties do not otherwise establish a contract." The code also recognizes suppliers' standard confirmation forms and acknowledgment forms as a valid acceptance, *even if the terms stated thereon are different from the terms of the offer.*

When the terms of an acceptance differ from the terms of the offer—the so-called battle of the forms—the terms of the acceptance will automatically be incorporated in the contract unless one of three conditions exists: (1) They materially alter the intent of the offer, (2) the offeror objects in writing, or (3) the offer explicitly states that no different terms will be accepted. What happens when an offer and an acceptance contain *conflicting terms,* and yet none of the preceding conditions exist? All terms except the conflicting terms become part of the contract, and the conflicting terms are simply omitted from the contract. The buyer and the supplier subsequently are expected to resolve the issues covered by the conflicting terms. This provision of the code substantially clarifies the legal position of many such purchase orders. Moreover, as a consequence, it is clear that a wise buyer should carefully review the terms contained in a supplier's acceptance.

The code contains another important provision relating to the acceptance of an offer to buy. It recognizes as valid the communication of an acceptance in "any manner and by any medium reasonable to the circumstances." Consequently, when a supplier receives an order for the purchase of material for immediate delivery, it can accept the offer either by prompt acknowledgment of the order or by prompt shipment of the material. The code thus permits *prompt supplier performance* of such proposed contracts to constitute acceptance of the offer. The contract becomes effective when the supplier ships the material.

A hitherto longstanding principle of commercial law stated that an offer could be revoked by the offeror at any time before it had been accepted, regardless of the time period stipulated in the offer. The UCC has changed this principle with respect to the purchase or sale of goods. The code states that a *written* offer to buy or sell material must give the offeree assurance that the offer will be held open for the time period stipulated in the offer. If no time period is stipulated, the offer can be assumed firm for a "reasonable" period of time, not to exceed three months.

This provision of the code has significant implications for industrial purchasers and their potential suppliers. Purchasers can use suppliers' quotations in making precise manufacturing cost calculations and rely on the fact that the quotations cannot be revoked before a certain date. Without the code, no such assurance existed. On the other hand, this provision prevents a buyer from canceling an order, without legal obligation, prior to acceptance. An offer to buy, like an offer to sell, must also remain firm for a stated or a reasonable period of time. To maintain firm control, it is now doubly important that the buyer state in the order the length of time for which the offer is valid (or the date by which acceptance of the order is required).

Consideration   In addition to a meeting of minds, a valid contract must also contain the element of obligation. Most purchase contracts are bilateral; that is, *both parties* agree to do something they would not otherwise be required to do. The buyer promises to buy from the supplier certain material at a stated price; the supplier promises to deliver the material in accordance with stated contract conditions. The important point is the *mutuality of obligation.* The contract must be drawn so that each party (or promisor) is bound. If both are not bound, in the eyes of the law neither is bound. Hence, no contract exists.

A buyer is confronted with the practical significance of the "mutual obligation" concept when he or she formulates the terms of purchase. The statements regarding material quantity, price, delivery, and so on must be specific enough to bind both the buyer's firm and the supplier to definable levels of performance. In writing a blanket purchase order for pipe fittings, for example, it is not sufficient to state the quantity as "all company X desires." Such a statement is too indefinite to bind company X to any specific purchase. However, if the requirement were stated as "the quantity company X uses during the month of March," most courts would consider this sufficient to define X's purchase obligation. It is also prudent to qualify such a statement by indicating approximate minimum and maximum levels of consumption.

Similar situations arise in specifying prices and delivery dates. Some companies, for example, occasionally issue unpriced purchase orders. Aside from the questionable wisdom of such a business practice, a legal question concerning the definiteness of the offer also exists. From a legal standpoint, the question which must be answered is: Under existing conditions, can the price be determined precisely enough to define the obligations of both parties? The UCC provides more latitude in answering this question than did the Uniform Sales Act. The code specifically says that a buyer and a supplier can make a binding contract without agreeing on an exact price until a later date. If at the time of shipment a price cannot be agreed on, the code includes provisions by which a fair price shall be determined. On such orders, however, a buyer should protect his or her firm by noting a precise price range or by stating how the price is to be determined.

Competent Parties   A valid contract must be made by persons having full contractual capacity. A contract made by a minor or by an insane or intoxicated person is usually entirely void or voidable at the option of the incompetent party.

Legality of Purpose   A contract whose purpose is illegal is automatically illegal and void. A contract whose primary purpose is legal, but one of whose ancillary terms is illegal, may be either void or valid, depending on the seriousness of the illegality and the extent to which the illegal part can be separated from the legal part of the contract. The latter situation may occasionally have relevance for buyers. Such would be the case, for example, if a material were purchased at a price which violated restraint of trade or price discrimination laws.

The Written and the Spoken Word   Buyers should be aware of several basic concepts concerning the construction of a contract. Contrary to common belief, a contract is not a physical thing. It is actually a relationship which exists between the parties making the contract. When a contract is reduced to writing, the written document is not in fact the contract; it is simply evidence of the contract. Hence, a contract may be supported by either written or oral evidence. In most cases, courts hold an oral contract to be just as binding as a written one, although it may be substantially more difficult to prove the facts on which an oral contract is based. However, the law currently requires some types of agreements to be in writing. In the case of sales transactions between qualified "merchants,"[2] for example, the UCC specifically states that when a

---

[2]Section 2-104 of the UCC defines a "merchant" as one who deals in goods; one who holds himself out as having particular skill in the subject matter; or one who uses a person who holds himself out as having such knowledge or skill. Hence, it is generally held under this broad definition that almost every person in business, including a purchasing officer, is a "merchant." Even a person not in business may be classified as a "merchant" if he or she employs a purchasing officer or broker.

selling price of $500 or more is involved, the contract must be reduced to writing to be enforceable.[3] As noted earlier, though, provisions of the UCC are studied on a continuing basis to detect the need for possible changes or updating. As a result of this action, it is likely that the requirement for contracts exceeding $500 to be in written form may be modified somewhat in the near future.[4] Purchasing professionals should stay abreast of such potential changes.

In the event an oral contract between a supplier and buyer is later confirmed in writing, the *written confirmation* is binding on both parties if no objection is raised within ten days. Hence, it is important to note that when a contract is reduced to writing, the written evidence supersedes all prior oral evidence. The courts generally hold that a contract expressed in writing embodies all preceding oral discussion pertinent to the agreement. Generally speaking, this means that a buyer cannot legally rely on a supplier's oral statements concerning a material's performance or warranty unless the statements have been included in the written agreement. Consequently, from a legal standpoint, a buyer should consider carefully the content of his or her oral negotiations with a supplier and ensure that all relevant data to be included in the contract have been reduced to writing. The buyer should also be aware that courts have ruled that written or typed statements take precedence over printed statements on the contract form, should conflicting statements appear in the document.

Finally, in signing a written contract, a buyer or purchasing manager should specifically indicate on the document that he or she is acting in the capacity of an agent for his or her firm. This avoids any possible misinterpretation as to the identity of the parties making the contract. Moreover, all data to be included as part of the contract should appear above the agent's signature. Courts have ruled that data appearing below the signature are informational only and not part of the contract.

SPECIAL LEGAL CONSIDERATIONS

Inspection Rights

If a purchaser has not previously inspected the material purchased to ensure that it conforms with the terms of the contract, the law gives him or her a reasonable period of time to inspect the material after it is received. If the purchaser raises no objection to the material within a reasonable period of time, he or she is deemed to have accepted it. In court decisions on this matter, it has been largely industry practice which sets the standard for "reasonable" time.

---

[3]Prior to enactment of the UCC, the Statute of Frauds required contracts relating to personal property, for which neither delivery nor payment had been made, to be in writing if the value of the sale exceeded a specified amount; this specified amount varied widely among states.

[4]Gaylord A. Jentz, "More on the UCC Revisions," *NAPM Insights*, November 1993, p. 18.

Rights of Rejection

A purchaser has the right to reject material that does not conform with the terms of the contract. If an overshipment is received, the purchaser can either reject the complete shipment or reject the quantity in excess of the contract. When a buyer does not wish to accept wrongly delivered material, he or she is required only to notify the supplier of this fact, describing specifically the nature of the defect or default. The buyer is not legally bound to return the rejected material. However, the buyer's firm is obligated to protect and care for the material in a reasonable manner. If the buyer neither returns the material nor notifies the supplier of rejection within a reasonable period of time, however, the buying firm is then obligated to pay for the material.

Title

From a legal point of view, the question of which party has title to purchased materials is normally answered by defining the F.O.B. point of purchase. In the case of an F.O.B. origin shipment, the buying firm becomes the owner when the material is loaded into the carrier's vehicle. When material is shipped F.O.B. destination, the supplier owns the material until it is off-loaded at the buyer's receiving dock. A complete discussion of this matter is presented in Chapter 25, "Traffic."

Warranties

The UCC identifies four specific types of warranties:

1 Warranty of title
2 Implied warranty of merchantability
3 Implied warranty of fitness for a particular purpose
4 Express warranty

When a supplier agrees to sell a particular item, the firm implies that it (or its principal) has title to the item and hence has legal authority to sell it. This is the *warranty of title*. The supplier also implies that the item is free from defects in material and workmanship—that it is at least of "fair average quality." This means that the item meets the standards of the trade and that its quality is appropriate for ordinary use. This legal provision is the *implied warranty of merchantability*.

Another implied warranty a buyer *may* receive under certain circumstances is an *implied warranty of fitness for a particular purpose*. If a buyer communicates to a supplier the requirements the purchased material must satisfy, and subsequently relies on the skill or judgment of the supplier in selecting a specific material for the job, the material usually carries an implied warranty of fitness for the stated need. This assumes that the supplier is fully aware of the buyer's need and knows that the buyer is relying on guidance from the supplier's personnel. Hence, it should be amply clear why buyers must insist that purchase orders and related material specifications be written clearly and completely.

If a supplier accepts a purchase order without qualification, descriptions of the material included on the order form—model number, size, capacity, chemical composition, technical specifications, and so on—in fact become an *express warranty*. The supplier warrants that the material delivered will conform to these descriptions. Additionally, suppliers frequently make express warranties for their products in sales and technical literature. Such warranties typically refer to the material's performance characteristics, physical composition, appearance, and so on. If a buyer has no way of determining the facts of the matter and consequently relies on such warranties, the supplier normally is held liable for them. The buyer should also recognize that an express warranty nullifies an implied warranty to the extent that it conflicts with the implied warranty (with the exception of an implied warranty of fitness for a particular purpose).

Numerous variable factors influence the extent to which a buyer can rely on an implied warranty in a specific situation. The knowledge and conduct of both buyer and seller, as well as the specific conditions surrounding a transaction, are taken into consideration by the court in resolving a dispute over warranty. Generally speaking, if a buyer acts in good faith and has no knowledge of conditions contrary to an implied warranty, the law holds a supplier liable for such implied warranties, unless otherwise stated in the contract.

Recent legislation[5] has tended to increase warranty protection for buyers by strengthening and expanding the liability of manufacturers and sellers with respect to warranty performance. A buyer should recognize, however, that the UCC permits a seller to exclude or modify the implied warranty for a product. A supplier can do this by including a *conspicuous* written statement in the sales contract. Statements commonly used to accomplish warranty exclusion are: "This item is offered for sale 'as is,'" or "There are no warranties which extend beyond the description on the face hereof." Interestingly, in several states such warranty disclaimers have been declared to be contrary to public policy—and, hence, invalid. As a general rule, however, a prudent buyer adopts a caveat emptor attitude in verifying the warranty protection he or she actually has in any given purchase.

Order Cancellation and Breach of Contract

If a supplier fails to deliver an order by the delivery date agreed on in the contract, or if it fails to perform in accordance with contract provisions, legally the supplier has breached the contract. The breach usually gives the purchaser the right to cancel the order. In addition, the purchaser can sue for damages if he or she wishes. In practice, the latter right is infrequently exercised because a

---

[5]The Consumer Product Safety Act and the Federal Warranties Act, as well as the UCC.

more effective settlement can usually be negotiated directly with the supplier. Nevertheless, under the law, a buyer may be able to recover damages if injury is actually suffered as a result of a breach of contract. In the case of delivery failure, if the buyer subsequently purchases the material elsewhere, damages are generally limited to the difference between the contract price and the price paid the new supplier. If the material is not available elsewhere, actual damages may be difficult to determine. In any case, the courts usually follow the general rule of attempting to place the injured party in the same financial position he or she would have been in had the contract not been breached.

When no specific delivery date is stated in a contract, the law requires the supplier to deliver within a reasonable period of time. What the buyer thinks is a reasonable period of time may or may not coincide with what the supplier or the court deems to be a reasonable period of time. Hence, in such a situation, a buyer may be on uncertain ground if he or she decides to cancel an order because of nondelivery and subsequently places the order with another supplier. The buying firm may or may not have the legal right to do so. The desirability of including a specific delivery date in the contract thus becomes amply clear.

Situations sometimes arise that compel a buyer to cancel an order before the supplier is obligated to supply the material. In making such a cancellation, the *buyer* breaches the purchase contract. This act legally is termed *anticipatory breach*, and it makes the purchaser liable for any resulting injury to the supplier. If the cancellation results in no real injury to the supplier (as is often the case with orders for standard materials), the supplier can collect no damages. On the other hand, if the cancellation leaves the supplier with partially finished goods in its shop, the firm frequently does suffer injury. In such cases, if the in-process material is salable, the purchaser is usually held liable for the difference between the prorated contract value and the market value of the in-process material. If the material is not salable, the purchaser's liability usually covers the supplier's costs prior to termination plus a reasonable profit[6] on the contract.

Liquidated Damages Provision   If it is evident at the time a major contract is drawn that breach of the contract would severely injure one or both parties and that damages would be difficult to determine, it is wise to include in the contract itself a termination or liquidated damages provision. Such provisions stipulate *in advance* the procedures to be used in determining costs and damages. In some cases, specific damage payments are stated. For example, if the contract is for the purchase of power-generating equipment to be used on a large construction project, the date of delivery may be critical for the purchaser. Perhaps installation of the equipment must precede other important

---

[6]A "reasonable profit" generally is calculated using the same profit margin (percentage rate) as was included in the original contract.

phases of the construction work. If the project is delayed by late delivery of the generating equipment, the purchaser might well incur heavy financial losses. It is therefore normally sound practice on such a contract to include a liquidated damages clause that requires the supplier to pay the purchaser damages of x dollars per day for late delivery. It is essential, however, that the damage figure specified be a reasonable estimate of the probable loss to the buyer, and not be calculated simply to impose a penalty on the supplier. Courts generally refuse to enforce a penalty provision.

A termination or liquidated damages provision represents prior agreement by both parties on the ground rules to be followed in case the contract is breached. If such a breach actually occurs, the provision minimizes the possibility of misunderstandings and the generation of ill will between the two firms.

JIT Contracts

Because just-in-time purchasing and manufacturing operations are somewhat unique, they occasionally generate unexpected legal difficulties. The most common problems are reviewed briefly in the following paragraphs.

The major factor a buyer should keep in mind is that in most cases a JIT purchasing agreement requires different levels of supplier performance than the supplier typically has been used to. Consequently, it is important that communications be clear and complete. This includes oral discussions prior to the purchase, as well as the final written documents. Requirements for quality, quality control, delivery scheduling, inventory levels, and any other key factors should be spelled out in unequivocal terms, so there is little opportunity for misunderstanding that might lead to litigation.

Consider the following illustration. Assume that a buyer and a supplier have been doing business satisfactorily for several years. During the past year, approximately one-third of the shipments from the supplier arrived a week or so late, but the buyer accepted them without serious complaints. In the eyes of the law, these acceptances by the buyer may well have set a precedent which *waives the buyer's rights* to timely delivery on future contracts—not good for a new JIT contract. What must the buyer do to regain his or her rights? The two legal requirements are:

1 Give explicit written notice to the supplier.
2 Provide the supplier a reasonable period of time to gear up to meet the new delivery requirements.

With respect to the timing of design or configuration changes, the contract should always specify the minimal lead time, in terms of days or weeks of material usage, that the supplier will accept prior to supplying the modified material. Both parties should know what the supplier's planned inventory levels are so the firm is not likely to be left with an unusable stock of items built to the buyer's specifications. By the same token, the two must also agree on the minimum practical lead-time requirements for a delivery lot size increase or an accelerated delivery schedule.

The point is that JIT systems must be able to respond quickly to demand changes because of their tight scheduling and low inventory characteristics on the buyer's side. These requirements for flexibility must be built into the purchase contract to the extent possible. Although meshing the buyer's needs with the supplier's capability may be difficult, it is these issues that should be discussed ahead of time, agreed on, and stated in the contract.

Inspection and acceptance is another area that can pose problems. Many JIT shipments are delivered directly to the point of use, without first going through incoming inspection. In many cases, detection of nonconforming items does not occur until some time later, after the item has entered the production process. If no provision for this situation is made in the contract, legally the material may be considered to have been accepted when delivered. Consequently, this modified operating procedure should be detailed clearly in the contract. A satisfactory time frame for acceptance and the responsibility for subsequent rework costs should be stipulated.

In structuring JIT purchase orders and contracts, common sense tells the buyer to be conservative and to include ample detail about these unique issues in the contractual documents.

Arbitration

Serious contract disputes are a rarity in the lives of most purchasing managers. But in a complex business operation, they do arise from time to time. When a dispute does arise, after doing the appropriate "homework," the first step in the resolution process is to discuss the problem with the supplier. Happily, most disputes are resolved at this step through negotiation and compromise. In most cases, the executives involved want to avoid further confrontation simply because it is too time-consuming and too costly.

In the event a satisfactory solution cannot be worked out by the two parties, however, two alternatives remain. They can go to court, or they can employ an impartial arbitrator to settle the dispute. In the latter case, a professional arbitrator will hear testimony and study evidence from both sides, then make an impartial decision based on the facts. This alternative is the one usually chosen because it is much faster and less expensive, and produces less visibility and fuss outside the organization. In the settlement of commercial contract disputes, litigation is usually the last resort.

To avoid the possibility of future litigation on an important contract, buyers sometimes include in the purchase order an arbitration clause. The clause simply says, in effect, that any dispute arising out of the contract will be settled by arbitration, and that both parties will be bound by the decision. Normally, administration of the matter is handled through the American Arbitration Association. If upheld by law, this is an easy and convenient mechanism to use in establishing in advance the ground rules to be followed in the event a serious dispute arises.

To ensure that the ruling of an arbitrator will be legally binding, before preparing the order the buyer should seek assistance from the firm's legal counsel on two points. First, state statutes must be reviewed to determine whether the states in question do in fact have such legal provisions (most, but not all, do). Second, wording of the arbitration clause must be developed carefully in consonance with the state law and guidelines of the American Arbitration Association.

Honest Mistakes

When an honest mistake is made in drawing up a purchase contract, the conditions surrounding each specific case weigh heavily in determining whether the contract is valid or void. As a general rule, a mistake made by only one party does not render a contract void, unless the other party is aware or should be aware of the mistake. To affect a contract, the mistake usually must be made by both parties. Even then, not every mutual mistake invalidates the contract.

Assume, for example, that a supplier intends to submit a quotation with a price of $260. Through an error, the price is typed on the quotation as $250 and is so transmitted to the buyer. In such cases, courts have held that if the buyer accepts the offer, without knowledge of the error, a valid contract exists. The magnitude of the error is deemed insufficient to affect agreement materially. On the other hand, if the $260 price were incorrectly typed as $26, the court would probably hold that a competent buyer should recognize the error, and if one party knows or should know of the other's error, the contract is void.

Mutual mistakes concerning matters of opinion usually do not affect a contract. Neither is a contract affected by immaterial mutual mistakes about matters of fact. However, a mutual mistake concerning *matters of fact that materially affect agreement* usually renders a contract void. Assume, for example, that a buyer and a supplier agree on the sale of specific machinery. If, unknown to either, the machinery has been destroyed or for some other reason is not available for sale, the contract is void.

Generally speaking, a buyer should not assume that a mistake, however innocent, will release his or her firm from a contractual obligation. In the majority of cases, it will not do so. A prudent buyer employs all reasonable means to minimize the possibility of committing contractual mistakes.

Patent Infringement

The law gives a patent holder the exclusive right to manufacture, sell, and use the patented device for a specified number of years. A purchaser who engages in any of these activities during the period of patent protection, without permission from the patent holder, is guilty of patent infringement and can be sued for damages by the patent holder.

Buyers frequently have no way of knowing whether their suppliers are selling patented materials with or without authorization from the patent holder. If a purchaser unknowingly buys an item from a supplier who has infringed the patent holder's rights, the purchaser is also guilty of infringement if the firm uses the item. To protect against such unintentional violations, most companies include a protective clause in their purchase orders which states that the seller will indemnify the purchaser for all expenses and damages resulting from patent infringement. Clauses of this type do not prevent the patent holder from suing the user. If properly stated, however, they can require the seller to defend the user in such legal proceedings and can give the user legal recourse to recover any resulting losses from the seller.

Infringement suits are rare in the normal course of business activities. However, one area where most manufacturing firms frequently encounter potential infringement problems is in the maintenance of productive equipment. In some cases, a complete machine is patented, but its individual parts are not. In other cases, individual parts are patented. In cases where the individual part is not patented, the owner of the machine usually has the right to make a replacement part or to have it made by an outside shop. When the individual part is patented, however, this cannot be done legally without permission from the patent holder.

On the other hand, if the owner of a patented machine wishes to rebuild the machine substantially, such activity is not considered within the range of normal maintenance and repair activity. To accomplish a rebuilding job, the owner must either have it done by the patent holder or obtain the patent holder's permission to do the job himself or herself.

Restraint of Trade Laws

The *Robinson-Patman Act,* a 1936 amendment to the Clayton Act, is designed to prevent price discrimination that reduces competition in interstate commerce. Generally speaking, the act prevents a supplier from offering the same quantity of a specific material to competing buyers at different prices, unless (1) one buyer is offered a lower price because his or her purchases entail lower manufacturing or distribution costs for the supplier, or (2) one buyer is offered a lower price in order to meet the legitimate bid of a competing supplier.[7]

It is important that all buyers be familiar with the detailed provisions of the act, because it also makes it *unlawful for any buyer knowingly to induce or receive a discriminatory price.* Thus, if a buyer accepts a price that he or she knows is in fact discriminatory, the buyer violates the law to the same extent as the supplier. The act does not prevent a buyer from seeking legitimate price conces-

---

[7]A third condition also permits the offering of a discriminatory price—namely, one in which the marketability of goods is affected. Seasonal goods or those approaching obsolescence or deterioration fall into this category.

sions. It is imperative, however, for a buyer to ensure that any price concessions gained are in fact justifiable under the act.

In practice, the act has been enforced primarily in questionable situations involving retail industry purchases for resale to consumers. Historically, less than 5 percent of the Robinson-Patman case investigations have involved industrial materials and equipment. As a practical matter, then, while industrial purchasers clearly should operate within the provisions of the act, it is unlikely that this legislation will produce significant difficulties for them.[8]

Nearly every state also has its own price discrimination legislation applicable to intrastate transactions. Since these laws vary widely from state to state, each buyer likewise should be familiar with the regulations in his or her state.

Product Liability and Purchasing

Product liability is the responsibility held by manufacturers and downstream sales organizations to pay for injuries to users (or bystanders) caused by defective or unreasonably hazardous products. During the past several decades court decisions and interpretations of legal theories have produced a marked change in the legal environment surrounding such issues. Not only are business firms now placed at greater risk—so are their purchasing departments.

Two things, for the most part, have acted as catalysts to produce the sensitive situation that exists in this area today. The first was a decision handed down by the California Supreme Court in 1963. The decision concluded that "a manufacturer is *strictly liable* when an article he places on the market, knowing that it may be used without inspection, proves to have a defect that causes injury to a human being."[9] The practical result of this decision was that to obtain legal redress an injured user had to prove *only* that the product was defective and that it caused the injury. The earlier requirement that the manufacturer be proved negligent was eliminated. Since then, a majority of the states have followed the precedent set by the California court. Additionally, over the years the strict liability concept has been extended to cover all goods, not just consumer items.

The second major occurrence was the gradual elimination of the longstanding requirement for "privity of contract" in product liability cases. Originally, if an injured user sued the manufacturer on the grounds that it had breached the product warranty, the user was required to have a purchase contract directly with the manufacturer. Since this often was not the case, the elimination of this requirement facilitated the user's access to the courts for recovery. Subsequently, court interpretations frequently extended liability also to the

---

[8]Recent research into industrial applications of the Robinson-Patman Act is available in Richard L. Pinkerton and Deborah J. Kemp, *The Industrial Buyer and the Robinson-Patman Act*, a paper presented at the 79th Annual International Purchasing Conference, Atlanta, Ga., May 4, 1994.

[9]*Greenbaum v. Yuba Power Products, Inc.*, California Supreme Court, 1963.

wholesalers and retailers of the manufacturer's product. Thus, the injured party could seek redress at any point in the manufacturer-distribution chain.

For professional purchasing people, the bottom line of this evolutionary pattern of events is very clear—and important. Product liability suits have literally skyrocketed during the past decade. Most manufacturing and distribution firms now assume a much greater potential risk than in earlier years. Whether a buyer is purchasing a chemical compound for use within the organization, or buying component parts that go into the firm's finished product, he or she often has a magnified responsibility to safeguard the interests of the firm. This requires an added emphasis on the following activities:

1 Initial supplier investigation—with respect to quality capability, quality control, and reliability.
2 Purchase order or contract preparation—with respect to clear and complete communication of specification, operating, and safety requirements, as well as test and inspection procedures.
3 Coordination with quality control and inspection personnel—to ensure jointly that adequate procedures are being used. Further, the buyer must ensure adequate coordination between the QC personnel of both firms on problem issues.
4 In the case of potentially hazardous materials—clear communication to all users within the organization of information dealing with warnings, safety measures, usage instructions, and so on. (Material safety data sheets.)
5 Documentation for all the preceding activities. Even though the buyer's performance may have been first-rate, it is imperative that the purchasing and QC records *show clearly* what was done, and that it *was* done prudently and well.

In summary, from a materials point of view, purchasing managers assume an added responsibility to minimize the exposure of their firms to potential product liability litigation.[10]

INTERNATIONAL CONSIDERATIONS

When a buyer sources outside the United States, the chances are very good that a different set of laws will govern the related purchasing transactions. If stipulated and agreed on in the contract, the governing law *could be* U.S. law, or it *could be* the law of the supplier's country. *More commonly*, though, today it is usually the United Nations' Convention on Contracts for the International Sale of Goods (CISG).

---

[10]For a thorough analysis of purchasing's responsibility in the area of product liability, see R. J. Adams and John R. Browning, "Purchasing and Product Liability," *Journal of Purchasing and Materials Management*, Summer 1989, pp. 2–9.

In any case, in international or global procurement, it is particularly important to stipulate in the purchase order or contract which body of law is acceptable to both the buyer and the seller—and subsequently will govern the transaction. Likewise, it is important also to stipulate a mutually acceptable "choice of forum"—that is, the location at which the lawsuit will be heard, in the event a legal dispute arises.

As pointed out earlier, litigation is a time-consuming and costly way to solve domestic disputes. In the case of international disputes, litigation is even more time-consuming and more costly. Consequently, it is usually more sensible to settle such disputes by means of arbitration. Most, though not all, lawyers recommend that international contracts contain a provision for the settlement of a potential dispute through private arbitration, rather than resorting to court action.

The following sections provide an overview of two key topics for international purchasers—the CISG and the Foreign Corrupt Practices Act.

The CISG

During the early 1980s, the United Nations facilitated the development of a uniform body of law to govern contracts for the international sales of commercial goods. As noted above, the title given to this body of law is the United Nations' Convention on Contracts for the International Sale of Goods, commonly known as the CISG. Its objective is much like the objective of the Uniform Commercial Code, projected to the international level. The CISG does not apply to the purchase of services or to personal purchases of consumer goods.

Generally speaking, the CISG and the UCC have many more similarities than differences. However, there are five significant differences that purchasing and supply professionals should know about:

- *Acceptance of an offer.* The CISG requires that an offer be accepted in identical terms—the mirror image concept. If an acceptance contains terms that conflict with those in the offer, no contract exists.
- *Contract price.* An offer must contain a firm price or a precise procedure for determining a price. Without this provision, no contract exists under the CISG. The UCC is somewhat more lenient on this issue.
- *Revocation of an offer.* The CISG permits an offer to be revoked any time before an acceptance is received. One exception is "if it was reasonable for the offeree to rely on the offer as being irrevocable and the offeree acted in reliance on the offer," then the offer cannot be revoked. This revocation provision is less stringent than its counterpart in the UCC.
- *Formation of a contract.* Under the CISG, a contract is created at the time the acceptance is received by the offeror. Under the UCC, the contract is created when the acceptance is mailed or transmitted to the offeror.
- *Oral contracts.* The CISG recognizes oral contracts as being valid and enforceable. In contrast with the UCC, contracts exceeding $500 in value do not require written evidence.

The United States adopted the CISG in 1988. Canada, Mexico, and most of the major European trading nations have also adopted the CISG; by late 1993, thirty-four countries had ratified the convention. Thus, it is rapidly becoming a major piece of international business legislation. *Unless a contract specifically provides for the application of another body of law, the CISG will automatically apply if both the buyer's and the seller's countries have adopted it.*

CISG use by American purchasers is placed in focus by the following statement of an internationally known legal authority:

> The similarities between the CISG and the UCC are sufficient enough so business executives do not have to make an issue out of which set of rules applies. On the other hand, one should always be aware that there are these two sets of rules, and in specific cases one may be preferable to the other. In any event, the CISG would appear to be preferable (from the U.S. standpoint) to agreeing to (the use of) another country's law.[11]

The Foreign Corrupt Practices Act[12]

In the early 1970s Congress and the American public learned about a number of questionable payments made by U.S. multinational corporations to foreign government officials to gain an advantage in bidding for business contracts awarded by those governments. As a result of the strong negative public reaction to these shady business dealings, appropriate federal agencies investigated the international activities of U.S. firms that appeared to involve the possibility of commercial bribery. The investigation identified several hundred major firms that had been involved in such questionable dealings with potential international customers.

As a result of these findings, in 1977 Congress passed the Foreign Corrupt Practices Act (FCPA) as an amendment to the Securities Exchange Act of 1934. The objective of the new act was to curtail U.S. corporate involvement in foreign commercial bribery activities—and more generally to enhance the image of the United States throughout the world.

The FCPA contains three major sections focusing on (1) antibribery issues, (2) record-keeping requirements, and (3) penalty provisions. The antibribery section makes it a crime for a U.S. firm to offer or to make payments or gifts of *substantial value* to foreign officials. The intent is to prohibit payments in any form to influence a major decision of a foreign government official.

Somewhat to the contrary, however, is the fact that the act *does allow some forms of bribery*—those that are considered to be minor and inconsequential in influencing important government decisions. It is permissible to make pay-

---

[11]W. A. Hancock, "The UN Convention on the International Sale of Goods," *Executive Legal Summary,* May 1993, p. 100.004.

[12]This discussion is based on material presented by Glenn A. Pitman and James P. Sanford, "The Foreign Corrupt Practices Act Revisited: Attempting to Regulate Ethical Bribes in Global Business," *The International Journal of Purchasing and Materials Management,* Summer 1994, pp. 15–20.

ments to operating officials with ministerial or clerical duties. Although the FCPA is vague with respect to the details of application, the Omnibus Trade Act of 1988 specifies what types of payments are acceptable and who may receive them. Such payments are termed "transaction bribes" and are intended to accelerate the performance of a routine function, such as loading and unloading cargo, processing goods through customs promptly, moving goods across country, processing papers, and so on. It is expected that these types of payments may speed up governmental actions by lower-level officials that, in time, would have occurred anyway.

All other types of bribes are considered illegal. As the law now stands, the Omnibus Trade Act holds a firm criminally liable if evidence indicates that one of its representatives had actual knowledge that an illegal payment was made to a foreign government official to secure a favorable decision on a major issue.

Clearly, the FCPA and the related Omnibus Trade Act were designed primarily to curb unacceptable international sales practices. At the same time, however, they apply to international procurement practices. Purchasing professionals engaged in international buying should understand the provisions of these acts, and they must know the difference between acceptable transaction bribes and bribes whose intent and motivation are illegal.

CONCLUSION

The purpose of this chapter is to alert buyers and potential purchasing professionals to the most basic legal considerations that relate to the purchasing and supply function. Yet there is danger in doing this. No author can briefly accomplish this objective without simplifying the issues. And such simplification may at times leave the reader with an incomplete understanding which lulls him or her into a false feeling of security.

Even though adoption of the UCC by all but one of the states creates greater uniformity among state commercial laws than ever before, it is unreasonable to assume that interpretations of the laws by the various states will not vary. Only time can reveal how significant such variations will be. Moreover, the interpretation of circumstances surrounding each specific case weighs heavily in the analysis of that particular case. These factors virtually defy a definite and unqualified analysis of a legal controversy by anyone who is not a highly skilled professional in the legal field. Heinritz, Farrell, Guinipero, and Kolchin state the matter cogently in saying that "the person who tries to be his or her own lawyer has a fool for a client."[13] Perhaps the most important function of this chapter is to underscore the fact that purchasing professionals should seek sound legal counsel whenever potential legal problems arise.

Just as a lawyer is expected to exhibit skill in extricating his or her client from legal entanglements, so a purchasing and supply executive is expected to

---

[13]Stuart Heinritz, Paul Farrell, Larry Guinipero, and Michael Kolchin, *Purchasing Principles and Applications*, Prentice-Hall, Englewood Cliffs, N.J., 1991, p. 241.

exhibit skill in avoiding legal controversies. A purchasing manager must understand basic legal concepts well enough to detect potential problems before they become realities. At the same time, the most powerful tool he or she can utilize to avoid legal problems is skill in selecting sound, cooperative, and reliable suppliers. Vigilance in this area of responsibility minimizes the need for legal assistance.

FOR DISCUSSION

30-1 "A highly legalistic approach to purchasing is both unnecessary and unprofitable." Comment on this statement.

30-2 It has been said that the purchasing manager who tries to be his or her own lawyer has a fool for a client. If this is true, why do purchasing professionals study commercial law? Discuss.

30-3 Discuss the legal responsibilities of a buyer to his or her firm. To what extent are buyers liable for their actions?

30-4 What is the Foreign Corrupt Practices Act? How does it affect an industrial buyer?

30-5 Purchasing professionals and sales representatives are both "agents" for their respective firms. Is there usually any significant difference in the authority they possess as agents? Explain.

30-6 List and discuss the four essential elements of a contract.

30-7 When a purchase (or sales) contract is created, what specific actions constitute the "offer" and the "acceptance"? Explain.

30-8 What is the Uniform Sales Act? Discuss.

30-9 What is the Uniform Commercial Code? Discuss.

30-10 What is the CISG? Discuss.

30-11 What is the legal status of a purchase order which has been accepted by a supplier who used an acceptance form containing terms that conflict with the terms stated on the purchase order? Explain.

30-12 Would the answer to question 30-11 be different if the Uniform Sales Act were still in effect? Explain.

30-13 What is product liability?

30-14 What is meant by the term "mutuality of obligation"? What is its significance for normal purchasing transactions?

30-15 What inspection rights does a buyer have? Explain.

30-16 Under what conditions can buyers reject materials they have purchased?

30-17 Discuss the warranty protection buyers have when they make a purchase.

30-18 What are a buyer's legal rights and obligations when canceling an order if:
  a The supplier has failed to make delivery by the agreed delivery date?
  b The delivery date is three weeks in the future?
  c No delivery date has been specified on the order?

30-19 Discuss "liquidated damages" in relation to purchase contracts.

30-20 What is a contract? Explain.

30-21 Is an oral contract valid? Is it legally enforceable? Explain.

30-22 What is a warranty? What warranties usually accompany the purchase of production materials and equipment?

30-23 In what ways are JIT contracts different from contracts for the purchase of materials used in a traditional purchasing system?

30-24 What factors should a buyer pay particular attention to when preparing a JIT purchase order or contract?

30-25 What has been the impact of the legal aspect of product liability on purchasing activities? Discuss.

30-26 Why might a purchasing manager be interested in arbitration? Discuss.

30-27 How do "honest mistakes" affect purchase contracts? Discuss.

30-28 How can a purchaser infringe the rights of a patent holder?

30-29 Discuss the significance of the Robinson-Patman Act for the industrial buyer.

30-30 What are the major differences between the CISG and the UCC?

CASES FOR CHAPTER 30

31

ETHICAL AND PROFESSIONAL STANDARDS

KEY CONCEPTS

- Ethics in society
- Professional purchasing ethics
  - NAPM's Principles and Standards of Purchasing Practice
  - Avoiding sharp practices
  - Competitive bidding
  - Negotiation
  - Samples
  - Treating salespeople with respect
  - Substandard materials and services
  - Gifts and gratuities
  - Free lunches
- Management responsibilities
  - Written standards
  - Ethics training
  - Professional training
  - The department environment
- The responsibilities of a purchasing professional
  - Guidelines in gray areas; The Four Way Test
- Ethics and true professionalism

Ethics are the guidelines or rules of conduct by which we aim to live. Organizations, like individuals, have ethical standards and, frequently, ethics codes. The ethical standards of an organization are judged by its actions and the actions of its employees, not by pious statements of intent put out in its name. The *character* of an organization is a matter of importance to its employees and managers, to those who do business with it as customers and suppliers, and to those who are considering joining it in any of these capacities.

Marks and Spencer, the highly regarded U.K. retailer, is an example of an organization whose character is held in high regard. Some years ago, when the British pound had declined in value, Marks and Spencer reopened a contract which it had with a U.S. supplier, Burlington Mills, to see whether Burlington was making an adequate profit. A Burlington official commented that this was the first time in Burlington's history that a customer had been concerned over the effect of unforeseen economic events on Burlington's ability to make a profit. Marks and Spencer's *character* undoubtedly makes it a highly desirable customer!

One of the classic dilemmas facing management at all levels of any organization is the issue of "time focus": Do we focus on the short run or the long haul? Recent events on Wall Street demonstrate that expediency may be rewarding in the short run, but not in the long run. Dr. Clarence Walton, professor of ethics and the professions at the American College, adds, "Studies have indicated that companies which adhere to a set of ethical standards are healthier in the long run."[1]

Gary Edwards, executive director of the Ethics Resource Center of Washington, D.C., states, "Surveys show that corporations are paying more attention to the institutionalization of ethics within their organizations. This is happening, in part, because they've become aware of the *enormous costs of unethical activity*—in fines and penalties, in increased government regulations, and in *damage to their public image*. But they also believe that ethical behavior is good business."[2]

There is little doubt that in the minds of the American public, including responsible business men and women, ethical conduct is a more substantive and relevant issue today than it was several decades ago. Unfortunately, however, this is not a unanimous view. There are still a fairly significant number of individuals who are willing to "operate on the margin," or sacrifice long-term values for short-term gains. Figure 31-1 illustrates this situation. The newspaper headlines included in this collage represent a sample of those collected from two leading business papers in a recent study by one of the authors. During the three-month study, articles dealing with questionable ethical practices appeared at the rate of one to two a day. Two inescapable conclusions stand out: (1) Our society is genuinely concerned about individual and organiza-

---

[1]"Greater Concern for Ethics and the 'Bigger Backyard,'" *Management Review,* July 1986, p. 28.
[2]Gary Edwards, quoted in "Is Ethics Good Business?" by Abbey Brown, *Personnel Administrator,* February 1987, p. 67.

FIGURE 31-1
A sample of recent newspaper headlines dealing with matters of ethics.

tional ethical behavior, and (2) We have a long way to go, as a society, to achieve what many think is an acceptable goal in this area.

PROFESSIONAL PURCHASING ETHICS

We live and work in a highly competitive market economy with emphasis on results. There is pressure for sales, pressure to compromise, pressure to succeed in an environment of both internal and external competition, and pressure resulting from government mandates. The *pressures* which the marketplace exerts on purchasing departments and on individual buyers make it essential that top management, purchasing and supply managers, buyers, and all other members of the procurement system recognize and understand both the professional and ethical standards required in the performance of their duties.

The National Association of Purchasing Management, the major professional association representing U.S. industrial purchasers, has addressed this issue since its inception over eighty years ago. Its published *NAPM Standards of Conduct* have been updated on a continuing basis over the years. The current version of this document, *Principles and Standards of Purchasing Practice*, was developed by an NAPM standing committee in 1992 and addresses the matter of professional ethical behavior in the context of the contemporary business environment. Because this body of material is regarded by purchasing professionals as the benchmark work in the field, its key concepts are reproduced on the following pages for the benefit of readers and potential purchasing professionals who may not be familiar with them.

PRINCIPLES AND STANDARDS OF PURCHASING PRACTICE[3]

- **Loyalty To Your Organization**
- **Justice To Those With Whom You Deal**
- **Faith In Your Profession**

From these principles are derived the NAPM standards of purchasing practice.

1. ETHICAL PERCEPTIONS

Avoid the intent and appearance of unethical or compromising practice in relationships, actions, and communications.

The results of a perceived impropriety may become, over time, more disruptive or damaging than an actual transgression. It is essential that any activity or involvement between purchasing professionals and active or

---

[3]National Association of Purchasing Management, Tempe, Ariz., January 1992. This document is used with the permission of NAPM, and is edited slightly to assist student readers in interpreting the statements.

potential suppliers which in any way diminishes, or even appears to diminish, open and fair treatment of suppliers be strictly avoided. Those who do not know us will judge us on appearances. We must consider this—and act accordingly. If a situation is perceived as real, then it is in fact real in its consequences.

2. RESPONSIBILITIES TO THE EMPLOYER

Demonstrate loyalty to the employer by diligently following the lawful instructions of the employer, using reasonable care and only the authority granted.

The purchasing professional's foremost responsibility is to achieve the legitimate goals established by the employer. It is his or her duty to ensure that actions taken as an agent for the employer will benefit the best interests of the employer, *to the exclusion of personal gain*. This requires application of sound judgment and consideration of both the legal and the ethical implications of one's actions.

3. CONFLICT OF INTEREST

Refrain from any private business or professional activity that would create a conflict between personal interests and the interests of the employer.

Purchasing professionals have the right to engage in activities which are of a private nature outside of their employment. However, they must not use their positions in any way to induce another person to provide any benefit to themselves, or persons with whom they have family, business, personal, or financial ties. Even though technically a conflict may not exist, purchasing professionals must avoid the *appearance* of such a conflict. Whenever a potential conflict of interest arises, a purchasing professional should notify his or her supervisor for guidance or resolution.

4. GRATUITIES

Refrain from soliciting or accepting money, loans, credits, or prejudicial discounts, and the acceptance of gifts, entertainment, favors, or services from present or potential suppliers that might influence, or appear to influence, purchasing decisions.

Gratuities include any material goods or services offered with the intent of, or providing the potential for, influencing a buying decision. As such, gratuities may be offered to a buyer, or to other persons involved in purchasing decisions (or members of their immediate families). Having any influence on the purchasing process constitutes involvement. Those in a position to influence the purchasing process must be dedicated to the best interests of their employer. It is essential to avoid any activity which may diminish, or even appear to diminish, the objectivity of the purchasing decision-making process.

Gratuities may be offered in various forms. Common examples are monies, credits, discounts, supplier contests, sales promotion items, product test samples, seasonal or personal gifts, edibles, drinks, household appliances and furnishings, clothing, loans of goods or money, tickets to sporting or other events, dinners, parties, transportation, vacations, cabins, travel and hotel expenses, and various forms of entertainment. Although it does not occur as frequently, the offering of gratuities *by a purchaser to a supplier* is as unethical as the acceptance of gratuities from a supplier. Extreme caution must be used in evaluating the acceptance of any gratuities (even if of nominal value), and the frequency of such actions, to ensure that one is abiding by the spirit of these guidelines.

The following are selected guidelines in dealing with gratuities:

Business Meals

Occasionally during the course of business it may be appropriate to conduct business during meals.

- Such meals shall be for a specific business purpose.
- Frequent meals with the same supplier should be avoided.
- A purchasing professional should be in a position to pay for meals as frequently as the supplier. Purchasing professionals are encouraged to budget for this business activity.

International Purchasing

In some foreign cultures, *business* gifts, meals, and entertainment are considered to be part of the development of the business relationship and the buying and selling process. Acceptance of business gifts, meals, and entertainment of nominal value may be appropriate in accordance with country customs and your company's policies.

- In many foreign cultures, business is frequently conducted in the evenings and over weekends, which may be the only time key executives are available. Under these circumstances, it is understood that purchasers would be expected to accept or provide for meals and entertainment when business matters are conducted. This is typically a more sensitive issue during the initial phase of the business relationship and may be tempered as the relationship progresses.
- Reciprocal gift giving of nominal value is often an acceptable part of the international buying and selling process. When confronted with this— when company policy does not exist—an appropriate guide would be to

ensure that actions are in the best interest of your employer, *never for personal gain.*

- The definition of nominal value may be higher or lower than U.S. nominal value, due to custom, currency, and cost-of-living considerations and is often guided by the duration and scope of the relationship. A purchasing professional must carefully evaluate nominal value in terms of what is reasonable and customary. When in doubt, consult company managers, professional colleagues, and your conscience.

5. CONFIDENTIAL INFORMATION

Handle confidential or proprietary information belonging to employers or suppliers with due care and proper consideration of ethical and legal ramifications and governmental regulations.

Purchasing professionals and others in positions that influence buying decisions deal with confidential or proprietary information of both the employer and the supplier. It is the responsibility of a purchasing professional to ensure that such information, which includes information that may not be confidential in the strictest sense but is not generally known, is treated in a confidential manner.

Proprietary information requires protection of the name, composition, process of manufacture, or rights to unique or exclusive information which has marketable value and is upheld by patent, copyright, or nondisclosure agreement. Others in the organization may be unaware of the possible consequences of the misuse of such information. The purchasing professional should therefore avoid releasing information to other parties until assured that they understand and accept the responsibility for maintaining the confidentiality of the material. Extreme care and good judgment should be used if confidential information is communicated verbally. Such information should be shared only on a need-to-know basis.

Although some of the types of information listed below must be shared with others within the purchasing professional's own company, this should be done only on a need-to-know basis. Information of one supplier must never be shared with another supplier, unless laws or government regulations require that such information be disclosed. If one is unclear regarding disclosure requirements, an attorney should be consulted. When a purchasing professional is privy to cost or profit data, or other supplier information not generally known, it is his or her responsibility to maintain the confidentiality of that information.

Examples of information that may be considered confidential or proprietary are:

1 Pricing and cost data
2 Bid or quotation information

3 Formulas and process information
4 Design information (drawings, blueprints, etc.)
5 Company plans, goals, strategies, etc.
6 Personal information about employees or trustees
7 Supply sources and supplier information
8 Customer lists and customer information
9 Computer software programs

6. TREATMENT OF SUPPLIERS

Promote positive supplier relationships through courtesy and impartiality in all phases of the purchasing cycle.

It is the responsibility of a purchasing professional to promote mutually acceptable business relationships with all suppliers. The reputation and good standing of the employer, the purchasing profession, and the individual will be enhanced by affording all supplier representatives the same courtesy and impartiality in all phases of business transactions. Indications of rudeness, discourtesy, or disrespect in the treatment of a supplier will result in barriers to free and open communications between buyer and seller, and ultimately in a breakdown of the business relationship.

In addition to courtesy, a purchasing professional should extend the same fairness and impartiality to all legitimate business concerns that wish to compete for orders. It is natural and even desirable to build long-term relationships with suppliers based upon a history of trust and respect. However, such relationships should not cause a purchasing professional to ignore the potential to establish similar working relationships with new or previously untested suppliers.

7. RECIPROCITY

Refrain from reciprocal agreements that restrain competition.

Transactions which favor a specific customer as a supplier, or influence a supplier to become a customer, constitute reciprocity, as does a specific commitment to buy, in exchange for a specific commitment to sell. However, the true test for reciprocity is in the motive, since the process may be less vague than a written or formal commitment. In any such transactions the additional issue of restraint of trade places both the individual's and company's reputation for fair competitive procurement and high ethical standards under increased scrutiny. In organization structures where the purchasing and marketing functions report directly to the same individual, the potential for reciprocity may be greater.

Purchasing professionals must be especially careful when dealing with suppliers who are customers. Cross-dealings between suppliers and customers are not antitrust violations, per se. However, giving preference to a supplier who is also a customer should occur only when all other factors are equal. Dealing with a supplier who is also a customer may not constitute a problem if, in fact, the supplier is the best source. However, a company is engaging in reciprocity when it deals with a supplier solely because of the customer relationship. A professional purchaser must be able to recognize reciprocity and its ethical and legal implications.

8. FEDERAL AND STATE LAWS

Know and obey the letter and spirit of laws governing the purchasing function, and remain alert to the legal ramifications of purchasing decisions.

Purchasing professionals should pursue and retain an understanding of the essential legal concepts governing our conduct as agents of our companies.

Key laws and regulations a purchasing professional should be aware of are:

- Uniform Commercial Code
- The Sherman Act
- The Clayton Act
- The Robinson-Patman Act
- The Federal Trade Commission Act
- The Federal Acquisition Regulations
- The Defense Acquisition Regulations
- Patent, Copyright, and Trademark Laws
- OSHA, EPA, and EEOC Laws
- Foreign Corrupt Practices Act
- United Nations' Convention on Contracts for the International Sale of Goods (UNCISG)

9. SMALL, DISADVANTAGED, AND MINORITY-OWNED BUSINESSES

Encourage all segments of society to participate by demonstrating support for small, disadvantaged, and minority-owned businesses.

It is generally recognized that all business concerns, large or small, majority- or minority-owned, should be afforded an equal opportunity to compete. However, most government entities and many corporations have developed specific procedures to enforce policies designed to support and stimulate the growth of small, disadvantaged, and minority-owned businesses. Such businesses are dependent for their survival and expansion upon being given the opportunity to compete in the marketplace with larger firms.

10. PERSONAL PURCHASES FOR EMPLOYEES

Discourage purchasing's involvement in employer-sponsored programs of personal purchases that are not business related.

The function of purchasing is to supply the material requirements of the employer. Personal purchase programs divert organizational resources and dilute the effectiveness of the purchasing function. In certain states, trade diversion laws prohibit personal purchases for employees when such materials are not manufactured by the employer or required for the health or safety of the employee. Situations in which personal purchase programs are justifiable involve items such as work-related safety gear, hand tools, and computer hardware or software for business-related work performed at home.

If management decides to establish such programs, the following are recommended guidelines in dealing with purchases for employees:

- Avoid using an employer's purchasing power to make special purchases for an individual's nonbusiness use.
- If personal purchase programs exist, the purchasing professional should make certain that the arrangements are fair to suppliers, employees, and employers, and that the programs are equally available to all employees.
- Use caution to ensure that employer-sponsored programs do not force special concessions on the supplier.
- If a firm does utilize such a program, suppliers should be made aware that such purchases are not for the employer, but for the firm's employees.

11. RESPONSIBILITIES TO THE PROFESSION

Enhance the proficiency and stature of the purchasing profession by acquiring and maintaining current technical knowledge and the highest standards of ethical behavior.

Purchasing professionals have an obligation to master the basic skills of the profession, as well as keep abreast of current developments in the field.

It is equally imperative that purchasing professionals reflect those same standards through their combined actions in professional groups or associations. Since the activities of groups are highly visible, attention needs to center on actions taken as a group. Each member of a group should consider it an obligation to support only those activities which uphold the high ethical standards of our profession.

12. INTERNATIONAL PURCHASING

Conduct international purchasing in accordance with the laws, customs, and practices of foreign countries, consistent with United States laws, your organization's policies, and these Ethical Standards and Guidelines.

Purchasing professionals must be particularly cautious when operating in the international arena. Numerous customs are different from those in the United States, but the differences typically are only a matter of degree rather than basic substantive differences. Although important in all business dealings, international business transactions dictate a need for a knowledgeable, commonsense approach, with close scrutiny to the intent of each party's actions.

IMPORTANT AREAS REQUIRING AMPLIFICATION

Avoid Sharp Practices

In business, the term "sharp practices" has been used for years—and it is particularly relevant for purchasing professionals. One of the standards in an earlier version of NAPM's *Standards of Conduct* reads, "Avoid sharp practices." Section 4.7 of the NAPM *Guide to Purchasing*, authored by Dr. Robert Felch, provides a definition: "The term 'sharp practices' typically is illustrated as evasion and indirect misrepresentation, just short of actual fraud." These unscrupulous practices focus on short-term gains and ignore the long-term implications for a business relationship.

Some examples of sharp practices are:

- A buyer talks in terms of large quantities to encourage a price quote on that basis. However, the forthcoming order is smaller than the amount on which the price was based. The smaller order does not legitimately deserve the low price thus developed.
- A large number of bids are solicited in hope that the buyer will be able to take advantage of a quotation error.
- Bids are obtained from unqualified suppliers that the buyer would not patronize in any case. These bids are then played against the bids of responsible suppliers in order to gain a price or other advantage. The preparation of bids is a costly undertaking which deserves buyer sincerity in the solicitation stage.
- A market is misrepresented by a buyer who places in competition the prices of seconds, odd lots, or distress merchandise.
- An attempt is made to influence a seller by leaving copies of bids, or other confidential correspondence, where a supplier can see them.
- A concession may be forced by dealing only with "hungry" suppliers. The *current* philosophy is that a purchase order should create a mutual advantage with a price that is fair and reasonable.

- Obscure contract terms of benefit to the buyer's firm are buried in the small type of contract articles.
- A buyer may take advantage of a supplier who is short of cash and who may seek only to cover his/her out-of-pocket costs. Such a situation poses a dilemma, since the supplier may be saved from borrowing at a disadvantage and may look upon such an order as a blessing![4]

Acurex Corporation adds the following items to the preceding list of practices to be avoided:[5]

- Allowing one or more suppliers to have information about their competitor's quotations and *allowing such suppliers to requote*
- Making statements to an existing supplier that exaggerate the seriousness of a problem in order to obtain better prices or other concessions
- Giving preferential treatment to suppliers that higher levels of the firm's own management prefer to recommend
- Canceling a purchase order for parts already in process while also seeking to avoid cancellation charges
- Getting together with other buyers to take united action against another group of people or a company
- Lying to or grossly misleading a salesperson in a negotiation
- Allowing a supplier to become dependent on the purchasing organization for most of its business

While many of these practices were once commonplace, Dr. Felch notes that they are now replaced by a philosophy which holds that mutual confidence and integrity are far more desirable ends than the short-term gains obtained through willful misrepresentation.

Competitive Bidding[6]

Purchasing professionals respect and maintain the integrity of the competitive bidding process. They:

- Invite only firms to whom they are willing to award a contract to submit bids.
- Normally, award the contract to the lowest *responsive*, responsible bidder. If the buyer anticipates the possibility of awarding to other than the low bidder, then he or she notifies prospective bidders that other factors will be considered. (Ideally, these factors will be listed.)

---

[4]Robert I. Felch, "Proprieties and Ethics in Purchasing Management," *Guide to Purchasing*, NAPM, Oradell, N.J. 1986, p. 4.7–3&4.

[5]Richard E. Trevisan, "Developing a Statement of Ethics: A Case Study," *Journal of Purchasing and Materials Management*, Fall 1986, p. 13.

[6]Much of the discussion included on pages 732 and 733 is based on material in NAPM's *Guide to Purchasing*, section 4.7: "Proprieties and Ethics in Purchasing Management," authored by Dr. Robert I. Felch. Specific footnotes are utilized where appropriate.

- Keep competitive price information confidential.
- Notify unsuccessful bidders promptly so that they may reallocate reserved production capacity.
- Treat all bidders alike. Clarifying information is given to *all* potential bidders.
- Do not accept bids after the announced bid closing date and time.
- Do not take advantage of apparent mistakes in the supplier's bid.
- Do not "shop" or conduct auctions for low prices. Although this approach is used in several industries, the unfortunate result frequently is a contract in which the supplier cuts corners in order to avoid a loss.

On the other hand, it *is* ethical for a buyer to work with the low bidder in an effort to identify possible areas of savings. Such identified savings allow the potential supplier to reduce its *costs* and its price.

Negotiation

Professional buyers maintain high ethical standards during all negotiated purchasing activities.

- Competitors are informed of the factors which will be involved in source selection.
- All potential suppliers are given equal access to information and are afforded the same treatment.
- Professional buyers strive to negotiate terms which are fair to both parties. They do not take advantage of mistakes in the supplier's proposal.[7]

Samples

Many potential suppliers offer, even push, the acceptance of samples—"Just try it and see if it doesn't do a superior job for you." When a sample is accepted, professional buyers ensure that appropriate tests are conducted in a timely manner. The potential supplier then should be informed of the test results and suitability of the item in meeting the buyer's needs.

Treating Salespeople with Respect

As noted earlier, the use of courtesy and consideration by purchasing personnel can influence the effectiveness of supplier relationships, and it clearly produces overtones in the area of professional standards of conduct.[8]

[7]Felch, op. cit., pp. 4–5.
[8]Felch, op. cit., p. 7.

- Salespeople should not be kept waiting for protracted periods of time; appointments should be meticulously kept. The power that is attached to the patronage position of a buyer must not be abused so that the long-run interests of the buyer's company will be advanced.
- A mutually effective policy is for purchasing personnel to see every salesperson on his or her first call. The appropriateness of follow-up visits should be determined by the potential strength of the buyer's need for the supplier's product.

Substandard Materials and Services

When substandard materials or services are received, two proprieties should be observed:[9]

1 The supplier should be given prompt notice.
2 Negotiations for adjustments should be carried out by the appropriate purchaser with the appropriate sales personnel in the supplier's organization.

Gifts and Gratuities

Nothing can undermine respect for the purchasing profession more than improper action on the part of its members with regard to gifts, gratuities, favors, and so forth. People engaged in purchasing should not accept from any supplier or prospective supplier any substantive gifts or favors (as defined in NAPM Standard 4). All members of the procurement system must decline to accept or must return any such items offered them or members of their immediate family. The refusal of gifts and favors should be done discreetly and courteously. When the return of a gift is impractical for some reason, disposition should be made to a charitable institution, and the donor should be informed of the disposition.

Personal business transactions with suppliers or prospective suppliers should be scrupulously avoided. Offers of hospitality, business courtesies, or favors, no matter how innocent in appearance, can be a source of embarrassment to all parties concerned.

The purchasing firm's representatives should not allow themselves to become involved in situations where unnecessary embarrassment results from refusal of a hospitality or a business courtesy from suppliers. Generally, the best policy is to decline any sort of favor, hospitality, or entertainment in order to *ensure that all relationships are above reproach at all times.*

Clearly, all situations require the use of common sense and good judgment. For example, acceptance of company-provided luncheons during the course of a visit to a supplier's plant located in a remote area certainly is reasonable. Likewise, the acceptance of supplier-provided automobile transportation on a tem-

---

[9]Felch, op. cit., p. 7.

porary basis where other means are not readily available is a reasonable course of action for a buyer, expediter, or inspector to take.

Purchasing personnel may ethically attend periodic meetings or dinners of trade associations, professional and technical societies, or other industrial organizations as the guest of a supplier, where the meetings are of an educational and informative nature, and where it is considered to be in the professional interest of the buyer-seller relationship. However, the repeated appearance of an individual at such regularly scheduled meetings, as the guest of the same company, is the type of situation which should be tactfully avoided.

The simple casual lunch or cocktail with a supplier's representative typically is merely a normal expression of a friendly business relationship, or frequently a timesaving expediency. It would be prudish to raise any serious question on this score. The individual, himself or herself, is in the best position to judge when this point has been exceeded. Any breach of ethics can be rationalized. But members of the procurement system can avoid embarrassment or possible unethical behavior by asking, How would this look if reported in the company newsletter? It is the desire to continue to talk shop or to resolve a business issue that accounts for most buyer-supplier lunches. Since the buying firm's prestige also is involved, *there is good reason why an adequate expense account should be available to the buyer.* This permits him or her to reciprocate in picking up the bill for lunch! It is a small price to pay for maintaining a position free from any taint of obligation.

"There's No Such Thing as a Free Lunch"   Several years ago, Mike Darby of the NAPM-Silicon Valley organization addressed the issue of free lunches. His comments were so appropriate, they are included below for the benefit of our readers.

> The person who came up with this quote many years ago was probably a materials manager. There are many pro's and con's about buyers going to lunch with their suppliers. I don't propose to advocate one or the other, but I would like to point out some ideas that may help you to make up your own mind.
>
> First and foremost in my mind is, *WHY* would a company want to spend some of its dollars that would normally flow directly to the bottom line to have me join them for lunch? I've asked this question of many suppliers. Some of the answers I've received include: "I have to take somebody to lunch every day, and it might as well be somebody I like"; "If I take you to lunch, then my lunch is free also"; "It will give us an opportunity to get to know each other better." These are all good answers, some of them more honest than I expected.
>
> When I asked the same question of the buyers, the answer changed slightly. "We may need this supplier in the future, and I want to develop a close relationship with him"; "We have some serious problems to discuss"; "This will give me a good opportunity to negotiate a better deal with them."

Whatever the justification, the bottom line to me gets down to this. The supplier is willing to commit some of his profit dollars to this form of entertainment in *the belief that it will help him generate more profit in the future.* He may be in hope that the relationship he is building will help sustain him in your company through rough times, such as poor delivery performance or bad quality. He may be expecting to increase his prices, and a friend will never complain about a small change in price. He may ask you to lunch expecting that the slight social obligation he has just obtained from you may be paid back by getting another crack at a quote, first look at a new drawing, etc. Or he may join you for lunch hoping to obtain some information that will be useful to him in future negotiations.

All the above tend to add up to a one-sided deal, favoring the supplier and putting the buyer in the position of having to be very careful. Let's face it, the sales force of the supplier is being paid to perform a service to the supplier, and this is a good tool for him to use. He gets your undivided attention for a good hour or so, to use as he sees fit. Remember, it's impolite in our society to refuse to answer a question. A question as simple as "How's business?" provides the supplier with important information as to its market share within your company, business trends, and helps to set his expectations in future negotiations. It's also very difficult as a buyer not to show a slight amount of favoritism toward the supplier that you had lunch with last Friday. Should he ask, "Where do I stand on that quote, and what do I need to do to get the job?", it gets difficult to be firm and say no to such a request.

Now before I get blasted out of the water for being one-sided, let me say that there are times when a business meal is appropriate. If you have a supplier in from out of town, and your business discussions extend through lunch or past business hours, a meal is probably appropriate. In this circumstance, I like to use the Host rule—If the meeting is in your territory, then you should be the host. If you are visiting the supplier's territory, then he can be the host. Make it fair and equitable, and the supplier loses any advantage he might have held from an obligation point of view. Remember, an obligation is in the mind of the person who received the favor. If, because of the manner in which you handle your conduct, there was no potential for a favor, then there can also be no obligation.

As a buyer, picking up the check can quickly change a supplier's expectations, and as such is a very useful negotiation tactic. If he thought he had a contract in the bag, he suddenly begins to think that he may not be as secure as he thought. It also sends the message that you too are a professional and certainly not an easy target.[10]

Mature purchasing people know that they are quickly classified among the sales fraternity by the amount of entertainment they expect or will accept.

[10]*Pacific Purchaser,* November–December 1988, p. 11.

Salespeople usually speak with real respect of the buyer who pays his or her share of entertainment expenses. The purchasing expense account is the most effective answer to this ethical problem.

Traditional Sales Techniques   Many purchasing personnel feel that any form of gratuity constitutes a conflict with ethical standards. Others—in fact the majority, according to NAPM studies—consider many of these items to be traditional sales tools. They do not, therefore, believe that such gratuities are offered with the expectation of favorable consideration.[11]

There are two common ways of controlling the acceptance of these kinds of gifts. The first is by placing a dollar limit on what can be accepted. In this case, a purchasing department may have a stated policy of refusing any gratuity with a value in excess of, say, $10 or $15. Such policies provide a very simple, measurable guideline as to how a buyer should decide acceptance.

The other common policy is to forbid acceptance of any gratuity *the buying firm is not in a position to reciprocate.* Thus, if a firm's buyers accept sales promotion items such as pens or planning calendars, they should be in a position to reciprocate with similar items from their own firm.

Cultural Ramifications   Executives of many foreign suppliers expect that buyers will exchange gifts with them. Such action is an accepted part of many foreign cultures. Some buyers encounter situations where refusing a gift would interfere with the development of relations prerequisite to consummating a successful transaction. In such cases, professional buyers *report* the situation to their superiors and arrive at a solution that may include acceptance *and* a reciprocal gift.[12] If a buyer hides his or her action, he or she automatically knows that the action is unethical.

MANAGEMENT RESPONSIBILITIES

Written Standards

Management's first responsibility is to develop a set of written ethical and professional standards applicable to all members of the organization's procurement system. Purchasing supervisors, buyers, expediters, design engineers, manufacturing engineers, quality assurance personnel, maintenance supervisors, receivers, and accounts payable personnel all must accept these standards. The standards should address the topics discussed in this chapter. Research has shown clearly that *written* policies dealing with ethical issues have a strong positive influence on the behavior of a firm's purchasing professionals.[13]

[11]Michael H. Thomas, "Know Where You Stand on Ethics," *Purchasing World,* October 1984, p. 90.

[12]Somerby Dowst, "Taking the Mystery Out of Conflict of Interest," *Purchasing,* Sept. 11, 1986, p. 70A1.

[13]G. B. Turner, G. S. Taylor, and M. F. Hartley, "Ethics Policies and Gratuity Acceptance by Purchasers," *International Journal of Purchasing and Materials Management,* Summer 1994, p. 46.

Ethics Training and Professional Training

Professional purchasing and supply managers, with the *assistance of top management* and their colleagues in other functional areas, must ensure that appropriate personnel receive periodic training with respect to the organization's ethical and professional standards. Such training cannot address all issues. It can, however, increase the sensitivity of those attending. All members of the procurement system must respect their roles as agents of their employer and must represent the best interest of their organization. Subsequent to such training, many organizations require the attendees to sign *a statement to the effect that they have taken the training and understand and will honor the standards.*

Supply managers also should ensure that their personnel receive training on current thinking and techniques in the areas of requirements planning, source selection, pricing, cost analysis, negotiation, and supplier management, as well as ethical and professional standards.

The vast majority of buyers and their supervisors in U.S. firms are dedicated and conscientious people. Accordingly, it is almost shocking to see how little high-quality training many of these individuals have received. Procurement system reviews conducted by the authors indicate that a substantial number of buyers are being asked to perform tasks for which they have received little current training, including training in the area of ethical and professional conduct.

Departmental Environment

Departmental policy should make it clear that buying personnel engage in any unethical activity at the risk of losing their jobs. It is a generally accepted view that a small percentage of Americans are dishonest, that an equally small percentage are completely honest, and that most of us are honest *or* dishonest, *depending on the circumstances.* Consequently, after the basic policy and training frameworks have been established, it appears that the surest way to encourage ethical conduct is to create a working environment where unethical temptations seldom become realities.

The foundation for such an environment consists of the people themselves. Management will be repaid many times for the effort put into thorough, careful investigation and selection of buying personnel. Habits and attitudes are "catching" in the close working environment of a purchasing and supply department. If most of the personnel are basically honest, departmental management has the major part of the ethics battle won.

One businessman has said that "the way to keep employees honest is to pay them enough to pursue a satisfying life style." There is obviously room for debate about the exact definition of a "satisfying life style," but the idea is basically sound. It makes little sense to place a person who has major unfilled material needs in a position where he or she is confronted regularly with the temptation inherent in an industrial purchasing job. The implication for salaries is clear.

The age-old adage "Monkey see, monkey do" is certainly applicable in the matter of ethical conduct. Departmental management and supervisory people must *live,* to the letter, the department's policies and ideals. Numerous studies have confirmed beyond doubt that the actions and attitudes of supervisors are the most influential single factor in determining the attitudes of a work group.

Miscellaneous Factors

Two concluding thoughts are worthy of consideration. First, some progressive organizations have established an internal or external ombudsman who can be contacted with impunity about ethical issues. Once accepted, the practice seems to work well.

Finally, the president of Seldon Associates suggests greater utilization of postpurchase audits as desirable safeguards. He writes, "When every buyer knows that his or her purchases may be audited, there is a built-in safeguard tending to assure ethical purchasing."[14]

CONCLUSION

All purchasing and supply professionals have ethical obligations to three groups of people—*employers, suppliers, and colleagues:*

- *Employer.* Guidance should focus on the characteristics of loyalty, analytical objectivity, and a drive to achieve results that are in the very best interest of the employing organization.
- *Suppliers.* The essence of the guiding spirit in dealing with the supplier community is honesty and fair play.
- *Colleagues.* All individuals engaged in purchasing work are regarded by outside observers as members of an emerging profession. As such, they have an obligation to protect and enhance the reputation of that body of professionals.

When purchasing professionals must take action in a "gray area" not clearly covered by policy, they may find guidance by seeking answers to the following questions:

1 Is this action acceptable to everyone in my organization?
2 Is the action compatible with the firm's responsibilities to its customers, suppliers, and stockholders?
3 What would happen if *all* buyers and salespeople behaved this way?
4 If I were in the other person's shoes, how would I feel about this action if it were directed toward me?

[14]Doyle Seldon, "Ethics, an Additional Look," *Purchasing Management,* December 1988, p. 41.

A follow-up of four questions is provided by the business men and women of the Rotary International organization. They apply *The Four Way Test* to the things they think, say, or do:[15]

- Is it the TRUTH?
- Is it FAIR to all concerned?
- Will it build GOODWILL?
- Will it be BENEFICIAL to all concerned?

In making the final decision, a few moments' thought may well be devoted to the following lines, entitled "What Makes a Profession."[16]

If there is such a thing as a profession as a concept distinct from a vocation, it must consist in the ideals which its members maintain, the dignity of character which they bring to the performance of their duties, and the austerity of the self-imposed ethical standards. To constitute a true profession, there must be ethical tradition so potent as to bring into conformity members whose personal standards of conduct are at a lower level, and to have an elevating and ennobling effect on those members. A profession cannot be created by resolution, or become such overnight. It requires many years for its development, and they must be years of self-denial, years when success by base means is scorned, years when no results bring honor except those free from the taint of unworthy methods.

FOR DISCUSSION

31-1 Define "ethics."
31-2 How are the ethical standards of an organization judged?
31-3 To whom is the character of an organization important? Why?
31-4 What are the costs of unethical behavior?
31-5 To whom does a purchasing professional have ethical obligations? In a nutshell, what are the basic obligations he or she has to each group?
31-6 Define and describe "sharp practices."
31-7 Is it ethical to allow one or more suppliers to have information on their competitors' quotations and to allow such suppliers to requote? Discuss.
31-8 Is it ethical for the buyer to work with the low bidder in an effort to identify possible areas of savings? Discuss.
31-9 Describe three ethical guidelines to be followed during negotiations.
31-10 What are the ethical implications of purchasing departments' making personal purchases for company employees?
31-11 What are the ethical implications of gifts, gratuities, and favors? Discuss.
31-12 Should buyers have expense accounts? Discuss.
31-13 What are management's responsibilities in the area of ethics?
31-14 One of NAPM's standards of purchasing practice deals with ethical per-

[15]Author unknown, *Manual of Procedures*, Rotary International, Evanston, Ill., 1992, p. 94.
[16]Author unknown, quoted in *NAPM Standards of Conduct*, 1959.

ceptions. Discuss the significance of this standard for a purchasing professional.

31-15 Discuss NAPM's conflict-of-interest standard as it applies to a professional buyer.

31-16 What is the role of an ombudsman?

31-17 What is the relationship between ethics and true professionalism?

31-18 Assume you are the purchasing and supply manager for a machinery manufacturing firm of 700 employees. Every year you use approximately $1,000,000 worth of lubricants, which you purchase from one supplier who is selected on the basis of competitive bids every January.

The sales representative for your current supplier makes his usual monthly call to your office on the first day of October. After discussing the normal business problems, he extends an invitation (through your office) to a group of your company executives and supervisors to attend a party.

Those invited are:

- The purchasing and supply manager, her assistant, and three buyers
- The plant manager and his assistant
- The chief design engineer and four engineering section heads
- The maintenance superintendent and his three foremen
- The production manager and his staff assistant
- The controller and her assistant
- The sales manager
- The industrial relations manager

Supplier's personnel attending are:

- Two corporate sales managers and the district manager
- Several sales representatives
- A representative from the corporate research department
- Two representatives from the corporate technical applications department

The party is planned for a Friday evening in the private dining room of a local hotel and includes the following program:

6:30–7:30	Cocktail hour
7:30–8:30	Dinner
8:30–9:00	Informal discussion and a video of the supplier's technical research activities and achievements
9:00–9:30	Video of the Olympic Games
9:30–10:00	Video—"New Dimensions in Musical Entertainment"
10:00–	Adjourn for continuation of the cocktail hour

Discuss in detail how (and why) you would handle this situation.

CASES FOR CHAPTER 31

PART EIGHT

INSTITUTIONAL AND GOVERNMENT PURCHASING

32

PURCHASING FOR INSTITUTIONS AND GOVERNMENTAL ORGANIZATIONS

By Dr. Stephen B. Gordon*

KEY CONCEPTS

- Context
- Sources of authority and procedure
- Roles of the purchasing agency
- Responslblltles
    Products and services purchased
    Functions performed
- The purchasing cycle
    Planning and scheduling
    Requisitioning goods and services
    Identifying and organizing potential sources of supply
    Establishing sources of supply
    Contract administration
- Environmental factors
    External factors
    Internal factors
- Organizational issues
    Enabling authority
    Structure
    Internal organization
    Centralization and decentralization
    Performance measurement
- Ethics
- Professional development issues
- Socioeconomic issues

*This chapter was written by Stephen B. Gordon, Director of Purchasing for the Metropolitan Government of Nashville and Davidson County, Tennessee. The authors express their appreciation for the invaluable experience Dr. Gordon brings to this presentation of a specialized sector of professional purchasing activity.

Institutions and governments are key players in the service economy of postindustrial society. Among many useful functions, they educate, provide health care, protect, and otherwise maintain and enhance quality of life. Institutions are those established organizations or corporations "especially of a public character,"[1] and they include a variety of for-profit, not-for-profit, and governmental entities, such as colleges and universities, elementary and secondary schools, hospitals, and churches. Governments, which are the organizations through which "political units exercise authority and perform functions,"[2] include the massive federal government, the state and territorial governments, and some 84,000 different local government units. Institutions and governments perform many of the same functions, and depending on the specific circumstances may support, work with, or compete with one another. It can be difficult, in certain situations, to distinguish governmental organizations such as hospitals or universities from not-for-profit or even for-profit institutions.

The focus of this chapter is on purchasing by not-for-profit institutions and governmental organizations, with particular attention given to purchasing by not-for-profit educational and health care institutions and state and local governments. At least two reasons justify this overall focus. First, purchasing by institutions and governments can be clearly distinguished from that in for-profit, industrial organizations. Second, the dollar value of purchases by such organizations is significant and increasing.[3]

CONTEXT

Purchasing in not-for-profit institutions and governments is similar in many ways to purchasing in industrial organizations. The following paragraph, which describes the fundamental similarities between not-for-profit and industrial purchasing, describes equally well how not-for-profit institutional purchasing and governmental purchasing are like industrial purchasing.

> The fundamental objective is to identify sources of needed materials and to acquire those items when needed, as economically as possible within accepted standards of quality. The function must be able to react quickly, effectively, and efficiently to requirements, and policies and procedures must conform to sound business practice. . . . Purchasers utilize professional techniques and modern methods, and they

---

[1]*Webster's Ninth New Collegiate Dictionary,* Merriam-Webster, Inc., Publishers, Springfield, Mass., 1987, p. 627.

[2]Ibid., p. 529.

[3]See, for example, *National Center for Educational Statistics: Projections of Educational Statistics to 2000,* U.S. Department of Education, December 1989, table 36, "Current Expenditures and Current Expenditures per Pupil in Average Daily Attendance in Public Elementary and Secondary Schools, with Alternative Projections: 50 States and D.C., 1974–75 to 1999–2000"; *Business Statistics, 1963–91,* U.S. Department of Commerce, June 1992, table A-94, appendix II, "National Income and Products Account of the United States, 1960–91."

employ professional buyers and managers to assure that the purchasing program fully supports their organizations' needs.[4]

Notwithstanding the similarities, purchasing in not-for-profit institutions and governments differs from purchasing in industry in several respects. Most significantly, purchasing in the not-for-profit and governmental sectors is a stewardship function because in this arena hired administrators spend the money derived from someone else's contributions, fees, or taxes in support of activities that the employer has decided to provide on behalf of its clients or constituents. *Consequently the purchasing function in not-for-profit institutions and governments has become a regulated, yet open, process defined and controlled by innumerable laws, rules and regulations, judicial and administrative decisions, and policies and procedures.* Not-for-profit institutions and governments also tend to differ from industrial organizations in that they generally purchase a much broader range of items in order to support a wider spectrum of services by a large number of differentiated production subunits. In metropolitan Nashville and Davidson County, for example, the purchasing agency purchases tens of thousands of goods and services (including heavy construction) in support of services provided by more than sixty departments, offices, and agencies. The operating units include a water and sewerage department, a public works department, a police department, a hospitals department, a social services department, and many other activities that would be found in a typical city or county. *Purchasing in not-for-profit institutions tends to be less regulated than purchasing in governments, but the emphasis on accountability and stewardship is just as strong.*

Other noteworthy differences between purchasing in not-for-profit institutions and governments and purchasing in industrial organizations include the openness referred to previously and the frequency with which not-for-profit institutions and governments cooperate and share information. Generally speaking, the records of a not-for-profit institution or government are open to public review, and anyone who desires may ask questions and expect answers. Especially in government, aggrieved parties can file protests at any step in the procurement process. State governments, local governments, and institutions frequently pool their purchasing power through consolidated and cooperative arrangements, and the sharing of information is the rule rather than the exception.

SOURCES OF AUTHORITY AND PROCEDURE

Purchasing departments in not-for-profit institutions generally operate under authority granted to them by independent boards of directors or trustees. That authority usually is provided in charters, bylaws, and policies.

---

[4]Harold E. Fearon, Donald W. Dobler, and Kenneth H. Killen (eds.), *The Purchasing Handbook,* 5th ed., McGraw-Hill, Inc., New York, 1993, pp. 819–820.

Purchasing departments in government generally operate under authority granted to them by constitutional provisions, statutes, and, in the case of local governments, ordinances. Many state and local governments also operate in accordance with regulations developed by policy boards created specifically for that purpose. Purchasing by governmental organizations tends to be somewhat more regulated by legal requirements and more open to public scrutiny.

ROLES OF THE PURCHASING AGENCY

The purchasing agency or department in a not-for-profit institution or government plays several roles. These roles, which distinguish it from the purchasing department in an industrial organization, include those of:

- A supplier of a wide variety of goods and services to many departments and agencies, which, in turn, use those items to produce public services and support internal operations
- A decision maker, which must strike the appropriate balance between quality, total cost, timeliness, control, accountability, and politics
- A staff adviser, which assists management and line departments in developing budgets, planning projects, and making lease-or-buy and make-or-buy decisions
- An implementer of socioeconomic policy, which often is on the front line of economic development for local, small, and disadvantaged businesses
- A marketer of business opportunities and a provider of information and technical assistance, especially to small and disadvantaged businesses

RESPONSIBILITIES

Products and Services Purchased

As has been noted previously, the average institution or governmental organization purchases a much broader variety of goods and services than the average for-profit organization. Items purchased in significant volume by institutions and governments include fire trucks, police cars, pharmaceuticals, beds, desks, and numerous other items, ranging from personal computers to coffins and gravestones for the indigent. Services often purchased by institutions and governments include professional services such as architectural and engineering services, technical services such as examination preparation and systems design, operating services such as refuse collection and hazardous waste disposal, and human services such as counseling and day care. Institutions and governments purchase a considerable amount of construction, ranging from minor renovations to low-income housing to the construction of enormous utility plants. Major systems, which can involve goods and services as well as construction, also are purchased by many institutions and larger governmental entities.

Functions Performed

Functions performed by not-for-profit purchasing departments include:

- Developing and maintaining bidders' lists
- Working with end users to prepare invitations to bid, requests for proposals, and other written solicitations
- Evaluating bids and proposals in cooperation with end users and others
- Ensuring continuity of supply through planning and scheduling of purchases, term contracts, and other strategies and techniques
- Responding quickly to emergency situations when goods or services must be obtained immediately in order to protect life and/or property
- Assuring the quality of goods and services through standardization, specifications, and contract administration
- Documenting purchasing actions and making pricing and other nonproprietary data reasonably available to those who request it
- Advising management, departmental officials, and others on such matters as product improvements and new products, lease-or-buy and make-or-buy decisions, and economic development opportunities.

THE PURCHASING CYCLE

The purchasing cycle in a not-for-profit organization is shown in Figure 32 1. It includes a number of steps, beginning with the determination that a product or service is needed. For goods, the cycle ends when the organization has consumed or disposed of the item. For services, it generally ends when the final payment has been made. *Planning and scheduling, supplier selection,* and *contract administration* are the three principal phases in the cycle.

Planning and Scheduling

Planning and scheduling of purchases is no less important in institutions and governments than it is in industrial organizations. In fact, it may be more critical, because the public's health, safety, and welfare can be immediately and adversely affected by even a short-term disruption of supply. Many essential services such as police patrol, emergency medical services, and water and sewerage treatment are required on an around-the-clock basis, and an institution's or government's ability to deliver them can be severely crippled by a shortage of needed goods or services. Some services such as snow removal, de-icing of roads, or storm cleanup may be needed infrequently, but if and when the institution or government must provide them, it has to be equipped and supplied. In such cases, the public has no tolerance for a lack of preparedness.

Historically, institutional and governmental purchasing departments have not been particularly successful in enlisting the assistance of operating departments and personnel in planning and scheduling procurements. As a result,

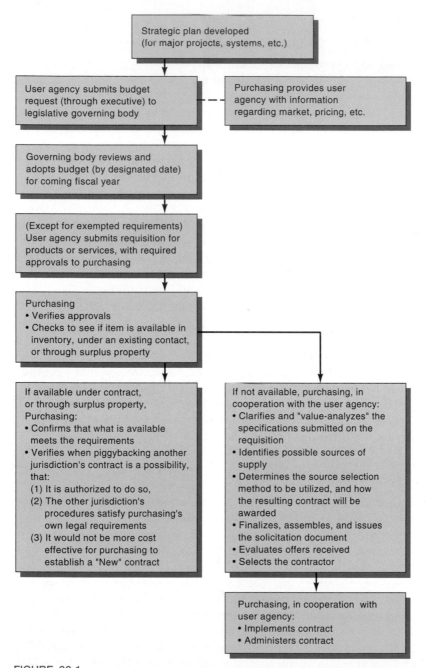

FIGURE 32-1
The purchasing cycle. [Source: *S. B. Gordon and R. L. Mooney in "Not-for-Profit Purchasing" in H. Fearon, D. Dobler, and K. Killen (eds.),* The Purchasing Handbook, *5th ed., McGraw-Hill, Inc., New York 1993.*]

urgent needs often have had to be addressed through emergency, rather than standard, procurement procedures. The effect has been disruptive, resulting in inefficient use of purchasing staff and delays in providing other needed goods and services. The increasing use of automated purchasing systems, growing professionalism within the work forces of institutions and governments, and better communication and cooperation between purchasing departments and operating units are facilitating procurement planning. Institutional and governmental purchasing departments are moving steadily from operating in a reactive manner to operating in a *proactive* mode.

Methods and strategies commonly used by institutions and governments to plan purchases more effectively include consolidation of requirements, term contracting, delegations of purchasing authority, and value analysis. By consolidating their requirements internally and sometimes with other entities, institutions and governments increase their buying power and, thus, obtain better pricing and service. By delegating to operating departments the authority to make small purchases, certain emergency purchases, and specialized purchases, institutional and governmental purchasing departments provide operating departments with greater flexibility and reduce the costs of the acquisition process.

Requisitioning Goods and Services

This step traditionally has been a major source of inefficiency and delay due primarily to a lack of understanding between the purchasing department and the operating departments of their respective needs. Purchasing departments are addressing the problem through training and efforts at better communications and cooperation with operating departments. Automation also is helping to remedy the problem by shortening cycle times and providing institutions and governments with an opportunity to reengineer their requisitioning processes. Most automated purchasing systems used by, or available to, institutions and governments provide for, or can be adapted to provide for, on-line requisitioning by operating departments.

Several factors complicate the challenge of improving the quality of requisitions submitted to institutional and governmental purchasing departments. One is the fact that in medium- to large-size organizations, there may be literally hundreds of requisitioners dispersed throughout a very complex organization. When so many different people are inputting data, and the data they are entering describe such a wide variety of products, it can be very difficult for purchasing managers and buyers to reduce variation in the quality of requisitions. Additionally, many of the requisitioners in institutions are professionals and technical specialists. Doctors, nurses, engineers, teachers, and professors, among others, sometimes have very definite ideas about what they want and when. Many also tend to have a very low tolerance for the competitive procurement process.

Identifying and Organizing Potential Sources of Supply

In most for-profit organizations, the emphasis is on reducing the number of suppliers. However, the thrust in most governments and many institutions still is (even in the wake of total quality management) on reaching out to as many suppliers as practicable. As a result, identifying and organizing potential sources of supply is a significant concern. Three aspects of this concern are addressed here, including outreach, classification, and list maintenance.

Reaching out to potential suppliers is important to many institutions and most governments. Their policies may include, for example, such goals as "to foster effective broad-based competition within the free enterprise system" and to "assure that small and disadvantaged businesses are solicited on each procurement for which such businesses may be suited."[5] Methods for reaching out to new suppliers typically include trade fairs, seminars, and other networking opportunities, as in the private sector. Some institutions and governments publish newsletters which list their bidding opportunities, while others are beginning to use electronic bulletin boards and EDI.

Classifying suppliers properly obviously is necessary if a purchasing department wants to fill in the holes in its bidders list, select the right set of potential suppliers for a particular procurement, or match certain suppliers with promising opportunities. Consequently, interested suppliers generally are asked to classify themselves according to products or services sold, type of business (corporation, partnership, etc.), size, and ownership or control. *The NIGP Commodity Code,* published by the National Institute of Governmental Purchasing, Inc., is the most commonly used code for classifying suppliers according to products or services sold. Business-type classifications are fairly consistent, but standards for size of business and organization and control vary from entity to entity.

Bidders lists can become very costly to maintain, cumbersome, or essentially useless if they are not purged and updated on an ongoing basis. Some suppliers may go out of business, others may lose interest, and still others may ask to receive information on far more products and services than they supply. Small and disadvantaged businesses generally are not purged from bidders lists, even when they do not respond to solicitations on a regular basis. Some institutions and governments "rotate" certain of their bidders lists for particular goods or services in order to offset the tendency for buyers to rely consistently on the same suppliers.

Establishing Sources of Supply

If a requisitioned good or service is not available through surplus property, or an eligible contract or a buying service to which the organization subscribes,

---

[5]The Metropolitan Government of Nashville and Davidson County, Code of Laws, Title 4, Procurement Code, Sec. 4.04.010, paragraph C.

the institutional or governmental purchaser must select the most appropriate source-selection method and the most appropriate type of contract. He or she also must seek to assure that the quality and content of the solicitation document are sufficient to secure acceptable offers.

If the item is available through surplus property, under contract, or through a buying service, the purchaser must confirm that the item meets specifications, is available at an acceptable price, and can be procured on a timely basis on acceptable terms and conditions. The issue of acceptable terms and conditions can be especially significant because an institution or governmental entity may be prohibited from agreeing to certain contract provisions. For example, a contract may stipulate that contract users must indemnify and hold harmless the supplier, a provision that is in conflict with many governmental units' procurement laws and policies.

Eligible contracts may include one of the organization's own contracts or a contract established by another institution or government. Before using another organization's contract, a purchaser must confirm that his or her organization has the authority to use that contract. This is especially true for governmental purchasers who can do only what they are authorized by law to do. In governmental procurement, the mere fact that an action is not prohibited does not necessarily make it acceptable.

If an item is not available in surplus, on contract, or through a buying service, the purchasing department has to make an open market purchase. That requires the purchasing department to work with the requisitioning department to:

- Clarify and value-analyze the specification submitted by the department
- Identify potential sources of supply
- Evaluate whether a joint-bid cooperative purchase would be advantageous
- Determine the method of source selection to be used and the way the resulting contract will be awarded
- Finalize, assemble, and issue the solicitation document
- Evaluate the offers received
- Award the contract
- Ensure that the contract is executed and fulfilled.

In general, the sourcing process represents a key area of difference between governmental purchasing and other types of purchasing. Laws and regulations define purchasing authority and responsibility, actions and documentation are public, and parties who believe they have been aggrieved generally have the legal right to file a formal protest at any step in the procurement process. In jurisdictions in which the protest process has been patterned after the one prescribed in *The Model Procurement Code for State and Local Governments* (hereafter, the *Model Procurement Code*), the procurement process stops until the protest has been resolved unless there is a compelling reason not to stop it.

Many state and local governments have used the *Model Procurement Code* and the *Recommended Regulations* to the code as a basis for updating and supplementing their procurement laws and regulations. The code provides for five principal methods of source selection: (1) *competitive sealed bidding,* (2) *competitive sealed proposals,* (3) *small purchases,* (4) *sole-source procurement,* and (5) *emergency procurement.* The sections of the Metropolitan Government of Nashville and Davidson County's 1992 Procurement Code which authorize the use of these five methods are reprinted in Figure 32-2. Additional details regarding the use of these five methods are provided in regulations which supplement these code provisions.

Provisions in the *Model Procurement Code* for the competitive sealed propos-

FIGURE 32-2
Five methods of source selection used by the Metropolitan Government of Nashville and Davidson County.

4.12.030   Competitive sealed bidding.

A.   Conditions for Use. Contracts shall be awarded by competitive sealed bidding except as otherwise provided in Section 4.12.020 of this code. Methods of source selection.

B.   Invitation to Bid. An invitation to bid shall be issued and shall include a purchase description and all contractual terms and conditions applicable to the procurement.

C.   Public Notice. Adequate public notice of the invitation to bid shall be given a reasonable time prior to the date set forth therein for the opening of bids, in accordance with regulations promulgated by the standards board. The standards board may require different types of public notice on the basis of the size of the purchase or contract, or the type of supplies, services or construction. Such notice may include, but is not limited to, publication in a newspaper of general circulation a reasonable time prior to bid opening, mailing to suppliers on a list of established suppliers, and/or posting notice.

D.   Bid Opening. Bids shall be publicly opened in the presence of one or more witnesses at the time and place designated in the invitation for bids. The amount of each bid and such other relevant information as may be specified by regulation, together with the name of each bidder, shall be read aloud and recorded and the record shall be open to public inspection.

E.   Bid Acceptance and Bid Evaluation. Bids shall be accepted without alteration or correction, except as authorized in this code. Bids shall be evaluated based on the requirements set forth in the invitation to bid, which may include criteria to determine acceptability such as inspection, testing, quality, workmanship, delivery and suitability for a particular purpose. Those criteria that will affect the bid price and be considered in evaluation for award shall be objectively measurable, such as discounts, transportation costs and total or life cycle costs. The invi-

tation to bid shall set forth the evaluation criteria to be used. No criteria may be used in bid evaluation that are not set forth in the invitation to bid.

F.   Correction or Withdrawal of Bids: Cancellation of Awards. Correction or withdrawal of inadvertently erroneous bids before or after reward, or cancellation of awards or contracts based on such bid mistakes, shall be permitted in accordance with regulations promulgated by the standards board. After bid opening no changes in bid prices or other provisions of bids prejudicial to the interest of the metropolitan government or fair competition shall be permitted. In accordance with regulations of the standards board, the purchasing division may correct mathematical errors. Except as otherwise provided by regulation, all decisions to permit the correction or withdrawal of bids, or to cancel awards or contracts based on bid mistakes, shall be supported by a written determination made by the purchasing agent.

G.   Multi-Step Sealed Bidding. When it is considered impractical to initially prepare a purchase description to support an award based on price, an invitation to bid may be issued requesting the submission of unpriced offers to be followed by an invitation to bid limited to those bidders whose offers have been qualified under the criteria set forth in the first solicitation. The standards board shall adopt regulations governing the use of multi-step sealed bidding and establishing procedures. Discussions conducted for the purposes of facilitating understanding of technical offers or specifications may result in the obtaining of supplemental information, amendments of technical offers, and/or amendments of the specifications.

H.   Award. The contract shall be awarded with reasonable promptness by written notice to the lowest responsible and responsive bidder whose bid meets the requirements and criteria set forth in the invitation for bids.

FIGURE 32-2 *(continued)*

I. Rejection. The purchasing agent may reject any and all bids received for purchasing or sales. (Ord. 92-210 § 1(3-202), 1992).

4.12.040   Competitive sealed proposals.

A. Conditions of Use. When, under regulations promulgated by the standards board, the purchasing agent determines that the use of competitive sealed bidding is either not practicable or not advantageous to the metropolitan government, a contract may be entered into by competitive sealed proposals. The standards board may provide by regulation that it is either not practical or not advantageous to the metropolitan government to procure specified types of supplies, services or construction by competitive sealed bidding.

B. Request for Proposals. Proposals shall be solicited through a request for proposals.

C. Public Notice. Adequate public notice of the request for proposals shall be given in the same manner as provided in Section 4.12.030(C), Competitive sealed bidding, public notice.

D. Receipt of Proposals. Proposals shall be opened so as to avoid disclosure of contents to competing offerors during the process of negotiation. A register of proposals shall be prepared in accordance with regulations promulgated by the standards board and shall be open for public inspection after contract award.

E. Evaluation Factors. The request for proposals shall state the relative importance of price and other evaluation factors.

F. Discussion with Responsible Offerors and Revisions to Proposals. As provided in the request for proposals and under regulations promulgated by the standards board, discussions may be conducted with responsible offerors who submit proposals determined to be reasonably susceptible of being selected for award for the purpose of clarification to assure full understanding of, and responsiveness to, the solicitation requirements. Offerors shall be accorded fair and equal treatment with respect to any opportunity for discussion and revision of proposals and such revisions may be permitted after submissions and prior to award for the purpose of obtaining best and final offers. In conducting discussions, there shall be no disclosure of any information derived from proposals submitted by competing offerors.

G. Award. Award shall be made to the responsible offeror whose proposal is determined to be the most advantageous to the metropolitan government taking into consideration price and the evaluation factors set forth in the request for proposals. No other factors or criteria shall be used in the evaluation. The contract file shall contain the basis on which the award is made. (Ord. 92-210 § 1 (3-203), 1992

4.12.050   Small purchases.

Any procurement *not exceeding the sum of one thousand dollars* or such greater amount as may be permitted by the Metropolitan Charter may be made in accordance with the small purchase procedures promulgated by the standards board. "Split bidding," or the artificial division of procurement requirements so as to constitute a small purchase, is prohibited. (Ord. 92-210 § 1 (3-204), 1992)

4.12.060   Sole source procurement.

A contract may be awarded for a supply, service or construction item without competition when, under regulations promulgated by the standards board, the purchasing agent determines in writing that there is only one source for the required supply, service or construction item. The standards board may, by regulation, establish specific categories of supplies, services, or construction items as sole source items. (Ord. 92-210 § 1 (3-205), 1992)

4.12.070   Emergency procurements.

Notwithstanding any other provision of this code, the purchasing agent may make or authorize others to make, emergency procurements when there exists a threat to public health, welfare or safety under emergency conditions as defined in regulations promulgated by the standards board; provided that such emergency procurements shall be made with such competition as is practical under the circumstances. A written determination of the basis for the emergency and for the selection of the particular contractor shall be included in the contract file. Any department head or other official who makes an emergency purchase without following the regulations of the standards board may be held personally liable for such purchase. (Ord. 92-219 § 1 (3-206), 1992)

---

als method have provided state and local governments and related institutions with a legal framework for acquiring complex systems and services which cannot be purchased practicably or advantageously through the competitive sealed bidding method. Examples of systems and services purchased through the competitive sealed proposals method include information technology systems and consultant services.

Provisions in the code for sole-source procurement have provided the same types of organizations with a legal framework for efficiently purchasing those goods and services which are available from only a single supplier. Educational and health care organizations require many sole-source items, including instructional materials and certain medical supplies, equipment, and systems. For example, a university involved in research may have to purchase a particular microscope or other piece of instrumentation manufactured by only one company so that an experiment conducted in one of the university's laboratories can be performed under the controlled conditions specified by the sponsor. Prior to adopting those portions of the *Model Procurement Code* relating to sole-source procurement, purchasers had to either act without legal authority or put out for bid items for which there was only one source. The latter approach wasted time, was not cost-effective, and was unfair to suppliers.

Not-for-profit institutions and state and local governments use several types of contracts, including:

- Fixed price contracts
- Cost reimbursement contracts
- Definite quantity and indefinite quantity contracts
- Contracts with and without a performance incentive for the suppliers
- Contracts for one-time requirements
- Term contracts
- Straight purchases, lease purchases, and true leases

Most purchases entered into by not-for-profit institutions and state and local governments are of the fixed price type, because a majority of the goods and services these organizations purchase are commercially available. With increasing automation, institutions and governmental units now are utilizing more indefinite quantity term contracts, usually with estimated quantities and provisions for price escalation. One-time, open market purchases generally are made with definite quantity contracts.

Some state and local governments are beginning to use performance incentives successfully. Examples of "value added" for which incentives are being provided include early completion (when that is desired) and the accomplishment of performance objectives such as small and disadvantaged business subcontractor participation above the minimum level required. A particularly impressive example is the state of California's inclusion of an early completion bonus for the reconstruction of the Santa Monica Freeway following the earthquake in that state in early 1994. The performance incentive motivated the contractor to complete the reconstruction significantly ahead of schedule; the contractor earned an early completion bonus of approximately $14 million.

In state and local government purchasing, in particular, the fundamental goals of economy and fairness come together when quotes, bids, and proposals are evaluated. Therefore, it is essential for all parties involved in the procurement process to understand precisely how contracts must be awarded.

The criteria used as a basis for award vary, depending on the source-selection method that is used. Procurement laws and policies which are based on the *Model Procurement Code* generally provide for a contract that is to be established through competitive sealed bidding to be awarded to the *responsible* bidder (see Figure 32-3) whose offer is *responsive* (see Figure 32-4) to the requirements at the lowest price. Those same laws and policies generally provide for a contract that is to be established through the competitive sealed proposals method to be awarded to the supplier whose offer is most advantageous to the purchasing organization—that is, the one that represents the *optimal combination* of responsiveness and responsibility. Factors which purchasers should consider when evaluating the responsibility of a bidder are detailed in Figure 32-3. Seven ways that bidders can cause their bids to be non-responsive are shown as examples in Figure 32-4.

Purchasers whose laws and regulations are based on the *Model Procurement Code* and *Recommended Regulations* determine the responsiveness of a

FIGURE 32-3
Determination of responsibility.

Definition of Responsibility:

"Responsible bidder" or "offeror" means a person who has the capability in all respects to perform fully the contract requirements and the integrity and reliability which will assure good faith performance.

Code of Laws of The Metropolitan Government of
Nashville and Davidson County, Section 4.12.010

Standards of Responsibility:

Factors to be considered in determining whether the standard of responsibility has been met include whether a prospective contractor has:

(a) available the appropriate financial, material, equipment, facility, and personnel resources and expertise, or the ability to obtain them, necessary to indicate its capability to meet all contractual requirements;
(b) a satisfactory record of performance;
(c) a satisfactory record of integrity;
(d) qualified legally to contract with Metro;
(e) supplied all necessary information in connection with the inquiry concerning responsibility.

REGULATIONS
R4.12.110.1

Definition of Responsive Bidder:

"Responsive bidder" means a person who has submitted a bid which conforms in all material respects to the invitation to bid.

Code of Laws of The Metropolitan Government of
Nashville and Davidson County, Section 4.12.010

Examples of nonresponsive bidders include those who:

- Substitute their standard terms and conditions for those included in the solicitation document
- Qualify their offers in such a manner as to nullify or limit their liability to the jurisdiction
- Fail to conform with required delivery schedules as set forth in the solicitation or the permissible alternatives
- Qualify their prices in such a manner that the bid price cannot be determined
- Make their bids contingent upon their receiving award on other bids of theirs that are currently under consideration
- Make the purchasing authority responsible for determining that the bidder's products or services conform to the specifications
- Limit the rights of the contracting authority under any contract clause

FIGURE 32-4
Determination of responsiveness. *(From National Institute of Governmental Purchasing, Falls Church, Va.*, Basics of Public Purchasing, *1977. Used with permission.)*

bid or proposal strictly in accordance with the requirements and criteria set forth in the invitation to bid. No bid can be evaluated for any requirement or criterion that is not disclosed in the invitation to bid. Only minor irregularities may be waived, and the determination of responsibility has to be objective.

Purchasers may determine the responsibility of an offeror any time after bids or proposals have been opened and prior to award. The determination of responsibility should be as objective as possible, but it may involve subjective elements which reflect the judgment of the purchaser. Without exception, bids and proposals must be evaluated *only* on the basis of criteria and requirements which are set forth in the solicitation document. Awards for more complex, high-dollar-value procurements generally are made based on the recommendation of an evaluation committee.

Contract Administration

This phase of the procurement process is receiving unprecedented attention due to increased purchases of high technology and services of all types by institutions and governments. It also is receiving particular attention in the area of construction, where a form of the "partnering" concept is reinforcing and, in some respects, supplementing the traditional principles of contract administration.

Contract administration programs based on the objectives shown in Figure 32-5 help not-for-profit institutions and state and local governments use resources as efficiently as possible. They also help those organizations assure the quality of the good, service, or construction purchases under a particular contract.

Partnering builds on traditional contract administration by providing a formal framework for all parties to a project to work together toward results in which everyone wins. Partners agree up front on a common set of project objectives. They also agree to meet regularly, to air their concerns openly and without posturing, and to escalate immediately a problem to the next level of partners if it cannot be resolved at the current level of discussion. There may be one or more levels of partners, including, for example, supervisors, middle management, and senior management. Typically, if a problem cannot be resolved through partnering, it then is escalated to a disputes review board (DRB) appointed by all parties. The DRB makes a nonbinding recommendation which an aggrieved partner can either accept or pursue through legal action.

ENVIRONMENTAL FACTORS

Not-for-profit institutions and state and local governments are affected by *external factors* emanating from the organizations' publics, constituents, and

FIGURE 32-5
Objectives of contract administration. [Source: *S. B. Gordon, "Purchasing," in J. Peterson and D. Strachota (eds.)*, Concepts and Practices in Local Government Finance, *1991*.]

- Ensure that all necessary contractual requirements are spelled out clearly, correctly, and concisely
- Ensure that the staffs of both the not-for-profit organization and the supplier understand their responsibilities under the contract
- Flush out and resolve as many potential problems as possible before the contract takes effect
- Check (after the contract becomes effective) to assure that the supplier provides goods or services in accordance with the contract
- Document problems and take the appropriate action to resolve and/or minimize their impact
- Take the lessons that are learned and utilize them (to the extent possible) to improve future contracting arrangements

others on the outside. They also are affected by *internal factors* arising from within the organizations themselves. These factors affect the organization of the purchasing function, its responses to ethical dilemmas, and the way it reacts to operational challenges.

External Factors

Not-for-profit institutions and state and local governments generally are more affected than industrial organizations by such external factors as laws and regulations, political processes, and economic conditions. If this is the case, it may be largely because these organizations tend to have constituencies which are much more organized than those of industrial organizations. For example, parent-teacher organizations generally exert a strong influence on school board decisions, including those directly affecting whether a contract will be entered into or to which firm a contract will be awarded. Other outside constituencies which also seek to influence decisions include state and federal agencies and other organizations which purchase research and other services. A variety of special-interest groups, including accrediting organizations and professional, technical, and educational societies and associations, also add pressure. And the media and various other groups strive for a say in decisions. Various governing bodies at all levels of government add their "strings." Purchasers in not-for-profit institutions and state and local governments have to deal with outside pressures on a daily basis, and they must do so tactfully and effectively.

Internal Factors

Several internal factors affect how purchasers in institutions and governmental units perform their responsibilities and tasks. They include the organization's sense of mission, its size, the power structure, internal restrictions on what can and cannot be purchased, and job security. The organization's sense of mission is the one characteristic that, more than any other single quality, distinguishes it from industrial organizations. The bottom line is that the focus in an institution or government should be on making a difference for people, and purchasers (like all other staff members) should operate with that goal in mind. Organizational size plays an important role because it affects the extent to which purchasers must deal with issues of control, policy, and enforcement. Power structure influences in many ways the purchasing function's clout and how it operates. And purchasers in most not-for-profit institutions and state and local governments are separated from the chief executive officer by at least one level of management. Internal restrictions on what can and cannot be purchased are less important now than in the past, but there still are pressures on purchasers not to buy luxury-grade items, except for senior management. Job security, on balance, is a positive factor, because the result in most cases is a committed, experienced, and skilled work force.

ORGANIZATIONAL ISSUES

Important organizational issues for not-for-profit institutions and state and local governments are things such as enabling authority, forms of organization, internal organization, centralization and decentralization, and performance measurement.

Enabling Authority

This issue has been addressed to a certain extent in a previous section. It is important to emphasize, however, that the authority to purchase for a state or local government, in particular, should be defined in writing, in some form of law. For each of the fifty state governments, that authority is defined in a unique set of constitutional, statutory, and regulatory provisions. For the 85,000 or so local governments in the United States, the authority generally has its foundation in state law, and in the medium- to large-size entities is supplemented by ordinances and, often, regulation. For not-for-profit institutions, the authority is found in policies created by governing boards. As a general rule, those boards seek to provide purchasers with maximum possible flexibility. Federal government grant-in-aid requirements establish minimum standards for purchases made with federal funds by governmental and not-for-profit organizations.

Forms of Organization

Colleges and Universities In general, the purchasing manager in both private and public institutions of higher learning reports, either directly or through an intermediary executive such as a materials manager, to the vice president or vice chancellor who is responsible for administrative affairs. That vice president or vice chancellor reports to the president or chancellor, who, in turn, reports to a board of directors, governors, or trustees.

Primary and Secondary Schools Purchasing in most medium- and large-size school systems is managed through a centralized purchasing department. The chief purchasing officer generally reports to the superintendent or a deputy superintendent for business affairs, who in turn is accountable to a school board.

Hospitals Hospitals are structured very similarly to colleges and universities. The purchasing manager reports directly or indirectly to a director, who, in turn, reports to a board.

Cities The chief procurement officer in a city may report to the director of finance, the director of general services, or the chief executive officer. A recent survey by the National Institute of Governmental Purchasing showed that the chief procurement officer reports to the finance director in more than half of the cities which responded.[6] In smaller cities, the director of finance, the director of general services, or the CEO may be the chief procurement officer.

Counties   The degree of centralization of purchasing in county government varies widely, as does the office to which the chief procurement officer (where there is one) reports. The number of elected constitutional offices within a county and the extent to which the holders of those offices are willing to cooperate has a major effect on the degree of centralization. Chief procurement officers in counties are almost equally likely to report to the chief executive officer, the director of finance, or the director of general services.[7]

States   As in cities and counties, the central state purchasing office often is a division of a department of administration or finance. In many states, departments of transportation and state-related universities have their own purchasing authority, independent of the central purchasing authority. Most states delegate varying amounts of purchasing authority to using agencies. The chief procurement officer who heads the central state purchasing office generally reports to an appointed official who, in turn, reports to the governor or lieutenant governor.

Federal   At a very high level of generality, federal government purchases can be viewed as either military purchases or civilian purchases, although many of the items purchased for the military either are or are very similar to commercially available goods and services. The Department of Defense is by far the largest single federal government buying department. Other large-dollar-volume purchasers at this level include the General Services Administration, the Veterans Department, and the U.S. Postal Service. The National Aeronautics and Space Administration, the Department of Transportation, and the Tennessee Valley Authority also are major federal purchasers of goods and services.

Internal Organization

Buyers in purchasing departments of not-for-profit institutions and governments typically are organized on the basis of the materials handled, the departments they serve, or some combination of the two. When internal organization is along departmental lines, buyers are assigned to work with specific departments; when it is by commodity, a buyer is responsible for a specific set of goods and/or services. In most large institutions and governments, internal

---

[6]National Institute of Governmental Purchasing, *1993 Survey of Procurement Practices*, The National Institute of Governmental Purchasing, Inc., Reston, Va., table 12, p. 5.
[7]Ibid.

organization typically is specialized by commodity. Smaller organizations often organize buyers on the basis of operating units served. Many institutions and governments are beginning to use satellite buyers, whose work stations are located in the departments to which they are assigned.

Centralization and Decentralization

Centralization refers to the degree to which the authority for performing purchasing and purchasing-related functions is vested in a single operating unit under the control of a director of materials management or purchasing. Purchasing in most medium- to large-size institutions and governments tends to be both centralized and decentralized. A central purchasing unit typically is responsible for establishing term contracts and for purchasing goods and services of high-dollar-value and/or complexity in the open market. Using agencies typically issue purchase orders as releases against term contracts and make low-dollar-value purchases under delegations of purchasing authority from central purchasing units.

Performance Measurement

The goals by which the performance of institutional and governmental purchasing units is measured typically include such common measures as economy, efficiency, and effectiveness. They also include such qualitative standards as public confidence in the procedures followed, fair and equitable treatment of all who deal with the procurement system, the extent to which broad-based competition is fostered, and the quality and integrity of the procurement system.[8]

The second set of goals, which is especially prevalent in governmental organizations, is often in conflict with the first set. Consequently, as one authority noted with regard to conflicting goals in general, institutional and governmental purchasing managers must cope with conflicting goals by setting priorities, attending to important goals for a period and then turning to other goals, accepting a "'satisfactory' rather than a maximum level of performance," and, when necessary, bargaining with other managers to achieve their ongoing interests.[9] The tricky part in government, as one purchasing manager has noted, is that "Purchasing and politics don't mix; but, in government they have to."[10]

---

[8]*Metropolitan Nashville Code of Laws*, Sec. 4.04.010, paragraph C.

[9]Richard L. Daft, *Organization Theory and Design*, 3d ed., West Publishing Company, St. Paul, Minn., 1989, p. 96.

[10]Often-repeated statement of Kevin J. (Beau) Grant, former manager of procurement, Arizona Department of Transportation.

ETHICS

Purchasers in not-for-profit institutions and governments routinely face ethical dilemmas. It comes with the territory; because these organizations are very open to public scrutiny, they are headed by elected or appointed officials who are very accessible to their constituencies, and they often spend a lot of money. Officials rarely ask purchasers to take actions that are illegal or unethical, but they frequently ask them to "find a way" to get something done. It is not unusual for officials to ask purchasers to favor particular groups of suppliers, such as local or in-state businesses or minority enterprises, even when there is no legal authority for giving such preference.

Purchasers can look to a variety of sources for guidance. These sources include codes of ethics developed by the National Association of Purchasing Management, other professional purchasing associations, and the sections on ethics based on the *Model Procurement Code* which have been added to many institutions and governmental entities' enabling laws and policies. The code of ethics of the National Institute of Governmental Purchasing is reprinted in Figure 32-6. Points addressed in one local government's procurement code with regard to ethics include:

- Definitions
- Statement of policy
- General standards of ethical conduct
- Criminal sanctions
- Employee conflict of interest
- Gratuities and kickbacks
- Prohibition against contingent fees
- Restrictions on employment of present or former employees
- Use of official information
- Civil and administrative remedies against employees who breach ethical standards
- Civil and administrative remedies against nonemployees who breach ethical standards
- Waiver by procurement appeals board[11]

One key difference between what is considered to be ethical in governmental organizations and what is considered to be right in other organizations is that governmental purchasers are expected and required to disclose pricing and related information. Such disclosure would be unethical in most other organizations.

PROFESSIONAL DEVELOPMENT ISSUES

Purchasing managers and buyers in not-for-profit institutions and governments should have, as a minimum, the knowledge, skills, and abilities needed

---

[11]*Metropolitan Nashville Code of Laws*, Sec. 4.48.

NIGP CODE OF ETHICS

The Institute believes and it is a condition of membership that the following ethical principles should govern the conduct of every person employed by any public sector procurement or materials management organization.

(1) Seeks or accepts a position as head or employee only when fully in accord with the professional principles applicable thereto, and when confident of possessing the qualifications to serve under those principles to the advantage of the employing organization.

(2) Believes in the dignity and worth of the services rendered by the organization and the societal responsibilities assumed as a trusted public servant.

(3) Is governed by the highest ideals of honor and integrity in all public and personal relationships in order to merit the respect and inspire the confidence of the organization and the public being served.

(4) Believes that personal aggrandizement or personal profit obtained through misuse of public or personal relationships is dishonest and not tolerable.

(5) Identifies and eliminates participation of any individual in operational situations where a conflict of interest may be involved.

(6) Believes that members of the Institute and its staff should at no time or under any circumstances, accept directly or indirectly, gifts, gratuities or other things of value from suppliers which might influence or appear to influence purchasing decisions.

(7) Keeps the governmental organization informed, through appropriate channels, on problems and progress of applicable operations by emphasizing the importance of the facts.

(8) Resists encroachment on control of personnel in order to preserve integrity as a professional manager. Handles all personal matters on a merit basis. Politics, religion, ethnicity, gender and age carry no weight in personnel administration in the agency being directed or served.

(9) Seeks or dispenses no personal favors. Handles each administrative problem objectively and empathetically without discrimination.

(10) Subscribes to and supports the professional aims and objectives of the National Institute of Governmental Purchasing, Inc.

FIGURE 32-6
Code of Ethics of the National Institute of Governmental Purchasing (NIGP).

by purchasing managers and buyers in any type of organization. They also should have the knowledge, skills, and abilities that are needed to operate effectively within not-for-profit institutions and governments.

Opportunities for education and training on issues and methods related to purchasing in not-for-profit institutions and state and local governments include courses, seminars, and conferences offered by a variety of purchasing associations and educational institutions. Groups such as the National Association of Educational Buyers, the American Hospital Association, and the National Institute of Governmental Purchasing provide professional development opportunities focused specifically on the information and skills required by purchasers in these sectors. The National Association of Purchasing Management also offers training for institutional and governmental purchasers.

Institutional and governmental purchasers who wish to obtain professional certification have several options. The Universal Public Purchasing Certification Council offers both a certified professional public buyer (CPPB) designation and a certified public purchasing officer (CPPO) designation. The National Contract Management Association offers certification as a certified associate contracts manager (CACM) and as a certified professional contracts manager (CPCM). The National Association of Purchasing Management confers the designation of certified purchasing manager (C.P.M.) on professionals who meet their standards. It is not uncommon for institutional and governmental purchasers to hold more than one certification.

Finally, most institutional and governmental purchasers value their participation in the national professional associations and their statewide and local chapters and affiliates. These organizations provide purchasers with relatively inexpensive opportunities to share ideas, information, and concerns with their peers.

SOCIOECONOMIC ISSUES

Institutional and governmental purchasers sometimes are required or asked to favor businesses owned by a particular segment of the population. The preferences that purchasers are required or asked to give may be either formal (based on law) or informal (a matter of practice), and they generally fall into two categories: (1) in-state and local preferences and (2) preferences for small, disadvantaged, and women-owned businesses. Many state and local government programs which previously were minority business programs have been changed to *small and disadvantaged* business programs as a result of a ruling in February 1989 by the U.S. Supreme Court in *Croson v. the City of Richmond, Virginia.* In that decision, the Court said that racially based affirmative action contracting programs established without prior findings of discrimination and "narrow tailoring" as to the remedies applied were unconstitutional. The four basic components of affirmative action contracting programs in not-for-profit institutions and state and local governments are described in Figure 32-7.

CONCLUDING REMARKS

Although purchasing in not-for-profit institutions and governments is similar in many ways to purchasing in industrial organizations, there are some fundamental differences. Purchasers generally are considered to be stewards of the funds they spend, and they usually operate in a more regulated and complex environment than their peers in industrial purchasing. To varying degrees, institutional and governmental purchasing departments are far

- *Outreach.* Outreach is the term for reaching out into the community to identify qualified targeted firms and encourage them to become part of the institution's supplier base. Outreach is business affirmative action's *external* marketing function.
- *In-reach.* In-reach, a word coined to go with outreach, describes the process of reaching inside the institution to train, educate, and indoctrinate those on whom business affirmative action depends for its success. In-reach is the program's *internal* marketing function. In-reach activities consist of training and motivational activities for both purchasing and using department staff.
- *Compliance monitoring.* Some business affirmative action programs are two-tiered, particularly in the construction sector, where most of the work is done by subcontractors rather than prime contractors. Those programs require prime contractors to develop affirmative action subcontracting plans to accompany their bids. The terms of the invitations to bid often specify a minimum level of business affirmative action subcontracting plans to accompany their bids for bids to be considered. In effect, this practice transfers a significant part of the business affirmative action responsibility from the buying institution to the prime contractor, who may or may not be appropriately aggressive in meeting, or making good faith efforts to meet, the goals of approved plans. The goal of the compliance monitoring function is to assure that prime contractors comply with the terms of their business affirmative action contractual obligations.
- *Reporting.* The objective of the reporting function is to describe in accurate numeric terms the institution's business affirmative action performance. The need for accuracy and honesty in reporting cannot be overemphasized. If the numbers—both awards to targeted firms and the total base of expenditures—are not accurate or if they have been manipulated in any way to inflate the award percentage bottom line, the institution's credibility can be seriously and irrevocably damaged.

FIGURE 32-7
Basic components of affirmative action contracting programs. [Source: *S. B. Gordon and R. L. Mooney, "Public/Not-for-Profit Purchasing," in H. Fearon, D. Dobler, and K. Killen (eds.),* The Purchasing Handbook, *5th ed., McGraw-Hill, Inc., New York, 1993.*]

more open than industrial purchasing offices to scrutiny and criticism by the general public, the media, suppliers, and others. Institutional and governmental purchasing generally purchase a much broader range of items in support of a greater variety of activity than do industrial purchasing departments. Institutional and governmental purchasers often share information and participate in cooperative, consolidated, and group purchasing programs; industrial purchasers historically have not done such things to a significant extent.

FOR DISCUSSION

32-1 Discuss the similarities of purchasing for an industrial organization and purchasing for institutions and state and local governments.

32-2 Discuss the differences between purchasing for industrial organizations and purchasing for institutions and state and local governments.

32-3 Discuss the significance and role of a governmental purchasing agency as "an implementor of socioeconomic policy."

32-4 "Historically, institutional and governmental purchasing departments have not been particularly successful in enlisting the assistance of operating departments and personnel in planning and scheduling procurements." Discuss the significance of this situation for an institutional or governmental purchasing unit.

32-5 "In most for-profit organizations, the emphasis today is on reducing the number of suppliers." Discuss the applicability of this strategy in not-for-profit organizations.

32-6 The *Model Procurement Code* provides for five principal methods of source selection. List and discuss briefly each of these methods.

32-7 What is the *Model Procurement Code?*

32-8 Although industry has utilized incentive contracts for many years, some state and local governments are just now beginning to use contract performance incentives. Why do you think state and local governments have just begun to utilize this procurement approach?

32-9 What is meant by the phrase *"responsible* bidder whose offer is *responsive"?*

32-10 Discuss the use of the partnering concept in state and local governmental purchasing.

32-11 "Not-for-profit institutions and state and local governments generally are more affected than industrial organizations by such external factors as laws and regulations, political processes, and economic conditions." Discuss.

32-12 What is the source of "enabling authority" for most not-for-profit institutions and state and local governments?

32-13 Discuss the use of centralized and decentralized purchasing in institutions and governments, as compared with centralized and decentralized purchasing in industry.

32-14 "Purchasers in not-for-profit institutions and governments routinely face ethical dilemmas; they come with the territory." Discuss.

32-15 Do the ethical issues faced by institutional and governmental purchasers differ significantly from those faced by purchasing managers in industrial organizations? Discuss.

CASES FOR CHAPTER 32

PART NINE

CASES FOR STUDY AND ANALYSIS

771

CASES FOR STUDY AND ANALYSIS

AAA, INC.

On March 1, 1995, All American Aluminum (AAA) authorized the expenditure of $81 million to modernize its sheet mill facility located in Evansville, Indiana. Because of this modernization's strategic importance, a very tight timetable was established—2½ years for completion of the project. Top managers within the company stated that the schedule, *not cost*, was to be given top priority. Marketing projections estimated that $1.2 million in lost opportunity would be incurred for every month this project went beyond its scheduled completion date. Senior management indicated that additional funding was available if needed to keep the project on schedule.

The company did not have in-house engineering resources to complete a project of this magnitude within the allotted timeframe. A project team of twelve AAA engineers was established to provide key technical direction and overall management, while the bulk of the design work was to be contracted out. Of these twelve engineers, ten were located at the plant site in Evansville and two were located at the company headquarters in Steubenville, Ohio.

In early April, a group consisting of two engineers and a senior facilities buyer visited prospective engineering companies to determine which firm was most capable of handling this project. Each firm was evaluated on three major points:

This case was developed by Pat Craychee, Tim Murphy, Peter Andrade, David Kraylow, and Bruce Gray under the direction of Professor David N. Burt.

1 Quality of engineering expertise
2 Number of engineers that could be made available for the project (sub-contracting would not be allowed)
3 Ability to coordinate with the AAA project team (located primarily in Evansville)

Each company visited was given an outline of the project, including scope of work, conceptual design requirements, and the project team's engineering man-hour estimate. Each firm was requested to submit a proposal outlining how it would handle the project.

Four firms appeared to have the quantity and quality of engineering capability required. Consequently, the final decision was based on which firm AAA felt could best coordinate with its project team in Evansville.

Comstock Engineering was selected to do the job. Although its price and quality were only average, Comstock was considered the best choice because it had offices in both Steubenville and Evansville. It was thought that offices in both locations would reduce the potential for coordination problems.

Comstock maintained that the project could be best handled by its larger office in Steubenville, with Evansville providing only those services that required work at the plant site. AAA disagreed, and stated that any contract award would be contingent on the following conditions:

1 All engineering services were to be managed out of the Evansville office. This would require Comstock to relocate a project manager and two project engineers to the Evansville office.
2 All project management services (planning, scheduling, material control) were to be done out of the Evansville office.
3 The engineering design services (electrical, mechanical, and civil) for certain portions of the project must be done out of the Evansville office. This constituted approximately 60 percent of the design required for the entire project.
4 Prior to placement of the order, Comstock must identify key personnel—the project manager and three project engineers (electrical, mechanical, and civil).

These conditions required the addition of fifteen people to the thirty people already in Comstock's Evansville office. Comstock agreed and submitted the names of the key personnel, which in turn were accepted by AAA. An order, including the noted conditions, was issued to Comstock on a cost plus percentage basis with a cap of $3.3 million. The order was dated April 18.

A chronological sequence of subsequent events is noted below.

- *May 1*—Comstock communicated to AAA that three of the four key personnel would not agree to transfer to the Evansville area.
- *May 15*—Comstock suggested that since the key personnel would not transfer to Evansville, the project should be managed from its Steubenville office.

- *May 20*—AAA rejected Comstock's offer. It was learned that Comstock had just finished a very large project in its Steubenville office and would have to lay off personnel if no work could be found. AAA believed this to be the motivation for Comstock's suggestion.
- *May 25*—Comstock suggested that the project be managed with personnel currently located in the Evansville office.
- *June 15*—AAA accepted Evansville personnel as temporary management only and applied pressure to Comstock to resolve the issue.
- *July 1*—As the scope of work became more defined, it became apparent that electrical engineering man-hours would be double the number estimated by the AAA project team.
- *August 1*—Comstock submitted the names of three people to fill the vacant management slots. AAA accepted one, but rejected the other two as unqualified. The most important position, project manager, was still unfilled.
- *August 15*—AAA was unsatisfied with the scheduler assigned to the project and requested that he be removed. Comstock agreed and replaced him with its best scheduler. The new scheduler was located in Evansville on a temporary basis. Comstock asked that AAA pay for his temporary living expenses.
- *September 1*—It was determined that the civil engineering man-hours required would only be one-third the number estimated by the AAA project team. Comstock claimed that it had adjusted its schedule to accommodate this work and hence was overstaffed with civil engineers.
- *September 1*—Comstock communicated to AAA that it was having difficulty staffing the Evansville office with a sufficient number of electrical engineers. The people within the company were refusing to transfer, and outside recruiting efforts were unsuccessful.
- *September 7*—Comstock requested that the bulk of the electrical engineering work be transferred to its Steubenville office. AAA rejected this request.
- *September 15*—Although the Evansville office was understaffed and overloaded, Comstock was forced to lay people off in its Steubenville office.
- *September 17*—Comstock was still unable to staff its Evansville office with sufficient electrical engineers. It requested that the electrical engineering schedule be extended. AAA did not agree to this.
- *September 21*—AAA verified that Comstock was actively trying to recruit electrical engineers for its Evansville office. However, AAA also discovered that Comstock had submitted a bid for another electrical engineering job, which would conflict with the AAA project.
- *October 1*—By this time, five months had passed without a project manager, and the electrical engineering schedule was slipping badly. Comstock claimed that these problems could be eliminated by transferring the bulk of the engineering work to its Steubenville office. AAA claimed that these conditions were made very clear in the contract and must be adhered to.

AAA has scheduled an internal meeting for October 2 to determine whether to cancel the contract with Comstock.

1 How could AAA have avoided the problems it experienced with Comstock?

2 What are the potential implications of the type of contract AAA used? Discuss.

3 How could AAA have improved its approach to sourcing in this case?

4 What should AAA do now? Discuss.

AGE BUILDERS INC.

AGE Builders Inc. is a family-operated business that has built tract homes for the past ten years. The firm is located in San Jacinto, a city in Riverside County. It builds between 200 and 300 homes per year ranging from 1,100 square feet to 1,900 square feet, priced from $100,000 to $125,000. Alan Carter, president of AGE, and key personnel (also family members)—George Carter, construction manager, and Edward Carter, superintendent—are the decision makers for the firm.

In contracting with Bayord Construction Company for framing and materials for the Mirasol Palms project (single-family homes, one-story), tract #21016, George included a value analysis (VA) provision which allowed for cost reductions. AGE Builders had been doing business with Bayord for several years and had established a trustworthy relationship with Bayord. In accordance with the VA provision, Bayord researched a new innovative product, waferboard, which can be substituted for plywood. In its recent proposal to AGE Builders, Bayord submitted two cost breakdowns for roof sheathing. One included traditional plywood and the other was with waferboard, as shown in Exhibit A.*

George had never heard of waferboard, so he got on the phone with the framer to discuss this new product. The framer proceeded to explain to George that waferboard was created by the lumber industry as an alternative to plywood. Waferboard is made of layers of cross-aligned wood strands that are blended with a tough phenolic resin (glue) and then are mixed together under intense heat and pressure. The strands are aligned along the length of the panel, which increases the board's stiffness and strength in the long direction and makes it consistently uniform.

Quality has always been a great concern of AGE Builders Inc., so George was a bit skeptical about the quality and safety of this new product. According to the framer, waferboard is as good as plywood, if not better. Its quality is consistent, while plywood may have core voids, knotholes, and so on. Due to

*The framer gets the savings from the lumber supplier and then passes the savings on to AGE Builders (the developer).

EXHIBIT A

VALUE ANALYSIS PROVISION
MIRASOL PALMS TRACT 21016 PHASE I
(32 Houses; 30 Homes + 2 Models)

BREAKDOWN COST OF SINGLE-STORY HOMES
PLANS 101, 102, & 103 FOR ROOF SHEATHING

	Plywood, $250/1,000 bd. ft.	Waferboard, $188/1,000 bd. ft.
Plan 101 MP 2,800 board ft. of roof sheathing	$700.00	$526.40
Plan 102 MP 3,100 board ft. of roof sheathing	$775.00	$582.00
Plan 103 MP 3,264 board ft. of roof sheathing	$816.00	$613.63
Plan 101 MP 10 homes	$7,000.00	$5,264.00
Plan 102 MP 12 homes	$9,300.00	$6,984.00
Plan 103 MP 10 homes	$8,160.00	$6,136.30
Total	$24,460.00	$18,384.30

these characteristics, waferboard lies flatter and stiffer than plywood, which makes it easier to work with. The framer added that in his opinion waferboard is more water-resistant than plywood because of the glue (wax impregnation) which holds the particles together.

George was hesitant, since plywood had been the traditional material for roof and wall sheathing and flooring. After seeing what the waferboard looked like, George was still in doubt, because this waferboard resembled another type of board in the construction industry called particleboard, which is only used under sink counters—and not for structural purposes. George became extremely concerned about what the customer might think if he or she saw this particle-type board, especially after being accustomed to seeing traditional plywood which has a much neater and a finished look. The architect for the project also questioned waferboard's appearance.

The framer, who had worked with AGE in the past, assured George that he was presenting him with a quality product that was less expensive than plywood and that provided the same if not better performance than the traditional plywood. Waferboard met the building code regulations. County inspectors were approving the houses constructed with waferboard, with no problems.

George was not quite sure what to do. The idea of reducing costs and having an equivalent product sounded good, but his fear of losing buyers due to this change disturbed him greatly. If George didn't like the way waferboard looked, imagine what the customer might think. George's company might not only lose sales, but also get a bad reputation for building cheap houses. Indecisive, he presented the bid to Uncle Alan and his brother Edward to help him make the decision.

1 What are the advantages and disadvantages of using waferboard?
2 If AGE Builders Inc. does not use waferboard, does it risk falling behind its competition?
3 In this situation how would you determine if value analysis could be beneficial for AGE?
4 How can AGE obtain additional information on this new product? What information would be useful?
5 Are there other alternatives for the use of waferboard which AGE may consider? Can AGE implement further value analysis studies on the use of waferboard?

THE APEX AVIATION CASE

The Apex Aviation Company, with annual sales of $600 million, is a leading supplier of mechanical subsystems to the aviation industry. The firm is in a highly competitive industry, being one of four firms that supply approximately 80 percent of all mechanical subsystems to aircraft manufacturers. Typically, Apex receives a functional or performance specification from an aircraft manufacturer for a subsystem or component from which it designs the required item or subsystem. Due to the cyclical nature of the aviation industry, Apex frequently subcontracts for the manufacture of items, which are then assembled in its own plants.

Recently, Apex received a follow-on order for 100 landing gears. The initial order had been for 50 landing gears, delivery of which was completed three months ago. As a result of heavy plant loading, and following a review by the Apex make-or-buy committee, it has been decided to have the machining of the aluminum outer cylinder struts subcontracted, using aluminum ingots supplied by Apex.

The procurement has been assigned to Mr. Raymond of the purchasing department. Mr. Raymond has sent requests for proposals (RFP) to a number of qualified suppliers. Copies of the design specification accompanied the RFP. The RFP calls for a delivery schedule to commence six months after award of the contract. Initial deliveries are to be scheduled for two struts per month, with subsequent delivery quantities increasing until all units are delivered over a period of thirty-nine months.

The roles for Richard Raymond, buyer for Apex, and Ralph Hawk, president of Hawk Manufacturing Co., are contained in the *Instructor's Guide*.

BACK BAY UNIVERSITY

Back Bay University is a large private university with a distinguished faculty. Enrollment at Back Bay currently is 12,000 students, of whom 6,200 are enrolled in the university's five outstanding graduate schools.

Ms. Sharon Davis has been the director of Back Bay's purchasing department for six years. Her department consists of twenty-two employees and is responsible for the purchase of supplies, services, and equipment that total $36 million. On one of her recent tours of the campus, Ms. Davis noticed a janitor outside the dental school loading used x-ray film, some fairly heavy small cartons, and some floor sweepings into a trash container.

Ms. Davis decided to conduct an informal survey into how the university disposed of its surplus material. In talking with the machine shop foreman, she learned he was selling the shop's scrap metal to a salvage firm. He used the proceeds for the annual shop picnic.

Administrative services disposed of surplus furniture by selling it to interested members of the Back Bay staff on an informal basis. The proceeds were donated to the woman's auxiliary at the university hospital. Surplus scientific and research equipment was either stored in a larger barn or sold to interested faculty. The proceeds were used to purchase research supplies.

1 What arguments are there in favor of a formal salvage program at Back Bay University?
2 What arguments are there in opposition to such a program?
3 Assume that a salvage program is to be implemented. Which department at the university should be responsible for it? Why?
4 Develop an implementation plan for such a salvage program.

THE BETTER-LATE-THAN-NEVER BID

Lisa Evans, Buyer for Central Teachers College, issued an Invitation to Bid covering furnishing and installing metal lockers in the men's gym. Three responsive bids were received from reputable suppliers, ranging from $32,500 to $37,300. There was no public bid opening.

Lisa was concerned that Prairie Manufacturing, Inc., which had done most of the other locker jobs at Central, failed to bid. Expecting that Prairie would have been the low bidder, Lisa decided to find out what happened. Upon talking to Prairie's sales manager, she learned that the bid request had been assigned to a new employee who had misplaced it and missed the closing date. Since Lisa felt that Prairie would have provided the winning bid—and certainly any savings would help Central's tight budget—she decided to declare all the bid prices unreasonable, cancel all bids, and rebid the job.

On the second round of bidding, a low bid of $26,750 was submitted by Prairie. Lisa was delighted that she had made the right decision, and proceeded to make the award to Prairie.

Copyrighted by the National Association of Educational Buyers. Reprinted by permission. This case was prepared by George Morrell and Richard L. Mooney, C.P.M.

1 Did Lisa do the right thing? Was it ethical? Should she be commended for saving $6,000?

2 Would it have made any difference if the original bid opening had been public?

3 How might this look to the original bidders?

THE BIG D COMPANY

The Big D Company of Dallas, Texas, was a family owned, conservatively managed company. For over forty years the company enjoyed slow, steady growth in reaching its current employment level of just over 200. All expansions were financed entirely out of earnings. As the company grew, its operating procedures were periodically re-examined and modified to cope with the complex problems that accompany growth. The company developed, manufactured, and sold metering and flow control devices used in the chemical industry. Recently, as a result of declining profits, management was considering the advisability of installing a more formal system for controlling its cost of materials.

The company's product line contained about forty items, ranging in size from gauges and simple fittings to large flow meters weighing up to 150 pounds. Most of these were made in a number of different models and sizes, so that the total number of separate products was about 300. About half were standard models whose design had not changed greatly in the last ten years; others were subject to considerable technological change; a few involved special features for different customers, sometimes being made of special alloys to resist corrosive action of certain chemicals. Some of the more complex items were supplied with or without certain fittings and refinements. The company's position in the industry depended on its ability to keep ahead of its competitors in design, quality of product, customer service, and price—roughly in that order.

It was the responsibility of the purchasing manager to obtain the castings, materials, and parts indicated. Castings were purchased in the exact quantity required for the manufacturing order. For the most part, the same was true as to bar stock, plate, and similar materials. On the highly standard material sizes, more than enough for one order might be purchased, and in most cases full lengths would be ordered, rather than the exact fraction required. On odd sizes of expensive alloys, the exact amount would be purchased even down to the inch. Standard nuts, bolts, studs, pipefittings, and similar items were usually bought in standard commercial lot quantities, but even here the quantities did not greatly exceed immediate requirements, and frequently even these items were bought by the piece. Molded plastics and special fittings or stamp-

Reprinted by permission of Prentice-Hall, Inc., from *Selected Case Problems in Industrial Management* (2d ed.), by Holden, Shallenberger, and Diehm.

ings were sometimes bought in excess of immediate needs, especially when costs of small lot procurement were prohibitive. The purchasing manager did not alter the quantities shown on the make-and-buy sheet without discussion with the superintendent.

When materials began to come in, they were checked off the make-and-buy sheet and taken to the storeroom, to the production floor, or, if they were finished parts, to assembly.

Little attempt was made to schedule work to the shop, and the machine shop foreman was free to work on any manufacturing orders on which materials had been received. It was up to him to keep his staff and machines busy and to meet the estimated completion dates. As parts were completed, they moved on to assembly, where they were placed in the tote box with other parts accumulated against that order. When all parts were completed, assembly could take place. Finished units were placed in stock in the shipping room or were shipped out immediately against orders.

Completion of the lot was not posted to the sales and production record until the entire lot was finished. Inasmuch as some units were often assembled well in advance of the completion of the entire lot, the sales and production record frequently indicated earliest delivery as some time in the future when, in fact, completed units were in storage on the shipping room shelves. In this way sales had been lost to competitors who quoted earlier deliveries. Other sales had been lost because in setting estimated completion dates the superintendent usually allowed himself more time than was necessary for ordering, machining, and assembly.

The company had no formal inventory control system. No record was kept of raw materials, purchased parts, or manufactured parts on hand. An informal tabulation of finished goods, the sales and production record, was maintained for each item. This showed the balance on hand, the amount currently being manufactured, orders received, customers' names, and dates of shipments made. It also showed the minimum stock balance and the standard manufacturing quantity. These had been determined at a top management level, taking into consideration past sales of the item, the time required for a production run, manufacturing economies, potential obsolescence, storage space available, and the financial resources of the company. In the last year, the minimum stock balance and the manufacturing quantity on most items had been revised upward because of a substantial increase in volume, delivery delays, and more frequent manufacturing runs. The company felt that about three to four runs per year was about right for each item. A typical manufacturing run required about nine to twelve weeks, most of which was consumed in obtaining castings. Actual processing in the plant required two to four weeks. Recently, it was found that jobs were frequently sold before completion and a second lot started before the first lot was finished. Currently, about fifty to sixty shop orders were initiated each month.

As customer orders were received, they were posted to the sales and production record. When such orders reduced the balance on hand and in process to the predetermined minimum, a notice of depletions was prepared, showing the balance on hand and the standard manufacturing quantity. This notice was sent to the plant superintendent.

Big D did not have a formal production planning and inventory control activity. The plant superintendent, in determining the exact quantity to manufacture, was guided by the previously set quantities but consulted informally with the engineer, development, sales, and finance departments before each run. He then made out a make-and-buy sheet showing for the item in question the various parts required, the shop print numbers, the materials from which the parts were made, the quantity of each part required per completed unit, and the estimated completion date.

The make-and-buy sheet was forwarded to the assembly foreman, who checked off for each part the quantity of that part which had been accumulated from overruns on previous orders. No records were kept on such accumulated parts. The parts were stored in bins in the assembly department, and those counted out against the make-and-buy sheet were separated in a tote box against the time when that order would be assembled.

The make-and-buy sheet was returned to the plant superintendent, who edited it to determine whether certain parts should be made or ordered in larger quantity than required for that particular order. Where parts were interchangeable, he might also consolidate them with other orders. The plant superintendent was familiar with the manufacturing process and set-ups involved, knew the price breaks on materials, and had a general knowledge of probable future demand. Before forwarding the make-and-buy sheet to the purchasing manager, the superintendent entered an estimated completion date, which in turn was posted to the sales and production record.

The traffic function was performed by the plant superintendent's secretary. Receiving and warehousing were performed by three young employees who were more or less under the control of the superintendent. Normally, when an incoming shipment arrived, the foreman would oversee its receipt. Purchasing reported to the plant superintendent.

Certain executives felt that the company should establish a more systematic control over raw material, manufactured and finished parts, and finished goods inventories. They pointed to the orders lost, the waste of purchasing and producing in small quantities, delays in production and assembly occasioned by absence of materials and parts, and losses by misplacement, breakage, and pilferage. These concerned officials also felt that Big D might be able to make significant savings through a systematic control of surplus and salvage. Two of the officials expressed concern over the amount of money spent on transportation. No survey had been made to evaluate potential savings in these areas since no records were kept. Inventory losses could not be measured. Pilferage was probably negligible, because the only items having real intrinsic value (thermometers and similar components) were kept in a locked cabinet by the assembly foreman. Transportation costs were estimated to be 12 percent of the cost of purchased material.

Those who opposed changing the inventory control procedure pointed out the risks of obsolescence in any inventory accumulation, and, more importantly, the amount of funds that might be tied up in inventory and the space that would be necessary if substantial stocks of materials, parts, or finished assemblies were to be built up. They resisted the introduction of changes in the areas of production planning and control, receiving, warehousing, and traffic. They also pointed out that other uses of company buildings, equipment, research, and development would yield greater returns.

1 What specific action should the company take in the area of inventory control? Support your proposal with an analysis of its strengths and weaknesses.
2 What is your reaction to the argument of those who oppose tighter controls?
3 How would your recommendation in answering question 1 differ if this company were making a single product?
4 How does the inventory control problem change as the company's overall volume of business increases?
5 Do you think that Big D could benefit from the establishment of a materials management operation? If so, what functions should it include?

THE BIG "O" COMPANY

The Big "O" Company manufactures large hydraulic units. One of the most difficult items to manufacture is the hydraulic cylinder. The cylinder housing is fabricated from a malleable iron casting. The housing is machined to close tolerances, and the slightest discrepancy in either material or machining means a total loss. Machine cycle time on a typical housing is approximately sixteen hours.

For several years, castings had been purchased from the Macon Foundries in Georgia. Macon had been a Big "O" supplier for many years, and during that time it produced thousands of castings at acceptable quality levels. Eight months ago, however, when its founder and president, George Chapel, died, Macon announced that it was discontinuing foundry operations.

The purchasing department at Big "O" undertook a search for new sources. At first, few suppliers could be found who were either capable or willing to meet the exacting specifications and tolerances required. Ultimately, however, three foundries were selected and invited to submit bids on 4,000 castings.

The low bidder, at $76.17 a unit, was the Barry Foundry of Muncie, Indiana. Barry was a small concern with a good reputation for doing quality work and fulfilling every delivery promise. Barry was given a purchase order for the full 4,000 units, with the stipulation that Big "O" approve the first 100 units.

Within two weeks the first 100 castings were received. They were subjected to initial inspection and then dispatched to the floor for machining. In the words of the shop foreman, "They machined like butter." Barry was told to proceed with the entire order and a four-month delivery schedule.

It was about this time that problems began to develop in the shop. Some hard castings had damaged both grinding wheels and cutting tools. Also, cracks from casting porosity appeared on newly machined surfaces and slots. Although these conditions were not present in all castings, they occurred in a sufficient number to warrant action. It was determined that quality standards tighter than those of the existing procurement standard would be required. All suppliers were to be notified immediately.

Accordingly, the buyer contacted Barry and told the supplier to stop production of castings to the old standard, advising that new specifications were now being developed and would be issued within the next two days. To the buyer's shock, he learned that Barry had completed all 4,000 castings. Having had approval on the first 100 units, Barry established production on a continuous-line basis and turned out castings at a fast, steady rate. Because the order called for deliveries to extend over the next four months, Barry was holding the castings and shipping them in accordance with the schedule. To meet the new procurement standard, it was obvious that Barry would have to either scrap all the old castings and produce new ones, or undergo an expensive process of reannealing.

1 What are Barry's legal obligations in this matter?
2 Comment on the fact that Barry had already produced the full-order quantity of 4,000 well in advance of actual delivery requirements.
3 What does the buyer do now?

BLOZIS COMPANY

The Blozis Company was a manufacturer of highly technical equipment. The $16 million gross sales of the company consisted primarily of units designed to customer specifications by the engineering department and produced on a job-shop basis by the production department. The engineering department also designed highly complex control equipment of general industrial application to be sold by the Blozis Company on an off-the-shelf basis.

The purchasing department consisted of the purchasing manager, a buyer, and two clerks who handled typing and filing. Although many of the items purchased were of a highly technical nature, the purchasing manager had no technical training. Through the years, he had picked up a fair grasp of the engineering terminology used in the field, but had made no attempt to keep up with the specialized design problems of the company. The buyer was a woman who was known in the trade as "hard-boiled but big-hearted" and was generally considered a competent general supplies buyer. Without great ingenuity, the buyer also successfully handled technical items if detailed specifications were supplied by engineering or production.

An expediter was attached to production. He formerly had been one of the technicians in the production shop and had picked up some technical training in the Army. Because he could understand verbal descriptions of items needed by engineering and production, these groups often contacted him on ordering problems before submitting a requisition to purchasing. He frequently would suggest substitute components that could be drawn immediately from the stock room; or he would convert the oral description into a commercial specification, type a requisition, and submit it to purchasing. The expediter had two primary responsibilities: to pick up rush orders and to supervise the stock room. He spent about 50 percent of each day picking up items at nearby suppliers, at truck terminals, or airports, or carrying materials to subcontractors, to platers, or to various carriers for shipment. In the stock room, a clerk kept up the facilities, issued supplies to engineering and production personnel, and kept stock records. The clerk reported to the expediter, who reviewed the stock records, prepared requisitions for items at their reorder points, and disposed of items that were turning too slowly or had deteriorated.

Frequent problems had arisen when suppliers claimed long overdue payments on materials that had been received by the Blozis Company. In these cases it always developed that someone had forgotten to make up a receiving report. Since purchasing only passed bills for payment after receipt of the receiving report, several sizable discounts had been missed and the company had been substantially tardy in meeting the net date on several bills. In these cases, the expediter was always sure that the item had come over the receiving dock, and the receiving clerk was just as sure that the expediter had brought it into the plant in the back of his station wagon.

A particularly unfortunate incident had occurred when two special micrometers disappeared within the plant after the Blozis Company had waited six months to receive them. The supplier could prove receipt by the bill of lading signed by the receiving clerk. The receiving clerk claimed the expediter had picked up the micrometers on the receiving dock to carry them to the engineers as quickly as possible. The expediter claimed he had never seen the micrometers. Both the production and plant maintenance managers had backed their respective men to the fullest. No disciplinary action had been taken since there were no signatures on the receiving reports to prove either case.

The expediter periodically typed up purchase orders for rush items. In other cases he picked up the desired items and informed the suppliers that they would receive "confirming orders" from the Blozis Company purchasing department. When the expediter forgot to ask purchasing for a confirming order, the purchasing department was occasionally distressed to be processing invoices for which it had no corresponding orders. Some suppliers were also mildly petulant when a promised purchase order was not forthcoming. Although suppliers had been warned not to honor an order from the Blozis Company unless it bore the purchasing manager's signature, it was considered poor business to penalize the suppliers who had honored the expediter's request in good faith. Consequently, purchase orders were often made up to match invoices if the material had obviously been received from the supplier.

The president liked to operate "informally" and allowed anyone in the company to initiate requisitions. The only approval signature required on orders up to $10,000 was the purchasing manager's. Orders over $10,000 required the president's approval on requisitions, but, in practice, all orders for more than $10,000 were approved by the president either in the materials budget or the capital budget long before requisitions were made out.

The president had heard something of the micrometer incident from his brother, but had dismissed the whole matter as "one of those unfortunate interdepartment squabbles." However, when his engineering manager and his production manager began to complain of the difficulties of staying within the materials budget, he looked further into the matter. In subsequent talks with both men he drew up the following summary list of complaints:

1 The managers did not know what materials were being charged to their departments until the monthly accounting statement came out.
2 The engineering and operating personnel were not notified when materials came in unless the expediter dropped the material on the desk of the requisitioner.
3 The purchasing department was entirely too slow in processing orders. It took almost a full day just to get the order to the telephone.
4 The purchasing department did not understand technical specifications, and the expediter was being overworked by handling all technical orders.

The president presented these complaints to the purchasing manager and asked him for a solution.

1 If you were the purchasing manager, what recommendations would you have made?
2 At what points does this purchasing department exhibit weak control over (a) materials and (b) overall purchasing performance?
3 How could these weaknesses be corrected?
4 What activities should the expediter be responsible for in this organization?
5 What is the purchasing department's responsibility in establishing and interpreting technical specifications?

THE BOARDROOM

In June 1995, Tom Dewey, purchasing manager for Builder's Bank, Inc.'s (BBI) New York office, wanted to resolve a set of problems arising from the purchase of eighty chairs for the executive boardroom.

GENERAL COMPANY BACKGROUND

BBI was a large international bank with operations throughout the world. It had recently purchased an office building and had hired the well-known architect Peter Tropper to do the major design and renovation plans.

THE PURCHASING DEPARTMENT

The purchasing department in the New York office was responsible for all local purchases, in addition to a few major purchases for the international offices. The bank did not have an approved supplier list; an invitation to bid was an indication that the potential supplier was considered qualified.

BUILDING RENOVATION

The architectural firm of Peter Tropper was hired to redesign the entire building, including the selection of furniture. Once the design was completed, a working group, including the president and vice president, had approved the design, including selection and color for all major furniture. The purchasing department did not participate in this process.

In June 1994, Peter Tropper sent a specification sheet to the purchasing department for all purchases, which included model number and manufacturer. Suppliers would bid on the same manufacturer, with no substitutions allowed. Although the department had the option to split the order between suppliers, Tom Dewey decided to order through a single source.

In late June, the working group asked Tom Dewey to submit a budget of what the bank would have to spend to complete the renovation during fiscal 1995. Therefore, in early July, Tom Dewey submitted a request for proposal (RFP) to ten potential suppliers, all of which responded.

When the bids were received in mid-August, the working group reviewed the bids and rejected them as being too high. The working group and Peter Tropper agreed to a scaling down of the work proposed. A week later, Tom Dewey sent new specifications to the same ten suppliers, of which eight responded. The low bid on the RFP was $1.3 million, submitted by ABCO Furniture, a large local furniture dealer. In September, the working group authorized Tom Dewey to purchase major furniture and the chairs for the executive boardroom totaling $400,000.

CHAIRS FOR THE BOARDROOM

Among the items on the RFP were eighty leather chairs for the executive boardroom. These chairs had a single pedestal and a fixed jury base, which would not allow the chairs to rock or swivel. Twelve of the chairs, costing $1,500 each, required installation in concrete, with the remaining sixty-eight chairs, costing $1,300 each, having bases that could be installed on wood flooring. The RFP made no mention of installation.

In February 1995, ABCO Furniture informed Tom Dewey that the chairs were ready. Since the boardroom was still under construction, he arranged to have ABCO store the chairs, with the agreement that he honor the invoice in March. The invoice was paid in late March and ABCO stored the chairs until they were delivered on the morning of April 22, 1995.

When the chairs were delivered, the construction manager talked with Peter Tropper regarding installation. The construction manager told Tom Dewey that the architect had said he would give detailed drawings regarding installation of the chairs, although the drawings had not been received. When Tom Dewey asked Peter Tropper about the problem, Peter indicated that Purchasing, having bought the chairs, was responsible for installation. Peter Tropper also stated that he had informed Purchasing, by letter in late March, that Purchasing was responsible for installation.

At the instruction of Tom Dewey, ABCO hired a local installer to install the chairs. The installer had seen neither the chairs nor the boardroom before. The installer arrived late on the 22d and discussed the installation procedure with the construction manager. They concluded that they would use expansion bolts in the concrete and wood screws in the platforms. Both the construction manager and the installer agreed that long lag screws could not be used since the platforms were elevated, with electrical conduit underneath.

After installing a few chairs on the morning of April 23d, the installer and construction manager concluded that the wood screws would not hold. Since the chairs were rigid, the smallness of the diameter of the base was insufficient for the torque applied to the base when the chair was used. Since no adequate support was designed into the floor when the room was remodeled, other support alternatives had to be evaluated.

The construction manager contacted the field representative of Peter Tropper and explained the problem. Peter Tropper indicated that toggle bolts were required. As a check on the architect, the construction manager called the furniture manufacturer in Pennsylvania. The call provided no additional information. The manufacturer's service representative stated that since they were not directly involved, they were unable to make suggestions. The representative did state, off the record, that the base was too small for the chair.

The installer, even after installing the toggle bolts, discovered that the chairs were still coming loose. In addition, the expansion bolts, installed in the concrete, would also eventually work loose. However, with the upcoming board meeting on May 6, 1995, the construction manager and installer agreed that the chairs could be used temporarily. The supplier, after discussing installation costs with the installer, told Tom Dewey that the current bill for setting up the chairs would be around $4,000. However, for the installer to do the job correctly would cost an additional $15,000.

The May 6 board meeting went smoothly, although many board members noted the instability of the chairs. In June, the executive directors expressed concern over the need to fix the chairs—and quickly. However, Tom Dewey's frequent discussions with Peter Tropper had yielded no results.

The installer billed ABCO Furniture at the end of May. In late June, Tom Dewey received a bill from ABCO for the installation of the chairs, and a copy of the invoice received by ABCO from the supplier. Tom Dewey recognized that BBI had not allowed for any additional installation costs and wondered what the best way to resolve the problem would be.

1 What alternatives are open to Tom?
2 What is the best course of action now?
3 Who is responsible for the present situation?
4 What should Tom have done to avoid the present situation?

BRONX BUSINESS MACHINES CORPORATION

The Bronx Business Machines Corporation (BBM) was in the process of developing a new, smart personal computer. The first working prototype was planned for release in ten months. The design-to-cost objective was $600 for the 5,000th unit, with a planned production run of 1 million units.

A thorough make-or-buy analysis had been conducted. One of the more costly items studied in the make-or-buy analysis was a radically new input/output (I/O) device. The design-to-cost analysis allocated $100 per unit for the device. The make-or-buy analysis concluded that BBM should buy the I/O device. Based on limited experience with similar but less sophisticated devices, it was estimated that contractual development costs would be in the range of a half million dollars.

Due to staffing problems, June Oster (a newly promoted procurement manager at BBM) was handling the procurement of the R&D work. She had contacted five firms that had the capability of developing the I/O device. Two firms declined to participate in the project. The third indicated that it would be delighted to proceed with the development on a no-cost basis, provided that BBM would purchase a minimum of 100,000 devices. Production costs for these units would be based on a fixed price redeterminable contract, with the ceiling price to be negotiated on completion of the R&D portion of the work.

Ms. Oster received proposals for the R&D work from the remaining two firms. One appeared to be either a get-rich-quick proposal or a courtesy bid (she was not sure which—and really did not care) of $1 million. The other proposal was from the Tigertronix Corporation of Skunk Hollow, Arkansas. Tigertronix had been founded five years before by four engineers who had worked together at a large electronics firm in Beaverton, Oregon. The new company had expanded to 450 employees, had sales of $50 million, and enjoyed an excellent reputation in the I/O industry.

EXHIBIT 1
TIGERTRONIX CORPORATION
Skunk Hollow, Arkansas

---

1 April 1995

Ms. June Oster
Procurement Manager
Bronx Business Machines Corp.
32 White Plains Avenue
New York, New York 10036

Dear Ms. Oster:

We are pleased to submit our proposal for development of a smart input/output device. If we are able to begin work by April 15, we will be able to provide two prototype models by February 1, 1996.

We understand the confidential nature of the work and agree not to release any data to individuals not employed by your company.

We have submitted the cost breakdown data you requested. The total of our projected costs and profit is $621,000. We will be pleased to answer any questions you may have, while being sensitive to the time constraint under which we both are working.

In the interest of time, we are willing to enter into a cost reimbursement production option with a target cost of $100 per unit for the first 10,000 units of production. With this cost history, we then would be in a position to enter into a firm fixed unit price contract based on our production experience with these first 10,000 units.

Very sincerely,

Ron Cox
President

Attachment: Proposal

ATTACHMENT
ESTIMATED R&D COSTS

Engineering

4,000 hours @ $30/hour	$120,000
Supervisory		
600 hours @ $50/hour	30,000
SUBTOTAL	$150,000
Overhead 250%	375,000
G&A 10%	15,000
SUBTOTAL	$540,000
Profit	81,000
TOTAL	$621,000

Ms. Oster met with Freddie Ready, vice president of marketing at Tigertronix, to discuss development of the new I/O device. She indicated BBM's desire to pay for the development so that it would own any patents and data rights, including procurement specifications. Ms. Oster also indicated her desire to enter into an R&D contract which included a fixed price incentive option for production. BBM would retain the right to complete the production work. Obviously, the R&D supplier would have good insight into the costs and nuances of production.

On April 1, Tigertronix submitted a proposal. (See Exhibit 1, page 790.)

1 If you were Ms. Oster, what action would you take? Why?

BROTHERS MOWERS

In 1958 the Stanley brothers pooled their efforts and experience to form Brothers Mowers. The company began with production of a single hand mower. The business has grown to include a full line of manual and motorized mowers and motorized gardening equipment including blowers, hedgers, and rototillers. Despite its growth, the company has remained virtually family-run; relatives and family friends have held important positions within the organizational structure. The company has never been an industry leader or even a top competitor. Yet it has managed to provide an adequate profit and retain its independence.

In January 1995, the company was given a shock. Uncle Phill, the head of procurement for the past twenty-two years, died unexpectedly from a heart attack early in the month. Rod Stanton, a graduate of the University of San Diego, was hired later in the month to replace Uncle Phill as the new procurement director. On his arrival, Rod observed that late supplies sometimes caused breaks in production. He also saw that rework and scrap seemed excessive. Rod figured he had three to four months to "clean up" the procurement function before the increased demand during the winter months became a burial rather than a harvest.

The corporate managers at Brothers are graying, and more new hires are expected. Employees are skeptical of, if not averse to, changes. They fear the company will lose sight of its family origins. The employees are comfortable with the current situation, and the corporate managers were satisfied with Uncle Phill's operation of the procurement function.

Rod Stanton saw an opportunity to clean up the procurement process. Brothers Mowers' limited use of standardized parts prompted Rod to review the numerous routine orders placed with suppliers. Rod found that many of the suppliers had been used for ten to twenty years and were directly linked

This case was developed by Mark A. Sonna and Susanne Thieback under the direction of Professor David N. Burt.

to one product or model. He sensed that efficiencies could be gained by using fewer suppliers of standardized parts. Realizing his relative newness at the company, he was cautious not to suggest anything that he couldn't support. Discussions with his cousin, Sam, who had worked in engineering for five years, indicated that minor redesign of each product line would allow utilization of many more standardized parts. Although this approach would be contrary to the current practice of ordering nonstandardized parts for specific models within each line, Rod realized that it would create an opportunity to decrease the variety of parts ordered as a result of the design simplification.

One month after assuming his new position, Rod now has a meeting with the department heads to review his first month on the job. Rod has what he feels are some valuable suggestions. He believes that design modifications are required to utilize simplification and standardization techniques; however, he realizes that his suggestions may fall on deaf ears because of the change-resistant nature of the company.

Rod seems to be in a sensitive position. What suggestions would you offer him in response to the problems he anticipates?

1 How can Rod suggest solutions to problems when the people whose cooperation he needs don't realize that the problems exist?
2 How can Rod get engineers to redesign a whole line of products when sales are healthy?
3 How can Rod propose changing from trusted suppliers of ten to twenty years to new suppliers of standardized products?

CAPITAL EQUIPMENT PURCHASING

James Sampson, manager of central purchasing, Celebrity Electronics Group, in Somerville, California, wondered what action to take. Supplier quotations had been reviewed for a vacuum chamber and significant differences existed among the four finalists.

CELEBRITY BACKGROUND DATA

Celebrity was a manufacturer of electronic equipment, systems, and components for markets in the United States and other countries. Last year, sales and revenues were $6.2 billion, with net earnings of $321 million.

The company was organized into sectors, groups, and divisions, with essentially a decentralized management structure.

The Celebrity Electronics Group specialized in the research, development, and production of advanced electronic systems and equipment for the U.S. Department of Defense, NASA, and commercial users, both domestic and off-shore. The Communications Division, Radar Operations Division, and Strategic Electronics Division, which made up the Group, each had a separate organization for purchasing production material. Because all operations were located in the greater Los Angeles area, a central purchasing organization bought capital equipment, new construction, maintenance, repair, and operating supplies.

For major capital equipment procurements, the manager of central purchasing and representatives from finance, quality assurance, and the test equipment facility organization made up a source-selection team. The team, under the leadership of the manager of purchasing, was responsible, according to procedure, to evaluate supplier proposals, select a supplier, and prepare an appropriate justification memorandum recommending the supplier.

An appropriation request was reviewed by the local general manager and his staff and, based on current approval levels, forwarded to the corporate offices in Los Angeles, California, for approval by a committee of senior corporate executives.

NEW FACILITY PROCUREMENTS

A new, large facility was to be constructed in the Somerville area to provide production capability for new projects. Central purchasing was deeply involved in purchasing equipment for the facility.

One important item was a thermal vacuum chamber, 10 feet in diameter, capable of simulating the vacuum, heat, and cold of deep outer space. The specifications were developed for this custom walk-in chamber by Celebrity engineers, and were within current technological understanding and capabilities. The chamber would test components and systems that would be sent into outer space. In addition to the 10^{-14} atmospheres vacuum, the chamber had to cycle between the extremes of heat and cold that hardware is subjected to in the deep space environment.

Because of the extreme vacuum involved, the speed in achieving the vacuum was important since the energy cost to operate the chamber increased rapidly as the time increased. There were also safety considerations. A catastrophic failure of the chamber could cause severe personal injury as well as heavy damage to the building.

The chamber had to be delivered in 14 months after release of the order. The building's last wall could not be completed before the chamber was installed. If delivery were late, construction would be halted on the building. It might be possible for "work-around" construction to continue in such a case, but additional costs would be involved.

SUPPLIER DATA

On receiving the specifications for the chamber, James Sampson prepared a request for bid for ten potential suppliers. Based on various input and evaluations, the list was pared to five companies. (The following table lists the suppliers' proposals.)

	Supplier	Location	Quotation in 000's	Delivery
A	Rayard Air Products Co.	Peabody, MA	$1,101.5	14 months
B	MRT Engineering Inc.	Chicago, IL	1,051.1	14 months
C	Houston Chambers Co.	Houston, TX	561.8	12 months
D	Engineered Environments	Danbury, CT	No bid	
E	The Wiston Group	San Diego, CA	1,008.0	14 months

Each of the suppliers reportedly had successfully constructed chambers similar in design and requirements to the one Celebrity was purchasing.

The evaluation team studied the technical proposals at some length. The Rayard submission was very complete and included photos of similar installations. The pump-down time was forecasted to be slightly better than the others. The MRT Engineering proposal was technically sound. Their conditions of sale, however, provided the customer little recourse in the case of late delivery. Six years earlier they had been five months late on a delivery of a critical system to Celebrity.

The Houston Chambers Company's technical proposal was not complete and could not be fully evaluated. Some team members questioned whether the supplier understood the specifications or had been unable to develop the full details in time for the proposal. The low price was also a concern.

The Wiston Group proposal had arrived somewhat late and seemed hastily prepared. Its technical proposal offered no advantages or disadvantages. It was technically less detailed than the Rayard Air Products proposal.

The evaluation team had been impressed with the presentation and completeness of the Rayard proposal. James Sampson was concerned about the spread in the pricing and the fact that a qualified supplier had not bid. He wondered if he should have the team probe further.

One thing was clear; in two weeks, a request for appropriation with a supplier recommendation was supposed to be submitted to the general manager. It would take four or five days to prepare. If construction were delayed, Sampson estimated added construction costs could run from $5,000 to $10,000 a day.

1 Outline in step-by-step fashion the actions you suggest James Sampson take in handling this matter. Discuss the significance of each.

THE CASE OF THE COSTLY ACCOMMODATION

Dollars are in short supply on our campus and have been for quite a while. In fact, our purchasing employees haven't had a raise for 30 months and an important buyer position has been caught in a hiring freeze for almost a year. Fortunately, campus-wide attrition has been greater than expected and the hiring freeze has just been lifted. It looks like there'll be raises soon, too.

As you might expect, we received a lot of resumes in response to the buyer position ad. I screened them and decided to interview five candidates. One dropped out, and I interviewed the remaining four. Both on paper and in person, the best qualified applicant is a disabled woman, for whom we'd have to make a one-time expenditure of about $15,000 to accommodate her disability. There would probably be some annual costs, too.

When I told my boss I wanted to hire this woman, he approved but said I would have to take the accommodation costs out of my department budget—and it would likely force cancellation of the raises we were planning. He suggested I reconsider my decision and stressed that the choice was mine.

This candidate is just what the purchasing department needs to be able, at long last, to handle major contract and grant purchases well. If I can't get her, it'll really hurt the department. But if getting her costs all the other employees their long-awaited raises, that'll hurt too.

I know we're supposed to hire the best candidates for open jobs and not discriminate against disabled people, but I don't know if I can comply in this case. One alternative is simply to make an argument for one of the other candidates. Or I could delay the recruitment until after the raises are announced and try again. Maybe she'll still be available and maybe not, but I just might have to take my chances on that. To whom should I be loyal: to the department, to the employees, or to the best candidate? What should I do?

1 Identify and discuss the basic issues in this case.

THE CASE OF THE ROTATING BIDS

Each year, Ridgefield University solicits bids on its letterhead stationery and envelope requirements. Typically, all three local suppliers respond—and the business is awarded to the low bidder. This year a fourth bid was received from a new firm that had recently been organized by J. W. Sprat, who previously had been the sales manager of one of the three old-line firms. Sprat was not the low bidder.

Not long after the bid opening, Sprat appeared in the purchasing office to go over the bid results, and also to review the history of the bidding over the past several years, with Henderson J. Rockwell, III, the director of purchasing. Sprat pointed out that the low bidder each year had been one of the "big three." And that, because of the obvious rotating pattern, collusion had to be suspected. Further, he claimed that, having been an insider until recently, he knew there was no real competitive bidding.

Sprat, therefore, demanded that Rockwell throw out the three bids and place the order with his own firm.

1 What should Henderson Rockwell do? Why?

THE CASE OF THE SECRET DISCOUNT

Dr. Smith, a researcher at Swampland University Medical Center, needed an expensive piece of complex research equipment, which would include a computer and related software. He based his specs on a device he was familiar with, manufactured by As Specified Enterprises, and sent his requisition to Purchasing. As their regulations required, Purchasing issued a "request for bids" for an "As Specified Enterprises *or equal*" device.

On the morning of the day bids were due to be opened, Dr. Smith called Mr. Buylow, the Director of Purchasing, to say that he had received a bid from another company, Alternate Technologies, and that he would walk it right over. When he arrived, it was discovered that he had received an information copy of the bid and that the original had already been received by purchasing. There was a letter attached to Dr. Smith's copy, which in part said:

> I am prepared to offer you, at no additional cost, one additional software package. However, this offer will not be shown on the bid which has been sent to the purchasing department.

According to an attached price list, the value of the additional software package was $18,500.

When the bids were opened, it was found that the Alternate Technologies price was substantially higher than the price bid by As Specified Enterprises and, sure enough, it made no mention of the extra software offered.

Dr. Smith recalled that he had been visited by the Alternate Technologies sales representative during the bidding period, who admitted that his bid would probably be high. But the rep expressed confidence that, if Dr. Smith were to do a proper technical evaluation, the Alternate Technologies equipment would be selected regardless of the high price.

As Dr. Smith related this story, his face clouded over and his eyes widened. "Does this sound like a bribe to you?" he asked Buylow. Buylow leaned back and pondered what he would do next.

1 Is there an ethical problem here?
2 What additional information does Buylow need, if any?
3 What are his options?
4 What advice would you give Buylow?

THE CASE OF THE SLEEPING DOGS

Phil Wrightman, Purchasing Director at Metropolitan University, didn't think he'd ever seen a year like this one. They'd cut his budget. He was short of staff. And now there were all those noises about environmental issues. Phil was known for his judgement, his loyalty to the institution and his can-do attitude, but this was too much.

First, there were those people from the Student Coalition for Environmental Action who wanted him to rebid his food service paper and plastics contract to drop all the plastic items and substitute biodegradable materials. He shuddered to think of the horrible problems he would have getting all the campus users to accept the substitute items, and anyway, biodegradable products were probably going to be more expensive.

The same was true about recycled xerographic bond. There had been an increasing number of inquiries recently from people in smaller departments who said they were interested in buying recycled paper. But he knew how particular the big paper users were about their copy quality and he was willing to bet that they wouldn't go along. He also suspected that they wouldn't tolerate any cost increases right now.

Then there was that freon he went ahead and bought for the physical plant people, even though he knew that freon was an environmental problem. But he hadn't had time to question it or look for an alternate product.

Finally, there was the pressure to add an office paper recycling project to his surplus property disposal program. He knew from long experience that the administration wouldn't tolerate any program that didn't pay for itself, and what with the added collection and sorting costs, coupled with the low price he would probably be able to get for scrap paper, he suspected such a venture didn't stand a chance of being approved.

Thank God the campus' purchasing activity was down a bit because of the budget situation. It was the only thing keeping his head above water. Phil saw these environmental issues as sleeping dogs, and he was glad he decided to let them lie.

1 Is it an ethical problem for a buyer to buy something he or she knows is bad for the environment, or to avoid buying something known to be environmentally safe?
2 What is a buyer's responsibility to the institution versus his or her responsibility to society in general?

A CASE OF TOO MUCH HELP

Nancy O'Leary, senior buyer at the Northfield Unified School District purchasing department, sat reflecting on a purchase requisition (P.R.) she had just received. The P.R. called for 1,000 model 2001 classroom armchairs, manufactured by the Twinsburg Chair Company. The P.R. was requested by Betsy Burns, instructor, and authorized by Rudolf Rupp, principal. Sufficient funds and the budget class were cited. A copy of a sales agreement for the chairs was attached. The price was $120 per chair, F.O.B. Northfield. Nancy reviewed three other chair suppliers' catalogues and learned that nearly identical chairs were available F.O.B. Northfield at prices ranging from $40 to $43.

Nancy called Betsy Burns and asked whose idea it was to specify the Twinsburg chairs, mentioning that this chair was nearly three times as expensive as three comparable chairs. Betsy responded in her Georgia drawl, "Why, Nancy, darlin', the superintendent's cabinet decided that at last week's meeting. They said that they wanted the best there was for our young people."

Nancy thanked Betsy for the information. Based on past experiences with the superintendent's cabinet, she knew that it would be futile to get authorization to buy the less expensive chairs. In a resigned manner, she called the Twinsburg rep and requested him to visit her to discuss the terms of the purchase.

Something did not seem right—but Nancy seemed powerless to do anything about it.

1 What courses of action are open to Nancy?
2 What are the advantages and disadvantages of each?
3 Write a policy for the school focusing on early purchasing involvement.

THE CENTENNIAL COMPANY

The Centennial Company manufactured small electrical appliances for the consumer market. Its major product line consisted of several models of electric shavers for both men and women. The shaver division generated over 90 percent of the firm's annual sales, which ran at approximately $30 million last year.

Several years ago the company introduced a new shaver model that proved to be extremely successful. The model utilized a new microscreen-type head that produced an extremely close shave. During the design stage of the new product, the marketing department had conducted an extensive consumer survey to determine exactly what style and color combinations best suited the market for this innovative new product. The style finally selected was an extremely modish plastic case with a sleek futuristic contour.

From a cost and pricing point of view, the new product fit the company's basic operating strategy very well. Over the years, Centennial had become known as a manufacturer of low-cost, high-quality products. The firm typically priced its products 15 to 20 percent below its major competitors. This pricing policy was made possible, in part, because Centennial was basically a design-and-assembly-type operation that purchased a majority of its parts and components in large volumes from specialty manufacturers and supply houses. Centennial's production facilities were highly automated so that its labor cost was relatively low; last year, material costs ran approximately 65 percent of net sales.

During the past six months, Centennial's material costs had been increasing at a level significantly higher than the producer price index for finished non-consumer goods. Indirect labor costs and overhead also had also begun to increase. Consequently, the firm's profit margin and its return on investment had begun to drop off noticeably. Several members of the firm's top management team thought that Centennial should reconsider its basic pricing policy. The possibility of a 5 to 10 percent price increase was being contemplated. The vice president for sales, however, resisted a price increase because he thought it might erode the low-cost, high-quality image the firm had developed in the marketplace. The result, he thought, could well be a significant loss of economy-minded customers.

Each of the Centennial department managers was asked to consider possible approaches to the resolution of the cost-price squeeze issue and also to prepare a brief report on possible cost cutting/productivity improvement measures that could be undertaken in their respective departments. The manager of the purchasing department was asked in his report to pay particular attention to the matter of material costs and efficient utilization of departmental personnel.

1 As a purchasing manager, what is your responsibility concerning top management's knowledge and expectation of the purchasing operation?
   a What performance data should management have been receiving?
   b What information is necessary to control material costs?
2 What types of suggestions might the purchasing manager make in his report that would be worth exploring? Making several reasonable operating assumptions (also assume the current profit margin is 5 percent), quantify the estimated results from a profitability point of view.

COLLIER COMPANY I

The Collier Company is a large electrical manufacturer. Recently, a new division of the company was started, and entirely new facilities were required. In equipping the new plant, it was decided that for certain subassembly operations it would be desirable to have production employees seated at high stools instead of standing at their work benches. Eight hundred and fifty employees were to be so seated in the new plant.

After investigating many possible stool designs, the plant engineering department and the personnel department agreed on a certain style of stool that was easily described to the trade as "Carter's 816 or equal." Bids were requested by purchasing from most major fabricators of this type of item, and bids from nine suppliers were received more than ten days before the announced closing date.

Several days before the final bid date these suppliers started to call the purchasing manager to see how they ranked. The purchasing manager answered their questions honestly with phrases like:

"You are not low bidder, but you are fairly competitive."

"You are not low bidder. You are way out of line."

"You are presently low bidder, but others seem to be revising their bids."

By April 23, the day originally chosen to close bidding, every supplier except supplier C had submitted at least one revised quotation. (See Exhibit 1.) In most cases, the prices quoted were substantially below the initial bids.

Late in the afternoon on April 23, two suppliers asked for special permission to make a final bid on April 24. Since these two firms had been satisfactory suppliers of the Collier Company for years, the purchasing manager was

---

EXHIBIT 1
UNIT PRICES QUOTED BY SUPPLIERS

	Original bid	April 23 bid	May 7 bid
Supplier A	$55.92	$41.10	$34.08
Supplier B	44.70	37.50	31.62
Supplier C	39.48	39.48	39.48
Supplier D	45.36	35.88	30.06
Supplier E	43.86	38.58	31.98
Supplier F	38.70*	37.92	29.88*
Supplier G	39.00	35.40*	30.60
Supplier H	42.78	39.60	31.50
Supplier I	48.60	41.34	33.18

*Indicates low bid.

anxious to give them any opportunity to keep their facilities operating in the depressed conditions that then characterized their industry. He gave them a special extension of one day. By the next afternoon, the purchasing manager had heard from three more firms who wanted the same privileges as the two concerns who had rebid. Firms kept asking for special extensions or equal bid privileges until the purchasing manager finally said to all who called that May 7 was the last day he would entertain bids. On May 7 several suppliers asked for special permission to bid late and were refused. Supplier C still had not called in to change its original bid.

By May 7, the purchasing manager felt that all the firms were bidding at less than their total costs in order to keep their facilities operating at the highest possible volume in this slack period. He also felt that further price adjustments would be negligible. However, not wanting any supplier to go "out of pocket" on the order, the purchasing manager asked the plant engineers to make a cost estimate on the chairs. The engineers estimated costs as follows:

Labor	$12.00
Materials	13.62
Overhead: 150% of direct labor	18.00
Total cost (excluding profit)	$43.62

Having satisfied himself that all suppliers were making some contribution to overhead at the quoted prices, the purchasing manager awarded the order to supplier D, who had done business with the Collier Company in the past and was considered one of the best fabricators in its field.

On May 9, two days after *making the award,* the purchasing manager heard from both supplier C and supplier F.

Supplier C was extremely angry that he had not been told of the acceptance of new bids. He said that he would write a letter to the vice president of material requesting a review of this "entire deplorable situation." The purchasing manager informed supplier C that reasonable follow-up on the latter's part would have given him any information available to other potential suppliers. Supplier C was not at all satisfied with this answer and again expressed his intention to contact the vice president of material.

Supplier F asked why the purchasing manager had requested bids at all if his "mind had been made up all along." Supplier F said that the order should have gone to the lowest bidder who could provide the object desired. He said he could meet the specifications and could deliver to any schedule supplier D could meet. He demanded the order, and when the purchasing manager informed supplier F that "final selection of the supplier is entirely my province," the supplier raged that he would "spread the word to the trade" and would write the Collier Company president, who "should know of such favoritism and incompetence." He further stated that he even suspected that money had passed hands for this order.

The purchasing manager was upset by these calls and did not enjoy his supper on May 9.

1 What suggestions might you have made in the purchasing manager's handling of this matter?
2 What would you recommend that he do now?
3 To what extent would you concur in the purchasing manager's belief that suppliers should at least be allowed to recover direct costs?
4 Who do you feel should have received the order?
5 What are the weaknesses inherent in the competitive bidding process?
6 Should this purchase have been negotiated? Discuss.

THE COUNTY WATER WORKS

INTRODUCTION

Rick Anderson was recently hired in the finance department of the County Water Works. One of the first things Rick noticed was the absence of and need for personal computers. He was not alone in his opinion; most department heads had included funds in their budgets to acquire personal computers in the next few months. As Rick spoke with others, he realized that most departments were getting different types of computers, with different types of software and operating systems, and were using different suppliers. Although some of the needs were specialized, most of the software packages performed one of three functions: spreadsheet, data base, or document processing. There also was the possible need to share information between departments in the not too distant future. Rick saw a potential to organize the needs of the different people in the hope of standardizing software applications and hardware platforms, obtaining government quantity discount prices, establishing a long-term relationship with a suitable supplier to facilitate support, and creating an environment where the electronic exchange of information between departments would be feasible.

THE COUNTY WATER WORKS

The County Water Works (CWW) is a regional water wholesaler. The government agency is responsible for delivering water to local cities and districts within its service area. Although the agency is forty-five years old, the agency hasn't grown in terms of personnel much until recently. Between 1995 and 2000, the personnel requirements will grow from 50 to over 100. Personal computer needs will grow faster since the CWW has historically not purchased personal computers for its employees, relying instead on pencil and paper.

This case was developed by Duane Mason and Ralph Williams under the direction of Professor David N. Burt.

During the same time span, estimates predict the installed personal computer base to grow from two personal computers to thirty.

Procurement issues generally revolve around price; all other things being equal, the supplier with the lowest price receives the order. However, if a supplier has proven reliability, this supplier can be used when warranted. For purchases in excess of $200, three bids must be obtained. There is no central purchasing department. Since all purchasing is a distributed function, the department wanting to buy a computer creates a requisition which describes the computer in full detail, listing all required specifications. When time permits, the requisitions are mailed to the suppliers and written bids are then mailed back to the initiating department. These written bids are used to complete a purchase order request. The purchase order request is used to complete the purchase order, which is made out to the selected supplier. There is no process to preapprove suppliers.

HISTORY OF THE PROJECT

Initial conversations with the department heads and the general manager went well. Everyone saw the potential benefits of standardization outlined by Rick. As a result, the general manager (who answers only to the board of directors) created a personal computer committee, made up of ten people representing most of the departments. This committee would act as a steering committee, its purpose being to create a personal computer standard and review all requests for personal computers.

The committee began by inventorying all the current and projected computer needs of all the departments. From this list, an application was selected to meet the need. As often as possible, the same application was selected to meet similar needs. Next, computers were selected that would run the applications needed. Again, as often as possible, the same type of computer (in terms of performance) was selected. During this process, two suppliers were requested to suggest what they thought were appropriate applications and computers, and to submit recommended solutions in writing to the committee. Their reports were also to include prices on the software, hardware, and any necessary installation and training they thought might be needed.

The committee compiled all the information, wrote a report, and, at the request of the general manager, distributed the report to all the department heads. The report cited applications considered, explained why a particular application was chosen, and met all the existing procurement concerns of the Water Works. A similar list showed all computers reviewed and gave reasons to support the decision on two types of computers. One type was described as a 777-based computer to meet light-to-moderate performance requirements, while the second type was an 888-based computer for some of the more processing-intensive applications. See Table 1 for a schedule showing products reviewed. The report also recommended a single software supplier and a single hardware supplier, explaining best price and service as the main reasons

TABLE 1

	Cost
Hardware:	
777 platform, 40 meg hard drive, 2 meg RAM, 1 1.2 floppy drive	
ARC 777	$2,400
Wyse 777	3,000
Zenith 777	3,200
*Compaq 777 Deskpro	4,000
IBM P/S 7, Model 50	4,800
888 platform, 60 meg hard drive, 4 meg RAM, 1 1.2 floppy drive	
ARC 888	$3,400
Wyse 888	4,000
Zenith 888	4,600
*Compaq 888 Deskpro	6,000
IBM P/S 7, Model 70	7,800
Software:	
Spreadsheet	
*Lotus 4-5-6	$200
Microsoft Universe	400
Borland Quarto	150
Data base	
Dabse III+	$400
*Rapid File	200
VP Info	75
Q & A	300
Document processing	
*WordPerfect 7.0	$225
Sprint	200
*Pagemaker	450
Q & A Write	200

*Recommended items.

for selection. By using one hardware supplier, the purchase price would be at least 20 percent less per purchase. By using one software supplier, the purchase price would be 15 percent less per purchase. GSA (Government Services Administration) pricing was not available. Warranties on computer equipment are similar among most manufacturers and valid only if purchased from an authorized dealer. Warranties on software vary between manufacturers but are the same regardless of the supplier.

At the department heads meeting, concern was expressed over the findings of the report. One concern was that, of the computers reviewed, the committee recommended the second most expensive machine. Comparably equipped machines from other manufacturers cost as much as 40 percent less than the recommended machines. The heads felt the additional cost was not fully justified. Further, they had budgeted based on the less expensive machines. In addition, some felt that other operating systems would more fully meet their needs and didn't see the loss of standardization as a problem for their particular department. The two main problems, then, were excessively high hardware costs and less than ultimate operating system platforms.

The general manager was pleased with the report. He thought he could justify the additional cost to the board because the report recommended a reputable manufacturer. He also believed integration and standardization were key issues. It was his experience that having various types of operating system platforms complicated training and maintenance issues unnecessarily. In regard to software, he believed it didn't make sense to have five different word processing programs, four different spreadsheet programs, and three different data-base programs. He asked Rick to attend the next department heads' meeting to try to fully address any questions. The meeting is at the end of the week. In getting prepared for the meeting, Rick wondered how to proceed.

1 What additional information should Rick obtain or develop in preparation for the meeting?
2 Identify improvements and/or additions to the procurement system that need to be implemented.
3 How important is the issue of computer standardization?
4 Rick feels unqualified to fully address the questions of the department heads. Who might be able to help?
5 How can the Water Works enter into a long-term relationship with a supplier and continue to fulfill the prerequisite of choosing the supplier with the lowest bid?

CROSSING THE BORDER

The North American Free Trade Agreement (NAFTA) had just passed. For Katie Dunhill it was good news because, she hoped, the paperwork would be reduced. Katie was the import/export coordinator for Tokisan America Inc. (TAI). She managed the process of obtaining and sending raw materials and finished goods to and from the Mexican maquiladora. The maquiladora was a Mexican company that processed and assembled labor-intensive parts. Companies from all over the world, including TAI, arranged for maquiladoras to do assembly work because of the low-cost labor.

Tokisan was a Japanese company with headquarters in Tokyo and subsidiary production facilities in the United States and Mexico. The U.S. subsidiary, TAI, was essentially autonomous, while the Mexican maquiladora was not. The maquiladora was managed entirely by TAI. For the last week there

This case was developed by Frederick terVeer under the direction of Professor David N. Burt.

had been ominous rumors of a future trucking strike in Mexico. Any trucking strike would slow or stop cross-border traffic since the truckers would most likely block major roads.

Katie knew the import/export process well. She was aware that the export paperwork at TAI took at least eight hours to process (Katie was sure it could be done faster). It took at least four hours for the trucks to be loaded and four hours for the trucks to reach the border. At the border, the trucks could clear in a minimum of five minutes, but sometimes the Mexican Customs officials would review the shipping documents with agonizing slowness. Sometimes the tactic was used to extract minor bribes, which TAI refused to pay, preferring up to one day of delay. Customs officials were slowly learning that TAI did not pay, and were resorting to tougher tactics such as questioning the shipping documents and refusing entry of material. Once across the border, it would take an additional six hours for the truck to reach the plant and get unloaded. Only then was the raw material available for the assembly work.

Recently the headquarters office in Japan had made the request to begin converting all manufacturing to a just-in-time basis. Katie knew this would be problematic, especially with the Mexican maquiladora as part of the manufacturing process. With all this in mind, she knew she had to make some quick decisions. Allowing production to stop was viewed poorly by management. Today was Wednesday, 7 a.m., and the trucker strike would probably start next Monday—and was expected to last a minimum of two days. She would attend the daily production meeting in fifteen minutes. She sat down, looked out the window, then looked down at her calendar, and decided what to do.

1 Identify and discuss the key issues in the case.

THE DEAR JOHN MOWER COMPANY

The Dear John Mower Company is an old-line manufacturer of gasoline-powered lawn mowers and riding mowers. Increased competition has resulted in Dear John's share of the mower market declining to 10 percent. Profits have declined to the point that many are questioning Dear John's ability to survive.

The firm employs three engineers who are responsible for the development and design of all new mowers. When the engineers are not involved in the development of new products, they apply their energy to value analysis work in an effort to engineer costs out of the firm's products.

Material costs at Dear John range from 55 to 65 percent of the cost of goods sold. Purchasing has been a routine function, responsible for issuing purchase orders confirming the sourcing decisions of the engineers and for issuing order releases against these purchase orders. Recently, Mr. Tom Dalton, CPM, was hired in an effort to reduce the cost of purchased materials. Mr. Dalton had some success through the application of price and cost analysis and professional negotiation concepts. Material costs have dropped an average of 12.5 percent. These savings have been the basis of a badly needed shot in the arm for Dear John's financial report.

Tom believes that he's done about all he can to reduce costs—short of getting himself and his key suppliers involved early in the design of new mowers. Tom has initiated discussions on this approach with John Steel, chief of engineering—to no avail. Mr. Steel is adamant that his engineers are the best in the industry and develop the industry's finest mowers. He acted insulted when Tom suggested that early purchasing and early supplier involvement would improve Dear John's profitability.

Having had no success with engineering, Tom has initiated discussions on the matter with Mr. Helmich, COO of Dear John. Mr. Helmich has requested Mr. Steel and Mr. Dalton to meet with him to discuss the merits and possible implementation of early purchasing and early supplier involvement.

1 Prepare a list of advantages of the inclusion of purchasing and prequalified suppliers.
2 Prepare a list of disadvantages of excluding purchasing and suppliers from the new product development process.
3 Assuming that the three executives agree on early involvement of purchasing and suppliers, develop a plan to implement this new way of doing business.

DONLEY BROTHERS

The Donley Brothers Company had encountered the problem of latent defects in some of its purchased castings. Being latent, the defects did not show up until after machining had taken place at Donley Brothers. This group of failures greatly irritated the manufacturing boss, who declared that "repairing those darn castings is eating up all our profits."

When the defects were discovered, the rough casting had to be taken off the machine, the defect chipped out and repair-welded, and the casting remachined when possible. Even with this process, almost 12 percent of the incoming castings ended up as scrap. Actually, 1,140 raw castings had to be purchased and machined in order to produce 1,000 good machined ones. The raw castings cost $600 each from either of two suppliers. Worse than the costs associated with rework and high scrap rates were the continual changes in production scheduling necessitated by a machined casting not being available as scheduled. These changes were costly because they required shop personnel to tear down the job they were working on and set up a new job. Marketing was constantly complaining about the firm's inability to meet delivery commitments for the finished machinery that incorporated the castings. Marketing claimed that many sales were lost as a result of this failure.

George Donley, the production manager, and Terry Donley, the vice president for marketing, asked Bob Donley, the purchasing manager, to investigate the costs involved in purchasing finished machined castings. If finished castings were purchased, the responsibility for finding hidden defects would be that of the supplier. Such action would encourage the supplier to improve the casting quality. Donley Brothers would accept and pay only for finished, usable castings.

The internal cost of machining each incoming rough casting and repair welding and remachining it, as necessary, was approximately $312 per casting. This figure included $156 of direct labor and $156 of overhead. The accounting department estimated that overhead, which was 100 percent of direct labor, consisted of 50 percent variable and 50 percent fixed costs. No estimate was available on the cost of disrupted production schedules and operations.

Bob approached all his major suppliers of castings in an attempt to generate interest for the supply of finished machined castings. Only one supplier, Akron Foundry, showed genuine interest. Of major concern to all the foundries was the $120,000 to $160,000 investment necessary to set themselves up to machine the raw castings. Akron was willing both to invest in the necessary machines and to guarantee delivery of up to 150 units per month—provided Donley Brothers would contract with it as a sole source for the castings for the next three years. The price per casting would be $1,000 the first year, with an annual increase or decrease in price tied to an appropriate economic index.

Bob was faced with the problem of deciding whether to recommend contracting with Akron Foundry for finished castings, continue as in the past buying rough castings, or developing a more attractive alternative. The Donley machine shop was currently operating at 90 percent of capacity, but it was not possible to make a reliable estimate of what would happen in the next few months, let alone the next three years. The decision of whether to buy finished castings was of major dollar importance to Donley Brothers because the firm used at least 1,000 finished castings per year and anticipated that this usage would continue for each of the next five years.

1 Should Bob Donley contract with Akron Foundry for finished castings?
2 Would there be any dollar savings by contracting with Akron Foundry if the Donley Brothers' machine shop were operating at full capacity?
3 What are the dangers involved if Akron Foundry becomes a single source for Donley Brothers' castings?
4 Who is responsible for the make-or-buy decision?
5 What other suggestions can you make for improving the situation at Donley Brothers?

DRIVE SHAFT DECISION: CASE A

On January 15, Robert Hardin, who was international sourcing manager for John Deere Des Moines Works, was interrupted. Bill Smith, QA manager, burst into Hardin's office, exclaiming "The report is back from the outside lab. BPT's shipment of shafts has been rejected due to inferior material!" Robert was surprised. While this was only BPT's second shipment of this part, BPT of Seoul, Korea, had been supplying excellent quality on raw and machined castings since late 1987.

COMPANY BACKGROUND

John Deere Company, a major international manufacturer and distributor of industrial, farm, and lawn equipment, had 16 plants worldwide. Last year's sales were $7.2 billion. Purchasing dollars were approximately 55 percent of cost of goods sold. Purchasing at John Deere was highly decentralized. Each plant had its own purchasing staff which reported to the general manager through the materials manager. The purchasing dollars of the Des Moines Works (DMW) plant accounted for approximately 57% of DMW's cost of goods sold.

INTERNATIONAL PURCHASING

In 1982, the world farming economy entered a major slump. To help offset declining sales and profitability, John Deere sought to reduce costs. Thus, overseas sourcing, particularly in the Far East, became an attractive option. To support the firm's objectives of reducing cost, DMW began actively to investigate international purchasing opportunities in 1985. By 1987, DMW was purchasing about $275,000 worth of parts from Korean suppliers. This grew to $2.7 million by 1993.

RELATIONSHIP WITH BPT

BPT was by far the largest Korean source for DMW, accounting for about 75 percent of its Korean purchases. DMW valued BPT as a supplier; BPT provided DMW with excellent quality and service on a number of raw and machined castings, at a price 40–60 percent below comparable U.S. sources. Delivery time averaged 30 days. Thus, in February of 1992, DMW requested that BPT provide a quotation on drum drive shaft number M5555, used in cotton picking equipment. These drive shafts required a special stress-relieved cold drawn steel rod, a material which was produced by only a few manufacturers.

Copyrighted by the National Association of Purchasing Management. Reproduced by permission. This case was written by Lisa M. Ellram during one of the NAPM-sponsored case writing workshops.

The part was currently being satisfactorily supplied by a U.S. supplier, but DMW desired a lower price.

BPT provided DMW with samples which met dimensional specifications, at a cost of about 50 percent of the current manufacturer. Thus, DMW's cost for this part would drop from over $40,000 a year to under $20,000, or around $9.00 each. However, the material used did not meet specifications. DMW faxed its concerns about the material used to BPT. DMW was assured, via return fax, that the proper material would be used on actual production. Thus, DMW approved the samples, again faxing the information that substitution of materials would not be acceptable.

CURRENT QUALITY PROBLEM

In mid-December, 1992, DMW received its first shipment of part M5555. A standard inspection at the DMW plant showed the dimensions and surface hardness of the part were acceptable. Thus, the parts were used in production.

On January 12, 1993, about 30 days after the initial shipment, the second shipment of shafts arrived from BPT. Standard QA testing at the DMW revealed that this shipment did not meet specifications; there were dimensional deficiencies. This failure concerned QA managers, who immediately sent samples to an outside lab for further testing.

On January 15, 1993, the results from the outside lab were received by QA manager Bill Smith. The tests revealed that the wrong kind of steel had been used. The steel was not "stress-relieved," but had been heat-treated after machining to provide a superficial outside hardness. If these parts were used in production, the product would be subject to early failure. Premature failure of a product was totally unacceptable to a quality company like John Deere.

The implications were staggering. Cotton pickers have highly seasonal sales, and DMW had no backup shafts. Picker production would be unable to proceed. DMW was no longer using its U.S. supplier for this particular item, although it was buying other parts from that supplier. Further, the shaft generally had a lead time of about three months. BPT also had a shipment of shafts in transit to DMW, somewhere on the Pacific Ocean.

1 Identify and discuss the major issues in the case.

THE DUTZEL DIESEL CASE

Jack Haley, a senior buyer for the Dynamite Truck Company, was confronted with an interesting predicament—and possibly a trip overseas. Rising gasoline costs and increased foreign competition had caused the management at Dynamite Truck to develop a new truck powered by an air-cooled diesel engine.

From bumper to tailgate, the new vehicle was designed as a full-performance diesel truck. It was heavy-duty throughout: frame, suspension, brakes, axles, and steering. It was built to endure. Under normal operating conditions, the new truck, using an efficient air-cooled diesel engine, was designed to yield 18 to 20 miles per gallon. The warranty was for 100,000 miles or two full years, whichever came first.

Jack had been actively involved in the development of the new truck. He provided the Dynamite engineers with information on the availability and cost implications of various materials, components, and subassemblies under consideration. From a technical, cost, availability, and service point of view, the diesel engine was the most crucial item to be purchased for the new truck.

Jack obtained technical data on four air-cooled diesel engines that appeared to satisfy Dynamite's requirements. Two of the manufacturers of these engines were located in Europe, one in Japan, and one in the United States.

Discussions with the program manager indicated that from a technical point of view, each of the diesel power plants was acceptable. Accordingly, all four manufacturers were invited to submit bids. The request for bids stipulated an estimated requirement of 10,000 engines per year for each of the next three years.

The date specified for the close of the bidding period was Friday, June 13. All four firms submitted bids by the established date. Dutzel Diesel of Gailsdorf, Germany, was the low bidder with an F.O.B. destination price of $14,263 for the first year, and a standard price escalation clause for the second and third years. The second lowest bidder was a U.S. firm, the Great American Diesel Company. Its price bid for the first year was $16,287 per engine. The price for the second and third years contained the same economic escalation clause as Dutzel's bid.

Jack sat contemplating a course of action. He wondered if the $2,024 per unit price differential required to buy the U.S. engines could be justified. He also wondered about the necessity of a trip to Gailsdorf to perform a survey on Dutzel prior to awarding the contract.

1 Do you believe that global purchasing is destined to give purchasing managers and buyers an increasing number of problems? Discuss.
2 What is the easiest way for buyers to start making international purchases?
3 If you were Jack, how would you decide this issue?

DYNAMIC AIRCRAFT

The Dynamic Aircraft Company was recently awarded a multibillion dollar contract for a new high-performance aircraft. This project required the use of new materials in many areas of the aircraft. The aircraft incorporated a state-of-the-art concept known as fly-by-wire.

Among the conventional materials no longer useful were many of the types of wire used in the electrical systems of aircraft. Fortunately, however, the electrical wire manufacturers had been brought in on the problem at an early date so that, before long, many of them could offer for sale a standard stock electrical wire capable of withstanding unusually high temperatures.

One leading electrical wire firm, Advanced Wire of Chattahoochee, Georgia, had developed a ceramic-coated wire. Other wire sources had tackled the problem in different ways. The representatives of all these companies were anxious to demonstrate their products to the engineering departments of the aircraft companies.

The engineers at the Dynamic Aircraft Company, a large airframe manufacturer, were quite favorably impressed with Advanced Wire's ceramic-coated wire. They knew from previous experience that Advanced Wire had a reputation as a quality supplier of electrical wiring for the aircraft industry. Believing that Advanced's wire was the highest quality obtainable, the engineers specified it on the bill of materials.

Bill Marshall bought wire and related items for the Dynamic Aircraft Company. An experienced buyer, Mr. Marshall had a reputation for being conscientious and knowledgeable concerning the commodities that he purchased. When the requisition came to him to buy Advanced's ceramic-coated wire, he immediately wondered why Advanced Wire had been designated as a sole source. From his experience in buying wire, he knew Advanced to be a high-cost producer. Moreover, he always attempted to follow the Dynamic Aircraft Company policy of dealing with more than one source whenever possible.

Believing that engineering may have been "sold a bill of goods" by the Advanced sales representative, Mr. Marshall decided to telephone the engineering department to learn what specifications governed the wire in question. Mr. Marshall did not want the engineer he was telephoning to think that, despite the fact that the current instance was typical of a number of similar instances, he was in any way censuring him for specifying Advanced Wire as a sole source. The engineer explained that the wire was of a special nature, designed to withstand extremely high temperatures. He also said that Advanced's wire was the highest quality obtainable and that in his judgment, it should be purchased to fill the current need.

Mr. Marshall pointed out to the engineer that there were many thousands of types of electrical wiring. He said that all of these types were made according to some sort of specification—either military specifications, wire industry specifications, or specifications established by the purchaser. Mr. Marshall also said that a rule of the Dynamic Aircraft purchasing department required a buyer to know about any governing specifications before issuing a purchase order. After a few more minutes of conversation, the engineer said that he would attempt to locate the governing specifications and send them over to Mr. Marshall.

In the meantime, Mr. Marshall got in touch with the local representative of Advanced Wire to request samples of its ceramic-coated wire and price quotations. When the quotations were submitted. Mr. Marshall observed that once again Advanced's prices were higher than those of the industry in general. Yet he realized that this particular wire might well be a more expensive item to manufacture as a result of its ceramic-coating feature.

Several days later, Mr. Marshall received the specifications for the wire. The specifications were of the military standard type and listed the performance requirements that the wire was to meet. They said nothing about whether the wire was to have a ceramic coating. Accordingly, Mr. Marshall solicited quotations from the other qualified suppliers and asked that samples be submitted to him that would meet the performance requirements of the specifications.

Five other suppliers submitted samples and price quotations. On receipt of the samples, Mr. Marshall forwarded the samples, along with Advanced's sample, to the production development laboratory of Dynamic Aircraft for analysis and evaluation. The production development laboratory was under the direction of Dynamic Aircraft's inspection department and was separated both physically and organizationally from the engineering department.

A week later the report of the production development laboratory was in Mr. Marshall's hands. The samples submitted by the six suppliers had undergone exhaustive tests, particularly with regard to their ability to withstand high temperatures for prolonged periods of time. One of the suppliers was eliminated from consideration when its product failed to meet performance specifications. The other five samples, including Advanced's, were found to exceed minimum performance requirements, and at extremely high temperature ranges the ceramic coating of Advanced's sample made it superior to the others.

With regard to the weight of the samples (another important consideration), Advanced's wire was found to be heavier than the others. Furthermore, the conductivity characteristics of Advanced's wire were rated as inferior to the other samples, although all the samples exceeded the minimum performance requirements and were rated as acceptable. On the abrasiveness test, Advanced's wire was found to be slightly less durable than the other suppliers' samples but, nevertheless, acceptable.

These laboratory findings tended to confirm Mr. Marshall's belief that the engineering department had been sold a bill of goods in specifying Advanced as the sole supplier. The samples submitted by four of the other suppliers had met the governing military specifications and in some ways were superior to Advanced's. While Advanced's wire withstood higher temperatures, Mr. Marshall saw no need to pay a premium price for it since the wire supplied by the other suppliers met the specifications that engineering had submitted to him. With regard to price, the Easternhouse Electric Company was the lowest bidder and Advanced was the highest. The high and low bidders compared dollarwise as shown in Exhibit 1 on the quantities to be purchased.

The delivery schedules required by Dynamic Aircraft posed no particular problem since all five of the qualified suppliers seemed capable of meeting required delivery dates.

EXHIBIT 1

Size	Advanced price (per 1,000 ft)	Eastern-house price (per 1,000 ft)	Quantity to be purchased (in 1,000 ft)	Advanced total price	Eastern-house total price	Difference in total price
20 gauge	$ 55.20	$ 21.00	100	$ 5,520.00	$2,100.00	$ 3,420.00
12 gauge	102.00	50.40	70	7,140.00	3,528.00	3,612.00
10 gauge	124.60	76.90	120	14,952.00	9,228.00	5,724.00
8 gauge	243.60	129.60	40	9,744.00	5,184.00	4,560.00
4 gauge	399.90	248.40	20	7,998.00	4,968.00	3,030.00
Totals				$45,354.00	$25,008.00	$20,346.00

The laboratory report and the price quotations were then sent by Mr. Marshall to the engineering department, along with a request that the purchasing department be authorized to place the order with any company that could meet the military specifications.

The engineering department refused Mr. Marshall's request, maintaining that Advanced was the only company that could manufacture wiring that would meet the requirements of Dynamic's engineering department. The engineers stated further that since Advanced had been the first company to develop this particular wire, the purchase order should be placed with it. In conclusion, they reiterated their claim that Advanced had a superior product that would justify any price differential.

1 If you were Mr. Marshall, what action would you take now?
2 Should Mr. Marshall have challenged the engineering department's specification of Advanced's wire?

EAGLE MACHINE COMPANY

The Eagle Machine Company has fallen on bad times. Eagle, a maker of specialty restaurant equipment, has sales totaling $72 million, but sales are declining while costs continue to increase. If things continue in this direction, Eagle soon may have to close its doors.

At a special management meeting, the president lays it on the line! He demands that the firm break even in the remaining quarter of the year. For next year, he calls for profits of 5 percent, a 20 percent increase in sales, and deeper cuts in labor, material, and overhead. Later in the day, the president calls Sally Stone, director of purchasing, in for a discussion.

"Sally, I want you purchasing people to carry the ball at the start of this game. We can't get sales moving for six months. But you can improve your housekeeping—and Eagle's profits—right away. Just think what you can do to that chart! Every penny you save is profit! So take a close look at what you buy. I don't care how you make your savings—by negotiations, inventories, imports, anything. But put the screws on tight—right away!

"Start with inventories, they're sky-high. So get together with manufacturing on a 10 percent cut! We've got $12 million worth of materials stashed away around here, and a 10 percent cut would save at least $300,000 a year in carrying charges. At the same time, get your payroll and operating expenses down 10 percent. That's in line with our companywide cutback. I know this hurts, Sally, because you've got some mighty fine people here in purchasing, but we can't be sentimental these days. Our overhead has got to come down—or we're dead!

"I'm having an executive committee meeting in one week. Have your plans ready by that time! We're betting on you, Sally. You've got to get us out of the hole. I know you can do it."

Sally Stone starts a review of her purchases, which total $43.2 million per year. Eagle buys a wide variety of materials, ranging from a few pounds of rare metals to sizable quantities of sheet metal. A big part of the dollar volume is in nonferrous castings, forgings, stampings, fasteners, and subassemblies.

Her department consists of Sally, three buyers, and four clerks. Salaries, fringes, and expenses come to $370,000 a year. The purchasing department is responsible only for buying and expediting; the manufacturing manager handles production, inventory control, receiving, and traffic. Sally reports to the president, as do other department heads.

Sally learns from inventory control that raw stock inventory is $12.2 million. The marketing manager controls finished goods stocks.

Sally wonders how she can deliver the cost reduction and still keep her department and supplier relations in shape for the long pull.

1 What actions should Sally take to reduce inventories by 10 percent?
2 What dangers, if any, are there in reducing inventories?
3 In what ways could the cost of goods purchased be reduced?
4 What position should Sally take on the president's plan to reduce the purchasing payroll by 10 percent?
5 Develop a list of arguments in support of, and another list in opposition to, the introduction of a materials management organization at Eagle.

ERIE MACHINE, INC.

Erie Machine, Inc., is a small machine shop that derives the bulk of its business from large- and medium-sized copy machine manufacturers. The major part of Erie's work is building prototypes from rough blueprints. From time to time, production runs have been undertaken; however, Erie's machines, layout, and space do not lend themselves to line production.

In the ten years of its life, Erie Machine, Inc., has grown continuously. Employment has increased from 35 to 282 employees, and the company is very successful. A new treasurer, Ray Grabit, has just been hired. Ray, a young man seven years out of college, is full of new ideas and questions. One of the questions bothering him is the company's method of disposing of its scrap metal.

Because of its type of specialized manufacturing, Erie Machine does not use a large quantity of metal. However, it does use several types including iron, steel, Monel, lead, copper, and brass. The total usage of all types generates about 12 tons of scrap per year. Roughly 10 percent of this total is brass and copper.

At the end of each day the metal scrap, together with wood and paper waste, is placed in a trash bin. The bin is emptied by the Lake Erie Sanitation Engineering Company three times a week.

Ray is curious about this procedure. Could the company realize some value by salvaging and selling its scrap?

1 Would a small quantity of metal be worth the trouble of setting up a good procedure to handle it?
2 If so, who should be responsible for managing such surplus material?

FAUQUIER GAS COMPANY

On April 14, Mr. Bill Murphy, manager of purchasing for the Fauquier Gas Company in the Carolinas, was concerned about being able to find a supplier who could deliver 3½ miles of large-diameter pipe for a new residential and commercial development.

COMPANY BACKGROUND

Fauquier Gas Company, as one of the nation's 440 gas companies, served an area where land use was changing from agricultural to residential and commercial. To meet the increased demand for gas resulting from this conversion, 3½ miles of new gas lines had to be ready for customer hookup by September. An additional 10 miles of new gas lines were planned for the next year.

THE PURCHASING AREA

Mr. Murphy, as the manager of purchasing, was responsible for the purchases of materials used in gas distribution such as pipe, meters, fittings, etc. Other major areas included the purchasing of furniture, systems and forms, stores management, and materials forecasting and control. The purchasing organization was under the management control of the vice-president for operations.

THE SPECIFICATION DECISION

In January, Mr. Murphy was having lunch in the company cafeteria when he heard Mr. Clive Byers, the construction project manager, talking about a new project. Fauquier Gas Company was going to add $3\frac{1}{2}$ miles of new gas lines and would start construction in June in order to "gas the line" that September. Murphy asked Byers for the purchase request so he could immediately contact suppliers (mills) and get quotations on prices and deliveries. Murphy knew from experience that the mills' schedules for pipe production required a substantial lead time. He was concerned that the mills would not be able to accommodate Fauquier's schedule. Byers told him that the purchase request would be sent over as soon as Pat Wilson, the design engineer, completed the pipe specification and Sam Law, the construction project engineer, approved it.

The design organization was headed by Mr. Charlie Buck, the design superintendent. Both the design and construction organizations were under the management control of the vice president of operations.

Mr. Murphy called Pat Wilson and asked about the pipe specification. Wilson told him that the diameter of the pipe would be 24 inches with a wall thickness of $\frac{3}{4}$ inches and that the length would be 57 feet. In prior purchases, the wall thickness was $\frac{3}{8}$ inches and the length was "random double normal" (40 feet plus or minus 5 feet). When Mr. Murphy inquired about the change in wall thickness and length, Wilson replied that the operation of the line would be governed by less stringent specifications if the wall thickness was $\frac{3}{4}$ inches. Wilson said welding costs would be reduced by using 57-foot-length pipe.

When asked which wrapper would be applied to the pipe, Wilson said that he had not yet gotten to that part of the specification. In past purchases, Fauquier had used two types of wrappers—coal tar and pry-tech. The mill supplying the pipe would apply the wrapper. The company which applied the coal tar wrapper was located in Philadelphia and the one applying pry-tech wrapper was in Atlanta.

Mr. Murphy was concerned about the economic consequences and the schedule impact of the proposed changes in wall thickness and length of the pipe. At lunchtime on April 14, he had not yet received the purchase request with the pipe specification.

1 What are the key facts?
2 What is the problem?
3 List and discuss three alternative solutions.
4 What is your recommended solution?

FOUR SQUARE LUMBER MILL

Jon Johansen was the supplies buyer at Four Square's Valdosta plant. One day he sat examining a traveling requisition (TR) card for ten carborundum saw blades. The specified blade was made in Switzerland and obtainable through a mill supply house in Birmingham at a cost of $225 each, F.O.B. Birmingham. Jon observed on the TR that some 110 blades were ordered a year. The requisition specified that no substitutes were permitted. Even so, Jon decided to see if any money could be saved through alternative sourcing. He contacted two of his better mill supply sources to see what they could do.

Both suppliers indicated that the Dipson 412 blade was every bit as good as its Swiss counterpart. Based on an annual purchase of eighty or more blades, one supplier quoted a unit price of $112.50 per blade. (The second supplier's price was $115.00.) Both prices were F.O.B. Valdosta.

Jon then contacted Sam Sharpe, the foreman of sawing operations at Four Square. Jon explained the potential savings and asked Sam to give the American blade a try. Sam was certain that the Dipson blade would not stand up to the Swiss blade. After several minutes of trying to convince Sam of the desirability of buying the Dipson 412, Jon said that he thought that they really should give it a try. Sam left in a good humor saying, "O.K., but I know it won't work."

Jon ordered ten Dipson blades. He included a provision that any unused blades could be returned for credit if the Dipson did not prove to be equal to the Swiss blade. Two days after the blades arrived, Sam entered Jon's office. Sam was grinning from ear to ear, holding a saw blade in each hand. Both blades were burned as a result of the excess heat generated during the cutting operation. Jon was convinced that the boys in the yard had treated the blades unfairly to ensure that they would fail.

1 What could Jon have done to avoid this situation?
2 What should Jon do now?

FRICH TURBO ENGINE COMPANY

Mr. Fingold, a buying supervisor at the Frich Turbo Engine Company, was responsible for the purchase of valves and other items for low-pressure assemblies in the company's engines. He had handled numerous valve procurements and had found that the designs were subject to considerable variation. He had found it useful, therefore, whenever he was required to initiate procurement of a new design, to make an estimate of the probable cost of the item from historical costs of similar equipment and from his own wide experience with machine shop practice and with conditions in the industry. He found that this method enabled him to question suppliers' cost estimates effectively and to negotiate good prices even on initial procurements, with a corresponding saving in subsequent purchases of the same item.

In February, Mr. Fingold received a purchase request for 10,000 low-pressure valves of a new design. The engineering department was proud of the new design, which called for a valve made largely of stamped parts to replace an older type of valve that had involved a number of casting and machining processes. The last procurement of the old valve in November had been at a unit price of $2.64, and it was anticipated that substitution of the new process would result in a considerably lower unit price.

Mr. Fingold realized that prospective suppliers for the procurement would include a group different from his usual suppliers and decided for that reason to make an extremely careful estimate of the probable cost. After performing research and analyzing the processes and materials to be used, he arrived at a figure of approximately $1.74 per unit as a reasonable price for the item, made up as follows:

Material	$0.448	
Direct labor	0.344	
Manufacturing overhead	0.516	(assumed to be 150% of direct labor)
Tooling	0.192	
General and administrative	0.0752	(assumed to be 5% of total cost)
Profit	0.1576	(assumed to be 10% of total cost)
Selling price	$1.7328	

Meanwhile, requests for proposals were sent out to eighteen companies. The closing date for submission of proposals was set at May 1. By the middle of April, Mr. Fingold had received thirteen proposals, of which nine were in the range from $1.84 to $2.08 per unit, while the other four ranged from $2.32 to $3.04. Mr. Fingold was pleased with the indication that his estimate had "pegged" the low range of quotations. As each of the quotations came in, he examined each supplier's cost breakdown with a view to points for questioning and negotiation. Between April 20 and 23, however, two more companies submitted proposals. One of these, the Bayfleet Machining Company, quoted a unit price of $1.232, and the other, the Union Stamping Company, $1.488. Mr. Fingold was surprised, to say the least, at these low figures, and was inclined to think that they represented unrealistic estimates. On investigation, however, he found that both suppliers were large, well-established metal forming companies with good reputations for satisfactory performance on previous contracts. The cost breakdowns for the two low proposals are reproduced below.

	Bayfleet Machining	Union Stamping	Mr. Fingold's estimate
Direct material	$0.344	$0.408	$0.448
Subcontracted parts	0.080	—	—
Direct labor	0.288	0.400	0.344
Manufacturing overhead	0.296 (103%)	0.304 (76%)	0.516 (150%)
Tooling	0.104	0.232	0.192
General and administrative	0.064 (6%)	0.024 (2%)	0.0752 (5%)
Profit	0.056 (5%)	0.120 (9%)	0.1576 (10%)
Selling price	$1.232	$1.488	$1.7328

1 What factors might have caused the variance between Bayfleet's quotation and Mr. Fingold's estimate? Between Bayfleet's quotation and Union's quotation?

2 In light of your answer to the above question, what conclusions can you draw concerning (a) the reliability and usefulness of cost estimates made by the buyer, and (b) the value to be gained from the comparison of one supplier's quotation with that of another?

FUTRONICS, INC.

Steve Hastell, purchasing manager of Futronics, Inc., was studying the replacement of the company's central office stores by an outside service. Futronics, located in Lexington, Massachusetts, was in the midst of a corporate overhead reduction program. As part of this program, Steve had been assigned the task of investigating opportunities for outsourcing selected in-house services. He was expected to report on the central stores issue at the next program meeting in three days.

FUTRONICS' COST REDUCTION PROGRAM

Futronics was a $2 billion firm with sales in consumer products and government systems and services. It enjoyed high overall growth until fierce competition flattened sales and decreased profits sharply two years ago. Since then, corporate cost and overhead reduction efforts had become wide-

Copyrighted by the National Association of Purchasing Management. Reprinted by permission. This case was written by Joseph L. Cavinato during one of the NAPM-sponsored case writing workshops.

spread. The purchasing department sought savings by increasing emphasis in existing areas as well as by participating in corporatewide cost reduction team programs. The central stores operation came under review when two outside firms approached Steve's department with initial proposals to replace Futronics' stores operation with their own inventory and delivery service.

CENTRAL STORES

Central stores at Futronics was created in the middle 1950s when a corporatewide study revealed that large savings would result from bulk buying and distribution of stationery and all other supplies. A central group was formed to serve Futronics' twenty-one area sites. While it represented an increase in manpower, facility, and delivery expenses, large savings resulted through reduction in individual office inventories, mass buying, and decreased purchase order expenses.

At the present time, central stores served forty-two area sites from a warehouse in Lexington. Annual throughput was about $900,000 and the average inventory was valued at $140,000. Over 500 items were stocked. A catalogue of items was updated and distributed every six months. Four people worked in the operation: two as pickers, one order entry clerk, and one to wrap, label, and load trucks. Activity was slightly seasonal, with peaks occurring in December when the demand for calendars was high, and at the end of quarter budget periods for other items. The cost of the personnel and space was about $200,000 per year. Deliveries were made on a daily basis with a corporate truck that handled corporate mail and other interplant movements. These deliveries were made to the building docks or reception areas. Corporate stores were part of Corporate Administrative Services, which also included food service contracting, security services, and personnel.

Service complaints in the form of lengthened order times (e.g., specific letterhead stationery took three to four weeks, while other items required ten to fourteen days) were common. It also took a long time for stores to implement the acquisition of new items. Post-Its, for example, were not added until five months after they were on the market. Split deliveries also were common. Up until this time it was generally believed by Steve and his boss that the economies of this system were still better than any other alternatives, but this conclusion had never been verified.

OUTSIDE SERVICES

The idea of investigating outside stores services arose in June when two firms approached Steve's shop with general proposals. These proposals coincided with a top-management mandate in May for all departments to seek and implement reportable savings by year end. Steve heard through outside contacts that other firms in the Boston area were reducing both expenditures and overhead costs by these means.

By June, Steve had in hand initial proposals from Litton, Boise-Cascade, L. E. Muran, Bay State Office, and New England Supply. The initial information provided by the suppliers included:

1 Sample catalogues
2 Price lists
3 Ranges of costs for certain delivery/volume configurations

A line item analysis by Steve's assistant showed that about 90 percent of the 500 currently stocked items would be available at less cost. On the average, the promised savings would be about 6 percent. Furthermore, the suppliers' proposed catalogues included about 600 items each.

All five firms sought three-year contracts with options for renewal. The firms would provide their own specially printed catalogues in unique binders. Order cycle times were promised to be no longer than ten working days, including specially printed letterheads. Deliveries would be made directly to each secretary. The use of special preprinted order forms with the most common items was suggested in all proposals.

Steve, his manager, and others in the review group had some concerns about the outside service idea. These ranged from the uncertainty and risk of the idea to the reduced control over the process. Questions arose over the profit to be made by the outside firms. Greater mass buying power gave these firms pricing advantages. Steve did notice, however, that overhead transparencies, an important item to Futronics, were priced in the $39–45 range in the proposed catalogues. Futronics currently enjoyed a better price of $23 per box. All the proposed contracts would lock in Futronics for three years. The four people in central stores either would be redeployed to other jobs in the company or laid off. One of these four people was physically handicapped and worked in a wheelchair.

DEADLINE

Steve's job was to develop an analysis of the concept behind the initial proposals and to recommend dropping the idea or requesting complete proposals. He felt that by this time there might be political momentum to adopt the idea of outsourcing and elimination of Futronics' central stores. He wanted to make sure the review group would not compare the worst features of the current situation to the best of the proposed ones. His deadline was the next meeting of the corporate cost reduction team, three days hence.

1 Assume you are Steve Hastell. Prepare an analysis and report on this issue for presentation at the next program meeting.

GAS TURBINES INCORPORATED

Gas Turbines Incorporated (GTI) has designed and manufactured small, high-quality gas turbine engines for over twenty years. The firm's engines are used primarily as auxiliary power units for airplanes and helicopters. The purpose of the auxiliary power unit is to provide compressed air for both passenger cabin cooling and aircraft main engine starting. GTI's main market has been the military helicopter market. Recently GTI was acquired by ATG Corporation, whose primary objective is to penetrate the lucrative large commercial air transport market.

GTI senior management has been directed by ATG to develop an auxiliary power unit for use in large commercial aircraft. In 1994, development was started on the APS 2000. This engine is based on GTI's proven design but with twice the horsepower of previous engines.

Marketing efforts commenced by contacting airlines which fly Boeing 737 aircraft. It soon became apparent that cost and schedule would be the critical factors. The APS 2000 would have to sell for approximately $115,000 and must receive Federal Aviation Administration certification within one year to meet the customer's specified delivery date. GTI engineering personnel estimate that certification can be completed within six months of the receipt of all component parts.

Bill Terry, a senior buyer in the purchasing department, has the responsibility of procuring all of the hydromechanical control devices for the APS 2000. Bill is particularly anxious to place an order for the main air bleed control valve. Years of experience have taught him that this valve is the most expensive component, with the longest lead time, of any that he buys. Several weeks ago he issued requests for quotation (RFQs) to the five valve manufacturers on GTI's approved source list. The RFQs requested price and delivery for a quantity of 100 valves based on marketing's sales plan of 100 engines per year for the next ten years. With each RFQ, Bill included GTI's standard form requesting cost reduction suggestions. Recently, Bill received the responses summarized below:

Supplier	Price	Delivery	Exceptions
Ajax Controls	—	—	Declined to bid
Lundy Pneumatics	$950	32 wks. ARO	See Note 1
H S Bender	—	—	Declined to bid
Valient Eng.	$724	20 wks. ARO	See Exhibit 1
Smith Controls	$1,085	16 wks. ARO	None

Note 1: A one-time nonrecurring engineering cost of $35,000 is required in addition to the per-piece price.

This case was developed by Barrie Gove and Carmen Lorduy under the direction of Professor David N. Burt.

EXHIBIT 1 VALIENT ENGINEERING CORPORATION
27 Rutherford Rd., Caldwell, NJ

Gas Turbines Incorporated
7709 Balboa Avenue
San Diego, CA 92123

Attention: Mr. Bill Terry, Senior Buyer

Reference: Gas Turbines Incorporated P/N 169783-100
Valve, Air Bleed Control
Valient Proposal #874-085

Dear Mr. Terry:

We are pleased to respond to your Request for Quotation #89-JH-031 as follows.

Proposal #1

We are able to provide a valve in total compliance with your drawing requirements. Delivery, however, would be approximately 42 weeks ARO. Also, a new design would cause us to incur a nonrecurring engineering expense of $24,000 due to the extensive design and testing work which would be required. The unit price for a quantity of 100 is $995 each.

Proposal #2

If, however, the following deviations can be given, we could offer 100 pieces at a unit price of $724 each. The deviations would be as follows:

1 Solenoid coil to be 1" square instead of 0.75" diam.
2 Total height from connector to bottom of body to be 3.50" instead of 2.70" estimated.
3 Electrical connector per Mil-C-5015 in lieu of Mil-C-38999.
4 Maximum weight to be 0.67 lb. instead of 0.521 lb.

These deviations would allow us to use an existing design which would help greatly with deliveries. I estimate delivery for 100 pieces of this configuration to be 20 weeks ARO.

If you have any questions, please contact me.

Sincerely,

VALIENT ENGINEERING CORPORATION

B. Don Roberts
Applications Engineer

Upon reviewing the quotations, Bill felt excited that Valient had an existing design which offered a substantial reduction in cost over his initial cost estimate. Bill decided that he would speak to the design engineer, Linda Mitchell, to get her opinion on Valient's proposal.

Bill found Linda at her computer graphic workstation. He said, "Linda, I've received responses to all of the RFQs on the bleed air valve for the APS 2000. It appears that Valient has an off-the-shelf valve which only requires some minor modifications to our design. Here is a copy of Valient's proposal."

After reading Valient's proposal, Linda said, "I don't know if we can live with these deviations. The weight estimate for the engine is 20 pounds over target. The whole department is working in a weight reduction program. The connector change will require us to revise the electrical harness design. I really don't think that we can use this valve."

Bill responded, "Linda, if we are going to make it in the commercial APU market, we're going to have to be a lot more innovative in reducing costs than we have been in the past."

Linda replied, "I worked closely with Julio Lopez, the applications engineer for Smith Controls. The valve which he has proposed is essentially the same as the one which is used on the Airbus Industries A320 aircraft, which has thousands of hours of field experience. Julio is one of the most knowledgeable engineers in the servo-valve field. I've benefited from his knowledge many times in the past and feel that he has a technically superior valve to Valient's. We may need lower costs but not at the expense of technology."

At this point, Bill wondered how he could more effectively present his case. He believed that while Valient's valve might not be as technically advanced as Smith Control's, it probably was more reliable. He knew for sure that Valient's supplier performance rating was higher than Smith's for both quality level and on-time deliveries. He said, "Somehow we need to evaluate all of the factors. Will you study the proposal, and I will call a meeting for next week. We can discuss the issue in more detail and decide which valve to buy."

With that, Bill walked back to his office, deep in thought about what he should do to prepare for the meeting.

1 What information would be useful for Bill to take with him to the meeting?
2 Who should Bill invite to the meeting?
3 What economic factors should be considered in arriving at the procurement decision?
4 Discuss the noneconomic factors involved in this case.
5 What organizational changes could be made at GTI to give greater emphasis to value analysis?

GENERATION DISK SYSTEMS INC.

Five members of the management team at Generation Disk Systems Inc. had gathered around the table in the board room: the president, Richard Bass; the vice president of engineering, Bill Northrop; the vice president of sales and marketing, Jane Engles; the vice president of purchasing, Norman Garvey; and the director of production, Alex Woodhue. Just the night before, Bass, Engles, and Garvey had returned from Las Vegas where they had attended COMDEX '94. COMDEX is a popular trade exposition for the computer industry which is held annually in November.

Although the company was incorporated less than a year ago, management had made the decision to do everything it could in order to display a prototype of its new product at COMDEX '94. The product was a type of Winchester computer disk drive. For the past several months all efforts were channeled in the production of this prototype. A successful model was completed by the end of October, and the company reps enthusiastically went off with prototype in hand to man their booth at the expo.

Generation Disk Systems Inc. (GDS), located near Santa Barbara, California, was incorporated in November 1993. It joined at least twenty other companies bidding for a piece of the Winchester disk drive market. The Winchester disk drive was named for the famous Winchester rifle because early prototypes had two drives that could store up to 30 megabytes of information each. These disk drives were currently one of the hottest pieces of equipment on the computer market because of their increased storage capacity over floppy disks. The GDS model—the Micro/Magnum 5/5"—offered new capabilities: It contained both a fixed disk and a removable disk cartridge which allowed the user backup protection against loss in case of a computer system malfunction.

Reaction to the GDS model at COMDEX '94 was extremely favorable. It seemed that the industry was in love with the Micro/Magnum 5/5". Bass and Engles busily recorded and made preliminary sales estimates: Within a few years they could expect $100 million in sales.

But before they could start to count sales dollars, they realized they had a long way to go from their design/prototype stage to actual production. This would be no simple task for a small company starting from scratch. Fortunately, though, some things were already in place. They had a new plant ready and waiting to start production. And Norman Garvey, vice president of purchasing, had done a thorough job of sourcing potential suppliers.

Garvey's procurement group began early in the project by checking on potential suppliers' histories of quality. The cost of the purchased materials that go into the GDS disk drives is estimated to be 72 percent of the cost of the finished drive. Trying to eliminate the unknowns, the group gathered information on tooling, production, delivery performance, lead times, costs, etc. This homework would give the company a substantial advantage in getting production started.

The sooner GDS could get to the market with the product, the better off it would be. Bass had called together his management team to address the issues involved in producing thousands of disk drives as soon as possible. The issues involved included:

- Gaining maximum benefit from the learning curve
- Facilitating the design planning process to determine what is economically feasible
- Getting the necessary credit with their suppliers
- Allocating responsibility for quality

GDS's top management team had worked together for more than ten years at another high-tech firm before starting on its own. Because of this long association, the group was able to unite around a definite management philosophy right from the start. All agreed that the only way they could accomplish their goals was to get their suppliers involved in their design process. Somehow they had to persuade their suppliers to *want* to be a part of GDS's success.

1 Who should be responsible for establishing and monitoring the supplier quality plan at GDS?
2 The effectiveness of GDS's supplier quality program will rely on Garvey's ability to persuade GDS's suppliers to *want* to perform satisfactorily. How can he motivate the suppliers so that GDS will meet the deadline and with a high-quality product?
3 Suppose goods received from one or more suppliers do not conform to GDS requirements. What actions can you suggest to motivate the supplier(s)?
4 Managing an effective supplier quality program requires the allocation of substantial time and money. How can Norman Garvey justify the program's costs compared with the contributions made to company objectives and profits?

GOLDEN BUFFALO, INC.

Ruben Gomez is the purchasing manager of Golden Buffalo, a publisher of textbooks. Golden Buffalo's sales were $45 million last year. Ruben's department purchases paper, printing equipment, and office and printing supplies. From time to time, it contracts for the printing of a Golden Buffalo book. Purchasing reports directly to the general manager. Ruben attends all weekly management meetings along with the manager of marketing, the director of operations, the director of acquisitions, and the finance manager. These weekly meetings are more or less "bull" sessions. Apparently, the general manager, George Zinke, is satisfied with the operating results and the information picked up in the meetings.

The purchasing department consists of Ruben, three buyers, an expediter, and three clerks. Department salaries and operating expenses run about $280,000 per year. Purchasing spent $18 million last year.

Ruben recently attended a National Association of Purchasing Management seminar where he became impressed with the need to market purchasing's contribution to the well-being of the organization. This need for marketing was emphasized when the speaker reported on two incidents wherein purchasing managers had seen their department reorganized under manufacturing. The speaker maintained that both purchasing managers were competent. The major problem appeared to be that they had failed to publicize their department's contributions to their firm's success. Even before returning from the seminar, Ruben began to wonder what information he should report and how he should report it.

1 What information should Ruben Gomez report to his fellow managers at the weekly meetings?
2 What information should Ruben report directly to the general manager?

HARDY COMPANY

The Hardy Company manufactures small electrical appliances, including electric shavers, electric mixers, blenders, and irons for the home. The company had recently introduced a new line of electric shavers for women. In the product design stage of the new product, the sales department had conducted an extensive marketing research survey to determine exactly what style-color combinations best suited the market for this new product. The style finally selected was an extremely modish plastic case with an entirely new shape of cutting head.

Unfortunately, no commercially available fractional horsepower motor could be fitted into the desired style of case. It was, therefore, necessary to have a supplier develop the required motor.

The vice president of purchasing of the Hardy Company, Mr. Monaghan, discussed the problem with the sales representatives of several of Hardy's best motor suppliers. One of the persons contacted was the sales vice president of the Centennial Electric Company, which had been one of Hardy's suppliers for years and was known to have one of the best developmental groups in the small motor field. In his conversation with Mr. Monaghan, the Centennial Electric vice president expressed confidence that his firm could do the job, and he even roughed out a proposed method of attacking the problem.

Mr. Monaghan and the engineering manager were so impressed by the approach of the Centennial Company, as compared to presentations of the other companies contacted, that it was decided to award the development work to Centennial. In setting up the contract for this development work, it was discovered that the Centennial Electric Company had a rigid policy of billing separately for developmental services only on government contracts. For all other work, the Company recovered development costs through sale of the motors developed. Consequently, the shaver motor was developed by Centennial on a "no charge" basis simultaneously with the product design work at Hardy. Centennial was very cooperative and made several modifications to the original design specifications. Finally, ten handmade motors of the final design passed rigorous quality control checks by Hardy engineers. These motors were also provided on a "no charge" basis.

A purchase contract was then placed with Centennial Electric for the first production run of 100,000 units. The price of the motors was slightly above the price of a standard motor of equivalent horsepower ratings, but Mr. Monaghan felt that the differential was certainly not enough for Centennial to recover the entire development cost over the run of 100,000. He knew that Centennial had also made a sizable additional investment in special tools, dies, and fixtures for this motor.

The shaver was a great success and another 100,000 units were produced in the first year. Centennial had been given the order for these motors on a proprietary basis when it quoted a price equal to the price of standard motors of the same horsepower rating. A blanket order of 150,000 units for the second year's production was also awarded to Centennial without competitive bids.

When the contract for the third year's production was being considered, sales representatives of four different companies requested the right to bid on motors for the shaver. One salesman was very indignant and said that his company had been discriminated against all along and that he knew that his company could make a better motor for the job and sell it for less than Centennial's price. Although Mr. Monaghan felt that Centennial had done an excellent development job and was providing good service on the contract, he wondered how long he should allow Centennial to have this business on a proprietary basis. He was certain Centennial's price was not substantially out of line, but he was not at all certain that Centennial had recovered all of its investment in development, tools, dies, and fixtures.

1 Do you feel that the purchasing of this motor was properly handled? How would you have handled it?
2 Should the Hardy Company have solicited competitive bids on this item?
3 What would you do if you were in Mr. Monaghan's position now?

HOLY CROSS HEALTH CARE, INC.

BACKGROUND

Holy Cross is the largest health care provider in the Pittsburgh area. It has over 1,100 beds and numerous outpatient clinics spread throughout the city. This dominant size has been achieved through extremely rapid growth during the past three years. All buildings are new or have been recently remodeled to meet state and federal safety requirements.

Current market conditions are extremely competitive. Contributing factors include: an increasing number of patients without health care coverage, a growing number of HMOs (Health Maintenance Organizations), and recent funding cutbacks by government and insurance companies. Technological advances have had a major impact as well, with each hospital seeking to obtain the most up-to-date equipment. State-of-the-art equipment is a major factor in attracting and maintaining a pool of qualified doctors who admit their patients for care. In spite of a growing population, all major area hospitals are feeling the cost/revenue crunch due to the number of organizations competing for a relatively limited amount of revenue.

This case was written by Alex Miskiewicz and Lisa Wiethorn under the direction of Professor David N. Burt.

Holy Cross is one of two area hospitals performing heart transplants. Although it is a nonteaching organization, the hospital encourages new procedures and readily acquires state-of-the-art equipment.

SUPPLIES

Holy Cross previously had utilized a JIT process in obtaining supplies. As the organization grew, problems of stock-outs and shortages plagued operations as demand outstripped the supply system.

Twenty suppliers were dealt with on a regular basis, but the majority of supplies were purchased from only five firms, usually at substantial quantity discounts. Further complications resulted when all but one major supplier relocated to Philadelphia, frequently extending delivery times to over seven days. Management decided that new procedures and personnel were needed to solve these continuing problems.

JOE JONES

One management tactic had been to establish an off-site warehouse for medical supplies. Joe Jones had been hired as the warehouse manager overseeing seven young high school graduates as stockroom personnel. A typical day consisted of $100,000 worth of supplies coming into the warehouse, with approximately 80 percent being distributed within the Holy Cross system. Several things accounted for the remaining $20,000 of supplies. Employee theft was a problem, though Joe had no idea how extensive. Other area hospitals frequently ran out of supplies and came to the warehouse, paying a 5 percent markup. Finally, some supplies were delivered damaged and were returned to the manufacturer.

When Joe first started working for Holy Cross, only 800 different items were delivered to the hospital. As the hospital grew through the acquisition of other institutions, the supplies used by the new facilities were kept in use following acquisition. An examination of warehouse inventory revealed over twenty different brands of tape, as well as duplication of a number of other items. Over 6,000 items were now stocked in the warehouse. Joe's only guidelines were to prevent shortages by keeping the warehouse adequately stocked, and to screen for items that were slow movers (those not used at least once in thirty days). A computer system was used to monitor inventory levels and to project reorder points for frequently used items. Periodically, Joe scanned a computer-generated master inventory list (nearly 5 inches thick) to identify materials not used within a thirty-day period. These items were then reported to the materials management coordinator, who acted as a liaison with the Joint Standards Committee.

The warehouse items were delivered to each facility in bulk on an "as required" basis.

JOINT STANDARDS COMMITTEE

The Joint Standards Committee consisted of twenty-five members from all the major departments of Holy Cross. (See Exhibit 1.) Several members had been

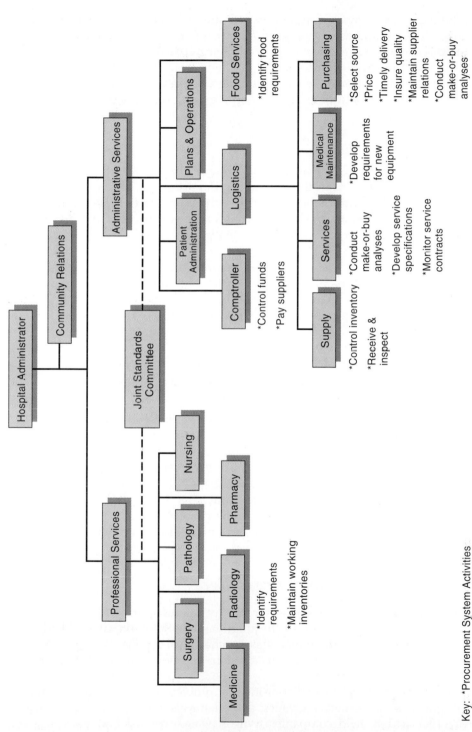

Key: *Procurement System Activities

EXHIBIT 1
Holy Cross organization structure.

on the committee since its inception and attended the monthly meetings regularly. Others found the meetings too time consuming and attended only when the discussions had a direct impact on their department. The committee exercised final approval prior to deleting an item from the master supply list, but this action was seldom taken. Political interests prevented committee members from effectively controlling the exploding growth of the warehouse.

SUPPLY PROCUREMENT

New items were added to the master inventory list by hospital staff, who submitted a request form to the purchasing department. The request form contained a brief description of the item and the intended use. These forms often were generated following visits from sales representatives to the various hospitals and doctor's offices within the Holy Cross system. Such requests frequently included specifications unique to a given sales representative's product, complete with all necessary ordering information conveniently included. Since the numerous requests were rarely for high-dollar amounts, purchasing tended to rubber stamp the majority of these requests to keep the medical personnel happy and to expedite the paperwork. To avoid political friction, the Standards Committee rarely raised any questions about the requests.

Joe had little time beyond his daily routine but felt that the current supply system was not the best fit for the needs of the hospital. He wanted to come up with some major cost-saving ideas to present to top management before being handed one that didn't include him.

1 Identify the major issues that need to be addressed in this situation.
2 What additional information would be useful in developing a solution to the materials management problems at Holy Cross?
3 Assume you are engaged as a consultant in this case. Prepare an outline for a report to management including:
   a A definition and analysis of the problems
   b Suggested solutions for each of the problems
   c Recommendations and suggested guidelines for implementation

JAY MANUFACTURING COMPANY

Charlie Wilson, purchasing director for Jay Manufacturing Company, had to make a decision that would tax the judgment of a Solomon. Charlie had found that Paul Hertz, Jay's top buyer, was purchasing components from New Technology, Inc., a firm of which his brother was vice president and chief of research and development.

Jay had never had a conflict-of-interest problem before, since the company bought most of its metals, plastics, and chemicals from giants of the industry or other widely held companies. Wilson was surprised that there was any family connection between one of his buyers and a supplier, but then he had not figured that such a relationship could enter the picture on Jay Manufacturing Company contracts. At a recent monthly dinner for purchasing and sales managers, Paul had introduced Wilson to his brother Harold. "Charlie, this is my brother Harold, the gee-whiz type of the family. He's the brains behind the control switch we're putting in the new 'Bluejay' line. Harold developed it for us right on our kitchen table over coffee after I told him what our problems were. It's great being able to tap a local outfit for research and development help. This development has saved us a good 35 *percent a year* on that product and given us a real jump on the competition!"

The product Paul Hertz had brought in had really met a definite need and added another cost-cutting laurel to Paul's already impressive record in value analysis and all-around good purchasing know-how. But Wilson began to have qualms about the situation, even though Paul's performance on the contract—and on all others—was above reproach.

He discussed the problem in conference with several fellow company executives.

Kingsby Blackstone, company attorney: "This is a serious case, Charlie. That buyer has entered a conspiracy to defraud this company by routing orders to his brother's outfit. He probably owns a good chunk of New Technology stock besides. We should fire him and take quick action to recover damages. You have to prohibit buyers from having any interest in supplier firms."

Roger Goodbody, manufacturing manager: "You're making a mountain out of a molehill! I grew up with the Hertz brothers and they are solid citizens. We're darn lucky to have one of them working for this firm. Besides, only Paul Hertz could have gotten that genius interested in our problem. It's a darn good thing when our buyers can get that close to a supplier."

Charlie Wilson: "If it were anybody else but Paul, I'd be suspicious of his intentions. But I am sure he has acted in the best interest of the company, even though the situation does look a bit fishy. If we unfairly crack down on him, it will look as if we are punishing initiative. Also, if we kick up a fuss over the situation, aren't we trying to close the barn door after the horse has been stolen? I'll check into the situation a bit further and talk it over with you next week."

1 What should Charlie do about Paul now?
2 What should Charlie do about this problem in the future?

JULBERG, INC.

Julberg, Inc., was a manufacturer of computer output microfilm (COM) devices. These devices transfer data from a computer directly onto microfiche storage and retrieval systems. Banks and insurance companies were the prin-

This case was developed by Julie Goldberg under the direction of Professor David Burt.

cipal users of COM. Julberg was the leading firm in this market, and sales were $150 million per year. Its product line included ten different models of processors, ranging in price from $75,000 to $500,000.

The purchasing department at Julberg was responsible for purchasing approximately 20,000 different parts needed to manufacture the firm's processors. Mechanical parts, tubes, resistors, transistors, and keyboards were typical of the items purchased. The department consisted of fifteen buyers, five purchasing services clerks, and the purchasing manager. The buyers' experience ranged from two to thirty years with varying levels of education. The younger members of the department had degrees in business or engineering while the senior buyers had less education. Several of the senior buyers had worked their way up from manufacturing, receiving, and inventory control. The purchasing manager possessed an M.B.A. and three years of purchasing experience. Previous to this job, he had held a supervisory position in inventory control. His current job required him to oversee the day-to-day functioning of the department and to perform some purchasing duties.

Under the present manual system, considerable time and effort were required to perform supplier selection and price analysis activities. Ideally, information would be gathered on potential suppliers' past performance, including their prices, their ability to meet delivery dates, and their history on quality (based largely on the number of defective parts received per shipment). In order to compile this historical data, the buyer would have to go through several file cabinets and manually combine separate reports from purchasing, receiving, inspection, and the stockroom. Often, if a decision on a source had to be made in a hurry (the normal situation at Julberg), the buyer would rely on his or her memory.

At the present time, due to the heavy workload, such detailed analyses were the rare exception. Very little research on alternate suppliers and little negotiation were taking place. Further, most purchases were being made using Julberg design specifications. There simply was no time or resources available to study the material specifications and perhaps search for alternative materials, as a good value analysis–oriented buyer should do. The purchasing manager believed that the present procedures were resulting in material costs that were approximately 10 percent higher than should be the case. (An outside consultant offered the observation that the firm was paying 25 percent more than it should for its purchased material.)

One bright day in January, after a careful analysis of potential cost savings, Julberg's parent corporation decided to purchase and implement an on-line microprocessing system for the materials functions at all of its subsidiaries. This data processing and storage system would aid management in decision making. Furthermore, the system would automate routine, repetitive tasks. For example, if a buyer wished to place an order for a part, he or she could have the computer list all the firms that had previously supplied the item. The computer would rank the suppliers' past performance based on price, ability to meet delivery schedules, and history of percentage rejects.

To develop this data base, purchasing, receiving, inspection, and stockroom personnel at each subsidiary would enter data regarding the price and status of all purchases as well as information resulting from receipt, inspection, and issuance of ordered material, into the computer databank through the use of a microprocessor (a "smart" terminal). Such a terminal would serve as an input/output device, with the capability of editing input and formatting output data. The data base then would be available instantaneously to all individuals requiring it. Purchasing, as a by-product of preparing the purchase order, would input data via the department's microprocessors into the computer data system. In effect, each such input would be the basis for developing a new data file. Purchasing's input would include the name and address of the supplier, the purchase quantity, price, and accepted delivery date. When the ordered material arrived, receiving would enter the date and quantity of material received. Inspection would check the material for compliance with purchasing specifications and enter the number of acceptable parts into the data base through its microprocessor. The stockroom would record the fact that the parts were available for distribution to manufacturing.

Robert Hanson, the purchasing manager, was charged with the responsibility of overseeing the implementation of the new system. Both the hardware and software had been purchased by Julberg's parent company from the EZ Computer Company of Chicago. In early September, Mr. Hanson, together with the chiefs of receiving, inspection, and stores, flew to Chicago for an intensive week of instruction on the new system. They all returned eager and enthusiastic to get the system implemented. Mr. Hanson felt confident that the new system would cut material costs by at least 10 percent.

During the time the team was in Chicago, rumors began flying concerning potential implications of the computerized system. None of the purchasing personnel had much experience or training in the use of computers. Previously, several individuals had worked in other companies that were in various stages of computerization. These employees spoke of the problems that had occurred during the changeover from manual to computerized purchasing. "That is one of the reasons why I finally left," recalled one of the younger buyers. He continued, "I never trusted the information the computer gave me. It seemed like the receiving and inspection departments were never up to date in entering the latest data about shipments into the computer."

A week after returning from the training session in Chicago, Mr. Hanson called a meeting of all purchasing personnel to inform them about the new computer-based system. He began by outlining some of the functions the new system would perform. He continually emphasized that the system would free the buyers from much routine paperwork and give them time to get out and talk with their users and suppliers, research their purchases, find substitutes, and negotiate with suppliers. The buyers appeared to be bewildered as Mr. Hanson talked about the new tasks they would be performing with the aid of the computer. They seemed totally lost when he used terms like "on-line," "CRT," "query the data base," and "end user." Mr. Hanson ended the meeting by saying that management expected the buyers to be able to reduce the prices paid by Julberg by 10 percent as a result of being freed from routine clerical tasks.

The purchasing manager was completely unprepared for the ensuing reactions. "Well, I for one sure would not like a machine telling me who to buy from," said one buyer. "I do not want to have to call a supplier I've been dealing with for years and tell him, 'Sorry, my computer tells me not to buy from you anymore.' So much for supplier relations!" Another buyer who had worked in the purchasing department for twenty years said, "What's wrong with the way we've been doing things? All management has ever wanted us to do was to get parts ordered and delivered on time. And now they want us to research materials, to go out and talk with our customers, and to become negotiators! I have no interest in such activities. It sounds to me like this computer is trying to put me out of a job!"

The chiefs of receiving, inspection, and stores were waiting to see Mr. Hanson when he returned to his office. Phil Woods, chief of inspection, said, "I just had a meeting with my staff to tell them about the computer and our new system. Boy, were they unenthusiastic. It seems they feel that they should not have to change the way they do their jobs in order to put data into a computer for your guys in purchasing. They're happy with just filling out all the old forms."

Sid Brown, chief of receiving, said, "Yeah, my people are afraid that they are going to become slaves to a machine."

Robert Hanson sat speechless, feeling the walls close in. The smart terminals would be arriving in three weeks. Suddenly, he did not feel at all well.

1 What weaknesses are evident in the present materials system?
2 How can these weaknesses be minimized or eliminated by the use of a computer-based operating system? Develop a plan.
3 What is the basic problem confronting Robert Hanson?
4 What should or could Mr. Hanson have done to improve communication with his subordinates?
5 How could the material personnel's resistance to the computer be overcome?

KOCH BROTHERS

After reading the year-end income statement, Richard Koch, president of Koch Brothers, a retail office supply business in Des Moines, Iowa was concerned about declining net income. He thought this was due to the increasing costs of maintaining high levels of inventory coupled with slow growth in sales and wanted an action plan to reverse these trends.

COMPANY BACKGROUND

Koch Brothers, a closely held corporation, had annual total sales of approximately $15 million. Koch had been in business for 102 years and located at their present headquarters in downtown Des Moines, Iowa since 1920. They employed 75 people, seven of whom were considered outside sales personnel. However, all 75 employees were seen as part of the sales team. Des Moines had predominantly white-collar workers due, in part, to the numbers of insurance firms headquartered there. Koch had an average net income of approximately 2.5% while the industry average was 2.1%. There were five commercial stationers in the area and Koch Brothers was considered the largest. Koch serviced approximately 5,000 accounts. The largest account purchased approximately $600,000 per year in office supplies while the smallest account could be opened for a minimum of a $25 order. Koch also competed with a catalog company located in Chicago. A new entrant in the market was the office supply super store, which offered a warehouse-style retail outlet where customers could browse through aisles of office supply merchandise stacked up to the ceiling. These stores captured 12% of the market nationally. They were considered a threat in small business sales (i.e., under 10 employees), which had been traditionally a good market. There were two super stores in Des Moines. Customers generally ordered office supplies on a daily basis and Koch Brothers offered next-day delivery.

PLANNING MEETING

In January, Richard Koch, president of Koch Brothers, set up a planning meeting to develop an action plan. Al Koch, vice president, and Blair Lawson, head of purchasing, were present. Richard started the meeting by expressing his concerns about declining sales and the interest and insurance cost of maintaining such high levels of inventory.

Richard: "It cost us $25,000 last year in interest to maintain $256,000 in inventory and another $2,000 in insurance in case it all burns up. We don't seem to be turning our inventory over very fast and we keep missing the big sale. We can't stay in business by making nickel and dime sales, we have to get the big orders. Why aren't we?"

Al: "I think the big sales are important, but don't forget most of our revenue comes from the small business buying a box of pencils here, a ream of paper there. Besides we have not been able to compete on price with the mail order catalogs to get the big sale."

Richard: "Don't they want the next-day delivery service that we offer?"

Al and Blair shrugged their shoulders.

Blair: "We supply some of the office needs at the local university but they buy from about 15 other suppliers. We need to convince them that it would be more efficient to buy from one supplier—us! We get some discounts now through volume buying from our wholesaler but when we add on our costs and some margin, our selling price is above the catalog and mass market discounter price, and the new super store in town is taking away some of our small business accounts. When our sales people are making calls, the main issue is price; they don't seem to be too concerned about next-day delivery."

Richard: "Well, we need to do something. We're only three hours from Kansas City and about 5 hours from the Twin Cities. The market is becoming saturated and I'm afraid larger suppliers from those cities will start sending their sales force into our market. With the state government and insurance companies headquartered here, this is a wide-open market for an aggressive supplier. Remember, the new 44-story office building is scheduled to be finished this year and there will be a lot of potentially large accounts to service."

Al: "Dad, we could increase our sales force, but that won't help our selling price. If we cut inventory and don't have the supplies on hand the customer wants, they'll get mad and go to another supplier. We could also open up a retail outlet with the same idea as the super stores and house our inventory there. Or what would you think of joining a buying group?"

Blair: "Yes, I've heard these buying groups are supposed to be the coming thing for companies our size. It's such a new idea that there are only two buying groups in existence that we could consider right now. One is called National Distribution System (NDS) and the other is Independent Stationers (IS)."

Richard too had been reading about buying groups in the industry trade journal but did not have much information on them.

Richard: "Do either of you know much about them?"

Both of the other men replied that they did not have enough information to make any recommendations.

Richard: "OK, I'll check into the retail outlet to house our inventory idea. Al, you get information on NDS, and Blair, you get the info on IS and we'll meet in two weeks to discuss alternatives."

Richard adjourned the meeting.

INFORMATION MEETING

Blair: "How was the game Saturday, Al?"

Al: "Not too good, Blair. Iowa played Indiana, and just got stomped. I didn't think Indiana was supposed to be too good, but they sure came to Iowa City with all their guns loaded."

Richard: "How's my granddaughter doing, Al. Is she over that cold yet? Your mother and I meant to come over Sunday, but it was such a beautiful day on the lake and we had some really good wind, for a change. We didn't want to take the sails down and come in, so we sailed into the sunset."

Al: "Sounds great, dad."

Richard: "Well, Blair, what did you find out about IS?"

Blair: "Independent Stationers is set up as a franchise. One 'dealer' per area. They seem to be pretty regional right now but they say they intend to grow. There is an up-front $6,000 fee and then a quarterly charge of 2% of your sales volume. Basically, they view themselves as a buyer group. In other words, they act as one buyer to buy selected high-turnover items such as paper stock, file folders, ring binders, paper clips, liquid paper, pins, pencils, etc., in volume and get quite a discount. We in turn get the advantage of the discount. I think this could make us competitive on price with the catalog shoppers and mass market merchandisers. Because of the computer setup we should be able to cut back on inventories, I would say, 25%. They are willing to let us in. In fact the representative has called back several times since I made the first inquiry."

Richard: "That sounds good, Blair, but I'm a little concerned with the $6,000 fee. That's a lot of money and I'm not sure we would be getting our money's worth. What did you find out, Al?"

Al: "Well, NDS is even more. They want $12,000 to join."

Richard: "What do you mean 'join,' Al?"

Al: "It's not a franchise fee. It's a co-op fee. We would actually be member-owners. The up-front fee is based on the total sales of the company and if we joined we would actually be the smallest member. Because the membership fee with basic-net is an ownership fee, we would in effect be part owners of the company. It's like buying stock. There is, however, a quarterly $10,000 fee to pay for operating expenses; they will add 2.5% onto our purchases. If the addition on our quarterly purchases does not add up to $10,000 we have to send them the deficit. In other words, if the 2.5% add-on totals only $7,000 we have to send them a check for $3,000. On the other hand if we exceed the $10,000 they send us the difference. They offer great discounts and are nationwide. There are board meetings twice a year where we could get information from some of the 'big boys.' In addition, there is a membership network to service each other's accounts. If we were to get an account with Firestone here in Des Moines, we could indirectly service all Firestone operations around the country. A Firestone plant in another area would order office supplies through a member and we get a percent of the sales. This would allow us, for the first time, to negotiate a large national account without having to move out of Des Moines. Because of the computer setup and factory-direct service we could cut the need to maintain the inventories of bulk items such as paper goods. It could cut our inventories more than in half and allow us to offer a competitive price. They say they intend to develop an EDI computer system for members, where the customer would place an order on their computer and the order would be placed through us but go directly to the supplier and the supplier would ship the order directly to the customer. All we have to do is send out the invoice."

Richard: "I checked on a retail outlet in order to store inventories, as a third option. They now store inventories on the second floor of the headquarters building. Opening a retail outlet would involve leasing property or buying a building. In addition, they would have to hire additional staff and, of course, operating expenses would go up. Also, this would not solve the problem of buying in enough volume to be price-competitive with the mass merchandisers or the super stores, since they are nationwide chains."

Richard concluded by thanking both Blair and Al for their efforts and said, "I don't know if this plan would keep the Kansas City or Twin Cities competitors out of our market." Then he promised he would think about each option further before he made his decision.

1 What facts should Richard Koch take into consideration in analyzing the situation?

KRAUSE CORPORATION

Steve Rothel was purchasing manager for the Midwest division of the Krause Corporation. Shortly before his company was to install an exhaust system in a new construction project, Steve was asked to compare fabricating the pipe with purchasing the pipe from an outside source.

KRAUSE CORPORATION

Krause Corporation, a mechanical and sheet metal contractor, was founded over 50 years ago. Although it had a number of branches in the United States, the majority of its metal fabrication work was performed in its Midwest facility. The company mission stressed quality workmanship, competitive pricing, and timely performance.

A LABORATORY EXHAUST SYSTEM

Krause recently was awarded the bid to provide the HVAC system in a corporate headquarters building that housed a research laboratory. This was a complex project with many nonstandard features due to the specialized use of the building.

The system included a need for over 6500 feet of 10-inch diameter, 16-gauge stainless steel pipe. This piping would be used for the venting of the laboratory exhaust. When the cost estimation department at Krause prepared the original bid, they had planned to fabricate this pipe at their Midwest facility.

A REQUEST FOR COST REDUCTION

As the project got underway, the vice president of sheet metal fabrication asked Steve Rothel "if it would be possible to provide the stainless steel pipe at a lower cost than the original estimate." Steve knew, of course, that any reduction in cost must not come at a sacrifice of quality. Because of toxins that would be present in the laboratory exhaust, it was critical that this system be absolutely leak proof. Every pipe run would be individually tested to insure integrity. If leaks were uncovered in the welds, it would require a time-consuming effort to reweld the joints on-site.

Steve realized that there were two approaches to providing the pipe. Krause could proceed as planned and fabricate the pipe in-house, using the lowest-cost, acceptable quality steel available on the market. The second possibility would be to find a supplier who could provide the pipe already formed at a better cost.

THE PURCHASE OPTION

Steve first explored the purchase option. He did a thorough search of the market, and found that most suppliers were asking from 23 to 28 dollars per linear foot (delivered) for 10-inch-diameter, 16-gauge stainless steel pipe. He was pleasantly surprised, however, to find a supplier who would provide the pipe for $18.10 per linear foot. This supplier provided the pipe in 20-foot sections and guaranteed the pipe to be sound (no leaks). In addition, their pipe was "perfectly" true (round), a trait that Krause's current equipment could not always provide. This feature would reduce the time needed to make connections between sections of pipe and reduce the likelihood of a bad weld joint.

Although this option sounded very attractive, Steve, a veteran in the purchasing area with almost 14 years of experience, knew he couldn't rely on first impressions to make important management decisions. He would have to subject his options to a thorough analysis to ensure a wise decision.

THE MAKE OPTION

Steve had access to the data necessary for manufacturing cost estimating. He knew that the process of making pipe required two steps. First, a flat sheet of steel is formed into a cylinder through the process of "rolling." Then the seam is joined in a welding process. For a 10-inch-diameter pipe of 16-gauge steel, it takes about six minutes per piece to roll, including loading and unloading the part. The equipment Krause had available for this process could roll lengths up to eight feet. The welding process was estimated to take ten minutes for an eight-foot section. The figure the company used for cost estimating purposes for hourly labor rate was $32.60 per hour. An overhead charge of 40 percent was added to the variable costs.

Stainless steel sheets were available in 36-inch, 48-inch, and 60-inch widths at any length up to 10 feet, with the best price being $1.80 per pound. A square foot of 16-gauge steel weighs two and one-half pounds. The welding process required welding wire and welding gas. Welding wire cost around $5.20 per pound and .03 pounds were needed per foot of weld. Welding gas cost around 25 cents per eight-foot seam.

Many of the lengths of pipe needed in the project were longer than eight feet. Thus, Steve thought it necessary to include the cost of an extra joint (which, for example, would make two eight-foot lengths into one sixteen-foot length) in the "make in-house" alternative. Such a joint required welding around the diameter of the pipe, a process that, with setup, would take around 18 minutes per joint.

Steve wondered which option would be best.

1 Should Steve recommend purchasing the pipe or making it?

LAXTEC, INC.

COMPANY BACKGROUND

Laxtec, Inc., is a subsidiary of a Texas-based company that manufactures surveillance cameras. Laxtec's main function is to manufacture the motor and arm that rotates the cameras. Laxtec is located in Illinois.

Laxtec, Inc., has no individual ethical regulations, nor does it have an ethics team within the organization. Laxtec's parent company, however, has an ethics staff within corporate headquarters that deals with questions of ethics for its employees. The corporate headquarters does not take an active part in exercising ethics requirements in its subsidiaries due to staff limitations.

SITUATION

Laxtec has been directed by its parent company to manufacture a new arm that will rotate 360 degrees instead of the present 180 degrees.

Since Laxtec is operating near full capacity and cannot extend its resources to design and manufacture the special motor and control unit needed for the 360-degree specification, it has decided to subcontract this project.

Knowing that there were only a few companies that would be able to design and manufacture the arm, Peter Ferdenzi, president of Laxtec, instructed Larry Morris, director of procurement, to inform the bidders that there were many companies bidding for the contract. This would insure that the bids received were competitive.

One out-of-town bid and three local bids were received. Mr. Ferdenzi called Larry into his office to discuss them. Larry told Mr. Ferdenzi that the out-of-town bid from Aster Company appeared to be the most favorable. But Mr. Ferdenzi told Larry to discard it because he wanted to subcontract the motor within the area to enhance business and social relationships with the community. Out-of-town contracting would only cause friction among the workers. The out-of-town bids, explained Mr. Ferdenzi, were simply to obtain pricing information.

Larry looked over the remaining bids and explained that Prextel was the next best choice, then Gordon, Inc., and lastly Tomos Corporation. Larry was

---

This case was developed by Brian Kopf and Debbie Sinopoli under the direction of Professor David N. Burt.

familiar with the Tomos Corporation and told Mr. Ferdenzi that it had been involved in questionable business activities and was being investigated by the local authorities.

Mr. Ferdenzi looked sternly at Larry when he heard the Prextel bid was the best and told Larry to discard it. Mr. Ferdenzi's ex-wife was the director of the research and design team at Prextel and relations between the two were difficult, to say the least.

Finally, Mr. Ferdenzi agreed to award the bid to Gordon, Inc. Mr. Ferdenzi told Larry to negotiate the specifics with Gordon. Mr. Ferdenzi also told Larry to delay notifying the other bidders of the award until two weeks after production had started with Gordon. In this way, it would not be necessary to listen to the other suppliers "beg" for more consideration.

Negotiations between Gordon and Laxtec were finalized and production started. A problem arose within the second week, however, when Laxtec's quality representative noticed that the materials being used were not of the quality standard stated in the contract.

Larry immediately called a meeting with Gordon, Inc. During the meeting it became apparent that there was a lack of honesty in the development of Gordon's bid. Further, Gordon's attempt to use substandard materials was an attempt to increase profit. Larry realized that Laxtec could not rely on Gordon, Inc. He stated that he would cancel the contract based on fraud. Gordon, wishing to avoid any litigation and bad publicity, agreed and passively backed out.

Luckily, at Mr. Ferdenzi's direction, Larry had not notified the other bidders of the award to Gordon. Larry met with Mr. Ferdenzi again and recommended that Prextel be awarded the contract. Mr. Ferdenzi refused and ordered Larry to meet with Tomos and negotiate a contract.

THE DILEMMA

Larry called Chuck Moore, president of Tomos, for a meeting the next day. Chuck knew that if Laxtec wanted him to negotiate a contract, it must be in desperate need of someone. Accordingly, Chuck told Larry that a donation to the Tomos pension fund would make things much smoother in the negotiations. Larry brushed the comment aside and finalized the meeting time. Larry told Mr. Ferdenzi about the pension fund. Mr. Ferdenzi simply shrugged his shoulders and told Larry to pay Chuck since it was essential to have Tomos accept the contract.

Larry was unsure of what to do. In his last two jobs, he had refused to participate in similar activities and was fired on both occasions. That was when he was single. Now Larry had a house and two children to support.

1 Is it ethical to:

- Tell suppliers that there are many bidders?
- Delay telling unsuccessful suppliers of an award?
- Void a contract on the basis of dishonesty?
- Allow companies to bid even though they would not be considered for the contract (out-of-towners)?
- Refuse to award on the basis of personal relationships?

2 How important is it to have written procedures dealing with ethics in a company?

3 What should Larry do?

LION INDUSTRIES

In early 1992, Lion Industries was awarded a $1 billion ten-year contract by the Boeing Aircraft Company. The contract stated that Lion was to provide specific engine components for the CF680C2 engine. The engines were to be used on the Boeing 767 and 777 aircraft.

The award was important for several reasons. First, it provided an opportunity to participate in what was anticipated to be a contract with significant follow-on potential. That potential was extremely important to Lion in its efforts to stabilize the cyclical nature of its commercial aircraft revenues. Additionally, Boeing represented approximately 32 percent of Lion's business. A sound performance by Lion would help solidify a strong business relationship.

The major assembly being supplied by Lion was the propulsion system casement, or nacelle. Part of the assembly consisted of a titanium precooler duct, used to direct the hot engine exhaust out of the engine into the atmosphere. Titanium was specified, since it functions well when subjected to high temperatures, as well as being lightweight.

However, titanium also possesses characteristics that make it difficult to work in manufacturing. It requires superordinate heat to get the metal from its elastic to its plastic state. The duct was made by using "hot form" technology. The process entails the application of heat to the metal such that it would assume the contour of the master tool. The manufacturing problem was to ensure that a sufficient amount of heat was applied for a sufficient duration. If the process was not exact, the metal would not assume the desired contour, because as it cools it tends to rebound to its original state. Additionally, the assembly, after "hot forming," must be welded. Titanium is difficult to weld. The welding environment must be purged of all atmospheric gases; otherwise, the integrity of the fusion would be jeopardized.

Lion performed a make-or-buy analysis on the duct shortly after receipt of the contract. For many years, Lion had the reputation of being a leader in sheet metal forming. However, Lion's production personnel privately stated that they "wouldn't touch" the precooler duct due to its "tricky" titanium configuration. The decision was made to competitively bid the project.

The duct was to be made according to Lion's drawing specifications. On reviewing these drawings, a number of sources declined to bid. Only two suppliers, Polytek and Sennes, submitted proposals for the part. The bids, F.O.B. Lion plant, were as follows:

This case was developed by John Araneo, Paul Bealman, Tom Donnelly, and Yuki Marsden under the direction of Professor David N. Burt.

	Unit price	Non-recurring	Lead time	Location	Union
Polytek	$4,500	$300,000	52 wks ARO	Grand Rapids, MI	UAW
Sennes	$6,500	$500,000	52 wks ARO	Moorpark, CA	AFL-CIO

Preaward surveys were performed on both suppliers. The source-selection team, composed of personnel from engineering, finance, quality, and purchasing, chose Polytek as supplier on the basis of submitting the low bid (as the two suppliers appeared to be fairly equal in other key areas of concern). Due to the excessive nonrecurring charges, Polytek was to be the single source of the item.

Due to the complexity of the unit, some problems were anticipated. Lion's production requirements called for only one unit per month through fiscal year 1994, to allow Polytek a lengthy developmental period before going into actual production. However, beginning January 1995, the production rate would be increased to six per month.

The initial units, as anticipated, had numerous quality and producibility problems. In spite of this, however, Lion was able to fulfill its commitments to Boeing through fiscal year 1994, primarily due to the low production rate. Various Lion engineering and quality personnel regularly visited Polytek to advise and instruct Polytek personnel, yet no real headway was made. Quality problems persisted, although the supplier contended that the problems were temporary in nature. However, months of "coaching" by Lion engineering failed to correct these inadequacies.

In October 1994, it became apparent that the supplier lacked the ability to produce at the rate of six per month, which Lion had promised to Boeing beginning in January of 1995. Polytek simply could not progress from the developmental phase to the production phase. A team of Lion employees, representing purchasing, engineering, and quality, was sent to the Polytek plant to review the situation and make recommendations. The team found that Polytek's basic tooling philosophy for manufacturing the parts was at fault. The errors were of sufficient magnitude to require rework, but it was agreed that Polytek did not have sufficient production expertise. Further, quality procedures were being circumvented. It also became clear that Polytek was having difficulty in supporting other customers, primarily due to quality and producibility problems.

Lion was less than three months away from being in a position where it could not support delivery requirements to Boeing due to lack of availability of the precooler ducts. Purchasing scrambled to identify options. Sennes was still interested in the program, but refused to shorten its lead time or decrease its $500,000 nonrecurring charge. In addition, the earliest it could supply units would be November 1, 1996.

The sentiment internally at Lion had shifted somewhat since 1992. While stating that the configuration was a troublesome one resulting in many uncertainties, production personnel felt that the duct could be made at a unit cost of

$5,000. Nonrecurring expenses would total $400,000, and the duct could be supplied at a rate of six per month in 40 weeks. The general consensus among nonproduction personnel was that these projections were ambitious and overly optimistic.

Lion purchasing once again solicited additional suppliers, but none showed interest in the design. The options seemed to be fairly clear—and very limited.

The buyer, Harvey Smidlapp, was perplexed by the situation. He had been given the assignment of reviewing the possibilities and providing a recommendation for upper management within forty-eight hours. Harvey wondered if it was possible to support Boeing's needs. And he wondered how he could best protect his company's liability and cost in doing so.

1 How should the buyer approach the situation with Polytek?
2 Should the company consider alternative sources of supply? Discuss.
3 What corrective actions would you recommend to preclude another occurrence of this situation?

MAINE-BARNES, LTD.

Maine-Barnes was a successful small firm that had carved out a profitable niche in the electronic office products field. A proposed new line of sophisticated professional calculators currently posed some manufacturing problems for the firm because of limited shop capacity. Josh Purdy, the firm's purchasing director, was asked to investigate the possibility of subcontracting one of the components to an outside source—and then to prepare a make-or-buy recommendation for the general manager.

Maine-Barnes was located near Boston in the heart of a high-tech manufacturing community. The firm's success was due primarily to its ability to produce high-quality specialty products designed for particular professional uses by engineers, architects, medical researchers, financial analysts, and so on. Product technology in the field was undergoing continual change. As a result, product prices had dropped markedly during the past two years, and competition in the market was keen and fast paced.

The proposed line of new calculators was designed to be highly price competitive. Consequently, the units were powered by a permanent rechargeable battery. This meant that each unit was sold with a small plug-in recharging unit. Although the recharger increased the initial cost of the unit somewhat, the user realized significant operating cost savings during the life of the product. In addition to an attractive life cycle cost, Maine-Barnes was banking on several unique proprietary design features of the calculator and the recharging unit to generate a high demand for the new product line. Unfortunately, the new design features were not patentable.

Despite the general manager's optimistic views for the new product line, the marketing manager was unable to forecast demand for the new units with what he considered to be a comfortable level of accuracy. Because of competition and rapidly changing technology in the industry, he was not willing to forecast first-year sales of more than 50,000 units. If the line was well received, he estimated that approximately 100,000 units could be sold in each of the two succeeding years.

Maine-Barnes had grown steadily during the past five years and was now operating near its manufacturing capacity. The shop manager cautioned that addition of the new calculator line would stretch the operation to its limit. In fact, further analysis revealed that the shop could handle no more than 75,000 new calculator units per year—and this was without producing the companion recharger units. If Maine-Barnes were to produce the recharger units too, it would have to invest approximately $84,000 in new equipment. The life of the equipment would be approximately twelve years. For tax purposes, however, the Internal Revenue Service would permit it to be depreciated over a seven-year period.

As a result of the preceding analysis, Josh Purdy requested bids from three former suppliers for the new recharger unit. All three were known to be competent and reliable; their bids are summarized below.

	Bids on the recharger unit ($ per unit)		
Purchase qty.	Eastern Mfg.	Boston Electrical	D & A Mfg.
50,000	$8.15	$7.45	$7.82
75,000	7.68	7.12	7.45
100,000	7.06	6.79	7.10

In response to Josh's inquiry, all three firms indicated an interest in discussing the possibility of a three-year, single-source contract. All were willing to discuss bid prices further if a three-year deal could be worked out.

After reviewing the bid figures, Josh discussed the possibility of making the recharger in-house with the shop manager and the firm's chief cost accountant. Several days later, Josh received the following estimated cost data from the controller's office.

In-house unit costs to make the recharger	
Direct labor	$1.50
Materials	3.00
Factory overhead (110% direct labor)	1.65
Factory cost	6.15
General administrative and selling expense (10% factory cost)	.62
	$6.77 per unit

Notes:
 1 Materials cost includes a 20 percent internal material handling cost.
 2 Factory overhead is estimated to be 35 percent variable and 65 percent fixed.

After studying the cost estimate, Josh was not certain that it was complete. For example, he wondered why an allowance of 15 percent had been made for scrap material but none for labor. He was also puzzled about the overhead figures. The controller indicated that there would be no reduction in overhead if the new equipment was purchased—and that the amortization of the new equipment would constitute an additional expense.

Josh was also aware that the firm's labor contract expired in several months. In the past, subcontracting work to outside suppliers had always been a sensitive issue with the union, although wage rates seemed to be particularly important this year.

1 What factors should Josh consider in conducting a make-or-buy analysis for this product?
2 Prepare a comparative cost analysis of the make/buy alternatives. Which cost elements should be investigated particularly carefully? Discuss thoroughly.
3 Prepare a complete report for the general manager, including the details of your analysis—and your recommendation.

MAZDA ELECTRONICS

Dennis Kwok had been with Mazda Electronics for twelve years, rising from a junior quality control technician to vice president, operations. He had seen the company grow as a manufacturer of monitor screens used in electrocardiometers. In 1992, Mazda produced and sold about 200,000 units of its current model, the ME1001, at an average price of $150 per unit. The firm operates on a net margin of 5 percent and is in a marginal tax bracket of 50 percent.

A few months ago, Dennis met with Jackie Brown (V.P., marketing) and her marketing research group. Jackie indicated that a recently incorporated medical group was interested in installing 1 million electrocardiogram monitors over the next five years if the screens and frames could be supplied at an all-in-cost of $100 per unit.

Dennis shared this news with Larry McDonald in the engineering R&D department. Larry called back with some exciting news. Engineering was confident that a new model under development, the ME2001, would meet the buyer's specifications and could be manufactured at a variable production cost of $65 per unit provided it could use a special plastic frame designed by Burton Plastics, Inc.

Burton had approached Mazda's engineers with a prototype of a 9-inch supertough frame coated with a special chemical that made the frame more elegant and economical. Burton could manufacture 20,000 such frames per

This case was developed by Jimmy Anklesaria and David N. Burt of the University of San Diego.

month, starting within three months, and offered a price of $30 per unit F.O.B. Mazda's plant, provided Mazda agreed to use the new frames exclusively for the next five years. This price of $30 per unit was incorporated in the $65 per unit variable cost estimate by engineering for the ME2001. The firm's cost accountant, Dirk Hageman, estimated that if 200,000 units of the ME2001 were sold, the allocation for fixed general, administrative, and marketing expenses of $4 million per annum would add approximately $20 to the cost per unit. This was based on the assumption that the ME1001 would be discontinued, which would have to be the case, since Mazda did not have the plant capacity to produce both the ME1001 and ME2001 simultaneously.

Dennis decided to call a meeting before a final decision was made on whether to replace the ME1001 with the new low-cost ME2001 model. He invited Jackie Brown, Larry McDonald, Patrice Regnier from manufacturing, and Jeff Meltzer of purchasing. Everyone seemed enthusiastic about the new low-priced model, which would also be the first of its kind in the market. Jeff, however, was not too happy that Burton would be the sole source of supply for the supertough 9-inch frame. As a former QC technician, Dennis expressed his concern about the quality of the new frame. On previous occasions he had experienced many unpleasant situations with exciting low-cost developments that had failed to meet quality standards over long periods of use. Components that appeared to function well initially would then, for no apparent reason, develop defects that sent the whole process out of control. In his opinion it would take at least a year to effectively test the new component and stabilize the process. Jackie wasn't sure Mazda could wait that long. If it didn't sign the five-year contract with the medical group within six months, chances were that someone else would develop a monitor screen and frame for less than $100 per unit.

Patrice agreed with Dennis and indicated that there was a 10 percent probability that considerable testing and rework might be required by the production department if Mazda's quality standards were to be maintained. In the event the low-cost frame turned out to be defective, the cost of rework would turn the estimated profit contribution into a loss. More disastrous was the possibility that promised delivery dates might not be met. As a result, current sales, customer goodwill, and future business could suffer.

At the end of the meeting, Dennis was in a predicament. There were so many unanswered questions. And a decision on whether or not to proceed with the ME2001 had to be made.

1 Should Mazda Electronics proceed with the low-cost ME2001, incorporating the new frame developed by Burton Plastics, Inc.? Explain.
2 Who should be involved in the decision-making process? Who is ultimately responsible for the decision?
3 What additional information would you require if you were in Dennis Kwok's place?
4 What other issues related to this problem are of concern to purchasing and materials management?

MICROCOMP, INC.

Microcomp, Inc. is a rapidly growing manufacturer of microcomputers located in the Silicon Valley of California. Since the company was incorporated in 1987 it has experienced an average annual growth in sales of 24 percent. The latest development in its product line is the MCD86, a 128-bit microcomputer that requires state-of-the-art microprocessors. Suppliers of microprocessors included Wedge Computers, Inc., Baker Bros., Synergistic Technologies, and La Playa. While Baker had just entered the market, Synergistic and La Playa had been in existence for over a decade, producing a range of computer peripherals. The firm expected to purchase its annual requirement of 100,000 microprocessors from Wedge Computers, Inc., which had recently developed a new microprocessor, the WC 8000. The main feature of the WC 8000 was that it reduced the number of chips necessary to process signals from three to one. This made it more cost-effective than most competing brands and also enhanced the marketability of the MCD86.

John Hunt, the purchasing manager, had been with Microcomp since its incorporation ten years ago. Because of the critical nature of the product, John decided to personally coordinate the preaward survey and participate in the negotiation process. To him, the preaward survey was a mere formality and he was not particularly excited about it. In his opinion, there was really nothing to interfere in negotiating a contract with Wedge Computers. Nevertheless, John realized that such an analysis was an essential step in preparing for negotiations. He decided to seek the assistance of Art Traynor, production manager, Ray Zogob from industrial relations, Shannon Richey from finance, and Christine Bugelli, a senior buyer. The group visited the supplier's facilities in Oregon and met with their respective counterparts. The next day, John sent out a memo to each of these persons requesting their individual opinion on the Wedge contract. (See Exhibit 1.)

A week later John received the various responses. (See Exhibits 2, 3, 4, and 5.) He was not surprised by what Art, Ray, and Christine had to say. But Shannon's observations worried him. He took a look at the balance sheets (Exhibit 6) and the income statements (Exhibit 7) that Shannon had sent him. Although John was not a finance person, he could see that the figures were not as rosy as one would have them appear to be. (For industry averages, see Exhibit 8.) What would happen if Wedge ran into a cash shortage during the term of the contract? Suppose lenders were not willing to advance more money to the firm? First, that company's suppliers would not be paid on time. Would they continue to supply the required raw material in that case? And what if the banks decided to foreclose on the loan secured by the new equipment? These were most disturbing thoughts. What appeared to be an open and shut case was now turning out to be a nightmare. And John had just another week to make the final decision.

This case was developed by Jimmy Anklesaria of the University of San Diego.

EXHIBIT 1
INTEROFFICE MEMO

TO: Art Traynor, Ray Zogob, Shannon Richey, Christine Bugelli
FROM: John Hunt, Purchasing Manager
SUBJECT: Preaward survey

We are about to enter into a contract with Wedge Computers, Inc., for the purchase of 100,000 microprocessors per annum over the next three years. Before entering into the final negotiation stage, I would appreciate your comments on the ability of Wedge to fulfill the terms of this contract, which you know is very important to us.

Please report back to me within a week. You will find copies of relevant documents pertaining to Wedge Computers with my secretary, Sandi Harrod.

EXHIBIT 2
INTEROFFICE MEMO

TO: John Hunt, Purchasing Manager
FROM: Art Traynor, Production Manager
SUBJECT: Wedge Computers

I have examined the documents available on file and sent a team of engineers to the Wedge plant. In my opinion, the firm is fully equipped to satisfy our demand over the next three years. I was particularly impressed with the new equipment installed at a cost of about $5 million. This will increase Wedge's capacity from 400,000 to around 600,000 units per year. The production and quality control systems appear to be adequate, and I believe the firm should have no difficulty meeting our specifications.

EXHIBIT 3
INTEROFFICE MEMO

TO: John Hunt, Purchasing Manager
FROM: Ray Zogob, Industrial Relations
SUBJECT: Wedge Computers

Thanks for soliciting my opinion on the Wedge deal. As far as industrial relations are concerned, the management of Wedge seems to enjoy a cordial relationship with its employees. To the best of my knowledge there is no history of labor unrest in the company. Just last month management increased wages by 3 percent and offered a wide range of incentives to all categories of employees. The employees are not organized, and there is little possibility that they will be in the near future.

EXHIBIT 4
INTEROFFICE MEMO

TO: John Hunt, Purchasing Manager
FROM: Shannon Richey, Financial Analyst
SUBJECT: Wedge Computers

I have studied the income statements and balance sheets of Wedge Computers, Inc., from 1990 till 1994 and wish to make some observations that I hope will be of use to you.

—Sales have grown rapidly from $18.7 million in 1990 to $43.1 million last year. This indicates an average annual growth of 23.21 percent.

—Gross margins have remained close to 20 percent, but I am a bit worried about the decline in the net income after taxes in 1994. While most companies in the industry work on an average net margin of 7 percent, Wedge has failed to meet this figure so far.

—In the past year the firm has spent over $5 million on plant expansion, which I understand has been financed by a $3 million 10.5 percent loan from a local bank. Wedge will need to make five payments of $772,380 each year from January 1, 1996. The balance has been financed through the sale of ten-year 8 percent bonds.

—I am very concerned about the dramatic increase in accounts receivable, which have grown from $2.6 million in 1990 to $21.5 million in 1994. I checked with other companies in the industry and understand that it is an industry practice to allow sixty-days credit to valued customers like us.

Overall, in my opinion Wedge may have some cash flow problems in the near future. The company is heavily leveraged and may find additional borrowing difficult and very costly. I don't know why it is not able to collect money from its customers. I would proceed with caution if I were in your position. Let me know if you need any further information or explanation.

EXHIBIT 5
INTEROFFICE MEMO

TO: John Hunt, Purchasing Manager
FROM: Christine Bugelli, Senior Buyer
SUBJECT: Wedge Computers

In response to your memo of June 21, 1995, I have no hesitation in recommending Wedge Computers, Inc., as a supplier of microprocessors for the next three years. We have studied the bids of three other firms and Wedge's bid of $103 per unit is 10 percent below the next lowest bidder. We investigated the sources of raw material used by the company and are confident that the firm has an adequate source of silicon wafers enhanced with aluminum oxide, which are the main raw materials used by it. I was very impressed with the procurement system at Wedge and especially by the purchasing manager, Richard Cleary, who has a proactive approach to purchasing. The new machines have been installed and are really great. Let me know how the negotiations go. We can't afford to lose this potential source.

EXHIBIT 6
WEDGE COMPUTERS, INC.

(dollar amounts in thousands)

Balance sheets as of December 31	1990	1991	1992	1993	1994
Cash	533.90	1232.00	1736.40	2328.70	594.30
Accounts receivable	2640.00	4686.50	5788.40	15749.70	21500.00
Inventories	2340.30	3379.80	6993.20	3914.30	5590.50
Total current assets	5514.20	9298.30	14518.00	2,1992.70	27684.80
Land, buildings, equipment	2253.50	2439.50	7364.60	8003.40	13370.20
Less: Accumulated deprcn.	544.00	650.00	1211.30	1687.10	2747.10
Net fixed assets	1709.50	1789.50	6153.30	6316.30	10623.10
Investments/advances	1165.60	28.90	232.30	462.00	633.60
Other assets	488.50	376.60	837.50	1132.00	937.80
Total assets	8877.80	11493.30	21741.10	29903.00	39879.30
Accounts payable	1540.80	2134.60	4140.20	2791.00	6239.20
Notes payable—banks	300.00		1000.00		2000.00
Accrued taxes, interest	674.30	1437.70	1900.70	1941.20	1507.70
Current sinking fund	77.00	173.90	324.30	382.50	512.50
Total current liabilities	2592.10	3746.20	7365.20	5114.70	10259.40
Long-term debt:					
From banks	2186.70	2059.70	1777.20	9000.00	12000.00
Bonds			5162.60	4649.50	7170.40
Total liabilities	4778.80	5805.90	14305.00	18764.20	29429.80
Preferred stock	1757.20	2432.20	2392.50	2347.50	2254.30
Common stock & surplus	2341.80	3255.20	5043.60	8791.30	8195.20
Total liab. & net worth	8877.80	11493.30	21741.10	29903.00	39879.30

EXHIBIT 7
WEDGE COMPUTERS, INC.

(dollar amounts in thousands)

Income statements for the years ending December 31	1990	1991	1992	1993	1994
Net sales	18675.90	23400.20	30563.70	38396.40	43140.10
Cost of goods sold	15500.90	18914.70	24119.50	30416.80	34331.70
Gross profit	3175.00	4485.50	6444.20	7979.60	8808.40
Gen. & admin. exps.	1817.20	2134.10	2499.30	2853.60	4350.70
Depreciation & amortzn.	263.20	185.90	377.60	584.20	1089.60
Interest charges	199.80	212.70	410.60	881.60	1791.50
Earnings before taxes	894.80	1952.80	3156.70	3660.20	1576.60
Taxes	443.50	1051.60	1671.20	1875.20	788.30
Net income after taxes	451.30	901.20	1485.50	1785.00	788.30

EXHIBIT 8
WEDGE COMPUTERS, INC.
Selected Financial Ratios

	Industry Average
Current ratio	2.13
Quick ratio	1.18
Inventory turnover	6.95
Average collection period	60.00
Fixed asset turnover	12.35
Total asset turnover	5.75
Debt ratio	0.50
Debt-equity ratio	1.00
Times interest earned	10.00
Gross profit margin	0.22
Net profit margin	0.07
Return on investment	0.09
Return on equity	0.25
Average stock price	N/A
Earnings per share	1.37
Price earnings ratio	N/A

1 Calculate the key financial ratios and comment briefly on each one.
2 Based on the information provided in the case, do you think John Hunt is justifiably worried?
3 What problems would you anticipate with the Wedge contract?
4 What additional sources could Shannon Richey use in order to assess the financial position of Wedge Computers?
5 Are there any disadvantages to using financial ratios in a preaward survey?
6 What specific action would you recommend? Would your recommendation be different if Wedge's price were only 1 or 2 percent lower than another supplier's?

MIDWEST OIL COMPANY

In April of 1993, Mr. Al Smith became director of a new surplus management program at the Midwest Oil Company headquarters in Chicago, Illinois. He was given a deadline of January 1994 by the director of purchasing to increase surplus transactions and dollar recovery. After a preliminary

Copyrighted by the National Association of Purchasing Management and the School of Government and Business Administration, George Washington University. Reprinted by permission. This case was written by E. M. Donnelly during one of the NAPM-sponsored case writing workshops.

study of his new assignment, Al concluded that he faced some significant obstacles.

Prior to 1993, responsibility for Midwest Oil's surplus equipment disposal program had been delegated to the plant level where surplus was generated. Procedures directed the 350 plants first to attempt to locate a need for the equipment at another plant within their division, and to transfer the equipment to the plant in need. If this effort failed, they were asked to attempt to identify a need at a plant in one of the other divisions of the company. Finally, the surplus items that remained were to be sold in the used equipment market.

A major obstacle in operating this program was in advertising the availability of surplus equipment to the plants managed by other divisions, where plant locations and personnel were unknown. Consequently, surplus assets were generally sold as scrap, rather than being transferred to other divisions.

A study of the worldwide corporate purchasing organization and its methods of operation was undertaken in 1993. Since corporate purchasing activities crossed all divisional lines on a regular basis, one result of the study was the formation of a Corporate Surplus Management group, headed by Al Smith. The intent was to serve all divisions and plants within the company with this new group.

Al's mission was to provide structure and coordination, and to develop procedures to facilitate conversion of non-productive assets to productive assets through voluntary transfer between divisions. His office became the central clearinghouse for surplus for all divisions desiring to use his network.

Since the program was voluntary, however, Al encountered some difficulties in obtaining reports on available surplus materials and equipment from the various plants throughout the organization. Internal rivalries produced obstacles rather than cooperation in the identification and interdivision communication phases of the program.

1 How should Al organize the program, and what should he do to obtain voluntary cooperation by the various divisions?

THE MISSISSIPPI MUTUAL LIFE INSURANCE COMPANY

In October, 1994, Frank Smithson, assistant director of Travel and Meeting Services in Mississippi Mutual Life's Administrative Services Division, was asked to develop an ethics training session to address inconsistencies in acceptable buyer behavior in dealing with suppliers. The training program was to be ready by January, 1995.

MISSISSIPPI MUTUAL LIFE

The Mississippi Mutual was a diversified family services organization offering a full range of insurance and financial products and services for businesses, groups, and individuals. The company had about 14,000 employees, with approximately 7,000 in one major Midwestern metropolitan area. It was the largest employer there. It had a strong financial position, with approximately $30 billion in total assets, and almost $11 billion total life insurance in force. Mississippi Mutual had a conservative culture with good morale, no extreme behaviors, and a respected image within both its local and state community. Most of the employees had been with the company for a number of years. Mississippi Mutual ranked in the upper 10 percent of all life insurance companies in assets and premium income. It had a number of affiliated companies and subsidiaries.

ADMINISTRATIVE SERVICES DIVISION

Mississippi Mutual's Administrative Services Division provided services within the company throughout the country, including purchasing outside services and products. The division's customers were the other departments and divisions within the company, including Pension, Group Insurance, Individual Insurance, Mutual Funds, and various subsidiaries. The division had about 500 employees, reporting to a vice president, in charge of eleven service departments, including mail, facilities management, graphic services, travel and meeting services, management services, and office services.

BUYERS' RELATIONSHIP WITH SUPPLIERS

Early in 1994, the division began a series of proactive training and improvement efforts under a program called "Mastering Our Commitment." In May, 1994, Frank Smithson met with division officers to discuss issues related to the program. At this meeting attention focused on acceptable buyer behavior in dealing with outside suppliers. A number of past situations, as well as questions, were discussed, including the following:

1 Buyers accepting gifts of value from suppliers.
2 Buyers having breakfast, lunch, or dinner with suppliers, at suppliers' expense.
3 Buyers having breakfast, lunch, or dinner with suppliers, but buyers picking up the costs.
4 Will other suppliers see the accepting of gifts, lunching, or fraternizing with their competitors by Mississippi's buyers as unfair?

There existed confusion and inconsistencies as to the meaning of ethics, and whether any of these past actions were possibly unethical. There was also a discussion that centered on internal company activities with regard to buyers' activities. For example, some suppliers were also customers of Mississippi Mutual. Thus, how should buyers handle a situation where a supplier directly or indirectly implied that its future business with the company might be contingent upon receiving business *from* the company? How should a buyer respond if there were pressures from within the company to grant a supplier a contract due to that supplier being a customer of the company, particularly when that supplier was not the most attractive supplier? There were inconsistencies among views held by supervisors and leaders with regard to what was considered acceptable behavior.

ETHICAL STANDARDS

The concern for these inconsistencies on the part of the managers and leaders led to an assignment to Smithson to define ethical behavior for buyers and to develop a program for communicating ethical standards. Consideration also had to be given to the reinforcement and enforcement of the standards. Smithson was to submit his recommended standards to the officers of the division, including the vice president, by January, 1995.

To some degree the ethics issue was also one of cultural differences. The changing culture of the division mirrored the changes in the company. About 40 percent of employees in the division had been in the company less than three years. Many newer employees did not share Mississippi Mutual's traditional values, and were beginning to question policies and practices, or chose not to operate "like in the past." There also were concerns that these newer employees might not readily accept the ethical standards. They might question Mississippi Mutual's attempts to impose its value system on them. Experienced employees who had operated without any hint of unethical behavior might resent the standards as questioning their professional judgement in dealing with suppliers. The ethical standards were to apply to everyone involved in buying activities for Mississippi Mutual. These standards were to address, among other issues, dealing with customers; supplier relations; and executing a fair bidding process.

In accepting the assignment, Mr. Smithson recognized the challenges that would have to be met. He was aware of the impact formal ethical standards might have within the company. The new standards would apply to all persons engaged in buying regardless of their location inside or outside of the Administrative Services Division. Mississippi Mutual's fairly recent reorganization into strategic business units (SBU) had fostered a degree of independence leading to the promulgation of different operating practices.

Smithson had to consider the acceptance of ethical standards within his division, and their acceptance and application within the SBUs. Smithson also had to consider a number of difficult questions and decisions that had broad internal and external applications. In reflecting on the task, Mr. Smithson concluded, "I have a tough job ahead."

1 Outline the process Frank Smithson should use in developing the ethical standards for the division.
2 In which key areas should ethical standards be developed?

MUENSTER PUMP BUYS A CAR

This is a negotiation role-playing case regarding the purchase of a company car. The case provides a negotiating experience that is both educational and fun. It offers students an opportunity to test their negotiating skills born from insight, analysis, and an understanding of the strengths, weaknesses, and objectives of both the buyer and seller.

In this case, each member of the class participates. Half the members are assigned the role of the buyer, the other half the role of the seller. Negotiations are one on one.

The role each student is to play will be assigned in class. Each student playing the buyer will be given the specific information that is known to the buyer at the time negotiations begin. Similarly, each student playing the seller will be given the information known to the seller at that time.

After passing out the role-playing information, the instructor will advise the class how to proceed with the negotiations.

THE MUENSTER PUMP COMPANY

The Muenster Pump Company has manufactured high-quality agricultural pumps for over forty years. The firm's only plant is located in the small midwestern city of Muenster. The company is Muenster's largest employer. Bob Dorf, president of the firm, is the grandson of Emil Dorf, the founder. Bob and his family, along with all key personnel, live in or near the city of Muenster. Cordial relations exist between the firm and the city officials.

Since its founding, the firm has always been as self-sufficient as possible. Shortly after setting up business, Emil Dorf established a foundry to cast pump housings and related items. Today, the foundry provides virtually all of the required pump housings.

Bob's cousin, Terry, is the purchasing manager for Muenster Pump. After graduating from State University, Terry worked as a buyer at a large appliance manufacturer in the southwestern corner of the state. But after two years of life in the big city, Terry returned to Muenster. Bob was delighted to have Terry back in town. He established the position of purchasing manager by consolidating the buying functions previously performed by himself and other members of the firm. As seen in Exhibit 1, Terry reports to her Uncle Ned, who is the vice president for manufacturing.

Muenster Pump Company

```
              ┌───────────────────────────────────┐
              │ President and Chief Executive Officer │
              │           Robert A. Dorf             │
              └───────────────────────────────────┘
```

| V.P. Engineering Samuel Dorf | V.P. Manufacturing Nathanial Dorf (Ned) | Comptroller Judy Dorf | V.P. Sales James Dorf |

| Operations Theodore Dorf | Purchasing Terry Dorf | Receiving Judy Dorf | Quality Anneta Dorf |

EXHIBIT 1

The internal organization of the Muenster Pump Company.

Terry is an aggressive and conscientious buyer. Materials costs have come down from 60 percent of the cost of sales to 50 percent in the two years since she assumed responsibility for purchasing.

Recently a representative of Union Foundry, a firm located in the southeastern part of the state, called on Terry. The rep was aware that Muenster Pump made its own cast pump housings. But he claimed that new developments in casting pouring allowed his firm to offer extremely attractive prices.

Terry requested a price on the L-1012 casting housing, Muenster's most popular size. The L-1012 represents 60 percent of Muenster's demand for casting housings. The pump that incorporates the L-1012 is sold to distributors for $500. Within a week of the meeting, a letter arrived from Union Foundry, quoting a price of $90 F.O.B. Muenster. Delivery was promised in 120 days after receipt of the first order. Thereafter, delivery would be made in sixty days after receipt of an order. Minimum orders were established as 100 units. Terry contacted two other foundries and obtained quotations for the L-1012 housing. The prices were $94 and $98 F.O.B. Muenster.

Terry met her Uncle Ned, discussed her findings with him, and asked how much it cost Muenster to produce the casting housings internally in its own foundry.

Ned Dorf was not at all enthusiastic about Terry's efforts in this area of the business. He said, "Terry, I appreciate your interest and efforts at reducing cost. But a lot more is involved here than meets the eye. We produce a quality housing that is not equaled in the industry. It's one of the primary keys to our success! Furthermore, we can respond to requirements much quicker than those city boys."

Terry responded, "Ned, let's assume that all your doubts could be overcome. How much does it cost us to make the housings?" Ned replied, "Terry, there is something else involved. We have sixteen men working in that foundry. If we stop making our own housings, we'll have to close down the foundry. And there's no other place in the firm where these men could work."

At this point, Terry thought that discretion would be the better part of valor. She thanked her Uncle Ned for the information and returned to her office.

Later that day, her cousin Bob stopped by. In the ensuing conversation, she learned that the L-1012 housing cost Muenster about $180. Total overhead at Muenster was calculated to be approximately 200 percent; hence, direct costs for materials and labor for the housings would be about $60. Approximately 70 percent of the overhead is for fixed costs such as depreciation, taxes, and executive salaries.

1 What other information would be useful in arriving at a make-or-buy decision?
2 Who should take part in the make-or-buy decision process?
3 What role should purchasing play?
4 How should the noneconomic factors be evaluated?
5 Should Muenster make or buy its casting housings?
6 What do you think of the organizational structure at Muenster?

NADIA DEVELOPS A COMMODITY STUDY

Nadia Aladray is a 1993 graduate of the University of San Diego, where she majored in purchasing. After two years at W, T & R, Inc., Nadia has been told that she is under consideration for promotion to a prestigious position as commodity manager of semiconductors. (Usually, such a position requires eight years of experience.) Mr. Lee Fredland, Nadia's boss, has asked her to develop a commodity study of semiconductors as a means of demonstrating her ability to handle the commodity management job.

1 What issues should Nadia address in her study?

NATIONAL COMPUTERS

Tom Jones, manager of purchased materials at the National Computers plant in San Diego, is introducing what the company has termed a "supply line management (SLM) strategy." Long-term goals of the SLM system include reducing production costs, improving product quality, and increasing the overall performance of the plant. The mission statement of supply line management is "to provide the lowest total cost of purchased materials" to the San Diego facility—and "to continuously improve product quality, supplier responsiveness, and delivery predictability of purchased materials." The following objectives were set forth by SLM:

- Develop long-term agreements on 95 percent of purchased material part numbers. Target date: 4th quarter 1996
- Reduce core supplier base to 125. Target date: 4th quarter 1996
- Target 100 percent of critical suppliers for "early supplier involvement." Target date: 4th quarter 1994
- Reduce part number base by 40 percent. Target date: 4th quarter 1996
- Maintain in-house quality levels at fewer than 500 defective parts per million (PPM). Target date: 4th quarter 1996
- 90 percent of purchased parts to be certified. Target date: 4th quarter 1996
- Maintain on-hand direct materials inventory at less than $10K. Target date: 4th quarter 1996
- Maintain on-time delivery greater than 95 percent. Target date: 4th quarter 1996
- Maintain planned order late starts at less than 3 percent. Target date: 4th quarter 1996
- Maintain reschedule left/right at less than 7 percent. Target date: 4th quarter 1996
- Reduce the largest supplier repeat lead time to four weeks. Target date: 4th quarter 1997

Out of all the stated position objectives, Tom believes reduction of the part number base by 40 percent to be the least attainable. He thinks that *convincing the engineering department* will prove to be the most important step in achieving the desired reduction—and therefore in achieving the objectives of supply line management. Tom understands that improved communications between the departments are necessary. Attached is a memo sent to the director of operations and the director of hardware engineering, explaining the need for part number reduction and subsequent target performance measurement. (See Exhibit 1.)

1 What specific techniques and methods should Tom use to convince engineering to reduce part numbers?
2 What kind of evidence should he use to support his case?
3 What suggestions could he give engineering to facilitate the reduction in part numbers?
4 Outline in general terms an overall inventory management program for National Computers.

EXHIBIT 1

Intracorporation Memo

Date: February 19, 1994

To: P. A. Why, Acting Director, Operations; R. W. Hart,
Director, Hardware Engineering

From: T. R. Jones, Manager, Purchased Materials Management

Extension: 2111

Subject: PURCHASED MATERIAL INVENTORY

The primary drivers of purchased material inventories are:

—The number of part numbers
—The lead time to obtain parts
—Schedule fluctuations
—On-time delivery

My concern is that total coordination does not exist to maximize the effectiveness of our materials inventory plan. At inventory meetings, the presentations represent what we are doing to specifically address existing purchasing inventory problems.

To ensure that we are maximizing our improvement potential, the following is recommended:

1. Part Number Reduction

Today we have $4.4M of purchased material in inventory, consisting of approximately 4,500 active part numbers ($1,000/part number). The foundation of part number reduction is part number standardization. Larry Lempke's group is attacking this impressively with two people involved part time; however, new part numbers still are being added daily.

Engineering controls need to be established to totally address part number reduction. When new part numbers are added, other part numbers need to be reviewed for deletion.

Target performance measurement needs to be implemented for engineering. It should include:

a. Part number reduction objectives. Recommended objectives for target commodities are as shown.

Commodity	Active P/Ns	Targeted reduction	Current inv. dollars
Active electronics	617	25	1,262,339
PCBs	279	25	724,681
Passive electronics	1275	250	662,833
Interconnect products	340	75	446,232
Sheet metal/plastics	785	50	244,833
Wire assemblies	214	25	207,820
Hardware/fasteners	664	140	202,052
Packaging	96	10	37,284
Tools/molds/castings	N/A	N/A	N/A
TOTALS:	4270	600	3.8M

b. Part number targets for new products.

It is recommended that engineering report part number additions and deletions monthly.

Long-term part number reduction objectives are as follows.

ACTIVE PART NUMBERS:	YE94	YE95	YE96
	3700	3200	2800

EXHIBIT 1 *(continued)*

2.   Lead-Time Reduction

Today lead times for unique parts are as shown (A). Targeted performance measurement for existing unique parts has been established (B) in purchasing. These lead times include one week for P.O. generation and signoff, supplier lead time, plus one week for receipt and processing to production.

	(A) Current lead times (wks)	(B) Lead-time targets—YE94 (purchasing)	(C) Future lead times (engr. targets)
Twisted pair wire	12	10	6
Back panels	12	10	6
Card cages	14–16	10	6
AWW	14	10	6
Sheet metal	9–15	10	6
PCBs	10–12	10	6
Wire assemblies	9–14	10	6
Plastic	8–12	10	6
Power supplies	14–22	12	9

For future production requirements, it is recommended that engineering implement target performance measurement for unique products as shown (C). Design attention with early supplier involvement can significantly contribute to further lead-time reduction. Our long-term lead-time objective for YE96 is *4 weeks.*

NATIONAL MACHINE AND ELECTRONICS

Early in 1995, Michael Phillips, C.P.M., purchasing director for National Machine and Electronics (NME), met with his company's president at the president's request to discuss reducing materials costs. In considering all possible alternatives, Mike knew that offshore sourcing appeared to offer interesting opportunities. The meeting centered on NME's historical position as a buyer only of domestic products, and concluded with Mike receiving authorization to explore the cost-saving potential of offshore sourcing.

NATIONAL MACHINE AND ELECTRONICS (NME)

NME is a division of a worldwide conglomerate that specializes in precision machined products and aerospace electronics. While largely government and defense oriented, NME has one commercial aviation electronics division among its fifteen autonomous operating groups. Total sales for NME during 1986 were approximately $2.5 billion, with over $1 billion being spent by the purchasing departments of the various groups.

The NME purchasing function is divided among the fifteen autonomous divisions. Each has its own purchasing department, which reports to division management but adheres to corporate policies and procedures. There is a relatively small corporate purchasing staff concerned with corporate policy and common goods and services.

THE COST REDUCTION OBJECTIVE

To maintain its competitive position, NME needed to explore all possible ways to reduce costs. In addition to analyzing and working with its domestic suppliers, Mike believed it was necessary at this time to begin considering offshore sources.

OFFSHORE SOURCING

Until 1995, NME had only purchased offshore as part of an offset countertrade requirement. The other exception was the Commercial Aviation Electronics (CAE) division, which had been acquired in 1994 as a means of diversifying NME's electronics markets. CAE not only had been buying from foreign sources but had established a factory in Singapore to source and manufacture one of its product lines.

CAE's offshore experience began before being acquired by NME. At first, parts were purchased from Singapore and other East Asian sources. These parts were then assembled in this country. Soon CAE began to buy assemblies in East Asia, and finally all factory operations were shifted to their own Singapore facility.

When Mike contacted each of the other divisions' purchasing managers, he was surprised to discover that each one had a collection of horror stories of past foreign purchasing attempts and was unwilling to try again. Most of these stories centered around problems of communication, quality control, credibility, and understanding.

Mike again contacted the CAE purchasing manager to discuss details of the Singapore operation. Not only did the Singapore factory build a product line, but the Singapore purchasing department sourced components for that product line from throughout East Asia. Initial cost savings from first buys (including engineering, test fixtures, and other startup costs) ranged from 10 to 18 percent. Subsequent purchases yielded savings in the 25 to 40 percent range compared to domestic sources. Quality and delivery problems were minimal.

Following that conversation, Mike wondered what he might do next.

1 What choices does Mike have for starting an international sourcing program?
2 What are the advantages and disadvantages of each?
3 Would NME benefit from an international procurement office in Asia?

NATIONWIDE TELEPHONE

BACKGROUND

Nationwide Telephone has been a manufacturer of quality low-cost telephones since 1988. The firm has based its business strategy on automation, fast deliveries, and reliable service. Nationwide is one of the first low-cost telephone manufacturers still producing and selling telephones in the United States. Competition, especially from the Far East, has made this an increasingly difficult endeavor.

The most important segment of Nationwide's sales has been the promotional "Gift with Purchase" market. Magazine publishers currently compose Nationwide's largest customer base. Positive growth has been forecasted in the promotional incentive market for the next five years. To meet market demand, Nationwide manufactures two models of telephones in a variety of colors.

The firm's plant is located in Nogales, Arizona. The plant was built near the major sources of supply, which are in Mexico. Nationwide procures all its components from Mexico except for the plastic items. The plastic components are purchased in the local domestic area. Nationwide has ruled out the use of a maquiladora,* due to the highly automated nature of its production process. As a capital-intensive firm, Nationwide also concluded a maquiladora was not a feasible alternative because of the increased risks of having its equipment in a foreign country.

Roger Stoga is the president and founder of the company. He has an engineering degree from Michigan Tech and an M.B.A. from Purdue University. He attributes Nationwide's ability to stay competitive to two factors: (1) automating its process and (2) procuring highly labor-intensive materials in Mexico.

The plant employs only twenty people, of which twelve are responsible for the actual assembly work. With the help of automated assembly machines, Nationwide has been able to meet market demand and keep labor and manufacturing costs down.

PURCHASING

Steven Young is the sales and purchasing manager. He employs two buyers, Jan Newman and Bill Bush. Jan has been with the company for a little over a year and is a graduate of Arizona State University. She has a strong background in price analysis. Bill is the eldest and most experienced member of the Nationwide staff. He is expected to retire later this year. Jan purchases all the electronics and wire harnesses, while Bill concentrates his efforts on the plastics and hardware.

This case was developed by Bruce Asbaugh and Sandra Sarmiento under the direction of Professor David N. Burt.

*Maquiladora plants are located in northern Mexico. Bascially, foreign materials are imported duty free, processed (using low-cost labor), and then returned to the country of origin without customs duties being imposed in either Mexico or the country of origin.

PROCUREMENT SYSTEM

The manufacturing process is highly dependent on timely deliveries from its suppliers. Local sourcing is used to assure prompt delivery and to keep supplier lead times short. Procurement focuses its efforts on maintaining a small supplier base.

The driving force of the procurement system is to obtain low-cost, high-quality materials as a means of staying competitive. As a standard procedure, purchasing prepares annual recosting reports of its suppliers. Currently, requests for quotations are sent to potential suppliers to compare with the current supplier's prices. The buyers are to sort through the various bids and choose the lowest one submitted to use as a basis for negotiating future part pricing.

DEVELOPING SITUATION

Over the last six months, Roger has been noticing a drop in sales, while expenses have begun to increase. A careful evaluation of production costs revealed a recent increase in the plastic component prices. Since plastic components account for 40 percent of the telephone's cost, the rise in price significantly impacted profit.

Plastic components are made by injection molding. Injection molding is a process whereby a thermoplastic material, usually in pellet form, is heated to its melting point. The melted material is then pushed into a mold via an injection molding machine and held in the closed mold while it is cooled into a solid shape. The solidified part is ejected from the mold and the process begins again.

On further investigation, Roger noticed Nationwide is sole-sourced by one injection molder in the local area, ABC Plastics. Nationwide has been purchasing solely from ABC since it consistently submitted the lowest bid. Quality and delivery have been generally good.

Roger called Steve into his office to discuss the situation. Roger said to Steve, "As you are aware, our sales this quarter have been weak and expenses have been increasing. I have gone through our material price sheets and noticed plastic part prices have been steadily increasing. Why is that?" Steve replied, "Bill has made me aware of the problem, but he has not been able to determine the cause of the price changes. He has stated that 'ABC refuses to divulge any cost information.'" Roger firmly said, "We have to understand what the problem is and get it fixed now!"

Steve was pondering his options and alternatives to solve this problem. He knew if he did nothing to rectify this situation quickly, Nationwide would not be able to price its telephones competitively.

Steve also knew that Jan had been successful in obtaining price reductions; therefore, Steve decided to ask Jan to work with Bill to develop an action plan to get the escalating plastic material prices under control.

1 What type of analytical tools can be used by the purchasing group to determine the right price?

2 How could Nationwide's purchasing department have prevented the price escalations?

3 How does the competitive condition of the plastic component industry impact the use of price analysis?

4 What kind of resistance might Jan encounter from Bill? How can Bill help facilitate the pricing analysis process?

5 What are some of the costs/benefits of continuing to source from the same local suppliers?

NEW VALLEY POWER CORPORATION

NEW VALLEY POWER CORPORATION (NVPC)

In early 1995, Joan Davis became project director for the Materials Management Information System (MMIS) at NVPC, located in the eastern part of the country. She found that the MMIS faced considerable opposition from several departments within the organization. She also found that the firm's inventory level was unusually high.

ORGANIZATION BACKGROUND

NVPC was incorporated as an electric utility in 1923. Over the next five decades, NVPC management focused on building a large number of generating plants and related distribution networks. By 1970, revenues had reached $250 million and the company had over 4,000 employees.

In 1973, just prior to the international energy crisis, 56% of NVPC's total electric output of four million kilowatts was produced by coal and 44% by oil. Due to the Mideast oil embargo, petroleum prices sky-rocketed. The increased demand for coal caused its price to increase as well.

Supply shortages, rising prices, and the double-digit inflation that followed placed added pressure on NVPC's financial resources. Needed rate increases of about 11% per year created severe reactions from consumers. Regulatory officials responded by demanding comprehensive cost justification studies before granting higher prices. NVPC management began to investigate cost-containment strategies within the major functional components of the firm (see Exhibit 1). David Chance, manager of the Materials Group, initiated a study of cost-saving and cost-containment alternatives available to the Materials Group.

THE MATERIALS GROUP AND OPERATIONS AT NVPC

The Materials Group served the other departments by purchasing requested goods and services, maintaining centralized inventories of common items, and

Copyrighted by the National Association of Purchasing Management and the School of Government and Business Administration, George Washington University. Reprinted by permission. This case was written by John M. Browning during one of the NAPM-sponsored case writing workshops.

performing store-keeping activities. The two largest using departments were the Generating Group and the Electric Systems Group. These two groups historically had also maintained their own large inventories for emergency situations.

To understand the general operating procedures in this type of business, consider how the Electric Systems Group does its job. This group is responsible for distribution of electric power; this involves the use of poles, towers, wire, transformers, customer hook-ups, etc. It is a common practice to requisition everything that *could be needed* on a job and load it onto trucks. The trucks are then dispatched to the job-site, which could be 100 miles away. The job could run from a few hours to over a month. When the job is completed, the trucks return and are unloaded, remaining materials are identified, forms are prepared to return the materials to storage, and the actual physical movement is accomplished. This entire process could span several months from the beginning to the end of a project.

David Chance's original investigation along with follow-up studies revealed the following useful information about inventory and existing MMIS operations.

1 Even the most current information contained in the MMIS system was *at least* one week old.
2 A physical inventory was taken once every 24 months to reconcile computer inventory records with actual inventory stock on hand.

EXHIBIT 1
Major functional groups.

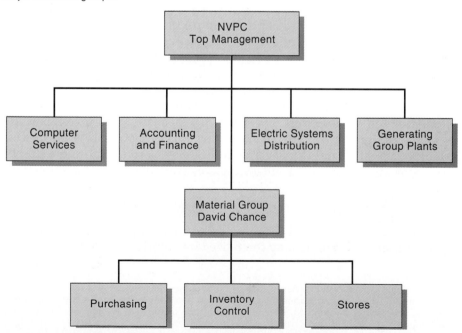

3 There was a 40–45 percent error rate between the physical inventory and the computer records.

4 Inventory investment had grown at an average rate of 14% per year over the last decade.

5 By the early 1990s, the inventory value had grown to over $100 million, with more than a third of the investment tied up in MRO items.

THE MATERIALS MANAGEMENT INFORMATION SYSTEM (MMIS)

David concluded that much better control over materials would have to be obtained for significant savings to be realized. He proposed that a fully integrated MMIS should consist of these activities: (1) purchasing; (2) accounts payable; (3) inventory control; (4) cash management; and (5) stores control.

The director of Computer Services, Sharon Johnson, believed that David's concept of the MMIS was sound, and assigned several of her computer specialists to the development effort. It took three years to design the system.

After the system was implemented, a cost/benefit study revealed that the MMIS had a savings potential of $3 million per year. Actual figures at the time, however, showed that the inventory investment figures were continuing their upward climb. Large stockpiles were still maintained by the Generating and Electric Systems Groups.

Early in 1995, David appointed Joan Davis to be the project director for the MMIS. Joan was given 90 days to interview key people in the using departments to determine what problems were present, if any, and to make recommendations on resolving the problems she found.

Her findings revealed that the departments did not like the MMIS. In fact, the Generating and Electric Systems Groups claimed that the MMIS did not suit their needs and, indeed, complicated their jobs unduly. Joan pondered how to resolve these issues in an expedient fashion.

1 Identify and analyze the key issues in this case.

NORTHEASTERN EQUIPMENT COMPANY

The Northeastern Equipment Company manufactured goods for the consumer, government, and industrial markets. The company was organized on a divisional basis according to product lines. Each of the four division managers reported to the executive vice president, as did the personnel director and controller. Each division manager was expected to operate his or her division as a separate business on a profitable basis. (See Exhibit 1.) Each division occupied a separate building containing its entire production facility, home marketing office, and so on. The divisional plants were all within a 15-mile radius of the executive offices where the president, vice president, personnel department, and accounting department were housed.

THE TEST EQUIPMENT DIVISION

The Test Equipment Division manufactured electrical and mechanical test equipment for industrial, government, and laboratory use. The products of the division fell into two broad classes: relatively inexpensive mass-produced units and expensive highly engineered units that were manufactured on a low-volume or single-unit basis. Manufacturing, therefore, was placed under two foremen: one who was responsible for low-volume or "specialty products" and another who was responsible for the high-volume or "mass production" items. These two groups were supported by a metal shop and a machine shop, each of which was responsible for fabrication of subassemblies for both the specialty products group and the mass production group. (See Exhibit 2.)

EXHIBIT 1
Northeastern Equipment Company organization chart.

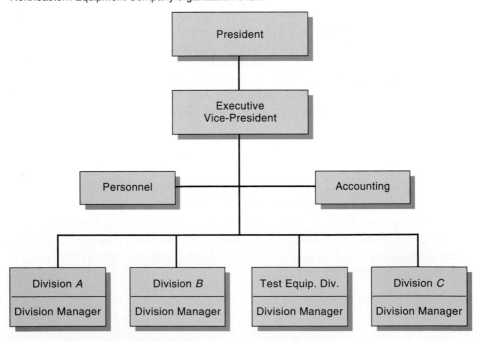

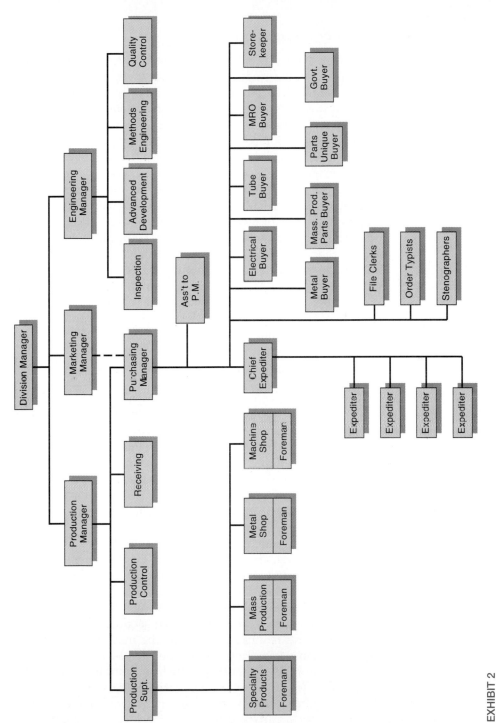

EXHIBIT 2
Northeastern Equipment Company organization chart, Test Equipment Division.

PURCHASING—TEST EQUIPMENT DIVISION

The purchasing manager, who was very competent and had twenty years' experience in production, engineering, and purchasing, reported to the production manager because the division manager felt that the purchasing manager's primary function was to "see that production had what it needed when it needed it." The production manager was held responsible by the division manager for keeping all production costs in line.

On the other hand the marketing manager exercised functional authority over the purchasing manager on all specialty products. These products, which were frequently large equipment installations such as automation devices and communication systems, were normally made on a job shop basis to customer specifications. Success in the sale of these products depended on the ability of the division to produce efficiently to tight customer specifications and to deliver more quickly than competitors. The marketing manager, therefore, could specify brands and suppliers for component parts, and he frequently negotiated directly with suppliers and supplier salesmen prior to placing an order through purchasing. The purchasing manager had repeatedly tried to eliminate these direct contacts between the marketing manager and the suppliers since several expensive duplicate orders and contract complications had arisen as a result of purchasing's not being properly consulted or informed.

As a result of his resistance to the marketing manager's activities, the purchasing manager and the marketing manager were hardly on speaking terms. Whenever the marketing manager did want purchasing assistance, he always went to the assistant to the purchasing manager. This individual was a very competent engineer and former lawyer and was known to be able to obtain excellent cooperation from all suppliers. Because of frequent favors asked by the marketing manager in expediting and straightening out orders, the assistant to the purchasing manager had only one other set of assigned activities. These duties were keeping up with special features of government contracts in process or negotiation, government regulations concerning procurement, and government liaison.

The internal organization of purchasing is shown in Exhibit 2. The metal buyer bought castings, bar, plate, and extruded stock for the four production groups. His responsibilities included all basic metals and alloys that were to be further fabricated in the division. The electrical buyer bought meters, wire, resistors, capacitors, and all similar fabricated electrical parts, except tubes, for both the specialty products and mass production sections. The mass production parts buyer bought all fabricated parts for the mass production section, other than electrical parts including tubes. The tube buyer bought cathode ray and miscellaneous tubes for both production sections. These tubes ranged in unit price from a few cents to $8,000, some being off-the-shelf items and others special development jobs. The parts unique buyer bought all fabricated parts other than electrical parts and tubes for the specialty products section. The MRO buyer handled all operating and clerical supplies for the entire division.

The government buyer handled subcontracts and purchase orders placed under government prime or subcontracts. Government work was handled by both production sections and accounted for 40 percent of the division's sales. Because government work was carried on in the production section simultaneously with civilian orders, and because many parts were interchangeable, the government buyer only placed orders for parts unique to government orders. For standard items that would be included in government orders, he merely ensured that the other buyers included proper clauses in the orders they placed. The government buyer worked closely with the assistant to the purchasing manager, with the marketing department, and with all other buyers. He was well thought of by the entire division and handled government contract materials with a minimum of friction.

The storekeeper kept all records on preproduction inventories and supervised the stock clerks in the various storerooms of the plant. The expediters helped the buyers by following up on material orders until they were received in the plant and by picking up rush orders, and so on, on request. Once materials were drawn from stores they became the responsibility of the production foreman who had drawn them from stock. Because some materials went directly from boxcars into production, rather than through stores, the receiving department was placed under the production manager. Inspection was performed by engineers assigned to the job by the engineering manager upon request by the purchasing manager. There was no full-time inspection department.

The Test Equipment Division had been operating at a low profit ratio for several years. Inventories of raw materials, goods in process, and final inventories were turning slowly, and orders were being lost because of high quoted prices and slow deliveries. A new division manager was appointed to clear up the situation.

1 What would you recommend the new division manager do to make the materials management operation more efficient?
2 What could be done to make purchasing operations more efficient?

THE OAKLAND SCHOOL DISTRICT

Gene Smith, purchasing manager for the Oakland School District, has just completed an analysis of his purchasing paper workload. His staff, consisting of an assistant, two buyers, a clerk, and a stenographer, had complained of the steadily growing number of orders that the department had to process. The school district had expanded to include another high school and two vo-tech schools during the last several years. This expansion, plus normal growth, had created a workload in which 31,164 purchase orders (exclusive of changes and adjustments) were placed, spending $5,405,678 with 1,296 suppliers. Another breakdown Gene developed showed that 15.2 percent of the suppliers received 82.5 percent of the dollar volume purchased.

A further analysis revealed that the average value of all orders placed was $482.21, and that 35 percent of them ranged between $30 and $100 and totaled 2.8 percent of the total dollars spent annually. In fact, 23 percent of the purchases were for less than $30 and added only 0.35 percent to the dollar volume. Purchase orders were evenly spread throughout the year, running about 2,600 per month.

One cause for the numerous orders, he told the district director for operations, was "daily need for rubber stamps, small equipment parts, special laboratory supplies, fluorescent tubes, MRO supplies, and other miscellaneous items." In Gene's words, "the school district seemed to be like a custom job shop type operation." In addition, the various departments wrote an excessive number of requisitions for purchasing because they needed detailed records for their files, which are required by the stringent district accounting control policies.

Gene had asked Harry Flint, the controller, to reduce some of the documentation required. He was told that "it's necessary to have proper records to control expenses, and the extra orders are not extra expenses because you would be on the payroll anyway."

Mr. Flint also pointed out that the stores supervisor, who initiated many of the orders, was following present district policy to keep only very active inventory items in stock and to make direct purchases of all others. Both the controller and the stores supervisor were under the treasurer's office, which in turn reported to the district superintendent.

Another problem was the unpredictable number of change orders issued by maintenance and by the district engineer's office. These modifications involved changes in quality specifications, actual amount delivered, and date of delivery originally specified by users or by inventory control. Accounting insisted that it would not approve invoices that did not completely match a confirmed purchase order or its supporting changes. During the past year, 5,678 change orders had been issued, of which 2,946 had been due to relatively minor variations.

Smith knew that local suppliers and distributors had complained of the burden of small orders and that some were considering a minimum charge of $40 per order. After further investigation, he concluded that small orders were not economical for either the buyer or the seller and had asked the accounting office and stores to help him solve this problem. But neither would suggest to his boss, the district treasurer, any change in policy or procedure. Smith's boss, the director for operations, also reported to the district superintendent and had expressed interest in trying to update the growing organization's management methods.

1 Identify the basic issues and management problems that Smith should consider in trying to improve the situation.
2 What additional information should Smith attempt to obtain?
3 How would you suggest Smith solve these problems?

THE OFFICE SUPPLIES HASSLE

In 1994 Gordon Harrison took over as director of purchasing for Iona University, a small private university in Des Moines, Iowa. Upon his arrival he discovered that the staff was spending too much time processing requisitions for office supplies. Consequently, he wanted to develop methods of increasing the effectiveness and the efficiency of handling the acquisition of office supplies for the university.

THE UNIVERSITY

Iona University offers both liberal arts education and professional and pre-professional programs. The university's 120-acre campus is a self-contained community just outside Des Moines. The population of the university includes approximately 8,000 students and about 400 full-time faculty and staff representing over 50 different academic and administrative departments.

THE PURCHASING DEPARTMENT

The purchasing department was directed by Mr. Harrison. His primary responsibility was to manage the procurement of materials requested by all university departments. Mr. Harrison's current purchasing staff consisted of himself and his secretary who assisted him in the daily purchasing activities. This involved the processing of approximately 1,000 requisitions and 3,500 invoices per month for over 500 suppliers. Mail room personnel also reported to him, and were responsible for maintaining the office supply store, which carried over $13,000 of office supply items in inventory.

OFFICE SUPPLIES AND REQUISITIONS

Mr. Harrison's research covering a 12-month period of the school's purchasing activity revealed that $57,000 was spent for office supplies—and that the requisitioning, invoicing, and related check issuing frequency for these purchases was uneconomical. Mr. Harrison discovered that much of the time spent maintaining the office supply store involved mail room personnel. Their daily responsibilities included putting away items received, filling campus orders, and pricing each item for accounting. Since most standard items were held in inventory, supplies were immediately issued as each requisitioner approached the service window.

Each month there were between 150 and 200 requisitions for office supplies and about twice as many invoices received and processed by purchasing and accounting personnel. This corresponded to the distribution of over 50 checks per month to seven different office supply firms, and an abundance of follow-up paperwork. Additionally, the discounts received from these suppliers for similar items ranged from 10 to 35 percent off of published prices.

In an attempt to relieve the mail room and the accounting department of some of the more repetitive processing tasks, Mr. Harrison sorted and organized the monthly invoices by each department's account number before releasing them for payment. Thus, he initiated an effort to find ways of streamlining the procedures and reducing the costs for procuring, inventorying, and managing office supplies. At the same time, he wanted to reduce the labor time associated with the effort.

While considering possible alternatives, Mr. Harrison recalled the increasing demand for space by the mail room and the printing department. The office supply store occupied considerable space—and he wondered if it could be better utilized by one of these departments.

1 Identify and analyze the key issues facing the new director of purchasing.

PACIFIC HEALTHCARE

Pacific Healthcare is the largest health care provider in Santa Barbara County. The institution consists of three hospitals: Pacific Memorial (415 beds), Pacific Cabrillo (250 beds), and Pacific Isla Vista (300 beds); also included are two nursing homes and ten outpatient clinics. All combined, Pacific Healthcare has over 1,500 beds.

Barney Rubble, corporate director of materials management for Pacific, is in charge of purchasing for all Pacific Healthcare subsidiaries.

Mr. Thurston Howell, director of radiology, had been in charge of supplier selection of X ray film at Pacific for the past fifteen years. In the past, Mr. Howell refused to authorize the use of any X ray film other than Kodak.

Recently, Mr. Howell passed away, leaving Barney Rubble the opportunity to change the policy on selecting the supplier of the film. After a detailed investigation, Mr. Rubble had reason to believe that the current Kodak price was above that of possible competition.

The existing agreement with Kodak calls for furnishing X ray equipment, along with maintenance and service, at a substantial discount for using Kodak as the single supplier of the X ray film. Kodak refused to provide these services if it were not the only source used for X ray film.

X ray film comes in different types and sizes for various uses. The three types of film used at Pacific hospitals are general X ray film, film for mammograms, and film for CAT scans. Pacific uses approximately 1,500 sheets of X ray film per day.

Kodak film has been the industry standard in the past. There are also four other companies that manufacture X ray film: Dupont, Agfa, Fuji, and 3M. The

APPENDIX A	
Manufacturer	X ray film, price per sheet
Kodak	$1.80
Agfa	$1.58
Dupont	$1.50
Fuji	$1.40
3M	$1.35

quality of Dupont and Agfa is consistent with Kodak. Fuji and 3M film is thought to be of lower quality; however, this film meets minimum spec requirements. The prices of each brand are listed in Appendix A.

Obtaining the highest quality with the best service at the lowest overall cost is Pacific Healthcare's purchasing strategy for medical supplies. Pacific's objective is to find a single-source supplier for a one-year contract.

1 What alternatives should Barney Rubble consider when addressing the problem?
2 Should Pacific's purchasing policy allow for any medical staff personnel to control purchasing decisions?
3 What are the advantages and disadvantages of staying with Kodak—or changing suppliers? How would you evaluate these?
4 What action could Mr. Rubble have taken prior to Mr. Howell's death to obtain reduced film prices?

A PARTNERING AGREEMENT AT I.M.C.

Mr. Jim Burton, purchasing manager of I.M.C. (Indiana Manufacturing Company) of Indianapolis, Indiana, a manufacturer of car hoist machinery, was offered a partnering agreement by Indiana Aluminum Company (I.A.C.) whereby I.M.C. and its suppliers could purchase aluminum at specified pricing and terms. I.M.C. had thirty days to accept or reject the offer.

GENERAL COMPANY BACKGROUND

I.M.C. had developed a good reputation for producing car hoist equipment. Its total sales in the last twelve months, from both its domestic and international distributors, was approximately $50 million. I.M.C., in its seventeenth year of operation, had seen its sales increase steadily over the last twelve months and it expected sales to continue to increase. Its total annual purchase of aluminum was approximately $27 million.

PURCHASING'S SOURCE SELECTION

The Indiana Aluminum Company (I.A.C.), one of eight suppliers of aluminum to I.M.C., supplied approximately seventy percent of I.M.C.'s aluminum needs. I.M.C. has purchased aluminum from I.A.C. for all seventeen years of its existence. Mr. Burton believed that while individual suppliers might at any one time provide the best pricing, delivery, quality or service, I.A.C. had consistently provided the best overall combination of these requirements. All aluminum suppliers were highly competitive and were always seeking to increase their share of I.M.C.'s business. Failure to receive a share of I.M.C.'s business at one point in time had not deterred them from seeking an increase in that share at the next opportunity. I.M.C. had recently considered reducing the number of its aluminum suppliers to one prime and two to three backup suppliers, solely for the purpose of efficiency. It had good working relationships with all of these suppliers. It had no annual requirements contracts or fixed price agreements with any of them, nor had it ever had any discussions with any of them to do so. Mr. Burton believed, but has not verified the fact, that no such agreements existed in the industry. All of I.M.C.'s purchasing of aluminum had been on the spot market, based solely on quality, pricing, and delivery available on any particular day.

   I.M.C. had four fabricator subcontractors that also independently purchased aluminum from one or all of its eight possible aluminum suppliers. The amount of aluminum purchased by I.M.C. and its four suppliers totaled approximately 1,700,000 pounds per year. Currently, two of the fabricators purchased all of their aluminum from I.A.C. while the other two purchased between 30% and 50% from I.A.C.

THE PARTNERING AGREEMENT

I.A.C. had approached I.M.C. with a proposal to enter into its first-ever partnering agreement. In this agreement, I.M.C. would be offered a firm, fixed price of $1.02 per pound for the aluminum it purchased over the next twelve months. The current price of aluminum on the open, highly competitive market was $0.98 per pound. The market is volatile. The price of aluminum in the last six months had been as high as $1.12 per pound and eighteen months ago it was $1.30 per pound. While there was no guarantee that prices would go either up or down in the next twelve months, Mr. Burton expected the prices to rise since current prices were the lowest he had experienced in his five years with I.M.C. In the event of a major price change during the agreement period, I.A.C. would agree to renegotiate, although not necessarily change, the established prices.

Also, I.A.C. would, at no cost, agree to put I.M.C.'s part numbers on its (I.A.C.'s) computer to ensure a more efficient ordering system.

MARKETING TO SUBCONTRACTORS

Another condition of this partnering agreement is that I.M.C. had to try to convince its four fabricator subcontractors to purchase all of their aluminum from I.A.C. Their guaranteed annual pricing per pound would be the same as I.A.C.'s. Additionally, I.A.C. would maintain inventory for these subcontractors in order to minimize their inventory investment. If a subcontractor were to agree to use I.A.C. as its single source for aluminum, it would receive the benefits noted, but there would be no punitive action in the event of their failure to do so. The subcontractors would have no individual contracts to sign.

An additional incentive for I.M.C. to accept this agreement is that I.M.C. would receive a $0.02 rebate for all combined purchases by them and the four listed subcontractors if such annual I.M.C.-related purchases exceeded 500,000 pounds. I.A.C. would regularly monitor and report to I.M.C. the amount of all such purchases.

SPECIAL CONDITIONS

I.A.C. did not want the subcontractors to receive and, in fact, did not want them even notified of the existence of the rebate incentive. Since they were the ones proposing this offer, I.A.C. did not believe that I.M.C. should question other suppliers as to their willingness to enter into the same or similar agreement.

I.A.C. allowed I.M.C. 30 days to respond. Jim Burton, therefore, had to recommend to I.M.C.'s president whether or not this agreement was in I.M.C.'s best interest.

1 Are any ethical or legal issues involved in I.A.C.'s proposal? Discuss.
2 How should Burton analyze the proposal? Is this a true partnering arrangement?

THE PEACH COMPUTER COMPANY

Donald Bright, purchasing manager at the Peach Computer Company, was preparing for a meeting to be held that afternoon. The meeting concerned the construction of a new $6 million, 120,000-square-foot building to be located near Dayton, Ohio. The principal issue to be discussed, and hopefully resolved, was what method of specification the firm should use in the purchase of its new building.

When the requirement for the building first arose, the plant engineer at Peach advocated the use of a design firm as the desired method of developing the specifications. Such firms were employed successfully by Peach on seven previous construction projects it had completed during the past five years. Under this approach, a design firm, traditionally referred to as an architect-engineer or simply A-E, is retained to develop the detailed plans and specifications for the new building. These specifications are identical in concept to the materials and method-of-manufacture specifications used in the manufacturing industry to purchase manufactured goods. After they are developed and approved, the construction plans and specifications in sequence become (1) the basis for solicitation of bid prices from qualified construction firms, (2) the cardinal part of the resulting construction contract, and (3) the standard against which inspections are performed.

Don had conducted some preliminary discussions with members of the Dayton Purchasing Management Association regarding the cost for A-E services. He learned that the fees for local projects similar to his were averaging 8 percent of estimated construction cost. This percentage was in line with Peach's experience on its own projects.

One of the members of the Dayton chapter with whom Don talked suggested that he read an article in an issue of the *California Management Review* (*CMR*). The article, entitled "Inflation, Recession, and Your Building Dollar," dealt with the purchase of building construction. Don learned that several alternative approaches to purchasing building construction were available. One approach particularly appealed to him. It provided for the use of performance specifications. Such specifications, instead of describing the building item by item in terms of its physical properties, describe in words the building's intended function, i.e., how large it must be; how well lighted, heated, and cooled it must be; its longevity; its operating costs; and so on. After the performance description is developed, it is used to solicit from qualified bidders a package proposal that includes (1) a design approach, (2) a firm agreed price, and (3) a guaranteed completion date.

The *CMR* article documented that when properly used, performance specifications for buildings can result in a significant savings in both dollars and time. Additionally, the article data revealed that when this method is correctly used, a considerable savings in both the cost and the time required to complete the project is a reasonable expectation. Furthermore, the article indicated that the buyers of buildings purchased under this method have experienced approximately equal satisfaction with their buildings as those who used A-E's.

In preparation for the afternoon meeting, Don decided to develop lists of advantages and disadvantages for each of the two approaches he was considering. After an evaluation of both lists, Don expected to be able to make a formal recommendation as to which method he thought Peach should employ.

1 Should Don get any additional information? Explain.
2 Discuss the inherent advantages and disadvantages of using performance specifications.
3 Discuss the inherent advantages and disadvantages of the plans and specifications method of describing quality.

4 Assuming that Don's investigation and analysis indicates that both methods are practical for use by Peach, discuss which approach Don should recommend.
5 Explain why one method will require more active involvement on Don's part than the other approach.

PEGASUS TECHNOLOGIES

In June 1995, Linda Wang, procurement specialist for Pegasus Technologies, Phoenix, Arizona, and three teammates were responsible for recommending which of four potential suppliers should receive a purchase order for the next year's requirement of 11-inch color monitors. The monitors were expected to be of exceptional quality, with extra high resolution. Pegasus was recognized as a well-established manufacturer of mainframe computers. More recently, the company had expanded its product line to include personal computers. The latest in this line of products was the PT 9000, a high-quality personal computer with two disk drives and an optional hard disk drive.

In its nearly three decades of operation, Pegasus had grown from a single product manufacturer with annual sales of around $250,000 to a multiproduct $5-billion firm. The company has always had a reputation for high quality. Funds have never been compromised where research and development is concerned.

In order to facilitate the sale of the PT 9000, it was decided that the computer would be sold as a package together with an 11-inch color monitor and a printer. While Pegasus manufactured its own CPU, printer, and keyboard, the firm intended to buy the 11-inch color monitor from one of the four potential suppliers. It was estimated that the demand for the next year would be in the region of 1 million monitors. Forecasts indicated that this demand was expected to grow at an annual rate of 20 percent over the next three years. In order to maintain a uniform quality, the company policy was to use a single source of supply as far as possible.

In determining the supplier for the color monitor, Linda was assisted by the following persons, who brought a varied line of expertise to the source-selection team:

- *Arno Berg*, the senior engineer, had been with the company for fourteen years and currently was its R&D chief. He held an engineering degree from a Norwegian university and an M.B.A. from the University of San Diego.
- *Kevin Rice*, financial analyst, had recently joined Pegasus after moving from Los Angeles, where he worked for three years with Pasadena Financial Corporation. He held an M.B.A. from UCLA.

This case was developed by Jimmy Anklesaria of the University of San Diego.

- *John Harper,* quality assurance, had been with the company for eight years. He had an engineering degree from MIT and had a reputation for being a very tough man when quality was in question.

The responsibilities of the team included:

1 Identifying potential suppliers.
2 Preparing a brief comparative statement of the key suppliers.
3 Developing a brief analysis of each potential supplier.
4 Recommending the supplier with whom the order should be placed. This recommendation was to be made to a corporate-level review board.

After a preliminary review, including visits to all potential suppliers and a detailed review of their facilities, equipment, management systems, and purchasing departments, the team had narrowed the list of potential suppliers to four manufacturers:

1 *Reese Corporation,* the largest manufacturer of color monitors under consideration, with annual sales of about $6.5 billion. The firm had been in existence since 1960 and was the industry price leader. Recently management had indicated that the company would not be interested in any order of less than $500 million per annum. This decision was made after Reese had put in a bid for the Pegasus contract. Reese's price was $245 per unit.
2 *Capozzi Manufacturing,* a fairly large and highly reputed manufacturer of computer equipment, including color monitors. With sales of nearly $2 billion, more than half of which were through the sale of monitors, the firm was the second largest of its kind in the area. Its price was $250.
3 *Kruger Corp.* had recently entered the market with a new range of color monitors. In its short life of four years, Kruger had established a reputation for quality and innovation. Kruger maintained that its success was largely based on heavy R&D expenditures. The firm quoted a price of $275 per unit.
4 *Payne Industries,* the smallest of the four potential suppliers, looked attractive since it quoted a price of $240, which was about 4 percent lower than Reese or Capozzi and 14 percent below that of Kruger. If selected, Payne would devote almost all of its production capacity to the Pegasus contract. Industry experts viewed the company as one of the most promising and dynamic new corporations in the industry.

Since the estimated contract was for about $250 million, Linda was aware of the critical nature of the decision. She had to turn in the team's recommendation within a week.

1 Briefly analyze the data provided in Exhibit 1 (on page 883) for each of the four potential suppliers. (Compare the figures with industry averages where necessary.)
2 On the basis of the information contained in Exhibit 1, which potential supplier looks most attractive? Why?

EXHIBIT 1
COMPARATIVE FINANCIAL AND OTHER DATA ON POTENTIAL SUPPLIERS

	Reese	Capozzi	Kruger	Payne	Ind. avg.
Previous year's sales (in millions)	6548.00	1850.05	593.70	253.80	
Net fixed assets (in millions)	1091.80	212.90	75.80	20.63	
Current stock price	$63.77	$55.98	$32.98	$11.63	
Price earnings ratio	18.50	6.45	7.15	34.5	12.00
Liquidity ratios:					
Current ratio	1.89	2.12	2.56	1.78	2.19
Quick ratio	1.14	1.02	1.28	0.99	1.08
Activity ratios:					
Average collection period	29 days	26 days	28 days	37 days	30 days
Inventory turnover	12.65	12.34	11.96	18.25	12.50
Fixed asset turnover	6.00	8.69	7.83	12.30	5.80
Profitability ratios:					
Gross profit margin	16.8%	15.8%	15.4%	13.8%	14.6%
Net profit margin	9.48%	6.78%	7.35%	8.6%	6.57%
Return on equity	16.6%	18.6%	12.8%	18.7%	N/A
Return on investment	14.56%	14.75%	8.7%	12.5%	14.2%
Debt ratio	0.14	0.5	0.45	0.65	0.5
Times interest earned	16.8	8.5	9.6	2.6	6.0
Other data:					
R&D expenditure					
(as a % of sales)	2.30	4.67	8.29	5.5	3.9
Installed capacity	97%	95%	88%	85%	N/A
Production efficiency	102%	91%	95.1%	97.3%	N/A
Sales growth (3 years)	8.2%	11.67%	18.82%	32.1%	N/A
Price quoted	$245.00	$250.00	$275.00	$240.00	

THE PERILS OF PRESUMPTION

This is the sad story of Tom Rogers, purchasing manager of the Buzzy Tool
Company, who found out that a little knowledge is a dangerous thing. His
company makes do-it-yourself power tools. After its president went on a cost-
cutting rampage, Tom desperately embraced value analysis.

Tom set up a lobby exhibit that showed the most important components
and subassemblies that Buzzy Tool bought. Sales representatives were invited
to come up with better ways of making these repetitive items. Whenever visiting suppliers showed interest in this new potential market, Tom gave them the
following clues, "Fellows, we used to make a lot of these items ourselves. But our
business grew so fast that we eventually had to farm them out. We're satisfied
with present designs and quality, but our potential is such that we now are shopping around in all directions for new suppliers, designs, price—everything."

The fancy Drill-A-Thon drew most attention. Made of castings, stampings,
and turnings, it had been designed and turned over to a supplier before purchasing became a separate profit center under the president.

Three firms promptly came up with proposals. The first company said, "Tom, the ABC Company can give you a really swell price if you accept plastics instead of metal. Quality will be tops."

The second company said, "Our engineers at XYZ Company have figured out a way to use fewer parts. You know what a cost saving that will be!"

The third company said, "Tom, we at PDQ Company feel your best bet is to do your own assembling again. We'll supply the parts and give you a rock-bottom price because, as you know, we can make all kinds of economies on a big, continuing order."

Tom then got a hot telephone call from the sales vice president of his present supplier, Dandy Products, Inc.: "Tom, I think Dandy Products has a right to get upset when you put an assembly we've been making a long time up for grabs—without even giving us a chance to discuss the situation with you. What do you think a newcomer could possibly offer you? You know we've tried to get your people to talk value analysis time and again. No soap. Now all of a sudden everybody is invited to the party. We understand your product better than anybody else. How about giving us a chance to put our know-how together with any ideas you have floating around and come up with a price—and a job—that you can depend on?"

Then the chief design engineer came in, "Say, Tom what's all that stuff you have rigged up out there in the lobby? Is it true that you have a bunch of unknowns fooling with the Drill-A-Thon design? Don't tell me you've got some of those plastic peddlers trying to cheapen our merchandise! Over my dead body!"

Tom saw that he was in the middle of a four-way crossfire, from his president, who wanted a 5 percent cost reduction; his company's design experts, who were uneasy about outside interference; would-be suppliers who were eager to re-engineer Drill-A-Thon to fit their own shops; and his current supplier, who could count on considerable loyalty throughout Buzzy Tool.

1 How can Tom start a sound value analysis program?
2 How should he inform the suppliers who can be genuinely helpful in this program?
3 What should Tom tell Dandy Products?

PLACIDO ENGINE COMPANY

It was four o'clock on Friday afternoon and Ronald Penson, senior buyer of castings for the Placido Engine Company of Detroit, Michigan, had just finished a telephone conversation with an upset supplier. It was the fourth such call Ronald had received in response to a letter he had sent to his magnesium castings suppliers concerning a severe corrosion problem. All four had told Ronald that they could not adhere to his request without a significant increase in their costs.

THE PLACIDO ENGINE COMPANY

The Placido Engine Company was a division of the General Products Corporation, a $2 billion company that enjoyed a worldwide reputation for quality and leadership in aviation, aerospace, and industrial products. In its nearly four decades of operations, Placido had built more than 45,000 gas engines for a wide variety of commercial, industrial, and military applications. While the most significant part of Placido's sales was in the commercial and general aviation markets, the company was attempting to move toward a balance between commercial and military sales.

THE EXECUTIVE CORROSION TASK FORCE

Last summer, Placido started receiving complaints from its customers concerning corroded gear boxes on engines. The problem was significant and serious enough to warrant the attention of Fred Thompson, senior vice president of the company. In order to resolve this problem and find a permanent solution, Fred created an Executive Corrosion Task Force. This task force immediately solicited inputs from purchasing, quality assurance, manufacturing, engineering, production control, materials, and the Magnesium Corrosion Task Circle* for suggested solutions to the corrosion problem, as well as recommendations for implementing suggested programs. The Executive Corrosion Task Force was under extreme pressure from Fred Thompson to take immediate steps to resolve the corrosion problem.

CORROSION-FREE MAGNESIUM CASTINGS

On investigation, it was determined that a large part of the corrosion problem centered in the Turbo 110 engine and its magnesium castings. It was also found that a significant proportion of these castings were already corroded on receipt from Placido's suppliers. However, instead of rejecting these castings, quality assurance was processing them through for rework. The basis for this action was the need for parts to meet production schedules. It was believed that the delay encountered by rejecting unacceptable castings would be more costly than the cost of reworking them internally.

The task force decided that this process of reworking unacceptable castings was no longer desirable and directed the purchasing department to take immediate steps to ensure that corrosion-free magnesium castings were

---

*The Magnesium Corrosion Task Circle was established in 1990 to deal with the general problem of magnesium corrosion. It was part of Placido's reliability circles program.

received by Placido. As a first step in this direction, the purchasing department was further instructed to notify its castings suppliers that strict adherence to the previously issued Mil Spec-M-3171 and the cleaning and corrosion prevention procedure prescribed by Placido would now be required. Failure to meet these specifications would result in rejection of unacceptable castings or, in cases where Placido elected to reprocess unacceptable castings in lieu of rejection, the supplier would be debited for the cost of the reprocessing work involved.

The responsibility for notifying the castings suppliers of this decision fell to Ronald Penson, who was the senior buyer for castings for Placido. Given the urgency of the situation and the political sensitivity of the issue, Ronald thought it best to send a letter to his current magnesium castings suppliers immediately. (See Exhibit 1.)

NEGATIVE REACTIONS FROM SUPPLIERS

Ronald was not prepared for the quick and negative responses he received from his suppliers. The general sense of the comments from the suppliers was that they were already properly treating the castings to prohibit corrosion and that they disagreed with the procedure Placido was requiring. Furthermore, they all told Ronald that if they were required to follow the procedure prescribed by Placido, it would be necessary for them to expend considerable amounts of time to retool their current processes and to purchase new equipment. These actions would result in substantially higher costs in producing the castings, which would be passed on to Placido.

Ronald was now facing a serious dilemma and was not sure what to do. One thing was certain. He had to act quickly, as Fred Thompson was demanding an immediate solution to the corrosion problem.

1 Define and discuss the basic issues in this case.
2 What should Ronald Penson do?

PRINTED CIRCUITS COMPONENTS FOR A JIT FACTORY

Mr. Carl Burger, buyer at Acacia Company, is faced with a problem of researching several electronic components for a new graphic plotter, manufactured in a just-in-time environment.

Acacia Company is a major producer of graphic plotters, renowned for top-quality and innovative products. The newest unit in the product line is the 440A, a relatively inexpensive eight-pen, A-size (8½" × 11") plotter, designed to be used with personal computers.

Thoughtful design of the component parts, along with a dedicated value engineering effort, resulted in substantially fewer component parts required for assembly. Extensive market research indicated that the plotter was priced lower than most of its competition, and provided more features, such as

---

EXHIBIT 1
LETTER SENT TO CASTINGS SUPPLIERS CONCERNING CORROSION-FREE CASTINGS

An intense corrosion prevention program for magnesium castings has recently been undertaken at Placido Engine Company. An integral part of this program is the assurance that castings are corrosion free on receipt of shipment from our suppliers. Your strict adherence to Mil Spec-M-3171 and the following is requested:

CLEAN & CORROSION PREVENTION PROCEDURES PER MIL SPEC-M-3171 AND AS FOLLOWS:

- After penetrative inspection, following heat treat, castings will be alkaline cleaned and hydrofluoric acid pickled.
- After hydrofluoric acid pickle, castings to chrome pickle treatment, rinse and bake to dry at 250°F ± 25°F.
- Dip castings in 7220 rust oil B and package for shipment.
- Package to ensure castings do not come into contact with each other, subsequently rubbing away protection.

The responsibility to deliver corrosion-free magnesium castings per casting drawing, engineering blueprint, or M.O.T. is placed with you, the supplier. Failure to do so necessitates an immediate rework at Placido to stop the corrosion process that may ultimately scrap parts. The cost incurred for the rework will be passed on to you in the form of a debit initiated by an Inspection Transfer Report (I.T.R.). The I.T.R. will also have a negative effect on your quality rating.

Your support in this effort is imperative. Please forward the aforementioned procedure to the appropriate personnel in your company.

Direct any questions regarding processing to Robert Dear, Quality Assurance Engineer, (405)876-1241.

Thank you.

Ronald Penson
Senior Buyer

RP:rr

cc: Executive Corrosion Task Force members

---

greater accuracy at higher speed. The marketing forecast estimated annual volume to exceed 60,000 units, far more than any other Acacia model. The combination of few component parts and very high volume made the 440A an excellent choice for implementing a JIT process.

Buyers at Acacia were traditionally organized by commodity, such as raw materials and motors. In an effort to improve the procurement process, buyers with technical backgrounds (such as Carl Burger) are now assigned to new products during product development, and are responsible for buying all parts unique to their instrument. Although this means that a motor manufacturer might interact with several Acacia buyers (one commodity buyer and one or more new product buyers), Acacia is satisfied that any confusion or overlap is more than compensated by significant improvements in new product procurement.

Many of the 440A's components are identical technically to components purchased by commodity buyers for other Acacia plotters, but have separate part numbers to differentiate JIT packaging and delivery requirements and to identify higher costs when they occur.

The JIT facility at Acacia is divided into two main production areas, the printed circuit cell (PC cell) and the assembly line. The PC cell contains state-of-the-art robotics equipment requiring little human intervention. The equipment is designed to select the component parts while still packaged, load its feeder bins, and automatically insert the components into PC boards based on a computerized XY insertion program. There is also a JIT stockroom facility near the production areas, and a separate MRP system.

Parts purchased for the 440A must meet special JIT requirements. Suppliers are requested to use bar-coded labels to identify their shipments for optical wanding into inventory, and the automatic equipment requires specially designed packaging tubes and parts for taping for auto-insertion of PC components. Furthermore, the delivery of most JIT parts must be weekly (instead of usual monthly delivery), in order to maintain a minimum of inventory in the stockroom. Deliveries must be highly reliable to prevent stock-outs and line shut-downs.

The parts which Carl is considering re-sourcing are four integrated circuits (ICs), seven diodes, and three transistors. These parts are all low-cost, industry-standard parts, with the exception of five of the diodes, which are manufactured by only one company, Monitor Inc. Monitor is the industry leader in diodes and transistors, and supplies Acacia with quality parts at competitive prices for other plotters.

While the 440A was still in the design phase, Carl and the electrical engineers began preliminary discussions with Monitor, which had never supplied parts to JIT customers. Monitor indicated that it was willing to meet the JIT requirements in order to get the 440A business and the promised follow-on JIT new product business. Monitor was selected as the single-source supplier for the fourteen PC components.

Acacia provided the necessary technical specifications, and over a period of many months Monitor struggled to satisfactorily meet the packaging and labeling specifications. Any label or package changes made by Acacia required extensive paperwork, conferences, and cross-country trips to Monitor's facility. In an effort to help Monitor understand the JIT concept, and why special treatment of parts was needed, Monitor engineers toured the Acacia facility and attended JIT presentations.

In July, the 440A entered production. In addition to the usual last-minute design changes one expects with a new product, the production team had to cope with new machinery, new employees, a new inventory method, and new computer systems. As the production process became more organized, Carl was pleased to see that nearly all his suppliers were complying with the JIT requirements. A critical exception to this was Monitor.

Monitor-supplied components were often marked with the wrong bar-code label, which resulted in repeated inventory problems. Packaging tubes were outside specifications and could not be handled by the automatic equipment. The components themselves sometimes had bent leads, preventing their insertion in PC boards. Also, the deliveries were often behind schedule, although unrelated production problems meant that this was less critical than it could have been. Through conferences with Monitor representatives, Carl began to realize that Monitor's focus on high-volume production made it ill-equipped to handle relatively small, special-order items. Monitor maintained that it was getting better at the JIT orders, but Carl was frustrated with the apparent lack of progress and began to examine his alternatives.

Five of the diodes could not be re-sourced, as Monitor was the sole manufacturer. United Semiconductors, a large U.S. firm, was willing to meet the JIT requirements for the four ICs, although JIT would be new to it. After talking with United management and engineers, Carl felt that the company showed greater administrative flexibility, which was Monitor's weak point. United offered to supply the parts at a price 10 percent above Monitor's current price. Acacia already purchases non-JIT parts from United and has experienced no problems.

The three transistors and two remaining diodes could be obtained from Taguchi Company, a Japanese-based firm. Taguchi mentioned that it was already supplying components to Japanese firms using JIT processes, and noted that its engineers were familiar with the robotics used at Acacia. Taguchi's price was about 10 percent higher than Monitor's. Taguchi was successfully supplying non-JIT parts to Acacia. Both United and Taguchi indicated they could be ready for delivery in approximately one month.

Carl sat at his desk, trying to weigh the benefits and disadvantages of switching suppliers now. He was worried about damaging relations with Monitor, and the impact on the commodity buyer's purchases from Monitor. He was also concerned about what finance would say about a significant price increase for several components. Just then Stan Ervin, PC cell supervisor, stormed in.

"Bent leads on your ICs shut my equipment down again! What do you intend to do about it?"

1 Compare the advantages and disadvantages of staying with Monitor versus switching to the new suppliers.
2 What should Carl do now?
3 How could Carl have avoided the problems he experienced with Monitor?

THE PRIVILEGED FLY

You are a privileged fly: You are allowed to be on the wall of a corporate boardroom during a high-powered discussion. The corporation is an engineering firm whose sales total approximately $140 million a year. Up to now, things appear to have been going well. Production does an efficient job, and inventories have been reduced. But danger signs are cropping up. Although no orders have been lost as yet, several shipments have missed their deadlines.

Customers are beginning to complain. In addition, transportation costs on incoming and outbound freight shipments are mushrooming. It is 9 a.m., and several people are nervously sitting at the conference table. A stern-looking individual enters.

THE CAST

- *Production manager:* Heinrich Holtz, former blue-collar worker. Loves his machines and hates to see them idle. But beneath his "good of the corporation" exterior lies the soul of a power maniac who seeks control over traffic and purchasing.
- *Marketing manager:* Harold Levi, a stereotype. Is afraid of losing sales because of late deliveries. Generally, echoes presidential statements. Appears ready to support Heinrich Holtz's power play.
- *President:* Joe Gish, old-line type. Extremely successful. Has just attended a National Industrial Conference Board (NICB) seminar and is throwing a lot of new buzz words and thoughts around. From his subordinates' point of view, he is dangerous.
- *Traffic manager:* Harold Tracks, another old-liner, but much less successful. Not good at verbalizing, except to quote percentage increases. His freight bills are going up, and he is being made to look bad by comparison.
- *Purchasing manager:* Joan Glass, much younger than her associates. Does her best. Understands president Gish's words and tries to put some of them into action. Extremely inventory conscious.
- *Director of finance:* Sol Stein, dedicated to cost reduction.

ACTION

(This is what the privileged fly observes and hears.)

President Gish brings the meeting to order. "Look at these air freight bills! Here's one for $955—more than the damn part is worth! I know, I *checked!* These things are murdering us. You must realize that in our business today, transportation has great cost-cutting potential!"

Traffic manager Tracks responds, "I know that freight bills have risen 30 percent in the last six months, but what can I do? Miss Glass here is cutting inventories so hard that she never has anything in stock. Her short lead times force me to use air freight. And the way she spreads small orders, I almost never find a way to consolidate them to get volume rates. And I'm having the same problems on outgoing shipments. I'm caught in a two-bladed buzzsaw!"

Purchasing manager Joan Glass interrupts to say, "Harold, we're operating on low inventories because we save money doing it. Many times air freight is the only way I can be sure of getting what I need on time."

Production manager Holtz comments, "And ven I need something, I need it. Take spares. This 'downtime' is an awfully expensive proposition, and ve all know it. Further, by the time Miss Glass here gets me needed production materials, ve are so late that the only way to meet delivery dates is mit overtime and the use of air freight."

Marketing manager Levi joins in, "Whatever the trouble, it seems there must be a way to get an efficient pipeline. If Heinrich is late, then I'm late. We're losing our image as a reliable supplier. Soon, we'll be losing sales!"

Traffic manager Tracks defends himself by saying, "I don't want to seem bitter, but it looks like I'm getting the short end of the stick."

President Gish interrupts to say, "No more excuses. I want action! Costs must come down."

Purchasing manager Glass defends herself by saying, "The lead-time problem goes right back through production and eventually to Harold's sales forecasts. I need earlier information."

Marketing manager Levi says, "I have to promise prompt delivery. We all know that the problem is at the other end."

Production manager Holtz suggests, "Like I've been zaying for a long time, ve should combine purchasing and traffic and get them closer to production."

At this point, purchasing manager Glass sounds frustrated when she says, "Heinrich, we're right back where we started. We need lower freight costs, but at the same time we must keep inventory down."

Director of finance Stein says, "Inventory carrying cost is over 30 percent a year. I think that Joan has done a great job. But I do agree with Mr. Gish that transportation costs are way over budget."

President Gish concludes the meeting by saying, "Heinrich's idea is a possibility. We could create a materials management setup. I understand it's the coming thing. I'll give each of you one week to put all your ideas on paper. Be prepared to deliver your reports at our next meeting. I want us out of this fix . . . and soon!"

1 Discuss the basic inventory problem confronting this firm.
2 Air freight bills keep growing both in numbers and in total dollar value of freight transported. What are the factors that have contributed to the development of this situation? Do they reflect efficient or inefficient management of purchasing, inventories, and production in firms such as this one? Discuss.
3 What should Joan Glass do?
4 Should Glass suggest a materials manager?
5 Should Glass build up her inventories?

A PROBLEM OF PRICE

Sue Jones sat at her desk reflecting on a pricing problem. Sue was a graduate of State University, where she majored in materials management. Since joining the small manufacturing firm of Prestige Plastics in Des Moines, she has been promoted from assistant buyer to buyer. She was responsible for purchasing the chemicals used in producing the firm's plastic products.

Sue was really perplexed by a particular procurement involving the purchase of X-pane, a chemical that was formulated specifically for Prestige Plastics. Thirty-one days ago, she forwarded a request for bids to six suppliers for Prestige's estimated annual requirement of 10,000 drums of X-pane. Yesterday morning, Sue opened the five bids that had been received. The bids, F.O.B. Des Moines, were as follows:

	Price per drum ($)	Total price ($) (for estimated annual requirement of 10,000 drums)
Greater Sandusky Chemical	312	3,120,000
Chicago Chemical Co.	297	2,970,000
Tri-Cities Chemical	323	3,230,000
St. Louis Industries	332	3,320,000
St. Paul Plastics	340	3,400,000

The Chicago Chemical Company was low bidder for the fifth straight year. On the face of it, a decision to award the annual requirements contract to Chicago Chemical looked obvious. The day after the bid opening, the sales engineer from Greater Sandusky Chemical threw Sue a ringer. He said that no one would ever be able to beat Chicago Chemical's price. His firm estimated that setup costs associated with producing X-pane would be approximately $750,000. He went on to say that due to the uncertainties of follow-on orders, his firm would have to amortize this cost over the one-year period of the contract to preclude a loss.

Sue checked with the other unsuccessful bidders. They said substantially the same thing: $700,000 to $850,000 in setup costs were included in their prices.

Next, Sue looked at the history of past purchases of X-pane. She saw that on the initial procurement five years ago, Chicago Chemical's bid was $202 per barrel, $3 lower than the second lowest price. Since that time, bid prices had increased, reflecting cost growth in the materials required to produce X-pane. Each year, Chicago Chemical's prices were $3 to $15 per drum lower than those of the unsuccessful competitors.

Sue knew from her purchasing course at State University that when five prerequisites were satisfied, under most conditions, competitive bidding normally resulted in the lowest price. She also knew that it was important to maintain the integrity of the competitive bidding process. But Sue felt a strong sense of uneasiness. Something did not seem right.

1 Under what conditions does competitive bidding normally assure the buyer of obtaining the lowest possible price?

2 Under what conditions may a buyer fall into the "competitive bidding trap"?

3 Which situation existed at Prestige Plastics for the *first* contract? Why?

4 Which situation existed at Prestige Plastics for the *current* buy? Why?

5 Describe three approaches to overcoming Sue's pricing problem. Support with a quantitative analysis.

Q-4: THE OUTSOURCING OF INFORMATION TECHNOLOGY

Q-4 is a developer and manufacturer of laser printers. Jim Perry, senior buyer at Q-4, is representing the purchasing department at the firm's quarterly strategic planning meeting. Mr. Bigelow, the firm's CEO, has just returned from an AME meeting at Kodak in upstate New York. One of Mr. Bigelow's action items resulting from the trip is to investigate the desirability and feasibility of outsourcing Q-4's information technology (IT) operations.

Mr. Bigelow requests that Jim and Gene Rathswold, the firm's CIO, work together to develop a list of pros and cons of outsourcing its IT. The report is to be ready at the next quarterly planning meeting.

1 What issues favor such outsourcing?

2 When would outsourcing not be appropriate?

3 What would be Mr. Rathswold's (CIO) role if IT were outsourced?

4 What fairly unique procurement issues must be addressed if Q-4 were to proceed with outsourcing?

RANDALL CORPORATION

Bill Huff was a subcontract buyer for Randall Corporation, located in Houston, Texas. His major supplier for mechanical subassemblies was Qualco Corporation of Los Angeles, California. In early 1995, Bill found out that Qualco was experiencing some financial difficulties. By May of 1995, these financial problems had worsened, and Bill wondered what, if anything, he should do.

RANDALL CORPORATION

Randall Corporation was a large supplier to the military, with total sales in excess of $3 billion. Depending on the nature of the contract and Randall's capabilities, some military work would be subcontracted. Bill Huff was responsible for a variety of subcontracts, including mechanical subassemblies to machine shops.

Because of the critical nature of the subcontracted subassemblies, Bill thought that quality was the most important criterion for selecting suppliers. The next most important criterion was on-time delivery. Delivery times were important to ensure that the prime contract was completed on time and to avoid penalties for late completion that were usually part of the prime military contract.

Randall's policy was to maintain a minimum of three suppliers, and this was frequently a requirement that was included in the prime military contract as well. Furthermore, Randall's policy was to add suppliers as the volume of purchases increased. The volume of purchases of mechanical subassemblies required five suppliers under this policy. A supplier could not be added without eliminating another; if a supplier were dropped, another had to be added.

SUPPLY MARKET

In Bill's opinion, there were many machine shops in the United States that could produce good-quality mechanical subassemblies of the type required by Randall. These companies were typically small businesses owned by independent entrepreneurs. The profit margins for these companies were typically 5 to 6 percent of sales. For the mechanical subassemblies that Bill bought, location was not an important consideration because the freight costs were very low in comparison to the price of the products.

When a military contract required mechanical subassemblies, Bill would award the business among his five suppliers. In 1994, Bill had placed 40 percent, or $2.5 million, of his total mechanical subassembly volume with Qualco; the remaining 60 percent was evenly divided among the other four suppliers. In 1990, just before Qualco became a supplier for Randall, Qualco's sales were $900,000.

Qualco had become Randall's major supplier for mechanical subassemblies because of its superior performance. The company always met its delivery schedule, and the quality of its products was unsurpassed. In addition, its prices were about 12 percent below competitive machine shops. When Bill originally started to contract with Qualco, he was concerned about these low prices. He wanted his suppliers to make reasonable profits and therefore become good, long-term sources of supply. He found that Qualco's labor rates, machinery, and capabilities were similar to other machine shops he was using. However, Qualco was able to obtain much lower scrap rates than the rest of the industry. As a result, Qualco could charge lower prices and still maintain healthy profit margins.

Over the last three years, Qualco had been an excellent supplier. Qualco had also helped Randall by producing prototypes of subassemblies, which were useful in evaluating military systems before production.

FINANCIAL PROBLEMS AT QUALCO

In December 1994, Bill was told by the sales representative for Qualco that Qualco was having difficulty paying its representatives. At the same time, Bill observed that Qualco had remodeled its offices in a luxurious style. The owner of the company had recently taken his family on two cruises, and he had purchased a new luxury automobile.

In April 1995, the sales representative for Qualco told Bill that Qualco owed him $18,000 for back salary and bonuses. At about the same time, the owner called Randall's accounts payable department. He complained that a $40,000 invoice was two days overdue. He said to them, "I need the money. I may have to shut down if you don't pay me now." In May 1995, Bill learned that Qualco had "factored" its accounts receivable at 3 percent with National Acceptance Corporation.

Based on these events, Bill was concerned about the financial management and stability of Qualco. He was worried that he would suddenly be faced with the loss of his major supplier of mechanical subassemblies. Bill also knew that he would have to award subcontracts for a new $320,000 mechanical subassembly within two weeks. This requirement could grow to $2 million worth of subassembly business.

1 What is the relationship between financial soundness and supplier performance?
2 What action should Bill take?

RIPLEY ENGINE COMPANY

In early 1995, Tom Kemp, procurement specialist for R&D at Ripley Engine Company, Birmingham, Alabama, and a three-man team were responsible for recommending which potential suppliers should receive a request for proposal (RFP) for an important new component for small turbine aircraft engines. One of the four potential suppliers in the market, Aerolog, Inc., had been disqualified as a supplier to Ripley in early 1993. Tom wondered whether to include Aerolog, Inc., on the RFP list.

RIPLEY ENGINE COMPANY

In its nearly four decades of operation, Ripley had built more than 45,000 turbine engines for a wide variety of commercial, industrial, and military applications. Annual sales were about $1 billion. Major product lines included aircraft propulsion systems, compact and powerful gas turbines for power generation systems, and larger, more rugged turbine systems for high-precision industrial applications. Noted for its research and development and innovation, Ripley led the very profitable market for small gas turbines. The company had a reputation for high quality and had always leaned on its suppliers for both quality products and on-time deliveries. The product lines all had worldwide applications in existing markets. Major customers looked to Ripley for research and development activities to improve overall operations.

In the mid-1990s, Ripley initiated actions to miniaturize the fabricated metallic components of certain engines to reduce both their weight and size. Several of these special efforts had progressed to the design and procurement phase.

PROCUREMENT AT RIPLEY

Procurement operations for turbo machinery projects were divided into four major activities under the management of David Nelson. (See Exhibit 1.)

Procurement to support research and development projects was accomplished by eight procurement specialists under the supervision of Joseph Moncreif. Typically, this work to support R&D was completed in very close coordination with the engineers and quality control personnel responsible for the research project. Indeed, for major projects, a two-step supplier selection process was used. Step 1 involved selecting potential suppliers to receive the RFP, while Step 2 involved evaluating the supplier proposals actually received.

EXHIBIT 1
Ripley Organization chart.

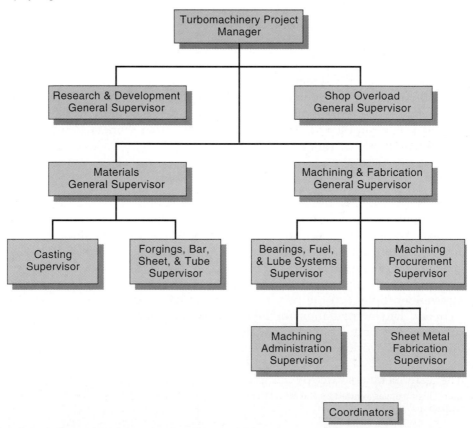

The two-step process was completed by a team of specialists representing engineering, procurement, and quality assurance. The procurement specialist was usually the team leader.

In early 1995, a supplier-selection team was appointed to select suppliers for an RFP for a highly complex fabricated metal component for small turbine engines for the aircraft market. The team was headed by Tom Kemp of R&D Procurement. The other members of the team were two engineers and a representative from quality control. The members of the team brought the following expertise to the task:

- *Tom Kemp*, team leader, had been with the company about two years. He graduated from Whittier College in 1980 with a major in physics. After college, he worked two years with the committee to re-elect President Reagan and then was a lobbyist in Washington, D.C. A contact with business led to a major job in purchasing with a California firm. In 1993, he moved to the Ripley Company in Birmingham, Alabama.
- *George Smith*, the senior engineer on the team, had been with the company for fifteen years. He was a highly respected R&D engineer. He held an undergraduate degree from MIT and had done graduate work at Cal Tech.
- *Fred Brown*, the other engineer, had been with the company about ten years. He held an engineering degree from Purdue University and had worked as an R&D engineer at Ripley since graduating from college.
- *Paul Logan*, quality control, had been with the company about four years. He was a quality control engineer by training with an M.B.A. from Case Western University. Paul had a reputation for being a very tough man when quality was in question.

PROCEDURES FOR SELECTING POTENTIAL SUPPLIERS TO RECEIVE THE RFP

Typically, the RFP team responsibilities included:

1 Identifying all potential suppliers.
2 Developing a detailed analysis of each potential supplier.
3 Recommending the potential list of suppliers to a corporate-level review board, consisting of the vice president of engineering, the director of purchasing, and the program manager. The board decided which firms were to be on the RFP list.
4 Conducting the analysis of the proposals actually received from the firms on the RFP list.
5 Recommending a firm for contract negotiations.

COMPLEX METAL FABRICATION INDUSTRY

The team members discovered rather quickly and somewhat to their surprise that the industry capable of supplying the needed fabricated metal components consisted of only four firms. Their initial research uncovered the fact that one of these four firms, Aerolog, Inc., had been disqualified two years earlier as a supplier to Ripley for both quality and delivery problems. The Aerolog incident had required extensive litigation in 1992–93. Aerolog had a bad reputation with the old timers at Ripley.

The team listed these facts about the firms:

1 Aerolog appeared to be fully qualified as a bidder based on the criteria developed for technology, plant capacity, utilization rates, managerial team, and finances.
2 Two other firms, Reck Aerospace and Crum Aerospace, also appeared to be fully qualified.
3 The fourth firm, Northeast Machine Works, was questionable in the context of plant capacity and utilization rates. The firm appeared to have a superior managerial team.
4 Many senior managers, engineers, and others were strongly opposed to considering Aerolog for anything at Ripley.
5 Word that Aerolog might get its foot back in the door spread throughout R&D, engineering, marketing, and quality control like a prairie fire.
6 Phone calls and comments to the team all seemed to say "not again," or more specifically, "You will be sorry you did that!" and "It's been nice knowing you."
7 See Exhibit 2 for comparative data on the suppliers developed by the team.

EXHIBIT 2
COMPARATIVE DATA ON POTENTIAL SUPPLIERS

	Aerolog, Inc.	Reck Aerospace	Crum Aerospace	Northeast Machine Works
Technology (scale 1 to 50)[a]	48	47	49	46
Capacity				
sufficient	Yes	Yes	Yes	Yes
utilization rate	80%	82%	79%	90%
Financial status				
current ratio	2.36	2.22	2.02	2.56
quick ratio	1.35	1.10	.93	1.50
debt to equity	.75	.73	.76	.76
Sales (millions)—1988	$41,759.9	$18,653.0	$9,653.4	$7,543.8
Sales growth over past year	10%	9.8%	11%	3%
Cost of goods sold	89.6%	88.7%	90.3%	89.3%
Change from last year	−3%	−.5%	+2%	+3.5%
Managerial team (scale 1 to 10)	9.4	9.2	9.1	9.6
Quality reputation[b] long term (scale 1 to 10)	5	9	8.5	9.3
Last two years	9.5	9	8.7	9.4

[a]All scales are based on big being best.
[b]Based on information collected from other customers.

As Tom and the team met early on July 21, 1995, they knew they had to bite the bullet on this issue. Should Aerolog be included on the list for the RFP? Their list and analysis was to be presented to the Corporate Review Board at 9 a.m. on July 23, 1995.

1 What are the arguments favoring Aerolog's inclusion on the list?
2 What are the arguments against Aerolog's inclusion?
3 What would you recommend?

ROBOTICS, INC.

Robotics, Inc., of Chicago placed an order for four automatic welders with the Michigan Manufacturing Company. The order was on a fixed price basis of $200,000 per unit, F.O.B. Detroit (shipping point). The Robotics traffic manager designated a carrier and routes, and Michigan Manufacturing acknowledged the order without change.

Within six months the welders were completed, and they were shipped by Michigan Manufacturing. However, instead of shipping via Conrail, Robotics' designated carrier, Michigan shipped by truck. As was customary, Michigan invoiced Robotics immediately. Robotics paid immediately to take advantage of the cash discount.

En route to Chicago, the truck, a common carrier, collided with a tractor-trailer. The truck rolled over an embankment causing total loss of the four automatic welders.

When the buyer contacted the Michigan Manufacturing Company concerning the loss-in-transit, he was told that Michigan Manufacturing disclaimed all responsibility. "The units were sold F.O.B. Detroit, and title passed to Robotics at that time." When the buyer pointed out that Michigan Manufacturing Company did not ship via Robotics' designated routes or carrier, he was told, "We saved Robotics transportation costs by shipping via a less expensive carrier. You approved of our method of shipment by paying our invoice. The responsibility of filing a claim with the trucker clearly must be yours."

1 What is the significance of the F.O.B. point? What are the advantages and disadvantages of F.O.B. point of delivery? F.O.B. shipping point?
2 Whose responsibility is it to file claim with the carrier? Discuss.

ROMMY PICKS A CAREER

Rommy Los, a junior at Poway University, has thoroughly enjoyed his first two years of college. But this summer, he had a rude awakening: His parents informed him that in two years he will be on his own. Previously, Rommy had assumed that he'd go on to graduate school—maybe even become a professor—anything to be able to remain at Poway University—affectionately known as P.U.

This fall, Rommy is enrolled in a course entitled Purchasing and Supply Management. The very first day of class, something clicked—this is it! "If I've got to work for a living (in contrast with being a professor), it should be in a profession with both challenges and the potential for great satisfaction . . . supply management."

With this momentous decision behind him, Rommy plans to take follow-on courses in cost and pricing and in negotiations, and he plans to take an internship in purchasing and supply management. Life is more interesting than ever now that Rommy has a direction and sense of purpose. There's only one fly in the ointment—Rommy's parents are both accountants, and they have always assumed that Rommy would be one too!

This weekend, Rommy's parents will be in town to see him and, he hopes, take his laundry home. Although Rommy is determined to pursue a career in purchasing and supply management, he'd like his parents' approval.

1 If you were Rommy, what arguments would you present in favor of such a decision?

RUHLING MANUFACTURING COMPANY

The Ruhling Manufacturing Company was founded in 1901 by Cyrus Ruhling. Until 1915, the firm made electric motors. In 1915, Mr. Ruhling was persuaded by the War Department to take on several defense contracts. Ruhling expanded rapidly. After World War I, Ruhling found itself the possessor of much excess capacity. Cyrus decided to cater to the small but growing home appliance industry. Today, Ruhling is one of the nation's largest appliance manufacturers.

Although appliances account for all the firm's sales, a small electric motor capacity has been retained, partly for historic purposes and partly to protect against unforeseen contingencies. Whenever feasible, Ruhling follows a dual sourcing policy. In some cases, three sources may be under contract.

Last month, purchasing issued an invitation for bids for $^{11}/_{32}$-horsepower motors for a six-month period. Ruhling's estimated price for the motors was $29. The quantity estimated was 48,000 motors over the six-month period. Orders were to be placed daily through the firm's automated material requirements planning system, with deliveries to be within one week of release of an order.

Three days ago, the bids were opened. They were as follows:

Able Electric	$30.00
Beta Products	28.00
Gamma Manufacturing	32.00
Delta Electric	29.25
Epsilon Products	30.00

Today, prior to the award of a purchase order, Epsilon Products contacted the buyer and submitted an alternative proposal. Under the proposal, Epsilon would reduce its bid to $23.75 if Ruhling would agree to purchase all its requirements for this size motor from Epsilon for a period of one year. Ruhling would be free to release delivery quantities at its own convenience, and Epsilon would guarantee to meet them within three days. Epsilon would carry one month of normal inventory (8,000 motors) and would increase its capacity if demand warranted.

1 Should Epsilon's alternative proposal be considered?
2 Comment on the practice of dual sourcing when part of the requirement is produced internally. Relate this practice to the advantages and disadvantages of a 100 percent requirements contract.

SAMPSON PRODUCTS

Sampson Products Corporation was a major manufacturer of electrical equipment used extensively by consumer goods manufacturers. The company sold most of its products to manufacturers of refrigerators, automatic washers, and electric stoves to be installed as original equipment that usually retained the Sampson brand name. In addition to the original equipment market, Sampson had obtained a significant portion of the replacement market for the products it manufactured. Sales of Sampson replacement parts were normally made through channels such as small hardware stores and other home repair retail outlets. Another substantial part of Sampson's revenue was derived from manufacturing electrical equipment for large electrical supply houses under the brand names of those outlets.

Sampson's annual sales averaged approximately $400 million. Of this total, the production and sale of small electric motors accounted for over $100 million. Although Sampson was one of the largest producers of small motors in the United States, there were four other competing companies of comparable size, as well as several smaller manufacturers. Approximately one-fourth of the company's production of motors was used to fill contracts with manufacturers of air conditioners, vacuum cleaners, and other power equipment for the home. These motors carried the brand name of the retailer; hence, Sampson referred to these contracts as "special brand business."

In 1990 Sampson Products obtained a special brand contract with General Company to manufacture $20 million of "General" motors. General was a major U.S. electrical products manufacturer with annual sales of approximately $750 million. Sampson had been awarded the contract after bidding competitively against one of the other large motor manufacturers and five of the smaller firms. Sampson's sales manager believed his bid had been accepted because of the excellent quality and reputation of the firm's motors, not because it offered the lowest price. Although the contract terminated annually, new contracts had been negotiated each year to the satisfaction of both parties, and Sampson had obtained the contract to manufacture motors for

General again during 1995. Sampson succeeded in making an average before-tax profit of 9 percent on this contract, which management considered very satisfactory for this type of business.

While General Company had become an important customer for Sampson Products, General also *sold* to Sampson small rotor shafts used in some of Sampson's small high-speed motors. General manufactured these shafts in its machine shop division, which had been acquired in a merger seven years ago. Mr. George Smithe, director of purchases for Sampson, estimated that his department had purchased approximately $200,000 of shafts a year since 1991. In February 1993, Mr. Smithe negotiated a five-year contract with General, which obligated General to sell $200,000 of shafts each year at a fixed price of $3.10 per shaft (with escalation for labor and materials provided these costs rose by more than 10 percent). When the contract was developed, it contained a clause that provided General with an option to cancel the agreement at any time, with a three-month notice to Sampson. However, Mr. Jones, sales manager for the machine shop division of General, assured Mr. Smithe that his company would exercise the option only in the case of highly unusual, unforeseen circumstances.

The shafts were made of a special alloy that was in very short supply. Moreover, there were strong indications that the U.S. government might restrict all nonmilitary applications of the material to conserve supplies for military use. Accordingly, Sampson decided to purchase several years' supply of shafts before any government regulations could materialize. Consequently, Mr. Smithe was working on the procurement of approximately $1 million of motor shafts during 1994. Although Sampson was impressed by the performance of General shafts, Mr. Smithe decided to solicit competitive bids from several prospective suppliers. After investigation, he selected four major motor shaft manufacturers that had outstanding reputations for quality, service, and efficient operations. General Company was one of the producers from whom a quotation was requested.

The day following the receipt of General's quotation, Mr. Smithe was visited by Mr. Jones and the president of the machine shop division of General. Mr. Smithe understood that the president had a widely recognized reputation as an extremely aggressive, hard-hitting, sales-minded executive. Smithe's impression was quickly confirmed. From the beginning of the conversation he was the target of the president's well-known pressure tactics. The president informed Smithe in no uncertain terms that he felt the "friendship" of the two companies was at stake and reciprocal considerations were in order. Smithe informed the president that his bid was the highest received, and he suggested that the president knew by approximately how much he was high. Smithe stated that normally second bids were not accepted, but because of previous friendship he would in this case accept a revised bid from General. The president's reaction was to leave the meeting in anger with the parting comment that Smithe had better think again about awarding the contract to General—and fast.

Mr. Smithe set aside the shaft contract during the ensuing two weeks, partly as a result of his offer to the General representatives and also because he wanted to devote time to other problems. At that point, the president of Sampson Products asked Mr. Smithe to come to his office. The president stated that he had "just had a lengthy conversation with the chairman of the board of directors of the General Company. The chairman appeared to be exceedingly interested in getting that motor shaft contract you are presently considering. It seems the president of the machine shop division needs the work and is eager to get the order. He told the chairman that General's case might be strengthened if he brought the situation to my personal attention."

Mr. Smithe proceeded to outline the events surrounding the contract to the president. He also stated that he had not decided what action should be taken, but thus far had been against awarding General any portion of the shaft contract for four reasons:

1 There was no economic basis for General to insist on a premium price. In his opinion, General was attempting to take advantage of its substantial motor purchases to obtain a higher shaft price than was economically justified.

2 Doing business on a reciprocal basis, in his opinion, was a dangerous precedent and presented difficult administrative and control problems. "People are buying our products because they feel we provide the best value at the best price. If we start paying premiums for purchased materials, regardless of the reason, we risk losing that reputation as well as sales to those who are not our suppliers."

3 Mr. Smithe also believed General was bluffing. In his opinion, General was well satisfied with the quality and price of the motors, which was or should be the primary consideration of its purchasing them.

4 Finally, Mr. Smithe stated that he felt the only repercussion would be a possible cancellation of the long-term shaft contract. However, he believed that even the possibility of General exercising this option was remote since it would practically shut the door on any future shaft business from Sampson.

The president concluded the conversation by saying, "I see you have a good grasp of all the facts involved, George. In my opinion, this is a purchasing problem. You are our director of purchases, so it's your decision to make—and I wish you luck."

During the next week, Mr. Smithe received a second visit from Mr. Jones and the president of the machine shop division of General. During this visit, the conversation became very heated. The president of the machine shop division of General stated, "You get $20 million of business from us and we get $1 million of business from you; you can't find a better deal than that!" The president also reminded Smithe that the long-term contract could be canceled. After making this statement, the machine shop division president abruptly stormed out of the room in a very angry mood. Mr. Jones was a few steps behind the president. Before they reached the door, Mr. Smithe reminded them that he was going to complete the motor shaft contract the next day. He added that he hoped General would submit a new price by 10 a.m. the following morning. Mr. Jones replied that they would see what could be done, but the president left the office without another word or an acknowledging glance.

By 3:00 p.m. the following day, Mr. Smithe had not received any communication from the representative of General Company.

1 What are the basic policy issues in this situation? Analyze and discuss each of them.
2 What action should Mr. Smithe take? Why?

SDC CORPORATION

SDC Corporation is a large, high-technology manufacturer of sophisticated electromechanical devices. Its current manufacturing operations are diversified between several major product lines. Recently, SDC developed a new product line centered around the production of an electronic tracking device. The tracking device is placed in fleet vehicles such as taxi cabs, delivery trucks, and courier vans. During operation, it emits an electronic signal that is monitored at a central tracking console located near the dispatcher.

To facilitate a rapid entry into the market, SDC decided to rely on Hangsu Manufacturing Company in Japan to provide four critical electromechanical switching devices. Hangsu has a proven track record in supplying these components for Japanese applications. Hangsu had produced 40,000 of these components used in a similar tracking device in Japan. At the time of the decision, the exchange rate was acceptable.

SDC had experience *selling* finished goods on the international market; however, this was the firm's first attempt to use foreign subcontractors. SDC decided to use MTC, a Japanese trading company, to negotiate the initial agreement with Hangsu. The agreement was negotiated, and Hangsu supplied the components in accordance with the SDC performance specification.

SDC has only one major competitor in the tracking device market. The total domestic market is estimated to be 100,000 units. SDC had already won one contract with Fleetway Trucking for 2,700 units, contingent on a successful pilot test of 100 units. Unfortunately, Fleetway subsequently terminated the contract due to nonperformance of the test units. The operating problem was attributed to failure of the Japanese components to perform according to specification.

Another contract for 1,000 units was awarded to SDC by Nationwide Cab Service. Having heard about Fleetway's problem, however, Nationwide placed the contract "on hold" pending the outcome of a more stringent pilot test to be performed by SDC.

This case was developed by Christine Grambling, Robert Balderas, David Guebert, and Loven Lasche under the direction of Professor David N. Burt.

SDC deals directly with Hangsu on technical and production problems. MTC operates as Hangsu's representative for all financial and contractual decisions. SDC feels that the device's operating problems are confined to the four components produced by Hangsu. To resolve the problem, SDC has requested that Hangsu rework the components contained in the original 2,700 units, and ensure that the next 1,000 units fully meet the performance specification.

Relations with MTC/Hangsu have deteriorated somewhat at this point in time. Hangsu feels that the SDC specification has been extensively modified and does not reflect the original design agreed on for the components. With over 40,000 similar tracking devices operating successfully in Japan—all using the Hangsu components—Hangsu is confident that it has met all specification requirements.

Frustrated by the inability to reach an agreement, Tom Decker, purchasing manager for SDC, has decided to withhold $1 million from MTC/Hangsu to establish a better negotiating position. In addition, deterioration of the yen/dollar exchange rate has made future dealings with Hangsu uncertain, at best. Tom Decker realizes that the Japanese will negotiate with a long-term perspective (four to five years) in mind, while he is being pressured to address SDC's current bottom-line difficulties.

1 How could Tom Decker have avoided the problems encountered with Hangsu? Discuss in detail.
2 What negotiation skills should Decker rely on to achieve SDC's objectives?
3 How can Decker get the 3,700 units reworked to meet specification?

SELECTION OF A PRESSURE VESSEL MANUFACTURER

On August 1, the engineering department hand-carried a purchase requisition to Jack Toole, buyer, purchasing department, Oceanics, Inc. The requisition covered the purchase of one pressure vessel to Oceanics' specifications as outlined in the requisition. Immediately, Jack went to work. He prepared a request for quotations asking twenty major pressure vessel manufacturers to have their proposals in his hands no later than Wednesday, August 31st. The response to Jack's request for quotations was amazing.

During the month of August, eighteen of the twenty companies hurriedly prepared their proposals and submitted them to Jack within the allotted bidding time. As each proposal was received on Jack's desk, copies were forwarded to the engineer and manufacturing engineer for preliminary evaluation. By September 5, Jack called a meeting in his office with the engineer, Mr. Holpine, and the manufacturing engineer, Mr. Grinn.

During the course of the meeting, proposals were carefully screened and bidders were eliminated one by one until two companies remained. It was a difficult decision for the group to decide which of the two companies submitted the better proposal. The advantages and disadvantages of each supplier appeared to be about equal. Jack pointed out that Atomic Products Company submitted a lower estimated price, guaranteed the equipment, was more suitably located, and would meet the required delivery date. Jack also pointed out to Grinn and Holpine that Nuclear Vessels, Inc., offered Oceanics lower hourly and overhead rates, a minimum amount of subcontracting, and excellent past experience in making similar vessels. Jack stated that a field trip would be necessary to talk with both suppliers to determine which one was best qualified. At this point the meeting was adjourned and plans were made to visit both companies the following week. (See Exhibits 1 and 2.)

In following through with purchasing policy, Jack called the vice president of Oceanics' New York sales office and advised him of the potential trip. Jack learned that Atomic Products was a potential customer for Oceanics' products, but Oceanics' sales representatives were unable to get into the plant to meet key people responsible for procurement of major equipment. The vice president of sales stated that a sales rep would be at the airport to meet Oceanics' representatives and take them to the Atomic Products Company first thing Monday morning. Jack phoned the president, Mr. Wilcox, and advised him

---

EXHIBIT 1
ATOMIC PRODUCTS COMPANY, NEW YORK, N.Y.

We are pleased to submit a proposal in accordance with your request for the manufacture of one pressure vessel in accordance with your sketch #835 and all referenced specifications pointed out in your letter of August 2.

Price. Because of the potential changes pointed out in your invitation to bid, and in line with your request, the work will be performed on a cost-plus-a-fixed-fee contract detailed as follows:

a. Total price:	Estimated cost	$1,120,000
	Fixed fee	112,000
	Total	$1,232,000
b. Costing rate:	Estimated shop rate	$24/hour
	Shop overhead	180%
	Material	Cost + 10% handling charge

Shop facilities. There are adequate facilities at our New York Plant to manufacture the vessel and meet the specification to the fullest extent possible. We invite you and your associates to visit our facilities.

Past experience. Our company has not made vessels of this size but does have the equipment and know-how necessary to perform the work. Our experience has been in working with vessels up to 60" in length, I.D. 30" and 3" wall.

Subcontracting. We will be able to fabricate the entire vessel without exception in our shop.

Organization. A total of 2,000 employees is directly associated with our division.

Delivery. The pressure vessel will be shipped f.o.b. shipping point via rail in 6 months providing there are no engineering changes.

Guarantee. We guarantee workmanship and materials to be in accordance with the specifications which were supplied to us at the time of this proposal.

EXHIBIT 2
NUCLEAR VESSELS, INC., HOUSTON, TEXAS

Reference is made to your invitation to bid dated August 2 to manufacture the pressure vessel in accordance with your negative #835, and referenced specifications and any future changes necessary.

Price. The work will be performed on a cost-plus-a-fixed-fee basis, broken down as follows:

a. Total price:	Estimated cost	$1,560,000
	Fixed fee	1
	Total	$1,560,001
b. Costing rates:	Estimated shop rate	$16/hour
	Shop overhead	160%
	Material	At cost

Shop facilities. We have adequate shop facilities to manufacture and deliver the vessel and would be pleased to have representatives from your company visit our facilities at any time.

Past experience. The company has had extensive experience in manufacturing pressure vessels of heavy plate. Vessels 80″ I.D., 40′ long, 5″ thick and many others have been handled by this company.

Subcontracting. It will not be necessary for the company to subcontract any of the forming, welding, machining, or testing for this work. However, forgings will be purchased from a competent supplier after he has satisfied the company's metallurgist that his forgings will meet the specifications.

Organization. The Purchasing, Expediting, Quality Control, Production and other departments will each have one man assigned to follow this project from start to finish. Forms and records are available for your review. Our organization is familiar with Oceanics' requirements from knowledge gained as a result of previous work accomplished for your division.

Delivery. The pressure vessel will be shipped f.o.b. shipping point, Houston, Texas, to your Pittsburgh location within your required delivery time of six months or shortly thereafter.

Guarantee. This company will guarantee only workmanship. The rigid material specifications make it difficult for our supplier to furnish plate without any inclusion of slag deposits. Oceanics will have to stand the costs of any plate rejected or repaired after being tested by ultrasonic methods. Such costs can be negotiated after such defects are found.

---

that representatives from Oceanics would like to be at his plant Monday morning to review his plant facilities and meet the responsible people. The president did not appear to be enthusiastic, but said that he would be pleased to see them when they arrived.

Another call was also made to Nuclear Vessels' president, Mr. Winninghoff, who was quite enthusiastic about the potential visit and asked if he could meet the group at the airport, make hotel reservations, or perform other courtesies. Jack advised Mr. Winninghoff that these matters were taken care of and that an Oceanics' sales representative for the Houston, Texas, area would accompany the group during the visit.

Monday morning, Messrs. Toole, Grinn, and Holpine took off from Pittsburgh and arrived at Kennedy Airport in New York. Mr. Morgan, the sales manager of Oceanics' New York office, met the group and drove them to the main office of the Atomic Products Company. The group registered, obtained passes, and went to the conference room. Shortly thereafter, the manager of production, Mr. Strickland, entered, introduced himself, and stated that the president was tied up but would see them later in the day. Jack Toole opened the meeting by stating that Atomic Products' proposal was among the top contenders for supplying the pressure vessel and it was Oceanics' desire to look over Atomic Products' facilities and meet the people responsible for the job. Jack Toole asked Holpine to explain in greater detail the use of the vessel in the reactor system and to give Mr. Strickland some background on the engineering work relating to the vessel. Mr. Grinn reviewed the manufacturing aspects of the vessel as required by the basic specifications. Near the end of this discussion, Jack Toole asked Mr. Strickland if Holpine's and Grinn's comments had the same meaning as Atomic Products' interpretation of the specifications. Mr. Strickland agreed, but was somewhat concerned over the rigid cleaning specification. As he told the group, "It is difficult for a shop our size to construct a temporary building around the pressure vessel, make such a building airtight, and compel our workmen to wear white coveralls and gloves, and to adhere to surgical cleanliness requirements. I doubt if we can erect such a building in our present shop area. Instead, we may add a lean-to to the outside of our existing buildings."

The meeting with the production manager lasted one hour; then the group commenced to tour the shop. Grinn noted that most of the machines, such as the vertical boring mill, horizontal mill planer, radial drills, and beam press, were comparatively new and well maintained.

Jack Toole wondered why Atomic Products' estimated cost was lower than Nuclear Vessels', yet Atomic Products' costing rates were somewhat higher. With this thought in mind, he asked Mr. Strickland, "Do you consider your shop to be better equipped than your competitors'?" Mr. Strickland replied that it was their management's feeling that this shop was the best equipped in the United States to handle such vessels, and that even though the shop rates were higher than other shops, they would turn out more work in less time than any competitor. Holpine asked Mr. Strickland why their past experience was limited to smaller-sized vessels, to which Mr. Strickland replied that they could handle any size vessel up to and beyond the one required by Oceanics, but had never received a contract for such vessels.

Atomic Products Company was a union shop that had had several major strikes during the past few years. There were a total of 2,000 people employed, and the plant covered approximately 470,000 square feet of floor area.

The general appearance of the shop was excellent. The group noticed that the aisles were clean; that there was ample lighting, adequate ventilation, up-to-date laboratories, and good inspection facilities; and that the overall appearance of the building was extremely neat and well ordered.

The group pointed out several items in production and asked Mr. Strickland the ultimate use of these products. They received a vague reply, such as,

"These are a number of special jobs we have in the shop that we can handle without any trouble."

Mr. Strickland interrupted a group of employees standing in a corner and asked one of them to show the group the inspection and quality control departments. Both departments were well staffed and had up-to-date equipment.

The group asked Mr. Strickland to show them control of incoming materials vital to potential Oceanics' work. Wrong material that might possibly get into such a pressure vessel would contaminate the entire nuclear system. Mr. Strickland did not offer the group any evidence of materials control, but stated that they had produced hundreds of smaller vessels and had no trouble in the segregation of materials.

The metallurgical and chemical laboratories were well staffed and could provide Oceanics with adequate test specimens required by the specifications.

At the end of the tour, the group met with the president, who asked, "Do you think that our facilities are adequate to do the job?" Jack Toole replied that the facilities were impressive, but that the final selection of the supplier would be determined by many factors and that facilities were only part of the total evaluation. The president then replied, "If you want us to do the work, let us know and we will commence contract negotiations."

Several days later, Messrs. Toole, Grinn, and Holpine left New York and flew to Houston, Texas, for a visit to Nuclear Vessels, Inc. When the group registered in the hotel at 5 p.m., they found a call waiting for them from Mr. Winninghoff, president of Nuclear Vessels. Mr. Winninghoff asked the group to meet that evening at the Houston Country Club for dinner and business discussions. At 1:30 a.m., the group returned to the hotel.

The following morning, the Nuclear Vessels' chauffeur met Oceanics' team and the representative from Oceanics' sales office at the hotel and took them to Mr. Winninghoff's office. In the office, Mr. Winninghoff was waiting with the vice president of engineering, vice president of marketing, vice president of manufacturing, and other key figures in the organization. Jack Toole opened the meeting in much the same manner as was done at Atomic Products Company. After the Oceanics' people had gone into detail on the vessel, Jack Toole asked Mr. Winninghoff if they had any questions concerning the specifications. There were no comments, so the entire group commenced to tour the shop.

Mr. Grinn immediately noticed that the company's machines were of considerable age and not of large capacity, but adequate for the job. Some outside subcontracting work for the close machining tolerances would be required. Mr. Winninghoff stated: "True, we may not have all the necessary machines here, but there are ample machines available at other divisions, such as the large vertical boring mill at our El Paso, Texas, subsidiary plant. The schedule is such that we can move work into other divisions without delay." It was noted that general working conditions such as heating, lighting, ventilation, and cleanliness were not as adequate as Atomic Products'. Jack Toole noted that the higher estimated cost resulted from more man-hours required to make the vessel because of less adequate machines.

Mr. Winninghoff stopped by one of the shop foremen and asked, "Say, Sam, how about giving these gentlemen from Oceanics an idea of what your group will be doing in the forming and rolling of the pressure vessel?" Sam had several of his men stop work to show the equipment available and its intended use. Mr. Winninghoff mentioned to the group that their plant had been on a profit-sharing plan since it was organized. The employees never organized a union.

There appeared to be effective control between management and the shop. For instance, to carry out the work fully, one member each from purchasing, expediting, quality control, and scheduling was assigned to a task force headed by a project engineer. It was the responsibility of this task force to follow the entire project through the shop and keep the project engineer informed on a day-to-day basis.

Nuclear Vessels had constructed one vessel considerably larger than the vessel required by Oceanics. Mr. Winninghoff claimed that they ran into numerous problems at the beginning of manufacturing and that the experience gained in the production of such a large vessel made them change their organization for closer follow-up. They also changed the type of paperwork and records for better control of material. The group noticed that each piece of material in the shop was marked for the project of its intended use. The metallurgical and chemical laboratories were very large, but much of their equipment was old. They appeared to have adequate room for the location of a cleaning room.

On Friday of the same week, Toole called a meeting of Holpine and Grinn to evaluate the two companies being considered. Holpine argued strongly that Nuclear Vessels should be given a contract because of their extreme enthusiasm to carry out the job, their past experience in manufacturing pressure vessels of equal size, and their previous Oceanics experience. Said Holpine, "Atomic Products has not had experience with our rigid specifications and the price and delivery will probably slip." Grinn argued that Atomic Products should be the company selected because of their adequate shop and laboratory facilities, location, ability to meet delivery date, and ability to guarantee the vessel.

Neither Holpine nor Grinn took into consideration the cost, the company's organization, guarantees, and other business considerations. It was Jack Toole's responsibility to evaluate both of these companies and show which company should be given the contract.

1 What specific areas and activities should the Oceanics group have investigated on its two visits?
2 Evaluate each supplier on each of the above items using information obtained on the field visits.
3 Based on the face value of the written proposals, which company appeared to submit the better offer?
4 Based on the proposal plus information obtained from the case history, which company is likely to be the better supplier?
5 What do you recommend?

SENATOR FOGHORN

Senator Foghorn was a powerful political figure from the South who secretly enjoyed Yankee land far more than he could ever let anybody know. During his stay in Washington, he made some important business and political connections. As a result, when he was not reelected, he was able to secure several positions as a director for large companies and banks. This served as a sufficient excuse to keep him in the Washington area.

It was not too long a time until he was able to acquire a majority interest in a plating plant in New Jersey. The plant had good facilities and some excellent customers. The former senator naturally wished to expand its operation and started to use some of his political influence in business contacts to that end.

He was also able to get himself enmeshed in a very large housing project in Washington. Through his business affiliations and political contacts at local, county, state, and national levels, Mr. Foghorn maintained that he could exert powerful pressures on the architect and contractors for the housing project to buy from manufacturers of his selection. He said they were very receptive to pressure of this type. His recommendations carried much weight, said Senator Foghorn, and would be the deciding factor in the selection of suppliers on the housing project. With this in mind he approached selected manufacturers to obtain business for his plating plant and offered them in return his help in obtaining orders for the housing project.

One of the companies he approached was Maryland Electric, a firm in a position to supply all the electrical equipment and all the electrical appliances that would be required for the housing project. Foghorn went to see several vice presidents of Maryland, as well as Mr. Selby (in charge of trade relations), and explained that he was in a position to influence greatly the placement of the electrical work. While he did not say so, he intimated that he could almost guarantee it. Knowing that such influence did not come gratuitously, Mr. Selby tried to probe the former senator for the amount and the form of the return favor. His answer was a detailed explanation of the fine plating plant Foghorn controlled and the excellent quality of the plating it produced.

Mr. Selby knew that the amount of business that Maryland would have to place with the plating plant would be considerable in view of the fact that the order for the electrical equipment and appliances would run into several million dollars. The completely decentralized operation of Maryland Electric posed a problem in such cases, because many division managers and purchasing managers would have to be sold on the advantages of such a move.

In addition, Maryland owned its own plating facility, which was currently producing more than 75 percent of the company's requirements. The plating facility was operating at 60 percent of capacity at best, and it was trying to secure more work. In spite of these problems, Mr. Selby decided to investigate the possibilities of using Senator Foghorn's plant. This investigation showed that the 25 percent of the company plating requirements that were bought "outside" were purchased from basic raw material producers or from highly specialized platers who did nothing but intricate work. All of them were good Maryland customers.

Several days passed and Mr. Selby was still unable to resolve the problem. Naturally, he wanted to participate in the housing development, but there was no easy way of giving Senator Foghorn's plating plant any of Maryland's business. During this period Senator Foghorn had produced a very good contract for Maryland in molded plastic parts. He had done this, he said, to prove his value and show his good intentions toward Maryland. In addition, he spoke of other contracts, including one for an extremely large hydroelectric project in Asia. About this time Mr. Selby learned that Mr. Johnson, a recently retired president of one of the largest mail-order companies in the world, had joined forces with Senator Foghorn. The mail-order company handled Maryland equipment exclusively, and the retired president had been singularly responsible for this purchasing agreement. Mr. Johnson visited Mr. Selby and reiterated the great influence that Senator Foghorn had with the housing project contracts, as well as his many other areas of influence.

1 Should Maryland Electric become involved with Senator Foghorn? If so, to what degree?
2 Should business be taken from Maryland's own plating plant or other good sources of supply to satisfy Senator Foghorn?

SHEER ELEGANCE (AN ISSUE OF POLLUTION AVOIDANCE)

Mr. Jürgen Scherer was recently promoted to manager of packaging for the procurement department of the Sheer Elegance Lotion Corporation. This morning, Mr. Scherer was requested to develop a systematic analysis to reduce or eliminate pollution in conjunction with Sheer Elegance's new line of body lotions.

1 Develop a chain from Mother Earth, through upstream suppliers, to Sheer Elegance, through its distributors, to the end user and, finally, return of the packaging to recycling or to Mother Earth.
2 Identify points at which pollution may enter the value chain which, to some extent, are under the control of Sheer Elegance.
3 How can pollution be avoided throughout Sheer Elegance's value chain?
4 If you were Mr. Scherer, what action would you recommend?
5 What is supply management's role in such an effort?

SIGNAL-TEK CORPORATION

BACKGROUND

Signal-Tek Corporation was founded in 1963. Following a series of new product developments, mergers, and acquisitions, the company evolved into an

This case was developed by Dana Collins and Christine Childers under the direction of Professor David N. Burt.

$82.5 million corporation with wholly owned subsidiaries operating in Colorado, Indiana, England, and Germany. The Denver division generates approximately $30 million in revenues, primarily from signal generators. These general-purpose test and measurement instrumentation products are used in a variety of industrial, laboratory, and defense applications.

The Denver division had enjoyed several years of market leadership in these products based on innovative design, low cost, and high product quality. However, in recent years, Signal-Tek's product brand recognition has begun to slip due to its inability to meet competition. Based on more timely introduction of newer, low-cost products, two larger instrument manufacturers have been taking some of the division's market share. Signal-Tek has been unable to respond quickly enough to these competitive pressures and, as a result, has had to reduce its work force by almost 15 percent recently. It has become clear that the division must regain its market position by refocusing on its goals of timely introduction of low-cost, solid-performance, high-reliability instruments.

THE OPPORTUNITY

In late July 1995, the U.S. Army released a request for sealed bid quotes on a new low-cost signal generator that would eventually replace several thousand pieces of test equipment that the Army had in the field. The company with the lowest unit cost for the instrument would get the award.

The division estimated that the design and testing requirements alone would cost between $1 and $1.2 million and, based on the Army's request, had to be completed within one year after the release of the contract. The initial award included a first-year commitment of 900 units with a second- and third-year requirement of an additional 900 units each year. These additional requirements were to be awarded at a future date. Since the request also included an option to double the requirements in each of years two and three, the contract could be worth 4,500 units over the next three years with the potential of even more as the Army eventually replaced its entire field stock.

In reviewing this request, the Denver division saw its opportunity to develop the most utility/cost-efficient signal generator that has been built to date. However, given the potential volume of product that was at stake, Signal-Tek also recognized that competition for the contract could be very heavy. Marketing inquiries confirmed that the two competitors that had recently been taking market share, plus one foreign competitor, were planning to bid the contract. The division felt that the price of the unit would have to be under $1,900 in order to have a real chance at winning the award.

The bids were to be opened by the Army on August 25, 1995. Thus, the division had only enough time to make cost estimates based on current materials and labor standards used in similar products, rather than on a detailed analysis of the new product design. Typically, the cost of the division's products was 50 percent materials and 50 percent labor and overhead. Costs, when compared with the estimated required selling price, left a very low margin on the product.

However, the decision was made to proceed with the bid with the expectation that somehow it would be possible to reduce the unit cost during the design and development stages. The price for the first 3,600 units was established at $1,799 each, with a reduction in price made available for units in excess of 3,600.

THE PROCUREMENT ENVIRONMENT

The purchasing department at the Denver division consisted of a purchasing manager named Barry Etcher and a staff of five buyers—two senior buyers and three junior buyers. Although this staff had experience in buying electronic components, neither Barry nor any of his buyers had any formal engineering background. Therefore, the engineering staff rarely worked with the purchasing group during the design and prototype stages of new products. Typically, the purchasing group would become involved at the point just prior to the new product being turned over to manufacturing for preproduction runs. By this time the design had been fairly well completed, frequently requiring parts that were not currently used by the division. In addition, the engineers had already spent a considerable amount of time talking with suppliers about new products that were being developed by these potential suppliers and how these items might enhance the new design.

After the Army reviewed the bids, Signal-Tek was awarded the contract. The division's management now had to focus on the issues of limited design time and the necessary cost reduction programs.

1 How can early purchasing involvement assist in low-cost and timely new product development?
2 How does purchasing's involvement enhance an early supplier involvement program? What are the potential benefits?
3 How can the division increase cooperation/communication between the engineering and purchasing departments?
4 How will standardization improve the new product development process?
5 How does more effective purchasing involvement change engineering's role?
6 What can the division do to help expand purchasing's contribution?

SMC TURBINES

SMC is a world leader in the design and manufacturing of industrial gas turbines. SMC has been in business for over sixty years, with a great reputation for high-quality products. Its repuration is maintained by customer satisfac-

This case was developed by Jason Chaffee and Deanna Ryan under the direction of Professor David N. Burt.

tion with its timeliness, quality, and design. The main goal of SMC's purchasing team is to maximize value at the lowest possible cost. Mutually beneficial supplier management has kept its goals a reality. SMC monitors price, quality, service, and annual improvements of each of its significant suppliers.

The purchasing department is divided into two subdivisions: direct material and indirect material. Greg Barnes is an associate buyer in the direct material division. Greg was recently contacted by his supervisor, Earl Lupton, regarding a quality problem in the procurement of sand castings. Sand castings are a very essential part of every turbine, costing between $6,000 and $10,000 per turbine, depending on the design. Sand castings are frequently purchased and, coupled with their relatively high price, represent a significant segment of SMC's procurement. Greg was assigned the task of finding the source of the quality problem and suggesting possible solutions.

After investigating the problem, Greg discovered that only three out of ten of the sand castings received were acceptable for the production process. SMC currently uses seven different suppliers of these crucial parts. Producing the sand castings is considered an age-old process; however, it seems that the problems cannot be assigned to any one specific cause. SMC often receives parts that are too small or too large for the particular turbine into which they are to be built.

When SMC receives a faulty sand casting, it must be either sent back to the supplier for rework or completely scrapped depending on the severity of the problem. The sand castings are such an integral part of the turbine that faulty sand castings slow down or even shut down production altogether. This can lead to late deliveries, high-dollar loss on scrapped materials, and ultimately customer dissatisfaction.

Greg considered the option of buying a higher grade of materials to replace the trouble-plagued sand castings. Unfortunately, prices on the better grades of material were over twice the price of the castings. SMC cannot realistically produce the sand casting itself due to extremely high tooling costs.

Greg has a meeting with Earl Lupton in one week and must have a viable proposal to alleviate the problem.

1 What options are available to Greg through basic supplier management? What actions do you recommend?

SMITH-JONES ELECTRONICS CORPORATION

Mr. George Brown was promoted in January to the position of senior procurement specialist, a procurement staff position at Smith-Jones Electronics Corporation, a *Fortune* 100 company in the northeastern United States. Within the first few months on the job, he found it difficult to do his work well and wondered what action to take.

COMPANY BACKGROUND

The Smith-Jones Electronics Corporation was a forty-year-old electronics manufacturing company selling in three primary markets: defense electronics, commercial aviation, and consumer appliances. The company was a financially sound multiplant organization. Current sales were $6 billion, and the company was enjoying a rapid growth rate, according to Mr. Brown. It was a multinational company with 77,000 employees worldwide.

PROCUREMENT PRACTICES

Procurement at Smith-Jones was conducted primarily in a decentralized mode. Staff functions such as large contract procurement, training, policy and procedure administration, and consulting on an as-needed basis were centralized in a corporate procurement department. Purchasing research was conducted using resources outside the company, mainly supplier surveys. Plants had a dotted line responsibility to the corporate procurement manager.

MR. GEORGE BROWN

Mr. George Brown was a purchasing professional with more than thirty years of procurement experience. Prior to joining Smith-Jones over fifteen years ago, he was employed by two large companies in the same industry. When his predecessor left Smith-Jones to work for another firm, Mr. Brown was promoted from purchasing manager in the data systems group to his current position as senior procurement specialist.

CHALLENGES TO IMPROVING PURCHASING'S OPERATIONS

A short time after Mr. Brown began his new assignment as senior procurement specialist he became disturbed about the difficulties he encountered in attempting to do his job well. Drawing on his substantial procurement experience to evaluate job performance, he was able to identify those areas that he felt needed improvement. He concluded that they could be classified as a lack of effective procurement methods. For example, he found that production was not being supported in a timely fashion. In general, production management perceived purchasing as conducting price auctions and not as professionals making a contribution. A lack of effective criteria for an in-depth evaluation of responses to requests for quotation resulted in bids being awarded to low bidders without considering other factors, such as quality, that impact on cost. This perception was further reinforced by an unusually large incidence of late deliveries. Cost comparisons with the then-current market activity revealed that prices being paid were too high. Buyers were reacting to requisitions as they were generated. Due to lack of coordination among plant buyers, they were not making effective use of the company's buying power since they were operating independently of each other. Consequently, they were left to buy at the mercy of the marketplace. He found that a major contributing factor was that there were too few internal resources available to procurement specialists and buyers. The company did not have a strategic purchasing plan to provide direction for the procurement group. Attempts to collect meaningful data were not successful because the collection of data was inconsistent and usually incomplete throughout the procurement community.

Requests for forecasts could not be complied with since there was no internal base for developing purchasing forecasts. The only forecast data available in the procurement group was that supplied in response to requests to potential suppliers. Markets were not monitored by buyers. The absence of current market status, prediction of future market conditions, and an accurate forecast prevented buyers from reacting to market conditions to assure consistent sources of supply at competitive prices. Difficulties in assessing department productivity were encountered because the lack of credible data did not allow measurement of performance. However, even if such data were generated, their usefulness would be restricted by lack of historical data on performance. Without historical data for use as a base or an index, any attempt to measure productivity would yield flawed results. Proper use of suppliers as resources could not be realized since no vehicle existed to obtain, verify, and use data obtained from them. There was no formal supplier recognition program to encourage and reward supplier participation in performance, achievements, product development, cost containment, market awareness, and, when appropriate, brainstorming.

Some internal resistance to change existed due to a lack of understanding of how to react to market conditions. The one encouraging area Mr. Brown discovered was quality. There were few complaints about incoming quality and it was not considered an issue.

He realized that any initiative for change would have to come from him—and he wondered where to start.

1 Identify and discuss the basic issues in this case.

SPRINGER-BRIGHTON ELECTRONICS

Springer-Brighton Electronics is a small firm located in Chicago. Its major product is a line of automobile electrical system analyzers. These analyzers are used by auto repair shops in tune-up work to identify and diagnose problems in a car's electrical system. Although the market is highly competitive, Springer-Brighton's products compete well, and the firm is reasonably profitable.

The firm's production operation is ideally suited for management with an MRP-type planning and control system. Consequently, three years ago such a system was installed. Initially it did not work well, because it was not properly coordinated with the purchasing operation, and the planning data used in the system were not reliable. In time, however, the bugs were worked out, the system was refined, and it is now working well.

One of the organizational changes Springer-Brighton implemented was the creation of a materials management department that includes purchasing, production control, traffic, inventory management, and the warehouse operations. This arrangement seemed to facilitate effective operation of the MRP system.

More recently, the firm has adopted the use of the buyer-planner concept. That is, a buyer's job and a production planner's job have been combined into a single job. The number of materials handled by each buyer-planner has been reduced, but the scope of the task has become more extensive and more integrated in nature. For a given group of materials, a single individual prepares the production schedule and works directly with suppliers to make it function correctly.

Like most MRP systems, the one used by Springer-Brighton is computer operated. However, when a new buyer-planner is hired, he or she is "broken in" to the planning portion of the job by developing and managing the plan for one or two materials *manually*. The purpose of this approach is to teach the newcomer how the operating routine works, so he or she can understand clearly what the computer does when it runs the MRP planning and operating system.

Assume that you have just joined the firm's materials management department as a junior buyer-planner. One of the materials you have been assigned to handle is the metal housing for the Model 48A analyzer. The housing is formed by stamping and fabricating operations—and is single-sourced with a large metalworking shop in a north Chicago suburb.

As you begin to get organized during your second day on the job, your boss gives you the Model 48A housing requirements projection for the next ten weeks. The data are shown in the table below.

MODEL 48A HOUSING REQUIREMENTS PROJECTION

Order quantity = 140 Lead time = 4 weeks Safety stock = 80		Weeks → Firm reqts.										Tentative	
		1	2	3	4	5	6	7	8	9	10	11	12
Requirements		40	40	50	40	40	50	40	40	60	50	50	50
Receipts			140										
OH-end of week	130												
Planned order releases													

1 Manually complete the ordering/operations plan for the Model 48A housing. Simultaneously, construct a table showing when you would expect order points to be reached during the first eight weeks.
2 List and discuss briefly the types of operating problems you might encounter that could require replanning and rescheduling work. What are the implications for supplier relations?

STANDARD TELE-LINK CORPORATION

Returning from a supplier site visit, John Franklin, procurement manager for New Jersey–based Standard Tele-Link Corporation (STC), realized that the supplier favored by the user group presented problems for him. He sat down to plan his price negotiation strategy, including consideration of the lease versus buy options. He also wondered if the financial stability of this small supplier was adequate.

GENERAL BACKGROUND

STC operated a large international telecommunications network as a common carrier. It used cutting-edge technology, and in some instances, the technological requirements of the network exceeded available technology. A record of reliable service to the existing customer base was both a strategic operations objective and a vital marketing tool.

THE PROCUREMENT PROCESS

John Franklin managed the procurement of hardware and software used to operate the network. He worked with the "user group" on the operations side and the treasury group on the financial side. His scope of responsibility called for integrating the recommendations of both groups. When the user group selected the supplier(s) most responsive to the technical specifications and the treasury group made either a lease or purchase recommendation, Mr. Franklin entered into negotiations with a supplier, or group of suppliers, to obtain the best possible contract from STC's viewpoint.

Supplier Preference

The purchase under consideration involved advanced equipment with a processor, channel and line adapters, a control program, and training. The user group strongly favored Channel-Net Products (CNP) as the supplier, in spite of pricing levels almost three times as high as competing suppliers. CNP's hardware and software handled fiber, data, and satellite links where the other suppliers' current products only handled fiber and data links. In addition, a major electronics supplier, Universal Semi-Conductors, was expected to announce a competing product within four months. All parties within STC realized that the Channel-Net product survived testing, but was yet to be proven in a live environment. Nevertheless, the user group people wanted the

CNP product and, if left on their own, would immediately purchase it and absorb its price over a 60-month life as opposed to leasing it.

Site Visit

Mr. Franklin's notes from his visit to Channel-Net's plant near Boston listed these points:

- They occupy a large barren leased building using about 20% of its space.
- I see testing facilities and equipment but no fabrication capability.
- There are 17 employees in all.
- Hardware assembly is performed by a contractor using standard parts and techniques with some custom firmware.
- Research and design of hardware/firmware/software is complete.
- The board of directors and investors are major figures in industry.
- Venture capital of $4,000,000 was invested in 1982.
- Additional capital of $3,000,000 was invested in 1994.
- $2,400,000 cash remains at present.
- The sale to STC, if approved, would represent about four times current sales volume.
- Venture capital investments pay for research/development/operations, but no profit yet.
- I don't know if they are here to stay. (Exhibit 1 shows data from Dun & Bradstreet reports on CNP).

CNP's Pricing Schedule

The pricing schedule, per unit, for the equipment under consideration is shown below. The Duplex Links are the hardware; the Control Program is the software.

	Purchase	Monthly* lease	Monthly maint.
Duplex Links			
Processor	$56,000	$1,881	$308
Channel adapter	$25,740	$1,030	$72
Line adapter	$57,000	$2,328	$112
	$138,740	$5,239	$492

*Normally a minimum of 12 months.

Control program	Basic license fee	Distributed system license fee
	$2,000	$1,500
Training	Type, amount, and pricing to be determined	

EXHIBIT 1
STANDARD TELE-LINK CORPORATION
EXCERPTS FROM DUN & BRADSTREET REPORT—CNP

Started 1982
MFG Electronic Communications EQPT

- 100% of capital stock owned by officers and outside directors
- Senior officers active since 1982 start-up
- Sales offices operated in New York, Chicago, Dallas
- Credit history:
    1 During the past two years, most payments have been prompt. Several have been over-due.
    2 Outstanding short-term debt has increased moderately during the past year.
    3 No past due payments during the past six months.

John Franklin's Viewpoint

As he examined the CNP pricing data, John considered the lease versus purchase choice as a subsidiary consideration. He focused on understanding CNP's cost structure and STC's operating environment as a means of establishing a range for negotiating down the published price schedule. If he was able to make a recommendation in favor of acquiring the CNP hardware and software, he wanted the contract to reflect the best possible terms for STC. He knew that the supplier's costs were essentially sunk costs; and that, if purchased, the supplier had agreed to extend the warranty to 12 months. Therefore, under a lease, CNP should be willing to absorb maintenance costs. Additionally, since CNP provided documentation and support only for the basic license, CNP may be willing to consider the distributed licenses as "fully paid up" at some point in time. Training expense was predominately a fixed cost from the supplier's viewpoint. STC's expert use of the equipment was key to an ongoing relationship with CNP and, perhaps, "life or death" in the marketplace. The initial purchase was planned to be for six units.

His colleagues expected a recommendation within a few days.

1 Should the equipment be acquired now? If so, from which supplier?
2 Should the equipment be leased or purchased?

SUNSPOT, INC.

Ms. Monica Foltz was appointed CEO of Sunspot, Inc., nine months ago. Sunspot is a $1 billion manufacturer of sunglasses. Margins at Sunspot are about half of industry averages. R.O.I. is 8.4 percent.

Recently, Ms. Foltz read an article in *Fortune* magazine which described a relatively new approach to purchasing known as partnering. Typically, costs and time to market are reduced through these partnerships, while quality of incoming materials normally increases. Since time, cost, and quality are all key issues at Sunspot, Ms. Foltz has asked her vice president of procurement, Mr. Bart Lyons, to develop a briefing on the pros and cons of partnering.

1   What are the most likely benefits of forming strategic supply alliances, or "partnerships," with Sunspot's key suppliers?
2   What are the disadvantages or risks of such partnerships?
3   How can these disadvantages be offset?

TEMPLETON ENGINE COMPANY

The Templeton Engine Company, located in eastern Wisconsin, was a major producer of aircraft jet engines. On December 15, Dave Giltner, sales manager for Precision Cutting Tools, called Neil Carlson, a purchasing supervisor for Templeton, to tell him that Precision planned to increase its prices 6 percent across the board on February 15. When he replaced the telephone, Neil wondered how to respond to this news in view of Templeton's plan to reemphasize its cost reduction program in January.

THE COMPANY

The Templeton Engine Company produced turbo-jet and turbo-prop engines for use on small- and medium-sized jet aircraft. It did not compete in the commercial jet engine market, although it did produce smaller engines used to power auxiliary equipment on commercial airliners. Templeton's sales totaled approximately $1 billion per year, divided roughly 80–20 among private and governmental purchasers. The firm employed 6,200 people, including approximately 50 professionals in the purchasing department. Because of the technical character of its products, over the years the company developed a strong engineering orientation which pervaded all aspects of its operations.

PURCHASING ACTIVITIES

Templeton spent approximately $600 million a year for materials, most of which were used in producing its finished products. All buying activities were based on material specifications generated in the firm's various design engineering departments. As a general rule, technical factors were the controlling considerations in specification development.

    When considering potential new suppliers for major purchases, the purchasing department coordinated an extremely thorough investigation of the operations and capabilities of each firm reviewed. In addition to an investigation of the normal commercial and service considerations, personnel from Templeton's quality assurance and manufacturing engineering departments carefully analyzed each supplier's production and quality control operations. The objective was to evaluate both effectiveness and efficiency, as well as compatibility with Templeton's requirements. After selection, when a supplier proved its ability to meet the buyer's requirements consistently, Templeton frequently utilized a supplier certification program that allowed the supplier to perform a great deal of its own part inspection and acceptance.

Templeton's buyers used both competitive bidding and negotiation techniques in determining price, depending on the prevailing buying and market conditions. Since some of Templeton's products were sold to federal agencies, buyers had to follow government regulation, which stipulated the use of competitive bidding and negotiation, and set guidelines for the use of each. The Defense Contract Audit Agency periodically audited such purchases to ensure compliance. Once a supplier was selected, however, buyers frequently negotiated numerous contract details and service arrangements with the supplier.

An additional complication faced by some buyers stemmed from a Federal Aviation Agency (FAA) requirement. Each of Templeton's products and related components produced by specific suppliers had to be tested and certified initially by the FAA. Whenever a new supplier for such a part was used, Templeton was required to subject the new item to a rigorous and costly 150-hour operating test. Hence, buyers did not change suppliers without considerable analysis and effort to rectify problems with existing sources.

Like many major firms, over the years Templeton's purchasing philosophy evolved to view suppliers as partners that, in reality, functioned as extensions of Templeton's own production operations. Thus, while buyers evaluated a supplier's performance rigorously, they worked closely with the supplier to optimize the benefit of the relationship for both organizations. When it was advantageous, buyers liked to utilize long-term contracts—often up to three years in duration—to assure compliance with quality and pricing objectives. As a rule, Templeton's buyers had responsibility for the full range of activities involved in their respective transactions—everything from market research to expediting.

COST AND QUALITY

For obvious reasons, quality requirements in the jet engine industry were stringent and extremely important. No producer of shoddy work survived for long. At the same time, however, competition among major producers had become increasingly intense. Consequently, the incentives to keep costs down were substantial. For this reason, buyers at Templeton diligently sought out potential opportunities to reduce material costs without jeopardizing quality. The company, in fact, was currently in the process of reemphasizing its corporatewide cost reduction program.

THE PURCHASE OF TOOLING

The Templeton manufacturing organization used approximately $1 million worth of tooling each year. Because of the tight tolerances required in the manufacturing process, tooling that performed with precision and reliability was essential.

The special tooling supplied by Precision Cutting Tools was a major dollar item for Templeton. In addition, after extensive testing Templeton's design engineers specified the Precision organization as a single-source supplier.

As Neil Carlson pondered the pending 6 percent price increase on Precision's special tooling, he was acutely aware that he had less than sixty days to resolve the problem.

1 What alternatives does Neil have?
2 What are the advantages and disadvantages of each?
3 What should Neil do?

A TIGHT BUDGET SOLUTION

At Midwest Tech, as at most mid-size engineering schools, budgets always seemed to be very tight—so tight, in fact, that the faculty never seemed to have the resources to attend all the technical conferences they felt were necessary to keep up with what their colleagues were doing. This was seen by the administration to be a detriment to the teaching and research mission, but more recently was recognized as a specific handicap in the recruitment of new faculty. It was well known that the administration was receptive to innovative ideas to help solve this problem.

This morning, when Joe Fleming, Midwest's purchasing manager, opened his mail, he found a letter from the Condor Corporation announcing a new buyer incentive program. Condor, a supplier of a broad line of vibration transducers and analyzers, which are widely used in doing seismic studies on older buildings, was offering "frequent buyer points" to all those purchasing its products over the next 12 months. At the end of that period, Condor offered to redeem points for hotel stays of one to three nights, and various registration and dinner packages in connection with next year's Structural Engineering Society meeting in Honolulu.

Believing that this might help solve the faculty's conference travel problem, Joe asked his secretary to get him on the academic vice president's calendar so he could help give this offer wide visibility.

1 Does Condor's incentive plan constitute an offer of a gratuity which the institution should avoid?
2 Are there better ways that Condor might help faculty conference travel?
3 If the same Condor notice has also been received by the Midwest faculty, does that change anything?
4 If any institutional response should be made to Condor, what should it be?

TOKISAN CORPORATION

Jack Bressler, salesman for Tokisan America Corporation, was pleased. He had sought and obtained approval for purchasing a cost-effective coolant for various customer applications. Tokisan America was the American subsidiary of the Japanese parent company. Although located in the United States, Tokisan America Inc. (TAI) used a mix of Japanese and American business practices. The staff of the plant was an equal mix of Japanese and Americans. Traditionally, the Japanese held the senior positions in the company, but this was changing. Jack was considered a good candidate for promotion to manager of company sales.

To get approval to purchase any major item (expressed in terms of dollar value or a substantive impact on the firm's operations), a purchasing proposal was sent around the division for scrutiny by personnel that had experience with or would be affected by the purchase. This was the typical Japanese "ringi" system of getting input on and evaluating purchase decisions. TAI had two purchasing departments. Jack was part of the Business Systems Group, which had its own purchasing department. The other purchasing department was used by the production divisions and support functions.

Jack had found a coolant that could be used in customer equipment. The equipment was not made by TAI, but was used in conjunction with TAI products. Jack found the coolant at a discount, realized that it would complement the TAI product offering, and negotiated a competitive price. The Business Systems Group could buy and resell anything that would complement TAI's product line. Jack's next step was to ask key personnel in the Business Systems Group what they thought about the possible deal. He got positive feedback. He then prepared a Business Systems "ringi" for circulation. He was virtually assured of success. Two weeks after its initiation, the "ringi" was approved. He had the O.K. to initiate the purchasing process.

One week later the coolant was received at the TAI receiving department. The shipping documents cleared accounting, and payment was made. One hundred thousand cans of coolant at a cost of $2 per can were now ready to repackage and sell. Jack was elated. He had notified customers of the coolant, and TAI product/coolant bundle packages were priced to sell.

This case was written by Frederick terVeer under the direction of Professor David N. Burt.

During the ever-important coffee break Tuesday afternoon, Bob O'Connel, head of the Production & Support Purchasing Department and Yoshio Tanabe, head of Business Systems Group Purchasing Department, were joined by Cyrill Williams of plant safety. Bob and Cyrill worked together often since production "ringis" required plant safety to be involved. Yoshio had just finished mentioning the purchase of the coolant (which was now in the warehouse) and how surprised he was at the price and how cost-effective this CFC 111 was in relation to other coolants.

Cyrill choked on his coffee, spilling it in a very messy way. Bob's face went white, then livid. TAI Business Systems had purchased and paid for a coolant that was banned for the intended application in the United States and was being phased out worldwide.

Jack heard about it the next day. He was not happy, nor was anyone else in Business Systems. The plant manager was reported to be furious. Jack needed to concentrate. How did this happen to him, and what in the world was he going to do? Loud and high-speed Japanese was heard down the hall. It was going to be one heck of a day.

1 Identify and analyze the basic issues in this case.

TRANSPORTATION SERVICE

Caterpillar, Inc., was incorporated in Delaware on May 22, 1936. It has fifteen plants across the United States which design, manufacture, and market earthmoving, construction, and materials handling equipment. It also manufactures engines for earthmoving vehicles and tractor-trailers. Caterpillar's products are distributed worldwide. Net income last year totaled $350,000,000.

Caterpillar has developed a "transportation quality" program in order to reduce shipping damages to its equipment and to ensure its just-in-time production and inventory system. The program consists of two parts. The first part ensures proper lifting and tie-down provisions by working with engineers in the design process. The second part focuses on internal practices to prepare the product for shipment.

The chief transportation quality engineer has developed a carrier certification program for both inbound and outbound freight. The program establishes standards requiring the carrier to adhere to 100 percent performance. Use of fewer certified carriers increases the amount of business given to each one. The price is obtained through competitive bidding. It is a function of the travel distance and the weight and density of the shipment.

At the present time, Caterpillar is considering one of three carriers to add to its list of certified carriers. Carrier X has 10,000 trucks and a claim rate of 1.5 percent payment to revenue.* The company's pickup/delivery time meets the

---

*Claim rate is the amount paid out for damages incurred by the carrier. It is the percentage of the dollar amount paid on claims to total revenue.

industry average of four days to transport from New York to St. Louis. Carrier Y implements a quality program for its 9,000 trucks to meet on-time delivery. It has a 1 percent claim rate. Carrier Z has 9,500 trucks and an excellent safety record, but it has not met the average pickup/delivery time. Its claim rate is 1 percent. (See Exhibit A for price estimates.)

EXHIBIT A
PRICE ESTIMATES

Carrier X
  Price per ton-mile $1.05
Carrier Y
  Price per ton-mile $1.15
Carrier Z
  Price per ton-mile $0.95

---

1 Develop a checklist of items that should be considered when selecting a carrier.
2 What are the advantages of certifying the carriers?
3 Is price the most important factor in evaluating carriers? Explain.
4 What are the key factors regarding Caterpillar's carrier needs?
5 If you were selecting the carrier, what are the alternatives? Which carrier would you select? Why?

THE UNIVERSAL MOTOR COMPANY ACQUIRES SEMICONDUCTORS

BACKGROUND

The Universal Motor Company is one of the world's largest manufacturers of automobiles and trucks. In 1980, purchase content was 65 percent of the cost of goods sold. The purchasing organization was well managed and staffed with seasoned, well-educated professionals.

During the late 1970s, the U.S. government began addressing the air pollution issue by establishing vehicle emissions standards and corporate average fuel consumption economy targets for vehicles sold in the United States. The auto industry was faced with major technical problems. The U.S. government–mandated standards could not be achieved with available technology. These manated standards required the auto industry to design engine control computers (fuel intake, spark timing, etc.) to manage engine efficiency more precisely.

Management was highly confident that established purchasing policies and procedures that had been used successfully for so many years would apply to the procurement of the new semiconductors required for the manufacture of the new engine control computers. By 1980, it was obvious to the individuals directly involved that something was wrong. The tried and true methods of purchasing stampings and plastic injection molded parts were not getting satisfactory results when applied to the purchase of semiconductors. The company purchased about $10 million worth of semiconductors in 1980 from twenty suppliers. Stock-outs leading to production disruptions (absolutely forbidden in the auto industry) were occurring regularly. In fact, semiconductors were a greater cause of production disruptions than were all other purchased materials. Semiconductor suppliers, for the most part, seemed uninterested in the firm's problems and did not react to these emergencies in the normal auto industry supplier fashion.

Those responsible for the procurement of semiconductors were under intense pressure from management to resolve these difficulties. But nothing they tried seemed to make a difference. During these dark days some important observations were made:

- The total 1980 worldwide auto industry semiconductor requirement represented less than 2 percent of the semiconductor market. Therefore, members of the semiconductor industry did not see the auto industry as an important market requiring or deserving any special service.
- The purchasing practice of sourcing from many suppliers (to ensure competition and a low purchase price) was aggravating an already difficult supplier relations issue and further complicating the situation.
- Purchasing management projected its semiconductor requirements out over the next five years. The projection was shocking: The current $10 million annual requirement was forecast to grow to over $90 million by 1985. It seemed likely that this growth would be replicated by the entire auto industry. Interestingly, however, this growth did not increase the market position of the auto industry, as the semiconductor industry was growing faster than the automotive industry market component.

Based on these observations, it became clear that something had to change. The 1980 semiconductor supply situation was intolerable. Of equal or greater concern, projected growth in electronics requirements appeared to be unsupportable.

FORWARD PLANNING

In 1980, the concept of forward planning, business planning, or strategic planning was not commonly associated with the purchasing function. Purchasing was most often thought of as a reactive function organized to support manufacturing. Marketing, on the other hand, was more often thought of as the proactive organization focused on the future of the firm. The failure of management to recognize the strategic and futuristic implementation of purchasing limited innovative actions when dealing with a firm's supply world.

The 1980 situation demanded new thinking and a new approach to the acquisition of semiconductors. The purchasing managers involved had little choice, given the circumstances. Purchasing had no experience with strategic planning. There were no guidelines to follow. The responsible purchasing managers started with a clean piece of paper, a mission, and a problem statement.

THE ENVIRONMENT

The first order of business was to develop a complete understanding of both the internal and external environments. The firm's engineers documented their future technology requirements in the form of a technology plan or road map. Once the internal requirements were understood and documented, the focus turned to the external environment, revealing an industry which was (and remains) dynamic, high growth, entrepreneurial focused, and technology driven—one that defies simple analysis.

AREAS OF STRATEGIC IMPORTANCE

Several major areas were identified as being of strategic importance to the firm's survival and future profitability: How can Universal ensure that it benefits from rapidly evolving technologies in the area? How can Universal obtain the desired/required quality? How can Universal best ensure a continuity of supply? What actions need to be taken to compress the time involved in going from concept to customer? Can manufacturing cycle time be compressed? How can Universal best minimize the "all-in-cost" associated with the acquisition and use of semiconductors?

THE MAKE-OR-BUY ISSUE

One of the major issues confronting the team had to do with whether the firm should make the required semiconductor devices or purchase them. (We will explore this issue in considerable detail since it is representative of the complexity of decisions in the areas of design, source selection, pricing, and related procurement issues. Further, the make-or-buy decision impacts on all six of the areas of strategic importance.)

In order to understand the make-or-buy question, management recognized the need for a complete environmental analysis of the semiconductor industry. A team of company experts including engineering, quality, purchasing, and manufacturing professionals was assigned to develop a program analyzing the semiconductor industry. Both primary and secondary research were conducted. The research led Universal executives to conclude that the decision was more complicated than simply deciding whether to acquire a semiconductor facility or buy the required components. It became apparent that the semiconductor make-or-buy issue consisted of many subissues. Accordingly, the entire process of designing, manufacturing, and testing semiconductors was broken down into stages.

The first stage (design) involved both human and computerized inputs. Computerized design was in its infancy. Carver Meade had recently written his book addressing cell-based design methodology. There was a CAD/CAM component to design. But most design was done without a lot of computer-aided blocks or cells by human design engineers.

The second phase consisted of the development of masks for the process. The third phase had to do with the actual manufacture of the semiconductor, including the manufacture of the silicon ingot and imprinting of the integrated circuits. The fourth phase involved testing the manufactured wafers. The fifth phase involved packaging the integrated circuits. The last phase had to do with testing the packaged circuits. Thus, detailed investigation revealed that there was a whole array of different manufacturing processes and engineering technologies involved, and that the make-or-buy issue was not quite as simple as was originally thought.

1982 Environment Scan

A 1982 environment scan revealed some very interesting facts. The first and most important was that design engineers were in incredibly short supply. There were fewer semiconductor design engineers in the world than there were professional football players in the NFL.

A second finding was that there was adequate mask-making and manufacturing capacity for making ingots and imprinting integrated circuits. Manufacturing capacity (equipment and clean rooms) is incredibly expensive. To exacerbate the situation, technology moves very quickly and the obsolescence rate of the required capital equipment is quite high. For these reasons, senior executives properly were concerned about manufacturing capacity. But the research indicated that there was adequate capacity available worldwide and that sufficient capacity was being added to meet future demand.

The research effort revealed that the packaging issue consisted of at least two subissues: industry capacity and packaging technology. Capacity did not appear to be a problem. But management had some concerns about packaging technology to which the semiconductor industry was not sensitive. The semiconductor industry's attitude toward packaging was that parts would be placed into standard packages that would be good for all of the industry to use. The semiconductor industry's attitude was in conflict with Universal's ideas on manufacturing efficiency and module packaging, broad layout, size, weight, and other design requirements. Universal's ideas would allow the production of customized packages for special opportunities on new models.

Packaging

The issue of testing of the packaged semiconductor devices was extremely critical to Universal. The issue had to do with the relative value of a semiconductor to the various suppliers and to Universal. A semiconductor sold for $1 to $3, while an automobile, dependent on the semiconductor's performance, sold for $10,000 to $30,000 (1980 dollars). A $1 to $3 component could easily (and all too frequently did) cause a $20,000 automobile to malfunction, requiring the owner of the automobile to call a tow truck, pay for the tow truck, and have the vehicle towed in for repairs costing several hundred dollars. This is not the basis of customer satisfaction or of increasing market share for the auto manufacturer. The importance of defect-free semiconductors was of far greater importance to Universal than to the semiconductor industry, whose liability was limited to replacing the defective part. Universal executives recognized that the semiconductor industry did not have the same motivation to quality as it had.

Technology Leadership

After the above analysis was completed, another issue influencing the make-or-buy issue came into focus: technology leadership. A chip might offer Universal technological leadership in the automobile industry and possibly some very important marketing advantages. Management became very nervous about its semiconductor supplier(s) being able to sell identical or similar chips to the firm's competitors. Universal wanted to own the technologies incorporated in these circuits. These technologies were viewed as strategic keys to Universal's future.

Management, with the assistance of legal council, determined that if Universal designed the chips in-house, for all practical purposes it would own the technology. The processing technology would be covered by contract license agreements.

Economics

The economics involved in the make-or-buy issue were unusually complex. In 1982, the manufacturing facilities that were required to make a meaningful volume of semiconductors for Universal would have cost in excess of $50 million. There was concern about Universal's ability to run a high-tech semiconductor facility effectively and efficiently. Further, there was the issue of culture. Would the auto industry culture and the semiconductor industry culture mesh? It became apparent that a decision to manufacture integrated circuits (ICs) was a very high cost strategy. It was likely that the resulting ICs (manufactured by Universal) would cost two to four times as much as purchased ones. However, management felt that the cost penalty might be a sound investment in quality and technology and give Universal a significant competitive advantage.

1 What are UMC's six strategic concerns?
2 Develop a one-sentence statement of the problem confronting UMC in this case.
3 What alternatives are available to Universal?
4 What are the advantages and disadvantages of each?

5 What action do you recommend?

6 If Universal were to buy all or a portion of the semiconductors from one or more outside suppliers, what specific characteristics must such a supplier possess?

WORLD-WIDE INDUSTRIES

Alice Baxter recently joined the purchasing department of World-Wide Industries (WWI). Alice had been a buyer in a machine shop in the nearby town of Clarence. While at the machine shop, she completed her A.A. degree with a major in materials management. Her new job with WWI resulted in a handsome increase in salary and a great potential for promotion. Alice's first assignment at WWI was buyer for all purchased components for WWI's line of power mowers. Alice's new boss and the individual responsible for hiring her was Gayton Hackman, the purchasing manager.

Alice received as her first major buying assignment the purchase of a metal housing for a 19-inch power mower. Her previous experience had given her a familiarity with drawings and specifications, particularly as they were related to sheet metal work. She was not disturbed at all by the magnitude of the assignment. It involved not only a high-priced assembly, but a major investment in tools. Alice requested advice from Mr. Hackman as to those sources that could fabricate the housing at low cost. Mr. Hackman gave her the names, addresses, and contacts for four companies currently in the business of manufacturing this type of product, and recommended that they be sent drawings and specifications.

On receipt of the drawings, all the potential suppliers visited Miss Baxter to make sure that all the details were understood and to offer helpful suggestions as to ways in which the housing could be made at a lower cost. In the meetings that ensued, both Miss Baxter and Mr. Hackman discussed the details with the suppliers and the design engineer. At that time it was pointed out very clearly by Miss Baxter that this housing purchase was highly competitive, that other sources were also quoting on the same drawings and specifications, and that the power mower was a low-profit-margin item. Accordingly, the company was forced to make every conceivable effort by negotiation of design and price to purchase the housing at the rock-bottom price. She also pointed out that there would be substantial volume over a period of twelve to eighteen months, which should make the business very attractive. In a few days following these separate meetings, quotations were received from the suppliers. They were carefully reviewed by Miss Baxter, with the resultant determination on her part to place the business with the lowest bidder who apparently would meet all the drawing and specification requirements. The low bidder, the Troy Iron Works, quoted $19.56. The next lowest bidder, the Tipton Machine Company, quoted $19.80. The other two companies were over $21.00 and were not given any consideration by Miss Baxter.

In the course of a discussion about the placement of this business, Miss Baxter was quite surprised to find that Mr. Hackman did not consider that the business was ready for placement. He contended that the price of $19.56 was too high, and that the business should really be placed with the Tipton Machine Company. Miss Baxter argued with Mr. Hackman that, inasmuch as the suppliers had been told that they must bid at the lowest possible price, they had negotiated out all of the design features possible. The price must be right. She saw no reason for procrastination or further discussion. Mr. Hackman, on the other hand, calmly stated that they were now in a position for the first time really to negotiate the purchase and that Miss Baxter should go back to the low bidders and tell them that their prices were too high and that they should submit new quotations. Miss Baxter stated that she was of the opinion that this was unfair to the Troy Iron Works. She felt the quotations were already based on the suppliers making a fair profit and that such a quotation might injure their opportunity to negotiate further business with these suppliers. Mr. Hackman agreed that any company that does not receive the business is apt to be unhappy regardless of the circumstances, but he would not agree that the question of profit should concern the buyer. After all, no consideration was being given to the profitability of the power mower, which had already been clearly defined as marginal.

Mr. Hackman further explained to Miss Baxter that it was highly desirable for the business to be placed with the Tipton Machine Company, as the Troy Iron Works was already making all the other mower housings. Unless the company provided some split of the business, it would lose its negotiating effectiveness for future business (it being accepted by the suppliers that no one but the Troy Iron Works could get business from World-Wide Industries). Mr. Hackman further explained that the company was not in a position to pay Tipton more than Troy and that the negotiations should be conducted to ensure not only that Tipton Machine Company received the business but that it was the low bidder. The degree of determination on the part of Mr. Hackman that this must be true, and the lack of acceptance by Miss Baxter of the fact that it either could or should be done, resulted in Mr. Hackman taking over the completion of the negotiations with both the Troy and Tipton companies.

The net result of this second-look negotiation was that the business *was placed* with the Tipton Machine Company at a price of $18.60. The initial and revised bids are as follows:

	Initial bid	Second bid	Change
Troy Iron Works	$19.56	$18.75	−$0.81
Tipton Machine Co.	$19.80	$18.60	−$1.20

Miss Baxter was very upset on two counts: Her supervisor had proved that additional costs could be taken out of the part, and supplier relations had in no way been disturbed.

1 Why was Mr. Hackman able to reduce the price? How did he know that a reduction was possible?
2 Did Mr. Hackman treat Miss Baxter fairly?
3 Can this type of buying approach be broadly applied to all commodities and industries?
4 Do you believe that either Miss Baxter or Mr. Hackman was right in disregarding the high initial bids submitted by the third and fourth companies?

WVC INDUSTRIAL CHEMICALS COMPANY

WVC Industrial Chemicals Company was a large producer of several industrial chemicals that were widely used in the manufacture of steel, glass, and rubber, and in various types of food processing operations. The WVC operation itself was a continuous, twenty-four-hour-a-day processing operation in which the ingredients for a finished chemical underwent a series of a dozen or more purifying, mixing, and concentrating operations. After each operation was completed, the chemical was put in liquid form and pumped to the next processing operation, in some cases at high temperatures and in others at low temperatures. In total, the plant had over 400 pumps and 50 major processing machines in operation.

WVC's purchasing department was organized into four sections: (1) operating materials, (2) capital equipment, (3) maintenance parts for capital equipment, and (4) MRO supplies. In terms of purchase order activity, the maintenance parts section was the largest of the four.

WVC had developed an extensive and carefully planned two-phase preventive maintenance program. In the first phase, each pump and each major piece of equipment was taken out of service for a short period of time each month and given preplanned, routine maintenance, such as replacement of bearings, seals, and other parts subject to predictable wear. The second phase involved a production shutdown and complete overhaul of each piece of equipment every eighteen months. Bills of material and engineering drawings for all machines were on file, and a list of specific parts required for the overhaul of each machine was available approximately four months before the work was to be done.

For the upcoming phase-two shutdown, maintenance parts buyer Jan Allen was handling the requirement for three large cast pump housings. The large housings were first cast using special alloy steel, and then machined to very close tolerances to meet WVC's precise operating requirements. Because of the high cost involved, Jan solicited bids from four area foundries. All of the foundries responded; their quoted prices and lead times varied considerably.

Because of the tight timing requirements, Jan elected to go with Western Foundry, which quoted a twelve-week delivery, even though Western's price was approximately 10 percent higher than the low bidder. Jan had done business with Western before and knew that it was a reliable, high-quality firm. In addition, the Western sales representative assured Jan that his firm could easily meet her twelve-week delivery requirement.

Four weeks before the scheduled delivery for the castings, Jan received a call from the inside sales department at Western. The young man on the other end of the line told her that two of the three castings had to be scrapped because of problems that developed during the machining operations. This unexpected turn of events left Jan speechless—she did not know what to say next.

1 What should Jan do now?
2 If you had been Jan, how would you have handled the follow-up function?

SELECTED
BIBLIOGRAPHY

GENERAL PURCHASING AND SUPPLY REFERENCES

Bossert, James L.: *Supplier Management Handbook,* ASQC Press, Milwaukee, WI, 1994.

Burt, David N., and Michael F. Doyle: *The American Keiretsu,* Business One Irwin, Homewood, IL, 1993.

Ellram, Lisa, and Laura Birou: *Purchasing for Bottom Line Impact,* Irwin Professional Publishing, Burr Ridge, IL, 1995.

Fearon, Harold E., Donald W. Dobler, and Kenneth H. Killen: *The Purchasing Handbook,* McGraw Hill, NY, 1992.

Hale, Roger L., R. E. Kowal, D. D. Carlton, and T. K. Sehnert: *Managing Supplier Quality,* Monochrome Press, Exeter, NH, 1994.

Harding, Michael, and Mary Lu Harding: *Purchasing,* Barrons, Hauppauge, NY, 1991.

Harris, George: *Purchasing Policies,* Business Laws Inc., Chesterland, OH, 1988.

Heinritz, Stuart, Paul V. Farrell, Larry Giunipero, and Michael G. Kolchin: *Purchasing Principles and Applications,* Prentice Hall, Englewood Cliffs, NJ, 1991.

Killen, Kenneth H., and Robert L. Janson: *Purchasing Managers' Guide to Model Letters, Memos, and Forms,* Prentice Hall, Englewood Cliffs, NJ, 1991.

Killen, Kenneth H., and John W. Kamauff: *Managing Purchasing: Making the Supply Team Work,* Irwin Professional Publishing, Burr Ridge, IL, 1995.

Lamming, Richard: *Beyond Partnership,* Prentice Hall, NY and London, 1993.

Leenders, Michiel R., and David L. Blenkhorn: *Reverse Marketing,* The Free Press, NY, 1988.

Leenders, Michiel R., and Harold E. Fearon: *Purchasing and Materials Management,* Irwin, Homewood, IL, 1993.

Leenders, Michiel R., and Anna E. Flynn: *Value-Driven Purchasing,* Irwin Professional Publishing, Burr Ridge, IL, 1995.

Maass, Richard A., John O. Brown, and James L. Bossert: *Supplier Certification,* ASQC Quality Press, Milwaukee, WI, 1990.

Moody, Patricia E.: *Breakthrough Partnering,* Omneo, Essex Junction, VT, 1993.

Muller, Eugene W., and Donald W. Dobler: *C.P.M. Study Guide,* Updated 6th ed., NAPM Inc., Tempe, AZ, 1994.

Nierenberg, Gerald I.: *The Complete Negotiator,* Nierenberg and Zeif Publishers, NY, 1991.

Parker, Glenn M.: *Cross-Functional Teams,* Jossey-Bass Publishers, San Francisco, 1994.

Perlman, K. I.: *The Leasing Handbook,* Probus Publishing, Chicago, 1992.

Raedels, Alan R.: *Value-Focused Supply Management,* Irwin Professional Publishing, Burr Ridge, IL, 1995.

Reck, Ross R., and Brian G. Long: *The Win-Win Negotiator,* Blanchard Training and Development, Inc., Escondido, CA, 1985.

Ritterskamp, James J. Jr., and Donald D. King: *Purchasing Managers' Desk Book of Purchasing Law,* 2d ed., Prentice Hall, Englewood Cliffs, NJ, 1993.

Scheuing, Eberhard E.: *Purchasing Management,* Prentice Hall, Englewood Cliffs, NJ, 1989.

van Weele, A. J.: *Purchasing Management: Analysis, Planning, And Practice,* Chapman and Hall, London, 1994.

Zenz, Gary J.: *Purchasing and the Management Of Materials,* 7th ed., John Wiley and Sons, NY, 1994.

SELECTED TOPICAL REFERENCES

Specialized Purchasing and Supply

Code of Federal Regulations; Protection of the Environment, Office of the Federal Register, National Archives and Records Administration, Washington D.C., 1989.

Elderkin, Kenton W., and Warren E. Norquist: *Creative Counter Trade,* Ballinger Publishing Company, Cambridge, MA, 1987.

Graw, LeRoy H., and Deidre M. Maples: *Service Purchasing,* Van Nostrand Reinhold, NY, 1994.

McDonald, Paul R.: *Government Prime Contracts and Subcontracts,* Procurement Associates, Glendora, CA, revised annually.

Monczka, Robert M., and Larry C. Giunipero: *Purchasing Internationally: Concepts and Principles,* Bookcrafters, Chelsea, MI, 1990.

Pooler, Victor H.: *Global Purchasing,* Van Nostrand Reinhold, NY, 1992.

Sherman, Stanley M.: *Government Procurement Management,* Woodcrafters Publications, Gaithersburg, Maryland, 1991.

Federal Acquisition Regulations (FAR): Superintendent of Documents, Washington D.C., published annually.

Try Us, 1995: National Minority Business Directories, Minneapolis, 1995.

Cost/Price, Finance, and Economics

Bandler, James: *How to Use Financial Statements,* Irwin Professional Publishing, Burr Ridge, IL, 1994.

Burt, David N., Warren E. Norquist, and Jimmy Anklesaria: *Zero Base Pricing,* Probus Publishing Company, Chicago, 1990.

Frumkin, Norman: *Guide to Economic Indicators,* 2d ed., M. E. Sharpe, Armonk, NY, 1994.

Graw, LeRoy H.: *Cost/Price Analysis,* Van Nostrand Reinhold, NY, 1994.

Horngrun, C. T.: *Cost Accounting: A Managerial Emphasis,* 7th ed., Prentice Hall, Englewood Cliffs, NJ, 1991.

Horngrun, C. T., Gary L. Sundem, and John A. Elliott: *Financial Accounting,* 5th ed., Prentice Hall, Englewood Cliffs, NJ, 1993.

O'Guin, Michael C.: *The Complete Guide to Activity-Based Costing,* Prentice Hall, Englewood Cliffs, NJ, 1991.

Samuelson, Paul S.: *Economics,* 13th ed., McGraw Hill, NY, 1989.

Forecasting and Commodities Markets

Angell, George: *Winning in the Futures Markets: A Money Making Guide to Trading, Hedging, and Speculating,* Probus Publishing Company, Chicago, 1990.

Babcock, Bruce Jr.: *The Dow Jones-Irwin Guide to Commodity Futures Trading Systems,* Irwin Professional Publishing, Burr Ridge, IL, 1989.

Bowerman, Bruce L., and Richard T. O'Connell: *Forecasting and Times Series: An Applied Approach,* 3d ed., Wadsworth Publishing, Belmont, CA, 1993.

Chaman, Jain L.: *A Managerial Guide to Judgmental Forecasting,* Graceway Publishers, NY, 1987.

Inventory and Production Planning

Carter, Joseph R., and Gary L. Ragatz: *Supplier Bar Coding: Closing the EDI Loop,* Graduate School of Business Administration, Michigan State University, East Lansing, MI, 1991.

Janson, Robert: *Handbook of Inventory Management,* Prentice Hall, Englewood Cliffs, NJ, 1987.

Kobert, Norman: *Managing Inventory for Cost Reduction,* Prentice Hall, Englewood Cliffs, NJ, 1992.

Schorr, John E.: *Purchasing in the Twenty-First Century,* Oliver Wight Publications, Essex Junction, VT, 1992.

Wight, Oliver W.: *The Executive's Guide to Successful MRP II,* Prentice Hall, Englewood Cliffs, NJ, 1983.

Management

Chase, R. B., and M. J. Aquilano: *Production and Operations Management,* 6th ed., Irwin, Homewood, IL, 1992.

Cohen, Stephen, and John Zysman: *Manufacturing Matters,* Basic Books, NY, 1987.

DeRose, Louis J.: *The Value Network—Integrating the Five Critical Processes That Create Customer Satisfaction,* ANACOM, NY, 1994.

Drucker, Peter F.: *Managing for Results,* Harper and Row, NY, 1964.

Emmelhainz, Margaret A.: *EDI: A Total Management Guide,* 2d ed., Van Nostrand Reinhold, NY, 1993.

Goldratt, E. M., and Jeff Cox: *The Goal,* 2d rev. ed., North River Press, Croton-On-Hudson, NY, 1992.

McGregor, D.: *The Human Side of Enterprise*, McGraw Hill, NY, 1960

McNair, C. J., and Kathleen H. J. Leibfried: *Benchmarking*, Omneo, Essex Junction, VT, 1992.

Monks, Joseph G.: *Operations Management*, McGraw Hill, NY, 1988.

Ouchi, William G.: *Theory Z*, Avon Publishing, NY, 1993.

Tompkins, J. A., and Dale Harmelink: *The Distribution Management Handbook*, McGraw Hill, NY, 1994.

Whybark, D. C., and Gyula Vastag, *Global Manufacturing Practices*, Elsevier, NY, 1993.

Quality

Cali, James F.: *TQM for Purchasing Management*, McGraw Hill, NY, 1993.

Crosby, Philip B.: *Quality Is Free*, McGraw Hill, NY, 1989.

Grant, Eugene L., and R. S. Leavenworth: *Statistical Quality Control*, McGraw Hill, NY, 1988.

Hutchins, Greg: *ISO 9000: A Comprehensive Guide to Registration, Audit Guidelines, and Successful Certification*, Oliver Wight Publications, Essex Junction, VT, 1993.

Imai, Masaaki: *Kaizen*, Random House Business Division, NY, 1986.

Transportation and Logistics

Cavinato, Joseph L.: "Buying Transportation", *Guide to Purchasing*, NAPM, Tempe, AZ, 1986.

National Motor Freight Classification, American Trucking Association, Washington, D.C., published annually.

Stock, J. R., and D. M. Lambert: *Strategic Logistics Management*, 2d ed., Irwin, Homewood, IL, 1993.

Uniform Freight Classification, Tariff Publishing Office, Chicago, published periodically.

Value Analysis/Engineering

Fallon, Carlos: *Value Analysis*, 2d ed., Wiley Interscience Publishers, NY, 1991.

Miles, Lawrence D.: *Techniques of Value Analysis and Engineering*, 3d ed., The Miles Value Foundation, Society of American Value Engineers, Northbrook, IL, 1989.

Mudge, Arthur E.: *Successful Program Management* (Value Engineering, Part II), J. Pohl Associates, Pittsburgh, PA, 1989.

Purchasing, annual value analysis issue, published each spring.

CASE INDEX

NAME INDEX

SUBJECT INDEX